Stan Lee
PRESENTS

THE INCREDIBLE
HULK

VOL. 1

le 25 décembre 2012

Bonne Fêtes, Erick

Bises,

Ta Mamie

W9-DBB-401

INCREDIBLE HULK #1-6
TALES TO ASTONISH #60-91

ESSENTIAL HULK VOL. 1. Contains material originally published in magazine form as HULK #1-6 and TALES TO ASTONISH #60-91. Third printing 2003. ISBN# 0-7851-0993-5. Published by MARVEL COMICS, a division of MARVEL ENTERTAINMENT GROUP, INC. OFFICE OF PUBLICATION: 10 East 40th Street, New York, NY 10016. Copyright © 1962, 1963, 1964, 1965, 1966, 1967 and 1999 Marvel Characters, Inc. All rights reserved. $14.99 per copy in the U.S. and $24.00 in Canada (GST #R127032852); Canadian Agreement #40668537. All characters featured in this issue and the distinctive names and likenesses thereof, and all related indicia are trademarks of Marvel Characters, Inc. No similarity between any of the names, characters, persons, and/or institutions in this magazine with those of any living or dead person or institution is intended, and any such similarity which may exist is purely coincidental. **Printed in Canada.** STAN LEE, Chairman Emeritus. For information regarding advertising in Marvel Comics or on Marvel.com, please contact Russell Brown, Executive Vice President, Consumer Products, Promotions and Media Sales at 212-576-8561 or rbrown@marvel.com

10 9 8 7 6 5 4 3

ESSENTIAL INCREDIBLE HULK

VOL. 1

THE INCREDIBLE HULK #4

WRITER: STAN LEE
PENCILER: JACK KIRBY
INKER: DICK AYERS
LETTERER: JOHN DUFFY

THE INCREDIBLE HULK #1

WRITER: STAN LEE
PENCILER: JACK KIRBY
INKER: PAUL REINMAN
LETTERER: ART SIMEK

THE INCREDIBLE HULK #5

WRITER: STAN LEE
PENCILER: JACK KIRBY
INKER: DICK AYERS
LETTERER: ART SIMEK

THE INCREDIBLE HULK #2

WRITER: STAN LEE
PENCILER: JACK KIRBY
INKER: STEVE DITKO
LETTERER: ART SIMEK

THE INCREDIBLE HULK #6

WRITER: STAN LEE
ILLUSTRATOR: STEVE DITKO
LETTERER: ART SIMEK

THE INCREDIBLE HULK #3

WRITER: STAN LEE
PENCILER: JACK KIRBY
INKER: DICK AYERS
LETTERER: ART SIMEK

TALES TO ASTONISH #60

WRITER: STAN LEE
PENCILER: STEVE DITKO
INKER: GEORGE ROUSSOS
LETTERER: SAM ROSEN

TALES TO ASTONISH #61

WRITER: STAN LEE
PENCILER: STEVE DITKO
INKER: GEORGE ROUSSOS
LETTERER: SAM ROSEN

TALES TO ASTONISH #62

WRITER: STAN LEE
PENCILER: STEVE DITKO
INKER: GEORGE ROUSSOS
LETTERER: SAM ROSEN

TALES TO ASTONISH #63

WRITER: STAN LEE
PENCILER: STEVE DITKO
INKER: GEORGE ROUSSOS
LETTERER: SAM ROSEN

TALES TO ASTONISH #64

WRITER: STAN LEE
PENCILER: STEVE DITKO
INKER: GEORGE ROUSSOS
LETTERER: ART SIMEK

TALES TO ASTONISH #65

WRITER: STAN LEE
PENCILER: STEVE DITKO
INKER: DICK AYERS
LETTERER: SAM ROSEN

TALES TO ASTONISH #66

WRITER: STAN LEE
PENCILER: STEVE DITKO
INKER: VINCE COLLETTA
LETTERER: ART SIMEK

TALES TO ASTONISH #67

WRITER: STAN LEE
PENCILER: STEVE DITKO
INKER: FRANK GIACOIA
LETTERER: ART SIMEK

TALES TO ASTONISH #68

WRITER: STAN LEE
PENCILER: JACK KIRBY
INKER: MIKE ESPOSITO
LETTERER: ART SIMEK

ESSENTIAL INCREDIBLE HULK

VOL. 1

TALES TO ASTONISH #72

WRITER: STAN LEE
PENCILERS: JACK KIRBY & MIKE ESPOSITO
INKER: MIKE ESPOSITO
LETTERER: SAM ROSEN

TALES TO ASTONISH #69

WRITER: STAN LEE
PENCILER: JACK KIRBY
INKER: MIKE ESPOSITO
LETTERER: ART SIMEK

TALES TO ASTONISH #73

WRITER: STAN LEE
PENCILERS: JACK KIRBY & BOB POWELL
INKER: BOB POWELL
LETTERER: ART SIMEK

TALES TO ASTONISH #70

WRITER: STAN LEE
PENCILER: JACK KIRBY
INKER: MIKE ESPOSITO
LETTERER: ART SIMEK

TALES TO ASTONISH #74

WRITER: STAN LEE
PENCILERS: JACK KIRBY & BOB POWELL
INKER: MIKE ESPOSITO
LETTERER: SAM ROSEN

TALES TO ASTONISH #71

WRITER: STAN LEE
PENCILERS: JACK KIRBY & MIKE ESPOSITO
INKER: MIKE ESPOSITO
LETTERER: ART SIMEK

TALES TO ASTONISH #75

WRITER: STAN LEE
PENCILERS: JACK KIRBY & MIKE ESPOSITO
INKER: MIKE ESPOSITO
LETTERER: SAM ROSEN

TALES TO ASTONISH #76

WRITER: STAN LEE
PENCILERS: JACK KIRBY & GIL KANE
INKER: MIKE ESPOSITO
LETTERER: ART SIMEK

TALES TO ASTONISH #77

WRITER: STAN LEE
PENCILERS: JACK KIRBY & JOHN ROMITA
INKER: JOHN ROMITA
LETTERER: SAM ROSEN

TALES TO ASTONISH #78

WRITER: STAN LEE
PENCILERS: JACK KIRBY & BILL EVERETT
INKER: BILL EVERETT
LETTERER: SAM ROSEN

TALES TO ASTONISH #79

WRITER: STAN LEE
PENCILERS: JACK KIRBY & BILL EVERETT
INKER: BILL EVERETT
LETTERER: ART SIMEK

TALES TO ASTONISH #80

WRITER: STAN LEE
PENCILERS: JACK KIRBY & BILL EVERETT
INKER: BILL EVERETT
LETTERER: ART SIMEK

TALES TO ASTONISH #81

WRITER: STAN LEE
PENCILERS: JACK KIRBY & BILL EVERETT
INKER: BILL EVERETT
LETTERER: SAM ROSEN

TALES TO ASTONISH #82

WRITER: STAN LEE
PENCILERS: JACK KIRBY & BILL EVERETT
INKER: BILL EVERETT
LETTERER: ART SIMEK

TALES TO ASTONISH #83

WRITER: STAN LEE
PENCILERS: JACK KIRBY & BILL EVERETT
INKER: BILL EVERETT
LETTERER: SAM ROSEN

ESSENTIAL INCREDIBLE HULK VOL. 1

TALES TO ASTONISH #84

WRITER: STAN LEE
ILLUSTRATOR: MARVEL BULLPEN
LETTERER: ART SIMEK

TALES TO ASTONISH #85

WRITER: STAN LEE
PENCILER: JOHN BUSCEMA
INKER: JOHN TARTAGLIONE
LETTERER: RAY HOLLOWAY

TALES TO ASTONISH #86

WRITER: STAN LEE
PENCILER: JOHN BUSCEMA
INKER: MIKE ESPOSITO
LETTERER: ART SIMEK

TALES TO ASTONISH #87

WRITER: STAN LEE
PENCILER: JOHN BUSCEMA
INKER: MIKE ESPOSITO
LETTERER: ART SIMEK

TALES TO ASTONISH #88

WRITER: STAN LEE
ILLUSTRATOR: GIL KANE
LETTERER: SAM ROSEN

TALES TO ASTONISH #89

WRITER: STAN LEE
ILLUSTRATOR: GIL KANE
LETTERER: SAM ROSEN

TALES TO ASTONISH #90

WRITER: STAN LEE
ILLUSTRATOR: GIL KANE
LETTERER: SAM ROSEN

TALES TO ASTONISH #91

WRITER: STAN LEE
ILLUSTRATOR: GIL KANE
LETTERER: ART SIMEK

MARVEL ESSENTIAL DESIGN:
JOHN "JG" ROSHELL OF COMICRAFT
REPRINT CREDITS:
COVER ART: BRUCE TIMM
COVER COLORS: MARIE JAVINS
SPECIAL THANKS:
TOM BREVOORT, JONATHAN BABCOCK, JARED OSBORN, JACK MORELLI, POND SCUM, JULIO HERRERA, REPRO, DAVE SHARPE AND ROGER STERN

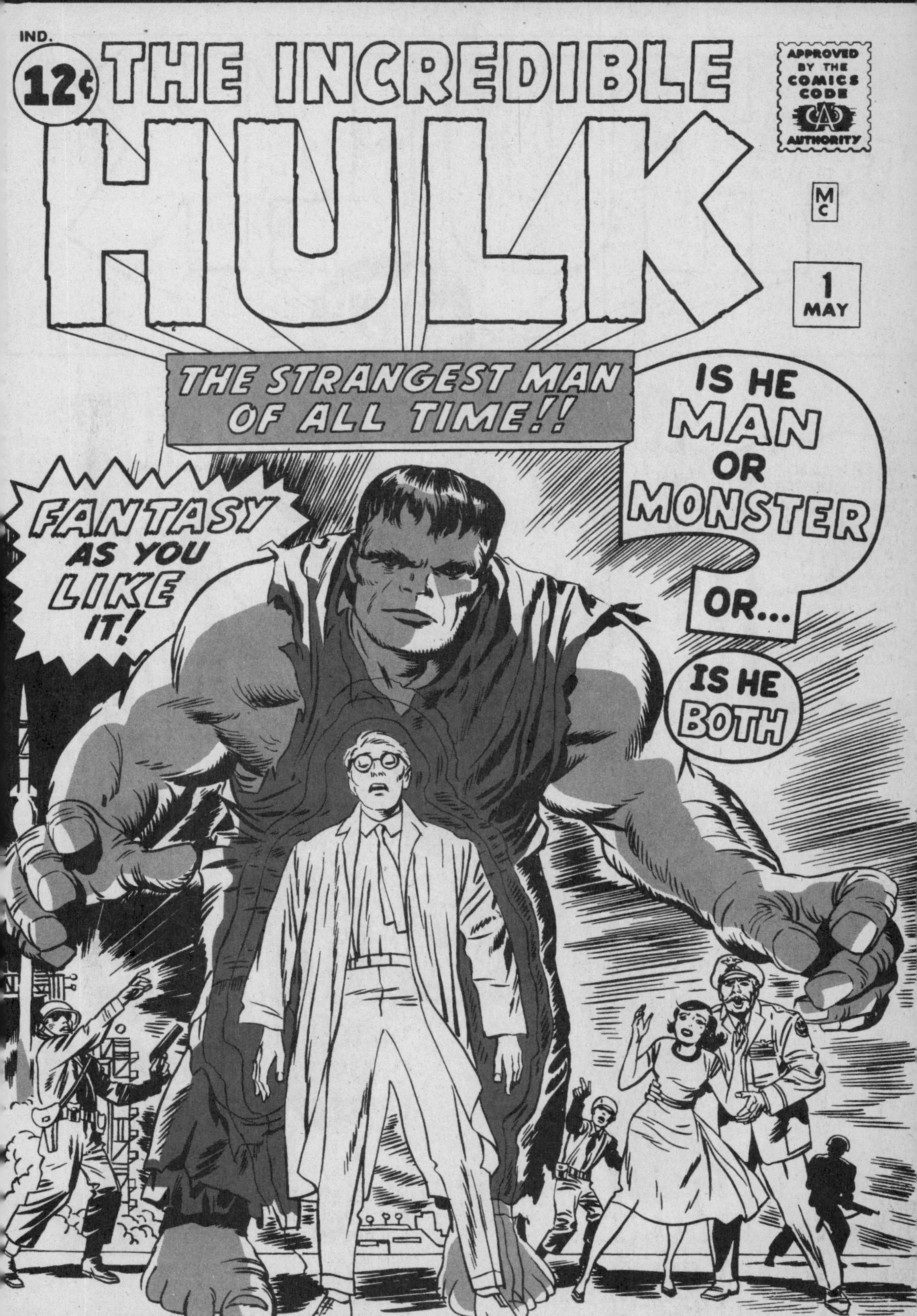
IND.
12¢
THE INCREDIBLE
HULK
APPROVED BY THE COMICS CODE AUTHORITY
MC
1
MAY
THE STRANGEST MAN OF ALL TIME!!
IS HE MAN OR MONSTER
OR...
IS HE BOTH
FANTASY AS YOU LIKE IT!

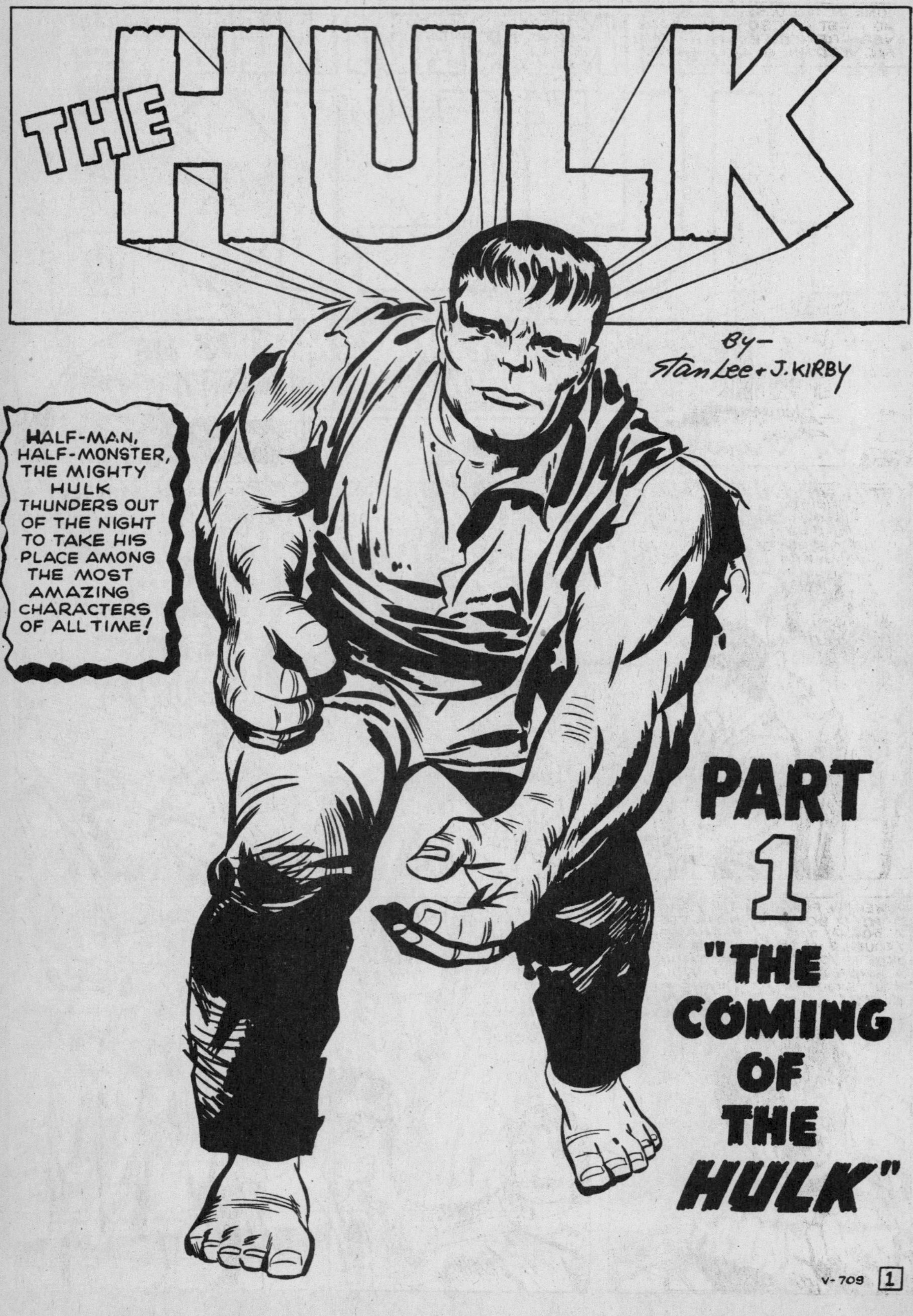
THE HULK
By- Stan Lee + J. KIRBY
HALF-MAN, HALF-MONSTER, THE MIGHTY HULK THUNDERS OUT OF THE NIGHT TO TAKE HIS PLACE AMONG THE MOST AMAZING CHARACTERS OF ALL TIME!
PART 1
"THE COMING OF THE HULK"

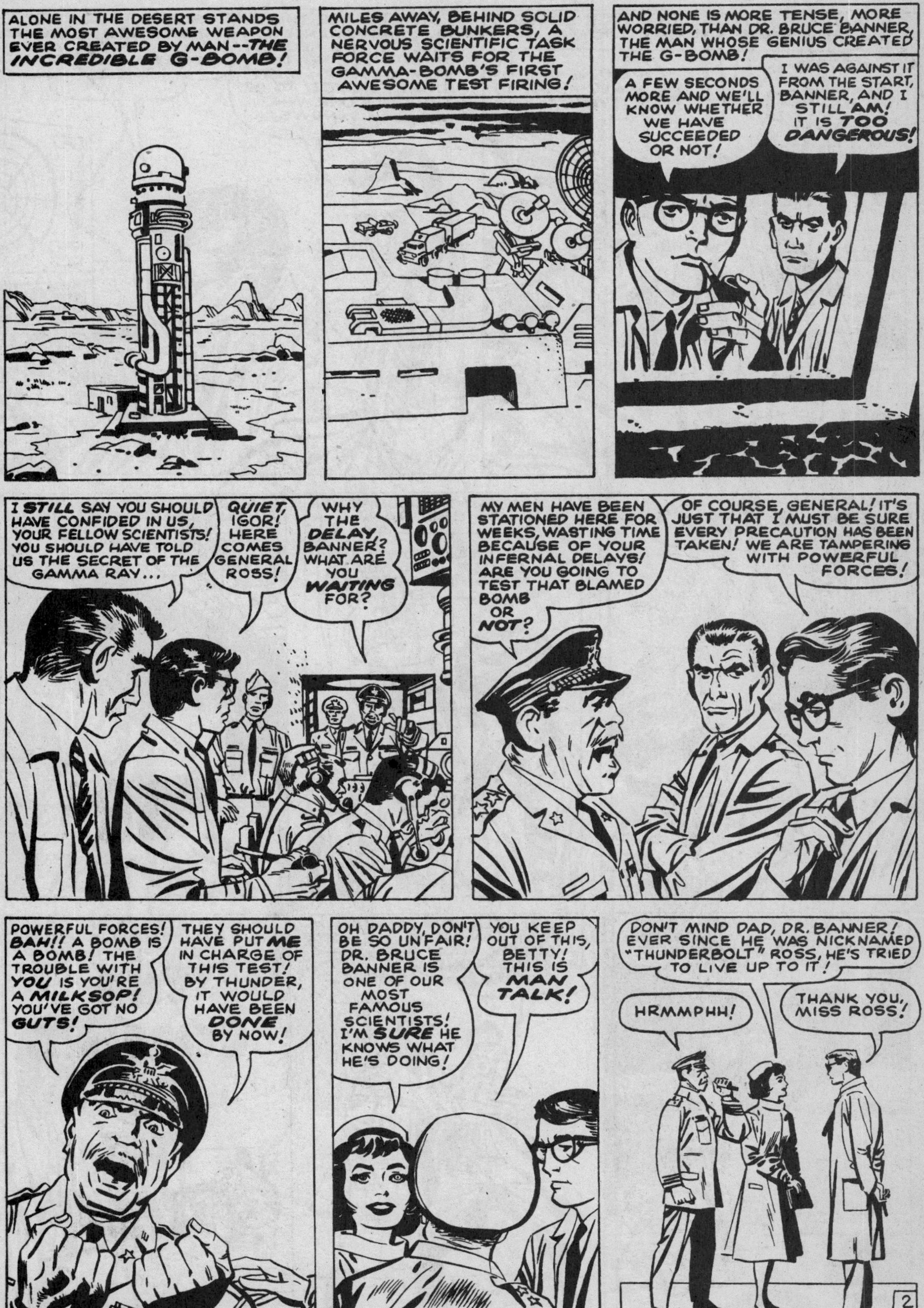

ALONE IN THE DESERT STANDS THE MOST AWESOME WEAPON EVER CREATED BY MAN--THE INCREDIBLE G-BOMB!
MILES AWAY, BEHIND SOLID CONCRETE BUNKERS, A NERVOUS SCIENTIFIC TASK FORCE WAITS FOR THE GAMMA-BOMB'S FIRST AWESOME TEST FIRING!
AND NONE IS MORE TENSE, MORE WORRIED, THAN DR. BRUCE BANNER, THE MAN WHOSE GENIUS CREATED THE G-BOMB!
A FEW SECONDS MORE AND WE'LL KNOW WHETHER WE HAVE SUCCEEDED OR NOT!
I WAS AGAINST IT FROM THE START, BANNER, AND I STILL AM! IT IS TOO DANGEROUS!
I STILL SAY YOU SHOULD HAVE CONFIDED IN US, YOUR FELLOW SCIENTISTS! YOU SHOULD HAVE TOLD US THE SECRET OF THE GAMMA RAY...
QUIET, IGOR! HERE COMES GENERAL ROSS!
WHY THE DELAY, BANNER? WHAT ARE YOU WAITING FOR?
MY MEN HAVE BEEN STATIONED HERE FOR WEEKS, WASTING TIME BECAUSE OF YOUR INFERNAL DELAYS! ARE YOU GOING TO TEST THAT BLAMED BOMB OR NOT?
OF COURSE, GENERAL! IT'S JUST THAT I MUST BE SURE EVERY PRECAUTION HAS BEEN TAKEN! WE ARE TAMPERING WITH POWERFUL FORCES!
POWERFUL FORCES! BAH!! A BOMB IS A BOMB! THE TROUBLE WITH YOU IS YOU'RE A MILKSOP! YOU'VE GOT NO GUTS!
THEY SHOULD HAVE PUT ME IN CHARGE OF THIS TEST! BY THUNDER, IT WOULD HAVE BEEN DONE BY NOW!
OH DADDY, DON'T BE SO UNFAIR! DR. BRUCE BANNER IS ONE OF OUR MOST FAMOUS SCIENTISTS! I'M SURE HE KNOWS WHAT HE'S DOING!
YOU KEEP OUT OF THIS, BETTY! THIS IS MAN TALK!
DON'T MIND DAD, DR. BANNER! EVER SINCE HE WAS NICKNAMED "THUNDERBOLT" ROSS, HE'S TRIED TO LIVE UP TO IT!
HRMMPHH!
THANK YOU, MISS ROSS!

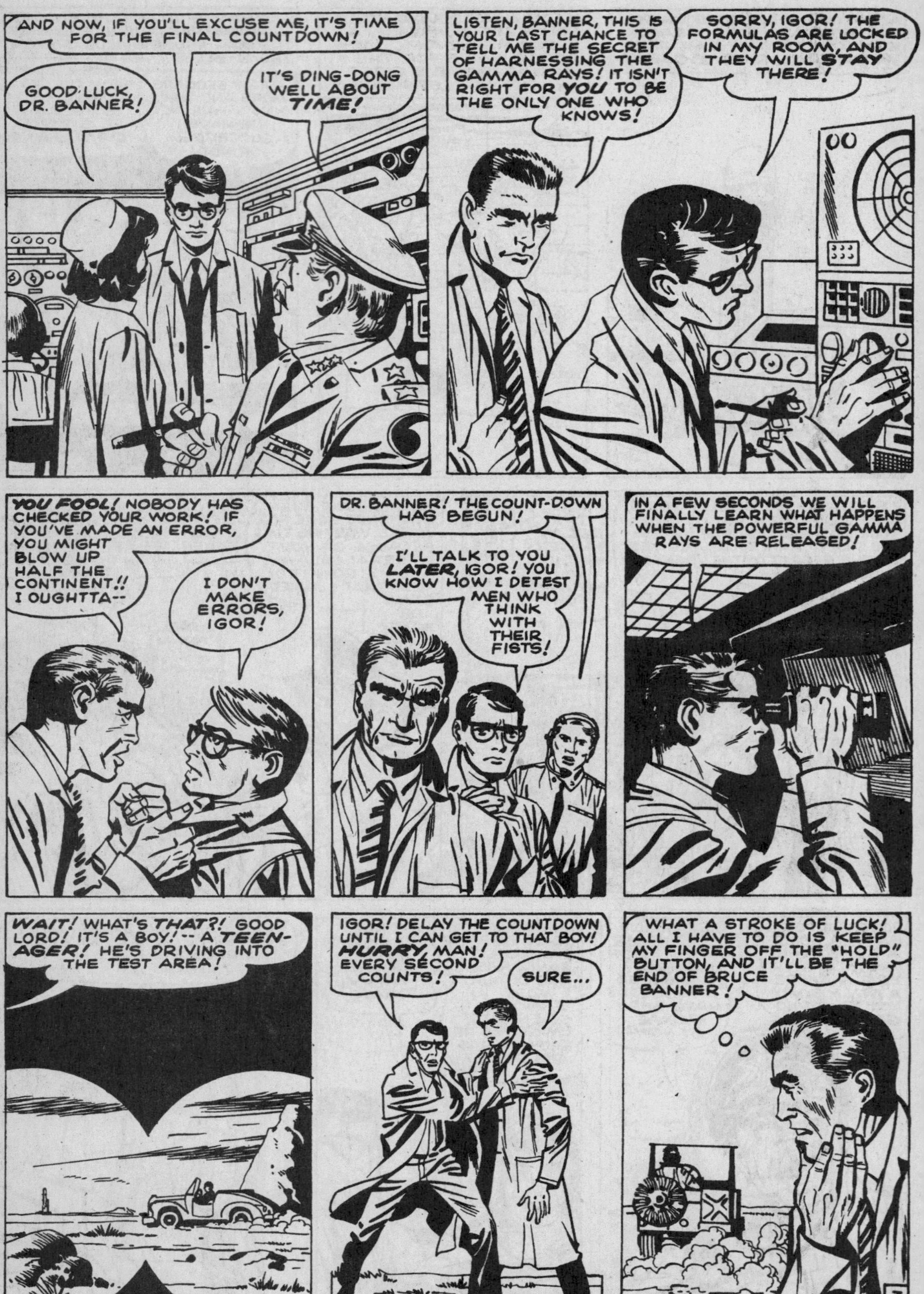
AND NOW, IF YOU'LL EXCUSE ME, IT'S TIME FOR THE FINAL COUNTDOWN!
GOOD LUCK, DR. BANNER!
IT'S DING-DONG WELL ABOUT TIME!
LISTEN, BANNER, THIS IS YOUR LAST CHANCE TO TELL ME THE SECRET OF HARNESSING THE GAMMA RAYS! IT ISN'T RIGHT FOR YOU TO BE THE ONLY ONE WHO KNOWS!
SORRY, IGOR! THE FORMULAS ARE LOCKED IN MY ROOM, AND THEY WILL STAY THERE!
YOU FOOL! NOBODY HAS CHECKED YOUR WORK! IF YOU'VE MADE AN ERROR, YOU MIGHT BLOW UP HALF THE CONTINENT!! I OUGHTTA--
I DON'T MAKE ERRORS, IGOR!
DR. BANNER! THE COUNT-DOWN HAS BEGUN!
I'LL TALK TO YOU LATER, IGOR! YOU KNOW HOW I DETEST MEN WHO THINK WITH THEIR FISTS!
IN A FEW SECONDS WE WILL FINALLY LEARN WHAT HAPPENS WHEN THE POWERFUL GAMMA RAYS ARE RELEASED!
WAIT! WHAT'S THAT?! GOOD LORD! IT'S A BOY! -- A TEEN-AGER! HE'S DRIVING INTO THE TEST AREA!
IGOR! DELAY THE COUNTDOWN UNTIL I CAN GET TO THAT BOY! HURRY, MAN! EVERY SECOND COUNTS!
SURE...
WHAT A STROKE OF LUCK! ALL I HAVE TO DO IS KEEP MY FINGER OFF THE "HOLD" BUTTON, AND IT'LL BE THE END OF BRUCE BANNER!
3

YOU! GET OUT OF THERE! YOU'RE IN A FORBIDDEN TEST AREA!

COOL IT, MAN! THE KIDS BET ME I WOULDN'T HAVE NERVE ENOUGH TO SNEAK PAST THE GUARDS...

HEY! WHAT ARE YA TRYIN' TO DO? MAKE THEM THINK I'M CHICKEN?

COME ON, YOU FOOL! WE'VE GOT TO REACH THE PROTECTIVE TRENCH BEFORE THE BOMB GOES OFF!

BOMB??

MEANWHILE, AT THE BUNKER, NOT HAVING BEEN TOLD TO DELAY THE FIRING, A FINGER TOUCHES THE FATAL BUTTON!

THREE TWO ONE ZERO

FIRE

THERE! YOU'RE SAFE!

AND NOW I'LL---

AHHH

ALTHO' MANY MILES FROM BOMB ZERO, DR. BRUCE BANNER IS BATHED IN THE FULL FORCE OF THE MYSTERIOUS GAMMA RAYS!

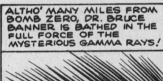

THE WORLD SEEMS TO STAND STILL, TREMBLING ON THE BRINK OF INFINITY, AS HIS EAR-SPLITTING SCREAM FILLS THE AIR...!

AND HE IS STILL SCREAMING, HOURS LATER, WHEN---

HE'S COMING OUT OF IT NOW!

THANK HEAVEN!

BANNER, IT'S A MIRACLE THAT YOU'RE STILL ALIVE! -- YOU ABSORBED THE FULL IMPACT OF THE GAMMA RAYS!

HOW-- HOW DID I GET HERE?

MY NAME IS RICK JONES... I BROUGHT YOU!

YOU SAVED MY DUMB LIFE... I FIGGERED IT WAS THE LEAST I COULD DO FOR YOU!... Y'KNOW, IT'S A FUNNY THING... I'M AN ORPHAN, AND NO ONE EVER DID ANYTHING FOR ME BEFORE--'CEPT YOU, A STRANGER!

4

IT'S GETTIN' DARK OUT! HOW LONG THEY GONNA **KEEP** US HERE, DOC?

I DON'T KNOW! I DON'T KNOW!! THEY MUST BE WAITING-- FOR ME TO DIE! IT ISN'T POSSIBLE TO TAKE SO MUCH GAMMA RADIATION AND NOT HAVE **SOMETHING** HAPPEN!

I--I'M BEGINNING TO FEEL STRANGE! MY HEAD IS THROBBING! THIS MUST BE --THE END...

THE WHOLE **WORLD'S** GOING BATTY! EVEN THIS KOOKIE RADIO-- IT WON'T PLAY! ALL IT GIVES OUT WITH IS **STATIC!**

CLICK-- CLICK--

THAT'S NO RADIO! IT'S A **GEIGER** COUNTER!

IT MEASURES RADIATION! **LISTEN** TO IT! IT--IT'S GOING **WILD!**

CLICK-CLICK CLICK CLICK CLICK CLICK CL CLICK CLICK CLICK CLICK

IT'S GETTING LOUDER-- AND LOUDER !!--FASTER AND FASTER !! WHAT'S HAPPENING ??

CLICK CLICK CLICK CLICK CK

WHAT IS HAPPENING ???

ARGHH

CLICK CLICK CLICK CLICK

HEY! **LOOK** AT YOU! YOU-- **CHANGED!**

GET OUT OF MY WAY, INSECT!

5

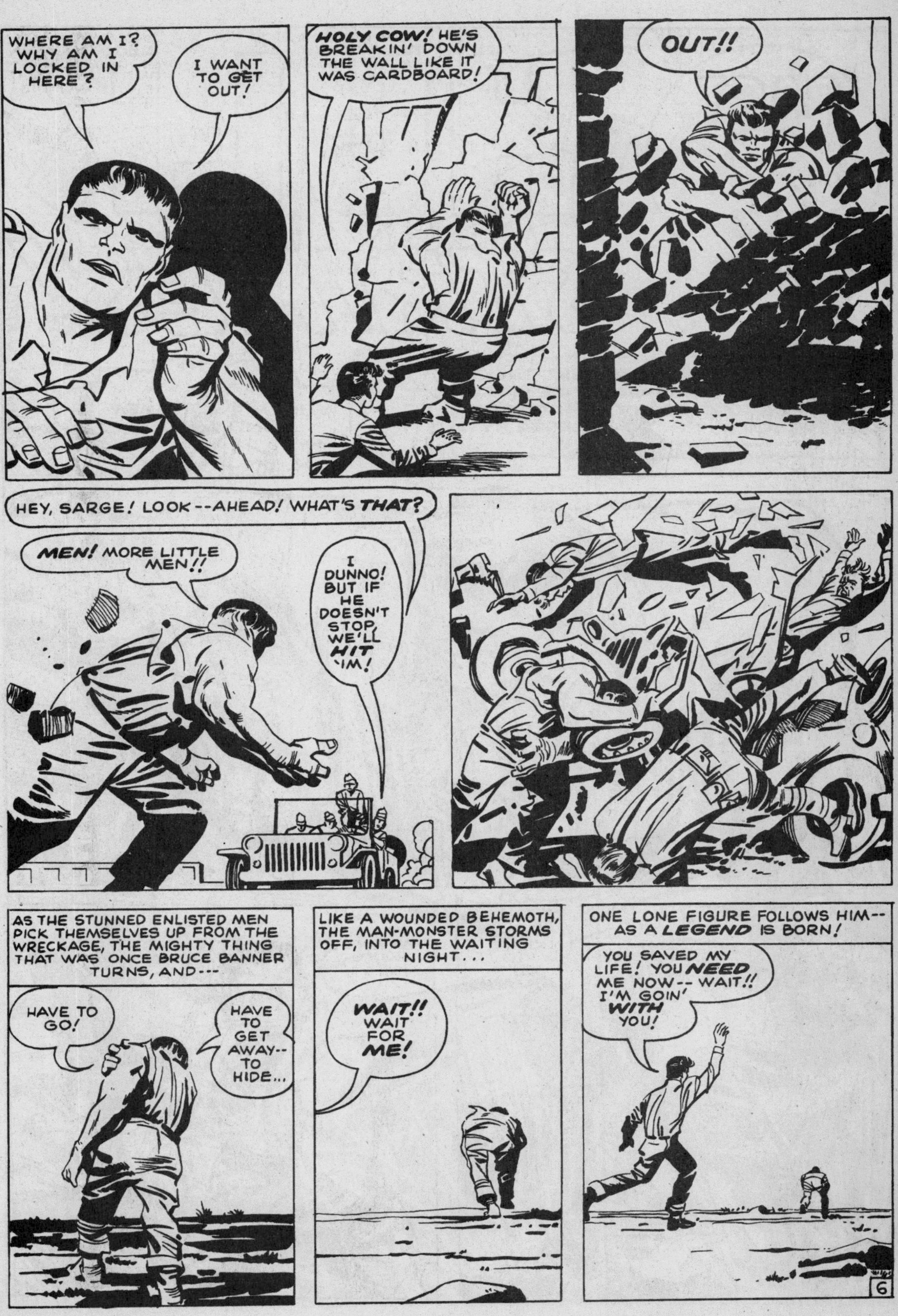
WHERE AM I? WHY AM I LOCKED IN HERE?
I WANT TO GET OUT!
HOLY COW! HE'S BREAKIN' DOWN THE WALL LIKE IT WAS CARDBOARD!
OUT!!
HEY, SARGE! LOOK--AHEAD! WHAT'S THAT?
MEN! MORE LITTLE MEN!!
I DUNNO! BUT IF HE DOESN'T STOP, WE'LL HIT 'IM!
AS THE STUNNED ENLISTED MEN PICK THEMSELVES UP FROM THE WRECKAGE, THE MIGHTY THING THAT WAS ONCE BRUCE BANNER TURNS, AND---
HAVE TO GO!
HAVE TO GET AWAY-- TO HIDE...
LIKE A WOUNDED BEHEMOTH, THE MAN-MONSTER STORMS OFF, INTO THE WAITING NIGHT...
WAIT!! WAIT FOR ME!
ONE LONE FIGURE FOLLOWS HIM-- AS A LEGEND IS BORN!
YOU SAVED MY LIFE! YOU NEED ME NOW-- WAIT!! I'M GOIN' WITH YOU!
6

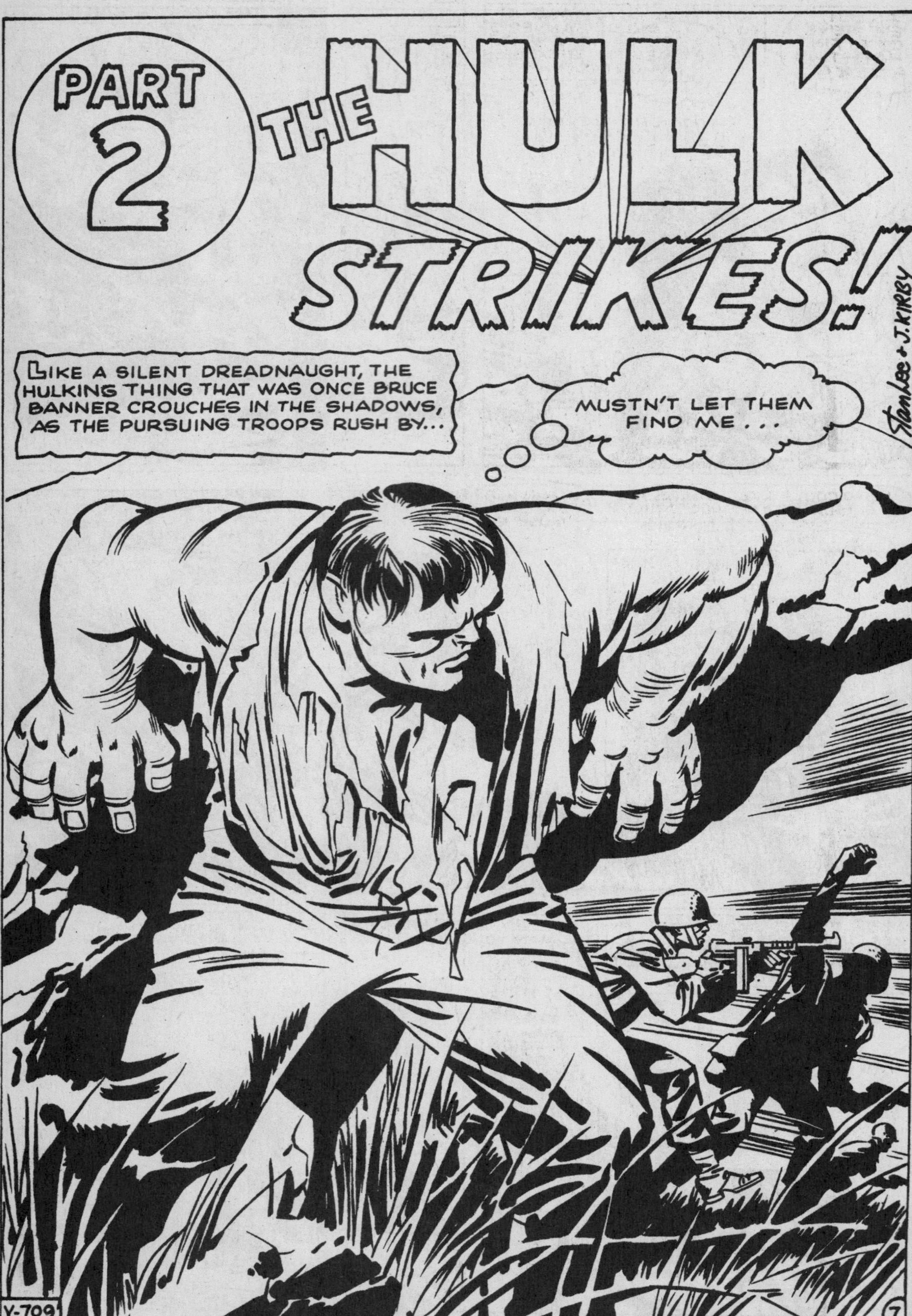
PART 2
THE HULK STRIKES!
Stan Lee + J. Kirby
LIKE A SILENT DREADNAUGHT, THE HULKING THING THAT WAS ONCE BRUCE BANNER CROUCHES IN THE SHADOWS, AS THE PURSUING TROOPS RUSH BY...
MUSTN'T LET THEM FIND ME . . .
V-709

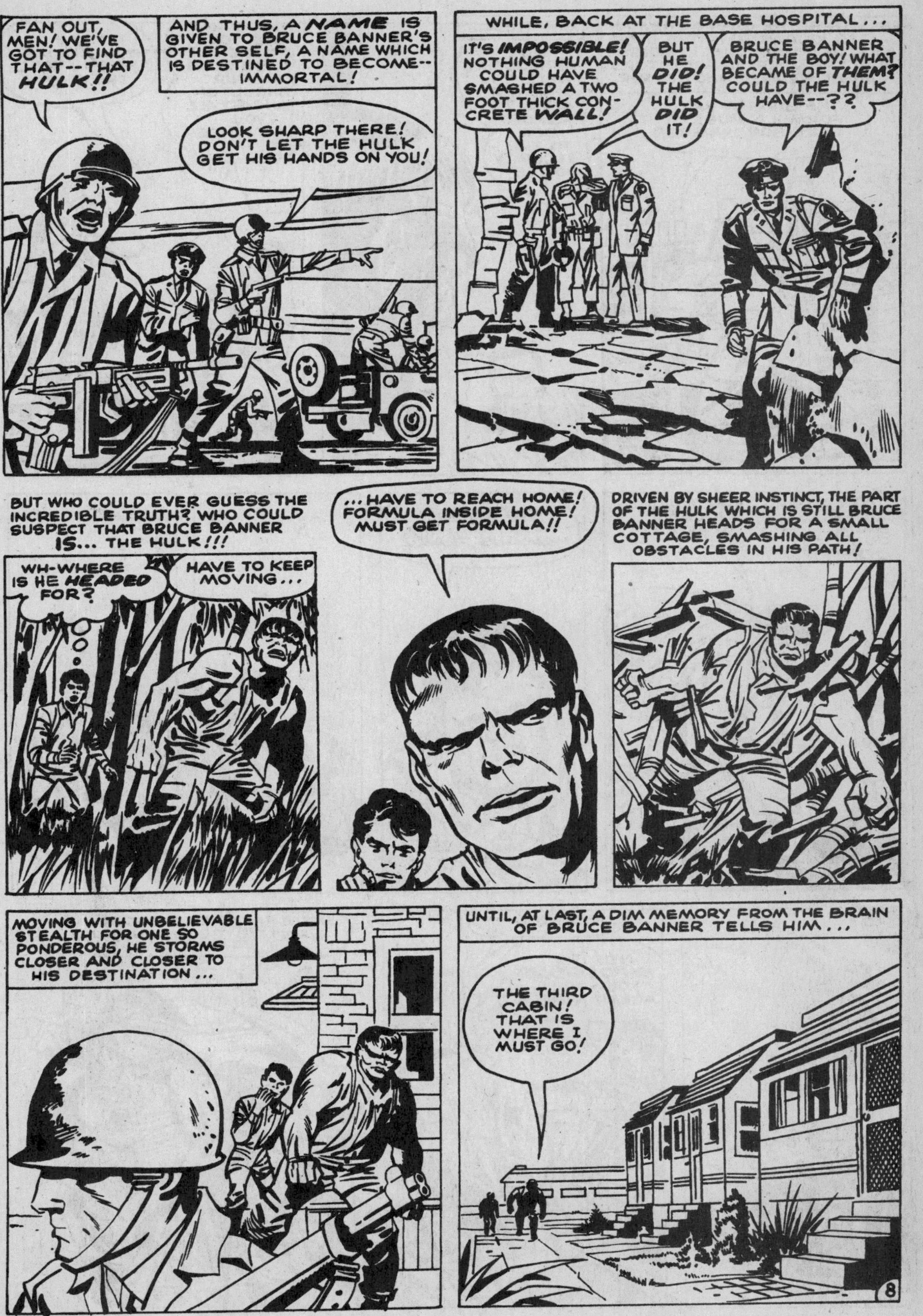
FAN OUT, MEN! WE'VE GOT TO FIND THAT--THAT HULK!!
AND THUS, A NAME IS GIVEN TO BRUCE BANNER'S OTHER SELF, A NAME WHICH IS DESTINED TO BECOME--IMMORTAL!
LOOK SHARP THERE! DON'T LET THE HULK GET HIS HANDS ON YOU!
WHILE, BACK AT THE BASE HOSPITAL...
IT'S IMPOSSIBLE! NOTHING HUMAN COULD HAVE SMASHED A TWO FOOT THICK CONCRETE WALL!
BUT HE DID! THE HULK DID IT!
BRUCE BANNER AND THE BOY! WHAT BECAME OF THEM? COULD THE HULK HAVE--??
BUT WHO COULD EVER GUESS THE INCREDIBLE TRUTH? WHO COULD SUSPECT THAT BRUCE BANNER IS... THE HULK!!!
WH-WHERE IS HE HEADED FOR?
HAVE TO KEEP MOVING...
...HAVE TO REACH HOME! FORMULA INSIDE HOME! MUST GET FORMULA!!
DRIVEN BY SHEER INSTINCT, THE PART OF THE HULK WHICH IS STILL BRUCE BANNER HEADS FOR A SMALL COTTAGE, SMASHING ALL OBSTACLES IN HIS PATH!
MOVING WITH UNBELIEVABLE STEALTH FOR ONE SO PONDEROUS, HE STORMS CLOSER AND CLOSER TO HIS DESTINATION...
UNTIL, AT LAST, A DIM MEMORY FROM THE BRAIN OF BRUCE BANNER TELLS HIM...
THE THIRD CABIN! THAT IS WHERE I MUST GO!

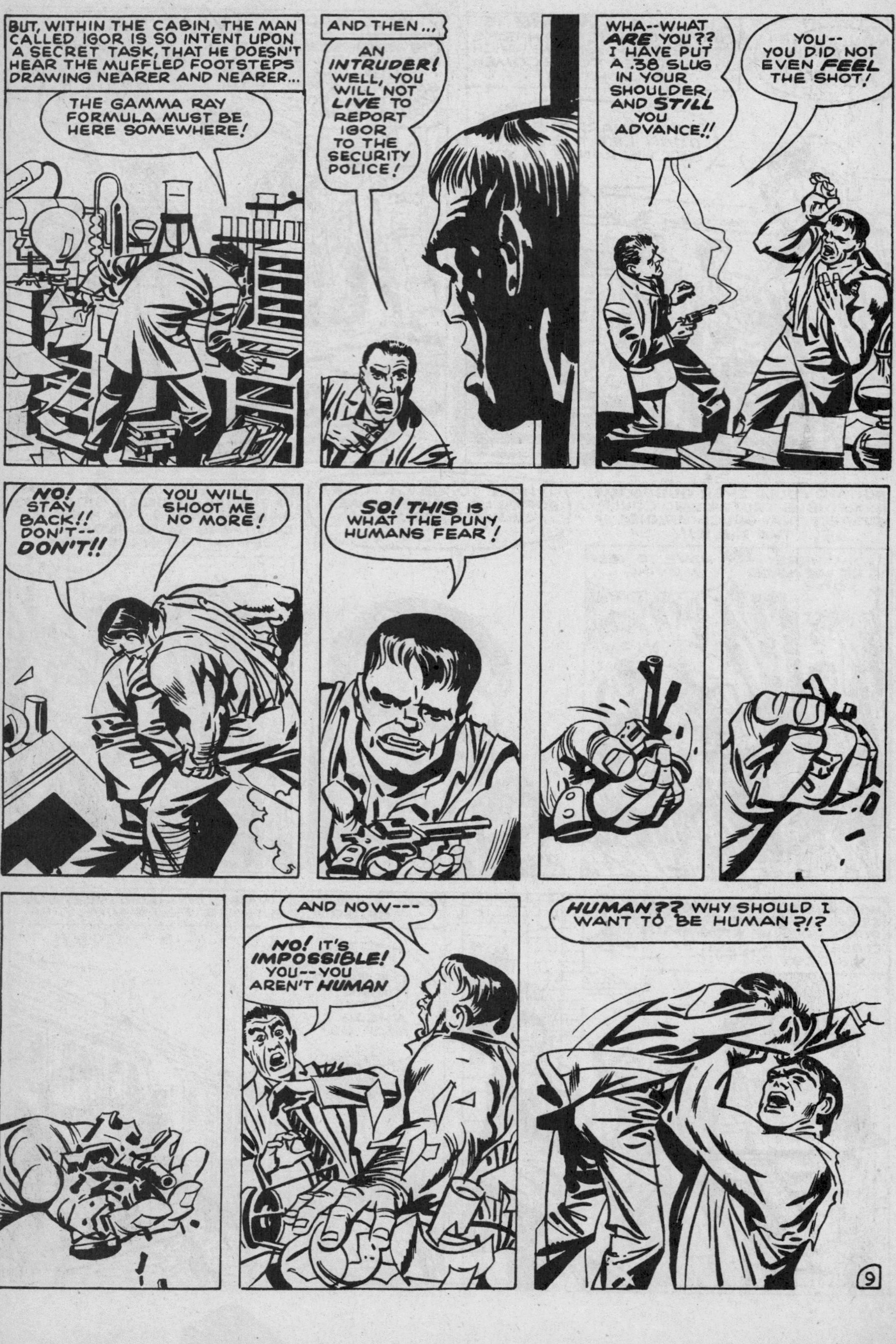
BUT, WITHIN THE CABIN, THE MAN CALLED IGOR IS SO INTENT UPON A SECRET TASK, THAT HE DOESN'T HEAR THE MUFFLED FOOTSTEPS DRAWING NEARER AND NEARER...
THE GAMMA RAY FORMULA MUST BE HERE SOMEWHERE!
AND THEN...
AN INTRUDER! WELL, YOU WILL NOT LIVE TO REPORT IGOR TO THE SECURITY POLICE!
WHA--WHAT ARE YOU?? I HAVE PUT A .38 SLUG IN YOUR SHOULDER, AND STILL YOU ADVANCE!!
YOU-- YOU DID NOT EVEN FEEL THE SHOT!
NO! STAY BACK!! DON'T-- DON'T!!
YOU WILL SHOOT ME NO MORE!
SO! THIS IS WHAT THE PUNY HUMANS FEAR!
AND NOW---
NO! IT'S IMPOSSIBLE! YOU--YOU AREN'T HUMAN
HUMAN?? WHY SHOULD I WANT TO BE HUMAN?!?

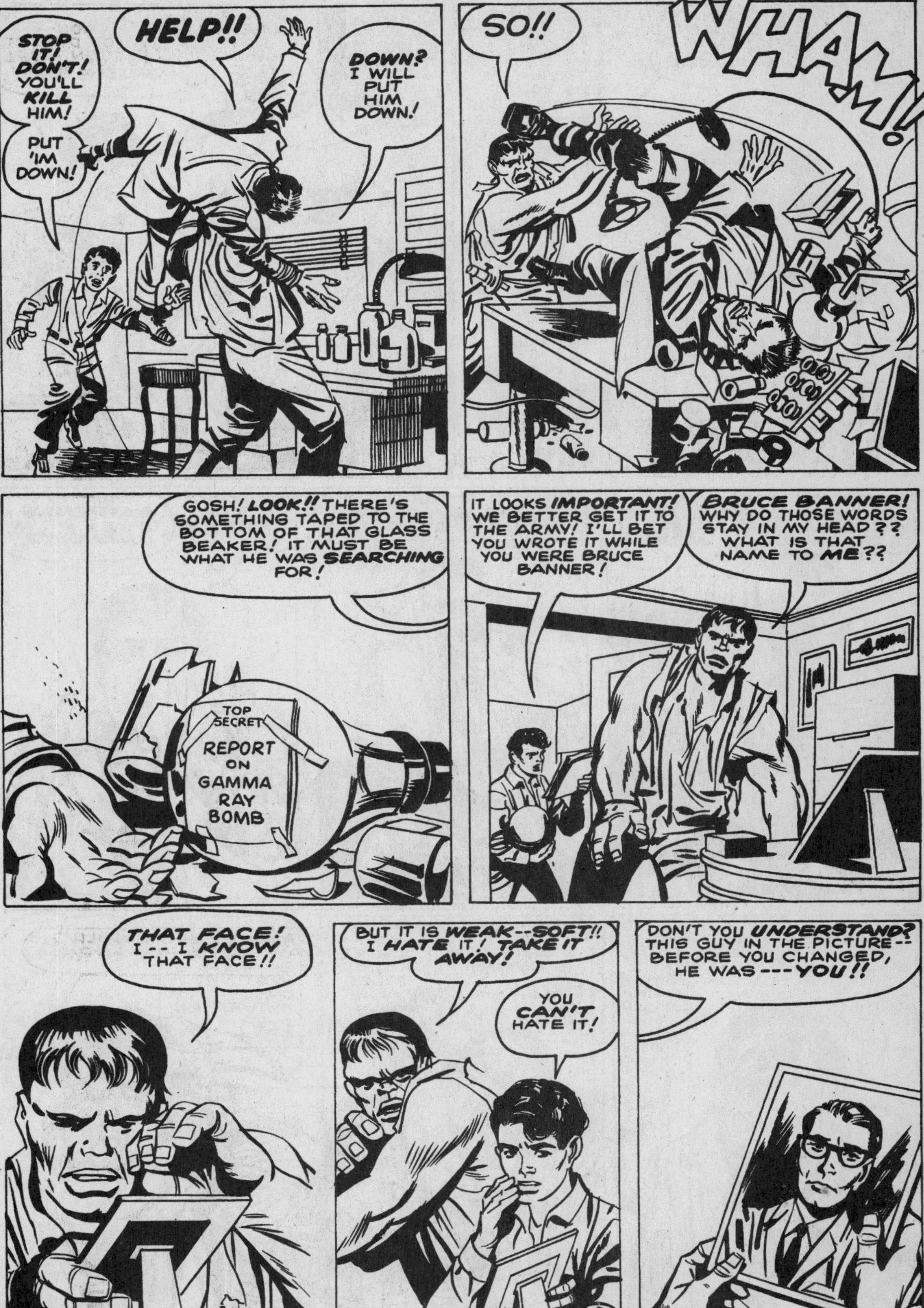
STOP IT! DON'T! YOU'LL KILL HIM!
HELP!!
PUT 'IM DOWN!
DOWN? I WILL PUT HIM DOWN!
SO!!
WHAM!!
GOSH! LOOK!! THERE'S SOMETHING TAPED TO THE BOTTOM OF THAT GLASS BEAKER! IT MUST BE WHAT HE WAS SEARCHING FOR!
TOP SECRET
REPORT ON GAMMA RAY BOMB
IT LOOKS IMPORTANT! WE BETTER GET IT TO THE ARMY! I'LL BET YOU WROTE IT WHILE YOU WERE BRUCE BANNER!
BRUCE BANNER! WHY DO THOSE WORDS STAY IN MY HEAD?? WHAT IS THAT NAME TO ME??
THAT FACE! I -- I KNOW THAT FACE!!
BUT IT IS WEAK--SOFT!! I HATE IT! TAKE IT AWAY!
YOU CAN'T HATE IT!
DON'T YOU UNDERSTAND? THIS GUY IN THE PICTURE-- BEFORE YOU CHANGED, HE WAS---YOU!!

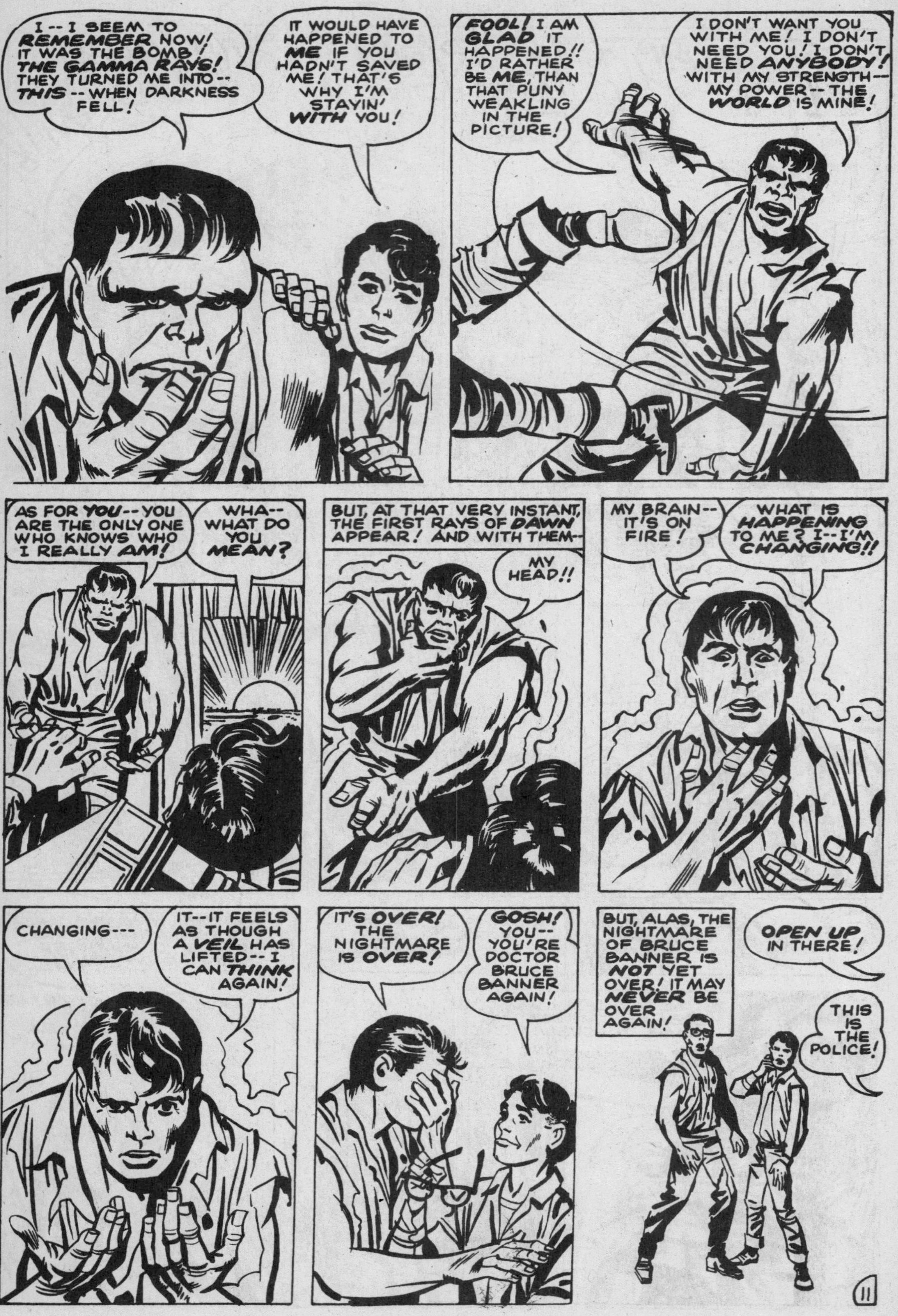
I -- I SEEM TO REMEMBER NOW! IT WAS THE BOMB! THE GAMMA RAYS! THEY TURNED ME INTO -- THIS -- WHEN DARKNESS FELL!
IT WOULD HAVE HAPPENED TO ME IF YOU HADN'T SAVED ME! THAT'S WHY I'M STAYIN' WITH YOU!
FOOL! I AM GLAD IT HAPPENED!! I'D RATHER BE ME, THAN THAT PUNY WEAKLING IN THE PICTURE!
I DON'T WANT YOU WITH ME! I DON'T NEED YOU! I DON'T NEED ANYBODY! WITH MY STRENGTH -- MY POWER -- THE WORLD IS MINE!
AS FOR YOU -- YOU ARE THE ONLY ONE WHO KNOWS WHO I REALLY AM!
WHA -- WHAT DO YOU MEAN?
BUT, AT THAT VERY INSTANT, THE FIRST RAYS OF DAWN APPEAR! AND WITH THEM --
MY HEAD!!
MY BRAIN -- IT'S ON FIRE!
WHAT IS HAPPENING TO ME? I -- I'M CHANGING!!
CHANGING ---
IT -- IT FEELS AS THOUGH A VEIL HAS LIFTED -- I CAN THINK AGAIN!
IT'S OVER! THE NIGHTMARE IS OVER!
GOSH! YOU -- YOU'RE DOCTOR BRUCE BANNER AGAIN!
BUT, ALAS, THE NIGHTMARE OF BRUCE BANNER IS NOT YET OVER! IT MAY NEVER BE OVER AGAIN!
OPEN UP IN THERE!
THIS IS THE POLICE!
11

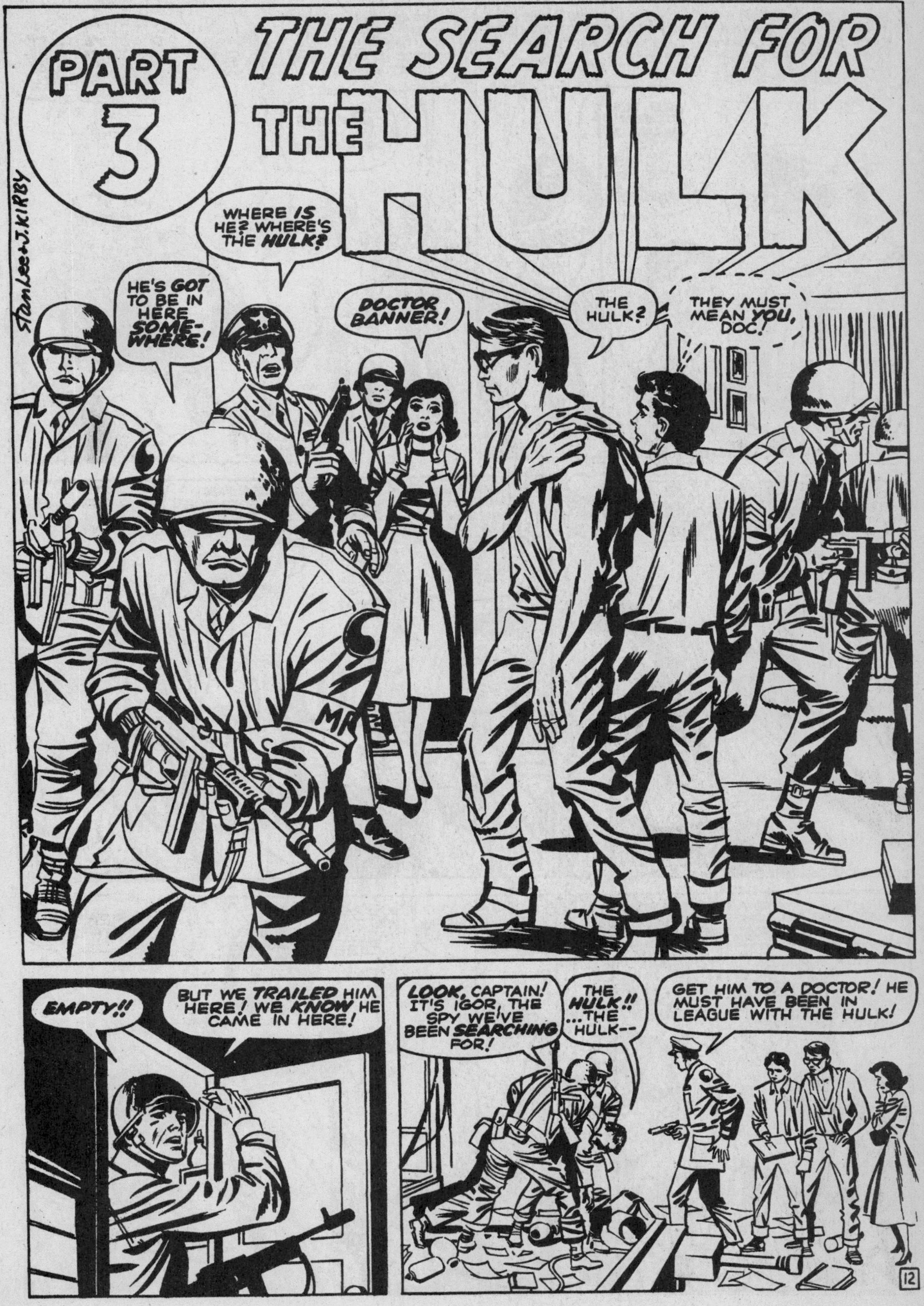

PART 3
THE SEARCH FOR THE HULK
Stan Lee + J. Kirby
WHERE IS HE? WHERE'S THE HULK?
HE'S GOT TO BE IN HERE SOME-WHERE!
DOCTOR BANNER!
THE HULK?
THEY MUST MEAN YOU, DOC!
MP
EMPTY!!
BUT WE TRAILED HIM HERE! WE KNOW HE CAME IN HERE!
LOOK, CAPTAIN! IT'S IGOR, THE SPY WE'VE BEEN SEARCHING FOR!
THE HULK!! ...THE HULK--
GET HIM TO A DOCTOR! HE MUST HAVE BEEN IN LEAGUE WITH THE HULK!
12

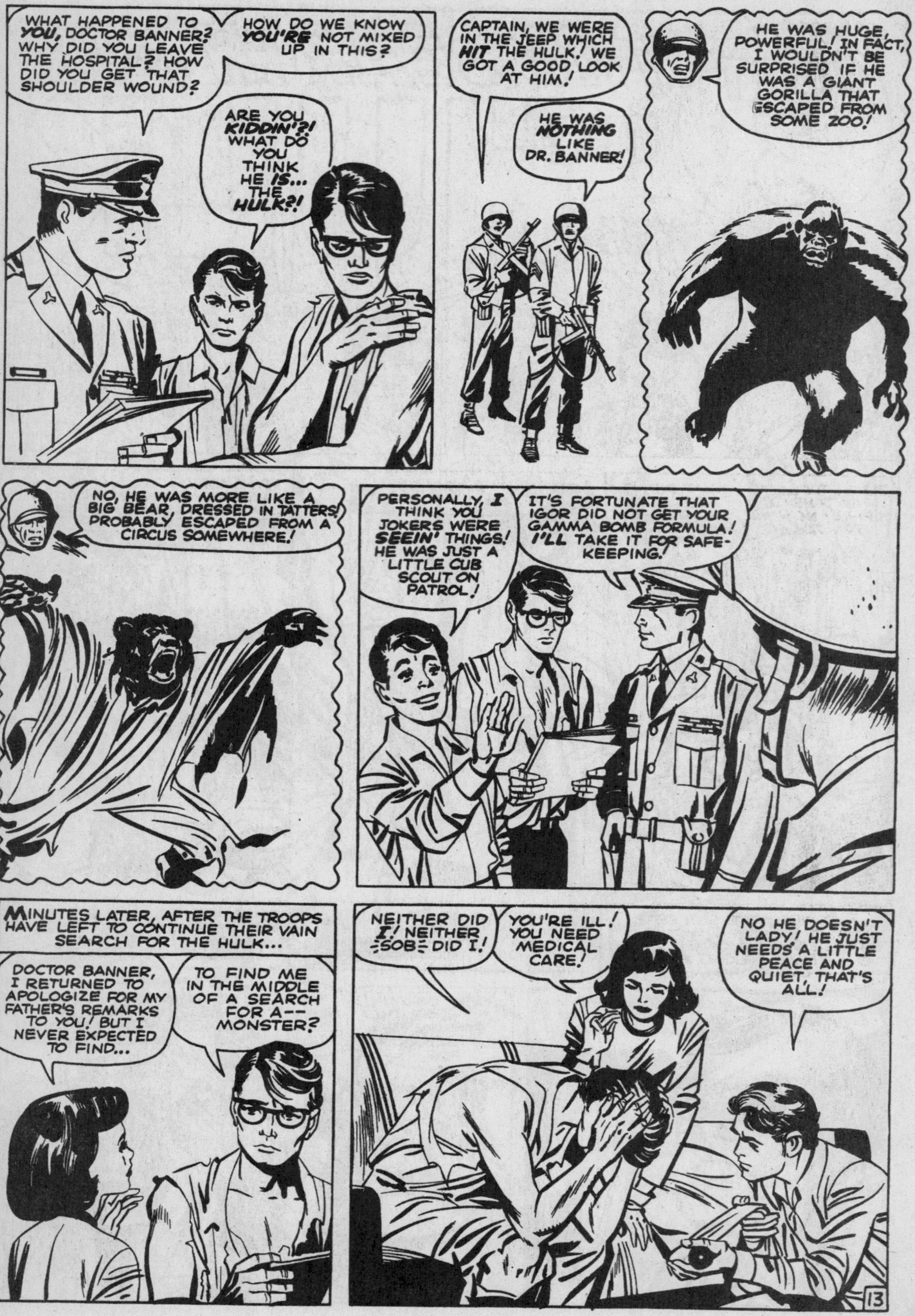
WHAT HAPPENED TO YOU, DOCTOR BANNER? WHY DID YOU LEAVE THE HOSPITAL? HOW DID YOU GET THAT SHOULDER WOUND?
HOW DO WE KNOW YOU'RE NOT MIXED UP IN THIS?
ARE YOU KIDDIN'?! WHAT DO YOU THINK HE IS... THE HULK?!
CAPTAIN, WE WERE IN THE JEEP WHICH HIT THE HULK! WE GOT A GOOD LOOK AT HIM!
HE WAS NOTHING LIKE DR. BANNER!
HE WAS HUGE, POWERFUL! IN FACT, I WOULDN'T BE SURPRISED IF HE WAS A GIANT GORILLA THAT ESCAPED FROM SOME ZOO!
NO, HE WAS MORE LIKE A BIG BEAR, DRESSED IN TATTERS! PROBABLY ESCAPED FROM A CIRCUS SOMEWHERE!
PERSONALLY, I THINK YOU JOKERS WERE SEEIN' THINGS! HE WAS JUST A LITTLE CUB SCOUT ON PATROL!
IT'S FORTUNATE THAT IGOR DID NOT GET YOUR GAMMA BOMB FORMULA! I'LL TAKE IT FOR SAFE-KEEPING!
MINUTES LATER, AFTER THE TROOPS HAVE LEFT TO CONTINUE THEIR VAIN SEARCH FOR THE HULK...
DOCTOR BANNER, I RETURNED TO APOLOGIZE FOR MY FATHER'S REMARKS TO YOU! BUT I NEVER EXPECTED TO FIND...
TO FIND ME IN THE MIDDLE OF A SEARCH FOR A-- MONSTER?
NEITHER DID I! NEITHER, -SOB- DID I!
YOU'RE ILL! YOU NEED MEDICAL CARE!
NO HE DOESN'T LADY! HE JUST NEEDS A LITTLE PEACE AND QUIET, THAT'S ALL!
13

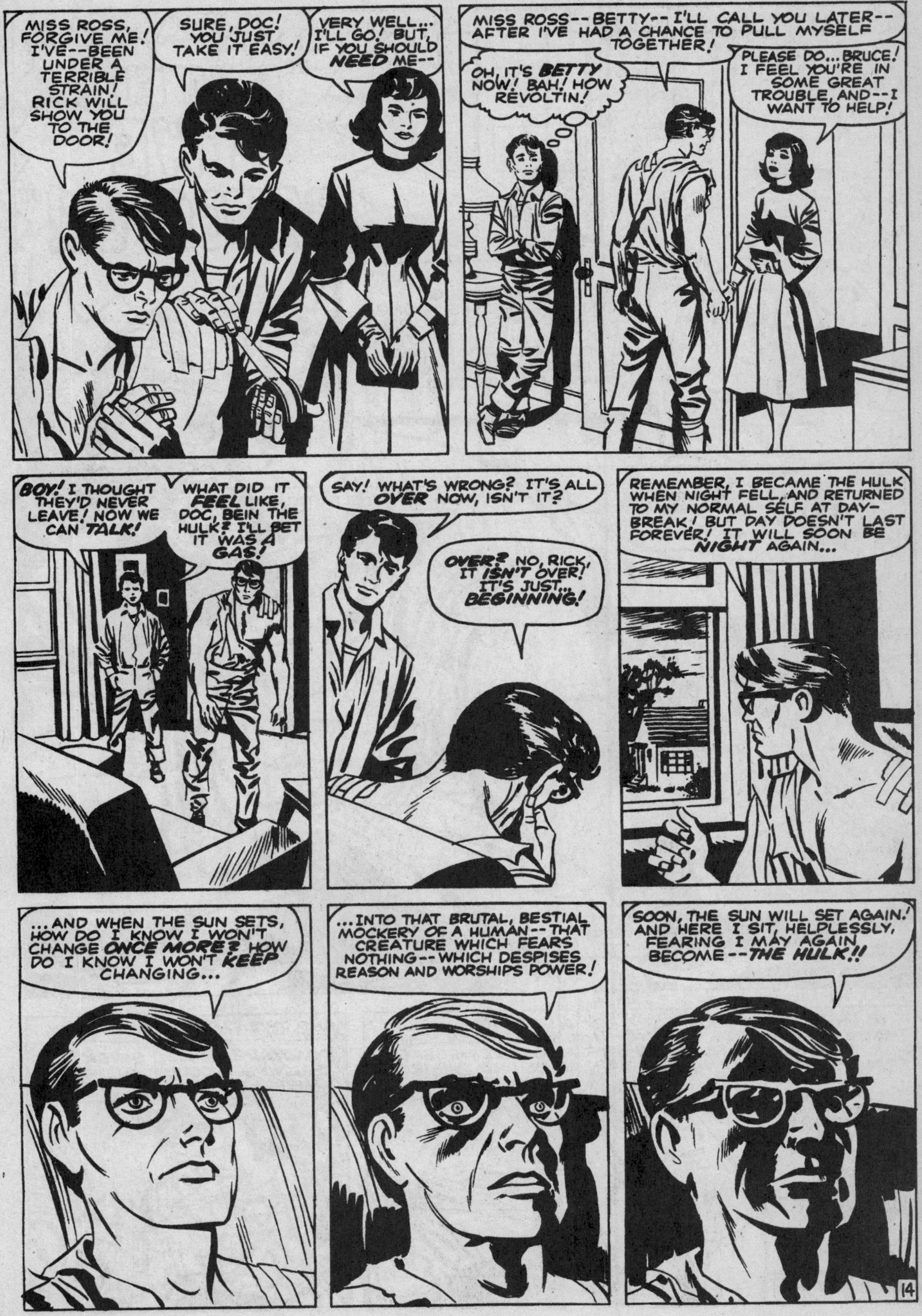
MISS ROSS, FORGIVE ME! I'VE--BEEN UNDER A TERRIBLE STRAIN! RICK WILL SHOW YOU TO THE DOOR!
SURE, DOC! YOU JUST TAKE IT EASY!
VERY WELL... I'LL GO! BUT, IF YOU SHOULD NEED ME--
MISS ROSS--BETTY--I'LL CALL YOU LATER--AFTER I'VE HAD A CHANCE TO PULL MYSELF TOGETHER!
OH, IT'S BETTY NOW! BAH! HOW REVOLTIN!
PLEASE DO... BRUCE! I FEEL YOU'RE IN SOME GREAT TROUBLE, AND--I WANT TO HELP!
BOY! I THOUGHT THEY'D NEVER LEAVE! NOW WE CAN TALK!
WHAT DID IT FEEL LIKE, DOC, BEIN THE HULK? I'LL BET IT WAS A GAS!
SAY! WHAT'S WRONG? IT'S ALL OVER NOW, ISN'T IT?
OVER? NO, RICK, IT ISN'T OVER! IT'S JUST... BEGINNING!
REMEMBER, I BECAME THE HULK WHEN NIGHT FELL, AND RETURNED TO MY NORMAL SELF AT DAY-BREAK! BUT DAY DOESN'T LAST FOREVER! IT WILL SOON BE NIGHT AGAIN...
...AND WHEN THE SUN SETS, HOW DO I KNOW I WON'T CHANGE ONCE MORE? HOW DO I KNOW I WON'T KEEP CHANGING...
...INTO THAT BRUTAL, BESTIAL MOCKERY OF A HUMAN--THAT CREATURE WHICH FEARS NOTHING--WHICH DESPISES REASON AND WORSHIPS POWER!
SOON, THE SUN WILL SET AGAIN! AND HERE I SIT, HELPLESSLY, FEARING I MAY AGAIN BECOME--THE HULK!!
14

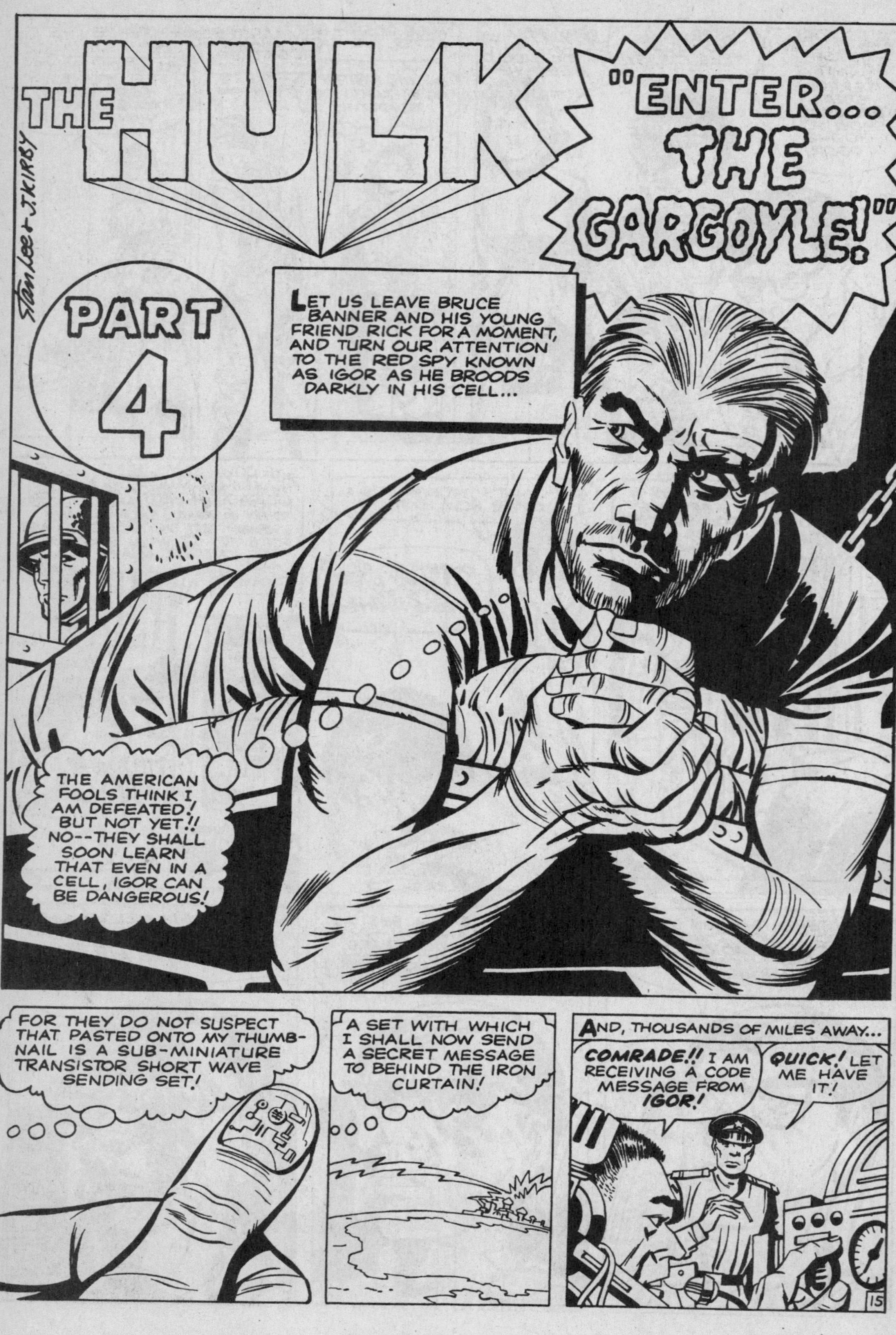
THE HULK
"ENTER... THE GARGOYLE!"
STAN LEE + J. KIRBY
PART 4
LET US LEAVE BRUCE BANNER AND HIS YOUNG FRIEND RICK FOR A MOMENT, AND TURN OUR ATTENTION TO THE RED SPY KNOWN AS IGOR AS HE BROODS DARKLY IN HIS CELL...
THE AMERICAN FOOLS THINK I AM DEFEATED! BUT NOT YET!! NO--THEY SHALL SOON LEARN THAT EVEN IN A CELL, IGOR CAN BE DANGEROUS!
FOR THEY DO NOT SUSPECT THAT PASTED ONTO MY THUMB-NAIL IS A SUB-MINIATURE TRANSISTOR SHORT WAVE SENDING SET!
A SET WITH WHICH I SHALL NOW SEND A SECRET MESSAGE TO BEHIND THE IRON CURTAIN!
AND, THOUSANDS OF MILES AWAY...
COMRADE!! I AM RECEIVING A CODE MESSAGE FROM IGOR!
QUICK! LET ME HAVE IT!
15

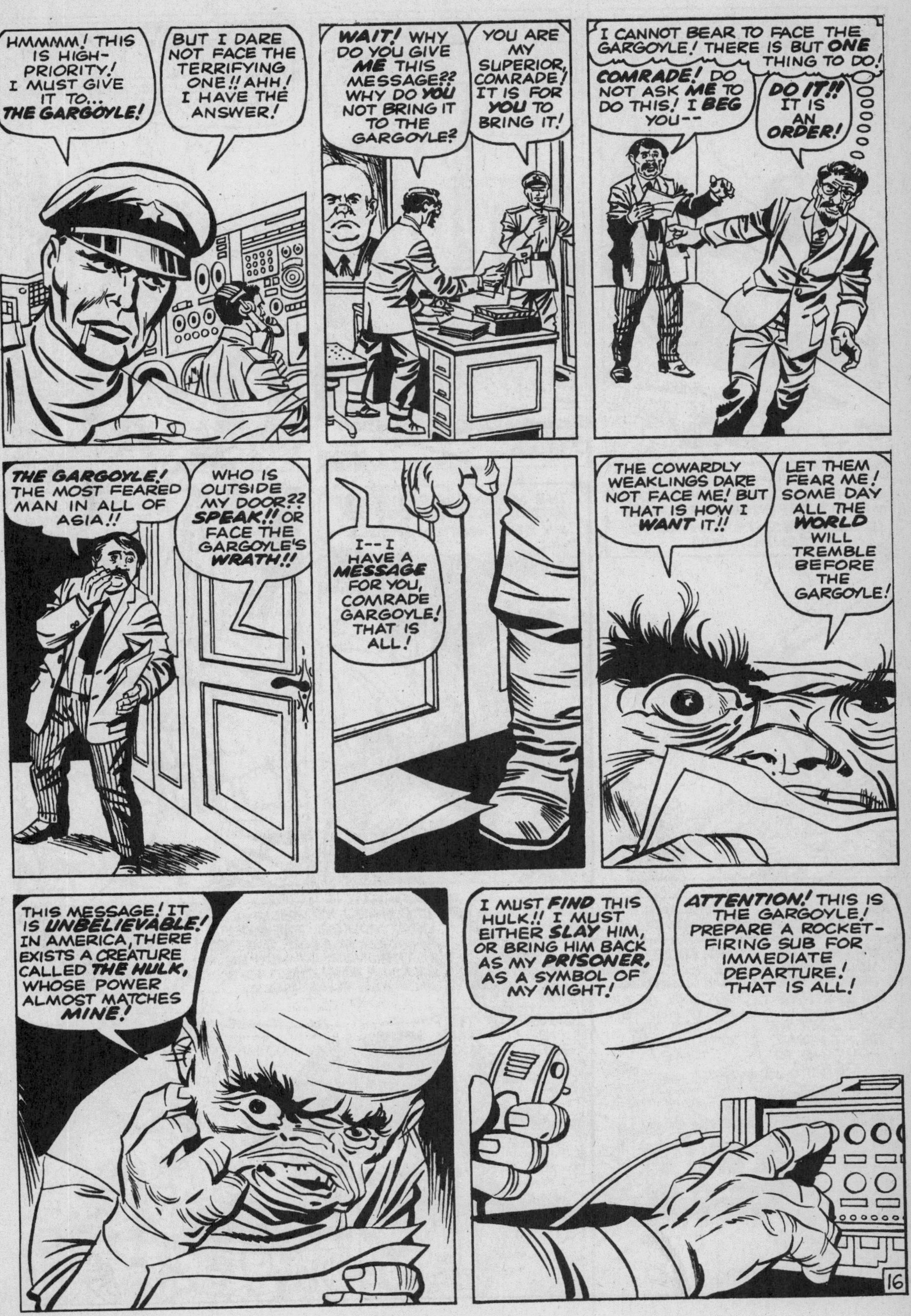
HMMMM! THIS IS HIGH-PRIORITY! I MUST GIVE IT TO... THE GARGOYLE!
BUT I DARE NOT FACE THE TERRIFYING ONE!! AHH! I HAVE THE ANSWER!
WAIT! WHY DO YOU GIVE ME THIS MESSAGE?? WHY DO YOU NOT BRING IT TO THE GARGOYLE?
YOU ARE MY SUPERIOR, COMRADE! IT IS FOR YOU TO BRING IT!
I CANNOT BEAR TO FACE THE GARGOYLE! THERE IS BUT ONE THING TO DO!
COMRADE! DO NOT ASK ME TO DO THIS! I BEG YOU--
DO IT!! IT IS AN ORDER!
THE GARGOYLE! THE MOST FEARED MAN IN ALL OF ASIA!!
WHO IS OUTSIDE MY DOOR?? SPEAK!! OR FACE THE GARGOYLE'S WRATH!!
I--I HAVE A MESSAGE FOR YOU, COMRADE GARGOYLE! THAT IS ALL!
THE COWARDLY WEAKLINGS DARE NOT FACE ME! BUT THAT IS HOW I WANT IT!!
LET THEM FEAR ME! SOME DAY ALL THE WORLD WILL TREMBLE BEFORE THE GARGOYLE!
THIS MESSAGE! IT IS UNBELIEVABLE! IN AMERICA, THERE EXISTS A CREATURE CALLED THE HULK, WHOSE POWER ALMOST MATCHES MINE!
I MUST FIND THIS HULK!! I MUST EITHER SLAY HIM, OR BRING HIM BACK AS MY PRISONER, AS A SYMBOL OF MY MIGHT!
ATTENTION! THIS IS THE GARGOYLE! PREPARE A ROCKET-FIRING SUB FOR IMMEDIATE DEPARTURE! THAT IS ALL!
16

BRIEF HOURS LATER, THE VERY LATEST MODEL RED SUB CUTS THRU THE MURKY DEPTHS OF THE SEA...

UNTIL, REACHING A PRE-ARRANGED AREA, IT UN-LEASHES AN EXPERIMENTAL MAN-CARRYING ROCKET!

WHAT'S THAT?? OUR RADAR HAS TRACKED AN UNIDENTIFIED MISSILE HEADING THIS WAY??!

UNLEASH OUR *HUNTER MISSILES!*

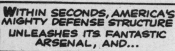

WITHIN SECONDS, AMERICA'S MIGHTY DEFENSE STRUCTURE UNLEASHES ITS FANTASTIC ARSENAL, AND...

THE MISSILE IS DESTROYED! BUT I HAVE LANDED AT MY DESTINATION SAFELY!

AND NOW... IT IS TIME FOR *THE GARGOYLE* TO MEET... *THE HULK!*

AND SO, FATE TWISTS THE THREADS OF OUR TALE TIGHTER AND TIGHTER, UNTIL...

WHERE ARE YOU GOING, DOC? IT'LL BE *EVENING* SOON! SHOULDN'T WE BE AT HOME, WAITING TO SEE--?

NO, RICK! IF I AM DESTINED TO BECOME THAT INHUMAN CREATURE AGAIN, LET IT HAPPEN OUT IN THE OPEN THIS TIME!

IT'S HARD TO BELIEVE, DOC! YOU'RE THE MOST FAMOUS MISSILE EXPERT IN THE WORLD! YOU'RE BRAINY AND CULTURED, AND ALL THAT JAZZ! AND YET...

AND YET, DUE TO THE FORCES UN-LEASHED BY THE GAMMA RAY, I TURN INTO A MARAUDING, SAVAGE BRUTE AT NIGHTFALL!

17

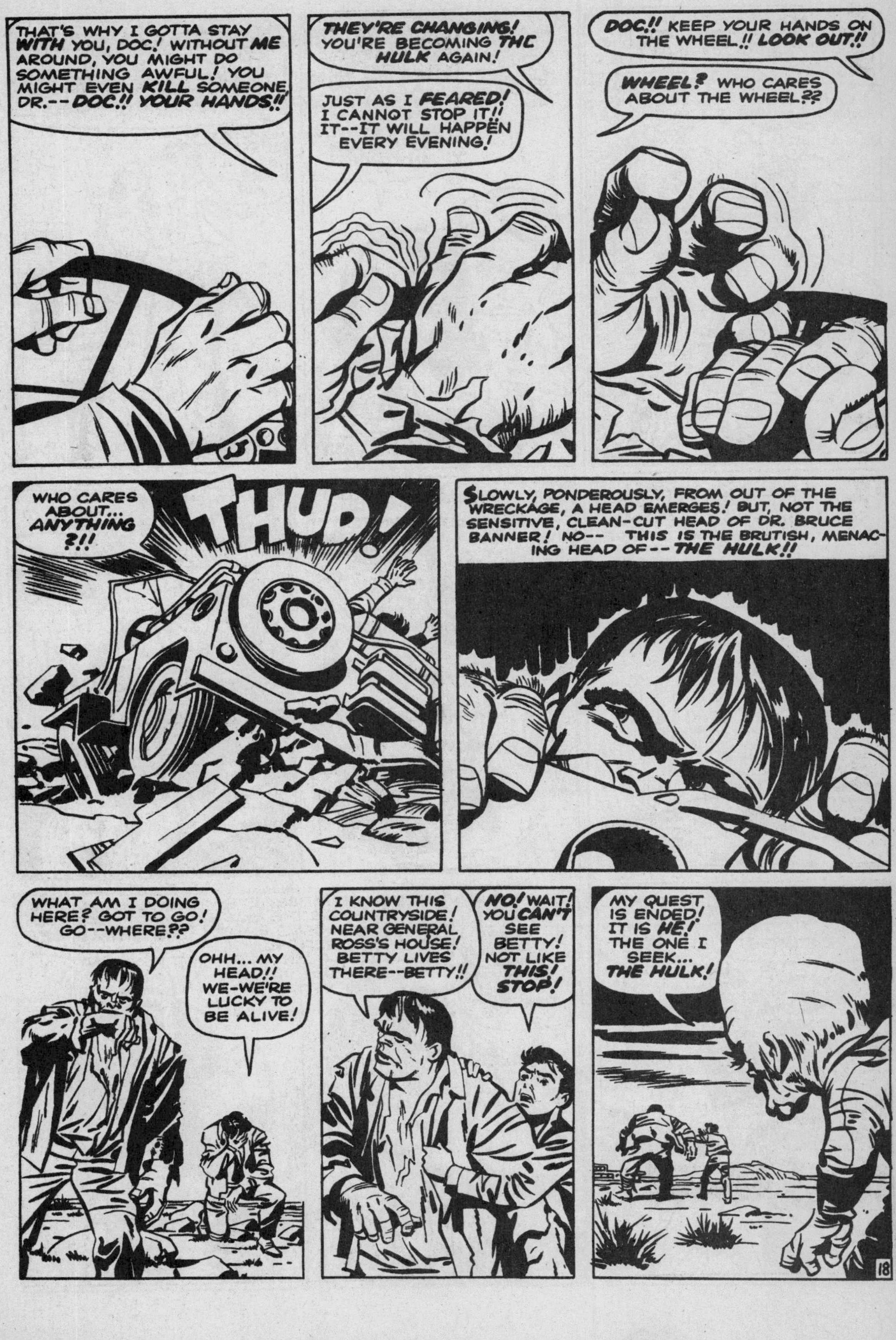
THAT'S WHY I GOTTA STAY WITH YOU, DOC! WITHOUT ME AROUND, YOU MIGHT DO SOMETHING AWFUL! YOU MIGHT EVEN KILL SOMEONE DR.--DOC!! YOUR HANDS!!
THEY'RE CHANGING! YOU'RE BECOMING THE HULK AGAIN!
JUST AS I FEARED! I CANNOT STOP IT!! IT--IT WILL HAPPEN EVERY EVENING!
DOC!! KEEP YOUR HANDS ON THE WHEEL!! LOOK OUT!!
WHEEL?? WHO CARES ABOUT THE WHEEL??
WHO CARES ABOUT... ANYTHING ?!!
THUD!
SLOWLY, PONDEROUSLY, FROM OUT OF THE WRECKAGE, A HEAD EMERGES! BUT, NOT THE SENSITIVE, CLEAN-CUT HEAD OF DR. BRUCE BANNER! NO-- THIS IS THE BRUTISH, MENACING HEAD OF--THE HULK!!
WHAT AM I DOING HERE? GOT TO GO! GO--WHERE??
OHH... MY HEAD!! WE-WE'RE LUCKY TO BE ALIVE!
I KNOW THIS COUNTRYSIDE! NEAR GENERAL ROSS'S HOUSE! BETTY LIVES THERE--BETTY!!
NO! WAIT! YOU CAN'T SEE BETTY! NOT LIKE THIS! STOP!
MY QUEST IS ENDED! IT IS HE! THE ONE I SEEK... THE HULK!
18

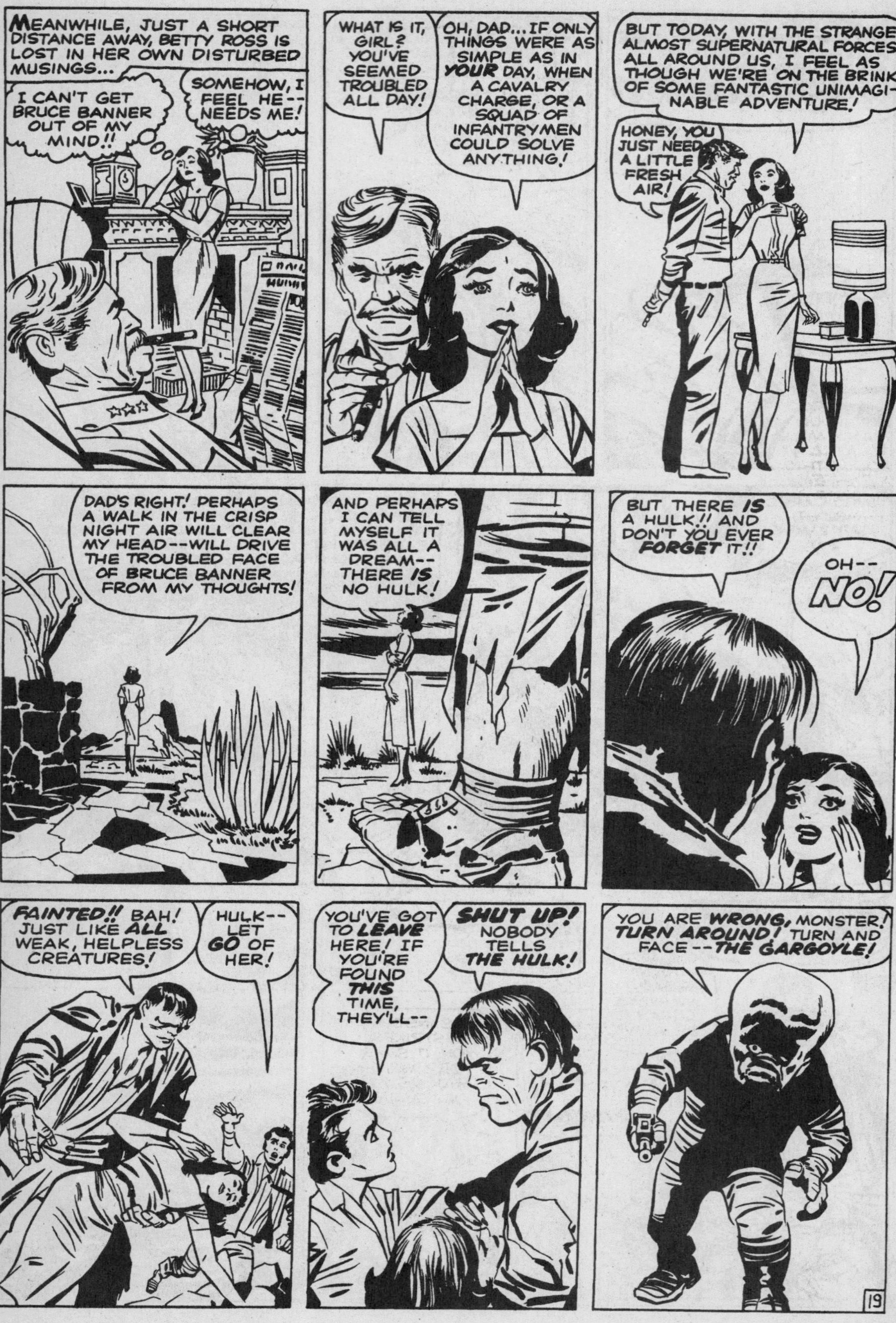
MEANWHILE, JUST A SHORT DISTANCE AWAY, BETTY ROSS IS LOST IN HER OWN DISTURBED MUSINGS...
I CAN'T GET BRUCE BANNER OUT OF MY MIND!!
SOMEHOW, I FEEL HE-- NEEDS ME!
WHAT IS IT, GIRL? YOU'VE SEEMED TROUBLED ALL DAY!
OH, DAD... IF ONLY THINGS WERE AS SIMPLE AS IN YOUR DAY, WHEN A CAVALRY CHARGE, OR A SQUAD OF INFANTRYMEN COULD SOLVE ANYTHING!
BUT TODAY, WITH THE STRANGE, ALMOST SUPERNATURAL FORCES ALL AROUND US, I FEEL AS THOUGH WE'RE ON THE BRINK OF SOME FANTASTIC UNIMAGI-NABLE ADVENTURE!
HONEY, YOU JUST NEED A LITTLE FRESH AIR!
DAD'S RIGHT! PERHAPS A WALK IN THE CRISP NIGHT AIR WILL CLEAR MY HEAD--WILL DRIVE THE TROUBLED FACE OF BRUCE BANNER FROM MY THOUGHTS!
AND PERHAPS I CAN TELL MYSELF IT WAS ALL A DREAM-- THERE IS NO HULK!
BUT THERE IS A HULK!! AND DON'T YOU EVER FORGET IT!!
OH-- NO!
FAINTED!! BAH! JUST LIKE ALL WEAK, HELPLESS CREATURES!
HULK-- LET GO OF HER!
YOU'VE GOT TO LEAVE HERE! IF YOU'RE FOUND THIS TIME, THEY'LL--
SHUT UP! NOBODY TELLS THE HULK!
YOU ARE WRONG, MONSTER! TURN AROUND! TURN AND FACE --THE GARGOYLE!

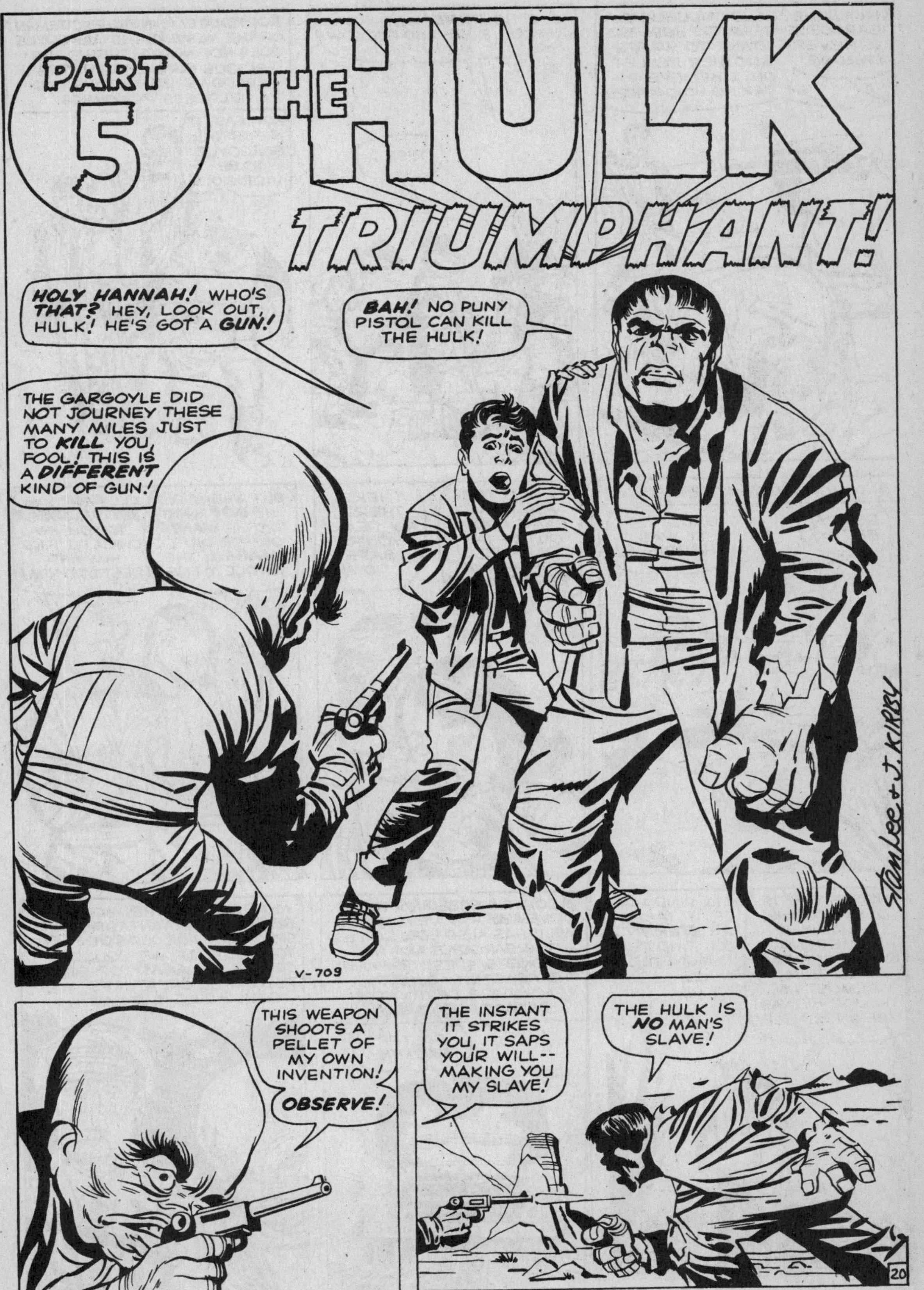
PART 5
THE HULK TRIUMPHANT!
HOLY HANNAH! WHO'S THAT? HEY, LOOK OUT, HULK! HE'S GOT A GUN!
BAH! NO PUNY PISTOL CAN KILL THE HULK!
THE GARGOYLE DID NOT JOURNEY THESE MANY MILES JUST TO KILL YOU, FOOL! THIS IS A DIFFERENT KIND OF GUN!
Stan Lee + J. Kirby
V-709
THIS WEAPON SHOOTS A PELLET OF MY OWN INVENTION! OBSERVE!
THE INSTANT IT STRIKES YOU, IT SAPS YOUR WILL-- MAKING YOU MY SLAVE!
THE HULK IS NO MAN'S SLAVE!
20

HAH! THE GARGOYLE IS NEVER WRONG! AND THOUGH *YOU* SEEM TOO UNIMPORTANT TO WASTE ANOTHER PELLET ON, I BELIEVE IN TAKING NO CHANCES!

IT IS *DONE!* BOTH OF YOU... RISE, AND FOLLOW ME!

RISE...

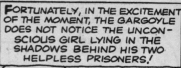

FORTUNATELY, IN THE EXCITEMENT OF THE MOMENT, THE GARGOYLE DOES NOT NOTICE THE UNCONSCIOUS GIRL LYING IN THE SHADOWS BEHIND HIS TWO HELPLESS PRISONERS!

HOW EASY IT IS FOR THE GARGOYLE TO BE VICTORIOUS!

AND MOMENTS LATER...

BETTY! BETTY!

DAD... IT-- IT WAS HORRIBLE!

IT WAS *THE HULK!* HE CAME FROM OUT OF THE DARKNESS! HE--HE WAS *TERRIFYING!*

THERE, THERE, MY DEAR! YOU'RE *SAFE* NOW!

BUT WHERE DID HE *GO?* WHAT DID HE *WANT?* OR--OR DID I *IMAGINE* THE WHOLE THING?

I'LL *FIND* HIM, BETTY! I *SWEAR* TO YOU, MY CHILD, I'LL FIND HIM AND DESTROY HIM!

AND YET, IN SPITE OF EVERYTHING, THERE WAS SOMETHING... SOMETHING *SAD* ABOUT HIM!! ALMOST AS THOUGH HE WAS SEEKING... HELP!

I'LL FIND HIM! IF IT TAKES AN *ETERNITY,* I'LL FIND THAT MONSTER!

AND, IN A SPEEDING TRUCK, DRIVEN BY A DRIVER WHOSE WILL HAS ALSO BEEN SAPPED, THE GARGOYLE AND HIS PRISONERS SPEED TOWARD THE COAST... RACING TO REACH THEIR DESTINATION BEFORE THE DAWN!

FASTER! *FASTER!*

WHAT A *PRIZE* THE HULK WILL BE!! WHAT A FANTASTIC SPECIMAN FOR OUR SCIENTISTS TO STUDY! IF WE COULD CREATE AN *ARMY* OF SUCH POWERFUL CREATURES, WE COULD RULE THE EARTH!

21

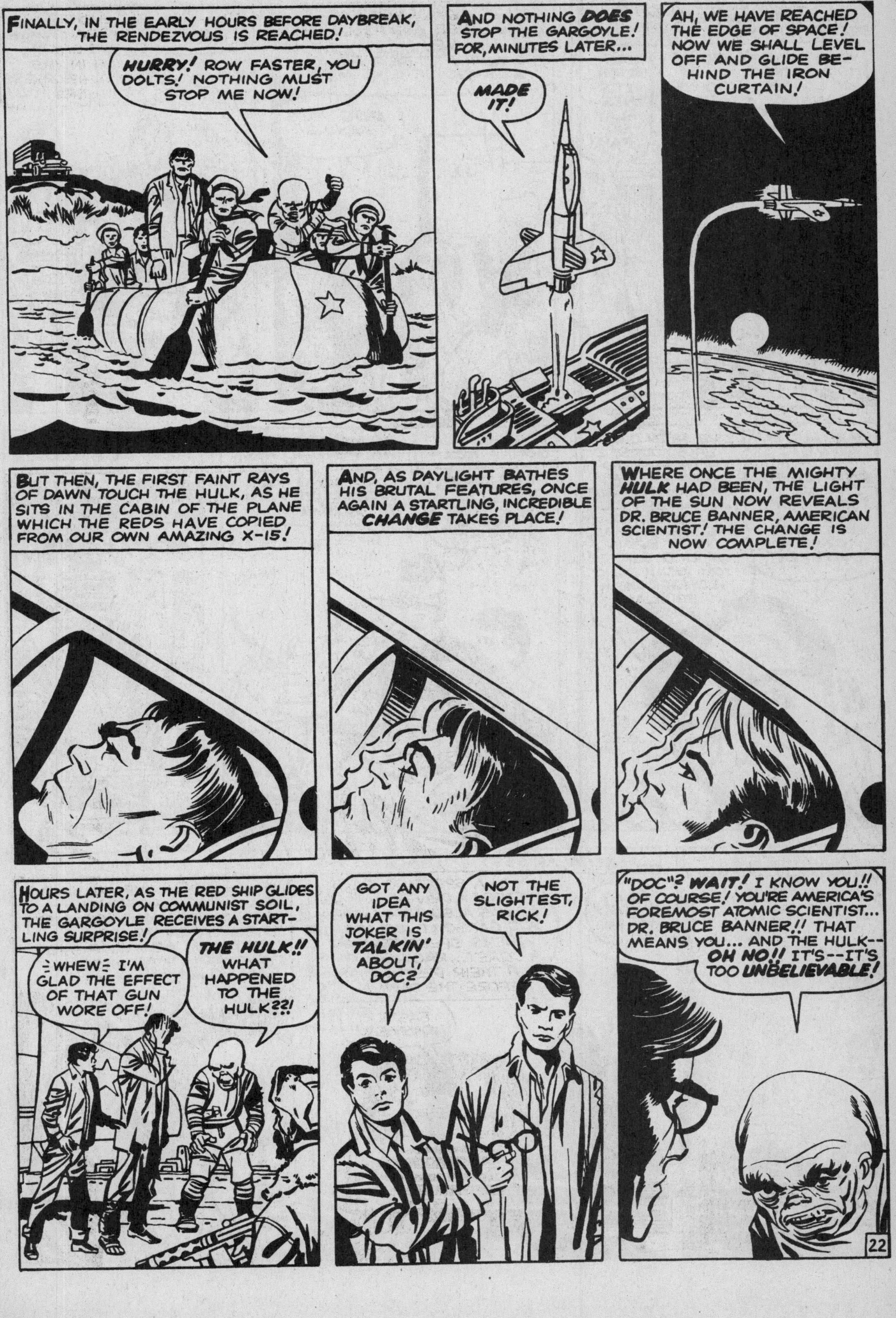
FINALLY, IN THE EARLY HOURS BEFORE DAYBREAK, THE RENDEZVOUS IS REACHED!
HURRY! ROW FASTER, YOU DOLTS! NOTHING MUST STOP ME NOW!
AND NOTHING DOES STOP THE GARGOYLE! FOR, MINUTES LATER...
MADE IT!
AH, WE HAVE REACHED THE EDGE OF SPACE! NOW WE SHALL LEVEL OFF AND GLIDE BEHIND THE IRON CURTAIN!
BUT THEN, THE FIRST FAINT RAYS OF DAWN TOUCH THE HULK, AS HE SITS IN THE CABIN OF THE PLANE WHICH THE REDS HAVE COPIED FROM OUR OWN AMAZING X-15!
AND, AS DAYLIGHT BATHES HIS BRUTAL FEATURES, ONCE AGAIN A STARTLING, INCREDIBLE CHANGE TAKES PLACE!
WHERE ONCE THE MIGHTY HULK HAD BEEN, THE LIGHT OF THE SUN NOW REVEALS DR. BRUCE BANNER, AMERICAN SCIENTIST! THE CHANGE IS NOW COMPLETE!
HOURS LATER, AS THE RED SHIP GLIDES TO A LANDING ON COMMUNIST SOIL, THE GARGOYLE RECEIVES A STARTLING SURPRISE!
WHEW I'M GLAD THE EFFECT OF THAT GUN WORE OFF!
THE HULK!! WHAT HAPPENED TO THE HULK??!
GOT ANY IDEA WHAT THIS JOKER IS TALKIN' ABOUT, DOC?
NOT THE SLIGHTEST, RICK!
"DOC"? WAIT! I KNOW YOU!! OF COURSE! YOU'RE AMERICA'S FOREMOST ATOMIC SCIENTIST... DR. BRUCE BANNER!! THAT MEANS YOU... AND THE HULK-- OH NO!! IT'S--IT'S TOO UNBELIEVABLE!

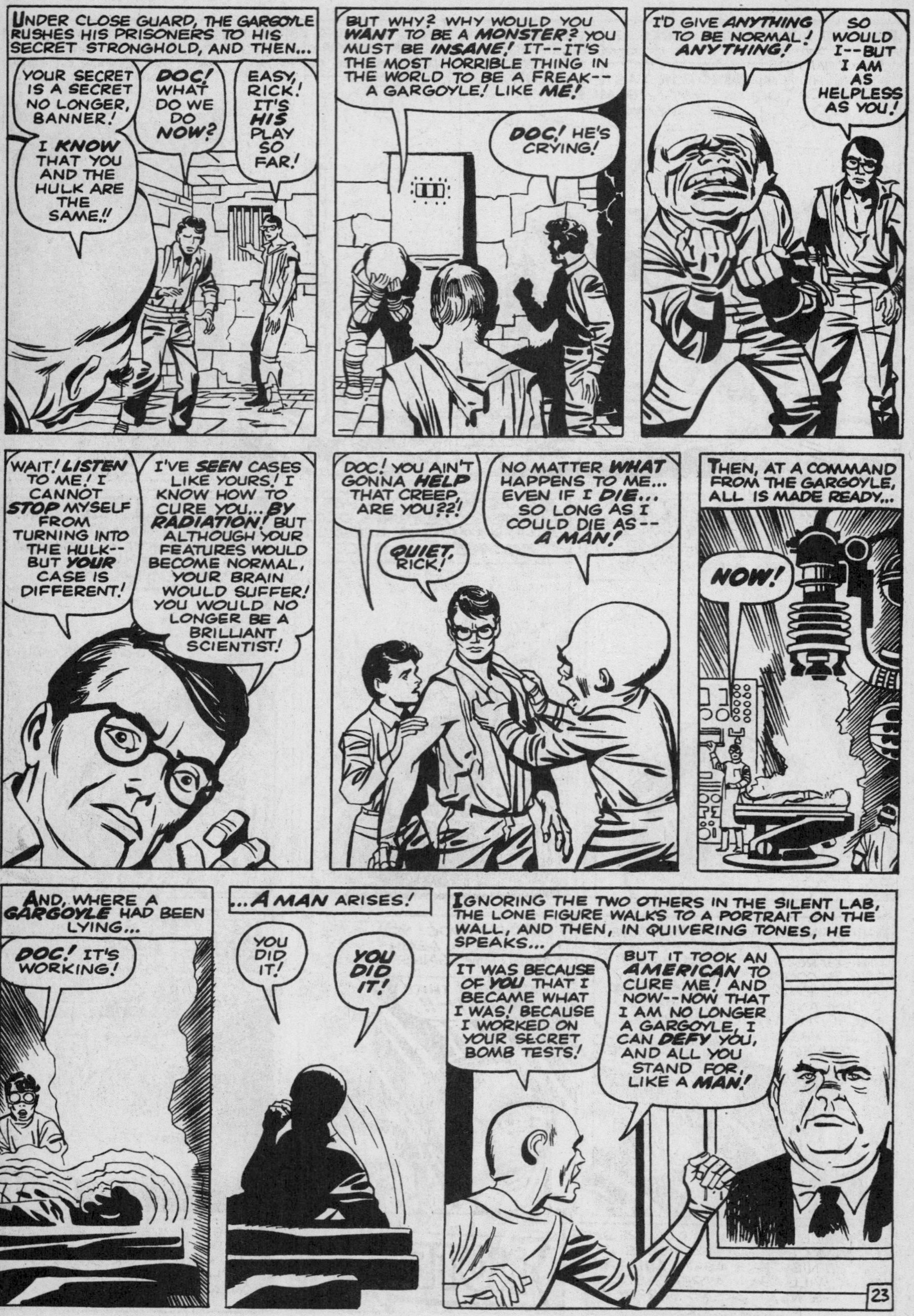
UNDER CLOSE GUARD, THE GARGOYLE RUSHES HIS PRISONERS TO HIS SECRET STRONGHOLD, AND THEN...
YOUR SECRET IS A SECRET NO LONGER, BANNER!
I KNOW THAT YOU AND THE HULK ARE THE SAME!!
DOC! WHAT DO WE DO NOW?
EASY, RICK! IT'S HIS PLAY SO FAR!
BUT WHY? WHY WOULD YOU WANT TO BE A MONSTER? YOU MUST BE INSANE! IT--IT'S THE MOST HORRIBLE THING IN THE WORLD TO BE A FREAK-- A GARGOYLE! LIKE ME!
DOC! HE'S CRYING!
I'D GIVE ANYTHING TO BE NORMAL! ANYTHING!
SO WOULD I--BUT I AM AS HELPLESS AS YOU!
WAIT! LISTEN TO ME! I CANNOT STOP MYSELF FROM TURNING INTO THE HULK-- BUT YOUR CASE IS DIFFERENT!
I'VE SEEN CASES LIKE YOURS! I KNOW HOW TO CURE YOU... BY RADIATION! BUT ALTHOUGH YOUR FEATURES WOULD BECOME NORMAL, YOUR BRAIN WOULD SUFFER! YOU WOULD NO LONGER BE A BRILLIANT SCIENTIST!
DOC! YOU AIN'T GONNA HELP THAT CREEP, ARE YOU??!
QUIET, RICK!
NO MATTER WHAT HAPPENS TO ME... EVEN IF I DIE... SO LONG AS I COULD DIE AS -- A MAN!
THEN, AT A COMMAND FROM THE GARGOYLE, ALL IS MADE READY...
NOW!
AND, WHERE A GARGOYLE HAD BEEN LYING...
DOC! IT'S WORKING!
...A MAN ARISES!
YOU DID IT!
YOU DID IT!
IGNORING THE TWO OTHERS IN THE SILENT LAB, THE LONE FIGURE WALKS TO A PORTRAIT ON THE WALL, AND THEN, IN QUIVERING TONES, HE SPEAKS...
IT WAS BECAUSE OF YOU THAT I BECAME WHAT I WAS! BECAUSE I WORKED ON YOUR SECRET BOMB TESTS!
BUT IT TOOK AN AMERICAN TO CURE ME! AND NOW--NOW THAT I AM NO LONGER A GARGOYLE, I CAN DEFY YOU, AND ALL YOU STAND FOR, LIKE A MAN!
23

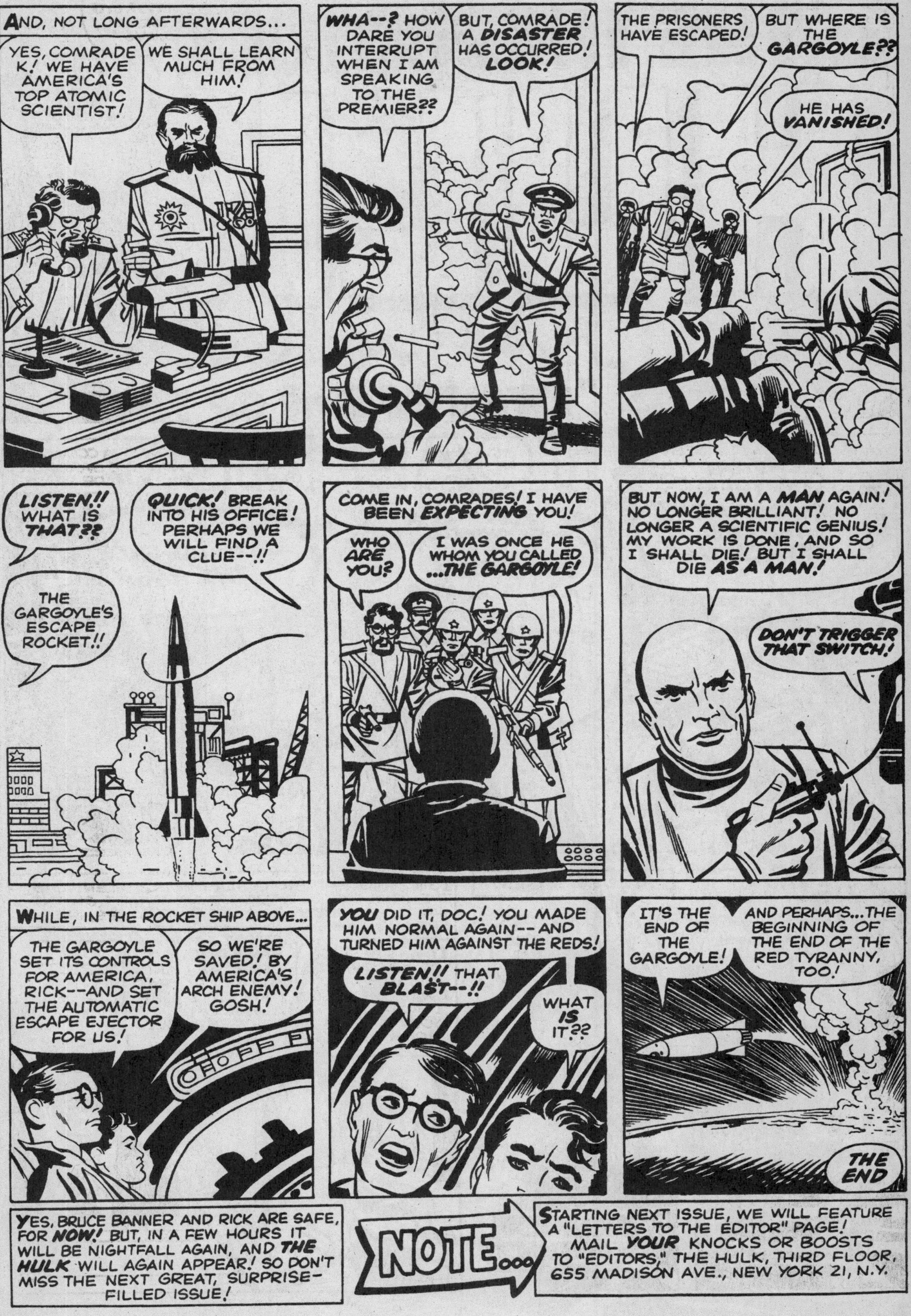
AND, NOT LONG AFTERWARDS...
YES, COMRADE K! WE HAVE AMERICA'S TOP ATOMIC SCIENTIST!
WE SHALL LEARN MUCH FROM HIM!
WHA--? HOW DARE YOU INTERRUPT WHEN I AM SPEAKING TO THE PREMIER??
BUT, COMRADE! A DISASTER HAS OCCURRED! LOOK!
THE PRISONERS HAVE ESCAPED!
BUT WHERE IS THE GARGOYLE??
HE HAS VANISHED!
LISTEN!! WHAT IS THAT??
QUICK! BREAK INTO HIS OFFICE! PERHAPS WE WILL FIND A CLUE--!!
THE GARGOYLE'S ESCAPE ROCKET!!
COME IN, COMRADES! I HAVE BEEN EXPECTING YOU!
WHO ARE YOU?
I WAS ONCE HE WHOM YOU CALLED ...THE GARGOYLE!
BUT NOW, I AM A MAN AGAIN! NO LONGER BRILLIANT! NO LONGER A SCIENTIFIC GENIUS! MY WORK IS DONE, AND SO I SHALL DIE! BUT I SHALL DIE AS A MAN!
DON'T TRIGGER THAT SWITCH!
WHILE, IN THE ROCKET SHIP ABOVE...
THE GARGOYLE SET ITS CONTROLS FOR AMERICA, RICK--AND SET THE AUTOMATIC ESCAPE EJECTOR FOR US!
SO WE'RE SAVED! BY AMERICA'S ARCH ENEMY! GOSH!
YOU DID IT, DOC! YOU MADE HIM NORMAL AGAIN-- AND TURNED HIM AGAINST THE REDS!
LISTEN!! THAT BLAST--!!
WHAT IS IT??
IT'S THE END OF THE GARGOYLE!
AND PERHAPS...THE BEGINNING OF THE END OF THE RED TYRANNY, TOO!
THE END
YES, BRUCE BANNER AND RICK ARE SAFE, FOR NOW! BUT, IN A FEW HOURS IT WILL BE NIGHTFALL AGAIN, AND THE HULK WILL AGAIN APPEAR! SO DON'T MISS THE NEXT GREAT, SURPRISE-FILLED ISSUE!
NOTE...
STARTING NEXT ISSUE, WE WILL FEATURE A "LETTERS TO THE EDITOR" PAGE! MAIL YOUR KNOCKS OR BOOSTS TO "EDITORS," THE HULK, THIRD FLOOR, 655 MADISON AVE., NEW YORK 21, N.Y.

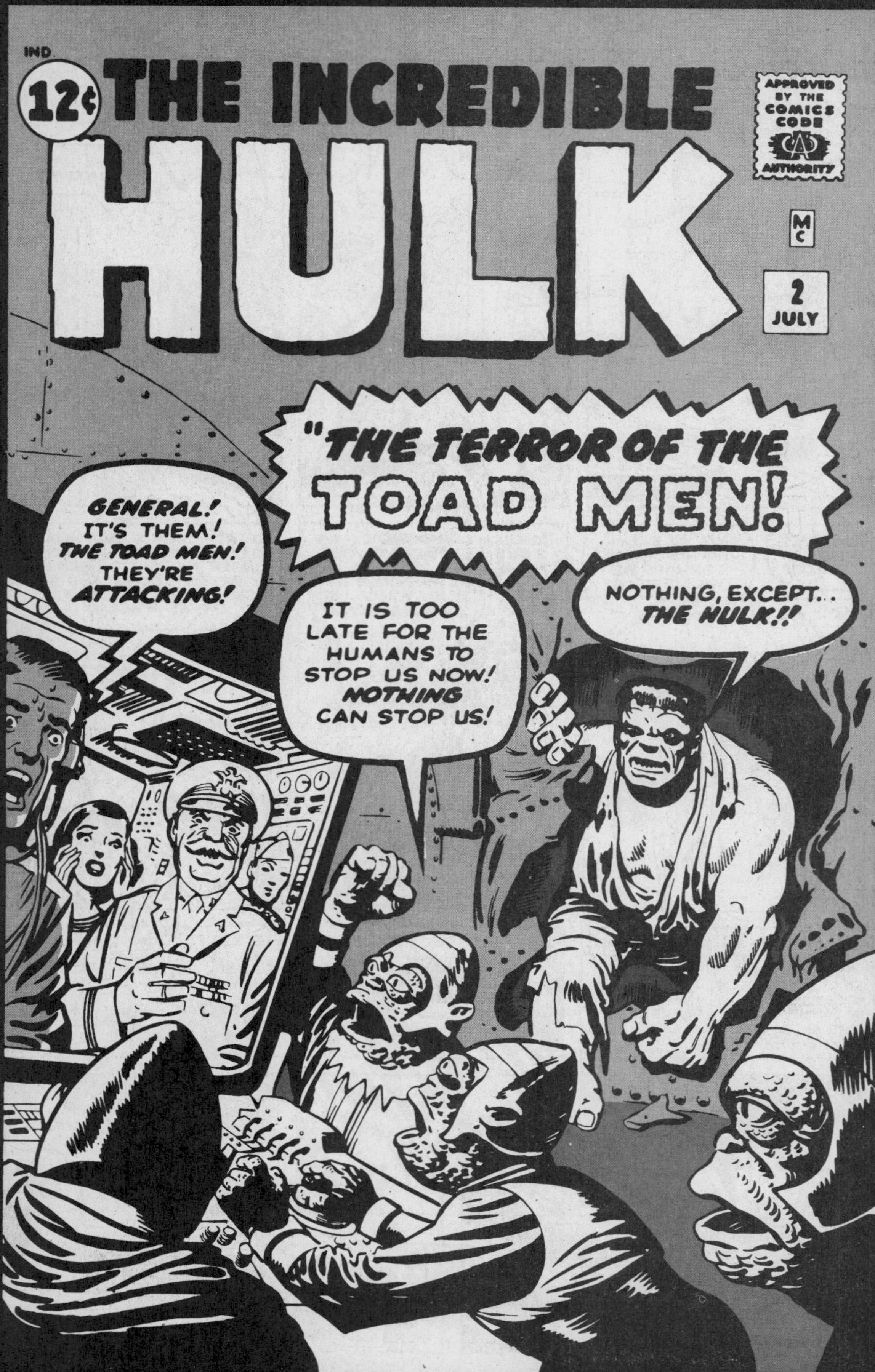
IND.
12¢
THE INCREDIBLE
HULK
APPROVED BY THE COMICS CODE AUTHORITY
MC
2
JULY
"THE TERROR OF THE TOAD MEN!
GENERAL! IT'S THEM! THE TOAD MEN! THEY'RE ATTACKING!
IT IS TOO LATE FOR THE HUMANS TO STOP US NOW! NOTHING CAN STOP US!
NOTHING, EXCEPT... THE HULK!!

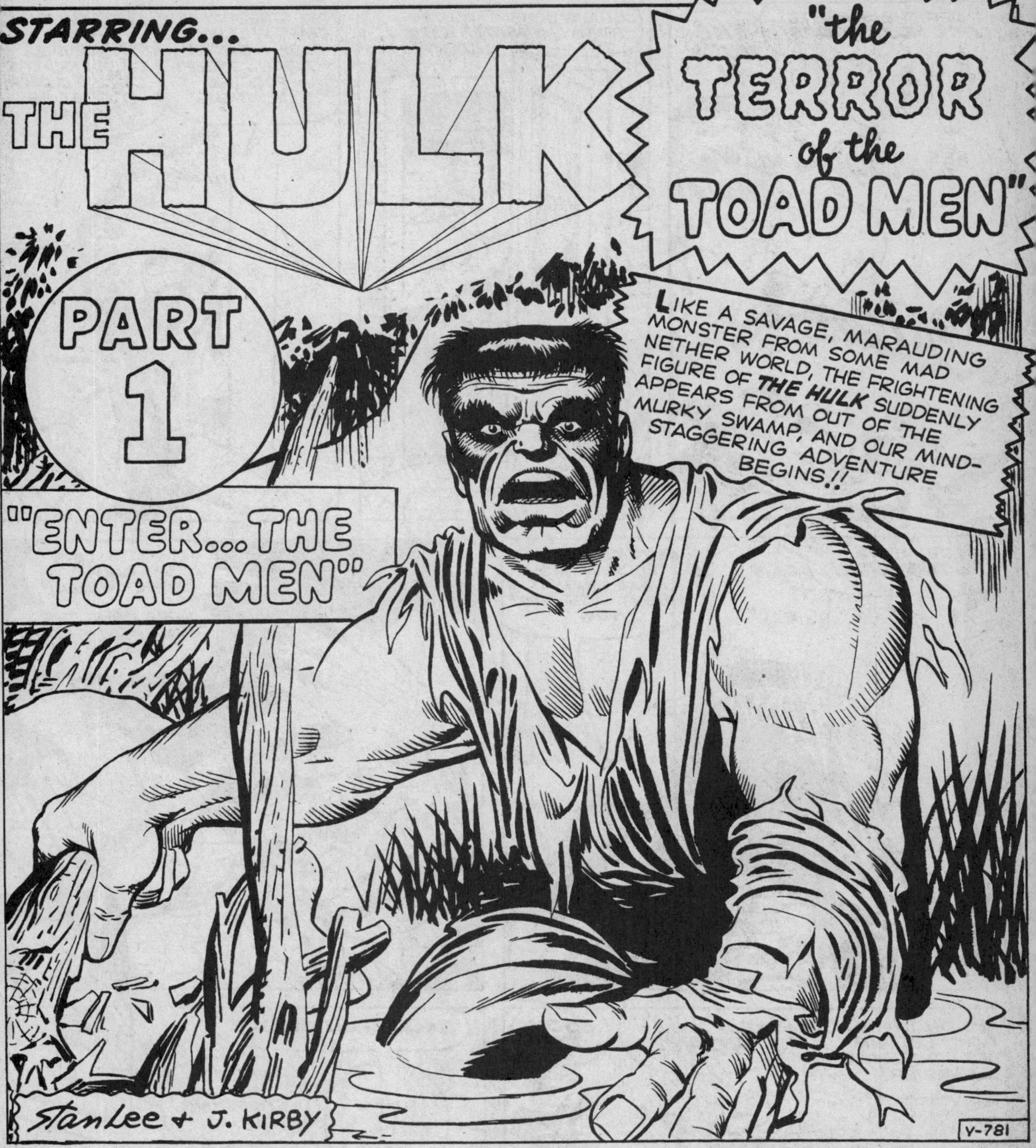
STARRING...
THE HULK
"the TERROR of the TOAD MEN"
PART 1
"ENTER... THE TOAD MEN"
LIKE A SAVAGE, MARAUDING MONSTER FROM SOME MAD NETHER WORLD, THE FRIGHTENING FIGURE OF THE HULK SUDDENLY APPEARS FROM OUT OF THE MURKY SWAMP, AND OUR MIND-STAGGERING ADVENTURE BEGINS!!
Stan Lee + J. KIRBY
V-781

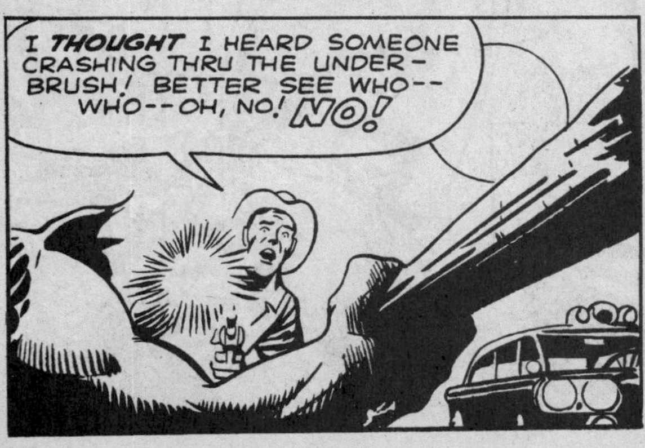
I THOUGHT I HEARD SOMEONE CRASHING THRU THE UNDER-BRUSH! BETTER SEE WHO-- WHO--OH, NO! NO!

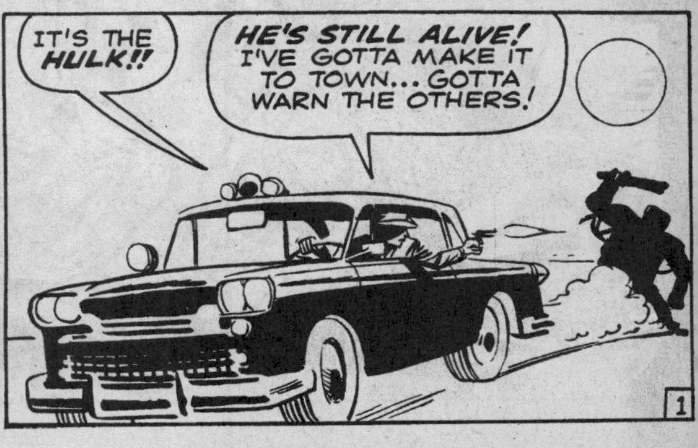
IT'S THE HULK!!
HE'S STILL ALIVE! I'VE GOTTA MAKE IT TO TOWN... GOTTA WARN THE OTHERS!

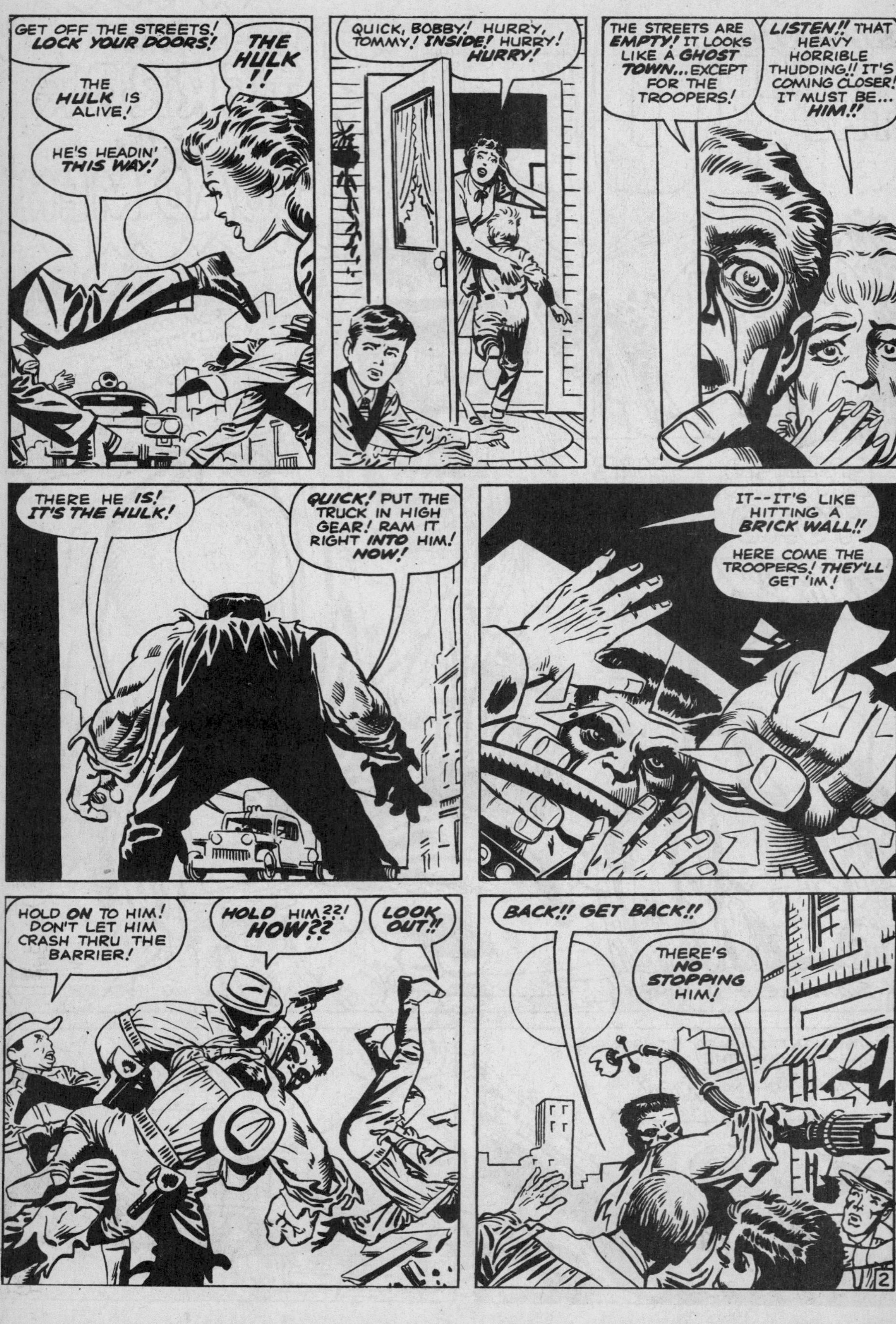
GET OFF THE STREETS! LOCK YOUR DOORS!
THE HULK!!
THE HULK IS ALIVE!
HE'S HEADIN' THIS WAY!
QUICK, BOBBY! HURRY, TOMMY! INSIDE! HURRY! HURRY!
THE STREETS ARE EMPTY! IT LOOKS LIKE A GHOST TOWN... EXCEPT FOR THE TROOPERS!
LISTEN!! THAT HEAVY HORRIBLE THUDDING!! IT'S COMING CLOSER! IT MUST BE... HIM!!
THERE HE IS! IT'S THE HULK!
QUICK! PUT THE TRUCK IN HIGH GEAR! RAM IT RIGHT INTO HIM! NOW!
IT--IT'S LIKE HITTING A BRICK WALL!!
HERE COME THE TROOPERS! THEY'LL GET 'IM!
HOLD ON TO HIM! DON'T LET HIM CRASH THRU THE BARRIER!
HOLD HIM??! HOW??
LOOK OUT!!
BACK!! GET BACK!!
THERE'S NO STOPPING HIM!
2

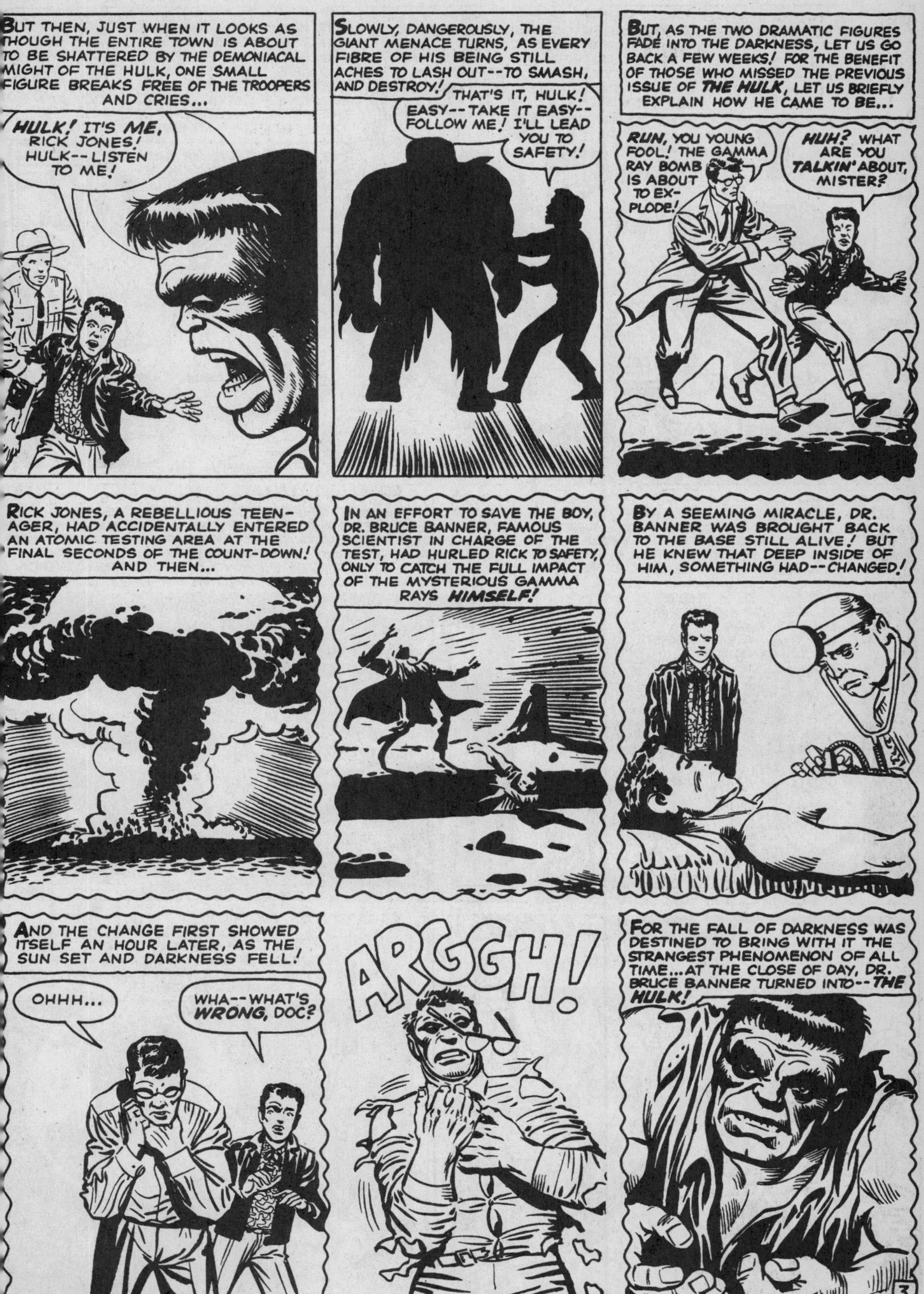
BUT THEN, JUST WHEN IT LOOKS AS THOUGH THE ENTIRE TOWN IS ABOUT TO BE SHATTERED BY THE DEMONIACAL MIGHT OF THE HULK, ONE SMALL FIGURE BREAKS FREE OF THE TROOPERS AND CRIES...
HULK! IT'S ME, RICK JONES! HULK-- LISTEN TO ME!
SLOWLY, DANGEROUSLY, THE GIANT MENACE TURNS, AS EVERY FIBRE OF HIS BEING STILL ACHES TO LASH OUT--TO SMASH, AND DESTROY!
THAT'S IT, HULK! EASY--TAKE IT EASY--FOLLOW ME! I'LL LEAD YOU TO SAFETY!
BUT, AS THE TWO DRAMATIC FIGURES FADE INTO THE DARKNESS, LET US GO BACK A FEW WEEKS! FOR THE BENEFIT OF THOSE WHO MISSED THE PREVIOUS ISSUE OF THE HULK, LET US BRIEFLY EXPLAIN HOW HE CAME TO BE...
RUN, YOU YOUNG FOOL! THE GAMMA RAY BOMB IS ABOUT TO EX-PLODE!
HUH? WHAT ARE YOU TALKIN' ABOUT, MISTER?
RICK JONES, A REBELLIOUS TEEN-AGER, HAD ACCIDENTALLY ENTERED AN ATOMIC TESTING AREA AT THE FINAL SECONDS OF THE COUNT-DOWN! AND THEN...
IN AN EFFORT TO SAVE THE BOY, DR. BRUCE BANNER, FAMOUS SCIENTIST IN CHARGE OF THE TEST, HAD HURLED RICK TO SAFETY, ONLY TO CATCH THE FULL IMPACT OF THE MYSTERIOUS GAMMA RAYS HIMSELF!
BY A SEEMING MIRACLE, DR. BANNER WAS BROUGHT BACK TO THE BASE STILL ALIVE! BUT HE KNEW THAT DEEP INSIDE OF HIM, SOMETHING HAD--CHANGED!
AND THE CHANGE FIRST SHOWED ITSELF AN HOUR LATER, AS THE SUN SET AND DARKNESS FELL!
OHHH...
WHA--WHAT'S WRONG, DOC?
ARGGH!
FOR THE FALL OF DARKNESS WAS DESTINED TO BRING WITH IT THE STRANGEST PHENOMENON OF ALL TIME...AT THE CLOSE OF DAY, DR. BRUCE BANNER TURNED INTO--THE HULK!
3

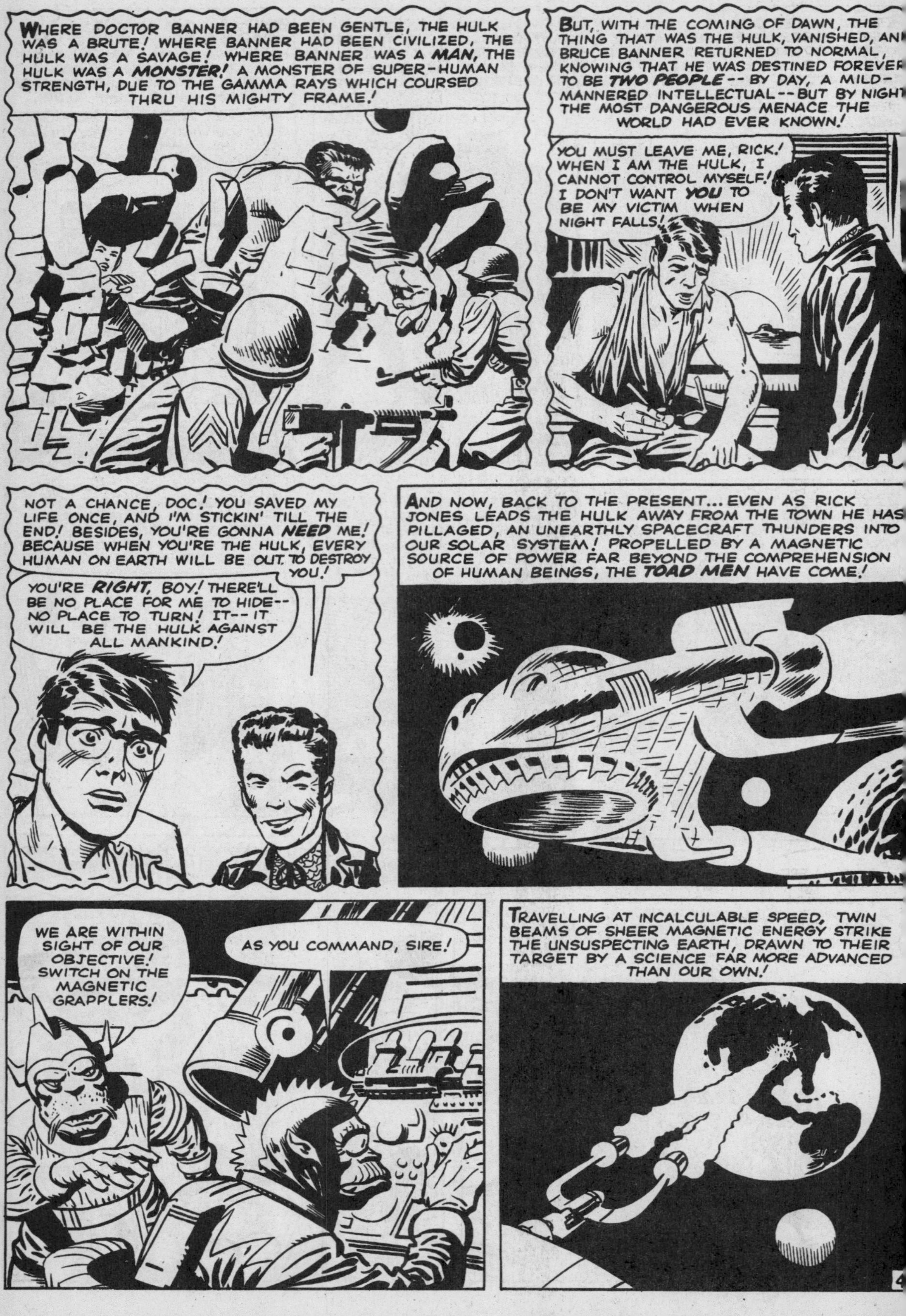
WHERE DOCTOR BANNER HAD BEEN GENTLE, THE HULK WAS A BRUTE! WHERE BANNER HAD BEEN CIVILIZED, THE HULK WAS A SAVAGE! WHERE BANNER WAS A MAN, THE HULK WAS A MONSTER! A MONSTER OF SUPER-HUMAN STRENGTH, DUE TO THE GAMMA RAYS WHICH COURSED THRU HIS MIGHTY FRAME!
BUT, WITH THE COMING OF DAWN, THE THING THAT WAS THE HULK, VANISHED, AN BRUCE BANNER RETURNED TO NORMAL, KNOWING THAT HE WAS DESTINED FOREVE TO BE TWO PEOPLE -- BY DAY, A MILD-MANNERED INTELLECTUAL -- BUT BY NIGH THE MOST DANGEROUS MENACE THE WORLD HAD EVER KNOWN!
YOU MUST LEAVE ME, RICK! WHEN I AM THE HULK, I CANNOT CONTROL MYSELF! I DON'T WANT YOU TO BE MY VICTIM WHEN NIGHT FALLS!
NOT A CHANCE, DOC! YOU SAVED MY LIFE ONCE, AND I'M STICKIN' TILL THE END! BESIDES, YOU'RE GONNA NEED ME! BECAUSE WHEN YOU'RE THE HULK, EVERY HUMAN ON EARTH WILL BE OUT TO DESTROY YOU!
YOU'RE RIGHT, BOY! THERE'LL BE NO PLACE FOR ME TO HIDE-- NO PLACE TO TURN! IT-- IT WILL BE THE HULK AGAINST ALL MANKIND!
AND NOW, BACK TO THE PRESENT... EVEN AS RICK JONES LEADS THE HULK AWAY FROM THE TOWN HE HAS PILLAGED, AN UNEARTHLY SPACECRAFT THUNDERS INTO OUR SOLAR SYSTEM! PROPELLED BY A MAGNETIC SOURCE OF POWER FAR BEYOND THE COMPREHENSION OF HUMAN BEINGS, THE TOAD MEN HAVE COME!
WE ARE WITHIN SIGHT OF OUR OBJECTIVE! SWITCH ON THE MAGNETIC GRAPPLERS!
AS YOU COMMAND, SIRE!
TRAVELLING AT INCALCULABLE SPEED, TWIN BEAMS OF SHEER MAGNETIC ENERGY STRIKE THE UNSUSPECTING EARTH, DRAWN TO THEIR TARGET BY A SCIENCE FAR MORE ADVANCED THAN OUR OWN!
4

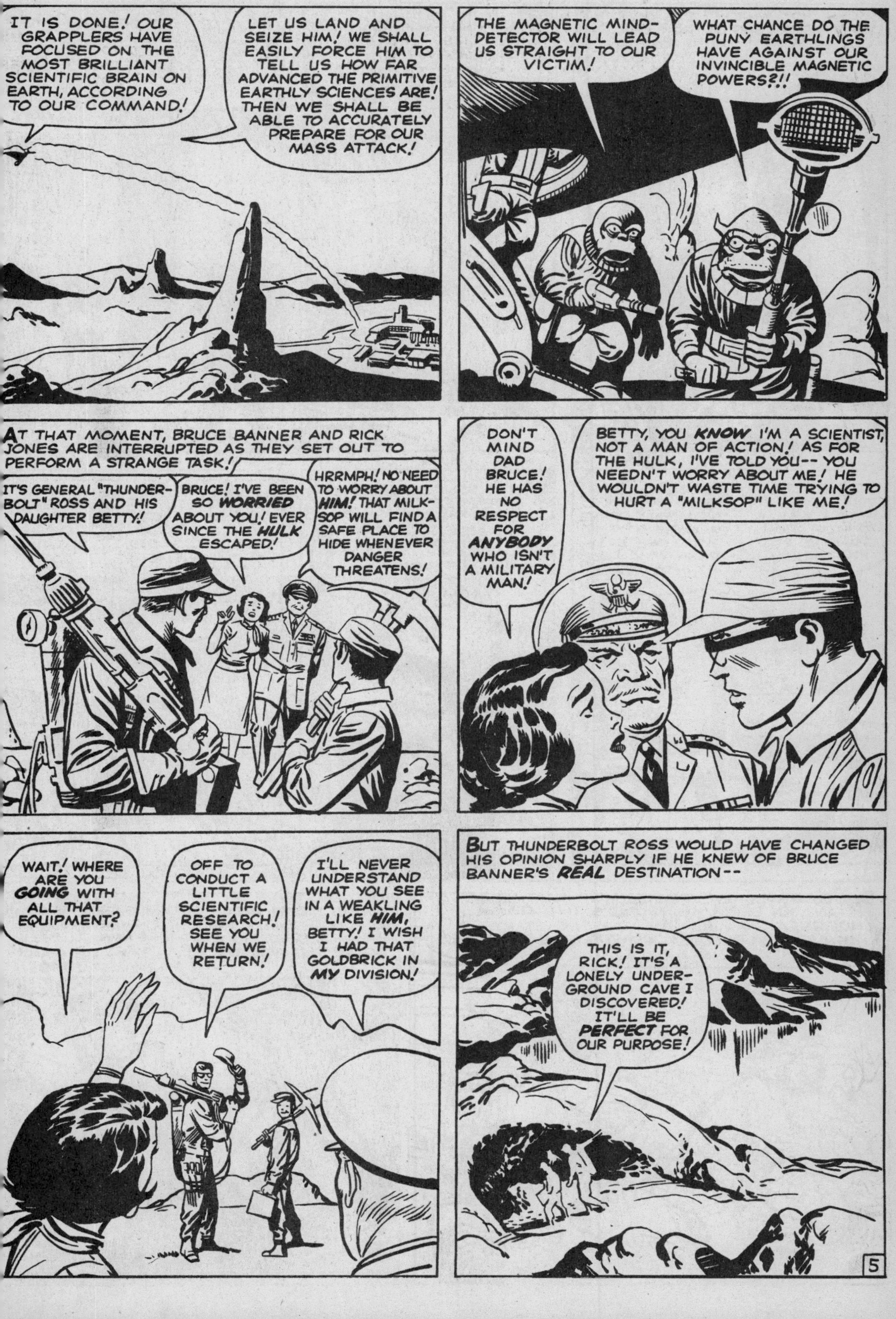
IT IS DONE! OUR GRAPPLERS HAVE FOCUSED ON THE MOST BRILLIANT SCIENTIFIC BRAIN ON EARTH, ACCORDING TO OUR COMMAND!
LET US LAND AND SEIZE HIM! WE SHALL EASILY FORCE HIM TO TELL US HOW FAR ADVANCED THE PRIMITIVE EARTHLY SCIENCES ARE! THEN WE SHALL BE ABLE TO ACCURATELY PREPARE FOR OUR MASS ATTACK!
THE MAGNETIC MIND-DETECTOR WILL LEAD US STRAIGHT TO OUR VICTIM!
WHAT CHANCE DO THE PUNY EARTHLINGS HAVE AGAINST OUR INVINCIBLE MAGNETIC POWERS?!!
AT THAT MOMENT, BRUCE BANNER AND RICK JONES ARE INTERRUPTED AS THEY SET OUT TO PERFORM A STRANGE TASK!
IT'S GENERAL "THUNDERBOLT" ROSS AND HIS DAUGHTER BETTY!
BRUCE! I'VE BEEN SO WORRIED ABOUT YOU! EVER SINCE THE HULK ESCAPED!
HRRMPH! NO NEED TO WORRY ABOUT HIM! THAT MILKSOP WILL FIND A SAFE PLACE TO HIDE WHENEVER DANGER THREATENS!
DON'T MIND DAD BRUCE! HE HAS NO RESPECT FOR ANYBODY WHO ISN'T A MILITARY MAN!
BETTY, YOU KNOW I'M A SCIENTIST, NOT A MAN OF ACTION! AS FOR THE HULK, I'VE TOLD YOU-- YOU NEEDN'T WORRY ABOUT ME! HE WOULDN'T WASTE TIME TRYING TO HURT A "MILKSOP" LIKE ME!
WAIT! WHERE ARE YOU GOING WITH ALL THAT EQUIPMENT?
OFF TO CONDUCT A LITTLE SCIENTIFIC RESEARCH! SEE YOU WHEN WE RETURN!
I'LL NEVER UNDERSTAND WHAT YOU SEE IN A WEAKLING LIKE HIM, BETTY! I WISH I HAD THAT GOLDBRICK IN MY DIVISION!
BUT THUNDERBOLT ROSS WOULD HAVE CHANGED HIS OPINION SHARPLY IF HE KNEW OF BRUCE BANNER'S REAL DESTINATION--
THIS IS IT, RICK! IT'S A LONELY UNDERGROUND CAVE I DISCOVERED! IT'LL BE PERFECT FOR OUR PURPOSE!

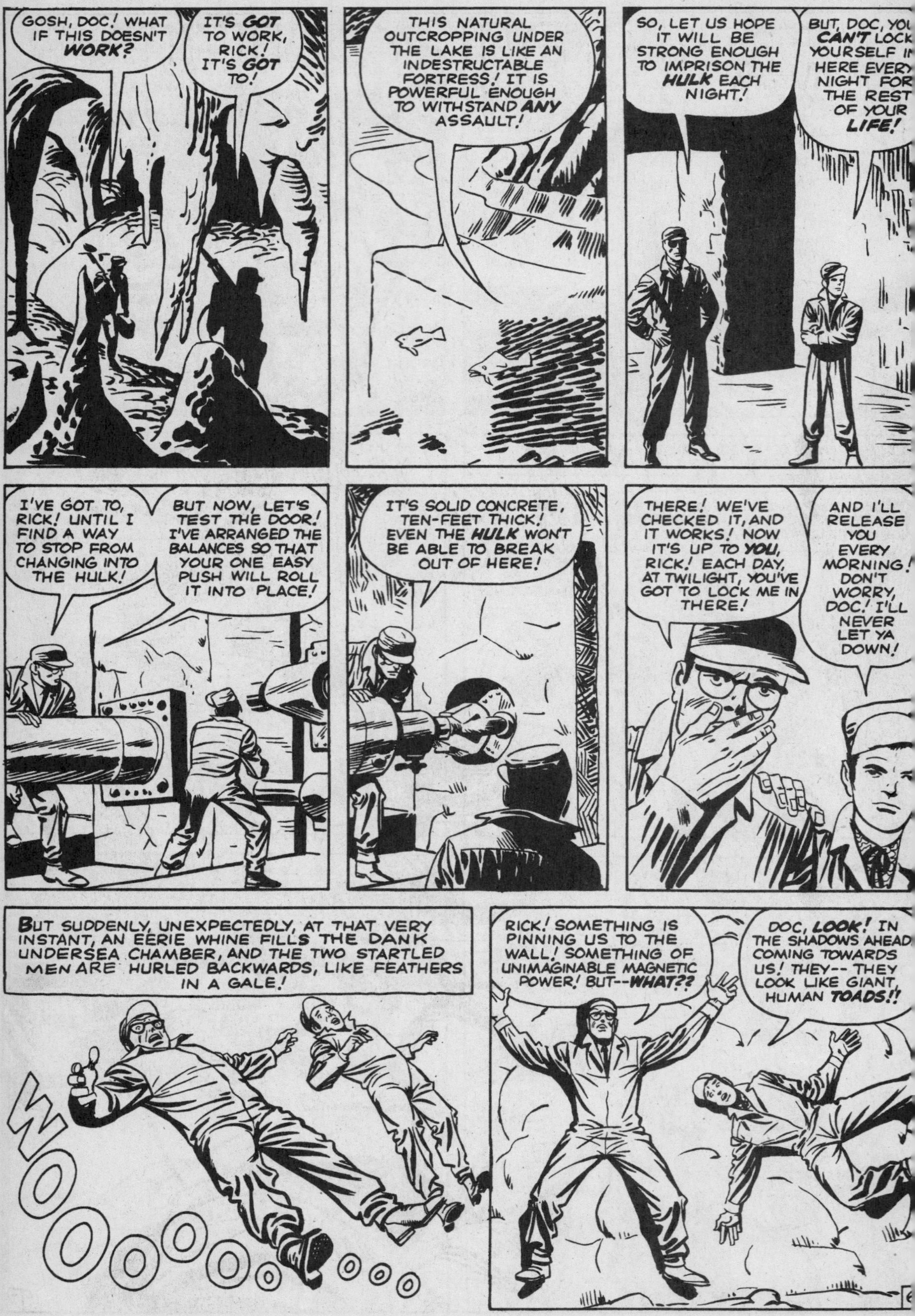

GOSH, DOC! WHAT IF THIS DOESN'T WORK?
IT'S GOT TO WORK, RICK! IT'S GOT TO!
THIS NATURAL OUTCROPPING UNDER THE LAKE IS LIKE AN INDESTRUCTABLE FORTRESS! IT IS POWERFUL ENOUGH TO WITHSTAND ANY ASSAULT!
SO, LET US HOPE IT WILL BE STRONG ENOUGH TO IMPRISON THE HULK EACH NIGHT!
BUT, DOC, YOU CAN'T LOCK YOURSELF IN HERE EVERY NIGHT FOR THE REST OF YOUR LIFE!
I'VE GOT TO, RICK! UNTIL I FIND A WAY TO STOP FROM CHANGING INTO THE HULK!
BUT NOW, LET'S TEST THE DOOR! I'VE ARRANGED THE BALANCES SO THAT YOUR ONE EASY PUSH WILL ROLL IT INTO PLACE!
IT'S SOLID CONCRETE, TEN-FEET THICK! EVEN THE HULK WON'T BE ABLE TO BREAK OUT OF HERE!
THERE! WE'VE CHECKED IT, AND IT WORKS! NOW IT'S UP TO YOU, RICK! EACH DAY, AT TWILIGHT, YOU'VE GOT TO LOCK ME IN THERE!
AND I'LL RELEASE YOU EVERY MORNING! DON'T WORRY, DOC! I'LL NEVER LET YA DOWN!
BUT SUDDENLY, UNEXPECTEDLY, AT THAT VERY INSTANT, AN EERIE WHINE FILLS THE DANK UNDERSEA CHAMBER, AND THE TWO STARTLED MEN ARE HURLED BACKWARDS, LIKE FEATHERS IN A GALE!
WOOOOOOOO...OOO
RICK! SOMETHING IS PINNING US TO THE WALL! SOMETHING OF UNIMAGINABLE MAGNETIC POWER! BUT--WHAT??
DOC, LOOK! IN THE SHADOWS AHEAD! COMING TOWARDS US! THEY-- THEY LOOK LIKE GIANT, HUMAN TOADS!!
6

PART 2
PRISONERS of the TOAD MEN!
DO NOT STRUGGLE AND YOU WILL NOT BE INJURED--YET! YOU ARE POWERLESS AGAINST OUR MAGNETIC RAY GUNS!
V-781 Stan Lee + J. KIRBY
7

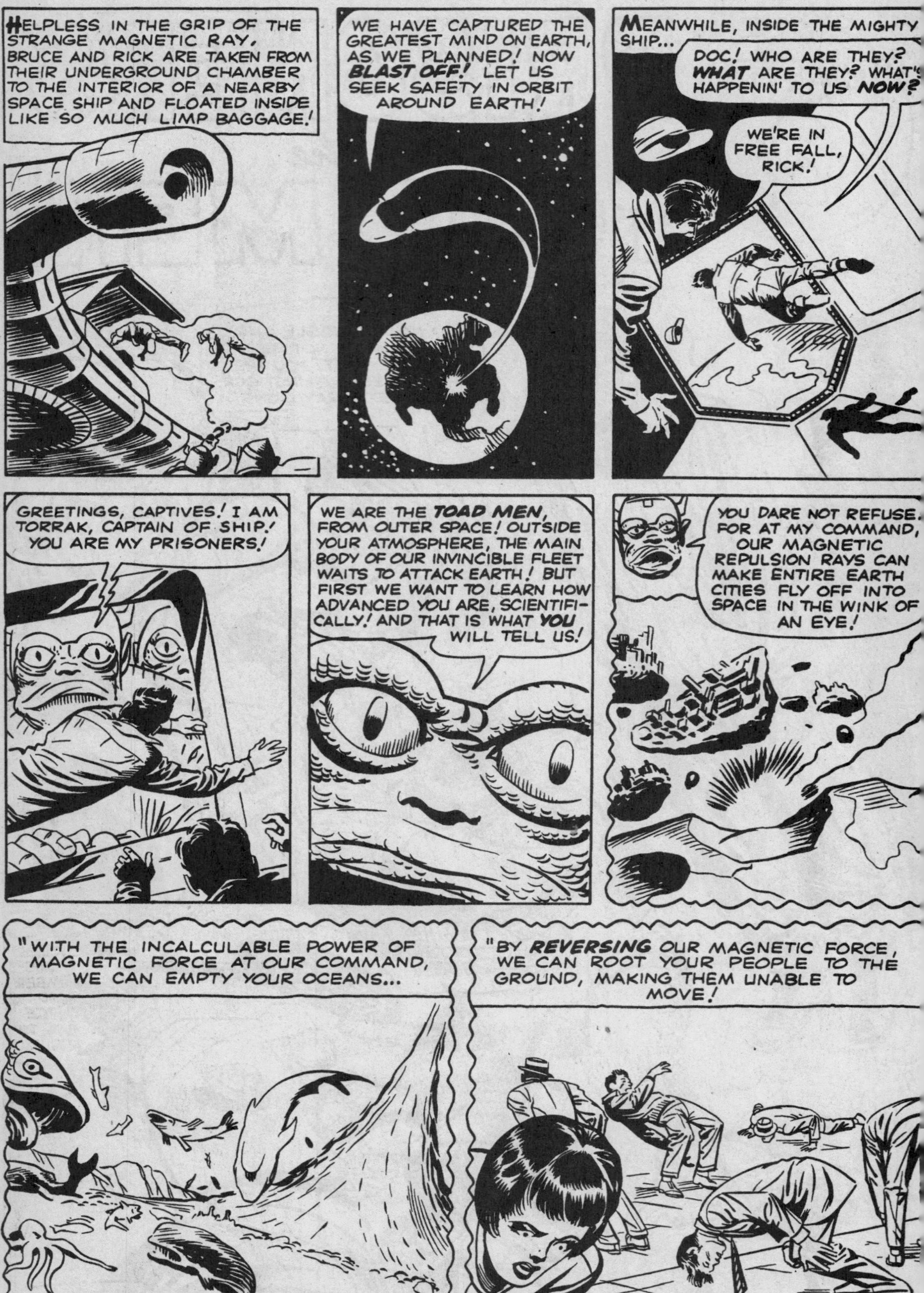
HELPLESS IN THE GRIP OF THE STRANGE MAGNETIC RAY, BRUCE AND RICK ARE TAKEN FROM THEIR UNDERGROUND CHAMBER TO THE INTERIOR OF A NEARBY SPACE SHIP AND FLOATED INSIDE LIKE SO MUCH LIMP BAGGAGE!
WE HAVE CAPTURED THE GREATEST MIND ON EARTH, AS WE PLANNED! NOW BLAST OFF! LET US SEEK SAFETY IN ORBIT AROUND EARTH!
MEANWHILE, INSIDE THE MIGHTY SHIP...
DOC! WHO ARE THEY? WHAT ARE THEY? WHAT'S HAPPENIN' TO US NOW?
WE'RE IN FREE FALL, RICK!
GREETINGS, CAPTIVES! I AM TORRAK, CAPTAIN OF SHIP! YOU ARE MY PRISONERS!
WE ARE THE TOAD MEN, FROM OUTER SPACE! OUTSIDE YOUR ATMOSPHERE, THE MAIN BODY OF OUR INVINCIBLE FLEET WAITS TO ATTACK EARTH! BUT FIRST WE WANT TO LEARN HOW ADVANCED YOU ARE, SCIENTIFICALLY! AND THAT IS WHAT YOU WILL TELL US!
YOU DARE NOT REFUSE. FOR AT MY COMMAND, OUR MAGNETIC REPULSION RAYS CAN MAKE ENTIRE EARTH CITIES FLY OFF INTO SPACE IN THE WINK OF AN EYE!
"WITH THE INCALCULABLE POWER OF MAGNETIC FORCE AT OUR COMMAND, WE CAN EMPTY YOUR OCEANS...
"BY REVERSING OUR MAGNETIC FORCE, WE CAN ROOT YOUR PEOPLE TO THE GROUND, MAKING THEM UNABLE TO MOVE!

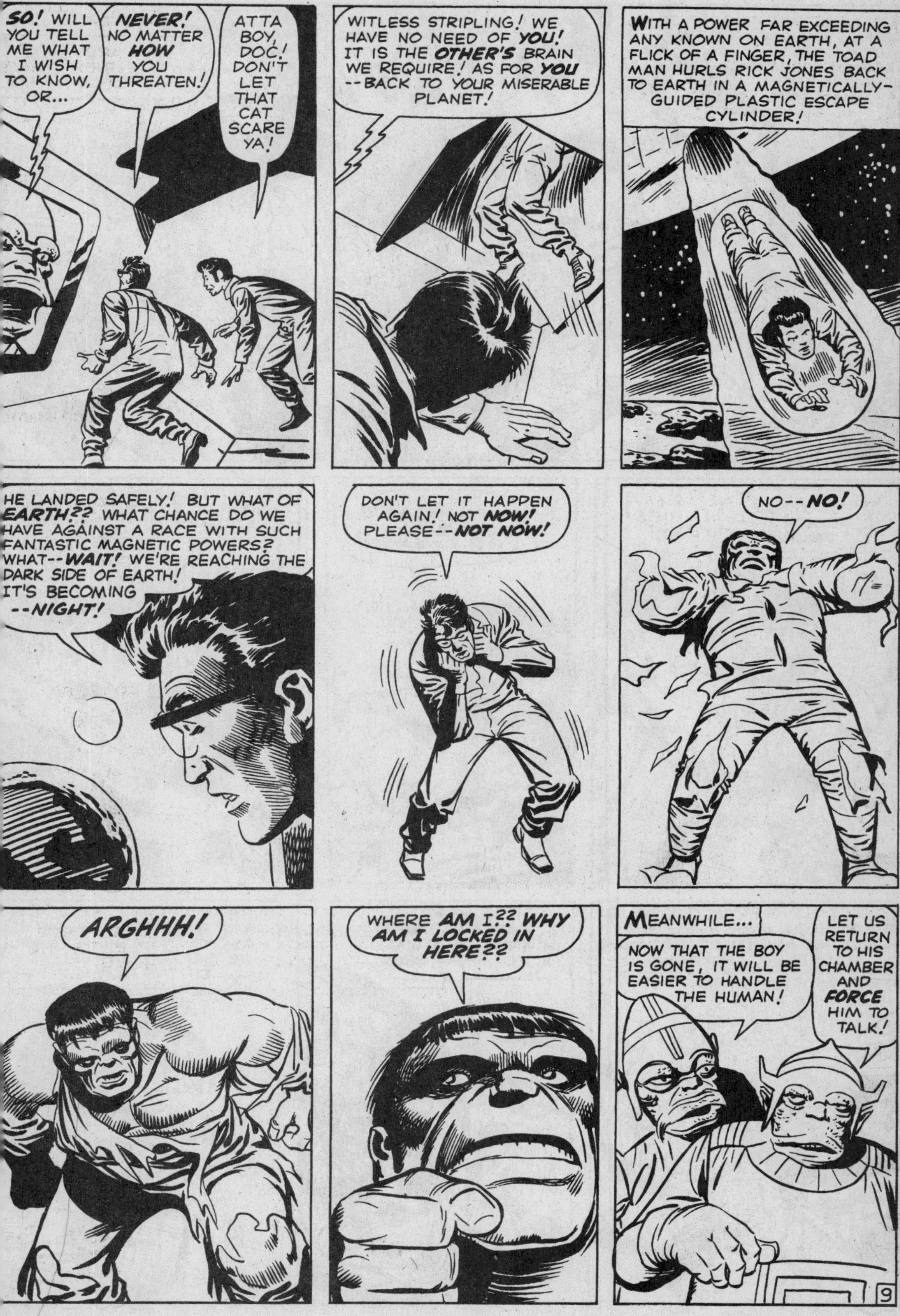
SO! WILL YOU TELL ME WHAT I WISH TO KNOW, OR...
NEVER! NO MATTER HOW YOU THREATEN!
ATTA BOY, DOC! DON'T LET THAT CAT SCARE YA!
WITLESS STRIPLING! WE HAVE NO NEED OF YOU! IT IS THE OTHER'S BRAIN WE REQUIRE! AS FOR YOU --BACK TO YOUR MISERABLE PLANET!
WITH A POWER FAR EXCEEDING ANY KNOWN ON EARTH, AT A FLICK OF A FINGER, THE TOAD MAN HURLS RICK JONES BACK TO EARTH IN A MAGNETICALLY-GUIDED PLASTIC ESCAPE CYLINDER!
HE LANDED SAFELY! BUT WHAT OF EARTH?? WHAT CHANCE DO WE HAVE AGAINST A RACE WITH SUCH FANTASTIC MAGNETIC POWERS? WHAT--WAIT! WE'RE REACHING THE DARK SIDE OF EARTH! IT'S BECOMING --NIGHT!
DON'T LET IT HAPPEN AGAIN! NOT NOW! PLEASE--NOT NOW!
NO--NO!
ARGHHH!
WHERE AM I?? WHY AM I LOCKED IN HERE??
MEANWHILE...
NOW THAT THE BOY IS GONE, IT WILL BE EASIER TO HANDLE THE HUMAN!
LET US RETURN TO HIS CHAMBER AND FORCE HIM TO TALK!
9

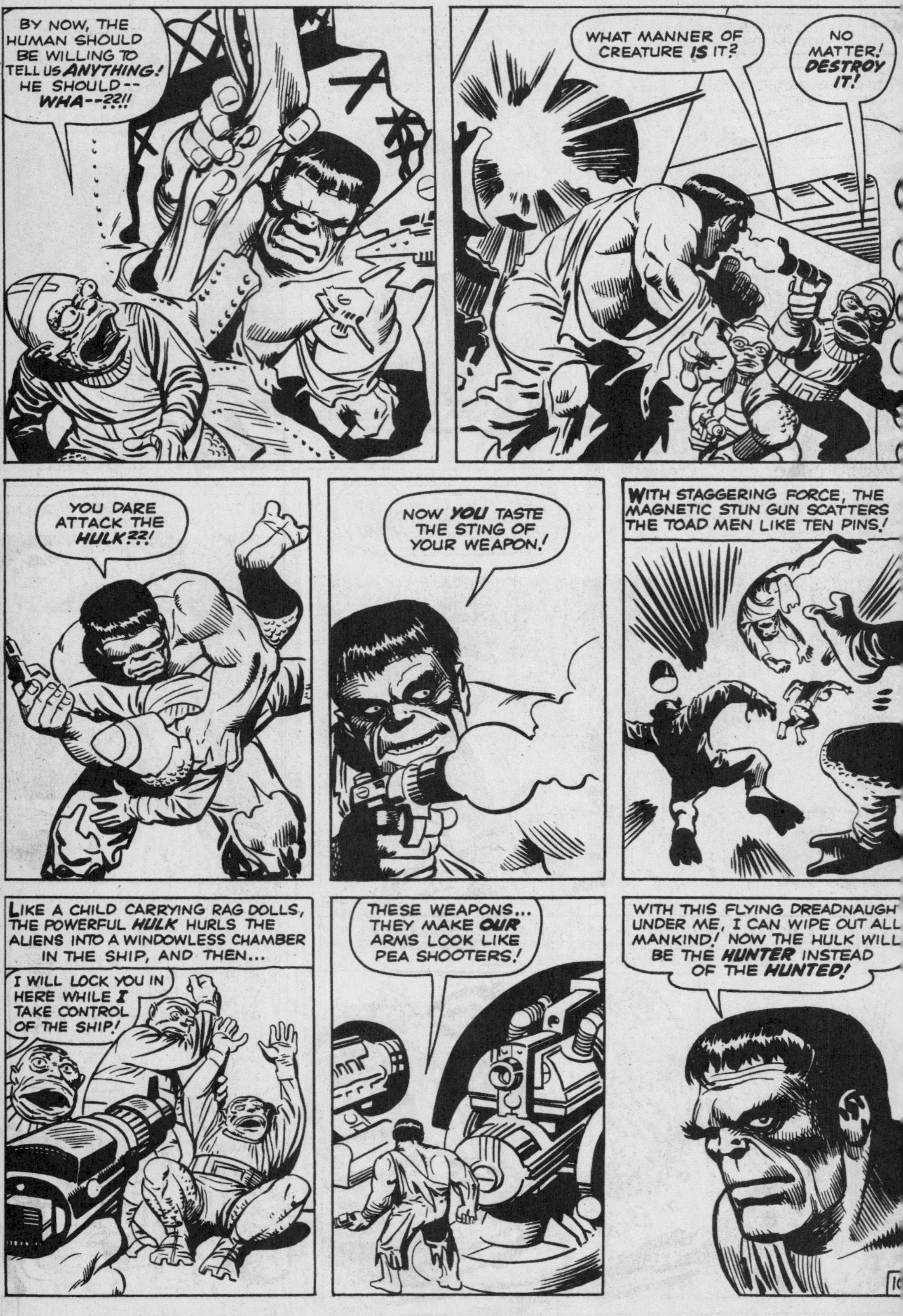

BY NOW, THE HUMAN SHOULD BE WILLING TO TELL US ANYTHING! HE SHOULD-- WHA--??!!
WHAT MANNER OF CREATURE IS IT?
NO MATTER! DESTROY IT!
YOU DARE ATTACK THE HULK??!
NOW YOU TASTE THE STING OF YOUR WEAPON!
WITH STAGGERING FORCE, THE MAGNETIC STUN GUN SCATTERS THE TOAD MEN LIKE TEN PINS!
LIKE A CHILD CARRYING RAG DOLLS, THE POWERFUL HULK HURLS THE ALIENS INTO A WINDOWLESS CHAMBER IN THE SHIP, AND THEN...
I WILL LOCK YOU IN HERE WHILE I TAKE CONTROL OF THE SHIP!
THESE WEAPONS... THEY MAKE OUR ARMS LOOK LIKE PEA SHOOTERS!
WITH THIS FLYING DREADNAUGHT UNDER ME, I CAN WIPE OUT ALL MANKIND! NOW THE HULK WILL BE THE HUNTER INSTEAD OF THE HUNTED!

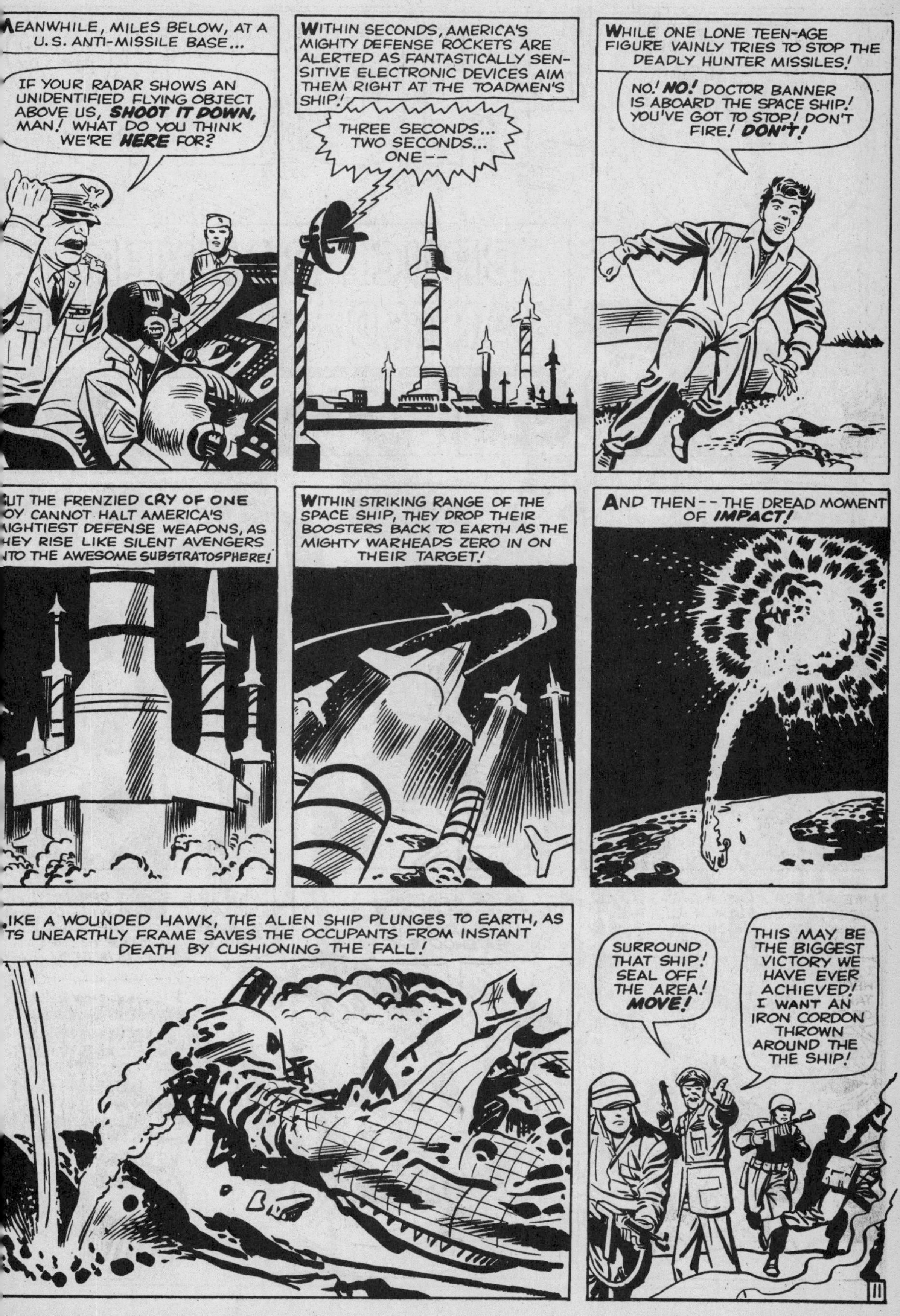

MEANWHILE, MILES BELOW, AT A U.S. ANTI-MISSILE BASE...
IF YOUR RADAR SHOWS AN UNIDENTIFIED FLYING OBJECT ABOVE US, SHOOT IT DOWN, MAN! WHAT DO YOU THINK WE'RE HERE FOR?
WITHIN SECONDS, AMERICA'S MIGHTY DEFENSE ROCKETS ARE ALERTED AS FANTASTICALLY SENSITIVE ELECTRONIC DEVICES AIM THEM RIGHT AT THE TOADMEN'S SHIP!
THREE SECONDS... TWO SECONDS... ONE--
WHILE ONE LONE TEEN-AGE FIGURE VAINLY TRIES TO STOP THE DEADLY HUNTER MISSILES!
NO! NO! DOCTOR BANNER IS ABOARD THE SPACE SHIP! YOU'VE GOT TO STOP! DON'T FIRE! DON'T!
BUT THE FRENZIED CRY OF ONE BOY CANNOT HALT AMERICA'S MIGHTIEST DEFENSE WEAPONS, AS THEY RISE LIKE SILENT AVENGERS INTO THE AWESOME SUBSTRATOSPHERE!
WITHIN STRIKING RANGE OF THE SPACE SHIP, THEY DROP THEIR BOOSTERS BACK TO EARTH AS THE MIGHTY WARHEADS ZERO IN ON THEIR TARGET!
AND THEN--THE DREAD MOMENT OF IMPACT!
LIKE A WOUNDED HAWK, THE ALIEN SHIP PLUNGES TO EARTH, AS ITS UNEARTHLY FRAME SAVES THE OCCUPANTS FROM INSTANT DEATH BY CUSHIONING THE FALL!
SURROUND THAT SHIP! SEAL OFF THE AREA! MOVE!
THIS MAY BE THE BIGGEST VICTORY WE HAVE EVER ACHIEVED! I WANT AN IRON CORDON THROWN AROUND THE THE SHIP!
11

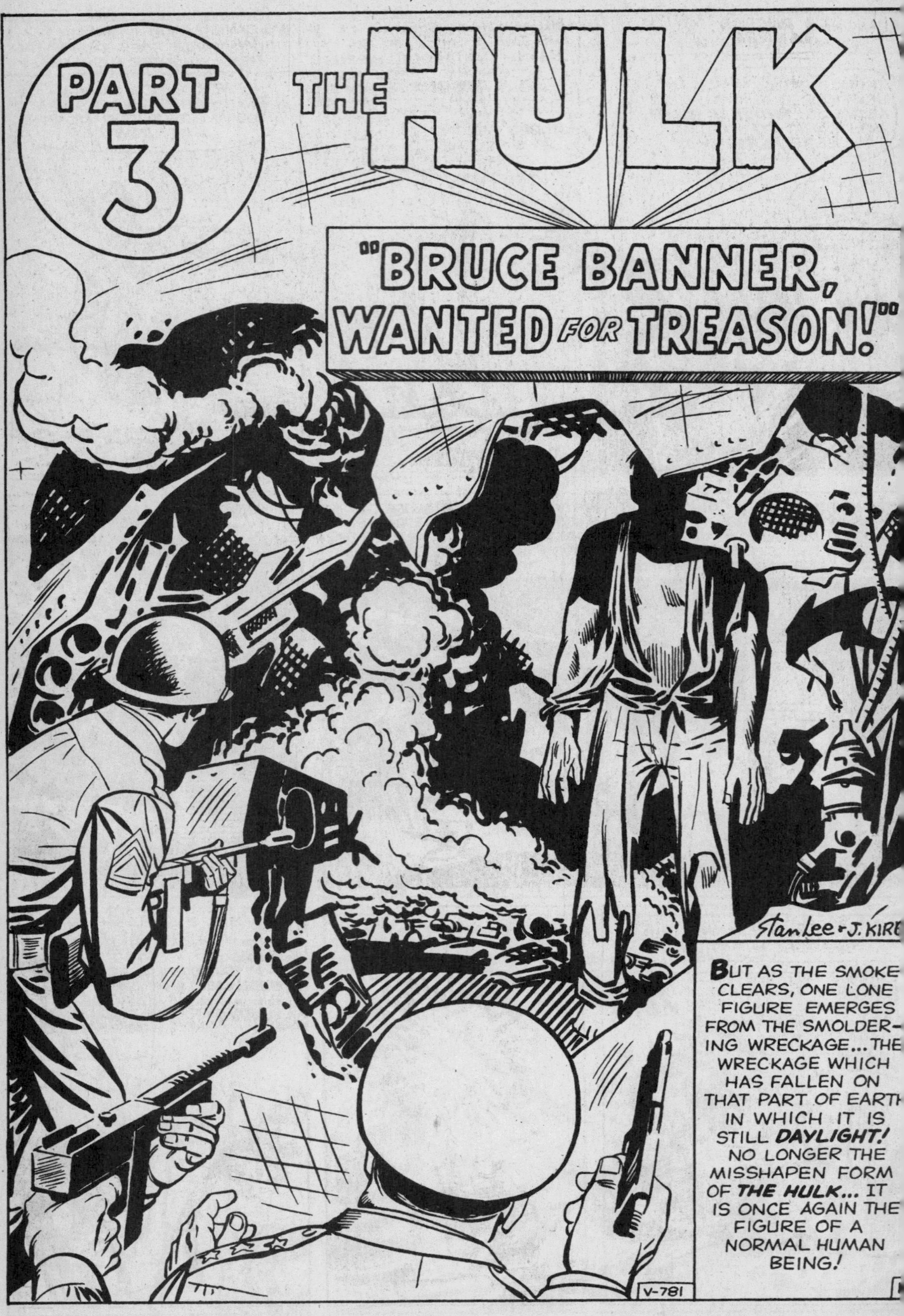
PART 3
THE HULK
"BRUCE BANNER, WANTED FOR TREASON!"
Stan Lee + J. Kirby
BUT AS THE SMOKE CLEARS, ONE LONE FIGURE EMERGES FROM THE SMOLDERING WRECKAGE... THE WRECKAGE WHICH HAS FALLEN ON THAT PART OF EARTH IN WHICH IT IS STILL DAYLIGHT! NO LONGER THE MISSHAPEN FORM OF THE HULK... IT IS ONCE AGAIN THE FIGURE OF A NORMAL HUMAN BEING!
V-781

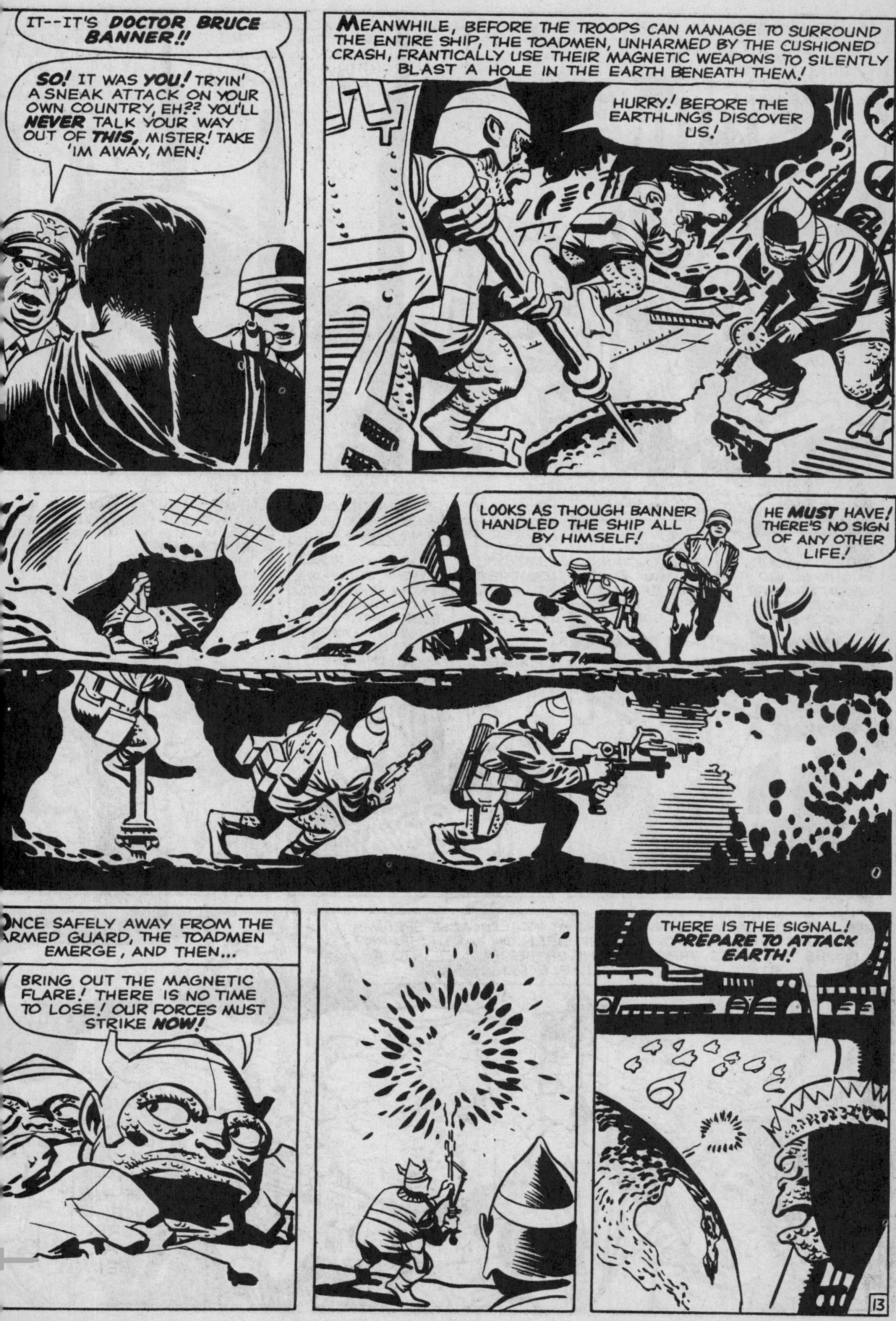
IT--IT'S DOCTOR BRUCE BANNER!!
SO! IT WAS YOU! TRYIN' A SNEAK ATTACK ON YOUR OWN COUNTRY, EH?? YOU'LL NEVER TALK YOUR WAY OUT OF THIS, MISTER! TAKE 'IM AWAY, MEN!
MEANWHILE, BEFORE THE TROOPS CAN MANAGE TO SURROUND THE ENTIRE SHIP, THE TOADMEN, UNHARMED BY THE CUSHIONED CRASH, FRANTICALLY USE THEIR MAGNETIC WEAPONS TO SILENTLY BLAST A HOLE IN THE EARTH BENEATH THEM!
HURRY! BEFORE THE EARTHLINGS DISCOVER US!
LOOKS AS THOUGH BANNER HANDLED THE SHIP ALL BY HIMSELF!
HE MUST HAVE! THERE'S NO SIGN OF ANY OTHER LIFE!
ONCE SAFELY AWAY FROM THE ARMED GUARD, THE TOADMEN EMERGE, AND THEN...
BRING OUT THE MAGNETIC FLARE! THERE IS NO TIME TO LOSE! OUR FORCES MUST STRIKE NOW!
THERE IS THE SIGNAL! PREPARE TO ATTACK EARTH!

MOMENTS LATER, AT A MAXIMUM SECURITY PRISON...

TAKE IT EASY, RICK! THERE'S NOTHING YOU CAN DO FOR ME NOW!

BUT, DOC, THESE JOES DON'T UNDER-STAND! THEY CAN'T CALL *YOU* A TRAITOR! NOT *YOU*!

DOC, AS SOON AS IT GETS DARK-- *THE HULK* CAN BUST OUTTA THIS JOINT EASY ENOUGH, CAN'T HE?

PERHAPS, RICK, BUT HE'S SO UNPREDICTABLE! IT MIGHT BE BETTER IF DARKNESS NEVER CAME!

WHILE, OUTSIDE THE CONCRETE PRISON...

I WANT A TWENTY-FOUR HOUR GUARD AROUND BANNER! UNDERSTAND, SOLDIER??

YES SIR, GENERAL ROSS! NOTHING HUMAN *EVER* CAN ESCAPE FROM HERE, SIR!

BUT GENERAL "THUNDERBOLT" ROSS CANNOT REST EASY, EVEN AFTER REACHING HIS HOME...

DAD, YOU CAN'T REALLY THINK THAT BRUCE BANNER IS A TRAITOR! IT'S IM-POSSIBLE!

I DON'T KNOW *WHAT* TO THINK, BETTY! ALL I KNOW IS HE BUZZED THIS CONTINENT IN A STRANGE, POWERFUL SHIP, WITH NO WARN-ING AND NO AUTHOR-IZATION! IT'S UP TO *WASHINGTON* TO DECIDE HIS FATE NOW!

BRINNG!

WHAT'S THAT?? AN INVASION?? AN ARMADA OF *SPACE SHIPS!* WHERE?? HOW? KEEP CALM, MAN! SOUND THE RED ALERT! I'M ON MY WAY!

DAD! IF EARTH IS IN DANGER WE'LL *NEED* BRUCE BANNER! WE'LL NEED H... KNOWLEDGE H... BRAINS...

AT THAT VERY MOMENT, TRAVELLING AT INCALCULABLE SPEED, THE MIGHTIEST SPACE FORCE EVER SEEN ON EARTH STREAKS ACROSS THE SKIES, THROWING THE ENTIRE PLANET INTO A STATE OF UNCONTROLLABLE PANIC!

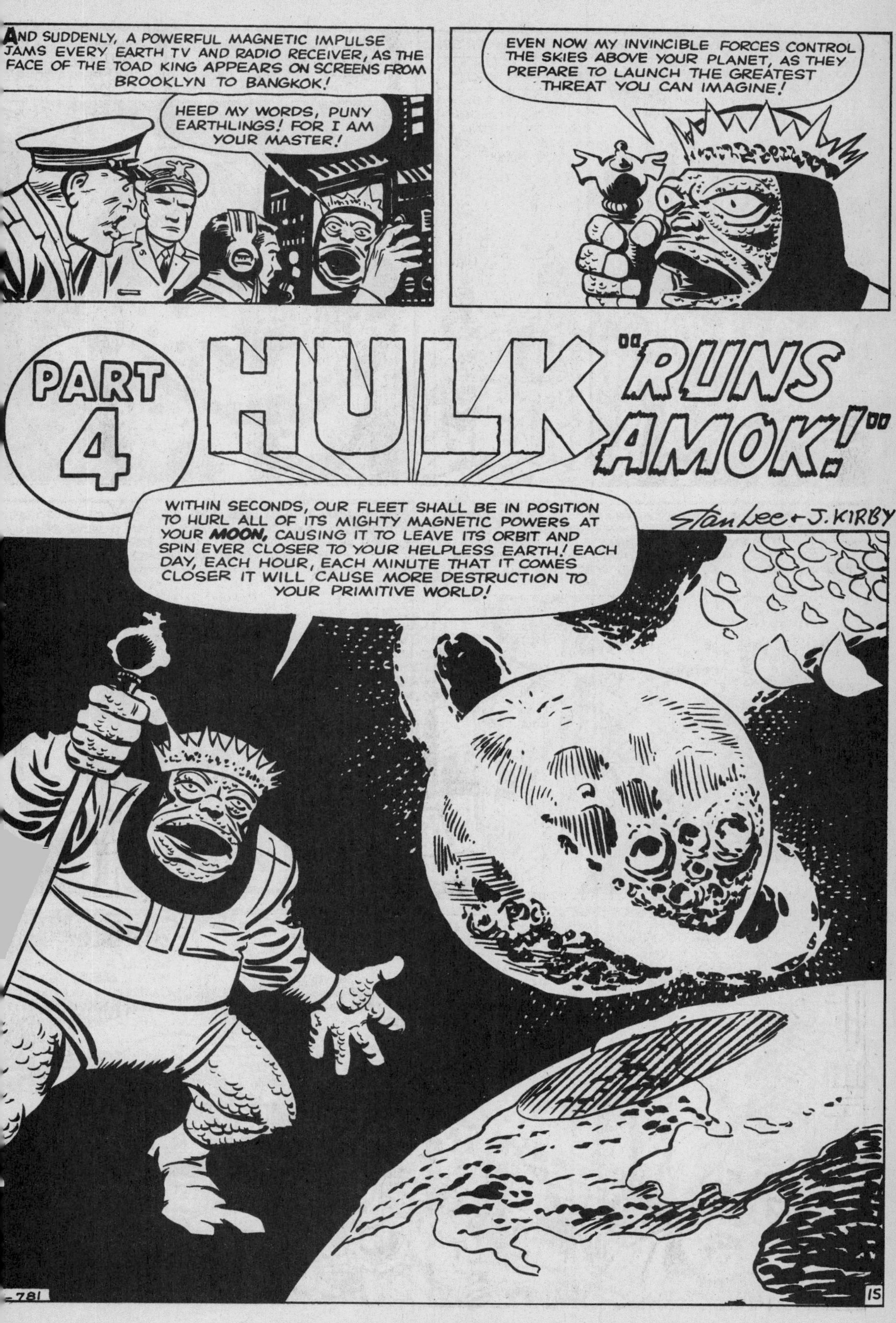
AND SUDDENLY, A POWERFUL MAGNETIC IMPULSE JAMS EVERY EARTH TV AND RADIO RECEIVER, AS THE FACE OF THE TOAD KING APPEARS ON SCREENS FROM BROOKLYN TO BANGKOK!
HEED MY WORDS, PUNY EARTHLINGS! FOR I AM YOUR MASTER!
EVEN NOW MY INVINCIBLE FORCES CONTROL THE SKIES ABOVE YOUR PLANET, AS THEY PREPARE TO LAUNCH THE GREATEST THREAT YOU CAN IMAGINE!
PART 4
HULK "RUNS AMOK!"
WITHIN SECONDS, OUR FLEET SHALL BE IN POSITION TO HURL ALL OF ITS MIGHTY MAGNETIC POWERS AT YOUR MOON, CAUSING IT TO LEAVE ITS ORBIT AND SPIN EVER CLOSER TO YOUR HELPLESS EARTH! EACH DAY, EACH HOUR, EACH MINUTE THAT IT COMES CLOSER IT WILL CAUSE MORE DESTRUCTION TO YOUR PRIMITIVE WORLD!
Stan Lee + J. KIRBY
-781
15

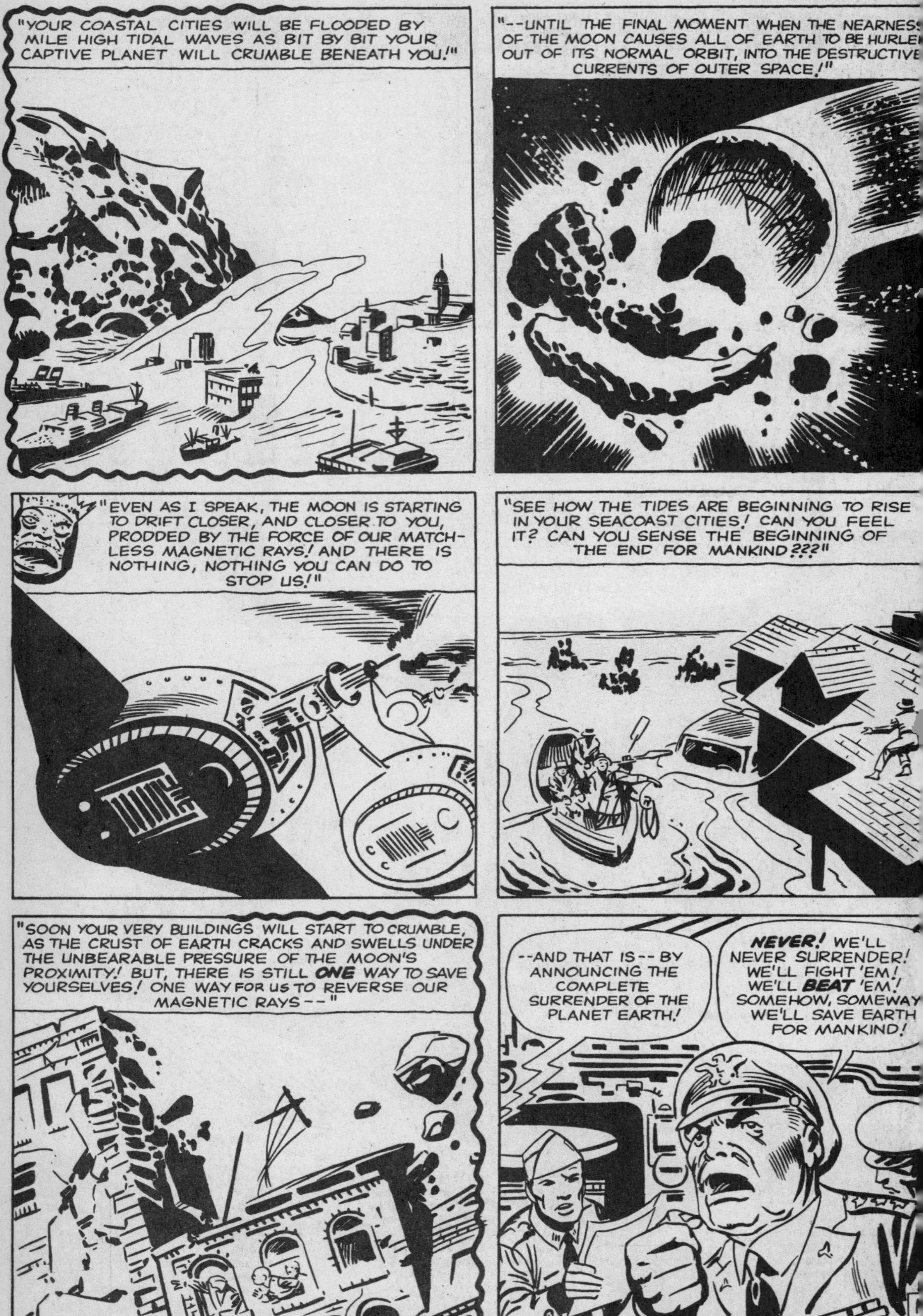

"YOUR COASTAL CITIES WILL BE FLOODED BY MILE HIGH TIDAL WAVES AS BIT BY BIT YOUR CAPTIVE PLANET WILL CRUMBLE BENEATH YOU!"
"--UNTIL THE FINAL MOMENT WHEN THE NEARNESS OF THE MOON CAUSES ALL OF EARTH TO BE HURLED OUT OF ITS NORMAL ORBIT, INTO THE DESTRUCTIVE CURRENTS OF OUTER SPACE!"
"EVEN AS I SPEAK, THE MOON IS STARTING TO DRIFT CLOSER, AND CLOSER TO YOU, PRODDED BY THE FORCE OF OUR MATCHLESS MAGNETIC RAYS! AND THERE IS NOTHING, NOTHING YOU CAN DO TO STOP US!"
"SEE HOW THE TIDES ARE BEGINNING TO RISE IN YOUR SEACOAST CITIES! CAN YOU FEEL IT? CAN YOU SENSE THE BEGINNING OF THE END FOR MANKIND???"
"SOON YOUR VERY BUILDINGS WILL START TO CRUMBLE, AS THE CRUST OF EARTH CRACKS AND SWELLS UNDER THE UNBEARABLE PRESSURE OF THE MOON'S PROXIMITY! BUT, THERE IS STILL ONE WAY TO SAVE YOURSELVES! ONE WAY FOR US TO REVERSE OUR MAGNETIC RAYS--"
--AND THAT IS--BY ANNOUNCING THE COMPLETE SURRENDER OF THE PLANET EARTH!
NEVER! WE'LL NEVER SURRENDER! WE'LL FIGHT 'EM! WE'LL BEAT 'EM! SOMEHOW, SOMEWAY WE'LL SAVE EARTH FOR MANKIND!

MEANWHILE, IN A LONELY, BARREN CELL, ONE FIGURE IS ALL BUT FORGOTTEN AS EARTH SEEMS TO TREMBLE IN ITS FINAL DEATH THROES! ONE LONE FIGURE WHO GRIMLY GRIPS THE IRON BARS AS HE WATCHES THE GATHERING TWILIGHT BEGIN TO CREEP OVER THE COUNTRYSIDE!

NOW I CAN FEEL IT! MY THROAT GROWS TIGHT! MY HEAD IS THROBBING! A BLACK HAZE SEEMS TO BE COVERING MY BRAIN...

I'M CHANGING! HEAVEN HELP ME, I CAN NO LONGER STOP IT--NO LONGER CONTROL MYSELF! I--I--

AHHHHHHH...

AND THERE IN THE CELL, UNNOTICED BY ANY HUMAN EYES, THE HULK AGAIN APPEARS!

SMASHING THRU THE CONCRETE WALL, THE STEEL BARS, AS THOUGH THEY ARE CARDBOARD, HE LUNGES OUT INTO THE OPEN!

LOOK! IT'S THE HULK!

HURRY! LOAD AND FIRE!

HE--HE'S RIPPING A RAIL RIGHT OUT OF THOSE TRACKS!

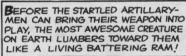

BEFORE THE STARTLED ARTILLARYMEN CAN BRING THEIR WEAPON INTO PLAY, THE MOST AWESOME CREATURE ON EARTH LUMBERS TOWARD THEM LIKE A LIVING BATTERING RAM!

RUN! NOTHIN' CAN HOLD HIM!!

17

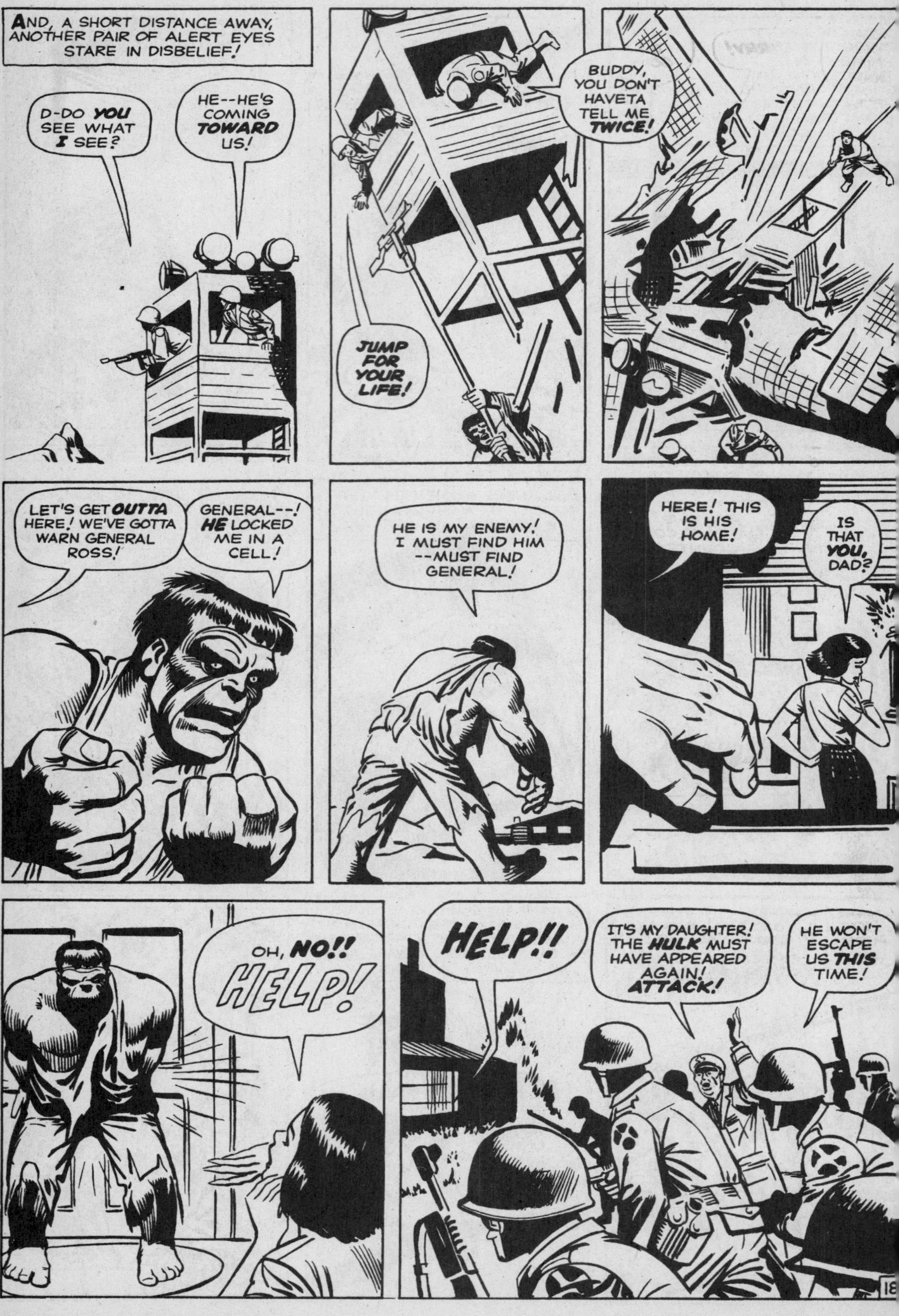
AND, A SHORT DISTANCE AWAY, ANOTHER PAIR OF ALERT EYES STARE IN DISBELIEF!
D-DO YOU SEE WHAT I SEE?
HE--HE'S COMING TOWARD US!
BUDDY, YOU DON'T HAVETA TELL ME TWICE!
JUMP FOR YOUR LIFE!
LET'S GET OUTTA HERE! WE'VE GOTTA WARN GENERAL ROSS!
GENERAL--! HE LOCKED ME IN A CELL!
HE IS MY ENEMY! I MUST FIND HIM --MUST FIND GENERAL!
HERE! THIS IS HIS HOME!
IS THAT YOU, DAD?
OH, NO!! HELP!
HELP!!
IT'S MY DAUGHTER! THE HULK MUST HAVE APPEARED AGAIN! ATTACK!
HE WON'T ESCAPE US THIS TIME!
18

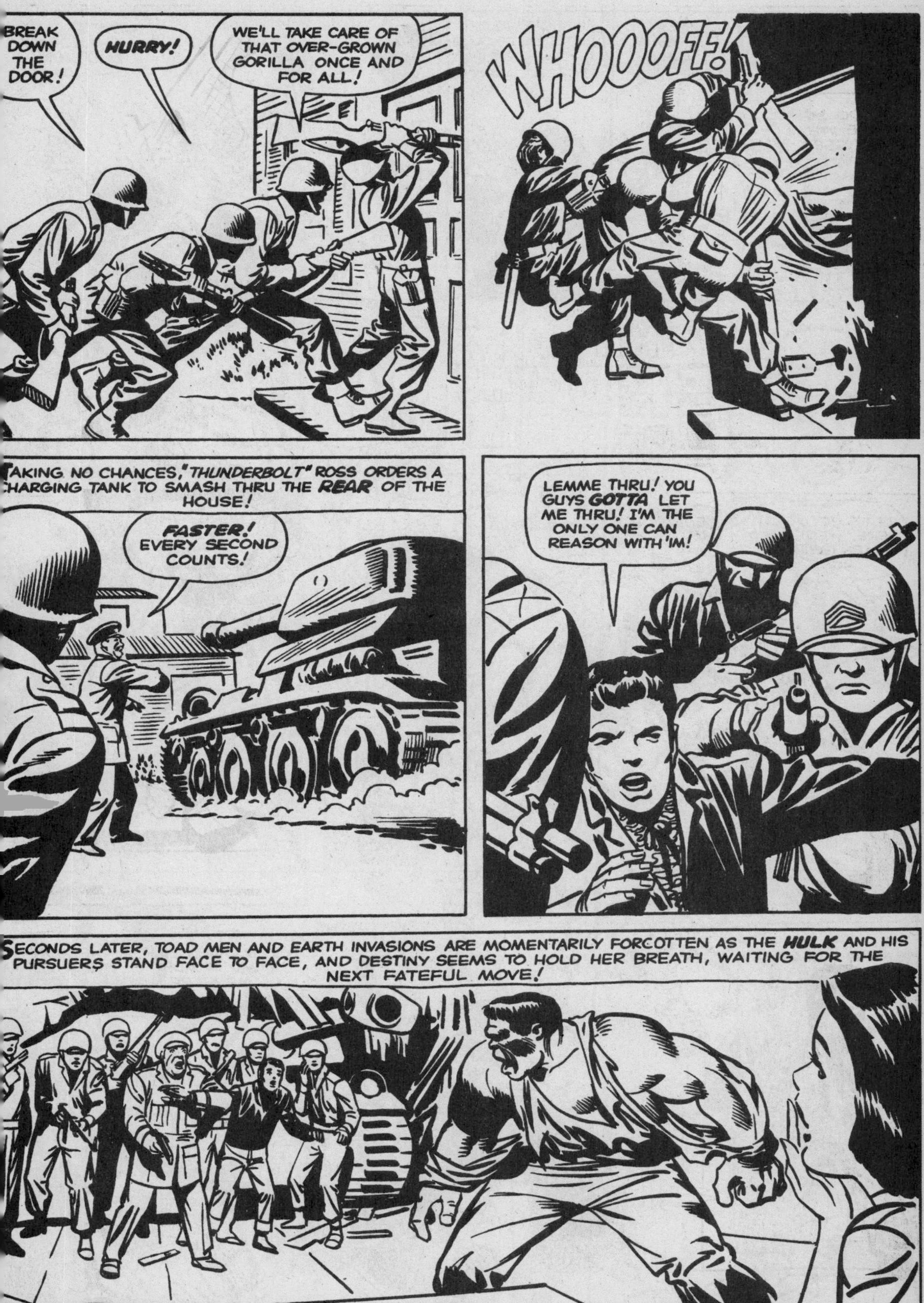
BREAK DOWN THE DOOR!
HURRY!
WE'LL TAKE CARE OF THAT OVER-GROWN GORILLA ONCE AND FOR ALL!
WHOOOFF!
TAKING NO CHANCES, "THUNDERBOLT" ROSS ORDERS A CHARGING TANK TO SMASH THRU THE REAR OF THE HOUSE!
FASTER! EVERY SECOND COUNTS!
LEMME THRU! YOU GUYS GOTTA LET ME THRU! I'M THE ONLY ONE CAN REASON WITH 'IM!
SECONDS LATER, TOAD MEN AND EARTH INVASIONS ARE MOMENTARILY FORGOTTEN AS THE HULK AND HIS PURSUERS STAND FACE TO FACE, AND DESTINY SEEMS TO HOLD HER BREATH, WAITING FOR THE NEXT FATEFUL MOVE!
19

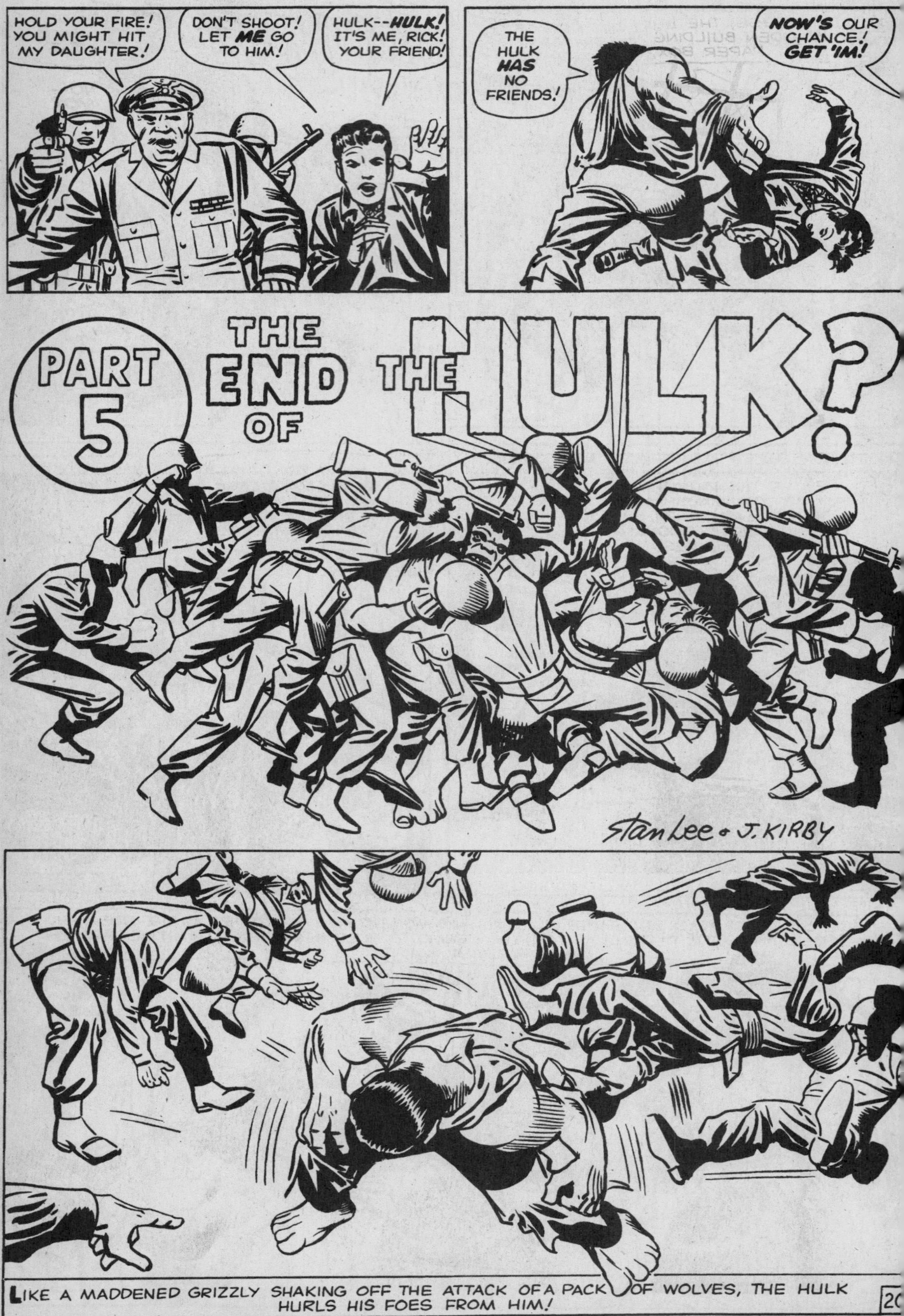
HOLD YOUR FIRE! YOU MIGHT HIT MY DAUGHTER!
DON'T SHOOT! LET **ME** GO TO HIM!
HULK--**HULK!** IT'S ME, RICK! YOUR FRIEND!
THE HULK **HAS** NO FRIENDS!
NOW'S OUR CHANCE! **GET 'IM!**
PART 5
THE END OF THE HULK?!
Stan Lee + J. KIRBY
LIKE A MADDENED GRIZZLY SHAKING OFF THE ATTACK OF A PACK OF WOLVES, THE HULK HURLS HIS FOES FROM HIM!

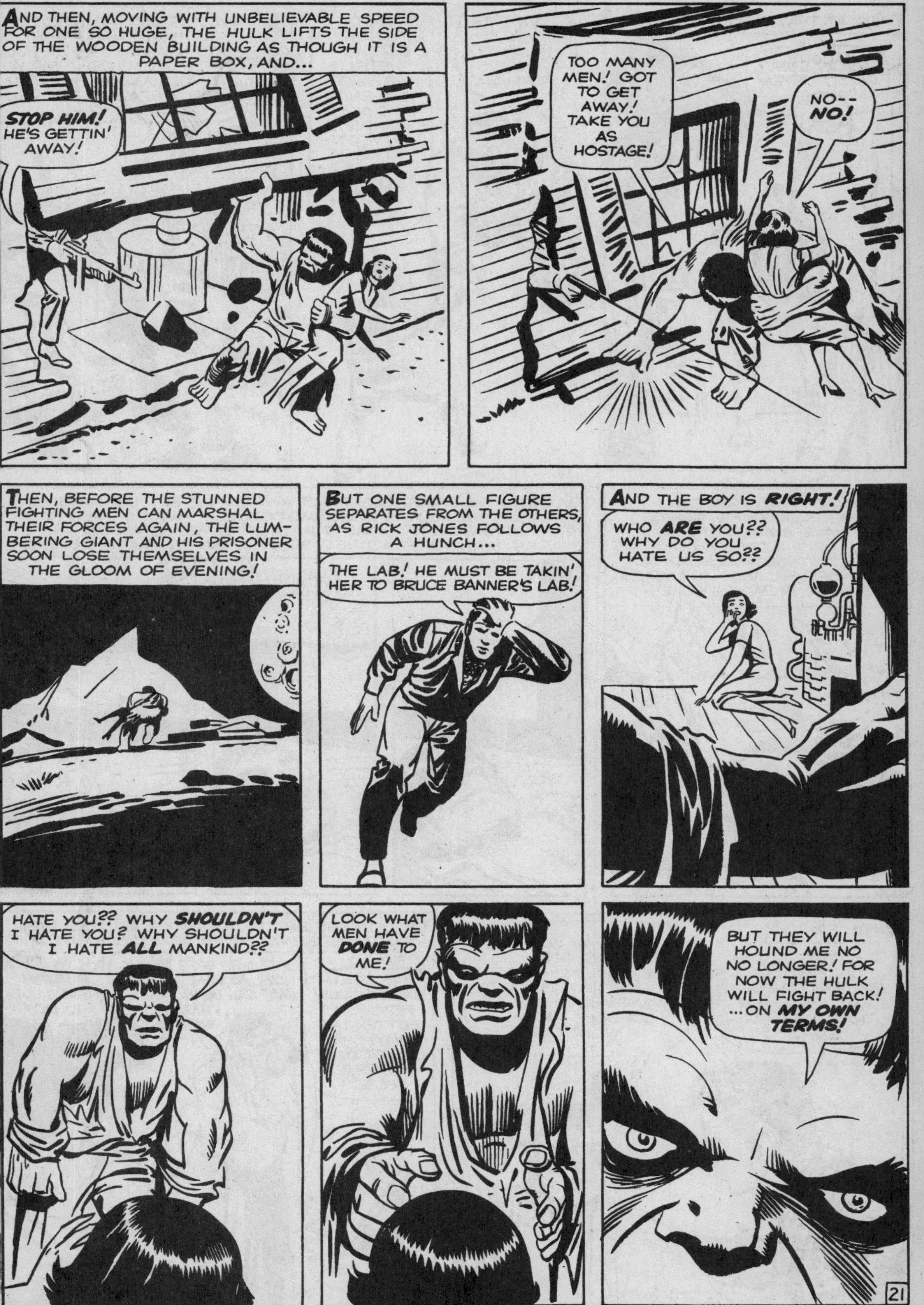

AND THEN, MOVING WITH UNBELIEVABLE SPEED FOR ONE SO HUGE, THE HULK LIFTS THE SIDE OF THE WOODEN BUILDING AS THOUGH IT IS A PAPER BOX, AND...
STOP HIM! HE'S GETTIN' AWAY!
TOO MANY MEN! GOT TO GET AWAY! TAKE YOU AS HOSTAGE!
NO-- NO!
THEN, BEFORE THE STUNNED FIGHTING MEN CAN MARSHAL THEIR FORCES AGAIN, THE LUMBERING GIANT AND HIS PRISONER SOON LOSE THEMSELVES IN THE GLOOM OF EVENING!
BUT ONE SMALL FIGURE SEPARATES FROM THE OTHERS, AS RICK JONES FOLLOWS A HUNCH...
THE LAB! HE MUST BE TAKIN' HER TO BRUCE BANNER'S LAB!
AND THE BOY IS RIGHT!
WHO ARE YOU?? WHY DO YOU HATE US SO??
HATE YOU?? WHY SHOULDN'T I HATE YOU? WHY SHOULDN'T I HATE ALL MANKIND??
LOOK WHAT MEN HAVE DONE TO ME!
BUT THEY WILL HOUND ME NO NO LONGER! FOR NOW THE HULK WILL FIGHT BACK! ...ON MY OWN TERMS!
21

Then, at that very instant...

HULK! STOP! DON'T! LISTEN TO ME--

YOU! THIS TIME I SILENCE YOU--FOREVER!

WAIT! YOU'VE GOT TO LISTEN! WE NEED YOU! EARTH IS IN DANGER! YOU'VE GOT TO HELP! YOU'VE GOT TO UNDERSTAND!

AND, EVEN AS RICK FRANTICALLY PLEADS WITH THE THING THAT CONFRONTS HIM--EVEN AS THE HULK GETS CLOSER, AND CLOSER, THRU'OUT THE LAND MORE AND MORE EARTHQUAKES AND UPHEAVELS BEGIN TO TAKE THEIR TOLL...

BUT WE CAN NEVER KNOW WHETHER RICK JONES' WORDS MIGHT HAVE SWAYED THE MIGHTY HULK, FOR THE OCCUPANTS OF THE SMALL COTTAGE ARE SUDDENLY FLUNG OFF BALANCE AS A VIOLENT EARTH TREMOR STRIKES!

SLOWLY, THE DAZED BOY PICKS HIMSELF UP, BUT THE MASSIVE FORM OF THE HULK IS STILL--MOTIONLESS--AS THE FIRST FAINT RAYS OF DAYLIGHT BATHE IT IN THEIR EERIE GLOW--AS THE HARSH, BRUTAL FEATURES BEGIN TO SOFTEN, AND CHANGE...

UNTIL FINALLY...

DOC! WOTTA RELIEF! I THOUGHT I WAS DONE FOR THAT TIME FOR SURE!

GIVE ME MY GLASSES, RICK! AND THEN--TELL ME--QUICKLY--WHAT HAPPENED! I-I CAN'T REMEMBER--IT'S LIKE AN UGLY, FADING NIGHTMARE!

QUICKLY, THE EXCITED TEEN-AGER RELATES THE FANTASTIC EVENTS OF THE PREVIOUS NIGHT, AND THEN...

SHE'S STILL UNCONSCIOUS! PERHAPS IT'S BETTER THIS WAY! SHE CANNOT KNOW MY TERRIBLE SECRET!

SHE'LL BE SAFE HERE NOW...AS SAFE AS ANYONE CAN BE IN THIS FEARFUL WORLD!

DOC, WE GOTTA HURRY! THERE'S LOTS TO DO!

2O

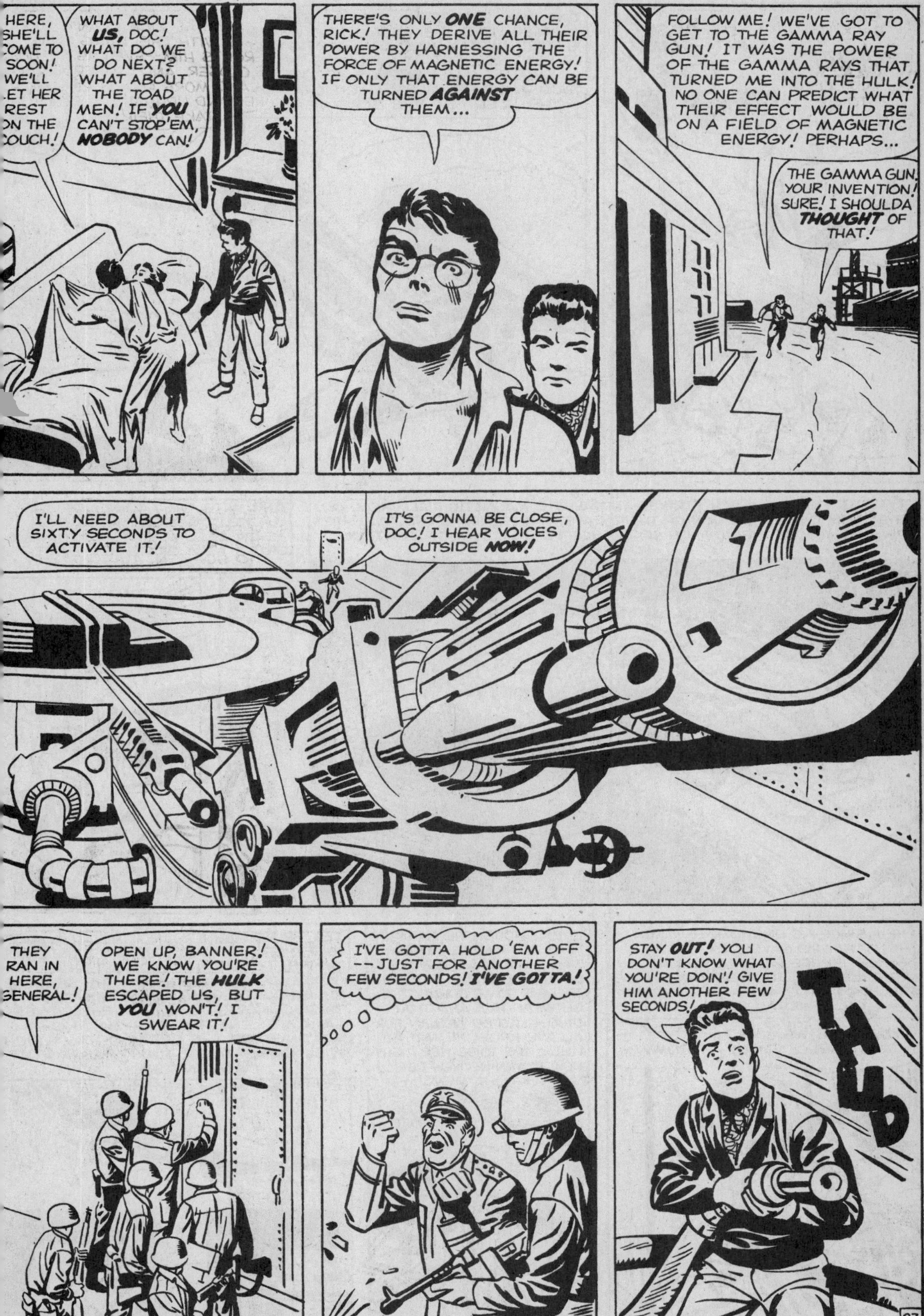

HERE, SHE'LL COME TO SOON! WE'LL LET HER REST ON THE COUCH!
WHAT ABOUT US, DOC! WHAT DO WE DO NEXT? WHAT ABOUT THE TOAD MEN! IF YOU CAN'T STOP 'EM, NOBODY CAN!
THERE'S ONLY ONE CHANCE, RICK! THEY DERIVE ALL THEIR POWER BY HARNESSING THE FORCE OF MAGNETIC ENERGY! IF ONLY THAT ENERGY CAN BE TURNED AGAINST THEM...
FOLLOW ME! WE'VE GOT TO GET TO THE GAMMA RAY GUN! IT WAS THE POWER OF THE GAMMA RAYS THAT TURNED ME INTO THE HULK! NO ONE CAN PREDICT WHAT THEIR EFFECT WOULD BE ON A FIELD OF MAGNETIC ENERGY! PERHAPS...
THE GAMMA GUN, YOUR INVENTION! SURE! I SHOULDA THOUGHT OF THAT!
I'LL NEED ABOUT SIXTY SECONDS TO ACTIVATE IT!
IT'S GONNA BE CLOSE, DOC! I HEAR VOICES OUTSIDE NOW!
THEY RAN IN HERE, GENERAL!
OPEN UP, BANNER! WE KNOW YOU'RE THERE! THE HULK ESCAPED US, BUT YOU WON'T! I SWEAR IT!
I'VE GOTTA HOLD 'EM OFF --JUST FOR ANOTHER FEW SECONDS! I'VE GOTTA!
STAY OUT! YOU DON'T KNOW WHAT YOU'RE DOIN'! GIVE HIM ANOTHER FEW SECONDS!
THUD
23

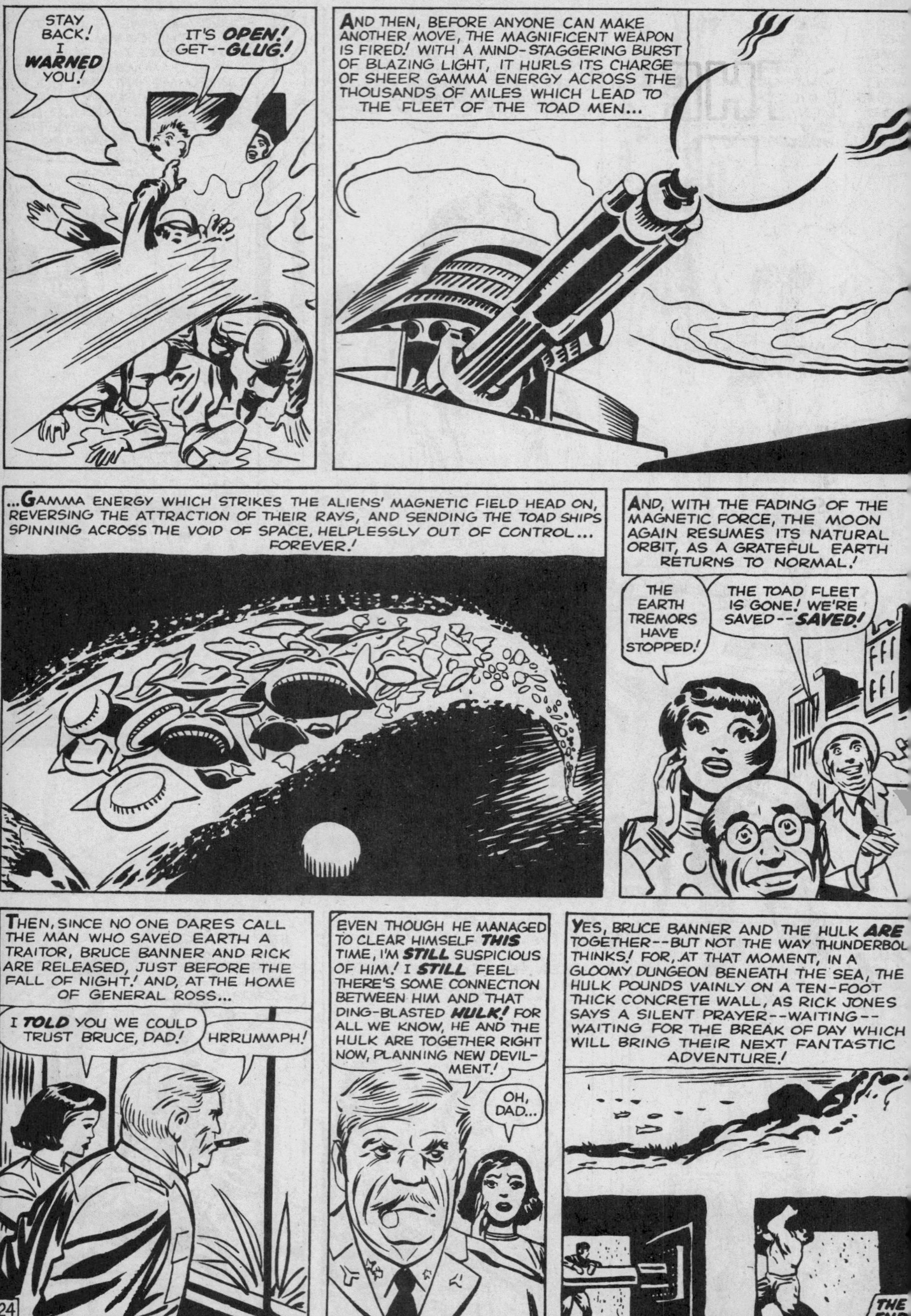
STAY BACK! I WARNED YOU!
IT'S OPEN! GET--GLUG!
AND THEN, BEFORE ANYONE CAN MAKE ANOTHER MOVE, THE MAGNIFICENT WEAPON IS FIRED! WITH A MIND-STAGGERING BURST OF BLAZING LIGHT, IT HURLS ITS CHARGE OF SHEER GAMMA ENERGY ACROSS THE THOUSANDS OF MILES WHICH LEAD TO THE FLEET OF THE TOAD MEN...
...GAMMA ENERGY WHICH STRIKES THE ALIENS' MAGNETIC FIELD HEAD ON, REVERSING THE ATTRACTION OF THEIR RAYS, AND SENDING THE TOAD SHIPS SPINNING ACROSS THE VOID OF SPACE, HELPLESSLY OUT OF CONTROL... FOREVER!
AND, WITH THE FADING OF THE MAGNETIC FORCE, THE MOON AGAIN RESUMES ITS NATURAL ORBIT, AS A GRATEFUL EARTH RETURNS TO NORMAL!
THE EARTH TREMORS HAVE STOPPED!
THE TOAD FLEET IS GONE! WE'RE SAVED--SAVED!
THEN, SINCE NO ONE DARES CALL THE MAN WHO SAVED EARTH A TRAITOR, BRUCE BANNER AND RICK ARE RELEASED, JUST BEFORE THE FALL OF NIGHT! AND, AT THE HOME OF GENERAL ROSS...
I TOLD YOU WE COULD TRUST BRUCE, DAD!
HRRUMMPH!
EVEN THOUGH HE MANAGED TO CLEAR HIMSELF THIS TIME, I'M STILL SUSPICIOUS OF HIM! I STILL FEEL THERE'S SOME CONNECTION BETWEEN HIM AND THAT DING-BLASTED HULK! FOR ALL WE KNOW, HE AND THE HULK ARE TOGETHER RIGHT NOW, PLANNING NEW DEVIL-MENT!
OH, DAD...
YES, BRUCE BANNER AND THE HULK ARE TOGETHER--BUT NOT THE WAY THUNDERBOL THINKS! FOR, AT THAT MOMENT, IN A GLOOMY DUNGEON BENEATH THE SEA, THE HULK POUNDS VAINLY ON A TEN-FOOT THICK CONCRETE WALL, AS RICK JONES SAYS A SILENT PRAYER--WAITING--WAITING FOR THE BREAK OF DAY WHICH WILL BRING THEIR NEXT FANTASTIC ADVENTURE!
THE END
24

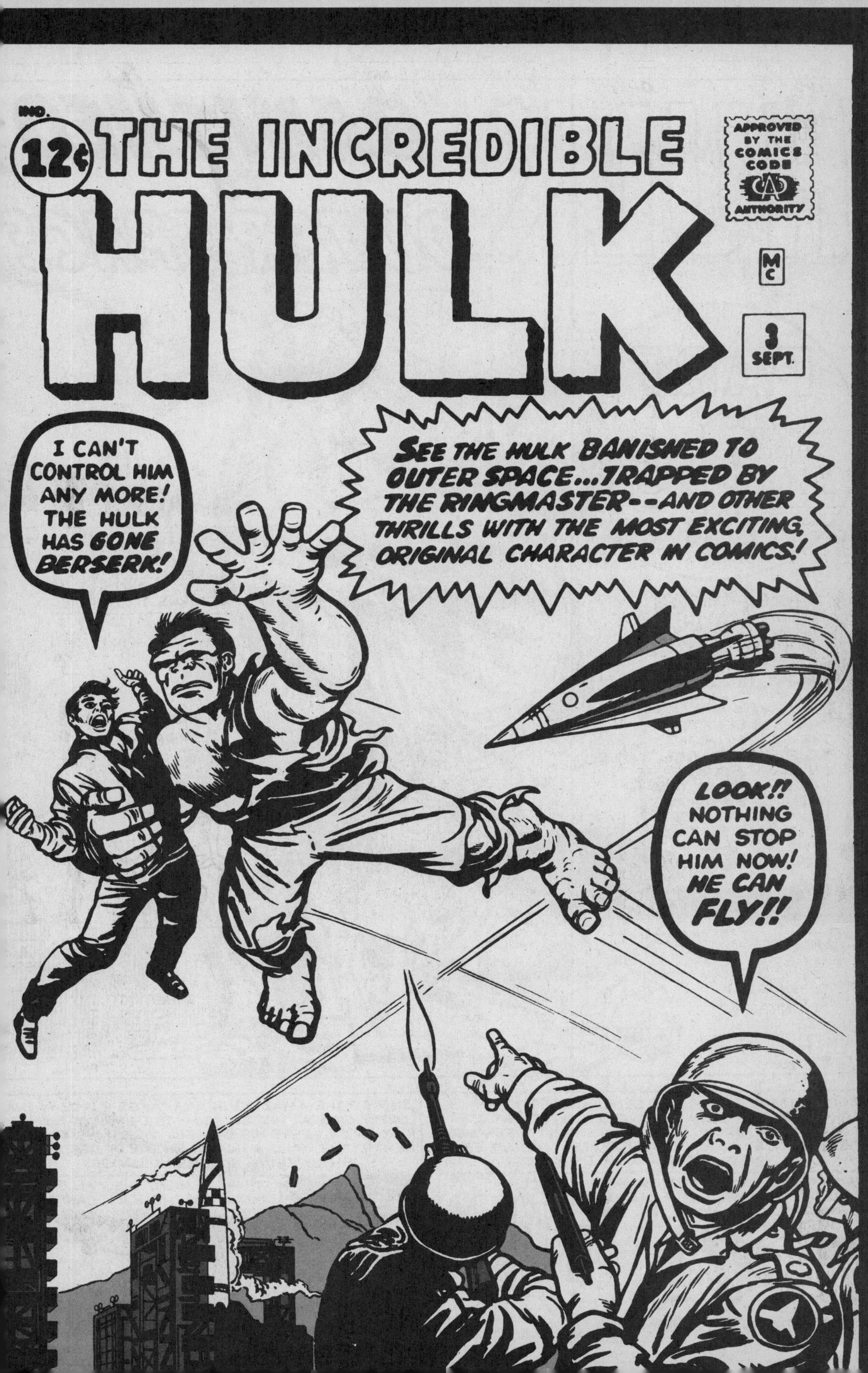

IND.
12¢
THE INCREDIBLE
HULK
APPROVED BY THE COMICS CODE AUTHORITY
MC
3
SEPT.
I CAN'T CONTROL HIM ANY MORE! THE HULK HAS GONE BERSERK!
SEE THE HULK BANISHED TO OUTER SPACE...TRAPPED BY THE RINGMASTER--AND OTHER THRILLS WITH THE MOST EXCITING, ORIGINAL CHARACTER IN COMICS!
LOOK!! NOTHING CAN STOP HIM NOW! HE CAN FLY!!

THE HULK "BANISHED TO OUTER SPACE"

PART 1

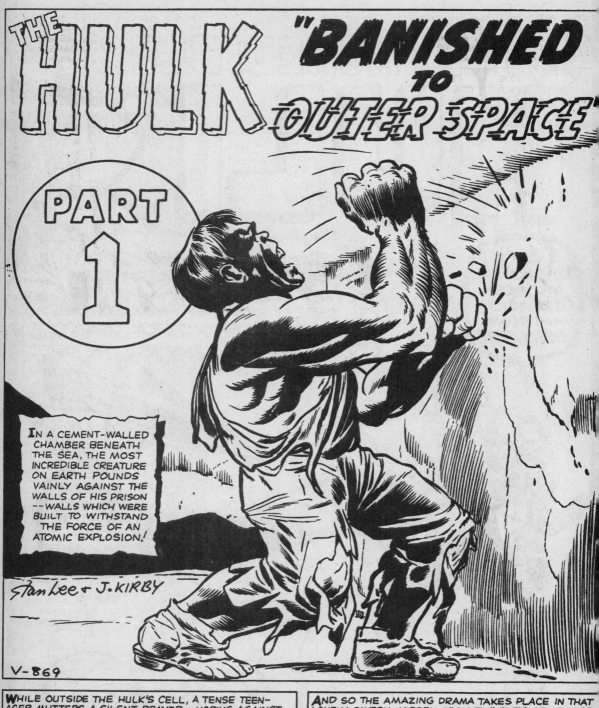

IN A CEMENT-WALLED CHAMBER BENEATH THE SEA, THE MOST INCREDIBLE CREATURE ON EARTH POUNDS VAINLY AGAINST THE WALLS OF HIS PRISON --WALLS WHICH WERE BUILT TO WITHSTAND THE FORCE OF AN ATOMIC EXPLOSION!

Stan Lee & J. KIRBY

V-869

WHILE OUTSIDE THE HULK'S CELL, A TENSE TEEN-AGER MUTTERS A SILENT PRAYER...HOPING AGAINST HOPE THAT DR. BRUCE BANNER HAS BUILT THE CHAMBER STRONG ENOUGH TO KEEP THE GREATEST MENACE EARTH HAS EVER KNOWN FROM ESCAPING!

ANOTHER FEW HOURS TILL DAYBREAK, AND THEN THE HULK WILL HAVE CHANGED BACK TO BRUCE BANNER, AND IT WILL BE SAFE FOR ME TO FREE HIM!

AND SO THE AMAZING DRAMA TAKES PLACE IN THAT LONELY CAVERN, HIDDEN FROM THE EYES OF MEN, AS RICK JONES KEEPS HIS FAITHFUL VIGIL, KNOWING THAT BEHIND THE WALL A HUMAN ENGINE OF DESTRUCTION IS QUIVERING TO BREAK LOOSE!

THANK HEAVEN! THE WALLS ARE HOLDING! THE HULK CAN'T ESCAPE!

1

ALONE WITH HIS THOUGHTS, THE BOY REMEMBERS THE EVENTS OF THE PAST FEW HOURS, AS HE AND DR. BANNER RUSHED TO THE HIDDEN CAVERN...

HURRY, RICK! IT'S GROWING DARK! THERE ISN'T MUCH TIME!

I'M COMIN', DOC!

WE'RE JUST IN TIME! NOW REMEMBER--DON'T OPEN THIS DOOR TILL DAYBREAK! NO MATTER WHAT!

BUT, DOC--WHAT IF SOMETHIN' *HAPPENS* TO ME?? WHAT IF I GET SICK OR SOMETHIN'? WHAT IF I *CAN'T* OPEN THE DOOR IN THE MORNING!

IT'S A CHANCE I HAVE TO TAKE, RICK! BETTER FOR ME TO SUFFOCATE IN THERE AS BRUCE BANNER, THAN TO ESCAPE AND MENACE THE WORLD AS -- THE *HULK!*

THE MASSIVE CONCRETE DOOR CLOSES BEHIND BRUCE BANNER AT THE EXACT MOMENT THAT EVENING BEGINS ON THE SURFACE! THEN, JUST AS IT HAS HAPPENED SO MANY TIMES BEFORE...

...A STARTLING *CHANGE* COMES OVER THE MILD, SCHOLARLY SCIENTIST...

...AND BEHOLD -- THE *HULK!!!*

SATISFIED THAT THE MONSTROUS CREATURE IS SAFELY IMPRISONED IN HIS CELL, RICK LEAVES THE CAVERN AS HE HEADS FOR BRUCE BANNER'S COTTAGE AND SOME MUCH-NEEDED SLEEP...

WHEW! I SURE CAN USE SOME SHUT-EYE!

BUT SUDDENLY!

HOLD ON, SON! YOU'RE RICK JONES, AREN'T YOU?

YEAH! WHAT'S IT TO *YOU*, NAPOLEON!

DON'T GET SMART, KID! WE'VE BEEN *LOOKIN'* FOR YOU!

2

WE'VE HAD THIS AREA UNDER SURVEILLANCE ALL DAY! WE KNEW YOU WERE BOUND TO SHOW UP SOONER OR LATER! AND OUR ORDERS FROM GENERAL "THUNDER-BOLT" ROSS ARE-- *BRING IN RICK JONES!* THE GENERAL KNOWS *YOU'RE* THE ONLY ONE WHO CAN LEAD US TO THE HULK!

AND, AT HIS HEADQUARTERS, A FEW MILES AWAY, THUNDERBOLT ROSS HOLDS A DRAMA[TIC] STAFF MEETING...

MY MEN WILL FIND RICK JONES -- YOU CA[N] *COUNT* ON IT! AND WHEN THEY DO, WE'[LL] GET THE HULK! HE WON'T ESCAPE US AGAIN! I *SWEAR* IT!

AND REMEMBER, WHEN THE BOY IS BROUGHT IN, WE BEGIN PLAN "H"! WE'LL *FORCE* HIM TO BRING THE HULK TO US!

HERE HE COMES *NOW*, GENERAL!

WHAT'S THE BIG IDEA, GENERAL? I AIN'T DONE NOTHIN'!

JONES, I'LL GET RIGHT TO THE POINT! YOU'VE GOT TO BRING THE HULK TO US! THERE'S NO TIME TO LOSE!

COOL IT, MISTER! *NOTHIN'* CAN MAKE ME RAT ON THE HULK!

LOOK, SON THIS IS BIGGER THA[N] YOU OR ME[!] THIS INVOLVE[S] THE SECURIT[Y] OF THE UNITE[D] STATE[S]

OUT THERE, ON THE LAUNCHING PAD, IS AMERICA'S NEWEST, MOST IMPORTANT MISSILE! IT *MUST* BE TESTED! BUT THERE ISN'T A MAN LIVING WHO COULD STAND THE FORCE OF ITS G-PULL-- EXCEPT THE HULK!

WE WANT THE HULK TO RIDE THAT ROCKET, IN THE INTERESTS OF NATIONAL SECURITY! NO ONE ELSE CAN DO IT! NOW, WHAT DO YOU SAY?

A SILENCE SO THICK THAT IT CAN ALMOST BE CUT DESCENDS UPON THE ROOM, AS THE SULLEN TEEN-AGER MAKES HIS DECISION..

IF IT'S SOMETHING THAT OUR COUNTRY NEEDS, HOW CAN I REFUSE? I-I'VE *GOTTA* BRING THE HULK HERE -- IF I *CAN!*

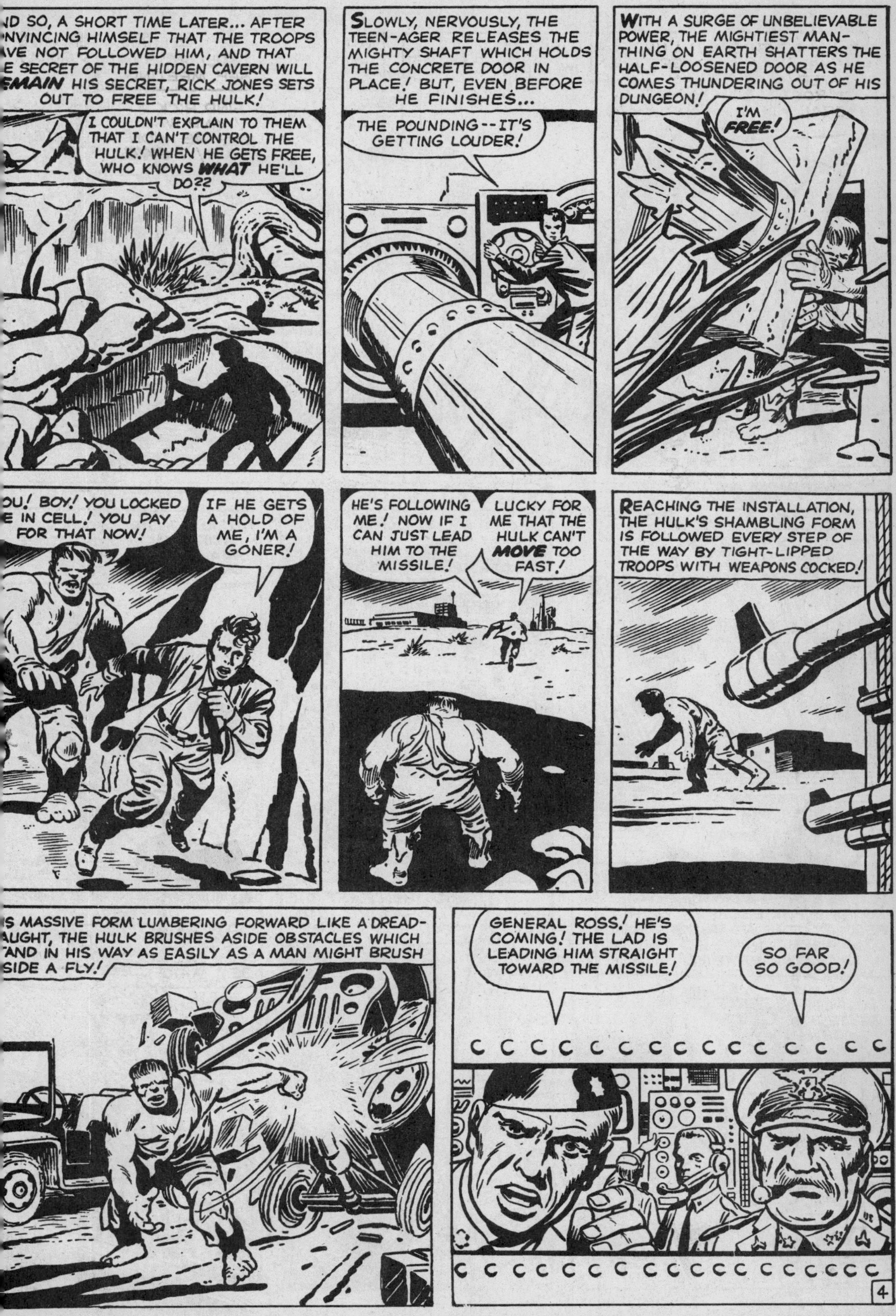
ND SO, A SHORT TIME LATER... AFTER NVINCING HIMSELF THAT THE TROOPS AVE NOT FOLLOWED HIM, AND THAT E SECRET OF THE HIDDEN CAVERN WILL EMAIN HIS SECRET, RICK JONES SETS OUT TO FREE THE HULK!
I COULDN'T EXPLAIN TO THEM THAT I CAN'T CONTROL THE HULK! WHEN HE GETS FREE, WHO KNOWS WHAT HE'LL DO??
SLOWLY, NERVOUSLY, THE TEEN-AGER RELEASES THE MIGHTY SHAFT WHICH HOLDS THE CONCRETE DOOR IN PLACE! BUT, EVEN BEFORE HE FINISHES...
THE POUNDING--IT'S GETTING LOUDER!
WITH A SURGE OF UNBELIEVABLE POWER, THE MIGHTIEST MAN-THING ON EARTH SHATTERS THE HALF-LOOSENED DOOR AS HE COMES THUNDERING OUT OF HIS DUNGEON!
I'M FREE!
OU! BOY! YOU LOCKED E IN CELL! YOU PAY FOR THAT NOW!
IF HE GETS A HOLD OF ME, I'M A GONER!
HE'S FOLLOWING ME! NOW IF I CAN JUST LEAD HIM TO THE MISSILE!
LUCKY FOR ME THAT THE HULK CAN'T MOVE TOO FAST!
REACHING THE INSTALLATION, THE HULK'S SHAMBLING FORM IS FOLLOWED EVERY STEP OF THE WAY BY TIGHT-LIPPED TROOPS WITH WEAPONS COCKED!
S MASSIVE FORM LUMBERING FORWARD LIKE A DREAD-AUGHT, THE HULK BRUSHES ASIDE OBSTACLES WHICH TAND IN HIS WAY AS EASILY AS A MAN MIGHT BRUSH SIDE A FLY!
GENERAL ROSS! HE'S COMING! THE LAD IS LEADING HIM STRAIGHT TOWARD THE MISSILE!
SO FAR SO GOOD!

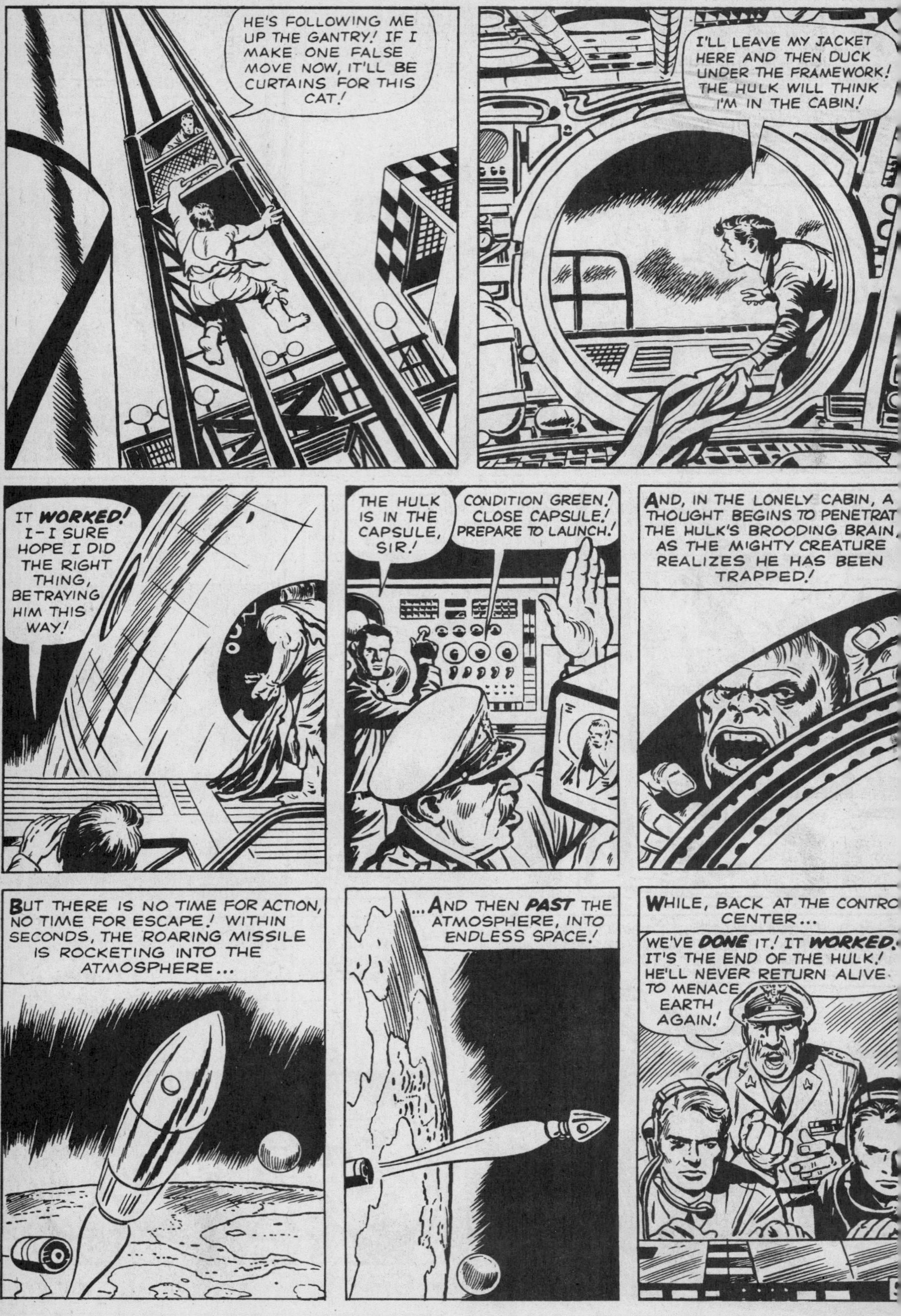
HE'S FOLLOWING ME UP THE GANTRY! IF I MAKE ONE FALSE MOVE NOW, IT'LL BE CURTAINS FOR THIS CAT!
I'LL LEAVE MY JACKET HERE AND THEN DUCK UNDER THE FRAMEWORK! THE HULK WILL THINK I'M IN THE CABIN!
IT WORKED! I-I SURE HOPE I DID THE RIGHT THING, BETRAYING HIM THIS WAY!
THE HULK IS IN THE CAPSULE, SIR!
CONDITION GREEN! CLOSE CAPSULE! PREPARE TO LAUNCH!
AND, IN THE LONELY CABIN, A THOUGHT BEGINS TO PENETRAT THE HULK'S BROODING BRAIN, AS THE MIGHTY CREATURE REALIZES HE HAS BEEN TRAPPED!
BUT THERE IS NO TIME FOR ACTION, NO TIME FOR ESCAPE! WITHIN SECONDS, THE ROARING MISSILE IS ROCKETING INTO THE ATMOSPHERE...
...AND THEN PAST THE ATMOSPHERE, INTO ENDLESS SPACE!
WHILE, BACK AT THE CONTRO CENTER...
WE'VE DONE IT! IT WORKED. IT'S THE END OF THE HULK! HE'LL NEVER RETURN ALIVE TO MENACE EARTH AGAIN!

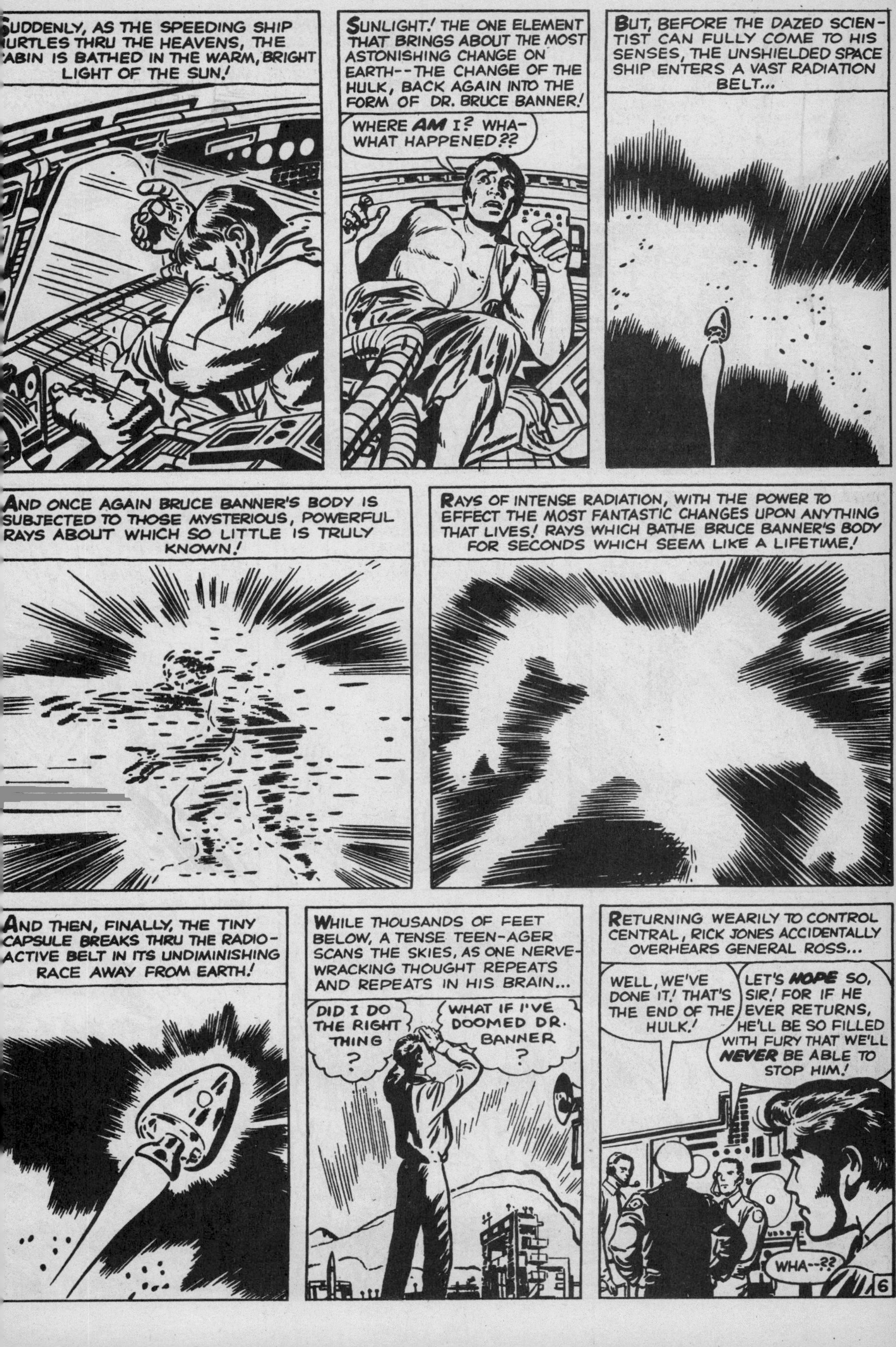
SUDDENLY, AS THE SPEEDING SHIP HURTLES THRU THE HEAVENS, THE CABIN IS BATHED IN THE WARM, BRIGHT LIGHT OF THE SUN!
SUNLIGHT! THE ONE ELEMENT THAT BRINGS ABOUT THE MOST ASTONISHING CHANGE ON EARTH--THE CHANGE OF THE HULK, BACK AGAIN INTO THE FORM OF DR. BRUCE BANNER!
WHERE AM I? WHA-WHAT HAPPENED??
BUT, BEFORE THE DAZED SCIENTIST CAN FULLY COME TO HIS SENSES, THE UNSHIELDED SPACE SHIP ENTERS A VAST RADIATION BELT...
AND ONCE AGAIN BRUCE BANNER'S BODY IS SUBJECTED TO THOSE MYSTERIOUS, POWERFUL RAYS ABOUT WHICH SO LITTLE IS TRULY KNOWN!
RAYS OF INTENSE RADIATION, WITH THE POWER TO EFFECT THE MOST FANTASTIC CHANGES UPON ANYTHING THAT LIVES! RAYS WHICH BATHE BRUCE BANNER'S BODY FOR SECONDS WHICH SEEM LIKE A LIFETIME!
AND THEN, FINALLY, THE TINY CAPSULE BREAKS THRU THE RADIO-ACTIVE BELT IN ITS UNDIMINISHING RACE AWAY FROM EARTH!
WHILE THOUSANDS OF FEET BELOW, A TENSE TEEN-AGER SCANS THE SKIES, AS ONE NERVE-WRACKING THOUGHT REPEATS AND REPEATS IN HIS BRAIN...
DID I DO THE RIGHT THING?
WHAT IF I'VE DOOMED DR. BANNER?
RETURNING WEARILY TO CONTROL CENTRAL, RICK JONES ACCIDENTALLY OVERHEARS GENERAL ROSS...
WELL, WE'VE DONE IT! THAT'S THE END OF THE HULK!
LET'S HOPE SO, SIR! FOR IF HE EVER RETURNS, HE'LL BE SO FILLED WITH FURY THAT WE'LL NEVER BE ABLE TO STOP HIM!
WHA--??
6

DON'T WORRY ABOUT THE HULK RETURNING! THAT MISSILE IS ON A FLIGHT TO INFINITY--AND IT'S A ONE-WAY JOURNEY!

IT WAS A TRAP! THEY *TRICKED* ME! IT WAS THE ONLY WAY THEY COULD REMOVE THE MENACE OF THE HULK!

BUT I CAN'T LET THEM DO IT! THEY DON'T REALIZE THAT HE ISN'T REALLY JUST AN INHUMAN MONSTER, TO BE DESTROYED BY ANY MEANS--HE'S BRUCE BANNER--AND I'VE GOT TO SAVE HIM!

HERE'S THE MISSILE CONTROL PANEL! THIS IS MY CHANCE! NO ONE'S LOOKING!

AT THAT SPLIT-SECOND, JUST AS RICK JONES TOUCHES THE CONTROL SWITCH, THE UNBELIEVABLE AMOUNT OF RADIATION WHICH THE SHIP HAS ABSORBED CAUSES A SHOCK TO TRAVEL THE MANY, MANY MILES BACK TO EARTH--AN ELECTRIC SHOCK WHICH WILL LINK THE HULK AND RICK JONES MORE CLOSELY TOGETHER THAN EVER BEFORE!

OWW!

THEN, THE DEED IS DONE! THE SHOCK IS GONE, AND DUE TO THE SWITCH BEING PULLED, THE ROCKET PACKAGE DROPS AWAY FROM THE MISSILE AND THE CAPSULE PLUMMETS BACK TO EARTH!

I'VE *DONE* IT! I'VE BROUGHT THE MISSILE BACK! THE AUTOMATIC CHUTE IS OPENING! BUT-- IT'S STILL FALLING TOO FAST!

IT'S DAYLIGHT NOW! BRUCE BANNER WILL BE IN THE CAPSULE, INSTEAD OF THE HULK! HE'LL NEVER BE ABLE TO SURVIVE A CRASH LANDING! =GASP= IT'S *TOO LATE!*

CRASH

I'VE KILLED HIM! I'VE KILLED THE ONLY REAL FRIEND I'VE EVER HAD! NO HUMAN BEING COULD HAVE LIVED THRU THAT CRASH! =SOB= I'VE KILLED HIM!

BUT, AT THAT MOMENT--

THE HULK! HOW?? HOW??

7

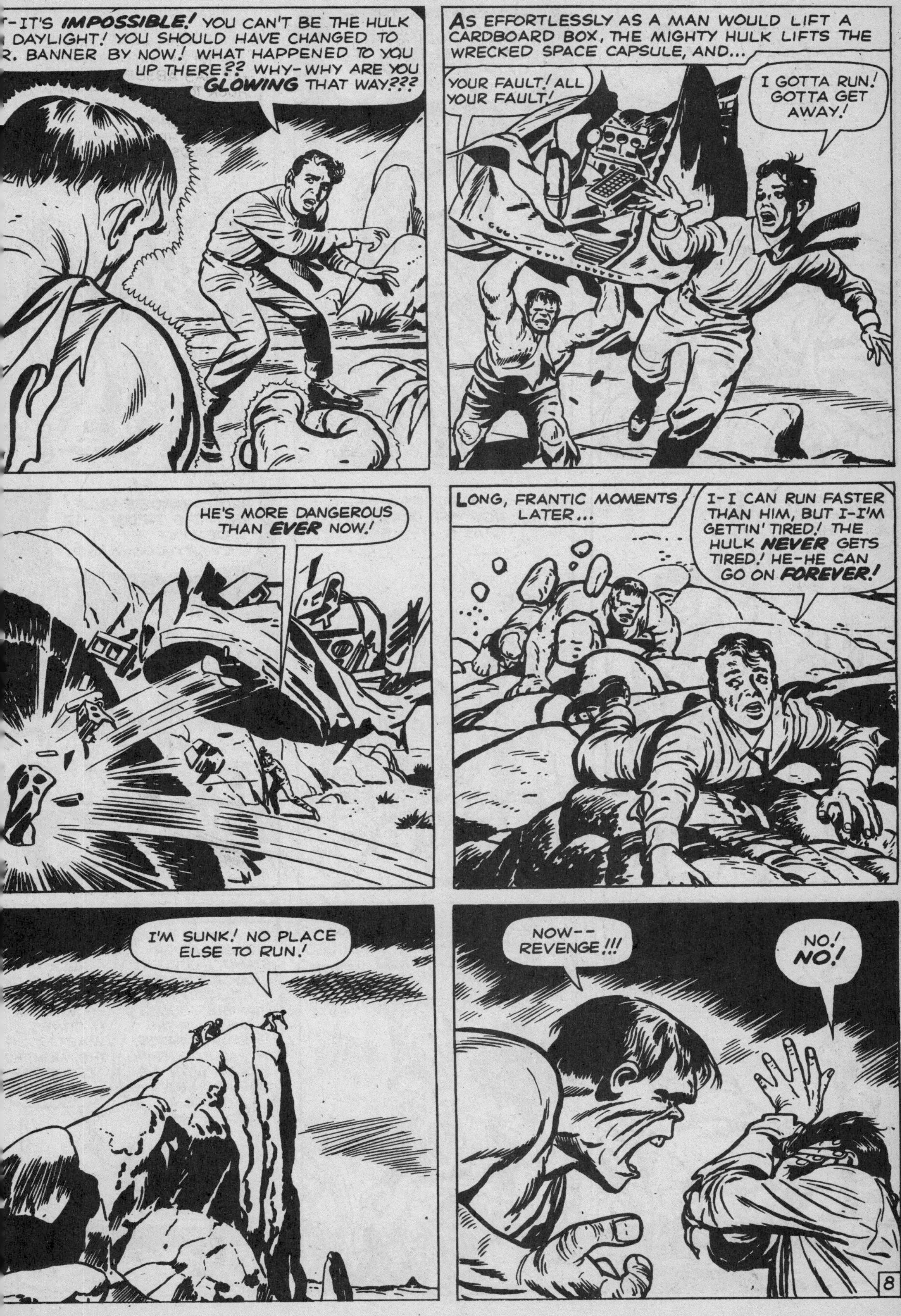
T-IT'S IMPOSSIBLE! YOU CAN'T BE THE HULK DAYLIGHT! YOU SHOULD HAVE CHANGED TO R. BANNER BY NOW! WHAT HAPPENED TO YOU UP THERE?? WHY-WHY ARE YOU GLOWING THAT WAY???
AS EFFORTLESSLY AS A MAN WOULD LIFT A CARDBOARD BOX, THE MIGHTY HULK LIFTS THE WRECKED SPACE CAPSULE, AND...
YOUR FAULT! ALL YOUR FAULT!
I GOTTA RUN! GOTTA GET AWAY!
HE'S MORE DANGEROUS THAN EVER NOW!
LONG, FRANTIC MOMENTS LATER...
I-I CAN RUN FASTER THAN HIM, BUT I-I'M GETTIN' TIRED! THE HULK NEVER GETS TIRED! HE-HE CAN GO ON FOREVER!
I'M SUNK! NO PLACE ELSE TO RUN!
NOW-- REVENGE!!!
NO! NO!

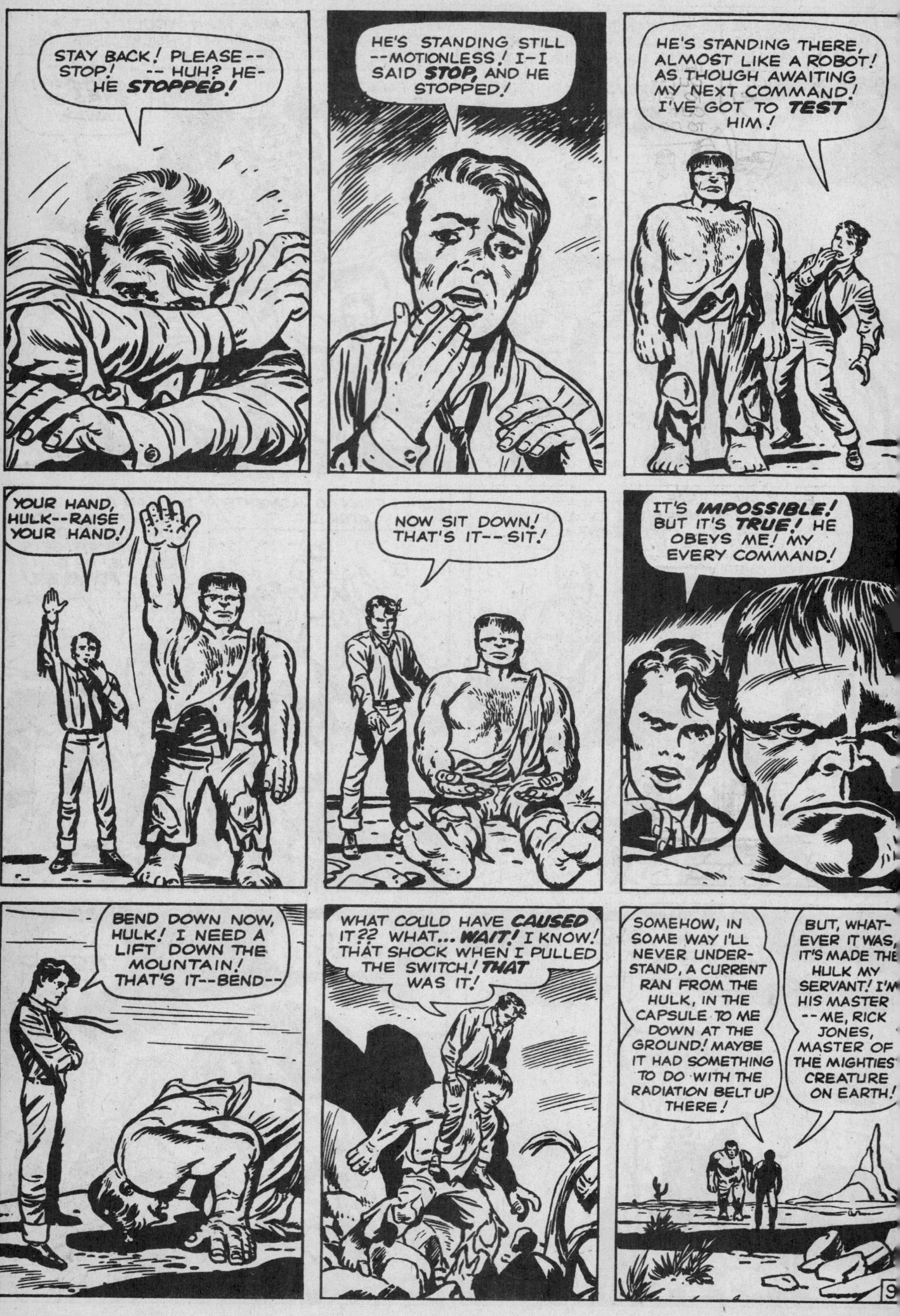
STAY BACK! PLEASE -- STOP! -- HUH? HE-HE STOPPED!
HE'S STANDING STILL --MOTIONLESS! I-I SAID STOP, AND HE STOPPED!
HE'S STANDING THERE, ALMOST LIKE A ROBOT! AS THOUGH AWAITING MY NEXT COMMAND! I'VE GOT TO TEST HIM!
YOUR HAND, HULK--RAISE YOUR HAND!
NOW SIT DOWN! THAT'S IT--SIT!
IT'S IMPOSSIBLE! BUT IT'S TRUE! HE OBEYS ME! MY EVERY COMMAND!
BEND DOWN NOW, HULK! I NEED A LIFT DOWN THE MOUNTAIN! THAT'S IT--BEND--
WHAT COULD HAVE CAUSED IT?? WHAT... WAIT! I KNOW! THAT SHOCK WHEN I PULLED THE SWITCH! THAT WAS IT!
SOMEHOW, IN SOME WAY I'LL NEVER UNDER-STAND, A CURRENT RAN FROM THE HULK, IN THE CAPSULE TO ME DOWN AT THE GROUND! MAYBE IT HAD SOMETHING TO DO WITH THE RADIATION BELT UP THERE!
BUT, WHAT-EVER IT WAS, IT'S MADE THE HULK MY SERVANT! I'M HIS MASTER --ME, RICK JONES, MASTER OF THE MIGHTIES' CREATURE ON EARTH!
9

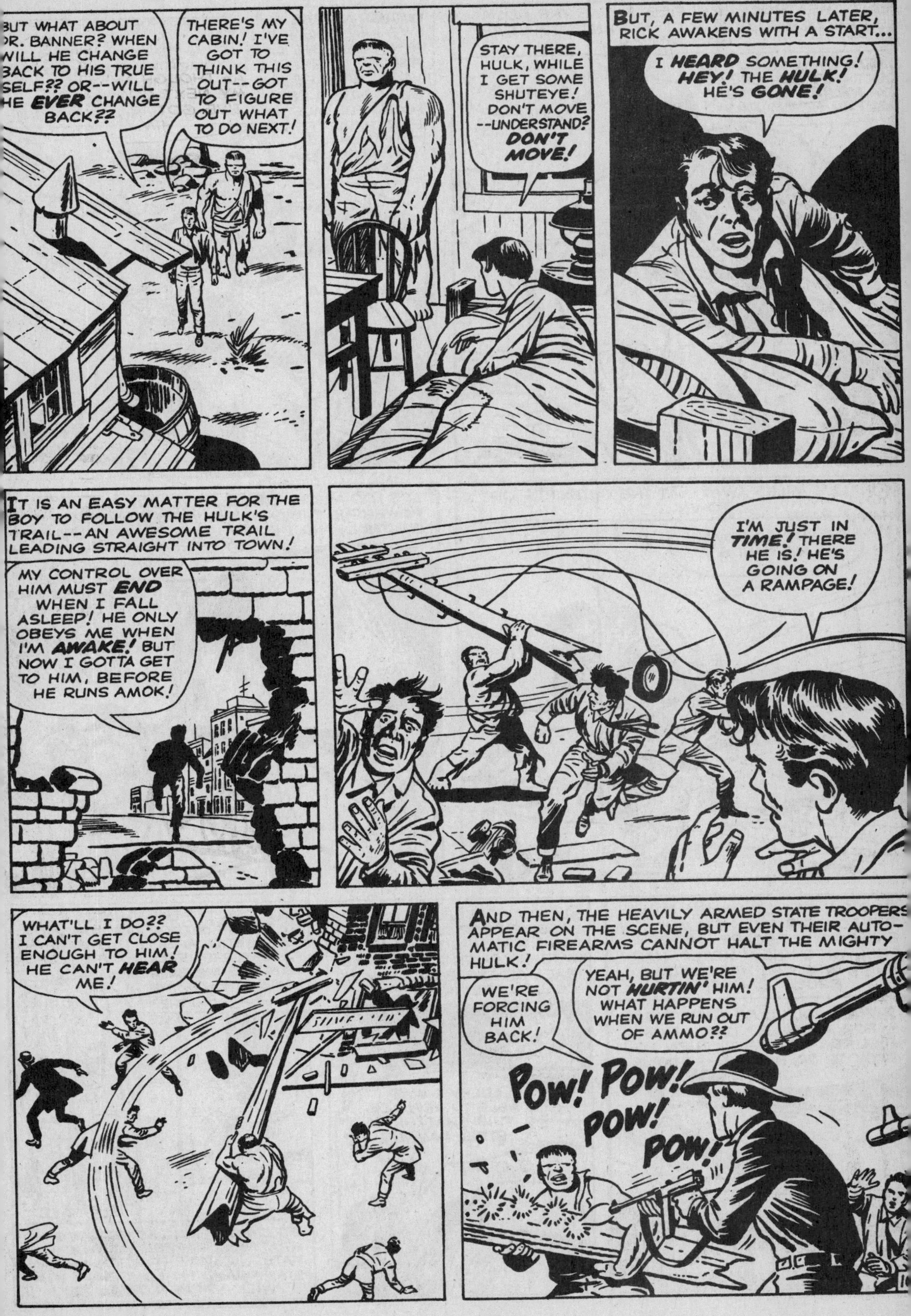
BUT WHAT ABOUT DR. BANNER? WHEN WILL HE CHANGE BACK TO HIS TRUE SELF?? OR--WILL HE EVER CHANGE BACK??
THERE'S MY CABIN! I'VE GOT TO THINK THIS OUT--GOT TO FIGURE OUT WHAT TO DO NEXT!
STAY THERE, HULK, WHILE I GET SOME SHUTEYE! DON'T MOVE --UNDERSTAND? DON'T MOVE!
BUT, A FEW MINUTES LATER, RICK AWAKENS WITH A START...
I HEARD SOMETHING! HEY! THE HULK! HE'S GONE!
IT IS AN EASY MATTER FOR THE BOY TO FOLLOW THE HULK'S TRAIL--AN AWESOME TRAIL LEADING STRAIGHT INTO TOWN!
MY CONTROL OVER HIM MUST END WHEN I FALL ASLEEP! HE ONLY OBEYS ME WHEN I'M AWAKE! BUT NOW I GOTTA GET TO HIM, BEFORE HE RUNS AMOK!
I'M JUST IN TIME! THERE HE IS! HE'S GOING ON A RAMPAGE!
WHAT'LL I DO?? I CAN'T GET CLOSE ENOUGH TO HIM! HE CAN'T HEAR ME!
AND THEN, THE HEAVILY ARMED STATE TROOPERS APPEAR ON THE SCENE, BUT EVEN THEIR AUTOMATIC FIREARMS CANNOT HALT THE MIGHTY HULK!
WE'RE FORCING HIM BACK!
YEAH, BUT WE'RE NOT HURTIN' HIM! WHAT HAPPENS WHEN WE RUN OUT OF AMMO??
POW! POW! POW! POW!

BUT THE TROOPERS' FIRE SLOWS THE HULK UP ENOUGH TO GIVE RICK A CHANCE TO LEAP INTO ACTION...

HULK! WE'VE GOT TO GET **OUT** OF HERE! DO YA **HEAR** ME?? **GET OUTTA HERE! FAST!**

I--HEAR!

GATHERING THE AWE-STRICKEN LAD IN ONE MASSIVE ARM, THE HULK LEAPS INTO THE AIR! BUT IT IS A LEAP THE LIKE OF WHICH HAS NEVER BEFORE BEEN SEEN BY MORTAL MAN!, A LEAP WHICH CARRIES HIM OVER THE TOP OF THE TALLES BUILDING! A LEAP PROPELLED BY THE MOST POWERFUL MUSCLES OF ANY LIVING THING ON EARTH!

WE-WE'RE **FLYIN'**!!!!

FINALLY, MILES AWAY--AT THE OUTSKIRTS OF TOWN...

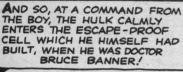

DOWN! GO DOWN, HULK! THAT'S IT!

IT'S TOO MUCH FOR ME! I'VE GOT THE MOST POWERFUL THING IN THE WORLD UNDER MY CONTROL, AND I DON'T KNOW WHAT TO **DO** WITH IT! BUT ONE THING I **DO** KNOW-- I DON'T DARE GO TO SLEEP AGAIN, UNLESS HE'S LOCKED UP BACK IN HIS DUNGEON!

AND SO, AT A COMMAND FROM THE BOY, THE HULK CALMLY ENTERS THE ESCAPE-PROOF CELL WHICH HE HIMSELF HAD BUILT, WHEN HE WAS DOCTOR BRUCE BANNER!

THERE! YOU'LL BE SAFE THERE -- FOR A WHILE! UNTIL I CAN FIGURE OUT HOW TO TURN YOU BACK TO DR. BANNER -- THAT IS, IF I EVER **CAN!**

SLOWLY, PONDEROUSLY, THE MASSIVE DOOR CLOSES, AS THE THING WHICH IS THE HULK WATCHES SILENTLY, WITH NO TRACE OF EXPRESSION ON HIS COLD, UNBLINKING EYES!

LUCKY I WAS ABLE TO REPLACE THIS SHATTERED STEEL RAMROD!

AND THRU THE LONG NIGHT, RICK JONES SITS OUTSIDE THE CONCRETE WALL....STILL AFRAID TO FALL ASLEEP, STILL NOT TRUSTING THE UNIMAGINABLE STRENGTH WHICH THE HULK POSSESSES!

STILL WONDERING AS HE WAITS-- WHAT WILL HAPPEN AT THAT FATEFUL MOMENT WHEN HE CAN STAY AWAKE NO LONGER ?? WHAT WILL HAPPEN **THEN** ???

11

.... AS RICK JONES SITS AGAINST THE COLD, DANK WALL, FIGHTING DESPERATELY TO KEEP FROM FALLING ASLEEP, HIS THOUGHTS GO RACING BACK...BACK TO THE BEGINNING... BACK TO

THE ORIGIN OF THE HULK!

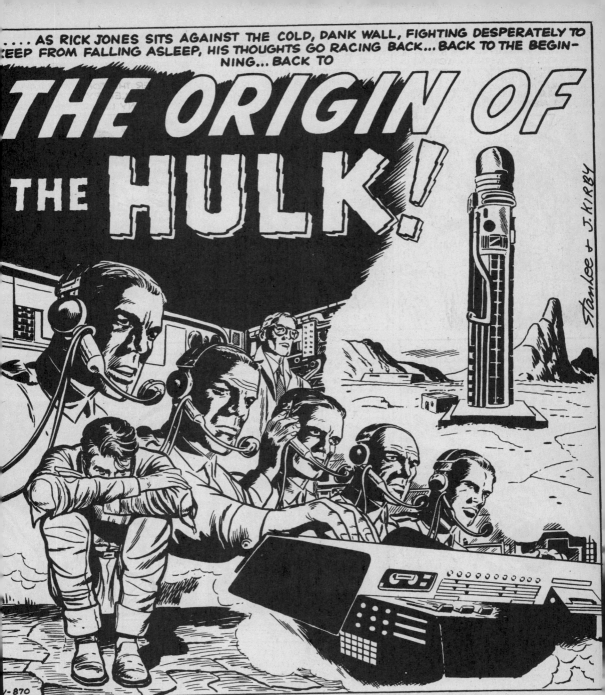

Stan Lee + J. Kirby

IT WAS A DAY THAT HAD STARTED LIKE ANY DAY, WHEN RICK HAD TAKEN A DARE FROM SOME FRIENDS AND DRIVEN INTO AN OFF-LIMITS ATOMIC TESTING RANGE!

I'LL SHOW THE GUYS I AIN'T CHICKEN! I'LL DRIVE RIGHT UP TO THE TEST AREA!

THEN, SECONDS BEFORE HIS POWERFUL GAMMA-RAY BOMB WAS DUE TO BE DETONATED, DOCTOR BRUCE BANNER SIGHTED THE BOY, FROM HIS VANTAGE POINT IN A SHIELDED BUNKER!

THERE'S SOMEONE *OUT* THERE! HE'LL BE *KILLED!*

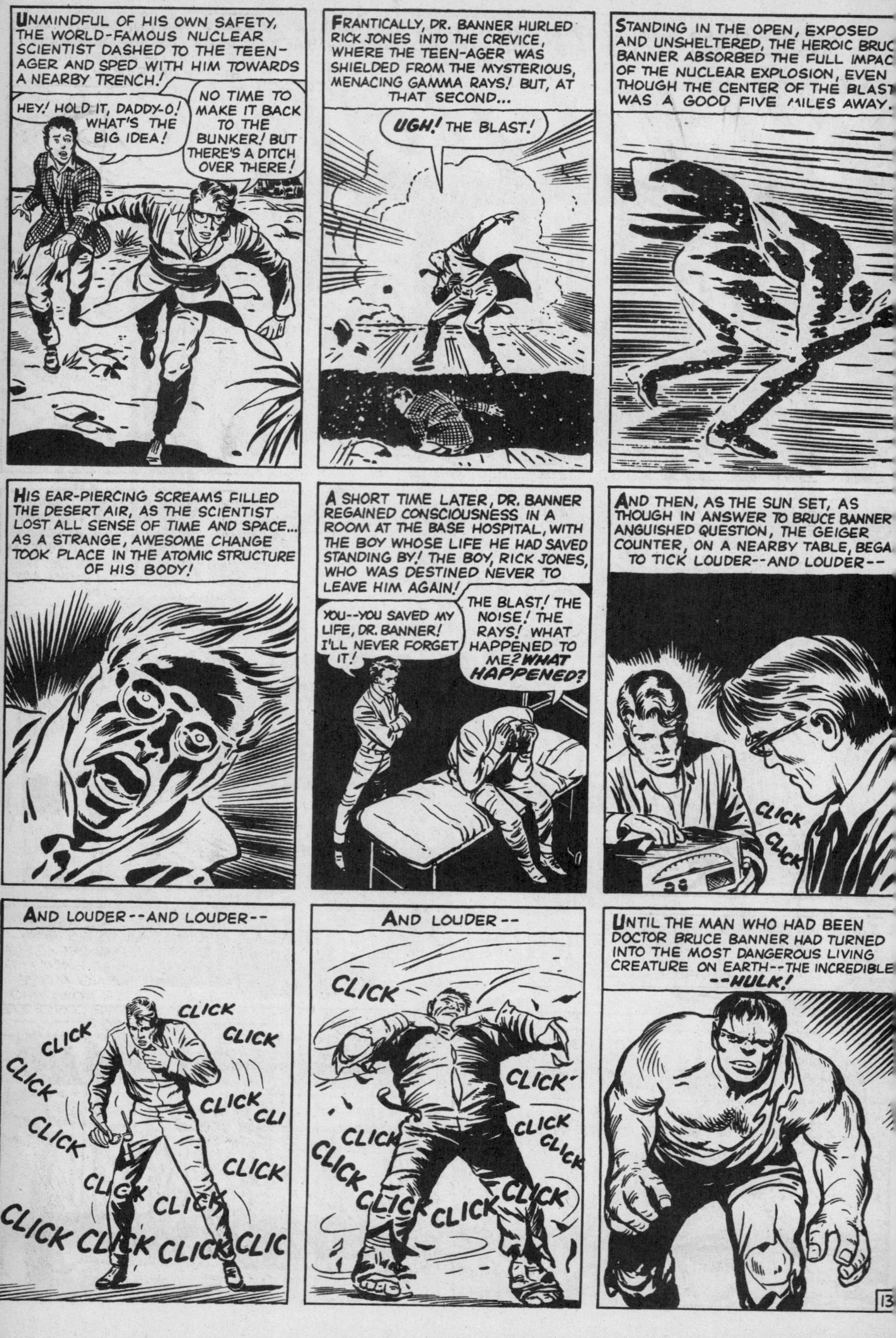
UNMINDFUL OF HIS OWN SAFETY, THE WORLD-FAMOUS NUCLEAR SCIENTIST DASHED TO THE TEEN-AGER AND SPED WITH HIM TOWARDS A NEARBY TRENCH!
HEY! HOLD IT, DADDY-O! WHAT'S THE BIG IDEA!
NO TIME TO MAKE IT BACK TO THE BUNKER! BUT THERE'S A DITCH OVER THERE!
FRANTICALLY, DR. BANNER HURLED RICK JONES INTO THE CREVICE, WHERE THE TEEN-AGER WAS SHIELDED FROM THE MYSTERIOUS, MENACING GAMMA RAYS! BUT, AT THAT SECOND...
UGH! THE BLAST!
STANDING IN THE OPEN, EXPOSED AND UNSHELTERED, THE HEROIC BRUC BANNER ABSORBED THE FULL IMPAC OF THE NUCLEAR EXPLOSION, EVEN THOUGH THE CENTER OF THE BLAST WAS A GOOD FIVE MILES AWAY.
HIS EAR-PIERCING SCREAMS FILLED THE DESERT AIR, AS THE SCIENTIST LOST ALL SENSE OF TIME AND SPACE... AS A STRANGE, AWESOME CHANGE TOOK PLACE IN THE ATOMIC STRUCTURE OF HIS BODY!
A SHORT TIME LATER, DR. BANNER REGAINED CONSCIOUSNESS IN A ROOM AT THE BASE HOSPITAL, WITH THE BOY WHOSE LIFE HE HAD SAVED STANDING BY! THE BOY, RICK JONES, WHO WAS DESTINED NEVER TO LEAVE HIM AGAIN!
YOU--YOU SAVED MY LIFE, DR. BANNER! I'LL NEVER FORGET IT!
THE BLAST! THE NOISE! THE RAYS! WHAT HAPPENED TO ME? WHAT HAPPENED?
AND THEN, AS THE SUN SET, AS THOUGH IN ANSWER TO BRUCE BANNER ANGUISHED QUESTION, THE GEIGER COUNTER, ON A NEARBY TABLE, BEGA TO TICK LOUDER--AND LOUDER--
CLICK
CLICK
AND LOUDER--AND LOUDER--
CLICK CLICK CLICK CLICK CLICK CLICK CLI CLICK CLICK CLICK CLICK CLICK CLICK CLICK CLICK CLIC
AND LOUDER--
CLICK CLICK CLICK CLICK CLICK CLICK CLICK CLICK CLICK CLICK
UNTIL THE MAN WHO HAD BEEN DOCTOR BRUCE BANNER HAD TURNED INTO THE MOST DANGEROUS LIVING CREATURE ON EARTH--THE INCREDIBLE --HULK!
13

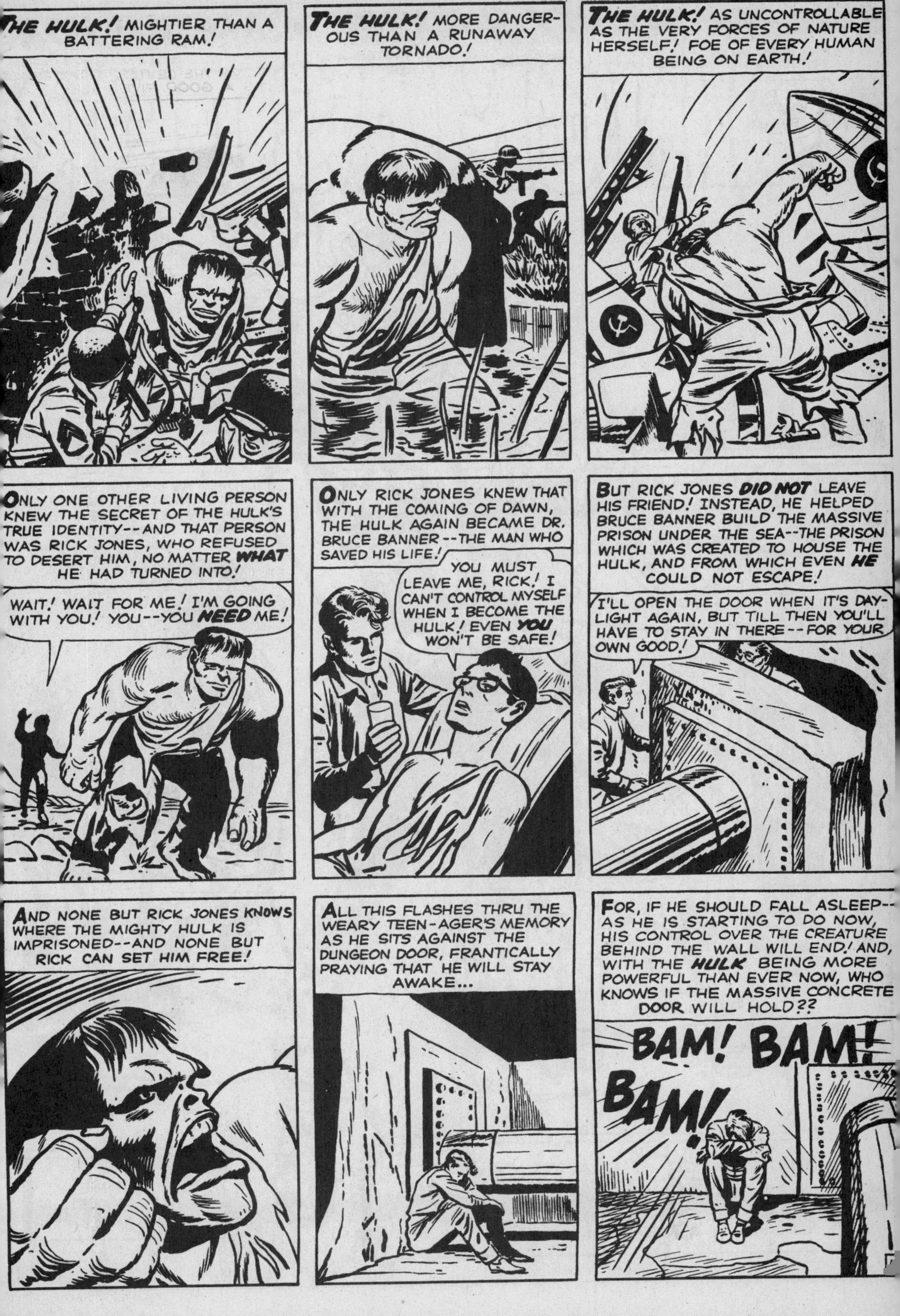
THE HULK! MIGHTIER THAN A BATTERING RAM!
THE HULK! MORE DANGER-OUS THAN A RUNAWAY TORNADO!
THE HULK! AS UNCONTROLLABLE AS THE VERY FORCES OF NATURE HERSELF! FOE OF EVERY HUMAN BEING ON EARTH!
ONLY ONE OTHER LIVING PERSON KNEW THE SECRET OF THE HULK'S TRUE IDENTITY--AND THAT PERSON WAS RICK JONES, WHO REFUSED TO DESERT HIM, NO MATTER WHAT HE HAD TURNED INTO!
WAIT! WAIT FOR ME! I'M GOING WITH YOU! YOU--YOU NEED ME!
ONLY RICK JONES KNEW THAT WITH THE COMING OF DAWN, THE HULK AGAIN BECAME DR. BRUCE BANNER--THE MAN WHO SAVED HIS LIFE!
YOU MUST LEAVE ME, RICK! I CAN'T CONTROL MYSELF WHEN I BECOME THE HULK! EVEN YOU WON'T BE SAFE!
BUT RICK JONES DID NOT LEAVE HIS FRIEND! INSTEAD, HE HELPED BRUCE BANNER BUILD THE MASSIVE PRISON UNDER THE SEA--THE PRISON WHICH WAS CREATED TO HOUSE THE HULK, AND FROM WHICH EVEN HE COULD NOT ESCAPE!
I'LL OPEN THE DOOR WHEN IT'S DAY-LIGHT AGAIN, BUT TILL THEN YOU'LL HAVE TO STAY IN THERE--FOR YOUR OWN GOOD!
AND NONE BUT RICK JONES KNOWS WHERE THE MIGHTY HULK IS IMPRISONED--AND NONE BUT RICK CAN SET HIM FREE!
ALL THIS FLASHES THRU THE WEARY TEEN-AGER'S MEMORY AS HE SITS AGAINST THE DUNGEON DOOR, FRANTICALLY PRAYING THAT HE WILL STAY AWAKE...
FOR, IF HE SHOULD FALL ASLEEP--AS HE IS STARTING TO DO NOW, HIS CONTROL OVER THE CREATURE BEHIND THE WALL WILL END! AND, WITH THE HULK BEING MORE POWERFUL THAN EVER NOW, WHO KNOWS IF THE MASSIVE CONCRETE DOOR WILL HOLD??
BAM! BAM!
BAM!

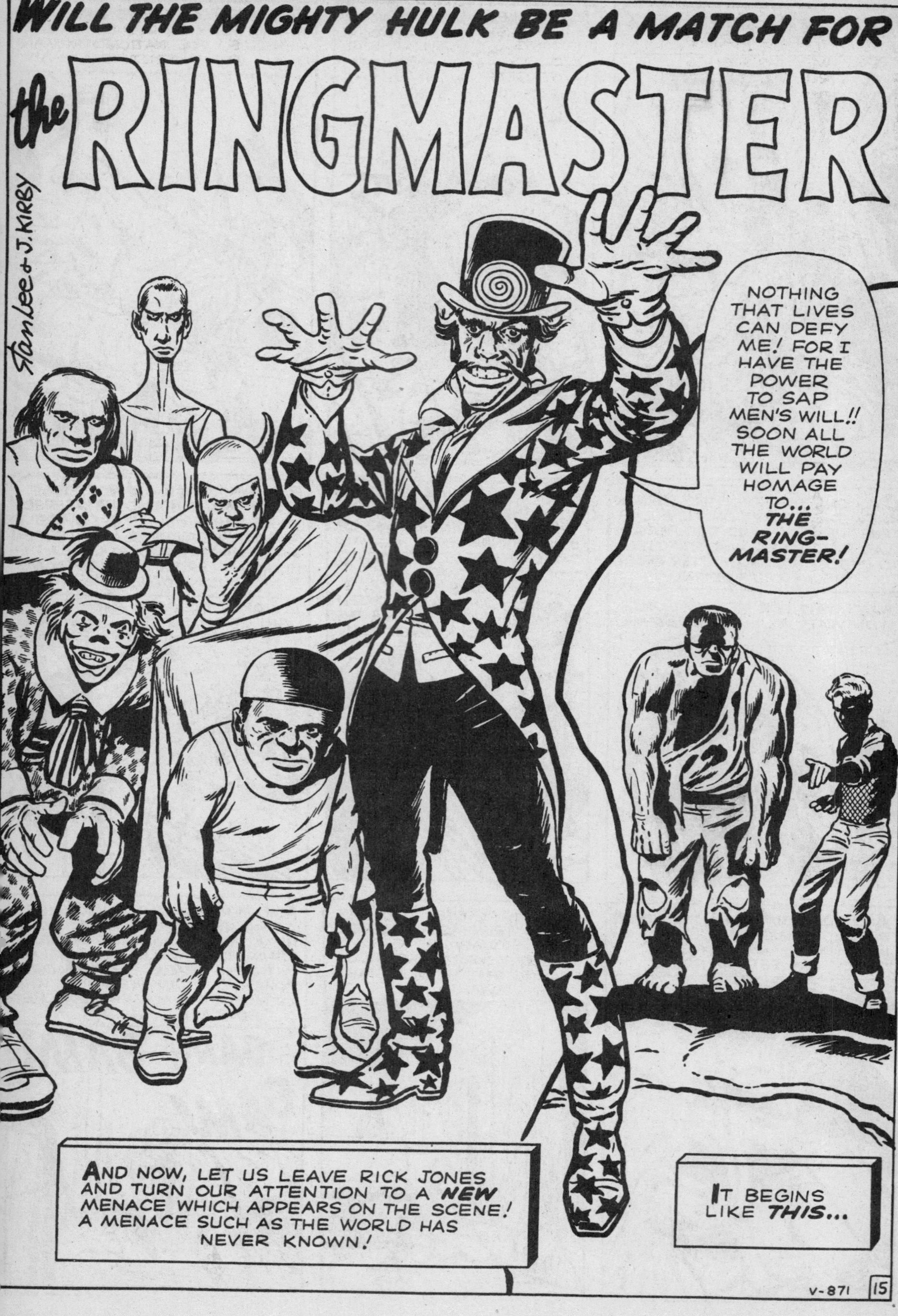
WILL THE MIGHTY HULK BE A MATCH FOR
the RINGMASTER
Stan Lee + J. Kirby
NOTHING THAT LIVES CAN DEFY ME! FOR I HAVE THE POWER TO SAP MEN'S WILL!! SOON ALL THE WORLD WILL PAY HOMAGE TO... THE RING-MASTER!
AND NOW, LET US LEAVE RICK JONES AND TURN OUR ATTENTION TO A NEW MENACE WHICH APPEARS ON THE SCENE! A MENACE SUCH AS THE WORLD HAS NEVER KNOWN!
IT BEGINS LIKE THIS...
V-871

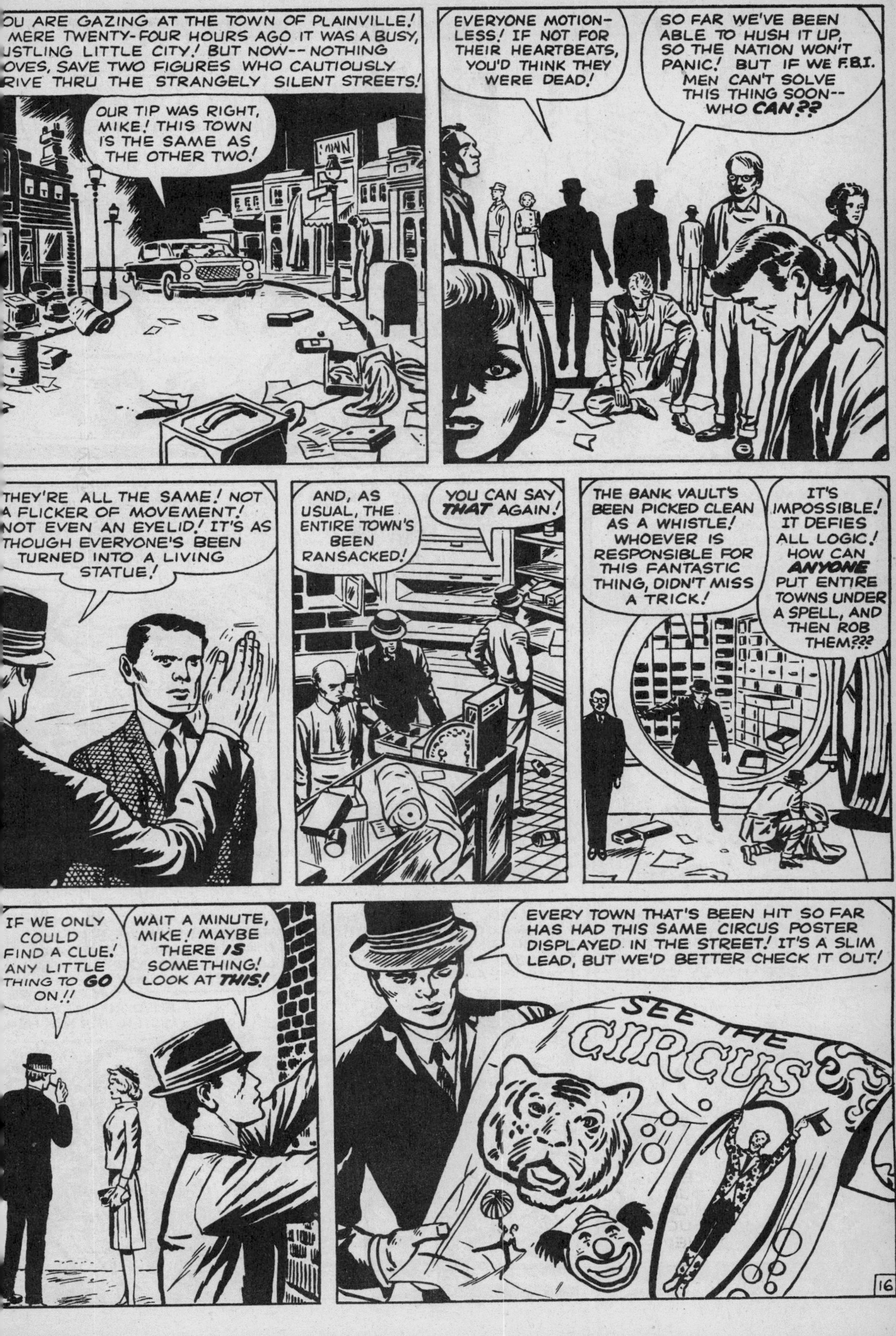

OU ARE GAZING AT THE TOWN OF PLAINVILLE! MERE TWENTY-FOUR HOURS AGO IT WAS A BUSY, USTLING LITTLE CITY! BUT NOW-- NOTHING OVES, SAVE TWO FIGURES WHO CAUTIOUSLY RIVE THRU THE STRANGELY SILENT STREETS!
OUR TIP WAS RIGHT, MIKE! THIS TOWN IS THE SAME AS THE OTHER TWO!
EVERYONE MOTIONLESS! IF NOT FOR THEIR HEARTBEATS, YOU'D THINK THEY WERE DEAD!
SO FAR WE'VE BEEN ABLE TO HUSH IT UP, SO THE NATION WON'T PANIC! BUT IF WE F.B.I. MEN CAN'T SOLVE THIS THING SOON-- WHO CAN??
THEY'RE ALL THE SAME! NOT A FLICKER OF MOVEMENT! NOT EVEN AN EYELID! IT'S AS THOUGH EVERYONE'S BEEN TURNED INTO A LIVING STATUE!
AND, AS USUAL, THE ENTIRE TOWN'S BEEN RANSACKED!
YOU CAN SAY THAT AGAIN!
THE BANK VAULT'S BEEN PICKED CLEAN AS A WHISTLE! WHOEVER IS RESPONSIBLE FOR THIS FANTASTIC THING, DIDN'T MISS A TRICK!
IT'S IMPOSSIBLE! IT DEFIES ALL LOGIC! HOW CAN ANYONE PUT ENTIRE TOWNS UNDER A SPELL, AND THEN ROB THEM???
IF WE ONLY COULD FIND A CLUE! ANY LITTLE THING TO GO ON!!
WAIT A MINUTE, MIKE! MAYBE THERE IS SOMETHING! LOOK AT THIS!
EVERY TOWN THAT'S BEEN HIT SO FAR HAS HAD THIS SAME CIRCUS POSTER DISPLAYED IN THE STREET! IT'S A SLIM LEAD, BUT WE'D BETTER CHECK IT OUT!
SEE THE CIRCUS

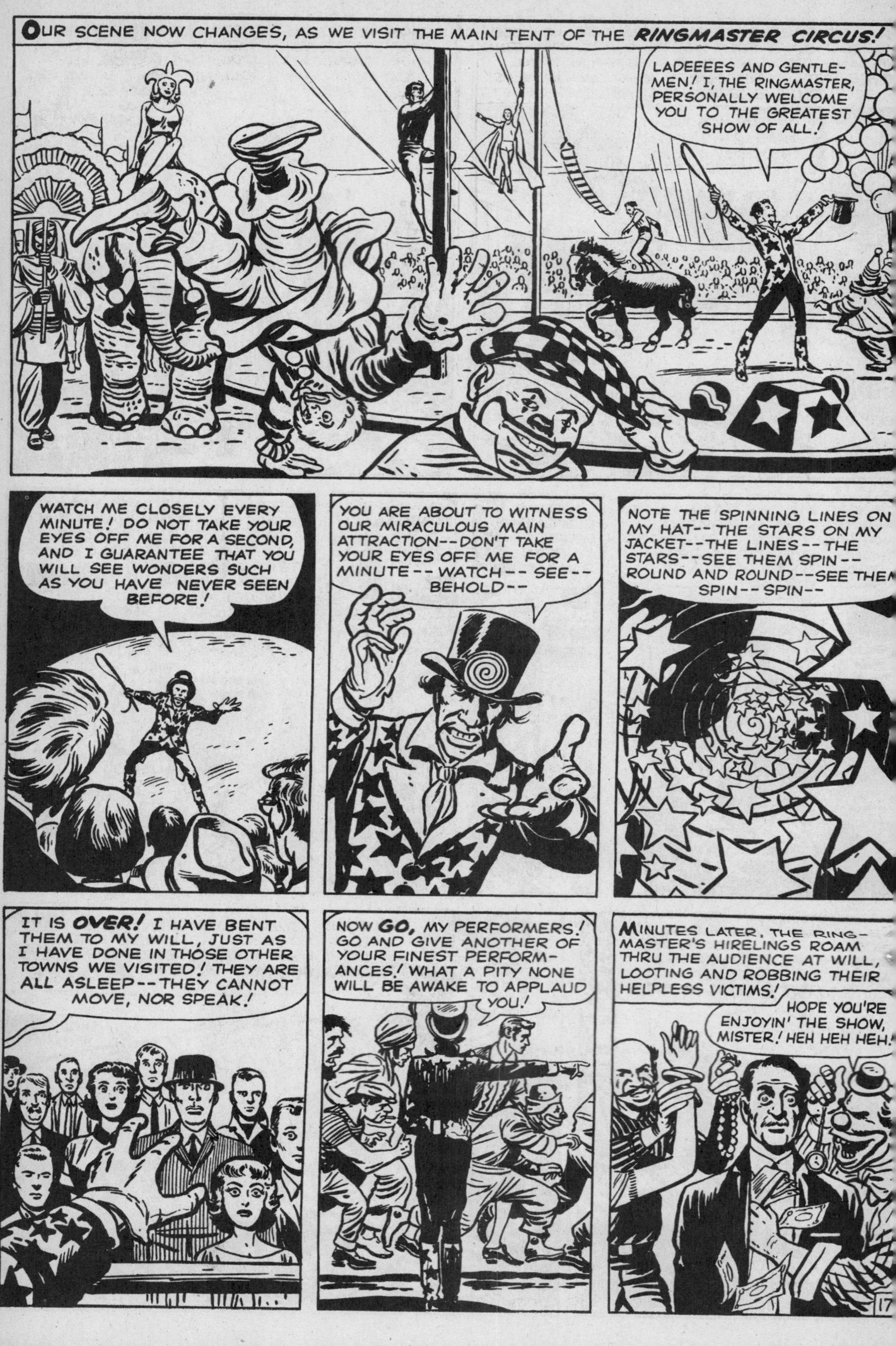
OUR SCENE NOW CHANGES, AS WE VISIT THE MAIN TENT OF THE RINGMASTER CIRCUS!
LADEEEES AND GENTLEMEN! I, THE RINGMASTER, PERSONALLY WELCOME YOU TO THE GREATEST SHOW OF ALL!
WATCH ME CLOSELY EVERY MINUTE! DO NOT TAKE YOUR EYES OFF ME FOR A SECOND, AND I GUARANTEE THAT YOU WILL SEE WONDERS SUCH AS YOU HAVE NEVER SEEN BEFORE!
YOU ARE ABOUT TO WITNESS OUR MIRACULOUS MAIN ATTRACTION--DON'T TAKE YOUR EYES OFF ME FOR A MINUTE--WATCH--SEE--BEHOLD--
NOTE THE SPINNING LINES ON MY HAT--THE STARS ON MY JACKET--THE LINES--THE STARS--SEE THEM SPIN--ROUND AND ROUND--SEE THEM SPIN--SPIN--
IT IS OVER! I HAVE BENT THEM TO MY WILL, JUST AS I HAVE DONE IN THOSE OTHER TOWNS WE VISITED! THEY ARE ALL ASLEEP--THEY CANNOT MOVE, NOR SPEAK!
NOW GO, MY PERFORMERS! GO AND GIVE ANOTHER OF YOUR FINEST PERFORMANCES! WHAT A PITY NONE WILL BE AWAKE TO APPLAUD YOU!
MINUTES LATER, THE RINGMASTER'S HIRELINGS ROAM THRU THE AUDIENCE AT WILL, LOOTING AND ROBBING THEIR HELPLESS VICTIMS!
HOPE YOU'RE ENJOYIN' THE SHOW, MISTER! HEH HEH HEH!
17

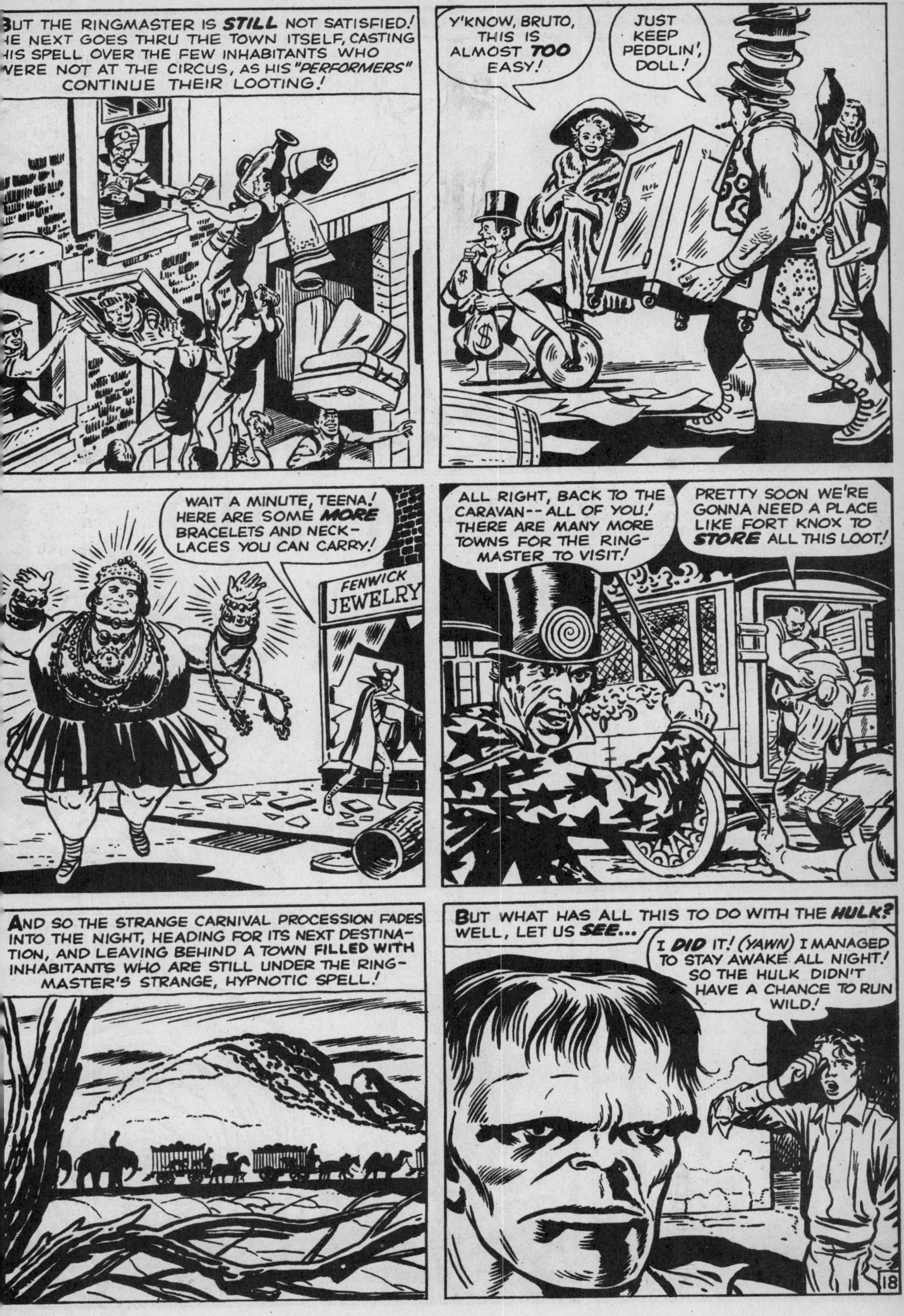

BUT THE RINGMASTER IS STILL NOT SATISFIED! HE NEXT GOES THRU THE TOWN ITSELF, CASTING HIS SPELL OVER THE FEW INHABITANTS WHO WERE NOT AT THE CIRCUS, AS HIS "PERFORMERS" CONTINUE THEIR LOOTING!
Y'KNOW, BRUTO, THIS IS ALMOST TOO EASY!
JUST KEEP PEDDLIN', DOLL!
WAIT A MINUTE, TEENA! HERE ARE SOME MORE BRACELETS AND NECKLACES YOU CAN CARRY!
FENWICK JEWELRY
ALL RIGHT, BACK TO THE CARAVAN--ALL OF YOU! THERE ARE MANY MORE TOWNS FOR THE RINGMASTER TO VISIT!
PRETTY SOON WE'RE GONNA NEED A PLACE LIKE FORT KNOX TO STORE ALL THIS LOOT!
AND SO THE STRANGE CARNIVAL PROCESSION FADES INTO THE NIGHT, HEADING FOR ITS NEXT DESTINATION, AND LEAVING BEHIND A TOWN FILLED WITH INHABITANTS WHO ARE STILL UNDER THE RINGMASTER'S STRANGE, HYPNOTIC SPELL!
BUT WHAT HAS ALL THIS TO DO WITH THE HULK? WELL, LET US SEE...
I DID IT! (YAWN) I MANAGED TO STAY AWAKE ALL NIGHT! SO THE HULK DIDN'T HAVE A CHANCE TO RUN WILD!
18

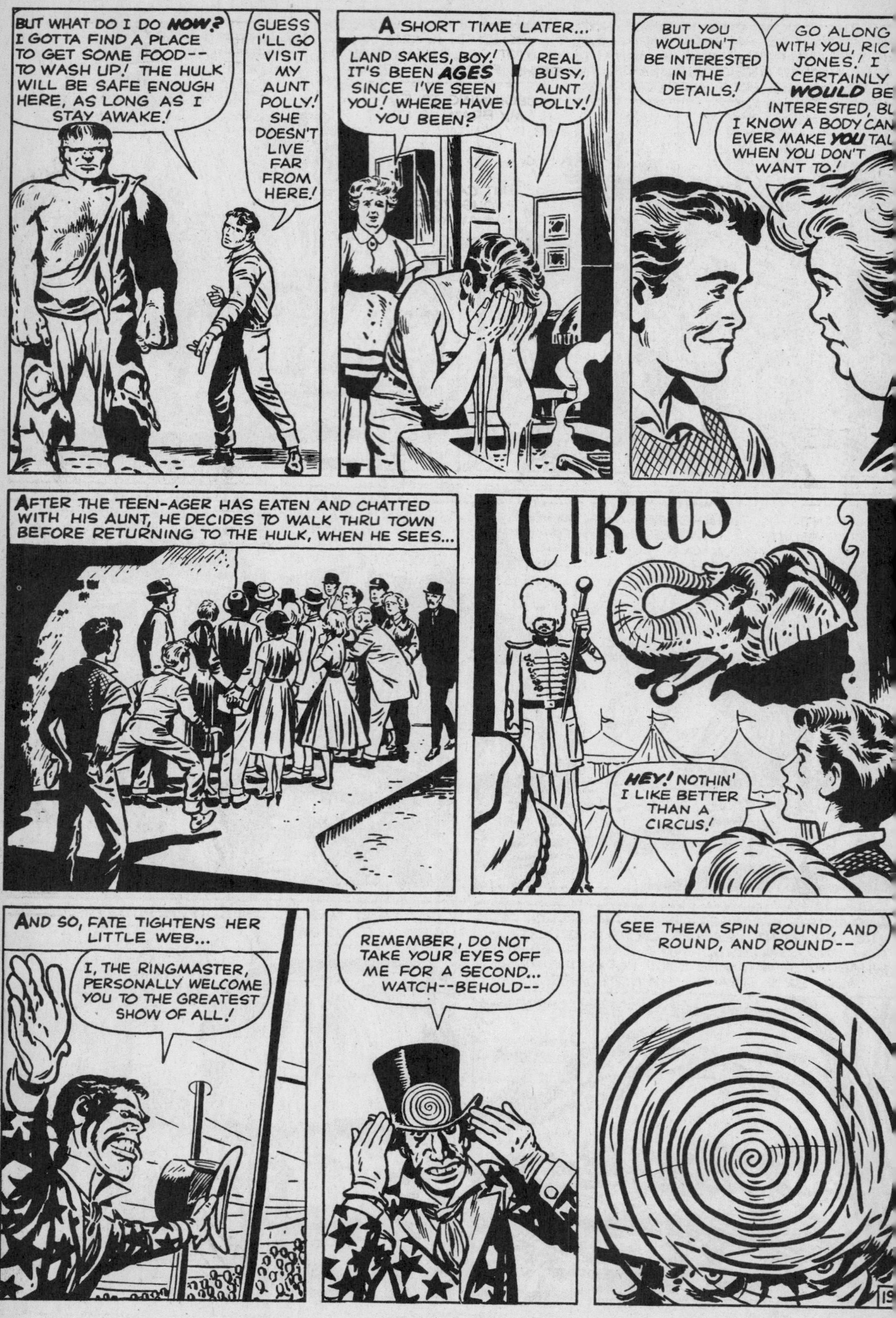

BUT WHAT DO I DO NOW? I GOTTA FIND A PLACE TO GET SOME FOOD-- TO WASH UP! THE HULK WILL BE SAFE ENOUGH HERE, AS LONG AS I STAY AWAKE!
GUESS I'LL GO VISIT MY AUNT POLLY! SHE DOESN'T LIVE FAR FROM HERE!
A SHORT TIME LATER...
LAND SAKES, BOY! IT'S BEEN AGES SINCE I'VE SEEN YOU! WHERE HAVE YOU BEEN?
REAL BUSY, AUNT POLLY!
BUT YOU WOULDN'T BE INTERESTED IN THE DETAILS!
GO ALONG WITH YOU, RIC JONES! I CERTAINLY WOULD BE INTERESTED, BU I KNOW A BODY CAN EVER MAKE YOU TAL WHEN YOU DON'T WANT TO!
AFTER THE TEEN-AGER HAS EATEN AND CHATTED WITH HIS AUNT, HE DECIDES TO WALK THRU TOWN BEFORE RETURNING TO THE HULK, WHEN HE SEES...
CIRCUS
HEY! NOTHIN' I LIKE BETTER THAN A CIRCUS!
AND SO, FATE TIGHTENS HER LITTLE WEB...
I, THE RINGMASTER, PERSONALLY WELCOME YOU TO THE GREATEST SHOW OF ALL!
REMEMBER, DO NOT TAKE YOUR EYES OFF ME FOR A SECOND... WATCH--BEHOLD--
SEE THEM SPIN ROUND, AND ROUND, AND ROUND--
19

ND, **THIS** TIME, AMONG HIS HELPLESS VICTIMS, THE RINGMASTER UNWITTINGLY NUMBERS NE TEEN-AGE BOY-- A BOY HO HAS **THE HULK** TO COMMAND!

I-I CAN'T MOVE! CAN'T SPEAK! HE-HE'S **HYPNOTIZED** US ALL!

BUT RICK JONES IS **NOT** HELPLESS! NOT SO LONG AS HE HAS THE POWER TO **THINK**!

I-I'M BEGINNING TO FEEL NUMB! MY BRAIN IS GETTING CLOUDED! I'VE GOT TO CALL THE HULK BEFORE I BLACK OUT! COME TO ME, HULK! **HELP!** COME, HULK!

BUT, CAN HE HEAR MY THOUGHTS FROM SO FAR AWAY?? HE MUST! **HE MUST!**

AND HE **DOES!**

BOY IN DANGER! MUST GO TO HIM!

IKE A FANTASTIC FLYING DREAD-AUGHT, THE MASSIVE CREATURE URTLES THRU THE AIR AND LUMMETS DOWN TOWARDS THE IRCUS TENT, DIRECTED BY RICK'S THOUGHT WAVES!

WHAT IS-- **THAT??!**

LOOK! THERE'S SOMEONE WHO THE RINGMASTER **DIDN'T** HYPNOTIZE!

JUST AIM ME TOWARDS HIM, PAL! **I'LL** TAKE CARE OF THE BIG OX!

HUMAN CANNONBALL

POW

20

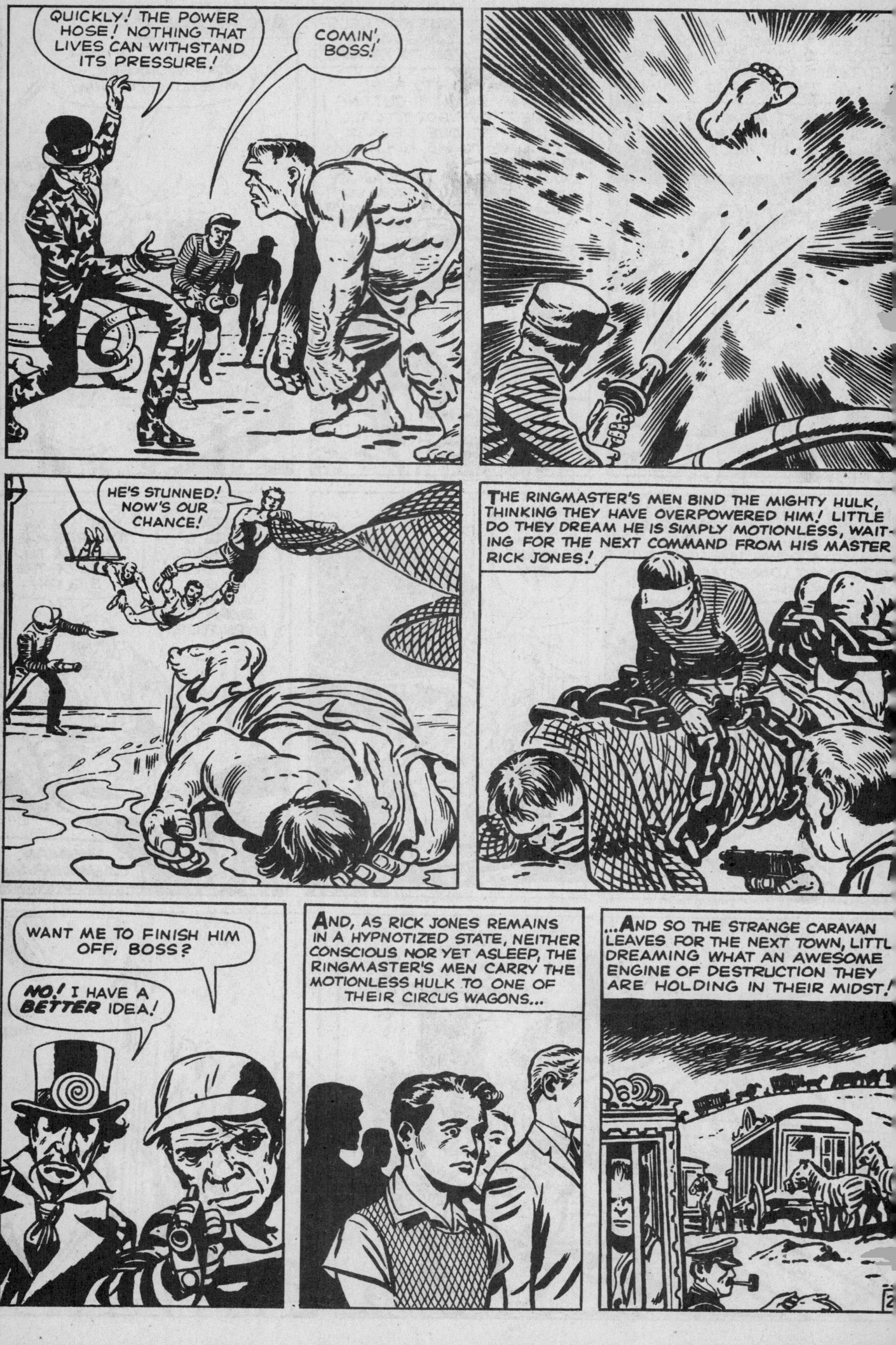
QUICKLY! THE POWER HOSE! NOTHING THAT LIVES CAN WITHSTAND ITS PRESSURE!
COMIN', BOSS!
HE'S STUNNED! NOW'S OUR CHANCE!
THE RINGMASTER'S MEN BIND THE MIGHTY HULK, THINKING THEY HAVE OVERPOWERED HIM! LITTLE DO THEY DREAM HE IS SIMPLY MOTIONLESS, WAITING FOR THE NEXT COMMAND FROM HIS MASTER RICK JONES!
WANT ME TO FINISH HIM OFF, BOSS?
NO! I HAVE A BETTER IDEA!
AND, AS RICK JONES REMAINS IN A HYPNOTIZED STATE, NEITHER CONSCIOUS NOR YET ASLEEP, THE RINGMASTER'S MEN CARRY THE MOTIONLESS HULK TO ONE OF THEIR CIRCUS WAGONS...
...AND SO THE STRANGE CARAVAN LEAVES FOR THE NEXT TOWN, LITTL DREAMING WHAT AN AWESOME ENGINE OF DESTRUCTION THEY ARE HOLDING IN THEIR MIDST!

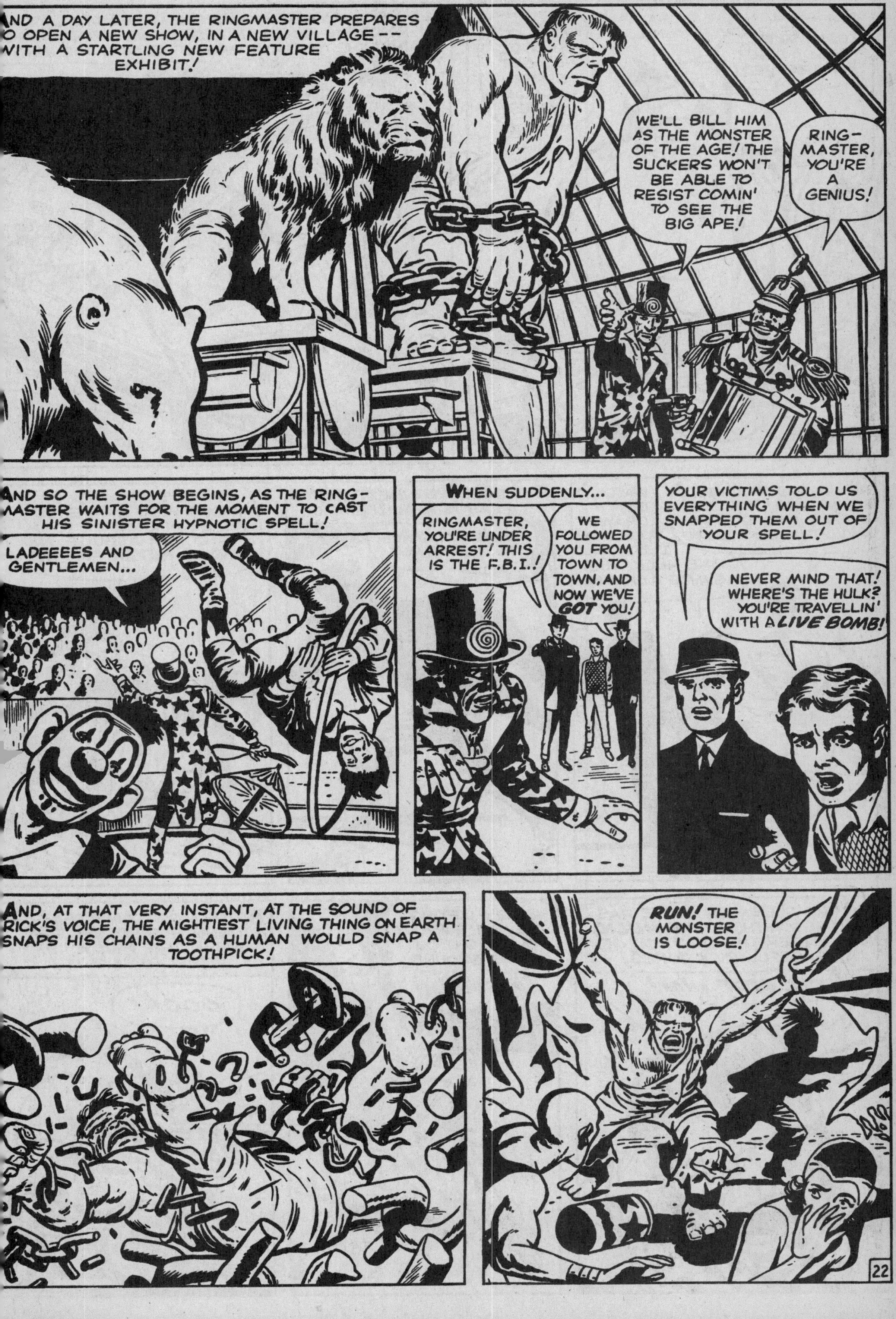
AND A DAY LATER, THE RINGMASTER PREPARES TO OPEN A NEW SHOW, IN A NEW VILLAGE -- WITH A STARTLING NEW FEATURE EXHIBIT!
WE'LL BILL HIM AS THE MONSTER OF THE AGE! THE SUCKERS WON'T BE ABLE TO RESIST COMIN' TO SEE THE BIG APE!
RING-MASTER, YOU'RE A GENIUS!
AND SO THE SHOW BEGINS, AS THE RING-MASTER WAITS FOR THE MOMENT TO CAST HIS SINISTER HYPNOTIC SPELL!
LADEEEES AND GENTLEMEN...
WHEN SUDDENLY...
RINGMASTER, YOU'RE UNDER ARREST! THIS IS THE F.B.I.!
WE FOLLOWED YOU FROM TOWN TO TOWN, AND NOW WE'VE GOT YOU!
YOUR VICTIMS TOLD US EVERYTHING WHEN WE SNAPPED THEM OUT OF YOUR SPELL!
NEVER MIND THAT! WHERE'S THE HULK? YOU'RE TRAVELLIN' WITH A LIVE BOMB!
AND, AT THAT VERY INSTANT, AT THE SOUND OF RICK'S VOICE, THE MIGHTIEST LIVING THING ON EARTH SNAPS HIS CHAINS AS A HUMAN WOULD SNAP A TOOTHPICK!
RUN! THE MONSTER IS LOOSE!
22

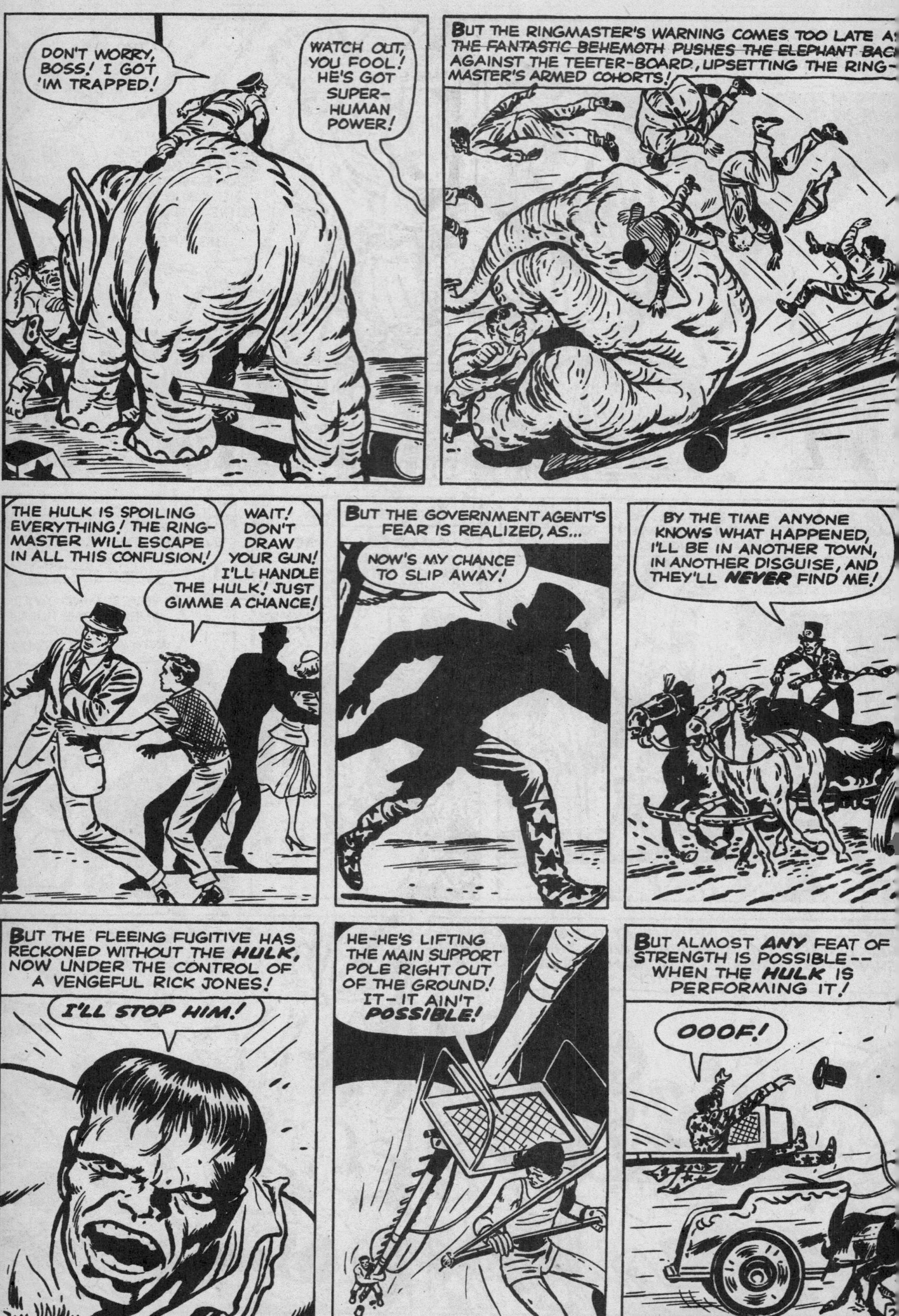

DON'T WORRY, BOSS! I GOT 'IM TRAPPED!
WATCH OUT, YOU FOOL! HE'S GOT SUPER-HUMAN POWER!
BUT THE RINGMASTER'S WARNING COMES TOO LATE AS THE FANTASTIC BEHEMOTH PUSHES THE ELEPHANT BACK AGAINST THE TEETER-BOARD, UPSETTING THE RING-MASTER'S ARMED COHORTS!
THE HULK IS SPOILING EVERYTHING! THE RING-MASTER WILL ESCAPE IN ALL THIS CONFUSION!
WAIT! DON'T DRAW YOUR GUN! I'LL HANDLE THE HULK! JUST GIMME A CHANCE!
BUT THE GOVERNMENT AGENT'S FEAR IS REALIZED, AS...
NOW'S MY CHANCE TO SLIP AWAY!
BY THE TIME ANYONE KNOWS WHAT HAPPENED, I'LL BE IN ANOTHER TOWN, IN ANOTHER DISGUISE, AND THEY'LL NEVER FIND ME!
BUT THE FLEEING FUGITIVE HAS RECKONED WITHOUT THE HULK, NOW UNDER THE CONTROL OF A VENGEFUL RICK JONES!
I'LL STOP HIM!
HE-HE'S LIFTING THE MAIN SUPPORT POLE RIGHT OUT OF THE GROUND! IT-IT AIN'T POSSIBLE!
BUT ALMOST ANY FEAT OF STRENGTH IS POSSIBLE--WHEN THE HULK IS PERFORMING IT!
OOOF!

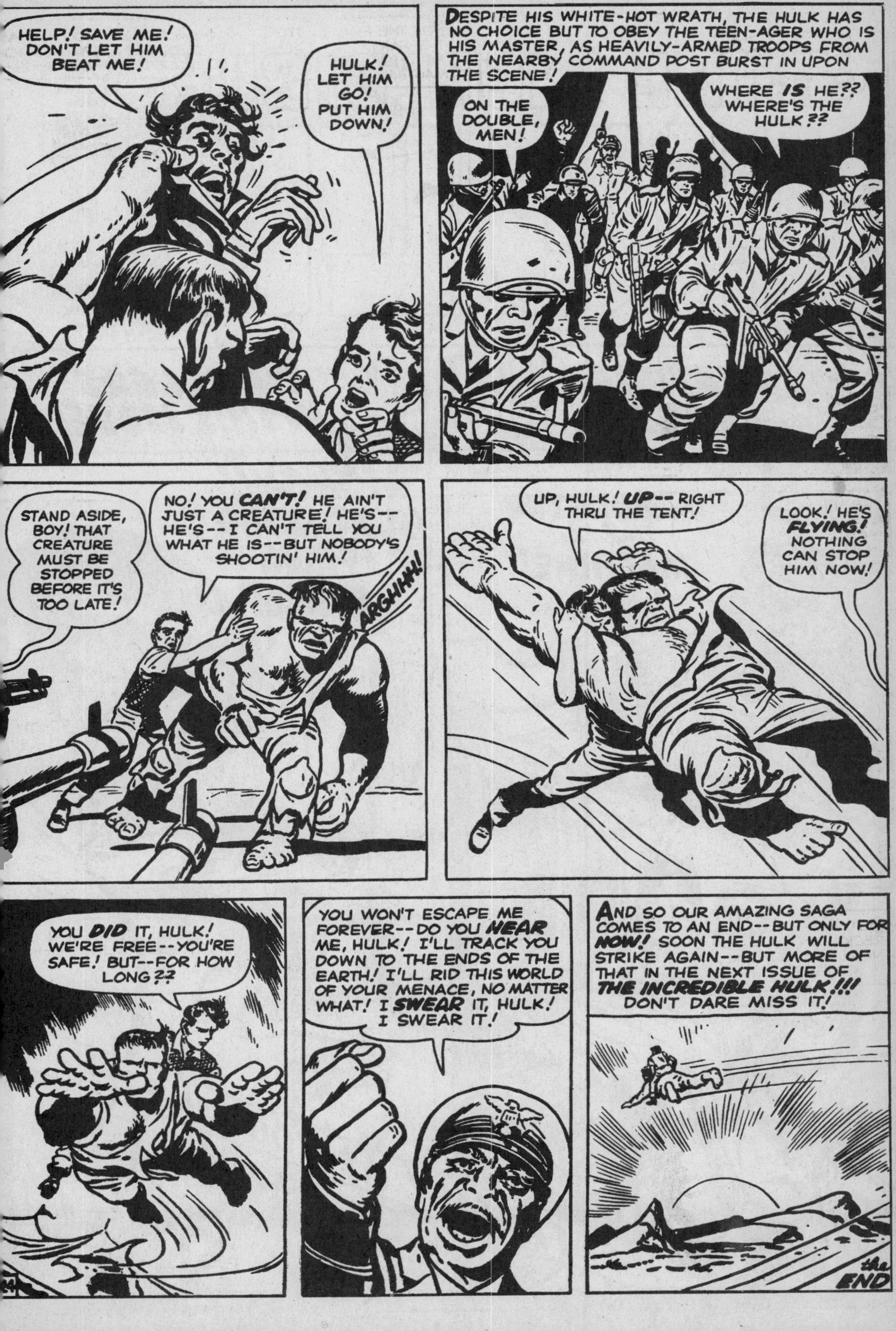
HELP! SAVE ME! DON'T LET HIM BEAT ME!
HULK! LET HIM GO! PUT HIM DOWN!
DESPITE HIS WHITE-HOT WRATH, THE HULK HAS NO CHOICE BUT TO OBEY THE TEEN-AGER WHO IS HIS MASTER, AS HEAVILY-ARMED TROOPS FROM THE NEARBY COMMAND POST BURST IN UPON THE SCENE!
ON THE DOUBLE, MEN!
WHERE IS HE?? WHERE'S THE HULK??
STAND ASIDE, BOY! THAT CREATURE MUST BE STOPPED BEFORE IT'S TOO LATE!
NO! YOU CAN'T! HE AIN'T JUST A CREATURE! HE'S-- HE'S--I CAN'T TELL YOU WHAT HE IS--BUT NOBODY'S SHOOTIN' HIM!
ARGHHH!
UP, HULK! UP-- RIGHT THRU THE TENT!
LOOK! HE'S FLYING! NOTHING CAN STOP HIM NOW!
YOU DID IT, HULK! WE'RE FREE--YOU'RE SAFE! BUT--FOR HOW LONG??
YOU WON'T ESCAPE ME FOREVER--DO YOU HEAR ME, HULK! I'LL TRACK YOU DOWN TO THE ENDS OF THE EARTH! I'LL RID THIS WORLD OF YOUR MENACE, NO MATTER WHAT! I SWEAR IT, HULK! I SWEAR IT!
AND SO OUR AMAZING SAGA COMES TO AN END--BUT ONLY FOR NOW! SOON THE HULK WILL STRIKE AGAIN--BUT MORE OF THAT IN THE NEXT ISSUE OF THE INCREDIBLE HULK!!! DON'T DARE MISS IT!
the END

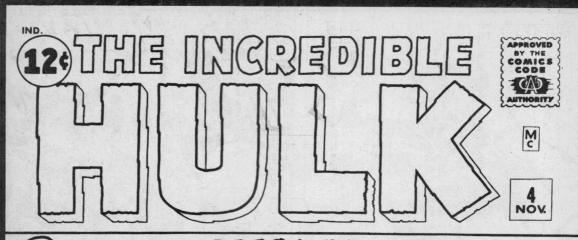

IND. 12¢

THE INCREDIBLE HULK.

APPROVED BY THE COMICS CODE AUTHORITY

4 NOV.

MC

2 FEATURE-LENGTH HULK THRILLERS IN THIS ISSUE!

"the MONSTER and the MACHINE!"

"MONGU!! GLADIATOR FROM SPACE!"

FANTASY AS YOU LIKE IT!

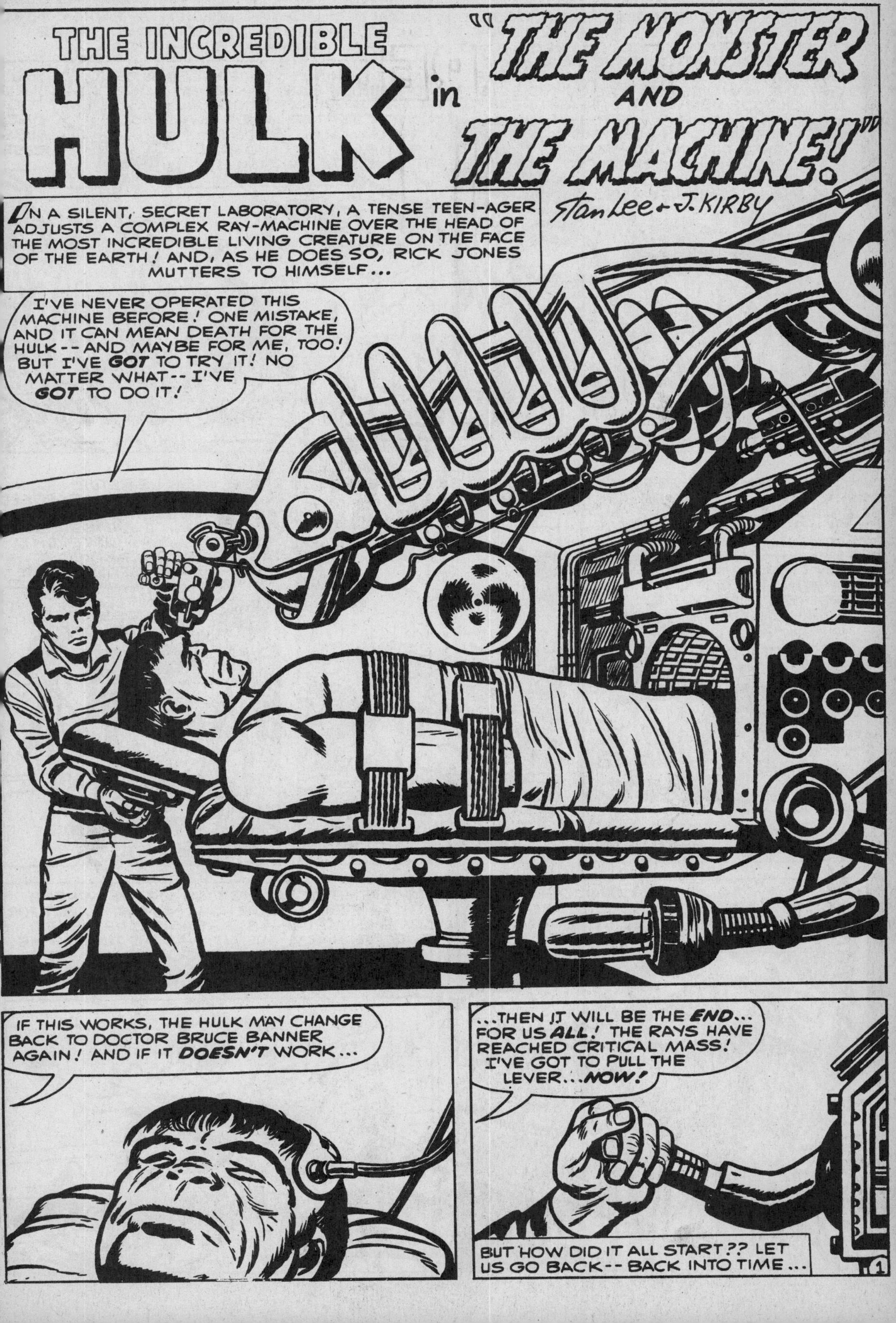
THE INCREDIBLE HULK in "THE MONSTER AND THE MACHINE!"
Stan Lee + J. Kirby
IN A SILENT, SECRET LABORATORY, A TENSE TEEN-AGER ADJUSTS A COMPLEX RAY-MACHINE OVER THE HEAD OF THE MOST INCREDIBLE LIVING CREATURE ON THE FACE OF THE EARTH! AND, AS HE DOES SO, RICK JONES MUTTERS TO HIMSELF...
I'VE NEVER OPERATED THIS MACHINE BEFORE! ONE MISTAKE, AND IT CAN MEAN DEATH FOR THE HULK--AND MAYBE FOR ME, TOO! BUT I'VE GOT TO TRY IT! NO MATTER WHAT--I'VE GOT TO DO IT!
IF THIS WORKS, THE HULK MAY CHANGE BACK TO DOCTOR BRUCE BANNER AGAIN! AND IF IT DOESN'T WORK...
...THEN IT WILL BE THE END... FOR US ALL! THE RAYS HAVE REACHED CRITICAL MASS! I'VE GOT TO PULL THE LEVER...NOW!
BUT HOW DID IT ALL START?? LET US GO BACK--BACK INTO TIME...
1

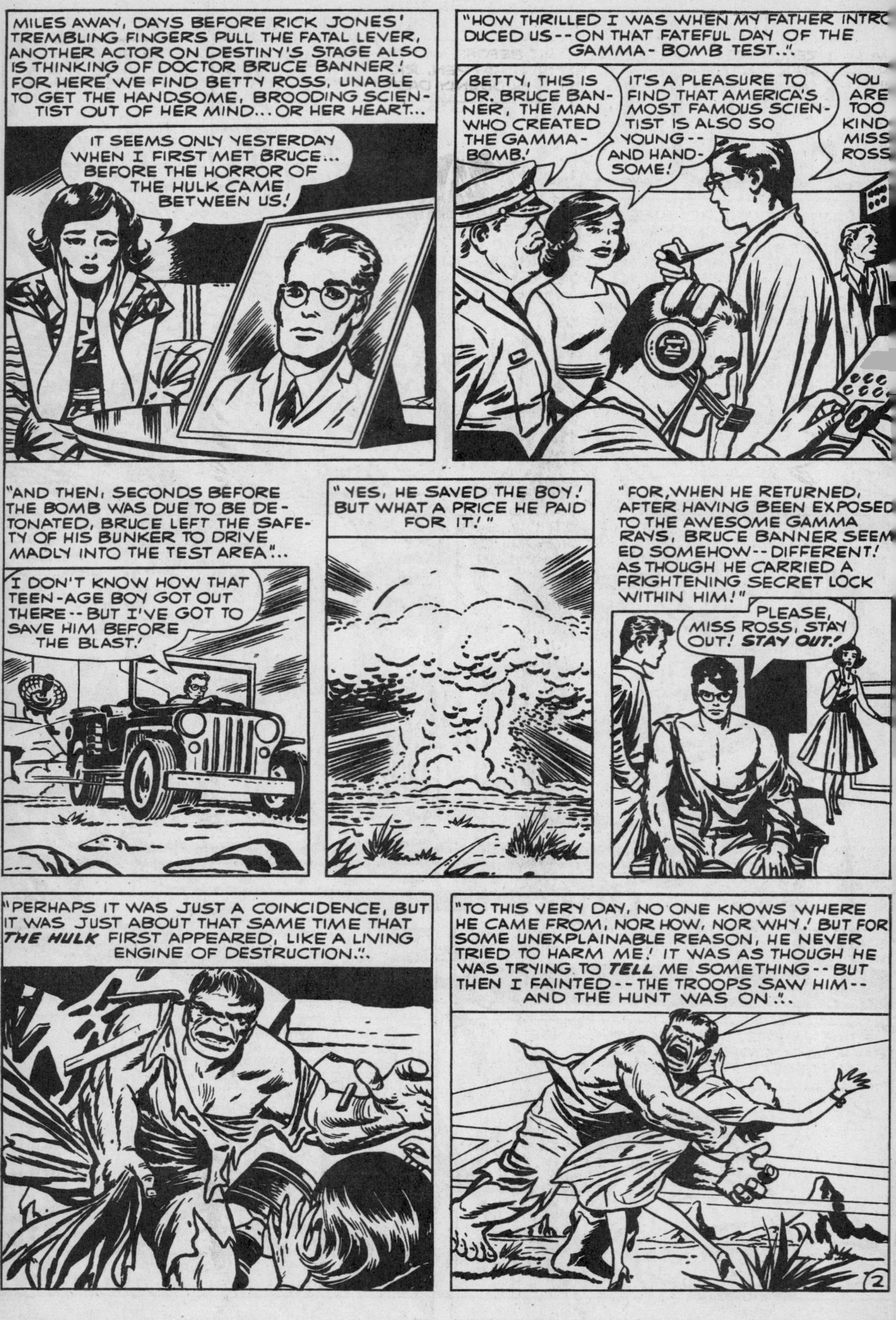

MILES AWAY, DAYS BEFORE RICK JONES' TREMBLING FINGERS PULL THE FATAL LEVER, ANOTHER ACTOR ON DESTINY'S STAGE ALSO IS THINKING OF DOCTOR BRUCE BANNER! FOR HERE WE FIND BETTY ROSS, UNABLE TO GET THE HANDSOME, BROODING SCIENTIST OUT OF HER MIND... OR HER HEART...
IT SEEMS ONLY YESTERDAY WHEN I FIRST MET BRUCE... BEFORE THE HORROR OF THE HULK CAME BETWEEN US!
"HOW THRILLED I WAS WHEN MY FATHER INTRODUCED US--ON THAT FATEFUL DAY OF THE GAMMA-BOMB TEST..".
BETTY, THIS IS DR. BRUCE BANNER, THE MAN WHO CREATED THE GAMMA-BOMB!
IT'S A PLEASURE TO FIND THAT AMERICA'S MOST FAMOUS SCIENTIST IS ALSO SO YOUNG-- AND HANDSOME!
YOU ARE TOO KIND MISS ROSS
"AND THEN, SECONDS BEFORE THE BOMB WAS DUE TO BE DETONATED, BRUCE LEFT THE SAFETY OF HIS BUNKER TO DRIVE MADLY INTO THE TEST AREA"...
I DON'T KNOW HOW THAT TEEN-AGE BOY GOT OUT THERE--BUT I'VE GOT TO SAVE HIM BEFORE THE BLAST!
"YES, HE SAVED THE BOY! BUT WHAT A PRICE HE PAID FOR IT!"
"FOR, WHEN HE RETURNED, AFTER HAVING BEEN EXPOSED TO THE AWESOME GAMMA RAYS, BRUCE BANNER SEEMED SOMEHOW--DIFFERENT! AS THOUGH HE CARRIED A FRIGHTENING SECRET LOCK WITHIN HIM!"
PLEASE, MISS ROSS, STAY OUT! STAY OUT!
"PERHAPS IT WAS JUST A COINCIDENCE, BUT IT WAS JUST ABOUT THAT SAME TIME THAT THE HULK FIRST APPEARED, LIKE A LIVING ENGINE OF DESTRUCTION..".
"TO THIS VERY DAY, NO ONE KNOWS WHERE HE CAME FROM, NOR HOW, NOR WHY! BUT FOR SOME UNEXPLAINABLE REASON, HE NEVER TRIED TO HARM ME! IT WAS AS THOUGH HE WAS TRYING TO TELL ME SOMETHING--BUT THEN I FAINTED--THE TROOPS SAW HIM--AND THE HUNT WAS ON..".

WHEN I RECOVERED, THE TOWERING MONSTER HAD BROUGHT ME TO BRUCE'S LAB! I LOOKED AROUND IN SHOCKED SURPRISE -- THE PLACE WAS A SHAMBLES!"

" BUT BEFORE ANYTHING ELSE COULD HAPPEN, RICK JONES SUDDENLY DASHED IN:"..

HULK! STOP!

"AND THIS IS THE MOST INCREDIBLE FACT OF ALL -- ONLY THAT ONE YOUNG TEEN-AGER, IN ALL THE WORLD, IS ABLE TO CONTROL THE SUPER-HUMAN HULK."

BACK, HULK -- YOU MUST GO BACK!

GO -- BACK --

RICK JONES AND BRUCE BANNER! RICK JONES AND THE HULK!

WHAT CONNECTION IS THERE BETWEEN ALL OF THEM?! SOMEHOW, IN SOME MYSTERIOUS WAY-- RICK JONES HOLDS THE KEY! IT HAS TO BE RICK JONES!

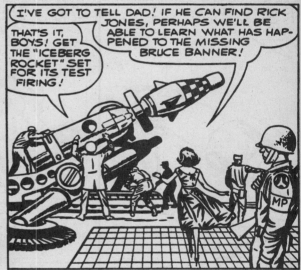

I'VE GOT TO TELL DAD! IF HE CAN FIND RICK JONES, PERHAPS WE'LL BE ABLE TO LEARN WHAT HAS HAPPENED TO THE MISSING BRUCE BANNER!

THAT'S IT, BOYS! GET THE "ICEBERG ROCKET" SET FOR ITS TEST FIRING!

STAY BACK, BETTY! THIS IS THE WEAPON WHICH SOME DAY CAPTURE THE HULK FOR US! WATCH!

READY ON THE FIRING LINE! FOLLOW PLAN B! RELEASE THE JET-POWERED FACSIMILE OF THE HULK!

YES, SIR!

FIRE FACSIMILE!

3

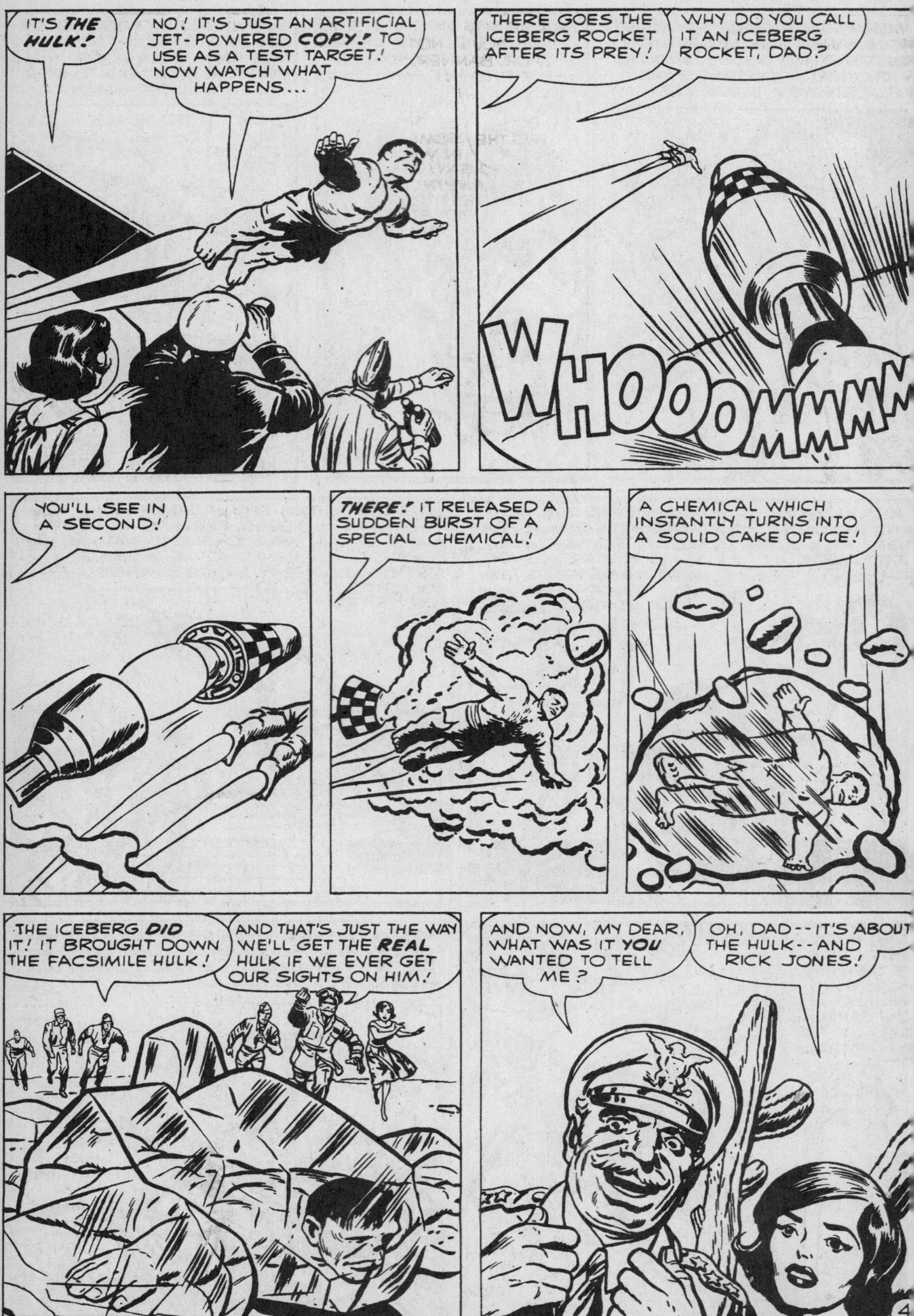
IT'S THE HULK!
NO! IT'S JUST AN ARTIFICIAL JET-POWERED COPY! TO USE AS A TEST TARGET! NOW WATCH WHAT HAPPENS...
THERE GOES THE ICEBERG ROCKET AFTER ITS PREY!
WHY DO YOU CALL IT AN ICEBERG ROCKET, DAD?
WHOOOOMMMMM
YOU'LL SEE IN A SECOND!
THERE! IT RELEASED A SUDDEN BURST OF A SPECIAL CHEMICAL!
A CHEMICAL WHICH INSTANTLY TURNS INTO A SOLID CAKE OF ICE!
THE ICEBERG DID IT! IT BROUGHT DOWN THE FACSIMILE HULK!
AND THAT'S JUST THE WAY WE'LL GET THE REAL HULK IF WE EVER GET OUR SIGHTS ON HIM!
AND NOW, MY DEAR, WHAT WAS IT YOU WANTED TO TELL ME?
OH, DAD--IT'S ABOUT THE HULK--AND RICK JONES!
4

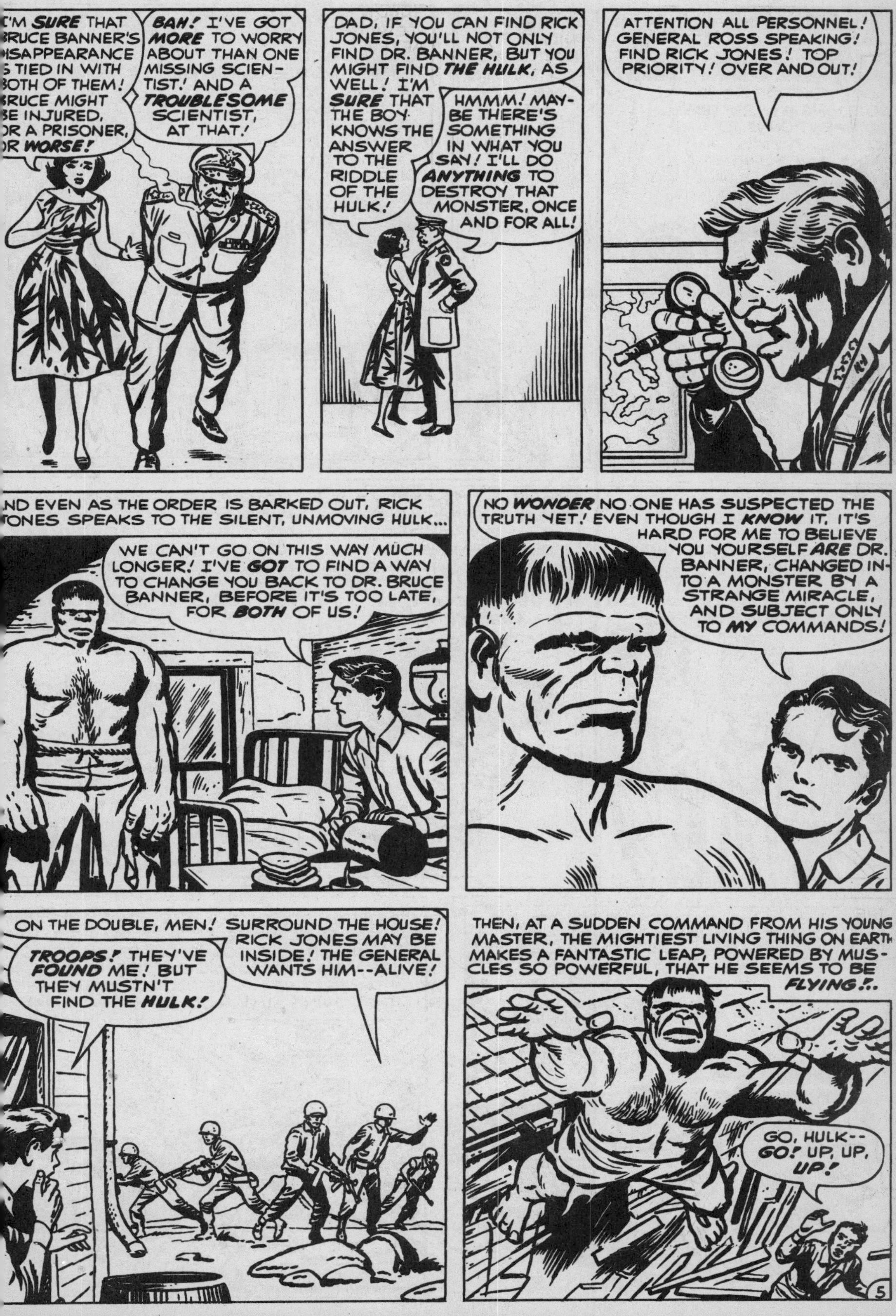
I'M SURE THAT BRUCE BANNER'S DISAPPEARANCE IS TIED IN WITH BOTH OF THEM! BRUCE MIGHT BE INJURED, OR A PRISONER, OR WORSE!
BAH! I'VE GOT MORE TO WORRY ABOUT THAN ONE MISSING SCIENTIST! AND A TROUBLESOME SCIENTIST, AT THAT!
DAD, IF YOU CAN FIND RICK JONES, YOU'LL NOT ONLY FIND DR. BANNER, BUT YOU MIGHT FIND THE HULK, AS WELL! I'M SURE THAT THE BOY KNOWS THE ANSWER TO THE RIDDLE OF THE HULK!
HMMM! MAYBE THERE'S SOMETHING IN WHAT YOU SAY! I'LL DO ANYTHING TO DESTROY THAT MONSTER, ONCE AND FOR ALL!
ATTENTION ALL PERSONNEL! GENERAL ROSS SPEAKING! FIND RICK JONES! TOP PRIORITY! OVER AND OUT!
AND EVEN AS THE ORDER IS BARKED OUT, RICK JONES SPEAKS TO THE SILENT, UNMOVING HULK...
WE CAN'T GO ON THIS WAY MUCH LONGER! I'VE GOT TO FIND A WAY TO CHANGE YOU BACK TO DR. BRUCE BANNER, BEFORE IT'S TOO LATE, FOR BOTH OF US!
NO WONDER NO ONE HAS SUSPECTED THE TRUTH YET! EVEN THOUGH I KNOW IT, IT'S HARD FOR ME TO BELIEVE YOU YOURSELF ARE DR. BANNER, CHANGED INTO A MONSTER BY A STRANGE MIRACLE, AND SUBJECT ONLY TO MY COMMANDS!
ON THE DOUBLE, MEN! SURROUND THE HOUSE! RICK JONES MAY BE INSIDE! THE GENERAL WANTS HIM--ALIVE!
TROOPS! THEY'VE FOUND ME! BUT THEY MUSTN'T FIND THE HULK!
THEN, AT A SUDDEN COMMAND FROM HIS YOUNG MASTER, THE MIGHTIEST LIVING THING ON EARTH MAKES A FANTASTIC LEAP, POWERED BY MUSCLES SO POWERFUL, THAT HE SEEMS TO BE FLYING!!..
GO, HULK--GO! UP, UP, UP!
5

SECONDS LATER...

STRANGE -- I COULD HAVE SWORN I SAW SOME SORT OF FIGURE GO FLYING BY! BETTER NOT MENTION IT TO ANYONE, THEY'LL THINK I'VE FLIPPED!

WADDA YOU GUYS WANT?

GENERAL THUNDER-BOLT ROSS WILL EXPLAIN! COME WITH US!

AND THEN, AT THE GENERAL'S HEADQUARTERS...

NOW HEAR THIS, JONES! DR. BANNER HAS BEEN MISSING FOR DAYS, AND WE SUSPECT THAT HIS DISAPPEARANCE HAS SOMETHING TO DO WITH YOU! IF HE DOESN'T SHOW UP SOON, I'M PLACING YOU UNDER ARREST!

HE WAS ASSIGNED TO MY COMMAND, AND I'VE GOT COMPLETE AUTHORITY IN THIS MATTER!

RICK, IF YOU KNOW WHAT'S HAPPENED TO BRUCE, YOU'VE GOT TO TELL US! HE MAY BE IN TROUBLE! PERHAPS WE CAN HELP HIM! I'VE GOT TO KNOW!

I'M SORRY, MISS ROSS! I CAN'T TELL YOU ANYTHING!

I'VE GOT TO!

HOW CAN I TELL THEM THAT BRUCE BANNER IS REALLY THE HULK!?? AND YET, IF I DON'T PRODUCE DOCTOR BANNER SOON, I'M GONNA BE IN BIG TROUBLE! THEY MAY EVEN ACCUSE ME OF -- MURDERING HIM!

MEANWHILE, PROPELLED BY HIS PRODIGIOUS LEAP, THE ONE LIVING CREATURE WHO HOLDS THE KEY TO THE MYSTERY OF BRUCE BANNER ZOOMS THRU THE AIR, MINDLESSLY, AIMLESSLY, TOO FAR FROM RICK JONES TO RECEIVE ANY FURTHER MENTAL COMMANDS...

AND THEN, AS HIS LEAP BEGINS TO LOSE MOMENTUM, HIS COLD, BRUTISH EYES SEE A FOREBODING SIGHT...

THE MOTOR'S STALLED! CAN'T MOVE THE BUS! AND -- THE EXPRESS IS BEARING DOWN -- TOO FAST FOR ME TO GET THE KIDS OFF!

SOMEWHERE, DEEP WITHIN THE MONSTER'S BRAIN, A TINY SPARK OF BRUCE BANNER COMES TO LIFE! AND THEN, WITHOUT CONSCIOUS THOUGHT, MOVING LIKE A GIGANTIC, LIVING BATTERING RAM, THE HULK TAKES OVER, PERFORMING A FEAT WHICH NO OTHER LIVING HUMAN COULD HAVE ACCOMPLISHED!

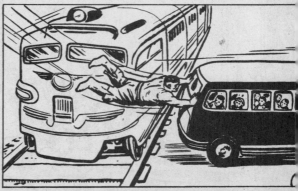

THE AMAZING INCIDENT OCCUPIED THE HEADLINES DURING THE NEXT 24 HOURS, BUT AFTER THAT, IT WAS SOON SWEPT AWAY BY THE RUSH OF OTHER EVENTS...

ENDSFORD GAZETTE

UNIDENTIFIED FLYING OBJECT AVERTS SCHOOL BUS TRAGEDY! DETAILS ON PG. 3

WAS IT SOMETHING HUMAN? CHILDREN'S DESCRIPTION PRONOUNCED AS HYSTERIA BY AUTHORITIES! EXTRA

LATER, ON A MOVIE SET, NOT FAR AWAY...

NO! NO! NO! YOU'RE NOT HAMMING IT UP ENOUGH! THIS IS SUPPOSED TO BE A MONSTER MOVIE! YOU'VE GOT TO LOOK SCARED!

NOW LET'S TRY IT AGAIN!

OKAY, MIKE! ROLL 'EM! NOW LET'S HEAR YOU REALLY SCREAM, KID!

EEEK!

THAT'S IT, BABY! YOU'RE DOIN' FINE! KEEP IT UP! NEVER KNEW YOU COULD ACT SO GOOD!

HELP! HELP!

HOLY HANNAH! SHE WASN'T ACTING! LEMME OUT OF HERE! RUN FOR THE HILLS, BOYS!

MINUTES LATER, AT THE STUDIO COMMISSARY, A SHORT DISTANCE AWAY...

STOP SHOVIN' BACK THERE! I WAS FIRST IN LINE!

C'MON, KEEP THE LINE MOVIN'! WHO'S NEXT?

FOOD!

URK!

I'M THRU WITH SHOW BUSINESS! IT'S BACK TO THE HASH HOUSE FOR ME!

7

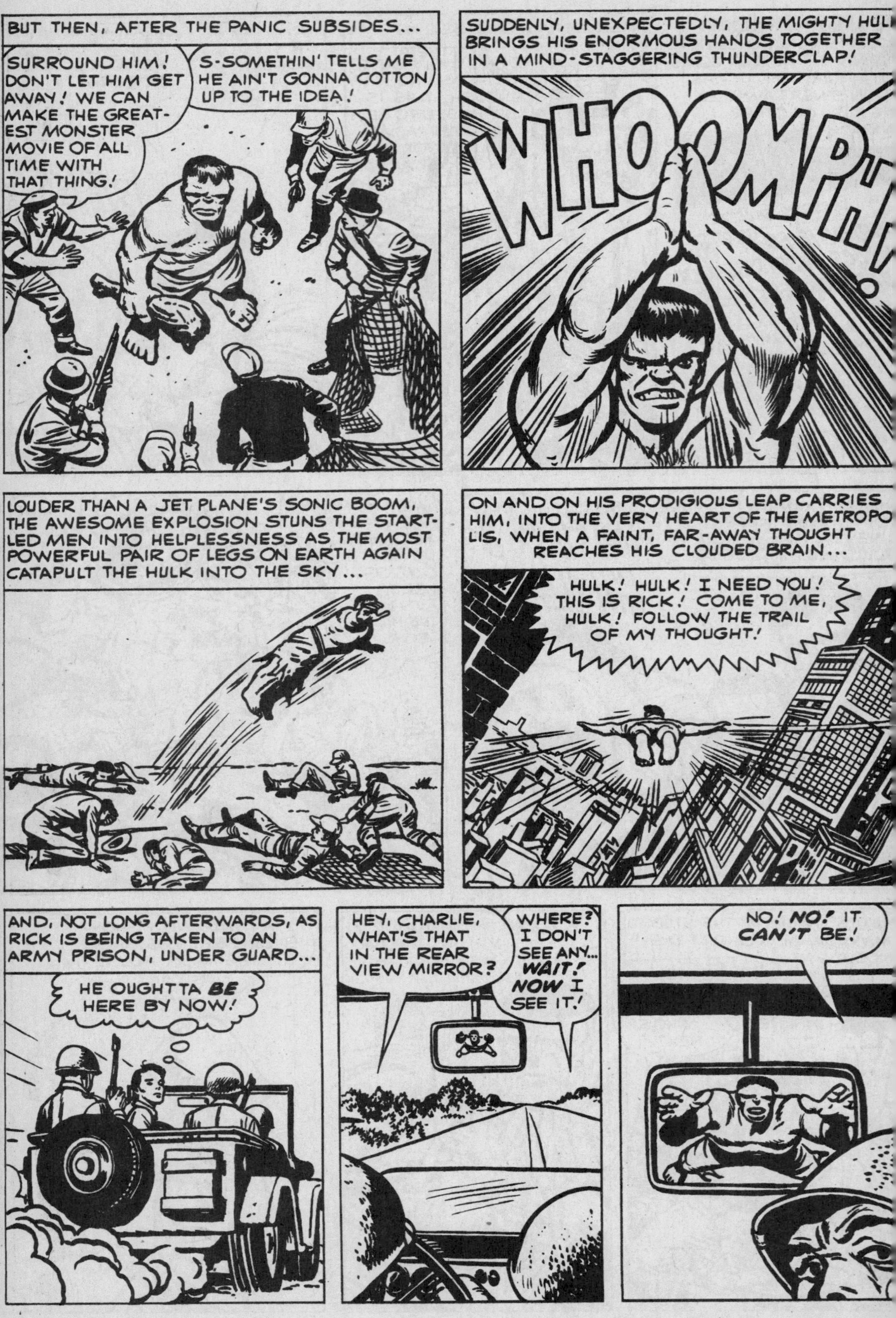

BUT THEN, AFTER THE PANIC SUBSIDES...
SURROUND HIM! DON'T LET HIM GET AWAY! WE CAN MAKE THE GREATEST MONSTER MOVIE OF ALL TIME WITH THAT THING!
S-SOMETHIN' TELLS ME HE AIN'T GONNA COTTON UP TO THE IDEA!
SUDDENLY, UNEXPECTEDLY, THE MIGHTY HULK BRINGS HIS ENORMOUS HANDS TOGETHER IN A MIND-STAGGERING THUNDERCLAP!
WHOOOMPH
LOUDER THAN A JET PLANE'S SONIC BOOM, THE AWESOME EXPLOSION STUNS THE STARTLED MEN INTO HELPLESSNESS AS THE MOST POWERFUL PAIR OF LEGS ON EARTH AGAIN CATAPULT THE HULK INTO THE SKY...
ON AND ON HIS PRODIGIOUS LEAP CARRIES HIM, INTO THE VERY HEART OF THE METROPOLIS, WHEN A FAINT, FAR-AWAY THOUGHT REACHES HIS CLOUDED BRAIN...
HULK! HULK! I NEED YOU! THIS IS RICK! COME TO ME, HULK! FOLLOW THE TRAIL OF MY THOUGHT!
AND, NOT LONG AFTERWARDS, AS RICK IS BEING TAKEN TO AN ARMY PRISON, UNDER GUARD...
HE OUGHTTA BE HERE BY NOW!
HEY, CHARLIE, WHAT'S THAT IN THE REAR VIEW MIRROR?
WHERE? I DON'T SEE ANY... WAIT! NOW I SEE IT!
NO! NO! IT CAN'T BE!

IT WAS THE *HULK!* HE GOT THE BOY!

LIKE A HUMAN CATAPULT, THE HULK SOARS THRU THE AIR WITH HIS TEEN-AGE BURDEN UNTIL HE REACHES A FAMILIAR LOCATION...

THIS IS IT, HULK! DOWN -- PUT ME DOWN!

SLOWLY, CAREFULLY, THE CREATURE AND THE BOY ENTER A HIDDEN CAVE AND NOISELESSLY PROCEED THRU THE DIMLY-LIT CAVERN...

FOLLOW ME, HULK! IT'S JUST A LITTLE FURTHER!

LUCKY FOR US YOU BUILT THIS HIDDEN LAB WHILE YOU WERE STILL BRUCE BANNER! IT'S MY ONLY CHANCE TO CLEAR MY-SELF NOW -- AND TO BRING YOU BACK TO NORMAL, TOO!

WELL, THERE IT IS! THE MACHINE YOU BUILT TO BOMBARD YOU WITH GAMMA RAYS! THE ONLY PROBLEM IS -- AM I SMART ENOUGH TO FIGURE OUT HOW IT STARTS!

I CAN'T EVEN UNDER-STAND HALF OF THE JAZZ YOU WROTE IN THIS INSTRUC-TION MANUAL! IF ONLY YOU COULD HELP ME! IF I MAKE A MISTAKE, ANYTHING CAN HAPPEN!

HULK, TRY TO THINK! SOME-WHERE IN THAT HEAD OF YOURS A SPARK OF BRUCE BANNER MUST STILL BE LISTENING! TELL ME, HULK-- SHOULD I TAKE THE CHANCE? SHOULD I TRY? YOU'VE *GOT* TO TELL ME!

...*TRY*... RICK!

9

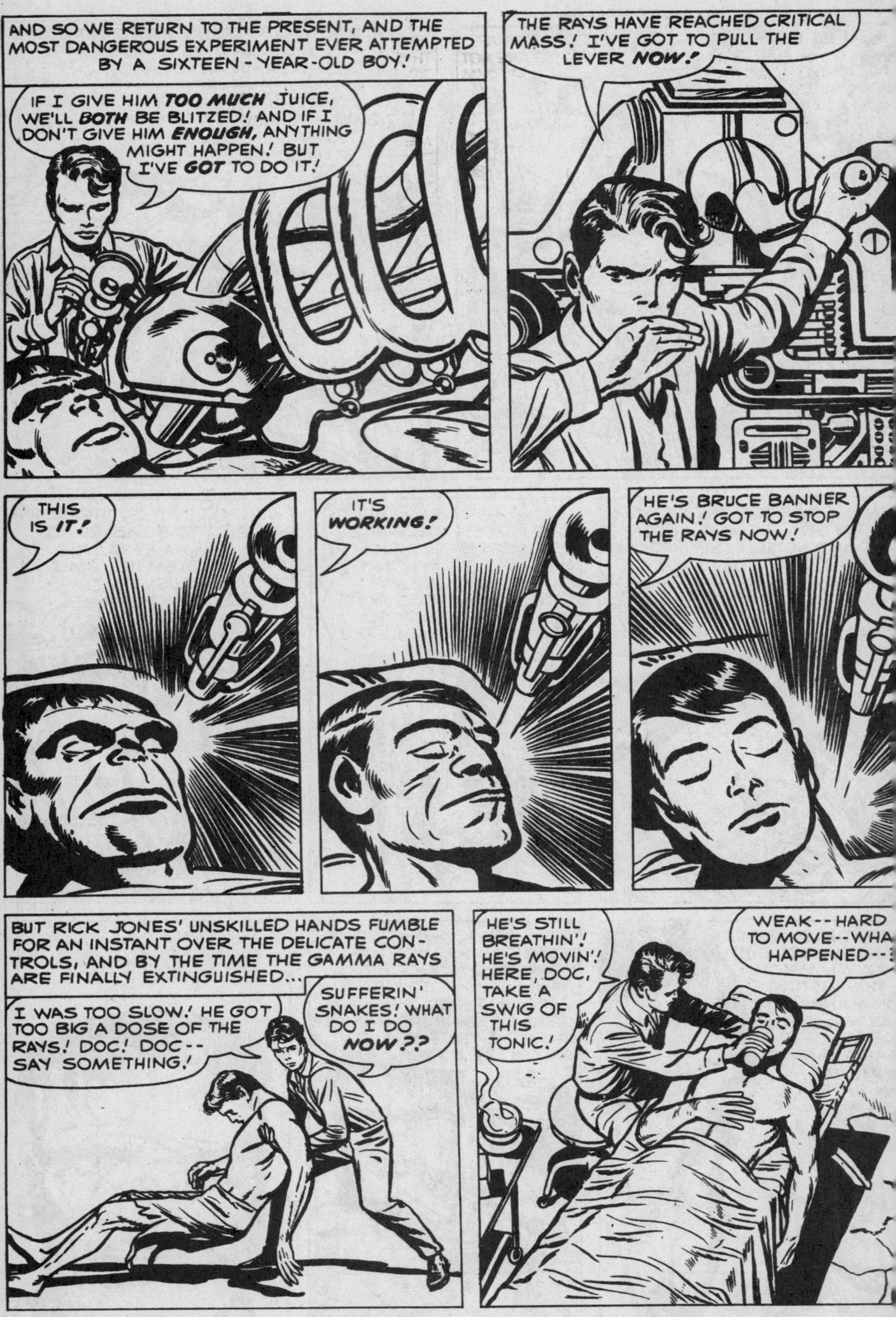
AND SO WE RETURN TO THE PRESENT, AND THE MOST DANGEROUS EXPERIMENT EVER ATTEMPTED BY A SIXTEEN-YEAR-OLD BOY!
IF I GIVE HIM TOO MUCH JUICE, WE'LL BOTH BE BLITZED! AND IF I DON'T GIVE HIM ENOUGH, ANYTHING MIGHT HAPPEN! BUT I'VE GOT TO DO IT!
THE RAYS HAVE REACHED CRITICAL MASS! I'VE GOT TO PULL THE LEVER NOW!
THIS IS IT!
IT'S WORKING!
HE'S BRUCE BANNER AGAIN! GOT TO STOP THE RAYS NOW!
BUT RICK JONES' UNSKILLED HANDS FUMBLE FOR AN INSTANT OVER THE DELICATE CONTROLS, AND BY THE TIME THE GAMMA RAYS ARE FINALLY EXTINGUISHED...
I WAS TOO SLOW! HE GOT TOO BIG A DOSE OF THE RAYS! DOC! DOC-- SAY SOMETHING!
SUFFERIN' SNAKES! WHAT DO I DO NOW??
HE'S STILL BREATHIN'! HE'S MOVIN'! HERE, DOC, TAKE A SWIG OF THIS TONIC!
WEAK--HARD TO MOVE--WHA HAPPENED--

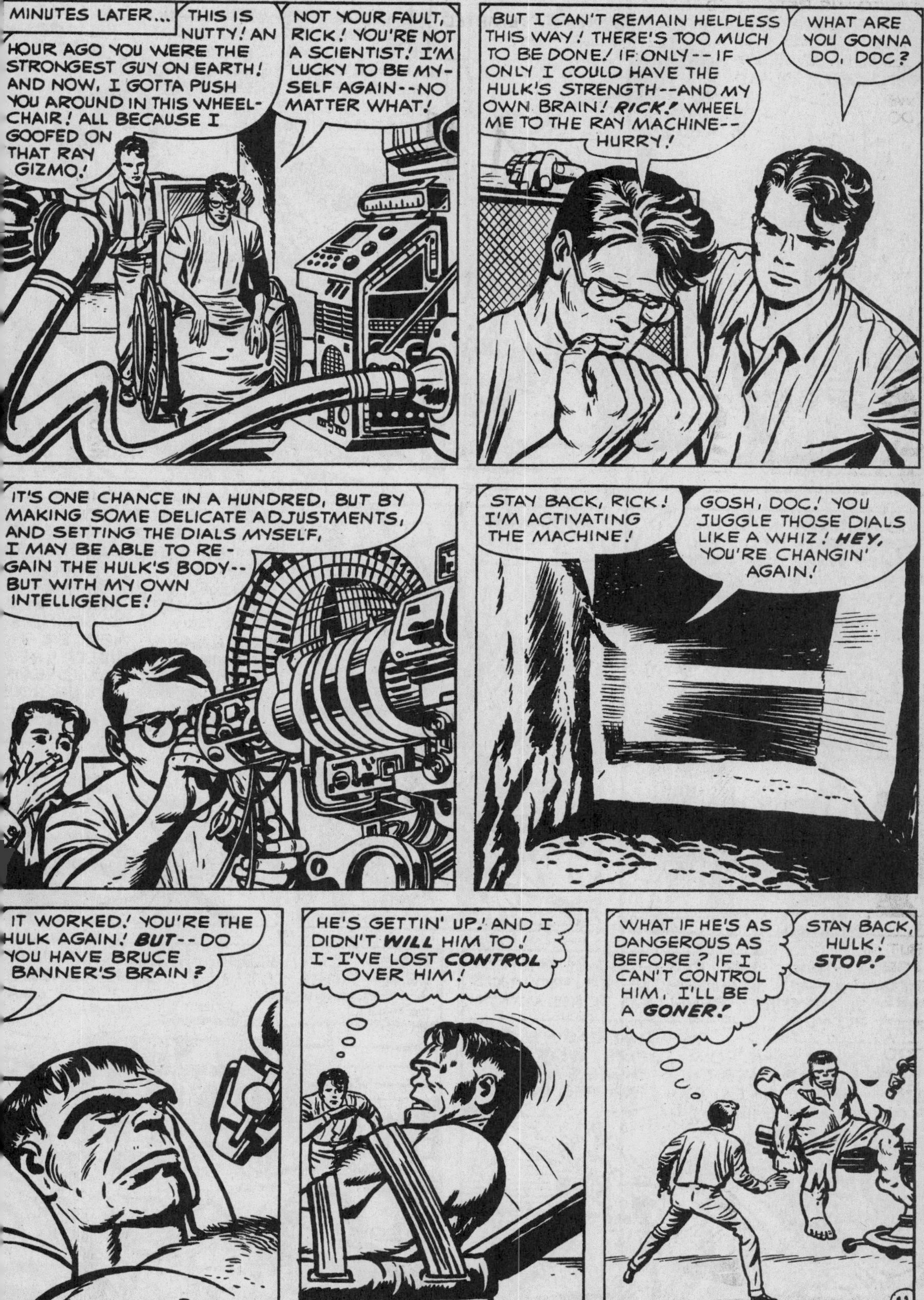

MINUTES LATER...
THIS IS NUTTY! AN HOUR AGO YOU WERE THE STRONGEST GUY ON EARTH! AND NOW, I GOTTA PUSH YOU AROUND IN THIS WHEEL-CHAIR! ALL BECAUSE I GOOFED ON THAT RAY GIZMO!
NOT YOUR FAULT, RICK! YOU'RE NOT A SCIENTIST! I'M LUCKY TO BE MY-SELF AGAIN--NO MATTER WHAT!
BUT I CAN'T REMAIN HELPLESS THIS WAY! THERE'S TOO MUCH TO BE DONE! IF ONLY--IF ONLY I COULD HAVE THE HULK'S STRENGTH--AND MY OWN BRAIN! RICK! WHEEL ME TO THE RAY MACHINE--HURRY!
WHAT ARE YOU GONNA DO, DOC?
IT'S ONE CHANCE IN A HUNDRED, BUT BY MAKING SOME DELICATE ADJUSTMENTS, AND SETTING THE DIALS MYSELF, I MAY BE ABLE TO RE-GAIN THE HULK'S BODY--BUT WITH MY OWN INTELLIGENCE!
STAY BACK, RICK! I'M ACTIVATING THE MACHINE!
GOSH, DOC! YOU JUGGLE THOSE DIALS LIKE A WHIZ! HEY, YOU'RE CHANGIN' AGAIN!
IT WORKED! YOU'RE THE HULK AGAIN! BUT--DO YOU HAVE BRUCE BANNER'S BRAIN?
HE'S GETTIN' UP! AND I DIDN'T WILL HIM TO! I-I'VE LOST CONTROL OVER HIM!
WHAT IF HE'S AS DANGEROUS AS BEFORE? IF I CAN'T CONTROL HIM, I'LL BE A GONER!
STAY BACK, HULK! STOP!

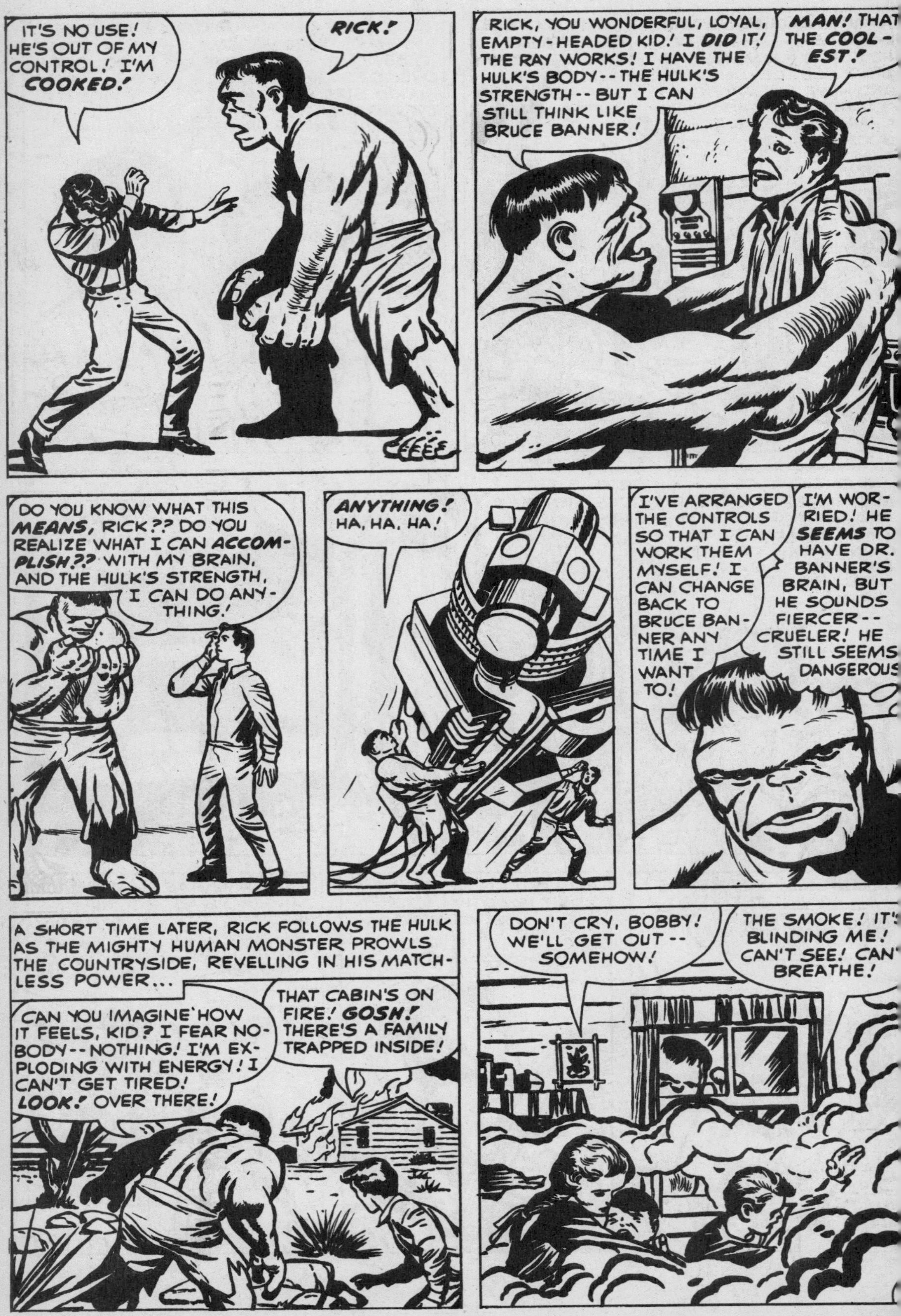
IT'S NO USE! HE'S OUT OF MY CONTROL! I'M COOKED!
RICK!
RICK, YOU WONDERFUL, LOYAL, EMPTY-HEADED KID! I DID IT! THE RAY WORKS! I HAVE THE HULK'S BODY -- THE HULK'S STRENGTH -- BUT I CAN STILL THINK LIKE BRUCE BANNER!
MAN! THAT THE COOL-EST!
DO YOU KNOW WHAT THIS MEANS, RICK?? DO YOU REALIZE WHAT I CAN ACCOMPLISH?? WITH MY BRAIN, AND THE HULK'S STRENGTH, I CAN DO ANYTHING!
ANYTHING! HA, HA, HA!
I'VE ARRANGED THE CONTROLS SO THAT I CAN WORK THEM MYSELF! I CAN CHANGE BACK TO BRUCE BANNER ANY TIME I WANT TO!
I'M WORRIED! HE SEEMS TO HAVE DR. BANNER'S BRAIN, BUT HE SOUNDS FIERCER -- CRUELER! HE STILL SEEMS DANGEROUS
A SHORT TIME LATER, RICK FOLLOWS THE HULK AS THE MIGHTY HUMAN MONSTER PROWLS THE COUNTRYSIDE, REVELLING IN HIS MATCHLESS POWER...
CAN YOU IMAGINE HOW IT FEELS, KID? I FEAR NOBODY -- NOTHING! I'M EXPLODING WITH ENERGY! I CAN'T GET TIRED! LOOK! OVER THERE!
THAT CABIN'S ON FIRE! GOSH! THERE'S A FAMILY TRAPPED INSIDE!
DON'T CRY, BOBBY! WE'LL GET OUT -- SOMEHOW!
THE SMOKE! IT'S BLINDING ME! CAN'T SEE! CAN'T BREATHE!

WITHOUT A SECOND THOUGHT, THE INCREDIBLE HULK GRASPS THE SECTION OF THE CABIN WHICH IS IN FLAME AND GIVES IT ONE MIGHTY FLING...

STAND BACK, KID!

THERE! THAT'S ONE WAY OF PUTTIN' OUT A FIRE!

THERE, THERE, CHILDREN -- DON'T CRY! THE FIRE IS OUT! WE'RE ALL SAFE NOW!

I DON'T UNDERSTAND! IT HAPPENED SO FAST! THE WALL -- IT JUST VANISHED!

IT DIDN'T VANISH, SONNY...

I GOT RID OF IT FOR YOU!

EEEK!

GOOD HEAVENS!

HELP!

HEARING THE CRIES, A LOCAL DEPUTY RACES ONTO THE SCENE, TO FIND...

I SAW A MASS OF FLAMING DEBRIS FLY THRU THE AIR, AND THEN -- LOOK!

I'LL BE BLAMED! IT'S THAT MONSTER THEY BEEN BROADCASTIN' AN ALARM ON RADIO ABOUT! I'LL GIT 'IM!

THE BRAINLESS IDIOTS! THEY'RE SHOOTING AT ME!

SAVE A MAN'S FAMILY AND THEY SHOOT AT YA! COME ON, RICK -- WE'RE TAKIN' OFF!

BAM!

BLAM!

BAM!

13

THAT'S RIGHT! SEND OUT AN ALL-POINTS ALARM! THE HULK IS IN THE AREA SOMEPLACE! NO ONE WILL BE SAFE UNTIL HE'S FOUND AND DESTROYED! HE - HE'S EVEN MORE TERRIFYING THAN I *HEARD* HE WAS!

WE BETTER HEAD BACK TO THE HID-DEN LAB, HULK!

WHERE DO YA *THINK* I'M GOIN'? I'M *SICK* OF BEIN' SHOT AT AND HOUNDED!

HERE, I RIGGED UP THIS GADGET SO ALL I GOTTA DO IS STEP ON THESE BUTTONS TO ACTIVATE THE GAMMA RAY!

THEY CAN LOOK FOR THE HULK FROM NOW TIL DOOMSDAY, BUT THEY'LL NEVER FIND ME!

AND ONCE AGAIN THE AWESOME RAYS WEAVE THEIR MAGIC ON THE BEING WHO STANDS BEFORE THEM...

BOY, DOC, IT'S A RELIEF TO HAVE YOU BACK AGAIN -- AS *YOU!* THAT HULK WAS BEGINNIN' TO EVEN SCARE *ME!*

CAN'T TALK, RICK -- TIRED -- VERY TIRED.

HAVE TO REST -- THE GAMMA RAYS -- CAN'T KEEP CHANGING TOO OFTEN -- NOT TOO QUICKLY -- RAYS ARE TOO STRONG! MUST REST NOW -- TIRED -- TIRED --

SURE, DOC... GO AHEAD! GRAB YOUR-SELF SOME SHUT-EYE!

EVEN THOUGH THE HULK NOW HAS MY BRAIN, HE IS STILL A RAGING GOLIATH! STILL HARD TO CONTROL! I PRAY HE NEVER TURNS ON ME -- OR ON MANKIND -- BUT MUSTN'T TELL RICK -- MUSTN'T WORRY THE BOY -- SO MUCH TO THINK ABOUT -- SO MUCH TO DO...

GO ON AND SLEEP, DOC -- YOU'VE *EARNED* IT! I KNOW YOU'RE WORRIED! I KNOW THE HULK IS *STILL* A PRO-BLEM! BUT I'LL SEE IT THRU WITH YA TILL THE END! I SWEAR IT, DOC -- NO MATTER WHAT!

CLICK

THE END

14

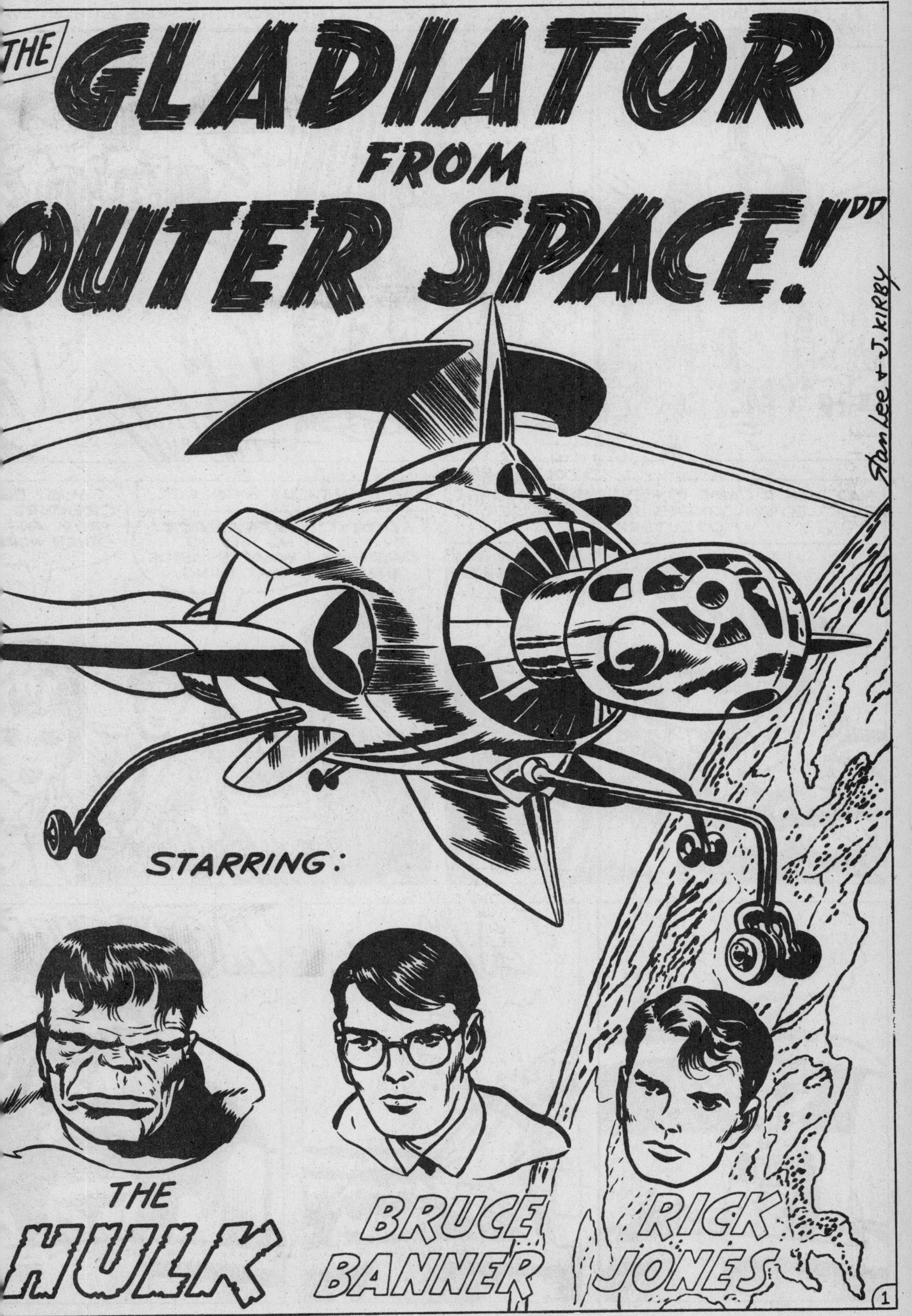
THE GLADIATOR FROM OUTER SPACE!"
Stan Lee + J. Kirby
STARRING:
THE HULK
BRUCE BANNER
RICK JONES
1

_I_T LANDED SUDDENLY, UNEXPECTEDLY, SWOOPING DOWN FROM THE SKIES WITHOUT WARNING!

AND THEN IT CAME TO REST! SLOWLY, THE STARTLED ONLOOKERS INCHED CLOSER AND CLOSER...

WHAT _IS_ IT? WHERE DID IT COME FROM?

UNTIL, WITHOUT WARNING...

LOOK! IT - IT'S _OPENING_ UP!

STAY BACK! NO TELLING _WHAT'S_ INSIDE THAT THING!

IT MUST BE CREATURE FROM AN- OTHER WORL

_I-_

_AM-_

MONGU!

...THAT MOMENT, IN ANOTHER PART OF TOWN, [R]CK JONES TURNS ON HIS TV SET, AND...

[D]OC! HEY, [D]OC! LOOK [A]T *THIS*! [S]OME KINDA *MONSTER* [J]UST LANDED [I]N THE PARK!

I SHOULD BE THE *LAST* ONE TO CALL ANYONE ELSE A MONSTER, RICK!

WHO *IS* HE? WHERE DID HE *COME* FROM?

LISTEN--- I HAVE COME TO EARTH TO ISSUE A *CHAL-LENGE!*

I CHALLENGE EARTH'S MIGHTIEST MORTAL TO MEET ME IN HAND-TO-HAND COMBAT! IF YOUR CHAMPION DEFEATS ME, I SHALL DEPART FOR-EVER...

BUT, IF *MONGU* IS VICTORIOUS, THEN EARTHLINGS *BE-WARE!* FOR THEN, THE WARRIORS OF MY WORLD WILL ATTACK THIS PUNY PLANET AND CON-QUER IT WITH-OUT MERCY!

SEND ME A CHAMPION WHO CAN WELD A *TWO-TON AX* LIKE ME!

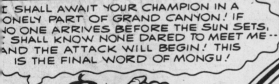

I SHALL AWAIT YOUR CHAMPION IN A [L]ONELY PART OF GRAND CANYON! IF [N]O ONE ARRIVES BEFORE THE SUN SETS, [I] SHALL KNOW NONE DARED TO MEET ME-- [A]ND THE ATTACK WILL BEGIN! THIS IS THE FINAL WORD OF MONGU!

THEN, WITHOUT FURTHER ADO, THE STRANGE, UNEARTHLY CRAFT RISES INTO THE AIR AND HEADS TOWARDS GRAND CANYON, AS THE WATCHING MULTITUDES HARDLY DARE TO DRAW A BREATH...

NO HUMAN ON EARTH CAN DEFEAT THAT BRUTE!

3

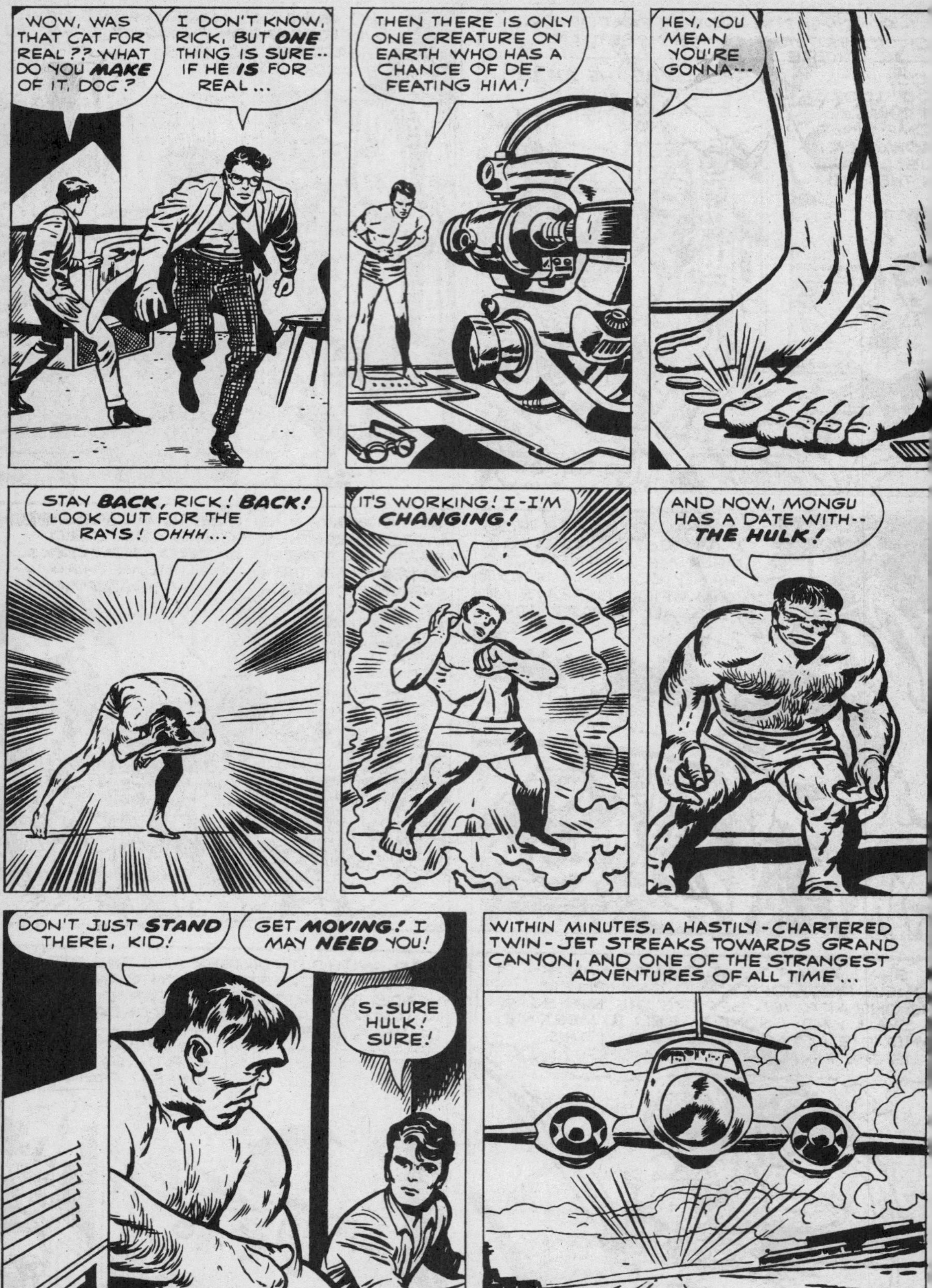

WOW, WAS THAT CAT FOR REAL ?? WHAT DO YOU MAKE OF IT, DOC ?
I DON'T KNOW, RICK, BUT ONE THING IS SURE -- IF HE IS FOR REAL ...
THEN THERE IS ONLY ONE CREATURE ON EARTH WHO HAS A CHANCE OF DE-FEATING HIM!
HEY, YOU MEAN YOU'RE GONNA ---
STAY BACK, RICK! BACK! LOOK OUT FOR THE RAYS! OHHH...
IT'S WORKING! I-I'M CHANGING!
AND NOW, MONGU HAS A DATE WITH -- THE HULK!
DON'T JUST STAND THERE, KID!
GET MOVING! I MAY NEED YOU!
S-SURE HULK! SURE!
WITHIN MINUTES, A HASTILY-CHARTERED TWIN-JET STREAKS TOWARDS GRAND CANYON, AND ONE OF THE STRANGEST ADVENTURES OF ALL TIME ...
4

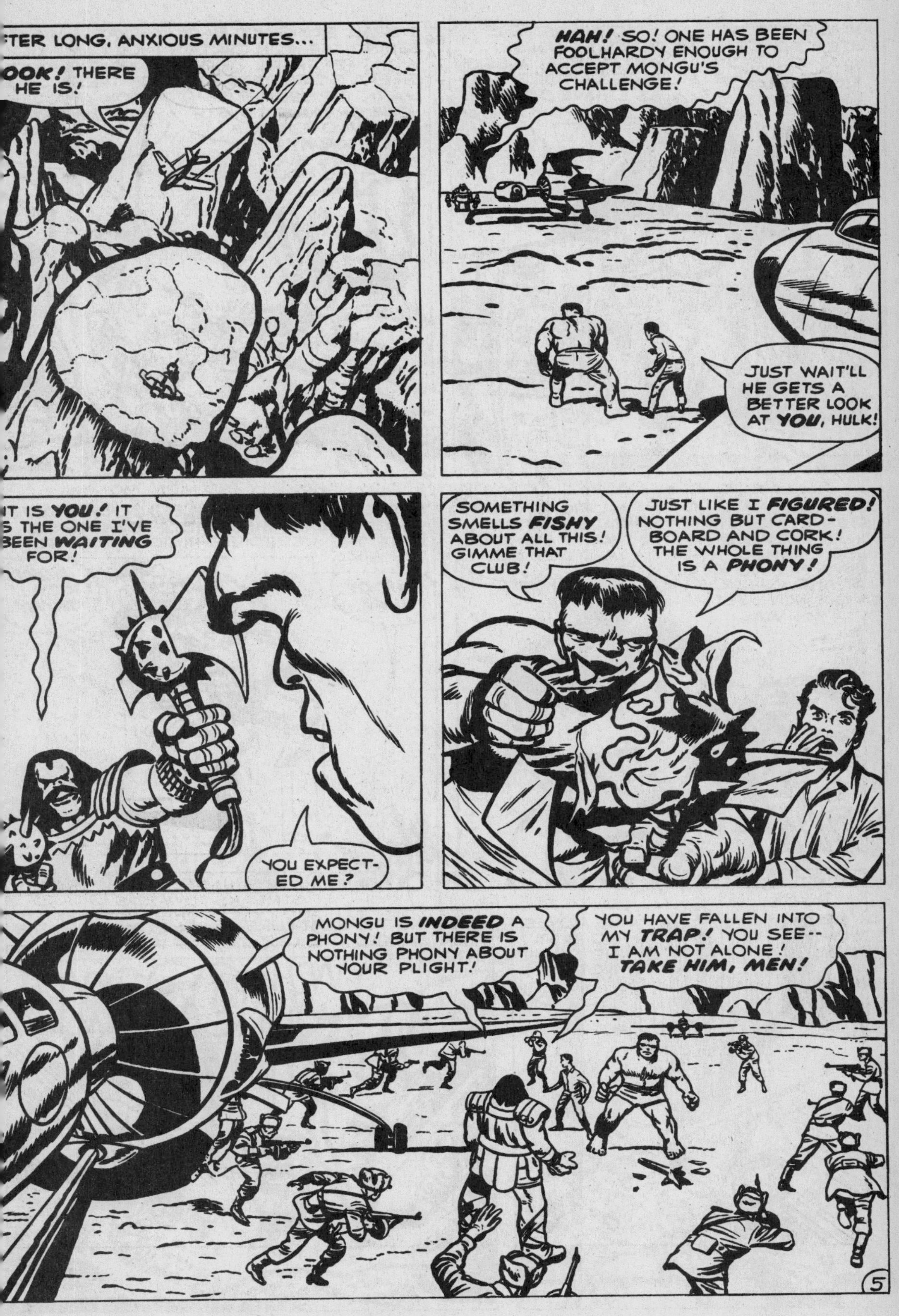
FTER LONG, ANXIOUS MINUTES...
OOK! THERE HE IS!
HAH! SO! ONE HAS BEEN FOOLHARDY ENOUGH TO ACCEPT MONGU'S CHALLENGE!
JUST WAIT'LL HE GETS A BETTER LOOK AT YOU, HULK!
IT IS YOU! IT S THE ONE I'VE BEEN WAITING FOR!
YOU EXPECTED ME?
SOMETHING SMELLS FISHY ABOUT ALL THIS! GIMME THAT CLUB!
JUST LIKE I FIGURED! NOTHING BUT CARDBOARD AND CORK! THE WHOLE THING IS A PHONY!
MONGU IS INDEED A PHONY! BUT THERE IS NOTHING PHONY ABOUT YOUR PLIGHT!
YOU HAVE FALLEN INTO MY TRAP! YOU SEE-- I AM NOT ALONE! TAKE HIM, MEN!

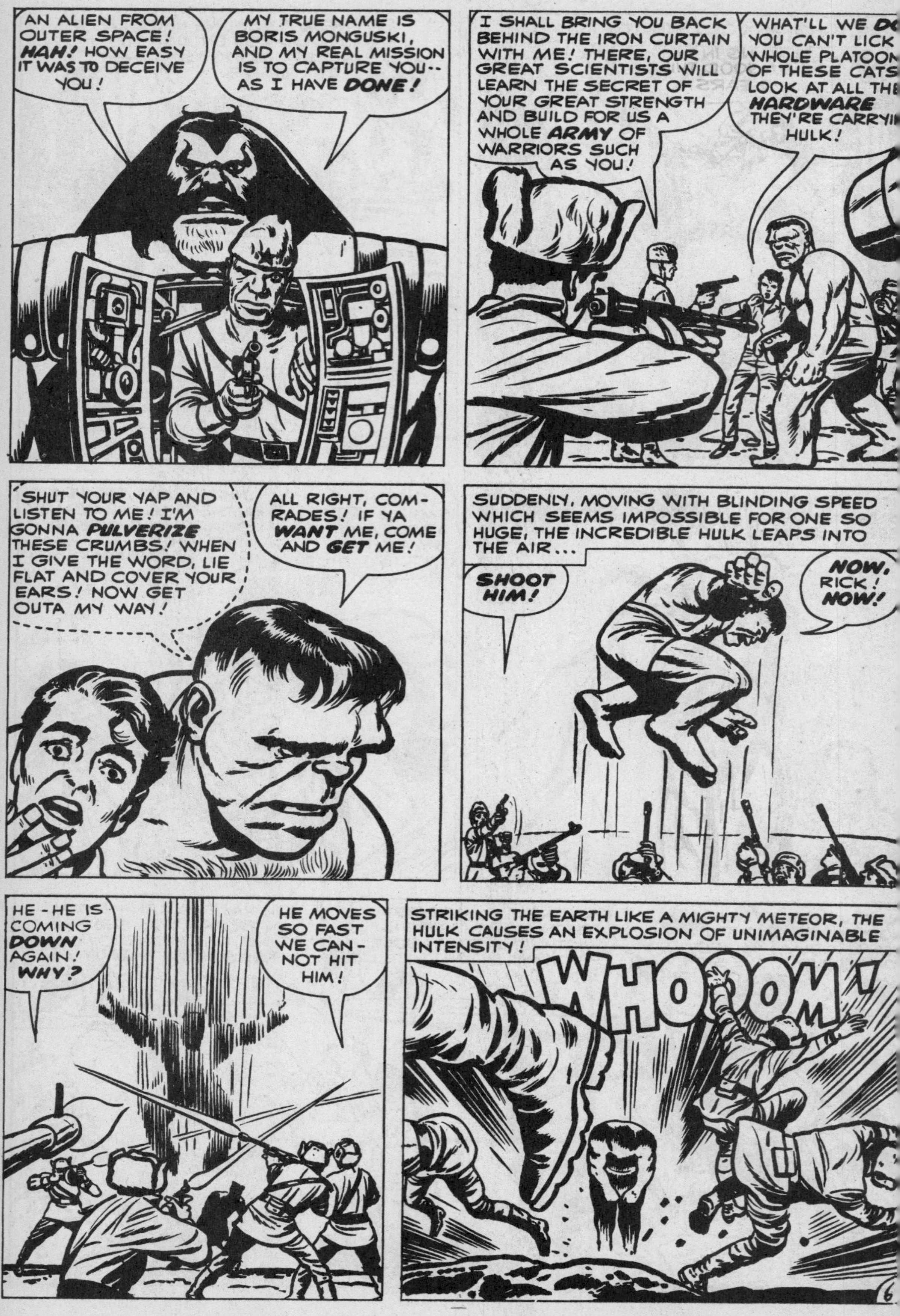
AN ALIEN FROM OUTER SPACE! HAH! HOW EASY IT WAS TO DECEIVE YOU!
MY TRUE NAME IS BORIS MONGUSKI, AND MY REAL MISSION IS TO CAPTURE YOU-- AS I HAVE DONE!
I SHALL BRING YOU BACK BEHIND THE IRON CURTAIN WITH ME! THERE, OUR GREAT SCIENTISTS WILL LEARN THE SECRET OF YOUR GREAT STRENGTH AND BUILD FOR US A WHOLE ARMY OF WARRIORS SUCH AS YOU!
WHAT'LL WE DO YOU CAN'T LICK WHOLE PLATOON OF THESE CATS LOOK AT ALL THE HARDWARE THEY'RE CARRYI HULK!
SHUT YOUR YAP AND LISTEN TO ME! I'M GONNA PULVERIZE THESE CRUMBS! WHEN I GIVE THE WORD, LIE FLAT AND COVER YOUR EARS! NOW GET OUTA MY WAY!
ALL RIGHT, COMRADES! IF YA WANT ME, COME AND GET ME!
SUDDENLY, MOVING WITH BLINDING SPEED WHICH SEEMS IMPOSSIBLE FOR ONE SO HUGE, THE INCREDIBLE HULK LEAPS INTO THE AIR...
SHOOT HIM!
NOW, RICK! NOW!
HE - HE IS COMING DOWN AGAIN! WHY?
HE MOVES SO FAST WE CAN-NOT HIT HIM!
STRIKING THE EARTH LIKE A MIGHTY METEOR, THE HULK CAUSES AN EXPLOSION OF UNIMAGINABLE INTENSITY!
WHOOOM!
6

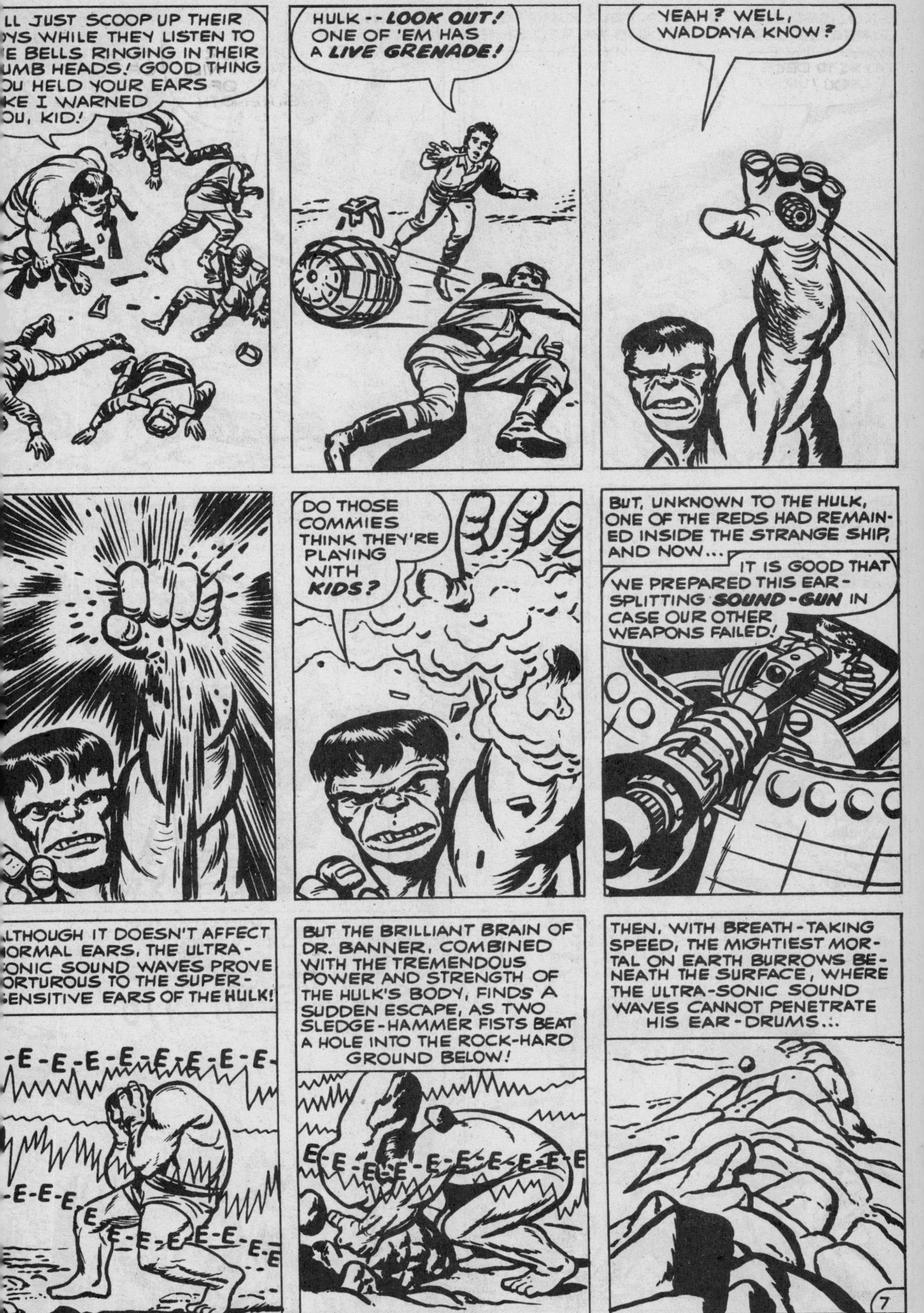
LL JUST SCOOP UP THEIR
OYS WHILE THEY LISTEN TO
E BELLS RINGING IN THEIR
UMB HEADS! GOOD THING
OU HELD YOUR EARS
KE I WARNED
OU, KID!
HULK--*LOOK OUT!* ONE OF 'EM HAS A *LIVE GRENADE!*
YEAH? WELL, WADDAYA KNOW?
DO THOSE COMMIES THINK THEY'RE PLAYING WITH *KIDS?*
BUT, UNKNOWN TO THE HULK, ONE OF THE REDS HAD REMAINED INSIDE THE *STRANGE SHIP,* AND NOW...
IT IS GOOD THAT WE PREPARED THIS EAR-SPLITTING *SOUND-GUN* IN CASE OUR OTHER WEAPONS FAILED!
LTHOUGH IT DOESN'T AFFECT
ORMAL EARS, THE ULTRA-
ONIC SOUND WAVES PROVE
ORTUROUS TO THE SUPER-
ENSITIVE EARS OF THE HULK!
-E-E-E-E-E-E-E-E-E-
-E-E-E-E-E-E-E-E-E-E-E-E-E
BUT THE BRILLIANT BRAIN OF DR. BANNER, COMBINED WITH THE TREMENDOUS POWER AND STRENGTH OF THE HULK'S BODY, FINDS A SUDDEN ESCAPE, AS TWO SLEDGE-HAMMER FISTS BEAT A HOLE INTO THE ROCK-HARD GROUND BELOW!
E-E-E-E-E-E-E-E-E-E-E-E
THEN, WITH BREATH-TAKING SPEED, THE MIGHTIEST MORTAL ON EARTH BURROWS BENEATH THE SURFACE, WHERE THE ULTRA-SONIC SOUND WAVES CANNOT PENETRATE HIS EAR-DRUMS...

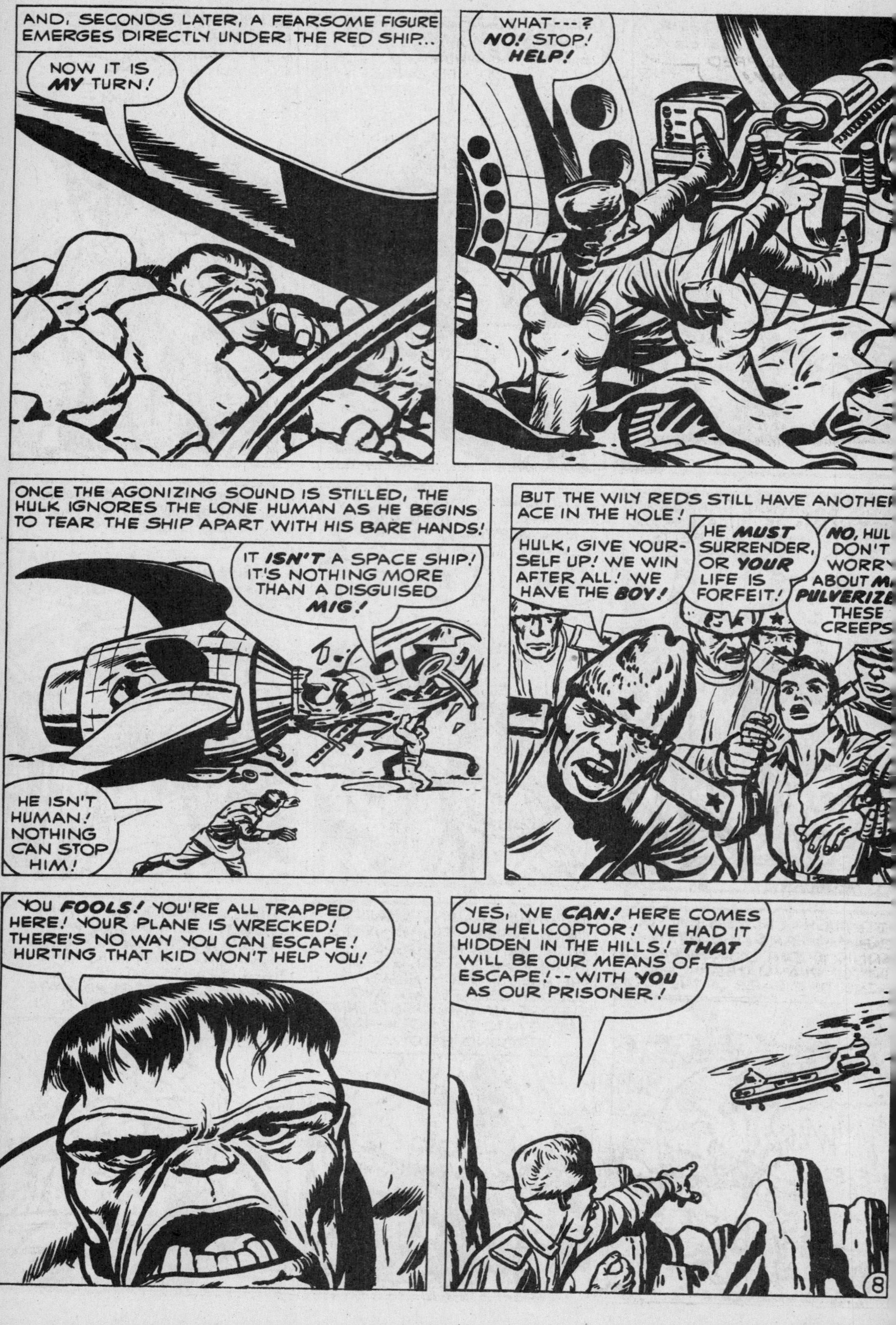
AND, SECONDS LATER, A FEARSOME FIGURE EMERGES DIRECTLY UNDER THE RED SHIP..
NOW IT IS MY TURN!
WHAT---? NO! STOP! HELP!
ONCE THE AGONIZING SOUND IS STILLED, THE HULK IGNORES THE LONE HUMAN AS HE BEGINS TO TEAR THE SHIP APART WITH HIS BARE HANDS!
IT ISN'T A SPACE SHIP! IT'S NOTHING MORE THAN A DISGUISED MIG!
HE ISN'T HUMAN! NOTHING CAN STOP HIM!
BUT THE WILY REDS STILL HAVE ANOTHER ACE IN THE HOLE!
HULK, GIVE YOURSELF UP! WE WIN AFTER ALL! WE HAVE THE BOY!
HE MUST SURRENDER, OR YOUR LIFE IS FORFEIT!
NO, HUL DON'T WORRY ABOUT M. PULVERIZE THESE CREEPS
YOU FOOLS! YOU'RE ALL TRAPPED HERE! YOUR PLANE IS WRECKED! THERE'S NO WAY YOU CAN ESCAPE! HURTING THAT KID WON'T HELP YOU!
YES, WE CAN! HERE COMES OUR HELICOPTOR! WE HAD IT HIDDEN IN THE HILLS! THAT WILL BE OUR MEANS OF ESCAPE!--WITH YOU AS OUR PRISONER!
8

GUESS AGAIN, LOUDMOUTH! THAT BIRD'S GONNA GET ITS WINGS CLIPPED RIGHT **NOW!**

BEFORE ANY OF THE REDS CAN MOVE A MUSCLE, THE MIGHTY HULK HURLS A PIECE OF THE WRECKED MIG SKYWARD TOWARDS THE HOVERING SHIP! SKIMMING THRU THE AIR LIKE A WHIRLING BLADE, IT SEVERS THE HELICOPTER'S LANDING GEAR, MAKING FURTHER DESCENT IMPOSSIBLE...

THAT TAKES CARE OF THAT! NOW I CAN FINISH OFF THESE COMMIES WITHOUT ANY MORE INTERRUPTIONS!

BUT THERE IS A LIMIT TO THE FRUSTRATIONS WHICH ANY MEN CAN ENDURE -- EVEN COMMUNISTS! AND SO...

TAKE HIM -- WE GIVE UP!

STAY BACK! DO NOT HARM US! WE ARE YOUR PRISONERS!

TAKE OFF ALL YOUR BELTS!

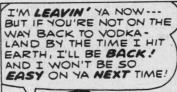

WH-WHAT IS HE **DOING?**

TYING US TOGETHER WITH OUR OWN BELTS!

BUT-- **WHY?**

THIS IS WHY, COMRADES, BECAUSE YOU'RE TAKIN' A LITTLE TRIP!

I'LL TIE YA ON TO THE TOW TABLE OF THIS EGG-BEATER, AND YOU CAN JOIN YOUR LITTLE PLAYMATES INSIDE!

I'M **LEAVIN'** YA NOW --- BUT IF YOU'RE NOT ON THE WAY BACK TO VODKA-LAND BY THE TIME I HIT EARTH, I'LL BE **BACK!** AND I WON'T BE SO **EASY** ON YA **NEXT** TIME!

HULK -- YOU **DID** IT! **YOU DID IT!** THEY'VE **GONE!**

WHAT DID YA **EXPECT**, HALF-PINT? I WASN'T PLAYIN' FOR **FUN!**

9

A FEW HOURS LATER, THE ONCE DESERTED PLATEAU IS A BEE-HIVE OF ACTIVITY...

THE "SPACE-SHIP" WAS NOTHING BUT A CAMO-FLAUGED MIG! THE "ALIEN" WAS A PHONY SUIT, IN WHICH A NORMAL MAN WAS CONCEALED!

THE WHOLE THING WAS JUST ONE GIGANTIC HOAX!

WE FOUND FOOT-PRINTS AND FINGER-PRINTS THAT CAN ONLY BELONG TO THE HULK! HE'S INVOLVED IN THIS SOMEHOW!

THE WHOLE THING MUS BE HIS DOING! HE WAN ED US TO THINK THAT H DEFEATED A MENACE FROM SPACE! HE WAN ED TO BE CONSIDERED A HERO!

WHATEVER THE HULK PLANNED TO ACCOMPLISH BY HIS PHONY SCHEME, IT SURE BACKFIRED! HE DIDN'T FOOL ANYBODY!

YEAH! NOW THE ARMY WANTS TO GET HIM MORE THAN EVER! HE WON'T BE ABLE TO ESCAPE OLD THUNDERBOLT ROSS MUCH LONGER!

METROPOLITAN HERALD
BATTLE WITH SPACE GLADIATOR RIGGED BY HULK!
EXTRA!
PUBLIC TAKEN IN BY BRAZEN HOAX!
"I'LL TRAP THE HULK YET!" SWEARS GENERAL ROSS

BUT, MILES AWAY, IN A HIDDEN CAVE BE-NEATH THE SEA, ONE OF THE WORLD'S MOS FANTASTIC TRANSFORMATIONS IS AGAIN TAKI PLACE, AS THE ANGRY, POWERFUL, BRUTAL HULK SUBJECTS HIMSELF TO THE MYSTERIOU GAMMA RAYS WHICH HE HAD DISCOVERED WHEN HE WAS DOCTOR BRUCE BANNER...

AND THEN, SLOWLY THE MAS-SIVE DOOR SWINGS OPEN, AND A WEARY SCIENTIST STAGGERS OUT...

IT'S OVER-- FOR NOW!

YOU CAME THRU IT OKAY! I WAS BEGINNIN' TO GET WORRIED ABOUT YOU!

BOY! IT SURE IS HARD TO BELIEVE THAT YOU WERE THE STRONGEST JOE ON EARTH JUST A LITTLE WHILE AGO!

LET ME LEAN ON YOUR SHOULDER, RICK! I-I'M TIRED! SO TIRED...

AND SO, THE WORLD'S MOST AMAZING HUMAN, AND THE BO WHO SHARES HIS AWESOME SECRET, SLOWLY WALK OUT IN THE LIGHT OF DAY...HOPING TO HAVE A LONG BREATHING SPEL A LONG REST...

...BEFORE THE INCREDIBLE HULK COMES TO LIFE AGAIN!

10

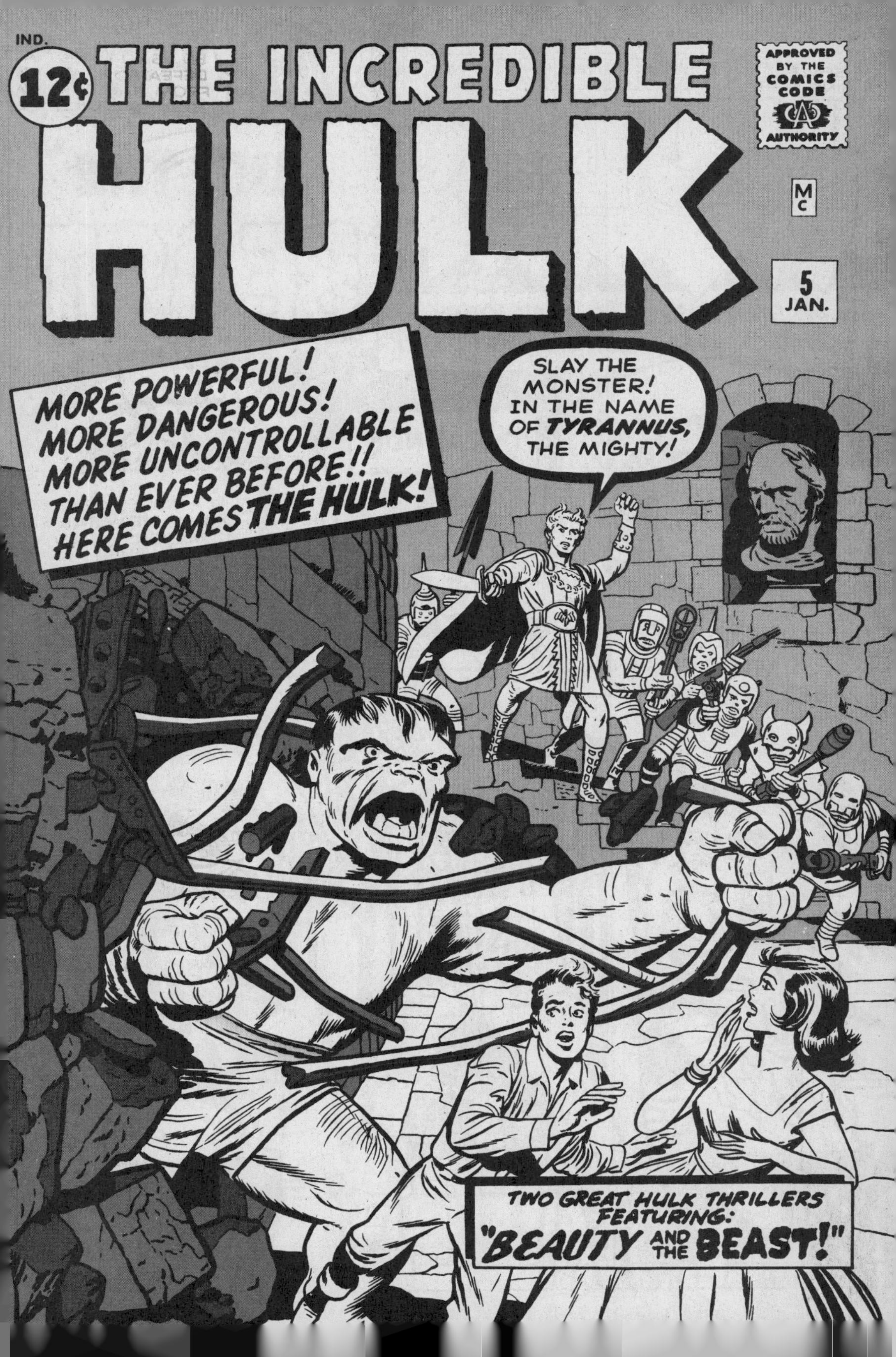
IND.
12¢
THE INCREDIBLE
HULK
APPROVED BY THE COMICS CODE AUTHORITY
MC
5
JAN.
MORE POWERFUL! MORE DANGEROUS! MORE UNCONTROLLABLE THAN EVER BEFORE!! HERE COMES THE HULK!
SLAY THE MONSTER! IN THE NAME OF TYRANNUS, THE MIGHTY!
TWO GREAT HULK THRILLERS FEATURING: "BEAUTY AND THE BEAST!"

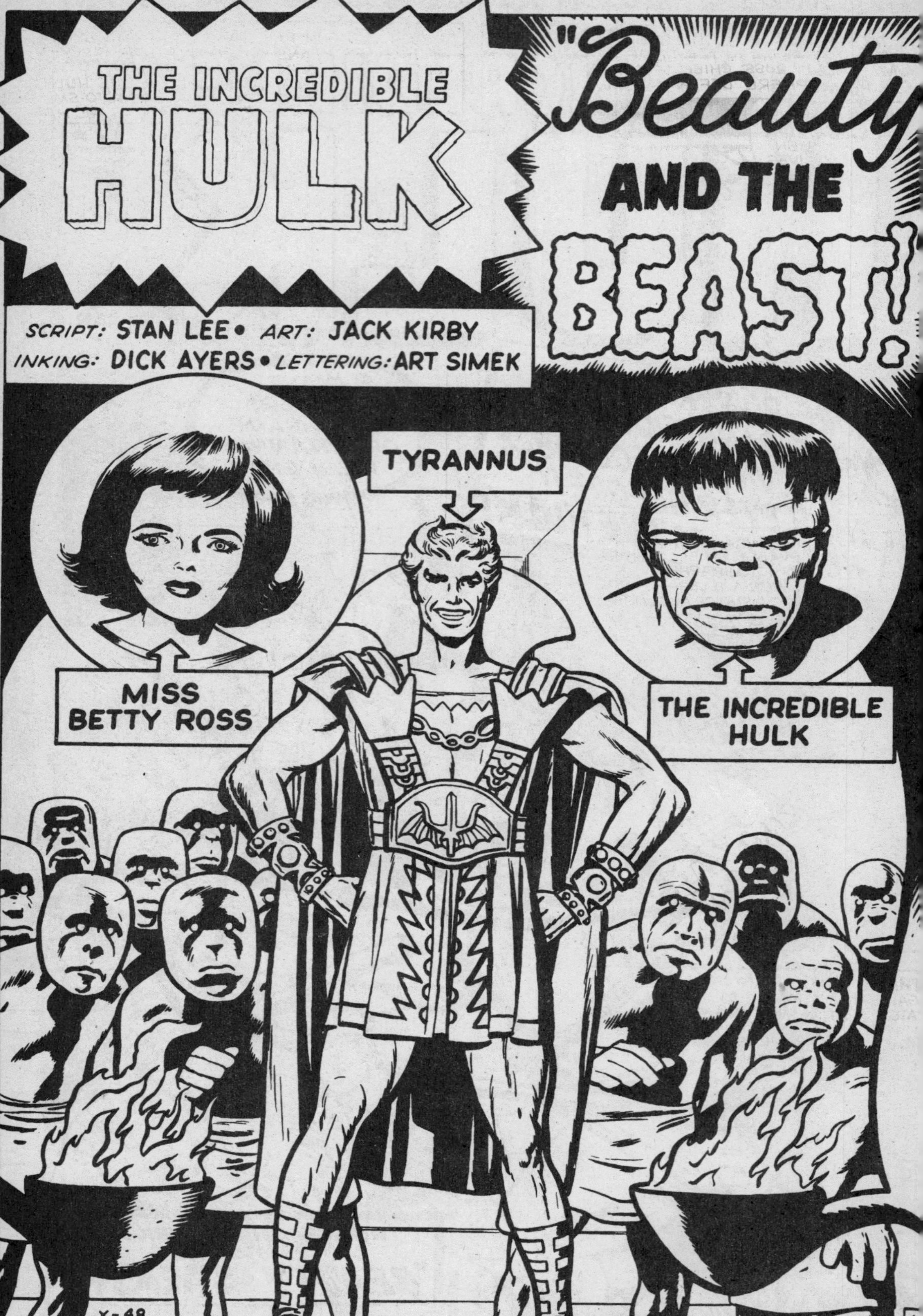
THE INCREDIBLE HULK
"Beauty AND THE BEAST!"
SCRIPT: STAN LEE • ART: JACK KIRBY
INKING: DICK AYERS • LETTERING: ART SIMEK
TYRANNUS
MISS BETTY ROSS
THE INCREDIBLE HULK
X-48
1

OUR TALE BEGINS WITH THE SHOWING OF TOP-SECRET ARMY FILMS IN THE HOME OF GENERAL "THUNDERBOLT" ROSS, CHIEF OF THE WESTERN HEMISPHERE DEFENSE COMMAND!

HERE HE IS--THE DEMONIACAL HULK! THREE BRAVE MEN RISKED THEIR LIVES TO GET THESE PICTURES!

"THIS SHOWS OUR FAILURE TO TRAP THE BRUTAL MONSTER BY MEANS OF A GIANT, SPECIALLY-CONSTRUCTED NEURON-MAGNET, DESIGNED TO ATTRACT AND HOLD LIVING BEINGS! THE HULK'S SUPER-HUMAN STRENGTH ENABLED HIM TO SMASH THE MAGNET JUST WHEN WE THOUGHT WE **HAD** HIM!"

"AS FURTHER EVIDENCE OF THE HULK'S UNBELIEVABLE STRENGTH, A FREE-LANCE PHOTOGRAPHER TOOK THIS FILM WITH A TELEPHOTO LENS FROM A SAFE DISTANCE AWAY!"

"AND **THIS** IS THE MOST INCREDIBLE OF ALL! THE ONLY FILM IN EXISTENCE WHICH SHOWS, IN VIVID DETAIL..."

"...THE HULK'S ABILITY TO SURVIVE ANY EXPLOSION SHORT OF AN ACTUAL ATOMIC DEVICE!"

THAT'S WHAT I'M UP AGAINST! IT'S **MY** JOB TO CATCH THAT RAMPAGING MONSTER! NO MATTER **HOW** POWERFUL HE IS, HIS GOVERNMENT WANTS HIM **STOPPED!**

BUT I CAN'T DO IT BY MILITARY MEANS ALONE, BANNER! I NEED **SCIENTIFIC** HELP--AND THAT'S WHERE **YOU** COME IN! AS TOP SCIENTIST ON MY STAFF, YOU'VE GOT TO THINK OF A WAY TO CONQUER THAT MAN-BEAST!

CAN'T MAKE ANY PROMISES, SIR, BUT RICK AND I WILL DO OUR BEST TO THINK OF SOMETHING!

RICK! **BAH!** I CAN'T SEE WHY YOU INSIST ON HAVING THAT INSOLENT TEEN-AGER AS YOUR ASSISTANT!

OH, DAD, DON'T BE SO GRUMPY! YOU KNOW THE DEFENSE DEPARTMENT HAS GIVEN BRUCE THE RIGHT TO SELECT ANY AIDES HE CHOOSES!

2

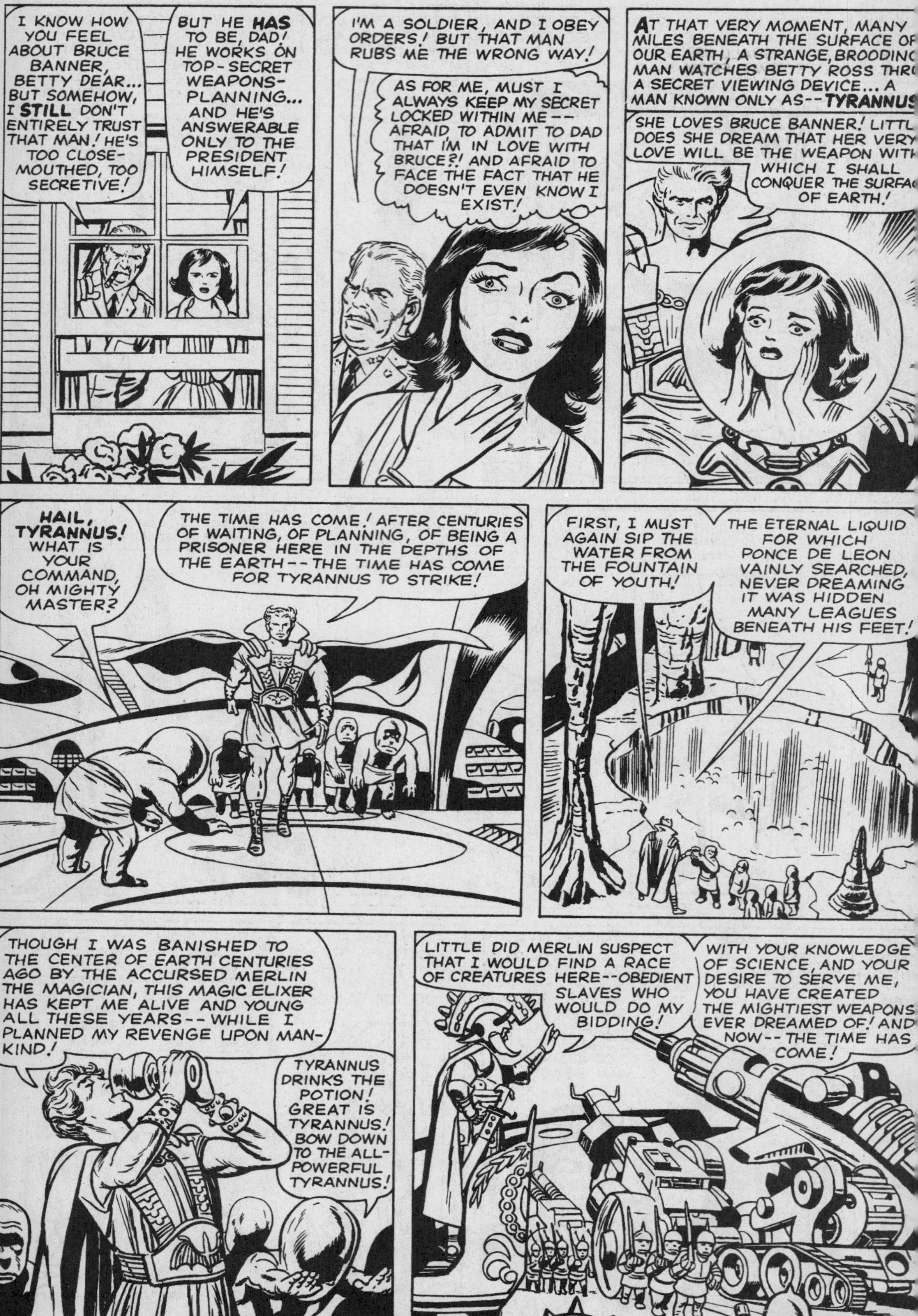
I KNOW HOW YOU FEEL ABOUT BRUCE BANNER, BETTY DEAR... BUT SOMEHOW, I STILL DON'T ENTIRELY TRUST THAT MAN! HE'S TOO CLOSE-MOUTHED, TOO SECRETIVE!
BUT HE HAS TO BE, DAD! HE WORKS ON TOP-SECRET WEAPONS-PLANNING... AND HE'S ANSWERABLE ONLY TO THE PRESIDENT HIMSELF!
I'M A SOLDIER, AND I OBEY ORDERS! BUT THAT MAN RUBS ME THE WRONG WAY!
AS FOR ME, MUST I ALWAYS KEEP MY SECRET LOCKED WITHIN ME -- AFRAID TO ADMIT TO DAD THAT I'M IN LOVE WITH BRUCE?! AND AFRAID TO FACE THE FACT THAT HE DOESN'T EVEN KNOW I EXIST!
AT THAT VERY MOMENT, MANY MILES BENEATH THE SURFACE OF OUR EARTH, A STRANGE, BROODING MAN WATCHES BETTY ROSS THRU A SECRET VIEWING DEVICE... A MAN KNOWN ONLY AS--TYRANNUS
SHE LOVES BRUCE BANNER! LITTLE DOES SHE DREAM THAT HER VERY LOVE WILL BE THE WEAPON WITH WHICH I SHALL CONQUER THE SURFACE OF EARTH!
HAIL, TYRANNUS! WHAT IS YOUR COMMAND, OH MIGHTY MASTER?
THE TIME HAS COME! AFTER CENTURIES OF WAITING, OF PLANNING, OF BEING A PRISONER HERE IN THE DEPTHS OF THE EARTH -- THE TIME HAS COME FOR TYRANNUS TO STRIKE!
FIRST, I MUST AGAIN SIP THE WATER FROM THE FOUNTAIN OF YOUTH!
THE ETERNAL LIQUID FOR WHICH PONCE DE LEON VAINLY SEARCHED, NEVER DREAMING IT WAS HIDDEN MANY LEAGUES BENEATH HIS FEET!
THOUGH I WAS BANISHED TO THE CENTER OF EARTH CENTURIES AGO BY THE ACCURSED MERLIN THE MAGICIAN, THIS MAGIC ELIXER HAS KEPT ME ALIVE AND YOUNG ALL THESE YEARS -- WHILE I PLANNED MY REVENGE UPON MAN-KIND!
TYRANNUS DRINKS THE POTION! GREAT IS TYRANNUS! BOW DOWN TO THE ALL-POWERFUL TYRANNUS!
LITTLE DID MERLIN SUSPECT THAT I WOULD FIND A RACE OF CREATURES HERE--OBEDIENT SLAVES WHO WOULD DO MY BIDDING!
WITH YOUR KNOWLEDGE OF SCIENCE, AND YOUR DESIRE TO SERVE ME, YOU HAVE CREATED THE MIGHTIEST WEAPONS EVER DREAMED OF! AND NOW -- THE TIME HAS COME!
3

...HAVE BEEN FEARFUL OF ONLY ONE THING -- THE ARMED ATOMIC MIGHT OF THE LAND CALLED AMERICA! BUT I SHALL USE BETTY ROSS TO PROTECT ME FROM THAT MIGHT!

MEANWHILE, NOT SUSPECTING WHAT FATE HAS IN STORE FOR THEM, BRUCE BANNER AND RICK RETURN TO THE GENERAL'S HOME THE NEXT DAY...

MAN, WHAT A GASSER! IMAGINE OL' THUNDERBOLT ROSS ORDERING YOU TO CAPTURE YOURSELF!

HE STILL DOESN'T SUSPECT THAT I MYSELF AM THE HULK, RICK -- AND I PRAY HE NEVER FINDS OUT!

IF ONLY MANKIND DIDN'T FEAR THE HULK! IF ONLY THEY WOULD TRUST HIM -- SO THAT I COULD REVEAL MY SECRET!

TRUST THE HULK?! LISTEN, DADDY-O, I KNOW YOUR SECRET -- AND I STILL TREMBLE WHEN I SEE 'IM!

THEN, AFTER REACHING THE GENERAL'S HOME...

...ORRY, BRUCE, DAD ISN'T IN YET! BUT MAY I INTRODUCE MR. TYRANNUS -- HE IS AN ARCHAEOLOGIST! I'M GOING TO SHOW HIM ...HE CLIFF CAVES NEARBY!

OH?

S'MATTER, BRUCE? WHAT'S BUGGIN' YA?

JUST A FEELING, KID! I DON'T LIKE HIS LOOKS!

IT'S WORKING! BRUCE LOOKS JEALOUS! I'M SO GLAD I MET MR. TYRANNUS! MAYBE THIS WILL MAKE BRUCE THINK OF ME AS A WOMAN!

...MINUTES LATER...

...IT DOESN'T SIT RIGHT WITH ME, RICK! WHY WOULD AN ARCHAEOLOGIST NEED A LOCAL GIRL TO SHOW HIM THE CAVES! THEIR TRACKS LEAD IN HERE...

AW, THIS IS FOR THE BIRDS, PAL! WHO WANTS TO FOLLOW A COUPLE OF CAVE-LOVERS AROUND?

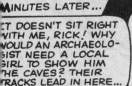

ANOTHER THING -- WHY DIDN'T TYRANNUS HAVE ANY ARCHEOLOGICAL EQUIPMENT WITH HIM? RICK -- LOOK AT THAT?

HOW'D THEY GET PAST THIS GIANT BOULDER?

WE CAN'T BUDGE IT -- AND YET THEIR TRACKS LEAD PAST IT! HOW--??

THAT'S WHAT WE'RE GOING TO FIND OUT -- WITH THE HELP OF SOMEONE WHO CAN BUDGE IT! QUICK -- BACK TO THE LAB!

4

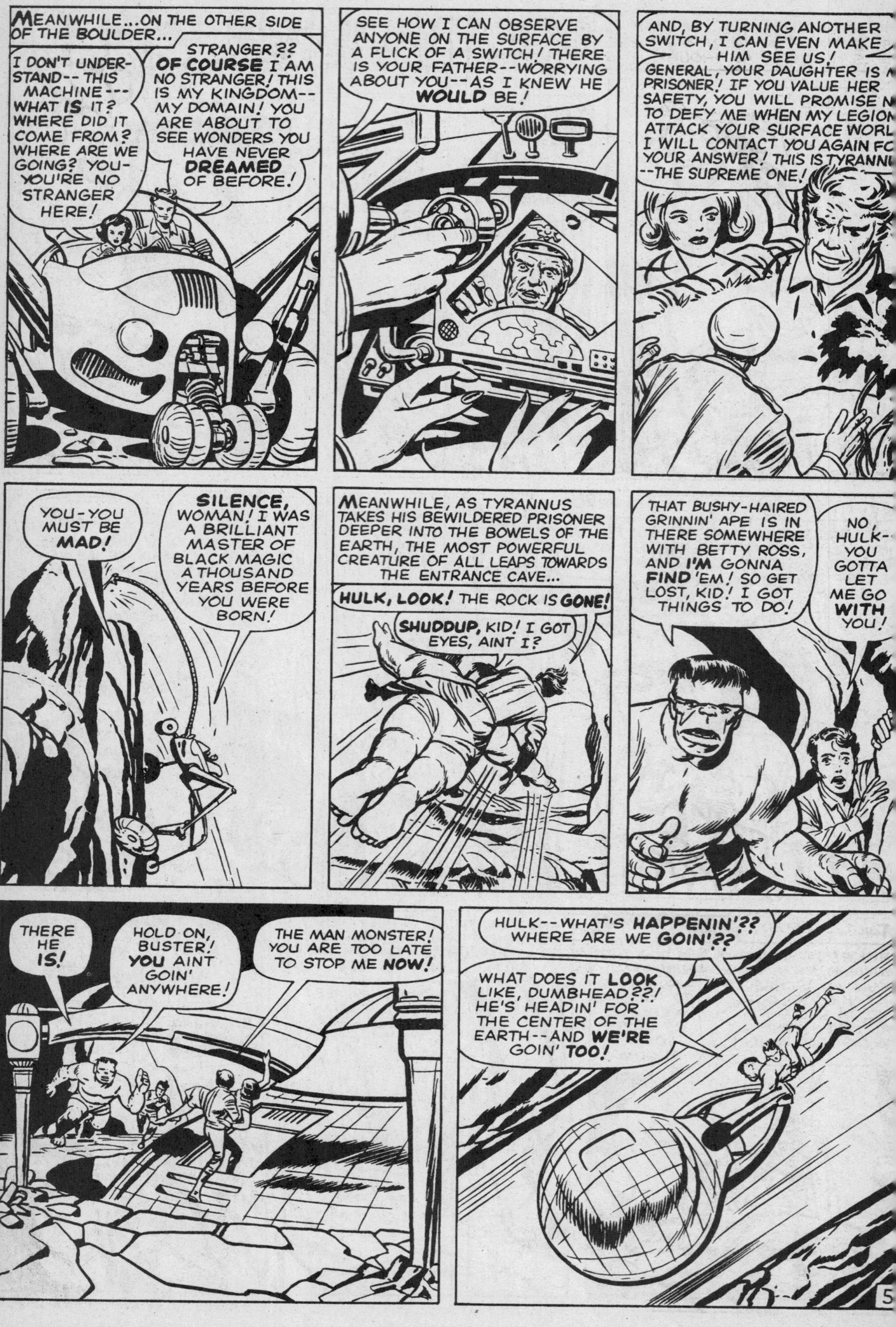
MEANWHILE...ON THE OTHER SIDE OF THE BOULDER...
I DON'T UNDERSTAND-- THIS MACHINE--- WHAT IS IT? WHERE DID IT COME FROM? WHERE ARE WE GOING? YOU-YOU'RE NO STRANGER HERE!
STRANGER?? OF COURSE I AM NO STRANGER! THIS IS MY KINGDOM-- MY DOMAIN! YOU ARE ABOUT TO SEE WONDERS YOU HAVE NEVER DREAMED OF BEFORE!
SEE HOW I CAN OBSERVE ANYONE ON THE SURFACE BY A FLICK OF A SWITCH! THERE IS YOUR FATHER--WORRYING ABOUT YOU--AS I KNEW HE WOULD BE!
AND, BY TURNING ANOTHER SWITCH, I CAN EVEN MAKE HIM SEE US!
GENERAL, YOUR DAUGHTER IS A PRISONER! IF YOU VALUE HER SAFETY, YOU WILL PROMISE N TO DEFY ME WHEN MY LEGION ATTACK YOUR SURFACE WORL I WILL CONTACT YOU AGAIN FO YOUR ANSWER! THIS IS TYRANNU --THE SUPREME ONE!
YOU-YOU MUST BE MAD!
SILENCE, WOMAN! I WAS A BRILLIANT MASTER OF BLACK MAGIC A THOUSAND YEARS BEFORE YOU WERE BORN!
MEANWHILE, AS TYRANNUS TAKES HIS BEWILDERED PRISONER DEEPER INTO THE BOWELS OF THE EARTH, THE MOST POWERFUL CREATURE OF ALL LEAPS TOWARDS THE ENTRANCE CAVE...
HULK, LOOK! THE ROCK IS GONE!
SHUDDUP, KID! I GOT EYES, AINT I?
THAT BUSHY-HAIRED GRINNIN' APE IS IN THERE SOMEWHERE WITH BETTY ROSS, AND I'M GONNA FIND 'EM! SO GET LOST, KID! I GOT THINGS TO DO!
NO, HULK-- YOU GOTTA LET ME GO WITH YOU!
THERE HE IS!
HOLD ON, BUSTER! YOU AINT GOIN' ANYWHERE!
THE MAN MONSTER! YOU ARE TOO LATE TO STOP ME NOW!
HULK--WHAT'S HAPPENIN'?? WHERE ARE WE GOIN'??
WHAT DOES IT LOOK LIKE, DUMBHEAD??! HE'S HEADIN' FOR THE CENTER OF THE EARTH--AND WE'RE GOIN' TOO!
5

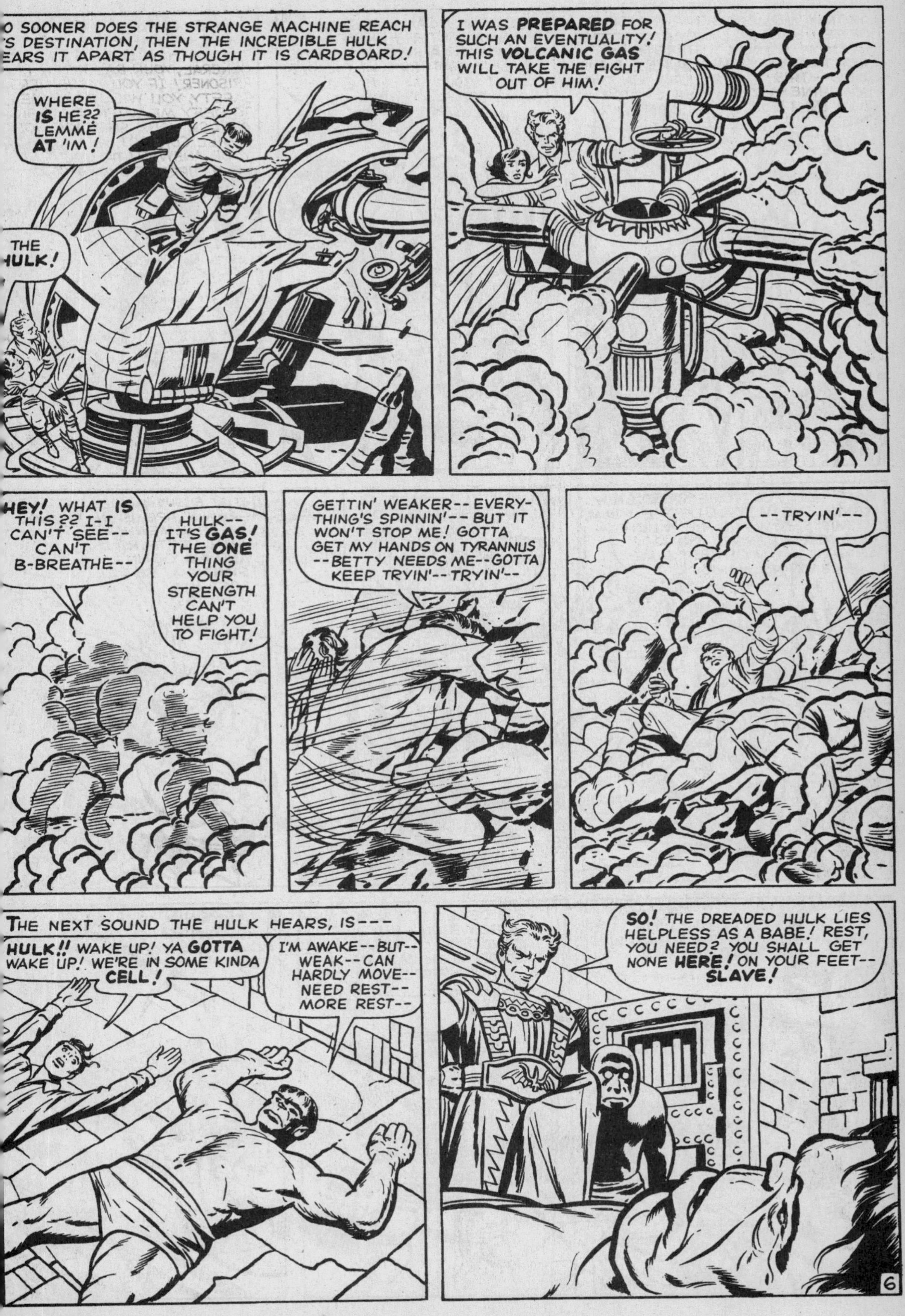
O SOONER DOES THE STRANGE MACHINE REACH 'S DESTINATION, THEN THE INCREDIBLE HULK EARS IT APART AS THOUGH IT IS CARDBOARD!
WHERE IS HE?? LEMMÉ AT 'IM!
THE HULK!
I WAS PREPARED FOR SUCH AN EVENTUALITY! THIS VOLCANIC GAS WILL TAKE THE FIGHT OUT OF HIM!
HEY! WHAT IS THIS?? I-I CAN'T SEE-- CAN'T B-BREATHE--
HULK-- IT'S GAS! THE ONE THING YOUR STRENGTH CAN'T HELP YOU TO FIGHT!
GETTIN' WEAKER-- EVERY-THING'S SPINNIN'-- BUT IT WON'T STOP ME! GOTTA GET MY HANDS ON TYRANNUS --BETTY NEEDS ME--GOTTA KEEP TRYIN'-- TRYIN'--
--TRYIN'--
THE NEXT SOUND THE HULK HEARS, IS---
HULK!! WAKE UP! YA GOTTA WAKE UP! WE'RE IN SOME KINDA CELL!
I'M AWAKE--BUT-- WEAK--CAN HARDLY MOVE-- NEED REST-- MORE REST--
SO! THE DREADED HULK LIES HELPLESS AS A BABE! REST, YOU NEED? YOU SHALL GET NONE HERE! ON YOUR FEET-- SLAVE!
6

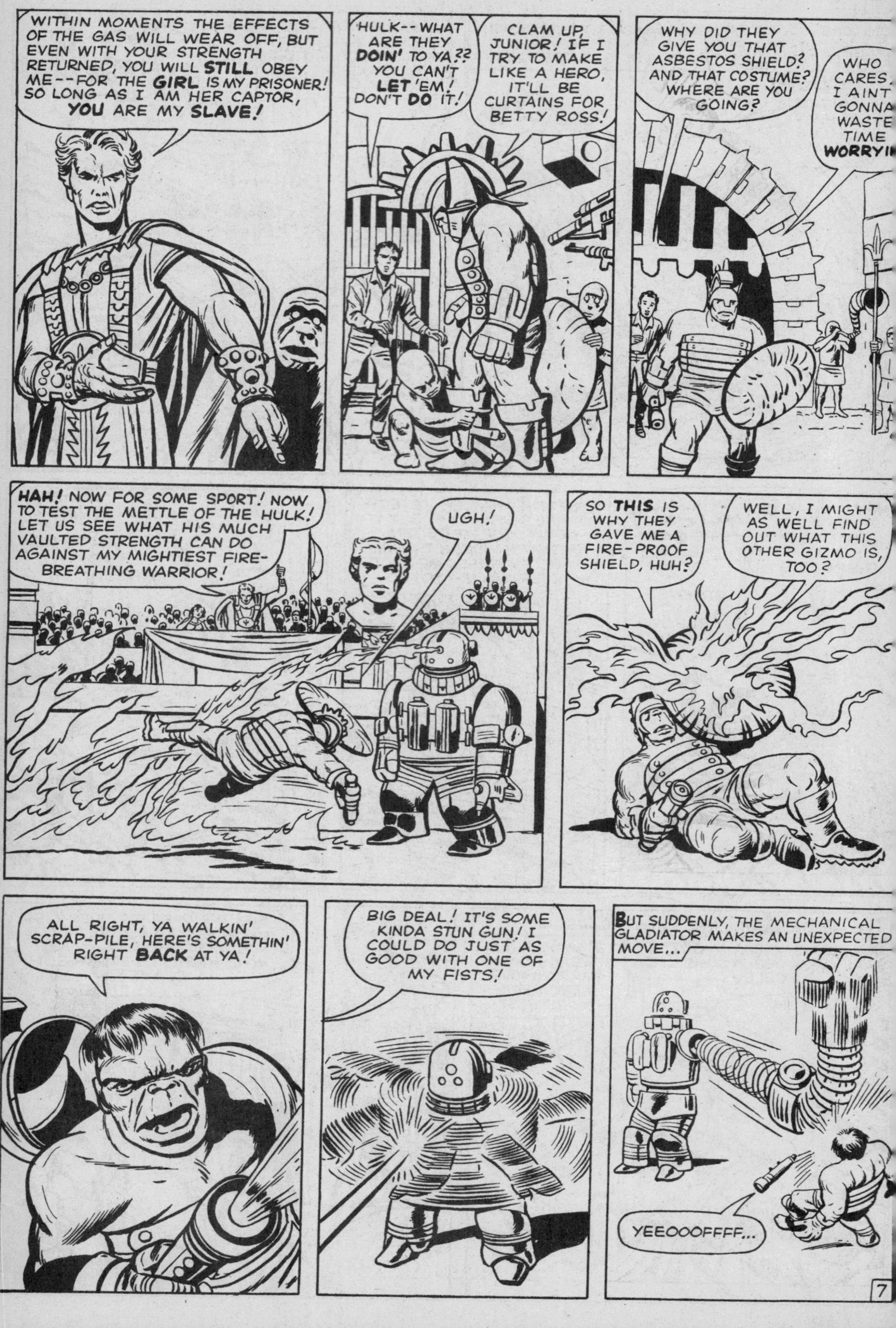
WITHIN MOMENTS THE EFFECTS OF THE GAS WILL WEAR OFF, BUT EVEN WITH YOUR STRENGTH RETURNED, YOU WILL STILL OBEY ME--FOR THE GIRL IS MY PRISONER! SO LONG AS I AM HER CAPTOR, YOU ARE MY SLAVE!
HULK--WHAT ARE THEY DOIN' TO YA?? YOU CAN'T LET 'EM! DON'T DO IT!
CLAM UP, JUNIOR! IF I TRY TO MAKE LIKE A HERO, IT'LL BE CURTAINS FOR BETTY ROSS!
WHY DID THEY GIVE YOU THAT ASBESTOS SHIELD? AND THAT COSTUME? WHERE ARE YOU GOING?
WHO CARES, I AINT GONNA WASTE TIME WORRYI
HAH! NOW FOR SOME SPORT! NOW TO TEST THE METTLE OF THE HULK! LET US SEE WHAT HIS MUCH VAULTED STRENGTH CAN DO AGAINST MY MIGHTIEST FIRE-BREATHING WARRIOR!
UGH!
SO THIS IS WHY THEY GAVE ME A FIRE-PROOF SHIELD, HUH?
WELL, I MIGHT AS WELL FIND OUT WHAT THIS OTHER GIZMO IS, TOO?
ALL RIGHT, YA WALKIN' SCRAP-PILE, HERE'S SOMETHIN' RIGHT BACK AT YA!
BIG DEAL! IT'S SOME KINDA STUN GUN! I COULD DO JUST AS GOOD WITH ONE OF MY FISTS!
BUT SUDDENLY, THE MECHANICAL GLADIATOR MAKES AN UNEXPECTED MOVE...
YEEOOOFFFF...
7

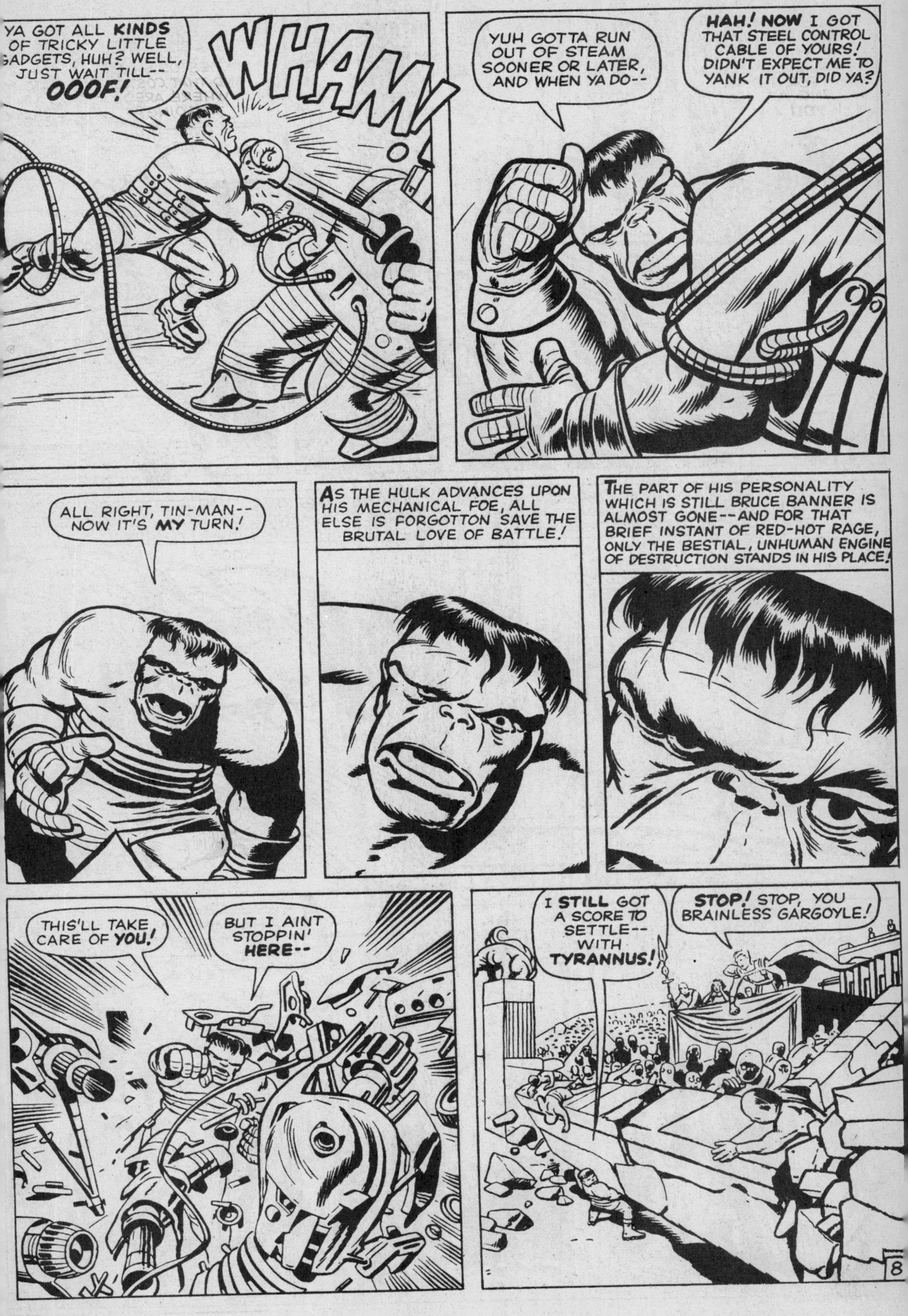
YA GOT ALL KINDS OF TRICKY LITTLE GADGETS, HUH? WELL, JUST WAIT TILL-- OOOF!
WHAM!
YUH GOTTA RUN OUT OF STEAM SOONER OR LATER, AND WHEN YA DO--
HAH! NOW I GOT THAT STEEL CONTROL CABLE OF YOURS! DIDN'T EXPECT ME TO YANK IT OUT, DID YA?
ALL RIGHT, TIN-MAN-- NOW IT'S MY TURN!
AS THE HULK ADVANCES UPON HIS MECHANICAL FOE, ALL ELSE IS FORGOTTON SAVE THE BRUTAL LOVE OF BATTLE!
THE PART OF HIS PERSONALITY WHICH IS STILL BRUCE BANNER IS ALMOST GONE--AND FOR THAT BRIEF INSTANT OF RED-HOT RAGE, ONLY THE BESTIAL, UNHUMAN ENGINE OF DESTRUCTION STANDS IN HIS PLACE!
THIS'LL TAKE CARE OF YOU!
BUT I AINT STOPPIN' HERE--
I STILL GOT A SCORE TO SETTLE-- WITH TYRANNUS!
STOP! STOP, YOU BRAINLESS GARGOYLE!
8

YOU HAVE FORGOTTEN THE GIRL! TAKE ANOTHER STEP, AND I **FIRE!**

NO-- **NO!** DON'T HURT **HER!**

I DIDN'T **INTEND** TO! I JUST NEEDED TIME TO AIM MY **PARALYZER RAY** AT YOU!

TYRANNUS FORGOT ABOUT **ME!** GUESS I'M NOT IMPORTANT ENOUGH FOR HIM TO WORRY ABOUT! BUT I GOTTA FIND **SOME** WAY TO FREE THE HULK, OR IT'LL BE CURTAINS FOR **ALL** OF US!

LIKE A STOLID, HELPLESS BEAST OF BURDON, THE HULK IS PUT TO WORK AS A SLAVE LABORER FOR THE TRIUMPHANT TYRANNUS!

FASTER, YOU CLOD! **FASTER,** I SAY!

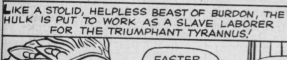

LIKE THE LEGENDARY LABORS OF HERCULES, NO TASK IS TOO MENIAL, NO FEAT TOO IMPOSSIBLE FOR THE MIGHTY HULK!

MUST DAM THE FLOOD-- MUST DO IT-- FOR **BETTY'S** SAKE!

YOU MUST NOT STOP YET! TYRANNUS COMMANDED THAT YOU DRIVE ALL THESE POSTS INTO THE GROUND WITH YOUR FISTS!

YOU HAVE ONLY DONE A THOUSAND OF THEM-- THERE ARE STILL FIVE HUNDRED MORE!

MUST NOT FAIL-- (GASP) MUST KEEP WORKING-- CAN'T LET TYRANNUS BEAT ME--

AND WHAT OF THE MAN CALLED TYRANNUS?

I NO LONGER FIND THE HULK'S LABORS AMUSING!

I GO NOW TO ORDER HIS **DOOM!**

9

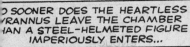

NO SOONER DOES THE HEARTLESS TYRANNUS LEAVE THE CHAMBER THAN A STEEL-HELMETED FIGURE IMPERIOUSLY ENTERS...

PRAISE TYRANNUS! I HAVE BEEN ORDERED TO BRING THE GIRL TO HIM!

OH NO-- NO!

THAT'S IT-- KEEP SCREAMING! MAKE IT LOOK GOOD! THIS IS A ONE-IN-A-MILLION GAMBLE, BUT IT HAS TO WORK!

WHAT--?? WHO ARE YOU? WHAT DO YOU MEAN??

OH! I SHOULD HAVE GUESSED! IT'S YOU!

YOU WERE EXPECTIN' MEBBE CHUBBY CHECKER?? KNOCK OFF THE DUMB REMARKS AND LET'S MOVE! TYRANNUS HAS ORDERED HIS GOONS TO GET RID OF THE HULK!

HULK--GET UP! DO YA HEAR ME?? GET UP!

GO 'WAY-- CAN'T DO ANYTHING-- CAN'T TAKE A CHANCE OF HIM HARMING BETTY ROSS!

NO, HULK--NO! I'M SAFE! YOU MUST SAVE YOURSELF! HURRY!

THEY'RE COMING FOR YOU NOW! YOU MUST FIGHT BACK! IT'S YOUR ONLY CHANCE! IT'S -SOB-OUR ONLY CHANCE!

YOU'RE SAFE!

STAND ASIDE, FEMALE! WE ARE HERE FOR THE HULK!

NOW, HULK-- NOW!

SHE'S SAFE! I DON'T HAVETA WORRY ABOUT HER!

THIS IS WHAT I BEEN WAITIN' FOR! GIT OUTTA MY WAY--ALL OF YA!

HAH! DID YA SEE 'EM RUN LIKE WHIPPED CURS?? AND THAT'S ONLY THE BEGINNING!

MEBBE SO, BUT WE AINT OUTTA THIS YET!

TYRANNUS WILL NEVER LET US ESCAPE!

10

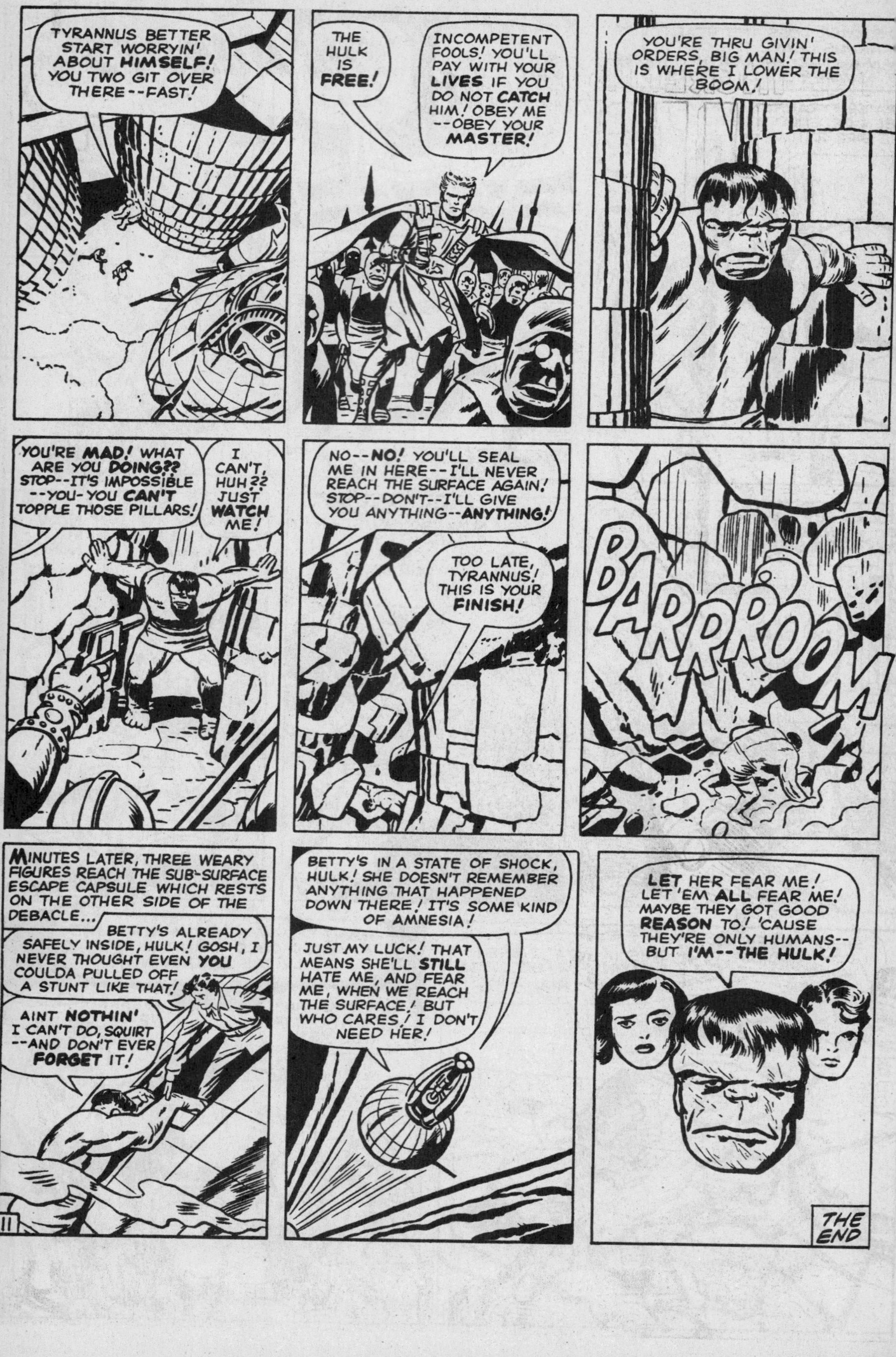

TYRANNUS BETTER START WORRYIN' ABOUT HIMSELF! YOU TWO GIT OVER THERE--FAST!
THE HULK IS FREE!
INCOMPETENT FOOLS! YOU'LL PAY WITH YOUR LIVES IF YOU DO NOT CATCH HIM! OBEY ME --OBEY YOUR MASTER!
YOU'RE THRU GIVIN' ORDERS, BIG MAN! THIS IS WHERE I LOWER THE BOOM!
YOU'RE MAD! WHAT ARE YOU DOING?? STOP--IT'S IMPOSSIBLE --YOU-YOU CAN'T TOPPLE THOSE PILLARS!
I CAN'T, HUH?? JUST WATCH ME!
NO--NO! YOU'LL SEAL ME IN HERE--I'LL NEVER REACH THE SURFACE AGAIN! STOP--DON'T--I'LL GIVE YOU ANYTHING--ANYTHING!
TOO LATE, TYRANNUS! THIS IS YOUR FINISH!
BARRROOM
MINUTES LATER, THREE WEARY FIGURES REACH THE SUB-SURFACE ESCAPE CAPSULE WHICH RESTS ON THE OTHER SIDE OF THE DEBACLE...
BETTY'S ALREADY SAFELY INSIDE, HULK! GOSH, I NEVER THOUGHT EVEN YOU COULDA PULLED OFF A STUNT LIKE THAT!
AINT NOTHIN' I CAN'T DO, SQUIRT --AND DON'T EVER FORGET IT!
BETTY'S IN A STATE OF SHOCK, HULK! SHE DOESN'T REMEMBER ANYTHING THAT HAPPENED DOWN THERE! IT'S SOME KIND OF AMNESIA!
JUST MY LUCK! THAT MEANS SHE'LL STILL HATE ME, AND FEAR ME, WHEN WE REACH THE SURFACE! BUT WHO CARES! I DON'T NEED HER!
LET HER FEAR ME! LET 'EM ALL FEAR ME! MAYBE THEY GOT GOOD REASON TO! 'CAUSE THEY'RE ONLY HUMANS-- BUT I'M--THE HULK!
THE END
11

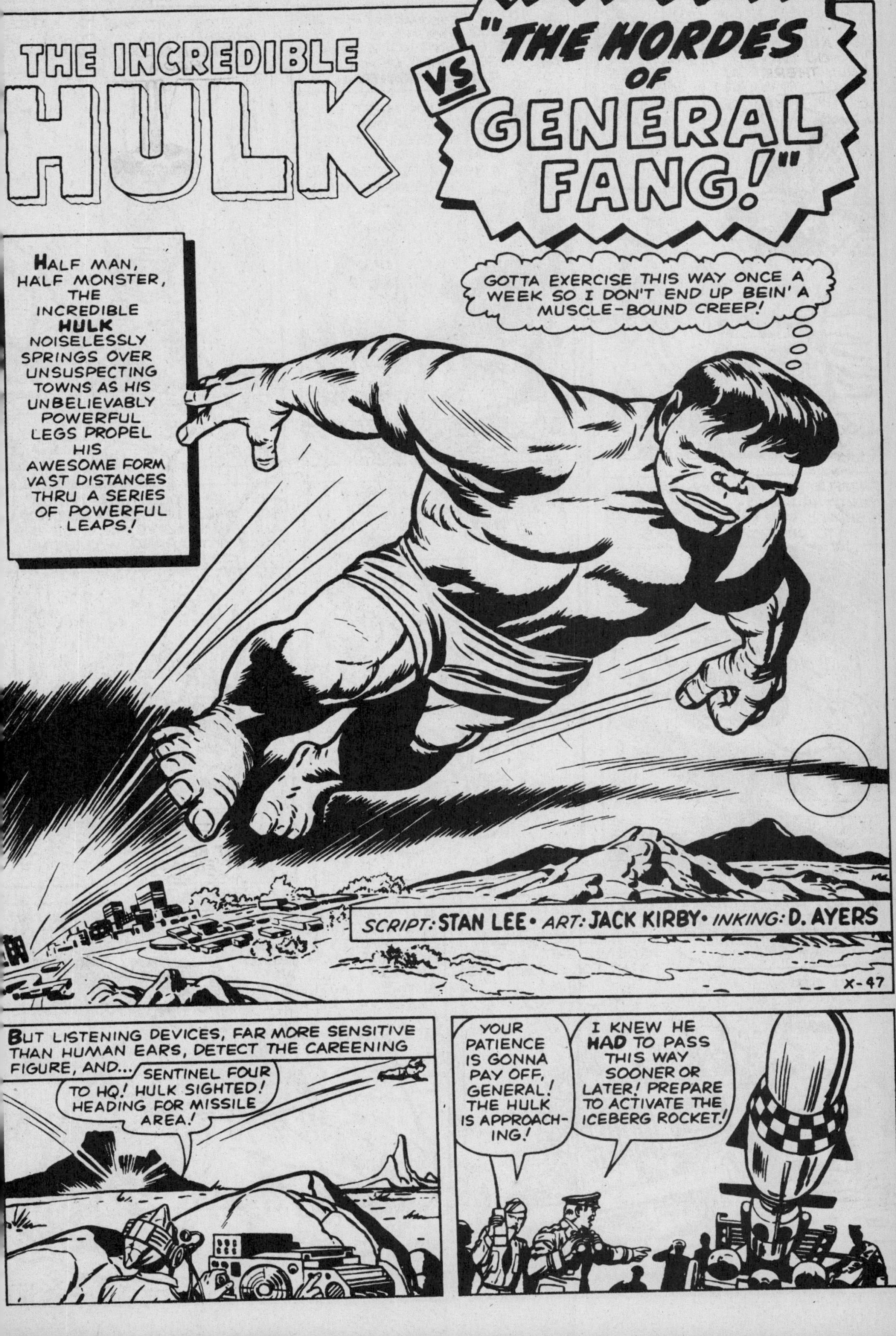
THE INCREDIBLE HULK
VS
"THE HORDES OF GENERAL FANG!"
HALF MAN, HALF MONSTER, THE INCREDIBLE HULK NOISELESSLY SPRINGS OVER UNSUSPECTING TOWNS AS HIS UNBELIEVABLY POWERFUL LEGS PROPEL HIS AWESOME FORM VAST DISTANCES THRU A SERIES OF POWERFUL LEAPS!
GOTTA EXERCISE THIS WAY ONCE A WEEK SO I DON'T END UP BEIN' A MUSCLE-BOUND CREEP!
SCRIPT: STAN LEE • ART: JACK KIRBY • INKING: D. AYERS
X-47
BUT LISTENING DEVICES, FAR MORE SENSITIVE THAN HUMAN EARS, DETECT THE CAREENING FIGURE, AND...
SENTINEL FOUR TO HQ! HULK SIGHTED! HEADING FOR MISSILE AREA!
YOUR PATIENCE IS GONNA PAY OFF, GENERAL! THE HULK IS APPROACH-ING!
I KNEW HE HAD TO PASS THIS WAY SOONER OR LATER! PREPARE TO ACTIVATE THE ICEBERG ROCKET!

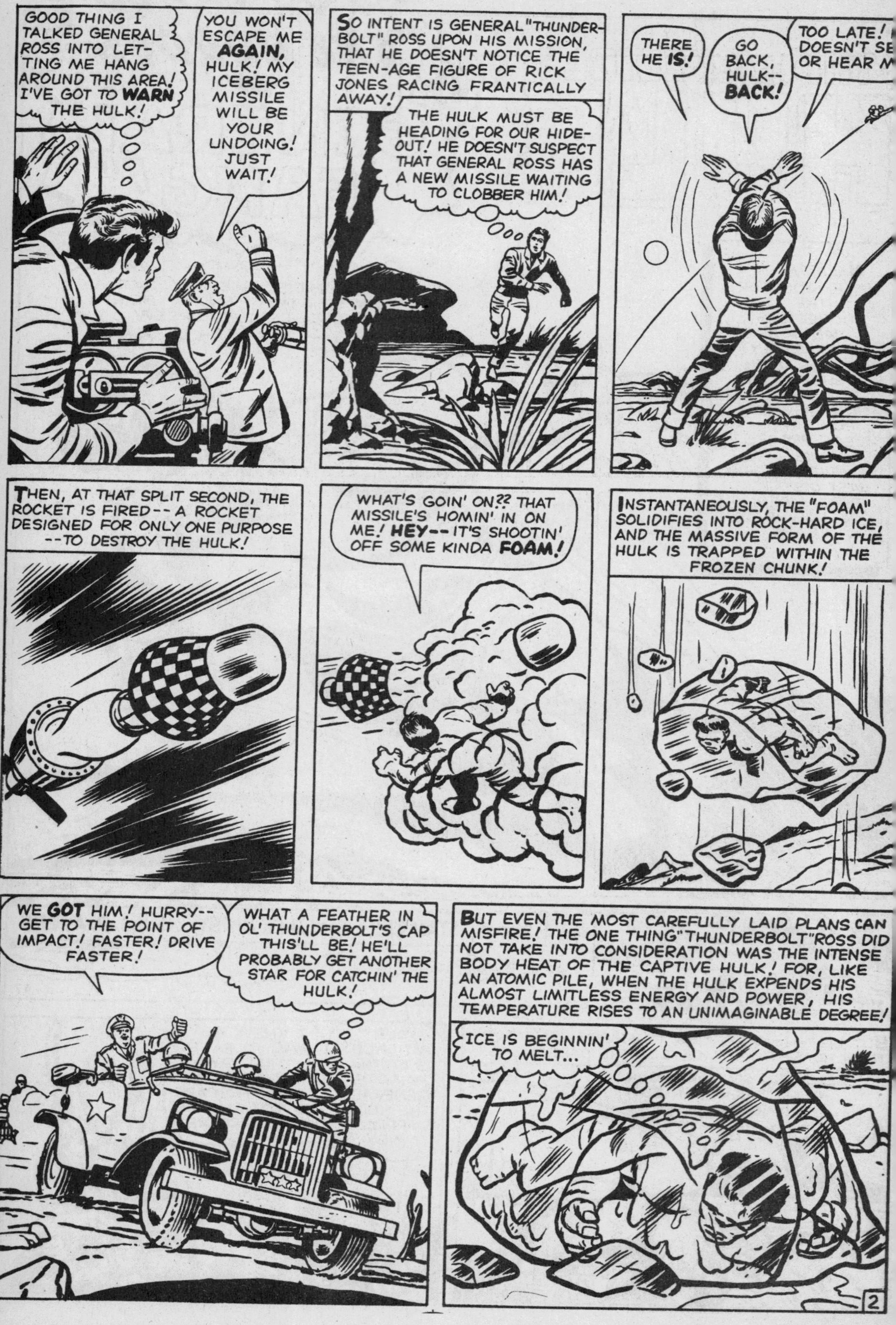

GOOD THING I TALKED GENERAL ROSS INTO LETTING ME HANG AROUND THIS AREA! I'VE GOT TO WARN THE HULK!
YOU WON'T ESCAPE ME AGAIN, HULK! MY ICEBERG MISSILE WILL BE YOUR UNDOING! JUST WAIT!
SO INTENT IS GENERAL "THUNDERBOLT" ROSS UPON HIS MISSION, THAT HE DOESN'T NOTICE THE TEEN-AGE FIGURE OF RICK JONES RACING FRANTICALLY AWAY!
THE HULK MUST BE HEADING FOR OUR HIDE-OUT! HE DOESN'T SUSPECT THAT GENERAL ROSS HAS A NEW MISSILE WAITING TO CLOBBER HIM!
THERE HE IS!
GO BACK, HULK-- BACK!
TOO LATE! DOESN'T SE OR HEAR M
THEN, AT THAT SPLIT SECOND, THE ROCKET IS FIRED-- A ROCKET DESIGNED FOR ONLY ONE PURPOSE --TO DESTROY THE HULK!
WHAT'S GOIN' ON?? THAT MISSILE'S HOMIN' IN ON ME! HEY-- IT'S SHOOTIN' OFF SOME KINDA FOAM!
INSTANTANEOUSLY, THE "FOAM" SOLIDIFIES INTO ROCK-HARD ICE, AND THE MASSIVE FORM OF THE HULK IS TRAPPED WITHIN THE FROZEN CHUNK!
WE GOT HIM! HURRY-- GET TO THE POINT OF IMPACT! FASTER! DRIVE FASTER!
WHAT A FEATHER IN OL' THUNDERBOLT'S CAP THIS'LL BE! HE'LL PROBABLY GET ANOTHER STAR FOR CATCHIN' THE HULK!
BUT EVEN THE MOST CAREFULLY LAID PLANS CAN MISFIRE! THE ONE THING "THUNDERBOLT" ROSS DID NOT TAKE INTO CONSIDERATION WAS THE INTENSE BODY HEAT OF THE CAPTIVE HULK! FOR, LIKE AN ATOMIC PILE, WHEN THE HULK EXPENDS HIS ALMOST LIMITLESS ENERGY AND POWER, HIS TEMPERATURE RISES TO AN UNIMAGINABLE DEGREE!
ICE IS BEGINNIN' TO MELT...
2

AND, BY THE TIME THE ASTONISHED PURSUERS REACH THEIR GOAL...

HE'S **FREE!** GET HIM-- BEFORE HE CAN LEAP AWAY!

SO-- IT WAS **ROSS** WHO DID THIS! I'LL **REMEMBER** THAT!

GRAB 'IM! OOOF!

COME **BACK**, YOU BLASTED FREAK!

WE'RE TOO LATE!

WHEW! THAT WAS A NARROW ONE! NOW I'D BETTER HUSTLE TO OUR HIDEOUT! THE HULK'LL BLOW HIS TOP IF I AIN'T THERE WAITIN' FOR HIM!

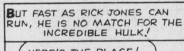

BUT FAST AS RICK JONES CAN RUN, HE IS NO MATCH FOR THE INCREDIBLE HULK!

HERE'S THE PLACE! BUT THE HULK MUSTA BEAT ME BY A MILE!

HE'S PROBABLY WAITIN' IN THE UNDERWATER DUNGEON FOR ME TO HELP HIM WORK THAT RAY MACHINE OF HIS, SO'S HE CAN TURN BACK TO DR. BRUCE BANNER!

THERE HE **IS**--BUT--

STAY BACK! THE HULK WAITS FOR **NO ONE!** LEAST OF ALL, A TEEN-AGED BRAT!

I CAN WORK THIS RAY BY JUST STEPPING ON THE CONTROL BUTTONS BENEATH MY FEET! **BAH!** HOW I HATE GIVING UP MY POWER--MY STRENGTH-- JUST TO RETURN TO THE DULL, ORDINARY HUMAN FORM OF...

...BRUCE BANNER!

3

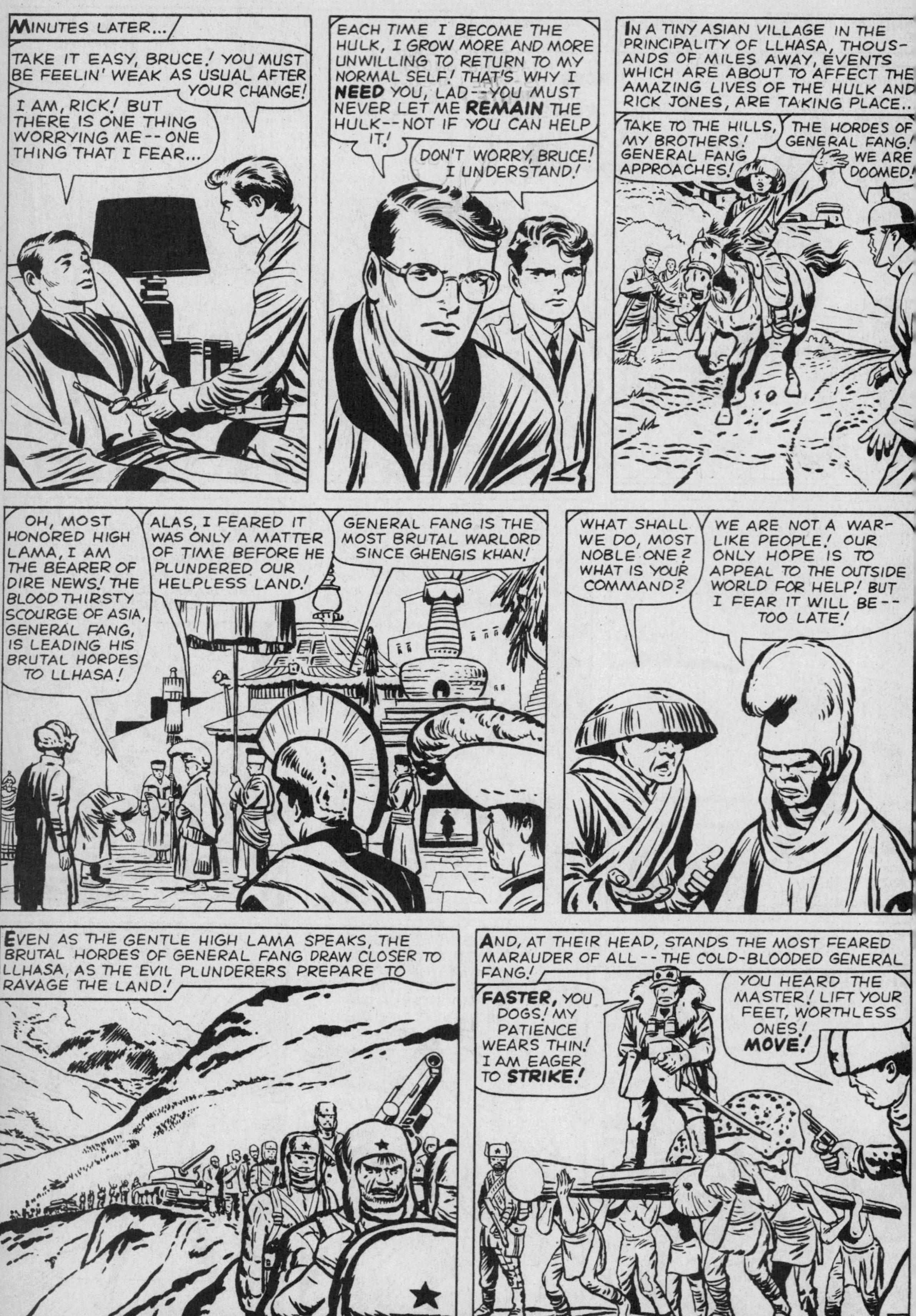
MINUTES LATER...
TAKE IT EASY, BRUCE! YOU MUST BE FEELIN' WEAK AS USUAL AFTER YOUR CHANGE!
I AM, RICK! BUT THERE IS ONE THING WORRYING ME-- ONE THING THAT I FEAR...
EACH TIME I BECOME THE HULK, I GROW MORE AND MORE UNWILLING TO RETURN TO MY NORMAL SELF! THAT'S WHY I NEED YOU, LAD--YOU MUST NEVER LET ME REMAIN THE HULK-- NOT IF YOU CAN HELP IT!
DON'T WORRY, BRUCE! I UNDERSTAND!
IN A TINY ASIAN VILLAGE IN THE PRINCIPALITY OF LLHASA, THOUSANDS OF MILES AWAY, EVENTS WHICH ARE ABOUT TO AFFECT THE AMAZING LIVES OF THE HULK AND RICK JONES, ARE TAKING PLACE..
TAKE TO THE HILLS, MY BROTHERS! GENERAL FANG APPROACHES!
THE HORDES OF GENERAL FANG! WE ARE DOOMED!
OH, MOST HONORED HIGH LAMA, I AM THE BEARER OF DIRE NEWS! THE BLOOD THIRSTY SCOURGE OF ASIA, GENERAL FANG, IS LEADING HIS BRUTAL HORDES TO LLHASA!
ALAS, I FEARED IT WAS ONLY A MATTER OF TIME BEFORE HE PLUNDERED OUR HELPLESS LAND!
GENERAL FANG IS THE MOST BRUTAL WARLORD SINCE GHENGIS KHAN!
WHAT SHALL WE DO, MOST NOBLE ONE? WHAT IS YOUR COMMAND?
WE ARE NOT A WAR-LIKE PEOPLE! OUR ONLY HOPE IS TO APPEAL TO THE OUTSIDE WORLD FOR HELP! BUT I FEAR IT WILL BE -- TOO LATE!
EVEN AS THE GENTLE HIGH LAMA SPEAKS, THE BRUTAL HORDES OF GENERAL FANG DRAW CLOSER TO LLHASA, AS THE EVIL PLUNDERERS PREPARE TO RAVAGE THE LAND!
AND, AT THEIR HEAD, STANDS THE MOST FEARED MARAUDER OF ALL -- THE COLD-BLOODED GENERAL FANG!
FASTER, YOU DOGS! MY PATIENCE WEARS THIN! I AM EAGER TO STRIKE!
YOU HEARD THE MASTER! LIFT YOUR FEET, WORTHLESS ONES! MOVE!
4

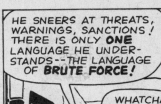

THUS DOES FATE SLOWLY, INEXORABLY DRAW HER WEB TIGHTER AND TIGHTER!

BULLETIN! AN URGENT PLEA FOR HELP HAS COME FROM THE TINY PRINCIPALITY LHASA! THE HORDES OF GENERAL FANG ARE POISED TO ATTACK...

GENERAL FANG! IF HE ISN'T STOPPED, HE'LL PLUNGE THE WORLD INTO WAR!

HE SNEERS AT THREATS, WARNINGS, SANCTIONS! THERE IS ONLY **ONE** LANGUAGE HE UNDERSTANDS--THE LANGUAGE OF **BRUTE FORCE!**

WHATCHA GONNA DO, BRUCE?

I? I SHALL DO NOTHING!

I AM MERELY ONE LONE MAN--POWERLESS TO AFFECT THE DEMONIAC GENERAL FANG!

BUT THERE IS **ANOTHER** WHO IS **NOT** POWERLESS!

IT'S TIME FOR **THE HULK** TO LIVE AGAIN!

B-BUT, HULK--YOU'RE **STILL** ONLY ONE GUY! WHAT CAN **YOU** DO AGAINST A WHOLE ARMY??

SHUT UP, YOU PUNY FOOL! STAY OUTTA MY HAIR WHILE I LOOK FOR SOMETHIN'!!

HERE IT IS! THIS BOOK'LL HELP ME **DEMOLISH** THAT CREEP AND HIS WHOLE CRUMMY RAT PACK! NOW CALL THE AIRPORT AND RESERVE A COUPLE OF SEATS HEADED EAST! **MOVE!**

HE-HE MUST BE CRACKIN' UP! BUT I GOTTA STRING ALONG WITH 'IM!

STRANGE MYTHS and LEGENDS

5

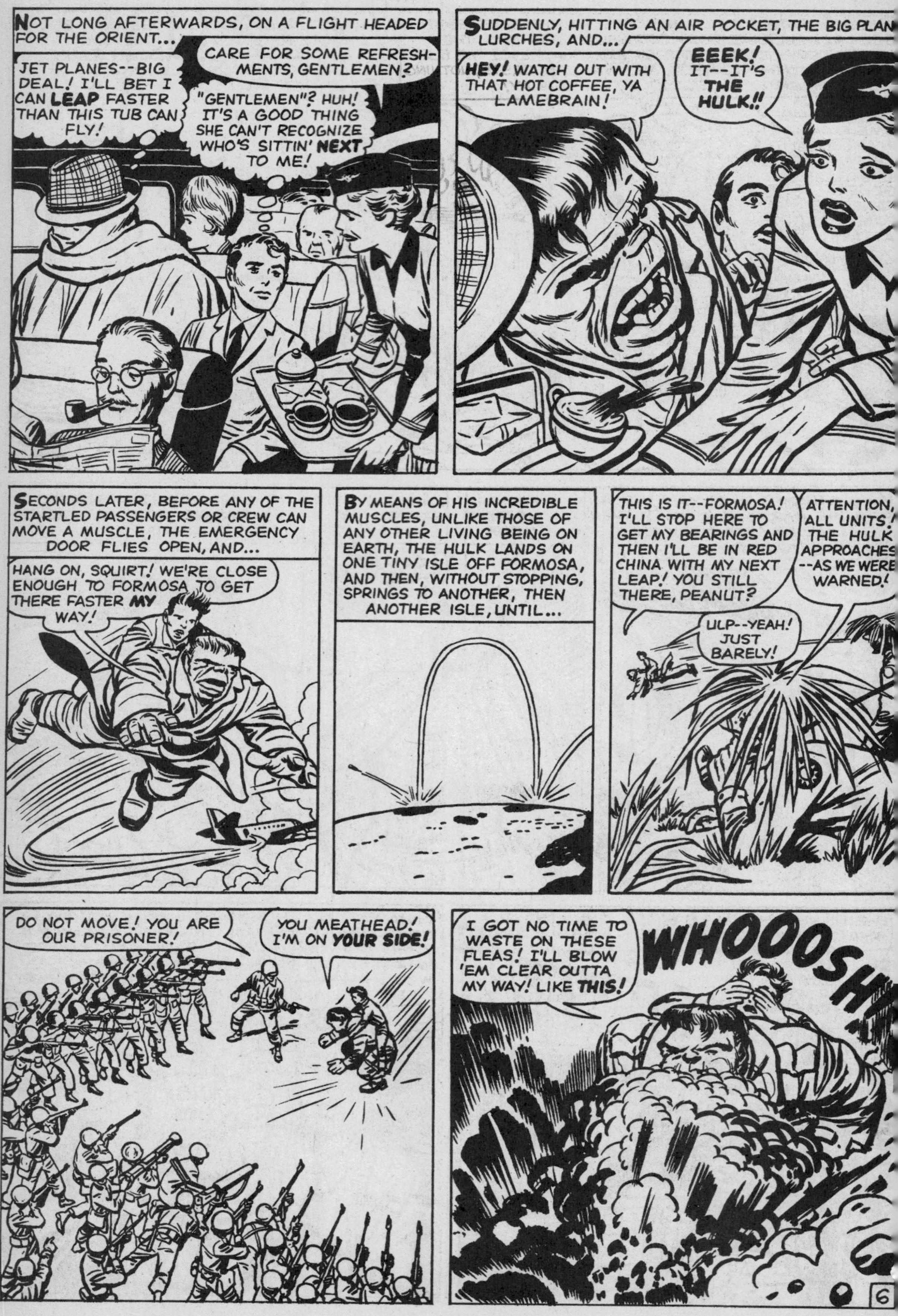
NOT LONG AFTERWARDS, ON A FLIGHT HEADED FOR THE ORIENT...
JET PLANES--BIG DEAL! I'LL BET I CAN LEAP FASTER THAN THIS TUB CAN FLY!
CARE FOR SOME REFRESHMENTS, GENTLEMEN?
"GENTLEMEN"? HUH! IT'S A GOOD THING SHE CAN'T RECOGNIZE WHO'S SITTIN' NEXT TO ME!
SUDDENLY, HITTING AN AIR POCKET, THE BIG PLAN LURCHES, AND...
HEY! WATCH OUT WITH THAT HOT COFFEE, YA LAMEBRAIN!
EEEK! IT--IT'S THE HULK!!
SECONDS LATER, BEFORE ANY OF THE STARTLED PASSENGERS OR CREW CAN MOVE A MUSCLE, THE EMERGENCY DOOR FLIES OPEN, AND...
HANG ON, SQUIRT! WE'RE CLOSE ENOUGH TO FORMOSA TO GET THERE FASTER MY WAY!
BY MEANS OF HIS INCREDIBLE MUSCLES, UNLIKE THOSE OF ANY OTHER LIVING BEING ON EARTH, THE HULK LANDS ON ONE TINY ISLE OFF FORMOSA, AND THEN, WITHOUT STOPPING, SPRINGS TO ANOTHER, THEN ANOTHER ISLE, UNTIL...
THIS IS IT--FORMOSA! I'LL STOP HERE TO GET MY BEARINGS AND THEN I'LL BE IN RED CHINA WITH MY NEXT LEAP! YOU STILL THERE, PEANUT?
ULP--YEAH! JUST BARELY!
ATTENTION, ALL UNITS! THE HULK APPROACHES --AS WE WERE WARNED!
DO NOT MOVE! YOU ARE OUR PRISONER!
YOU MEATHEAD! I'M ON YOUR SIDE!
I GOT NO TIME TO WASTE ON THESE FLEAS! I'LL BLOW 'EM CLEAR OUTTA MY WAY! LIKE THIS!
WHOOOSH

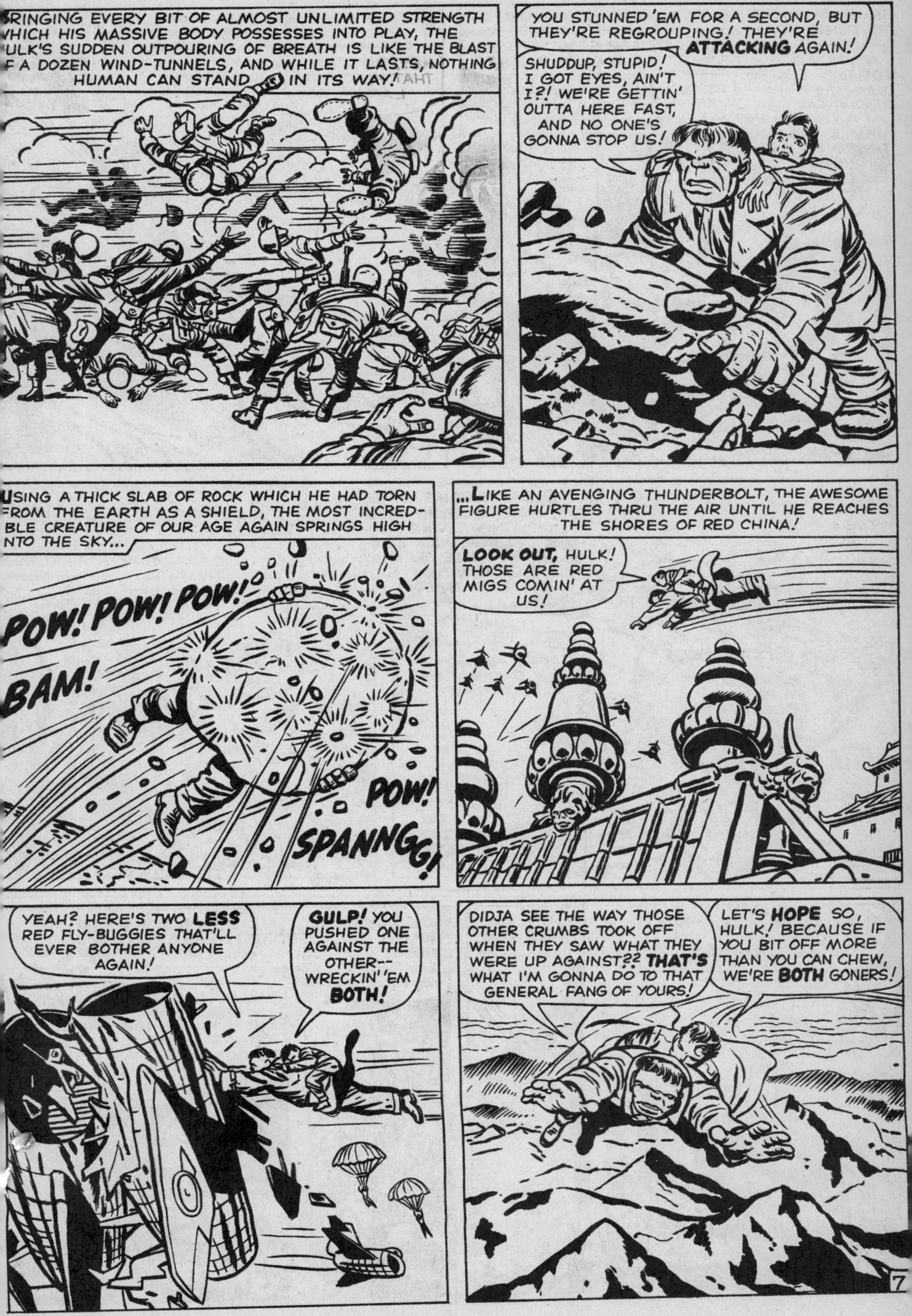
BRINGING EVERY BIT OF ALMOST UNLIMITED STRENGTH WHICH HIS MASSIVE BODY POSSESSES INTO PLAY, THE HULK'S SUDDEN OUTPOURING OF BREATH IS LIKE THE BLAST OF A DOZEN WIND-TUNNELS, AND WHILE IT LASTS, NOTHING HUMAN CAN STAND IN ITS WAY!
YOU STUNNED 'EM FOR A SECOND, BUT THEY'RE REGROUPING! THEY'RE ATTACKING AGAIN!
SHUDDUP, STUPID! I GOT EYES, AIN'T I?! WE'RE GETTIN' OUTTA HERE FAST, AND NO ONE'S GONNA STOP US!
USING A THICK SLAB OF ROCK WHICH HE HAD TORN FROM THE EARTH AS A SHIELD, THE MOST INCREDIBLE CREATURE OF OUR AGE AGAIN SPRINGS HIGH INTO THE SKY...
POW! POW! POW!
BAM!
POW!
SPANNGG!
...LIKE AN AVENGING THUNDERBOLT, THE AWESOME FIGURE HURTLES THRU THE AIR UNTIL HE REACHES THE SHORES OF RED CHINA!
LOOK OUT, HULK! THOSE ARE RED MIGS COMIN' AT US!
YEAH? HERE'S TWO LESS RED FLY-BUGGIES THAT'LL EVER BOTHER ANYONE AGAIN!
GULP! YOU PUSHED ONE AGAINST THE OTHER-- WRECKIN' 'EM BOTH!
DIDJA SEE THE WAY THOSE OTHER CRUMBS TOOK OFF WHEN THEY SAW WHAT THEY WERE UP AGAINST?? THAT'S WHAT I'M GONNA DO TO THAT GENERAL FANG OF YOURS!
LET'S HOPE SO, HULK! BECAUSE IF YOU BIT OFF MORE THAN YOU CAN CHEW, WE'RE BOTH GONERS!
7

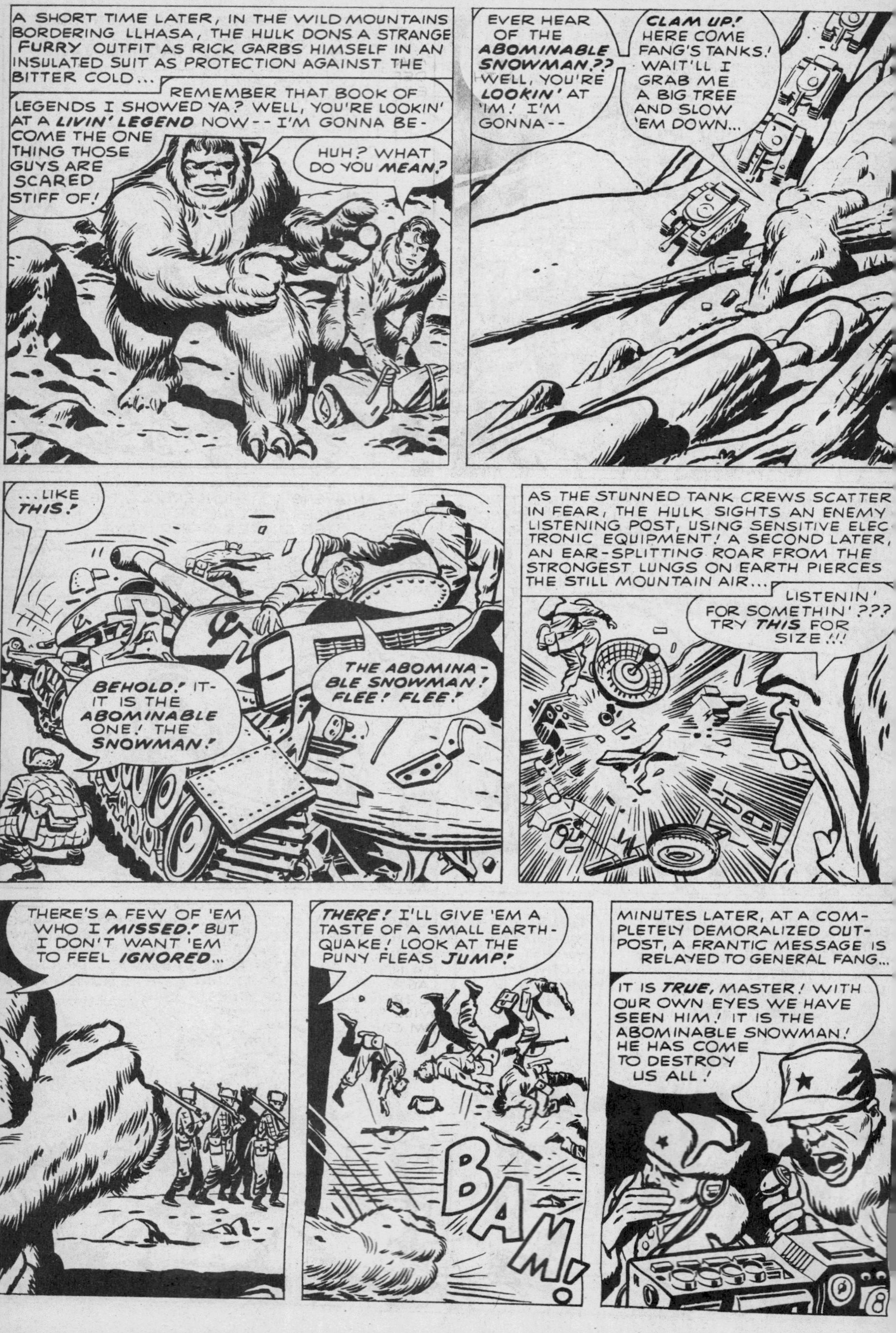

A SHORT TIME LATER, IN THE WILD MOUNTAINS BORDERING LLHASA, THE HULK DONS A STRANGE FURRY OUTFIT AS RICK GARBS HIMSELF IN AN INSULATED SUIT AS PROTECTION AGAINST THE BITTER COLD...
REMEMBER THAT BOOK OF LEGENDS I SHOWED YA? WELL, YOU'RE LOOKIN' AT A LIVIN' LEGEND NOW-- I'M GONNA BECOME THE ONE THING THOSE GUYS ARE SCARED STIFF OF!
HUH? WHAT DO YOU MEAN?
EVER HEAR OF THE ABOMINABLE SNOWMAN?? WELL, YOU'RE LOOKIN' AT 'IM! I'M GONNA--
CLAM UP! HERE COME FANG'S TANKS! WAIT'LL I GRAB ME A BIG TREE AND SLOW 'EM DOWN...
...LIKE THIS!
BEHOLD! IT-IT IS THE ABOMINABLE ONE! THE SNOWMAN!
THE ABOMINABLE SNOWMAN! FLEE! FLEE!
AS THE STUNNED TANK CREWS SCATTER IN FEAR, THE HULK SIGHTS AN ENEMY LISTENING POST, USING SENSITIVE ELECTRONIC EQUIPMENT! A SECOND LATER, AN EAR-SPLITTING ROAR FROM THE STRONGEST LUNGS ON EARTH PIERCES THE STILL MOUNTAIN AIR...
LISTENIN' FOR SOMETHIN'??? TRY THIS FOR SIZE!!!
THERE'S A FEW OF 'EM WHO I MISSED! BUT I DON'T WANT 'EM TO FEEL IGNORED...
THERE! I'LL GIVE 'EM A TASTE OF A SMALL EARTHQUAKE! LOOK AT THE PUNY FLEAS JUMP!
BAM!
MINUTES LATER, AT A COMPLETELY DEMORALIZED OUTPOST, A FRANTIC MESSAGE IS RELAYED TO GENERAL FANG...
IT IS TRUE, MASTER! WITH OUR OWN EYES WE HAVE SEEN HIM! IT IS THE ABOMINABLE SNOWMAN! HE HAS COME TO DESTROY US ALL!
8

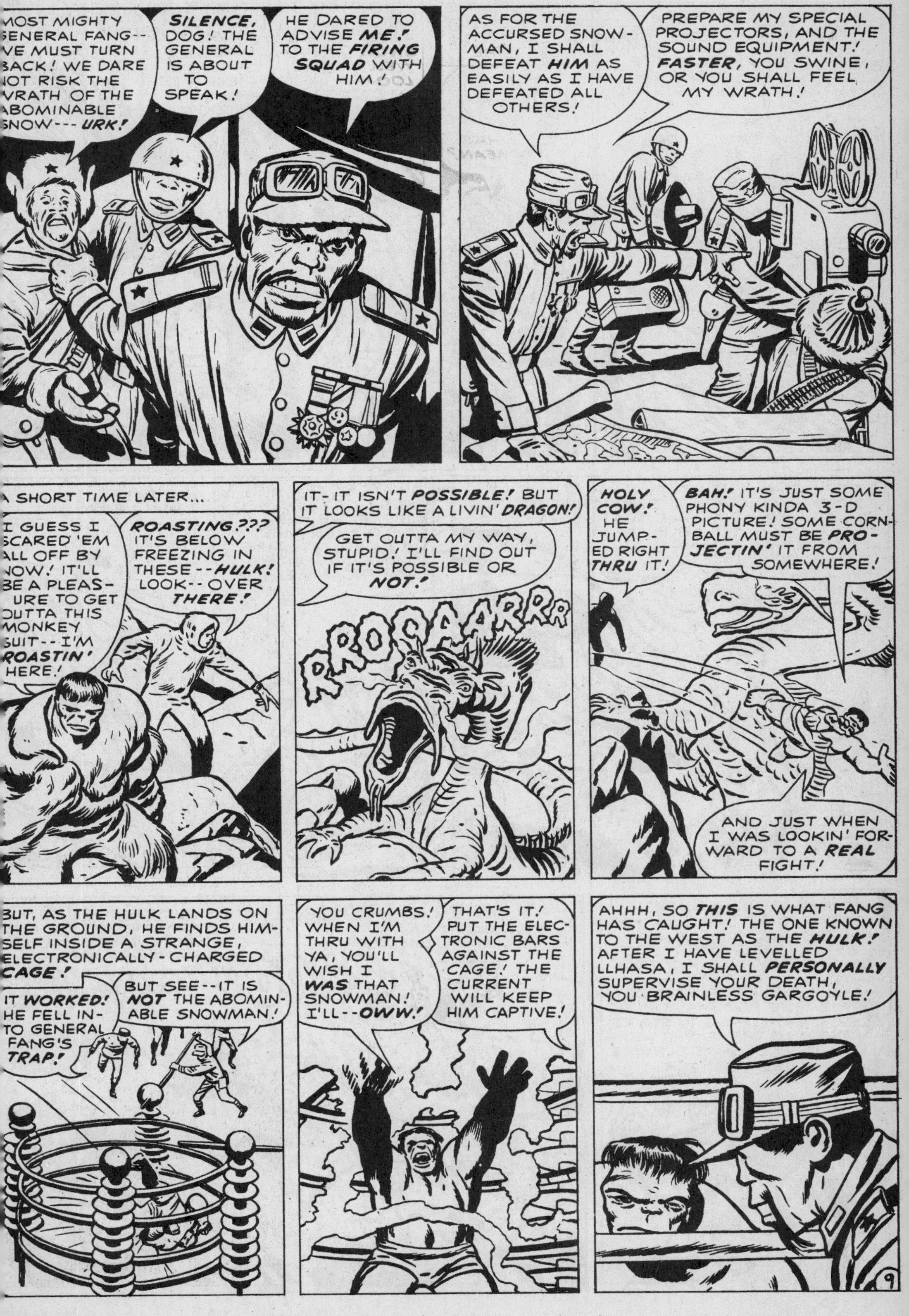
MOST MIGHTY GENERAL FANG-- WE MUST TURN BACK! WE DARE NOT RISK THE WRATH OF THE ABOMINABLE SNOW--- URK!
SILENCE, DOG! THE GENERAL IS ABOUT TO SPEAK!
HE DARED TO ADVISE ME! TO THE FIRING SQUAD WITH HIM!
AS FOR THE ACCURSED SNOW-MAN, I SHALL DEFEAT HIM AS EASILY AS I HAVE DEFEATED ALL OTHERS!
PREPARE MY SPECIAL PROJECTORS, AND THE SOUND EQUIPMENT! FASTER, YOU SWINE, OR YOU SHALL FEEL MY WRATH!
A SHORT TIME LATER...
I GUESS I SCARED 'EM ALL OFF BY NOW! IT'LL BE A PLEAS-URE TO GET OUTTA THIS MONKEY SUIT--I'M ROASTIN' HERE!
ROASTING??? IT'S BELOW FREEZING IN THESE--HULK! LOOK--OVER THERE!
IT-IT ISN'T POSSIBLE! BUT IT LOOKS LIKE A LIVIN' DRAGON!
GET OUTTA MY WAY, STUPID! I'LL FIND OUT IF IT'S POSSIBLE OR NOT!
RROOAARRR
HOLY COW! HE JUMP-ED RIGHT THRU IT!
BAH! IT'S JUST SOME PHONY KINDA 3-D PICTURE! SOME CORN-BALL MUST BE PRO-JECTIN' IT FROM SOMEWHERE!
AND JUST WHEN I WAS LOOKIN' FOR-WARD TO A REAL FIGHT!
BUT, AS THE HULK LANDS ON THE GROUND, HE FINDS HIM-SELF INSIDE A STRANGE, ELECTRONICALLY-CHARGED CAGE!
IT WORKED! HE FELL IN-TO GENERAL FANG'S TRAP!
BUT SEE--IT IS NOT THE ABOMIN-ABLE SNOWMAN!
YOU CRUMBS! WHEN I'M THRU WITH YA, YOU'LL WISH I WAS THAT SNOWMAN! I'LL--OWW!
THAT'S IT! PUT THE ELEC-TRONIC BARS AGAINST THE CAGE! THE CURRENT WILL KEEP HIM CAPTIVE!
AHHH, SO THIS IS WHAT FANG HAS CAUGHT! THE ONE KNOWN TO THE WEST AS THE HULK! AFTER I HAVE LEVELLED LLHASA, I SHALL PERSONALLY SUPERVISE YOUR DEATH, YOU BRAINLESS GARGOYLE!
9

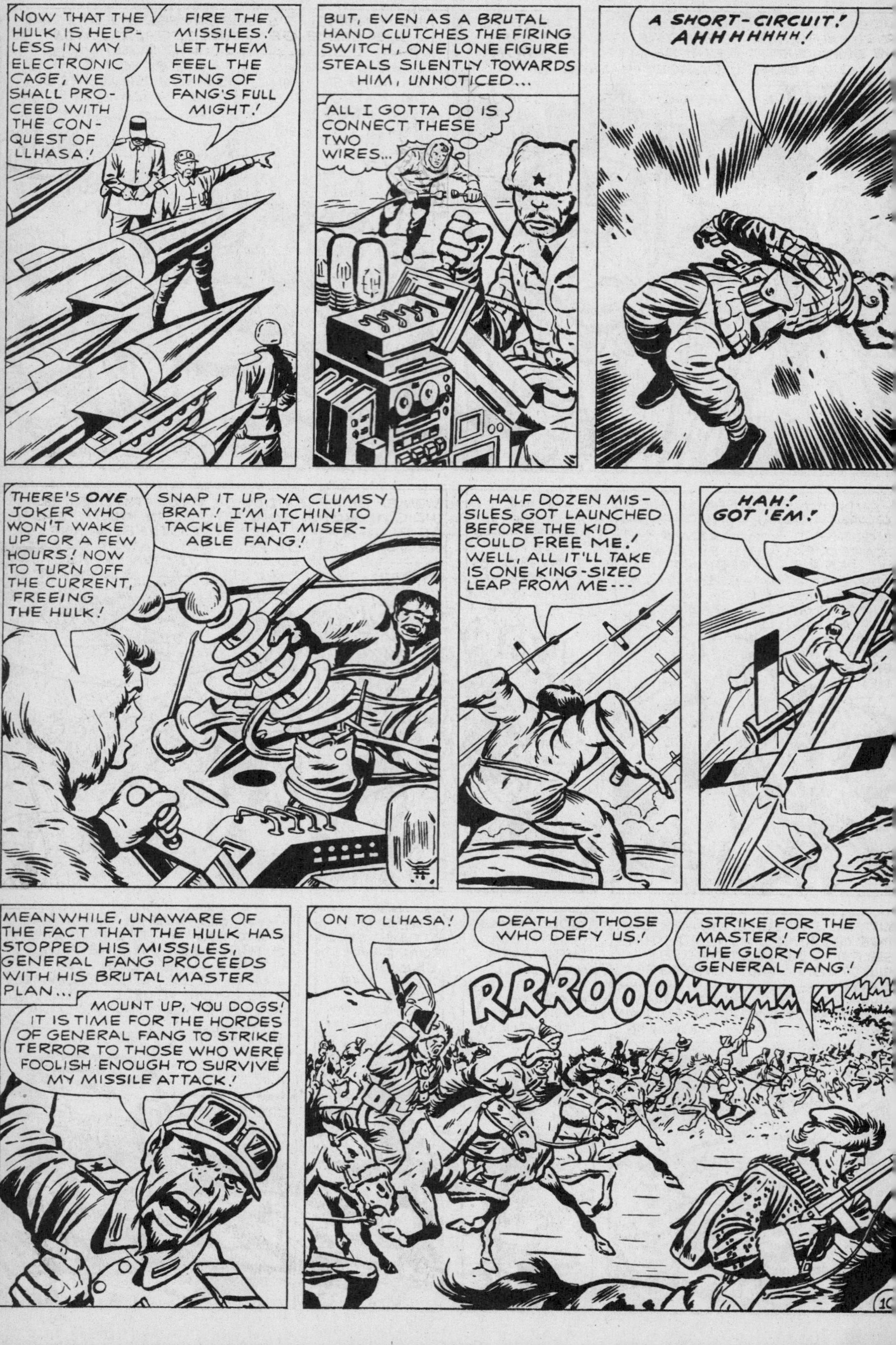

NOW THAT THE HULK IS HELPLESS IN MY ELECTRONIC CAGE, WE SHALL PROCEED WITH THE CONQUEST OF LLHASA!
FIRE THE MISSILES! LET THEM FEEL THE STING OF FANG'S FULL MIGHT!
BUT, EVEN AS A BRUTAL HAND CLUTCHES THE FIRING SWITCH, ONE LONE FIGURE STEALS SILENTLY TOWARDS HIM, UNNOTICED...
ALL I GOTTA DO IS CONNECT THESE TWO WIRES...
A SHORT-CIRCUIT! AHHHHHHH!
THERE'S ONE JOKER WHO WON'T WAKE UP FOR A FEW HOURS! NOW TO TURN OFF THE CURRENT, FREEING THE HULK!
SNAP IT UP, YA CLUMSY BRAT! I'M ITCHIN' TO TACKLE THAT MISERABLE FANG!
A HALF DOZEN MISSILES GOT LAUNCHED BEFORE THE KID COULD FREE ME! WELL, ALL IT'LL TAKE IS ONE KING-SIZED LEAP FROM ME---
HAH! GOT 'EM!
MEANWHILE, UNAWARE OF THE FACT THAT THE HULK HAS STOPPED HIS MISSILES, GENERAL FANG PROCEEDS WITH HIS BRUTAL MASTER PLAN...
MOUNT UP, YOU DOGS! IT IS TIME FOR THE HORDES OF GENERAL FANG TO STRIKE TERROR TO THOSE WHO WERE FOOLISH ENOUGH TO SURVIVE MY MISSILE ATTACK!
ON TO LLHASA!
DEATH TO THOSE WHO DEFY US!
STRIKE FOR THE MASTER! FOR THE GLORY OF GENERAL FANG!
RRROOOMMMMMMMM

...BUT EVEN THE MIGHTIEST LEGIONS IN THE ORIENT ARE NOT PREPARED TO COPE WITH THE GREATEST THREAT OF ALL -- THE FURY OF A FIGHTING MAD *HULK*...

ALL I GOTTA DO IS DROP THESE MISSILES ON THE RIGHT SPOT, AND...

...*NOW* LET'S SEE THOSE TOY SOLDIERS GET ACROSS THAT CHASM!

BUT, IN GENERAL FANG, THE HULK HAS AN *EQUALLY* DETERMINED AND DANGEROUS ENEMY...

THE GARGOYLE STILL LIVES! BUT HE SHALL NOT STOP ME!

WHERE MY *CAVALRY* CANNOT RIDE, MY *PARATROOPS* SHALL FLY! GIVE THE COMMAND!

MOMENTS LATER, THE SKY IS DARKENED BY THE OMINOUS BILLOWING OF COUNTLESS CHUTES, AS FANG'S WARRIORS DROP BEHIND THE NEWLY-FORMED CHASM...

BUT FANG AND HIS MINIONS ARE MERELY *MORTALS* -- AND THEY ARE RECKONING WITH THE MOST FEARSOME LIVING CREATURE OF ALL TIME -- THE INCREDIBLE *HULK!*

PARATROOPS! STAY BACK, KIDDO! I'M GONNA GIVE THOSE LAMEBRAINS A TASTE OF SOMETHING THEY'LL NEVER FORGET!

ALL I GOTTA DO IS LEAP PAST THE TREE-TOPS FAST ENOUGH TO BEND 'EM BACK, LIKE *THIS!*

11

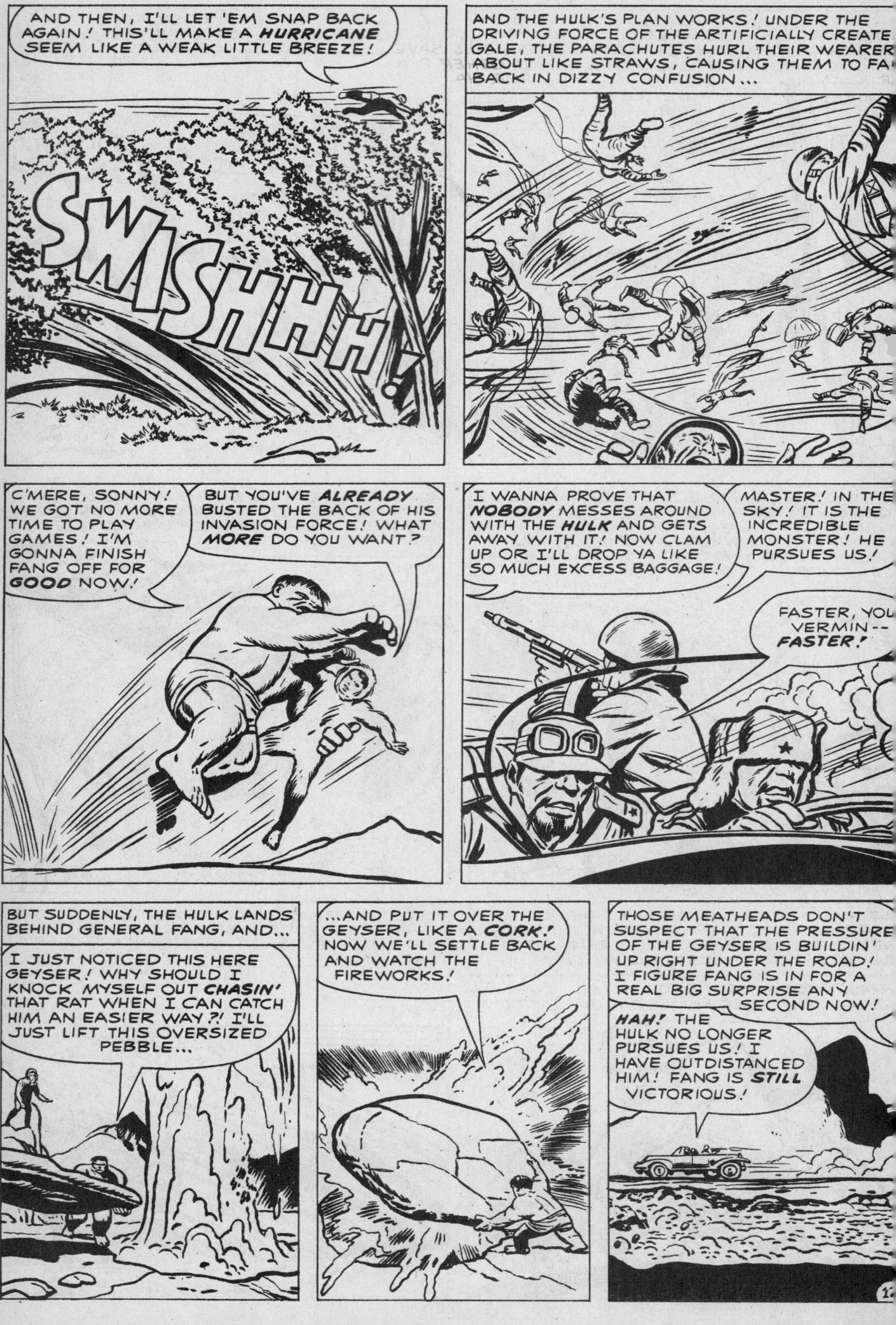
AND THEN, I'LL LET 'EM SNAP BACK AGAIN! THIS'LL MAKE A HURRICANE SEEM LIKE A WEAK LITTLE BREEZE!
SWISHHH!
AND THE HULK'S PLAN WORKS! UNDER THE DRIVING FORCE OF THE ARTIFICIALLY CREATE GALE, THE PARACHUTES HURL THEIR WEARER ABOUT LIKE STRAWS, CAUSING THEM TO FA BACK IN DIZZY CONFUSION...
C'MERE, SONNY! WE GOT NO MORE TIME TO PLAY GAMES! I'M GONNA FINISH FANG OFF FOR GOOD NOW!
BUT YOU'VE ALREADY BUSTED THE BACK OF HIS INVASION FORCE! WHAT MORE DO YOU WANT?
I WANNA PROVE THAT NOBODY MESSES AROUND WITH THE HULK AND GETS AWAY WITH IT! NOW CLAM UP OR I'LL DROP YA LIKE SO MUCH EXCESS BAGGAGE!
MASTER! IN THE SKY! IT IS THE INCREDIBLE MONSTER! HE PURSUES US!
FASTER, YOU VERMIN-- FASTER!
BUT SUDDENLY, THE HULK LANDS BEHIND GENERAL FANG, AND...
I JUST NOTICED THIS HERE GEYSER! WHY SHOULD I KNOCK MYSELF OUT CHASIN' THAT RAT WHEN I CAN CATCH HIM AN EASIER WAY?! I'LL JUST LIFT THIS OVERSIZED PEBBLE...
...AND PUT IT OVER THE GEYSER, LIKE A CORK! NOW WE'LL SETTLE BACK AND WATCH THE FIREWORKS!
THOSE MEATHEADS DON'T SUSPECT THAT THE PRESSURE OF THE GEYSER IS BUILDIN' UP RIGHT UNDER THE ROAD! I FIGURE FANG IS IN FOR A REAL BIG SURPRISE ANY SECOND NOW!
HAH! THE HULK NO LONGER PURSUES US! I HAVE OUTDISTANCED HIM! FANG IS STILL VICTORIOUS!

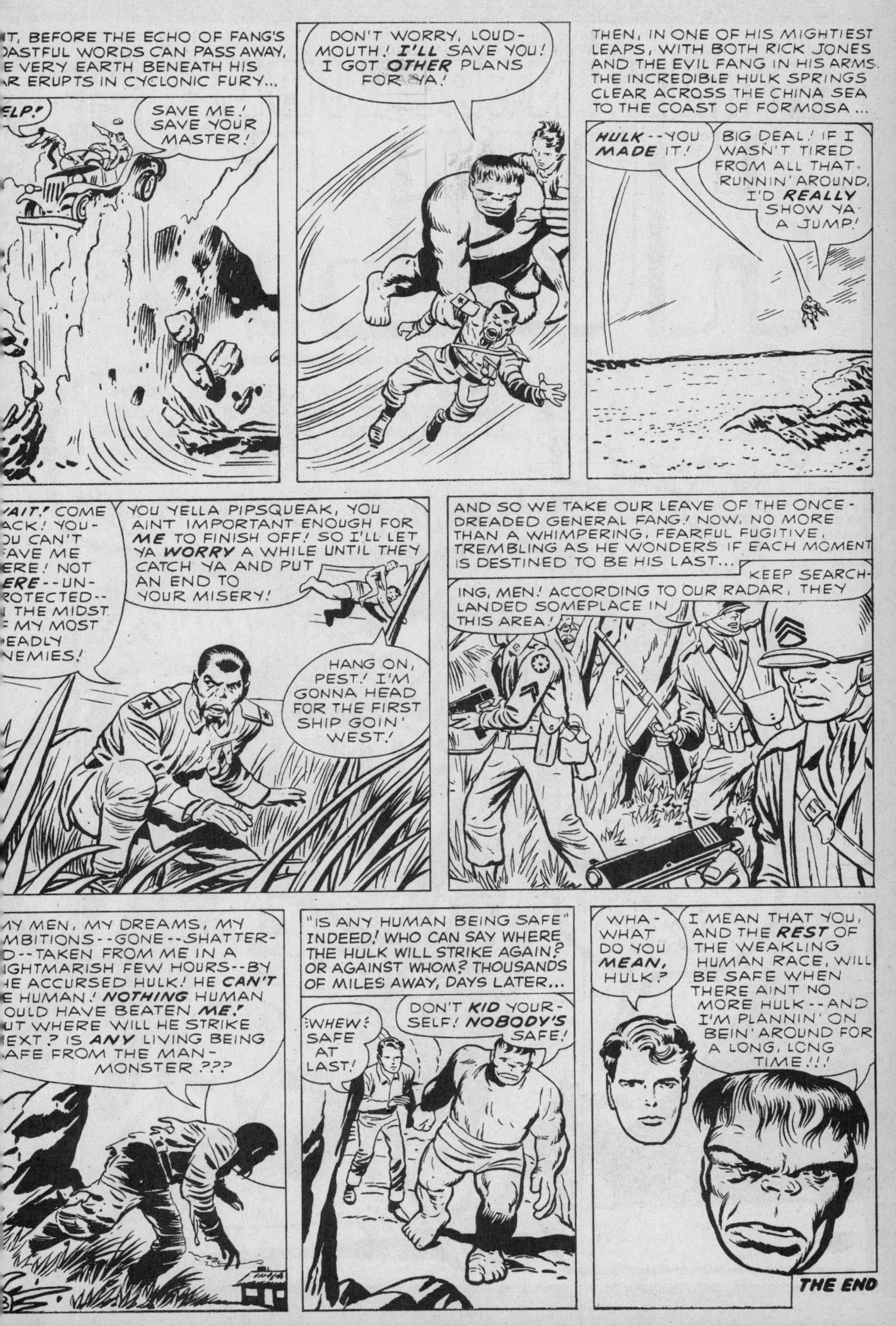

T, BEFORE THE ECHO OF FANG'S
OASTFUL WORDS CAN PASS AWAY,
E VERY EARTH BENEATH HIS
AR ERUPTS IN CYCLONIC FURY...
ELP!
SAVE ME! SAVE YOUR MASTER!
DON'T WORRY, LOUD-MOUTH! I'LL SAVE YOU! I GOT OTHER PLANS FOR YA!
THEN, IN ONE OF HIS MIGHTIEST LEAPS, WITH BOTH RICK JONES AND THE EVIL FANG IN HIS ARMS, THE INCREDIBLE HULK SPRINGS CLEAR ACROSS THE CHINA SEA TO THE COAST OF FORMOSA...
HULK--YOU MADE IT!
BIG DEAL! IF I WASN'T TIRED FROM ALL THAT RUNNIN' AROUND, I'D REALLY SHOW YA A JUMP!
AIT! COME
ACK! YOU-
OU CAN'T
AVE ME
ERE! NOT
ERE--UN-
ROTECTED--
THE MIDST
F MY MOST
EADLY
NEMIES!
YOU YELLA PIPSQUEAK, YOU AINT IMPORTANT ENOUGH FOR ME TO FINISH OFF! SO I'LL LET YA WORRY A WHILE UNTIL THEY CATCH YA AND PUT AN END TO YOUR MISERY!
HANG ON, PEST! I'M GONNA HEAD FOR THE FIRST SHIP GOIN' WEST!
AND SO WE TAKE OUR LEAVE OF THE ONCE-DREADED GENERAL FANG! NOW, NO MORE THAN A WHIMPERING, FEARFUL FUGITIVE, TREMBLING AS HE WONDERS IF EACH MOMENT IS DESTINED TO BE HIS LAST...
KEEP SEARCH-ING, MEN! ACCORDING TO OUR RADAR, THEY LANDED SOMEPLACE IN THIS AREA!
MY MEN, MY DREAMS, MY
MBITIONS--GONE--SHATTER-
D--TAKEN FROM ME IN A
IGHTMARISH FEW HOURS--BY
HE ACCURSED HULK! HE CAN'T
E HUMAN! NOTHING HUMAN
OULD HAVE BEATEN ME!
UT WHERE WILL HE STRIKE
EXT? IS ANY LIVING BEING
AFE FROM THE MAN-
MONSTER???
"IS ANY HUMAN BEING SAFE" INDEED! WHO CAN SAY WHERE THE HULK WILL STRIKE AGAIN? OR AGAINST WHOM? THOUSANDS OF MILES AWAY, DAYS LATER...
WHEW! SAFE AT LAST!
DON'T KID YOURSELF! NOBODY'S SAFE!
WHA-WHAT DO YOU MEAN, HULK?
I MEAN THAT YOU, AND THE REST OF THE WEAKLING HUMAN RACE, WILL BE SAFE WHEN THERE AINT NO MORE HULK--AND I'M PLANNIN' ON BEIN' AROUND FOR A LONG, LONG TIME!!!
THE END

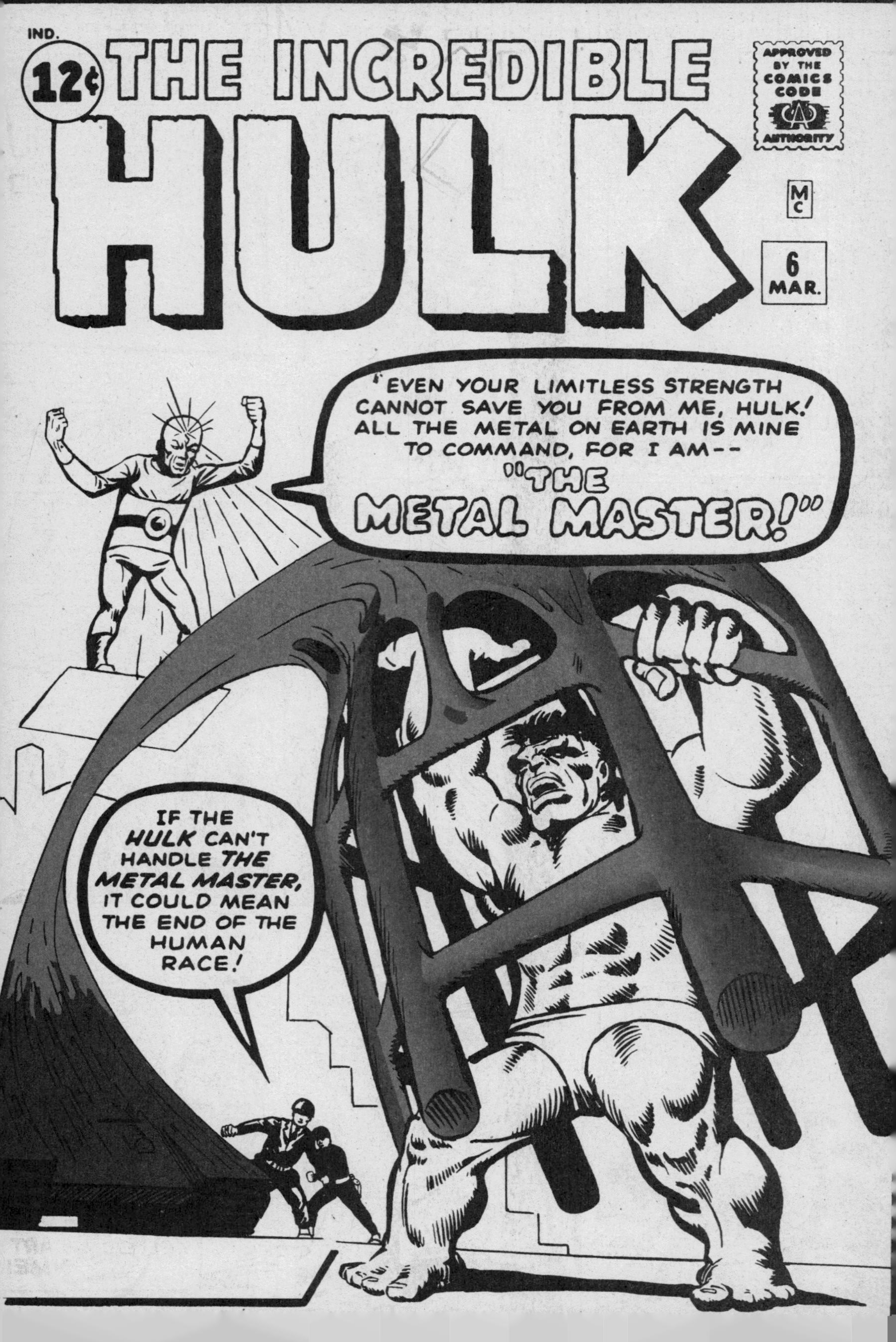
IND.
12¢
THE INCREDIBLE
HULK
APPROVED BY THE COMICS CODE AUTHORITY
MC
6
MAR.
"EVEN YOUR LIMITLESS STRENGTH CANNOT SAVE YOU FROM ME, HULK! ALL THE METAL ON EARTH IS MINE TO COMMAND, FOR I AM-- "THE METAL MASTER!"
IF THE HULK CAN'T HANDLE THE METAL MASTER, IT COULD MEAN THE END OF THE HUMAN RACE!

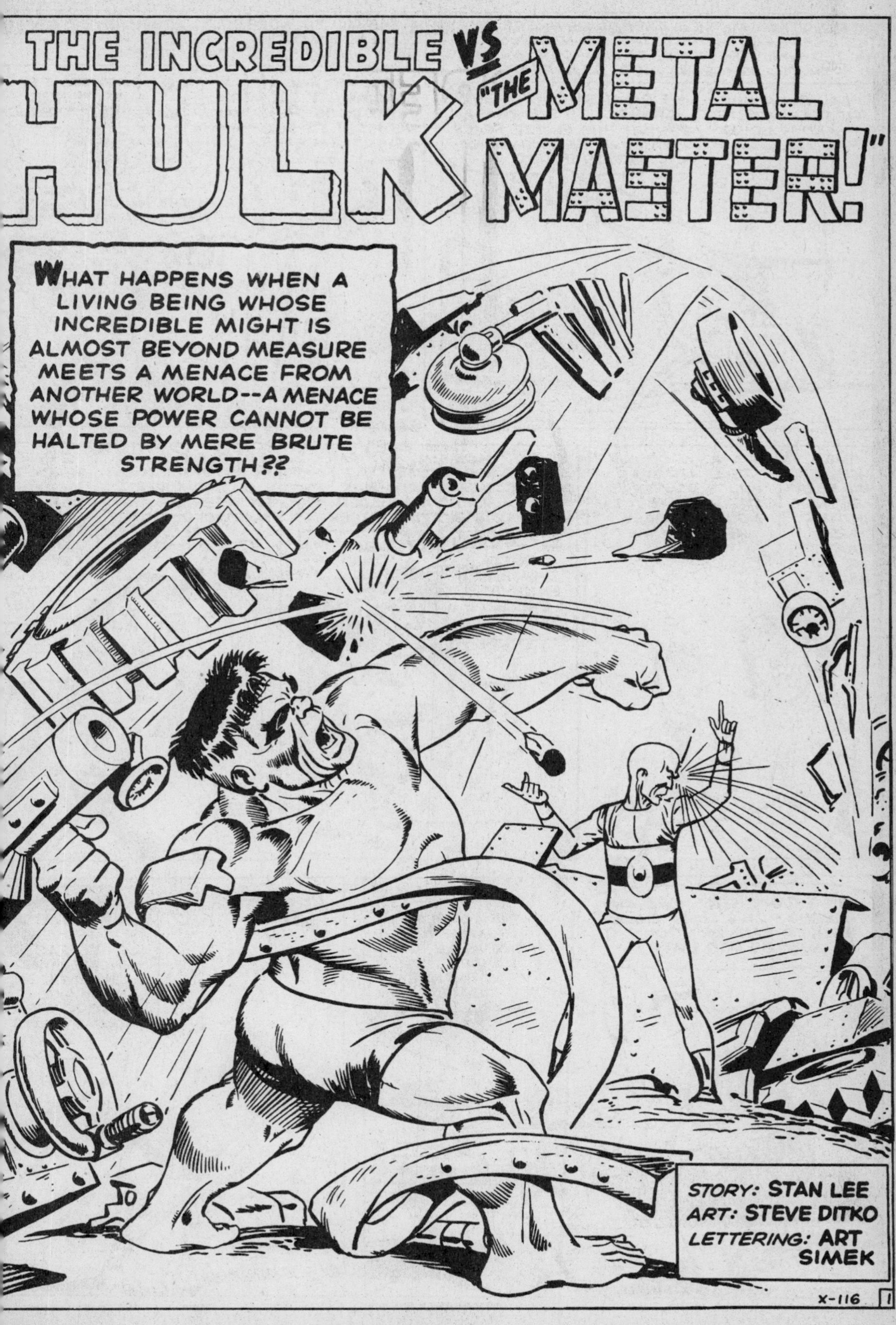

THE INCREDIBLE HULK VS "THE METAL MASTER!"
WHAT HAPPENS WHEN A LIVING BEING WHOSE INCREDIBLE MIGHT IS ALMOST BEYOND MEASURE MEETS A MENACE FROM ANOTHER WORLD--A MENACE WHOSE POWER CANNOT BE HALTED BY MERE BRUTE STRENGTH??
STORY: STAN LEE
ART: STEVE DITKO
LETTERING: ART SIMEK
X-116
1

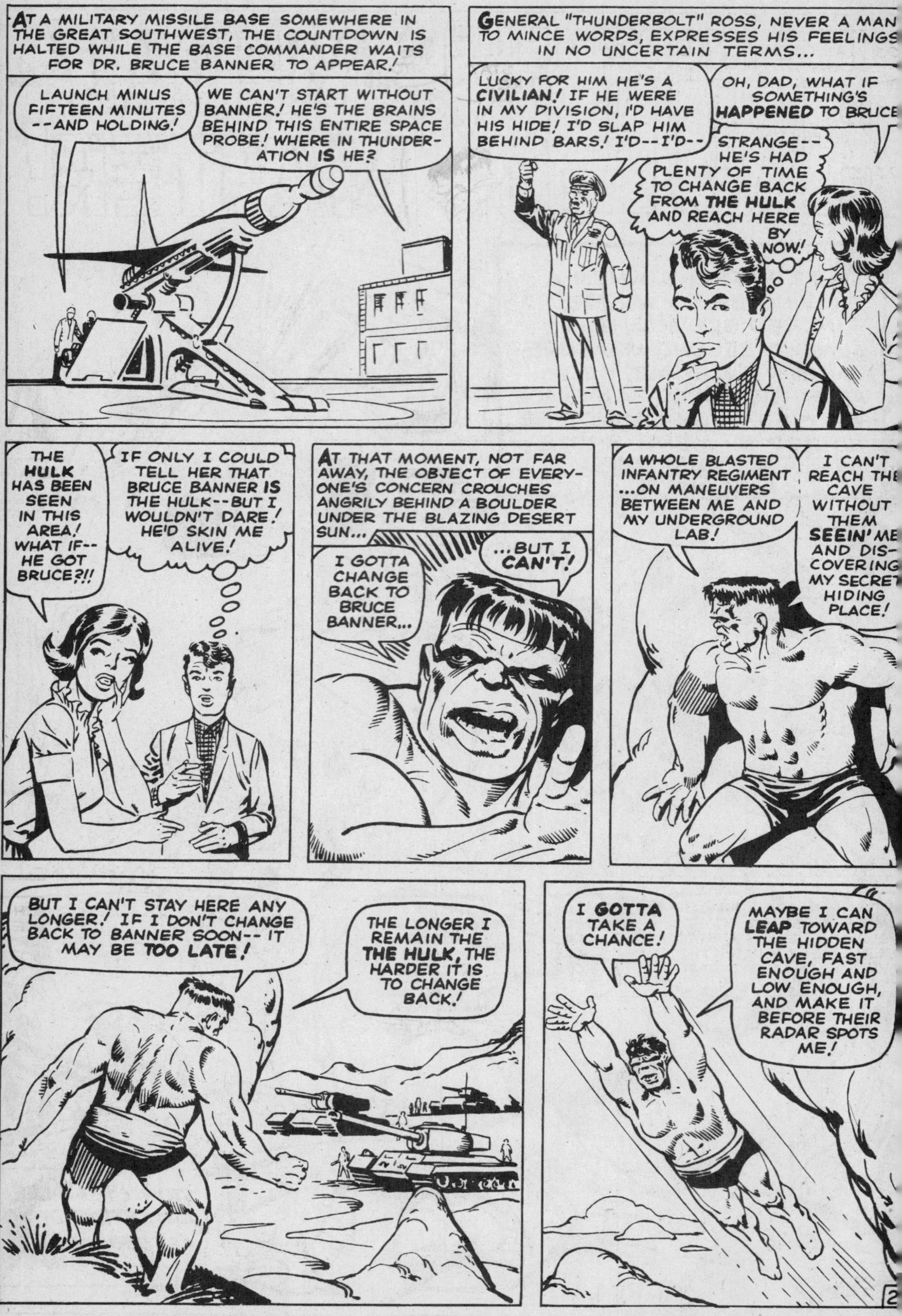
AT A MILITARY MISSILE BASE SOMEWHERE IN THE GREAT SOUTHWEST, THE COUNTDOWN IS HALTED WHILE THE BASE COMMANDER WAITS FOR DR. BRUCE BANNER TO APPEAR!
LAUNCH MINUS FIFTEEN MINUTES --AND HOLDING!
WE CAN'T START WITHOUT BANNER! HE'S THE BRAINS BEHIND THIS ENTIRE SPACE PROBE! WHERE IN THUNDERATION IS HE?
GENERAL "THUNDERBOLT" ROSS, NEVER A MAN TO MINCE WORDS, EXPRESSES HIS FEELINGS IN NO UNCERTAIN TERMS...
LUCKY FOR HIM HE'S A CIVILIAN! IF HE WERE IN MY DIVISION, I'D HAVE HIS HIDE! I'D SLAP HIM BEHIND BARS! I'D--I'D--
OH, DAD, WHAT IF SOMETHING'S HAPPENED TO BRUCE
STRANGE-- HE'S HAD PLENTY OF TIME TO CHANGE BACK FROM THE HULK AND REACH HERE BY NOW!
THE HULK HAS BEEN SEEN IN THIS AREA! WHAT IF-- HE GOT BRUCE?!!
IF ONLY I COULD TELL HER THAT BRUCE BANNER IS THE HULK--BUT I WOULDN'T DARE! HE'D SKIN ME ALIVE!
AT THAT MOMENT, NOT FAR AWAY, THE OBJECT OF EVERYONE'S CONCERN CROUCHES ANGRILY BEHIND A BOULDER UNDER THE BLAZING DESERT SUN...
I GOTTA CHANGE BACK TO BRUCE BANNER...
...BUT I CAN'T!
A WHOLE BLASTED INFANTRY REGIMENT ...ON MANEUVERS BETWEEN ME AND MY UNDERGROUND LAB!
I CAN'T REACH THE CAVE WITHOUT THEM SEEIN' ME AND DISCOVERING MY SECRET HIDING PLACE!
BUT I CAN'T STAY HERE ANY LONGER! IF I DON'T CHANGE BACK TO BANNER SOON-- IT MAY BE TOO LATE!
THE LONGER I REMAIN THE THE HULK, THE HARDER IT IS TO CHANGE BACK!
I GOTTA TAKE A CHANCE!
MAYBE I CAN LEAP TOWARD THE HIDDEN CAVE, FAST ENOUGH AND LOW ENOUGH, AND MAKE IT BEFORE THEIR RADAR SPOTS ME!
2

BLAST IT! IT'S NO GOOD! TOO MANY JETS! I ALMOST CRASHED INTO 'EM!

THEY'RE COMIN' THIS WAY! I CAN'T STAY HERE!

BUT THERE'S NO PLACE TO HIDE!

THEY GOTTA STAY BACK! WHY DON'T THEY KEEP AWAY?? I DON'T WANNA HURT ANYONE! BUT IF THEY COME ANY CLOSER -- IF THEY ATTACK ME -- IT'LL BE TOO BAD!

...BUT, AT THAT CRUCIAL SPLIT-SECOND, JUST BEFORE THE TROOPS CONFRONT THE DESPERATE HULK, AN EAR-SPLITTING WHINE FILLS THE HOT DESERT AIR...

WHEEEOOOOOOOOOOOOOOOO!

IT MEANS BACK TO THE BASE--ON THE DOUBLE!

IT'S THE EMERGENCY ALERT!

CONDITION RED!

WITHIN MINUTES, THE LAST DULL RUMBLE OF TANKS FADES INTO THE DISTANCE, AND A BEWILDERED HULK SAFELY ENTERS THE DANK CAVE WHICH LEADS TO HIS HIDDEN LAIR!

LUCKY FOR THEM THE ALARM SOUNDED! NOW I WON'T HAVETA BASH ANY HEADS TOGETHER!

MINUTES LATER, A GIANT FORM STANDS IN FRONT OF ONE OF EARTH'S MOST AWESOME RAY MACHINES...

I HATE HAVIN' TO BECOME THAT WEAKLING BANNER ALL THE TIME!

ARGHH!

-GASP- EACH TIME I MAKE THE CHANGE-- IT SEEMS MORE PAINFUL!

3

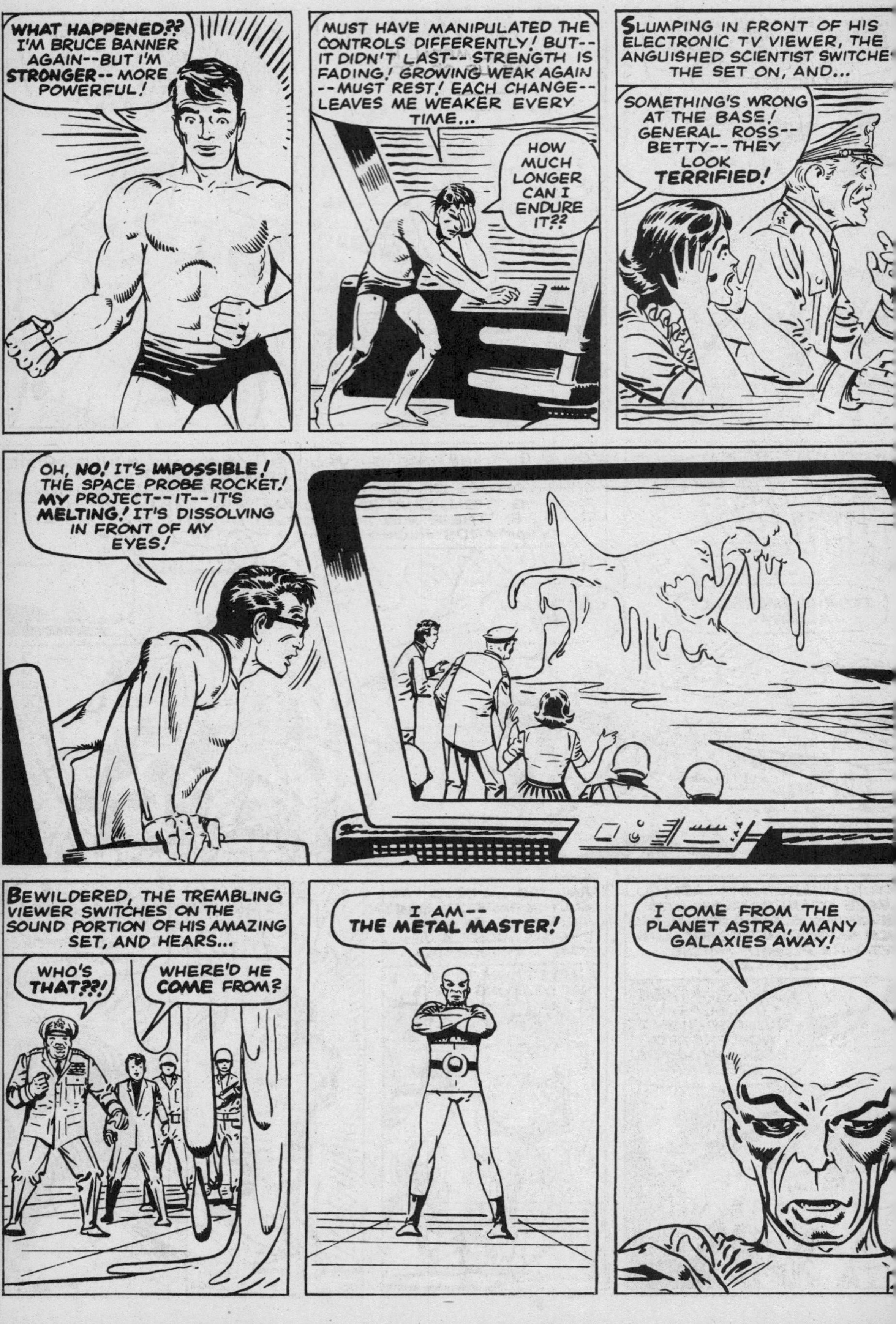
WHAT HAPPENED?? I'M BRUCE BANNER AGAIN--BUT I'M STRONGER-- MORE POWERFUL!
MUST HAVE MANIPULATED THE CONTROLS DIFFERENTLY! BUT--IT DIDN'T LAST-- STRENGTH IS FADING! GROWING WEAK AGAIN --MUST REST! EACH CHANGE--LEAVES ME WEAKER EVERY TIME...
HOW MUCH LONGER CAN I ENDURE IT??
SLUMPING IN FRONT OF HIS ELECTRONIC TV VIEWER, THE ANGUISHED SCIENTIST SWITCHES THE SET ON, AND...
SOMETHING'S WRONG AT THE BASE! GENERAL ROSS--BETTY-- THEY LOOK TERRIFIED!
OH, NO! IT'S IMPOSSIBLE! THE SPACE PROBE ROCKET! MY PROJECT--IT--IT'S MELTING! IT'S DISSOLVING IN FRONT OF MY EYES!
BEWILDERED, THE TREMBLING VIEWER SWITCHES ON THE SOUND PORTION OF HIS AMAZING SET, AND HEARS...
WHO'S THAT??!
WHERE'D HE COME FROM?
I AM-- THE METAL MASTER!
I COME FROM THE PLANET ASTRA, MANY GALAXIES AWAY!

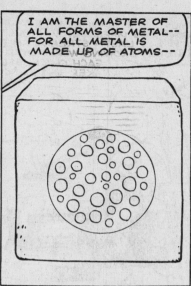

I MELTED YOUR PUNY ROCKET DEVICE THRU THE POWER OF MY BRAIN-- TO SHOW YOU HOW **INVINCIBLE** I AM!

I AM THE MASTER OF ALL FORMS OF METAL-- FOR ALL METAL IS MADE UP OF ATOMS--

--AND, WITH THE POWER OF MY BRAIN, I CAN **COMMAND** AND **CONTROL** EACH AND EVERY METALLIC ATOM!

I CAN CAUSE THEM TO MOVE, TO BE STILL, TO FLY APART, OR ADHERE TOGETHER!

"ON THE PLANET ASTRA, OUR SCULPTORS MAKE MAGNIFICENT STATUES OF METAL, FORMING THEM, SHAPING THEM, BY THEIR MENTAL COMMANDS ALONE!"

"BUT, OF ALL THE ASTRANS, ONLY I WAS JUDGED A CRIMINAL! ONLY I WAS SENTENCED TO EXTERNAL EXILE! FOR I WANTED TO USE MY GREAT POWER IN ORDER TO **CONQUER** ALL!"

OR TIME BEYOND MEASURE, I HAVE ROAMED THE GALAXIES, EEKING A PLANET WHICH WAS CH IN RESOURCES--RICH IN ETAL! A PLANET WHICH I COULD **RULE!**"

AND NOW, I HAVE FOUND SUCH A WORLD! EARTH SHALL BE MINE!

SOMEONE **GRAB** HIM! HE'S NUTTY AS A FRUIT CAKE!

SO! I SEE THAT **FURTHER** DEMONSTRATION IS NEEDED! VERY WELL, **BEHOLD!**

5

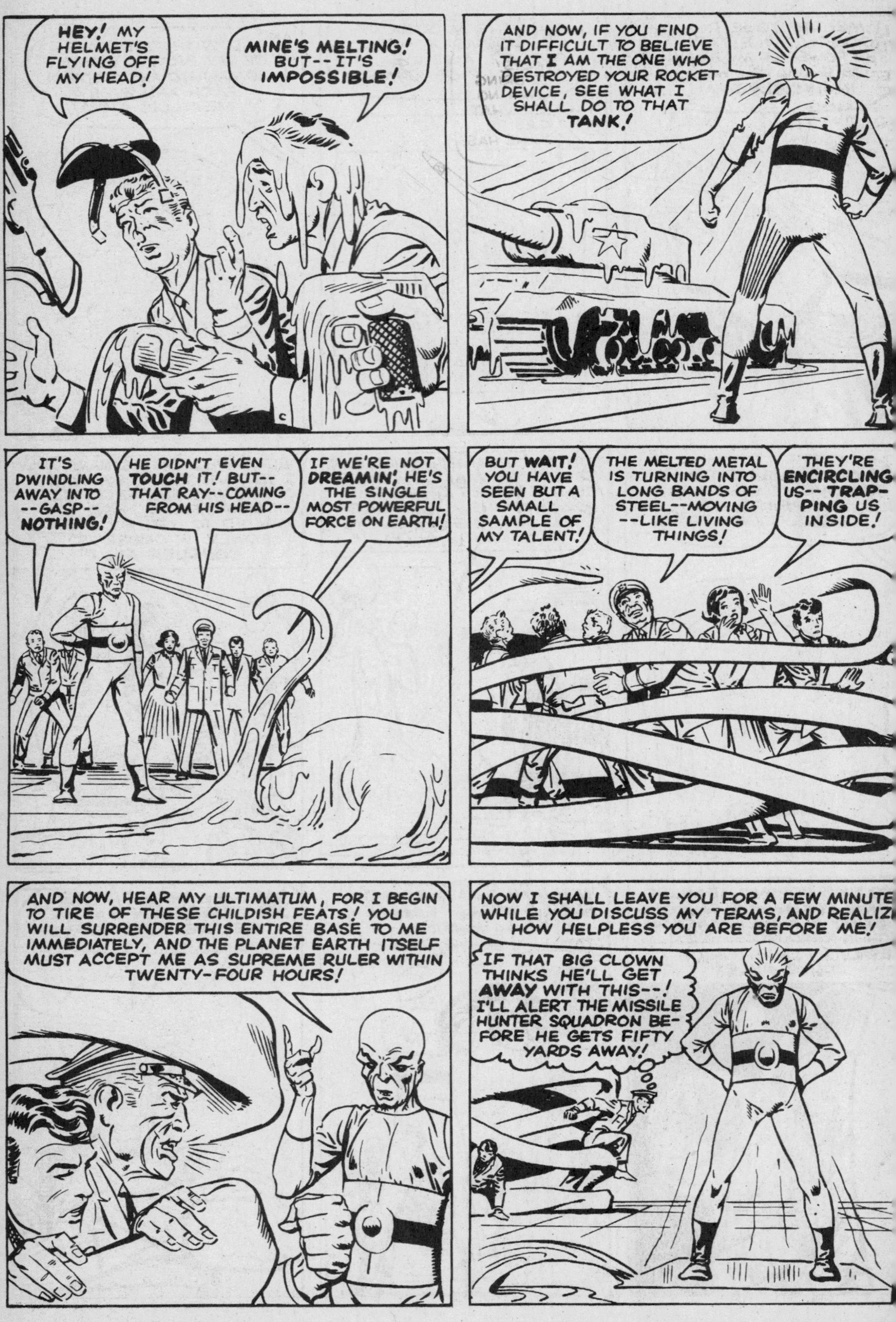
HEY! MY HELMET'S FLYING OFF MY HEAD!
MINE'S MELTING! BUT--IT'S IMPOSSIBLE!
AND NOW, IF YOU FIND IT DIFFICULT TO BELIEVE THAT I AM THE ONE WHO DESTROYED YOUR ROCKET DEVICE, SEE WHAT I SHALL DO TO THAT TANK!
IT'S DWINDLING AWAY INTO --GASP-- NOTHING!
HE DIDN'T EVEN TOUCH IT! BUT-- THAT RAY--COMING FROM HIS HEAD--
IF WE'RE NOT DREAMIN', HE'S THE SINGLE MOST POWERFUL FORCE ON EARTH!
BUT WAIT! YOU HAVE SEEN BUT A SMALL SAMPLE OF MY TALENT!
THE MELTED METAL IS TURNING INTO LONG BANDS OF STEEL--MOVING --LIKE LIVING THINGS!
THEY'RE ENCIRCLING US-- TRAPPING US INSIDE!
AND NOW, HEAR MY ULTIMATUM, FOR I BEGIN TO TIRE OF THESE CHILDISH FEATS! YOU WILL SURRENDER THIS ENTIRE BASE TO ME IMMEDIATELY, AND THE PLANET EARTH ITSELF MUST ACCEPT ME AS SUPREME RULER WITHIN TWENTY-FOUR HOURS!
NOW I SHALL LEAVE YOU FOR A FEW MINUTE WHILE YOU DISCUSS MY TERMS, AND REALIZ HOW HELPLESS YOU ARE BEFORE ME!
IF THAT BIG CLOWN THINKS HE'LL GET AWAY WITH THIS--! I'LL ALERT THE MISSILE HUNTER SQUADRON BEFORE HE GETS FIFTY YARDS AWAY!

LOOK! HE TURNED THAT PIECE OF STEEL PLATFORM TO A-A METAL FLYING CARPET!

BAH! THOSE PARLOR TRICKS DON'T IMPRESS THUNDERBOLT ROSS!

THERE GO MY HUNTER ROCKETS! THEY'LL BRING HIM DOWN NO MATTER WHAT POWERS HE CLAIMS HE HAS!

AND STILL THEY DO NOT BELIEVE!

DISINTEGRATE!

I'LL DIRECT THE REMAINING ROCKET TO RETURN TO THE BASE!

TAKE COVER!

THE ROCKET BACK-TRACKED IN MID-AIR! THAT GUY REALLY IS UNBEATABLE!

THERE'S A CHANCE -- JUST ONE SLIM CHANCE -- THAT THERE IS SOMEONE WHO CAN STOP THE METAL MASTER!

IF I CAN JUST GET TO THE HULK IN TIME!

BREATHLESS FROM HIS HEART-POUNDING RUN, RICK REACHES THE LAIR OF THE HULK, TO FIND...

STAY BACK! I KNOW ALL ABOUT IT -- SAW IT ON THE SCREEN! I'M CHANGING!

THERE! NOW THE HULK WILL -- WHAT ARE YOU STARIN' AT, BRAT??

YOUR FACE!! YOUR BODY IS THE HULK'S, BUT YOUR FACE--

SOMETHING WENT WRONG! I'VE GOT BANNER'S MILKSOP FACE!

YOU CAN'T GO OUT LIKE THAT! IT WOULD GIVE YOUR IDENTITY AWAY!

7

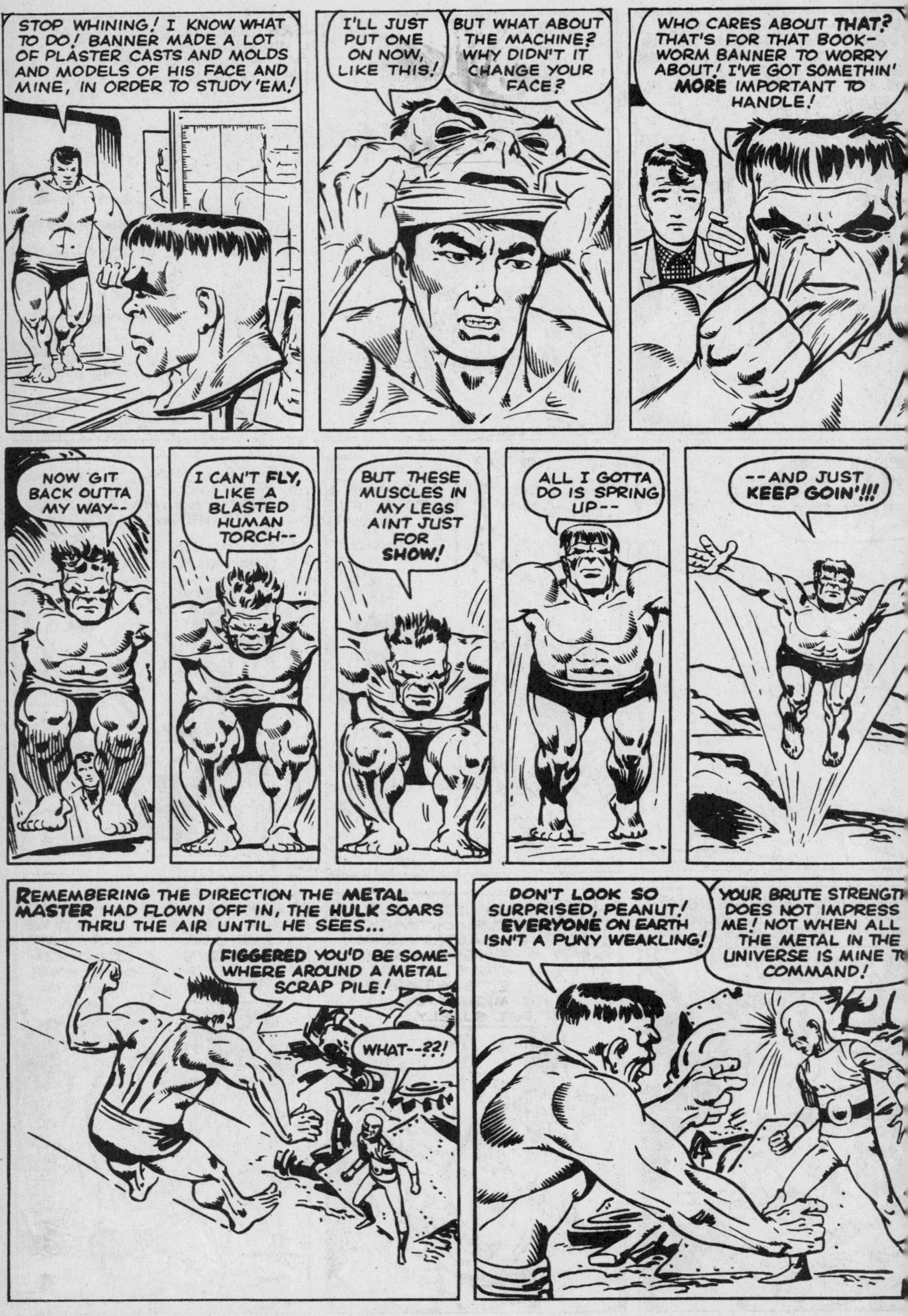
STOP WHINING! I KNOW WHAT TO DO! BANNER MADE A LOT OF PLASTER CASTS AND MOLDS AND MODELS OF HIS FACE AND MINE, IN ORDER TO STUDY 'EM!
I'LL JUST PUT ONE ON NOW, LIKE THIS!
BUT WHAT ABOUT THE MACHINE? WHY DIDN'T IT CHANGE YOUR FACE?
WHO CARES ABOUT THAT? THAT'S FOR THAT BOOK-WORM BANNER TO WORRY ABOUT! I'VE GOT SOMETHIN' MORE IMPORTANT TO HANDLE!
NOW GIT BACK OUTTA MY WAY--
I CAN'T FLY, LIKE A BLASTED HUMAN TORCH--
BUT THESE MUSCLES IN MY LEGS AINT JUST FOR SHOW!
ALL I GOTTA DO IS SPRING UP--
--AND JUST KEEP GOIN'!!!
REMEMBERING THE DIRECTION THE METAL MASTER HAD FLOWN OFF IN, THE HULK SOARS THRU THE AIR UNTIL HE SEES...
FIGGERED YOU'D BE SOME-WHERE AROUND A METAL SCRAP PILE!
WHAT--??!
DON'T LOOK SO SURPRISED, PEANUT! EVERYONE ON EARTH ISN'T A PUNY WEAKLING!
YOUR BRUTE STRENGTH DOES NOT IMPRESS ME! NOT WHEN ALL THE METAL IN THE UNIVERSE IS MINE TO COMMAND!

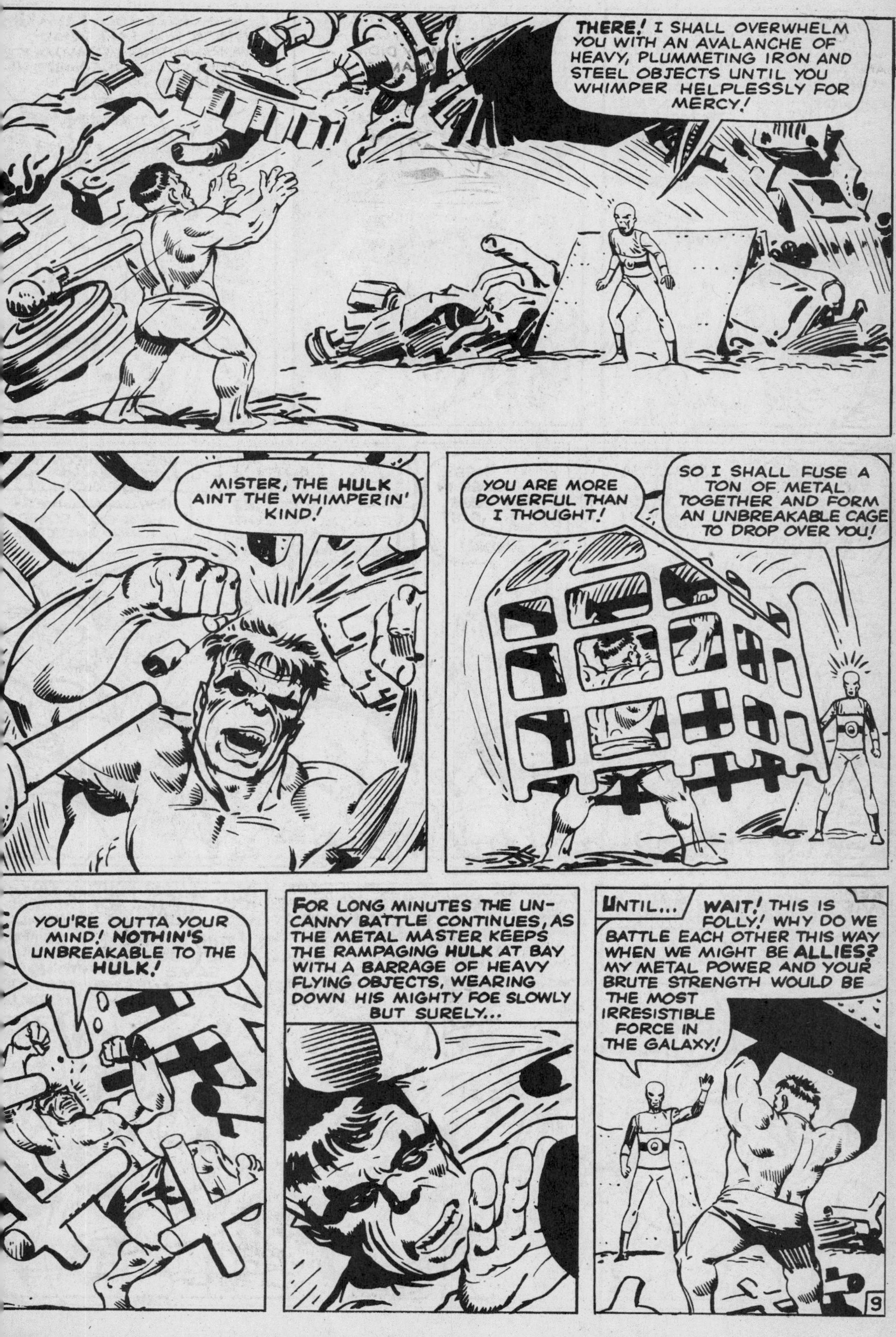
THERE! I SHALL OVERWHELM YOU WITH AN AVALANCHE OF HEAVY, PLUMMETING IRON AND STEEL OBJECTS UNTIL YOU WHIMPER HELPLESSLY FOR MERCY!
MISTER, THE HULK AINT THE WHIMPERIN' KIND!
YOU ARE MORE POWERFUL THAN I THOUGHT!
SO I SHALL FUSE A TON OF METAL TOGETHER AND FORM AN UNBREAKABLE CAGE TO DROP OVER YOU!
YOU'RE OUTTA YOUR MIND! NOTHIN'S UNBREAKABLE TO THE HULK!
FOR LONG MINUTES THE UNCANNY BATTLE CONTINUES, AS THE METAL MASTER KEEPS THE RAMPAGING HULK AT BAY WITH A BARRAGE OF HEAVY FLYING OBJECTS, WEARING DOWN HIS MIGHTY FOE SLOWLY BUT SURELY...
UNTIL...
WAIT! THIS IS FOLLY! WHY DO WE BATTLE EACH OTHER THIS WAY WHEN WE MIGHT BE ALLIES? MY METAL POWER AND YOUR BRUTE STRENGTH WOULD BE THE MOST IRRESISTIBLE FORCE IN THE GALAXY!
9

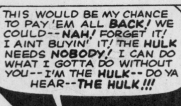

HUH? TEAM UP WITH **YOU**?! YOU'RE NUTS! I-- HEY, WHY **NOT**?

I DON'T OWE NOTHIN' TO THE HUMAN RACE! THEY'VE BEEN HOUNDIN' ME, HUNTIN' ME! TREATIN' ME LIKE AN ANIMAL!

THIS WOULD BE MY CHANCE TO PAY 'EM ALL **BACK**! WE COULD-- NAH! FORGET IT! I AINT BUYIN' IT! THE HULK NEEDS **NOBODY**! I CAN DO WHAT I GOTTA DO WITHOUT YOU-- I'M THE HULK-- DO YA HEAR-- **THE HULK!!!**

BUT, AT THAT SPLIT-SECOND, WHILE HIS FOE'S GUARD IS DOWN, THE METAL MASTER STRIKES AGAIN, SWIFTLY-- SURELY-- AND...

SO BE IT, THEN!

UGH

HE WAS **RIGHT**! WE DO NOT NEED EACH OTHER! FOR **I** AM THE STRONGER! I HAVE VANQUISHED HIM! NOW, ON ALL OF EARTH THERE ARE NONE WHO CAN DEFY ME! I AM SUPREME!

MINUTES LATER, A DETACHMENT OF RECON TROOPS STUMBLE ACROSS THE STUNNED FORM OF THE HULK...

LOOKS LIKE WE'RE ON THE RIGHT TRACK! THE METAL MASTER **MUST** HAVE BEEN IN THE VICINITY! ONLY **HE** COULD HAVE BEATEN THE HULK!

HEY! WHAT GIVES? HE'S GOT SOME KINDA **MASK** ON!

AT THAT MOMENT, THE **HULK** BEGINS TO REGAIN CONSCIOUSNESS...

LET'S SEE WHAT'S UNDERNEATH THIS THING...

WHA--? NO! NO!

GOT TO MOVE FAST, WHILE HE'S STILL WEAK AND DAZED! WHY WOULD THE HULK WEAR A MASK?? HAS HE ANOTHER IDENTITY??

IF THEY FIND OUT WHO I REALLY AM, IT'S THE END FOR ME!

BUT, WHEN THE MASK IS REMOVED...

THIS IS **CRAZY**! HE'S GOT THE SAME FACE UNDERNEATH!

BETTER TAKE HI... TO HQ! IT' TOO MUC FOR U!

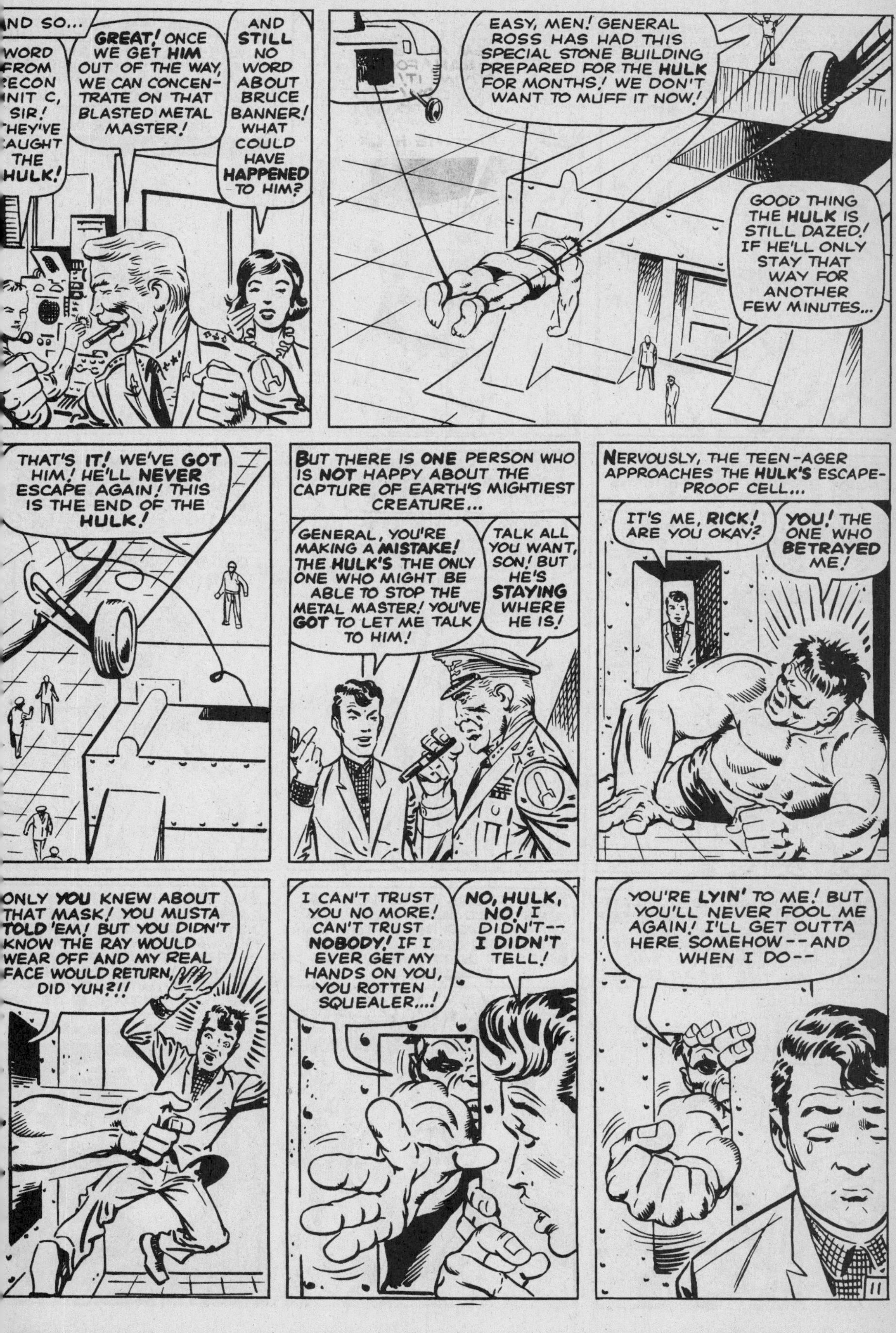

AND SO...
WORD FROM RECON UNIT C, SIR! THEY'VE CAUGHT THE HULK!
GREAT! ONCE WE GET HIM OUT OF THE WAY, WE CAN CONCENTRATE ON THAT BLASTED METAL MASTER!
AND STILL NO WORD ABOUT BRUCE BANNER! WHAT COULD HAVE HAPPENED TO HIM?
EASY, MEN! GENERAL ROSS HAS HAD THIS SPECIAL STONE BUILDING PREPARED FOR THE HULK FOR MONTHS! WE DON'T WANT TO MUFF IT NOW!
GOOD THING THE HULK IS STILL DAZED! IF HE'LL ONLY STAY THAT WAY FOR ANOTHER FEW MINUTES...
THAT'S IT! WE'VE GOT HIM! HE'LL NEVER ESCAPE AGAIN! THIS IS THE END OF THE HULK!
BUT THERE IS ONE PERSON WHO IS NOT HAPPY ABOUT THE CAPTURE OF EARTH'S MIGHTIEST CREATURE...
GENERAL, YOU'RE MAKING A MISTAKE! THE HULK'S THE ONLY ONE WHO MIGHT BE ABLE TO STOP THE METAL MASTER! YOU'VE GOT TO LET ME TALK TO HIM!
TALK ALL YOU WANT, SON! BUT HE'S STAYING WHERE HE IS!
NERVOUSLY, THE TEEN-AGER APPROACHES THE HULK'S ESCAPE-PROOF CELL...
IT'S ME, RICK! ARE YOU OKAY?
YOU! THE ONE WHO BETRAYED ME!
ONLY YOU KNEW ABOUT THAT MASK! YOU MUSTA TOLD 'EM! BUT YOU DIDN'T KNOW THE RAY WOULD WEAR OFF AND MY REAL FACE WOULD RETURN, DID YUH?!!
I CAN'T TRUST YOU NO MORE! CAN'T TRUST NOBODY! IF I EVER GET MY HANDS ON YOU, YOU ROTTEN SQUEALER...!
NO, HULK, NO! I DIDN'T-- I DIDN'T TELL!
YOU'RE LYIN' TO ME! BUT YOU'LL NEVER FOOL ME AGAIN! I'LL GET OUTTA HERE SOMEHOW--AND WHEN I DO--
11

AND WHEN I DO--WHEN I BREAK OUTTA HERE-- I'LL HAVE MY REVENGE! ON EVERYBODY! DO YA HEAR-- ON EVERYBODY!!

AND I **WILL** GET OUT! I WILL!

NO MATTER **HOW** LONG IT TAKES--I'LL GET OUT!

AND SO WE TAKE OUR LEAVE OF THE MOST INCREDIBLE CREATURE ON EARTH, FOR A SHORT TIME, AS HE POUNDS HIS UNBELIEVABLY POWERFUL FISTS AGAINST THE SILENT STONE WALL-- A WALL WHICH SLOWLY, EVER SO SLOWLY BEGINS TO CRUMBLE...

I'LL GET OUT!

BUT WHAT OF RICK JONES? HURT, BEWILDERED, HE TURNS TO THUNDERBOLT ROSS...

GENERAL, WHERE DO I GO TO ENLIST IN THE ARMY?

NOWHERE YET, SON! YOU'RE ONLY SIXTEEN! YOU'RE TOO YOUNG!

BUT I'M TIRED OF BEIN' JUST A **NOTHIN'!** I WANNA BE WHERE THE **ACTION** IS!

I KNOW HOW YOU FEEL, MY BOY, BUT IF YOU REALLY WANT TO SERVE YOUR COUNTRY...

...THE BEST THING TO DO IS STAY IN SCHOOL! AMERICA NEEDS TRAINED MEN, IN EVERY FIELD-- EVEN IN THE ARMY! AND **THEN**, WHEN YOU'RE OLD ENOUGH--

COOL IT, GENERAL! I GET THE MESSAGE!

AND SLOWLY, INEXORABLY, FATE DRAWS HER LITTLE WEB CLOSER AND CLOSER... FOR, AT THAT MOMENT, THE METAL MASTER DESTROYS OIL WELLS IN THE HEART OF THE NEAR EAST...

BEHOLD! IT IS THE METAL MASTER!

THEN SPEEDS ON TO TOPPLE CONSTRUCTION IN AFRICA, AFFECT SHIPPING IN THE MEDITERRANEAN, AND UPROOT BRIDGES IN THE HEART OF EUROPE!

ONLY THE METAL MASTER COULD DO ALL THIS!

AND, BEFORE LONG, THE ENTIRE EARTH HAS SEEN AWESOME DEMONSTRATIONS OF THE SEEMINGLY ENDLESS POWER OF THE MENACE FROM ANOTHER GALAXY! NOT A HUMAN BREATHES ON EARTH WHO DOES NOT TREMBLE AT THE NAME...

THE METAL MASTER

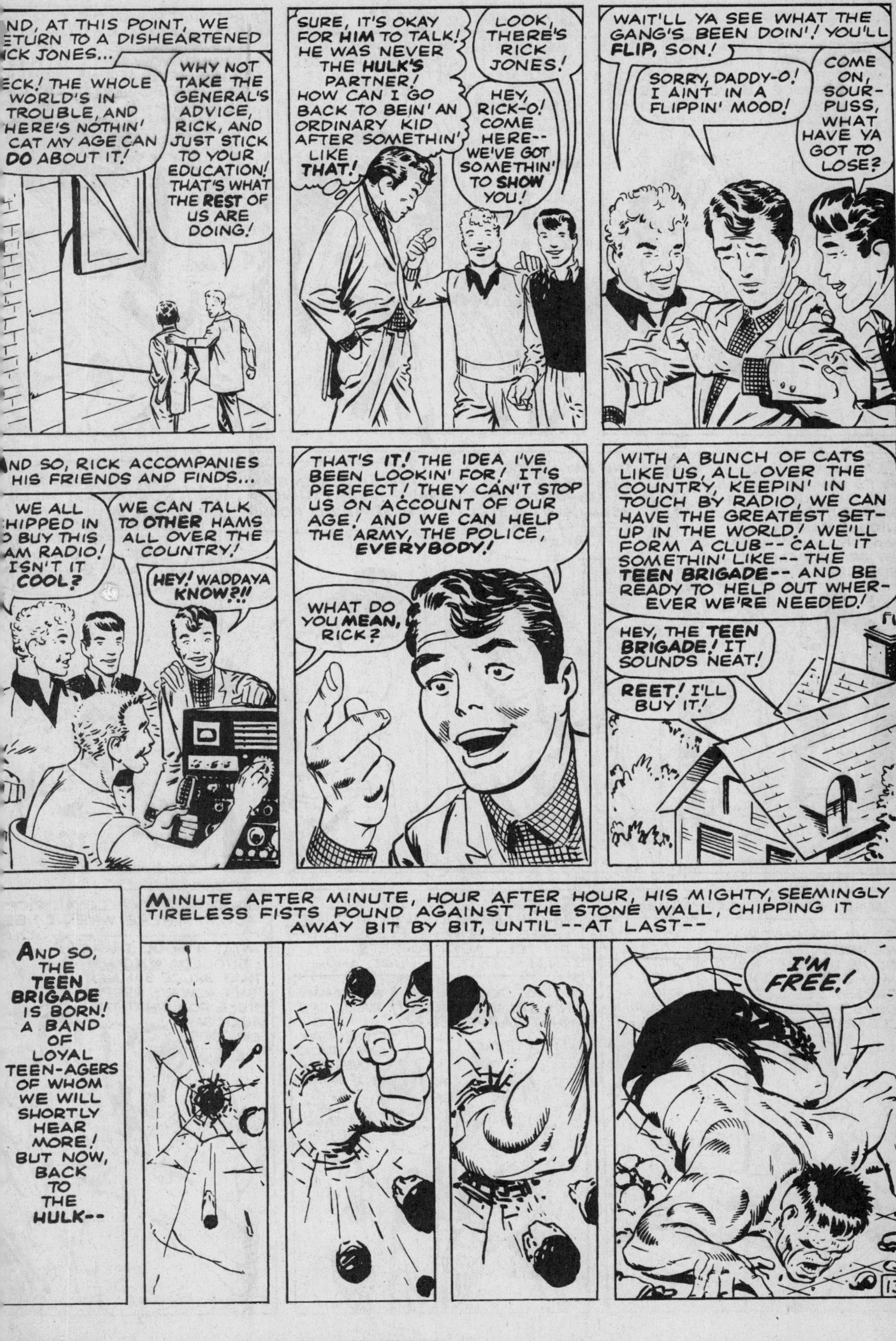

ND, AT THIS POINT, WE ETURN TO A DISHEARTENED ICK JONES...
ECK! THE WHOLE WORLD'S IN TROUBLE, AND HERE'S NOTHIN' CAT MY AGE CAN DO ABOUT IT!
WHY NOT TAKE THE GENERAL'S ADVICE, RICK, AND JUST STICK TO YOUR EDUCATION! THAT'S WHAT THE REST OF US ARE DOING!
SURE, IT'S OKAY FOR HIM TO TALK! HE WAS NEVER THE HULK'S PARTNER! HOW CAN I GO BACK TO BEIN' AN ORDINARY KID AFTER SOMETHIN' LIKE THAT!
LOOK, THERE'S RICK JONES!
HEY, RICK-O! COME HERE-- WE'VE GOT SOMETHIN' TO SHOW YOU!
WAIT'LL YA SEE WHAT THE GANG'S BEEN DOIN'! YOU'LL FLIP, SON!
SORRY, DADDY-O! I AINT IN A FLIPPIN' MOOD!
COME ON, SOUR-PUSS, WHAT HAVE YA GOT TO LOSE?
ND SO, RICK ACCOMPANIES HIS FRIENDS AND FINDS...
WE ALL HIPPED IN O BUY THIS AM RADIO! ISN'T IT COOL?
WE CAN TALK TO OTHER HAMS ALL OVER THE COUNTRY!
HEY! WADDAYA KNOW?!!
THAT'S IT! THE IDEA I'VE BEEN LOOKIN' FOR! IT'S PERFECT! THEY CAN'T STOP US ON ACCOUNT OF OUR AGE! AND WE CAN HELP THE ARMY, THE POLICE, EVERYBODY!
WHAT DO YOU MEAN, RICK?
WITH A BUNCH OF CATS LIKE US, ALL OVER THE COUNTRY, KEEPIN' IN TOUCH BY RADIO, WE CAN HAVE THE GREATEST SET-UP IN THE WORLD! WE'LL FORM A CLUB-- CALL IT SOMETHIN' LIKE-- THE TEEN BRIGADE-- AND BE READY TO HELP OUT WHEREVER WE'RE NEEDED!
HEY, THE TEEN BRIGADE! IT SOUNDS NEAT!
REET! I'LL BUY IT!
AND SO, THE TEEN BRIGADE IS BORN! A BAND OF LOYAL TEEN-AGERS OF WHOM WE WILL SHORTLY HEAR MORE! BUT NOW, BACK TO THE HULK--
MINUTE AFTER MINUTE, HOUR AFTER HOUR, HIS MIGHTY, SEEMINGLY TIRELESS FISTS POUND AGAINST THE STONE WALL, CHIPPING IT AWAY BIT BY BIT, UNTIL--AT LAST--
I'M FREE!
13

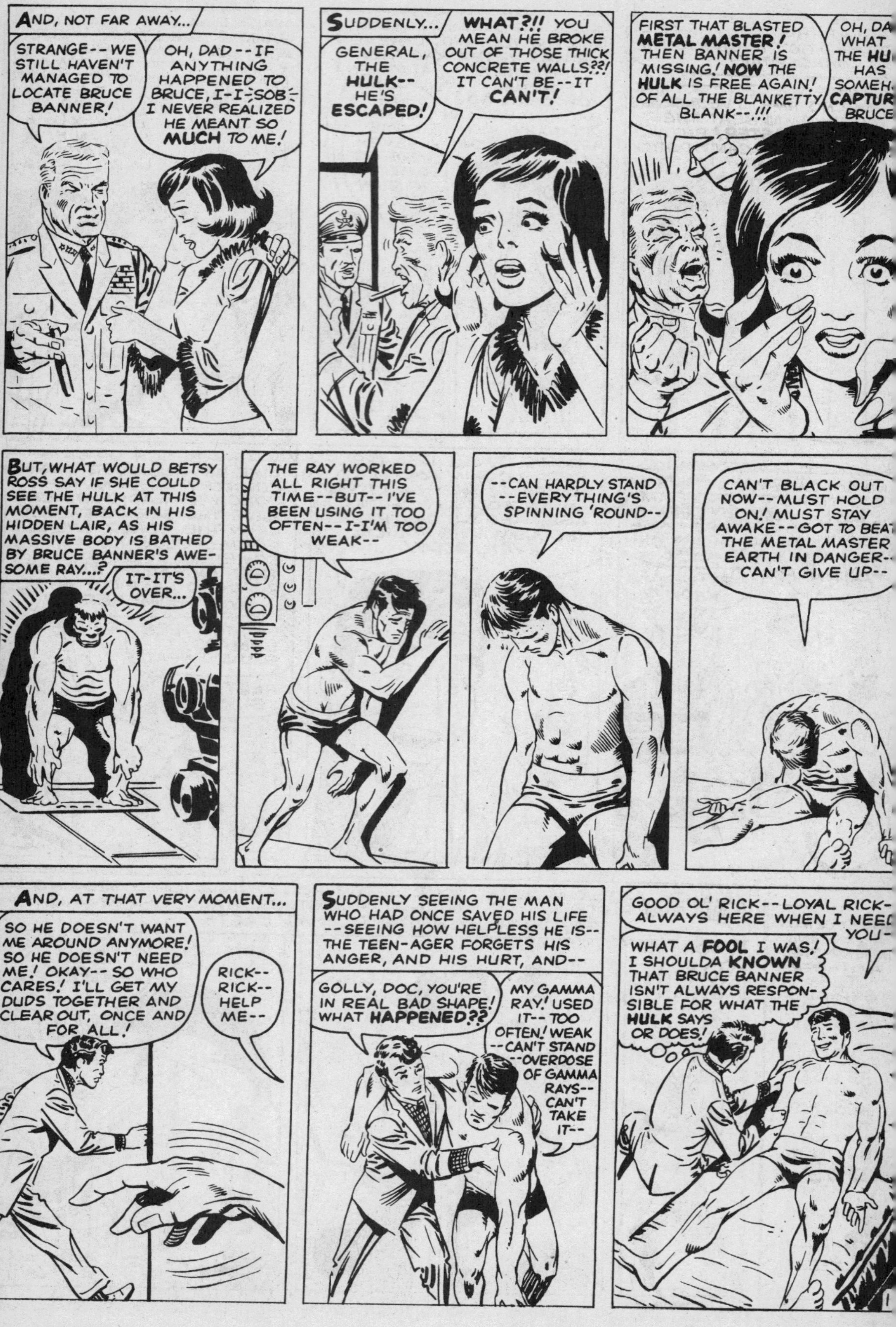
AND, NOT FAR AWAY...
STRANGE--WE STILL HAVEN'T MANAGED TO LOCATE BRUCE BANNER!
OH, DAD--IF ANYTHING HAPPENED TO BRUCE, I-I-SOB- I NEVER REALIZED HE MEANT SO MUCH TO ME!
SUDDENLY...
GENERAL, THE HULK--HE'S ESCAPED!
WHAT?!! YOU MEAN HE BROKE OUT OF THOSE THICK CONCRETE WALLS??! IT CAN'T BE--IT CAN'T!
FIRST THAT BLASTED METAL MASTER! THEN BANNER IS MISSING! NOW THE HULK IS FREE AGAIN! OF ALL THE BLANKETTY BLANK--!!!
OH, DA WHAT THE HU HAS SOMEH CAPTUR BRUCE
BUT, WHAT WOULD BETSY ROSS SAY IF SHE COULD SEE THE HULK AT THIS MOMENT, BACK IN HIS HIDDEN LAIR, AS HIS MASSIVE BODY IS BATHED BY BRUCE BANNER'S AWESOME RAY...?
IT-IT'S OVER...
THE RAY WORKED ALL RIGHT THIS TIME--BUT--I'VE BEEN USING IT TOO OFTEN--I-I'M TOO WEAK--
--CAN HARDLY STAND --EVERYTHING'S SPINNING 'ROUND--
CAN'T BLACK OUT NOW--MUST HOLD ON! MUST STAY AWAKE--GOT TO BEAT THE METAL MASTER EARTH IN DANGER-- CAN'T GIVE UP--
AND, AT THAT VERY MOMENT...
SO HE DOESN'T WANT ME AROUND ANYMORE! SO HE DOESN'T NEED ME! OKAY--SO WHO CARES! I'LL GET MY DUDS TOGETHER AND CLEAR OUT, ONCE AND FOR ALL!
RICK--RICK--HELP ME--
SUDDENLY SEEING THE MAN WHO HAD ONCE SAVED HIS LIFE --SEEING HOW HELPLESS HE IS-- THE TEEN-AGER FORGETS HIS ANGER, AND HIS HURT, AND--
GOLLY, DOC, YOU'RE IN REAL BAD SHAPE! WHAT HAPPENED??
MY GAMMA RAY! USED IT--TOO OFTEN! WEAK --CAN'T STAND --OVERDOSE OF GAMMA RAYS--CAN'T TAKE IT--
GOOD OL' RICK--LOYAL RICK-- ALWAYS HERE WHEN I NEED YOU-
WHAT A FOOL I WAS! I SHOULDA KNOWN THAT BRUCE BANNER ISN'T ALWAYS RESPONSIBLE FOR WHAT THE HULK SAYS OR DOES!

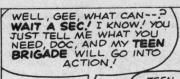

DOC, I'VE GOT TO GET YOU TO A HOSPITAL!

NO! NO TIME! I'VE THOUGHT OF A WAY TO BEAT THE METAL MASTER! BUT, NEED HELP! CAN'T DO IT ALONE!

WELL, GEE, WHAT CAN--? WAIT A SEC! I KNOW! YOU JUST TELL ME WHAT YOU NEED, DOC, AND MY TEEN BRIGADE WILL GO INTO ACTION!

TEEN BRIGADE--?

A SHORT TIME LATER, AFTER BEING SURE THAT BRUCE BANNER IS RESTING COMFORTABLY...

HERE'S THE PITCH, GANG! YOU'VE ALL HEARD OF DOCTOR BRUCE BANNER! WELL, HE'S GOT AN ANGLE ON HOW TO BEAT THE METAL MASTER, BUT IT'S UP TO US TO GET HIM THE EQUIPMENT HE NEEDS! NOW HERE'S WHAT WE WANT--

AND SO, EAGERLY, ENTHUSIASTICALLY, WITH ALL THE ENERGY OF TYPICAL AMERICAN TEEN-AGERS, THE NEWLY-FORMED **TEEN BRIGADE** RACES INTO ACTION!

WHAT ARE WE WAITIN' FOR?

LAST ONE BACK IS A ROTTEN EGG!

GANGWAY!

NORTH, SOUTH, EAST, AND WEST-- INTO EVERY CORNER OF THE UNITED STATES, THE TEEN BRIGADE RADIO THEIR MESSAGES! AND PARTS AND SUPPLIES START POURING IN FROM ALL OVER, IN A DESPERATE STRUGGLE TO STOP THE METAL MASTER!

JUST REACHED PITTSBURGH! OUR CONDENSERS ARE ON THE WAY!

HERE'S THE TUBES AND CIRCUITS RICK ASKED FOR--FROM SEATTLE!

BLUE-PRINTS ON THE WAY! OVER AND OUT!

AND, ONCE MORE, ALONE AND UNSUSPECTED, A SLENDER FIGURE STANDS IN FRONT OF THE GAMMA RAY MACHINE...

CAN'T AFFORD TO REST ANY LONGER! IT'S NOW OR NEVER!

IT'S WORKING!

AHHH-- I CAN FEEL THE POWER SURGING THRU MY BODY! I'M STRONG AGAIN! I'M THE HULK AGAIN!

AND SO OUR GRIPPING TALE GATHERS MOMENTUM AS IT RACES TOWARDS ITS INEVITABLE CLIMAX! FOR THE **METAL MASTER** IS STILL AT LARGE, AND EARTH HAS STILL FOUND NO WAY TO COPE WITH HIS DIRE MENACE!

WE'VE TRIED EVERY WEAPON-- EVERY SCHEME-- NOTHING CAN STOP THE METAL MASTER!

THE PEOPLE ARE GROWING PANICKY! SOMETHING MUST BE DONE SOON! BUT WHAT??

15

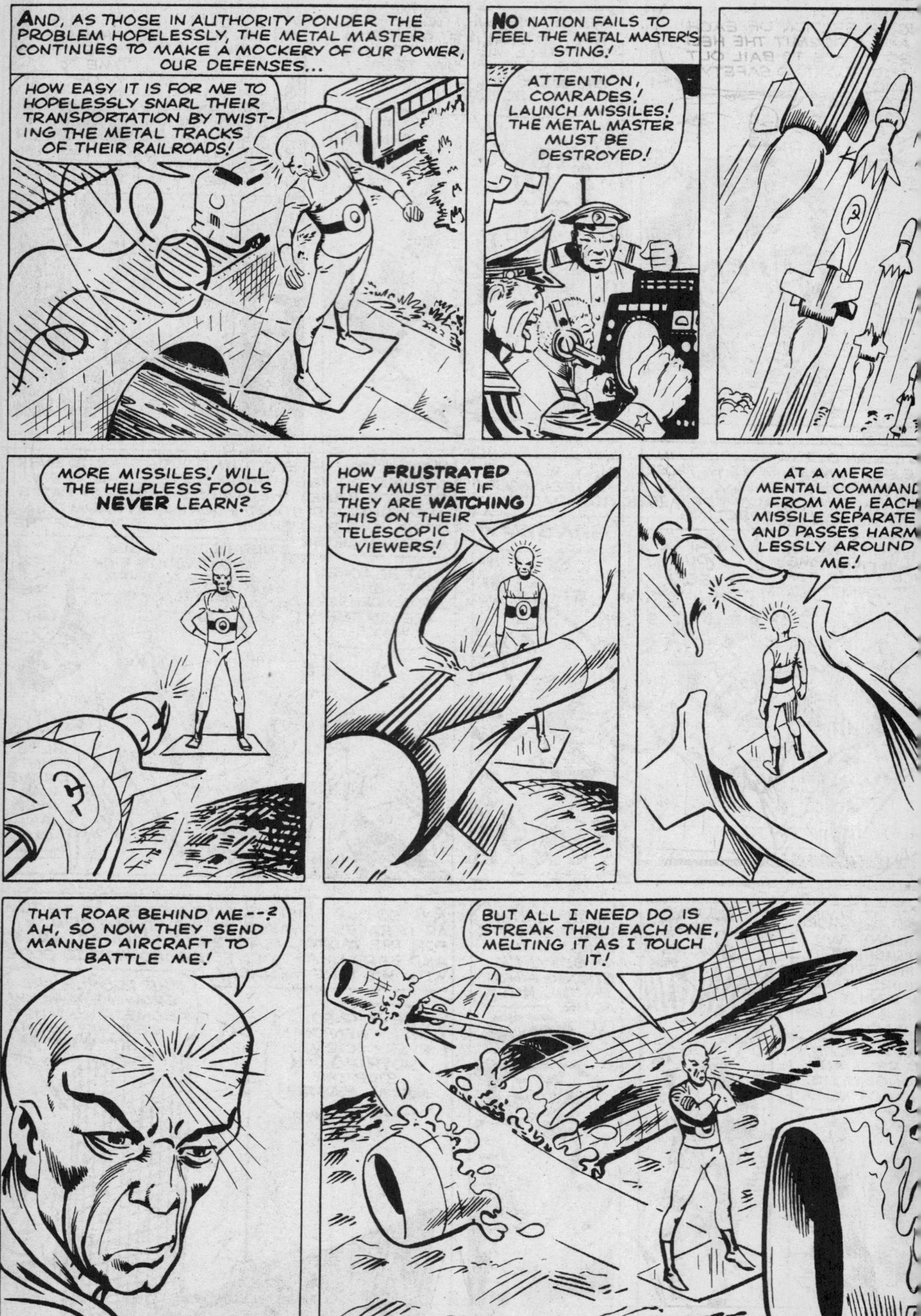
AND, AS THOSE IN AUTHORITY PONDER THE PROBLEM HOPELESSLY, THE METAL MASTER CONTINUES TO MAKE A MOCKERY OF OUR POWER, OUR DEFENSES...
HOW EASY IT IS FOR ME TO HOPELESSLY SNARL THEIR TRANSPORTATION BY TWISTING THE METAL TRACKS OF THEIR RAILROADS!
NO NATION FAILS TO FEEL THE METAL MASTER'S STING!
ATTENTION, COMRADES! LAUNCH MISSILES! THE METAL MASTER MUST BE DESTROYED!
MORE MISSILES! WILL THE HELPLESS FOOLS NEVER LEARN?
HOW FRUSTRATED THEY MUST BE IF THEY ARE WATCHING THIS ON THEIR TELESCOPIC VIEWERS!
AT A MERE MENTAL COMMAND FROM ME, EACH MISSILE SEPARATE AND PASSES HARMLESSLY AROUND ME!
THAT ROAR BEHIND ME--? AH, SO NOW THEY SEND MANNED AIRCRAFT TO BATTLE ME!
BUT ALL I NEED DO IS STREAK THRU EACH ONE, MELTING IT AS I TOUCH IT!

MERELY MELTING THE ENGINE SECTION OF EACH PLANE, I PERMIT THE HELPLESS PILOTS TO BAIL OUT AND FLOAT TO SAFETY!

IT IS NOT THAT I AM MERCIFUL! BUT I SHALL WANT EVERY EARTHLING **ALIVE**, SO THAT THERE WILL BE MANY TO **SERVE** ME! AND NOW, I SHALL SIMPLY LOSE MYSELF IN A BANK OF CLOUDS, FOR I GROW WEARY OF THIS CONFLICT...IT IS LIKE BATTLING **CHILDREN**!

THE **NEXT** TIME I APPEAR, I SHALL BE THRU **TOYING** WITH THESE PUNY HUMANS! WHEN NEXT THEY SEE ME, I SHALL HAVE COME TO TAKE POSSESSION OF ALL MANKIND!

BUT, IN AN OLD WAREHOUSE IN THE SOUTHWEST, SOME OF THOSE "PUNY HUMANS" ARE PLOTTING, AND PLANNING, AND WORKING TO DEFEAT THE UNSUSPECTING ALIEN!

WE BROUGHT ALL THE EQUIPMENT RICK ASKED FOR! HE'S LOCKED INSIDE NOW!

WHAT DO YOU SUPPOSE HE'S **DOIN'** WITH IT? AND WHERE'S DOCTOR BANNER?

DOCTOR BANNER **TOO** IS INSIDE -- BUT NOT IN THE FORM WHICH THE TEEN BRIGADE MIGHT EXPECT!

IT'S A GOOD THING YOU REMEMBER MOST OF BRUCE BANNER'S SCIENTIFIC KNOWLEDGE, HULK--

SHUDDUP AND LET ME THINK, BRAT!

THERE! THE MACHINE IS **FINISHED!** NOW OPEN THAT DOOR AND GIT OUTTA MY WAY!

Y-YOU BET, HULK!

NOW TO FIND THAT FLYIN' CREEP!

L-LOOK! IT'S-- IT'S THE **HULK!**

BUT HOW DID **HE** GET IN THERE??

AND WHAT WAS HE **CARRYIN'??** IT LOOKED LIKE SOME SORTA **GUN!**

IF HE'S LOOKIN' FOR THE **METAL MASTER**, HE'S WASTIN' HIS TIME! THAT GUN WON'T DO ANY GOOD!

17

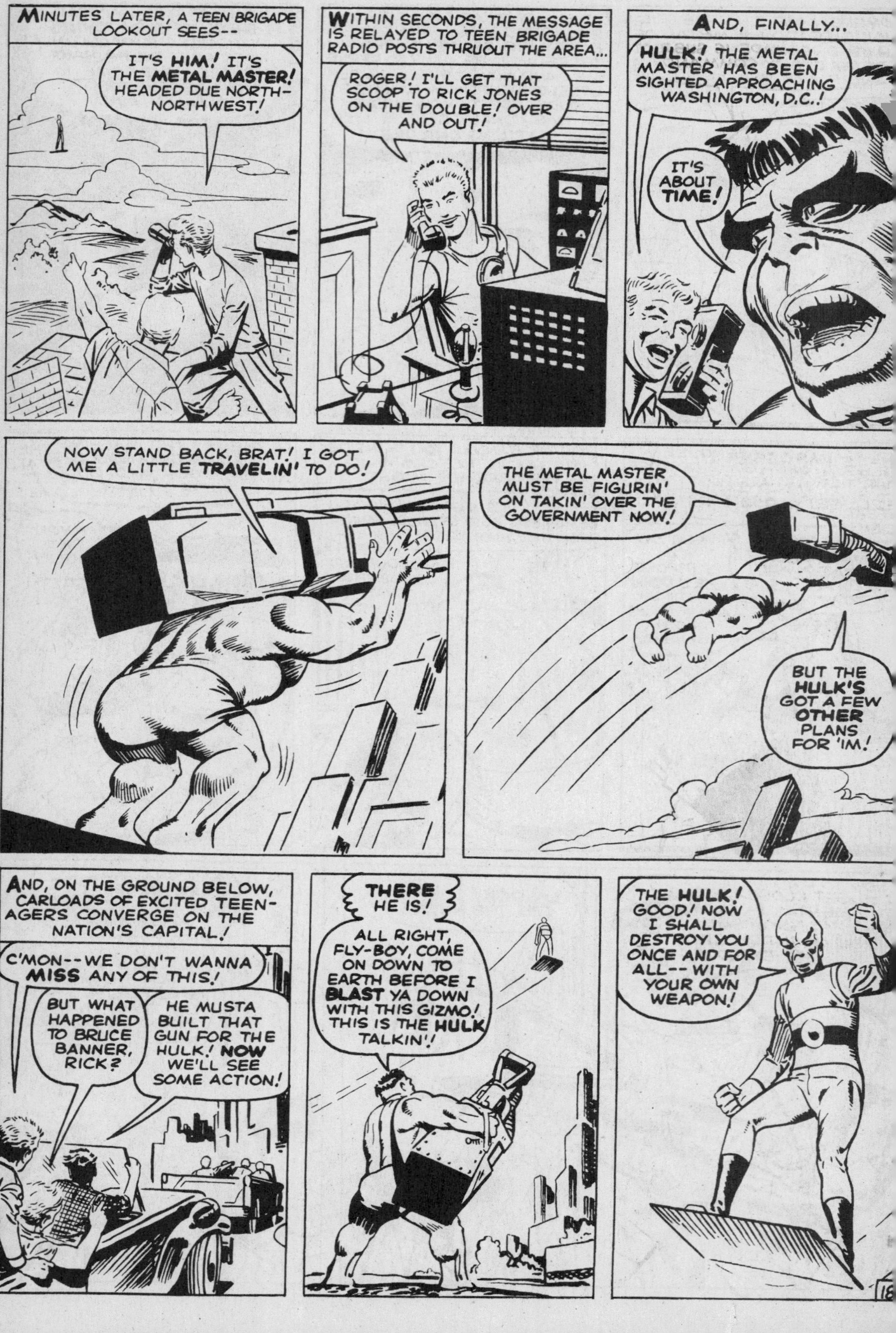
MINUTES LATER, A TEEN BRIGADE LOOKOUT SEES--
IT'S HIM! IT'S THE METAL MASTER! HEADED DUE NORTH-NORTHWEST!
WITHIN SECONDS, THE MESSAGE IS RELAYED TO TEEN BRIGADE RADIO POSTS THRUOUT THE AREA...
ROGER! I'LL GET THAT SCOOP TO RICK JONES ON THE DOUBLE! OVER AND OUT!
AND, FINALLY...
HULK! THE METAL MASTER HAS BEEN SIGHTED APPROACHING WASHINGTON, D.C.!
IT'S ABOUT TIME!
NOW STAND BACK, BRAT! I GOT ME A LITTLE TRAVELIN' TO DO!
THE METAL MASTER MUST BE FIGURIN' ON TAKIN' OVER THE GOVERNMENT NOW!
BUT THE HULK'S GOT A FEW OTHER PLANS FOR 'IM!
AND, ON THE GROUND BELOW, CARLOADS OF EXCITED TEEN-AGERS CONVERGE ON THE NATION'S CAPITAL!
C'MON--WE DON'T WANNA MISS ANY OF THIS!
BUT WHAT HAPPENED TO BRUCE BANNER, RICK?
HE MUSTA BUILT THAT GUN FOR THE HULK! NOW WE'LL SEE SOME ACTION!
THERE HE IS!
ALL RIGHT, FLY-BOY, COME ON DOWN TO EARTH BEFORE I BLAST YA DOWN WITH THIS GIZMO! THIS IS THE HULK TALKIN'!
THE HULK! GOOD! NOW I SHALL DESTROY YOU ONCE AND FOR ALL-- WITH YOUR OWN WEAPON!
18

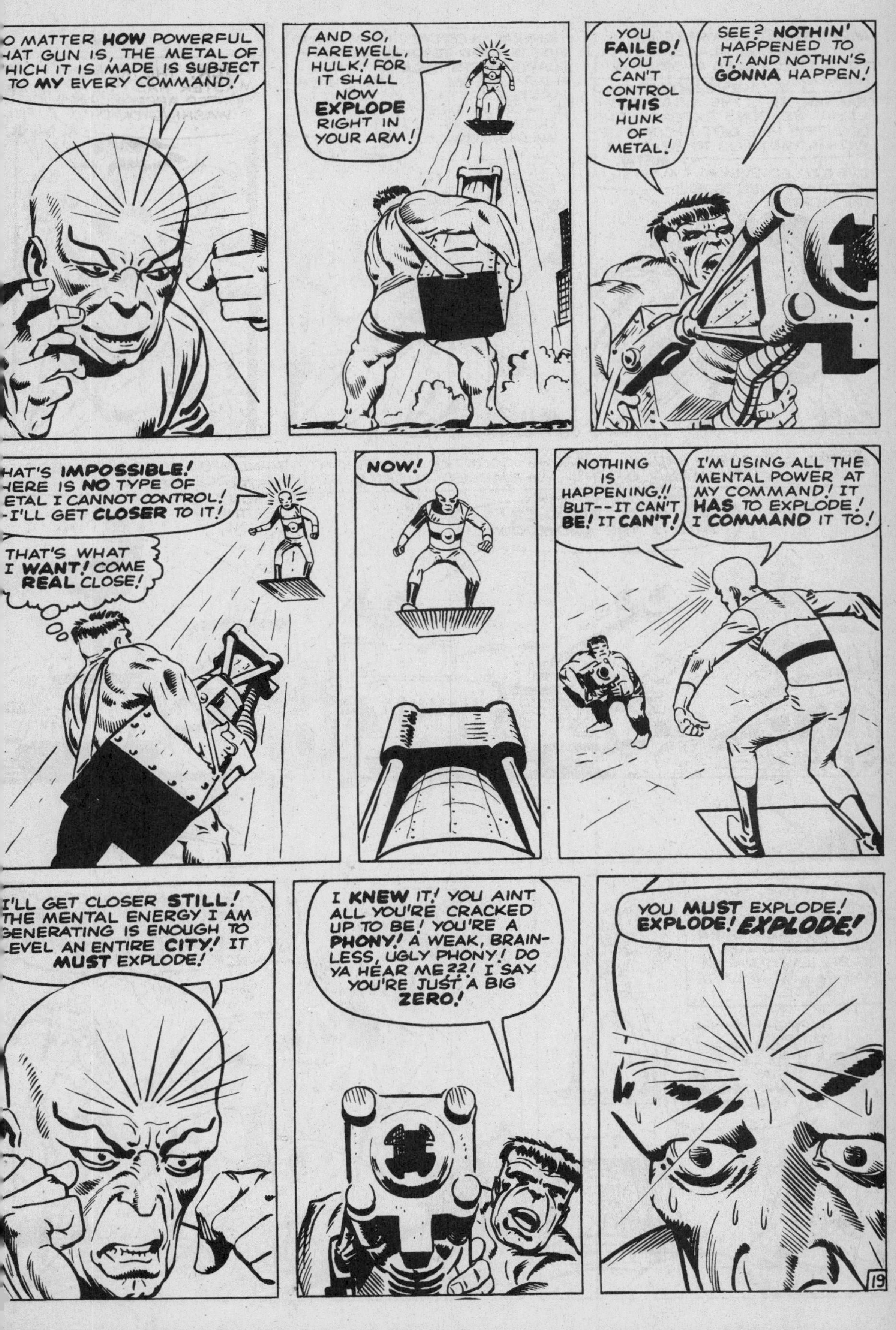
O MATTER HOW POWERFUL HAT GUN IS, THE METAL OF HICH IT IS MADE IS SUBJECT TO MY EVERY COMMAND!
AND SO, FAREWELL, HULK! FOR IT SHALL NOW EXPLODE RIGHT IN YOUR ARM!
YOU FAILED! YOU CAN'T CONTROL THIS HUNK OF METAL!
SEE? NOTHIN' HAPPENED TO IT! AND NOTHIN'S GONNA HAPPEN!
HAT'S IMPOSSIBLE! HERE IS NO TYPE OF ETAL I CANNOT CONTROL! -I'LL GET CLOSER TO IT!
THAT'S WHAT I WANT! COME REAL CLOSE!
NOW!
NOTHING IS HAPPENING!! BUT--IT CAN'T BE! IT CAN'T!
I'M USING ALL THE MENTAL POWER AT MY COMMAND! IT HAS TO EXPLODE! I COMMAND IT TO!
I'LL GET CLOSER STILL! THE MENTAL ENERGY I AM GENERATING IS ENOUGH TO LEVEL AN ENTIRE CITY! IT MUST EXPLODE!
I KNEW IT! YOU AINT ALL YOU'RE CRACKED UP TO BE! YOU'RE A PHONY! A WEAK, BRAIN-LESS, UGLY PHONY! DO YA HEAR ME?? I SAY YOU'RE JUST A BIG ZERO!
YOU MUST EXPLODE! EXPLODE! EXPLODE!
19

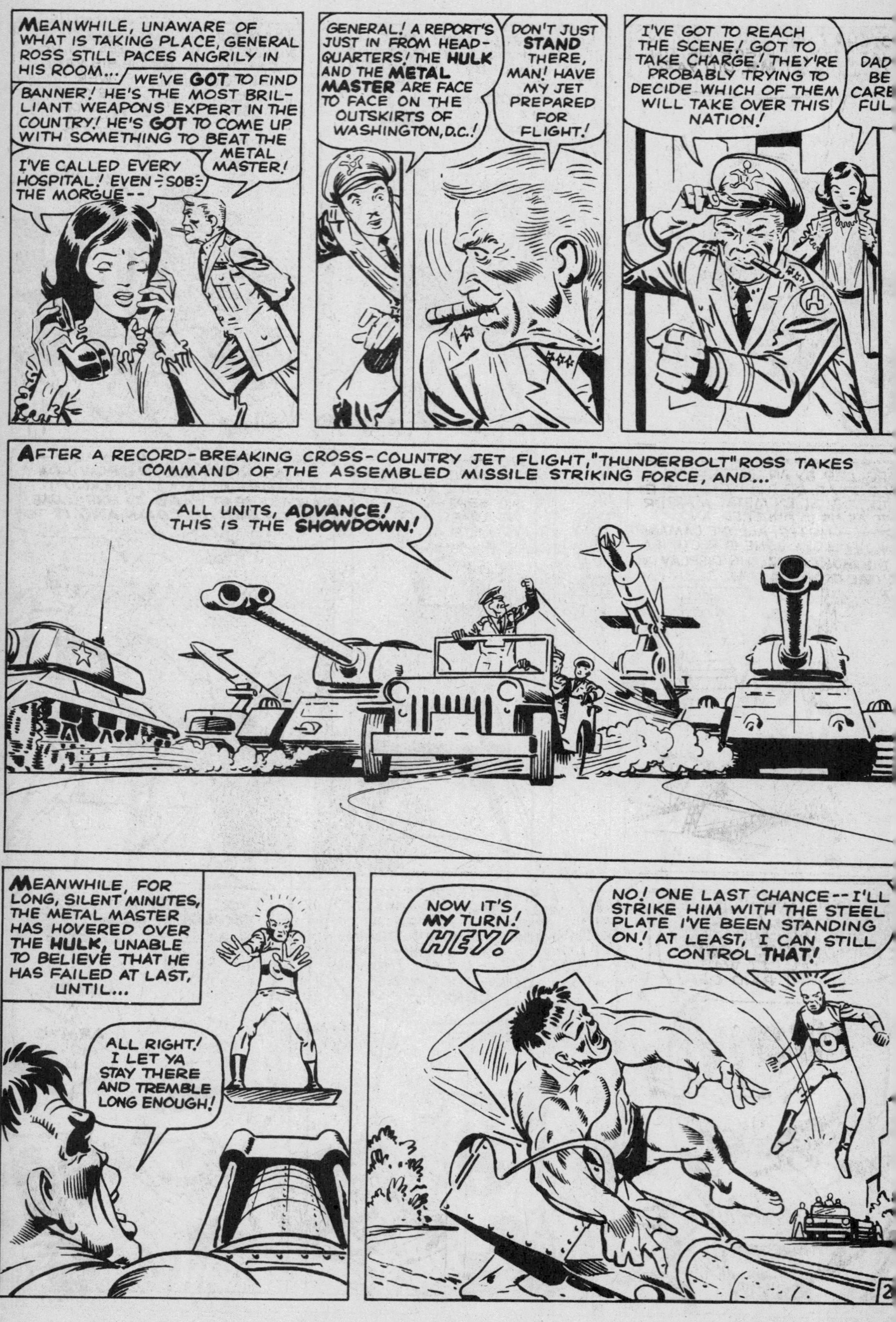

MEANWHILE, UNAWARE OF WHAT IS TAKING PLACE, GENERAL ROSS STILL PACES ANGRILY IN HIS ROOM...
WE'VE GOT TO FIND BANNER! HE'S THE MOST BRILLIANT WEAPONS EXPERT IN THE COUNTRY! HE'S GOT TO COME UP WITH SOMETHING TO BEAT THE METAL MASTER!
I'VE CALLED EVERY HOSPITAL! EVEN -SOB- THE MORGUE--
GENERAL! A REPORT'S JUST IN FROM HEADQUARTERS! THE HULK AND THE METAL MASTER ARE FACE TO FACE ON THE OUTSKIRTS OF WASHINGTON, D.C.!
DON'T JUST STAND THERE, MAN! HAVE MY JET PREPARED FOR FLIGHT!
I'VE GOT TO REACH THE SCENE! GOT TO TAKE CHARGE! THEY'RE PROBABLY TRYING TO DECIDE WHICH OF THEM WILL TAKE OVER THIS NATION!
DAD BE CAREFUL
AFTER A RECORD-BREAKING CROSS-COUNTRY JET FLIGHT, "THUNDERBOLT" ROSS TAKES COMMAND OF THE ASSEMBLED MISSILE STRIKING FORCE, AND...
ALL UNITS, ADVANCE! THIS IS THE SHOWDOWN!
MEANWHILE, FOR LONG, SILENT MINUTES, THE METAL MASTER HAS HOVERED OVER THE HULK, UNABLE TO BELIEVE THAT HE HAS FAILED AT LAST, UNTIL...
ALL RIGHT! I LET YA STAY THERE AND TREMBLE LONG ENOUGH!
NOW IT'S MY TURN! HEY!
NO! ONE LAST CHANCE--I'LL STRIKE HIM WITH THE STEEL PLATE I'VE BEEN STANDING ON! AT LEAST, I CAN STILL CONTROL THAT!

Panel 1:
OTCHA! YOU DIDN'T THINK HAT LITTLE PIECE OF TIN COULD HURT ME, DID YA??!

Panel 2:
THAT FIST! THAT ARM! DON'T! DON'T DO ANYTHING-- ANYTHING! BUT DON'T HIT ME!

ALL RIGHT, COWARD, I'LL GIVE YA A CHANCE! MAKE EVERYTHING THE WAY IT WAS BEFORE YA MESSED UP ALL THE METAL ON EARTH! AND I MEAN NOW!

Panel 3:

TREMBLINGLY, THE METAL MASTER CONCENTRATES AS HE SUMMONS UP ALL OF HIS VAST, AWESOME MENTAL POWER, SENDING BOUNDLESS WAVES OF PURE THOUGHT TO EVERY PART OF THE PLANET!

AND NO TRICKS, OR ELSE!

Panel 4:

PELLED BY AN UNCONTROLL- LE FEAR OF THE INCREDIBLE ULK, THE ALIEN METAL MASTER ES AS HE IS ORDERED, AND THIN MINUTES, ALL THE DAMAGE AT HAD BEEN DONE IS RECTIFIED, THE MOST DAZZLING DISPLAY OF ENTAL PROWESS EVER SEEN ON RTH!

Panel 5:

AND THEN, BEFORE ANYONE CAN MAKE A MOVE, THE HULK RE- LEASES THE BEATEN ALIEN, AND SILENTLY WATCHES AS THE METAL MASTER ROCKETS AWAY FROM EARTH--NEVER AGAIN TO RETURN!

HE'S GONE! WE'VE LICKED HIM! EARTH IS SAFE!

Panel 6:
YOU DID IT, HULK! YOU BEAT THE METAL MASTER! BUT--HOW? WHAT KIND OF METAL WAS THAT??

ANYBODY COULDA MADE IT! EXCEPT MOST OF YOU DUMB HUMANS ALWAYS LOSE YOUR HEADS WHEN SOMETHIN' HAPPENS!

Panel 7:

T WASN'T ANY KIND OF METAL AT ALL! JUST PLASTIC AND CARDBOARD! PAINTED IT TO LOOK LIKE METAL! IT WAS A BLUFF THAT PAID OFF!

HAH! LOOK--THE WHOLE THING'S A PHONY! IT'S ALL HOLLOW! BUT THE METAL MASTER NEVER SUSPECTED!

Panel 8:

I GUESS YOU KIDS DESERVE MOST OF THE CREDIT! IF YOU HADN'T ROUNDED UP ALL THE JUNK I NEEDED TO MAKE THAT GUN, IT WOULDA BEEN TOO LATE!

GOSH! IMAGINE THE HULK COMPLI- MENTING US! WOWEE!

HOLD ON! WE'VE GOT COMPANY COMIN'! THE ARMY'S MOVIN' IN!

21

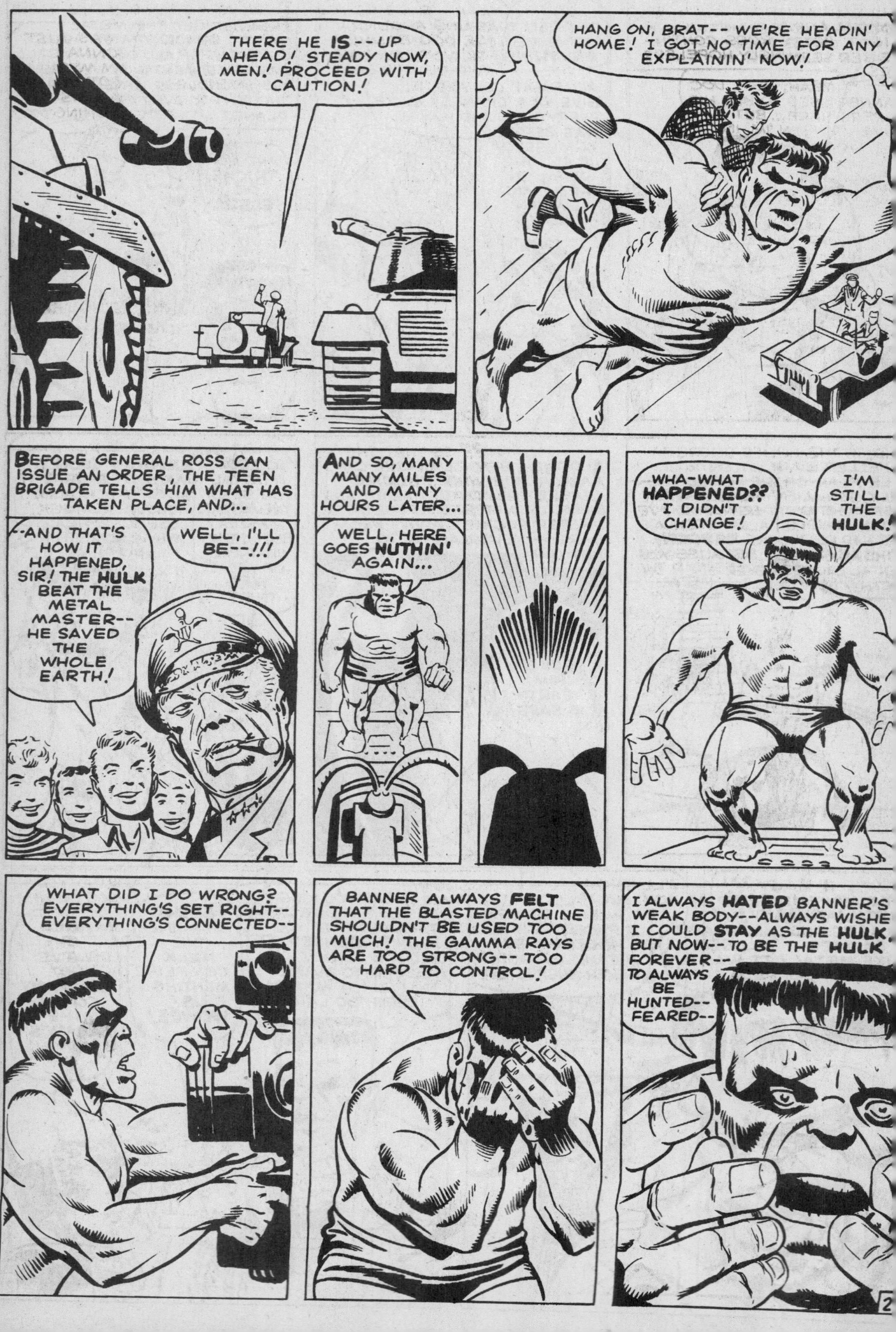

THERE HE IS--UP AHEAD! STEADY NOW, MEN! PROCEED WITH CAUTION!
HANG ON, BRAT--WE'RE HEADIN' HOME! I GOT NO TIME FOR ANY EXPLAININ' NOW!
BEFORE GENERAL ROSS CAN ISSUE AN ORDER, THE TEEN BRIGADE TELLS HIM WHAT HAS TAKEN PLACE, AND...
--AND THAT'S HOW IT HAPPENED, SIR! THE HULK BEAT THE METAL MASTER--HE SAVED THE WHOLE EARTH!
WELL, I'LL BE--!!!
AND SO, MANY MANY MILES AND MANY HOURS LATER...
WELL, HERE GOES NUTHIN' AGAIN...
WHA-WHAT HAPPENED?? I DIDN'T CHANGE!
I'M STILL THE HULK!
WHAT DID I DO WRONG? EVERYTHING'S SET RIGHT--EVERYTHING'S CONNECTED--
BANNER ALWAYS FELT THAT THE BLASTED MACHINE SHOULDN'T BE USED TOO MUCH! THE GAMMA RAYS ARE TOO STRONG--TOO HARD TO CONTROL!
I ALWAYS HATED BANNER'S WEAK BODY--ALWAYS WISHE I COULD STAY AS THE HULK. BUT NOW--TO BE THE HULK FOREVER--TO ALWAYS BE HUNTED--FEARED--
2

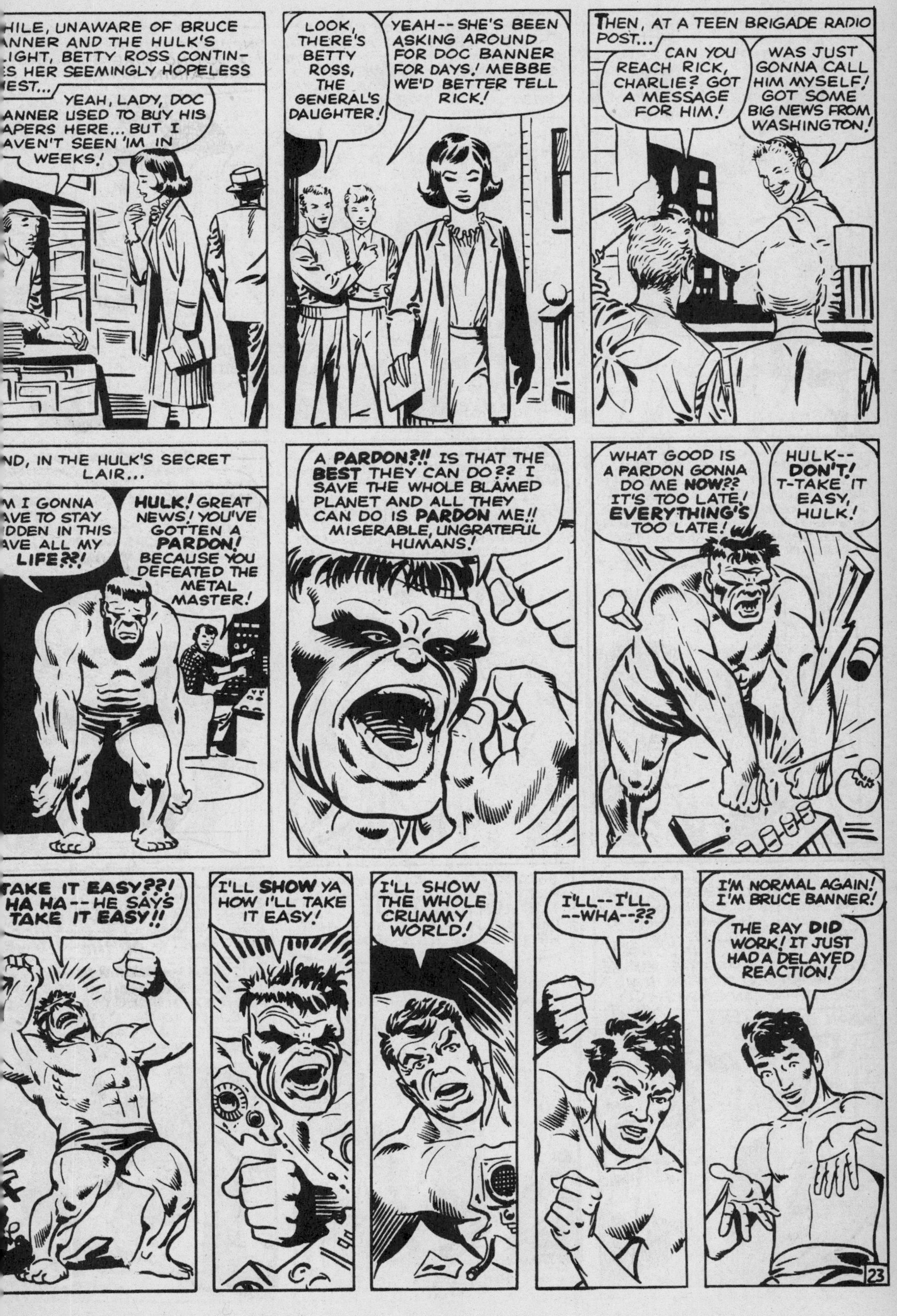

HILE, UNAWARE OF BRUCE ANNER AND THE HULK'S LIGHT, BETTY ROSS CONTIN- ES HER SEEMINGLY HOPELESS EST...
YEAH, LADY, DOC ANNER USED TO BUY HIS APERS HERE... BUT I AVEN'T SEEN 'IM IN WEEKS!
LOOK, THERE'S BETTY ROSS, THE GENERAL'S DAUGHTER!
YEAH--SHE'S BEEN ASKING AROUND FOR DOC BANNER FOR DAYS! MEBBE WE'D BETTER TELL RICK!
THEN, AT A TEEN BRIGADE RADIO POST...
CAN YOU REACH RICK, CHARLIE? GOT A MESSAGE FOR HIM!
WAS JUST GONNA CALL HIM MYSELF! GOT SOME BIG NEWS FROM WASHINGTON!
ND, IN THE HULK'S SECRET LAIR...
M I GONNA AVE TO STAY IDDEN IN THIS AVE ALL MY LIFE??!
HULK! GREAT NEWS! YOU'VE GOTTEN A PARDON! BECAUSE YOU DEFEATED THE METAL MASTER!
A PARDON?!! IS THAT THE BEST THEY CAN DO?? I SAVE THE WHOLE BLAMED PLANET AND ALL THEY CAN DO IS PARDON ME!! MISERABLE, UNGRATEFUL HUMANS!
WHAT GOOD IS A PARDON GONNA DO ME NOW?? IT'S TOO LATE! EVERYTHING'S TOO LATE!
HULK-- DON'T! T-TAKE IT EASY, HULK!
TAKE IT EASY??! HA HA--HE SAYS TAKE IT EASY!!
I'LL SHOW YA HOW I'LL TAKE IT EASY!
I'LL SHOW THE WHOLE CRUMMY WORLD!
I'LL--I'LL --WHA--??
I'M NORMAL AGAIN! I'M BRUCE BANNER!
THE RAY DID WORK! IT JUST HAD A DELAYED REACTION!

RICK, I HOPE I NEVER HAVE TO GO THRU THAT AGAIN! YOU-- YOU DON'T KNOW WHAT IT'S LIKE --THE PAIN--THE ANGUISH--

SURE, DOC, SURE-- I CAN IMAGINE! THAT'S WHAT MAKES YOU SO EDGY!

LATER, AFTER BRUCE BANNER HAS RESTED A WHILE...

BY THE WAY, DOC, I MEANT TO TELL YOU--BETTY ROSS HAS BEEN LOOKIN' FOR YOU! SHE'S REAL WORRIED ABOUT YOU BEIN' MISSIN' SO LONG!

POOR KID! I'LL GO TO SEE HER RIGHT AWAY!

AND, AT BETTY'S HOUSE...

SO THEY PARDONED THE HULK OF ALL THE LUNKHEAD DECISIONS! CAN'T THEY SEE HE'S TRICKED 'EM?? HE'S TRYIN' TO THROW US OFF-GUARD! HE'S AS DANGEROUS AS EVER!

THE DOORBELL! WHO--?

WHERE IN THUNDER HAVE YOU BEEN??! WE'VE TURNED THIS STATE UPSIDE DOWN SEARCHING FOR YOU!

SORRY, GENERAL! I-EH- WAS FEELING UNDER THE WEATHER! SO I TOOK A FEW DAYS REST IN BERMUDA!

BERMUDA! WHILE THE WHOLE WORLD TOTTERS ON THE BRINK, HE'S RESTIN' IN BERMUDA!!!

OH, BRUCE! BRUCE! THANK HEAVENS YOU'RE ALL RIGHT!

HELLO, BETTY! I'M SORRY I WORRIED YOU, DEAR!

"I'M SORRY I WORRIED YOU, DEAR!" BAH! HOW A DAUGHTER OF MINE COULD EVER FALL FOR SUCH A SPINELESS MILKSOP!

SOMETIMES I THINK SHE'D BE BETTER OFF MOONIN' OVER THE HULK! AT LEAST HE'S GOT A BACKBONE!

BRUCE, I KNOW THERE WAS MORE TO YOUR ABSENCE THAN THE FACT THAT YOU DIDN'T FEEL WELL! I-I HAVE THE STRANGEST FEELING THAT THERE IS SOME CONNECTION BETWEEN YOU AND THE HULK! WHY WON'T YOU CONFIDE IN ME? DON'T I--MEAN ENOUGH TO YOU??

MEAN ENOUGH??

I CAN'T TELL YOU ANY MORE, BETTY--BECAUSE YOU MEAN TOO MUCH TO ME! AS FOR THE HULK... LET'S HOPE THAT HE IS GONE NOW--FOREVER!

BUT ALAS, THE HOPE OF BRUCE BANNER IS NOT TO BE REALIZED! FOR THE HULK IS DESTINED TO LIVE AGAIN-- BUT THAT'S ANOTHER TALE!

THE GAMMA RAY MACHINE-- IT GROWS MORE UNPREDICTABLE EACH TIME IT'S USED! IF DOC HAS TO FACE IT AGAIN-- WHAT WILL HAPPEN NEXT TIME??!

THE END

24

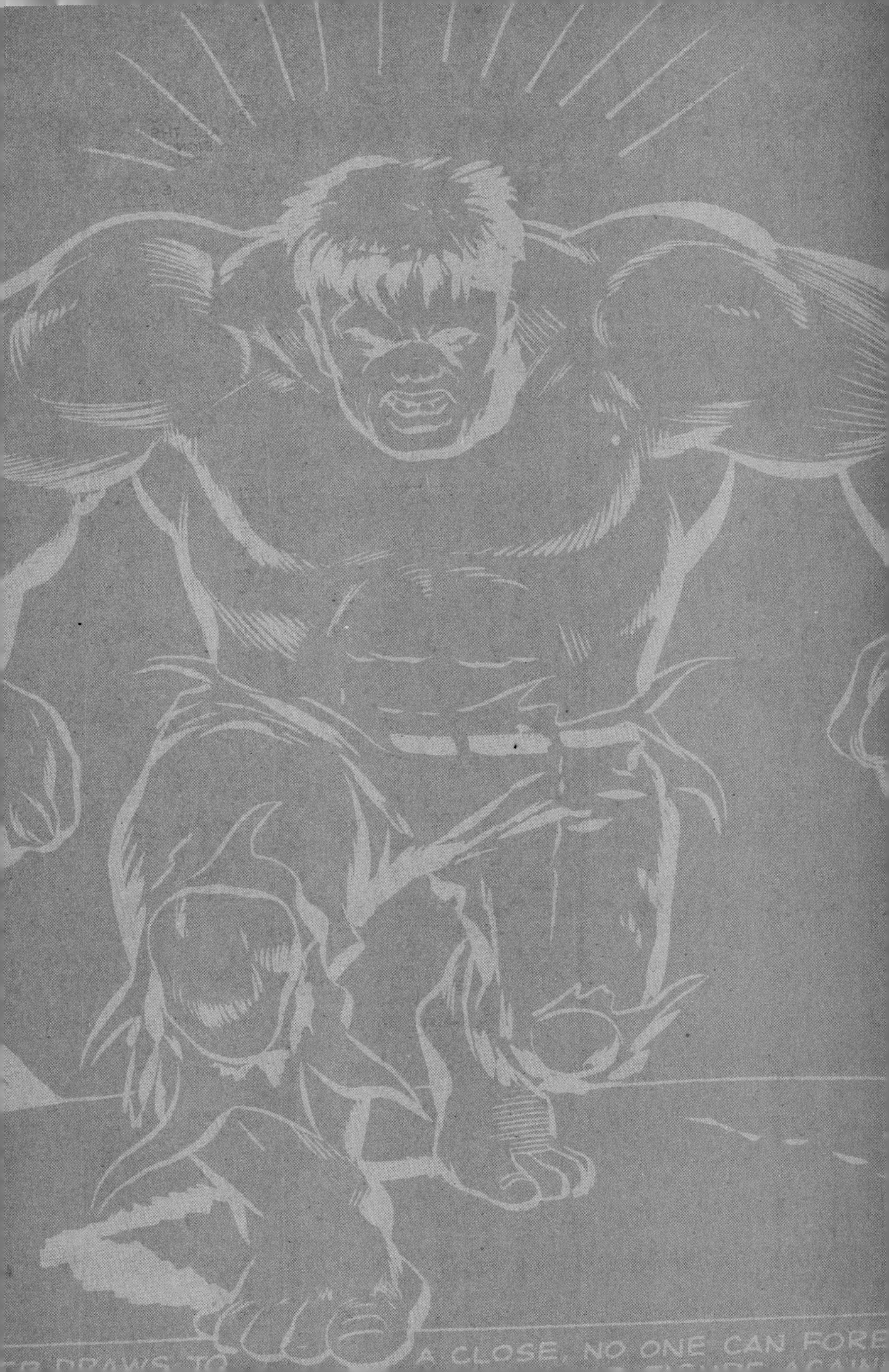
A CLOSE, NO ONE CAN FORE

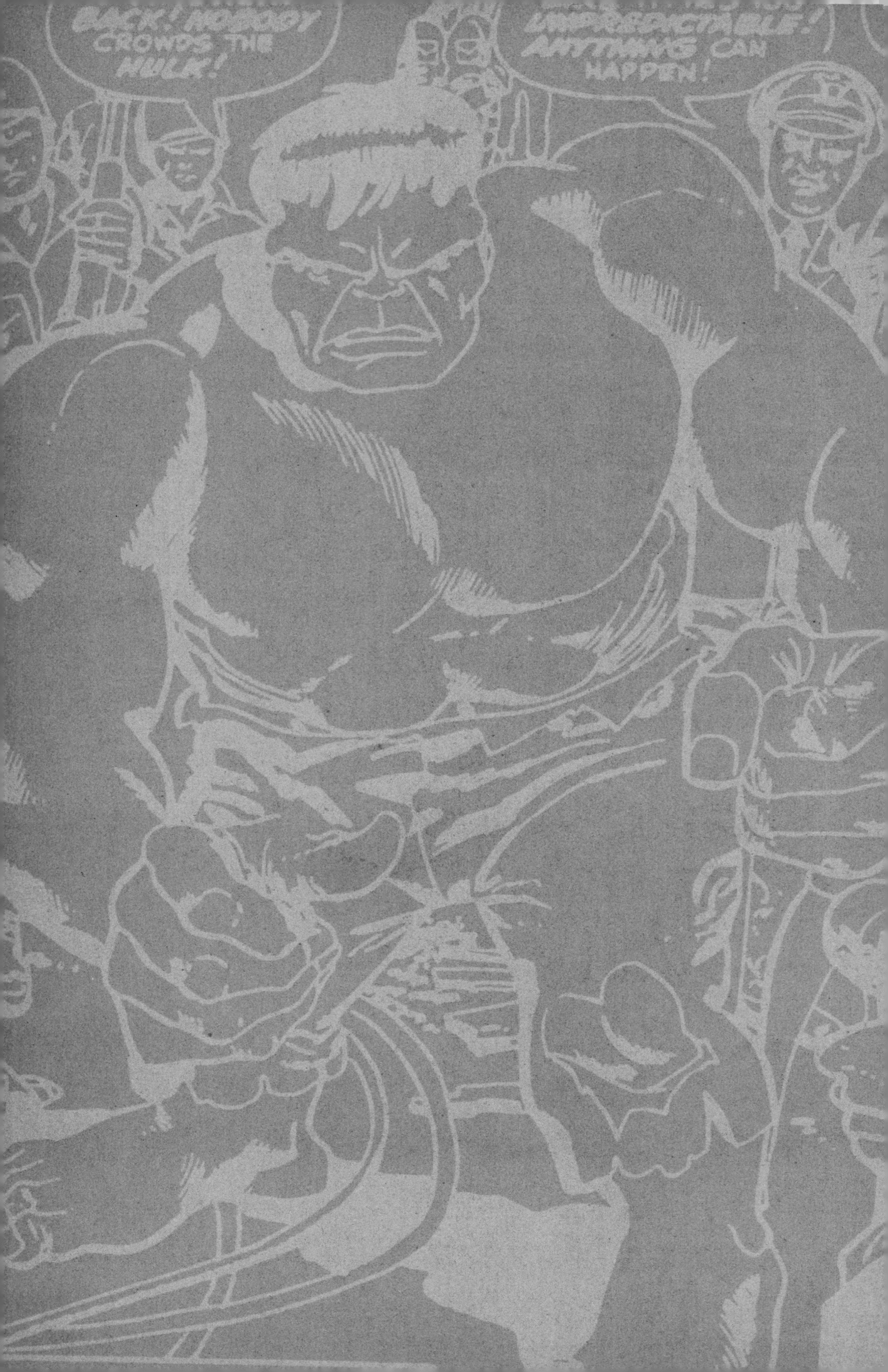
BACK! NOBODY CROWDS THE HULK!
UNPREDICTABLE! ANYTHING CAN HAPPEN!

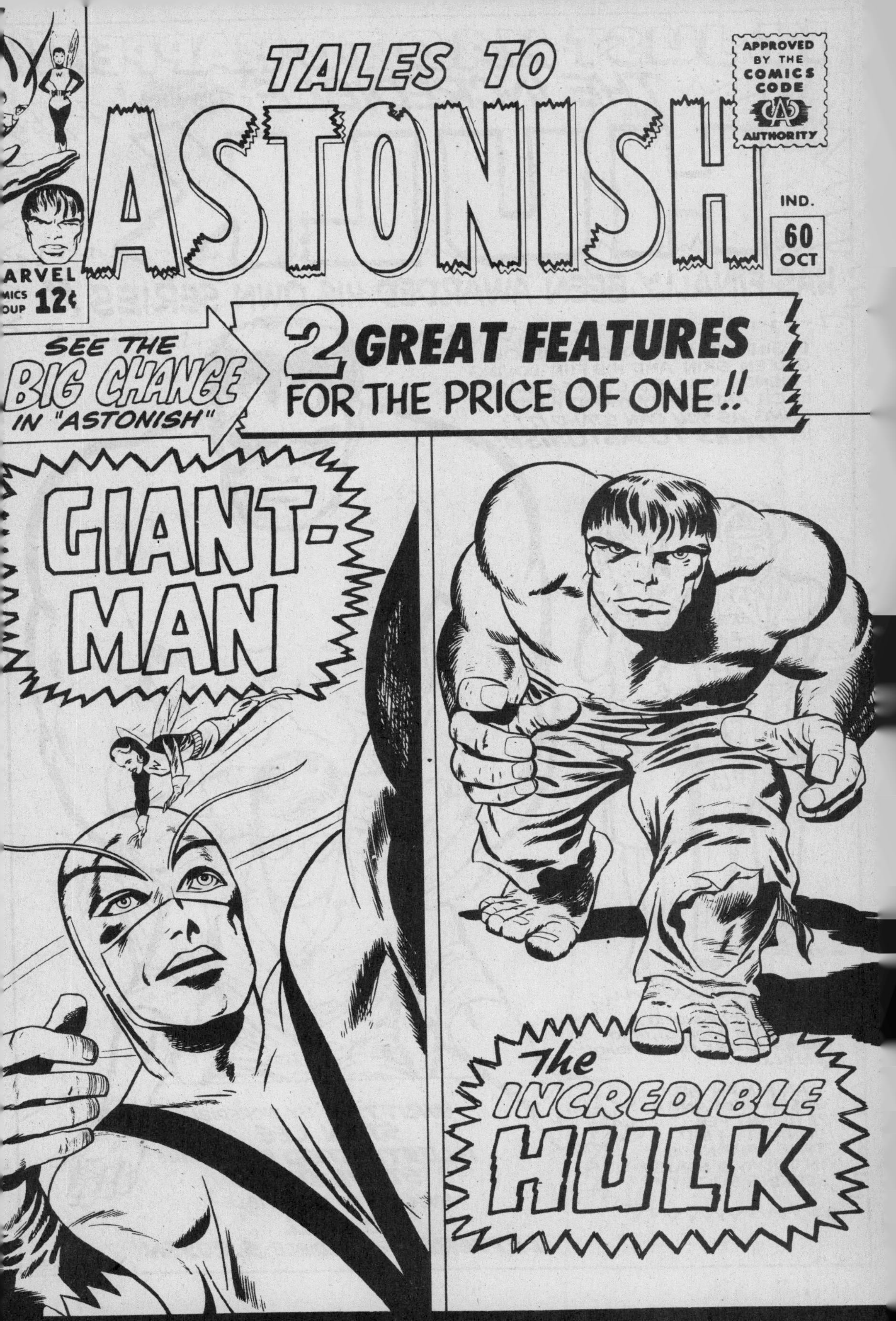

TALES TO ASTONISH
APPROVED BY THE COMICS CODE AUTHORITY
IND.
60 OCT
ARVEL MICS OUP 12¢
SEE THE BIG CHANGE IN "ASTONISH"
2 GREAT FEATURES FOR THE PRICE OF ONE!!
GIANT-MAN
The INCREDIBLE HULK

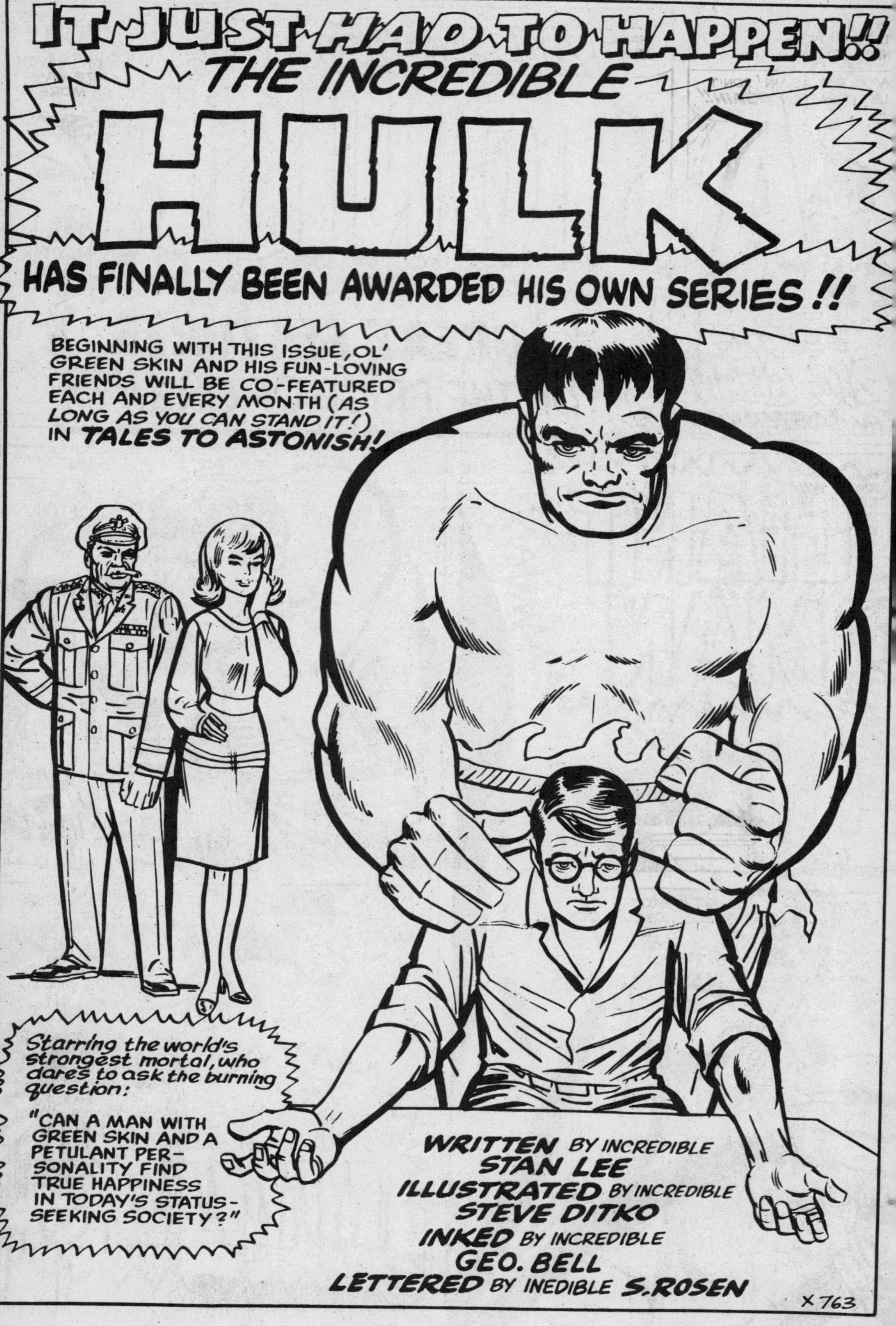
IT JUST HAD TO HAPPEN!!
THE INCREDIBLE
HULK
HAS FINALLY BEEN AWARDED HIS OWN SERIES!!
BEGINNING WITH THIS ISSUE, OL' GREEN SKIN AND HIS FUN-LOVING FRIENDS WILL BE CO-FEATURED EACH AND EVERY MONTH (AS LONG AS YOU CAN STAND IT!) IN TALES TO ASTONISH!
Starring the world's strongest mortal, who dares to ask the burning question:
"CAN A MAN WITH GREEN SKIN AND A PETULANT PERSONALITY FIND TRUE HAPPINESS IN TODAY'S STATUS-SEEKING SOCIETY?"
WRITTEN BY INCREDIBLE STAN LEE
ILLUSTRATED BY INCREDIBLE STEVE DITKO
INKED BY INCREDIBLE GEO. BELL
LETTERED BY INEDIBLE S.ROSEN
X 763

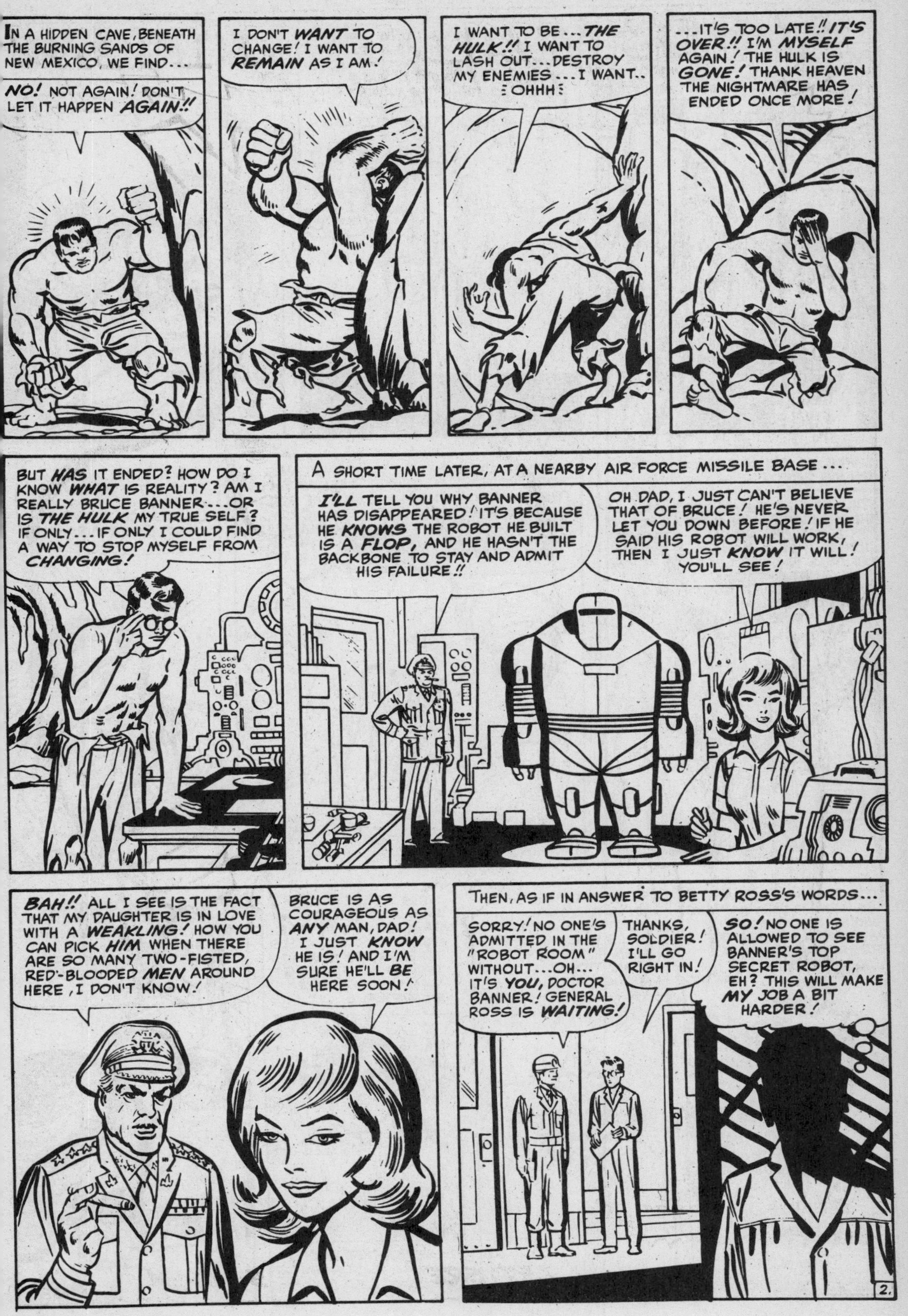

IN A HIDDEN CAVE, BENEATH THE BURNING SANDS OF NEW MEXICO, WE FIND...
NO! NOT AGAIN! DON'T LET IT HAPPEN AGAIN!!
I DON'T WANT TO CHANGE! I WANT TO REMAIN AS I AM!
I WANT TO BE... THE HULK!! I WANT TO LASH OUT... DESTROY MY ENEMIES... I WANT.. OHHH
...IT'S TOO LATE!! IT'S OVER!! I'M MYSELF AGAIN! THE HULK IS GONE! THANK HEAVEN THE NIGHTMARE HAS ENDED ONCE MORE!
BUT HAS IT ENDED? HOW DO I KNOW WHAT IS REALITY? AM I REALLY BRUCE BANNER... OR IS THE HULK MY TRUE SELF? IF ONLY... IF ONLY I COULD FIND A WAY TO STOP MYSELF FROM CHANGING!
A SHORT TIME LATER, AT A NEARBY AIR FORCE MISSILE BASE...
I'LL TELL YOU WHY BANNER HAS DISAPPEARED! IT'S BECAUSE HE KNOWS THE ROBOT HE BUILT IS A FLOP, AND HE HASN'T THE BACKBONE TO STAY AND ADMIT HIS FAILURE!!
OH DAD, I JUST CAN'T BELIEVE THAT OF BRUCE! HE'S NEVER LET YOU DOWN BEFORE! IF HE SAID HIS ROBOT WILL WORK, THEN I JUST KNOW IT WILL! YOU'LL SEE!
BAH!! ALL I SEE IS THE FACT THAT MY DAUGHTER IS IN LOVE WITH A WEAKLING! HOW YOU CAN PICK HIM WHEN THERE ARE SO MANY TWO-FISTED, RED-BLOODED MEN AROUND HERE, I DON'T KNOW!
BRUCE IS AS COURAGEOUS AS ANY MAN, DAD! I JUST KNOW HE IS! AND I'M SURE HE'LL BE HERE SOON!
THEN, AS IF IN ANSWER TO BETTY ROSS'S WORDS...
SORRY! NO ONE'S ADMITTED IN THE "ROBOT ROOM" WITHOUT... OH... IT'S YOU, DOCTOR BANNER! GENERAL ROSS IS WAITING!
THANKS, SOLDIER! I'LL GO RIGHT IN!
SO! NO ONE IS ALLOWED TO SEE BANNER'S TOP SECRET ROBOT, EH? THIS WILL MAKE MY JOB A BIT HARDER!
2.

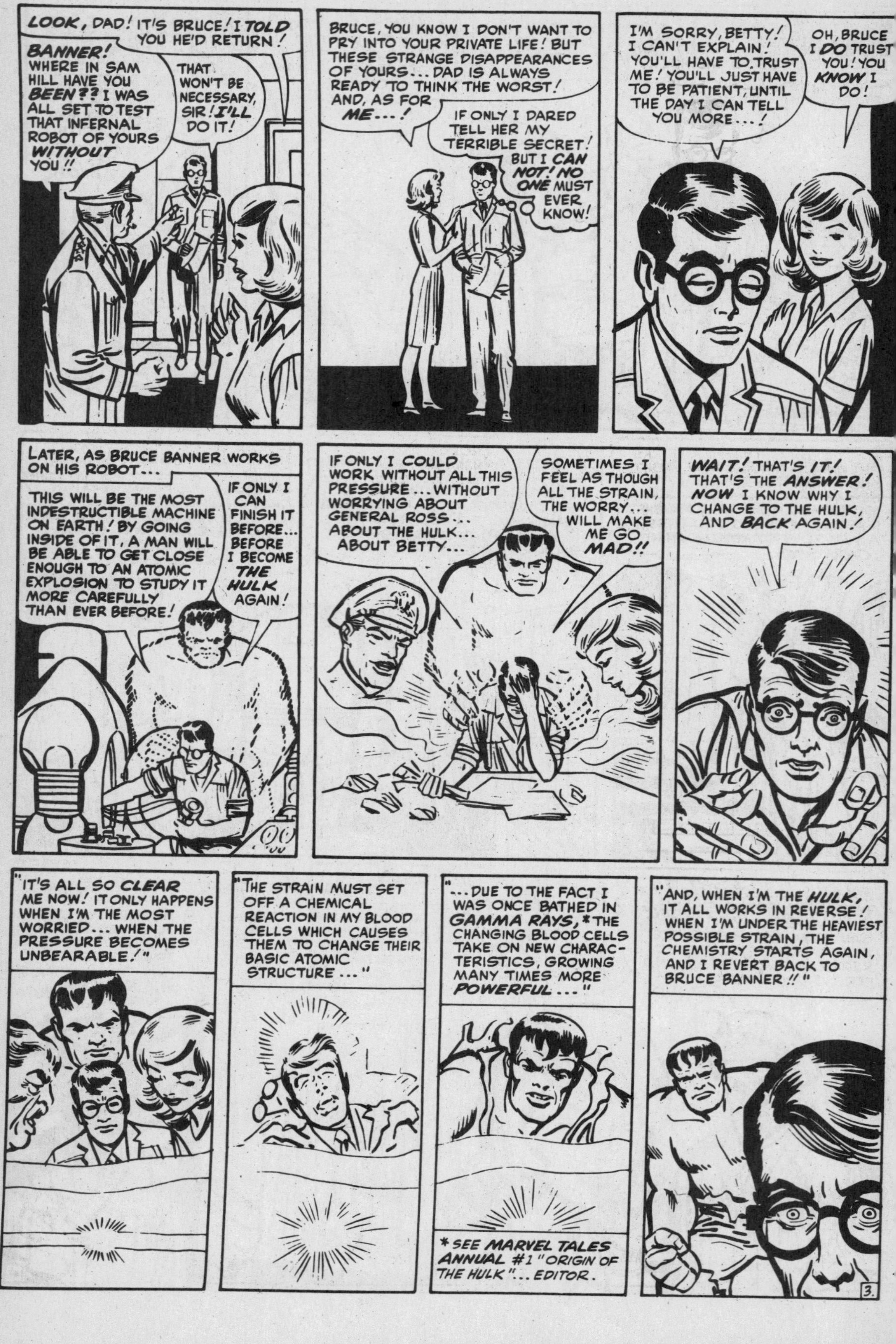
LOOK, DAD! IT'S BRUCE! I TOLD YOU HE'D RETURN!
BANNER! WHERE IN SAM HILL HAVE YOU BEEN?? I WAS ALL SET TO TEST THAT INFERNAL ROBOT OF YOURS WITHOUT YOU!!
THAT WON'T BE NECESSARY, SIR! I'LL DO IT!
BRUCE, YOU KNOW I DON'T WANT TO PRY INTO YOUR PRIVATE LIFE! BUT THESE STRANGE DISAPPEARANCES OF YOURS... DAD IS ALWAYS READY TO THINK THE WORST! AND, AS FOR ME...!
IF ONLY I DARED TELL HER MY TERRIBLE SECRET! BUT I CAN NOT! NO ONE MUST EVER KNOW!
I'M SORRY, BETTY! I CAN'T EXPLAIN! YOU'LL HAVE TO TRUST ME! YOU'LL JUST HAVE TO BE PATIENT, UNTIL THE DAY I CAN TELL YOU MORE...!
OH, BRUCE I DO TRUST YOU! YOU KNOW I DO!
LATER, AS BRUCE BANNER WORKS ON HIS ROBOT...
THIS WILL BE THE MOST INDESTRUCTIBLE MACHINE ON EARTH! BY GOING INSIDE OF IT, A MAN WILL BE ABLE TO GET CLOSE ENOUGH TO AN ATOMIC EXPLOSION TO STUDY IT MORE CAREFULLY THAN EVER BEFORE!
IF ONLY I CAN FINISH IT BEFORE... BEFORE I BECOME THE HULK AGAIN!
IF ONLY I COULD WORK WITHOUT ALL THIS PRESSURE... WITHOUT WORRYING ABOUT GENERAL ROSS... ABOUT THE HULK... ABOUT BETTY...
SOMETIMES I FEEL AS THOUGH ALL THE STRAIN, THE WORRY... WILL MAKE ME GO MAD!!
WAIT! THAT'S IT! THAT'S THE ANSWER! NOW I KNOW WHY I CHANGE TO THE HULK, AND BACK AGAIN!
"IT'S ALL SO CLEAR ME NOW! IT ONLY HAPPENS WHEN I'M THE MOST WORRIED... WHEN THE PRESSURE BECOMES UNBEARABLE!"
"THE STRAIN MUST SET OFF A CHEMICAL REACTION IN MY BLOOD CELLS WHICH CAUSES THEM TO CHANGE THEIR BASIC ATOMIC STRUCTURE..."
"...DUE TO THE FACT I WAS ONCE BATHED IN GAMMA RAYS,* THE CHANGING BLOOD CELLS TAKE ON NEW CHARACTERISTICS, GROWING MANY TIMES MORE POWERFUL..."
* SEE MARVEL TALES ANNUAL #1 "ORIGIN OF THE HULK"... EDITOR.
"AND, WHEN I'M THE HULK, IT ALL WORKS IN REVERSE! WHEN I'M UNDER THE HEAVIEST POSSIBLE STRAIN, THE CHEMISTRY STARTS AGAIN, AND I REVERT BACK TO BRUCE BANNER!!"
3.

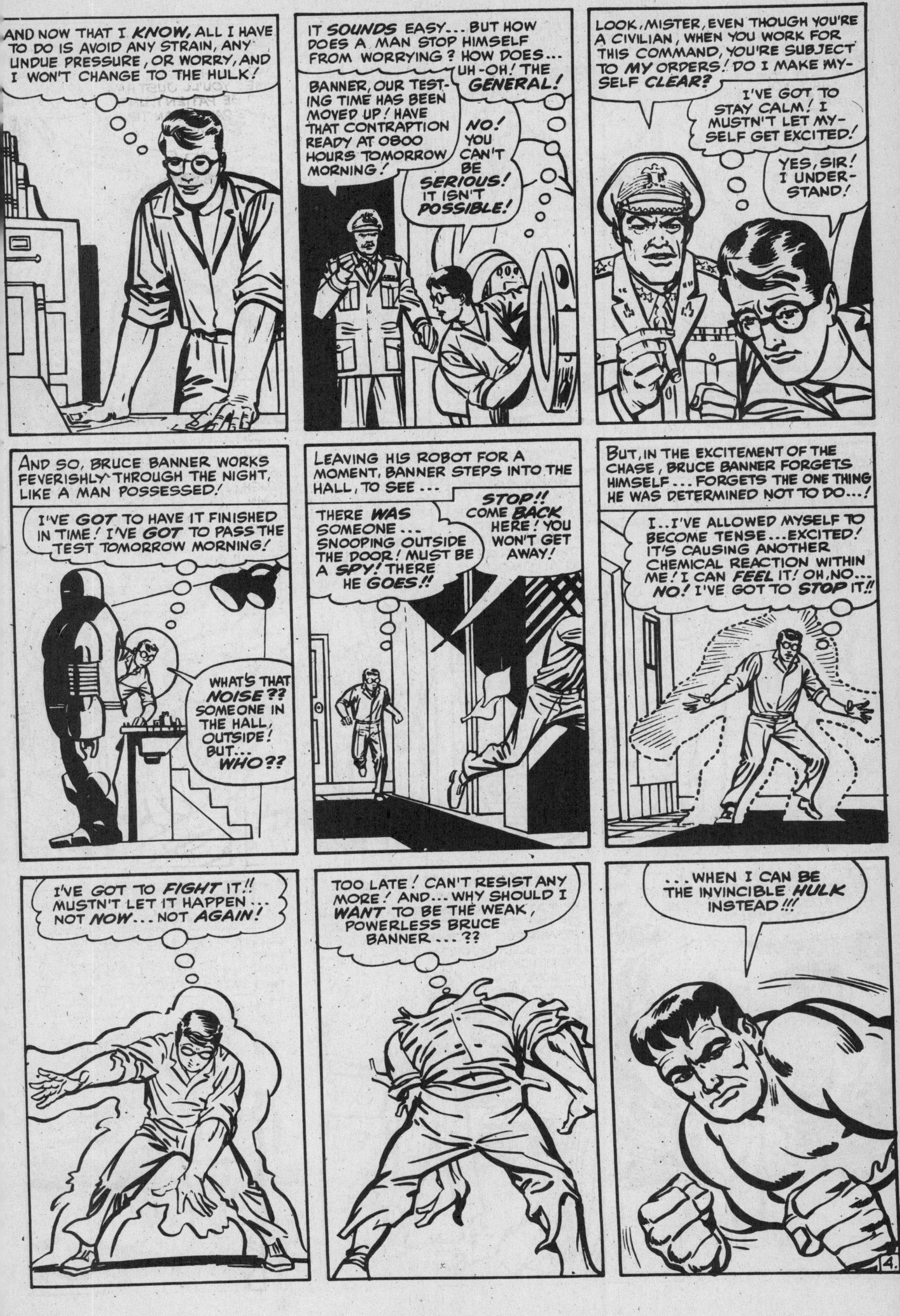
AND NOW THAT I KNOW, ALL I HAVE TO DO IS AVOID ANY STRAIN, ANY UNDUE PRESSURE, OR WORRY, AND I WON'T CHANGE TO THE HULK!
IT SOUNDS EASY... BUT HOW DOES A MAN STOP HIMSELF FROM WORRYING? HOW DOES... UH-OH! THE GENERAL!
BANNER, OUR TESTING TIME HAS BEEN MOVED UP! HAVE THAT CONTRAPTION READY AT 0800 HOURS TOMORROW MORNING!
NO! YOU CAN'T BE SERIOUS! IT ISN'T POSSIBLE!
LOOK, MISTER, EVEN THOUGH YOU'RE A CIVILIAN, WHEN YOU WORK FOR THIS COMMAND, YOU'RE SUBJECT TO MY ORDERS! DO I MAKE MYSELF CLEAR?
I'VE GOT TO STAY CALM! I MUSTN'T LET MYSELF GET EXCITED!
YES, SIR! I UNDERSTAND!
AND SO, BRUCE BANNER WORKS FEVERISHLY THROUGH THE NIGHT, LIKE A MAN POSSESSED!
I'VE GOT TO HAVE IT FINISHED IN TIME! I'VE GOT TO PASS THE TEST TOMORROW MORNING!
WHAT'S THAT NOISE?? SOMEONE IN THE HALL, OUTSIDE! BUT... WHO??
LEAVING HIS ROBOT FOR A MOMENT, BANNER STEPS INTO THE HALL, TO SEE...
THERE WAS SOMEONE... SNOOPING OUTSIDE THE DOOR! MUST BE A SPY! THERE HE GOES!!
STOP!! COME BACK HERE! YOU WON'T GET AWAY!
BUT, IN THE EXCITEMENT OF THE CHASE, BRUCE BANNER FORGETS HIMSELF... FORGETS THE ONE THING HE WAS DETERMINED NOT TO DO...!
I..I'VE ALLOWED MYSELF TO BECOME TENSE... EXCITED! IT'S CAUSING ANOTHER CHEMICAL REACTION WITHIN ME! I CAN FEEL IT! OH, NO... NO! I'VE GOT TO STOP IT!!
I'VE GOT TO FIGHT IT!! MUSTN'T LET IT HAPPEN... NOT NOW... NOT AGAIN!
TOO LATE! CAN'T RESIST ANY MORE! AND... WHY SHOULD I WANT TO BE THE WEAK, POWERLESS BRUCE BANNER...??
...WHEN I CAN BE THE INVINCIBLE HULK INSTEAD!!!
4

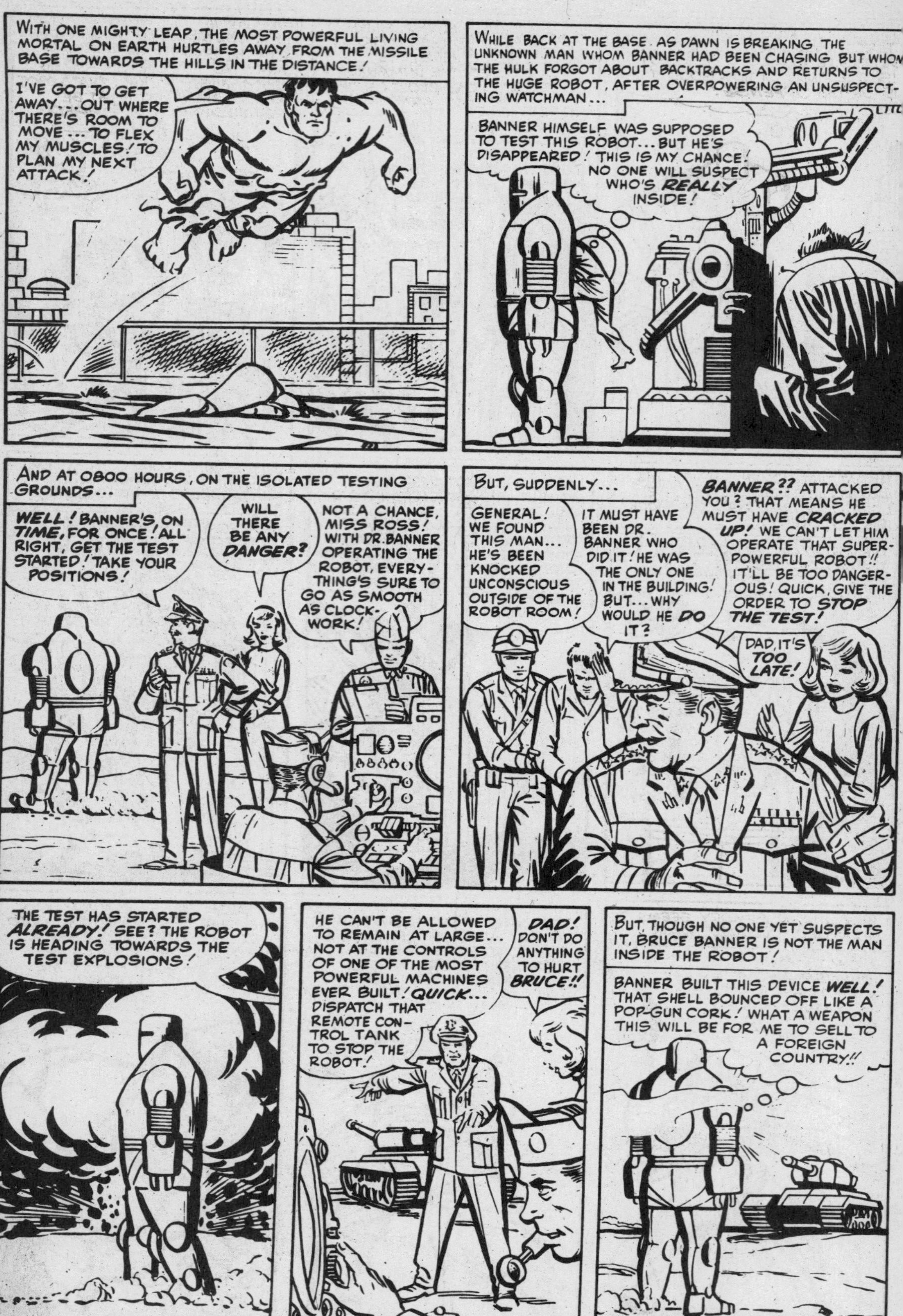
WITH ONE MIGHTY LEAP, THE MOST POWERFUL LIVING MORTAL ON EARTH HURTLES AWAY FROM THE MISSILE BASE TOWARDS THE HILLS IN THE DISTANCE!
I'VE GOT TO GET AWAY...OUT WHERE THERE'S ROOM TO MOVE...TO FLEX MY MUSCLES! TO PLAN MY NEXT ATTACK!
WHILE BACK AT THE BASE AS DAWN IS BREAKING THE UNKNOWN MAN WHOM BANNER HAD BEEN CHASING BUT WHOM THE HULK FORGOT ABOUT BACKTRACKS AND RETURNS TO THE HUGE ROBOT, AFTER OVERPOWERING AN UNSUSPECTING WATCHMAN...
BANNER HIMSELF WAS SUPPOSED TO TEST THIS ROBOT... BUT HE'S DISAPPEARED! THIS IS MY CHANCE! NO ONE WILL SUSPECT WHO'S REALLY INSIDE!
AND AT 0800 HOURS, ON THE ISOLATED TESTING GROUNDS...
WELL! BANNER'S ON TIME, FOR ONCE! ALL RIGHT, GET THE TEST STARTED! TAKE YOUR POSITIONS!
WILL THERE BE ANY DANGER?
NOT A CHANCE, MISS ROSS! WITH DR. BANNER OPERATING THE ROBOT, EVERYTHING'S SURE TO GO AS SMOOTH AS CLOCKWORK!
BUT, SUDDENLY...
GENERAL! WE FOUND THIS MAN... HE'S BEEN KNOCKED UNCONSCIOUS OUTSIDE OF THE ROBOT ROOM!
IT MUST HAVE BEEN DR. BANNER WHO DID IT! HE WAS THE ONLY ONE IN THE BUILDING! BUT... WHY WOULD HE DO IT?
BANNER?? ATTACKED YOU? THAT MEANS HE MUST HAVE CRACKED UP! WE CAN'T LET HIM OPERATE THAT SUPER-POWERFUL ROBOT!! IT'LL BE TOO DANGEROUS! QUICK, GIVE THE ORDER TO STOP THE TEST!
DAD, IT'S TOO LATE!
THE TEST HAS STARTED ALREADY! SEE? THE ROBOT IS HEADING TOWARDS THE TEST EXPLOSIONS!
HE CAN'T BE ALLOWED TO REMAIN AT LARGE... NOT AT THE CONTROLS OF ONE OF THE MOST POWERFUL MACHINES EVER BUILT! QUICK... DISPATCH THAT REMOTE CONTROL TANK TO STOP THE ROBOT!
DAD! DON'T DO ANYTHING TO HURT BRUCE!!
BUT, THOUGH NO ONE YET SUSPECTS IT, BRUCE BANNER IS NOT THE MAN INSIDE THE ROBOT!
BANNER BUILT THIS DEVICE WELL! THAT SHELL BOUNCED OFF LIKE A POP-GUN CORK! WHAT A WEAPON THIS WILL BE FOR ME TO SELL TO A FOREIGN COUNTRY!!
5.

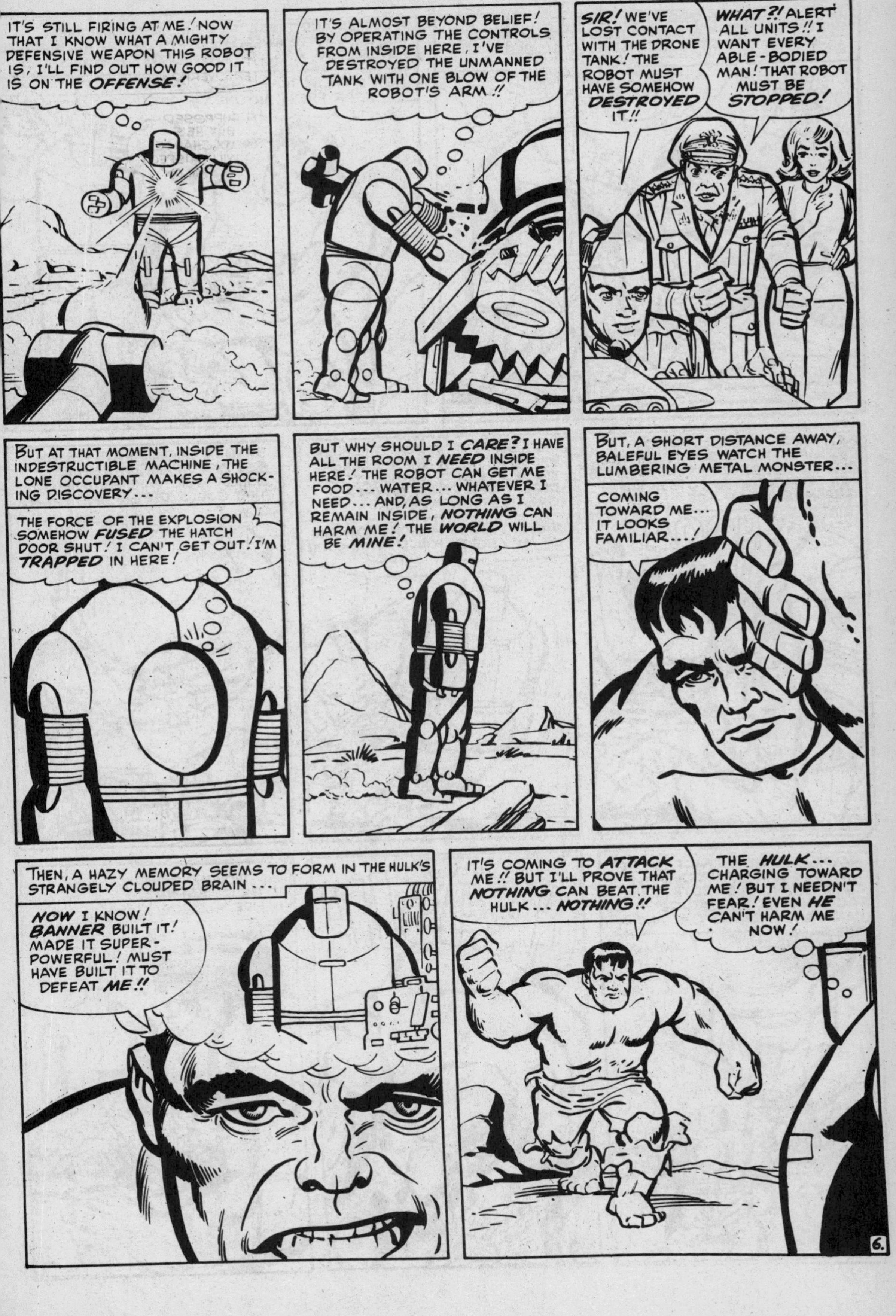
IT'S STILL FIRING AT ME! NOW THAT I KNOW WHAT A MIGHTY DEFENSIVE WEAPON THIS ROBOT IS, I'LL FIND OUT HOW GOOD IT IS ON THE OFFENSE!
IT'S ALMOST BEYOND BELIEF! BY OPERATING THE CONTROLS FROM INSIDE HERE, I'VE DESTROYED THE UNMANNED TANK WITH ONE BLOW OF THE ROBOT'S ARM!!
SIR! WE'VE LOST CONTACT WITH THE DRONE TANK! THE ROBOT MUST HAVE SOMEHOW DESTROYED IT!!
WHAT?! ALERT ALL UNITS!! I WANT EVERY ABLE-BODIED MAN! THAT ROBOT MUST BE STOPPED!
BUT AT THAT MOMENT, INSIDE THE INDESTRUCTIBLE MACHINE, THE LONE OCCUPANT MAKES A SHOCKING DISCOVERY...
THE FORCE OF THE EXPLOSION SOMEHOW FUSED THE HATCH DOOR SHUT! I CAN'T GET OUT! I'M TRAPPED IN HERE!
BUT WHY SHOULD I CARE? I HAVE ALL THE ROOM I NEED INSIDE HERE! THE ROBOT CAN GET ME FOOD... WATER... WHATEVER I NEED... AND, AS LONG AS I REMAIN INSIDE, NOTHING CAN HARM ME! THE WORLD WILL BE MINE!
BUT, A SHORT DISTANCE AWAY, BALEFUL EYES WATCH THE LUMBERING METAL MONSTER...
COMING TOWARD ME... IT LOOKS FAMILIAR...!
THEN, A HAZY MEMORY SEEMS TO FORM IN THE HULK'S STRANGELY CLOUDED BRAIN...
NOW I KNOW! BANNER BUILT IT! MADE IT SUPER-POWERFUL! MUST HAVE BUILT IT TO DEFEAT ME!!
IT'S COMING TO ATTACK ME!! BUT I'LL PROVE THAT NOTHING CAN BEAT THE HULK... NOTHING!!
THE HULK... CHARGING TOWARD ME! BUT I NEEDN'T FEAR! EVEN HE CAN'T HARM ME NOW!

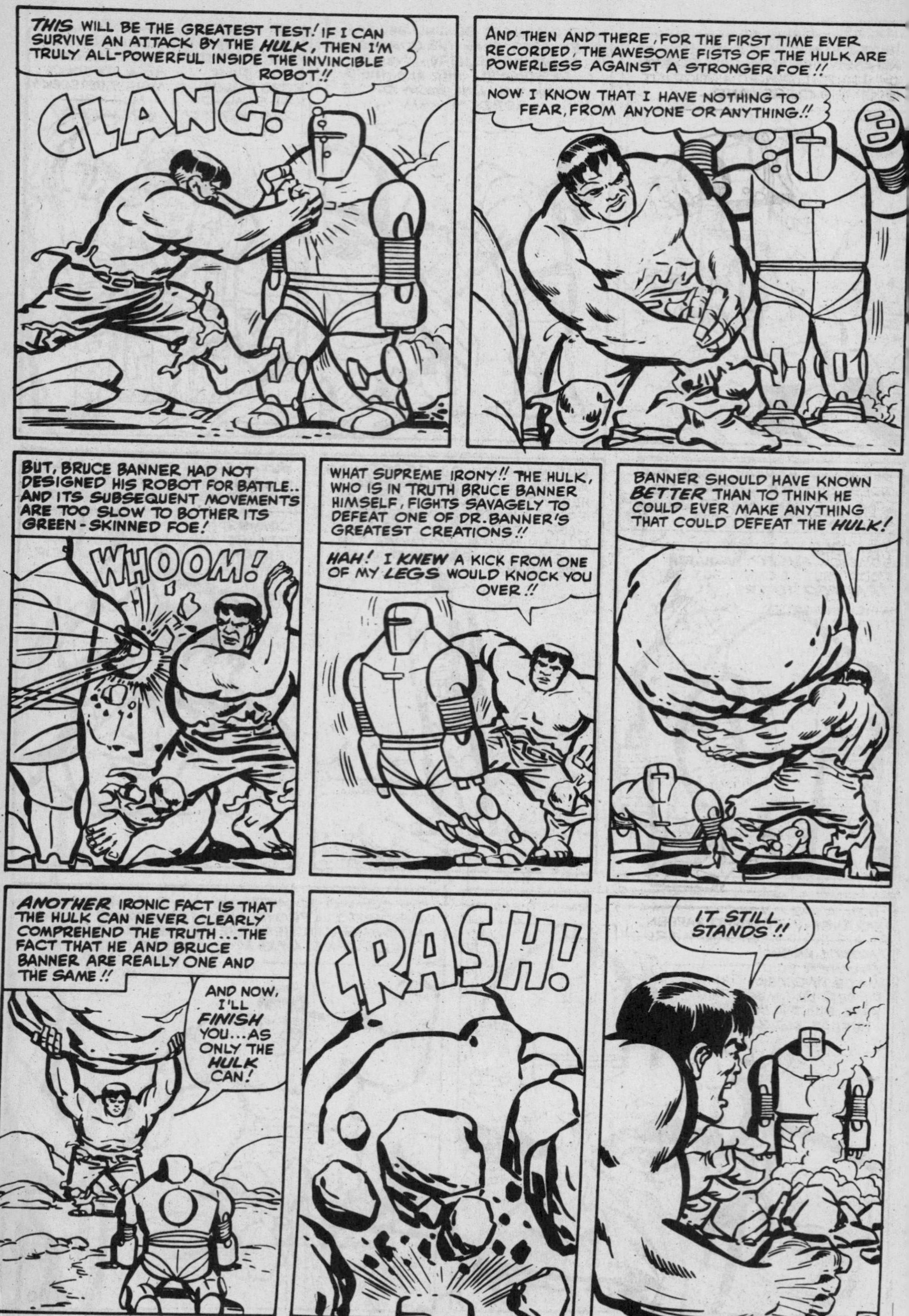
THIS WILL BE THE GREATEST TEST! IF I CAN SURVIVE AN ATTACK BY THE HULK, THEN I'M TRULY ALL-POWERFUL INSIDE THE INVINCIBLE ROBOT!!
CLANG!
AND THEN AND THERE, FOR THE FIRST TIME EVER RECORDED, THE AWESOME FISTS OF THE HULK ARE POWERLESS AGAINST A STRONGER FOE!!
NOW I KNOW THAT I HAVE NOTHING TO FEAR, FROM ANYONE OR ANYTHING!!
BUT, BRUCE BANNER HAD NOT DESIGNED HIS ROBOT FOR BATTLE.. AND ITS SUBSEQUENT MOVEMENTS ARE TOO SLOW TO BOTHER ITS GREEN-SKINNED FOE!
WHOOM!
WHAT SUPREME IRONY!! THE HULK, WHO IS IN TRUTH BRUCE BANNER HIMSELF, FIGHTS SAVAGELY TO DEFEAT ONE OF DR. BANNER'S GREATEST CREATIONS!!
HAH! I KNEW A KICK FROM ONE OF MY LEGS WOULD KNOCK YOU OVER!!
BANNER SHOULD HAVE KNOWN BETTER THAN TO THINK HE COULD EVER MAKE ANYTHING THAT COULD DEFEAT THE HULK!
ANOTHER IRONIC FACT IS THAT THE HULK CAN NEVER CLEARLY COMPREHEND THE TRUTH... THE FACT THAT HE AND BRUCE BANNER ARE REALLY ONE AND THE SAME!!
AND NOW, I'LL FINISH YOU... AS ONLY THE HULK CAN!
CRASH!
IT STILL STANDS!!
7.

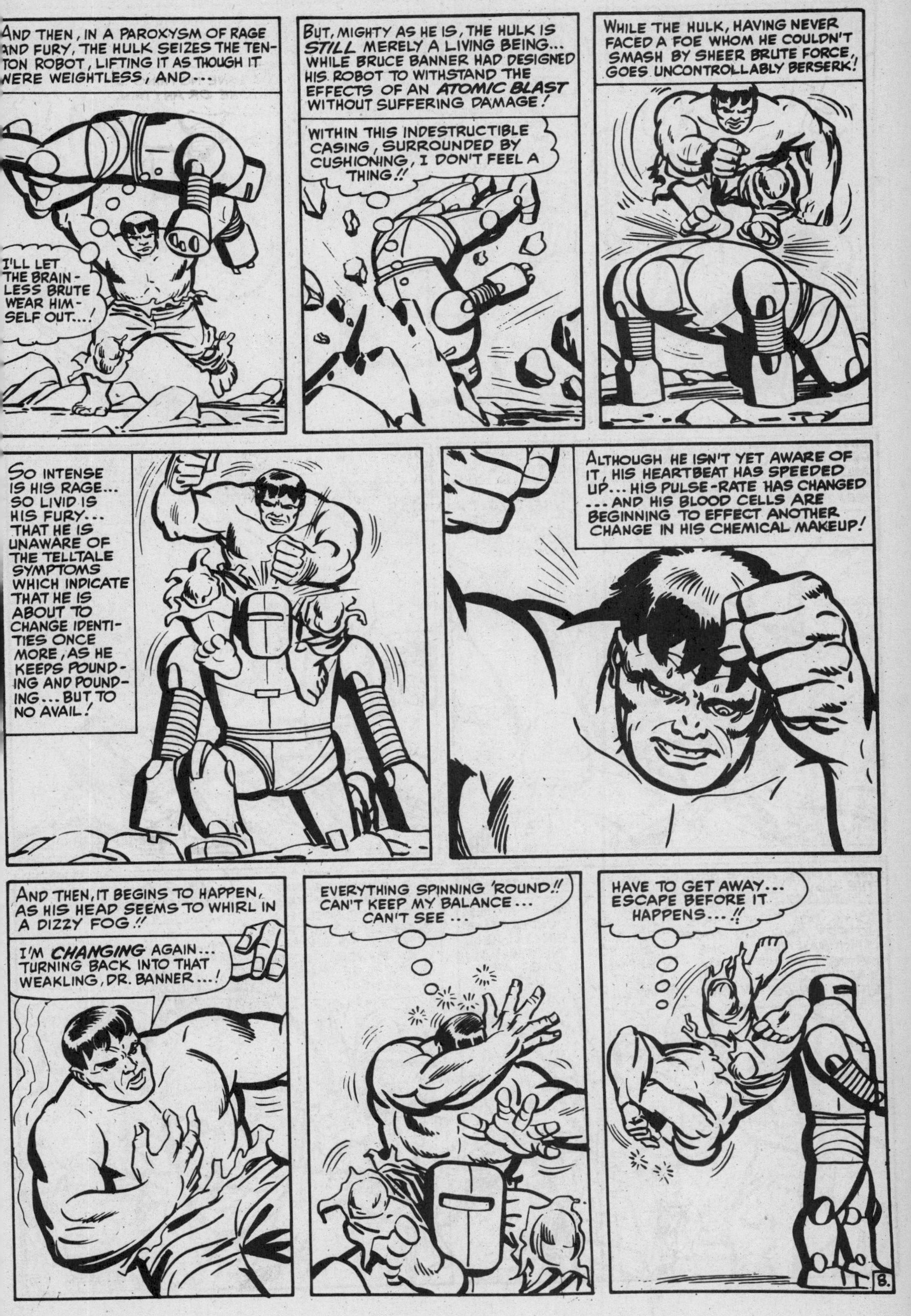
AND THEN, IN A PAROXYSM OF RAGE AND FURY, THE HULK SEIZES THE TEN-TON ROBOT, LIFTING IT AS THOUGH IT WERE WEIGHTLESS, AND...
I'LL LET THE BRAIN-LESS BRUTE WEAR HIM-SELF OUT...!
BUT, MIGHTY AS HE IS, THE HULK IS STILL MERELY A LIVING BEING... WHILE BRUCE BANNER HAD DESIGNED HIS ROBOT TO WITHSTAND THE EFFECTS OF AN ATOMIC BLAST WITHOUT SUFFERING DAMAGE!
WITHIN THIS INDESTRUCTIBLE CASING, SURROUNDED BY CUSHIONING, I DON'T FEEL A THING!!
WHILE THE HULK, HAVING NEVER FACED A FOE WHOM HE COULDN'T SMASH BY SHEER BRUTE FORCE, GOES UNCONTROLLABLY BERSERK!
SO INTENSE IS HIS RAGE... SO LIVID IS HIS FURY... THAT HE IS UNAWARE OF THE TELLTALE SYMPTOMS WHICH INDICATE THAT HE IS ABOUT TO CHANGE IDENTI-TIES ONCE MORE, AS HE KEEPS POUND-ING AND POUND-ING... BUT, TO NO AVAIL!
ALTHOUGH HE ISN'T YET AWARE OF IT, HIS HEARTBEAT HAS SPEEDED UP... HIS PULSE-RATE HAS CHANGED ... AND HIS BLOOD CELLS ARE BEGINNING TO EFFECT ANOTHER CHANGE IN HIS CHEMICAL MAKEUP!
AND THEN, IT BEGINS TO HAPPEN, AS HIS HEAD SEEMS TO WHIRL IN A DIZZY FOG!!
I'M CHANGING AGAIN... TURNING BACK INTO THAT WEAKLING, DR. BANNER...!
EVERYTHING SPINNING 'ROUND!! CAN'T KEEP MY BALANCE... CAN'T SEE...
HAVE TO GET AWAY... ESCAPE BEFORE IT HAPPENS...!!
8.

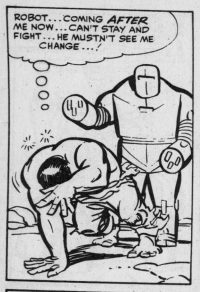

ROBOT...COMING *AFTER* ME NOW...CAN'T STAY AND FIGHT...HE MUSTN'T SEE ME CHANGE...!

NOW IT'S *MY* TURN, HULK! YOU'VE WORN YOURSELF *OUT!* YOU WON'T BE ABLE TO DODGE MY BLOWS!!

STILL A FEW SECONDS BEFORE THE CHANGE HAPPENS!! I'VE GOT TO ROLL AWAY NOW...DOWN THE HILL...BEFORE HE GRABS ME!

MADE IT!!

I'VE *BEATEN* YOU! NOW I NEED FEAR NOTHING THAT LIVES!

NOT LONG AFTERWARDS, A DETAIL OF SEARCHING TROOPS MAKES AN IMPORTANT DISCOVERY...

IT'S *DOCTOR BANNER!!* HE'S STILL ALIVE!!

BETTER CALL THE *GENERAL!* HE'LL WANT TO KNOW WE'VE *FOUND* HIM!

AND, A FEW MINUTES LATER...

SO *THERE* YOU ARE! WHAT HAPPENED TO THE *ROBOT?* WHERE IS IT??

BRUCE! ARE YOU *HURT??* ARE YOU ALL RIGHT?

I-I'M ALL RIGHT! BUT...I DON'T KNOW *WHERE* THE ROBOT IS! I WASN'T *IN* IT!!

THEN, AFTER BRUCE BANNER HAS EXPLAINED ABOUT THE *SPY...*

DON'T *LIE* TO ME, BOY!! THERE WAS NO SPY, AND YOU *KNOW* IT! IT WAS *YOU* ALONE INSIDE THAT INFERNAL MACHINE! NOW WHERE DID YOU *HIDE* IT? TALK!!

DAD!! PLEASE DON'T! CAN'T YOU SEE HE ISN'T *WELL?!*

WHAT?!! YES, I UNDERSTAND, SIR! I'LL TELL THE GENERAL! OVER AND OUT!

SIR, IT SEEMS BANNER IS TELLING THE *TRUTH!* THE ROBOT HAS BEEN SIGHTED IN THE DESERT! IT'S MOVING UNDER ITS OWN POWER, SO SOMEBODY ELSE *MUST* BE INSIDE!

WELL, DON'T JUST *STAND* THERE! ORDER A *PURSUIT...*ON THE DOUBLE!

OH, BRUCE, ISN'T THAT *WONDERFUL!* YOU'RE IN THE CLEAR!

AM I? I WONDER!

9.

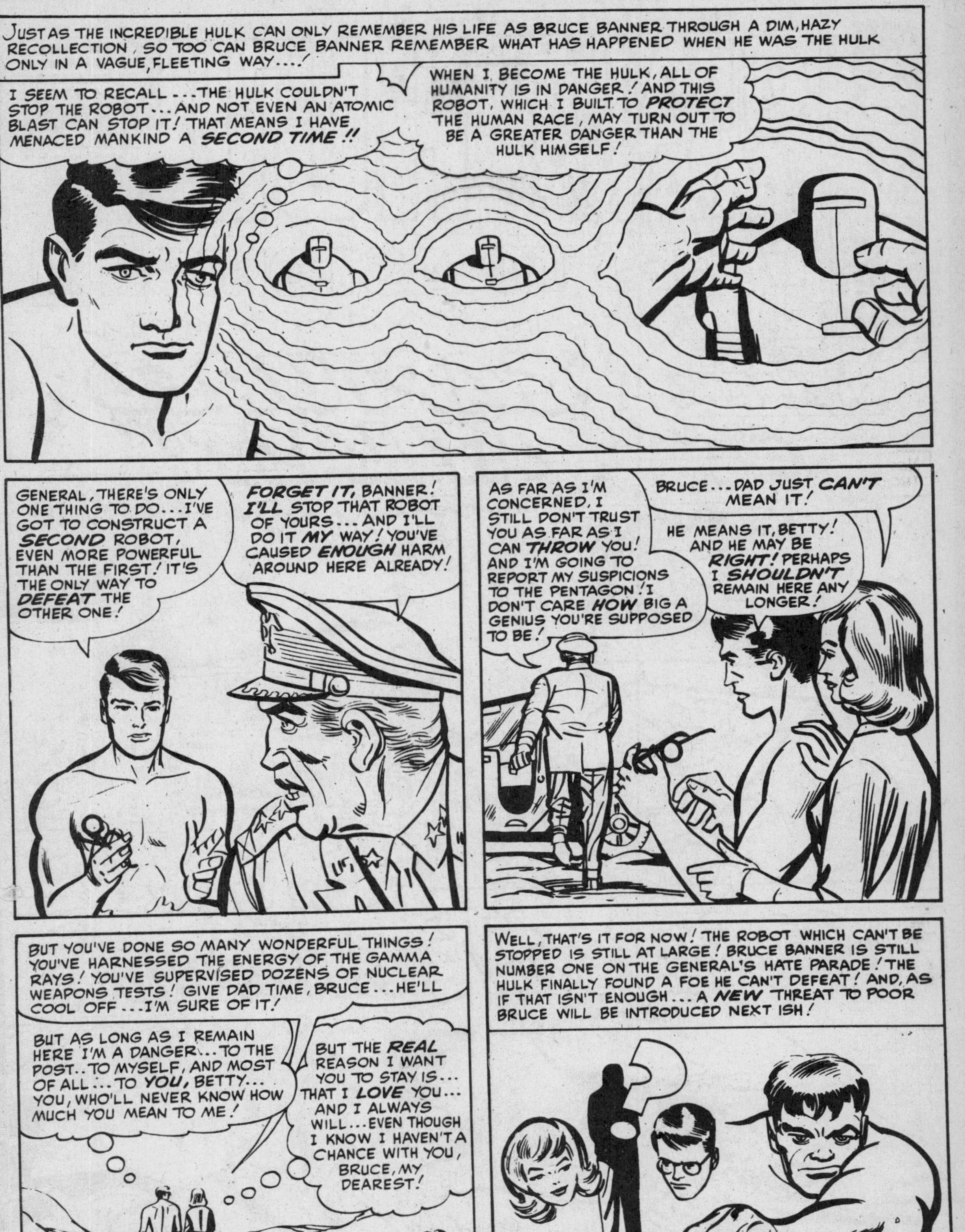

JUST AS THE INCREDIBLE HULK CAN ONLY REMEMBER HIS LIFE AS BRUCE BANNER THROUGH A DIM, HAZY RECOLLECTION, SO TOO CAN BRUCE BANNER REMEMBER WHAT HAS HAPPENED WHEN HE WAS THE HULK ONLY IN A VAGUE, FLEETING WAY...!
I SEEM TO RECALL ... THE HULK COULDN'T STOP THE ROBOT... AND NOT EVEN AN ATOMIC BLAST CAN STOP IT! THAT MEANS I HAVE MENACED MANKIND A SECOND TIME!!
WHEN I BECOME THE HULK, ALL OF HUMANITY IS IN DANGER! AND THIS ROBOT, WHICH I BUILT TO PROTECT THE HUMAN RACE, MAY TURN OUT TO BE A GREATER DANGER THAN THE HULK HIMSELF!
GENERAL, THERE'S ONLY ONE THING TO DO... I'VE GOT TO CONSTRUCT A SECOND ROBOT, EVEN MORE POWERFUL THAN THE FIRST! IT'S THE ONLY WAY TO DEFEAT THE OTHER ONE!
FORGET IT, BANNER! I'LL STOP THAT ROBOT OF YOURS... AND I'LL DO IT MY WAY! YOU'VE CAUSED ENOUGH HARM AROUND HERE ALREADY!
AS FAR AS I'M CONCERNED, I STILL DON'T TRUST YOU AS FAR AS I CAN THROW YOU! AND I'M GOING TO REPORT MY SUSPICIONS TO THE PENTAGON! I DON'T CARE HOW BIG A GENIUS YOU'RE SUPPOSED TO BE!
BRUCE... DAD JUST CAN'T MEAN IT!
HE MEANS IT, BETTY! AND HE MAY BE RIGHT! PERHAPS I SHOULDN'T REMAIN HERE ANY LONGER!
BUT YOU'VE DONE SO MANY WONDERFUL THINGS! YOU'VE HARNESSED THE ENERGY OF THE GAMMA RAYS! YOU'VE SUPERVISED DOZENS OF NUCLEAR WEAPONS TESTS! GIVE DAD TIME, BRUCE... HE'LL COOL OFF... I'M SURE OF IT!
BUT AS LONG AS I REMAIN HERE I'M A DANGER... TO THE POST.. TO MYSELF, AND MOST OF ALL... TO YOU, BETTY... YOU, WHO'LL NEVER KNOW HOW MUCH YOU MEAN TO ME!
BUT THE REAL REASON I WANT YOU TO STAY IS... THAT I LOVE YOU... AND I ALWAYS WILL... EVEN THOUGH I KNOW I HAVEN'T A CHANCE WITH YOU, BRUCE, MY DEAREST!
WELL, THAT'S IT FOR NOW! THE ROBOT WHICH CAN'T BE STOPPED IS STILL AT LARGE! BRUCE BANNER IS STILL NUMBER ONE ON THE GENERAL'S HATE PARADE! THE HULK FINALLY FOUND A FOE HE CAN'T DEFEAT! AND, AS IF THAT ISN'T ENOUGH... A NEW THREAT TO POOR BRUCE WILL BE INTRODUCED NEXT ISH!
SO, FOR MORE OF THE SAME, DON'T MISS THE NEXT CHAPTER OF THE ONLY COMIC MAG SUPER-HERO SOAP OPERA IN EXISTENCE! SEE YOU IN THE NEXT TALES TO ASTONISH! 'NUFF SAID!
10.

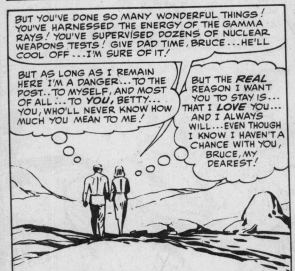

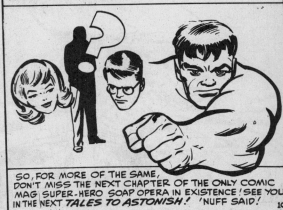

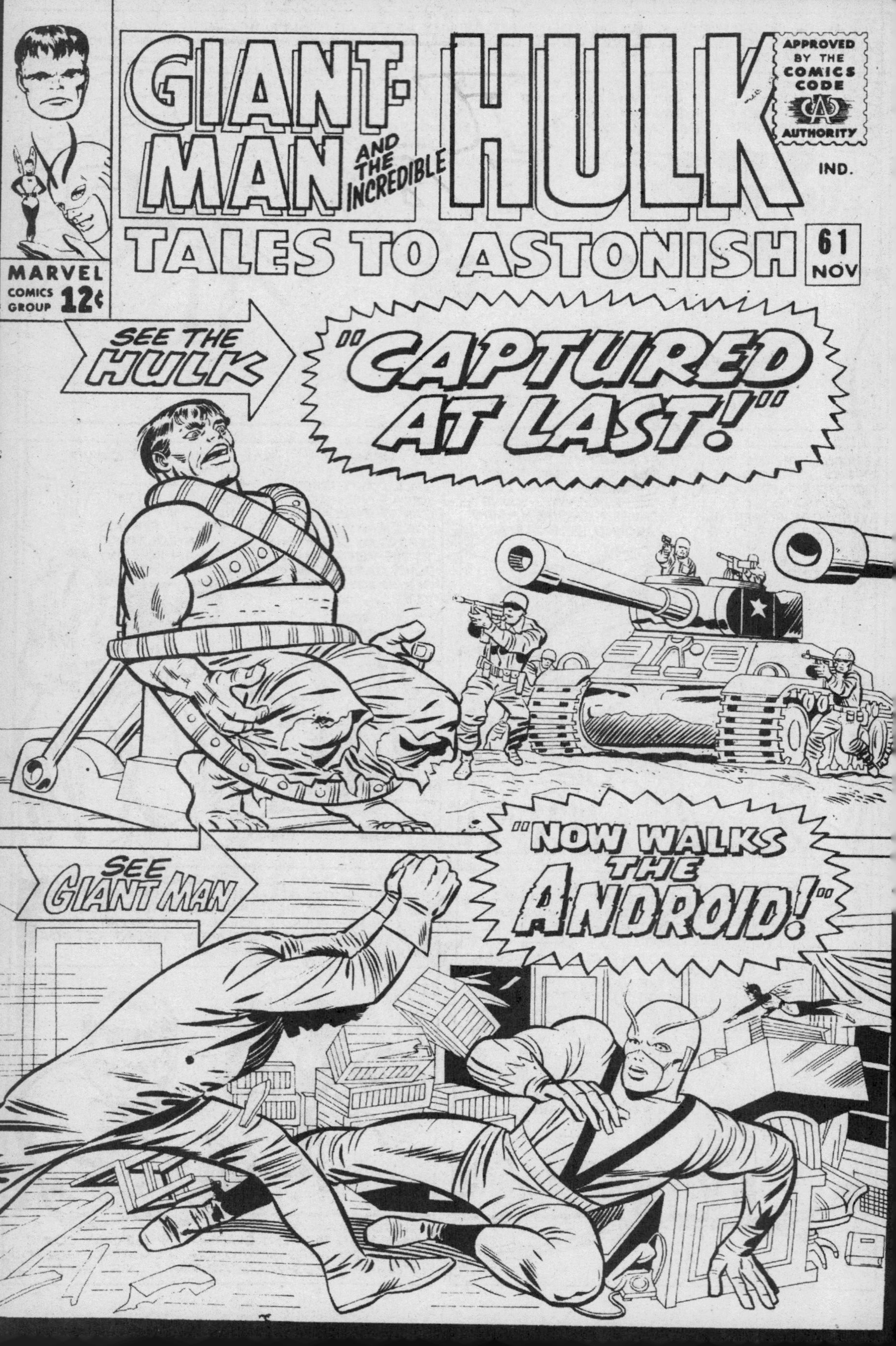
GIANT-MAN AND THE INCREDIBLE HULK
APPROVED BY THE COMICS CODE AUTHORITY
IND.
TALES TO ASTONISH
61
NOV
MARVEL COMICS GROUP 12¢
SEE THE HULK
"CAPTURED AT LAST!"
SEE GIANT MAN
"NOW WALKS THE ANDROID!"

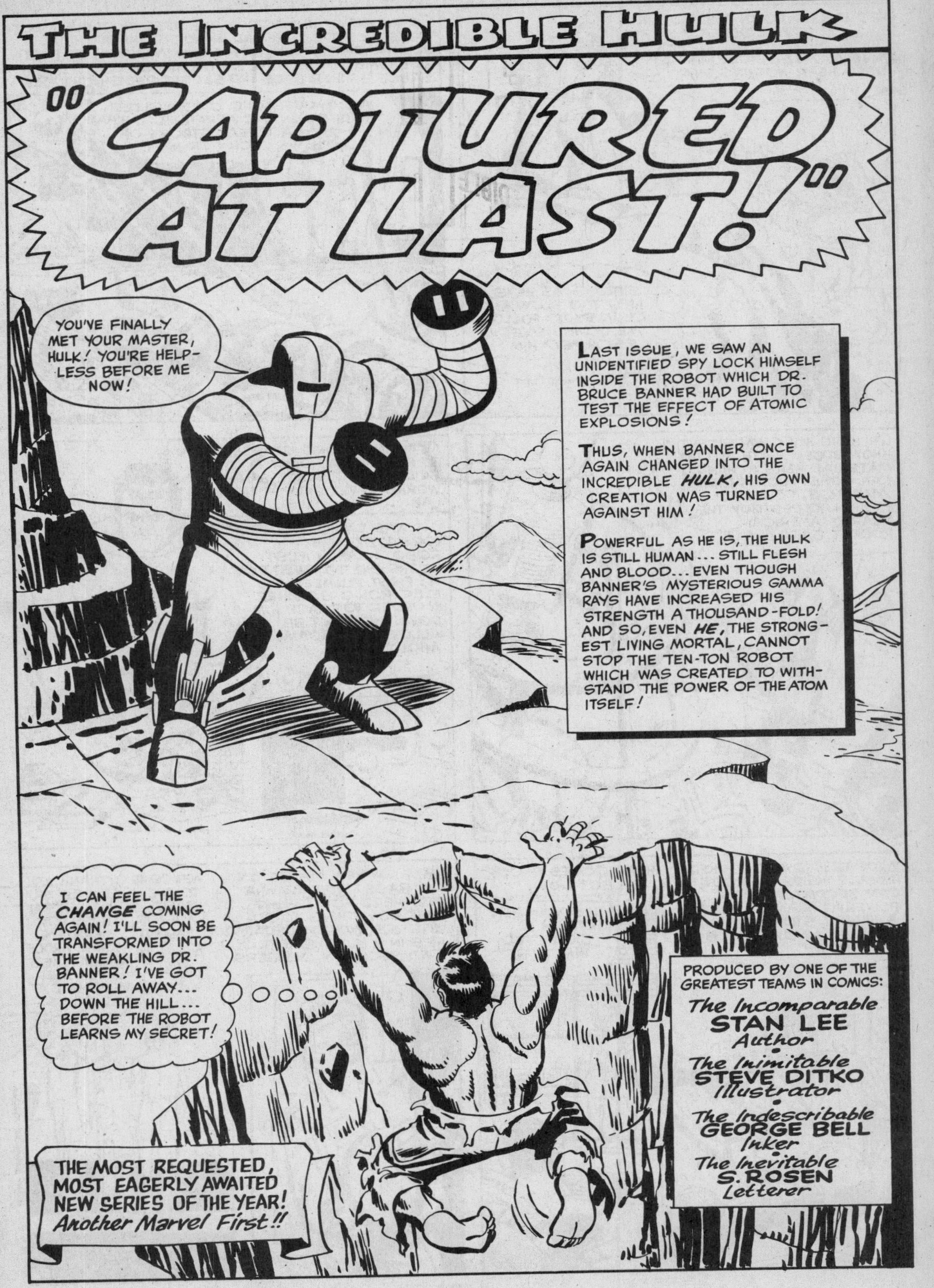
THE INCREDIBLE HULK
"CAPTURED AT LAST!"
YOU'VE FINALLY MET YOUR MASTER, HULK! YOU'RE HELPLESS BEFORE ME NOW!
LAST ISSUE, WE SAW AN UNIDENTIFIED SPY LOCK HIMSELF INSIDE THE ROBOT WHICH DR. BRUCE BANNER HAD BUILT TO TEST THE EFFECT OF ATOMIC EXPLOSIONS!
THUS, WHEN BANNER ONCE AGAIN CHANGED INTO THE INCREDIBLE HULK, HIS OWN CREATION WAS TURNED AGAINST HIM!
POWERFUL AS HE IS, THE HULK IS STILL HUMAN... STILL FLESH AND BLOOD... EVEN THOUGH BANNER'S MYSTERIOUS GAMMA RAYS HAVE INCREASED HIS STRENGTH A THOUSAND-FOLD! AND SO, EVEN HE, THE STRONGEST LIVING MORTAL, CANNOT STOP THE TEN-TON ROBOT WHICH WAS CREATED TO WITHSTAND THE POWER OF THE ATOM ITSELF!
I CAN FEEL THE CHANGE COMING AGAIN! I'LL SOON BE TRANSFORMED INTO THE WEAKLING DR. BANNER! I'VE GOT TO ROLL AWAY... DOWN THE HILL... BEFORE THE ROBOT LEARNS MY SECRET!
PRODUCED BY ONE OF THE GREATEST TEAMS IN COMICS: The Incomparable STAN LEE Author • The Inimitable STEVE DITKO Illustrator • The Indescribable GEORGE BELL Inker • The Inevitable S. ROSEN Letterer
THE MOST REQUESTED, MOST EAGERLY AWAITED NEW SERIES OF THE YEAR! Another Marvel First!!

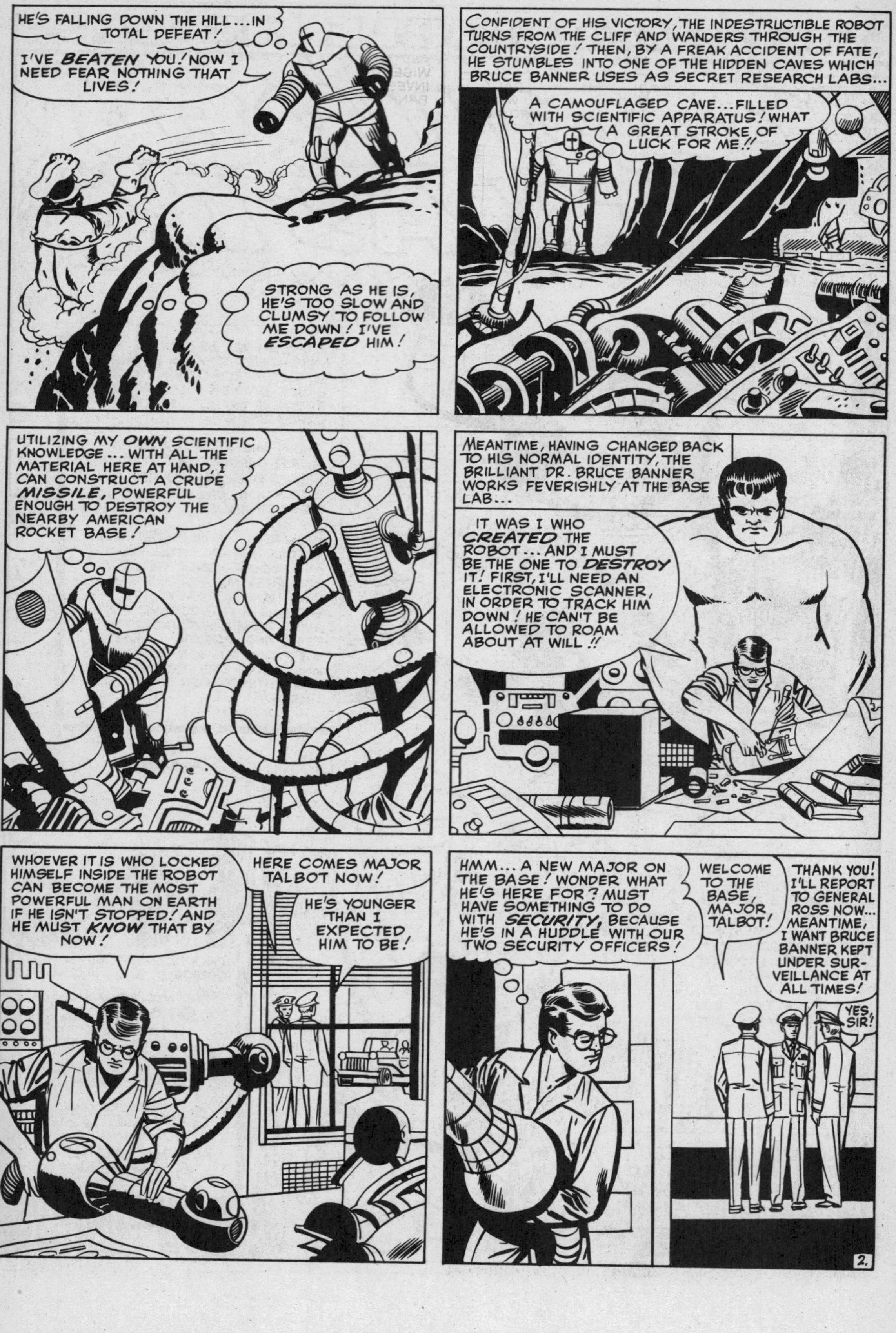
HE'S FALLING DOWN THE HILL... IN TOTAL DEFEAT!
I'VE BEATEN YOU! NOW I NEED FEAR NOTHING THAT LIVES!
STRONG AS HE IS, HE'S TOO SLOW AND CLUMSY TO FOLLOW ME DOWN! I'VE ESCAPED HIM!
CONFIDENT OF HIS VICTORY, THE INDESTRUCTIBLE ROBOT TURNS FROM THE CLIFF AND WANDERS THROUGH THE COUNTRYSIDE! THEN, BY A FREAK ACCIDENT OF FATE, HE STUMBLES INTO ONE OF THE HIDDEN CAVES WHICH BRUCE BANNER USES AS SECRET RESEARCH LABS...
A CAMOUFLAGED CAVE... FILLED WITH SCIENTIFIC APPARATUS! WHAT A GREAT STROKE OF LUCK FOR ME!!
UTILIZING MY OWN SCIENTIFIC KNOWLEDGE... WITH ALL THE MATERIAL HERE AT HAND, I CAN CONSTRUCT A CRUDE MISSILE, POWERFUL ENOUGH TO DESTROY THE NEARBY AMERICAN ROCKET BASE!
MEANTIME, HAVING CHANGED BACK TO HIS NORMAL IDENTITY, THE BRILLIANT DR. BRUCE BANNER WORKS FEVERISHLY AT THE BASE LAB...
IT WAS I WHO CREATED THE ROBOT... AND I MUST BE THE ONE TO DESTROY IT! FIRST, I'LL NEED AN ELECTRONIC SCANNER, IN ORDER TO TRACK HIM DOWN! HE CAN'T BE ALLOWED TO ROAM ABOUT AT WILL!!
WHOEVER IT IS WHO LOCKED HIMSELF INSIDE THE ROBOT CAN BECOME THE MOST POWERFUL MAN ON EARTH IF HE ISN'T STOPPED! AND HE MUST KNOW THAT BY NOW!
HERE COMES MAJOR TALBOT NOW!
HE'S YOUNGER THAN I EXPECTED HIM TO BE!
HMM... A NEW MAJOR ON THE BASE! WONDER WHAT HE'S HERE FOR? MUST HAVE SOMETHING TO DO WITH SECURITY, BECAUSE HE'S IN A HUDDLE WITH OUR TWO SECURITY OFFICERS!
WELCOME TO THE BASE, MAJOR TALBOT!
THANK YOU! I'LL REPORT TO GENERAL ROSS NOW... MEANTIME, I WANT BRUCE BANNER KEPT UNDER SURVEILLANCE AT ALL TIMES!
YES, SIR!
2.

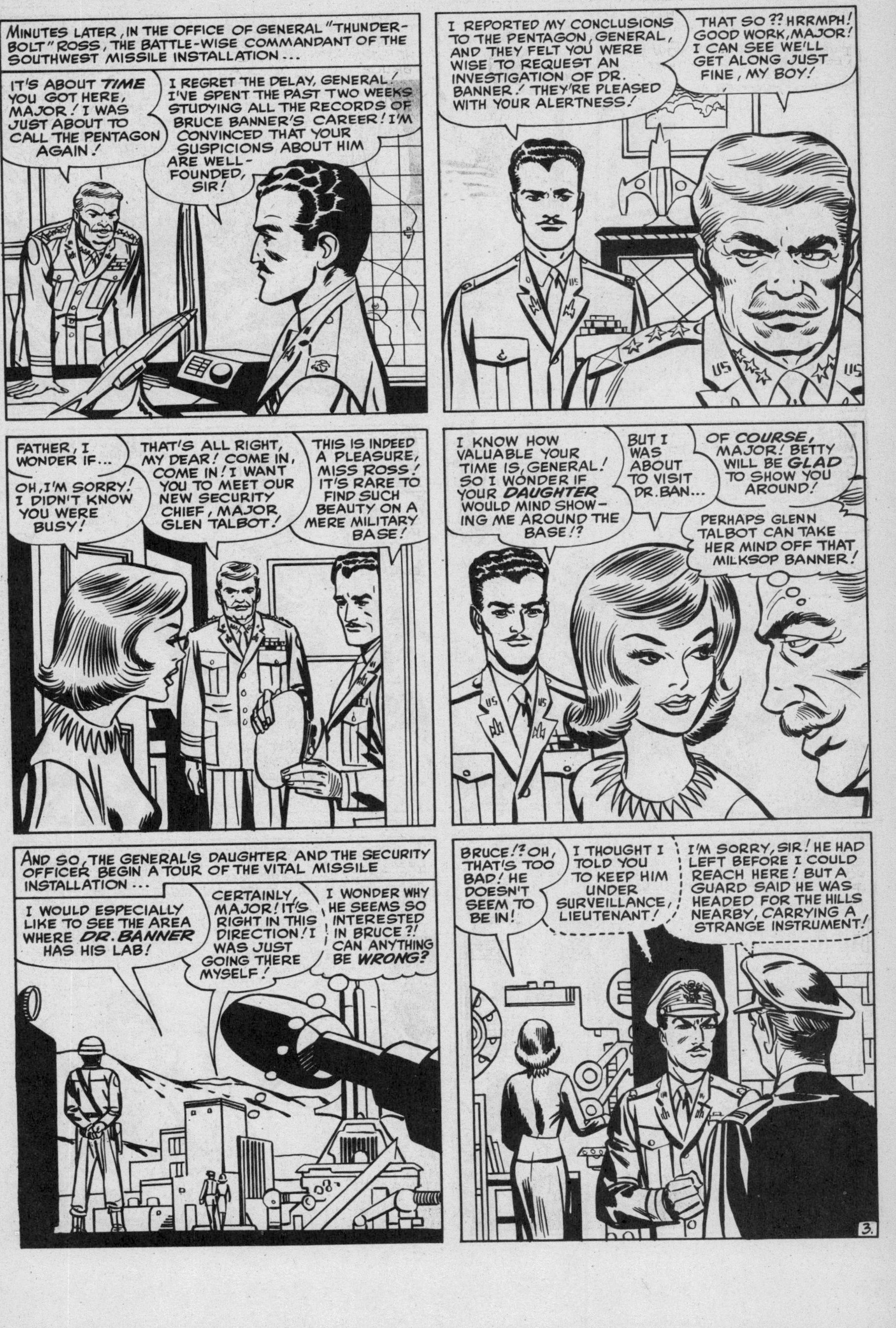
MINUTES LATER, IN THE OFFICE OF GENERAL "THUNDER-BOLT" ROSS, THE BATTLE-WISE COMMANDANT OF THE SOUTHWEST MISSILE INSTALLATION...
IT'S ABOUT TIME YOU GOT HERE, MAJOR! I WAS JUST ABOUT TO CALL THE PENTAGON AGAIN!
I REGRET THE DELAY, GENERAL! I'VE SPENT THE PAST TWO WEEKS STUDYING ALL THE RECORDS OF BRUCE BANNER'S CAREER! I'M CONVINCED THAT YOUR SUSPICIONS ABOUT HIM ARE WELL-FOUNDED, SIR!
I REPORTED MY CONCLUSIONS TO THE PENTAGON, GENERAL, AND THEY FELT YOU WERE WISE TO REQUEST AN INVESTIGATION OF DR. BANNER! THEY'RE PLEASED WITH YOUR ALERTNESS!
THAT SO?? HRRMPH! GOOD WORK, MAJOR! I CAN SEE WE'LL GET ALONG JUST FINE, MY BOY!
FATHER, I WONDER IF...
OH, I'M SORRY! I DIDN'T KNOW YOU WERE BUSY!
THAT'S ALL RIGHT, MY DEAR! COME IN, COME IN! I WANT YOU TO MEET OUR NEW SECURITY CHIEF, MAJOR GLEN TALBOT!
THIS IS INDEED A PLEASURE, MISS ROSS! IT'S RARE TO FIND SUCH BEAUTY ON A MERE MILITARY BASE!
I KNOW HOW VALUABLE YOUR TIME IS, GENERAL! SO I WONDER IF YOUR DAUGHTER WOULD MIND SHOW-ING ME AROUND THE BASE!?
BUT I WAS ABOUT TO VISIT DR. BAN...
OF COURSE, MAJOR! BETTY WILL BE GLAD TO SHOW YOU AROUND!
PERHAPS GLENN TALBOT CAN TAKE HER MIND OFF THAT MILKSOP BANNER!
AND SO, THE GENERAL'S DAUGHTER AND THE SECURITY OFFICER BEGIN A TOUR OF THE VITAL MISSILE INSTALLATION...
I WOULD ESPECIALLY LIKE TO SEE THE AREA WHERE DR. BANNER HAS HIS LAB!
CERTAINLY, MAJOR! IT'S RIGHT IN THIS DIRECTION! I WAS JUST GOING THERE MYSELF!
I WONDER WHY HE SEEMS SO INTERESTED IN BRUCE?! CAN ANYTHING BE WRONG?
BRUCE!? OH, THAT'S TOO BAD! HE DOESN'T SEEM TO BE IN!
I THOUGHT I TOLD YOU TO KEEP HIM UNDER SURVEILLANCE, LIEUTENANT!
I'M SORRY, SIR! HE HAD LEFT BEFORE I COULD REACH HERE! BUT A GUARD SAID HE WAS HEADED FOR THE HILLS NEARBY, CARRYING A STRANGE INSTRUMENT!
3.

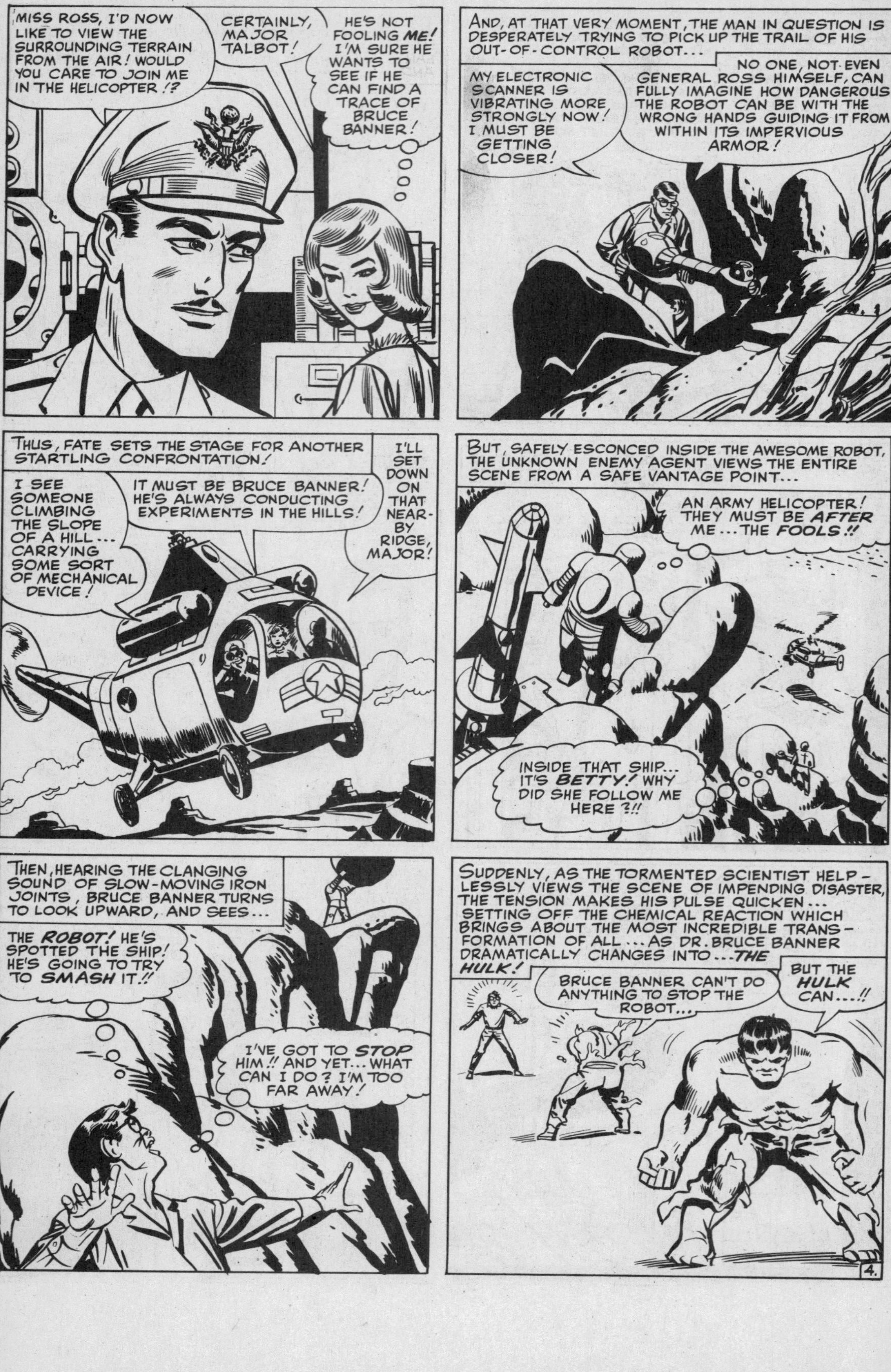
MISS ROSS, I'D NOW LIKE TO VIEW THE SURROUNDING TERRAIN FROM THE AIR! WOULD YOU CARE TO JOIN ME IN THE HELICOPTER !?
CERTAINLY, MAJOR TALBOT!
HE'S NOT FOOLING ME! I'M SURE HE WANTS TO SEE IF HE CAN FIND A TRACE OF BRUCE BANNER!
AND, AT THAT VERY MOMENT, THE MAN IN QUESTION IS DESPERATELY TRYING TO PICK UP THE TRAIL OF HIS OUT-OF-CONTROL ROBOT...
NO ONE, NOT EVEN GENERAL ROSS HIMSELF, CAN FULLY IMAGINE HOW DANGEROUS THE ROBOT CAN BE WITH THE WRONG HANDS GUIDING IT FROM WITHIN ITS IMPERVIOUS ARMOR!
MY ELECTRONIC SCANNER IS VIBRATING MORE STRONGLY NOW! I MUST BE GETTING CLOSER!
THUS, FATE SETS THE STAGE FOR ANOTHER STARTLING CONFRONTATION!
I SEE SOMEONE CLIMBING THE SLOPE OF A HILL... CARRYING SOME SORT OF MECHANICAL DEVICE!
IT MUST BE BRUCE BANNER! HE'S ALWAYS CONDUCTING EXPERIMENTS IN THE HILLS!
I'LL SET DOWN ON THAT NEAR-BY RIDGE, MAJOR!
BUT, SAFELY ESCONCED INSIDE THE AWESOME ROBOT, THE UNKNOWN ENEMY AGENT VIEWS THE ENTIRE SCENE FROM A SAFE VANTAGE POINT...
AN ARMY HELICOPTER! THEY MUST BE AFTER ME... THE FOOLS!!
INSIDE THAT SHIP... IT'S BETTY! WHY DID SHE FOLLOW ME HERE ?!!
THEN, HEARING THE CLANGING SOUND OF SLOW-MOVING IRON JOINTS, BRUCE BANNER TURNS TO LOOK UPWARD, AND SEES...
THE ROBOT! HE'S SPOTTED THE SHIP! HE'S GOING TO TRY TO SMASH IT!!
I'VE GOT TO STOP HIM!! AND YET... WHAT CAN I DO? I'M TOO FAR AWAY!
SUDDENLY, AS THE TORMENTED SCIENTIST HELP-LESSLY VIEWS THE SCENE OF IMPENDING DISASTER, THE TENSION MAKES HIS PULSE QUICKEN... SETTING OFF THE CHEMICAL REACTION WHICH BRINGS ABOUT THE MOST INCREDIBLE TRANS-FORMATION OF ALL... AS DR. BRUCE BANNER DRAMATICALLY CHANGES INTO... THE HULK!
BRUCE BANNER CAN'T DO ANYTHING TO STOP THE ROBOT...
BUT THE HULK CAN...!!
4.

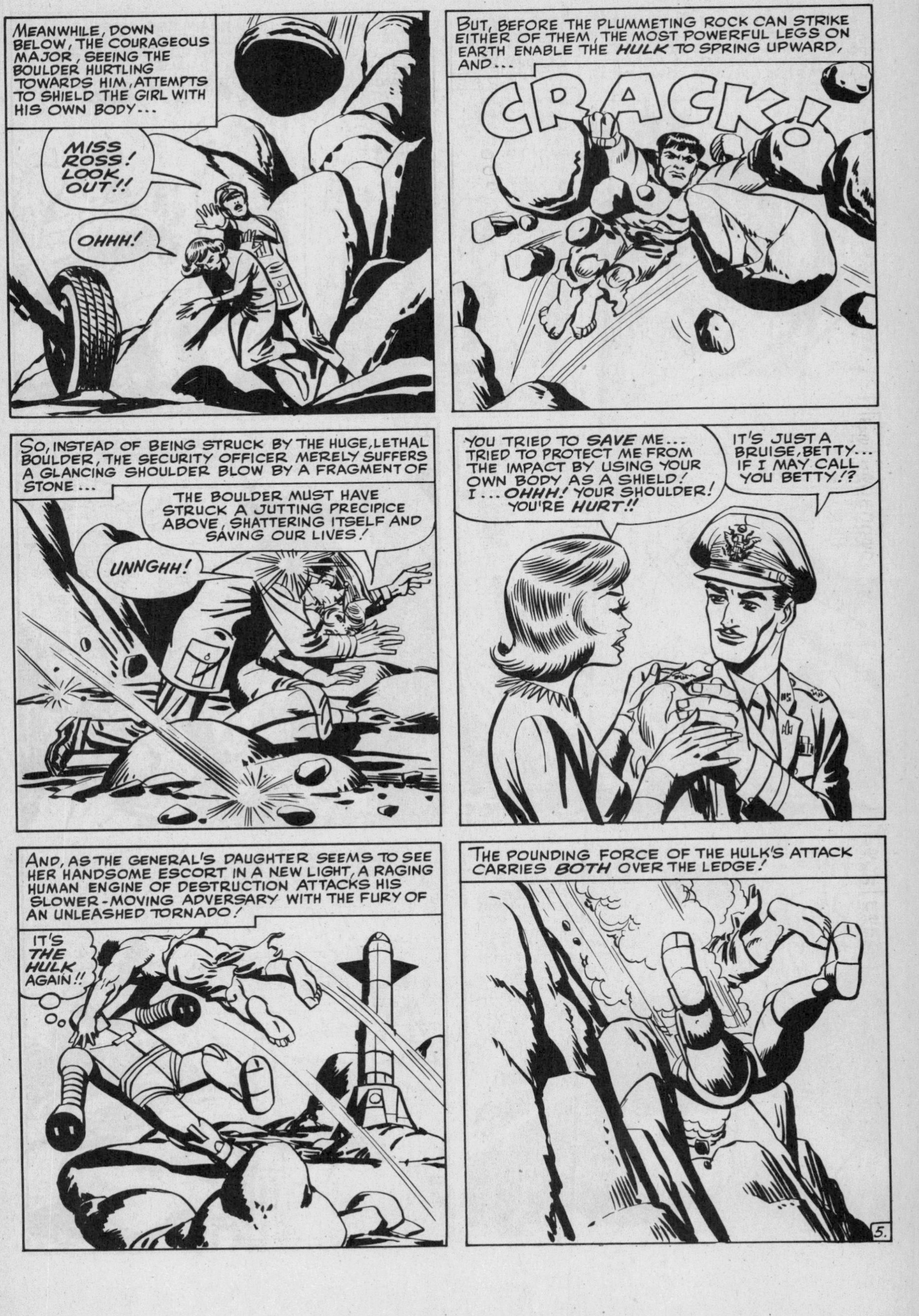
MEANWHILE, DOWN BELOW, THE COURAGEOUS MAJOR, SEEING THE BOULDER HURTLING TOWARDS HIM, ATTEMPTS TO SHIELD THE GIRL WITH HIS OWN BODY...
MISS ROSS! LOOK OUT!!
OHHH!
BUT, BEFORE THE PLUMMETING ROCK CAN STRIKE EITHER OF THEM, THE MOST POWERFUL LEGS ON EARTH ENABLE THE HULK TO SPRING UPWARD, AND...
CRACK!
SO, INSTEAD OF BEING STRUCK BY THE HUGE, LETHAL BOULDER, THE SECURITY OFFICER MERELY SUFFERS A GLANCING SHOULDER BLOW BY A FRAGMENT OF STONE...
THE BOULDER MUST HAVE STRUCK A JUTTING PRECIPICE ABOVE, SHATTERING ITSELF AND SAVING OUR LIVES!
UNNGHH!
YOU TRIED TO SAVE ME... TRIED TO PROTECT ME FROM THE IMPACT BY USING YOUR OWN BODY AS A SHIELD! I... OHHH! YOUR SHOULDER! YOU'RE HURT!!
IT'S JUST A BRUISE, BETTY... IF I MAY CALL YOU BETTY!?
AND, AS THE GENERAL'S DAUGHTER SEEMS TO SEE HER HANDSOME ESCORT IN A NEW LIGHT, A RAGING HUMAN ENGINE OF DESTRUCTION ATTACKS HIS SLOWER-MOVING ADVERSARY WITH THE FURY OF AN UNLEASHED TORNADO!
IT'S THE HULK AGAIN!!
THE POUNDING FORCE OF THE HULK'S ATTACK CARRIES BOTH OVER THE LEDGE!
5.

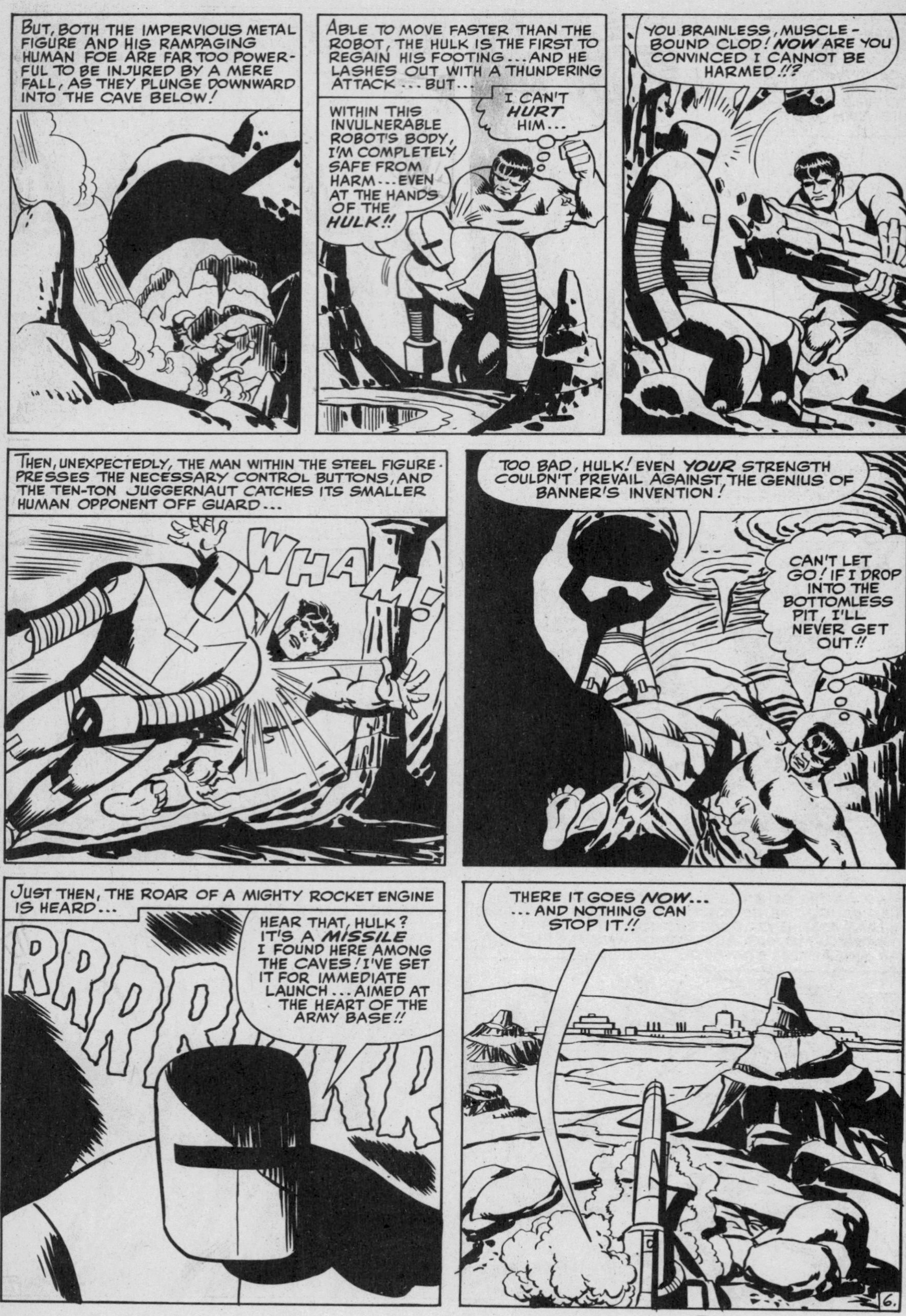

BUT, BOTH THE IMPERVIOUS METAL FIGURE AND HIS RAMPAGING HUMAN FOE ARE FAR TOO POWERFUL TO BE INJURED BY A MERE FALL, AS THEY PLUNGE DOWNWARD INTO THE CAVE BELOW!
ABLE TO MOVE FASTER THAN THE ROBOT, THE HULK IS THE FIRST TO REGAIN HIS FOOTING... AND HE LASHES OUT WITH A THUNDERING ATTACK... BUT...
I CAN'T HURT HIM...
WITHIN THIS INVULNERABLE ROBOT'S BODY, I'M COMPLETELY SAFE FROM HARM... EVEN AT THE HANDS OF THE HULK!!
YOU BRAINLESS, MUSCLE-BOUND CLOD! NOW ARE YOU CONVINCED I CANNOT BE HARMED!!?
THEN, UNEXPECTEDLY, THE MAN WITHIN THE STEEL FIGURE PRESSES THE NECESSARY CONTROL BUTTONS, AND THE TEN-TON JUGGERNAUT CATCHES ITS SMALLER HUMAN OPPONENT OFF GUARD...
WHAM!
TOO BAD, HULK! EVEN YOUR STRENGTH COULDN'T PREVAIL AGAINST THE GENIUS OF BANNER'S INVENTION!
CAN'T LET GO! IF I DROP INTO THE BOTTOMLESS PIT, I'LL NEVER GET OUT!!
JUST THEN, THE ROAR OF A MIGHTY ROCKET ENGINE IS HEARD...
RRRR
HEAR THAT, HULK? IT'S A MISSILE I FOUND HERE AMONG THE CAVES! I'VE SET IT FOR IMMEDIATE LAUNCH... AIMED AT THE HEART OF THE ARMY BASE!!
THERE IT GOES NOW... ... AND NOTHING CAN STOP IT!!
6.

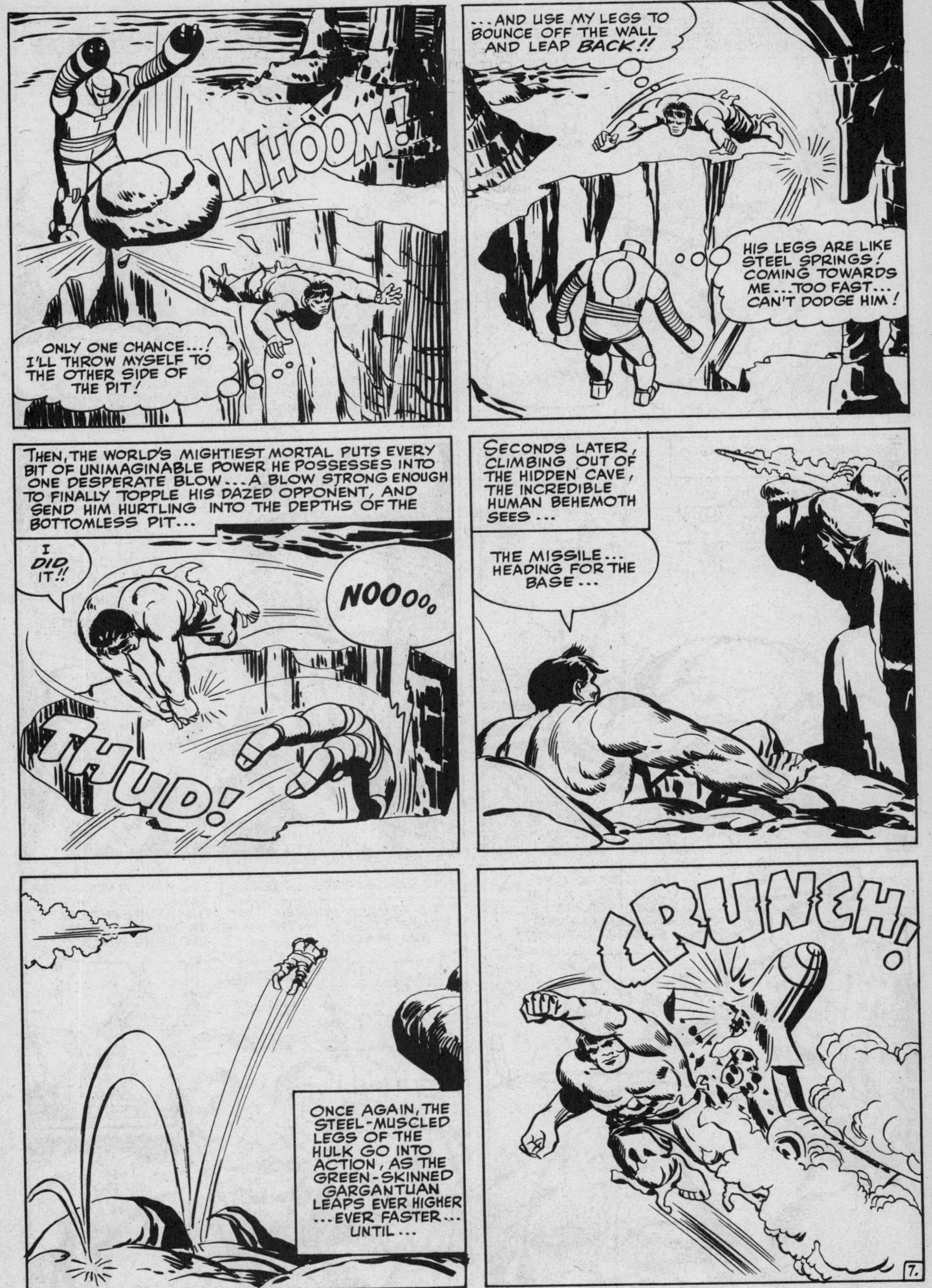
WHOOM!
ONLY ONE CHANCE...! I'LL THROW MYSELF TO THE OTHER SIDE OF THE PIT!
...AND USE MY LEGS TO BOUNCE OFF THE WALL AND LEAP BACK!!
HIS LEGS ARE LIKE STEEL SPRINGS! COMING TOWARDS ME...TOO FAST... CAN'T DODGE HIM!
THEN, THE WORLD'S MIGHTIEST MORTAL PUTS EVERY BIT OF UNIMAGINABLE POWER HE POSSESSES INTO ONE DESPERATE BLOW...A BLOW STRONG ENOUGH TO FINALLY TOPPLE HIS DAZED OPPONENT, AND SEND HIM HURTLING INTO THE DEPTHS OF THE BOTTOMLESS PIT...
I DID IT!!
NOOOoo
THUD!
SECONDS LATER, CLIMBING OUT OF THE HIDDEN CAVE, THE INCREDIBLE HUMAN BEHEMOTH SEES...
THE MISSILE... HEADING FOR THE BASE...
ONCE AGAIN, THE STEEL-MUSCLED LEGS OF THE HULK GO INTO ACTION, AS THE GREEN-SKINNED GARGANTUAN LEAPS EVER HIGHER ...EVER FASTER... UNTIL...
CRUNCH!
7.

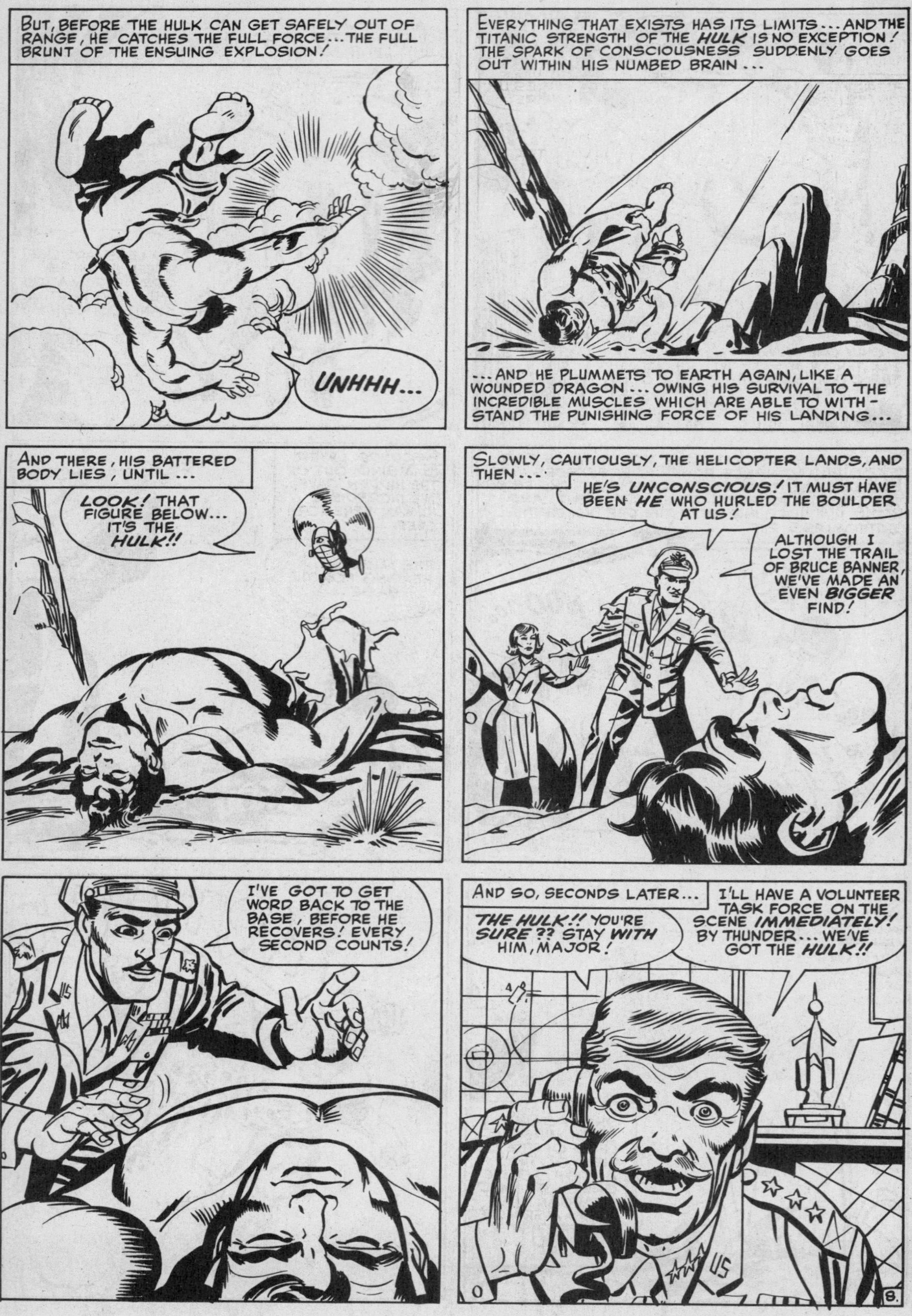
BUT, BEFORE THE HULK CAN GET SAFELY OUT OF RANGE, HE CATCHES THE FULL FORCE... THE FULL BRUNT OF THE ENSUING EXPLOSION!
UNHHH...
EVERYTHING THAT EXISTS HAS ITS LIMITS... AND THE TITANIC STRENGTH OF THE HULK IS NO EXCEPTION! THE SPARK OF CONSCIOUSNESS SUDDENLY GOES OUT WITHIN HIS NUMBED BRAIN...
...AND HE PLUMMETS TO EARTH AGAIN, LIKE A WOUNDED DRAGON... OWING HIS SURVIVAL TO THE INCREDIBLE MUSCLES WHICH ARE ABLE TO WITH-STAND THE PUNISHING FORCE OF HIS LANDING...
AND THERE, HIS BATTERED BODY LIES, UNTIL...
LOOK! THAT FIGURE BELOW... IT'S THE HULK!!
SLOWLY, CAUTIOUSLY, THE HELICOPTER LANDS, AND THEN...
HE'S UNCONSCIOUS! IT MUST HAVE BEEN HE WHO HURLED THE BOULDER AT US!
ALTHOUGH I LOST THE TRAIL OF BRUCE BANNER, WE'VE MADE AN EVEN BIGGER FIND!
I'VE GOT TO GET WORD BACK TO THE BASE, BEFORE HE RECOVERS! EVERY SECOND COUNTS!
AND SO, SECONDS LATER...
THE HULK!! YOU'RE SURE?? STAY WITH HIM, MAJOR!
I'LL HAVE A VOLUNTEER TASK FORCE ON THE SCENE IMMEDIATELY! BY THUNDER... WE'VE GOT THE HULK!!
8.

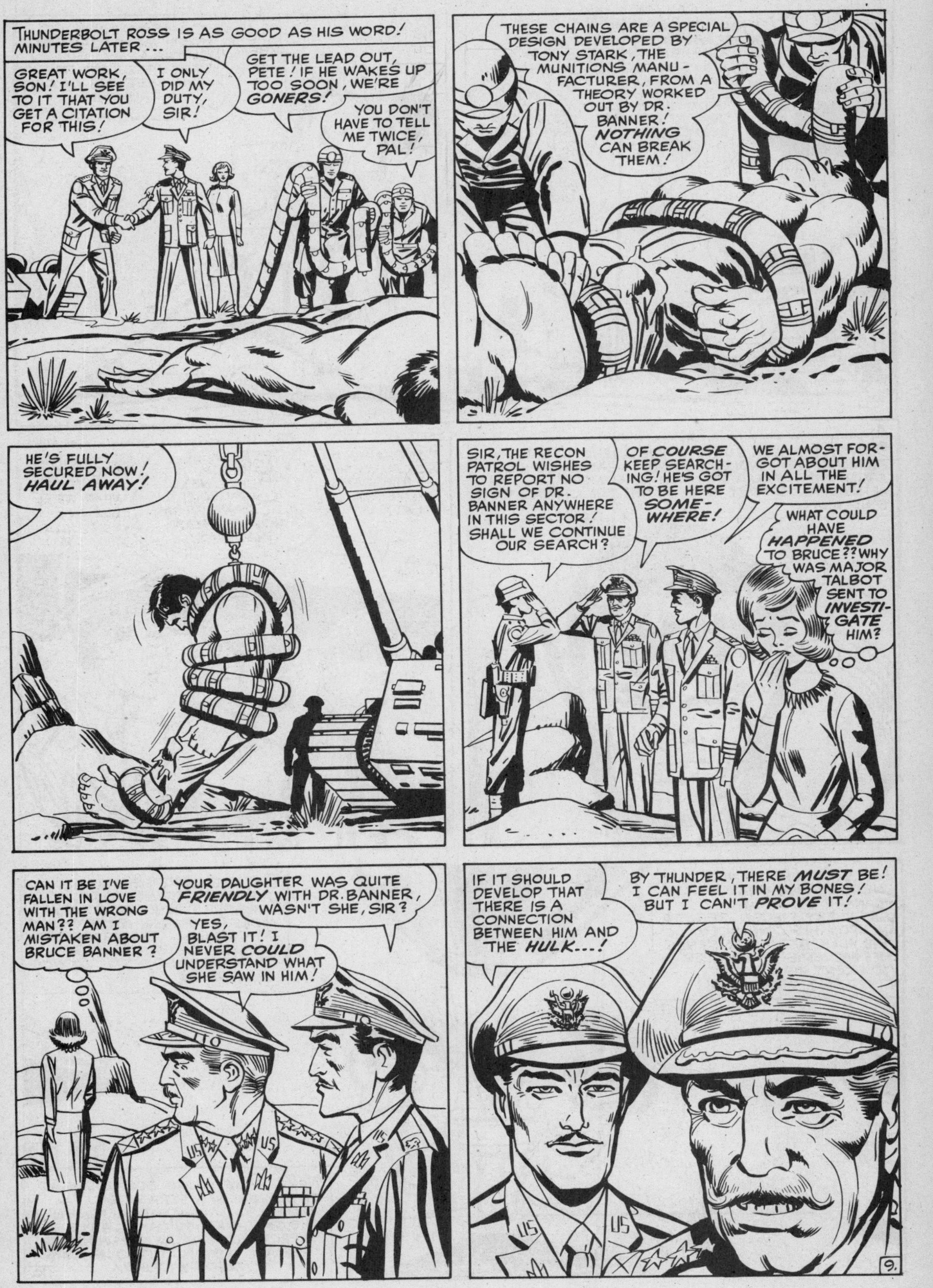
THUNDERBOLT ROSS IS AS GOOD AS HIS WORD! MINUTES LATER ...
GREAT WORK, SON! I'LL SEE TO IT THAT YOU GET A CITATION FOR THIS!
I ONLY DID MY DUTY, SIR!
GET THE LEAD OUT, PETE! IF HE WAKES UP TOO SOON, WE'RE GONERS!
YOU DON'T HAVE TO TELL ME TWICE, PAL!
THESE CHAINS ARE A SPECIAL DESIGN DEVELOPED BY TONY STARK, THE MUNITIONS MANU-FACTURER, FROM A THEORY WORKED OUT BY DR. BANNER! NOTHING CAN BREAK THEM!
HE'S FULLY SECURED NOW! HAUL AWAY!
SIR, THE RECON PATROL WISHES TO REPORT NO SIGN OF DR. BANNER ANYWHERE IN THIS SECTOR! SHALL WE CONTINUE OUR SEARCH?
OF COURSE KEEP SEARCH-ING! HE'S GOT TO BE HERE SOME-WHERE!
WE ALMOST FOR-GOT ABOUT HIM IN ALL THE EXCITEMENT!
WHAT COULD HAVE HAPPENED TO BRUCE?? WHY WAS MAJOR TALBOT SENT TO INVESTI-GATE HIM?
CAN IT BE I'VE FALLEN IN LOVE WITH THE WRONG MAN?? AM I MISTAKEN ABOUT BRUCE BANNER?
YOUR DAUGHTER WAS QUITE FRIENDLY WITH DR. BANNER, WASN'T SHE, SIR?
YES, BLAST IT! I NEVER COULD UNDERSTAND WHAT SHE SAW IN HIM!
IF IT SHOULD DEVELOP THAT THERE IS A CONNECTION BETWEEN HIM AND THE HULK...!
BY THUNDER, THERE MUST BE! I CAN FEEL IT IN MY BONES! BUT I CAN'T PROVE IT!
9.

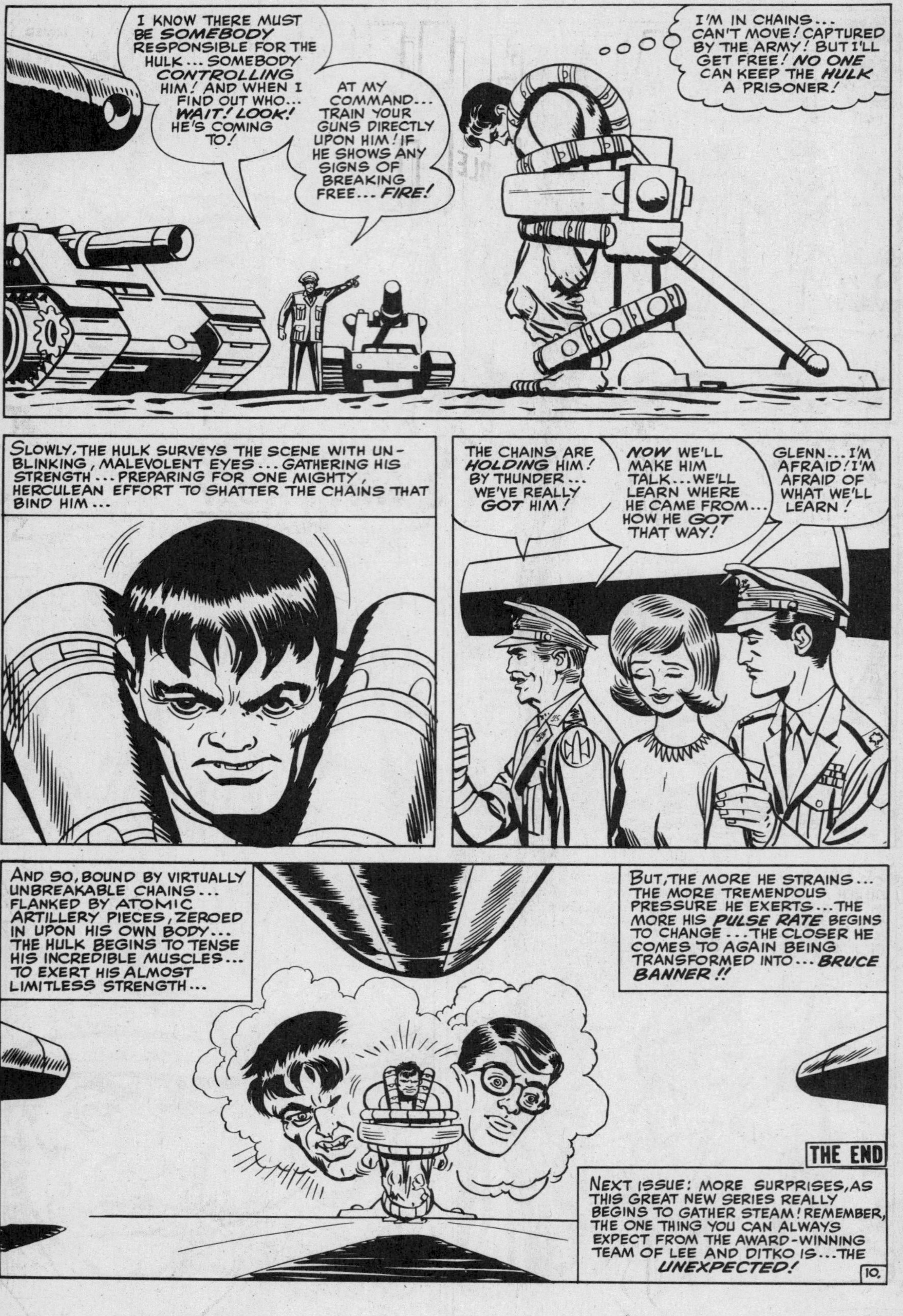
I KNOW THERE MUST BE SOMEBODY RESPONSIBLE FOR THE HULK... SOMEBODY CONTROLLING HIM! AND WHEN I FIND OUT WHO... WAIT! LOOK! HE'S COMING TO!
AT MY COMMAND... TRAIN YOUR GUNS DIRECTLY UPON HIM! IF HE SHOWS ANY SIGNS OF BREAKING FREE... FIRE!
I'M IN CHAINS... CAN'T MOVE! CAPTURED BY THE ARMY! BUT I'LL GET FREE! NO ONE CAN KEEP THE HULK A PRISONER!
SLOWLY, THE HULK SURVEYS THE SCENE WITH UN-BLINKING, MALEVOLENT EYES... GATHERING HIS STRENGTH... PREPARING FOR ONE MIGHTY, HERCULEAN EFFORT TO SHATTER THE CHAINS THAT BIND HIM...
THE CHAINS ARE HOLDING HIM! BY THUNDER... WE'VE REALLY GOT HIM!
NOW WE'LL MAKE HIM TALK... WE'LL LEARN WHERE HE CAME FROM... HOW HE GOT THAT WAY!
GLENN... I'M AFRAID! I'M AFRAID OF WHAT WE'LL LEARN!
AND SO, BOUND BY VIRTUALLY UNBREAKABLE CHAINS... FLANKED BY ATOMIC ARTILLERY PIECES, ZEROED IN UPON HIS OWN BODY... THE HULK BEGINS TO TENSE HIS INCREDIBLE MUSCLES... TO EXERT HIS ALMOST LIMITLESS STRENGTH...
BUT, THE MORE HE STRAINS... THE MORE TREMENDOUS PRESSURE HE EXERTS... THE MORE HIS PULSE RATE BEGINS TO CHANGE... THE CLOSER HE COMES TO AGAIN BEING TRANSFORMED INTO... BRUCE BANNER!!
THE END
NEXT ISSUE: MORE SURPRISES, AS THIS GREAT NEW SERIES REALLY BEGINS TO GATHER STEAM! REMEMBER, THE ONE THING YOU CAN ALWAYS EXPECT FROM THE AWARD-WINNING TEAM OF LEE AND DITKO IS... THE UNEXPECTED!
10.

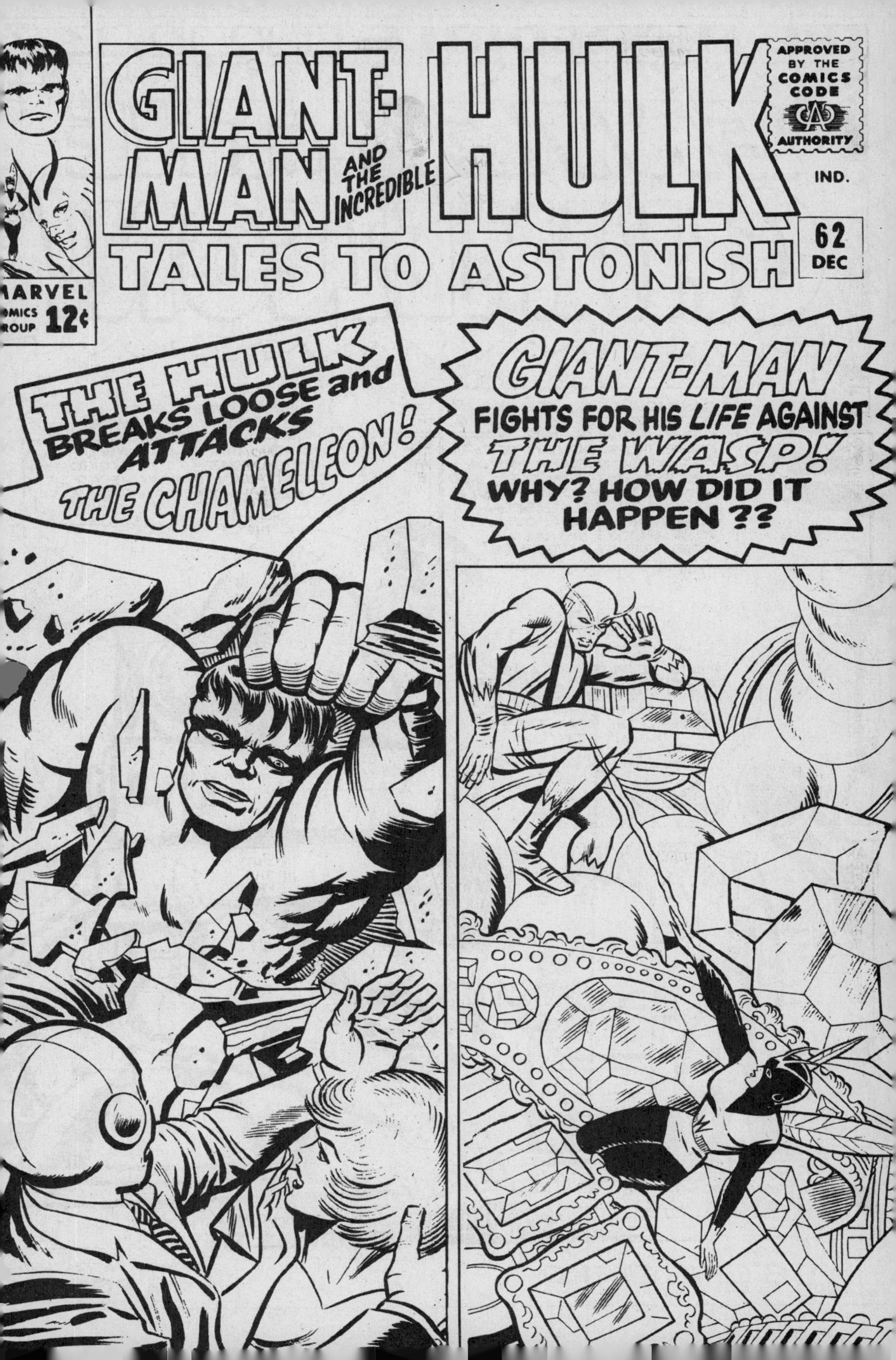

GIANT-MAN AND THE INCREDIBLE HULK
APPROVED BY THE COMICS CODE AUTHORITY
IND.
TALES TO ASTONISH
62 DEC
MARVEL COMICS GROUP 12¢
THE HULK BREAKS LOOSE and ATTACKS THE CHAMELEON!
GIANT-MAN FIGHTS FOR HIS LIFE AGAINST THE WASP! WHY? HOW DID IT HAPPEN ??

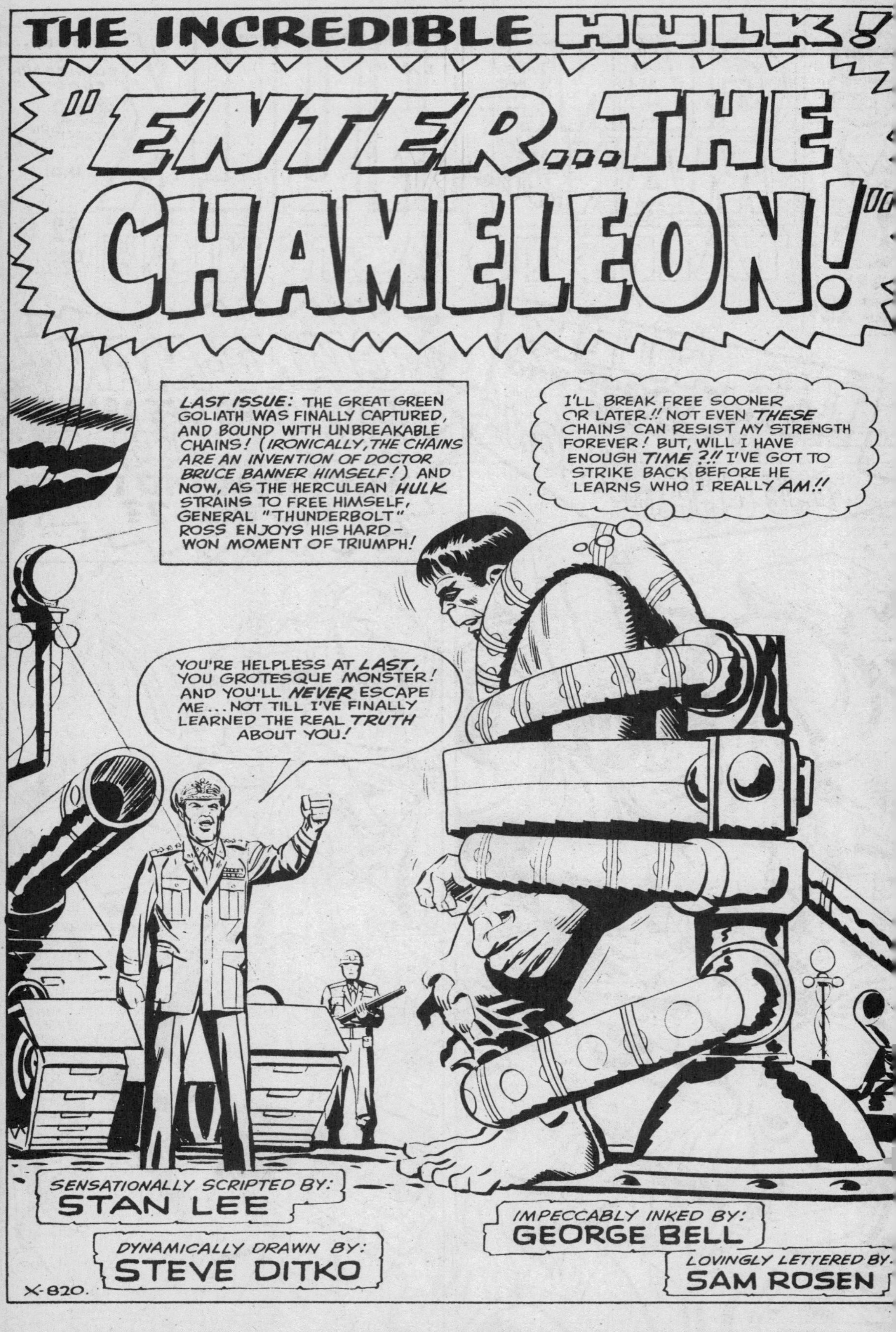
THE INCREDIBLE HULK!
"ENTER...THE CHAMELEON!"
LAST ISSUE: THE GREAT GREEN GOLIATH WAS FINALLY CAPTURED, AND BOUND WITH UNBREAKABLE CHAINS! (IRONICALLY, THE CHAINS ARE AN INVENTION OF DOCTOR BRUCE BANNER HIMSELF!) AND NOW, AS THE HERCULEAN HULK STRAINS TO FREE HIMSELF, GENERAL "THUNDERBOLT" ROSS ENJOYS HIS HARD-WON MOMENT OF TRIUMPH!
I'LL BREAK FREE SOONER OR LATER!! NOT EVEN THESE CHAINS CAN RESIST MY STRENGTH FOREVER! BUT, WILL I HAVE ENOUGH TIME?!! I'VE GOT TO STRIKE BACK BEFORE HE LEARNS WHO I REALLY AM!!
YOU'RE HELPLESS AT LAST, YOU GROTESQUE MONSTER! AND YOU'LL NEVER ESCAPE ME... NOT TILL I'VE FINALLY LEARNED THE REAL TRUTH ABOUT YOU!
SENSATIONALLY SCRIPTED BY: STAN LEE
DYNAMICALLY DRAWN BY: STEVE DITKO
IMPECCABLY INKED BY: GEORGE BELL
LOVINGLY LETTERED BY: SAM ROSEN
X-820.

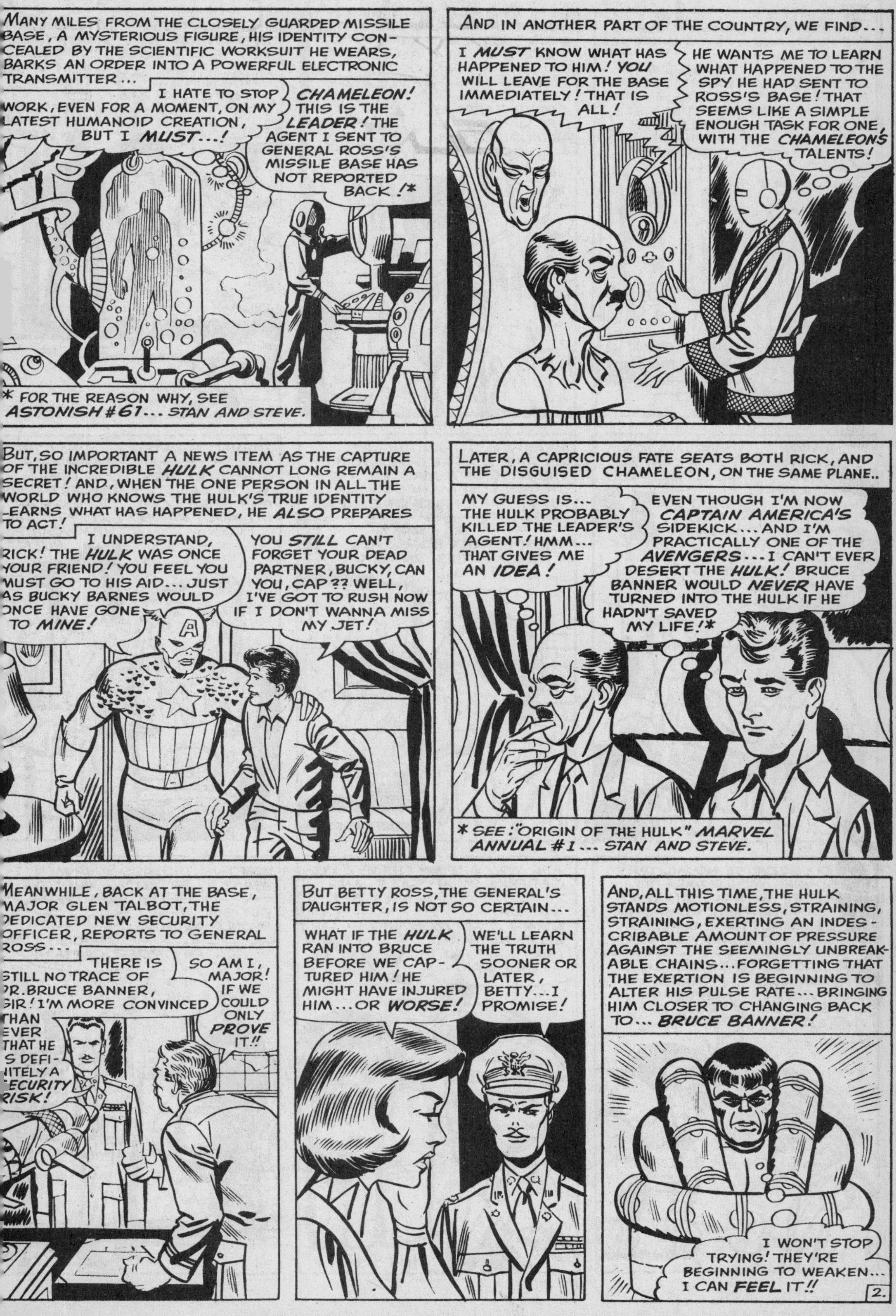
MANY MILES FROM THE CLOSELY GUARDED MISSILE BASE, A MYSTERIOUS FIGURE, HIS IDENTITY CONCEALED BY THE SCIENTIFIC WORKSUIT HE WEARS, BARKS AN ORDER INTO A POWERFUL ELECTRONIC TRANSMITTER...
I HATE TO STOP WORK, EVEN FOR A MOMENT, ON MY LATEST HUMANOID CREATION, BUT I MUST...!
CHAMELEON! THIS IS THE LEADER! THE AGENT I SENT TO GENERAL ROSS'S MISSILE BASE HAS NOT REPORTED BACK!*
* FOR THE REASON WHY, SEE ASTONISH #61... STAN AND STEVE.
AND IN ANOTHER PART OF THE COUNTRY, WE FIND...
I MUST KNOW WHAT HAS HAPPENED TO HIM! YOU WILL LEAVE FOR THE BASE IMMEDIATELY! THAT IS ALL!
HE WANTS ME TO LEARN WHAT HAPPENED TO THE SPY HE HAD SENT TO ROSS'S BASE! THAT SEEMS LIKE A SIMPLE ENOUGH TASK FOR ONE, WITH THE CHAMELEON'S TALENTS!
BUT, SO IMPORTANT A NEWS ITEM AS THE CAPTURE OF THE INCREDIBLE HULK CANNOT LONG REMAIN A SECRET! AND, WHEN THE ONE PERSON IN ALL THE WORLD WHO KNOWS THE HULK'S TRUE IDENTITY LEARNS WHAT HAS HAPPENED, HE ALSO PREPARES TO ACT!
I UNDERSTAND, RICK! THE HULK WAS ONCE YOUR FRIEND! YOU FEEL YOU MUST GO TO HIS AID... JUST AS BUCKY BARNES WOULD ONCE HAVE GONE TO MINE!
YOU STILL CAN'T FORGET YOUR DEAD PARTNER, BUCKY, CAN YOU, CAP?? WELL, I'VE GOT TO RUSH NOW IF I DON'T WANNA MISS MY JET!
LATER, A CAPRICIOUS FATE SEATS BOTH RICK, AND THE DISGUISED CHAMELEON, ON THE SAME PLANE..
MY GUESS IS... THE HULK PROBABLY KILLED THE LEADER'S AGENT! HMM... THAT GIVES ME AN IDEA!
EVEN THOUGH I'M NOW CAPTAIN AMERICA'S SIDEKICK... AND I'M PRACTICALLY ONE OF THE AVENGERS... I CAN'T EVER DESERT THE HULK! BRUCE BANNER WOULD NEVER HAVE TURNED INTO THE HULK IF HE HADN'T SAVED MY LIFE!*
* SEE: "ORIGIN OF THE HULK" MARVEL ANNUAL #1... STAN AND STEVE.
MEANWHILE, BACK AT THE BASE, MAJOR GLEN TALBOT, THE DEDICATED NEW SECURITY OFFICER, REPORTS TO GENERAL ROSS...
THERE IS STILL NO TRACE OF DR. BRUCE BANNER, SIR! I'M MORE CONVINCED THAN EVER THAT HE IS DEFINITELY A SECURITY RISK!
SO AM I, MAJOR! IF WE COULD ONLY PROVE IT!!
BUT BETTY ROSS, THE GENERAL'S DAUGHTER, IS NOT SO CERTAIN...
WHAT IF THE HULK RAN INTO BRUCE BEFORE WE CAPTURED HIM! HE MIGHT HAVE INJURED HIM... OR WORSE!
WE'LL LEARN THE TRUTH SOONER OR LATER, BETTY... I PROMISE!
AND, ALL THIS TIME, THE HULK STANDS MOTIONLESS, STRAINING, STRAINING, EXERTING AN INDESCRIBABLE AMOUNT OF PRESSURE AGAINST THE SEEMINGLY UNBREAKABLE CHAINS... FORGETTING THAT THE EXERTION IS BEGINNING TO ALTER HIS PULSE RATE... BRINGING HIM CLOSER TO CHANGING BACK TO... BRUCE BANNER!
I WON'T STOP TRYING! THEY'RE BEGINNING TO WEAKEN... I CAN FEEL IT!!
2.

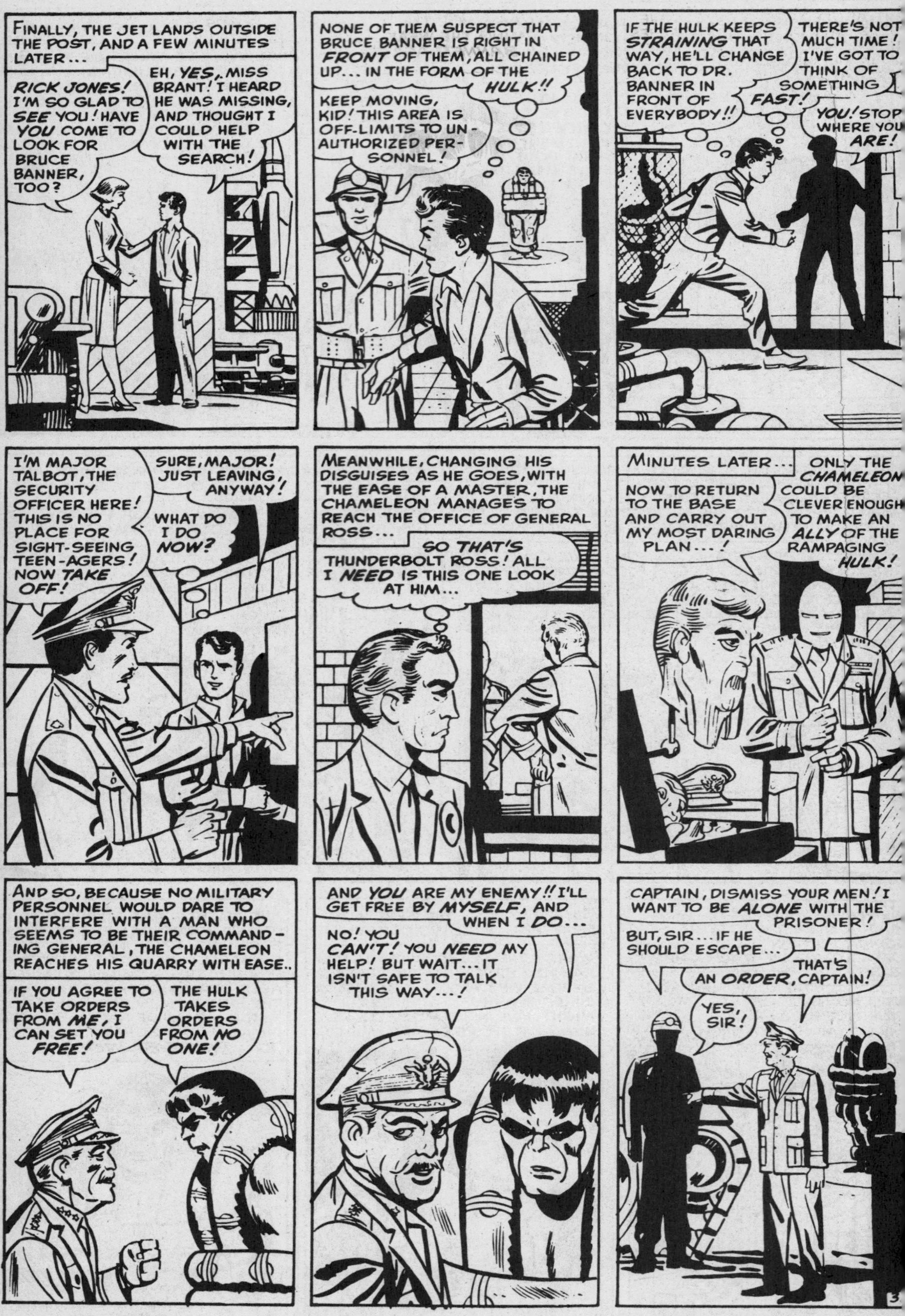
FINALLY, THE JET LANDS OUTSIDE THE POST, AND A FEW MINUTES LATER...
RICK JONES! I'M SO GLAD TO SEE YOU! HAVE YOU COME TO LOOK FOR BRUCE BANNER, TOO?
EH, YES, MISS BRANT! I HEARD HE WAS MISSING, AND THOUGHT I COULD HELP WITH THE SEARCH!
NONE OF THEM SUSPECT THAT BRUCE BANNER IS RIGHT IN FRONT OF THEM, ALL CHAINED UP... IN THE FORM OF THE HULK!!
KEEP MOVING, KID! THIS AREA IS OFF-LIMITS TO UN-AUTHORIZED PER-SONNEL!
IF THE HULK KEEPS STRAINING THAT WAY, HE'LL CHANGE BACK TO DR. BANNER IN FRONT OF EVERYBODY!!
THERE'S NOT MUCH TIME! I'VE GOT TO THINK OF SOMETHING FAST!
YOU! STOP WHERE YOU ARE!
I'M MAJOR TALBOT, THE SECURITY OFFICER HERE! THIS IS NO PLACE FOR SIGHT-SEEING TEEN-AGERS! NOW TAKE OFF!
SURE, MAJOR! JUST LEAVING, ANYWAY!
WHAT DO I DO NOW?
MEANWHILE, CHANGING HIS DISGUISES AS HE GOES, WITH THE EASE OF A MASTER, THE CHAMELEON MANAGES TO REACH THE OFFICE OF GENERAL ROSS...
SO THAT'S THUNDERBOLT ROSS! ALL I NEED IS THIS ONE LOOK AT HIM...
MINUTES LATER...
NOW TO RETURN TO THE BASE AND CARRY OUT MY MOST DARING PLAN...!
ONLY THE CHAMELEON COULD BE CLEVER ENOUGH TO MAKE AN ALLY OF THE RAMPAGING HULK!
AND SO, BECAUSE NO MILITARY PERSONNEL WOULD DARE TO INTERFERE WITH A MAN WHO SEEMS TO BE THEIR COMMAND-ING GENERAL, THE CHAMELEON REACHES HIS QUARRY WITH EASE..
IF YOU AGREE TO TAKE ORDERS FROM ME, I CAN SET YOU FREE!
THE HULK TAKES ORDERS FROM NO ONE!
AND YOU ARE MY ENEMY!! I'LL GET FREE BY MYSELF, AND WHEN I DO...
NO! YOU CAN'T! YOU NEED MY HELP! BUT WAIT... IT ISN'T SAFE TO TALK THIS WAY...!
CAPTAIN, DISMISS YOUR MEN! I WANT TO BE ALONE WITH THE PRISONER!
BUT, SIR... IF HE SHOULD ESCAPE...
THAT'S AN ORDER, CAPTAIN!
YES, SIR!
3

BUT, AS THE TROOPS DEPART, THE PULSE RATE OF THE HULK REACHES THE CRITICAL PEAK...AND ONCE AGAIN THE INCREDIBLE TRANSFORMATION BEGINS...

I'M CHANGING! I'M BECOMING THE WEAK BRUCE BANNER AGAIN!

SECONDS LATER, HUNDREDS OF POUNDS LIGHTER, AND FAR THINNER THAN HE WAS, BRUCE BANNER IS ABLE TO SLIP EASILY THROUGH THE CHAINS WHICH WERE INTENDED TO HOLD THE AWESOME HULK!

I'M FREE!

THEN, WHEN THE CHAMELEON RETURNS WITH A FLASHLIGHT AND A BOTTLE OF POWERFUL ACID, HE IS ASTONISHED TO FIND...

HE'S GONE!

BUT THE CHAINS ARE STILL INTACT! SOMEONE ELSE FREED HIM! BUT...WHO?!

AND AS BANNER RACES ACROSS THE FIELD...

IT'S DOCTOR BANNER! HE'S CHANGED AGAIN! I'VE GOT TO HELP HIM!

RICK JONES!!

OVER HERE... QUICK!

I DON'T THINK ANYONE SAW MY TRANSFORMATION! BUT, IF THEY FIND ME LIKE THIS... RICK! A SEARCH PATROL IS COMING!!

THROUGH THAT DOOR ... QUICK, DOC! LET ME HANDLE IT!

JUST SAW SOMEONE RACE PAST HERE...HEADING IN THAT DIRECTION!

THANKS, SON! LET'S GO MEN!!

YOU'RE SAFE NOW, DOC! GOOD THING I STASHED SOME EXTRA CLOTHES AWAY FOR YOU, JUST IN CASE!

BUT HOW DID YOU GET HERE, RICK? WHY DID YOU COME?

DID YOU THINK I COULD EVER FORGET HOW YOU ONCE SAVED MY LIFE, DOC? I'D NEVER HAVE LEFT YOU ... I'D HAVE STAYED WITH YOU ... IF YOU HADN'T DRIVEN ME OFF YOURSELF... WHEN YOU WERE THE HULK!!

4

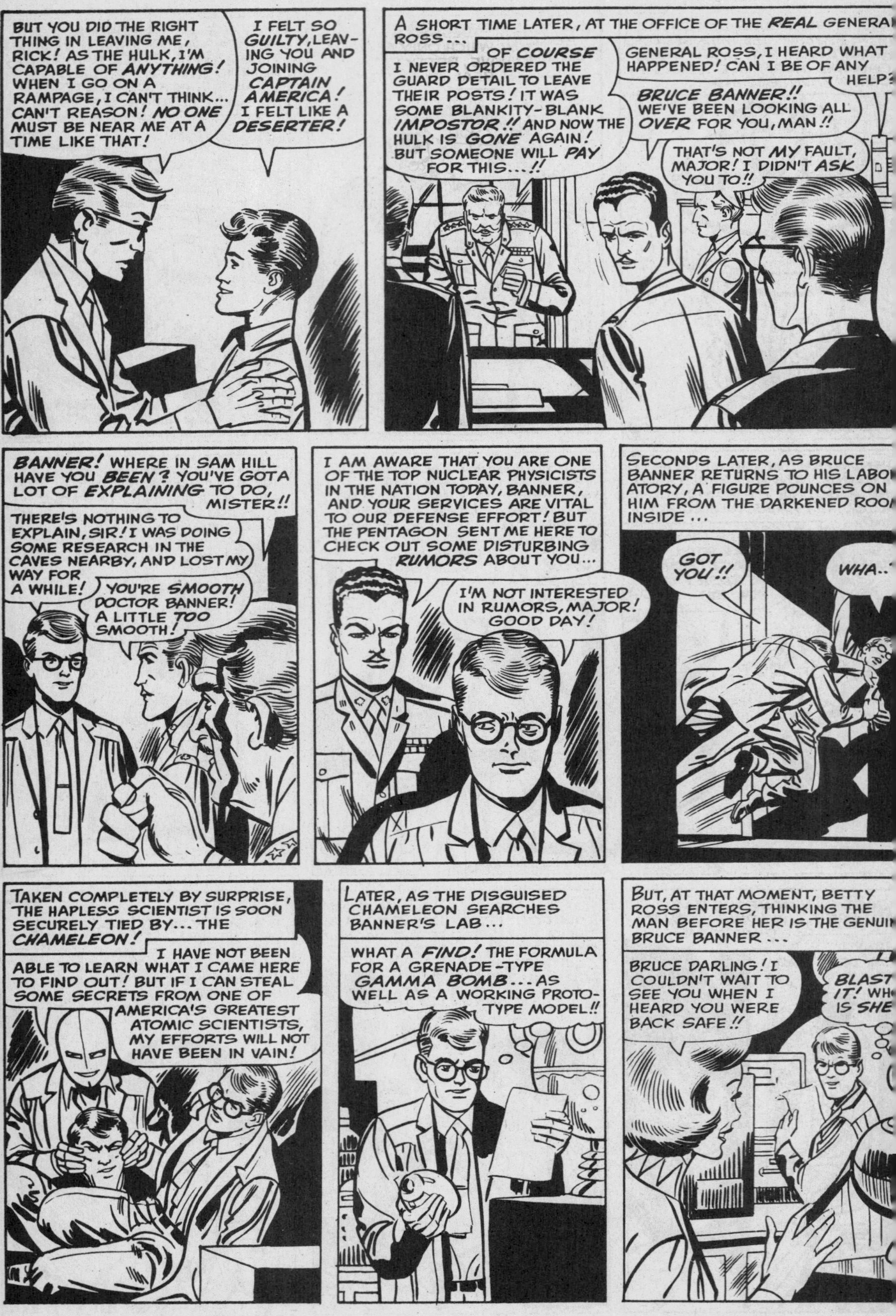
BUT YOU DID THE RIGHT THING IN LEAVING ME, RICK! AS THE HULK, I'M CAPABLE OF ANYTHING! WHEN I GO ON A RAMPAGE, I CAN'T THINK... CAN'T REASON! NO ONE MUST BE NEAR ME AT A TIME LIKE THAT!
I FELT SO GUILTY, LEAVING YOU AND JOINING CAPTAIN AMERICA! I FELT LIKE A DESERTER!
A SHORT TIME LATER, AT THE OFFICE OF THE REAL GENERA ROSS...
OF COURSE I NEVER ORDERED THE GUARD DETAIL TO LEAVE THEIR POSTS! IT WAS SOME BLANKITY-BLANK IMPOSTOR!! AND NOW THE HULK IS GONE AGAIN! BUT SOMEONE WILL PAY FOR THIS...!!
GENERAL ROSS, I HEARD WHAT HAPPENED! CAN I BE OF ANY HELP?
BRUCE BANNER!! WE'VE BEEN LOOKING ALL OVER FOR YOU, MAN!!
THAT'S NOT MY FAULT, MAJOR! I DIDN'T ASK YOU TO!!
BANNER! WHERE IN SAM HILL HAVE YOU BEEN? YOU'VE GOTA LOT OF EXPLAINING TO DO, MISTER!!
THERE'S NOTHING TO EXPLAIN, SIR! I WAS DOING SOME RESEARCH IN THE CAVES NEARBY, AND LOST MY WAY FOR A WHILE!
YOU'RE SMOOTH DOCTOR BANNER! A LITTLE TOO SMOOTH!
I AM AWARE THAT YOU ARE ONE OF THE TOP NUCLEAR PHYSICISTS IN THE NATION TODAY, BANNER, AND YOUR SERVICES ARE VITAL TO OUR DEFENSE EFFORT! BUT THE PENTAGON SENT ME HERE TO CHECK OUT SOME DISTURBING RUMORS ABOUT YOU...
I'M NOT INTERESTED IN RUMORS, MAJOR! GOOD DAY!
SECONDS LATER, AS BRUCE BANNER RETURNS TO HIS LABO ATORY, A FIGURE POUNCES ON HIM FROM THE DARKENED ROO INSIDE...
GOT YOU!!
WHA..
TAKEN COMPLETELY BY SURPRISE, THE HAPLESS SCIENTIST IS SOON SECURELY TIED BY... THE CHAMELEON!
I HAVE NOT BEEN ABLE TO LEARN WHAT I CAME HERE TO FIND OUT! BUT IF I CAN STEAL SOME SECRETS FROM ONE OF AMERICA'S GREATEST ATOMIC SCIENTISTS, MY EFFORTS WILL NOT HAVE BEEN IN VAIN!
LATER, AS THE DISGUISED CHAMELEON SEARCHES BANNER'S LAB...
WHAT A FIND! THE FORMULA FOR A GRENADE-TYPE GAMMA BOMB... AS WELL AS A WORKING PROTOTYPE MODEL!!
BUT, AT THAT MOMENT, BETTY ROSS ENTERS, THINKING THE MAN BEFORE HER IS THE GENUI BRUCE BANNER...
BRUCE DARLING! I COULDN'T WAIT TO SEE YOU WHEN I HEARD YOU WERE BACK SAFE!!
BLAST IT! WH IS SHE

LOOK...I'M BUSY NOW! COME BACK LATER!

SOMETHING'S *WRONG!!* YOU... YOU'VE *CHANGED!* YOU'D NEVER HAVE SPOKEN TO ME THAT WAY *BEFORE!*

AND THEN, POSSESSED BY AN *INTUITION* WHICH ONLY *FEMALES* SEEM TO HAVE, BETTY ROSS SUDDENLY REALIZES...

YOU'RE *NOT* BRUCE BANNER! YOU'RE AN *IMPOSTOR!* YOU MUST BE THE ONE WHO IMPERSONATED MY FATHER!!

YOU ARE CLEVER, YOUNG LADY! FAR *TOO* CLEVER... FOR YOUR OWN GOOD!

WHILE, A MERE FEW HEARTBEATS AWAY, BRUCE HEARS THE GIRL HE LOVES BEING THREATENED, AND SUDDENLY ALL IS FORGOTTEN SAVE THE DESPERATE NEED TO SAVE HER!!

I'VE GOT TO BREAK FREE!! THE CHAMELEON WON'T LET HER LEAVE HERE ALIVE!

AND SO, ONCE AGAIN BANNER'S PULSE RATE CHANGES UNDER THE SEVERE STRESS AND STRAIN OF HIS SEETHING EMOTIONS...CHANGES ENOUGH TO TRIGGER ONE OF THE GREATEST REACTIONS OF ALL...AS THE *HULK* COMES TO LIFE ONCE MORE!!

NO PUNY ROPES CAN HOLD *ME!!*

CRASH!

THE *HULK!!*

HOW??!

STAY BACK!! THIS IS A *GAMMA GRENADE* BOMB I'M HOLDING! IF I DROP IT, WE ALL DIE!!

LET ME GO!! WE'VE GOT TO *RUN!!* A MERE BOMB WON'T STOP *HIM!!*

BUT, IN A DIM RECESS IN HIS CLOUDED BRAIN, ONE SMALL PART WHICH IS STILL BRUCE BANNER REMEMBERS THE *POWER* OF THE GAMMA BOMB...AND THAT SAME SMALL PART OF DR. BANNER CANNOT LET THE ENTIRE BASE BE WIPED OUT!!

AND SO, THE HULK PAUSES... UNSURE...UNABLE TO DECIDE UPON HIS NEXT MOVE...UNTIL HE SEES...

A *PATROL* COMING!

THEY MUSTN'T CHAIN ME AGAIN!!

6.

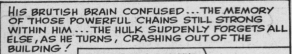

HIS BRUTISH BRAIN CONFUSED...THE MEMORY OF THOSE POWERFUL CHAINS STILL STRONG WITHIN HIM...THE HULK SUDDENLY FORGETS ALL ELSE, AS HE TURNS, CRASHING OUT OF THE BUILDING!

I'VE DRIVEN OFF THE *HULK!* IF I CAN DEFY HIM, THEN *NO ONE* CAN STOP ME!!

IT'S THE *HULK!!*

BUT THE PART OF HIM WHICH IS STILL BRUCE BANNER HAS *ANOTHER* MOTIVE FOR HURTLING PAST THE GUARD DETAIL! FOR, IF THEY SHOULD ATTACK THE CHAMELEON, THEY MIGHT CAUSE HIM TO DROP THE DEADLY GAMMA BOMB...

IF THEY FOLLOW *ME,* HE WON'T USE THAT BOMB!

IT'S THE *HULK!!*

QUICK! RADIO H.Q.

MEANTIME, AS THE CHAMELEON DASHES FOR FREEDOM WITH HIS HELPLESS CAPTIVE...

NO YOU *DON'T,* BANNER! IT'S A GOOD THING I *FOLLOWED* YOU! WHERE DO YOU THINK... *UNHHHH!*

NOBODY'S GOING TO STOP ME *NOW!* WITH THE GIRL AS A HOSTAGE, I'LL BE ABLE TO FLEE THE POST AND BRING THE GAMMA BOMB TO THE LEADER!

A ROCKET SPEED-VELOCITY TEST SLED!! JUST THE THING TO HIDE A MEDDLING FEMALE IN!

IT DOESN'T MATTER *WHAT* HAPPENED TO THE OTHER AGENT WHOSE FATE I WAS SUPPOSED TO LEARN! WITH A PRIZE SUCH AS THE GAMMA GRENADE, *I'LL* BE THE MOST IMPORTANT SPY OF ALL!

BUT THEN, THE CHAMELEON SEES ONE OF THE MOST FRIGHTENING SIGHTS OF ALL...

IT'S THE *HULK* AGAIN! HE LANDED IN FRONT OF ME, FROM A THOUSAND-YARD LEAP!!

WHAT IF THE THREAT OF THE BOMB WON'T *STOP* HIM THIS TIME ??

MOVING WITH DESPERATE SPEED, THE MERCILESS CHAMELEON PLACES HIS CAPTIVE INSIDE THE NEARBY ROCKET TEST SLED, AND...

THERE! THIS WILL KEEP HIM OCCUPIED LONG ENOUGH FOR ME TO ESCAPE!!

ONCE AGAIN, THE PART OF THE HULK WHICH IS STILL BRUCE BANNER REACTS TO THE THREAT AGAINST THE GIRL BANNER LOVES... AS THE INCREDIBLY POWERFUL HULK STOPS THE SPEEDING ROCKET SLED WITH HIS BARE HANDS!

WHOOM

BLAST IT!! I HOPED THE ROCKET SLED WOULD *CRUSH* THE LUMBERING BRUTE!! WELL, NO MATTER! IT *STILL* GAVE ME A HEAD START!

BUT, A HEAD START MEANS *NOTHING* WHEN FIGHTING THE *HULK!* FOR, HAVING STOPPED THE SPEEDING ROCKET SLED, HE REACHES THE CHAMELEON AGAIN WITH ONE MIGHTY LEAP...!

NOTHING CAN STOP HIM!

WAIT! STAY *BACK!* BEFORE I LET *YOU* TOUCH ME, I'LL BLOW US *ALL* TO SMITHEREENS!!

AND AGAIN THE STRANGELY TORTURED BRAIN OF THE INCREDIBLE HULK HAS TO MAKE A DIFFICULT CHOICE! BUT, WHILE HE PONDERS DARKLY...

FOOTSTEPS BEHIND ME!! A PATROL IS ATTACKING!! *BAH!!* I'LL SCATTER THEM LIKE GNATS!

UNABLE TO RETAIN ONE THOUGHT FOR TOO LONG A PERIOD OF TIME IN HIS BESTIAL BRAIN, THE HULK FORGETS ABOUT THE THREAT OF THE CHAMELEON, AS HE PREPARES TO BATTLE THE MEN WHO ARE SURROUNDING HIM!

LOOK! WHAT'S HE DOING??

STEADY! HE... HE'S ACTUALLY STARTING TO LIFT UP THE ENTIRE CONCRETE ROCKET TRACK BED!

NOW! NOW YOU'LL FEEL THE POWER OF THE HULK!!

BUT THE CHAMELEON, ALSO HALF CRAZED WITH FEAR AND UNCERTAINTY, DECIDES ON ONE LAST DESPERATE MOVE...

HE'S STRONGER THAN I *DREAMED!* I'VE GOT TO GET AWAY! EVEN THE *BOMB* DOESN'T MATTER ANY MORE! I'LL USE IT TO *DESTROY* HIM!

8.

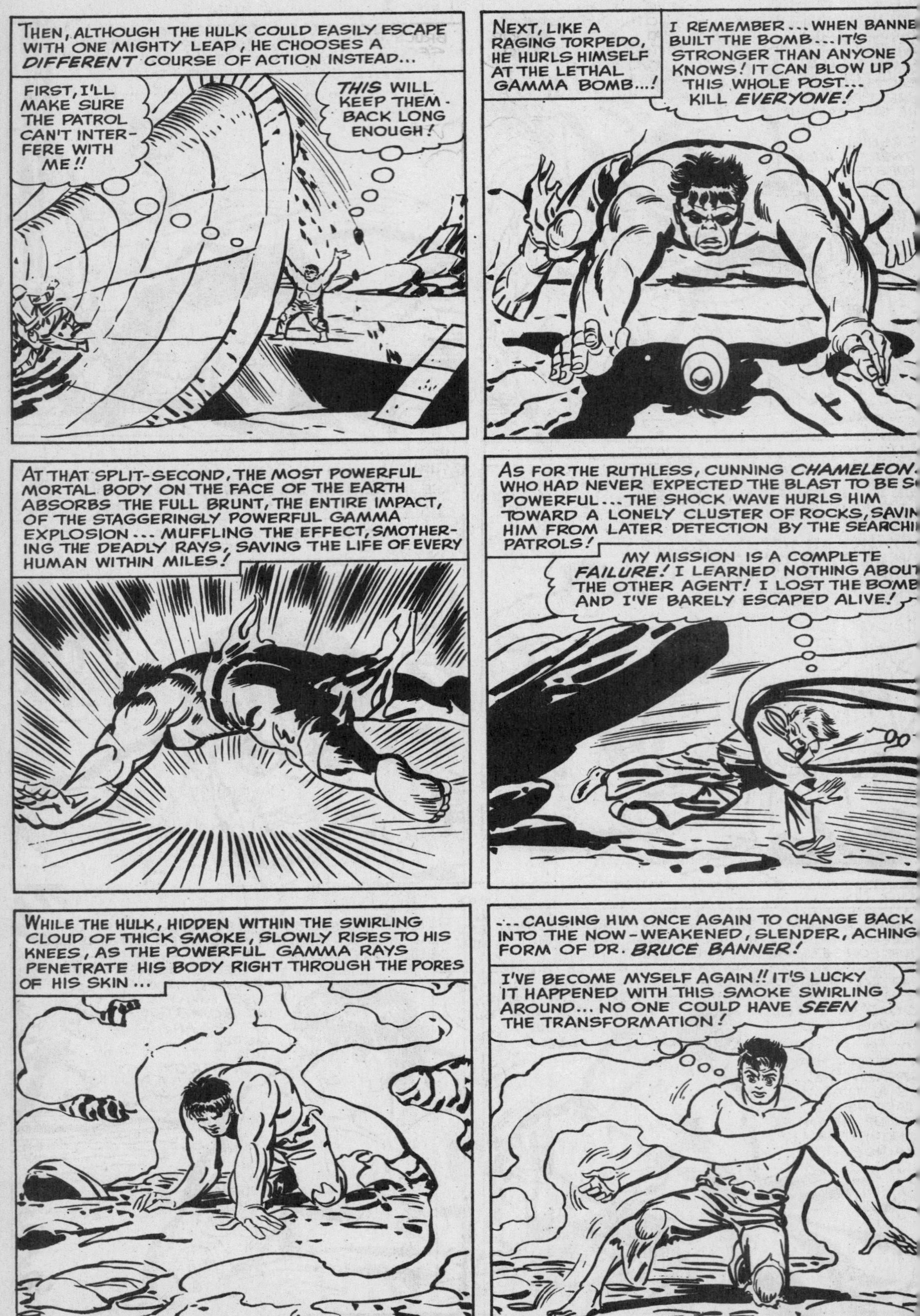

THEN, ALTHOUGH THE HULK COULD EASILY ESCAPE WITH ONE MIGHTY LEAP, HE CHOOSES A *DIFFERENT* COURSE OF ACTION INSTEAD...
FIRST, I'LL MAKE SURE THE PATROL CAN'T INTERFERE WITH ME!!
THIS WILL KEEP THEM BACK LONG ENOUGH!
NEXT, LIKE A RAGING TORPEDO, HE HURLS HIMSELF AT THE LETHAL GAMMA BOMB...!
I REMEMBER... WHEN BANNE BUILT THE BOMB... IT'S STRONGER THAN ANYONE KNOWS! IT CAN BLOW UP THIS WHOLE POST... KILL *EVERYONE!*
AT THAT SPLIT-SECOND, THE MOST POWERFUL MORTAL BODY ON THE FACE OF THE EARTH ABSORBS THE FULL BRUNT, THE ENTIRE IMPACT, OF THE STAGGERINGLY POWERFUL GAMMA EXPLOSION... MUFFLING THE EFFECT, SMOTHERING THE DEADLY RAYS, SAVING THE LIFE OF EVERY HUMAN WITHIN MILES!
AS FOR THE RUTHLESS, CUNNING *CHAMELEON*... WHO HAD NEVER EXPECTED THE BLAST TO BE S POWERFUL... THE SHOCK WAVE HURLS HIM TOWARD A LONELY CLUSTER OF ROCKS, SAVIN HIM FROM LATER DETECTION BY THE SEARCHI PATROLS!
MY MISSION IS A COMPLETE *FAILURE!* I LEARNED NOTHING ABOUT THE OTHER AGENT! I LOST THE BOMB AND I'VE BARELY ESCAPED ALIVE!
WHILE THE HULK, HIDDEN WITHIN THE SWIRLING CLOUD OF THICK SMOKE, SLOWLY RISES TO HIS KNEES, AS THE POWERFUL GAMMA RAYS PENETRATE HIS BODY RIGHT THROUGH THE PORES OF HIS SKIN...
...CAUSING HIM ONCE AGAIN TO CHANGE BACK INTO THE NOW-WEAKENED, SLENDER, ACHING FORM OF DR. *BRUCE BANNER!*
I'VE BECOME MYSELF AGAIN!! IT'S LUCKY IT HAPPENED WITH THIS SMOKE SWIRLING AROUND... NO ONE COULD HAVE *SEEN* THE TRANSFORMATION!

I'LL MAKE IT BACK TO MY LAB NOW WHILE I CAN, UNDER COVER OF THE SMOKE! AT LEAST I KNOW THAT BETTY IS SAFE FOR THE TIME BEING!!

I'VE GOT TO CHANGE CLOTHES BEFORE THAT SECURITY MAJOR PUTS TWO AND TWO TOGETHER AND REALIZES WHO THE HULK REALLY IS!

LATER, AS THE SMOKE CLEARS...

BRUCE BANNER WAS SEEN PUTTING YOU IN THAT ROCKET SLED, BETTY! THIS TIME I'VE REALLY GOT THE GOODS ON HIM!

SHE CAN'T SPEAK TO YOU JUST YET, MAJOR! SHE'S STILL IN A STATE OF SHOCK!

BUT LATER, AT A FORMAL BOARD OF INQUIRY HEARING...

DUE TO MISS BRANT'S TESTIMONY THAT IT WASN'T REALLY YOU WHO MENACED HER AND WHO THREW THAT BOMB, WE HAVE TO DISMISS THE CHARGES AGAINST YOU, BANNER!

BUT MAJOR TALBOT AND I ARE STILL NOT CERTAIN·MY DAUGHTER ISN'T TRYING TO PROTECT YOU IN SOME WAY! YOUR ACTIONS HAVE BEEN TOO MYSTERIOUS, YOUR FREQUENT DISAPPEARANCES TOO SUSPICIOUS! I STILL FEEL THERE'S SOME TIE-IN BETWEEN YOU AND THAT BLASTED HULK!

I HAVE NOTHING MORE TO SAY, SIR!

BUT WHY DO YOU STILL HATE THE HULK SO? I THOUGHT HE HAD SAVED THE POST!

THAT'S WHAT HE WANTED US TO THINK! HE WAS ONLY CONCERNED WITH SAVING HIMSELF!

IS THERE A CONNECTION BETWEEN BRUCE AND THE HULK?

IF SO, WHAT ON EARTH CAN IT BE??

AND, HALFWAY ACROSS THE COUNTRY, THE ONE WHO CALLS HIMSELF THE LEADER PLANS A NEW MOVE... ONE WHICH WILL HAVE A DRAMATIC EFFECT UPON THE LIVES OF OUR LITTLE CAST OF CHARACTERS...AND ESPECIALLY UPON...THE INCREDIBLE HULK...!

MY FIRST AGENT DISAPPEARED! THE CHAMELEON WAS NOT POWERFUL ENOUGH TO DEFEAT THE HULK! BUT, NOW THAT MY HUMANOID CREATION IS COMPLETED, IT IS TIME FOR THE LEADER TO TAKE OVER, PERSONALLY!

NEXT ISSUE:

WE SHALL LEARN MORE ABOUT THE MYSTERIOUS MENACING CHARACTER WHO CALLS HIMSELF---

THE LEADER!

SO, BE SURE TO BE WITH US AGAIN FOR THE FOLLOWING INSTALLMENT OF MARVEL'S NEW ADULT FANTASY SOAP-OPERA, STARRING THE MOST POWERFUL, MOST RAMPAGING MORTAL OF ALL TIME...

THE INCREDIBLE **HULK!**

10.

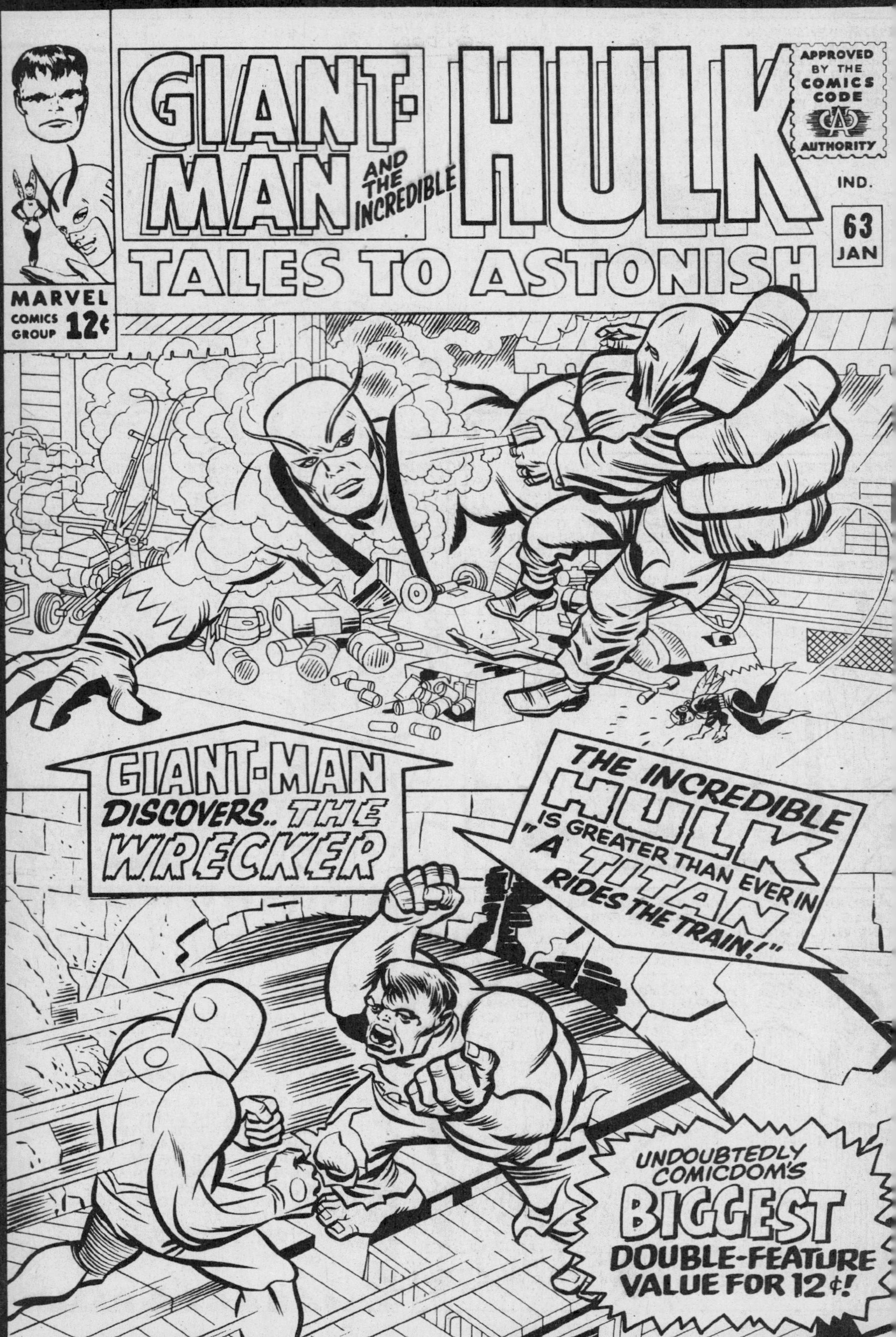
GIANT-MAN AND THE INCREDIBLE HULK
TALES TO ASTONISH
APPROVED BY THE COMICS CODE AUTHORITY
IND.
63 JAN
MARVEL COMICS GROUP 12¢
GIANT-MAN DISCOVERS.. THE WRECKER
THE INCREDIBLE HULK IS GREATER THAN EVER IN "A TITAN RIDES THE TRAIN!"
UNDOUBTEDLY COMICDOM'S BIGGEST DOUBLE-FEATURE VALUE FOR 12¢!

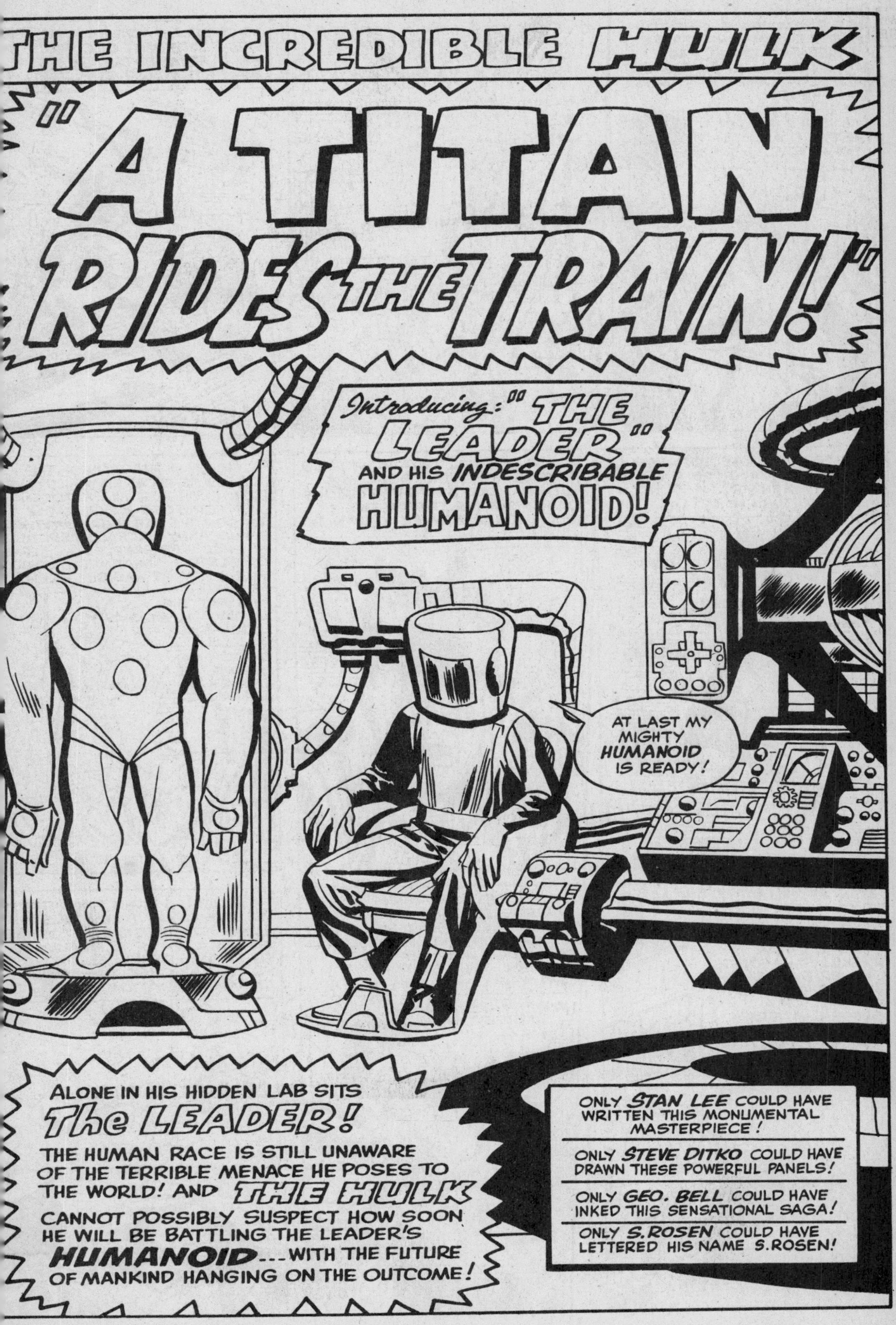
THE INCREDIBLE HULK
"A TITAN RIDES THE TRAIN!"
Introducing: "THE LEADER" AND HIS INDESCRIBABLE HUMANOID!
AT LAST MY MIGHTY HUMANOID IS READY!
ALONE IN HIS HIDDEN LAB SITS The LEADER! THE HUMAN RACE IS STILL UNAWARE OF THE TERRIBLE MENACE HE POSES TO THE WORLD! AND THE HULK CANNOT POSSIBLY SUSPECT HOW SOON HE WILL BE BATTLING THE LEADER'S HUMANOID... WITH THE FUTURE OF MANKIND HANGING ON THE OUTCOME!
ONLY STAN LEE COULD HAVE WRITTEN THIS MONUMENTAL MASTERPIECE!
ONLY STEVE DITKO COULD HAVE DRAWN THESE POWERFUL PANELS!
ONLY GEO. BELL COULD HAVE INKED THIS SENSATIONAL SAGA!
ONLY S.ROSEN COULD HAVE LETTERED HIS NAME S.ROSEN!

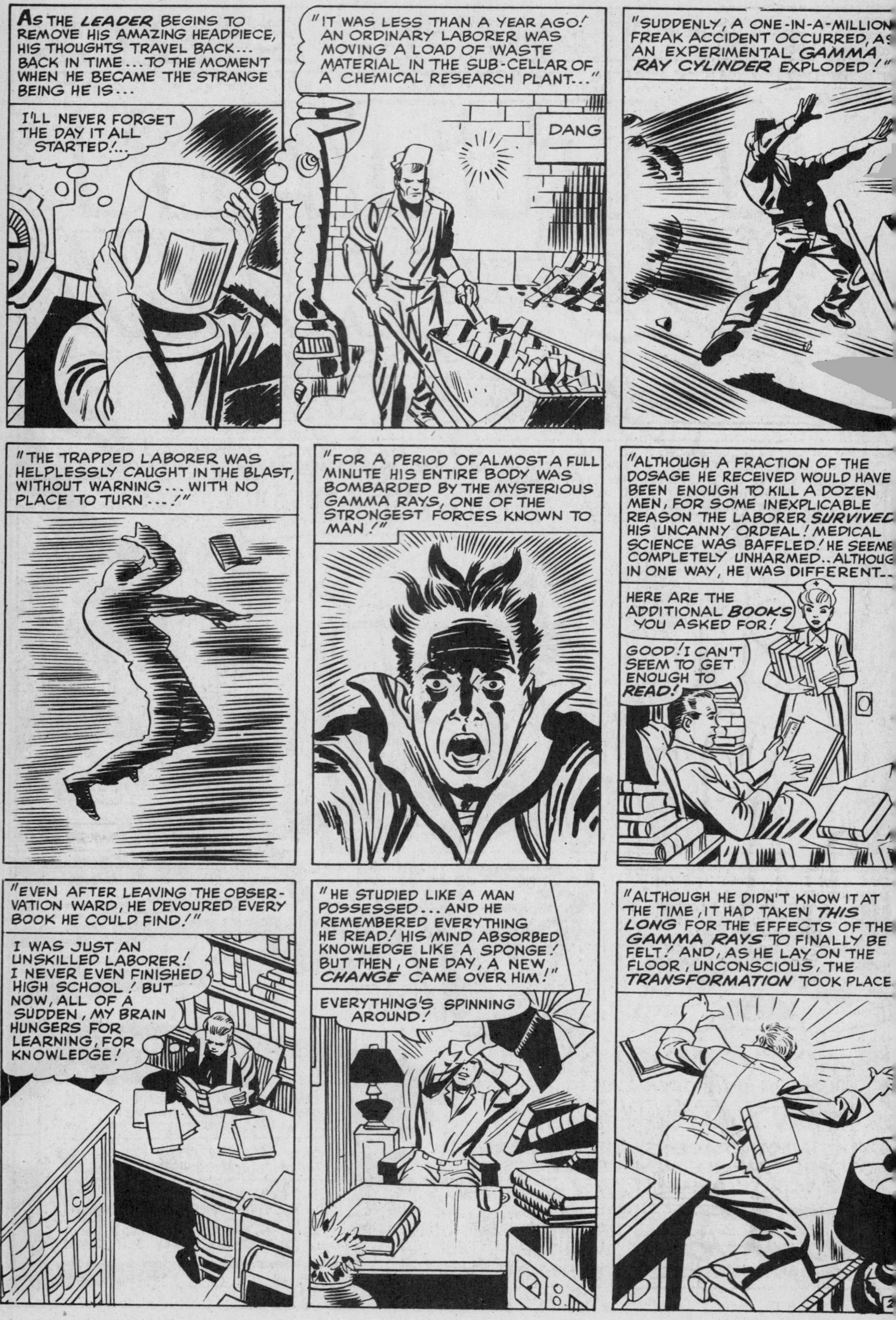
AS THE LEADER BEGINS TO REMOVE HIS AMAZING HEADPIECE, HIS THOUGHTS TRAVEL BACK... BACK IN TIME... TO THE MOMENT WHEN HE BECAME THE STRANGE BEING HE IS...
I'LL NEVER FORGET THE DAY IT ALL STARTED!...
"IT WAS LESS THAN A YEAR AGO! AN ORDINARY LABORER WAS MOVING A LOAD OF WASTE MATERIAL IN THE SUB-CELLAR OF A CHEMICAL RESEARCH PLANT..."
DANG
"SUDDENLY, A ONE-IN-A-MILLION FREAK ACCIDENT OCCURRED, AS AN EXPERIMENTAL GAMMA RAY CYLINDER EXPLODED!"
"THE TRAPPED LABORER WAS HELPLESSLY CAUGHT IN THE BLAST, WITHOUT WARNING... WITH NO PLACE TO TURN...!"
"FOR A PERIOD OF ALMOST A FULL MINUTE HIS ENTIRE BODY WAS BOMBARDED BY THE MYSTERIOUS GAMMA RAYS, ONE OF THE STRONGEST FORCES KNOWN TO MAN!"
"ALTHOUGH A FRACTION OF THE DOSAGE HE RECEIVED WOULD HAVE BEEN ENOUGH TO KILL A DOZEN MEN, FOR SOME INEXPLICABLE REASON THE LABORER SURVIVED HIS UNCANNY ORDEAL! MEDICAL SCIENCE WAS BAFFLED! HE SEEME COMPLETELY UNHARMED.. ALTHOUG IN ONE WAY, HE WAS DIFFERENT...
HERE ARE THE ADDITIONAL BOOKS YOU ASKED FOR!
GOOD! I CAN'T SEEM TO GET ENOUGH TO READ!
"EVEN AFTER LEAVING THE OBSERVATION WARD, HE DEVOURED EVERY BOOK HE COULD FIND!"
I WAS JUST AN UNSKILLED LABORER! I NEVER EVEN FINISHED HIGH SCHOOL! BUT NOW, ALL OF A SUDDEN, MY BRAIN HUNGERS FOR LEARNING, FOR KNOWLEDGE!
"HE STUDIED LIKE A MAN POSSESSED... AND HE REMEMBERED EVERYTHING HE READ! HIS MIND ABSORBED KNOWLEDGE LIKE A SPONGE! BUT THEN, ONE DAY, A NEW CHANGE CAME OVER HIM!"
EVERYTHING'S SPINNING AROUND!
"ALTHOUGH HE DIDN'T KNOW IT AT THE TIME, IT HAD TAKEN THIS LONG FOR THE EFFECTS OF THE GAMMA RAYS TO FINALLY BE FELT! AND, AS HE LAY ON THE FLOOR, UNCONSCIOUS, THE TRANSFORMATION TOOK PLACE.

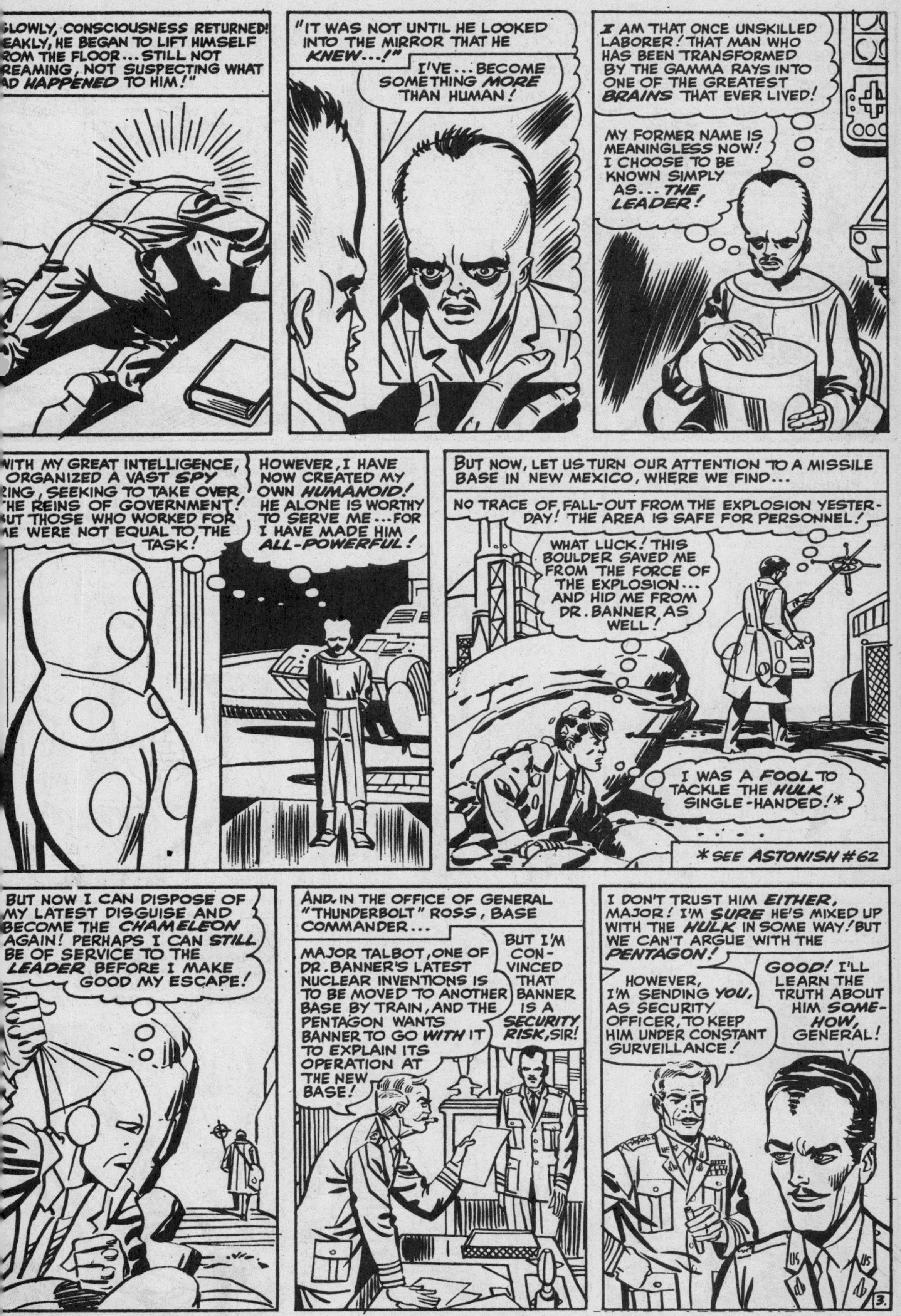
SLOWLY, CONSCIOUSNESS RETURNED! EAKLY, HE BEGAN TO LIFT HIMSELF ROM THE FLOOR... STILL NOT REAMING, NOT SUSPECTING WHAT AD HAPPENED TO HIM!"
"IT WAS NOT UNTIL HE LOOKED INTO THE MIRROR THAT HE KNEW...!"
I'VE... BECOME SOMETHING MORE THAN HUMAN!
I AM THAT ONCE UNSKILLED LABORER! THAT MAN WHO HAS BEEN TRANSFORMED BY THE GAMMA RAYS INTO ONE OF THE GREATEST BRAINS THAT EVER LIVED!
MY FORMER NAME IS MEANINGLESS NOW! I CHOOSE TO BE KNOWN SIMPLY AS... THE LEADER!
WITH MY GREAT INTELLIGENCE, ORGANIZED A VAST SPY RING, SEEKING TO TAKE OVER THE REINS OF GOVERNMENT! BUT THOSE WHO WORKED FOR ME WERE NOT EQUAL TO THE TASK!
HOWEVER, I HAVE NOW CREATED MY OWN HUMANOID! HE ALONE IS WORTHY TO SERVE ME... FOR I HAVE MADE HIM ALL-POWERFUL!
BUT NOW, LET US TURN OUR ATTENTION TO A MISSILE BASE IN NEW MEXICO, WHERE WE FIND...
NO TRACE OF FALL-OUT FROM THE EXPLOSION YESTERDAY! THE AREA IS SAFE FOR PERSONNEL!
WHAT LUCK! THIS BOULDER SAVED ME FROM THE FORCE OF THE EXPLOSION... AND HID ME FROM DR. BANNER, AS WELL!
I WAS A FOOL TO TACKLE THE HULK SINGLE-HANDED!*
* SEE ASTONISH #62
BUT NOW I CAN DISPOSE OF MY LATEST DISGUISE AND BECOME THE CHAMELEON AGAIN! PERHAPS I CAN STILL BE OF SERVICE TO THE LEADER BEFORE I MAKE GOOD MY ESCAPE!
AND, IN THE OFFICE OF GENERAL "THUNDERBOLT" ROSS, BASE COMMANDER...
MAJOR TALBOT, ONE OF DR. BANNER'S LATEST NUCLEAR INVENTIONS IS TO BE MOVED TO ANOTHER BASE BY TRAIN, AND THE PENTAGON WANTS BANNER TO GO WITH IT TO EXPLAIN ITS OPERATION AT THE NEW BASE!
BUT I'M CONVINCED THAT BANNER IS A SECURITY RISK, SIR!
I DON'T TRUST HIM EITHER, MAJOR! I'M SURE HE'S MIXED UP WITH THE HULK IN SOME WAY! BUT WE CAN'T ARGUE WITH THE PENTAGON!
HOWEVER, I'M SENDING YOU, AS SECURITY OFFICER, TO KEEP HIM UNDER CONSTANT SURVEILLANCE!
GOOD! I'LL LEARN THE TRUTH ABOUT HIM SOMEHOW, GENERAL!
3.

AND SO... YOU'RE NOT TO LEAVE THE TRAIN UNTIL IT REACHES ITS DESTINATION, BANNER! AND MAJOR TALBOT WILL HAVE HIS EYE ON YOU AT ALL TIMES! THEY MAY THINK YOU'RE A TOP SCIENTIST IN WASHINGTON, BUT I *STILL* DON'T TRUST YOU!

YOU'VE MANAGED TO MAKE ME VERY *AWARE* OF THAT, GENERAL!

HMM! I'M GLAD THAT I REMAINED HERE, DISGUISED AS A WORKER! THE *LEADER* WILL WANT TO KNOW ABOUT THIS SHIPMENT!

THEN, AFTER THE CHAMELEON HAS CONTACTED THE MASTER SPY...

BANNER'S NUCLEAR DEVICE MUST NOT REACH ITS DESTINATION! AND *YOU*, MY HUMANOID, WILL SEE THAT IT *DOESN'T*!

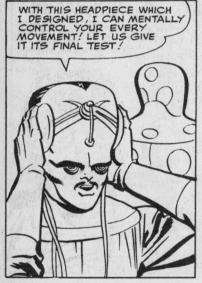

WITH THIS HEADPIECE WHICH I DESIGNED, I CAN MENTALLY CONTROL YOUR EVERY MOVEMENT! LET US GIVE IT ITS FINAL TEST!

WALK SLOWLY TOWARDS ME! AHH, GOOD! GOOD!

THERE IS AN IRON BAR ON THE FLOOR IN FRONT OF YOU! ...PICK IT UP!

NOW *BEND* IT! AHHH, *WONDERFUL*! THE *STRENGTH* I HAVE GIVEN YOU IS ALMOST UNBELIEVABLE!

THROUGH THIS SPECTROSCOPIC TRANSCEIVER, I CAN SEE EVERYTHING THAT *YOU* SEE, MY HUMANOID!

THERE I AM NOW... EXACTLY AS *YOU* SEE ME!

NOW WALK TO MY REMOTE CONTROL HELICOPTER, AND THEN ENTER IT! IT WILL TAKE YOU TO YOUR OBJECTIVE!

AN HOUR LATER...

PERFECT TIMING!... BANNER'S TRAIN IS BELOW! SOON, HIS NEWEST NUCLEAR SECRETS SHALL BE *MINE*!

NOW DESCEND! SLOWLY... SLOWLY...!!

LOOK! A WHIRLYBIRD! IT'S NOT ONE OF OURS!

STOP! STOP, OR I'LL SHOOT!

THE BULLET WENT *THROUGH* HIM...WITHOUT *AFFECTING* HIM! IT'S LIKE HE'S A LIVING *SPONGE!*

CRACK!

SECONDS LATER...

BETTER COME *QUICK,* MAJOR! LOOKS LIKE BIG *TROUBLE!*

MY *DEVICE!* IT MUSTN'T FALL INTO ENEMY HANDS!!

AT *EASE,* BANNER! YOU STAY PUT! I'LL HANDLE THIS!

I'M ORDERING YOU TO STAY IN THIS CAR UNTIL I SEE WHAT'S GOING *ON* OUT THERE! IF IT'S SOME SORT OF SCHEME OF *YOURS,* IT WON'T *WORK,* MISTER!

BUT, IF MY NUCLEAR DEVICE IS IN DANGER, I SHOULD *BE* THERE! IT REPRE- SENTS YEARS OF WORK!

SLAM!

I'M LOCKED *IN!* BUT I'VE *GOT* TO KNOW WHAT'S GOING ON! IF ANY- THING HAPPENS TO MY MACHINE...!!

BUT THEN, DUE TO THE STRAIN AND WORRY, DR. BRUCE BANNER'S PULSE RATE CHANGES, HIS HEART- BEAT SPEEDS UP, TRIGGERING THE INCREDIBLE CHANGE WHICH HE CAN NEVER CONTROL...

OH, NO!! NOT *AGAIN!*

DON'T... DON'T LET IT HAPPEN *AGAIN!!*

BUT, HAPPEN IT *DOES!!* WHERE SECONDS BEFORE A NORMAL SCIENTIST HAD STOOD, *NOW* THE RAMPAGING FORM OF THE INCREDIBLE *HULK* EXPLODES INTO ACTION!!

NO ONE LOCKS THE *HULK* IN!!

WHAK!

5

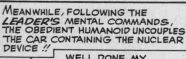

MEANWHILE, FOLLOWING THE *LEADER'S* MENTAL COMMANDS, THE OBEDIENT HUMANOID UNCOUPLES THE CAR CONTAINING THE NUCLEAR DEVICE!!

WELL DONE, MY MINDLESS ONE! NOW, THE MILITARY GUARDS IN THE OTHER SECTION ARE HELPLESS TO INTERFERE!

PREPARE FOR FURTHER INSTRUCTIONS! THE OTHER SECTION IS ALREADY BEGINNING TO LOSE SPEED AND LAG BEHIND! THEY CANNOT AFFECT YOU!

BUT, THE LEADER IS *WRONG!* THERE IS ONE WHO *CAN* AFFECT THE HUMANOID...

ONE KNOWN AS THE *HULK*... WHOSE INCREDIBLE LEGS ARE POWERFUL ENOUGH TO HURL HIM TO THE OTHER SECTION OF THE TRAIN...

MEANWHILE, NOT YET AWARE OF THE ONRUSHING HULK, THE LEADER ORDERS HIS HUMANOID TO UNCOVER THE NUCLEAR DEVICE, SO HE CAN STUDY IT!

A FEW SECONDS OF OBSERVATION WILL BE ALL I NEED!

BUT EVEN THOSE FEW SECONDS ARE DESTINED TO BE DENIED HIM, AS THE HULK ATTACKS!!

HOWEVER, FOR ONCE THE GREEN GOLIATH'S STRENGTH ACTS *AGAINST* HIM, AS THE FORCE OF HIS LUNGE CAUSES HIM TO *BOUNCE BACK* FORCIBLY DUE TO THE SPONGE-LIKE COMPOSITION OF THE HUMANOID'S BODY!!!

AND THEN, FOR THE FIRST TIME, THE LEADER REALLY *SEES* THE HULK, THROUGH THE EYES OF HIS HUMANOID...

I THOUGHT I WAS THE ONLY ONE... BUT I'M *NOT!* THERE IS *ANOTHER!!*

...THAT TITANIC MONSTER *ALSO* HAS GREEN SKIN! CAN IT BE THAT HIS *STRENGTH* IS THE RESULT OF GAMMA RAYS, AS MY *INTELLECT* IS??

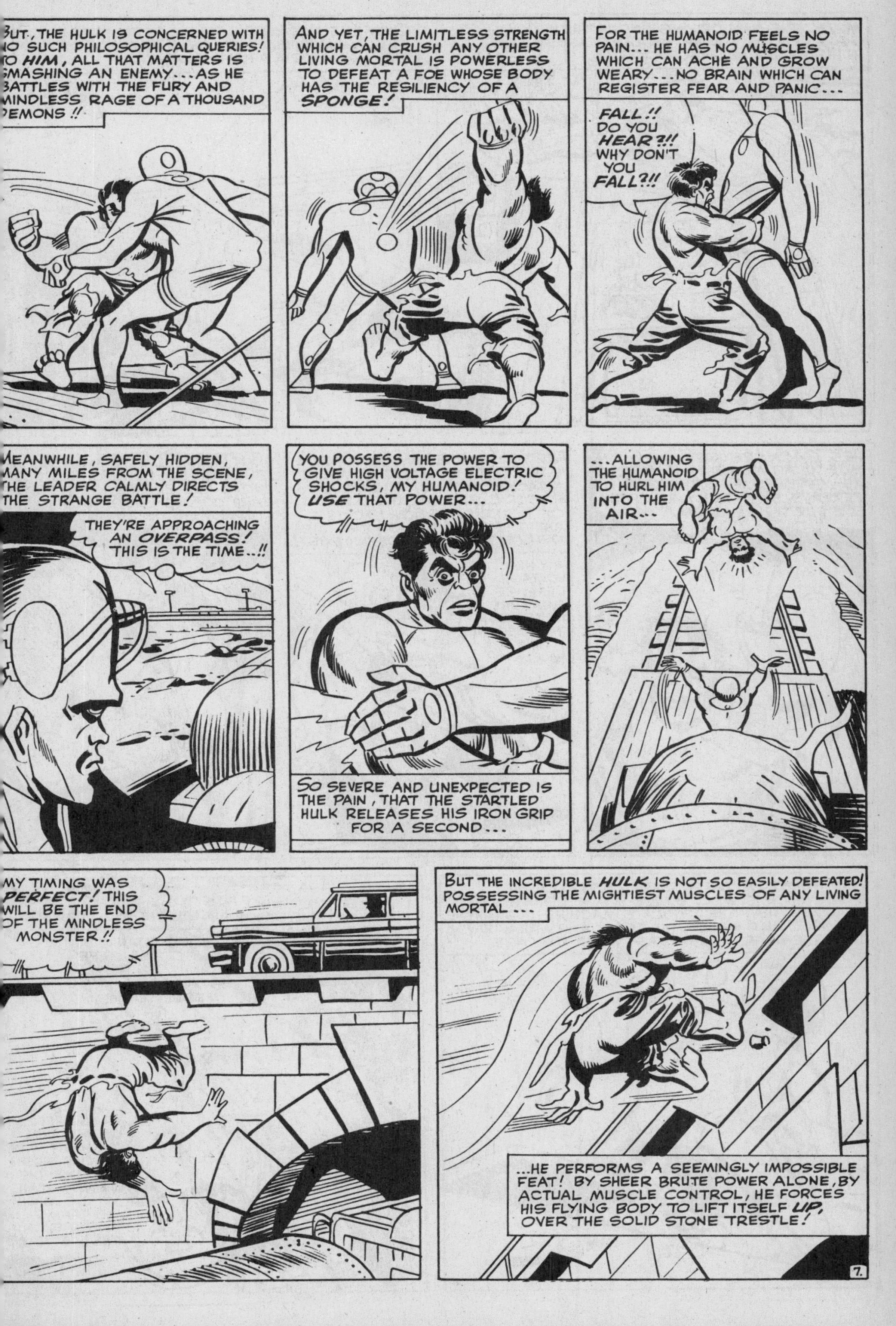
BUT, THE HULK IS CONCERNED WITH NO SUCH PHILOSOPHICAL QUERIES! TO HIM, ALL THAT MATTERS IS SMASHING AN ENEMY... AS HE BATTLES WITH THE FURY AND MINDLESS RAGE OF A THOUSAND DEMONS!!
AND YET, THE LIMITLESS STRENGTH WHICH CAN CRUSH ANY OTHER LIVING MORTAL IS POWERLESS TO DEFEAT A FOE WHOSE BODY HAS THE RESILIENCY OF A SPONGE!
FOR THE HUMANOID FEELS NO PAIN... HE HAS NO MUSCLES WHICH CAN ACHE AND GROW WEARY... NO BRAIN WHICH CAN REGISTER FEAR AND PANIC...
FALL!! DO YOU HEAR?!! WHY DON'T YOU FALL?!!
MEANWHILE, SAFELY HIDDEN, MANY MILES FROM THE SCENE, THE LEADER CALMLY DIRECTS THE STRANGE BATTLE!
THEY'RE APPROACHING AN OVERPASS! THIS IS THE TIME..!!
YOU POSSESS THE POWER TO GIVE HIGH VOLTAGE ELECTRIC SHOCKS, MY HUMANOID! USE THAT POWER...
SO SEVERE AND UNEXPECTED IS THE PAIN, THAT THE STARTLED HULK RELEASES HIS IRON GRIP FOR A SECOND...
...ALLOWING THE HUMANOID TO HURL HIM INTO THE AIR...
MY TIMING WAS PERFECT! THIS WILL BE THE END OF THE MINDLESS MONSTER!!
BUT THE INCREDIBLE HULK IS NOT SO EASILY DEFEATED! POSSESSING THE MIGHTIEST MUSCLES OF ANY LIVING MORTAL...
...HE PERFORMS A SEEMINGLY IMPOSSIBLE FEAT! BY SHEER BRUTE POWER ALONE, BY ACTUAL MUSCLE CONTROL, HE FORCES HIS FLYING BODY TO LIFT ITSELF UP, OVER THE SOLID STONE TRESTLE!
7.

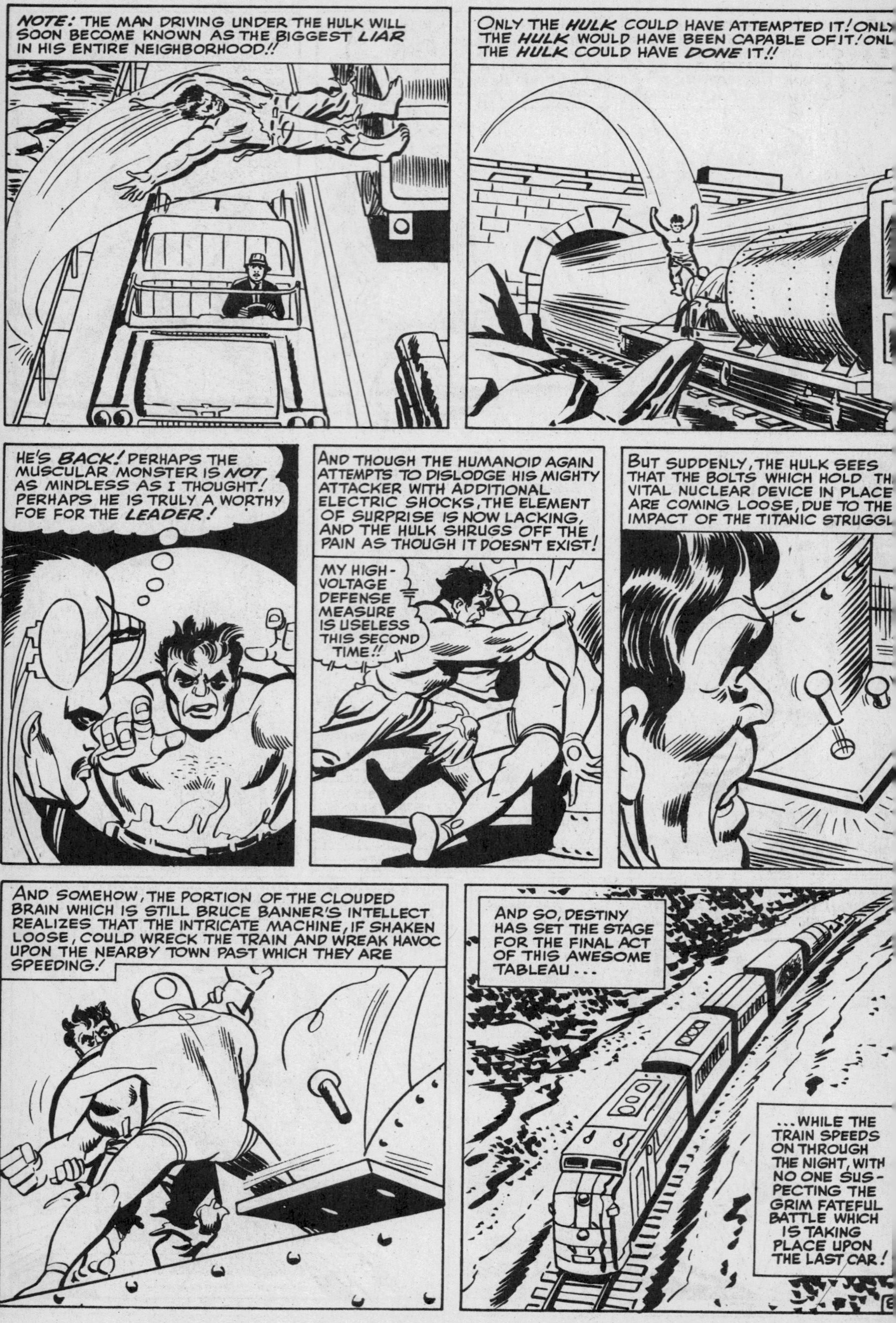
NOTE: THE MAN DRIVING UNDER THE HULK WILL SOON BECOME KNOWN AS THE BIGGEST LIAR IN HIS ENTIRE NEIGHBORHOOD!!
ONLY THE HULK COULD HAVE ATTEMPTED IT! ONLY THE HULK WOULD HAVE BEEN CAPABLE OF IT! ONL THE HULK COULD HAVE DONE IT!!
HE'S BACK! PERHAPS THE MUSCULAR MONSTER IS NOT AS MINDLESS AS I THOUGHT! PERHAPS HE IS TRULY A WORTHY FOE FOR THE LEADER!
AND THOUGH THE HUMANOID AGAIN ATTEMPTS TO DISLODGE HIS MIGHTY ATTACKER WITH ADDITIONAL ELECTRIC SHOCKS, THE ELEMENT OF SURPRISE IS NOW LACKING, AND THE HULK SHRUGS OFF THE PAIN AS THOUGH IT DOESN'T EXIST!
MY HIGH-VOLTAGE DEFENSE MEASURE IS USELESS THIS SECOND TIME!!
BUT SUDDENLY, THE HULK SEES THAT THE BOLTS WHICH HOLD TH VITAL NUCLEAR DEVICE IN PLACE ARE COMING LOOSE, DUE TO THE IMPACT OF THE TITANIC STRUGGL
AND SOMEHOW, THE PORTION OF THE CLOUDED BRAIN WHICH IS STILL BRUCE BANNER'S INTELLECT REALIZES THAT THE INTRICATE MACHINE, IF SHAKEN LOOSE, COULD WRECK THE TRAIN AND WREAK HAVOC UPON THE NEARBY TOWN PAST WHICH THEY ARE SPEEDING!
AND SO, DESTINY HAS SET THE STAGE FOR THE FINAL ACT OF THIS AWESOME TABLEAU...
...WHILE THE TRAIN SPEEDS ON THROUGH THE NIGHT, WITH NO ONE SUSPECTING THE GRIM FATEFUL BATTLE WHICH IS TAKING PLACE UPON THE LAST CAR!

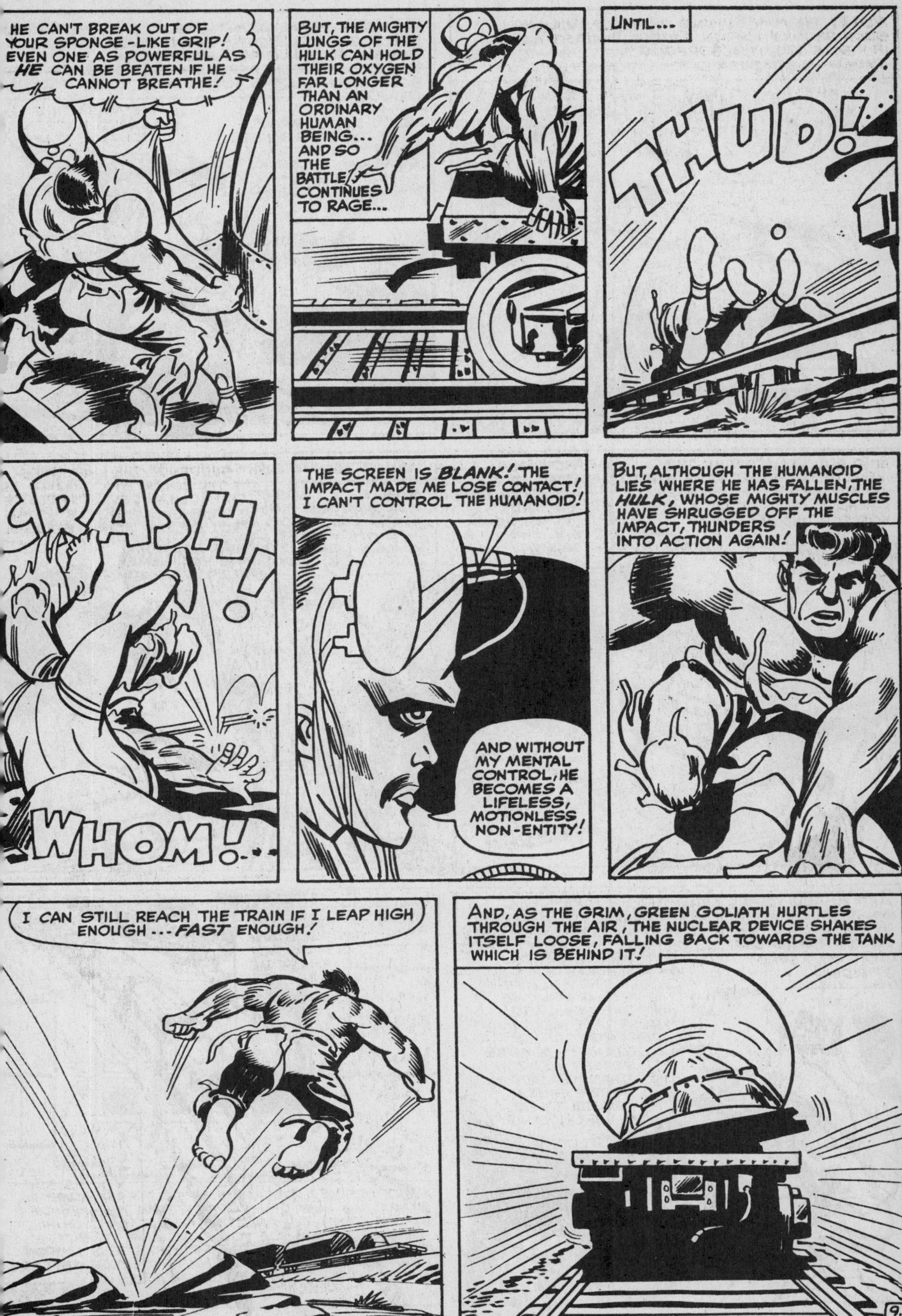

HE CAN'T BREAK OUT OF YOUR SPONGE-LIKE GRIP! EVEN ONE AS POWERFUL AS HE CAN BE BEATEN IF HE CANNOT BREATHE!
BUT, THE MIGHTY LUNGS OF THE HULK CAN HOLD THEIR OXYGEN FAR LONGER THAN AN ORDINARY HUMAN BEING... AND SO THE BATTLE CONTINUES TO RAGE...
UNTIL...
THUD!
CRASH!
WHOM!..
THE SCREEN IS BLANK! THE IMPACT MADE ME LOSE CONTACT! I CAN'T CONTROL THE HUMANOID!
AND WITHOUT MY MENTAL CONTROL, HE BECOMES A LIFELESS, MOTIONLESS NON-ENTITY!
BUT, ALTHOUGH THE HUMANOID LIES WHERE HE HAS FALLEN, THE HULK, WHOSE MIGHTY MUSCLES HAVE SHRUGGED OFF THE IMPACT, THUNDERS INTO ACTION AGAIN!
I CAN STILL REACH THE TRAIN IF I LEAP HIGH ENOUGH ... FAST ENOUGH!
AND, AS THE GRIM, GREEN GOLIATH HURTLES THROUGH THE AIR, THE NUCLEAR DEVICE SHAKES ITSELF LOOSE, FALLING BACK TOWARDS THE TANK WHICH IS BEHIND IT!
9.

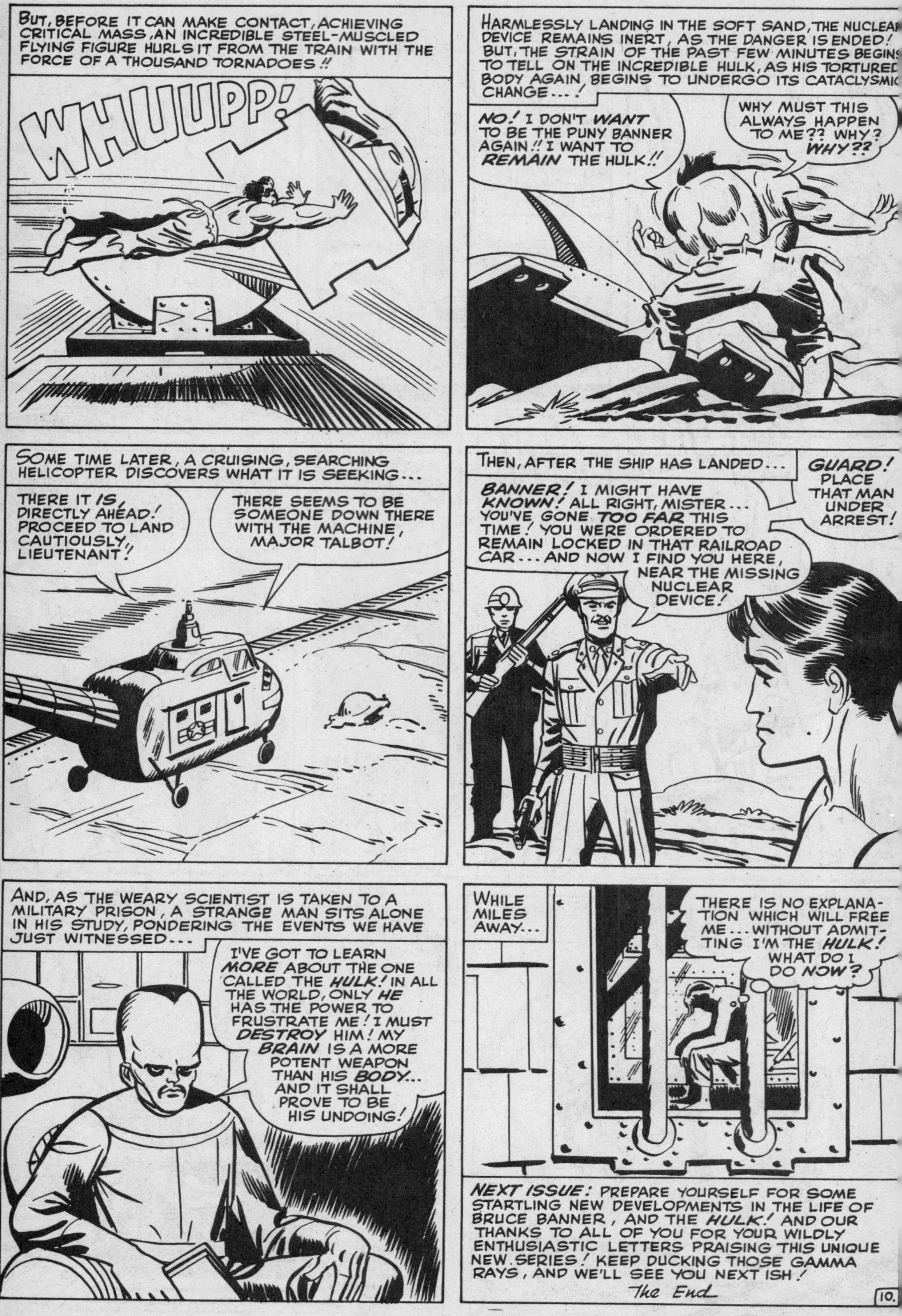
BUT, BEFORE IT CAN MAKE CONTACT, ACHIEVING CRITICAL MASS, AN INCREDIBLE STEEL-MUSCLED FLYING FIGURE HURLS IT FROM THE TRAIN WITH THE FORCE OF A THOUSAND TORNADOES!!
WHUUUPP!
HARMLESSLY LANDING IN THE SOFT SAND, THE NUCLEAR DEVICE REMAINS INERT, AS THE DANGER IS ENDED! BUT, THE STRAIN OF THE PAST FEW MINUTES BEGINS TO TELL ON THE INCREDIBLE HULK, AS HIS TORTURED BODY AGAIN BEGINS TO UNDERGO ITS CATACLYSMIC CHANGE...!
NO! I DON'T WANT TO BE THE PUNY BANNER AGAIN!! I WANT TO REMAIN THE HULK!!
WHY MUST THIS ALWAYS HAPPEN TO ME?? WHY? WHY??
SOME TIME LATER, A CRUISING, SEARCHING HELICOPTER DISCOVERS WHAT IT IS SEEKING...
THERE IT IS, DIRECTLY AHEAD! PROCEED TO LAND CAUTIOUSLY, LIEUTENANT!
THERE SEEMS TO BE SOMEONE DOWN THERE WITH THE MACHINE, MAJOR TALBOT!
THEN, AFTER THE SHIP HAS LANDED...
BANNER! I MIGHT HAVE KNOWN! ALL RIGHT, MISTER... YOU'VE GONE TOO FAR THIS TIME! YOU WERE ORDERED TO REMAIN LOCKED IN THAT RAILROAD CAR... AND NOW I FIND YOU HERE, NEAR THE MISSING NUCLEAR DEVICE!
GUARD! PLACE THAT MAN UNDER ARREST!
AND, AS THE WEARY SCIENTIST IS TAKEN TO A MILITARY PRISON, A STRANGE MAN SITS ALONE IN HIS STUDY, PONDERING THE EVENTS WE HAVE JUST WITNESSED...
I'VE GOT TO LEARN MORE ABOUT THE ONE CALLED THE HULK! IN ALL THE WORLD, ONLY HE HAS THE POWER TO FRUSTRATE ME! I MUST DESTROY HIM! MY BRAIN IS A MORE POTENT WEAPON THAN HIS BODY... AND IT SHALL PROVE TO BE HIS UNDOING!
WHILE MILES AWAY...
THERE IS NO EXPLANATION WHICH WILL FREE ME... WITHOUT ADMITTING I'M THE HULK! WHAT DO I DO NOW?
NEXT ISSUE: PREPARE YOURSELF FOR SOME STARTLING NEW DEVELOPMENTS IN THE LIFE OF BRUCE BANNER, AND THE HULK! AND OUR THANKS TO ALL OF YOU FOR YOUR WILDLY ENTHUSIASTIC LETTERS PRAISING THIS UNIQUE NEW SERIES! KEEP DUCKING THOSE GAMMA RAYS, AND WE'LL SEE YOU NEXT ISH!
The End
10.

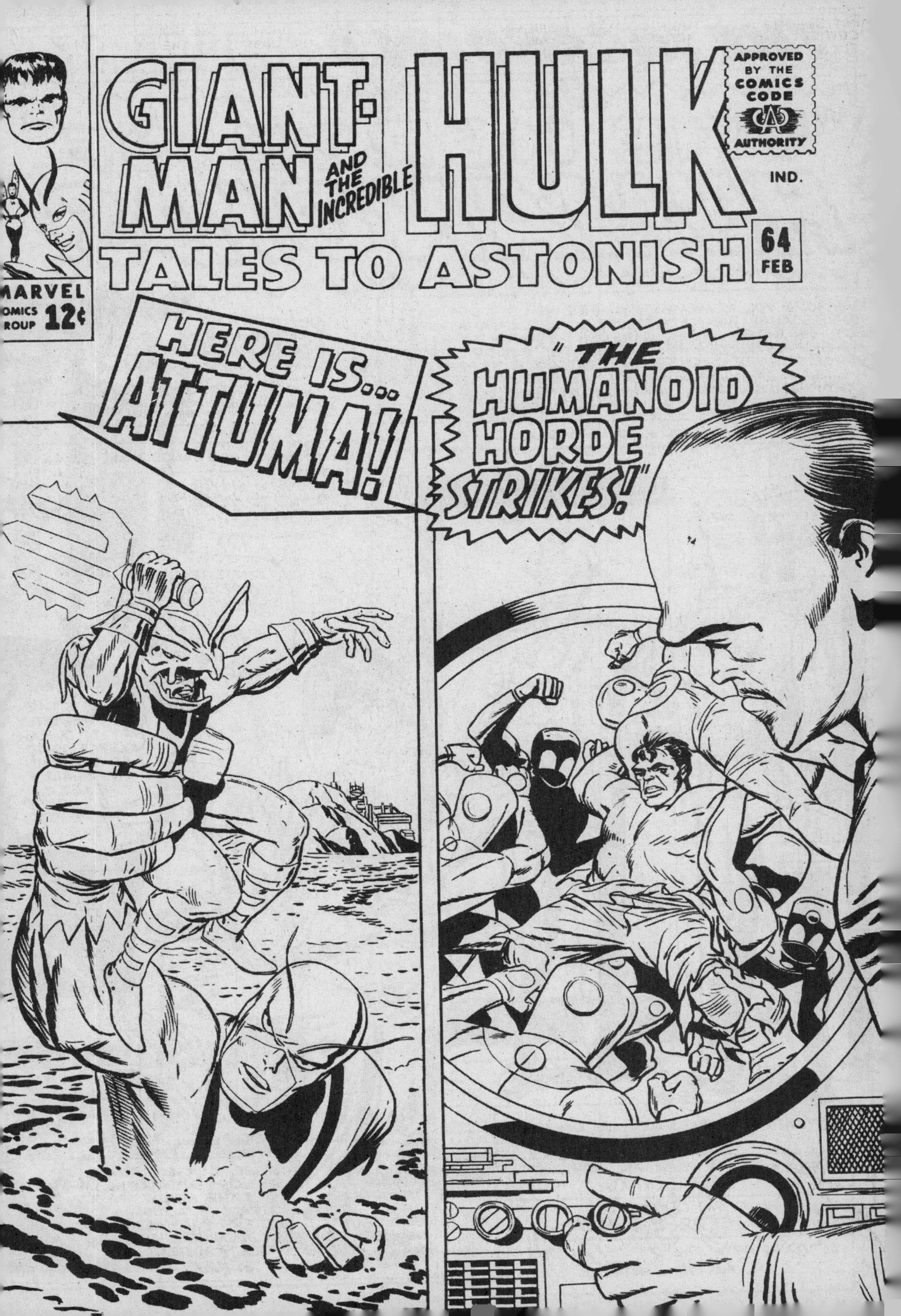

GIANT-MAN AND THE INCREDIBLE HULK
APPROVED BY THE COMICS CODE AUTHORITY
IND.
TALES TO ASTONISH
64 FEB
MARVEL COMICS GROUP 12¢
HERE IS... ATTUMA!
"THE HUMANOID HORDE STRIKES!"

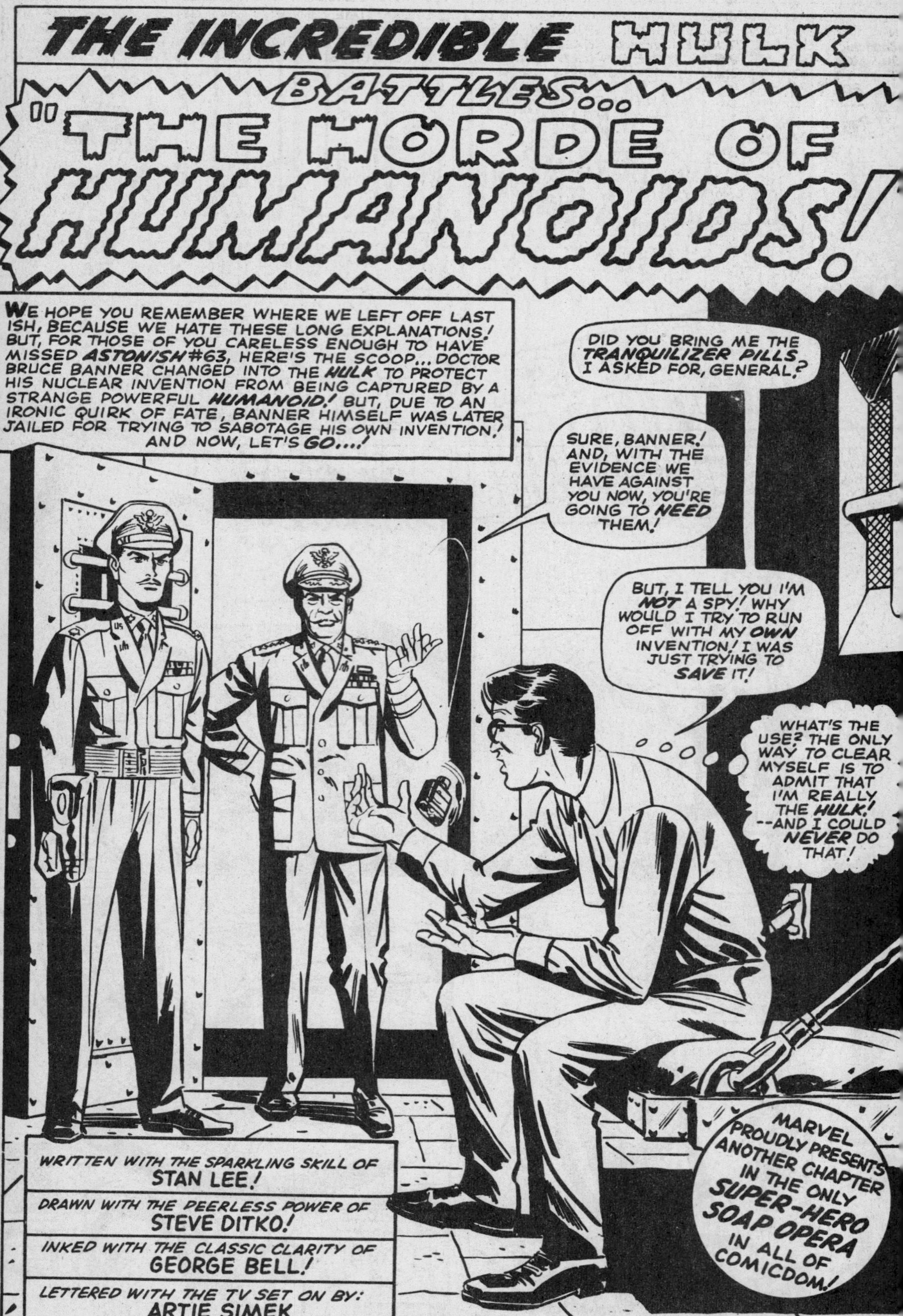
THE INCREDIBLE HULK
BATTLES...
"THE HORDE OF HUMANOIDS!"
WE HOPE YOU REMEMBER WHERE WE LEFT OFF LAST ISH, BECAUSE WE HATE THESE LONG EXPLANATIONS! BUT, FOR THOSE OF YOU CARELESS ENOUGH TO HAVE MISSED ASTONISH #63, HERE'S THE SCOOP... DOCTOR BRUCE BANNER CHANGED INTO THE HULK TO PROTECT HIS NUCLEAR INVENTION FROM BEING CAPTURED BY A STRANGE POWERFUL HUMANOID! BUT, DUE TO AN IRONIC QUIRK OF FATE, BANNER HIMSELF WAS LATER JAILED FOR TRYING TO SABOTAGE HIS OWN INVENTION! AND NOW, LET'S GO....!
DID YOU BRING ME THE TRANQUILIZER PILLS I ASKED FOR, GENERAL?
SURE, BANNER! AND, WITH THE EVIDENCE WE HAVE AGAINST YOU NOW, YOU'RE GOING TO NEED THEM!
BUT, I TELL YOU I'M NOT A SPY! WHY WOULD I TRY TO RUN OFF WITH MY OWN INVENTION! I WAS JUST TRYING TO SAVE IT!
WHAT'S THE USE? THE ONLY WAY TO CLEAR MYSELF IS TO ADMIT THAT I'M REALLY THE HULK! --AND I COULD NEVER DO THAT!
WRITTEN WITH THE SPARKLING SKILL OF STAN LEE!
DRAWN WITH THE PEERLESS POWER OF STEVE DITKO!
INKED WITH THE CLASSIC CLARITY OF GEORGE BELL!
LETTERED WITH THE TV SET ON BY: ARTIE SIMEK
MARVEL PROUDLY PRESENTS ANOTHER CHAPTER IN THE ONLY SUPER-HERO SOAP OPERA IN ALL OF COMICDOM!

YOU SURE ARE A **COOL** ONE, BANNER! BUT, THOSE TRANQUILIZERS WON'T KEEP YOU FROM **BREAKING** WHEN YOU STAND TRIAL FOR **TREASON!**

I WONDER WHAT HE'D SAY IF HE KNEW THE **REAL** REASON I TAKE THESE PILLS IS TO TRY TO KEEP CALM-- SO THAT I WON'T CHANGE INTO-- THE **HULK?!!**

A SHORT TIME LATER...

I STILL CAN'T BELIEVE THAT BRUCE IS A TRAITOR! I COULDN'T **LOVE** HIM AS I DO IF HE WERE! I JUST **COULDN'T!**

YOU GET YOUR **PROOF** AT THE TRIAL, BETTY! AND THEN PERHAPS YOU'LL LOOK AT **ME** IN A DIFFERENT LIGHT!

WITH BANNER OUT OF THE WAY, I'LL DO EVERYTHING I CAN TO WIN HER HEART!

MEANWHILE, MILES AWAY IN A CAREFULLY HIDDEN LABORATORY, A STRANGE, GREEN-SKINNED MAN KNOWN AS THE **THE LEADER** RECEIVES A REPORT FROM ONE OF HIS VAST NETWORK OF SECRET ESPIONAGE AGENTS...

THIS IS THE **CHAMELEON!** BRUCE BANNER UNDER ARREST! THE ARMY STILL PLANS TO TEST HIS NUCLEAR DEVICE ON A DESERTED ISLE! THAT IS ALL!

GOOD! THEN I **STILL** HAVE A CHANCE TO LEARN THE SECRET OF BANNER'S INVENTION! MY HUMANOIDS WILL ATTACK IT **AGAIN!**

BUT, THE THING I **MOST** WANT TO DO IS-- LEARN MORE ABOUT THE **HULK!** INASMUCH AS **HIS** SKIN ALSO IS GREEN, THEN **HE** MIGHT BE A VICTIM OF A GAMMA RAY EXPLOSION, AS **I** WAS! AND, WHERE THE RAYS INCREASED MY **BRAIN POWER**, THEY REACTED DIFFERENTLY WITH HIM-- INCREASING HIS **STRENGTH!**

I **MUST** STUDY HIM!

THUS, WHILE THE MYSTERIOUS **LEADER** WONDERS ABOUT THE **HULK**, WE TURN OUR ATTENTION TO THE NATION'S CAPITOL, WHERE DR. ROBERT BRUCE BANNER, ONE OF AMERICA'S TOP ATOMIC SCIENTISTS, IS UNDER INVESTIGATION. ON SUSPICION OF **TREASON!**

DR. BANNER, AS YOUR LAWYER, I MUST TELL YOU THAT I **CANNOT** HELP YOU IF YOU WON'T GIVE ME ALL THE FACTS!

BUT I **CAN'T** TELL YOU ANY MORE! I'M **INNOCENT!** I'M **NOT** A SPY! BUT-- I DON'T KNOW HOW TO **PROVE** IT!

NOT WITHOUT ADMITTING THAT I'M THE HULK!

THEN YOU HAVEN'T MUCH CHANCE...!

BUT SUDDENLY, AN EAGER TEEN-AGER ENTERS...

RICK! WHAT ARE **YOU** DOING HERE?

WHAT KINDA QUESTION IS **THAT**, DOC! YOU'RE IN A **JAM**, AREN'T YA?

2

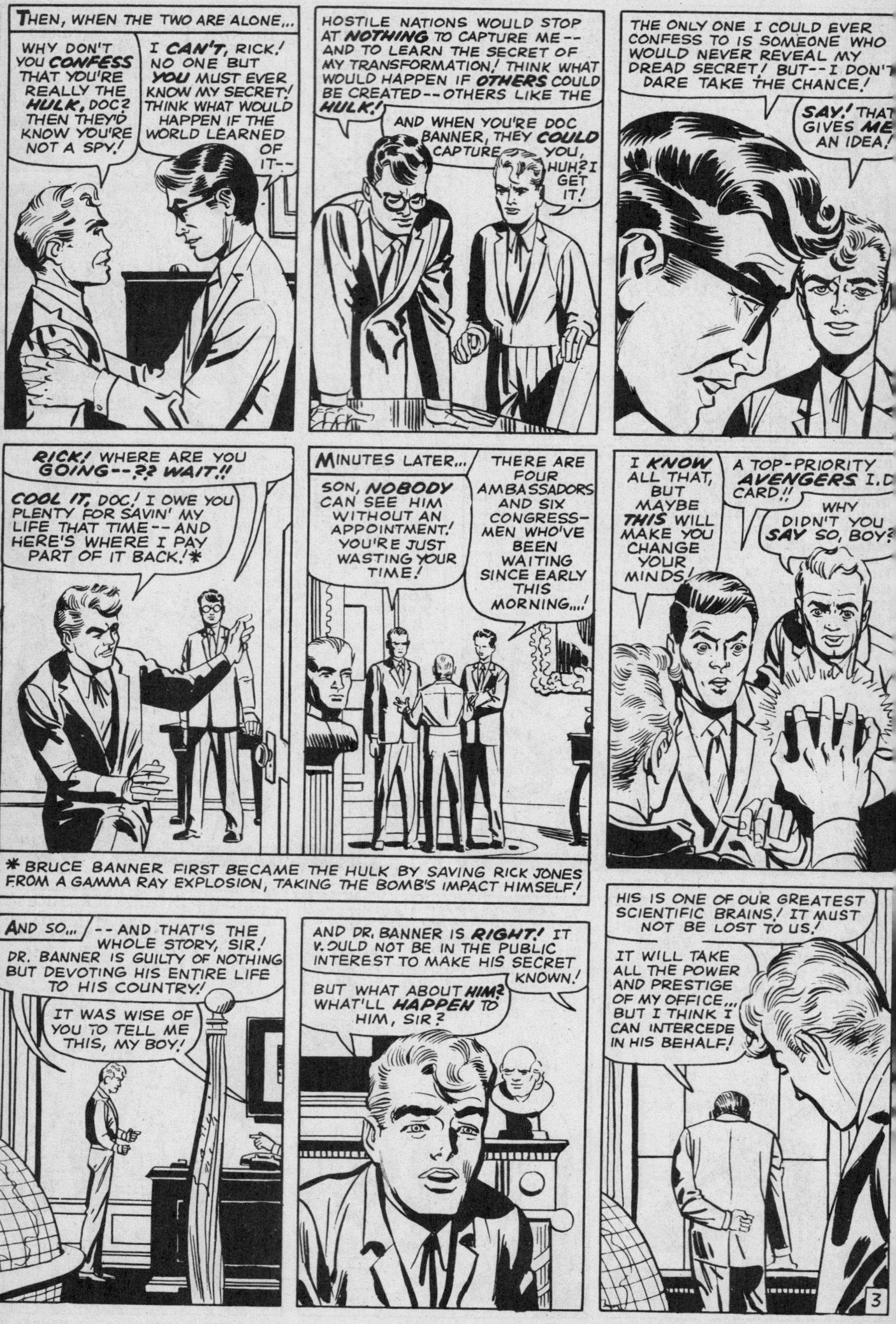
THEN, WHEN THE TWO ARE ALONE,..
WHY DON'T YOU CONFESS THAT YOU'RE REALLY THE HULK, DOC? THEN THEY'D KNOW YOU'RE NOT A SPY!
I CAN'T, RICK! NO ONE BUT YOU MUST EVER KNOW MY SECRET! THINK WHAT WOULD HAPPEN IF THE WORLD LEARNED OF IT--
HOSTILE NATIONS WOULD STOP AT NOTHING TO CAPTURE ME-- AND TO LEARN THE SECRET OF MY TRANSFORMATION! THINK WHAT WOULD HAPPEN IF OTHERS COULD BE CREATED--OTHERS LIKE THE HULK!
AND WHEN YOU'RE DOC BANNER, THEY COULD CAPTURE YOU, HUH? I GET IT!
THE ONLY ONE I COULD EVER CONFESS TO IS SOMEONE WHO WOULD NEVER REVEAL MY DREAD SECRET! BUT--I DON'T DARE TAKE THE CHANCE!
SAY! THAT GIVES ME AN IDEA!
RICK! WHERE ARE YOU GOING--?? WAIT!!
COOL IT, DOC! I OWE YOU PLENTY FOR SAVIN' MY LIFE THAT TIME--AND HERE'S WHERE I PAY PART OF IT BACK!*
MINUTES LATER...
SON, NOBODY CAN SEE HIM WITHOUT AN APPOINTMENT! YOU'RE JUST WASTING YOUR TIME!
THERE ARE FOUR AMBASSADORS AND SIX CONGRESS-MEN WHO'VE BEEN WAITING SINCE EARLY THIS MORNING...!
I KNOW ALL THAT, BUT MAYBE THIS WILL MAKE YOU CHANGE YOUR MINDS!
A TOP-PRIORITY AVENGERS I.D. CARD!!
WHY DIDN'T YOU SAY SO, BOY?
* BRUCE BANNER FIRST BECAME THE HULK BY SAVING RICK JONES FROM A GAMMA RAY EXPLOSION, TAKING THE BOMB'S IMPACT HIMSELF!
AND SO...
--AND THAT'S THE WHOLE STORY, SIR! DR. BANNER IS GUILTY OF NOTHING BUT DEVOTING HIS ENTIRE LIFE TO HIS COUNTRY!
IT WAS WISE OF YOU TO TELL ME THIS, MY BOY!
AND DR. BANNER IS RIGHT! IT WOULD NOT BE IN THE PUBLIC INTEREST TO MAKE HIS SECRET KNOWN!
BUT WHAT ABOUT HIM? WHAT'LL HAPPEN TO HIM, SIR?
HIS IS ONE OF OUR GREATEST SCIENTIFIC BRAINS! IT MUST NOT BE LOST TO US!
IT WILL TAKE ALL THE POWER AND PRESTIGE OF MY OFFICE... BUT I THINK I CAN INTERCEDE IN HIS BEHALF!
3

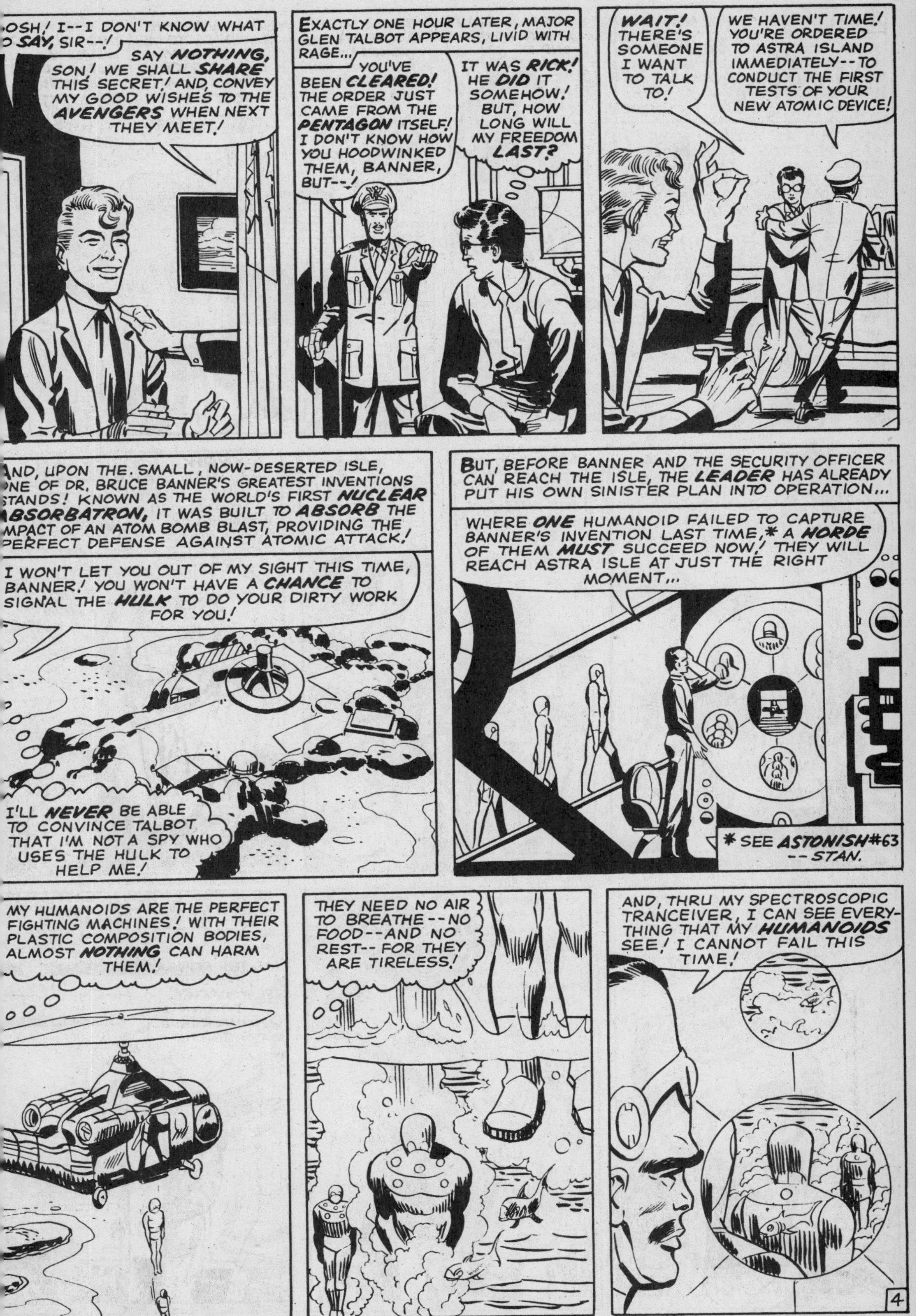

OSH! I--I DON'T KNOW WHAT O SAY, SIR--!
SAY NOTHING, SON! WE SHALL SHARE THIS SECRET! AND, CONVEY MY GOOD WISHES TO THE AVENGERS WHEN NEXT THEY MEET!
EXACTLY ONE HOUR LATER, MAJOR GLEN TALBOT APPEARS, LIVID WITH RAGE...
YOU'VE BEEN CLEARED! THE ORDER JUST CAME FROM THE PENTAGON ITSELF! I DON'T KNOW HOW YOU HOODWINKED THEM, BANNER, BUT--!
IT WAS RICK! HE DID IT SOMEHOW! BUT, HOW LONG WILL MY FREEDOM LAST?
WAIT! THERE'S SOMEONE I WANT TO TALK TO!
WE HAVEN'T TIME! YOU'RE ORDERED TO ASTRA ISLAND IMMEDIATELY--TO CONDUCT THE FIRST TESTS OF YOUR NEW ATOMIC DEVICE!
AND, UPON THE SMALL, NOW-DESERTED ISLE, ONE OF DR. BRUCE BANNER'S GREATEST INVENTIONS STANDS! KNOWN AS THE WORLD'S FIRST NUCLEAR ABSORBATRON, IT WAS BUILT TO ABSORB THE IMPACT OF AN ATOM BOMB BLAST, PROVIDING THE PERFECT DEFENSE AGAINST ATOMIC ATTACK!
I WON'T LET YOU OUT OF MY SIGHT THIS TIME, BANNER! YOU WON'T HAVE A CHANCE TO SIGNAL THE HULK TO DO YOUR DIRTY WORK FOR YOU!
I'LL NEVER BE ABLE TO CONVINCE TALBOT THAT I'M NOT A SPY WHO USES THE HULK TO HELP ME!
BUT, BEFORE BANNER AND THE SECURITY OFFICER CAN REACH THE ISLE, THE LEADER HAS ALREADY PUT HIS OWN SINISTER PLAN INTO OPERATION...
WHERE ONE HUMANOID FAILED TO CAPTURE BANNER'S INVENTION LAST TIME,* A HORDE OF THEM MUST SUCCEED NOW! THEY WILL REACH ASTRA ISLE AT JUST THE RIGHT MOMENT...
* SEE ASTONISH #63 --STAN.
MY HUMANOIDS ARE THE PERFECT FIGHTING MACHINES! WITH THEIR PLASTIC COMPOSITION BODIES, ALMOST NOTHING CAN HARM THEM!
THEY NEED NO AIR TO BREATHE--NO FOOD--AND NO REST--FOR THEY ARE TIRELESS!
AND, THRU MY SPECTROSCOPIC TRANCEIVER, I CAN SEE EVERYTHING THAT MY HUMANOIDS SEE! I CANNOT FAIL THIS TIME!
4

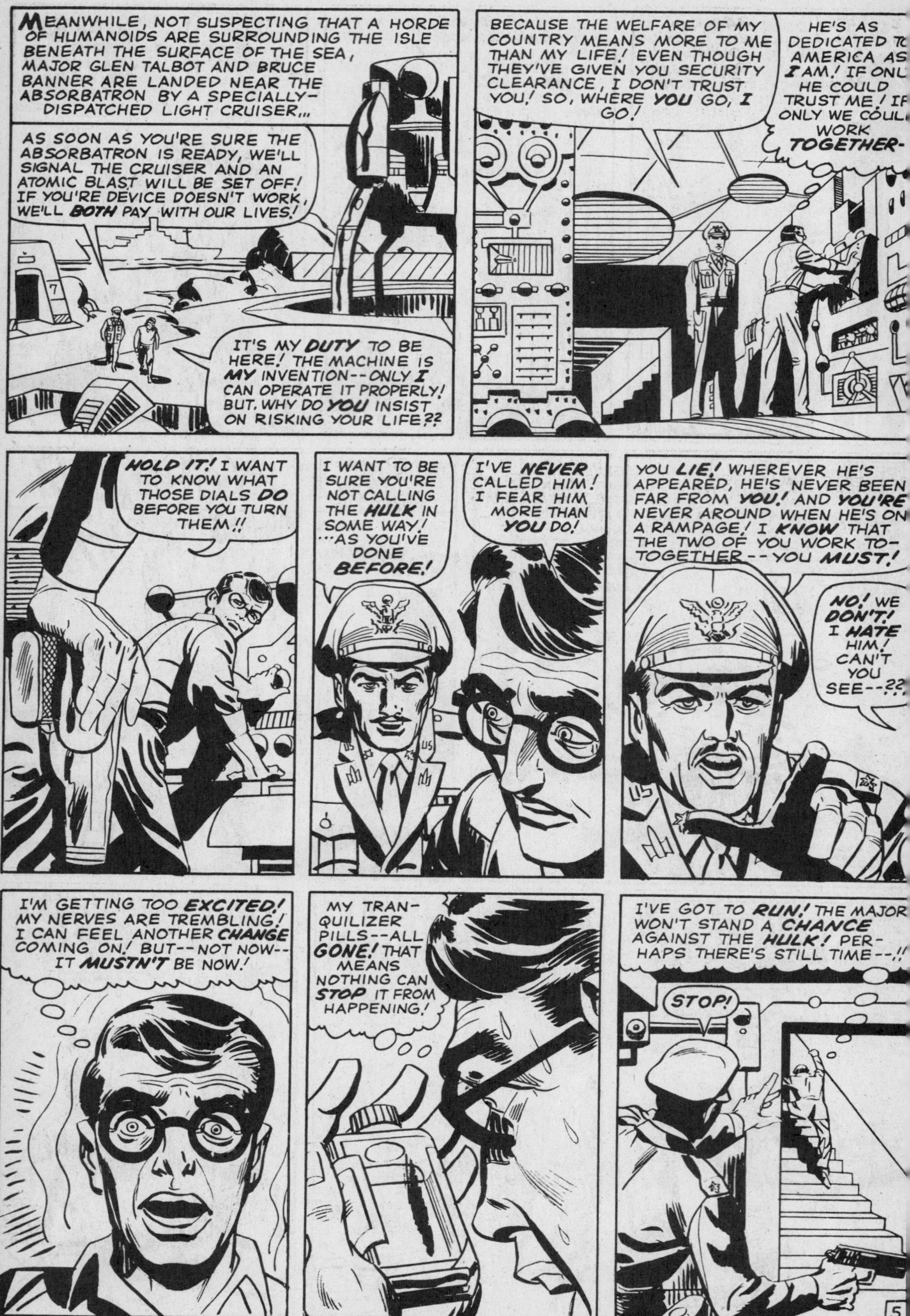
MEANWHILE, NOT SUSPECTING THAT A HORDE OF HUMANOIDS ARE SURROUNDING THE ISLE BENEATH THE SURFACE OF THE SEA, MAJOR GLEN TALBOT AND BRUCE BANNER ARE LANDED NEAR THE ABSORBATRON BY A SPECIALLY-DISPATCHED LIGHT CRUISER...
AS SOON AS YOU'RE SURE THE ABSORBATRON IS READY, WE'LL SIGNAL THE CRUISER AND AN ATOMIC BLAST WILL BE SET OFF! IF YOU'RE DEVICE DOESN'T WORK, WE'LL BOTH PAY WITH OUR LIVES!
IT'S MY DUTY TO BE HERE! THE MACHINE IS MY INVENTION--ONLY I CAN OPERATE IT PROPERLY! BUT, WHY DO YOU INSIST ON RISKING YOUR LIFE??
BECAUSE THE WELFARE OF MY COUNTRY MEANS MORE TO ME THAN MY LIFE! EVEN THOUGH THEY'VE GIVEN YOU SECURITY CLEARANCE, I DON'T TRUST YOU! SO, WHERE YOU GO, I GO!
HE'S AS DEDICATED TO AMERICA AS I AM! IF ONLY HE COULD TRUST ME! IF ONLY WE COULD WORK TOGETHER--
HOLD IT! I WANT TO KNOW WHAT THOSE DIALS DO BEFORE YOU TURN THEM!!
I WANT TO BE SURE YOU'RE NOT CALLING THE HULK IN SOME WAY! ...AS YOU'VE DONE BEFORE!
I'VE NEVER CALLED HIM! I FEAR HIM MORE THAN YOU DO!
YOU LIE! WHEREVER HE'S APPEARED, HE'S NEVER BEEN FAR FROM YOU! AND YOU'RE NEVER AROUND WHEN HE'S ON A RAMPAGE! I KNOW THAT THE TWO OF YOU WORK TO-TOGETHER--YOU MUST!
NO! WE DON'T! I HATE HIM! CAN'T YOU SEE--??
I'M GETTING TOO EXCITED! MY NERVES ARE TREMBLING! I CAN FEEL ANOTHER CHANGE COMING ON! BUT--NOT NOW--IT MUSTN'T BE NOW!
MY TRANQUILIZER PILLS--ALL GONE! THAT MEANS NOTHING CAN STOP IT FROM HAPPENING!
I'VE GOT TO RUN! THE MAJOR WON'T STAND A CHANCE AGAINST THE HULK! PERHAPS THERE'S STILL TIME--!!
STOP!
5

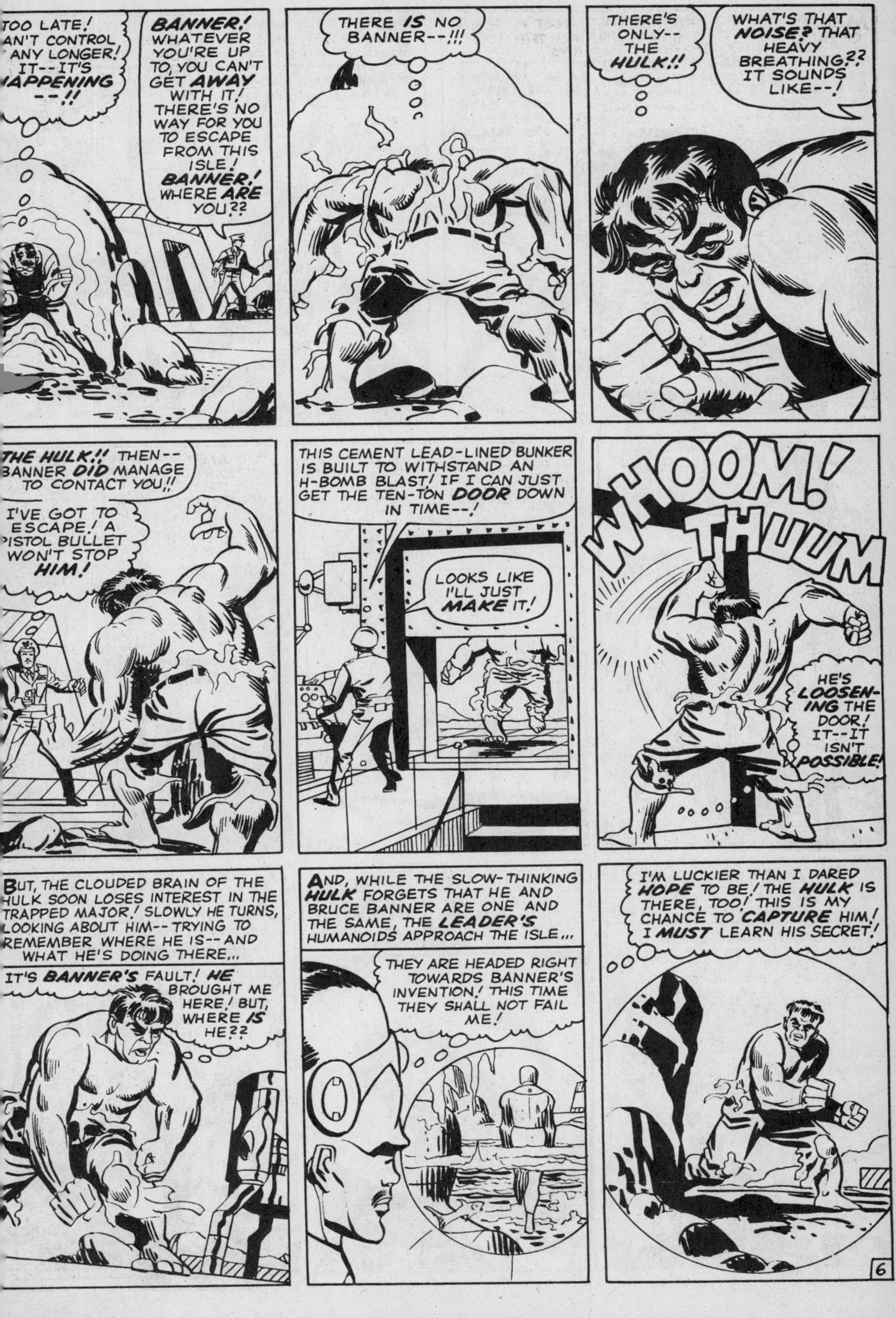
TOO LATE! CAN'T CONTROL IT ANY LONGER! IT--IT'S HAPPENING--!!
BANNER! WHATEVER YOU'RE UP TO, YOU CAN'T GET AWAY WITH IT! THERE'S NO WAY FOR YOU TO ESCAPE FROM THIS ISLE! BANNER! WHERE ARE YOU??
THERE IS NO BANNER--!!!
THERE'S ONLY--THE HULK!!
WHAT'S THAT NOISE? THAT HEAVY BREATHING?? IT SOUNDS LIKE--!
THE HULK!! THEN--BANNER DID MANAGE TO CONTACT YOU!!
I'VE GOT TO ESCAPE! A PISTOL BULLET WON'T STOP HIM!
THIS CEMENT LEAD-LINED BUNKER IS BUILT TO WITHSTAND AN H-BOMB BLAST! IF I CAN JUST GET THE TEN-TON DOOR DOWN IN TIME--!
LOOKS LIKE I'LL JUST MAKE IT!
WHOOM!
THUUM
HE'S LOOSENING THE DOOR! IT--IT ISN'T POSSIBLE!
BUT, THE CLOUDED BRAIN OF THE HULK SOON LOSES INTEREST IN THE TRAPPED MAJOR! SLOWLY HE TURNS, LOOKING ABOUT HIM--TRYING TO REMEMBER WHERE HE IS--AND WHAT HE'S DOING THERE...
IT'S BANNER'S FAULT! HE BROUGHT ME HERE! BUT, WHERE IS HE??
AND, WHILE THE SLOW-THINKING HULK FORGETS THAT HE AND BRUCE BANNER ARE ONE AND THE SAME, THE LEADER'S HUMANOIDS APPROACH THE ISLE...
THEY ARE HEADED RIGHT TOWARDS BANNER'S INVENTION! THIS TIME THEY SHALL NOT FAIL ME!
I'M LUCKIER THAN I DARED HOPE TO BE! THE HULK IS THERE, TOO! THIS IS MY CHANCE TO CAPTURE HIM! I MUST LEARN HIS SECRET!
6

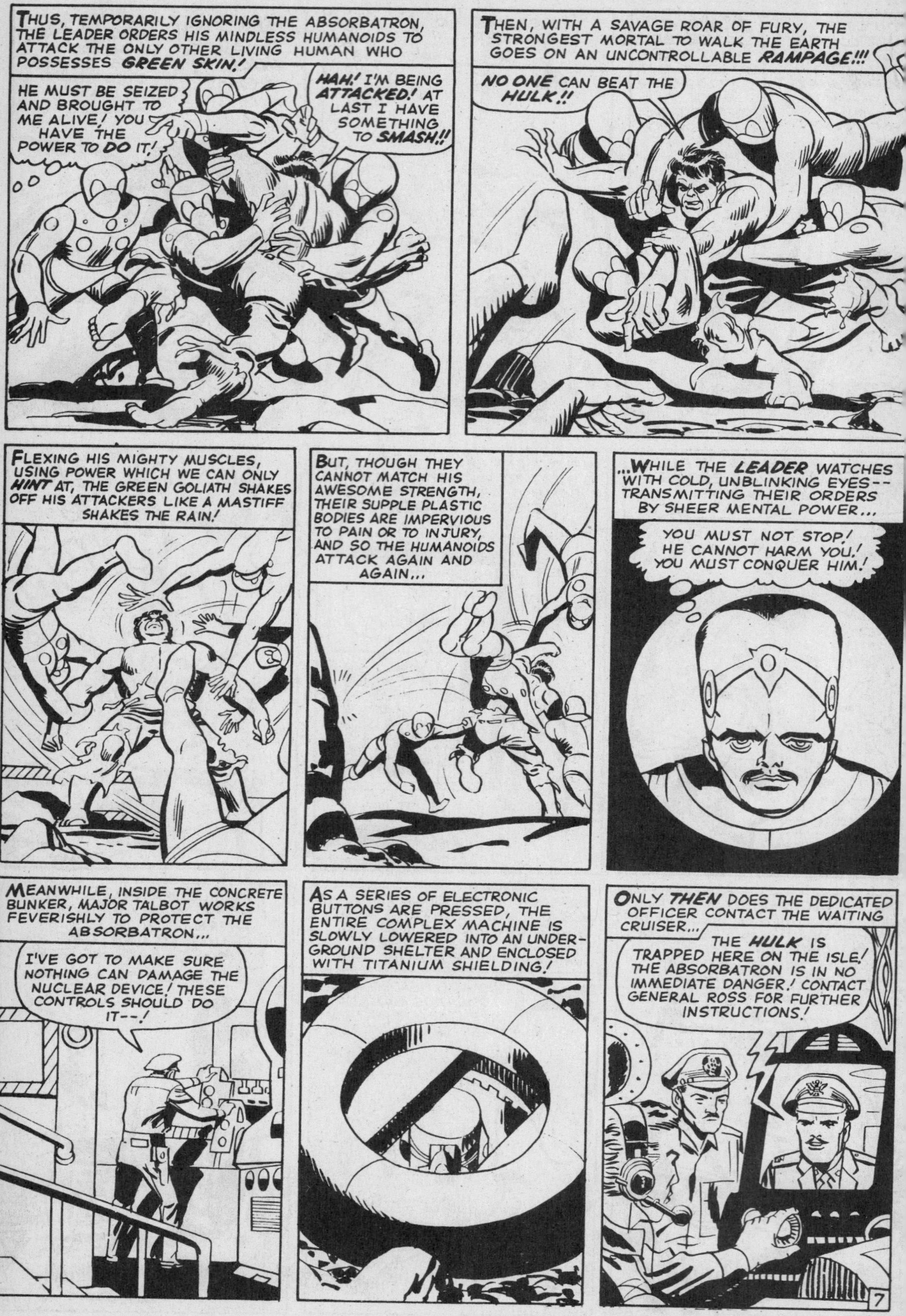
THUS, TEMPORARILY IGNORING THE ABSORBATRON, THE LEADER ORDERS HIS MINDLESS HUMANOIDS TO ATTACK THE ONLY OTHER LIVING HUMAN WHO POSSESSES GREEN SKIN!
HE MUST BE SEIZED AND BROUGHT TO ME ALIVE! YOU HAVE THE POWER TO DO IT!
HAH! I'M BEING ATTACKED! AT LAST I HAVE SOMETHING TO SMASH!!
THEN, WITH A SAVAGE ROAR OF FURY, THE STRONGEST MORTAL TO WALK THE EARTH GOES ON AN UNCONTROLLABLE RAMPAGE!!!
NO ONE CAN BEAT THE HULK!!
FLEXING HIS MIGHTY MUSCLES, USING POWER WHICH WE CAN ONLY HINT AT, THE GREEN GOLIATH SHAKES OFF HIS ATTACKERS LIKE A MASTIFF SHAKES THE RAIN!
BUT, THOUGH THEY CANNOT MATCH HIS AWESOME STRENGTH, THEIR SUPPLE PLASTIC BODIES ARE IMPERVIOUS TO PAIN OR TO INJURY, AND SO THE HUMANOIDS ATTACK AGAIN AND AGAIN...
...WHILE THE LEADER WATCHES WITH COLD, UNBLINKING EYES-- TRANSMITTING THEIR ORDERS BY SHEER MENTAL POWER...
YOU MUST NOT STOP! HE CANNOT HARM YOU! YOU MUST CONQUER HIM!
MEANWHILE, INSIDE THE CONCRETE BUNKER, MAJOR TALBOT WORKS FEVERISHLY TO PROTECT THE ABSORBATRON...
I'VE GOT TO MAKE SURE NOTHING CAN DAMAGE THE NUCLEAR DEVICE! THESE CONTROLS SHOULD DO IT--!
AS A SERIES OF ELECTRONIC BUTTONS ARE PRESSED, THE ENTIRE COMPLEX MACHINE IS SLOWLY LOWERED INTO AN UNDERGROUND SHELTER AND ENCLOSED WITH TITANIUM SHIELDING!
ONLY THEN DOES THE DEDICATED OFFICER CONTACT THE WAITING CRUISER...
THE HULK IS TRAPPED HERE ON THE ISLE! THE ABSORBATRON IS IN NO IMMEDIATE DANGER! CONTACT GENERAL ROSS FOR FURTHER INSTRUCTIONS!
7

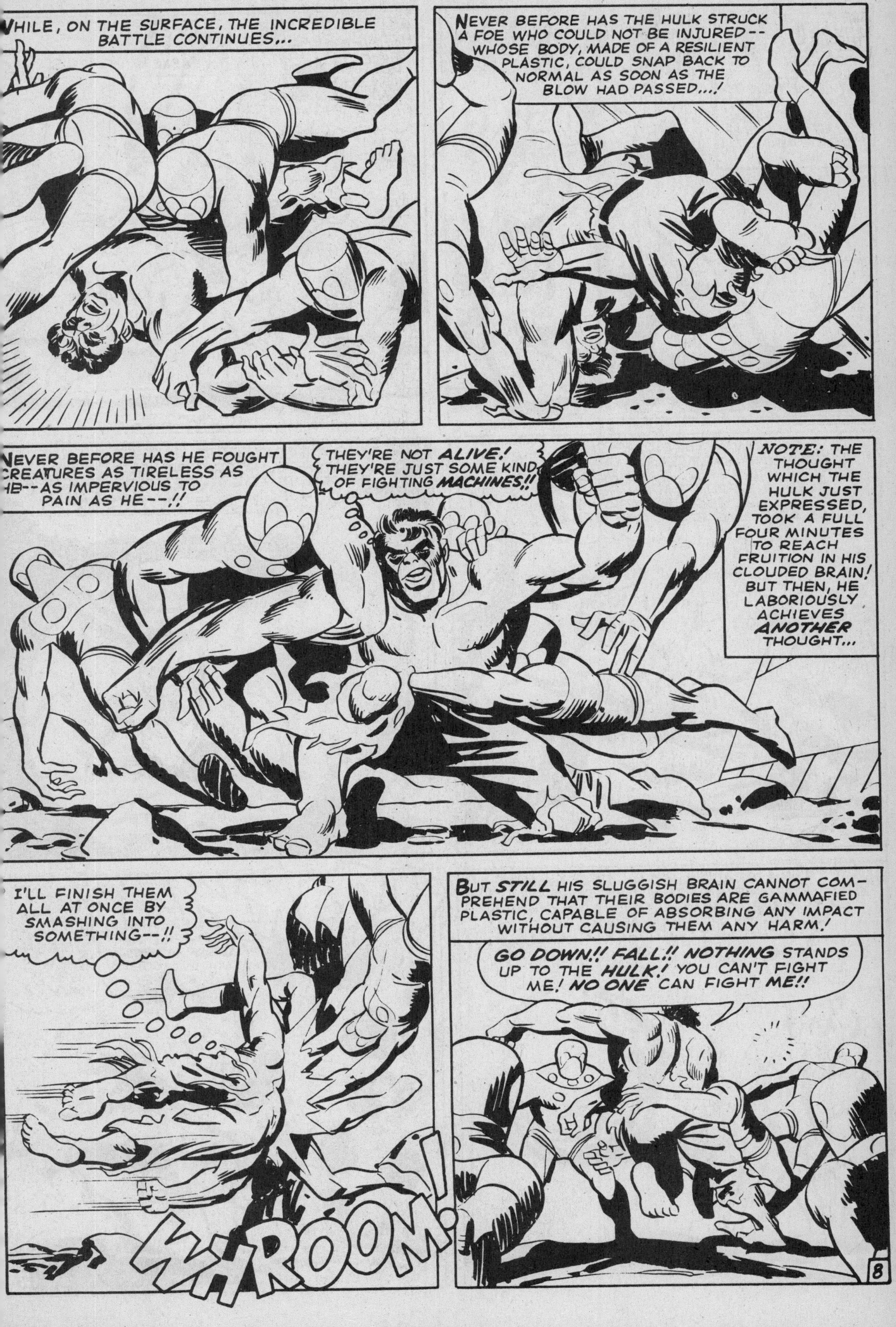
WHILE, ON THE SURFACE, THE INCREDIBLE BATTLE CONTINUES...
NEVER BEFORE HAS THE HULK STRUCK A FOE WHO COULD NOT BE INJURED-- WHOSE BODY, MADE OF A RESILIENT PLASTIC, COULD SNAP BACK TO NORMAL AS SOON AS THE BLOW HAD PASSED...!
NEVER BEFORE HAS HE FOUGHT CREATURES AS TIRELESS AS HE--AS IMPERVIOUS TO PAIN AS HE--!!
THEY'RE NOT ALIVE! THEY'RE JUST SOME KIND OF FIGHTING MACHINES!!
NOTE: THE THOUGHT WHICH THE HULK JUST EXPRESSED, TOOK A FULL FOUR MINUTES TO REACH FRUITION IN HIS CLOUDED BRAIN! BUT THEN, HE LABORIOUSLY ACHIEVES ANOTHER THOUGHT...
I'LL FINISH THEM ALL AT ONCE BY SMASHING INTO SOMETHING--!!
WHROOM!
BUT STILL HIS SLUGGISH BRAIN CANNOT COMPREHEND THAT THEIR BODIES ARE GAMMAFIED PLASTIC, CAPABLE OF ABSORBING ANY IMPACT WITHOUT CAUSING THEM ANY HARM!
GO DOWN!! FALL!! NOTHING STANDS UP TO THE HULK! YOU CAN'T FIGHT ME! NO ONE CAN FIGHT ME!!
8

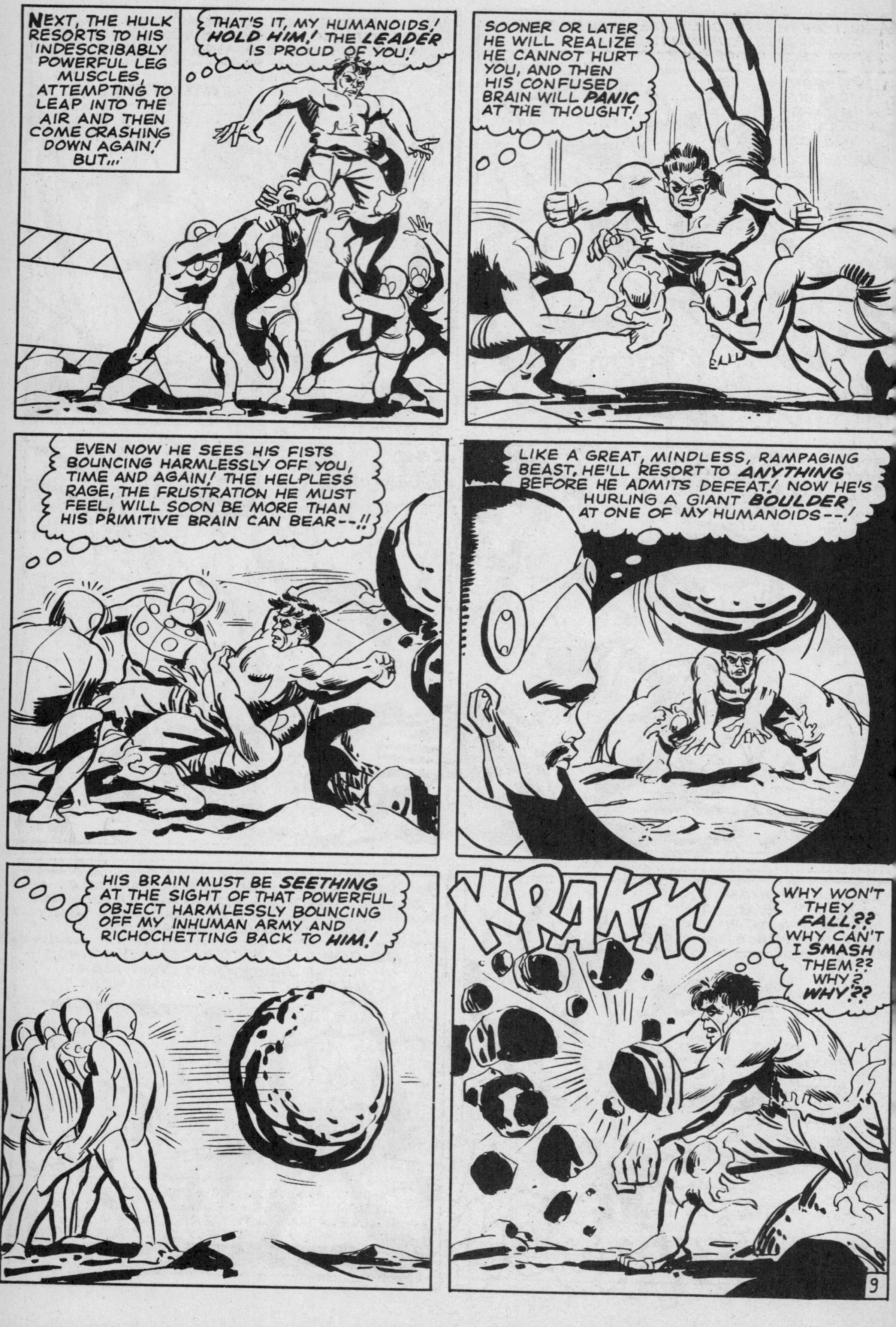
NEXT, THE HULK RESORTS TO HIS INDESCRIBABLY POWERFUL LEG MUSCLES, ATTEMPTING TO LEAP INTO THE AIR AND THEN COME CRASHING DOWN AGAIN! BUT...
THAT'S IT, MY HUMANOIDS! HOLD HIM! THE LEADER IS PROUD OF YOU!
SOONER OR LATER HE WILL REALIZE HE CANNOT HURT YOU, AND THEN HIS CONFUSED BRAIN WILL PANIC AT THE THOUGHT!
EVEN NOW HE SEES HIS FISTS BOUNCING HARMLESSLY OFF YOU, TIME AND AGAIN! THE HELPLESS RAGE, THE FRUSTRATION HE MUST FEEL, WILL SOON BE MORE THAN HIS PRIMITIVE BRAIN CAN BEAR--!!
LIKE A GREAT, MINDLESS, RAMPAGING BEAST, HE'LL RESORT TO ANYTHING BEFORE HE ADMITS DEFEAT! NOW HE'S HURLING A GIANT BOULDER AT ONE OF MY HUMANOIDS--!
HIS BRAIN MUST BE SEETHING AT THE SIGHT OF THAT POWERFUL OBJECT HARMLESSLY BOUNCING OFF MY INHUMAN ARMY AND RICHOCHETTING BACK TO HIM!
KRAKK!
WHY WON'T THEY FALL?? WHY CAN'T I SMASH THEM?? WHY? WHY??

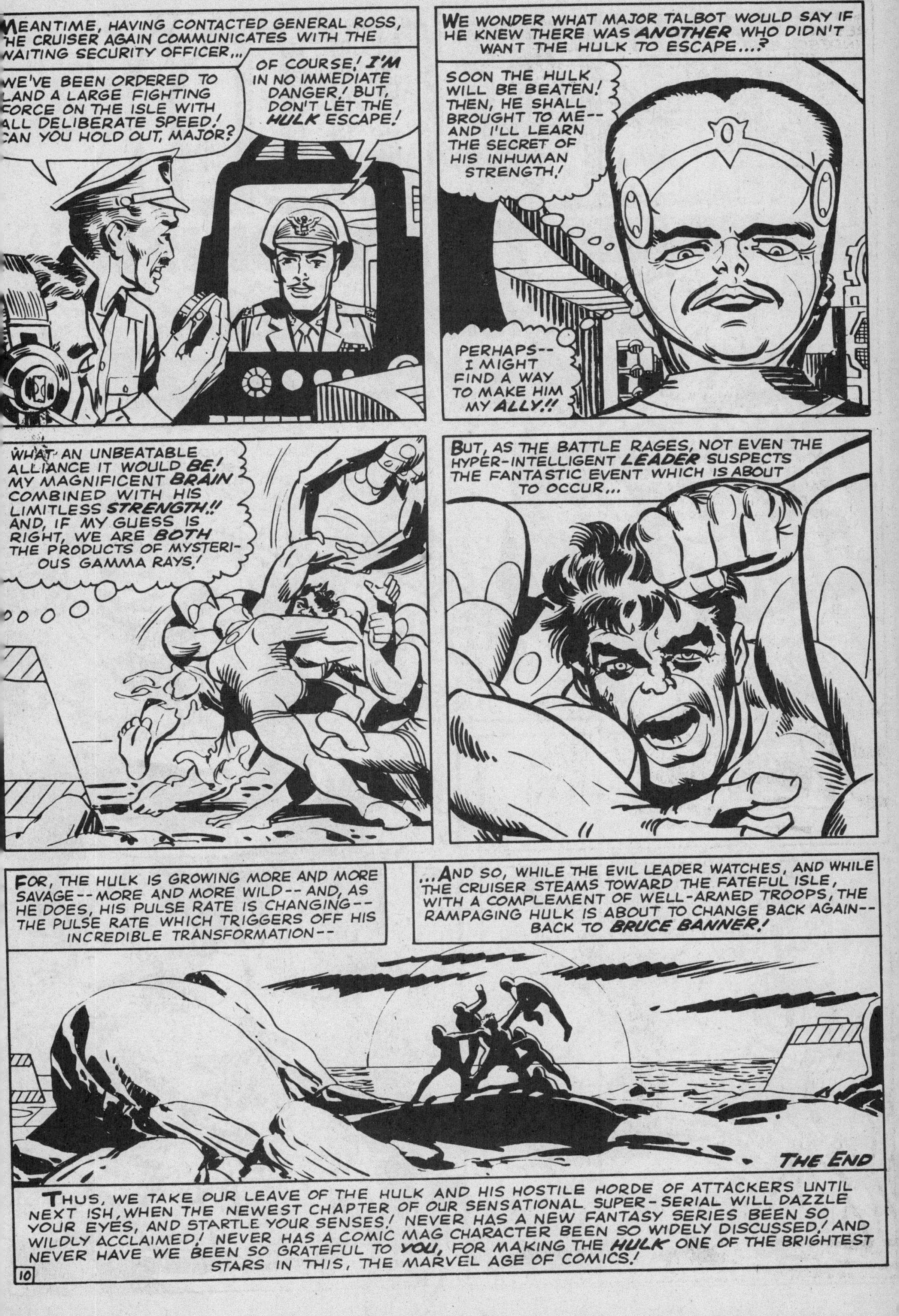
MEANTIME, HAVING CONTACTED GENERAL ROSS, THE CRUISER AGAIN COMMUNICATES WITH THE WAITING SECURITY OFFICER...
WE'VE BEEN ORDERED TO LAND A LARGE FIGHTING FORCE ON THE ISLE WITH ALL DELIBERATE SPEED! CAN YOU HOLD OUT, MAJOR?
OF COURSE! I'M IN NO IMMEDIATE DANGER! BUT, DON'T LET THE HULK ESCAPE!
WE WONDER WHAT MAJOR TALBOT WOULD SAY IF HE KNEW THERE WAS ANOTHER WHO DIDN'T WANT THE HULK TO ESCAPE...?
SOON THE HULK WILL BE BEATEN! THEN, HE SHALL BROUGHT TO ME--AND I'LL LEARN THE SECRET OF HIS INHUMAN STRENGTH!
PERHAPS--I MIGHT FIND A WAY TO MAKE HIM MY ALLY!!
WHAT AN UNBEATABLE ALLIANCE IT WOULD BE! MY MAGNIFICENT BRAIN COMBINED WITH HIS LIMITLESS STRENGTH!! AND, IF MY GUESS IS RIGHT, WE ARE BOTH THE PRODUCTS OF MYSTERIOUS GAMMA RAYS!
BUT, AS THE BATTLE RAGES, NOT EVEN THE HYPER-INTELLIGENT LEADER SUSPECTS THE FANTASTIC EVENT WHICH IS ABOUT TO OCCUR...
FOR, THE HULK IS GROWING MORE AND MORE SAVAGE--MORE AND MORE WILD--AND, AS HE DOES, HIS PULSE RATE IS CHANGING--THE PULSE RATE WHICH TRIGGERS OFF HIS INCREDIBLE TRANSFORMATION--
...AND SO, WHILE THE EVIL LEADER WATCHES, AND WHILE THE CRUISER STEAMS TOWARD THE FATEFUL ISLE, WITH A COMPLEMENT OF WELL-ARMED TROOPS, THE RAMPAGING HULK IS ABOUT TO CHANGE BACK AGAIN--BACK TO BRUCE BANNER!
THE END
THUS, WE TAKE OUR LEAVE OF THE HULK AND HIS HOSTILE HORDE OF ATTACKERS UNTIL NEXT ISH, WHEN THE NEWEST CHAPTER OF OUR SENSATIONAL SUPER-SERIAL WILL DAZZLE YOUR EYES, AND STARTLE YOUR SENSES! NEVER HAS A NEW FANTASY SERIES BEEN SO WILDLY ACCLAIMED! NEVER HAS A COMIC MAG CHARACTER BEEN SO WIDELY DISCUSSED! AND NEVER HAVE WE BEEN SO GRATEFUL TO YOU, FOR MAKING THE HULK ONE OF THE BRIGHTEST STARS IN THIS, THE MARVEL AGE OF COMICS!
10

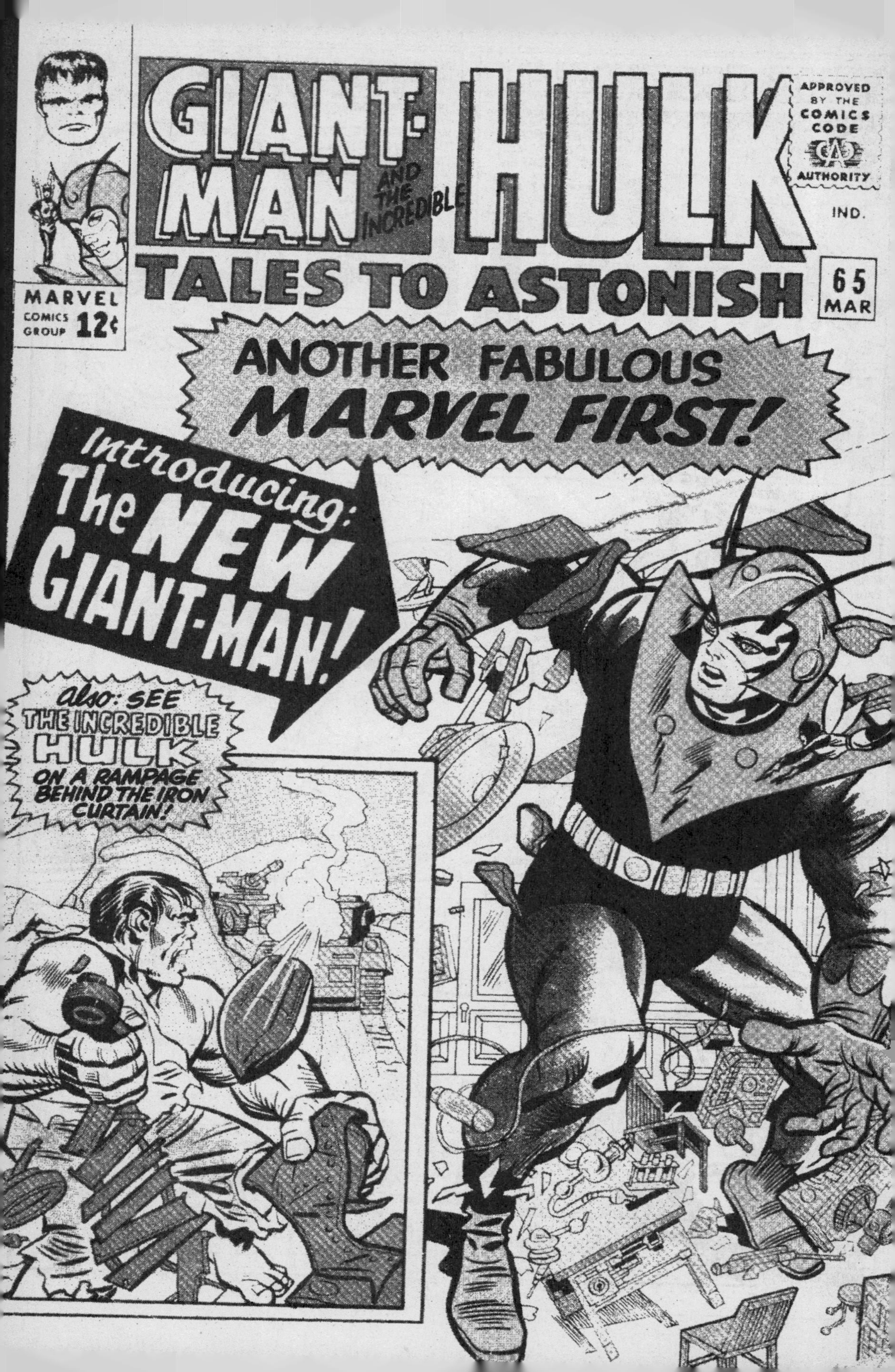

GIANT-MAN AND THE INCREDIBLE HULK
TALES TO ASTONISH
MARVEL COMICS GROUP 12¢
APPROVED BY THE COMICS CODE AUTHORITY
IND.
65 MAR
ANOTHER FABULOUS MARVEL FIRST!
Introducing: The NEW GIANT-MAN!
also: SEE THE INCREDIBLE HULK ON A RAMPAGE BEHIND THE IRON CURTAIN!

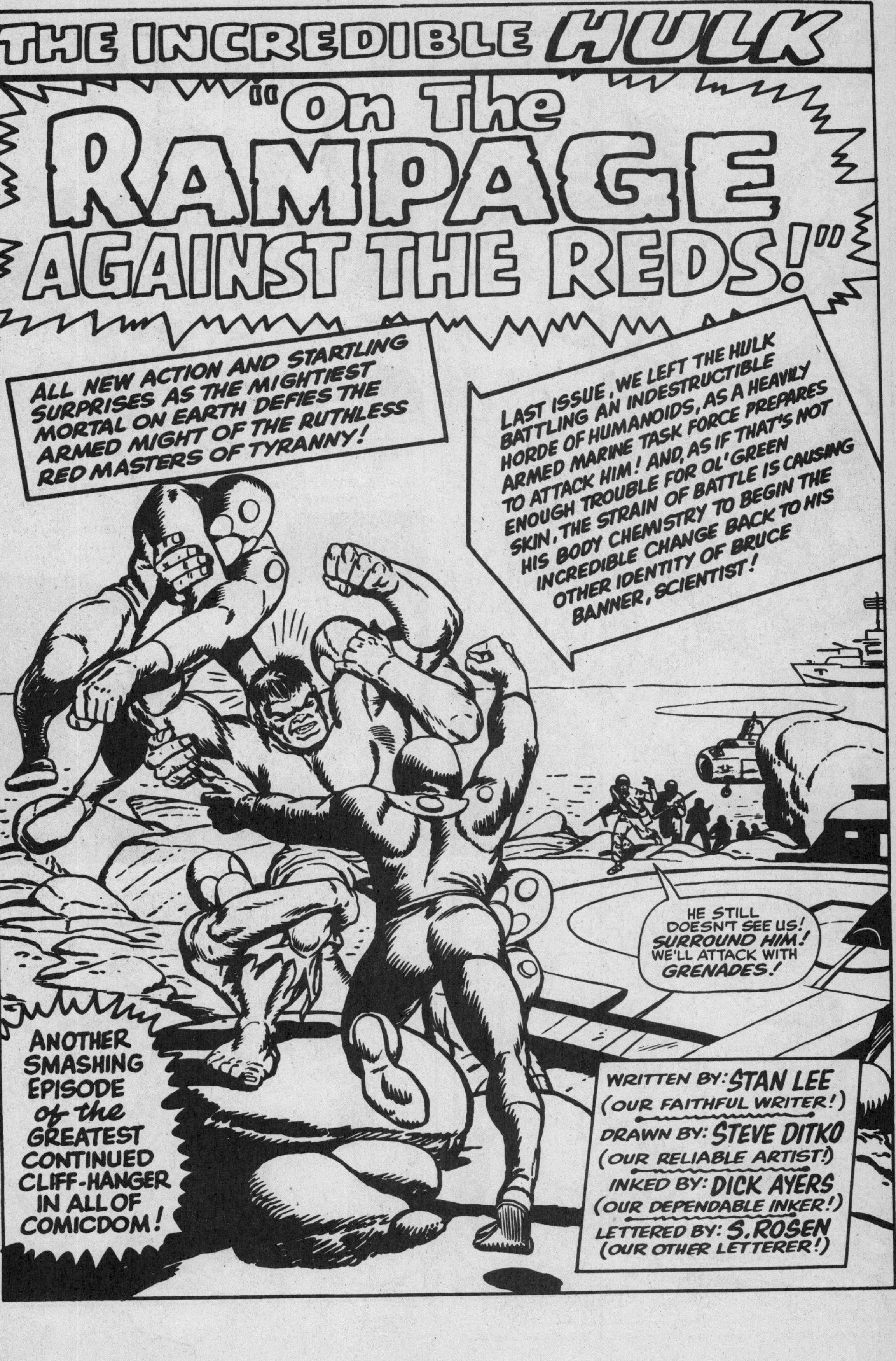
THE INCREDIBLE HULK
"On The RAMPAGE AGAINST THE REDS!"
ALL NEW ACTION AND STARTLING SURPRISES AS THE MIGHTIEST MORTAL ON EARTH DEFIES THE ARMED MIGHT OF THE RUTHLESS RED MASTERS OF TYRANNY!
LAST ISSUE, WE LEFT THE HULK BATTLING AN INDESTRUCTIBLE HORDE OF HUMANOIDS, AS A HEAVILY ARMED MARINE TASK FORCE PREPARES TO ATTACK HIM! AND, AS IF THAT'S NOT ENOUGH TROUBLE FOR OL' GREEN SKIN, THE STRAIN OF BATTLE IS CAUSING HIS BODY CHEMISTRY TO BEGIN THE INCREDIBLE CHANGE BACK TO HIS OTHER IDENTITY OF BRUCE BANNER, SCIENTIST!
HE STILL DOESN'T SEE US! SURROUND HIM! WE'LL ATTACK WITH GRENADES!
ANOTHER SMASHING EPISODE of the GREATEST CONTINUED CLIFF-HANGER IN ALL OF COMICDOM!
WRITTEN BY: STAN LEE (OUR FAITHFUL WRITER!)
DRAWN BY: STEVE DITKO (OUR RELIABLE ARTIST!)
INKED BY: DICK AYERS (OUR DEPENDABLE INKER!)
LETTERED BY: S. ROSEN (OUR OTHER LETTERER!)

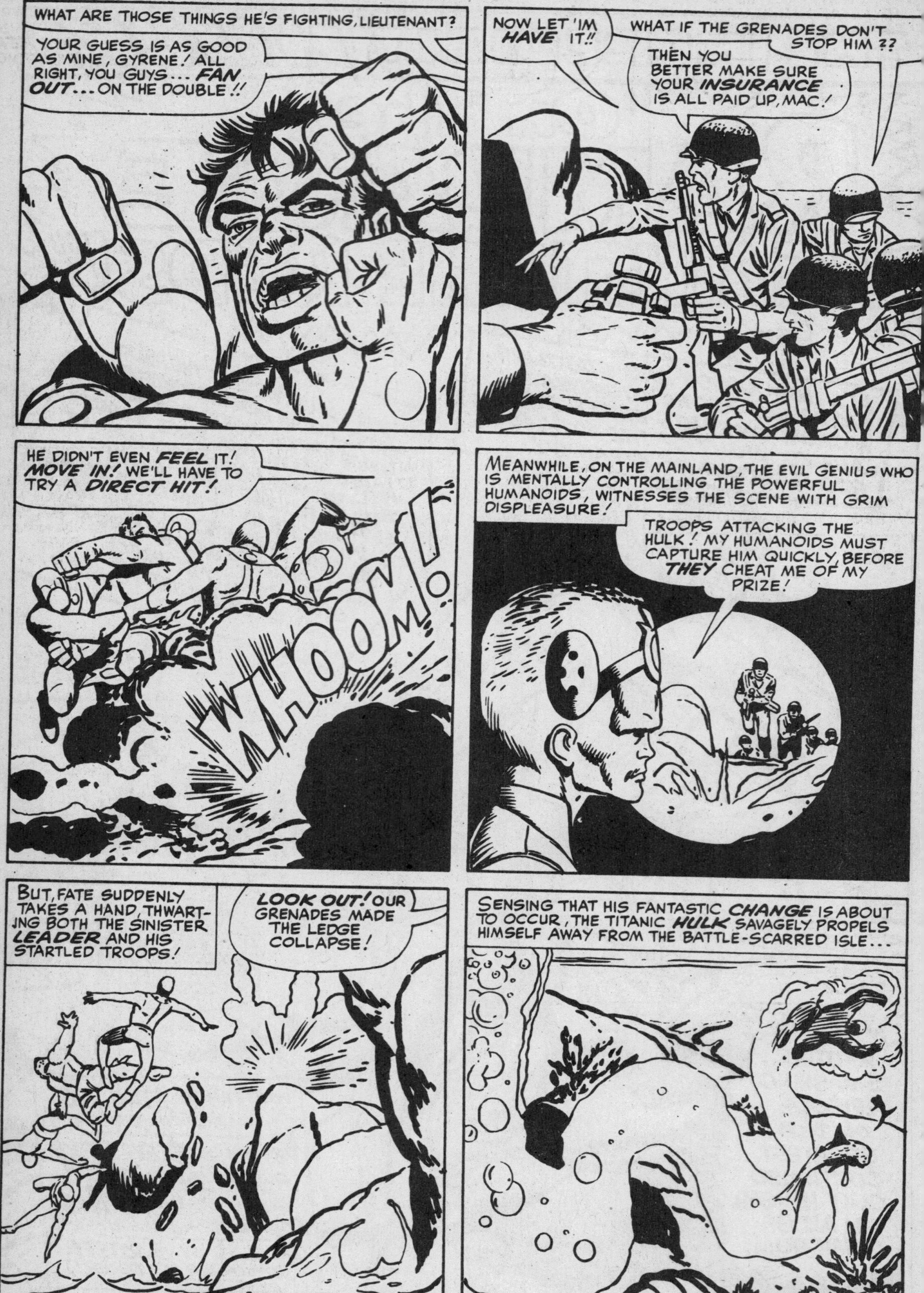

WHAT ARE THOSE THINGS HE'S FIGHTING, LIEUTENANT?
YOUR GUESS IS AS GOOD AS MINE, GYRENE! ALL RIGHT, YOU GUYS... FAN OUT... ON THE DOUBLE!!
NOW LET 'IM HAVE IT!!
WHAT IF THE GRENADES DON'T STOP HIM??
THEN YOU BETTER MAKE SURE YOUR INSURANCE IS ALL PAID UP, MAC!
HE DIDN'T EVEN FEEL IT! MOVE IN! WE'LL HAVE TO TRY A DIRECT HIT!
WHOOOM!
MEANWHILE, ON THE MAINLAND, THE EVIL GENIUS WHO IS MENTALLY CONTROLLING THE POWERFUL HUMANOIDS, WITNESSES THE SCENE WITH GRIM DISPLEASURE!
TROOPS ATTACKING THE HULK! MY HUMANOIDS MUST CAPTURE HIM QUICKLY, BEFORE THEY CHEAT ME OF MY PRIZE!
BUT, FATE SUDDENLY TAKES A HAND, THWARTING BOTH THE SINISTER LEADER AND HIS STARTLED TROOPS!
LOOK OUT! OUR GRENADES MADE THE LEDGE COLLAPSE!
SENSING THAT HIS FANTASTIC CHANGE IS ABOUT TO OCCUR, THE TITANIC HULK SAVAGELY PROPELS HIMSELF AWAY FROM THE BATTLE-SCARRED ISLE...
2.

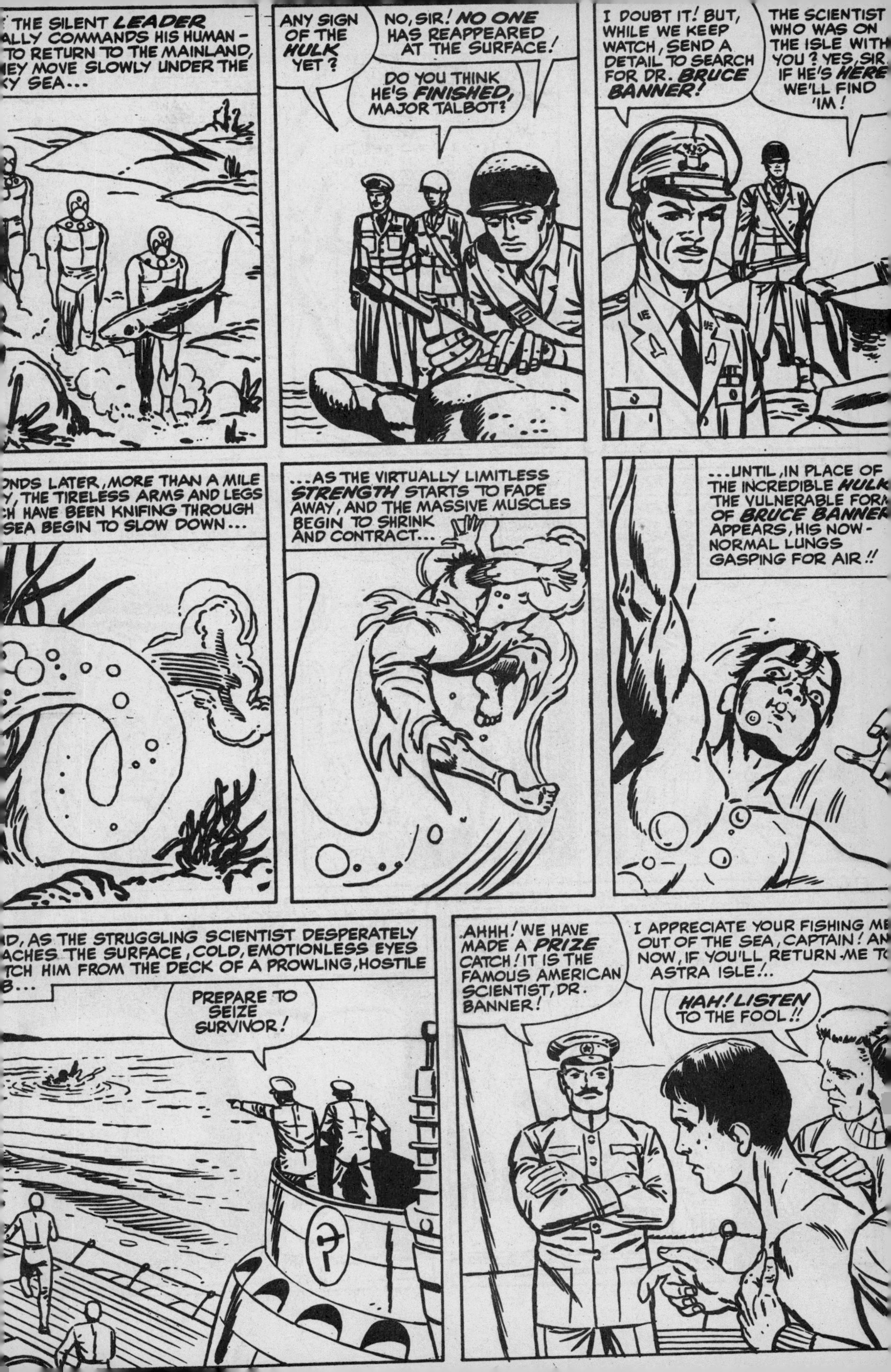

T THE SILENT LEADER
ALLY COMMANDS HIS HUMAN-
TO RETURN TO THE MAINLAND,
EY MOVE SLOWLY UNDER THE
KY SEA...
ANY SIGN OF THE HULK YET?
NO, SIR! NO ONE HAS REAPPEARED AT THE SURFACE!
DO YOU THINK HE'S FINISHED, MAJOR TALBOT?
I DOUBT IT! BUT, WHILE WE KEEP WATCH, SEND A DETAIL TO SEARCH FOR DR. BRUCE BANNER!
THE SCIENTIST WHO WAS ON THE ISLE WITH YOU? YES, SIR. IF HE'S HERE WE'LL FIND 'IM!
ONDS LATER, MORE THAN A MILE
Y, THE TIRELESS ARMS AND LEGS
CH HAVE BEEN KNIFING THROUGH
SEA BEGIN TO SLOW DOWN...
...AS THE VIRTUALLY LIMITLESS STRENGTH STARTS TO FADE AWAY, AND THE MASSIVE MUSCLES BEGIN TO SHRINK AND CONTRACT...
...UNTIL, IN PLACE OF THE INCREDIBLE HULK THE VULNERABLE FORM OF BRUCE BANNER APPEARS, HIS NOW-NORMAL LUNGS GASPING FOR AIR!!
ND, AS THE STRUGGLING SCIENTIST DESPERATELY
ACHES THE SURFACE, COLD, EMOTIONLESS EYES
TCH HIM FROM THE DECK OF A PROWLING, HOSTILE
B...
PREPARE TO SEIZE SURVIVOR!
AHHH! WE HAVE MADE A PRIZE CATCH! IT IS THE FAMOUS AMERICAN SCIENTIST, DR. BANNER!
I APPRECIATE YOUR FISHING ME OUT OF THE SEA, CAPTAIN! AN NOW, IF YOU'LL RETURN ME TO ASTRA ISLE!..
HAH! LISTEN TO THE FOOL!!

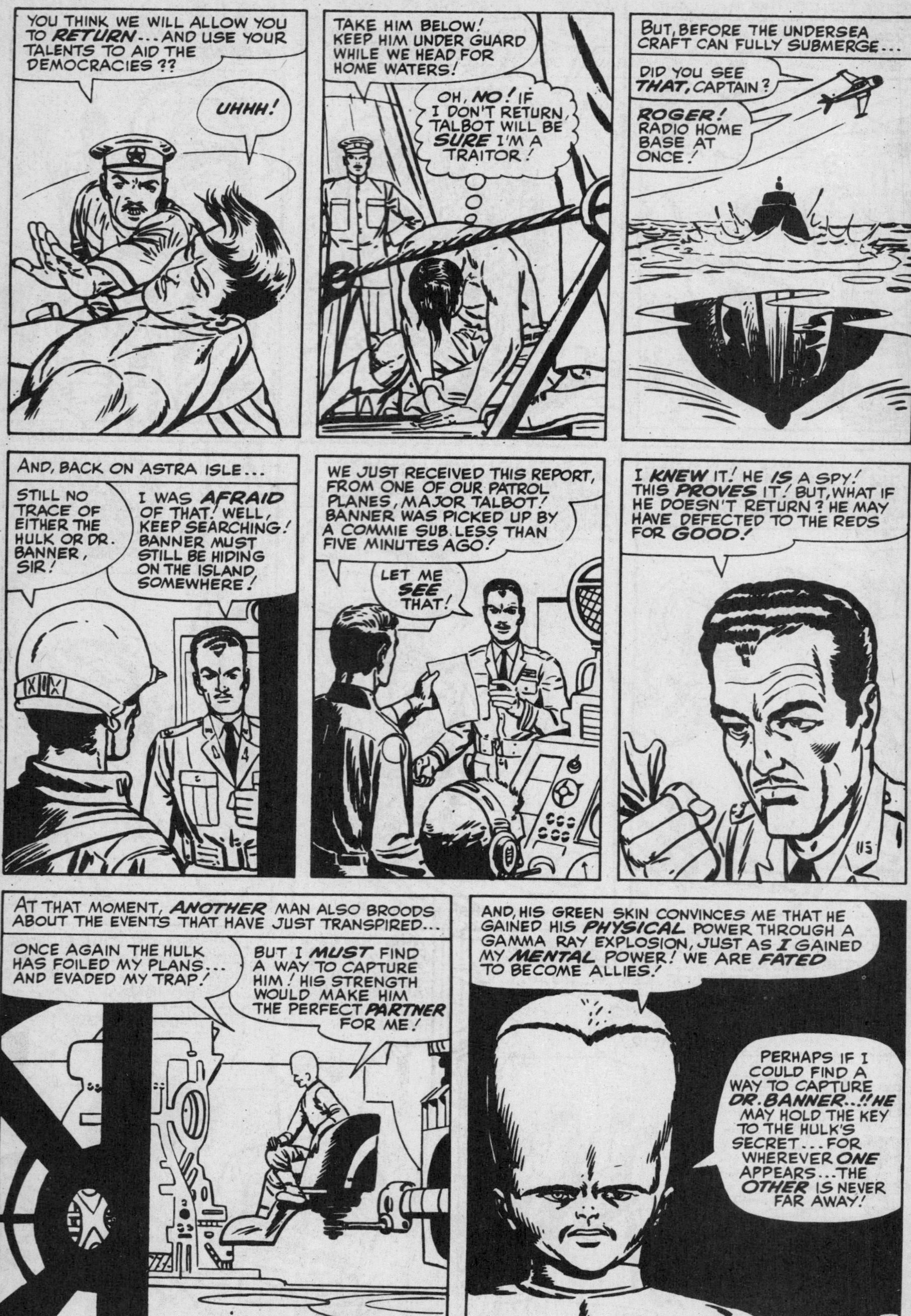
YOU THINK WE WILL ALLOW YOU TO RETURN... AND USE YOUR TALENTS TO AID THE DEMOCRACIES ??
UHHH!
TAKE HIM BELOW! KEEP HIM UNDER GUARD WHILE WE HEAD FOR HOME WATERS!
OH, NO! IF I DON'T RETURN, TALBOT WILL BE SURE I'M A TRAITOR!
BUT, BEFORE THE UNDERSEA CRAFT CAN FULLY SUBMERGE...
DID YOU SEE THAT, CAPTAIN?
ROGER! RADIO HOME BASE AT ONCE!
AND, BACK ON ASTRA ISLE...
STILL NO TRACE OF EITHER THE HULK OR DR. BANNER, SIR!
I WAS AFRAID OF THAT! WELL, KEEP SEARCHING! BANNER MUST STILL BE HIDING ON THE ISLAND SOMEWHERE!
WE JUST RECEIVED THIS REPORT, FROM ONE OF OUR PATROL PLANES, MAJOR TALBOT! BANNER WAS PICKED UP BY A COMMIE SUB LESS THAN FIVE MINUTES AGO!
LET ME SEE THAT!
I KNEW IT! HE IS A SPY! THIS PROVES IT! BUT, WHAT IF HE DOESN'T RETURN? HE MAY HAVE DEFECTED TO THE REDS FOR GOOD!
AT THAT MOMENT, ANOTHER MAN ALSO BROODS ABOUT THE EVENTS THAT HAVE JUST TRANSPIRED...
ONCE AGAIN THE HULK HAS FOILED MY PLANS... AND EVADED MY TRAP!
BUT I MUST FIND A WAY TO CAPTURE HIM! HIS STRENGTH WOULD MAKE HIM THE PERFECT PARTNER FOR ME!
AND, HIS GREEN SKIN CONVINCES ME THAT HE GAINED HIS PHYSICAL POWER THROUGH A GAMMA RAY EXPLOSION, JUST AS I GAINED MY MENTAL POWER! WE ARE FATED TO BECOME ALLIES!
PERHAPS IF I COULD FIND A WAY TO CAPTURE DR. BANNER..!! HE MAY HOLD THE KEY TO THE HULK'S SECRET... FOR WHEREVER ONE APPEARS... THE OTHER IS NEVER FAR AWAY!
4.

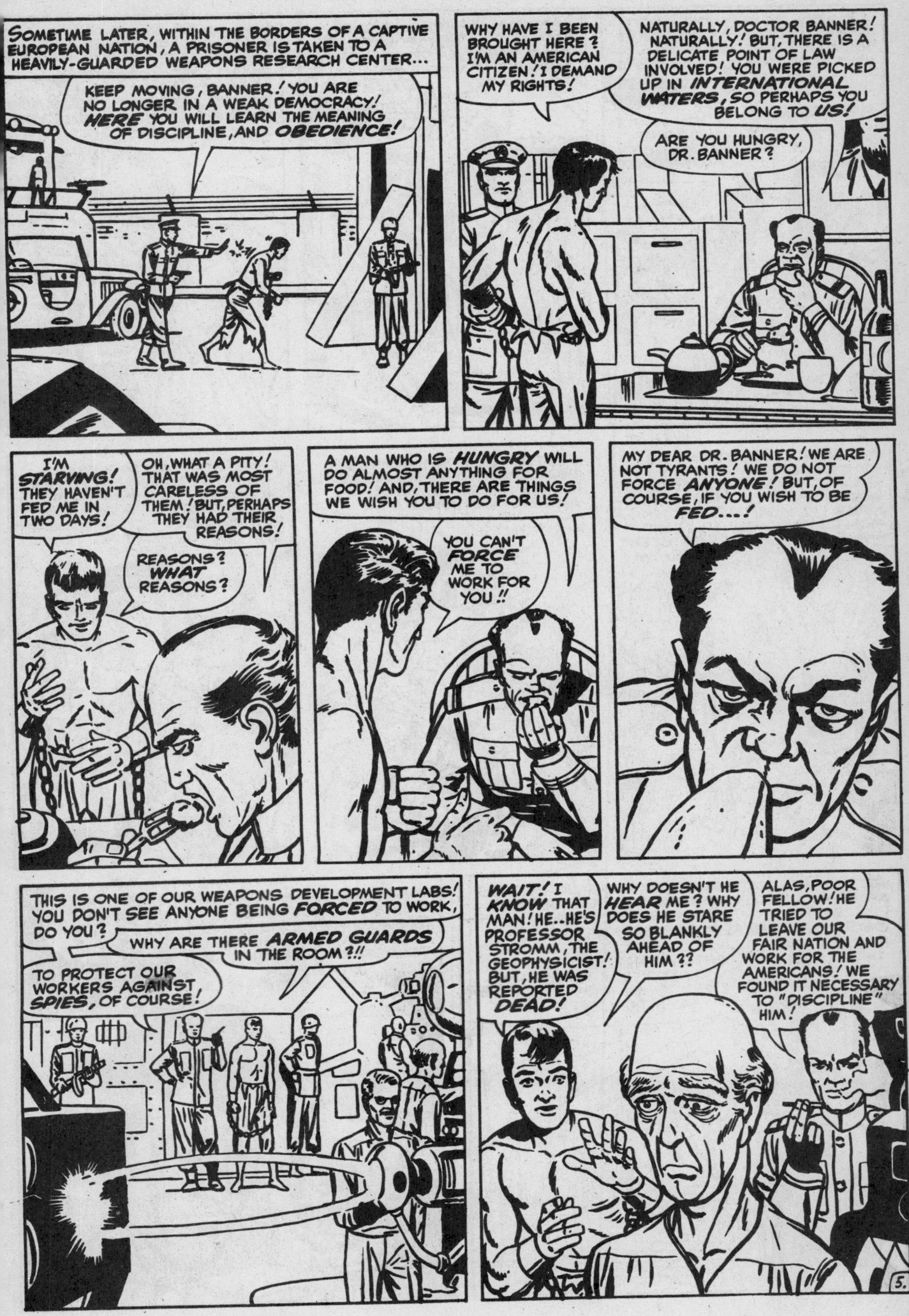

SOMETIME LATER, WITHIN THE BORDERS OF A CAPTIVE EUROPEAN NATION, A PRISONER IS TAKEN TO A HEAVILY-GUARDED WEAPONS RESEARCH CENTER...
KEEP MOVING, BANNER! YOU ARE NO LONGER IN A WEAK DEMOCRACY! HERE YOU WILL LEARN THE MEANING OF DISCIPLINE, AND OBEDIENCE!
WHY HAVE I BEEN BROUGHT HERE? I'M AN AMERICAN CITIZEN! I DEMAND MY RIGHTS!
NATURALLY, DOCTOR BANNER! NATURALLY! BUT, THERE IS A DELICATE POINT OF LAW INVOLVED! YOU WERE PICKED UP IN INTERNATIONAL WATERS, SO PERHAPS YOU BELONG TO US!
ARE YOU HUNGRY, DR. BANNER?
I'M STARVING! THEY HAVEN'T FED ME IN TWO DAYS!
OH, WHAT A PITY! THAT WAS MOST CARELESS OF THEM! BUT, PERHAPS THEY HAD THEIR REASONS!
REASONS? WHAT REASONS?
A MAN WHO IS HUNGRY WILL DO ALMOST ANYTHING FOR FOOD! AND, THERE ARE THINGS WE WISH YOU TO DO FOR US!
YOU CAN'T FORCE ME TO WORK FOR YOU!!
MY DEAR DR. BANNER! WE ARE NOT TYRANTS! WE DO NOT FORCE ANYONE! BUT, OF COURSE, IF YOU WISH TO BE FED...!
THIS IS ONE OF OUR WEAPONS DEVELOPMENT LABS! YOU DON'T SEE ANYONE BEING FORCED TO WORK, DO YOU?
WHY ARE THERE ARMED GUARDS IN THE ROOM?!!
TO PROTECT OUR WORKERS AGAINST SPIES, OF COURSE!
WAIT! I KNOW THAT MAN! HE..HE'S PROFESSOR STROMM, THE GEOPHYSICIST! BUT, HE WAS REPORTED DEAD!
WHY DOESN'T HE HEAR ME? WHY DOES HE STARE SO BLANKLY AHEAD OF HIM??
ALAS, POOR FELLOW! HE TRIED TO LEAVE OUR FAIR NATION AND WORK FOR THE AMERICANS! WE FOUND IT NECESSARY TO "DISCIPLINE" HIM!

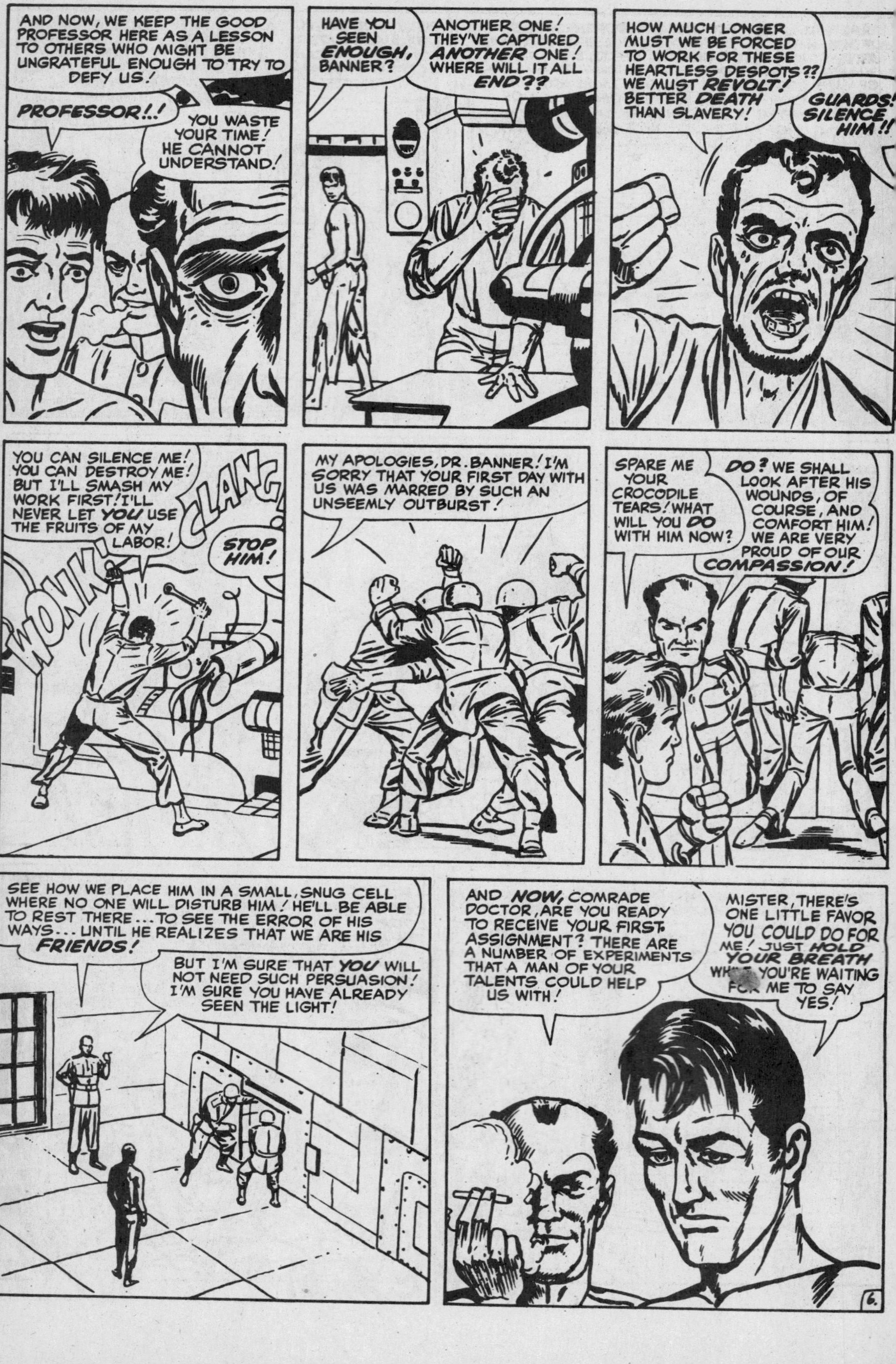

AND NOW, WE KEEP THE GOOD PROFESSOR HERE AS A LESSON TO OTHERS WHO MIGHT BE UNGRATEFUL ENOUGH TO TRY TO DEFY US!
PROFESSOR!.!
YOU WASTE YOUR TIME! HE CANNOT UNDERSTAND!
HAVE YOU SEEN ENOUGH, BANNER?
ANOTHER ONE! THEY'VE CAPTURED ANOTHER ONE! WHERE WILL IT ALL END??
HOW MUCH LONGER MUST WE BE FORCED TO WORK FOR THESE HEARTLESS DESPOTS?? WE MUST REVOLT! BETTER DEATH THAN SLAVERY!
GUARDS! SILENCE HIM!!
YOU CAN SILENCE ME! YOU CAN DESTROY ME! BUT I'LL SMASH MY WORK FIRST! I'LL NEVER LET YOU USE THE FRUITS OF MY LABOR!
CLANG!
WONK!
STOP HIM!
MY APOLOGIES, DR. BANNER! I'M SORRY THAT YOUR FIRST DAY WITH US WAS MARRED BY SUCH AN UNSEEMLY OUTBURST!
SPARE ME YOUR CROCODILE TEARS! WHAT WILL YOU DO WITH HIM NOW?
DO? WE SHALL LOOK AFTER HIS WOUNDS, OF COURSE, AND COMFORT HIM! WE ARE VERY PROUD OF OUR COMPASSION!
SEE HOW WE PLACE HIM IN A SMALL, SNUG CELL WHERE NO ONE WILL DISTURB HIM! HE'LL BE ABLE TO REST THERE... TO SEE THE ERROR OF HIS WAYS... UNTIL HE REALIZES THAT WE ARE HIS FRIENDS!
BUT I'M SURE THAT YOU WILL NOT NEED SUCH PERSUASION! I'M SURE YOU HAVE ALREADY SEEN THE LIGHT!
AND NOW, COMRADE DOCTOR, ARE YOU READY TO RECEIVE YOUR FIRST ASSIGNMENT? THERE ARE A NUMBER OF EXPERIMENTS THAT A MAN OF YOUR TALENTS COULD HELP US WITH!
MISTER, THERE'S ONE LITTLE FAVOR YOU COULD DO FOR ME! JUST HOLD YOUR BREATH WH YOU'RE WAITING FOR ME TO SAY YES!
6.

THAT WAS MOST FOOLISH OF YOU, BANNER! BUT, A BRIEF STAY IN YOUR NEW QUARTERS WILL SOON CHANGE YOUR MIND! USHER HIM IN, COMRADES!

BEFORE LONG, HE'LL BE BEGGING US TO LET HIM WORK FOR US! HE'LL DO ANYTHING TO BE LET OUT OF THERE!

WELL, BANNER, IT LOOKS LIKE THIS IS IT! I'LL NEVER AGREE TO WORK FOR THE COMMIES!... AND THEY'LL NEVER LET ME GO UNTIL I DO!!

AT ANY RATE, ONCE I'M DONE FOR, IT'LL SOLVE THE PROBLEM OF HOW TO STOP THE HULK FROM INJURING ANYBODY!

WAIT A MINUTE!! THE HULK! OF COURSE! THAT'S THE ANSWER! DR. BANNER HASN'T A CHANCE... BUT THE HULK MIGHT BE ABLE TO BREAK OUT OF HERE!

THUS, FIRED WITH NEW HOPE, THE CAPTIVE SCIENTIST CONCENTRATES ON THE CRUEL, MERCILESS THINGS HE HAS WITNESSED, AS HIS BODY CHEMISTRY GETS CLOSER TO THE BOILING POINT....!

UNTIL, FINALLY...

IT'S WORKING!! HA HA! I'M CHANGING! GROWING STRONGER... STRONGER!! NO CHAINS CAN HOLD ME NOW!

AND, UNNOTICED ON THE OTHER SIDE OF THE WALL, A SMALL CRACK APPEARS IN THE SOLID STONE MASONRY...

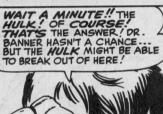

A CRACK WHICH GROWS LARGER, AND LARGER, UNTIL AT LAST...

WHUM!

...THE MIGHTIEST LIVING MORTAL ON EARTH IS FREE!

COMRADES!! LOOK! IT--IT'S THE HULK!

QUICK!! WHEEL IN THE NEW HIGH-INTENSITY FIELD CANNON!

WHERE DID HE COME FROM? HOW...??

7.

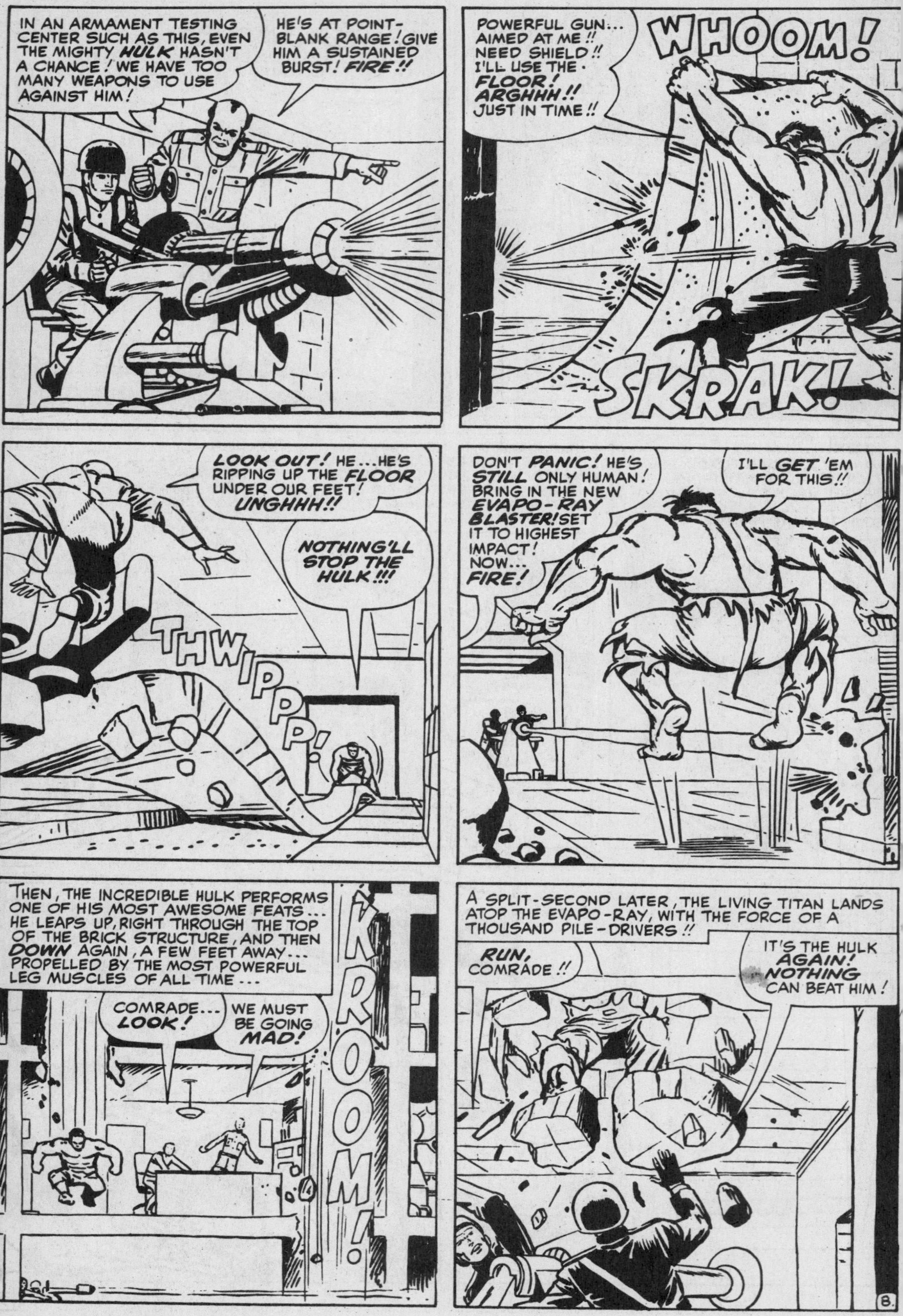
IN AN ARMAMENT TESTING CENTER SUCH AS THIS, EVEN THE MIGHTY HULK HASN'T A CHANCE! WE HAVE TOO MANY WEAPONS TO USE AGAINST HIM!
HE'S AT POINT-BLANK RANGE! GIVE HIM A SUSTAINED BURST! FIRE!!
POWERFUL GUN... AIMED AT ME!! NEED SHIELD!! I'LL USE THE FLOOR! ARGHHH!! JUST IN TIME!!
WHOOM!
SKRAK!
LOOK OUT! HE...HE'S RIPPING UP THE FLOOR UNDER OUR FEET! UNGHHH!!
NOTHING'LL STOP THE HULK!!!
THWIPPPP!
DON'T PANIC! HE'S STILL ONLY HUMAN! BRING IN THE NEW EVAPO-RAY BLASTER! SET IT TO HIGHEST IMPACT! NOW... FIRE!
I'LL GET 'EM FOR THIS!!
THEN, THE INCREDIBLE HULK PERFORMS ONE OF HIS MOST AWESOME FEATS... HE LEAPS UP, RIGHT THROUGH THE TOP OF THE BRICK STRUCTURE, AND THEN DOWN AGAIN, A FEW FEET AWAY... PROPELLED BY THE MOST POWERFUL LEG MUSCLES OF ALL TIME...
COMRADE... LOOK!
WE MUST BE GOING MAD!
KROOOM!
A SPLIT-SECOND LATER, THE LIVING TITAN LANDS ATOP THE EVAPO-RAY, WITH THE FORCE OF A THOUSAND PILE-DRIVERS!!
RUN, COMRADE!!
IT'S THE HULK AGAIN! NOTHING CAN BEAT HIM!
8.

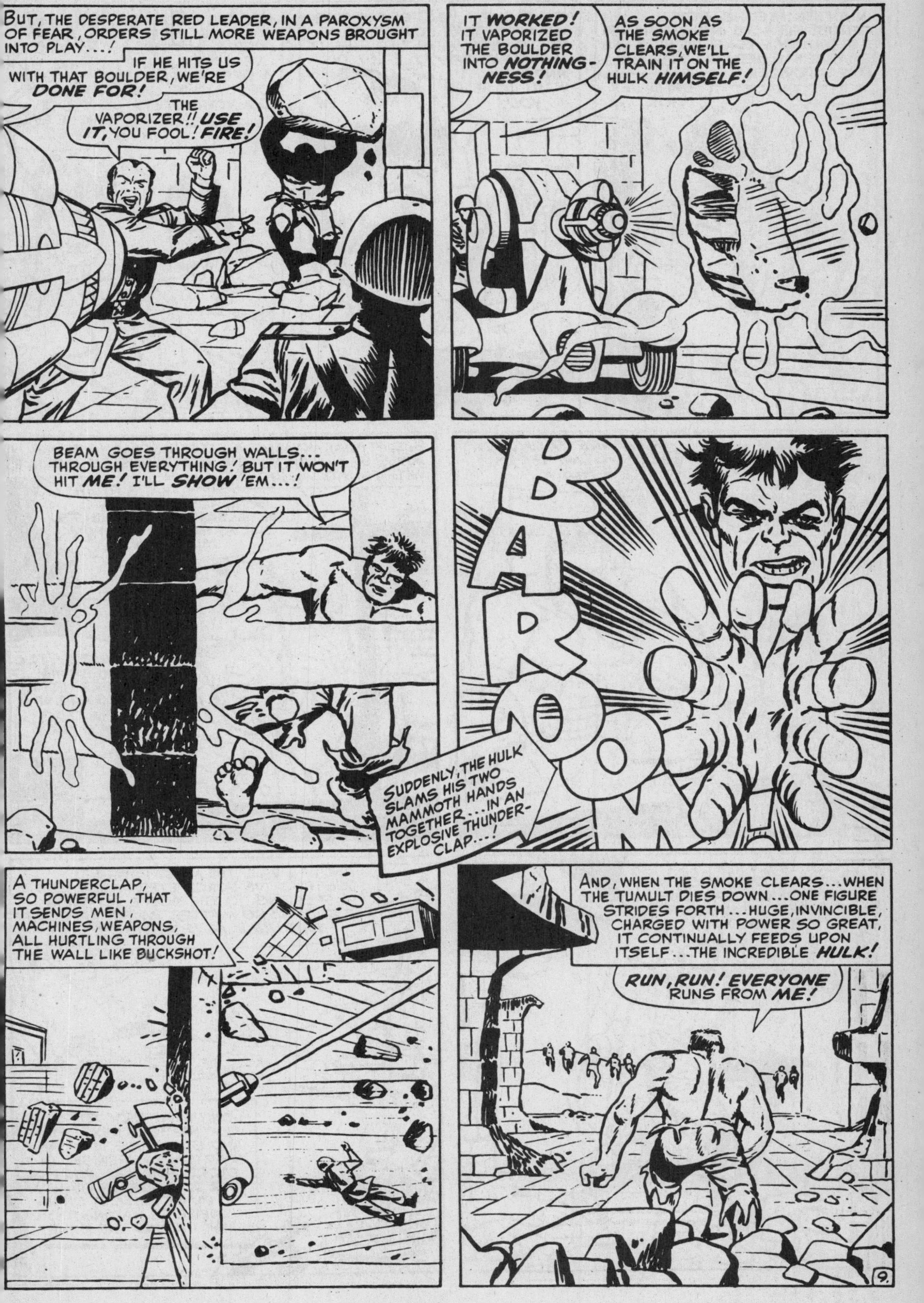
BUT, THE DESPERATE RED LEADER, IN A PAROXYSM OF FEAR, ORDERS STILL MORE WEAPONS BROUGHT INTO PLAY...!
IF HE HITS US WITH THAT BOULDER, WE'RE DONE FOR!
THE VAPORIZER!! USE IT, YOU FOOL! FIRE!
IT WORKED! IT VAPORIZED THE BOULDER INTO NOTHING-NESS!
AS SOON AS THE SMOKE CLEARS, WE'LL TRAIN IT ON THE HULK HIMSELF!
BEAM GOES THROUGH WALLS... THROUGH EVERYTHING! BUT IT WON'T HIT ME! I'LL SHOW 'EM...!
SUDDENLY, THE HULK SLAMS HIS TWO MAMMOTH HANDS TOGETHER...IN AN EXPLOSIVE THUNDER-CLAP...!
BAROOM!
A THUNDERCLAP, SO POWERFUL, THAT IT SENDS MEN, MACHINES, WEAPONS, ALL HURTLING THROUGH THE WALL LIKE BUCKSHOT!
AND, WHEN THE SMOKE CLEARS...WHEN THE TUMULT DIES DOWN...ONE FIGURE STRIDES FORTH...HUGE, INVINCIBLE, CHARGED WITH POWER SO GREAT, IT CONTINUALLY FEEDS UPON ITSELF...THE INCREDIBLE HULK!
RUN, RUN! EVERYONE RUNS FROM ME!
9.

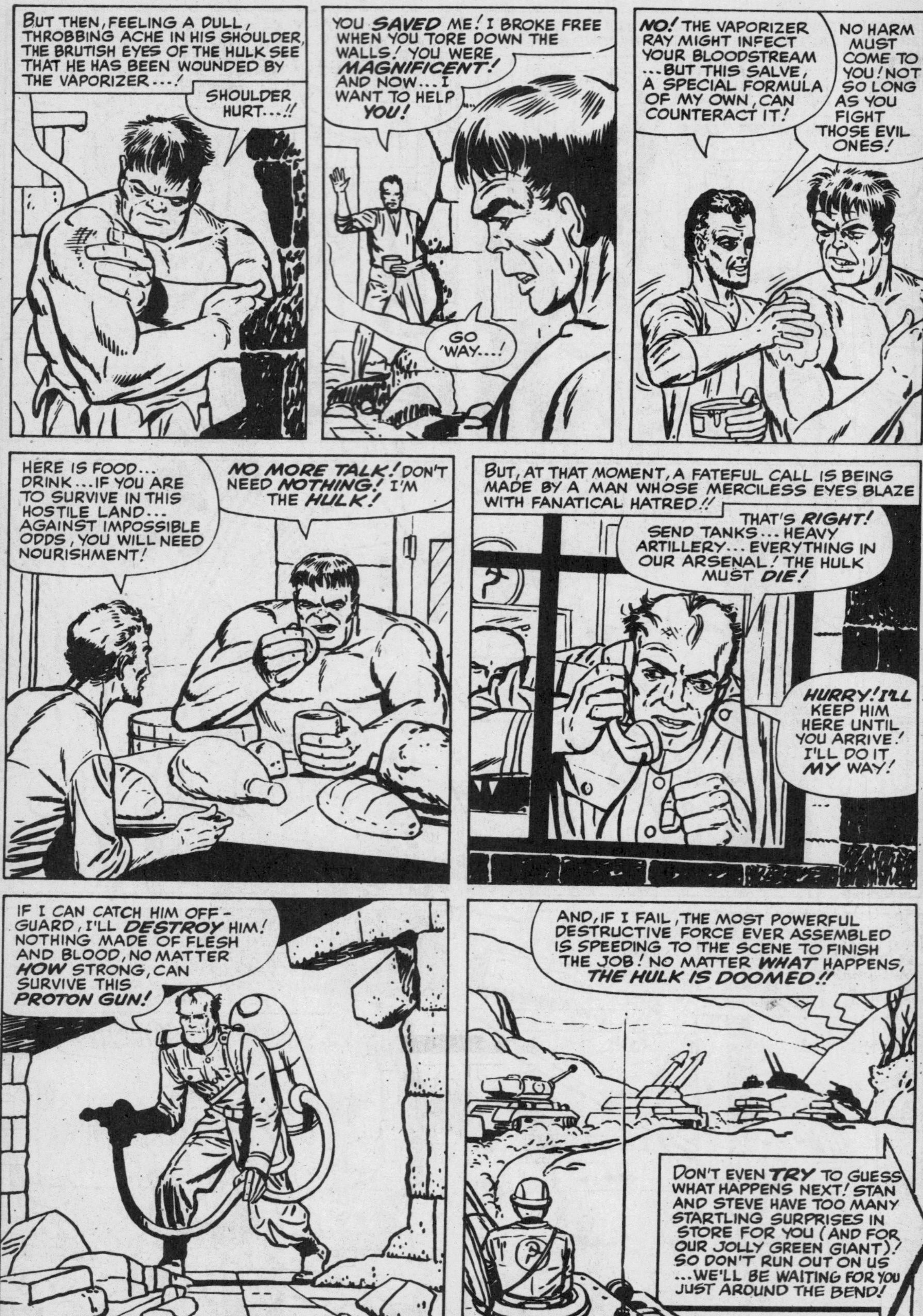

BUT THEN, FEELING A DULL, THROBBING ACHE IN HIS SHOULDER, THE BRUTISH EYES OF THE HULK SEE THAT HE HAS BEEN WOUNDED BY THE VAPORIZER...!
SHOULDER HURT...!!
YOU SAVED ME! I BROKE FREE WHEN YOU TORE DOWN THE WALLS! YOU WERE MAGNIFICENT! AND NOW... I WANT TO HELP YOU!
GO 'WAY...!
NO! THE VAPORIZER RAY MIGHT INFECT YOUR BLOODSTREAM ...BUT THIS SALVE, A SPECIAL FORMULA OF MY OWN, CAN COUNTERACT IT!
NO HARM MUST COME TO YOU! NOT SO LONG AS YOU FIGHT THOSE EVIL ONES!
HERE IS FOOD... DRINK... IF YOU ARE TO SURVIVE IN THIS HOSTILE LAND... AGAINST IMPOSSIBLE ODDS, YOU WILL NEED NOURISHMENT!
NO MORE TALK! DON'T NEED NOTHING! I'M THE HULK!
BUT, AT THAT MOMENT, A FATEFUL CALL IS BEING MADE BY A MAN WHOSE MERCILESS EYES BLAZE WITH FANATICAL HATRED!!
THAT'S RIGHT! SEND TANKS... HEAVY ARTILLERY... EVERYTHING IN OUR ARSENAL! THE HULK MUST DIE!
HURRY! I'LL KEEP HIM HERE UNTIL YOU ARRIVE! I'LL DO IT MY WAY!
IF I CAN CATCH HIM OFF-GUARD, I'LL DESTROY HIM! NOTHING MADE OF FLESH AND BLOOD, NO MATTER HOW STRONG, CAN SURVIVE THIS PROTON GUN!
AND, IF I FAIL, THE MOST POWERFUL DESTRUCTIVE FORCE EVER ASSEMBLED IS SPEEDING TO THE SCENE TO FINISH THE JOB! NO MATTER WHAT HAPPENS, THE HULK IS DOOMED!!
DON'T EVEN TRY TO GUESS WHAT HAPPENS NEXT! STAN AND STEVE HAVE TOO MANY STARTLING SURPRISES IN STORE FOR YOU (AND FOR OUR JOLLY GREEN GIANT)! SO DON'T RUN OUT ON US ...WE'LL BE WAITING FOR YOU JUST AROUND THE BEND!
10.

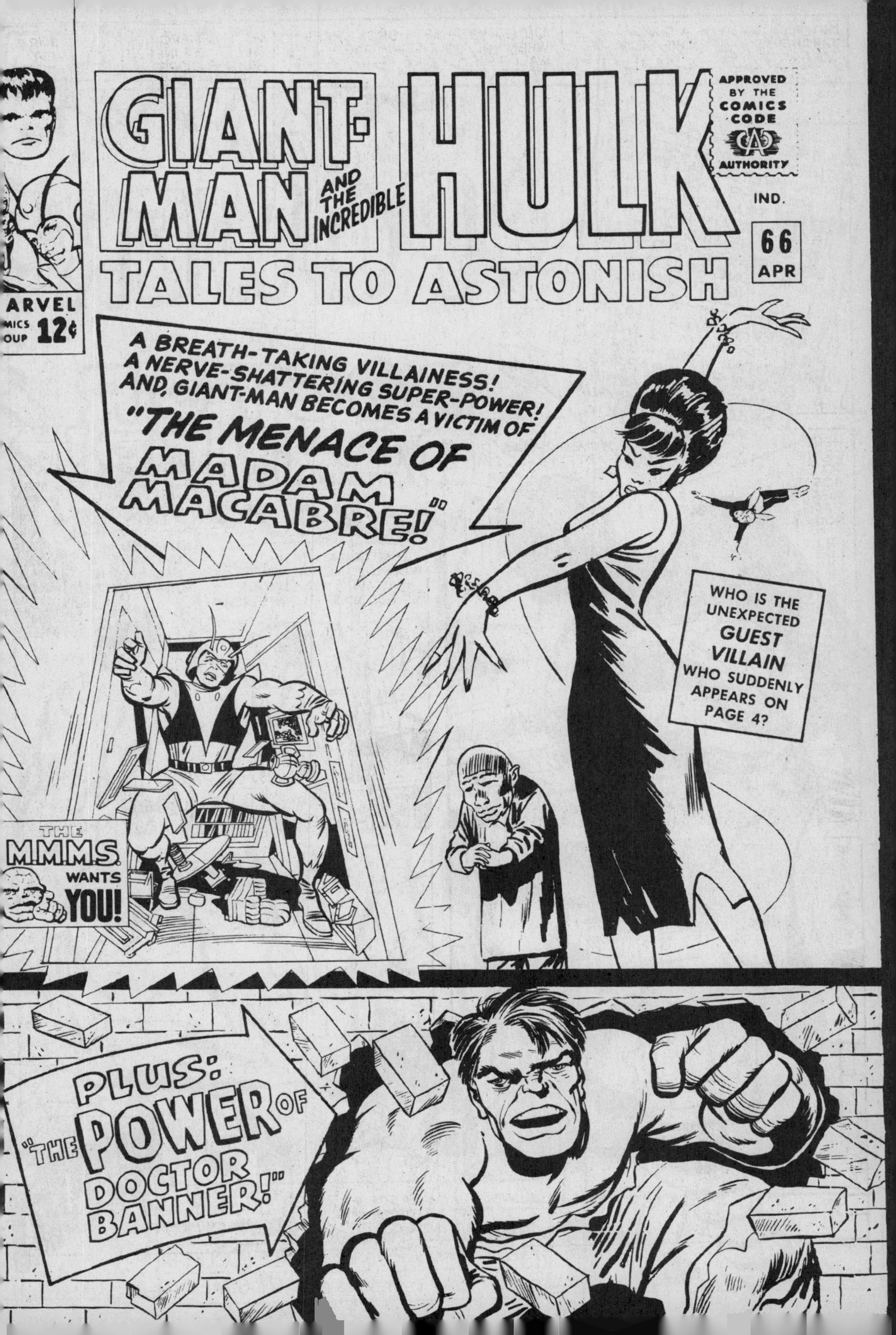
GIANT-MAN AND THE INCREDIBLE HULK
TALES TO ASTONISH
APPROVED BY THE COMICS CODE AUTHORITY
IND.
66
APR
ARVEL MICS OUP 12¢
A BREATH-TAKING VILLAINESS! A NERVE-SHATTERING SUPER-POWER! AND, GIANT-MAN BECOMES A VICTIM OF "THE MENACE OF MADAM MACABRE!"
WHO IS THE UNEXPECTED GUEST VILLAIN WHO SUDDENLY APPEARS ON PAGE 4?
THE M.M.M.S. WANTS YOU!
PLUS: "THE POWER OF DOCTOR BANNER!"

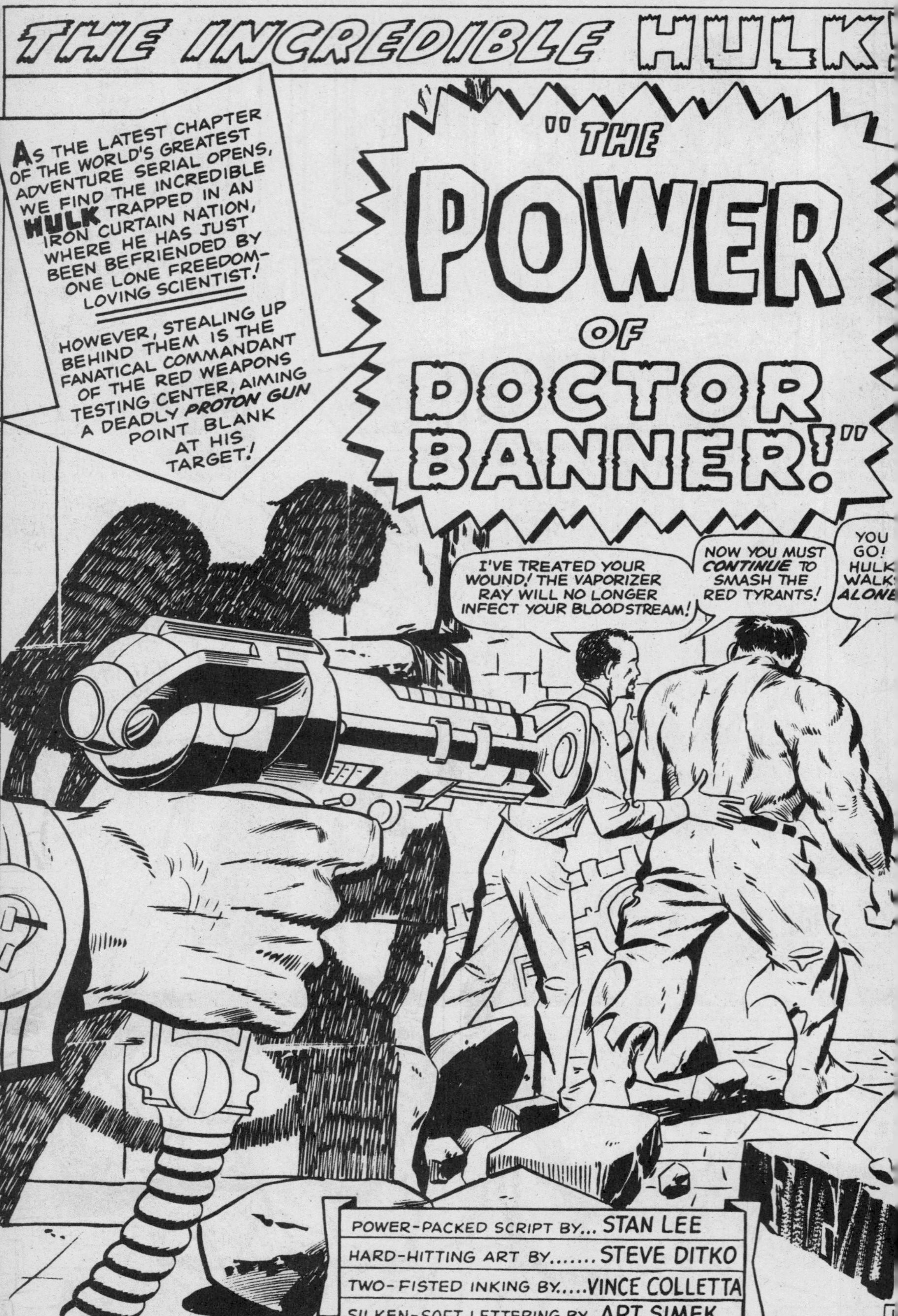
THE INCREDIBLE HULK!
AS THE LATEST CHAPTER OF THE WORLD'S GREATEST ADVENTURE SERIAL OPENS, WE FIND THE INCREDIBLE HULK TRAPPED IN AN IRON CURTAIN NATION, WHERE HE HAS JUST BEEN BEFRIENDED BY ONE LONE FREEDOM-LOVING SCIENTIST!
HOWEVER, STEALING UP BEHIND THEM IS THE FANATICAL COMMANDANT OF THE RED WEAPONS TESTING CENTER, AIMING A DEADLY PROTON GUN POINT BLANK AT HIS TARGET!
"THE POWER OF DOCTOR BANNER!"
I'VE TREATED YOUR WOUND! THE VAPORIZER RAY WILL NO LONGER INFECT YOUR BLOODSTREAM!
NOW YOU MUST CONTINUE TO SMASH THE RED TYRANTS!
YOU GO! HULK WALKS ALONE
POWER-PACKED SCRIPT BY... STAN LEE
HARD-HITTING ART BY....... STEVE DITKO
TWO-FISTED INKING BY.....VINCE COLLETTA
SILKEN-SOFT LETTERING BY.. ART SIMEK

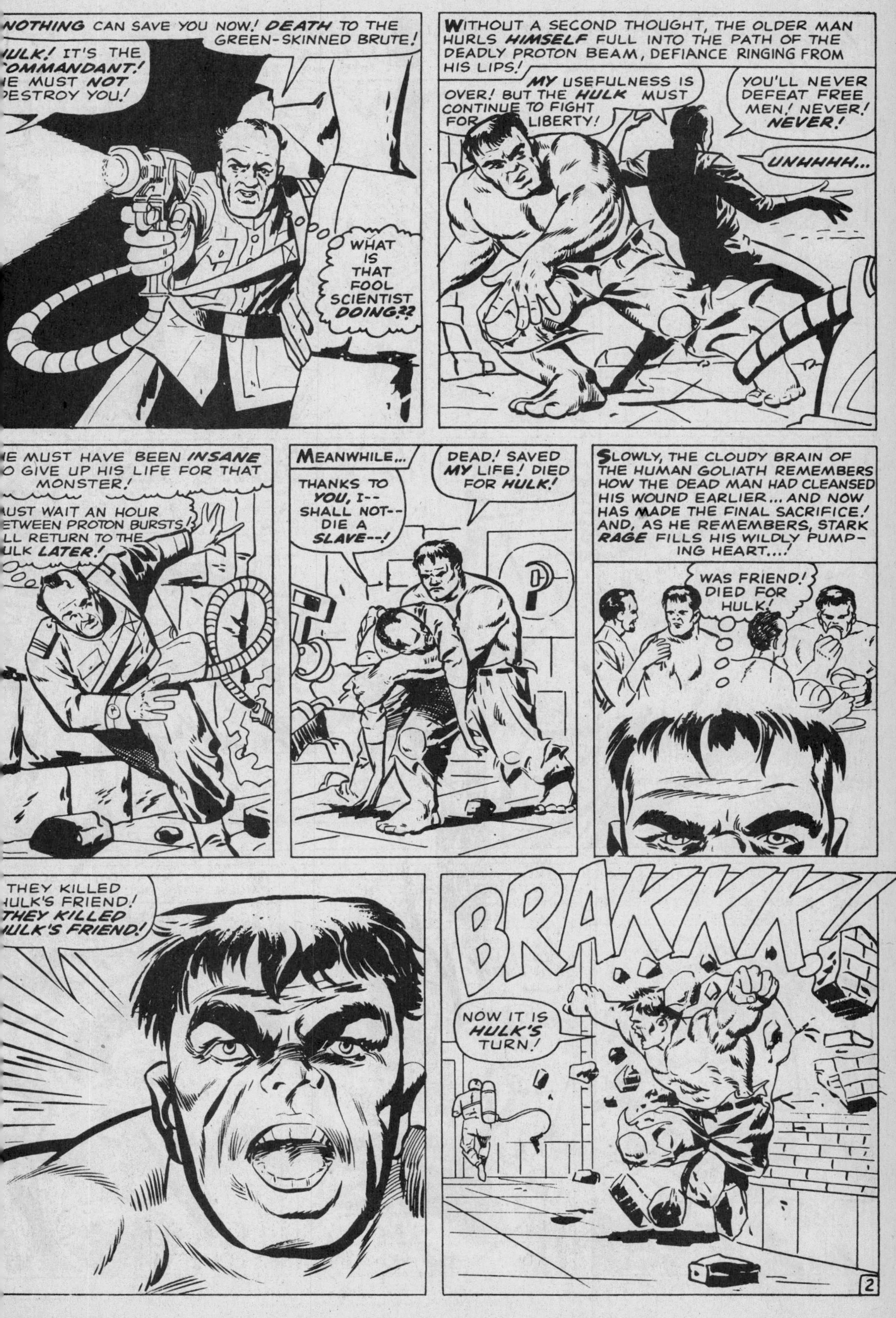

NOTHING CAN SAVE YOU NOW! DEATH TO THE GREEN-SKINNED BRUTE!
HULK! IT'S THE COMMANDANT! HE MUST NOT DESTROY YOU!
WHAT IS THAT FOOL SCIENTIST DOING??
WITHOUT A SECOND THOUGHT, THE OLDER MAN HURLS HIMSELF FULL INTO THE PATH OF THE DEADLY PROTON BEAM, DEFIANCE RINGING FROM HIS LIPS!
MY USEFULNESS IS OVER! BUT THE HULK MUST CONTINUE TO FIGHT FOR LIBERTY!
YOU'LL NEVER DEFEAT FREE MEN! NEVER! NEVER!
UNHHHH...
HE MUST HAVE BEEN INSANE TO GIVE UP HIS LIFE FOR THAT MONSTER!
MUST WAIT AN HOUR BETWEEN PROTON BURSTS! I'LL RETURN TO THE HULK LATER!
MEANWHILE...
THANKS TO YOU, I-- SHALL NOT-- DIE A SLAVE--!
DEAD! SAVED MY LIFE! DIED FOR HULK!
SLOWLY, THE CLOUDY BRAIN OF THE HUMAN GOLIATH REMEMBERS HOW THE DEAD MAN HAD CLEANSED HIS WOUND EARLIER... AND NOW HAS MADE THE FINAL SACRIFICE! AND, AS HE REMEMBERS, STARK RAGE FILLS HIS WILDLY PUMPING HEART...!
WAS FRIEND! DIED FOR HULK!
THEY KILLED HULK'S FRIEND! THEY KILLED HULK'S FRIEND!
BRAKKK!
NOW IT IS HULK'S TURN!

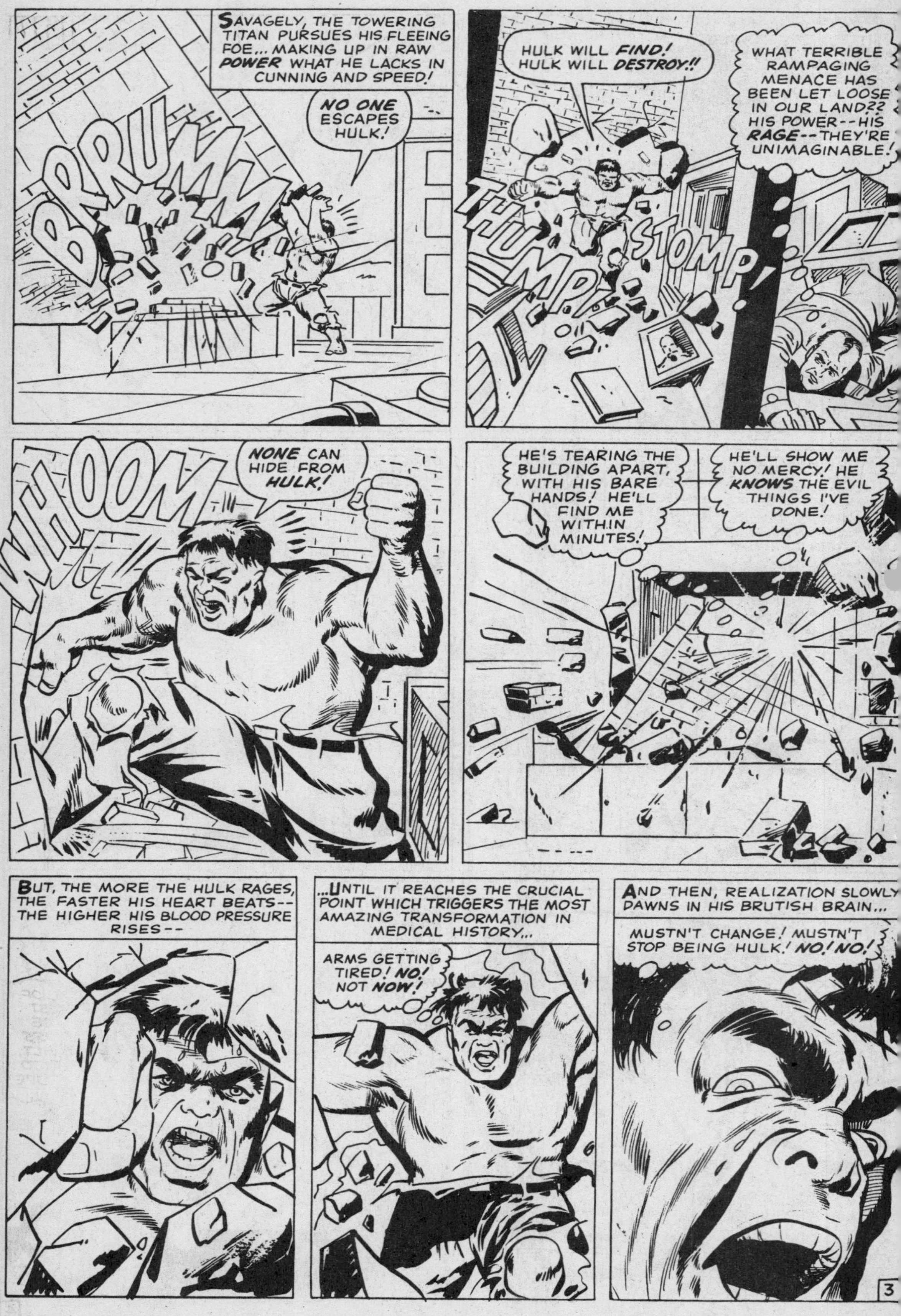
SAVAGELY, THE TOWERING TITAN PURSUES HIS FLEEING FOE... MAKING UP IN RAW POWER WHAT HE LACKS IN CUNNING AND SPEED!
NO ONE ESCAPES HULK!
BRRUMM
HULK WILL FIND! HULK WILL DESTROY!!
WHAT TERRIBLE RAMPAGING MENACE HAS BEEN LET LOOSE IN OUR LAND?? HIS POWER--HIS RAGE--THEY'RE UNIMAGINABLE!
THUMP!
STOMP!
NONE CAN HIDE FROM HULK!
WHOOM
HE'S TEARING THE BUILDING APART, WITH HIS BARE HANDS! HE'LL FIND ME WITHIN MINUTES!
HE'LL SHOW ME NO MERCY! HE KNOWS THE EVIL THINGS I'VE DONE!
BUT, THE MORE THE HULK RAGES, THE FASTER HIS HEART BEATS--THE HIGHER HIS BLOOD PRESSURE RISES--
...UNTIL IT REACHES THE CRUCIAL POINT WHICH TRIGGERS THE MOST AMAZING TRANSFORMATION IN MEDICAL HISTORY...
ARMS GETTING TIRED! NO! NOT NOW!
AND THEN, REALIZATION SLOWLY DAWNS IN HIS BRUTISH BRAIN...
MUSTN'T CHANGE! MUSTN'T STOP BEING HULK! NO! NO!
3

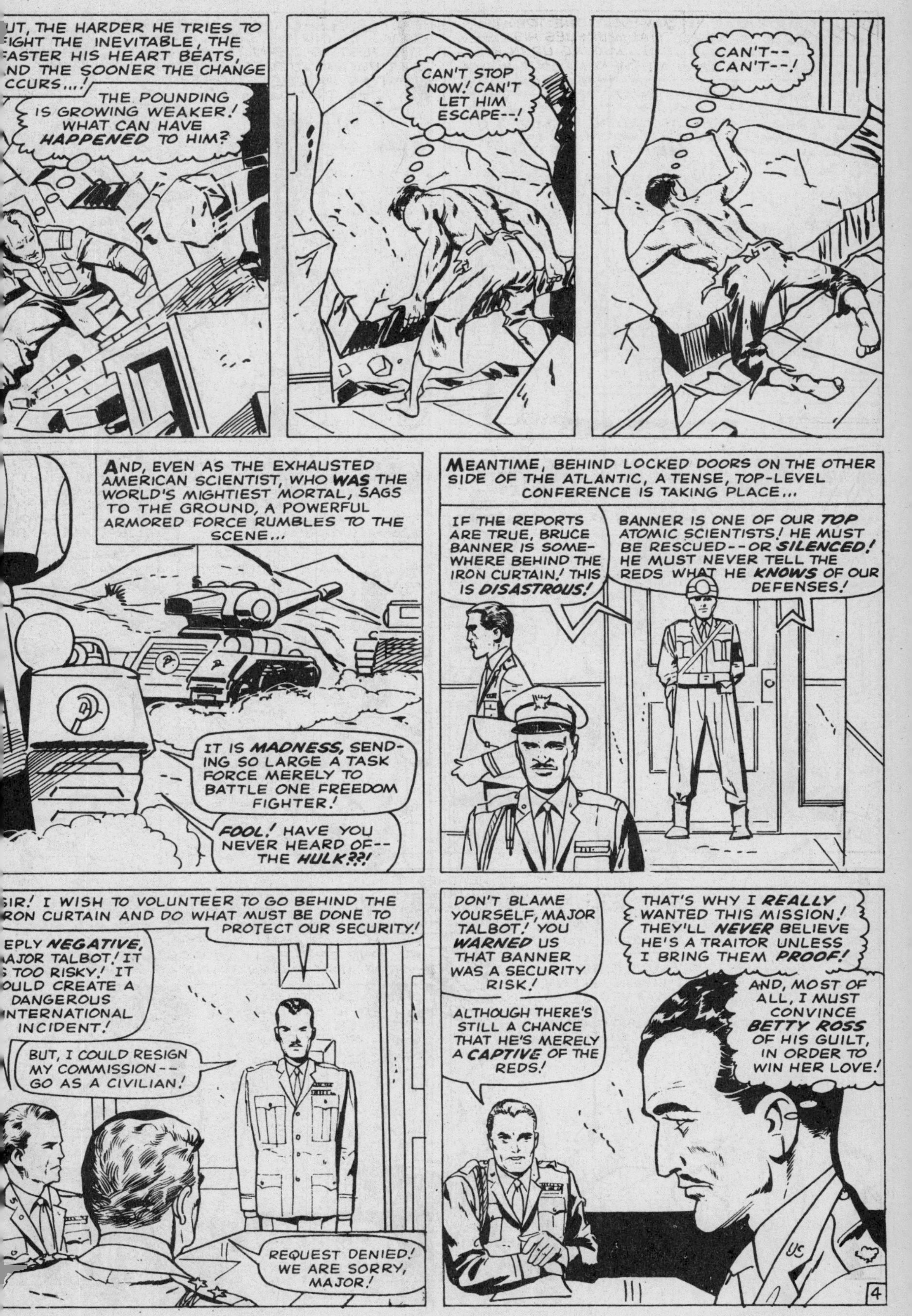

UT, THE HARDER HE TRIES TO FIGHT THE INEVITABLE, THE FASTER HIS HEART BEATS, AND THE SOONER THE CHANGE CCURS....!
THE POUNDING IS GROWING WEAKER! WHAT CAN HAVE HAPPENED TO HIM?
CAN'T STOP NOW! CAN'T LET HIM ESCAPE--!
CAN'T-- CAN'T--!
AND, EVEN AS THE EXHAUSTED AMERICAN SCIENTIST, WHO WAS THE WORLD'S MIGHTIEST MORTAL, SAGS TO THE GROUND, A POWERFUL ARMORED FORCE RUMBLES TO THE SCENE...
IT IS MADNESS, SENDING SO LARGE A TASK FORCE MERELY TO BATTLE ONE FREEDOM FIGHTER!
FOOL! HAVE YOU NEVER HEARD OF-- THE HULK??!
MEANTIME, BEHIND LOCKED DOORS ON THE OTHER SIDE OF THE ATLANTIC, A TENSE, TOP-LEVEL CONFERENCE IS TAKING PLACE...
IF THE REPORTS ARE TRUE, BRUCE BANNER IS SOMEWHERE BEHIND THE IRON CURTAIN! THIS IS DISASTROUS!
BANNER IS ONE OF OUR TOP ATOMIC SCIENTISTS! HE MUST BE RESCUED--OR SILENCED! HE MUST NEVER TELL THE REDS WHAT HE KNOWS OF OUR DEFENSES!
SIR! I WISH TO VOLUNTEER TO GO BEHIND THE RON CURTAIN AND DO WHAT MUST BE DONE TO PROTECT OUR SECURITY!
EPLY NEGATIVE, AJOR TALBOT! IT S TOO RISKY! IT OULD CREATE A DANGEROUS NTERNATIONAL INCIDENT!
BUT, I COULD RESIGN MY COMMISSION-- GO AS A CIVILIAN!
REQUEST DENIED! WE ARE SORRY, MAJOR!
DON'T BLAME YOURSELF, MAJOR TALBOT! YOU WARNED US THAT BANNER WAS A SECURITY RISK!
ALTHOUGH THERE'S STILL A CHANCE THAT HE'S MERELY A CAPTIVE OF THE REDS!
THAT'S WHY I REALLY WANTED THIS MISSION! THEY'LL NEVER BELIEVE HE'S A TRAITOR UNLESS I BRING THEM PROOF!
AND, MOST OF ALL, I MUST CONVINCE BETTY ROSS OF HIS GUILT, IN ORDER TO WIN HER LOVE!
4

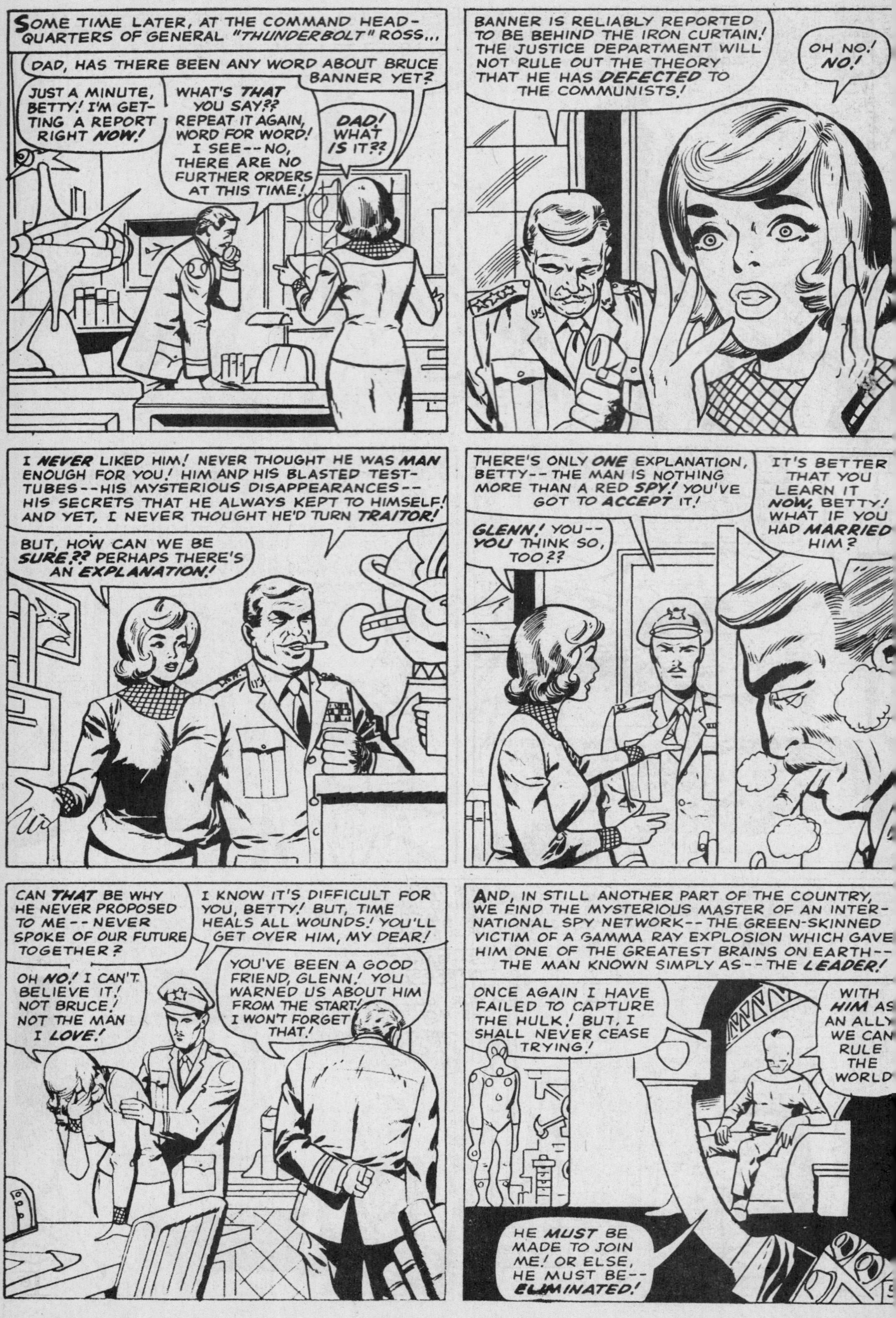
SOME TIME LATER, AT THE COMMAND HEAD-QUARTERS OF GENERAL "THUNDERBOLT" ROSS...
DAD, HAS THERE BEEN ANY WORD ABOUT BRUCE BANNER YET?
JUST A MINUTE, BETTY! I'M GETTING A REPORT RIGHT NOW!
WHAT'S THAT YOU SAY?? REPEAT IT AGAIN, WORD FOR WORD! I SEE--NO, THERE ARE NO FURTHER ORDERS AT THIS TIME!
DAD! WHAT IS IT??
BANNER IS RELIABLY REPORTED TO BE BEHIND THE IRON CURTAIN! THE JUSTICE DEPARTMENT WILL NOT RULE OUT THE THEORY THAT HE HAS DEFECTED TO THE COMMUNISTS!
OH NO! NO!
I NEVER LIKED HIM! NEVER THOUGHT HE WAS MAN ENOUGH FOR YOU! HIM AND HIS BLASTED TEST-TUBES--HIS MYSTERIOUS DISAPPEARANCES--HIS SECRETS THAT HE ALWAYS KEPT TO HIMSELF! AND YET, I NEVER THOUGHT HE'D TURN TRAITOR!
BUT, HOW CAN WE BE SURE?? PERHAPS THERE'S AN EXPLANATION!
THERE'S ONLY ONE EXPLANATION, BETTY--THE MAN IS NOTHING MORE THAN A RED SPY! YOU'VE GOT TO ACCEPT IT!
GLENN! YOU--YOU THINK SO, TOO??
IT'S BETTER THAT YOU LEARN IT NOW, BETTY! WHAT IF YOU HAD MARRIED HIM?
CAN THAT BE WHY HE NEVER PROPOSED TO ME--NEVER SPOKE OF OUR FUTURE TOGETHER?
I KNOW IT'S DIFFICULT FOR YOU, BETTY! BUT, TIME HEALS ALL WOUNDS! YOU'LL GET OVER HIM, MY DEAR!
OH NO! I CAN'T BELIEVE IT! NOT BRUCE! NOT THE MAN I LOVE!
YOU'VE BEEN A GOOD FRIEND, GLENN! YOU WARNED US ABOUT HIM FROM THE START! I WON'T FORGET THAT!
AND, IN STILL ANOTHER PART OF THE COUNTRY, WE FIND THE MYSTERIOUS MASTER OF AN INTERNATIONAL SPY NETWORK--THE GREEN-SKINNED VICTIM OF A GAMMA RAY EXPLOSION WHICH GAVE HIM ONE OF THE GREATEST BRAINS ON EARTH--THE MAN KNOWN SIMPLY AS--THE LEADER!
ONCE AGAIN I HAVE FAILED TO CAPTURE THE HULK! BUT, I SHALL NEVER CEASE TRYING!
WITH HIM AS AN ALLY WE CAN RULE THE WORLD
HE MUST BE MADE TO JOIN ME! OR ELSE, HE MUST BE--ELIMINATED!
5

WE ARE THE ONLY TWO GREEN-SKINNED MEN ON EARTH! HIS POWER, TOO, MUST STEM FROM GAMMA EXPLOSION! WE WERE DESTINED TO BECOME ALLIES! MY SUPREME INTELLECT MUST COMBINE WITH HIS LIMITLESS STRENGTH!

WHEREVER THE HULK IS, BANNER IS ALWAYS NEAR AT HAND! IN SOME STRANGE WAY, BRUCE BANNER IS THE KEY TO THE HULK!

I'LL CONTACT MY TOP LIEUTENANT, THE CHAMELEON! HE HAS BEEN ASSIGNED TO STEAL MILITARY SECRETS FROM BANNER'S AERO-SPACE UNIT!

HE SHOULD KNOW OF THE SCIENTIST'S WHEREABOUTS!

SECONDS LATER...

I WAS JUST ABOUT TO CONTACT YOU, LEADER! BANNER IS MISSING! HE IS REPORTED BEHIND THE IRON CURTAIN! THE HIGH COMMAND BELIEVES HE MIGHT HAVE DEFECTED!

WITHOUT A WORD, THE EVIL GENIUS BREAKS TV CONTACT, HAVING LEARNED WHAT HE WISHED TO KNOW...

IF MY THEORY IS CORRECT, THE HULK MUST ALSO BE BEHIND THE IRON CURTAIN, SOMEWHERE NEAR BANNER! THUS, I MUST TURN MY ATTENTION EASTWARD,...!

I SHALL CONTACT THE WOULD-BE CONQUERORS WHO ARE FOOLISH ENOUGH TO THINK THAT THE LEADER WORKS ONLY FOR THEM!

AHH! COMRADE LEADER! WHAT HAVE YOU TO REPORT?

NOTHING, AT THIS TIME, COMMISSAR! I REQUIRE INFORMATION ABOUT THE AMERICAN SCIENTIST, DR. BANNER!

AH YES--BANNER! A MOST INTERESTING CASE! YOU MIGHT CONSIDER HIM OUR "GUEST" AT THE MOMENT!

HE IS AT OUR WEAPONS TESTING CENTER NEAR THE SEA!

GOOD! THEN THAT IS WHERE I SHALL FIND THE HULK, AS WELL!

WHAT? HOW DID YOU KNOW?? IT IS OUR MOST CLOSELY GUARDED SECRET!

THERE CAN BE NO SECRETS FROM THE LEADER!

6

WAIT! DO NOT BREAK CONTACT! I MUST FIND OUT HOW YOU-- *ARROGANT DOG!* NOBODY ELSE WOULD *DARE* TO TREAT ME SO! SOME DAY HE SHALL GO *TOO FAR!* WITH HIS *SUPER-BRILLIANT BRAIN,* HE COULD BE MORE OF A THREAT TO US THAN AN *ARMY!*

BUT, THE MAN KNOWN AS THE *LEADER* CAN WASTE NO TIME WITH MERE COMMUNIST COMMISSARS! HE HAS MORE CHALLENGING MATTERS TO CONSIDER....!

I HAVE REACHED A *DECISION!* I SHALL TAKE NO ACTION YET! SOONER OR LATER BANNER AND THE HULK WILL ESCAPE THE REDS-- AND I CAN DEAL WITH THEM MORE EASILY WHEN THEY RETURN TO THESE SHORES!

I SHALL CONTENT MYSELF TO MERELY *WAIT-- AND OBSERVE* FUTURE DEVELOPMENTS.

MEANTIME, RED SEARCH PLANES COMB THE WEAPONS TESTING AREA, IN A FUTILE ATTEMPT TO FIND THE INCREDIBLE HULK...

THERE IS NO *TRACE* OF HIM! HE HAS SIMPLY *VANISHED!*

IMPOSSIBLE! HE IS SO *HUGE*-- WITH GREEN SKIN --IN A FOREIGN LAND! THERE IS *NO WAY* FOR HIM TO ELUDE US!

BUT, THERE *IS* ONE WAY-- A WAY THAT NO RATIONAL MAN WOULD EVER DREAM OF! THE *HULK* HAS RETURNED TO HIS PERFECT HIDING PLACE ONCE MORE-- HE HAS RETURNED TO THE IDENTITY OF *BRUCE BANNER,* WHO IS JUST REGAINING CONSCIOUSNESS...!

THIS IS *ONE* TIME I'D HAVE BEEN BETTER OFF TO REMAIN AS THE *HULK!*

AT LEAST IN THAT FORM I'D HAVE LIMITLESS *STRENGTH* TO HELP ME!

BUT, WHAT CHANCE CAN I HAVE FOR SURVIVAL *NOW*--? I'M *ALONE,* DEFENSELESS, IN A HOSTILE LAND!

RED *JETS!* THEY MUST BE SEARCHING FOR THE *HULK!*

THEY'VE *SIGHTED* ME! I'VE GOT TO GET *AWAY!*

THEY MUST HAVE ORDERS TO DESTROY ANYTHING THAT MOVES! AFTER THE HULK'S LAST RAMPAGE, THEY'RE TAKING NO CHANCES WITH *ANYONE!*

WEEEOW

7

CAN'T KEEP RUNNING MUCH [L]ONGER! IT LOOKS LIKE THIS IS [T]HE END OF THE LINE FOR ME!

[I]F ONLY I HAD [B]EEN ABLE TO [CL]EAR MY NAME! [IF] ONLY I COULD [H]AVE EXPLAINED [T]O BETTY! BUT [N]OW--IT'S TOO LATE!

IT'S TOO LATE FOR ANYTHING -- EXCEPT TRYING TO DIE AS BRAVELY AS-- WAIT!

THAT MAN! THAT FACE! I KNOW HIM! BUT, FROM WHERE? HOW??

AND THEN, A FAINT VESTIGE OF THE HULK'S MEMORY STEALS INTO DR. BANNER'S SUBCONSCIOUS, AS HE RECALLS THE HEROIC EURO-PEAN SCIENTIST WHO HAD DARED TO DEFY HIS RED MASTERS--

YES! YES! NOW I REMEMBER!

[T]HUS UNLEASHED, THE FLOOD OF MEMORIES [S]URGES INTO THE TORMENTED FUGITIVE'S MIND-- [M]EMORIES OF THE DEAD MAN HAVING SAVED HIS [O]WN LIFE, WHILE HE WAS FIGHTING AS THE HULK!

[H]E GAVE HIS LIFE [F]OR MINE! AND [N]OW HE'S DEAD! [KI]LLED BY THE [S]AME MERCILESS [O]NES WHO ARE [N]OW PURSUING ME!

AND, AS A WAVE OF UNCONTROLLABLE RAGE SURGES IN BANNER'S BREAST, THE INCREDIBLE CHEMICAL CHANGE WITHIN HIS BODY BEGINS ANEW--JUST AS THE GROUND IS ROCKED BY A THUNDEROUS ARTILLERY BLAST!

BAR-OOOOOM!

[LI]KE A LEAF IN A STORM, THE VALIANT SCIENTIST [IS] HURLED TOWARD A NEARBY STONE WALL--AND [T]HAT SEEMS TO BE HIS INEVITABLE DOOM!

BUT, IT IS NOT BRUCE BANNER WHO SMASHES INTO THE WALL WITH THE FORCE OF A PROJECTILE! INSTEAD, IT IS THE MIGHTIEST MORTAL TO WALK THE EARTH--THE INCREDIBLE HULK!

8

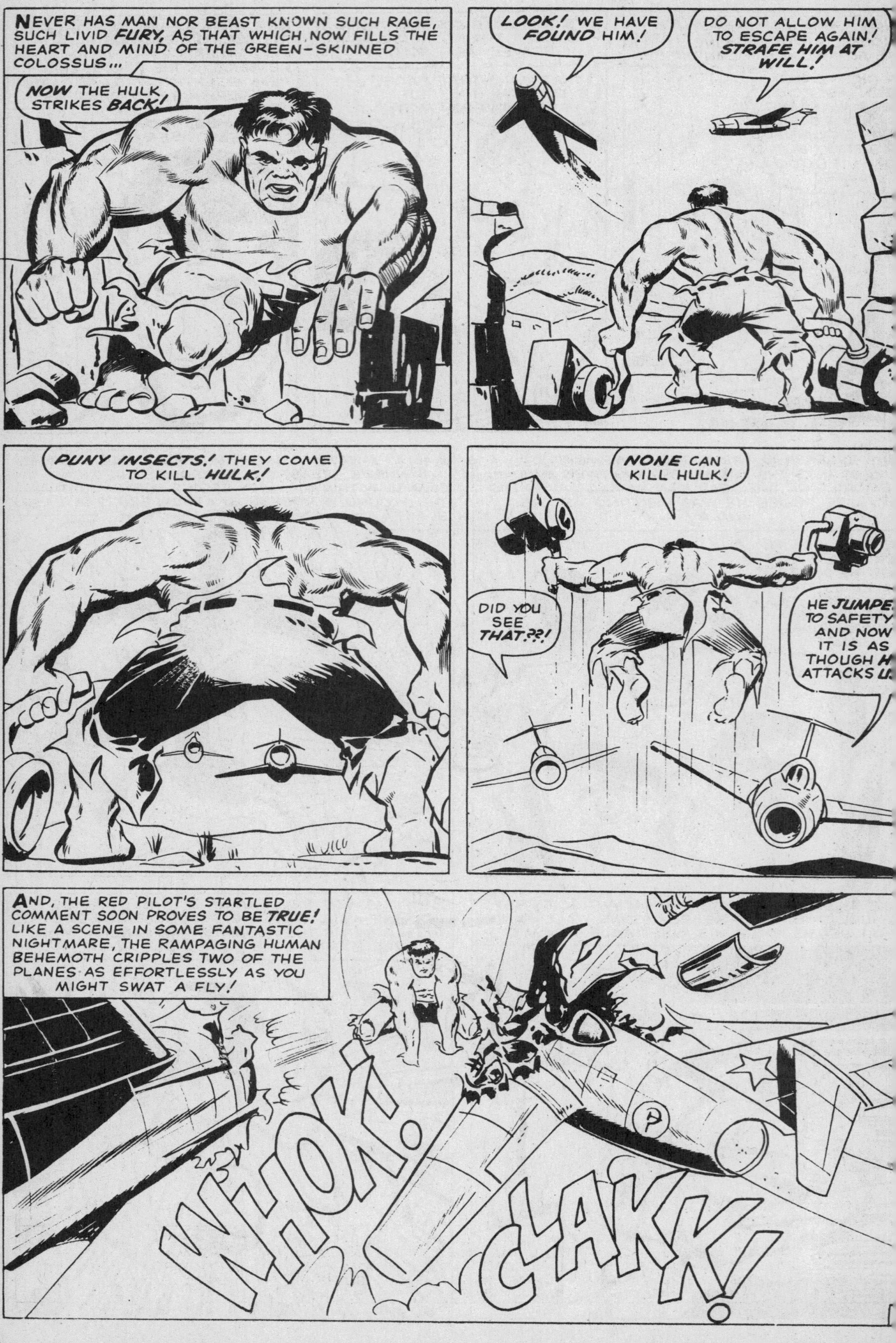
NEVER HAS MAN NOR BEAST KNOWN SUCH RAGE, SUCH LIVID FURY, AS THAT WHICH NOW FILLS THE HEART AND MIND OF THE GREEN-SKINNED COLOSSUS...
NOW THE HULK STRIKES BACK!
LOOK! WE HAVE FOUND HIM!
DO NOT ALLOW HIM TO ESCAPE AGAIN! STRAFE HIM AT WILL!
PUNY INSECTS! THEY COME TO KILL HULK!
NONE CAN KILL HULK!
DID YOU SEE THAT??!
HE JUMPE TO SAFETY AND NOW IT IS AS THOUGH H ATTACKS U
AND, THE RED PILOT'S STARTLED COMMENT SOON PROVES TO BE TRUE! LIKE A SCENE IN SOME FANTASTIC NIGHTMARE, THE RAMPAGING HUMAN BEHEMOTH CRIPPLES TWO OF THE PLANES AS EFFORTLESSLY AS YOU MIGHT SWAT A FLY!
WHOK!
CLAKK!

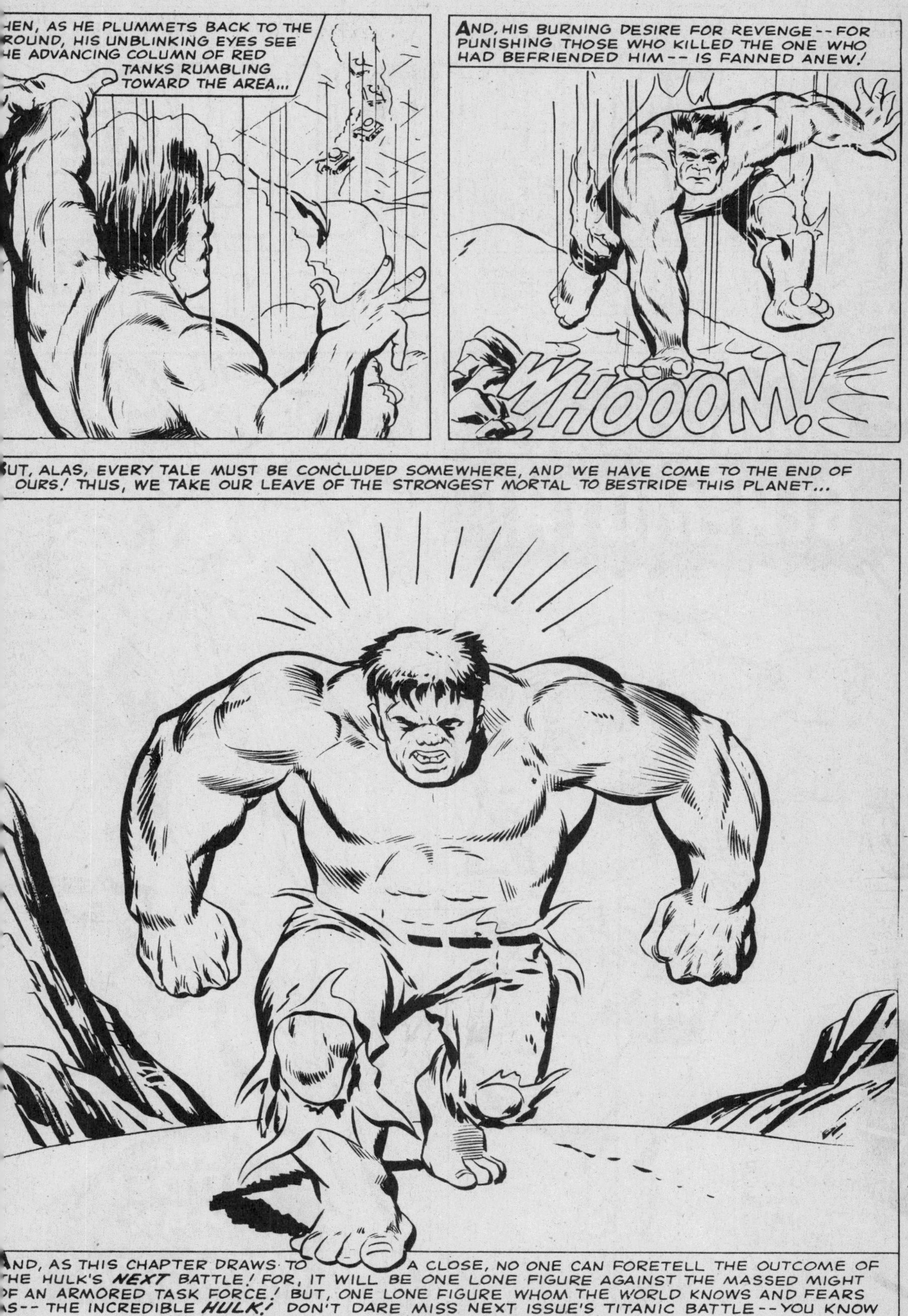
HEN, AS HE PLUMMETS BACK TO THE ROUND, HIS UNBLINKING EYES SEE HE ADVANCING COLUMN OF RED TANKS RUMBLING TOWARD THE AREA...
AND, HIS BURNING DESIRE FOR REVENGE--FOR PUNISHING THOSE WHO KILLED THE ONE WHO HAD BEFRIENDED HIM--IS FANNED ANEW!
WHOOOM!
UT, ALAS, EVERY TALE MUST BE CONCLUDED SOMEWHERE, AND WE HAVE COME TO THE END OF OURS! THUS, WE TAKE OUR LEAVE OF THE STRONGEST MORTAL TO BESTRIDE THIS PLANET...
AND, AS THIS CHAPTER DRAWS TO A CLOSE, NO ONE CAN FORETELL THE OUTCOME OF HE HULK'S NEXT BATTLE! FOR, IT WILL BE ONE LONE FIGURE AGAINST THE MASSED MIGHT OF AN ARMORED TASK FORCE! BUT, ONE LONE FIGURE WHOM THE WORLD KNOWS AND FEARS AS-- THE INCREDIBLE HULK! DON'T DARE MISS NEXT ISSUE'S TITANIC BATTLE--YOU KNOW HOW INSECURE YOUR ABSENCE MAKES US FEEL!

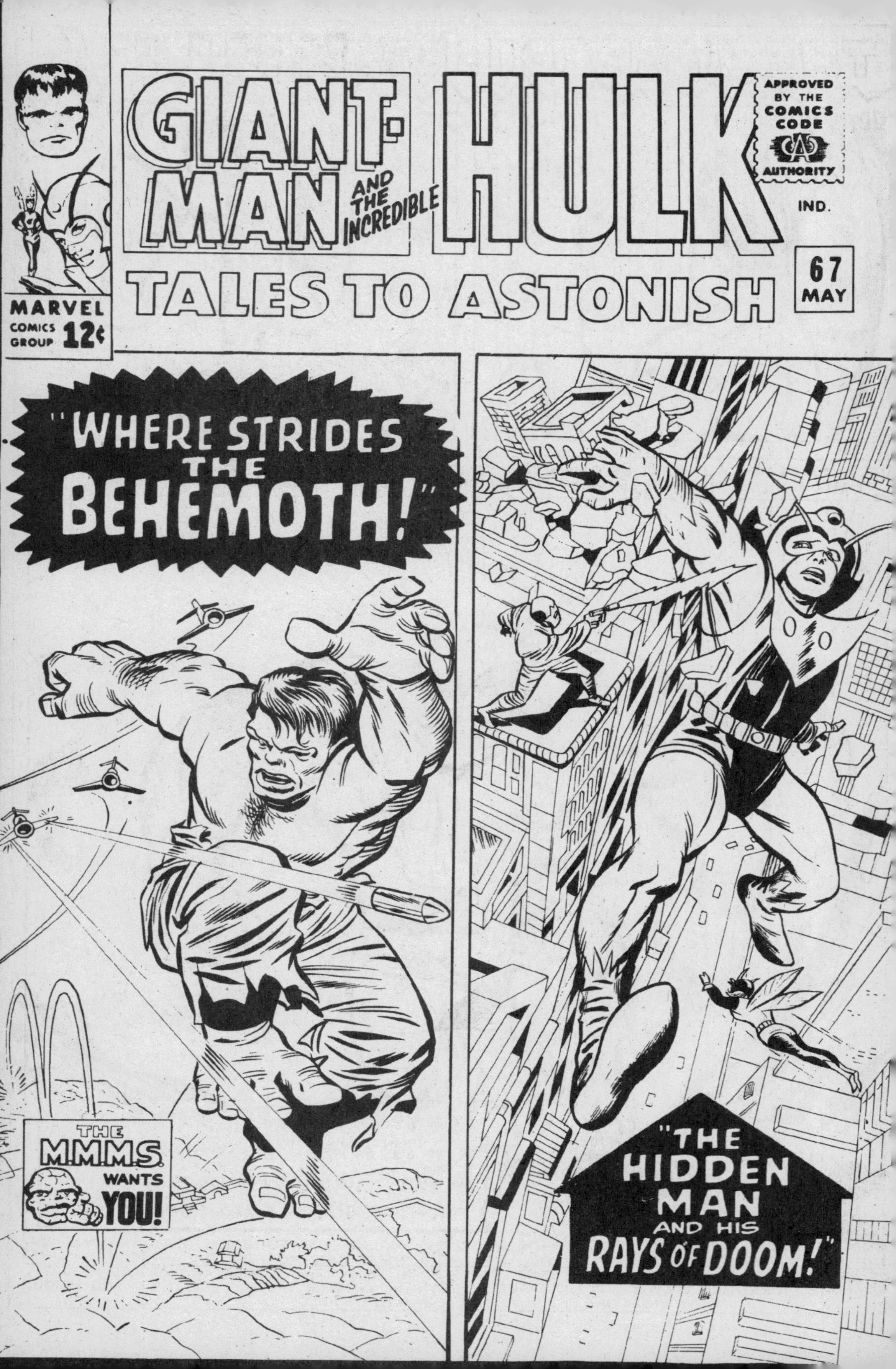

GIANT-MAN AND THE INCREDIBLE HULK
APPROVED BY THE COMICS CODE CA AUTHORITY
IND.
TALES TO ASTONISH
67 MAY
MARVEL COMICS GROUP 12¢
"WHERE STRIDES THE BEHEMOTH!"
THE M.M.M.S. WANTS YOU!
"THE HIDDEN MAN AND HIS RAYS OF DOOM!"

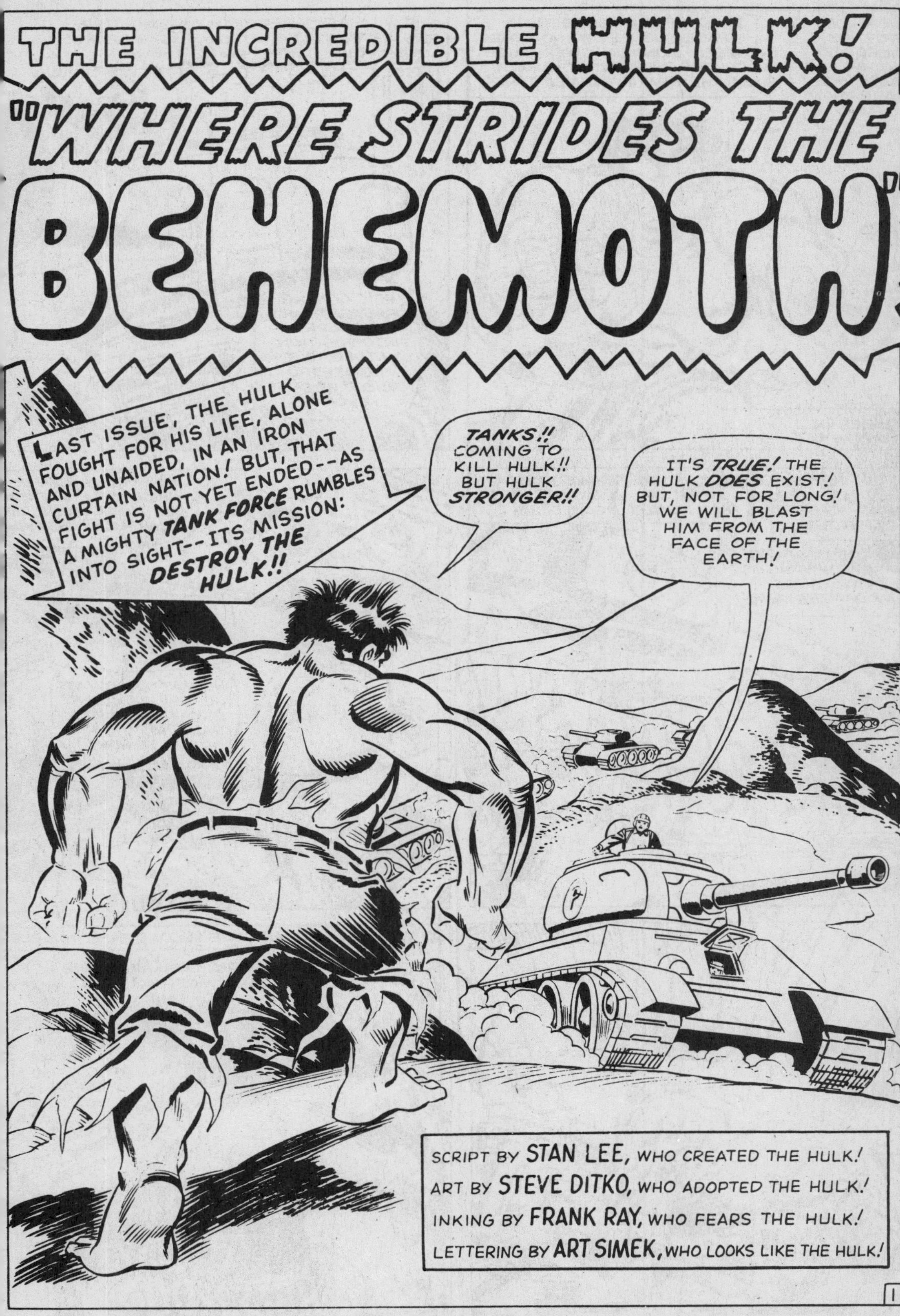

THE INCREDIBLE HULK!
"WHERE STRIDES THE BEHEMOTH"
LAST ISSUE, THE HULK FOUGHT FOR HIS LIFE, ALONE AND UNAIDED, IN AN IRON CURTAIN NATION! BUT, THAT FIGHT IS NOT YET ENDED--AS A MIGHTY TANK FORCE RUMBLES INTO SIGHT--ITS MISSION: DESTROY THE HULK!!
TANKS!! COMING TO KILL HULK!! BUT HULK STRONGER!!
IT'S TRUE! THE HULK DOES EXIST! BUT, NOT FOR LONG! WE WILL BLAST HIM FROM THE FACE OF THE EARTH!
SCRIPT BY STAN LEE, WHO CREATED THE HULK!
ART BY STEVE DITKO, WHO ADOPTED THE HULK!
INKING BY FRANK RAY, WHO FEARS THE HULK!
LETTERING BY ART SIMEK, WHO LOOKS LIKE THE HULK!
1

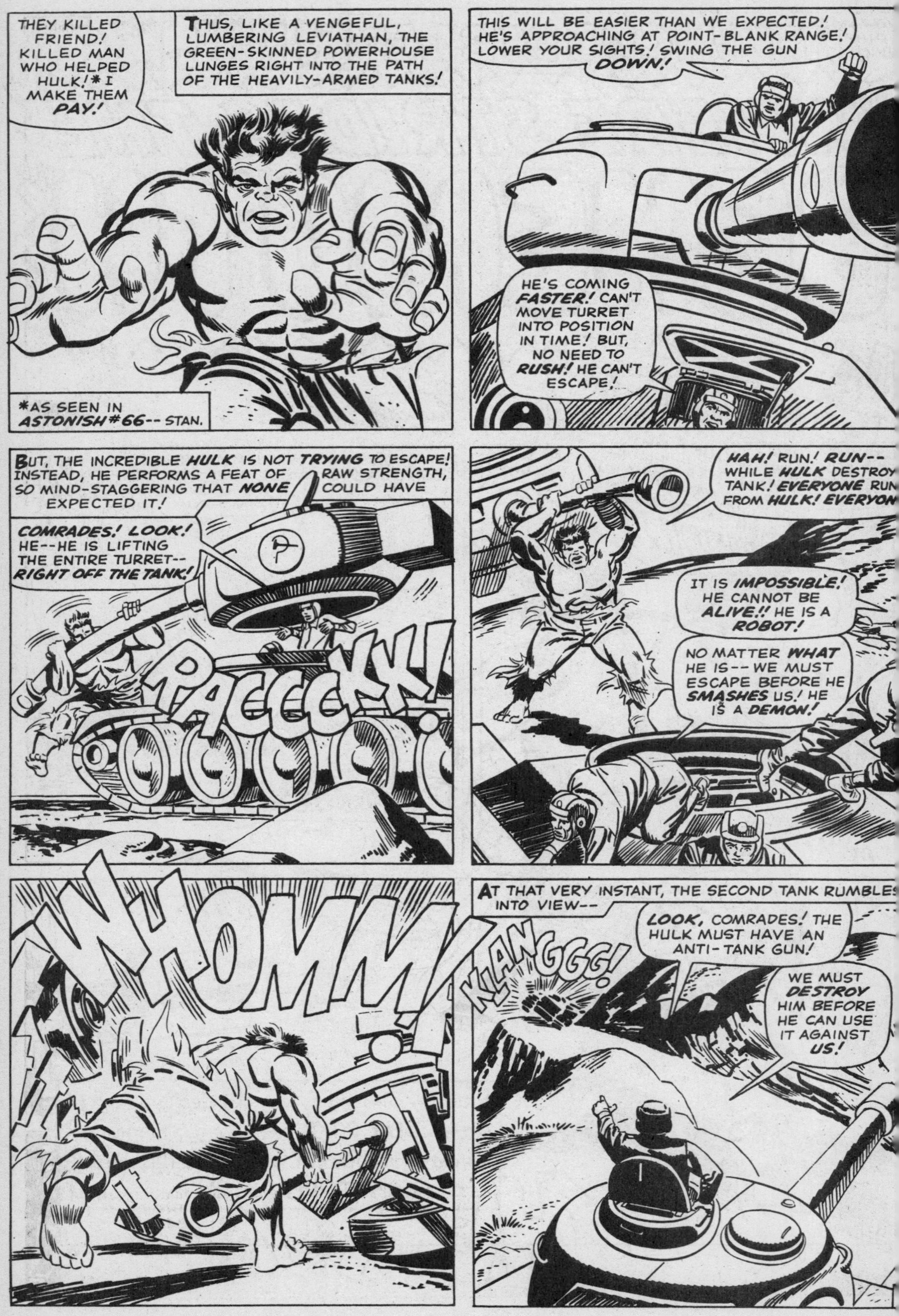

THEY KILLED FRIEND! KILLED MAN WHO HELPED HULK!* I MAKE THEM PAY!
THUS, LIKE A VENGEFUL, LUMBERING LEVIATHAN, THE GREEN-SKINNED POWERHOUSE LUNGES RIGHT INTO THE PATH OF THE HEAVILY-ARMED TANKS!
*AS SEEN IN ASTONISH #66-- STAN.
THIS WILL BE EASIER THAN WE EXPECTED! HE'S APPROACHING AT POINT-BLANK RANGE! LOWER YOUR SIGHTS! SWING THE GUN DOWN!
HE'S COMING FASTER! CAN'T MOVE TURRET INTO POSITION IN TIME! BUT, NO NEED TO RUSH! HE CAN'T ESCAPE!
BUT, THE INCREDIBLE HULK IS NOT TRYING TO ESCAPE! INSTEAD, HE PERFORMS A FEAT OF RAW STRENGTH, SO MIND-STAGGERING THAT NONE COULD HAVE EXPECTED IT!
COMRADES! LOOK! HE--HE IS LIFTING THE ENTIRE TURRET-- RIGHT OFF THE TANK!
RACCCKK!
HAH! RUN! RUN-- WHILE HULK DESTROY TANK! EVERYONE RUN FROM HULK! EVERYONE
IT IS IMPOSSIBLE! HE CANNOT BE ALIVE!! HE IS A ROBOT!
NO MATTER WHAT HE IS-- WE MUST ESCAPE BEFORE HE SMASHES US! HE IS A DEMON!
WHOMM!
AT THAT VERY INSTANT, THE SECOND TANK RUMBLES INTO VIEW--
KLANGGG!
LOOK, COMRADES! THE HULK MUST HAVE AN ANTI-TANK GUN!
WE MUST DESTROY HIM BEFORE HE CAN USE IT AGAINST US!

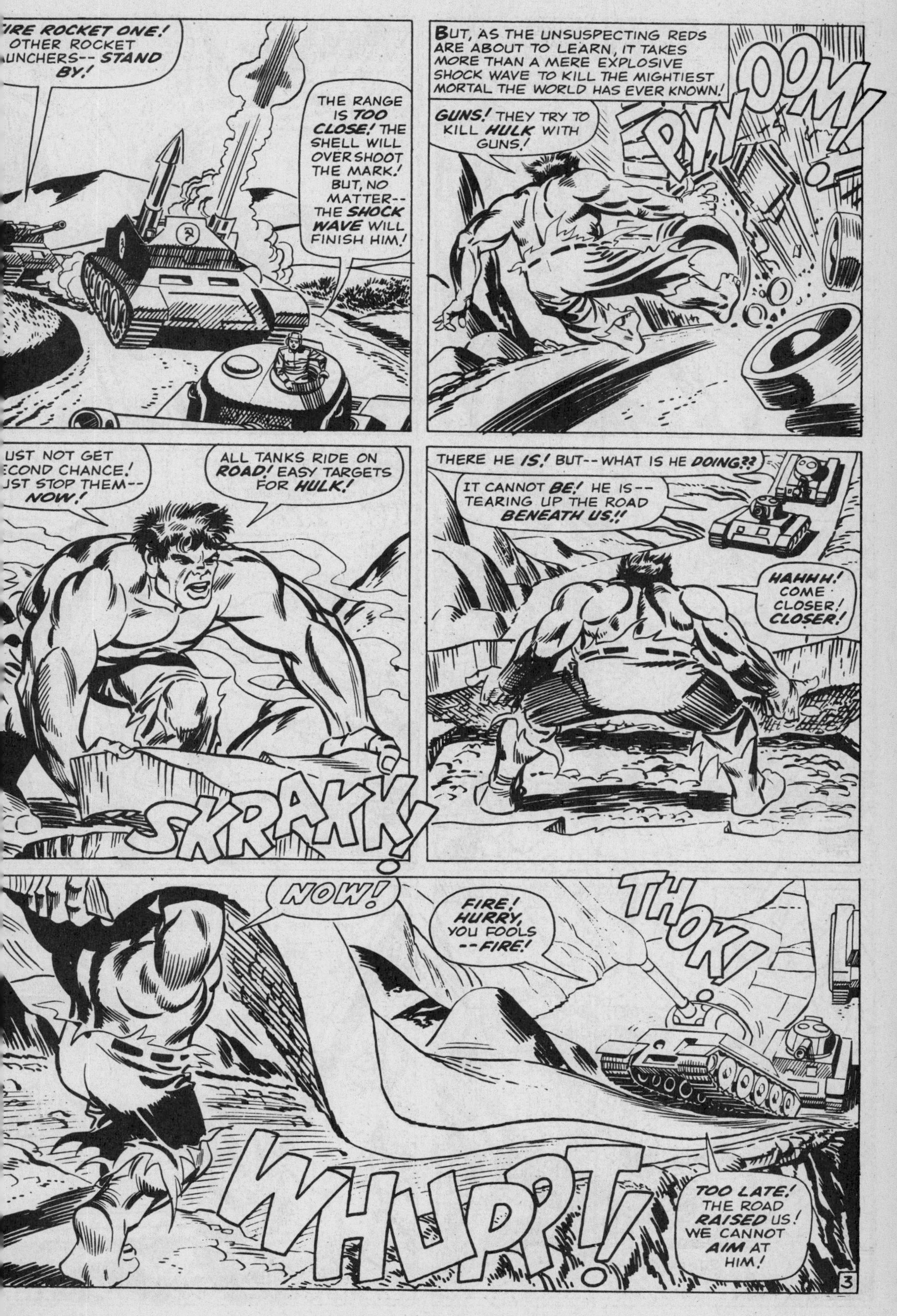

FIRE ROCKET ONE! OTHER ROCKET LAUNCHERS-- STAND BY!
THE RANGE IS TOO CLOSE! THE SHELL WILL OVERSHOOT THE MARK! BUT, NO MATTER-- THE SHOCK WAVE WILL FINISH HIM!
BUT, AS THE UNSUSPECTING REDS ARE ABOUT TO LEARN, IT TAKES MORE THAN A MERE EXPLOSIVE SHOCK WAVE TO KILL THE MIGHTIEST MORTAL THE WORLD HAS EVER KNOWN!
GUNS! THEY TRY TO KILL HULK WITH GUNS!
PYYOOOM!
MUST NOT GET SECOND CHANCE! MUST STOP THEM-- NOW!
ALL TANKS RIDE ON ROAD! EASY TARGETS FOR HULK!
SKRAKK!
THERE HE IS! BUT--WHAT IS HE DOING??
IT CANNOT BE! HE IS-- TEARING UP THE ROAD BENEATH US!!
HAHHH! COME CLOSER! CLOSER!
NOW!
FIRE! HURRY, YOU FOOLS --FIRE!
THOK!
WHUPPT!
TOO LATE! THE ROAD RAISED US! WE CANNOT AIM AT HIM!
3

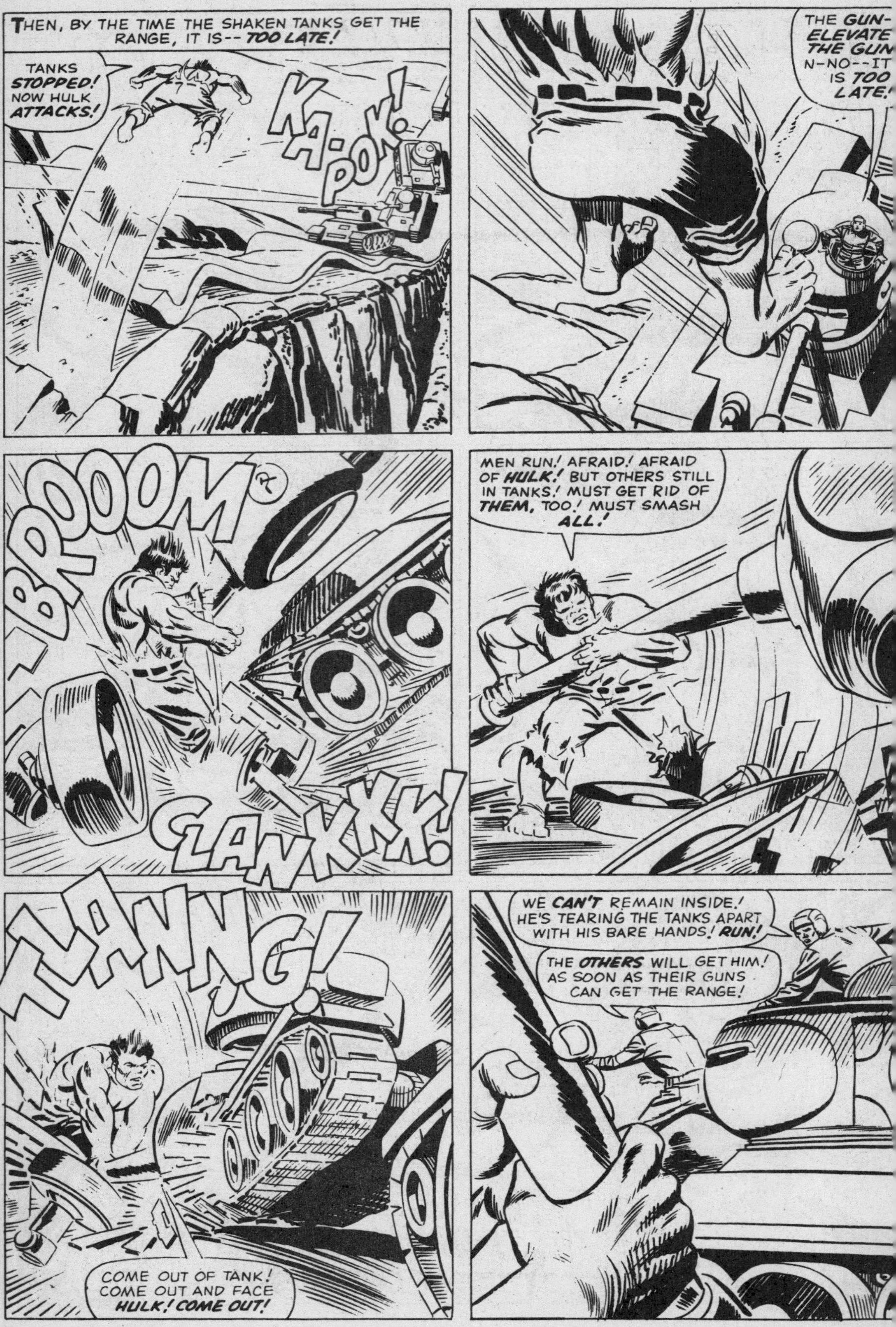
THEN, BY THE TIME THE SHAKEN TANKS GET THE RANGE, IT IS-- TOO LATE!
TANKS STOPPED! NOW HULK ATTACKS!
KA-POK!
THE GUN-ELEVATE THE GUN N-NO--IT IS TOO LATE!
BROOOM
CLANKKK!
MEN RUN! AFRAID! AFRAID OF HULK! BUT OTHERS STILL IN TANKS! MUST GET RID OF THEM, TOO! MUST SMASH ALL!
TLANNG!
COME OUT OF TANK! COME OUT AND FACE HULK! COME OUT!
WE CAN'T REMAIN INSIDE! HE'S TEARING THE TANKS APART WITH HIS BARE HANDS! RUN!
THE OTHERS WILL GET HIM! AS SOON AS THEIR GUNS CAN GET THE RANGE!

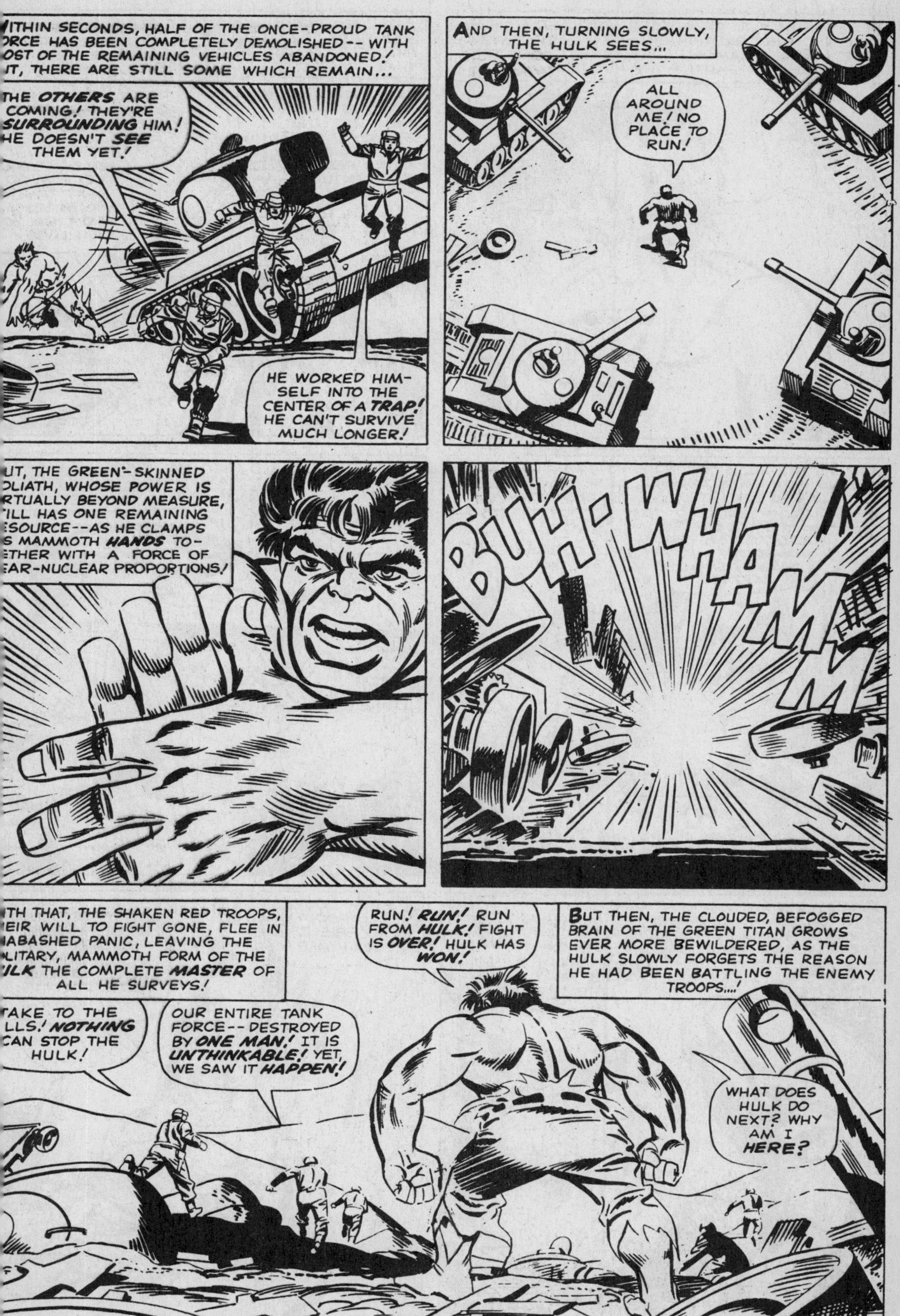

VITHIN SECONDS, HALF OF THE ONCE-PROUD TANK ORCE HAS BEEN COMPLETELY DEMOLISHED-- WITH OST OF THE REMAINING VEHICLES ABANDONED! UT, THERE ARE STILL SOME WHICH REMAIN...
THE OTHERS ARE COMING! THEY'RE SURROUNDING HIM! HE DOESN'T SEE THEM YET!
HE WORKED HIMSELF INTO THE CENTER OF A TRAP! HE CAN'T SURVIVE MUCH LONGER!
AND THEN, TURNING SLOWLY, THE HULK SEES...
ALL AROUND ME! NO PLACE TO RUN!
UT, THE GREEN-SKINNED OLIATH, WHOSE POWER IS RTUALLY BEYOND MEASURE, TILL HAS ONE REMAINING ESOURCE--AS HE CLAMPS S MAMMOTH HANDS TOETHER WITH A FORCE OF EAR-NUCLEAR PROPORTIONS!
BUH-WHAMMM
ITH THAT, THE SHAKEN RED TROOPS, EIR WILL TO FIGHT GONE, FLEE IN ABASHED PANIC, LEAVING THE OLITARY, MAMMOTH FORM OF THE ULK THE COMPLETE MASTER OF ALL HE SURVEYS!
TAKE TO THE LLS! NOTHING CAN STOP THE HULK!
OUR ENTIRE TANK FORCE-- DESTROYED BY ONE MAN! IT IS UNTHINKABLE! YET, WE SAW IT HAPPEN!
RUN! RUN! RUN FROM HULK! FIGHT IS OVER! HULK HAS WON!
BUT THEN, THE CLOUDED, BEFOGGED BRAIN OF THE GREEN TITAN GROWS EVER MORE BEWILDERED, AS THE HULK SLOWLY FORGETS THE REASON HE HAD BEEN BATTLING THE ENEMY TROOPS...!
WHAT DOES HULK DO NEXT? WHY AM I HERE?
5

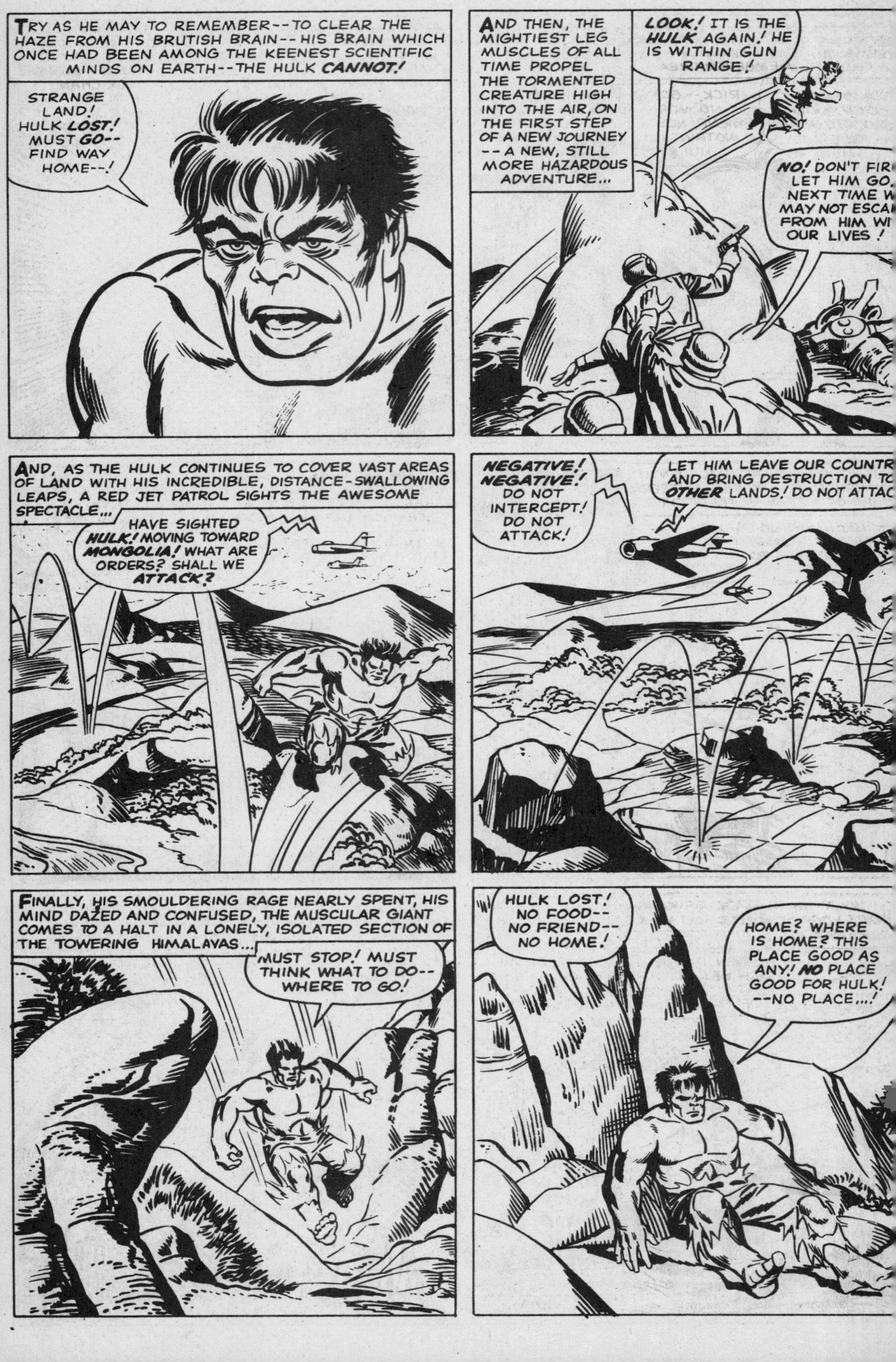
TRY AS HE MAY TO REMEMBER--TO CLEAR THE HAZE FROM HIS BRUTISH BRAIN--HIS BRAIN WHICH ONCE HAD BEEN AMONG THE KEENEST SCIENTIFIC MINDS ON EARTH--THE HULK CANNOT!
STRANGE LAND! HULK LOST! MUST GO-- FIND WAY HOME--!
AND THEN, THE MIGHTIEST LEG MUSCLES OF ALL TIME PROPEL THE TORMENTED CREATURE HIGH INTO THE AIR, ON THE FIRST STEP OF A NEW JOURNEY --A NEW, STILL MORE HAZARDOUS ADVENTURE...
LOOK! IT IS THE HULK AGAIN! HE IS WITHIN GUN RANGE!
NO! DON'T FIR LET HIM GO. NEXT TIME W MAY NOT ESCA FROM HIM WI OUR LIVES!
AND, AS THE HULK CONTINUES TO COVER VAST AREAS OF LAND WITH HIS INCREDIBLE, DISTANCE-SWALLOWING LEAPS, A RED JET PATROL SIGHTS THE AWESOME SPECTACLE...
HAVE SIGHTED HULK! MOVING TOWARD MONGOLIA! WHAT ARE ORDERS? SHALL WE ATTACK?
NEGATIVE! NEGATIVE! DO NOT INTERCEPT! DO NOT ATTACK!
LET HIM LEAVE OUR COUNTR AND BRING DESTRUCTION T OTHER LANDS! DO NOT ATTAC
FINALLY, HIS SMOULDERING RAGE NEARLY SPENT, HIS MIND DAZED AND CONFUSED, THE MUSCULAR GIANT COMES TO A HALT IN A LONELY, ISOLATED SECTION OF THE TOWERING HIMALAYAS...
MUST STOP! MUST THINK WHAT TO DO-- WHERE TO GO!
HULK LOST! NO FOOD-- NO FRIEND-- NO HOME!
HOME? WHERE IS HOME? THIS PLACE GOOD AS ANY! NO PLACE GOOD FOR HULK! --NO PLACE...!

AND THEN, A GLIMMER OF MEMORY SEEMS TO RETURN--FAINTLY--LIKE A DIMLY-REMEMBERED DREAM...

HULK ONCE HAD FRIEND--RICK--RICK! BOY--RAN AWAY!

RICK--GONE! NO MORE FRIEND! NOTHING! NOTHING FOR HULK--!

BUT, THE GAMMA-RAY-AFFECTED BRAIN OF THE GREEN-SKINNED CREATURE CANNOT RETAIN ANY THOUGHT FOR LONG--AND, WITHIN MINUTES, THE MEMORY LEAVES, AS THE TRAGEDY-RIDDEN FIGURE BEGINS TO SLUMBER...

THERE IS NOTHING FOR HULK--NOTHING BUT RUNNING--FIGHTING! NOTHING--

THEN, WITH SLEEP, COMES COMPLETE FORGETFULNESS, AS THE STORM WITHIN HIS BREAST STOPS RAGING, AND THE HULK CHANGES --BACK TO THE PERSON OF **BRUCE BANNER**...

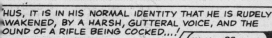

THUS, IT IS IN HIS NORMAL IDENTITY THAT HE IS RUDELY AWAKENED, BY A HARSH, GUTTERAL VOICE, AND THE SOUND OF A RIFLE BEING COCKED...!

HE HAS NOTHING WORTH STEALING! HE IS USELESS TO US!

SHOOT HIM, THEN! WE HAVE NO TIME TO WASTE WITH SUCH AS HE!

WHA--?? WHO **ARE** YOU?

CLICK!

YOU SPEAK TO **KANGA KHAN**, INFIDEL! I AM BANDIT CHIEFTON HERE! BUT, YOUR VOICE--YOU ARE **AMERICAN**!

AN AMERICAN--**HERE**! THIS IS WONDROUS STRANGE, MY CHIEFTON!

I'VE GOT TO THINK FAST! THEY'D SHOOT ME AS SOON AS LOOK AT ME!

LISTEN--I'LL MAKE YOU AN **OFFER**! TAKE ME TO THE NEAREST AMERICANS, AND YOU'LL BE REWARDED HANDSOMELY!

YOU TRY TO MAKE **FOOL** OF KANGA KHAN?!! YOU ARE **POOR**! LOOK AT **RAGS** YOU WEAR! WHY WOULD ANY PAY REWARD?

I'VE **GOT** TO CONVINCE THEM--OR ELSE, I'M **FINISHED**!

BUT, MIGHTY ONE--HAVE YOU FORGOTTEN THAT **ALL** AMERICANS ARE RICH BEYOND OUR POOR IMAGINATIONS?! IS IT NOT SO WRITTEN IN THE PAPERS OF THE PEOPLE'S GOVERNMENT?

THE REASON MY CLOTHES ARE IN TATTERS IS THAT I HAVE BEEN **LOST** HERE! WITHOUT FOOD, OR WATER--OTHER BANDITS TOOK MY MONEY--BUT I HAVE MORE--I CAN **GET** IT--!

PERHAPS HE ESCAPED FROM THE LAND OF THE SOVIETS! THEY WOULD PAY US FOR HIS RETURN!

PERHAPS--BUT THE AMERICANS ARE MORE GENEROUS WITH THEIR WEALTH! **THEY** WOULD PAY MORE HANDSOMELY!

7

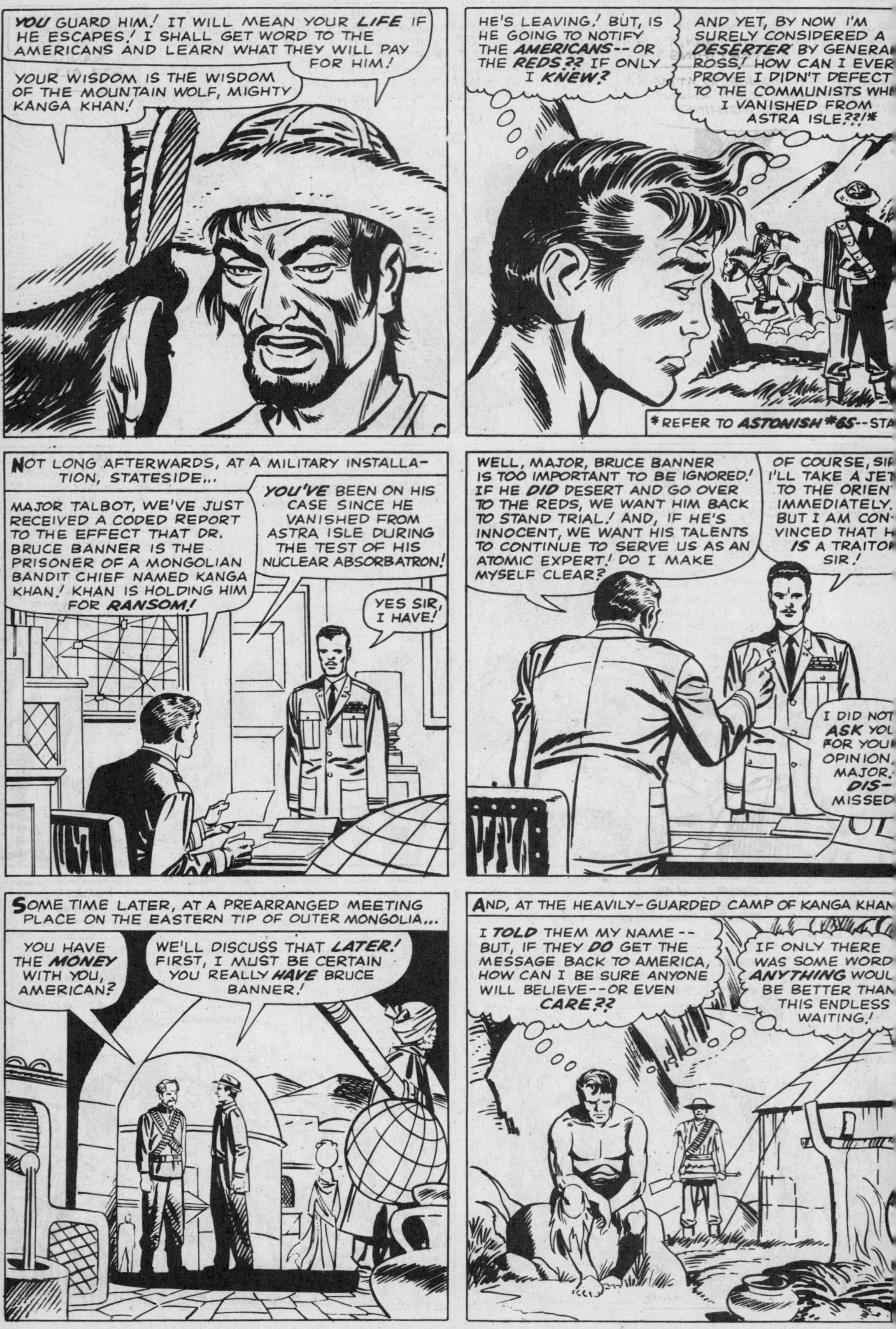
YOU GUARD HIM! IT WILL MEAN YOUR LIFE IF HE ESCAPES! I SHALL GET WORD TO THE AMERICANS AND LEARN WHAT THEY WILL PAY FOR HIM!
YOUR WISDOM IS THE WISDOM OF THE MOUNTAIN WOLF, MIGHTY KANGA KHAN!
HE'S LEAVING! BUT, IS HE GOING TO NOTIFY THE AMERICANS--OR THE REDS?? IF ONLY I KNEW?
AND YET, BY NOW I'M SURELY CONSIDERED A DESERTER BY GENERAL ROSS! HOW CAN I EVER PROVE I DIDN'T DEFECT TO THE COMMUNISTS WHEN I VANISHED FROM ASTRA ISLE??!*
*REFER TO ASTONISH #65--STA
NOT LONG AFTERWARDS, AT A MILITARY INSTALLATION, STATESIDE...
MAJOR TALBOT, WE'VE JUST RECEIVED A CODED REPORT TO THE EFFECT THAT DR. BRUCE BANNER IS THE PRISONER OF A MONGOLIAN BANDIT CHIEF NAMED KANGA KHAN! KHAN IS HOLDING HIM FOR RANSOM!
YOU'VE BEEN ON HIS CASE SINCE HE VANISHED FROM ASTRA ISLE DURING THE TEST OF HIS NUCLEAR ABSORBATRON!
YES SIR, I HAVE!
WELL, MAJOR, BRUCE BANNER IS TOO IMPORTANT TO BE IGNORED! IF HE DID DESERT AND GO OVER TO THE REDS, WE WANT HIM BACK TO STAND TRIAL! AND, IF HE'S INNOCENT, WE WANT HIS TALENTS TO CONTINUE TO SERVE US AS AN ATOMIC EXPERT! DO I MAKE MYSELF CLEAR?
OF COURSE, SIR! I'LL TAKE A JET TO THE ORIENT IMMEDIATELY. BUT I AM CONVINCED THAT HE IS A TRAITOR, SIR!
I DID NOT ASK YOU FOR YOUR OPINION, MAJOR. DISMISSED!
SOME TIME LATER, AT A PREARRANGED MEETING PLACE ON THE EASTERN TIP OF OUTER MONGOLIA...
YOU HAVE THE MONEY WITH YOU, AMERICAN?
WE'LL DISCUSS THAT LATER! FIRST, I MUST BE CERTAIN YOU REALLY HAVE BRUCE BANNER!
AND, AT THE HEAVILY-GUARDED CAMP OF KANGA KHAN
I TOLD THEM MY NAME -- BUT, IF THEY DO GET THE MESSAGE BACK TO AMERICA, HOW CAN I BE SURE ANYONE WILL BELIEVE--OR EVEN CARE??
IF ONLY THERE WAS SOME WORD! ANYTHING WOULD BE BETTER THAN THIS ENDLESS WAITING!

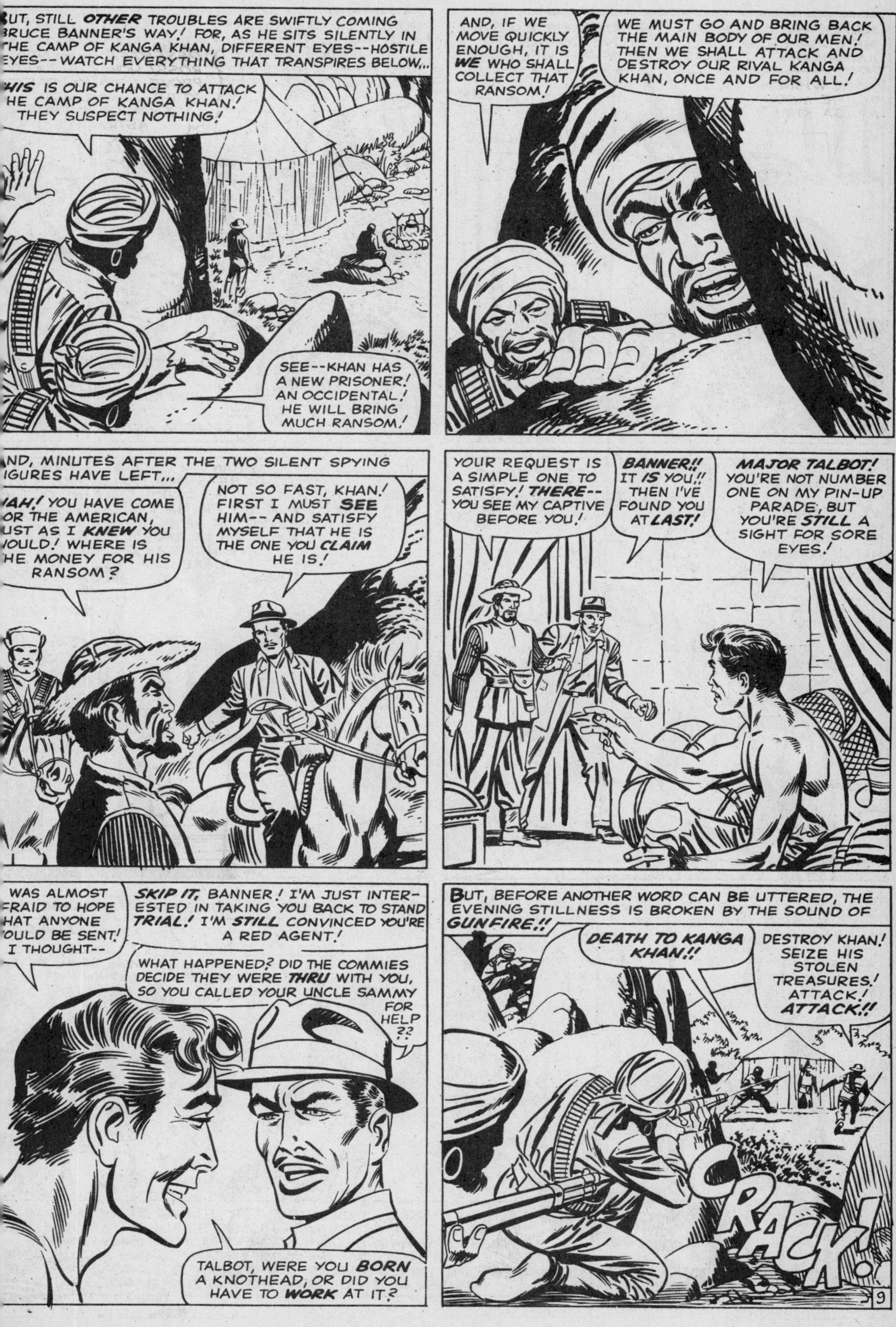
BUT, STILL OTHER TROUBLES ARE SWIFTLY COMING BRUCE BANNER'S WAY! FOR, AS HE SITS SILENTLY IN THE CAMP OF KANGA KHAN, DIFFERENT EYES--HOSTILE EYES--WATCH EVERYTHING THAT TRANSPIRES BELOW...
THIS IS OUR CHANCE TO ATTACK THE CAMP OF KANGA KHAN! THEY SUSPECT NOTHING!
SEE--KHAN HAS A NEW PRISONER! AN OCCIDENTAL! HE WILL BRING MUCH RANSOM!
AND, IF WE MOVE QUICKLY ENOUGH, IT IS WE WHO SHALL COLLECT THAT RANSOM!
WE MUST GO AND BRING BACK THE MAIN BODY OF OUR MEN! THEN WE SHALL ATTACK AND DESTROY OUR RIVAL KANGA KHAN, ONCE AND FOR ALL!
AND, MINUTES AFTER THE TWO SILENT SPYING FIGURES HAVE LEFT...
AHAH! YOU HAVE COME FOR THE AMERICAN, JUST AS I KNEW YOU WOULD! WHERE IS THE MONEY FOR HIS RANSOM?
NOT SO FAST, KHAN! FIRST I MUST SEE HIM-- AND SATISFY MYSELF THAT HE IS THE ONE YOU CLAIM HE IS!
YOUR REQUEST IS A SIMPLE ONE TO SATISFY! THERE-- YOU SEE MY CAPTIVE BEFORE YOU!
BANNER!! IT IS YOU!! THEN I'VE FOUND YOU AT LAST!
MAJOR TALBOT! YOU'RE NOT NUMBER ONE ON MY PIN-UP PARADE, BUT YOU'RE STILL A SIGHT FOR SORE EYES!
I WAS ALMOST AFRAID TO HOPE THAT ANYONE WOULD BE SENT! I THOUGHT--
SKIP IT, BANNER! I'M JUST INTERESTED IN TAKING YOU BACK TO STAND TRIAL! I'M STILL CONVINCED YOU'RE A RED AGENT!
WHAT HAPPENED? DID THE COMMIES DECIDE THEY WERE THRU WITH YOU, SO YOU CALLED YOUR UNCLE SAMMY FOR HELP??
TALBOT, WERE YOU BORN A KNOTHEAD, OR DID YOU HAVE TO WORK AT IT?
BUT, BEFORE ANOTHER WORD CAN BE UTTERED, THE EVENING STILLNESS IS BROKEN BY THE SOUND OF GUNFIRE!!
DEATH TO KANGA KHAN!!
DESTROY KHAN! SEIZE HIS STOLEN TREASURES! ATTACK! ATTACK!!
CRACK!
9

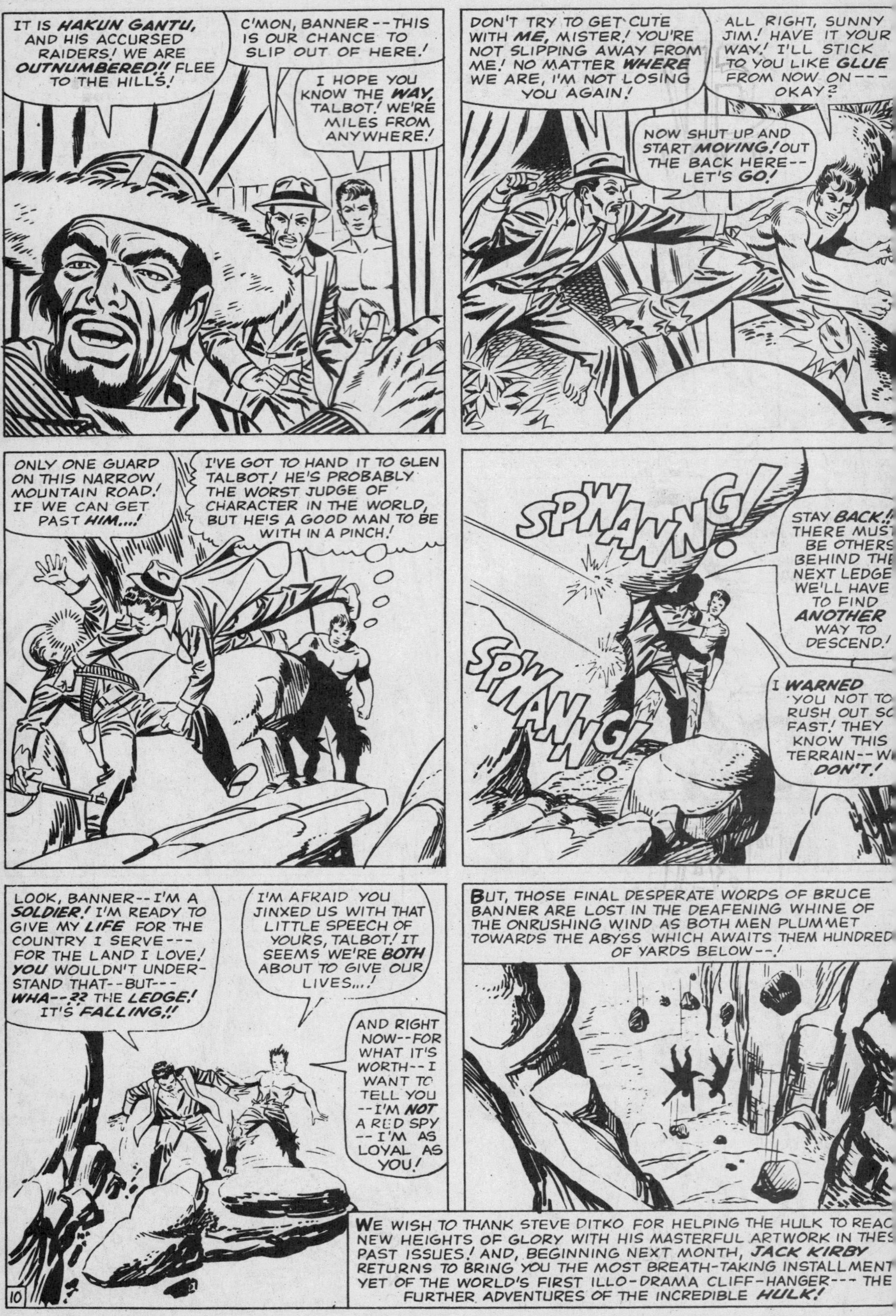

IT IS HAKUN GANTU, AND HIS ACCURSED RAIDERS! WE ARE OUTNUMBERED!! FLEE TO THE HILLS!
C'MON, BANNER--THIS IS OUR CHANCE TO SLIP OUT OF HERE!
I HOPE YOU KNOW THE WAY, TALBOT! WE'RE MILES FROM ANYWHERE!
DON'T TRY TO GET CUTE WITH ME, MISTER! YOU'RE NOT SLIPPING AWAY FROM ME! NO MATTER WHERE WE ARE, I'M NOT LOSING YOU AGAIN!
ALL RIGHT, SUNNY JIM! HAVE IT YOUR WAY! I'LL STICK TO YOU LIKE GLUE FROM NOW ON--- OKAY?
NOW SHUT UP AND START MOVING! OUT THE BACK HERE-- LET'S GO!
ONLY ONE GUARD ON THIS NARROW MOUNTAIN ROAD! IF WE CAN GET PAST HIM...!
I'VE GOT TO HAND IT TO GLEN TALBOT! HE'S PROBABLY THE WORST JUDGE OF CHARACTER IN THE WORLD, BUT HE'S A GOOD MAN TO BE WITH IN A PINCH!
SPWANNG!
SPWANNG!
STAY BACK!! THERE MUST BE OTHERS BEHIND THE NEXT LEDGE WE'LL HAVE TO FIND ANOTHER WAY TO DESCEND!
I WARNED YOU NOT TO RUSH OUT SO FAST! THEY KNOW THIS TERRAIN--WE DON'T!
LOOK, BANNER--I'M A SOLDIER! I'M READY TO GIVE MY LIFE FOR THE COUNTRY I SERVE--- FOR THE LAND I LOVE! YOU WOULDN'T UNDERSTAND THAT--BUT--- WHA--?? THE LEDGE! IT'S FALLING!!
I'M AFRAID YOU JINXED US WITH THAT LITTLE SPEECH OF YOURS, TALBOT! IT SEEMS WE'RE BOTH ABOUT TO GIVE OUR LIVES...!
AND RIGHT NOW--FOR WHAT IT'S WORTH--I WANT TO TELL YOU --I'M NOT A RED SPY --I'M AS LOYAL AS YOU!
BUT, THOSE FINAL DESPERATE WORDS OF BRUCE BANNER ARE LOST IN THE DEAFENING WHINE OF THE ONRUSHING WIND AS BOTH MEN PLUMMET TOWARDS THE ABYSS WHICH AWAITS THEM HUNDREDS OF YARDS BELOW--!
WE WISH TO THANK STEVE DITKO FOR HELPING THE HULK TO REACH NEW HEIGHTS OF GLORY WITH HIS MASTERFUL ARTWORK IN THESE PAST ISSUES! AND, BEGINNING NEXT MONTH, JACK KIRBY RETURNS TO BRING YOU THE MOST BREATH-TAKING INSTALLMENT YET OF THE WORLD'S FIRST ILLO-DRAMA CLIFF-HANGER--- THE FURTHER ADVENTURES OF THE INCREDIBLE HULK!

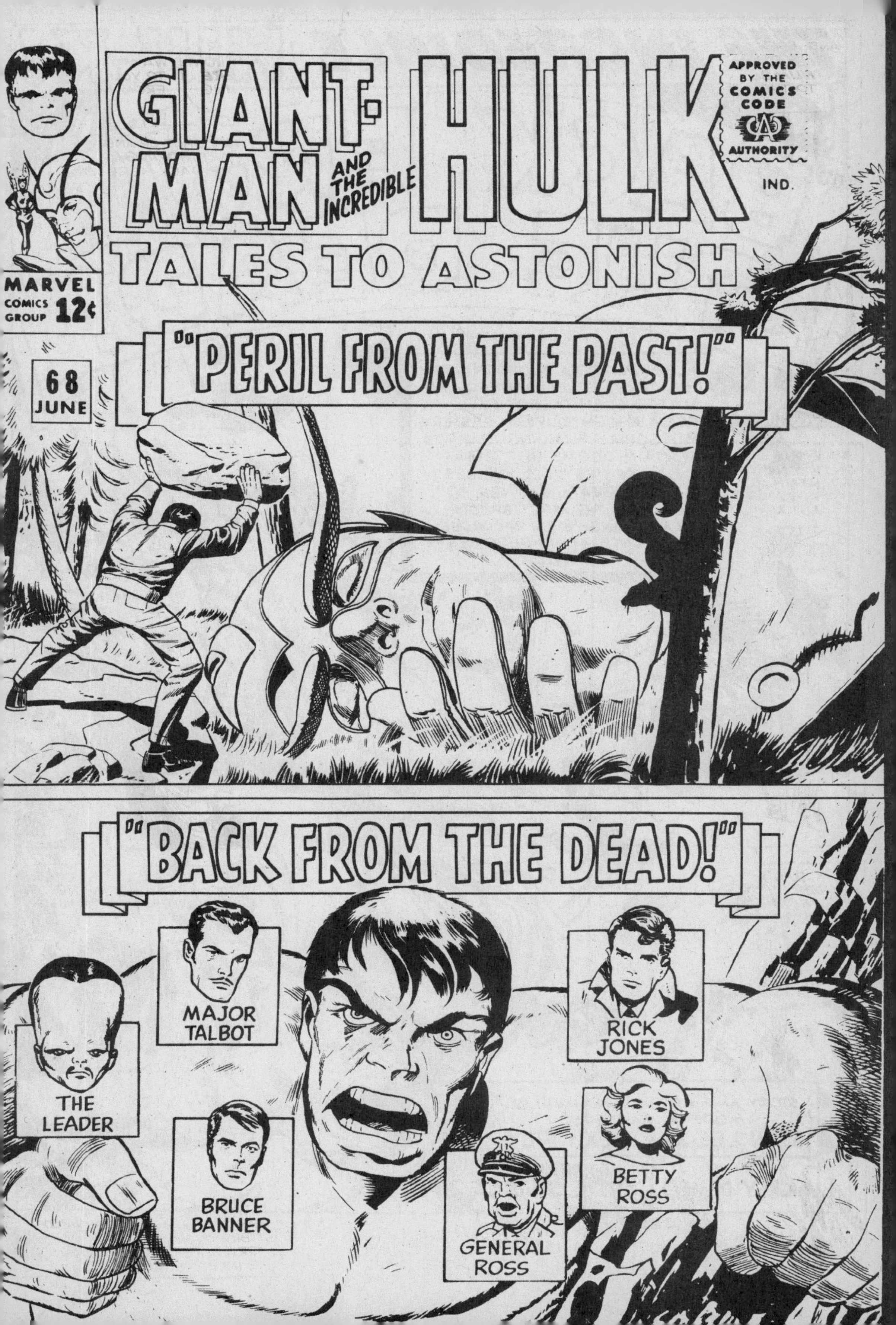
GIANT-MAN AND THE INCREDIBLE HULK
TALES TO ASTONISH
APPROVED BY THE COMICS CODE CA AUTHORITY
IND.
MARVEL COMICS GROUP 12¢
68 JUNE
"PERIL FROM THE PAST!"
"BACK FROM THE DEAD!"
MAJOR TALBOT
RICK JONES
THE LEADER
BETTY ROSS
BRUCE BANNER
GENERAL ROSS

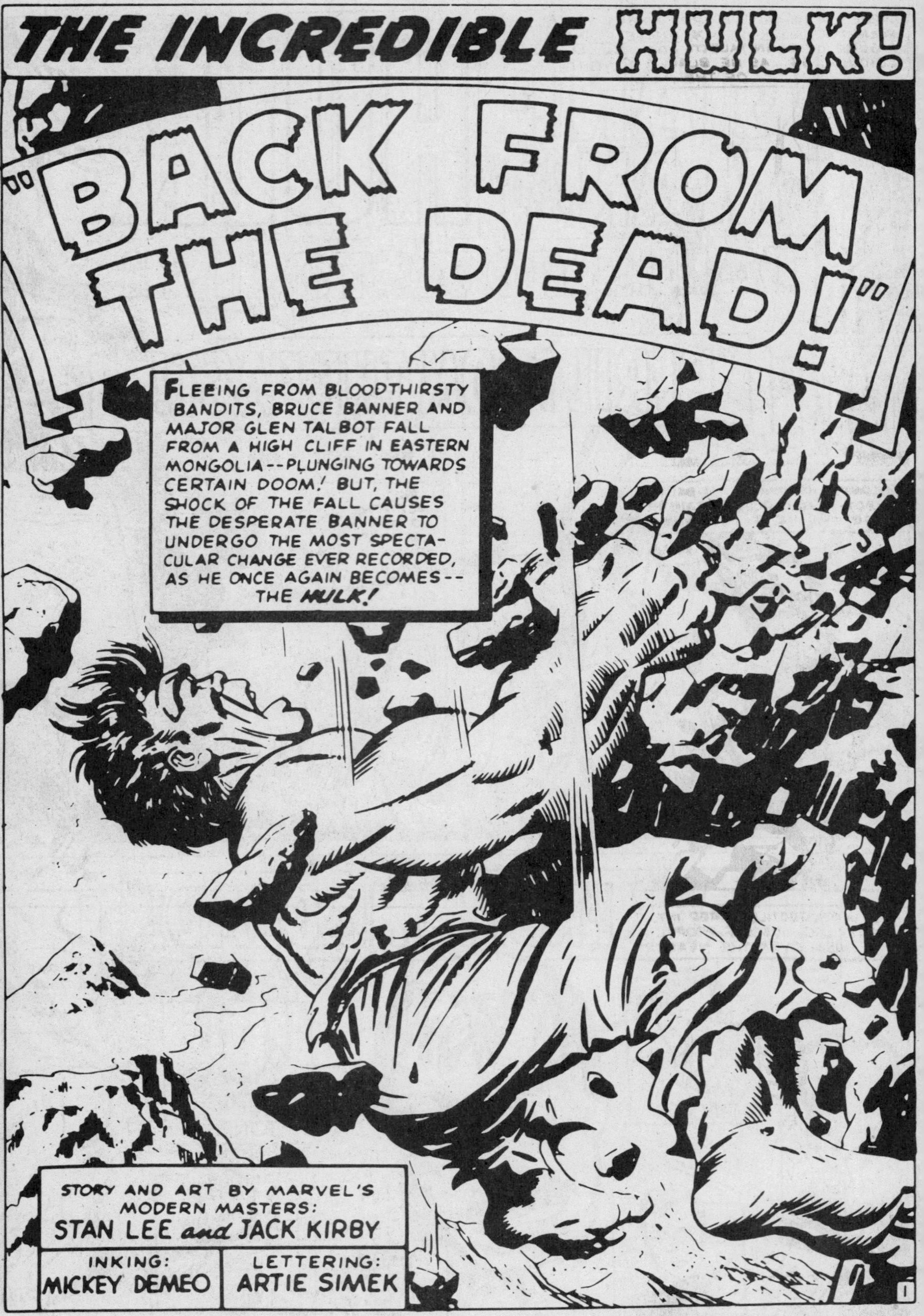

THE INCREDIBLE HULK!
"BACK FROM THE DEAD!"
FLEEING FROM BLOODTHIRSTY BANDITS, BRUCE BANNER AND MAJOR GLEN TALBOT FALL FROM A HIGH CLIFF IN EASTERN MONGOLIA--PLUNGING TOWARDS CERTAIN DOOM! BUT, THE SHOCK OF THE FALL CAUSES THE DESPERATE BANNER TO UNDERGO THE MOST SPECTACULAR CHANGE EVER RECORDED, AS HE ONCE AGAIN BECOMES-- THE HULK!
STORY AND ART BY MARVEL'S MODERN MASTERS: STAN LEE and JACK KIRBY
INKING: MICKEY DEMEO
LETTERING: ARTIE SIMEK
1

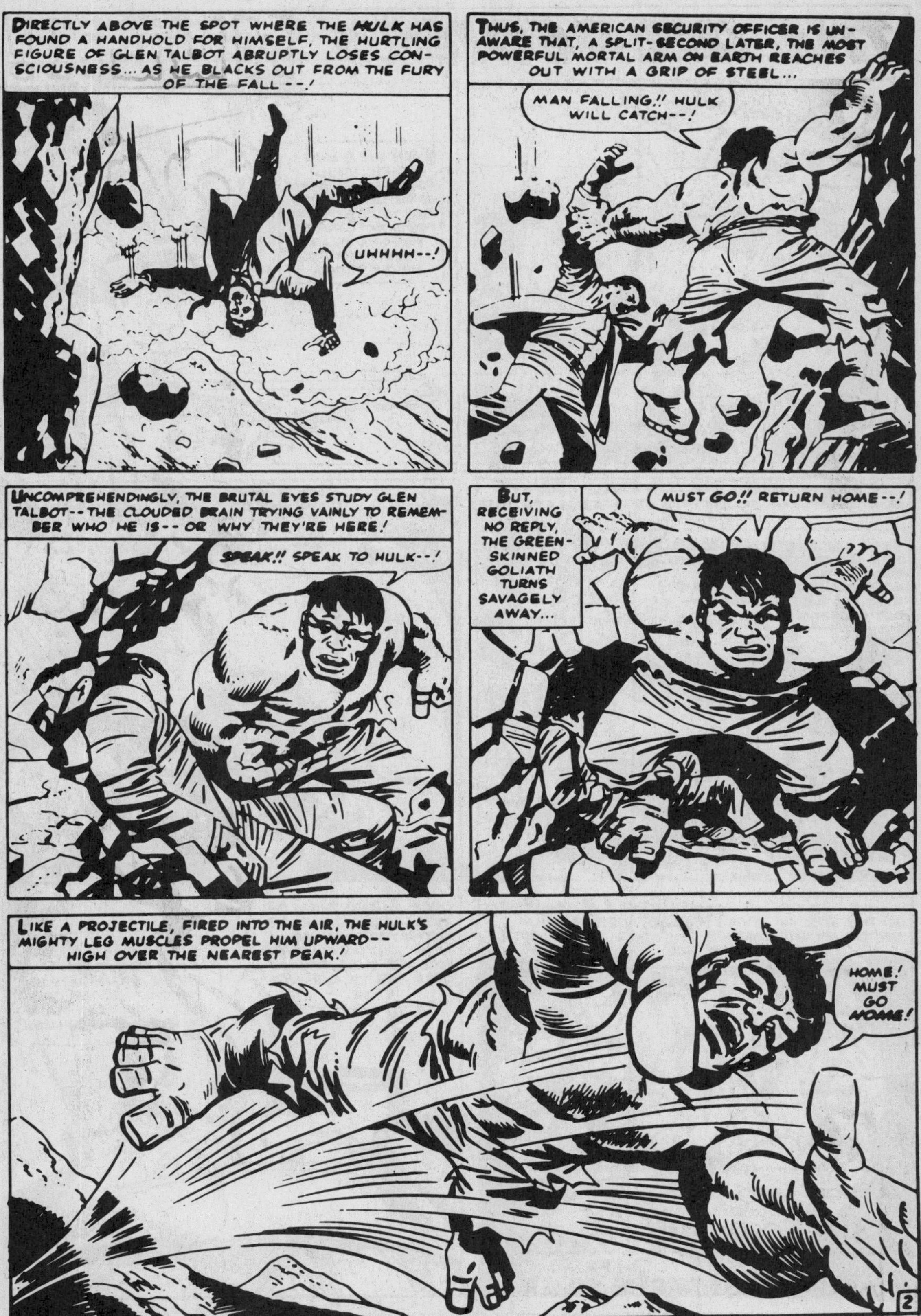

DIRECTLY ABOVE THE SPOT WHERE THE HULK HAS FOUND A HANDHOLD FOR HIMSELF, THE HURTLING FIGURE OF GLEN TALBOT ABRUPTLY LOSES CONSCIOUSNESS... AS HE BLACKS OUT FROM THE FURY OF THE FALL--!
UHHHH--!
THUS, THE AMERICAN SECURITY OFFICER IS UNAWARE THAT, A SPLIT-SECOND LATER, THE MOST POWERFUL MORTAL ARM ON EARTH REACHES OUT WITH A GRIP OF STEEL...
MAN FALLING!! HULK WILL CATCH--!
UNCOMPREHENDINGLY, THE BRUTAL EYES STUDY GLEN TALBOT--THE CLOUDED BRAIN TRYING VAINLY TO REMEMBER WHO HE IS--OR WHY THEY'RE HERE!
SPEAK!! SPEAK TO HULK--!
BUT, RECEIVING NO REPLY, THE GREEN-SKINNED GOLIATH TURNS SAVAGELY AWAY...
MUST GO!! RETURN HOME--!
LIKE A PROJECTILE, FIRED INTO THE AIR, THE HULK'S MIGHTY LEG MUSCLES PROPEL HIM UPWARD-- HIGH OVER THE NEAREST PEAK!
HOME! MUST GO HOME!
2

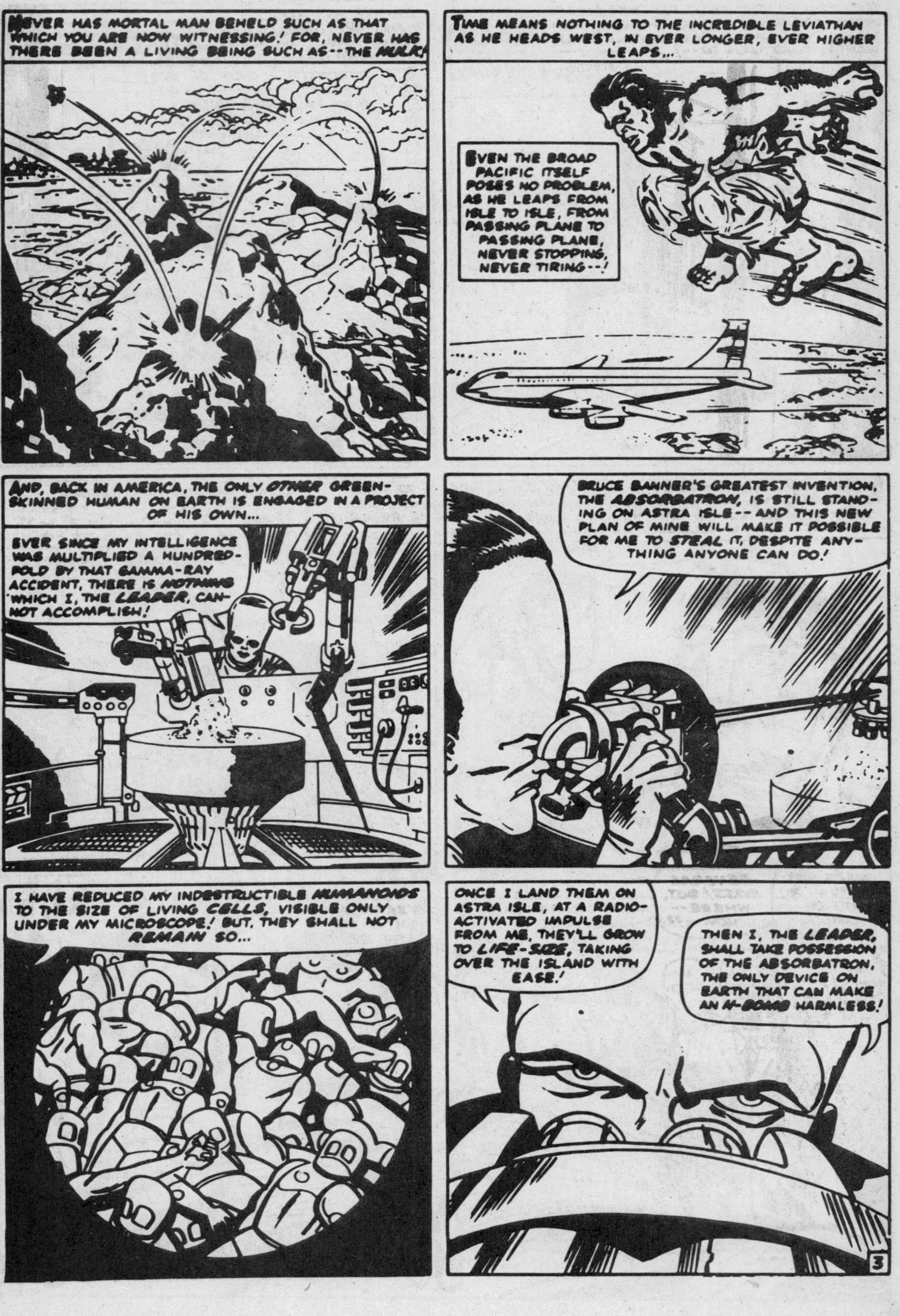
NEVER HAS MORTAL MAN BEHELD SUCH AS THAT WHICH YOU ARE NOW WITNESSING! FOR, NEVER HAS THERE BEEN A LIVING BEING SUCH AS--THE HULK!
TIME MEANS NOTHING TO THE INCREDIBLE LEVIATHAN AS HE HEADS WEST, IN EVER LONGER, EVER HIGHER LEAPS...
EVEN THE BROAD PACIFIC ITSELF POSES NO PROBLEM, AS HE LEAPS FROM ISLE TO ISLE, FROM PASSING PLANE TO PASSING PLANE, NEVER STOPPING, NEVER TIRING--!
AND, BACK IN AMERICA, THE ONLY OTHER GREEN-SKINNED HUMAN ON EARTH IS ENGAGED IN A PROJECT OF HIS OWN...
EVER SINCE MY INTELLIGENCE WAS MULTIPLIED A HUNDRED-FOLD BY THAT GAMMA-RAY ACCIDENT, THERE IS NOTHING WHICH I, THE LEADER, CANNOT ACCOMPLISH!
BRUCE BANNER'S GREATEST INVENTION, THE ABSORBATRON, IS STILL STANDING ON ASTRA ISLE--AND THIS NEW PLAN OF MINE WILL MAKE IT POSSIBLE FOR ME TO STEAL IT, DESPITE ANYTHING ANYONE CAN DO!
I HAVE REDUCED MY INDESTRUCTIBLE HUMANOIDS TO THE SIZE OF LIVING CELLS, VISIBLE ONLY UNDER MY MICROSCOPE! BUT, THEY SHALL NOT REMAIN SO...
ONCE I LAND THEM ON ASTRA ISLE, AT A RADIO-ACTIVATED IMPULSE FROM ME, THEY'LL GROW TO LIFE-SIZE, TAKING OVER THE ISLAND WITH EASE!
THEN I, THE LEADER, SHALL TAKE POSSESSION OF THE ABSORBATRON, THE ONLY DEVICE ON EARTH THAT CAN MAKE AN H-BOMB HARMLESS!
3

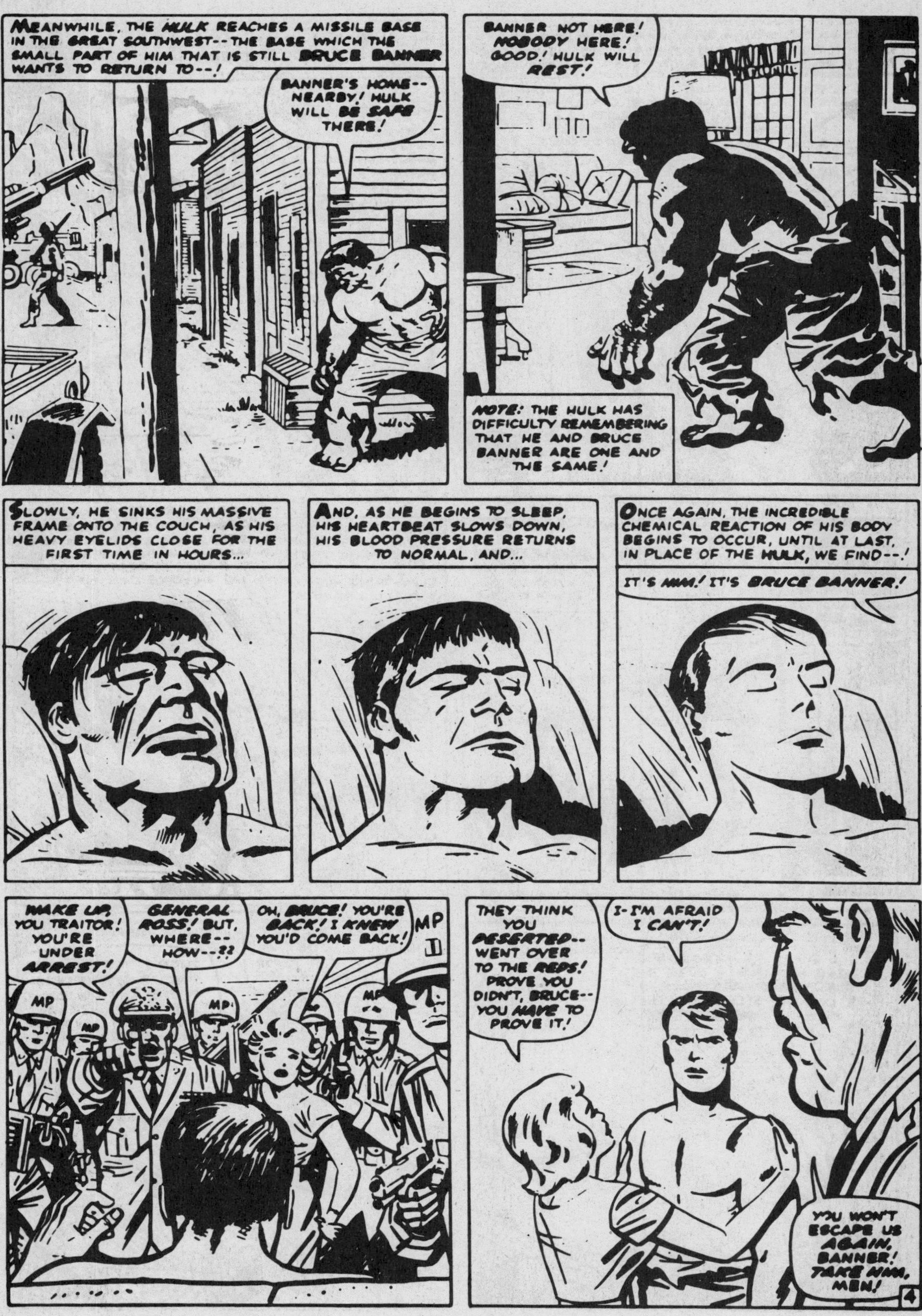
MEANWHILE, THE HULK REACHES A MISSILE BASE IN THE GREAT SOUTHWEST--THE BASE WHICH THE SMALL PART OF HIM THAT IS STILL BRUCE BANNER WANTS TO RETURN TO--!
BANNER'S HOME--NEARBY! HULK WILL BE SAFE THERE!
BANNER NOT HERE! NOBODY HERE! GOOD! HULK WILL REST!
NOTE: THE HULK HAS DIFFICULTY REMEMBERING THAT HE AND BRUCE BANNER ARE ONE AND THE SAME!
SLOWLY, HE SINKS HIS MASSIVE FRAME ONTO THE COUCH, AS HIS HEAVY EYELIDS CLOSE FOR THE FIRST TIME IN HOURS...
AND, AS HE BEGINS TO SLEEP, HIS HEARTBEAT SLOWS DOWN, HIS BLOOD PRESSURE RETURNS TO NORMAL, AND...
ONCE AGAIN, THE INCREDIBLE CHEMICAL REACTION OF HIS BODY BEGINS TO OCCUR, UNTIL AT LAST, IN PLACE OF THE HULK, WE FIND--!
IT'S HIM! IT'S BRUCE BANNER!
WAKE UP, YOU TRAITOR! YOU'RE UNDER ARREST!
GENERAL ROSS! BUT, WHERE--HOW--??
OH, BRUCE! YOU'RE BACK! I KNEW YOU'D COME BACK!
MP
THEY THINK YOU DESERTED--WENT OVER TO THE REDS! PROVE YOU DIDN'T, BRUCE--YOU HAVE TO PROVE IT!
I-I'M AFRAID I CAN'T!
YOU WON'T ESCAPE US AGAIN, BANNER! TAKE HIM, MEN!
4

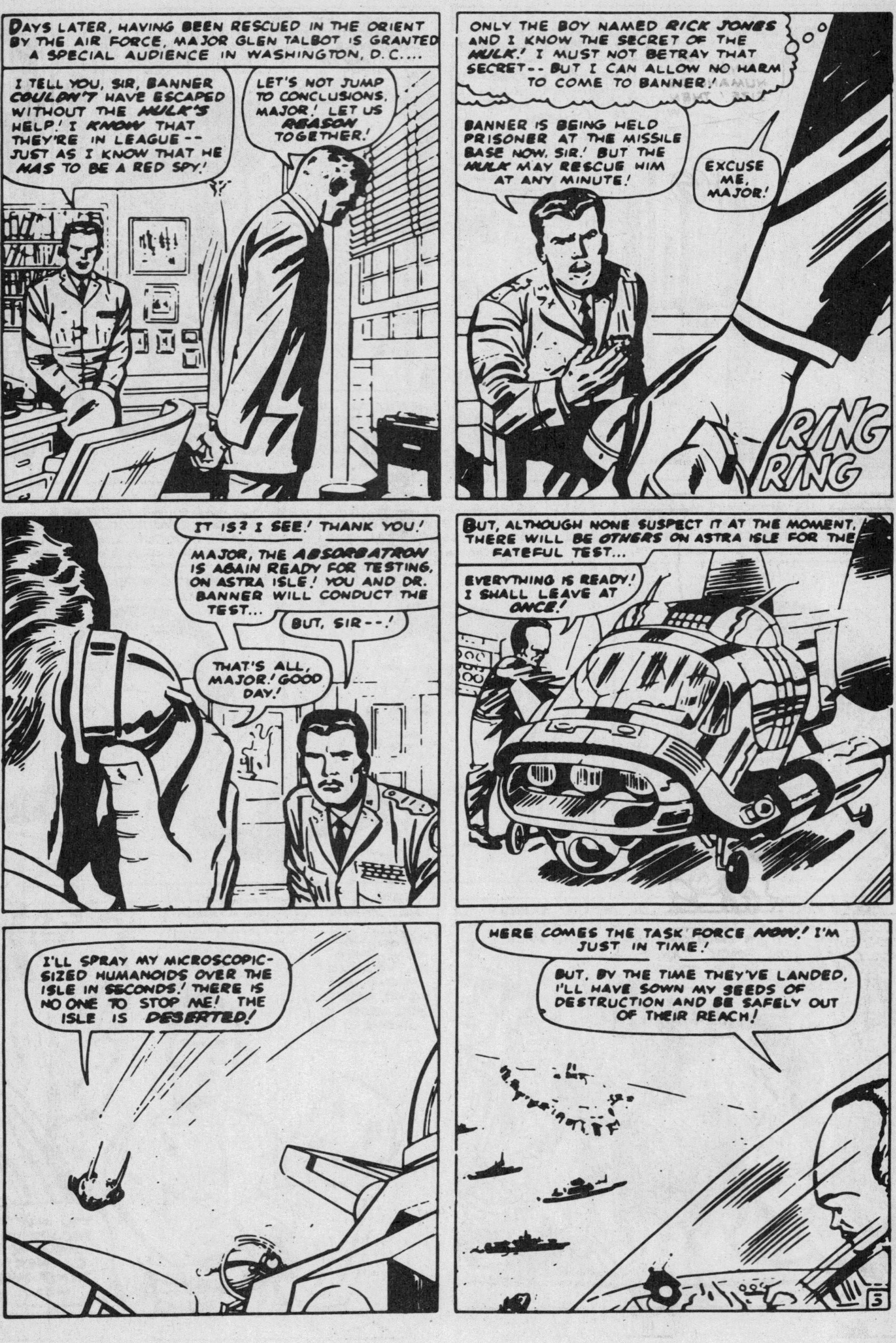
DAYS LATER, HAVING BEEN RESCUED IN THE ORIENT BY THE AIR FORCE, MAJOR GLEN TALBOT IS GRANTED A SPECIAL AUDIENCE IN WASHINGTON, D.C....
I TELL YOU, SIR, BANNER COULDN'T HAVE ESCAPED WITHOUT THE HULK'S HELP! I KNOW THAT THEY'RE IN LEAGUE -- JUST AS I KNOW THAT HE HAS TO BE A RED SPY!
LET'S NOT JUMP TO CONCLUSIONS, MAJOR! LET US REASON TOGETHER!
ONLY THE BOY NAMED RICK JONES AND I KNOW THE SECRET OF THE HULK! I MUST NOT BETRAY THAT SECRET -- BUT I CAN ALLOW NO HARM TO COME TO BANNER!
BANNER IS BEING HELD PRISONER AT THE MISSILE BASE NOW, SIR! BUT THE HULK MAY RESCUE HIM AT ANY MINUTE!
EXCUSE ME, MAJOR!
RING RING
IT IS? I SEE! THANK YOU!
MAJOR, THE ABSORBATRON IS AGAIN READY FOR TESTING, ON ASTRA ISLE! YOU AND DR. BANNER WILL CONDUCT THE TEST...
BUT, SIR--!
THAT'S ALL, MAJOR! GOOD DAY!
BUT, ALTHOUGH NONE SUSPECT IT AT THE MOMENT, THERE WILL BE OTHERS ON ASTRA ISLE FOR THE FATEFUL TEST...
EVERYTHING IS READY! I SHALL LEAVE AT ONCE!
I'LL SPRAY MY MICROSCOPIC-SIZED HUMANOIDS OVER THE ISLE IN SECONDS! THERE IS NO ONE TO STOP ME! THE ISLE IS DESERTED!
HERE COMES THE TASK FORCE NOW! I'M JUST IN TIME!
BUT, BY THE TIME THEY'VE LANDED, I'LL HAVE SOWN MY SEEDS OF DESTRUCTION AND BE SAFELY OUT OF THEIR REACH!
5

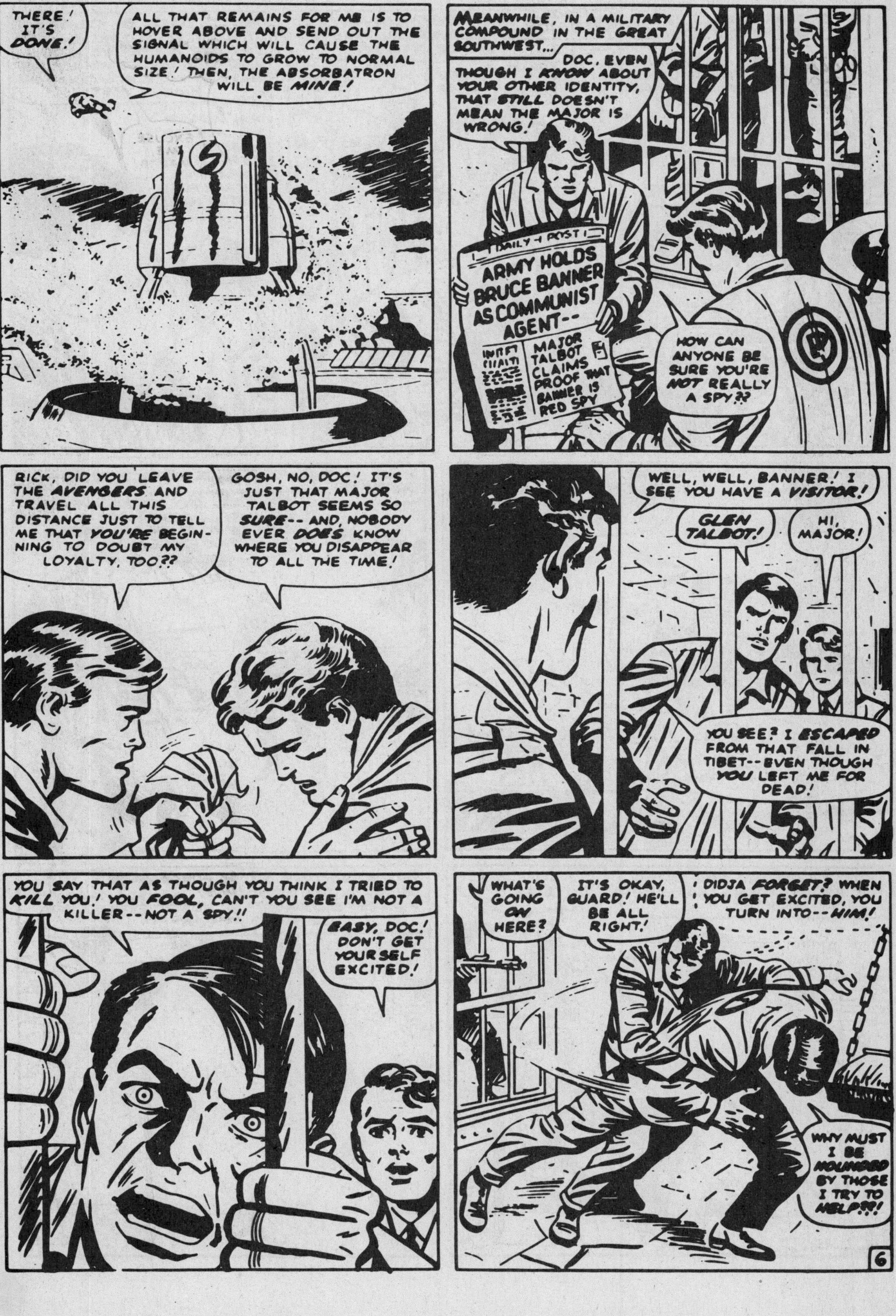
THERE! IT'S DONE!
ALL THAT REMAINS FOR ME IS TO HOVER ABOVE AND SEND OUT THE SIGNAL WHICH WILL CAUSE THE HUMANOIDS TO GROW TO NORMAL SIZE! THEN, THE ABSORBATRON WILL BE MINE!
MEANWHILE, IN A MILITARY COMPOUND IN THE GREAT SOUTHWEST...
DOC, EVEN THOUGH I KNOW ABOUT YOUR OTHER IDENTITY, THAT STILL DOESN'T MEAN THE MAJOR IS WRONG!
DAILY POST
ARMY HOLDS BRUCE BANNER AS COMMUNIST AGENT--
MAJOR TALBOT CLAIMS PROOF THAT BANNER IS RED SPY
HOW CAN ANYONE BE SURE YOU'RE NOT REALLY A SPY??
RICK, DID YOU LEAVE THE AVENGERS AND TRAVEL ALL THIS DISTANCE JUST TO TELL ME THAT YOU'RE BEGINNING TO DOUBT MY LOYALTY, TOO??
GOSH, NO, DOC! IT'S JUST THAT MAJOR TALBOT SEEMS SO SURE-- AND, NOBODY EVER DOES KNOW WHERE YOU DISAPPEAR TO ALL THE TIME!
WELL, WELL, BANNER! I SEE YOU HAVE A VISITOR!
GLEN TALBOT!
HI, MAJOR!
YOU SEE? I ESCAPED FROM THAT FALL IN TIBET--EVEN THOUGH YOU LEFT ME FOR DEAD!
YOU SAY THAT AS THOUGH YOU THINK I TRIED TO KILL YOU! YOU FOOL, CAN'T YOU SEE I'M NOT A KILLER--NOT A SPY!!
EASY, DOC! DON'T GET YOURSELF EXCITED!
WHAT'S GOING ON HERE?
IT'S OKAY, GUARD! HE'LL BE ALL RIGHT!
DIDJA FORGET? WHEN YOU GET EXCITED, YOU TURN INTO--HIM!
WHY MUST I BE HOUNDED BY THOSE I TRY TO HELP??!
6

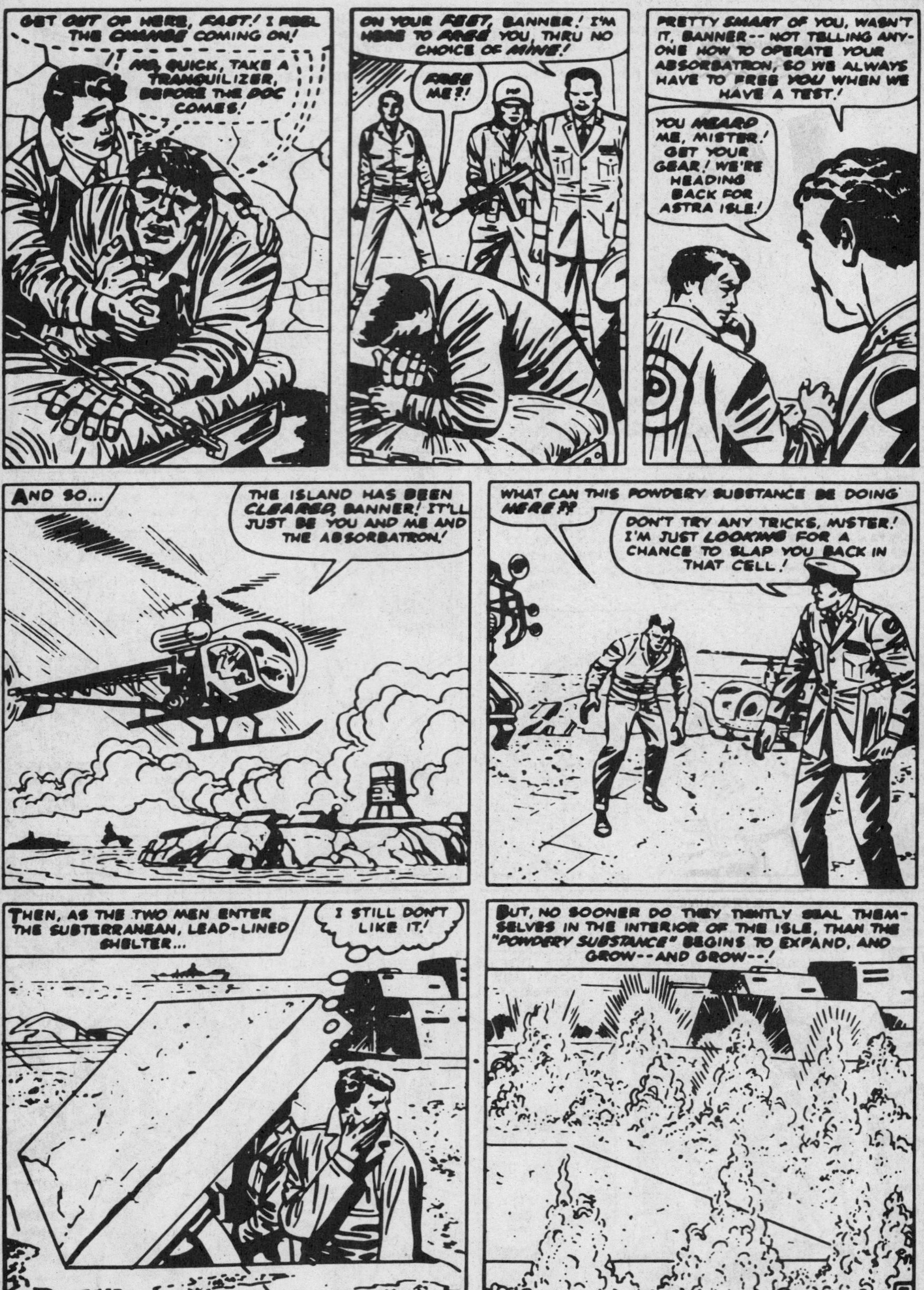

GET OUT OF HERE, FAST! I FEEL THE CHANGE COMING ON!
MR. QUICK, TAKE A TRANQUILIZER, BEFORE THE DOC COMES!
ON YOUR FEET, BANNER! I'M HERE TO FREE YOU, THRU NO CHOICE OF MINE!
FREE ME?!
PRETTY SMART OF YOU, WASN'T IT, BANNER-- NOT TELLING ANYONE HOW TO OPERATE YOUR ABSORBATRON, SO WE ALWAYS HAVE TO FREE YOU WHEN WE HAVE A TEST!
YOU HEARD ME, MISTER! GET YOUR GEAR! WE'RE HEADING BACK FOR ASTRA ISLE!
AND SO...
THE ISLAND HAS BEEN CLEARED, BANNER! IT'LL JUST BE YOU AND ME AND THE ABSORBATRON!
WHAT CAN THIS POWDERY SUBSTANCE BE DOING HERE??
DON'T TRY ANY TRICKS, MISTER! I'M JUST LOOKING FOR A CHANCE TO SLAP YOU BACK IN THAT CELL!
THEN, AS THE TWO MEN ENTER THE SUBTERRANEAN, LEAD-LINED SHELTER...
I STILL DON'T LIKE IT!
BUT, NO SOONER DO THEY TIGHTLY SEAL THEMSELVES IN THE INTERIOR OF THE ISLE, THAN THE "POWDERY SUBSTANCE" BEGINS TO EXPAND, AND GROW--AND GROW--!
7

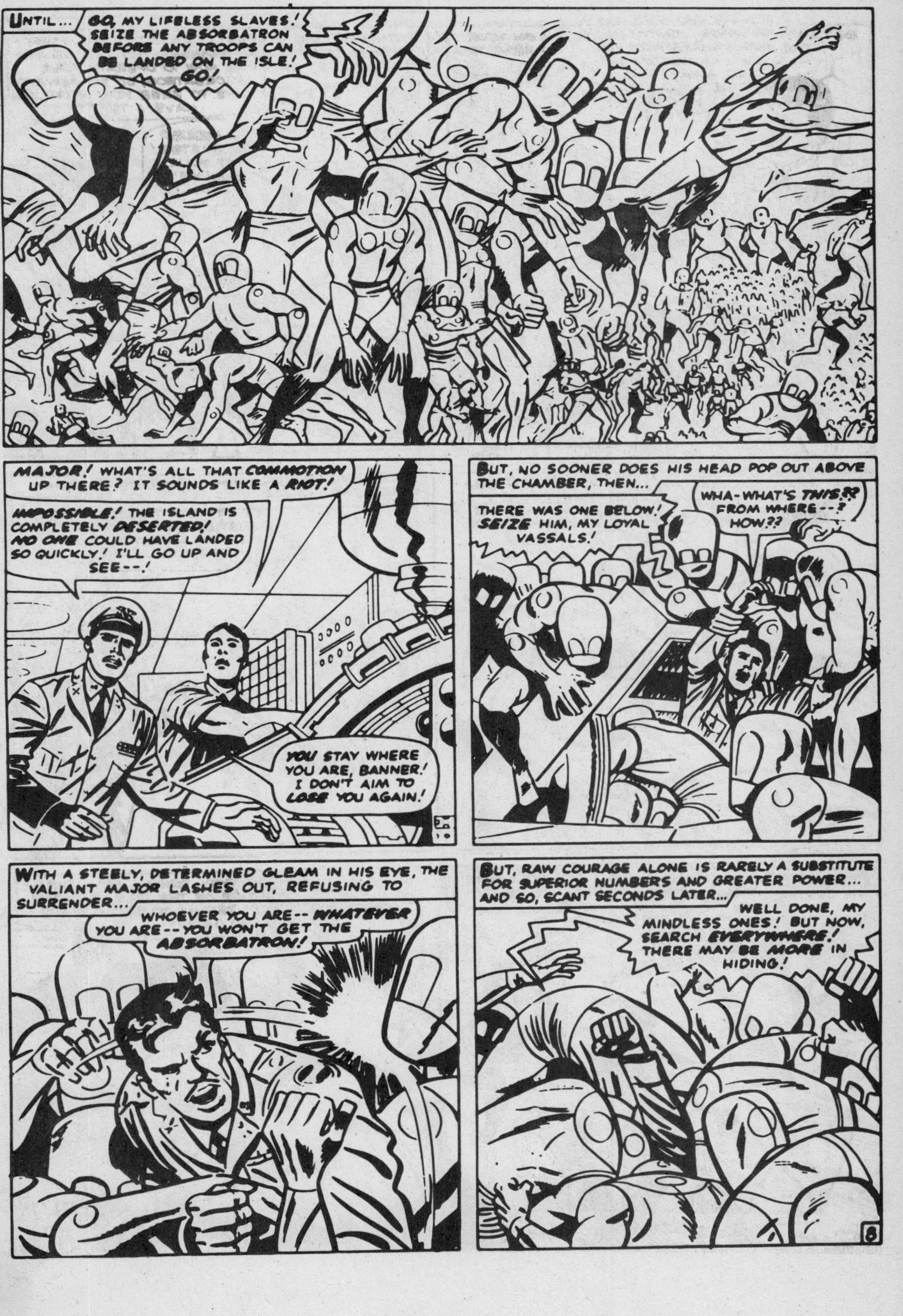
UNTIL...
GO, MY LIFELESS SLAVES! SEIZE THE ABSORBATRON BEFORE ANY TROOPS CAN BE LANDED ON THE ISLE! GO!
MAJOR! WHAT'S ALL THAT COMMOTION UP THERE? IT SOUNDS LIKE A RIOT!
IMPOSSIBLE! THE ISLAND IS COMPLETELY DESERTED! NO ONE COULD HAVE LANDED SO QUICKLY! I'LL GO UP AND SEE--!
YOU STAY WHERE YOU ARE, BANNER! I DON'T AIM TO LOSE YOU AGAIN!
BUT, NO SOONER DOES HIS HEAD POP OUT ABOVE THE CHAMBER, THEN...
THERE WAS ONE BELOW! SEIZE HIM, MY LOYAL VASSALS!
WHA-WHAT'S THIS?? FROM WHERE--? HOW??
WITH A STEELY, DETERMINED GLEAM IN HIS EYE, THE VALIANT MAJOR LASHES OUT, REFUSING TO SURRENDER...
WHOEVER YOU ARE-- WHATEVER YOU ARE--YOU WON'T GET THE ABSORBATRON!
BUT, RAW COURAGE ALONE IS RARELY A SUBSTITUTE FOR SUPERIOR NUMBERS AND GREATER POWER... AND SO, SCANT SECONDS LATER...
WELL DONE, MY MINDLESS ONES! BUT NOW, SEARCH EVERYWHERE! THERE MAY BE MORE IN HIDING!
8

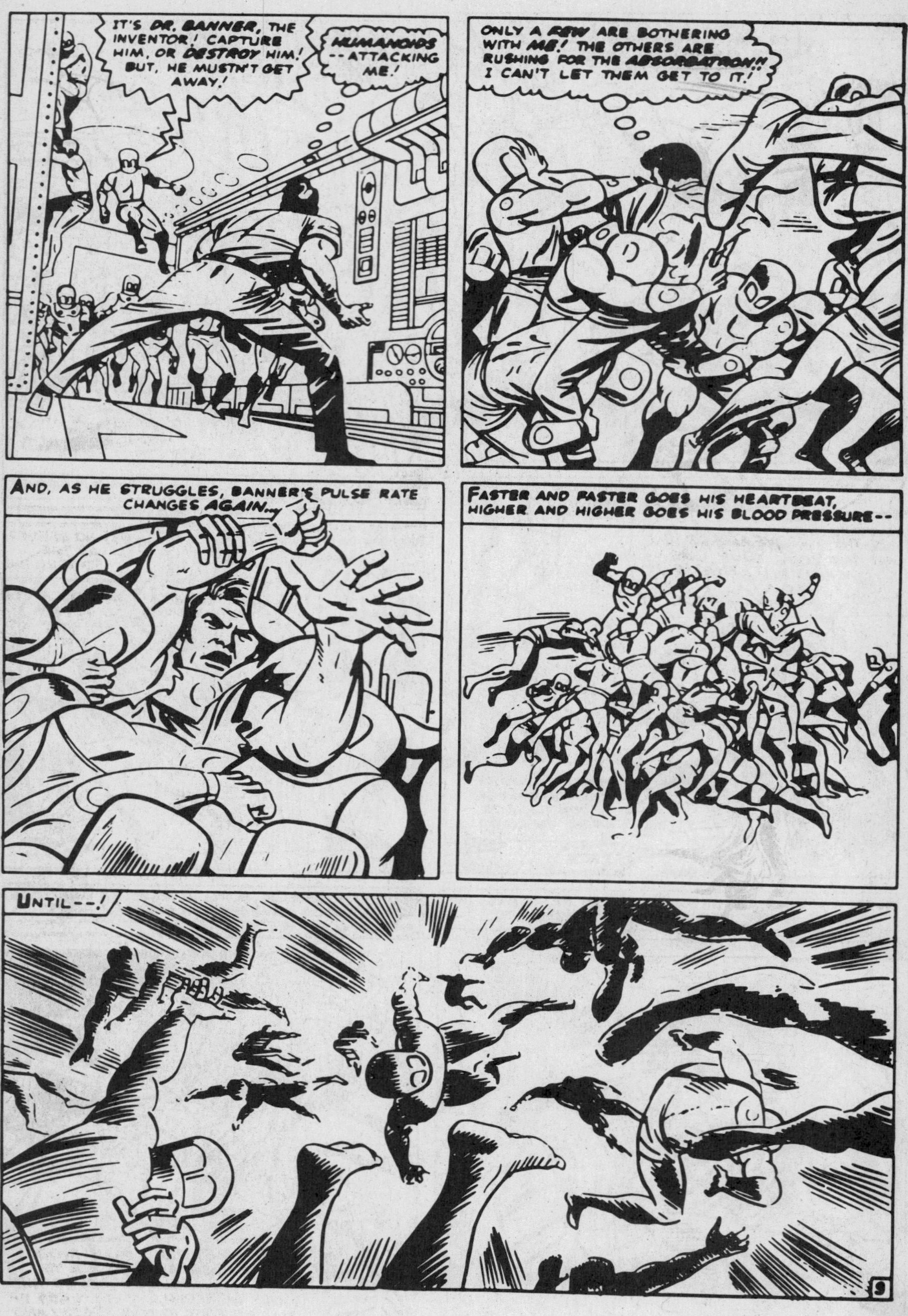

IT'S DR. BANNER, THE INVENTOR! CAPTURE HIM, OR DESTROY HIM! BUT, HE MUSTN'T GET AWAY!
HUMANOIDS -- ATTACKING ME!
ONLY A FEW ARE BOTHERING WITH ME! THE OTHERS ARE RUSHING FOR THE ABSORBATRON!! I CAN'T LET THEM GET TO IT!
AND, AS HE STRUGGLES, BANNER'S PULSE RATE CHANGES AGAIN...
FASTER AND FASTER GOES HIS HEARTBEAT, HIGHER AND HIGHER GOES HIS BLOOD PRESSURE--
UNTIL--!
9

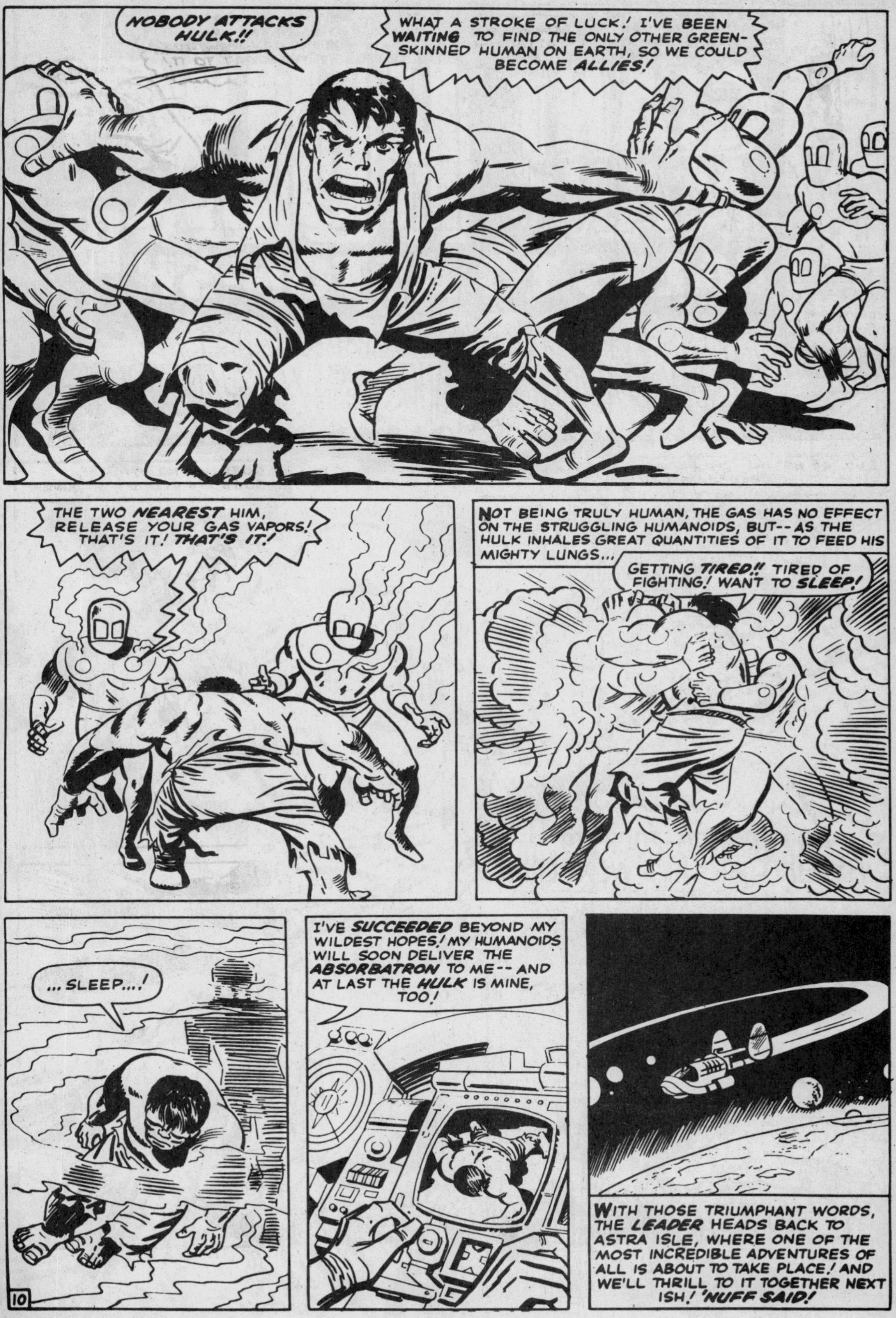
NOBODY ATTACKS HULK!!
WHAT A STROKE OF LUCK! I'VE BEEN WAITING TO FIND THE ONLY OTHER GREEN-SKINNED HUMAN ON EARTH, SO WE COULD BECOME ALLIES!
THE TWO NEAREST HIM, RELEASE YOUR GAS VAPORS! THAT'S IT! THAT'S IT!
NOT BEING TRULY HUMAN, THE GAS HAS NO EFFECT ON THE STRUGGLING HUMANOIDS, BUT-- AS THE HULK INHALES GREAT QUANTITIES OF IT TO FEED HIS MIGHTY LUNGS...
GETTING TIRED!! TIRED OF FIGHTING! WANT TO SLEEP!
... SLEEP....!
10
I'VE SUCCEEDED BEYOND MY WILDEST HOPES! MY HUMANOIDS WILL SOON DELIVER THE ABSORBATRON TO ME-- AND AT LAST THE HULK IS MINE, TOO!
WITH THOSE TRIUMPHANT WORDS, THE LEADER HEADS BACK TO ASTRA ISLE, WHERE ONE OF THE MOST INCREDIBLE ADVENTURES OF ALL IS ABOUT TO TAKE PLACE! AND WE'LL THRILL TO IT TOGETHER NEXT ISH! 'NUFF SAID!

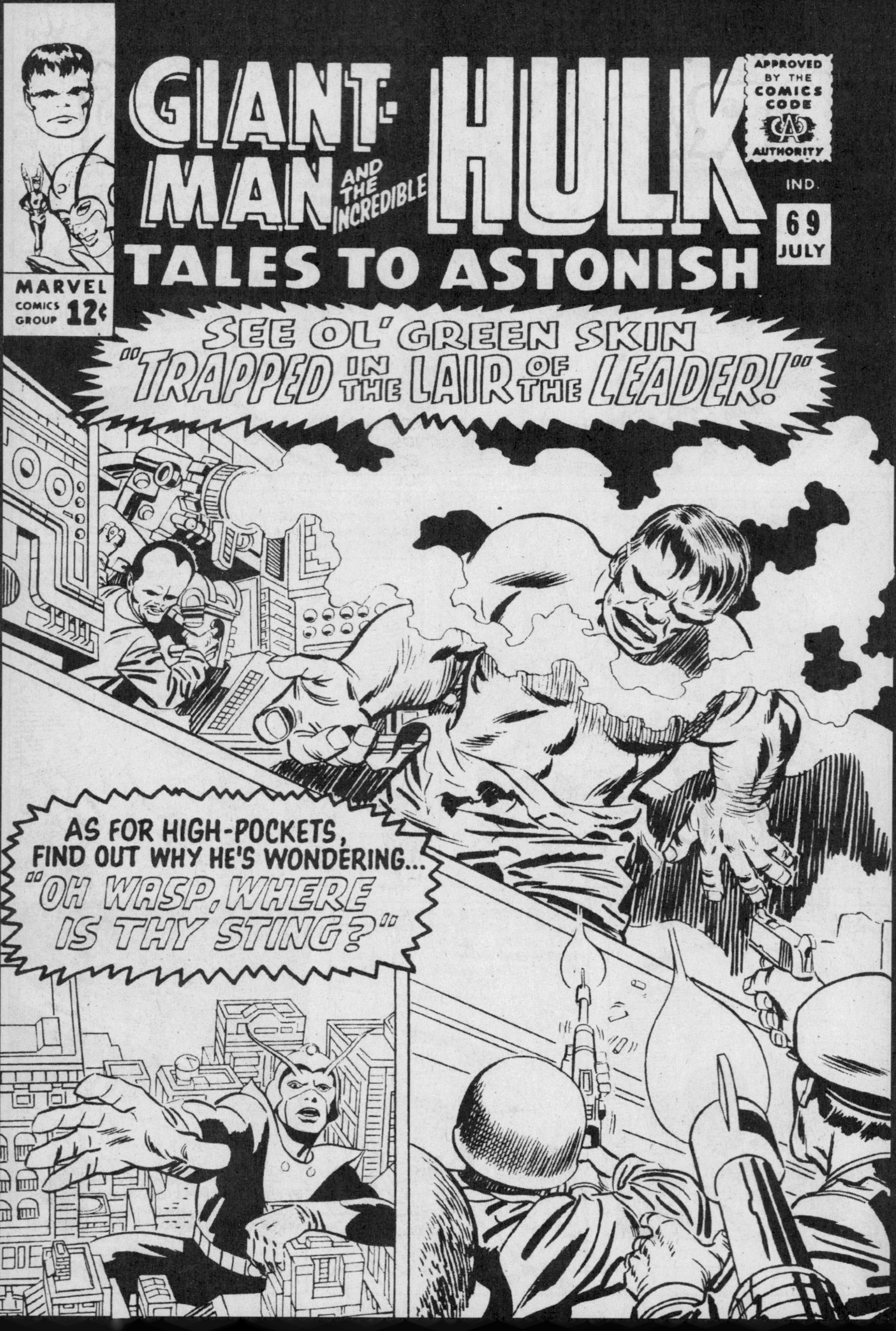
GIANT-MAN AND THE INCREDIBLE HULK
TALES TO ASTONISH
MARVEL COMICS GROUP 12¢
APPROVED BY THE COMICS CODE AUTHORITY
IND.
69 JULY
SEE OL' GREEN SKIN "TRAPPED IN THE LAIR OF THE LEADER!"
AS FOR HIGH-POCKETS, FIND OUT WHY HE'S WONDERING... "OH WASP, WHERE IS THY STING?"

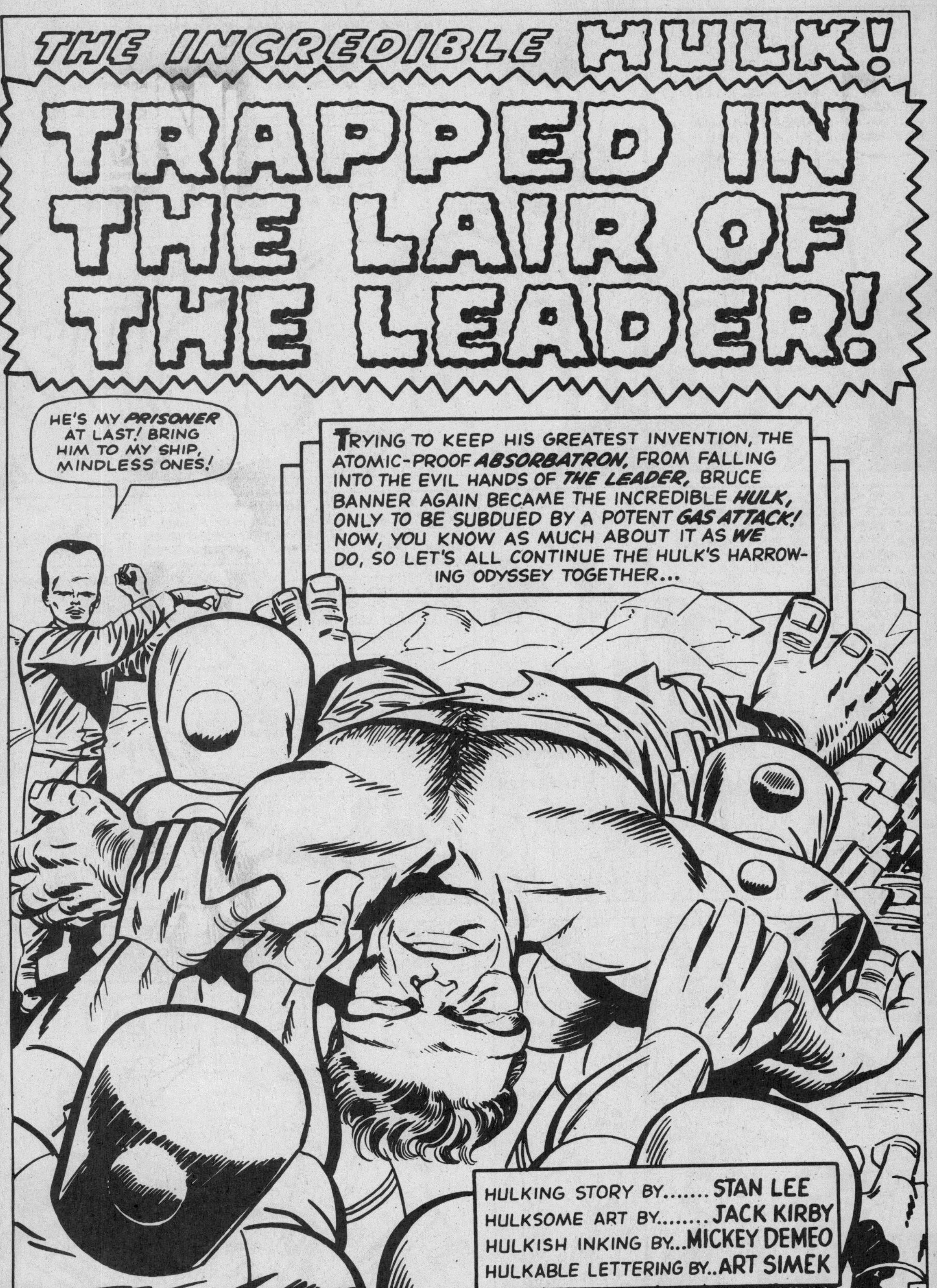
THE INCREDIBLE HULK!
TRAPPED IN THE LAIR OF THE LEADER!
HE'S MY PRISONER AT LAST! BRING HIM TO MY SHIP, MINDLESS ONES!
TRYING TO KEEP HIS GREATEST INVENTION, THE ATOMIC-PROOF ABSORBATRON, FROM FALLING INTO THE EVIL HANDS OF THE LEADER, BRUCE BANNER AGAIN BECAME THE INCREDIBLE HULK, ONLY TO BE SUBDUED BY A POTENT GAS ATTACK! NOW, YOU KNOW AS MUCH ABOUT IT AS WE DO, SO LET'S ALL CONTINUE THE HULK'S HARROWING ODYSSEY TOGETHER...
HULKING STORY BY....... STAN LEE
HULKSOME ART BY........ JACK KIRBY
HULKISH INKING BY...MICKEY DEMEO
HULKABLE LETTERING BY..ART SIMEK
1

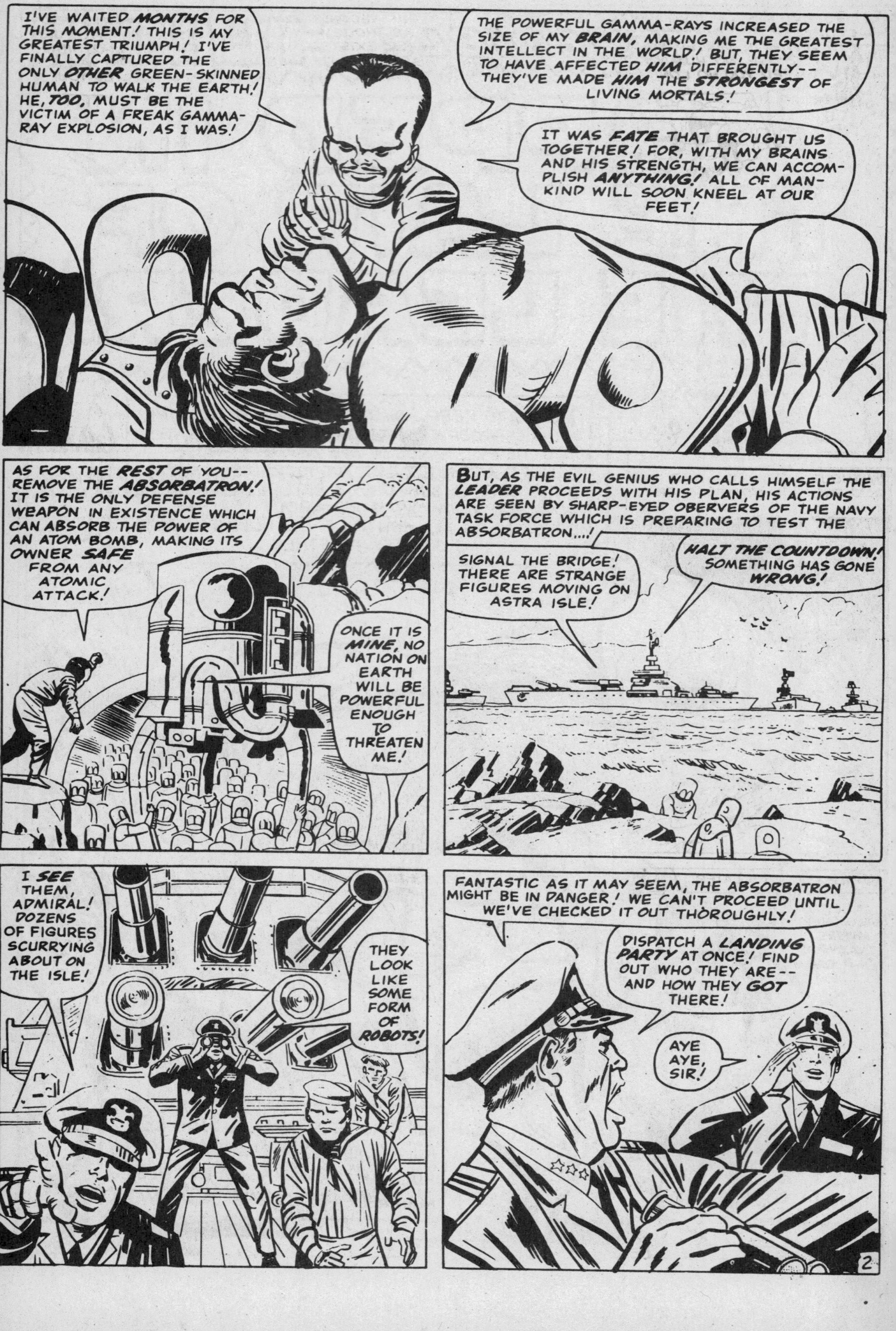
I'VE WAITED MONTHS FOR THIS MOMENT! THIS IS MY GREATEST TRIUMPH! I'VE FINALLY CAPTURED THE ONLY OTHER GREEN-SKINNED HUMAN TO WALK THE EARTH! HE, TOO, MUST BE THE VICTIM OF A FREAK GAMMA-RAY EXPLOSION, AS I WAS!
THE POWERFUL GAMMA-RAYS INCREASED THE SIZE OF MY BRAIN, MAKING ME THE GREATEST INTELLECT IN THE WORLD! BUT, THEY SEEM TO HAVE AFFECTED HIM DIFFERENTLY-- THEY'VE MADE HIM THE STRONGEST OF LIVING MORTALS!
IT WAS FATE THAT BROUGHT US TOGETHER! FOR, WITH MY BRAINS AND HIS STRENGTH, WE CAN ACCOMPLISH ANYTHING! ALL OF MANKIND WILL SOON KNEEL AT OUR FEET!
AS FOR THE REST OF YOU-- REMOVE THE ABSORBATRON! IT IS THE ONLY DEFENSE WEAPON IN EXISTENCE WHICH CAN ABSORB THE POWER OF AN ATOM BOMB, MAKING ITS OWNER SAFE FROM ANY ATOMIC ATTACK!
ONCE IT IS MINE, NO NATION ON EARTH WILL BE POWERFUL ENOUGH TO THREATEN ME!
BUT, AS THE EVIL GENIUS WHO CALLS HIMSELF THE LEADER PROCEEDS WITH HIS PLAN, HIS ACTIONS ARE SEEN BY SHARP-EYED OBERVERS OF THE NAVY TASK FORCE WHICH IS PREPARING TO TEST THE ABSORBATRON...!
SIGNAL THE BRIDGE! THERE ARE STRANGE FIGURES MOVING ON ASTRA ISLE!
HALT THE COUNTDOWN! SOMETHING HAS GONE WRONG!
I SEE THEM, ADMIRAL! DOZENS OF FIGURES SCURRYING ABOUT ON THE ISLE!
THEY LOOK LIKE SOME FORM OF ROBOTS!
FANTASTIC AS IT MAY SEEM, THE ABSORBATRON MIGHT BE IN DANGER! WE CAN'T PROCEED UNTIL WE'VE CHECKED IT OUT THOROUGHLY!
DISPATCH A LANDING PARTY AT ONCE! FIND OUT WHO THEY ARE-- AND HOW THEY GOT THERE!
AYE AYE, SIR!
2

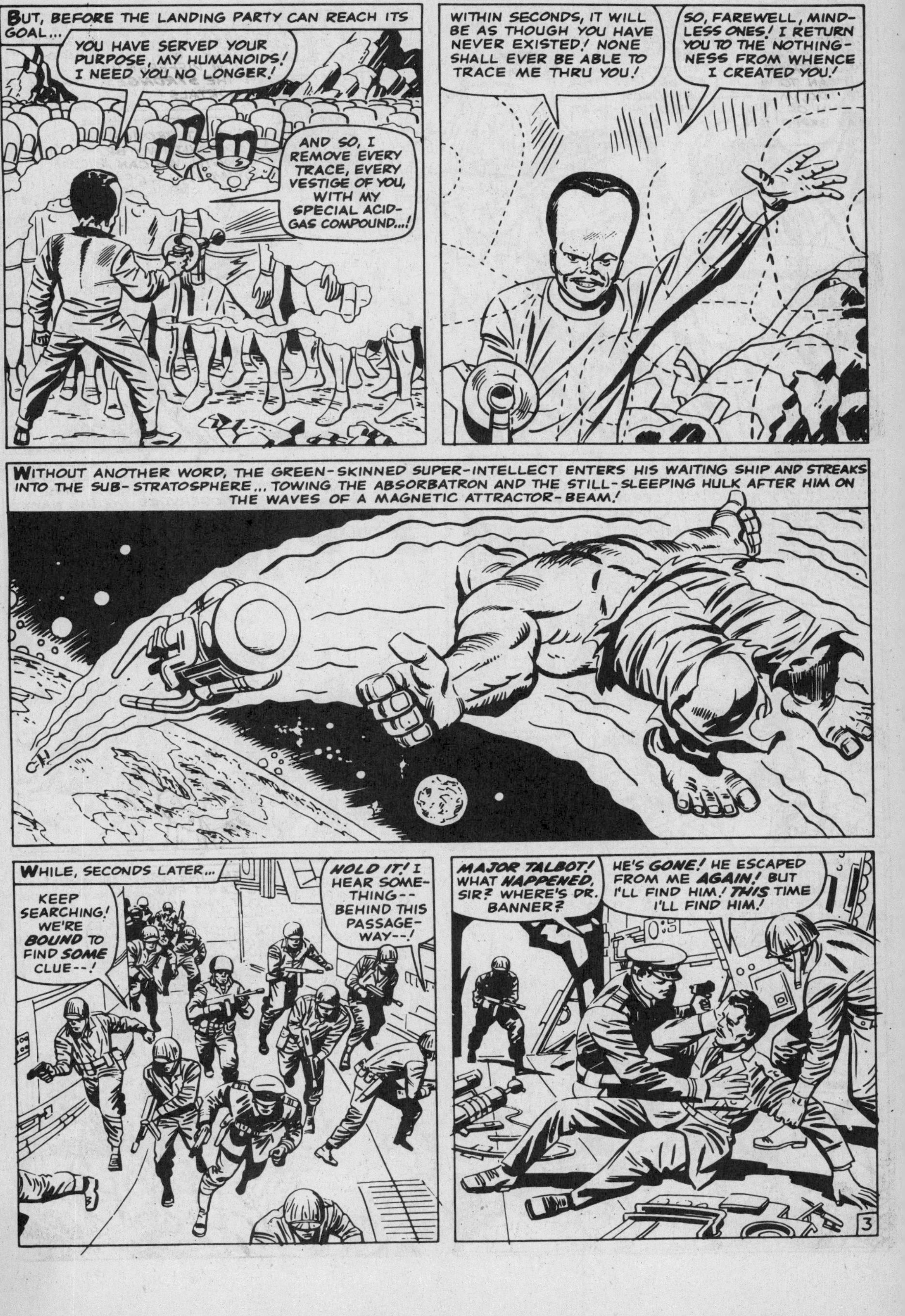
BUT, BEFORE THE LANDING PARTY CAN REACH ITS GOAL...
YOU HAVE SERVED YOUR PURPOSE, MY HUMANOIDS! I NEED YOU NO LONGER!
AND SO, I REMOVE EVERY TRACE, EVERY VESTIGE OF YOU, WITH MY SPECIAL ACID-GAS COMPOUND...!
WITHIN SECONDS, IT WILL BE AS THOUGH YOU HAVE NEVER EXISTED! NONE SHALL EVER BE ABLE TO TRACE ME THRU YOU!
SO, FAREWELL, MINDLESS ONES! I RETURN YOU TO THE NOTHINGNESS FROM WHENCE I CREATED YOU!
WITHOUT ANOTHER WORD, THE GREEN-SKINNED SUPER-INTELLECT ENTERS HIS WAITING SHIP AND STREAKS INTO THE SUB-STRATOSPHERE... TOWING THE ABSORBATRON AND THE STILL-SLEEPING HULK AFTER HIM ON THE WAVES OF A MAGNETIC ATTRACTOR-BEAM!
WHILE, SECONDS LATER...
KEEP SEARCHING! WE'RE BOUND TO FIND SOME CLUE--!
HOLD IT! I HEAR SOMETHING-- BEHIND THIS PASSAGEWAY--!
MAJOR TALBOT! WHAT HAPPENED, SIR? WHERE'S DR. BANNER?
HE'S GONE! HE ESCAPED FROM ME AGAIN! BUT I'LL FIND HIM! THIS TIME I'LL FIND HIM!
3

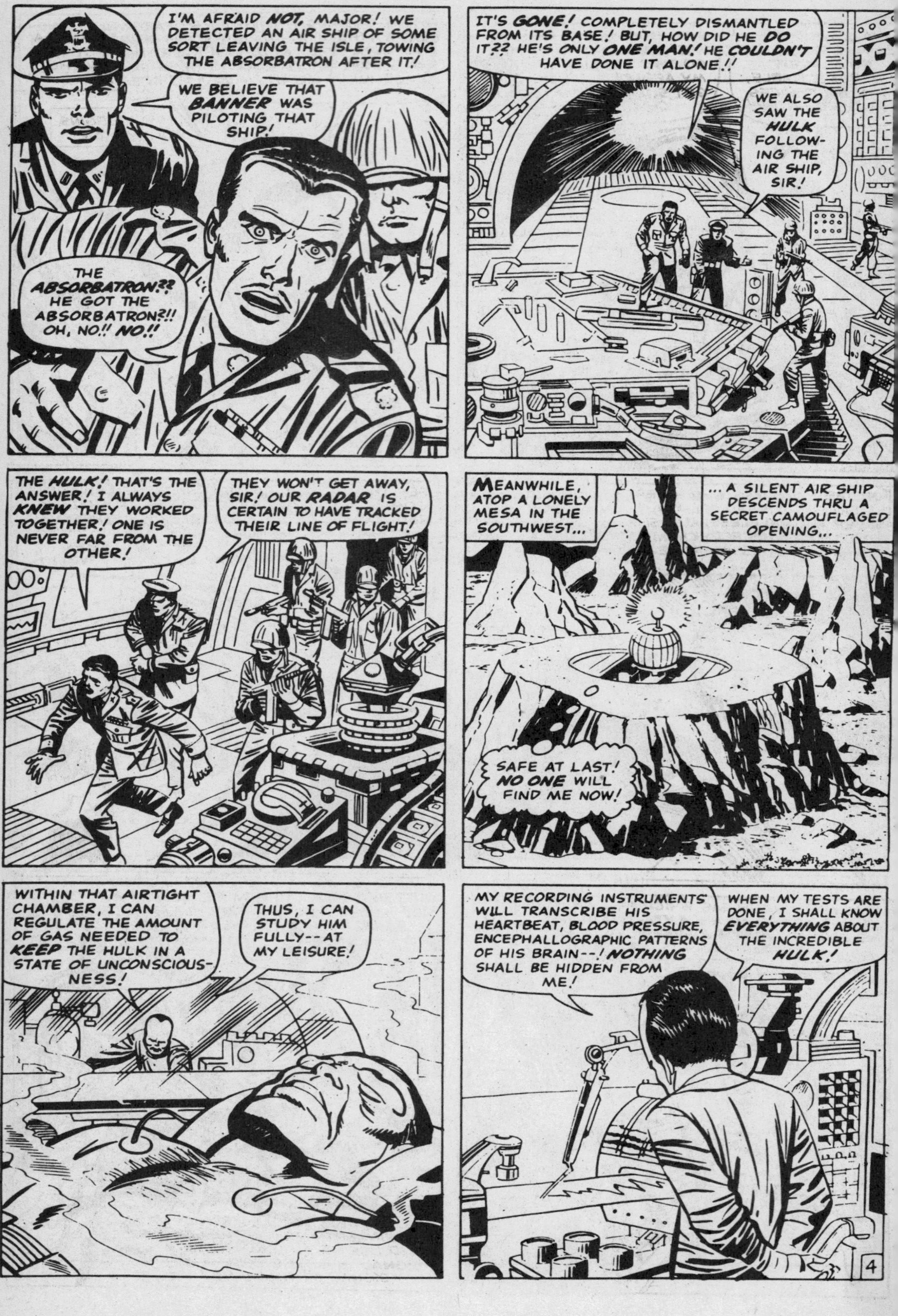
I'M AFRAID NOT, MAJOR! WE DETECTED AN AIR SHIP OF SOME SORT LEAVING THE ISLE, TOWING THE ABSORBATRON AFTER IT!
WE BELIEVE THAT BANNER WAS PILOTING THAT SHIP!
THE ABSORBATRON?? HE GOT THE ABSORBATRON?!! OH, NO!! NO!!
IT'S GONE! COMPLETELY DISMANTLED FROM ITS BASE! BUT, HOW DID HE DO IT?? HE'S ONLY ONE MAN! HE COULDN'T HAVE DONE IT ALONE!!
WE ALSO SAW THE HULK FOLLOWING THE AIR SHIP, SIR!
THE HULK! THAT'S THE ANSWER! I ALWAYS KNEW THEY WORKED TOGETHER! ONE IS NEVER FAR FROM THE OTHER!
THEY WON'T GET AWAY, SIR! OUR RADAR IS CERTAIN TO HAVE TRACKED THEIR LINE OF FLIGHT!
MEANWHILE, ATOP A LONELY MESA IN THE SOUTHWEST...
...A SILENT AIR SHIP DESCENDS THRU A SECRET CAMOUFLAGED OPENING...
SAFE AT LAST! NO ONE WILL FIND ME NOW!
WITHIN THAT AIRTIGHT CHAMBER, I CAN REGULATE THE AMOUNT OF GAS NEEDED TO KEEP THE HULK IN A STATE OF UNCONSCIOUSNESS!
THUS, I CAN STUDY HIM FULLY--AT MY LEISURE!
MY RECORDING INSTRUMENTS WILL TRANSCRIBE HIS HEARTBEAT, BLOOD PRESSURE, ENCEPHALLOGRAPHIC PATTERNS OF HIS BRAIN--! NOTHING SHALL BE HIDDEN FROM ME!
WHEN MY TESTS ARE DONE, I SHALL KNOW EVERYTHING ABOUT THE INCREDIBLE HULK!
4

AMAZING! HIS SKIN IS SO TOUGH-- SO ALMOST IMPENETRABLE, THAT MY DEVICES DON'T REGISTER!

BUT, THAT WON'T DELAY ME FOR LONG! I'LL MERELY GO TWO LEVELS BELOW TO MY APPARATUS LAB, AND GET SOME NEW, STRONGER COMPONENT PARTS!

BUT, AS THE LEADER LEAVES THE CHAMBER, A ONE-IN-A-MILLION CHANCE SIDE-EFFECT OF HIS SLEEP GAS OCCURS -- THE ONE THING HE COULD NEVER HAVE EXPECTED...

THE HULK BEGINS TO AWAKEN!

FOR, THE SAME GAS WHICH KEPT THE GREEN-SKINNED GOLIATH ASLEEP AND HELPLESS, ALSO SLOWLY TRANSFORMED HIS BODY CHEMISTRY, SLOWING DOWN HIS HEARTBEAT, UNTIL...

-- HE WHO HAD BEEN THE HULK FINALLY BECOMES THE BRILLIANT, TORTURED BRUCE BANNER ONCE AGAIN!

A BRUCE BANNER WHO AWAKENS WITH THE MEMORY OF WHAT HAS OCCURRED CLEARLY IMPRESSED UPON HIS BRAIN!

I'VE BEEN CAPTURED BY THE SPY WHO CALLS HIM- SELF THE LEADER!

HE DOESN'T YET SUSPECT THAT THE HULK IS ALSO BRUCE BANNER!

LUCKILY, THE SLEEP GAS WHICH FELLED THE HULK IS ACTING AS AN ANTI-TOXIN IN THE BODY OF BRUCE BANNER, SO IT NO LONGER AFFECTS ME!

BUT, I'VE GOT TO MOVE FAST! HE'S ALSO CAPTURED THE ABSORBATRON! IN HIS HANDS, IT'S A THREAT TO ALL OF MANKIND!

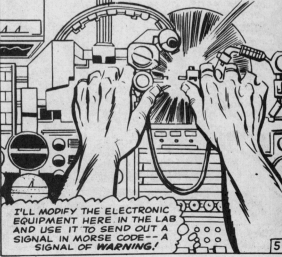

I'LL MODIFY THE ELECTRONIC EQUIPMENT HERE IN THE LAB AND USE IT TO SEND OUT A SIGNAL IN MORSE CODE -- A SIGNAL OF WARNING!

5

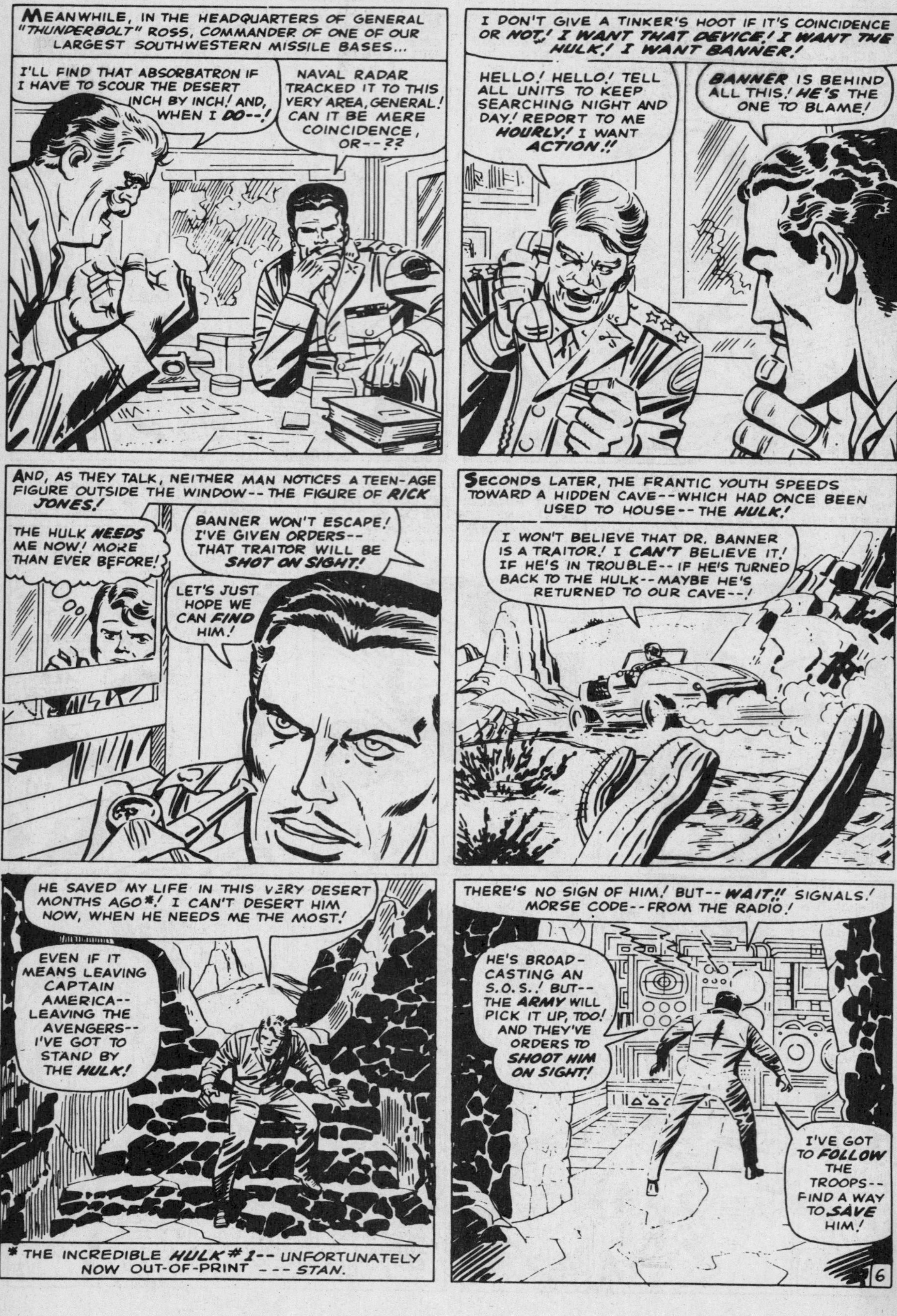

MEANWHILE, IN THE HEADQUARTERS OF GENERAL "THUNDERBOLT" ROSS, COMMANDER OF ONE OF OUR LARGEST SOUTHWESTERN MISSILE BASES...
I'LL FIND THAT ABSORBATRON IF I HAVE TO SCOUR THE DESERT INCH BY INCH! AND, WHEN I DO--!
NAVAL RADAR TRACKED IT TO THIS VERY AREA, GENERAL! CAN IT BE MERE COINCIDENCE, OR--??
I DON'T GIVE A TINKER'S HOOT IF IT'S COINCIDENCE OR NOT! I WANT THAT DEVICE! I WANT THE HULK! I WANT BANNER!
HELLO! HELLO! TELL ALL UNITS TO KEEP SEARCHING NIGHT AND DAY! REPORT TO ME HOURLY! I WANT ACTION!!
BANNER IS BEHIND ALL THIS! HE'S THE ONE TO BLAME!
AND, AS THEY TALK, NEITHER MAN NOTICES A TEEN-AGE FIGURE OUTSIDE THE WINDOW-- THE FIGURE OF RICK JONES!
THE HULK NEEDS ME NOW! MORE THAN EVER BEFORE!
BANNER WON'T ESCAPE! I'VE GIVEN ORDERS-- THAT TRAITOR WILL BE SHOT ON SIGHT!
LET'S JUST HOPE WE CAN FIND HIM!
SECONDS LATER, THE FRANTIC YOUTH SPEEDS TOWARD A HIDDEN CAVE--WHICH HAD ONCE BEEN USED TO HOUSE-- THE HULK!
I WON'T BELIEVE THAT DR. BANNER IS A TRAITOR! I CAN'T BELIEVE IT! IF HE'S IN TROUBLE-- IF HE'S TURNED BACK TO THE HULK--MAYBE HE'S RETURNED TO OUR CAVE--!
HE SAVED MY LIFE IN THIS VERY DESERT MONTHS AGO*! I CAN'T DESERT HIM NOW, WHEN HE NEEDS ME THE MOST!
EVEN IF IT MEANS LEAVING CAPTAIN AMERICA-- LEAVING THE AVENGERS-- I'VE GOT TO STAND BY THE HULK!
* THE INCREDIBLE HULK # 1-- UNFORTUNATELY NOW OUT-OF-PRINT --- STAN.
THERE'S NO SIGN OF HIM! BUT-- WAIT!! SIGNALS! MORSE CODE--FROM THE RADIO!
HE'S BROAD-CASTING AN S.O.S.! BUT-- THE ARMY WILL PICK IT UP, TOO! AND THEY'VE ORDERS TO SHOOT HIM ON SIGHT!
I'VE GOT TO FOLLOW THE TROOPS-- FIND A WAY TO SAVE HIM!
6

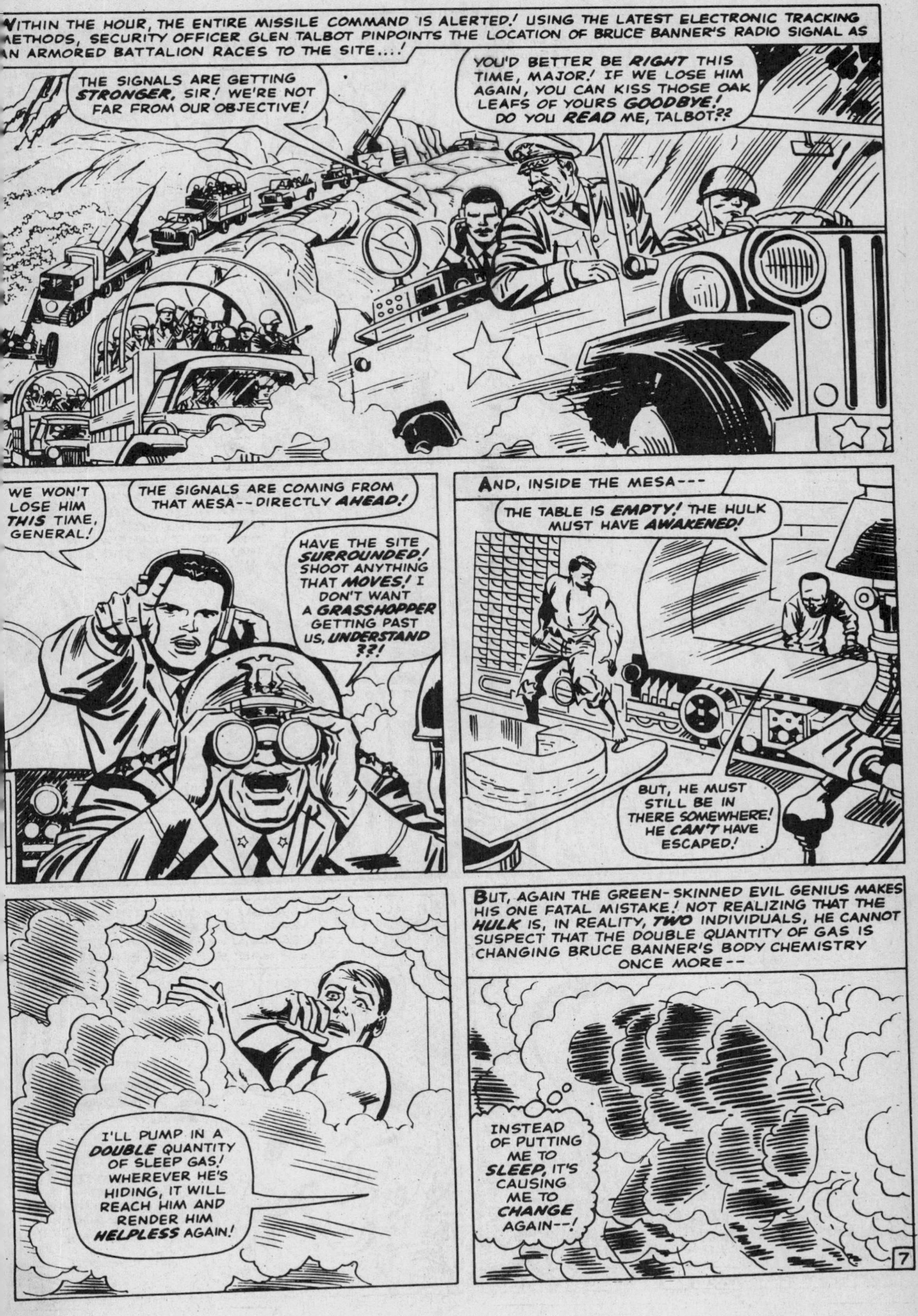

WITHIN THE HOUR, THE ENTIRE MISSILE COMMAND IS ALERTED! USING THE LATEST ELECTRONIC TRACKING METHODS, SECURITY OFFICER GLEN TALBOT PINPOINTS THE LOCATION OF BRUCE BANNER'S RADIO SIGNAL AS AN ARMORED BATTALION RACES TO THE SITE...!
THE SIGNALS ARE GETTING STRONGER, SIR! WE'RE NOT FAR FROM OUR OBJECTIVE!
YOU'D BETTER BE RIGHT THIS TIME, MAJOR! IF WE LOSE HIM AGAIN, YOU CAN KISS THOSE OAK LEAFS OF YOURS GOODBYE! DO YOU READ ME, TALBOT??
WE WON'T LOSE HIM THIS TIME, GENERAL!
THE SIGNALS ARE COMING FROM THAT MESA--DIRECTLY AHEAD!
HAVE THE SITE SURROUNDED! SHOOT ANYTHING THAT MOVES! I DON'T WANT A GRASSHOPPER GETTING PAST US, UNDERSTAND??!
AND, INSIDE THE MESA---
THE TABLE IS EMPTY! THE HULK MUST HAVE AWAKENED!
BUT, HE MUST STILL BE IN THERE SOMEWHERE! HE CAN'T HAVE ESCAPED!
I'LL PUMP IN A DOUBLE QUANTITY OF SLEEP GAS! WHEREVER HE'S HIDING, IT WILL REACH HIM AND RENDER HIM HELPLESS AGAIN!
BUT, AGAIN THE GREEN-SKINNED EVIL GENIUS MAKES HIS ONE FATAL MISTAKE! NOT REALIZING THAT THE HULK IS, IN REALITY, TWO INDIVIDUALS, HE CANNOT SUSPECT THAT THE DOUBLE QUANTITY OF GAS IS CHANGING BRUCE BANNER'S BODY CHEMISTRY ONCE MORE--
INSTEAD OF PUTTING ME TO SLEEP, IT'S CAUSING ME TO CHANGE AGAIN--!
7

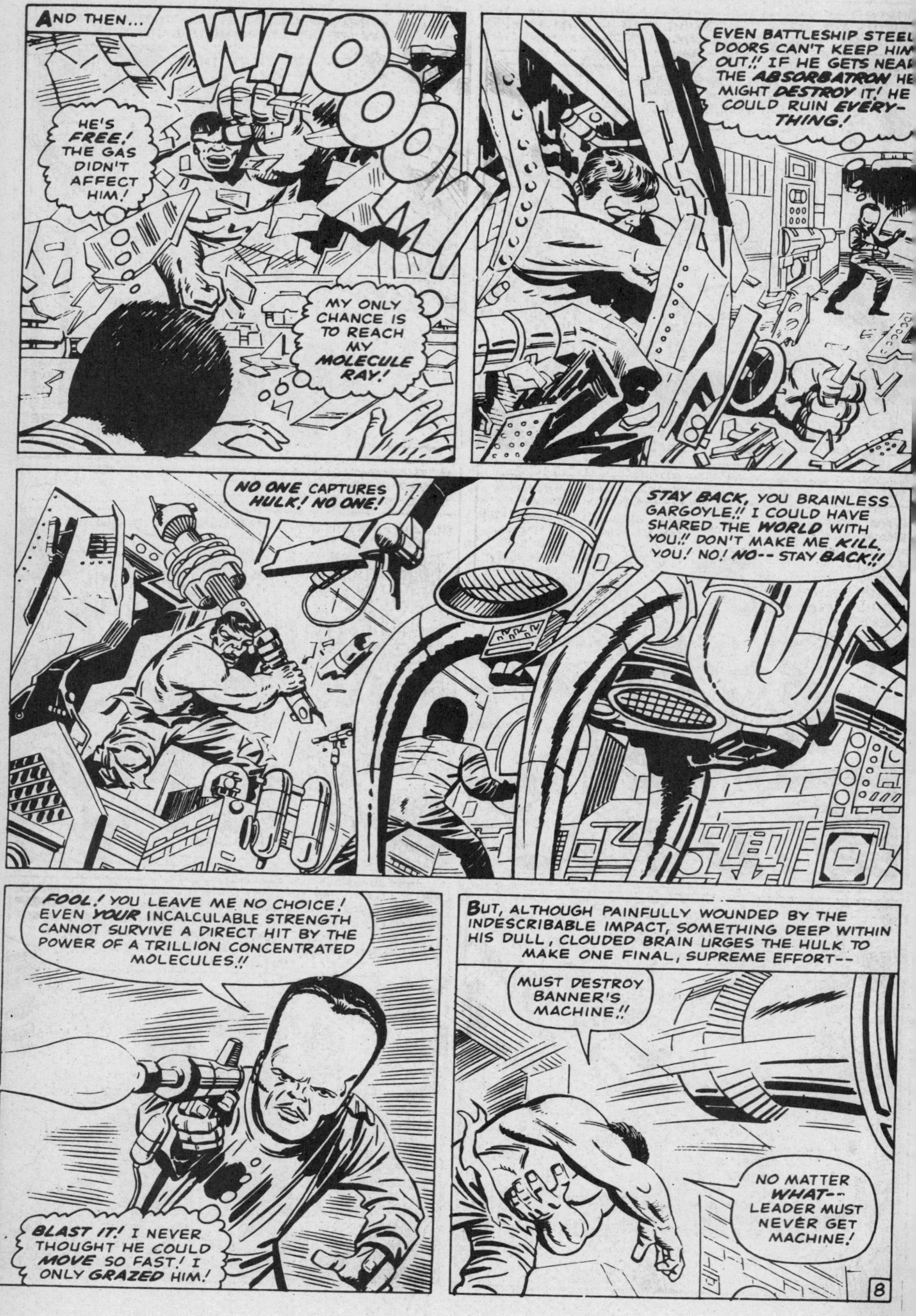
AND THEN...
WHOOOOM
HE'S FREE! THE GAS DIDN'T AFFECT HIM!
MY ONLY CHANCE IS TO REACH MY MOLECULE RAY!
EVEN BATTLESHIP STEEL DOORS CAN'T KEEP HIM OUT!! IF HE GETS NEAR THE ABSORBATRON HE MIGHT DESTROY IT! HE COULD RUIN EVERY-THING!
NO ONE CAPTURES HULK! NO ONE!
STAY BACK, YOU BRAINLESS GARGOYLE!! I COULD HAVE SHARED THE WORLD WITH YOU!! DON'T MAKE ME KILL YOU! NO! NO-- STAY BACK!!
FOOL! YOU LEAVE ME NO CHOICE! EVEN YOUR INCALCULABLE STRENGTH CANNOT SURVIVE A DIRECT HIT BY THE POWER OF A TRILLION CONCENTRATED MOLECULES!!
BLAST IT! I NEVER THOUGHT HE COULD MOVE SO FAST! I ONLY GRAZED HIM!
BUT, ALTHOUGH PAINFULLY WOUNDED BY THE INDESCRIBABLE IMPACT, SOMETHING DEEP WITHIN HIS DULL, CLOUDED BRAIN URGES THE HULK TO MAKE ONE FINAL, SUPREME EFFORT--
MUST DESTROY BANNER'S MACHINE!!
NO MATTER WHAT-- LEADER MUST NEVER GET MACHINE!
8

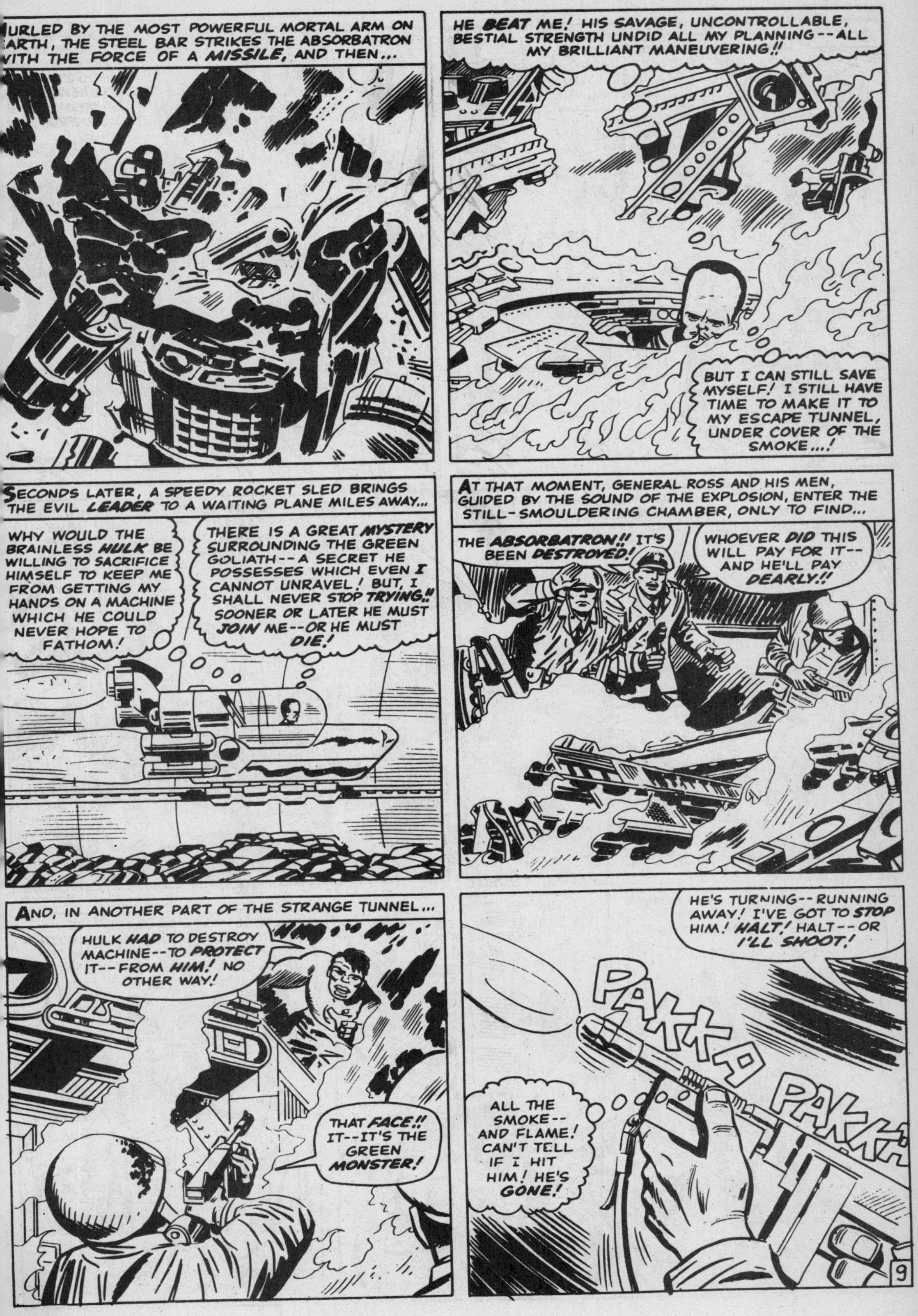
HURLED BY THE MOST POWERFUL MORTAL ARM ON EARTH, THE STEEL BAR STRIKES THE ABSORBATRON WITH THE FORCE OF A MISSILE, AND THEN...
HE BEAT ME! HIS SAVAGE, UNCONTROLLABLE, BESTIAL STRENGTH UNDID ALL MY PLANNING--ALL MY BRILLIANT MANEUVERING!!
BUT I CAN STILL SAVE MYSELF! I STILL HAVE TIME TO MAKE IT TO MY ESCAPE TUNNEL, UNDER COVER OF THE SMOKE...!
SECONDS LATER, A SPEEDY ROCKET SLED BRINGS THE EVIL LEADER TO A WAITING PLANE MILES AWAY...
WHY WOULD THE BRAINLESS HULK BE WILLING TO SACRIFICE HIMSELF TO KEEP ME FROM GETTING MY HANDS ON A MACHINE WHICH HE COULD NEVER HOPE TO FATHOM!
THERE IS A GREAT MYSTERY SURROUNDING THE GREEN GOLIATH--A SECRET HE POSSESSES WHICH EVEN I CANNOT UNRAVEL! BUT, I SHALL NEVER STOP TRYING!! SOONER OR LATER HE MUST JOIN ME--OR HE MUST DIE!
AT THAT MOMENT, GENERAL ROSS AND HIS MEN, GUIDED BY THE SOUND OF THE EXPLOSION, ENTER THE STILL-SMOULDERING CHAMBER, ONLY TO FIND...
THE ABSORBATRON!! IT'S BEEN DESTROYED!
WHOEVER DID THIS WILL PAY FOR IT--AND HE'LL PAY DEARLY!!
AND, IN ANOTHER PART OF THE STRANGE TUNNEL...
HULK HAD TO DESTROY MACHINE--TO PROTECT IT--FROM HIM! NO OTHER WAY!
THAT FACE!! IT--IT'S THE GREEN MONSTER!
HE'S TURNING--RUNNING AWAY! I'VE GOT TO STOP HIM! HALT!--OR I'LL SHOOT!
PAKKA PAKKA
ALL THE SMOKE--AND FLAME! CAN'T TELL IF I HIT HIM! HE'S GONE!
9

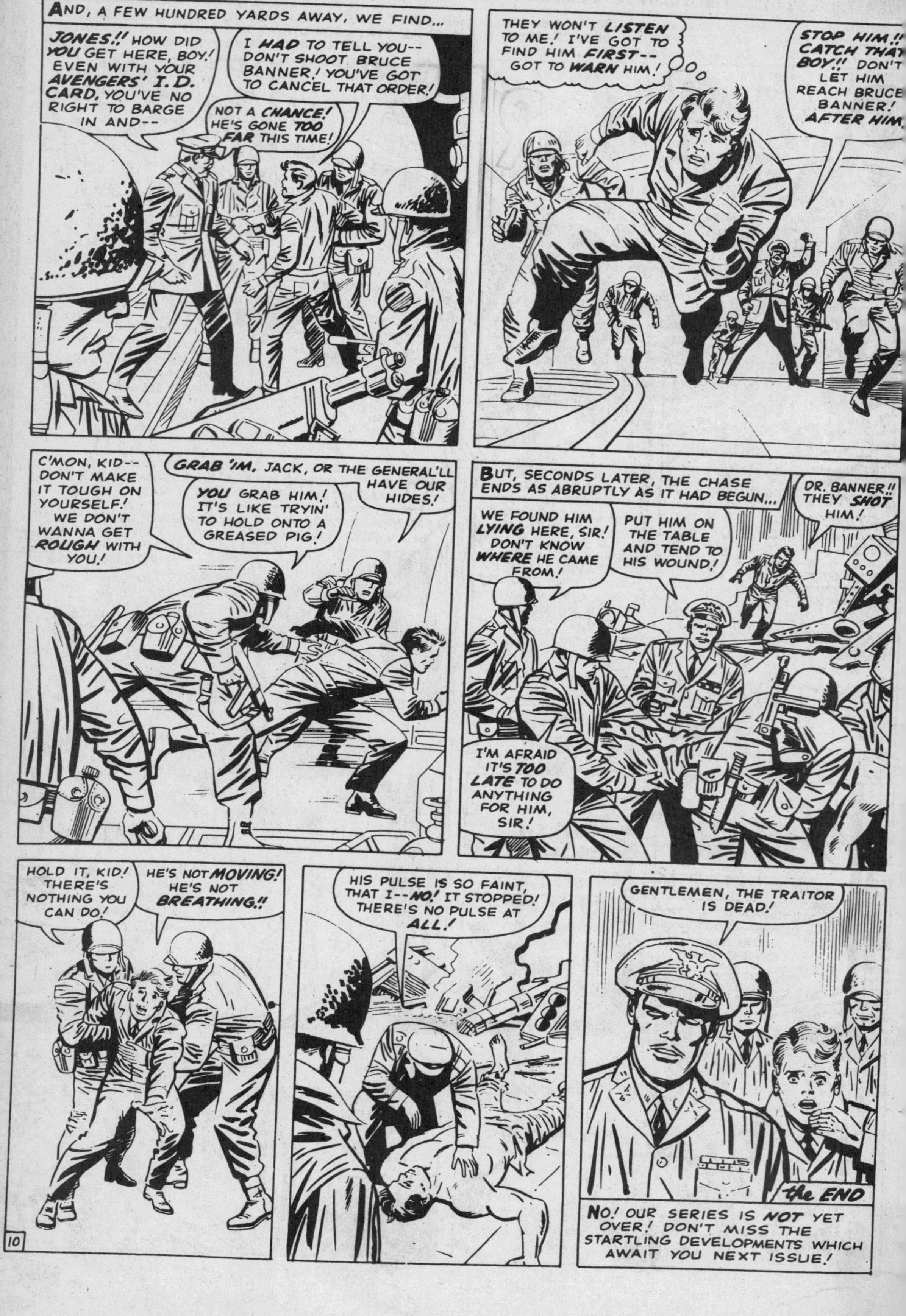
AND, A FEW HUNDRED YARDS AWAY, WE FIND...
JONES!! HOW DID YOU GET HERE, BOY! EVEN WITH YOUR AVENGERS' I.D. CARD, YOU'VE NO RIGHT TO BARGE IN AND--
I HAD TO TELL YOU-- DON'T SHOOT BRUCE BANNER! YOU'VE GOT TO CANCEL THAT ORDER!
NOT A CHANCE! HE'S GONE TOO FAR THIS TIME!
THEY WON'T LISTEN TO ME! I'VE GOT TO FIND HIM FIRST-- GOT TO WARN HIM!
STOP HIM!! CATCH THAT BOY!! DON'T LET HIM REACH BRUCE BANNER! AFTER HIM!
C'MON, KID-- DON'T MAKE IT TOUGH ON YOURSELF! WE DON'T WANNA GET ROUGH WITH YOU!
GRAB 'IM, JACK, OR THE GENERAL'LL HAVE OUR HIDES!
YOU GRAB HIM! IT'S LIKE TRYIN' TO HOLD ONTO A GREASED PIG!
BUT, SECONDS LATER, THE CHASE ENDS AS ABRUPTLY AS IT HAD BEGUN...
WE FOUND HIM LYING HERE, SIR! DON'T KNOW WHERE HE CAME FROM!
PUT HIM ON THE TABLE AND TEND TO HIS WOUND!
DR. BANNER!! THEY SHOT HIM!
I'M AFRAID IT'S TOO LATE TO DO ANYTHING FOR HIM, SIR!
HOLD IT, KID! THERE'S NOTHING YOU CAN DO!
HE'S NOT MOVING! HE'S NOT BREATHING!!
HIS PULSE IS SO FAINT, THAT I--NO! IT STOPPED! THERE'S NO PULSE AT ALL!
GENTLEMEN, THE TRAITOR IS DEAD!
the END
NO! OUR SERIES IS NOT YET OVER! DON'T MISS THE STARTLING DEVELOPMENTS WHICH AWAIT YOU NEXT ISSUE!
10

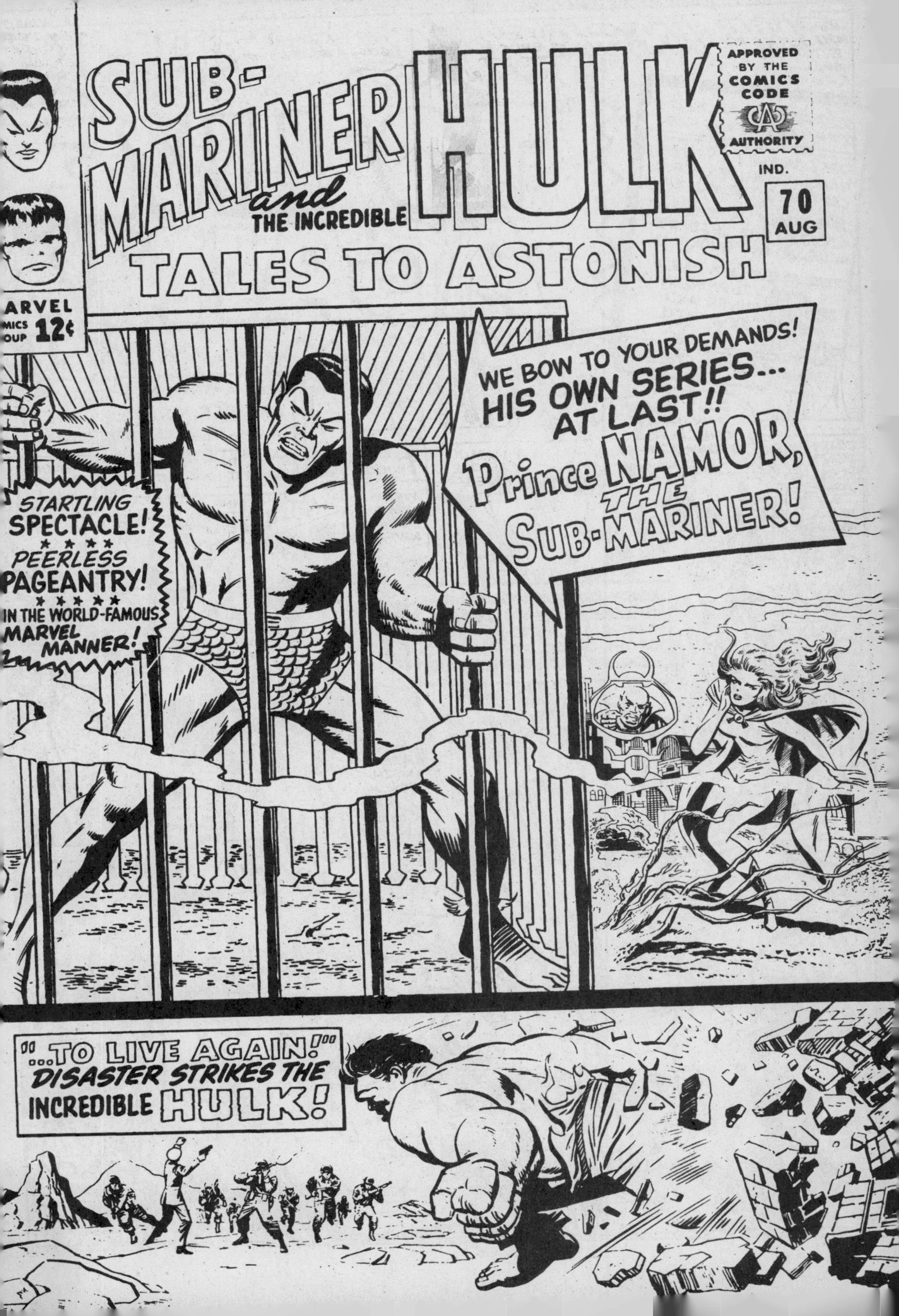

SUB-MARINER and THE INCREDIBLE HULK
TALES TO ASTONISH
APPROVED BY THE COMICS CODE AUTHORITY
IND.
70 AUG
ARVEL
12¢
WE BOW TO YOUR DEMANDS! HIS OWN SERIES... AT LAST!! Prince NAMOR, THE SUB-MARINER!
STARTLING SPECTACLE! PEERLESS PAGEANTRY! IN THE WORLD-FAMOUS MARVEL MANNER!
"...TO LIVE AGAIN!" DISASTER STRIKES THE INCREDIBLE HULK!

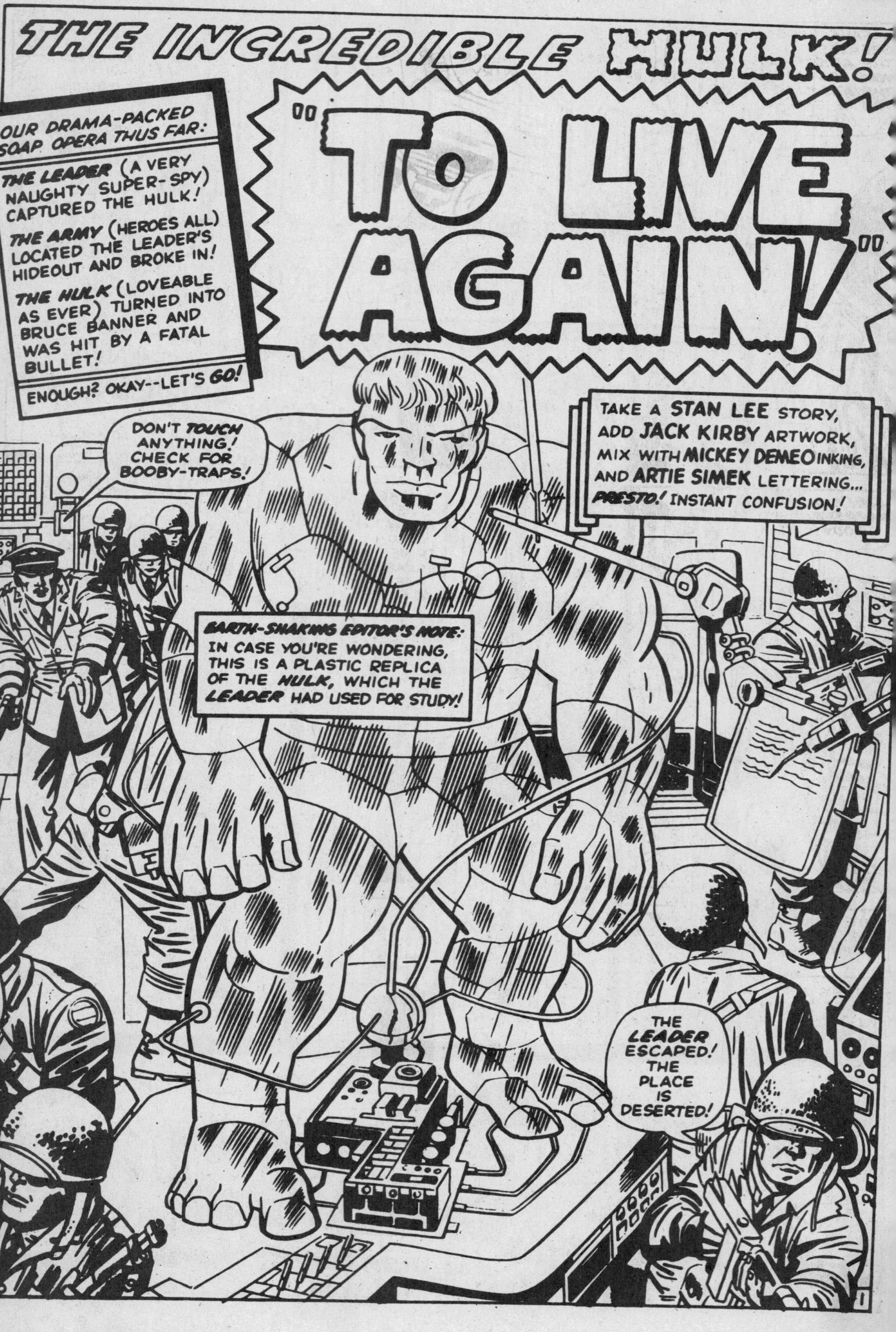
THE INCREDIBLE HULK!
"TO LIVE AGAIN!"
OUR DRAMA-PACKED SOAP OPERA THUS FAR:
THE LEADER (A VERY NAUGHTY SUPER-SPY) CAPTURED THE HULK!
THE ARMY (HEROES ALL) LOCATED THE LEADER'S HIDEOUT AND BROKE IN!
THE HULK (LOVEABLE AS EVER) TURNED INTO BRUCE BANNER AND WAS HIT BY A FATAL BULLET!
ENOUGH? OKAY--LET'S GO!
TAKE A STAN LEE STORY, ADD JACK KIRBY ARTWORK, MIX WITH MICKEY DEMEO INKING, AND ARTIE SIMEK LETTERING... PRESTO! INSTANT CONFUSION!
DON'T TOUCH ANYTHING! CHECK FOR BOOBY-TRAPS!
EARTH-SHAKING EDITOR'S NOTE: IN CASE YOU'RE WONDERING, THIS IS A PLASTIC REPLICA OF THE HULK, WHICH THE LEADER HAD USED FOR STUDY!
THE LEADER ESCAPED! THE PLACE IS DESERTED!
1

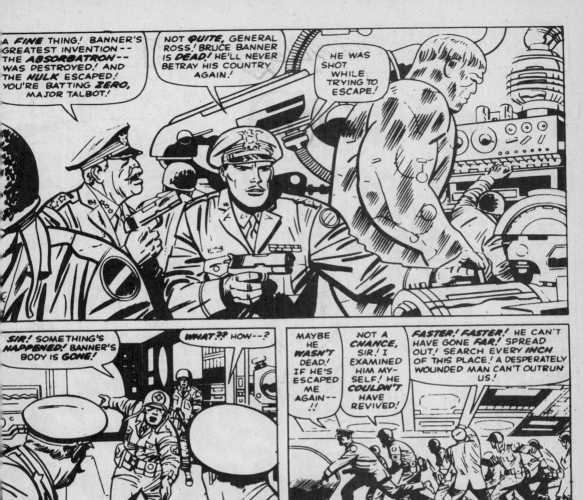

A *FINE* THING! BANNER'S GREATEST INVENTION -- THE *ABSORBATRON* -- WAS DESTROYED! AND THE *HULK* ESCAPED! YOU'RE BATTING *ZERO,* MAJOR TALBOT!

NOT *QUITE,* GENERAL ROSS! BRUCE BANNER IS *DEAD!* HE'LL NEVER BETRAY HIS COUNTRY AGAIN!

HE WAS SHOT WHILE TRYING TO ESCAPE!

SIR! SOMETHING'S *HAPPENED!* BANNER'S BODY IS *GONE!*

WHAT?? HOW--?

DON'T JUST *STAND* THERE! LET'S CHECK *INTO* IT!

MAYBE HE *WASN'T* DEAD! IF HE'S ESCAPED ME AGAIN--!!

NOT A *CHANCE,* SIR! I EXAMINED HIM MY-SELF! HE *COULDN'T* HAVE REVIVED!!

FASTER! FASTER! HE CAN'T HAVE GONE *FAR!* SPREAD OUT! SEARCH EVERY *INCH* OF THIS PLACE! A DESPERATELY WOUNDED MAN CAN'T OUTRUN US!

BUT, BRUCE BANNER IS *NOT* "OUTRUNNING" ANY-ONE! HIS LIFELESS BODY LIES ON THE SEAT OF A RACING TRUCK, SLUMPED NEXT TO A FRANTIC *RICK JONES*--!

THERE'S *STILL* A CHANCE OF SAVING DR. BANNER! IF I CAN JUST REACH HIS HIDDEN UNDERGROUND LABORATORY IN TIME--!

I'VE READ CASES OF MEN WHO RETURNED TO LIFE-- EVEN THOUGH THEIR HEARTS HAD STOPPED BEATING-- JUST SO LONG AS TOO MUCH TIME HADN'T PASSED!

BANNER IS REALLY *TWO* MEN! *ONE* OF THEM STOPPED A BULLET--BUT, IF I CAN BRING THE *OTHER* BACK TO LIFE....!

2

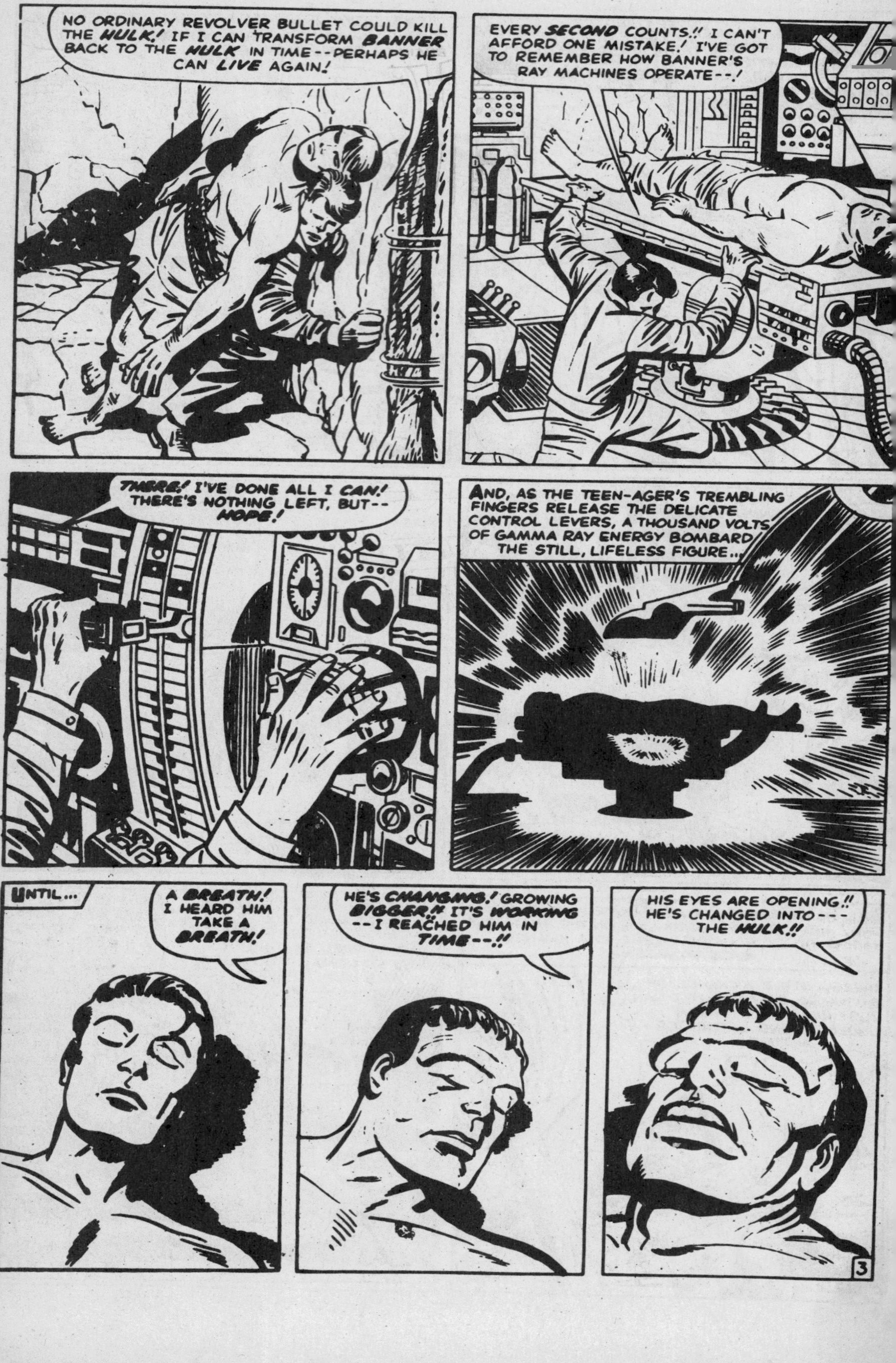
NO ORDINARY REVOLVER BULLET COULD KILL THE HULK! IF I CAN TRANSFORM BANNER BACK TO THE HULK IN TIME--PERHAPS HE CAN LIVE AGAIN!
EVERY SECOND COUNTS!! I CAN'T AFFORD ONE MISTAKE! I'VE GOT TO REMEMBER HOW BANNER'S RAY MACHINES OPERATE--!
THERE! I'VE DONE ALL I CAN! THERE'S NOTHING LEFT, BUT-- HOPE!
AND, AS THE TEEN-AGER'S TREMBLING FINGERS RELEASE THE DELICATE CONTROL LEVERS, A THOUSAND VOLTS OF GAMMA RAY ENERGY BOMBARD THE STILL, LIFELESS FIGURE...
UNTIL...
A BREATH! I HEARD HIM TAKE A BREATH!
HE'S CHANGING! GROWING BIGGER!! IT'S WORKING --I REACHED HIM IN TIME--!!
HIS EYES ARE OPENING!! HE'S CHANGED INTO--- THE HULK!!
3

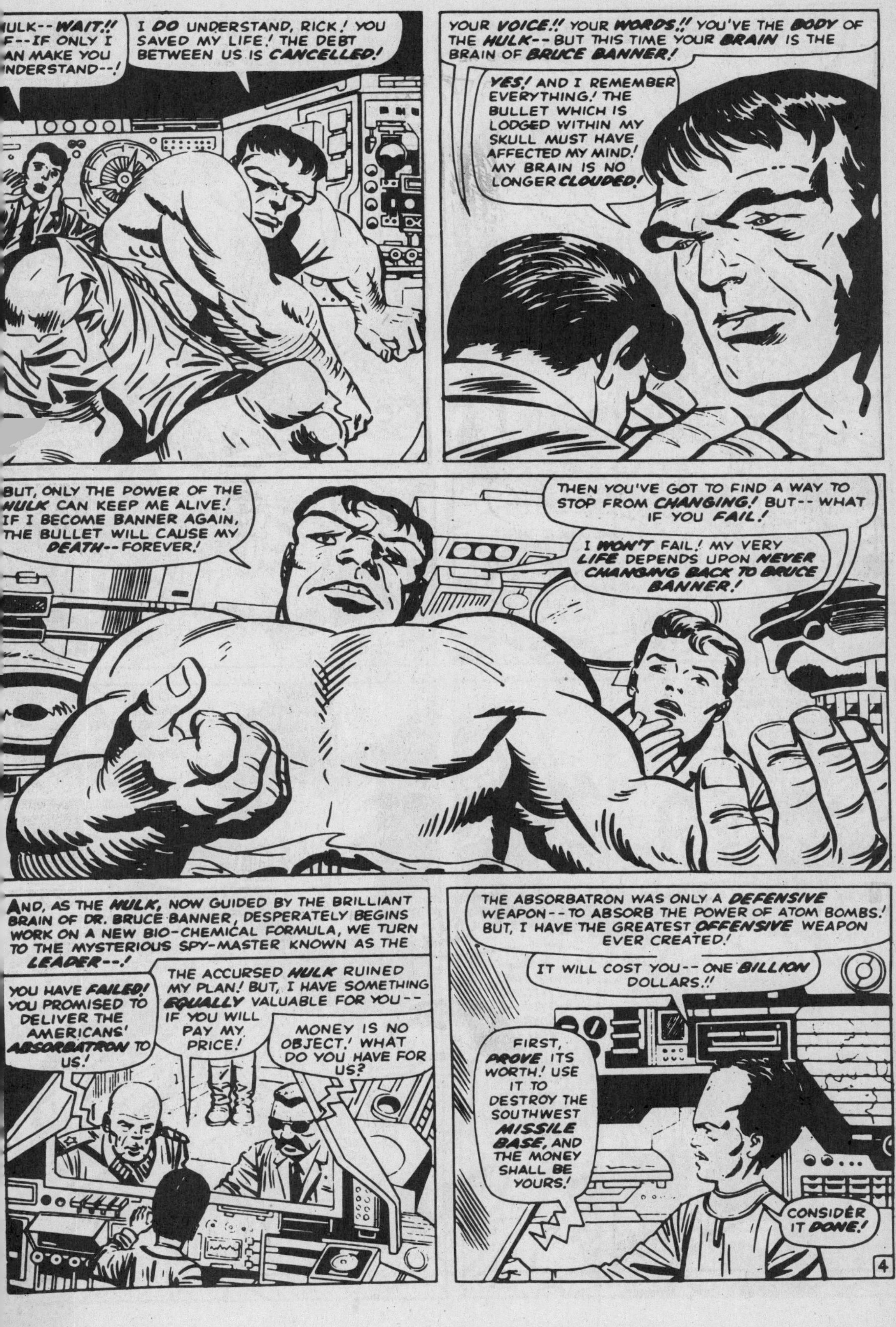
HULK--WAIT!! IF--IF ONLY I CAN MAKE YOU UNDERSTAND--!
I DO UNDERSTAND, RICK! YOU SAVED MY LIFE! THE DEBT BETWEEN US IS CANCELLED!
YOUR VOICE!! YOUR WORDS!! YOU'VE THE BODY OF THE HULK--BUT THIS TIME YOUR BRAIN IS THE BRAIN OF BRUCE BANNER!
YES! AND I REMEMBER EVERYTHING! THE BULLET WHICH IS LODGED WITHIN MY SKULL MUST HAVE AFFECTED MY MIND! MY BRAIN IS NO LONGER CLOUDED!
BUT, ONLY THE POWER OF THE HULK CAN KEEP ME ALIVE! IF I BECOME BANNER AGAIN, THE BULLET WILL CAUSE MY DEATH--FOREVER!
THEN YOU'VE GOT TO FIND A WAY TO STOP FROM CHANGING! BUT--WHAT IF YOU FAIL!
I WON'T FAIL! MY VERY LIFE DEPENDS UPON NEVER CHANGING BACK TO BRUCE BANNER!
AND, AS THE HULK, NOW GUIDED BY THE BRILLIANT BRAIN OF DR. BRUCE BANNER, DESPERATELY BEGINS WORK ON A NEW BIO-CHEMICAL FORMULA, WE TURN TO THE MYSTERIOUS SPY-MASTER KNOWN AS THE LEADER--!
YOU HAVE FAILED! YOU PROMISED TO DELIVER THE AMERICANS' ABSORBATRON TO US!
THE ACCURSED HULK RUINED MY PLAN! BUT, I HAVE SOMETHING EQUALLY VALUABLE FOR YOU--IF YOU WILL PAY MY PRICE!
MONEY IS NO OBJECT! WHAT DO YOU HAVE FOR US?
THE ABSORBATRON WAS ONLY A DEFENSIVE WEAPON--TO ABSORB THE POWER OF ATOM BOMBS! BUT, I HAVE THE GREATEST OFFENSIVE WEAPON EVER CREATED!
IT WILL COST YOU--ONE BILLION DOLLARS!!
FIRST, PROVE ITS WORTH! USE IT TO DESTROY THE SOUTHWEST MISSILE BASE, AND THE MONEY SHALL BE YOURS!
CONSIDER IT DONE!
4

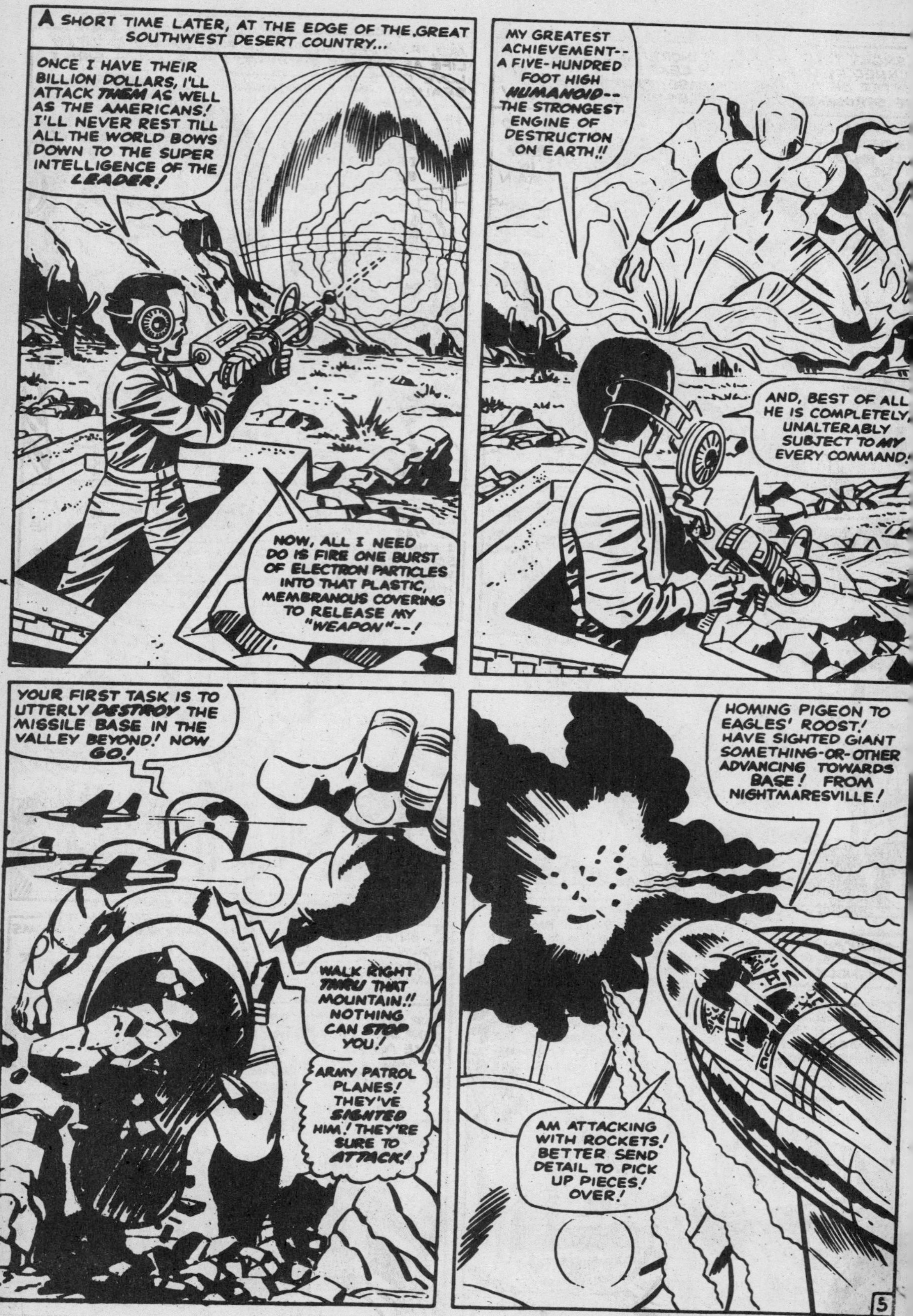
A SHORT TIME LATER, AT THE EDGE OF THE GREAT SOUTHWEST DESERT COUNTRY...
ONCE I HAVE THEIR BILLION DOLLARS, I'LL ATTACK THEM AS WELL AS THE AMERICANS! I'LL NEVER REST TILL ALL THE WORLD BOWS DOWN TO THE SUPER INTELLIGENCE OF THE LEADER!
NOW, ALL I NEED DO IS FIRE ONE BURST OF ELECTRON PARTICLES INTO THAT PLASTIC, MEMBRANOUS COVERING TO RELEASE MY "WEAPON"--!
MY GREATEST ACHIEVEMENT-- A FIVE-HUNDRED FOOT HIGH HUMANOID-- THE STRONGEST ENGINE OF DESTRUCTION ON EARTH!!
AND, BEST OF ALL HE IS COMPLETELY, UNALTERABLY SUBJECT TO MY EVERY COMMAND!
YOUR FIRST TASK IS TO UTTERLY DESTROY THE MISSILE BASE IN THE VALLEY BEYOND! NOW GO!
WALK RIGHT THRU THAT MOUNTAIN!! NOTHING CAN STOP YOU!
ARMY PATROL PLANES! THEY'VE SIGHTED HIM! THEY'RE SURE TO ATTACK!
HOMING PIGEON TO EAGLES' ROOST! HAVE SIGHTED GIANT SOMETHING-OR-OTHER ADVANCING TOWARDS BASE! FROM NIGHTMARESVILLE!
AM ATTACKING WITH ROCKETS! BETTER SEND DETAIL TO PICK UP PIECES! OVER!
5

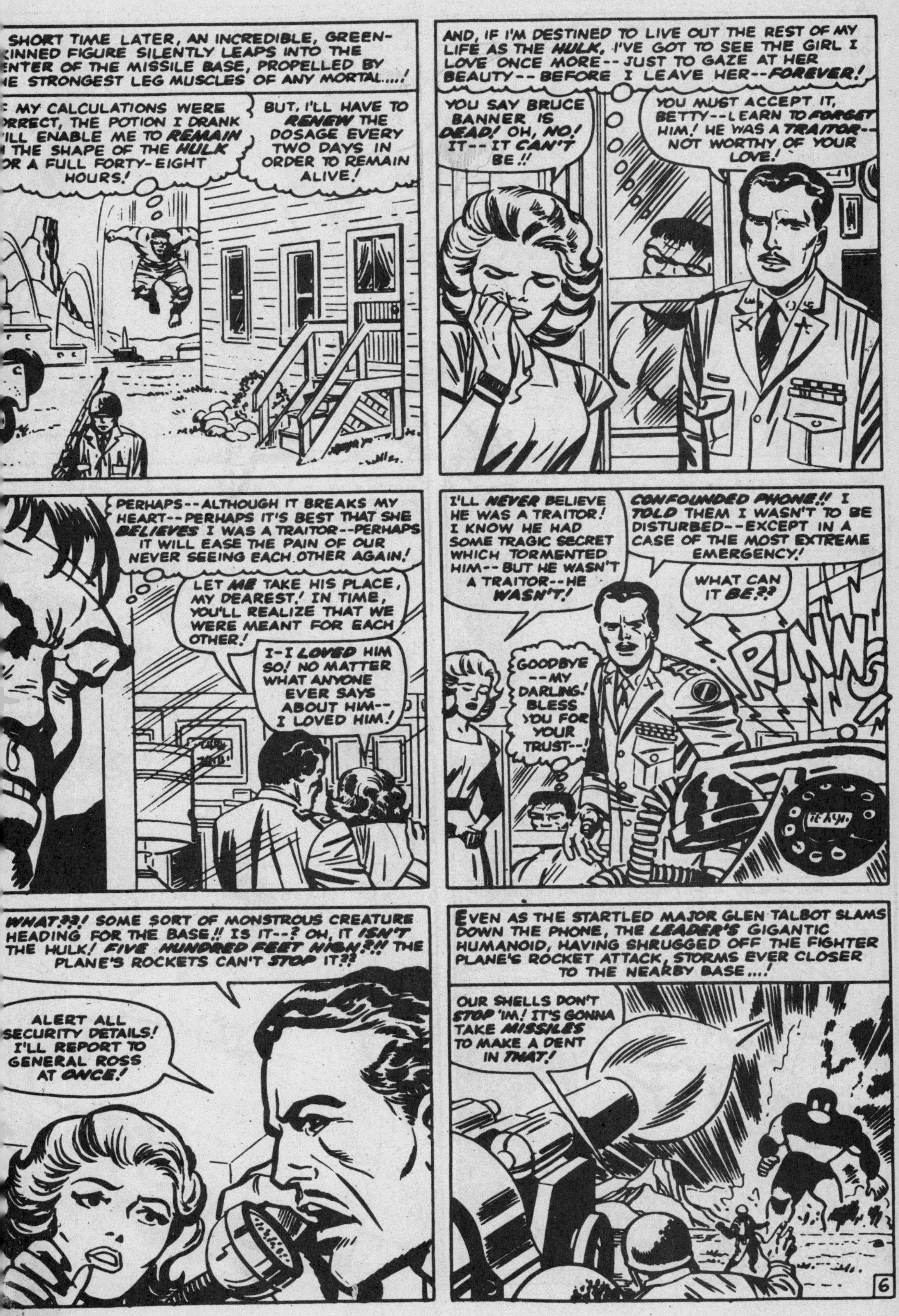
SHORT TIME LATER, AN INCREDIBLE, GREEN-KINNED FIGURE SILENTLY LEAPS INTO THE ENTER OF THE MISSILE BASE, PROPELLED BY HE STRONGEST LEG MUSCLES OF ANY MORTAL....!
MY CALCULATIONS WERE ORRECT, THE POTION I DRANK WILL ENABLE ME TO REMAIN N THE SHAPE OF THE HULK OR A FULL FORTY-EIGHT HOURS!
BUT, I'LL HAVE TO RENEW THE DOSAGE EVERY TWO DAYS IN ORDER TO REMAIN ALIVE!
AND, IF I'M DESTINED TO LIVE OUT THE REST OF MY LIFE AS THE HULK, I'VE GOT TO SEE THE GIRL I LOVE ONCE MORE--JUST TO GAZE AT HER BEAUTY--BEFORE I LEAVE HER--FOREVER!
YOU SAY BRUCE BANNER IS DEAD! OH, NO! IT--IT CAN'T BE!!
YOU MUST ACCEPT IT, BETTY--LEARN TO FORGET HIM! HE WAS A TRAITOR--NOT WORTHY OF YOUR LOVE!
PERHAPS--ALTHOUGH IT BREAKS MY HEART--PERHAPS IT'S BEST THAT SHE BELIEVES I WAS A TRAITOR--PERHAPS IT WILL EASE THE PAIN OF OUR NEVER SEEING EACH OTHER AGAIN!
LET ME TAKE HIS PLACE, MY DEAREST! IN TIME, YOU'LL REALIZE THAT WE WERE MEANT FOR EACH OTHER!
I-I LOVED HIM SO! NO MATTER WHAT ANYONE EVER SAYS ABOUT HIM--I LOVED HIM!
I'LL NEVER BELIEVE HE WAS A TRAITOR! I KNOW HE HAD SOME TRAGIC SECRET WHICH TORMENTED HIM--BUT HE WASN'T A TRAITOR--HE WASN'T!
GOODBYE--MY DARLING! BLESS YOU FOR YOUR TRUST--!
CONFOUNDED PHONE!! I TOLD THEM I WASN'T TO BE DISTURBED--EXCEPT IN A CASE OF THE MOST EXTREME EMERGENCY!
WHAT CAN IT BE??
RINNNG!
WHAT??! SOME SORT OF MONSTROUS CREATURE HEADING FOR THE BASE!! IS IT--? OH, IT ISN'T THE HULK! FIVE HUNDRED FEET HIGH??!! THE PLANE'S ROCKETS CAN'T STOP IT??
ALERT ALL SECURITY DETAILS! I'LL REPORT TO GENERAL ROSS AT ONCE!
EVEN AS THE STARTLED MAJOR GLEN TALBOT SLAMS DOWN THE PHONE, THE LEADER'S GIGANTIC HUMANOID, HAVING SHRUGGED OFF THE FIGHTER PLANE'S ROCKET ATTACK, STORMS EVER CLOSER TO THE NEARBY BASE....!
OUR SHELLS DON'T STOP 'IM! IT'S GONNA TAKE MISSILES TO MAKE A DENT IN THAT!
6

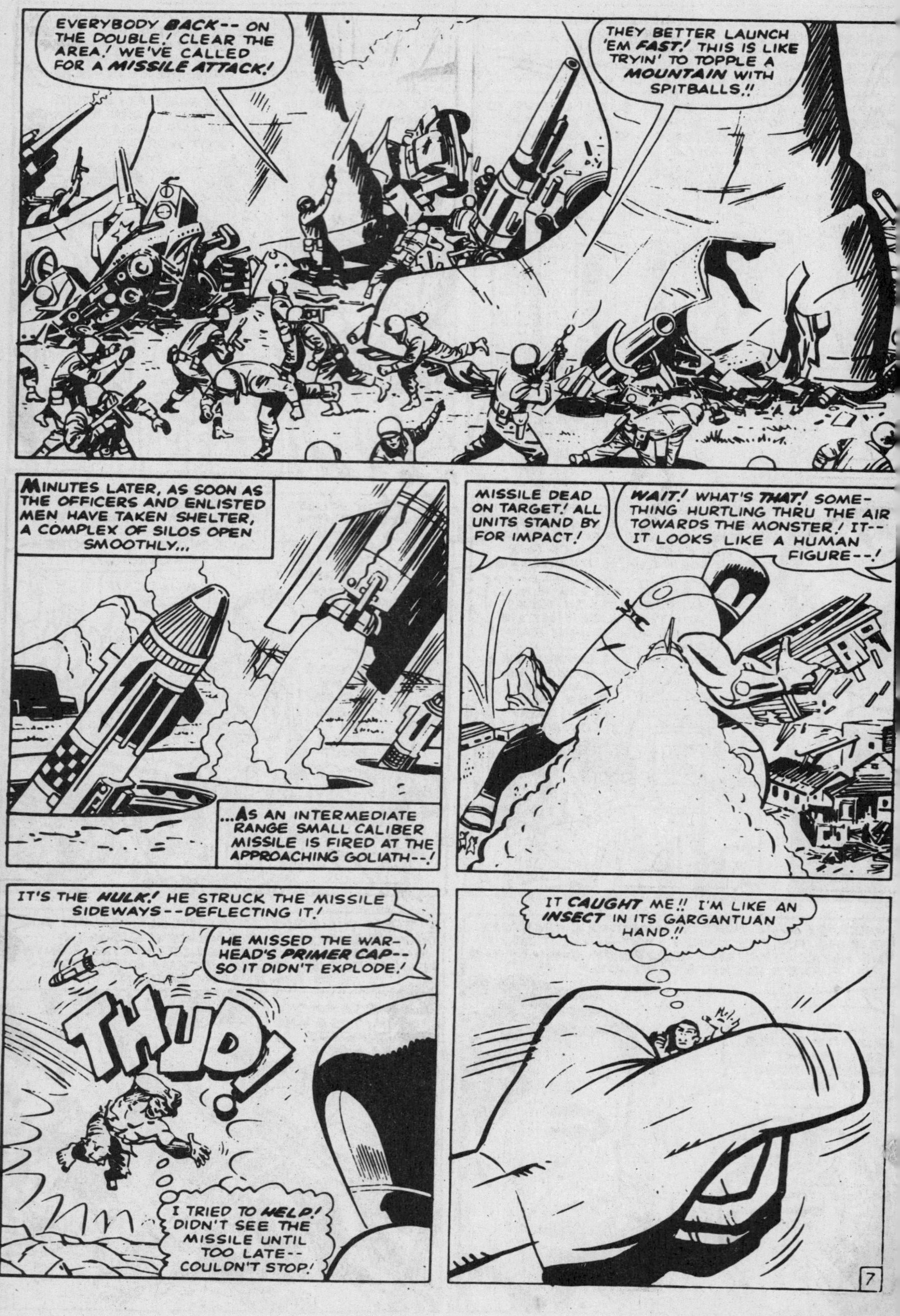
EVERYBODY BACK-- ON THE DOUBLE! CLEAR THE AREA! WE'VE CALLED FOR A MISSILE ATTACK!
THEY BETTER LAUNCH 'EM FAST! THIS IS LIKE TRYIN' TO TOPPLE A MOUNTAIN WITH SPITBALLS!!
MINUTES LATER, AS SOON AS THE OFFICERS AND ENLISTED MEN HAVE TAKEN SHELTER, A COMPLEX OF SILOS OPEN SMOOTHLY...
...AS AN INTERMEDIATE RANGE SMALL CALIBER MISSILE IS FIRED AT THE APPROACHING GOLIATH--!
MISSILE DEAD ON TARGET! ALL UNITS STAND BY FOR IMPACT!
WAIT! WHAT'S THAT! SOMETHING HURTLING THRU THE AIR TOWARDS THE MONSTER! IT-- IT LOOKS LIKE A HUMAN FIGURE--!
IT'S THE HULK! HE STRUCK THE MISSILE SIDEWAYS--DEFLECTING IT!
HE MISSED THE WAR-HEAD'S PRIMER CAP-- SO IT DIDN'T EXPLODE!
THUD!
I TRIED TO HELP! DIDN'T SEE THE MISSILE UNTIL TOO LATE-- COULDN'T STOP!
IT CAUGHT ME!! I'M LIKE AN INSECT IN ITS GARGANTUAN HAND!!

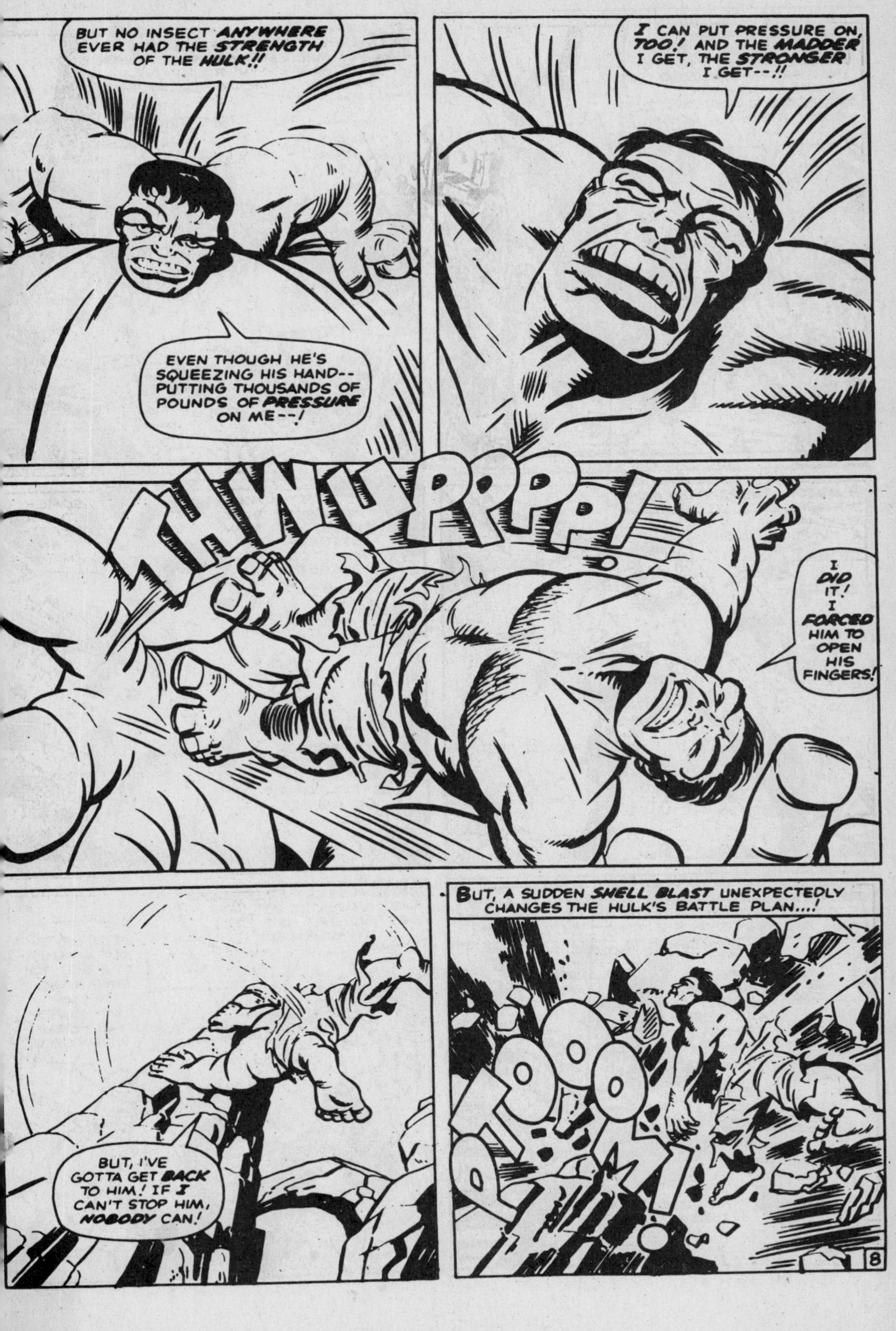
BUT NO INSECT ANYWHERE EVER HAD THE STRENGTH OF THE HULK!!
EVEN THOUGH HE'S SQUEEZING HIS HAND--PUTTING THOUSANDS OF POUNDS OF PRESSURE ON ME--!
I CAN PUT PRESSURE ON, TOO! AND THE MADDER I GET, THE STRONGER I GET--!!
THWUPPPP!
I DID IT! I FORCED HIM TO OPEN HIS FINGERS!
BUT, I'VE GOTTA GET BACK TO HIM! IF I CAN'T STOP HIM, NOBODY CAN!
BUT, A SUDDEN SHELL BLAST UNEXPECTEDLY CHANGES THE HULK'S BATTLE PLAN...!
POOOOM!
8

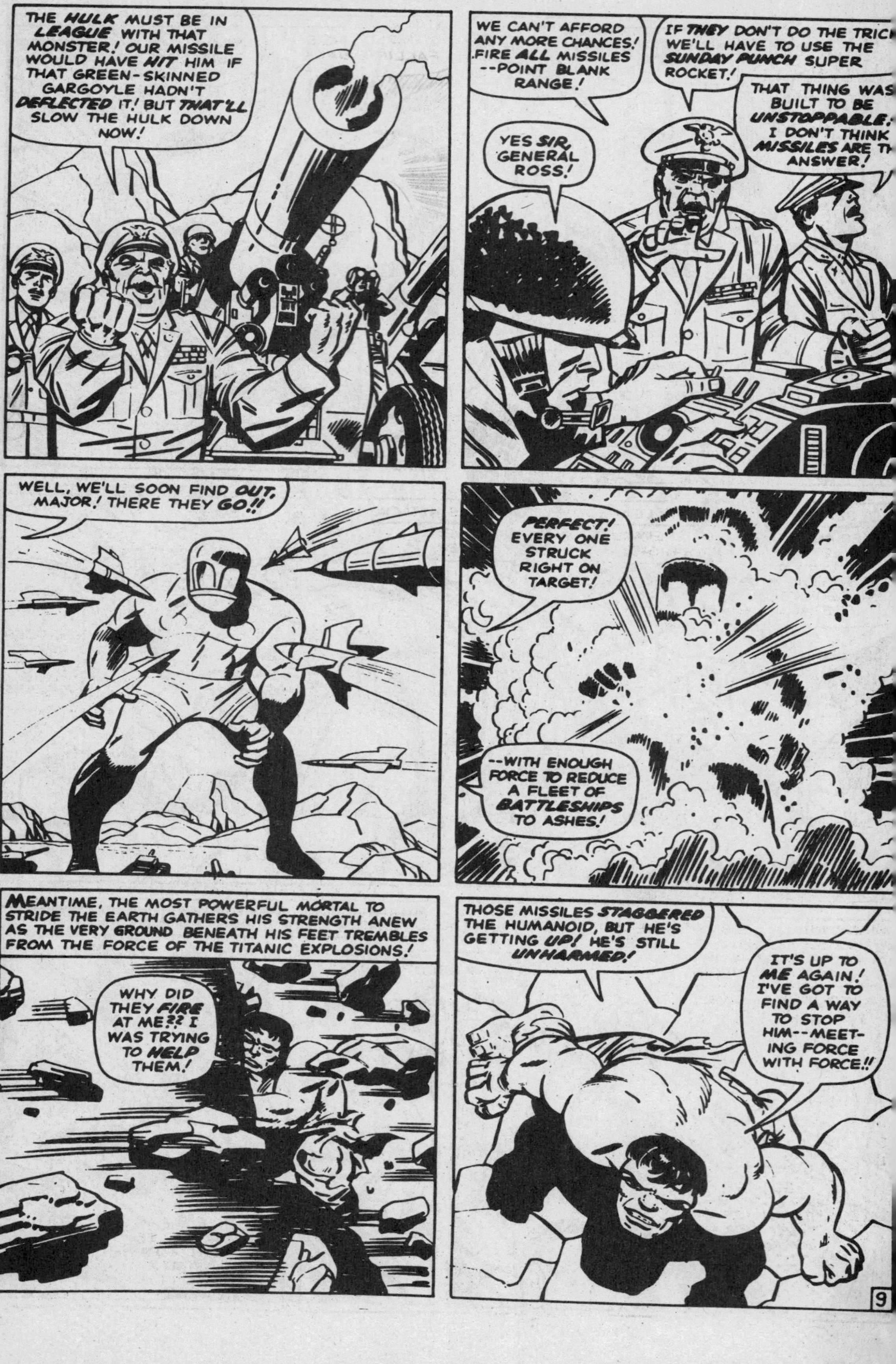
THE HULK MUST BE IN LEAGUE WITH THAT MONSTER! OUR MISSILE WOULD HAVE HIT HIM IF THAT GREEN-SKINNED GARGOYLE HADN'T DEFLECTED IT! BUT THAT'LL SLOW THE HULK DOWN NOW!
WE CAN'T AFFORD ANY MORE CHANCES! FIRE ALL MISSILES --POINT BLANK RANGE!
YES SIR, GENERAL ROSS!
IF THEY DON'T DO THE TRICK WE'LL HAVE TO USE THE SUNDAY PUNCH SUPER ROCKET!
THAT THING WAS BUILT TO BE UNSTOPPABLE! I DON'T THINK MISSILES ARE THE ANSWER!
WELL, WE'LL SOON FIND OUT, MAJOR! THERE THEY GO!!
PERFECT! EVERY ONE STRUCK RIGHT ON TARGET!
--WITH ENOUGH FORCE TO REDUCE A FLEET OF BATTLESHIPS TO ASHES!
MEANTIME, THE MOST POWERFUL MORTAL TO STRIDE THE EARTH GATHERS HIS STRENGTH ANEW AS THE VERY GROUND BENEATH HIS FEET TREMBLES FROM THE FORCE OF THE TITANIC EXPLOSIONS!
WHY DID THEY FIRE AT ME?? I WAS TRYING TO HELP THEM!
THOSE MISSILES STAGGERED THE HUMANOID, BUT HE'S GETTING UP! HE'S STILL UNHARMED!
IT'S UP TO ME AGAIN! I'VE GOT TO FIND A WAY TO STOP HIM--MEETING FORCE WITH FORCE!!

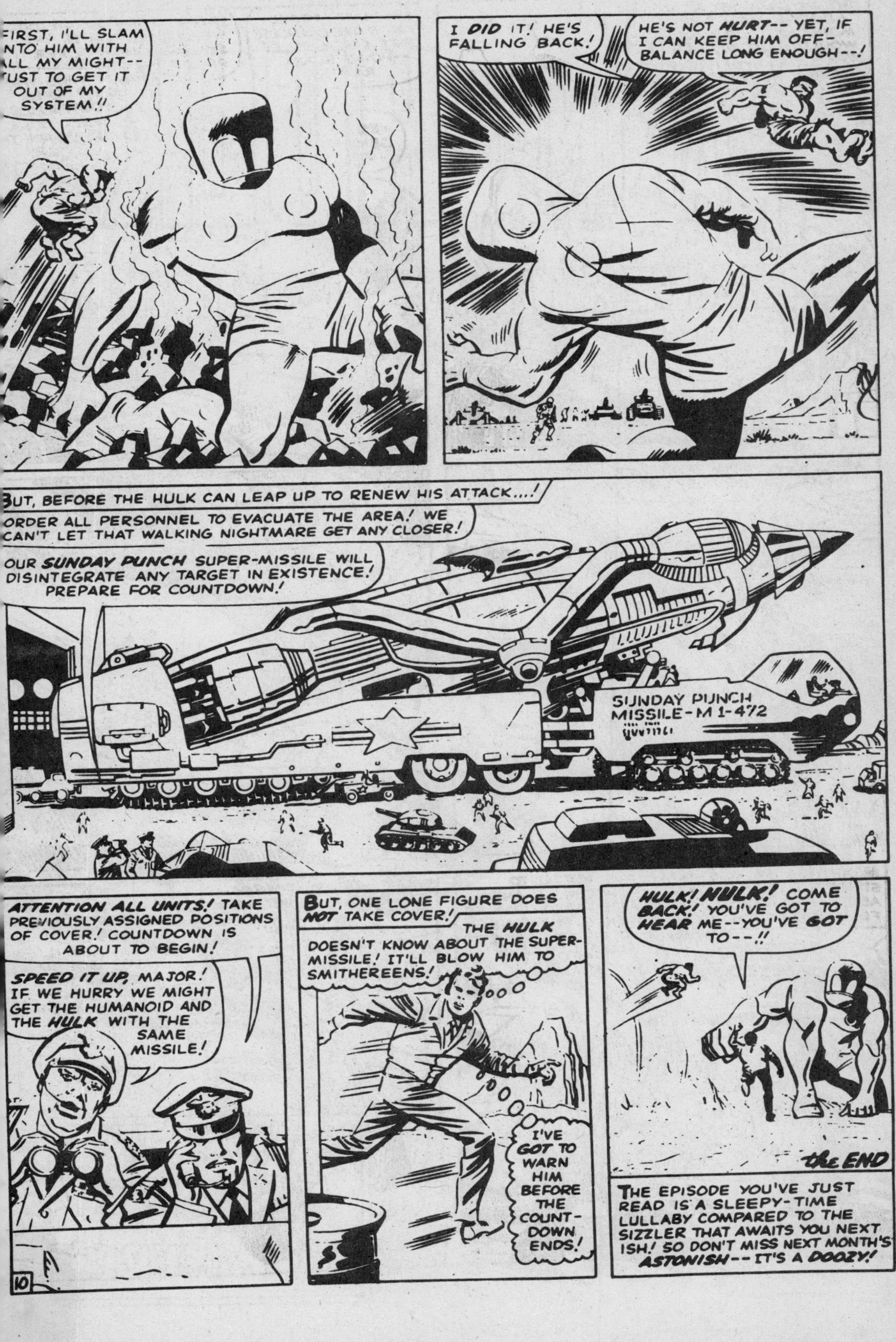

FIRST, I'LL SLAM INTO HIM WITH ALL MY MIGHT-- JUST TO GET IT OUT OF MY SYSTEM.!!
I DID IT! HE'S FALLING BACK.!
HE'S NOT HURT-- YET, IF I CAN KEEP HIM OFF-BALANCE LONG ENOUGH--!
BUT, BEFORE THE HULK CAN LEAP UP TO RENEW HIS ATTACK....!
ORDER ALL PERSONNEL TO EVACUATE THE AREA! WE CAN'T LET THAT WALKING NIGHTMARE GET ANY CLOSER!
OUR SUNDAY PUNCH SUPER-MISSILE WILL DISINTEGRATE ANY TARGET IN EXISTENCE! PREPARE FOR COUNTDOWN!
SUNDAY PUNCH MISSILE-M 1-472
ATTENTION ALL UNITS! TAKE PREVIOUSLY ASSIGNED POSITIONS OF COVER! COUNTDOWN IS ABOUT TO BEGIN!
SPEED IT UP, MAJOR! IF WE HURRY WE MIGHT GET THE HUMANOID AND THE HULK WITH THE SAME MISSILE!
BUT, ONE LONE FIGURE DOES NOT TAKE COVER!
THE HULK DOESN'T KNOW ABOUT THE SUPER-MISSILE! IT'LL BLOW HIM TO SMITHEREENS!
I'VE GOT TO WARN HIM BEFORE THE COUNT-DOWN ENDS!
HULK! HULK! COME BACK! YOU'VE GOT TO HEAR ME--YOU'VE GOT TO--!!
THE END
THE EPISODE YOU'VE JUST READ IS A SLEEPY-TIME LULLABY COMPARED TO THE SIZZLER THAT AWAITS YOU NEXT ISH! SO DON'T MISS NEXT MONTH'S ASTONISH-- IT'S A DOOZY!

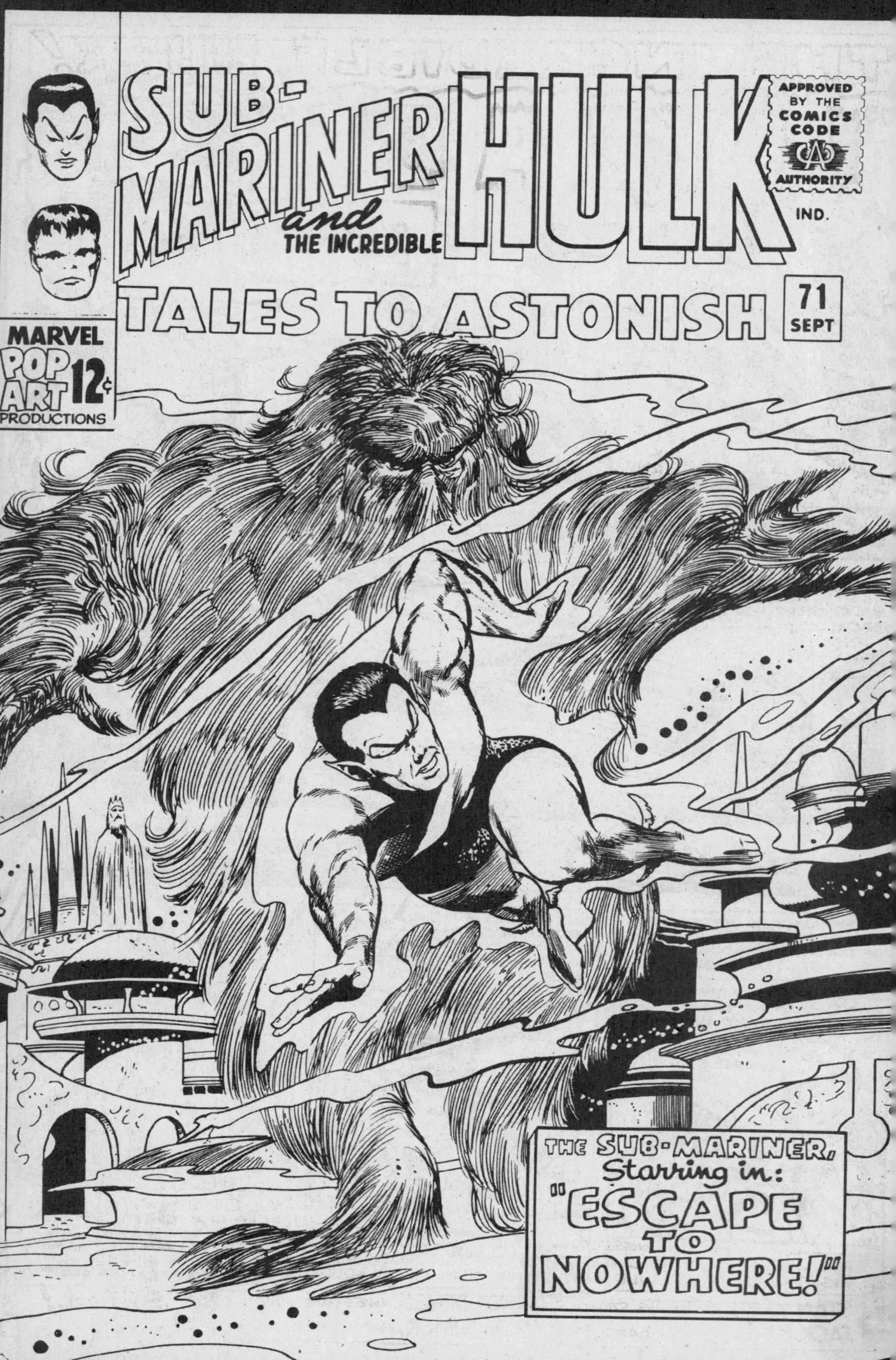
SUB-MARINER and THE INCREDIBLE HULK
TALES TO ASTONISH
71
SEPT
APPROVED BY THE COMICS CODE AUTHORITY
IND.
MARVEL POP ART PRODUCTIONS
12¢
THE SUB-MARINER, Starring in: "ESCAPE TO NOWHERE!"

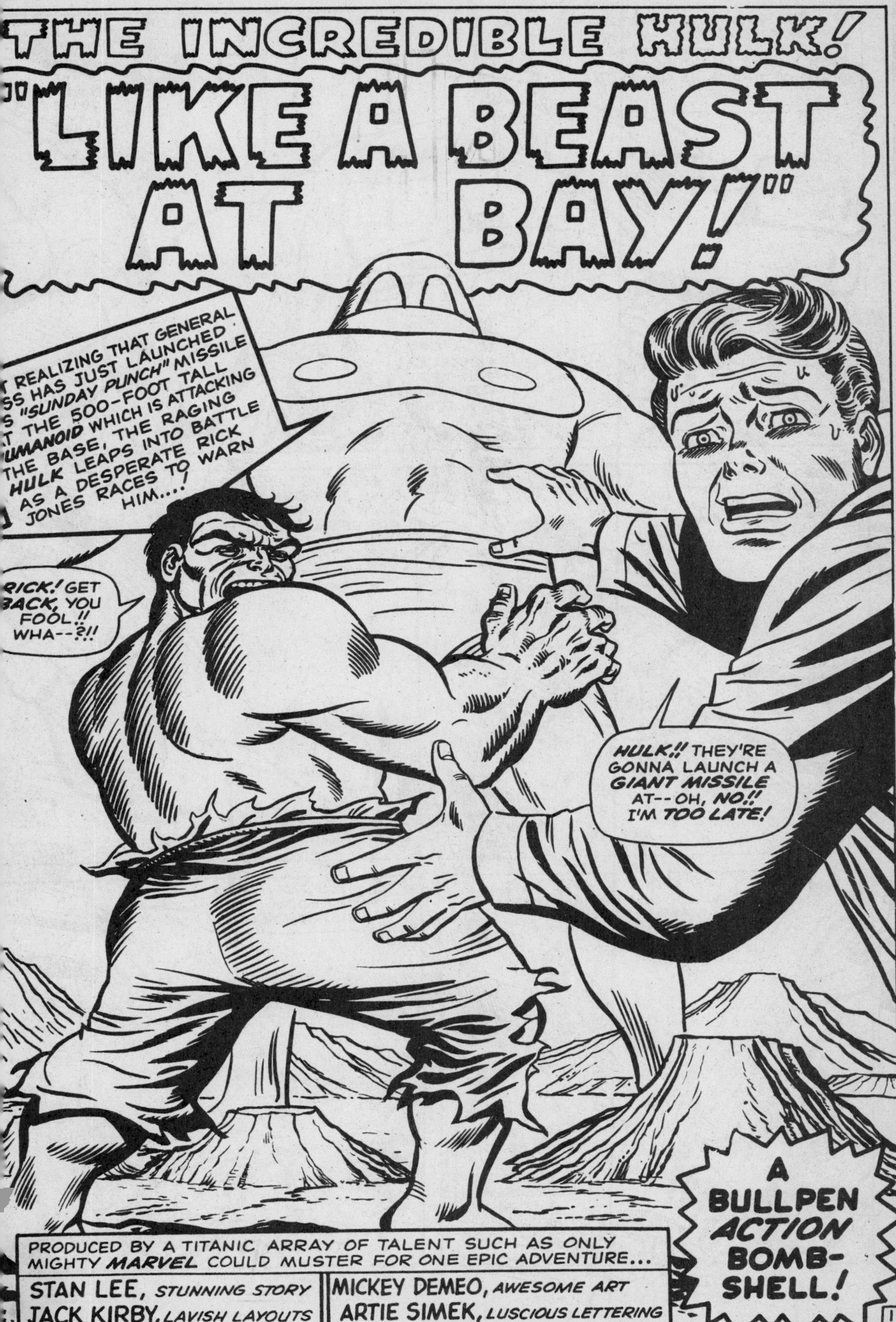
THE INCREDIBLE HULK!
"LIKE A BEAST AT BAY!"
T REALIZING THAT GENERAL SS HAS JUST LAUNCHED S "SUNDAY PUNCH" MISSILE T THE 500-FOOT TALL UMANOID WHICH IS ATTACKING THE BASE, THE RAGING HULK LEAPS INTO BATTLE AS A DESPERATE RICK JONES RACES TO WARN HIM....!
RICK! GET BACK, YOU FOOL!! WHA--?!!
HULK!! THEY'RE GONNA LAUNCH A GIANT MISSILE AT--OH, NO!! I'M TOO LATE!
A BULLPEN ACTION BOMB-SHELL!
PRODUCED BY A TITANIC ARRAY OF TALENT SUCH AS ONLY MIGHTY MARVEL COULD MUSTER FOR ONE EPIC ADVENTURE...
STAN LEE, STUNNING STORY
JACK KIRBY, LAVISH LAYOUTS
MICKEY DEMEO, AWESOME ART
ARTIE SIMEK, LUSCIOUS LETTERING
1

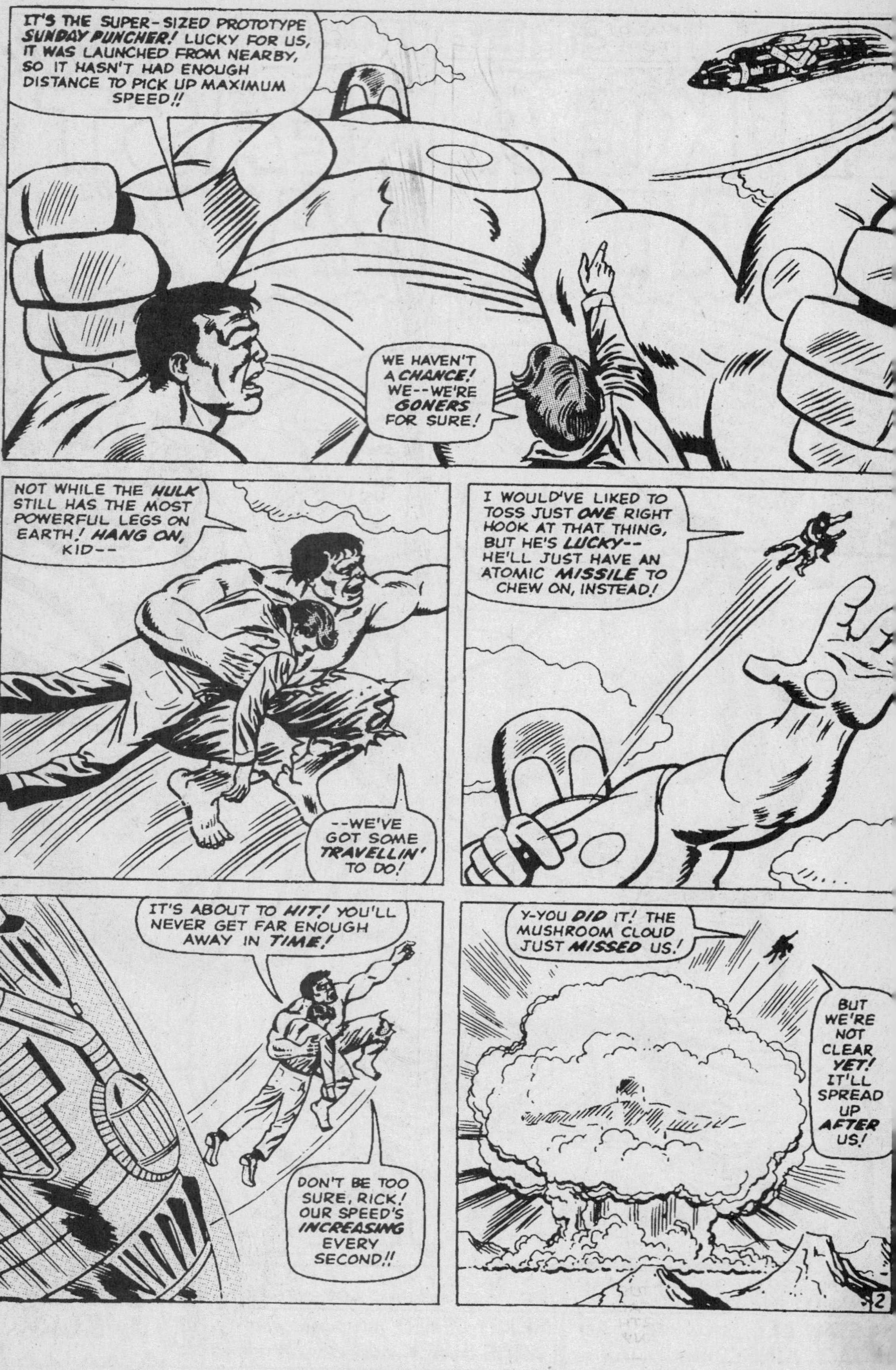

IT'S THE SUPER-SIZED PROTOTYPE SUNDAY PUNCHER! LUCKY FOR US, IT WAS LAUNCHED FROM NEARBY, SO IT HASN'T HAD ENOUGH DISTANCE TO PICK UP MAXIMUM SPEED!!
WE HAVEN'T A CHANCE! WE--WE'RE GONERS FOR SURE!
NOT WHILE THE HULK STILL HAS THE MOST POWERFUL LEGS ON EARTH! HANG ON, KID--
--WE'VE GOT SOME TRAVELLIN' TO DO!
I WOULD'VE LIKED TO TOSS JUST ONE RIGHT HOOK AT THAT THING, BUT HE'S LUCKY-- HE'LL JUST HAVE AN ATOMIC MISSILE TO CHEW ON, INSTEAD!
IT'S ABOUT TO HIT! YOU'LL NEVER GET FAR ENOUGH AWAY IN TIME!
DON'T BE TOO SURE, RICK! OUR SPEED'S INCREASING EVERY SECOND!!
Y-YOU DID IT! THE MUSHROOM CLOUD JUST MISSED US!
BUT WE'RE NOT CLEAR YET! IT'LL SPREAD UP AFTER US!
2

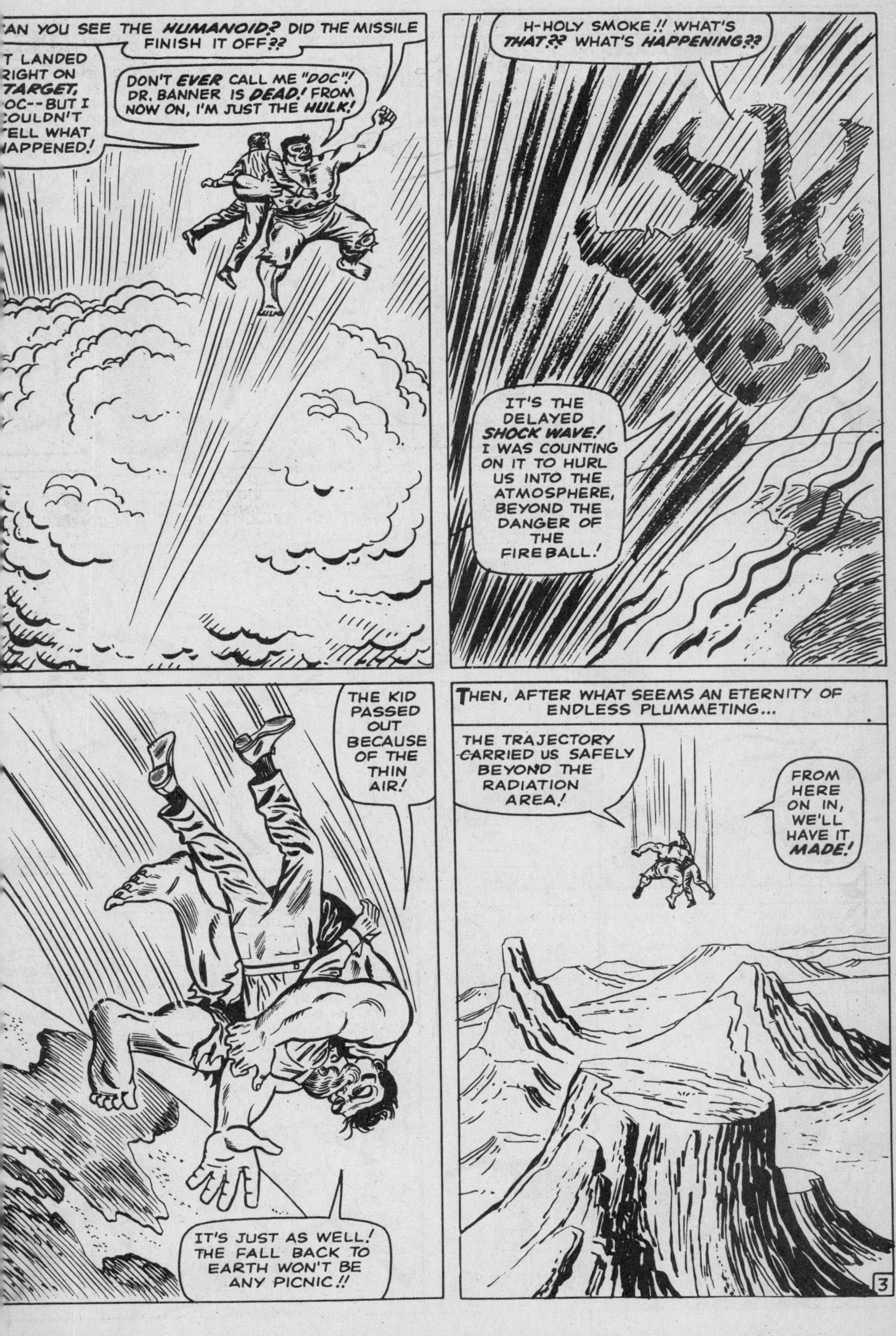
CAN YOU SEE THE HUMANOID? DID THE MISSILE FINISH IT OFF??
IT LANDED RIGHT ON TARGET, DOC--BUT I COULDN'T TELL WHAT HAPPENED!
DON'T EVER CALL ME "DOC"! DR. BANNER IS DEAD! FROM NOW ON, I'M JUST THE HULK!
H-HOLY SMOKE!! WHAT'S THAT?? WHAT'S HAPPENING??
IT'S THE DELAYED SHOCK WAVE! I WAS COUNTING ON IT TO HURL US INTO THE ATMOSPHERE, BEYOND THE DANGER OF THE FIREBALL!
THE KID PASSED OUT BECAUSE OF THE THIN AIR!
IT'S JUST AS WELL! THE FALL BACK TO EARTH WON'T BE ANY PICNIC!!
THEN, AFTER WHAT SEEMS AN ETERNITY OF ENDLESS PLUMMETING...
THE TRAJECTORY CARRIED US SAFELY BEYOND THE RADIATION AREA!
FROM HERE ON IN, WE'LL HAVE IT MADE!
3

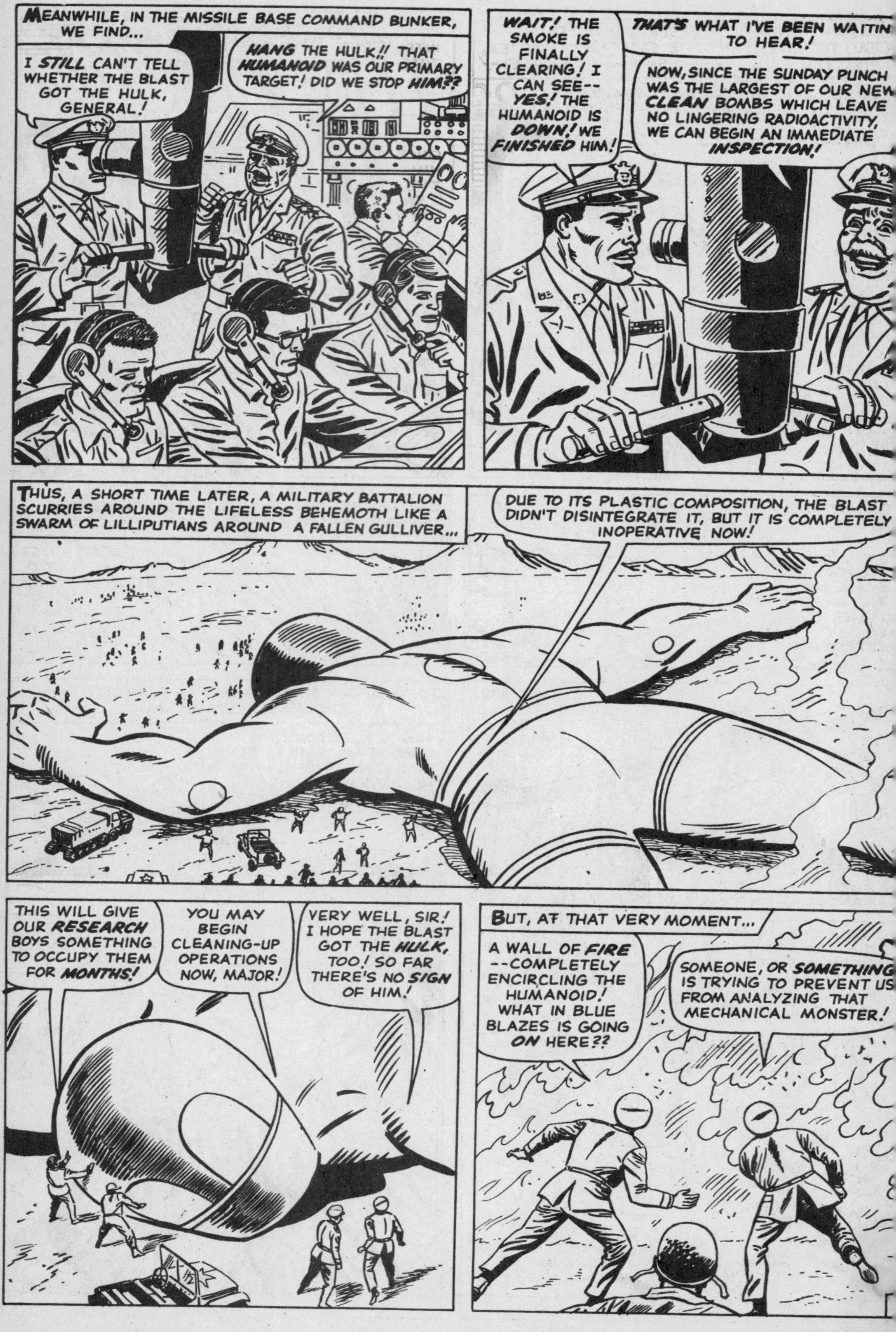

MEANWHILE, IN THE MISSILE BASE COMMAND BUNKER, WE FIND...
I STILL CAN'T TELL WHETHER THE BLAST GOT THE HULK, GENERAL!
HANG THE HULK!! THAT HUMANOID WAS OUR PRIMARY TARGET! DID WE STOP HIM??
WAIT! THE SMOKE IS FINALLY CLEARING! I CAN SEE-- YES! THE HUMANOID IS DOWN! WE FINISHED HIM!
THAT'S WHAT I'VE BEEN WAITIN TO HEAR!
NOW, SINCE THE SUNDAY PUNCH WAS THE LARGEST OF OUR NEW CLEAN BOMBS WHICH LEAVE NO LINGERING RADIOACTIVITY, WE CAN BEGIN AN IMMEDIATE INSPECTION!
THUS, A SHORT TIME LATER, A MILITARY BATTALION SCURRIES AROUND THE LIFELESS BEHEMOTH LIKE A SWARM OF LILLIPUTIANS AROUND A FALLEN GULLIVER...
DUE TO ITS PLASTIC COMPOSITION, THE BLAST DIDN'T DISINTEGRATE IT, BUT IT IS COMPLETELY INOPERATIVE NOW!
THIS WILL GIVE OUR RESEARCH BOYS SOMETHING TO OCCUPY THEM FOR MONTHS!
YOU MAY BEGIN CLEANING-UP OPERATIONS NOW, MAJOR!
VERY WELL, SIR! I HOPE THE BLAST GOT THE HULK, TOO! SO FAR THERE'S NO SIGN OF HIM!
BUT, AT THAT VERY MOMENT...
A WALL OF FIRE --COMPLETELY ENCIRCLING THE HUMANOID! WHAT IN BLUE BLAZES IS GOING ON HERE??
SOMEONE, OR SOMETHING IS TRYING TO PREVENT US FROM ANALYZING THAT MECHANICAL MONSTER!

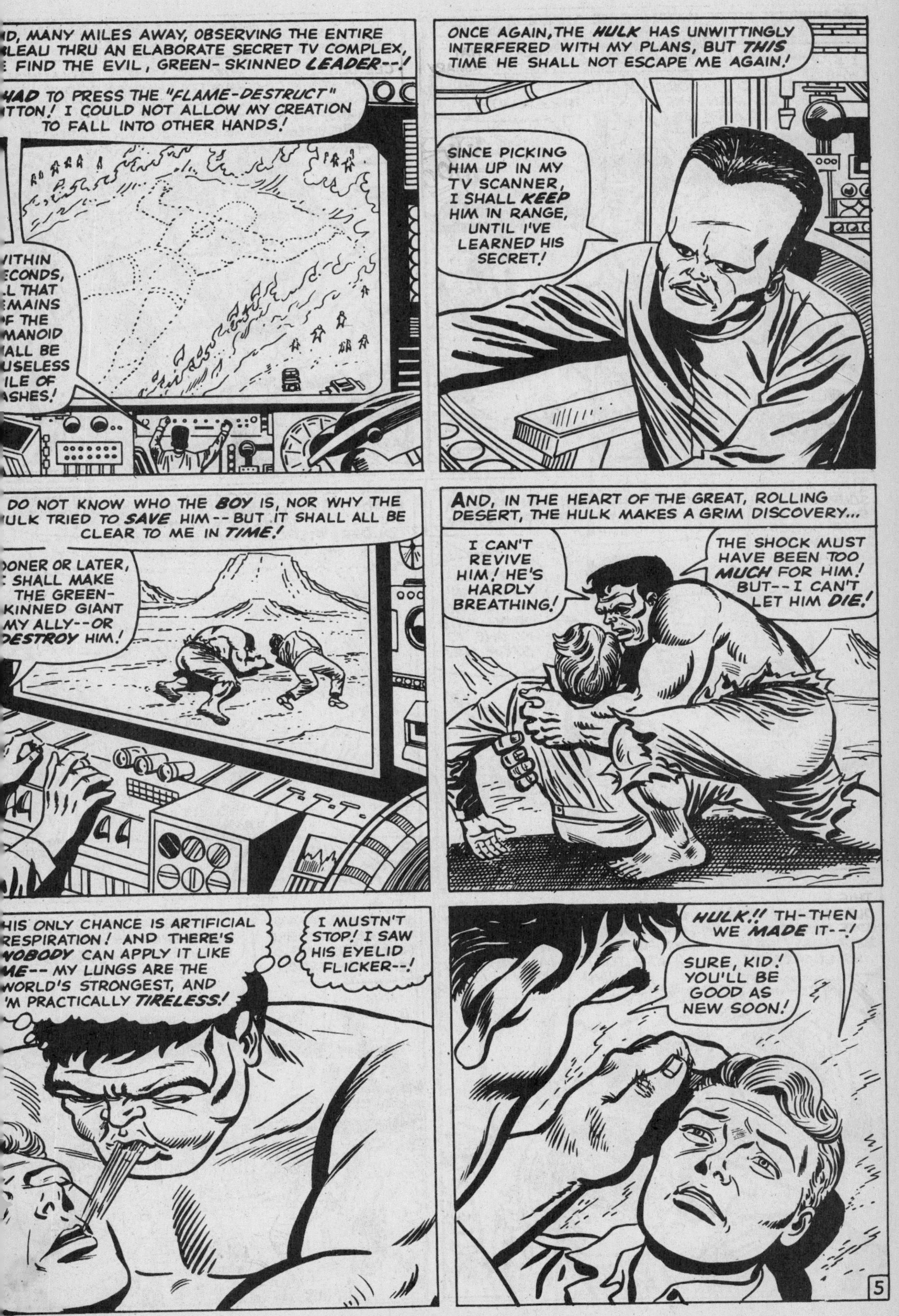

ND, MANY MILES AWAY, OBSERVING THE ENTIRE
BLEAU THRU AN ELABORATE SECRET TV COMPLEX,
E FIND THE EVIL, GREEN-SKINNED LEADER--!
HAD TO PRESS THE "FLAME-DESTRUCT" UTTON! I COULD NOT ALLOW MY CREATION TO FALL INTO OTHER HANDS!
WITHIN ECONDS, LL THAT EMAINS OF THE MANOID HALL BE USELESS ILE OF ASHES!
ONCE AGAIN, THE HULK HAS UNWITTINGLY INTERFERED WITH MY PLANS, BUT THIS TIME HE SHALL NOT ESCAPE ME AGAIN!
SINCE PICKING HIM UP IN MY TV SCANNER, I SHALL KEEP HIM IN RANGE, UNTIL I'VE LEARNED HIS SECRET!
DO NOT KNOW WHO THE BOY IS, NOR WHY THE ULK TRIED TO SAVE HIM--BUT IT SHALL ALL BE CLEAR TO ME IN TIME!
OONER OR LATER, SHALL MAKE THE GREEN-KINNED GIANT MY ALLY--OR DESTROY HIM!
AND, IN THE HEART OF THE GREAT, ROLLING DESERT, THE HULK MAKES A GRIM DISCOVERY...
I CAN'T REVIVE HIM! HE'S HARDLY BREATHING!
THE SHOCK MUST HAVE BEEN TOO MUCH FOR HIM! BUT--I CAN'T LET HIM DIE!
HIS ONLY CHANCE IS ARTIFICIAL RESPIRATION! AND THERE'S NOBODY CAN APPLY IT LIKE ME-- MY LUNGS ARE THE WORLD'S STRONGEST, AND I'M PRACTICALLY TIRELESS!
I MUSTN'T STOP! I SAW HIS EYELID FLICKER--!
HULK!! TH-THEN WE MADE IT--!
SURE, KID! YOU'LL BE GOOD AS NEW SOON!
5

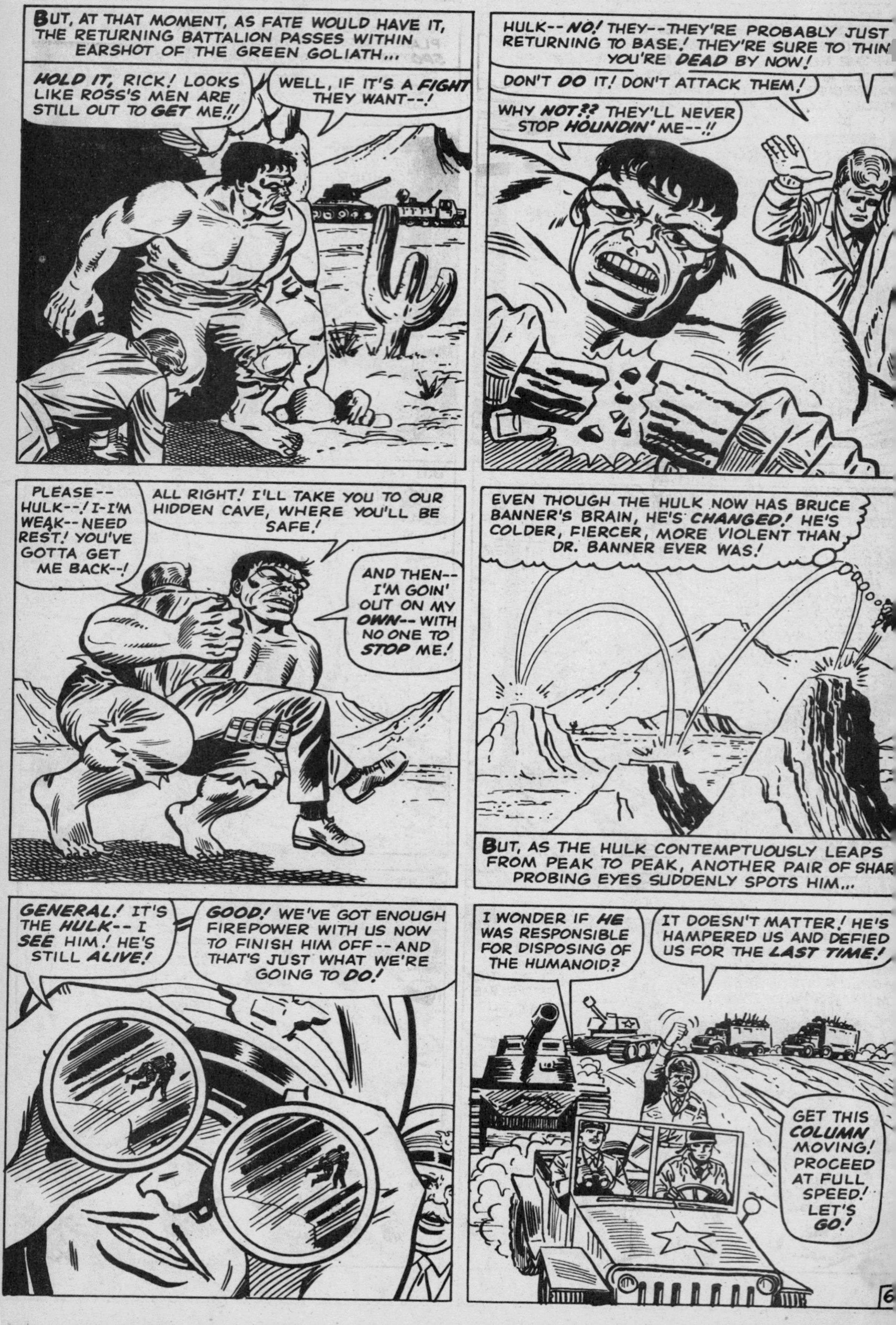
BUT, AT THAT MOMENT, AS FATE WOULD HAVE IT, THE RETURNING BATTALION PASSES WITHIN EARSHOT OF THE GREEN GOLIATH...
HOLD IT, RICK! LOOKS LIKE ROSS'S MEN ARE STILL OUT TO GET ME!!
WELL, IF IT'S A FIGHT THEY WANT--!
HULK--NO! THEY--THEY'RE PROBABLY JUST RETURNING TO BASE! THEY'RE SURE TO THIN YOU'RE DEAD BY NOW!
DON'T DO IT! DON'T ATTACK THEM!
WHY NOT?? THEY'LL NEVER STOP HOUNDIN' ME--!!
PLEASE-- HULK--! I-I'M WEAK--NEED REST! YOU'VE GOTTA GET ME BACK--!
ALL RIGHT! I'LL TAKE YOU TO OUR HIDDEN CAVE, WHERE YOU'LL BE SAFE!
AND THEN-- I'M GOIN' OUT ON MY OWN-- WITH NO ONE TO STOP ME!
EVEN THOUGH THE HULK NOW HAS BRUCE BANNER'S BRAIN, HE'S CHANGED! HE'S COLDER, FIERCER, MORE VIOLENT THAN DR. BANNER EVER WAS!
BUT, AS THE HULK CONTEMPTUOUSLY LEAPS FROM PEAK TO PEAK, ANOTHER PAIR OF SHAR PROBING EYES SUDDENLY SPOTS HIM...
GENERAL! IT'S THE HULK-- I SEE HIM! HE'S STILL ALIVE!
GOOD! WE'VE GOT ENOUGH FIREPOWER WITH US NOW TO FINISH HIM OFF -- AND THAT'S JUST WHAT WE'RE GOING TO DO!
I WONDER IF HE WAS RESPONSIBLE FOR DISPOSING OF THE HUMANOID?
IT DOESN'T MATTER! HE'S HAMPERED US AND DEFIED US FOR THE LAST TIME!
GET THIS COLUMN MOVING! PROCEED AT FULL SPEED! LET'S GO!

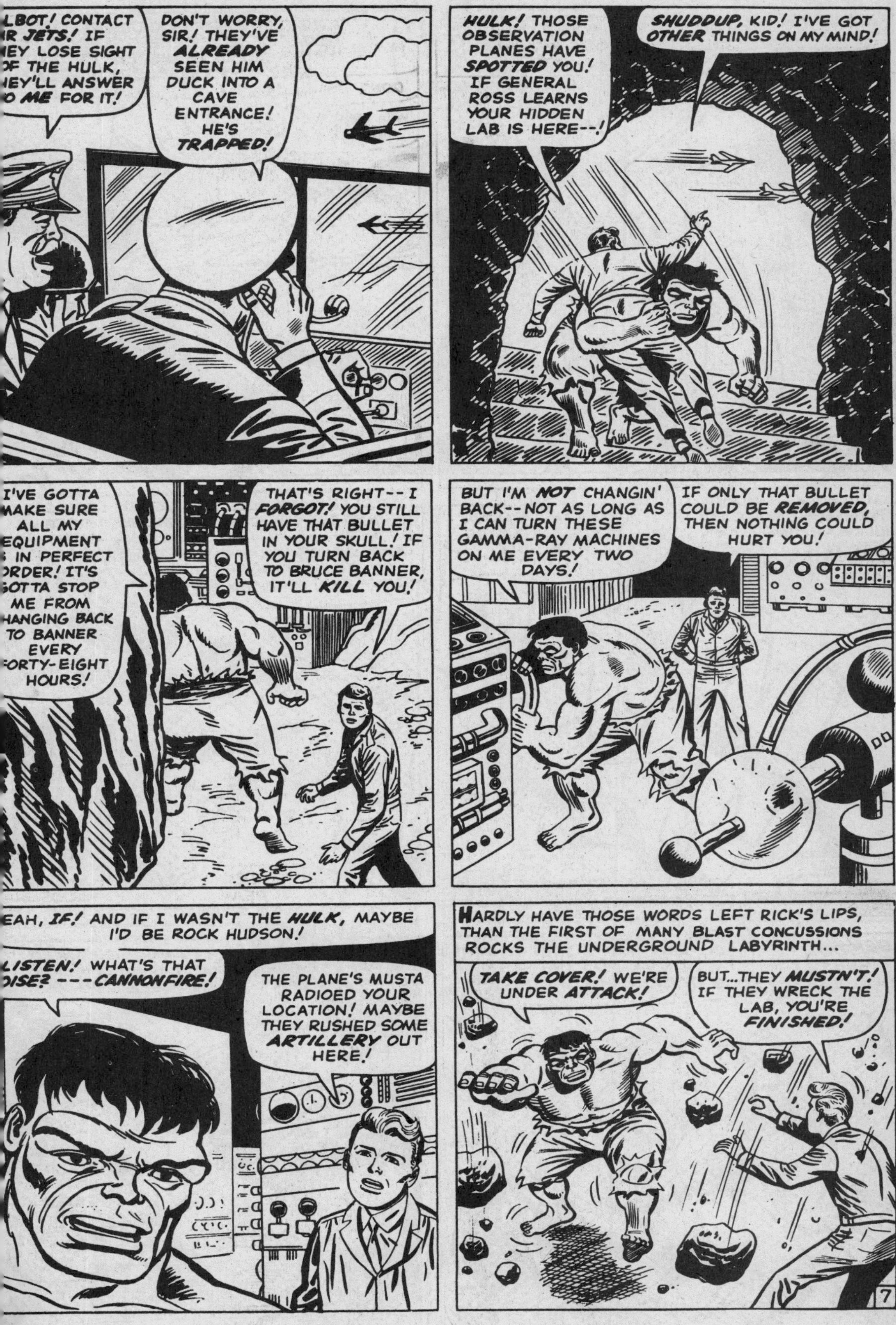
LBOT! CONTACT R JETS! IF EY LOSE SIGHT OF THE HULK, EY'LL ANSWER O ME FOR IT!
DON'T WORRY, SIR! THEY'VE ALREADY SEEN HIM DUCK INTO A CAVE ENTRANCE! HE'S TRAPPED!
HULK! THOSE OBSERVATION PLANES HAVE SPOTTED YOU! IF GENERAL ROSS LEARNS YOUR HIDDEN LAB IS HERE--!
SHUDDUP, KID! I'VE GOT OTHER THINGS ON MY MIND!
I'VE GOTTA AKE SURE ALL MY EQUIPMENT S IN PERFECT ORDER! IT'S GOTTA STOP ME FROM HANGING BACK TO BANNER EVERY FORTY-EIGHT HOURS!
THAT'S RIGHT-- I FORGOT! YOU STILL HAVE THAT BULLET IN YOUR SKULL! IF YOU TURN BACK TO BRUCE BANNER, IT'LL KILL YOU!
BUT I'M NOT CHANGIN' BACK--NOT AS LONG AS I CAN TURN THESE GAMMA-RAY MACHINES ON ME EVERY TWO DAYS!
IF ONLY THAT BULLET COULD BE REMOVED, THEN NOTHING COULD HURT YOU!
EAH, IF! AND IF I WASN'T THE HULK, MAYBE I'D BE ROCK HUDSON!
LISTEN! WHAT'S THAT OISE? ---CANNONFIRE!
THE PLANE'S MUSTA RADIOED YOUR LOCATION! MAYBE THEY RUSHED SOME ARTILLERY OUT HERE!
HARDLY HAVE THOSE WORDS LEFT RICK'S LIPS, THAN THE FIRST OF MANY BLAST CONCUSSIONS ROCKS THE UNDERGROUND LABYRINTH...
TAKE COVER! WE'RE UNDER ATTACK!
BUT...THEY MUSTN'T! IF THEY WRECK THE LAB, YOU'RE FINISHED!

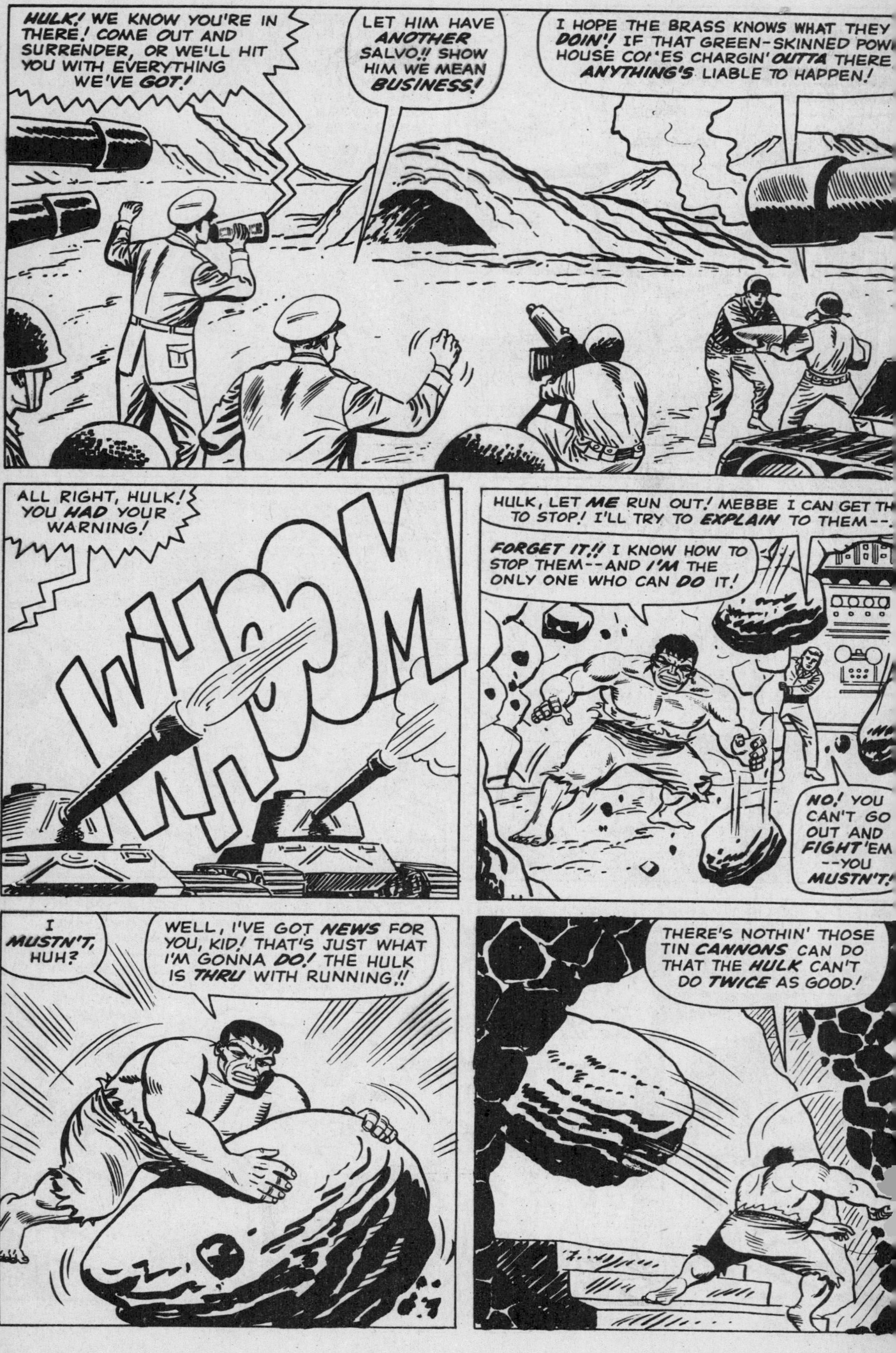
HULK! WE KNOW YOU'RE IN THERE! COME OUT AND SURRENDER, OR WE'LL HIT YOU WITH EVERYTHING WE'VE GOT!
LET HIM HAVE ANOTHER SALVO!! SHOW HIM WE MEAN BUSINESS!
I HOPE THE BRASS KNOWS WHAT THEY DOIN'! IF THAT GREEN-SKINNED POW HOUSE COMES CHARGIN' OUTTA THERE ANYTHING'S LIABLE TO HAPPEN!
ALL RIGHT, HULK! YOU HAD YOUR WARNING!
WHOOM
HULK, LET ME RUN OUT! MEBBE I CAN GET TH TO STOP! I'LL TRY TO EXPLAIN TO THEM--
FORGET IT!! I KNOW HOW TO STOP THEM--AND I'M THE ONLY ONE WHO CAN DO IT!
NO! YOU CAN'T GO OUT AND FIGHT 'EM --YOU MUSTN'T!
I MUSTN'T, HUH?
WELL, I'VE GOT NEWS FOR YOU, KID! THAT'S JUST WHAT I'M GONNA DO! THE HULK IS THRU WITH RUNNING!!
THERE'S NOTHIN' THOSE TIN CANNONS CAN DO THAT THE HULK CAN'T DO TWICE AS GOOD!

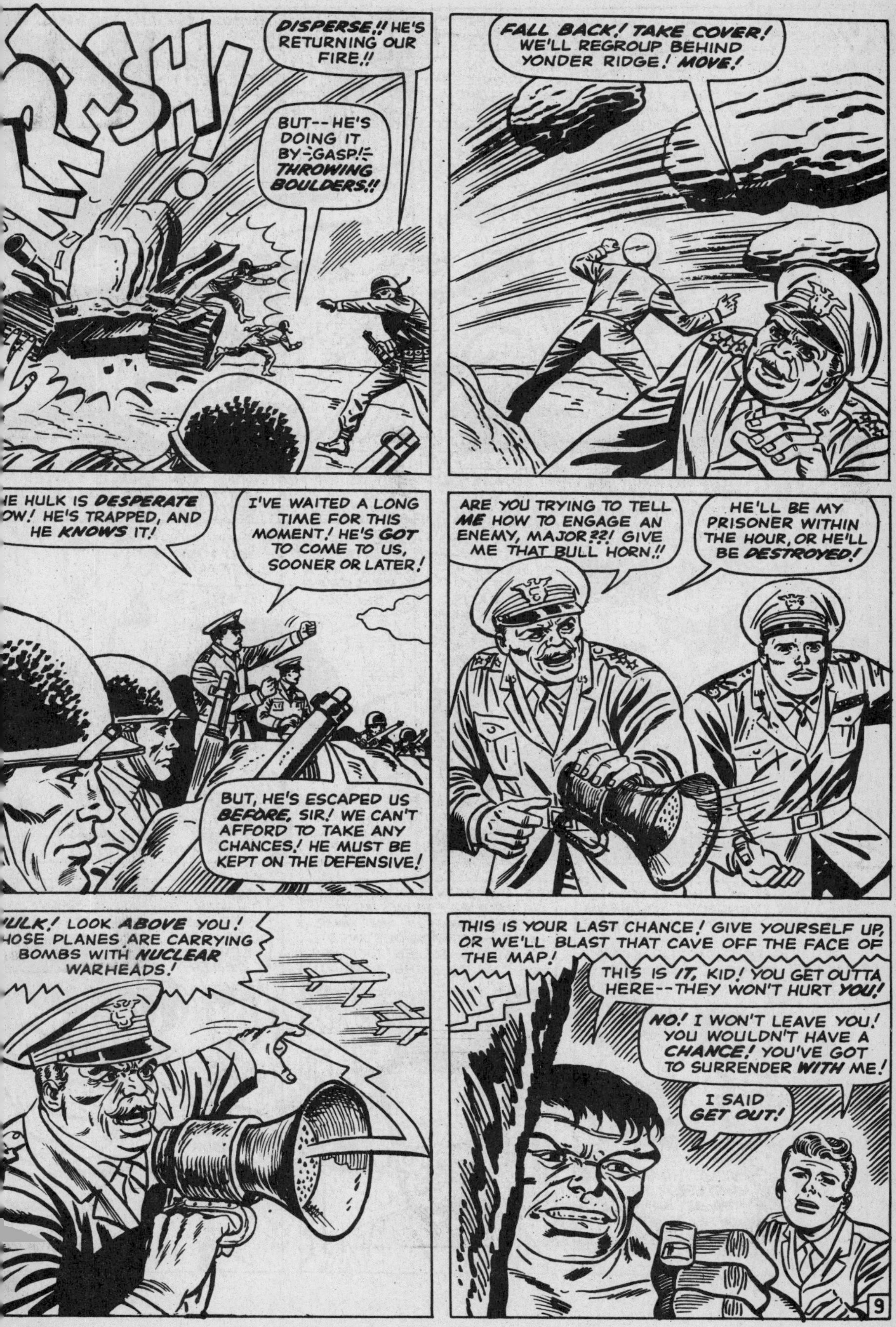
DISPERSE!! HE'S RETURNING OUR FIRE!!
BUT--HE'S DOING IT BY--GASP!--THROWING BOULDERS!!
FALL BACK! TAKE COVER! WE'LL REGROUP BEHIND YONDER RIDGE! MOVE!
HE HULK IS DESPERATE OW! HE'S TRAPPED, AND HE KNOWS IT!
I'VE WAITED A LONG TIME FOR THIS MOMENT! HE'S GOT TO COME TO US, SOONER OR LATER!
BUT, HE'S ESCAPED US BEFORE, SIR! WE CAN'T AFFORD TO TAKE ANY CHANCES! HE MUST BE KEPT ON THE DEFENSIVE!
ARE YOU TRYING TO TELL ME HOW TO ENGAGE AN ENEMY, MAJOR??! GIVE ME THAT BULL HORN!!
HE'LL BE MY PRISONER WITHIN THE HOUR, OR HE'LL BE DESTROYED!
ULK! LOOK ABOVE YOU! HOSE PLANES ARE CARRYING BOMBS WITH NUCLEAR WARHEADS!
THIS IS YOUR LAST CHANCE! GIVE YOURSELF UP, OR WE'LL BLAST THAT CAVE OFF THE FACE OF THE MAP!
THIS IS IT, KID! YOU GET OUTTA HERE--THEY WON'T HURT YOU!
NO! I WON'T LEAVE YOU! YOU WOULDN'T HAVE A CHANCE! YOU'VE GOT TO SURRENDER WITH ME!
I SAID GET OUT!

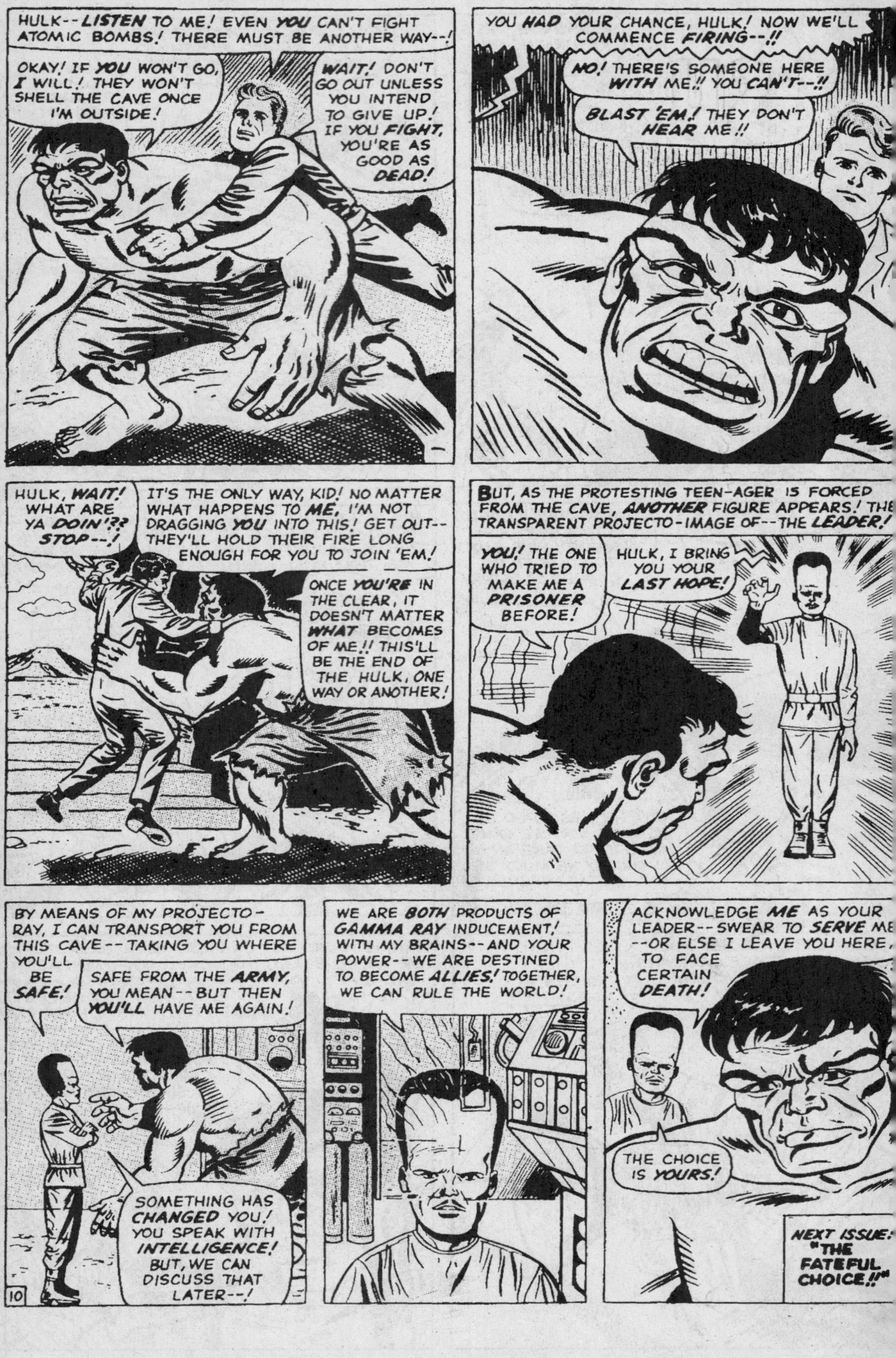
HULK--LISTEN TO ME! EVEN YOU CAN'T FIGHT ATOMIC BOMBS! THERE MUST BE ANOTHER WAY--!
OKAY! IF YOU WON'T GO, I WILL! THEY WON'T SHELL THE CAVE ONCE I'M OUTSIDE!
WAIT! DON'T GO OUT UNLESS YOU INTEND TO GIVE UP! IF YOU FIGHT, YOU'RE AS GOOD AS DEAD!
YOU HAD YOUR CHANCE, HULK! NOW WE'LL COMMENCE FIRING--!!
NO! THERE'S SOMEONE HERE WITH ME!! YOU CAN'T--!!
BLAST 'EM! THEY DON'T HEAR ME!!
HULK, WAIT! WHAT ARE YA DOIN'!?? STOP--!
IT'S THE ONLY WAY, KID! NO MATTER WHAT HAPPENS TO ME, I'M NOT DRAGGING YOU INTO THIS! GET OUT-- THEY'LL HOLD THEIR FIRE LONG ENOUGH FOR YOU TO JOIN 'EM!
ONCE YOU'RE IN THE CLEAR, IT DOESN'T MATTER WHAT BECOMES OF ME!! THIS'LL BE THE END OF THE HULK, ONE WAY OR ANOTHER!
BUT, AS THE PROTESTING TEEN-AGER IS FORCED FROM THE CAVE, ANOTHER FIGURE APPEARS! THE TRANSPARENT PROJECTO-IMAGE OF--THE LEADER!
YOU! THE ONE WHO TRIED TO MAKE ME A PRISONER BEFORE!
HULK, I BRING YOU YOUR LAST HOPE!
BY MEANS OF MY PROJECTO-RAY, I CAN TRANSPORT YOU FROM THIS CAVE--TAKING YOU WHERE YOU'LL BE SAFE!
SAFE FROM THE ARMY, YOU MEAN--BUT THEN YOU'LL HAVE ME AGAIN!
SOMETHING HAS CHANGED YOU! YOU SPEAK WITH INTELLIGENCE! BUT, WE CAN DISCUSS THAT LATER--!
10
WE ARE BOTH PRODUCTS OF GAMMA RAY INDUCEMENT! WITH MY BRAINS--AND YOUR POWER--WE ARE DESTINED TO BECOME ALLIES! TOGETHER, WE CAN RULE THE WORLD!
ACKNOWLEDGE ME AS YOUR LEADER--SWEAR TO SERVE ME --OR ELSE I LEAVE YOU HERE, TO FACE CERTAIN DEATH!
THE CHOICE IS YOURS!
NEXT ISSUE: "THE FATEFUL CHOICE!!"

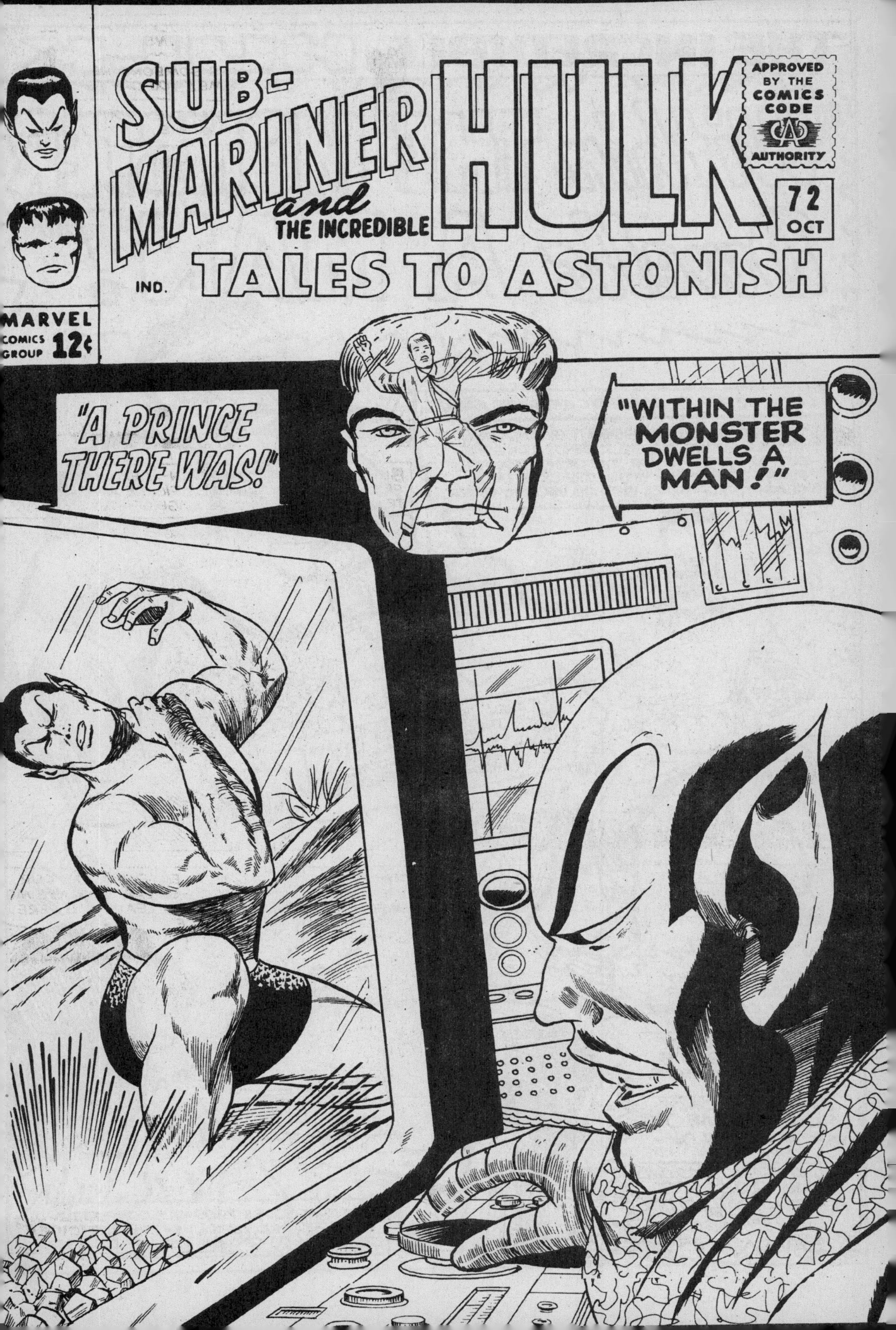
SUB-MARINER
and
THE INCREDIBLE
HULK
APPROVED BY THE COMICS CODE AUTHORITY
72
OCT
IND.
TALES TO ASTONISH
MARVEL COMICS GROUP 12¢
"A PRINCE THERE WAS!"
"WITHIN THE MONSTER DWELLS A MAN!"

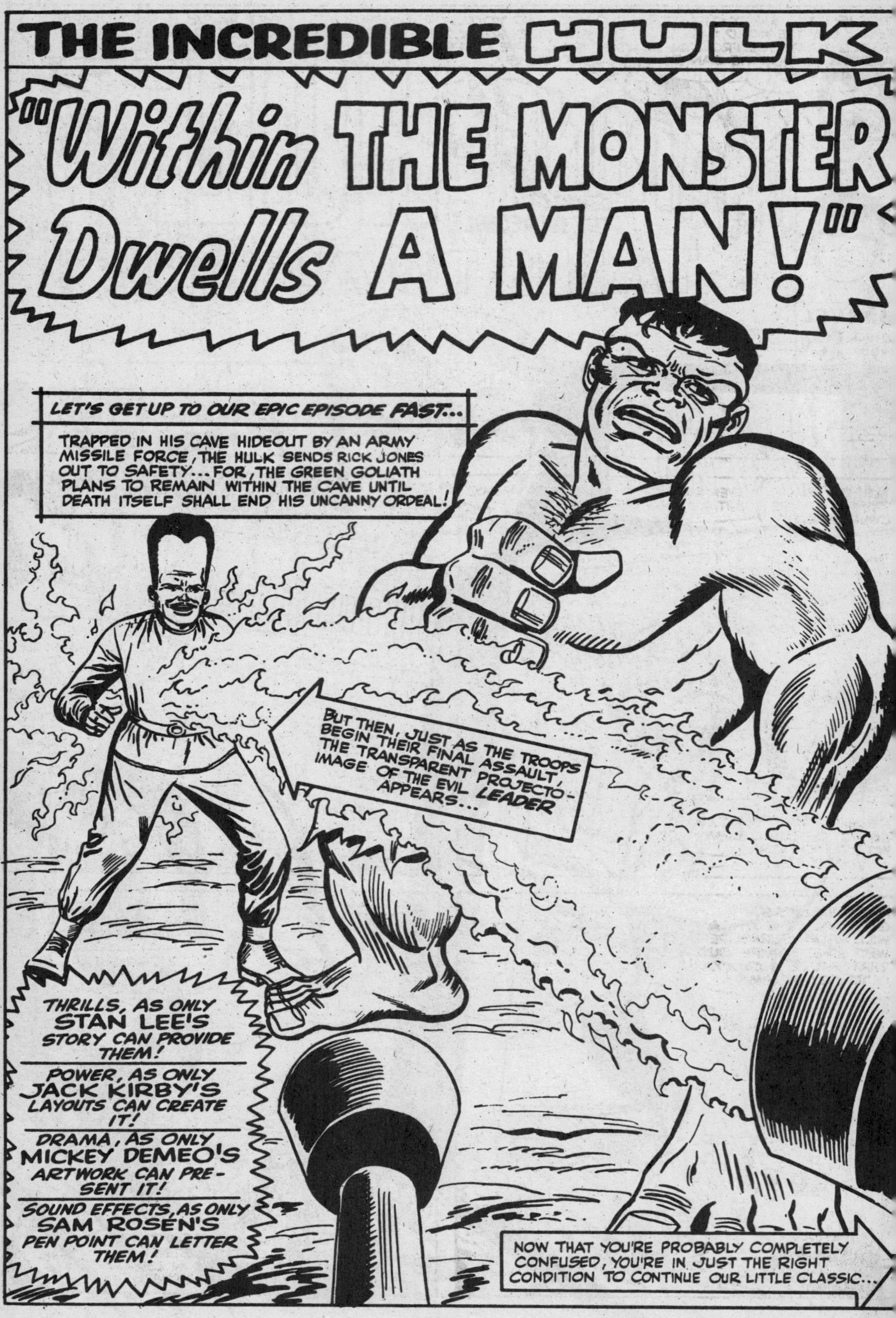
THE INCREDIBLE HULK
"Within THE MONSTER Dwells A MAN!"
LET'S GET UP TO OUR EPIC EPISODE FAST...
TRAPPED IN HIS CAVE HIDEOUT BY AN ARMY MISSILE FORCE, THE HULK SENDS RICK JONES OUT TO SAFETY... FOR, THE GREEN GOLIATH PLANS TO REMAIN WITHIN THE CAVE UNTIL DEATH ITSELF SHALL END HIS UNCANNY ORDEAL!
BUT THEN, JUST AS THE TROOPS BEGIN THEIR FINAL ASSAULT, THE TRANSPARENT PROJECTO-IMAGE OF THE EVIL LEADER APPEARS...
THRILLS, AS ONLY STAN LEE'S STORY CAN PROVIDE THEM!
POWER, AS ONLY JACK KIRBY'S LAYOUTS CAN CREATE IT!
DRAMA, AS ONLY MICKEY DEMEO'S ARTWORK CAN PRE-SENT IT!
SOUND EFFECTS, AS ONLY SAM ROSEN'S PEN POINT CAN LETTER THEM!
NOW THAT YOU'RE PROBABLY COMPLETELY CONFUSED, YOU'RE IN JUST THE RIGHT CONDITION TO CONTINUE OUR LITTLE CLASSIC...

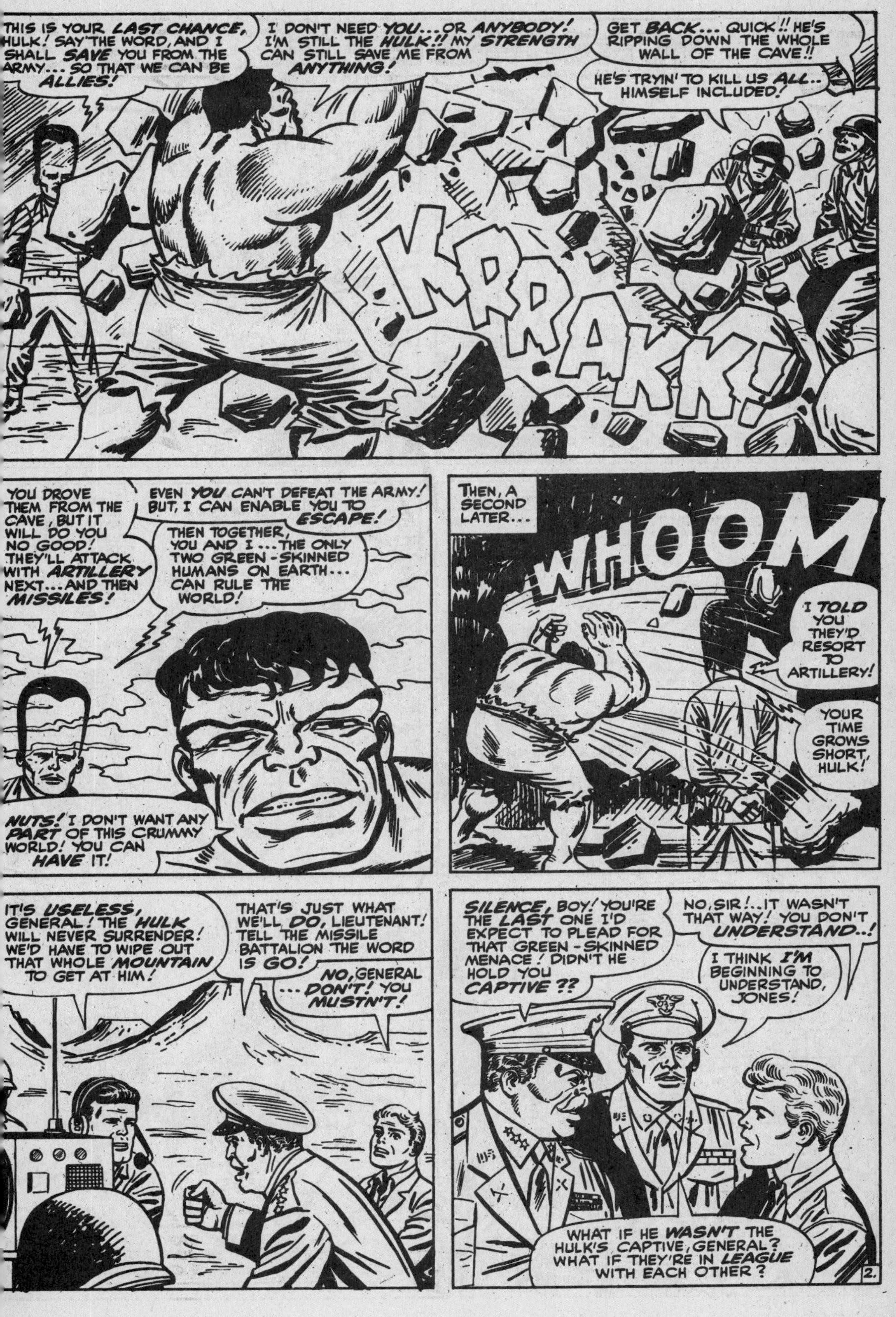
THIS IS YOUR LAST CHANCE, HULK! SAY THE WORD, AND I SHALL SAVE YOU FROM THE ARMY... SO THAT WE CAN BE ALLIES!
I DON'T NEED YOU... OR ANYBODY! I'M STILL THE HULK!! MY STRENGTH CAN STILL SAVE ME FROM ANYTHING!
GET BACK... QUICK!! HE'S RIPPING DOWN THE WHOLE WALL OF THE CAVE!!
HE'S TRYIN' TO KILL US ALL.. HIMSELF INCLUDED!
KRRAKK!
YOU DROVE THEM FROM THE CAVE, BUT IT WILL DO YOU NO GOOD! THEY'LL ATTACK WITH ARTILLERY NEXT... AND THEN MISSILES!
EVEN YOU CAN'T DEFEAT THE ARMY! BUT, I CAN ENABLE YOU TO ESCAPE!
THEN TOGETHER, YOU AND I... THE ONLY TWO GREEN-SKINNED HUMANS ON EARTH... CAN RULE THE WORLD!
NUTS! I DON'T WANT ANY PART OF THIS CRUMMY WORLD! YOU CAN HAVE IT!
THEN, A SECOND LATER...
WHOOM
I TOLD YOU THEY'D RESORT TO ARTILLERY!
YOUR TIME GROWS SHORT, HULK!
IT'S USELESS, GENERAL! THE HULK WILL NEVER SURRENDER! WE'D HAVE TO WIPE OUT THAT WHOLE MOUNTAIN TO GET AT HIM!
THAT'S JUST WHAT WE'LL DO, LIEUTENANT! TELL THE MISSILE BATTALION THE WORD IS GO!
NO, GENERAL ... DON'T! YOU MUSTN'T!
SILENCE, BOY! YOU'RE THE LAST ONE I'D EXPECT TO PLEAD FOR THAT GREEN-SKINNED MENACE! DIDN'T HE HOLD YOU CAPTIVE ??
NO, SIR!... IT WASN'T THAT WAY! YOU DON'T UNDERSTAND..!
I THINK I'M BEGINNING TO UNDERSTAND, JONES!
WHAT IF HE WASN'T THE HULK'S CAPTIVE, GENERAL? WHAT IF THEY'RE IN LEAGUE WITH EACH OTHER?
2.

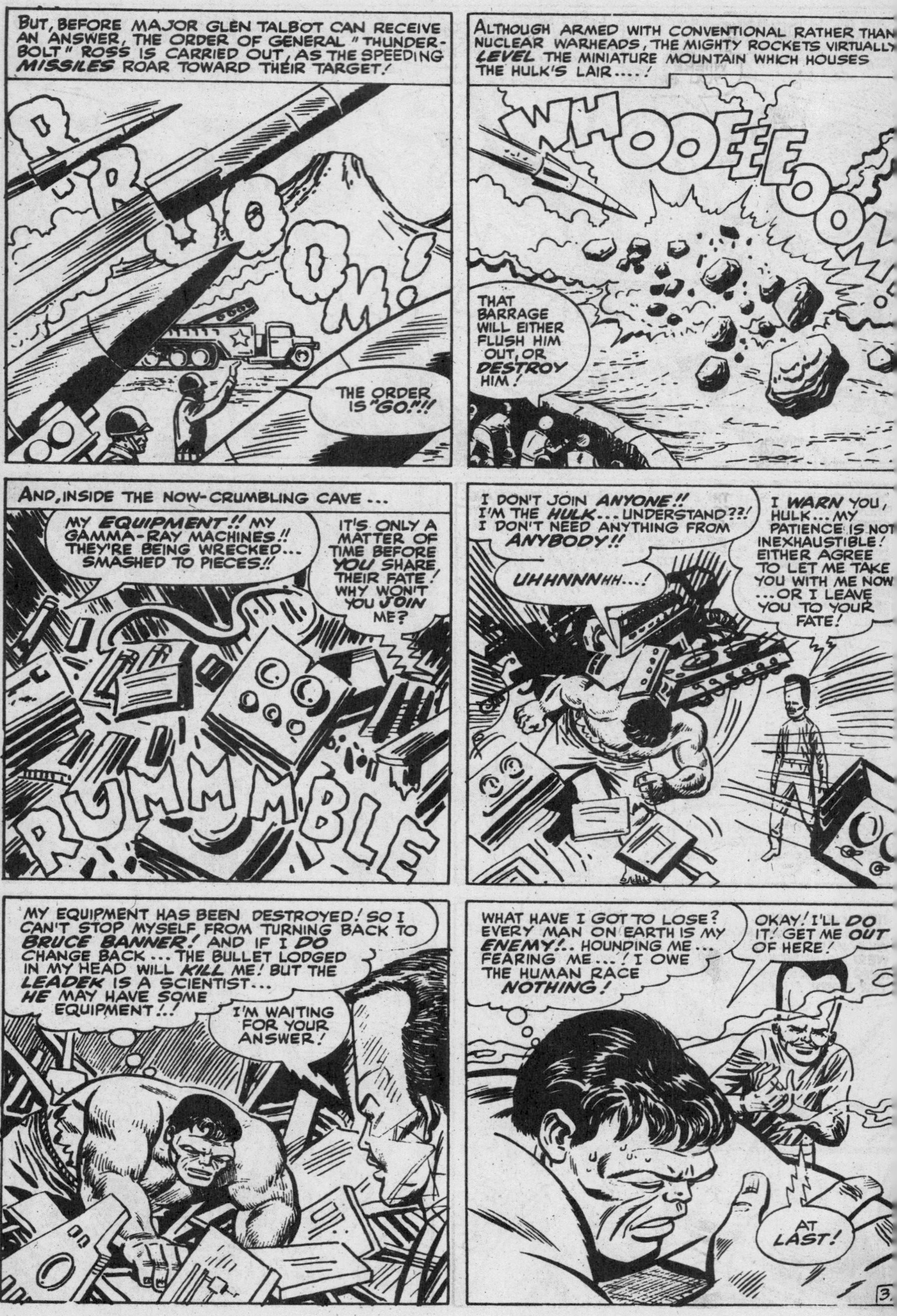

BUT, BEFORE MAJOR GLEN TALBOT CAN RECEIVE AN ANSWER, THE ORDER OF GENERAL "THUNDER-BOLT" ROSS IS CARRIED OUT, AS THE SPEEDING MISSILES ROAR TOWARD THEIR TARGET!
BRROOOM!
THE ORDER IS "GO!"!!
ALTHOUGH ARMED WITH CONVENTIONAL RATHER THAN NUCLEAR WARHEADS, THE MIGHTY ROCKETS VIRTUALLY LEVEL THE MINIATURE MOUNTAIN WHICH HOUSES THE HULK'S LAIR....!
WHOOEEEOOM!
THAT BARRAGE WILL EITHER FLUSH HIM OUT, OR DESTROY HIM!
AND, INSIDE THE NOW-CRUMBLING CAVE ...
MY EQUIPMENT!! MY GAMMA-RAY MACHINES!! THEY'RE BEING WRECKED... SMASHED TO PIECES!!
IT'S ONLY A MATTER OF TIME BEFORE YOU SHARE THEIR FATE! WHY WON'T YOU JOIN ME?
RUMMMBLE
I DON'T JOIN ANYONE!! I'M THE HULK... UNDERSTAND??! I DON'T NEED ANYTHING FROM ANYBODY!!
I WARN YOU, HULK... MY PATIENCE IS NOT INEXHAUSTIBLE! EITHER AGREE TO LET ME TAKE YOU WITH ME NOW ...OR I LEAVE YOU TO YOUR FATE!
UHHNNNHH...!
MY EQUIPMENT HAS BEEN DESTROYED! SO I CAN'T STOP MYSELF FROM TURNING BACK TO BRUCE BANNER! AND IF I DO CHANGE BACK ... THE BULLET LODGED IN MY HEAD WILL KILL ME! BUT THE LEADER IS A SCIENTIST... HE MAY HAVE SOME EQUIPMENT!..!
I'M WAITING FOR YOUR ANSWER!
WHAT HAVE I GOT TO LOSE? EVERY MAN ON EARTH IS MY ENEMY!.. HOUNDING ME... FEARING ME...! I OWE THE HUMAN RACE NOTHING!
OKAY! I'LL DO IT! GET ME OUT OF HERE!
AT LAST!
3

HIS IMAGE *VANISHED!* IT JUST FADED AWAY!

HEY! WHERE DID YOU *GO* ??

SUDDENLY, THE FIGURE THAT HAD BEEN THE *HULK,* JUST A MICRO-SECOND BEFORE, IS TRANSFORMED INTO FLOWING *ELECTRO-WAVES...!*

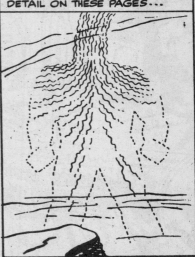

THE SCIENTIFIC PRINCIPLE INVOLVED IN WHAT YOU ARE SEEING IS TOO COMPLICATED TO EXPLAIN IN DETAIL ON THESE PAGES...

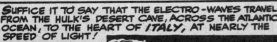

SUFFICE IT TO SAY THAT THE ELECTRO-WAVES TRAVEL FROM THE HULK'S DESERT CAVE, ACROSS THE ATLANTIC OCEAN, TO THE HEART OF *ITALY,* AT NEARLY THE SPEED OF LIGHT!

THERE IS NO CAUSE FOR ALARM, HULK! THIS METHOD, WHICH I CALL *MATTER-PORTATION,* IS AS HARMLESS AS IT IS SPECTACULAR!

HEY...WHEN YOU CALLED YOURSELF A *GENIUS,* YOU WEREN'T JUST WHISTLIN' IN THE DARK!

NATURALLY! THE GAMMA-RAY EXPLOSION WHICH TURNED MY SKIN THE COLOR OF *YOURS,* GAVE ME THE STRONGEST BRAIN ON EARTH!

JUST AS A *SIMILAR* GAMMA-RAY ACCIDENT MUST HAVE GIVEN *YOU* THE STRONGEST *BODY* ON EARTH!

BUT, IN THE CAVE YOU SAID THE SHELLS WERE DESTROYING *YOUR* EQUIPMENT! SURELY A BRUTE LIKE *YOU* CAN HAVE NO KNOWLEDGE OF SCIENCE!

I WAS *CARELESS!* GOTTA *WATCH* MYSELF!

SKIP THAT! FIRST TELL ME WHERE I AM....AND WHY I'M *HERE?*

4.

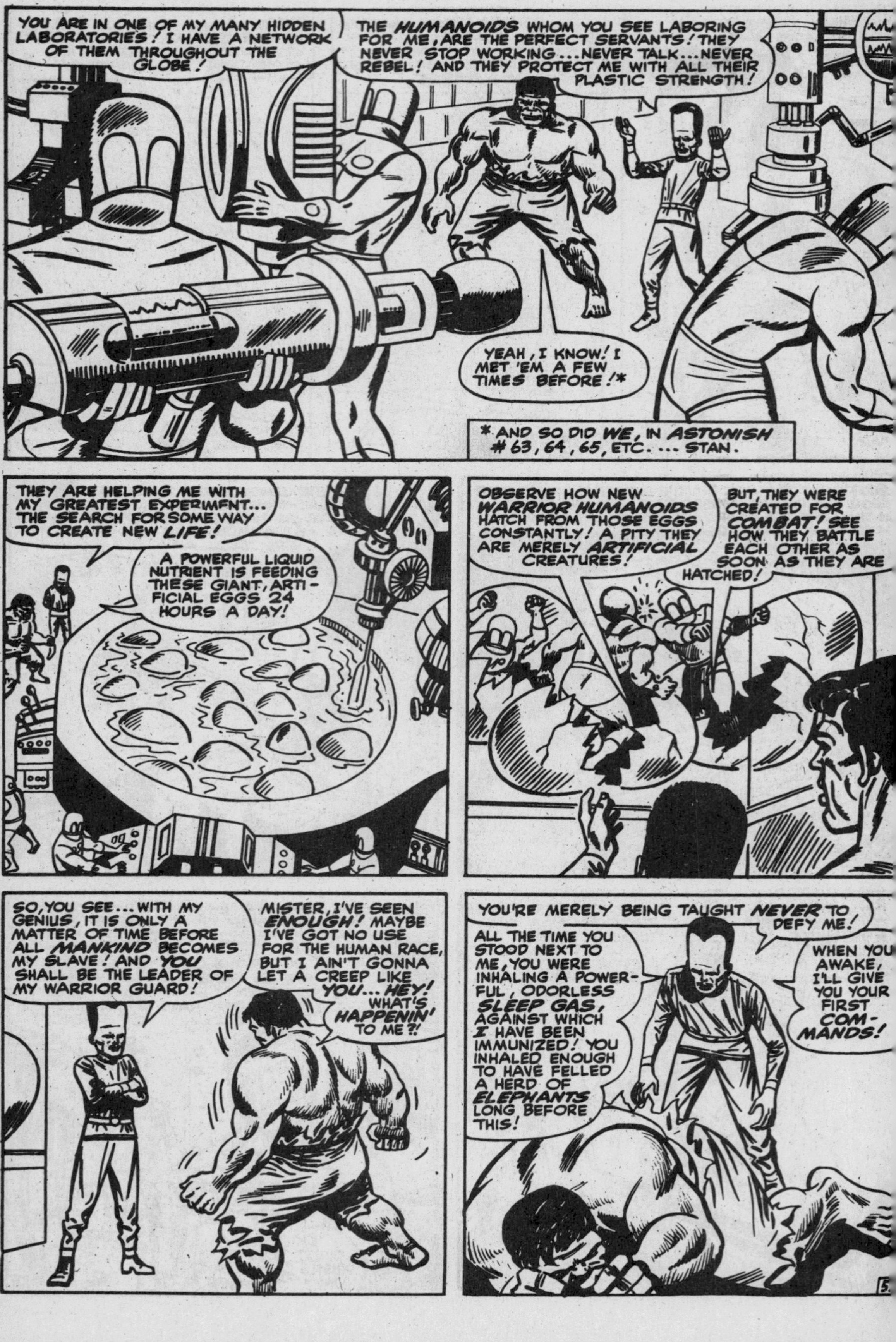
YOU ARE IN ONE OF MY MANY HIDDEN LABORATORIES! I HAVE A NETWORK OF THEM THROUGHOUT THE GLOBE!
THE HUMANOIDS WHOM YOU SEE LABORING FOR ME, ARE THE PERFECT SERVANTS! THEY NEVER STOP WORKING... NEVER TALK... NEVER REBEL! AND THEY PROTECT ME WITH ALL THEIR PLASTIC STRENGTH!
YEAH, I KNOW! I MET 'EM A FEW TIMES BEFORE!*
*AND SO DID WE, IN ASTONISH #63, 64, 65, ETC. ... STAN.
THEY ARE HELPING ME WITH MY GREATEST EXPERIMENT... THE SEARCH FOR SOME WAY TO CREATE NEW LIFE!
A POWERFUL LIQUID NUTRIENT IS FEEDING THESE GIANT, ARTI-FICIAL EGGS 24 HOURS A DAY!
OBSERVE HOW NEW WARRIOR HUMANOIDS HATCH FROM THOSE EGGS CONSTANTLY! A PITY THEY ARE MERELY ARTIFICIAL CREATURES!
BUT, THEY WERE CREATED FOR COMBAT! SEE HOW THEY BATTLE EACH OTHER AS SOON AS THEY ARE HATCHED!
SO, YOU SEE... WITH MY GENIUS, IT IS ONLY A MATTER OF TIME BEFORE ALL MANKIND BECOMES MY SLAVE! AND YOU SHALL BE THE LEADER OF MY WARRIOR GUARD!
MISTER, I'VE SEEN ENOUGH! MAYBE I'VE GOT NO USE FOR THE HUMAN RACE, BUT I AIN'T GONNA LET A CREEP LIKE YOU... HEY! WHAT'S HAPPENIN' TO ME?!
YOU'RE MERELY BEING TAUGHT NEVER TO DEFY ME!
ALL THE TIME YOU STOOD NEXT TO ME, YOU WERE INHALING A POWER-FUL, ODORLESS SLEEP GAS, AGAINST WHICH I HAVE BEEN IMMUNIZED! YOU INHALED ENOUGH TO HAVE FELLED A HERD OF ELEPHANTS LONG BEFORE THIS!
WHEN YOU AWAKE, I'LL GIVE YOU YOUR FIRST COM-MANDS!
5

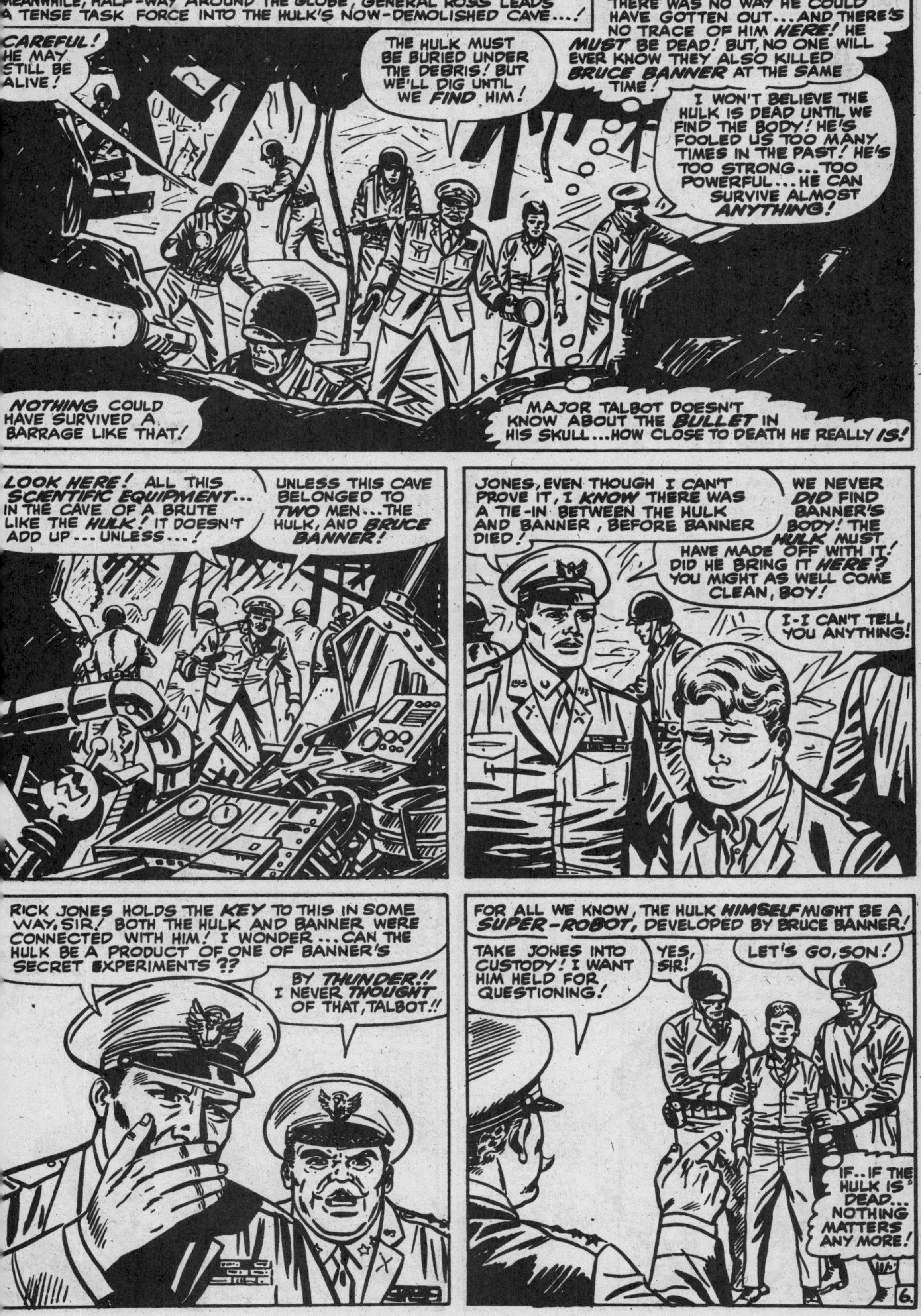
MEANWHILE, HALF-WAY AROUND THE GLOBE, GENERAL ROSS LEADS A TENSE TASK FORCE INTO THE HULK'S NOW-DEMOLISHED CAVE...!
CAREFUL! HE MAY STILL BE ALIVE!
THE HULK MUST BE BURIED UNDER THE DEBRIS! BUT WE'LL DIG UNTIL WE FIND HIM!
THERE WAS NO WAY HE COULD HAVE GOTTEN OUT...AND THERE'S NO TRACE OF HIM HERE! HE MUST BE DEAD! BUT, NO ONE WILL EVER KNOW THEY ALSO KILLED BRUCE BANNER AT THE SAME TIME!
I WON'T BELIEVE THE HULK IS DEAD UNTIL WE FIND THE BODY! HE'S FOOLED US TOO MANY TIMES IN THE PAST! HE'S TOO STRONG...TOO POWERFUL...HE CAN SURVIVE ALMOST ANYTHING!
NOTHING COULD HAVE SURVIVED A BARRAGE LIKE THAT!
MAJOR TALBOT DOESN'T KNOW ABOUT THE BULLET IN HIS SKULL...HOW CLOSE TO DEATH HE REALLY IS!
LOOK HERE! ALL THIS SCIENTIFIC EQUIPMENT... IN THE CAVE OF A BRUTE LIKE THE HULK! IT DOESN'T ADD UP...UNLESS...!
UNLESS THIS CAVE BELONGED TO TWO MEN...THE HULK, AND BRUCE BANNER!
JONES, EVEN THOUGH I CAN'T PROVE IT, I KNOW THERE WAS A TIE-IN BETWEEN THE HULK AND BANNER, BEFORE BANNER DIED!
WE NEVER DID FIND BANNER'S BODY! THE HULK MUST HAVE MADE OFF WITH IT! DID HE BRING IT HERE? YOU MIGHT AS WELL COME CLEAN, BOY!
I-I CAN'T TELL YOU ANYTHING!
RICK JONES HOLDS THE KEY TO THIS IN SOME WAY, SIR! BOTH THE HULK AND BANNER WERE CONNECTED WITH HIM! I WONDER...CAN THE HULK BE A PRODUCT OF ONE OF BANNER'S SECRET EXPERIMENTS ??
BY THUNDER!! I NEVER THOUGHT OF THAT, TALBOT!!
FOR ALL WE KNOW, THE HULK HIMSELF MIGHT BE A SUPER-ROBOT, DEVELOPED BY BRUCE BANNER!
TAKE JONES INTO CUSTODY! I WANT HIM HELD FOR QUESTIONING!
YES, SIR!
LET'S GO, SON!
IF..IF THE HULK IS DEAD... NOTHING MATTERS ANY MORE!
6.

AND, IN A VERY SPECIAL BUILDING, ON THE OUTSKIRTS OF ROME...

HERE, IN THE ETERNAL CITY, I HAVE FOUND THE PERFECT HIDEOUT!

TO THE UNSUSPECTING THRONGS PASSING BELOW, THIS IS AN INNOCENT-LOOKING BUILDING WHICH HOUSES AN EXPENSIVE ART GALLERY!

YET, HOW LITTLE THEY KNOW OF THE REAL TREASURES WHICH ARE LOCKED WITHIN THESE SILENT HALLS!

BUT, IT IS TIME FOR ME TO CHECK ON THE HULK AGAIN! I MUST FIND A WAY TO BRING HIM COMPLETELY UNDER MY CONTROL!

THERE IS STILL MUCH ABOUT HIM THAT PUZZLES ME! HIS INTELLIGENCE SEEMS TO HAVE INCREASED SINCE FIRST I SAW HIM! I MUST LEARN WHY!

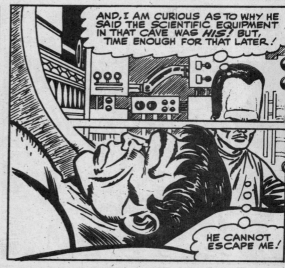

AND, I AM CURIOUS AS TO WHY HE SAID THE SCIENTIFIC EQUIPMENT IN THAT CAVE WAS HIS! BUT, TIME ENOUGH FOR THAT LATER!

HE CANNOT ESCAPE ME!

THEN, JUST AS THE LEADER TURNS AND EXITS FROM THE ROOM...

HE WILL SLEEP FOR AT LEAST TWO HOURS LONGER! NO HUMAN BODY COULD THROW OFF THE EFFECTS OF SO MUCH SLEEP GAS IN LESS TIME!

BUT, EVEN HIS BRILLIANT CAPTOR CANNOT GUESS HOW POWERFUL THE HULK'S BODY REALLY IS... AS HE STIRS... AND AWAKES...!

HOWEVER, THE SLEEP GAS, WHICH HIS TITANIC LUNGS SHRUGGED OFF IN RECORD TIME, HAD AN UNEXPECTED EFFECT ON THE GREEN GOLIATH... ONE WHICH COULD PROVE FATAL...!

THE GAS SET OFF A REACTION! MY BODY CHEMISTRY IS CHANGING... CHANGING BACK TO BRUCE BANNER!!

7.

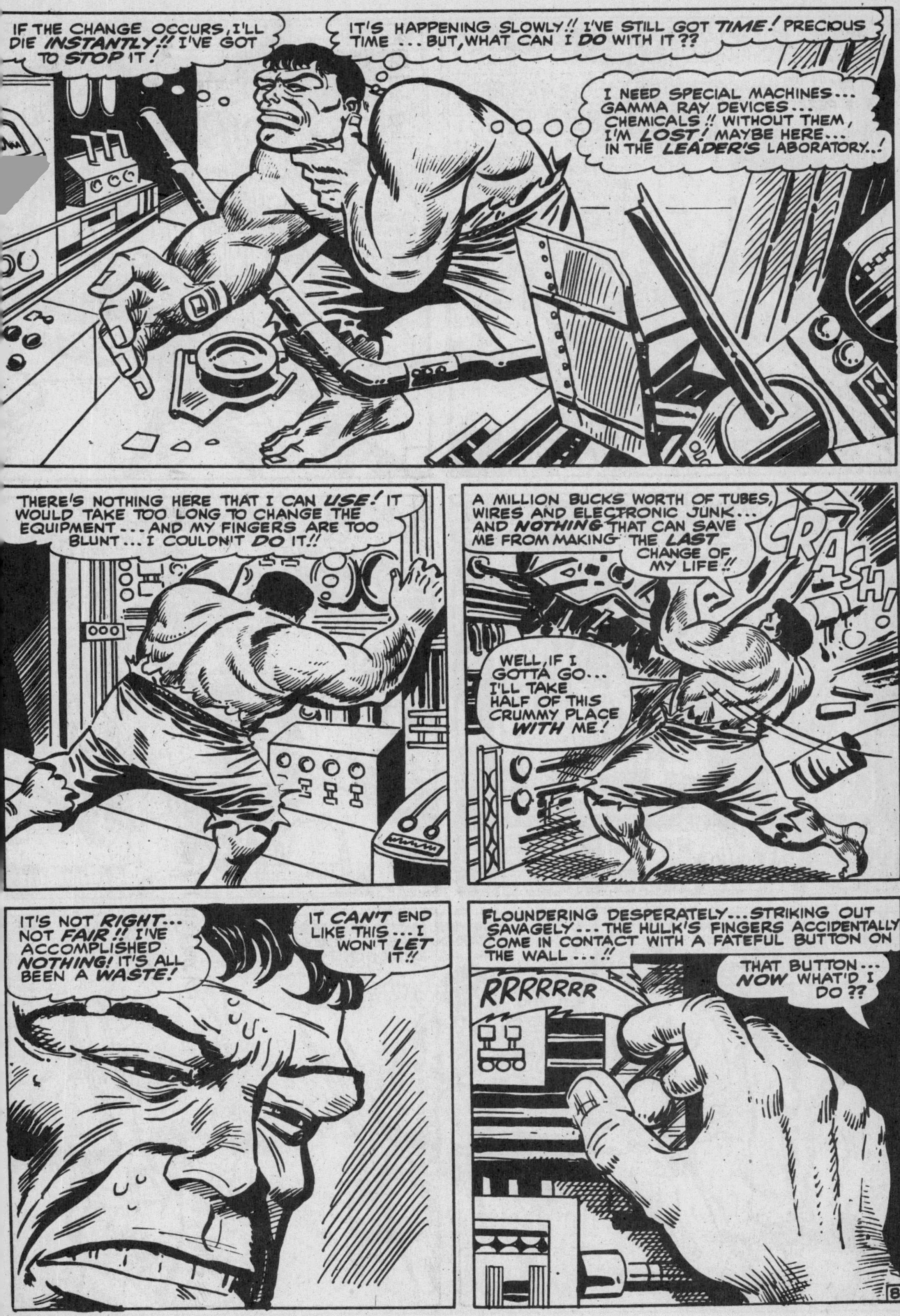
IF THE CHANGE OCCURS, I'LL DIE INSTANTLY!! I'VE GOT TO STOP IT!
IT'S HAPPENING SLOWLY!! I'VE STILL GOT TIME! PRECIOUS TIME ... BUT, WHAT CAN I DO WITH IT??
I NEED SPECIAL MACHINES... GAMMA RAY DEVICES... CHEMICALS!! WITHOUT THEM, I'M LOST! MAYBE HERE... IN THE LEADER'S LABORATORY..!
THERE'S NOTHING HERE THAT I CAN USE! IT WOULD TAKE TOO LONG TO CHANGE THE EQUIPMENT--- AND MY FINGERS ARE TOO BLUNT ... I COULDN'T DO IT!!
A MILLION BUCKS WORTH OF TUBES, WIRES AND ELECTRONIC JUNK... AND NOTHING THAT CAN SAVE ME FROM MAKING THE LAST CHANGE OF MY LIFE!!
CRASH!
WELL, IF I GOTTA GO... I'LL TAKE HALF OF THIS CRUMMY PLACE WITH ME!
IT'S NOT RIGHT... NOT FAIR!! I'VE ACCOMPLISHED NOTHING! IT'S ALL BEEN A WASTE!
IT CAN'T END LIKE THIS ... I WON'T LET IT!!
FLOUNDERING DESPERATELY... STRIKING OUT SAVAGELY --- THE HULK'S FINGERS ACCIDENTALLY COME IN CONTACT WITH A FATEFUL BUTTON ON THE WALL ... !!
RRRRRRR
THAT BUTTON... NOW WHAT'D I DO??
8.

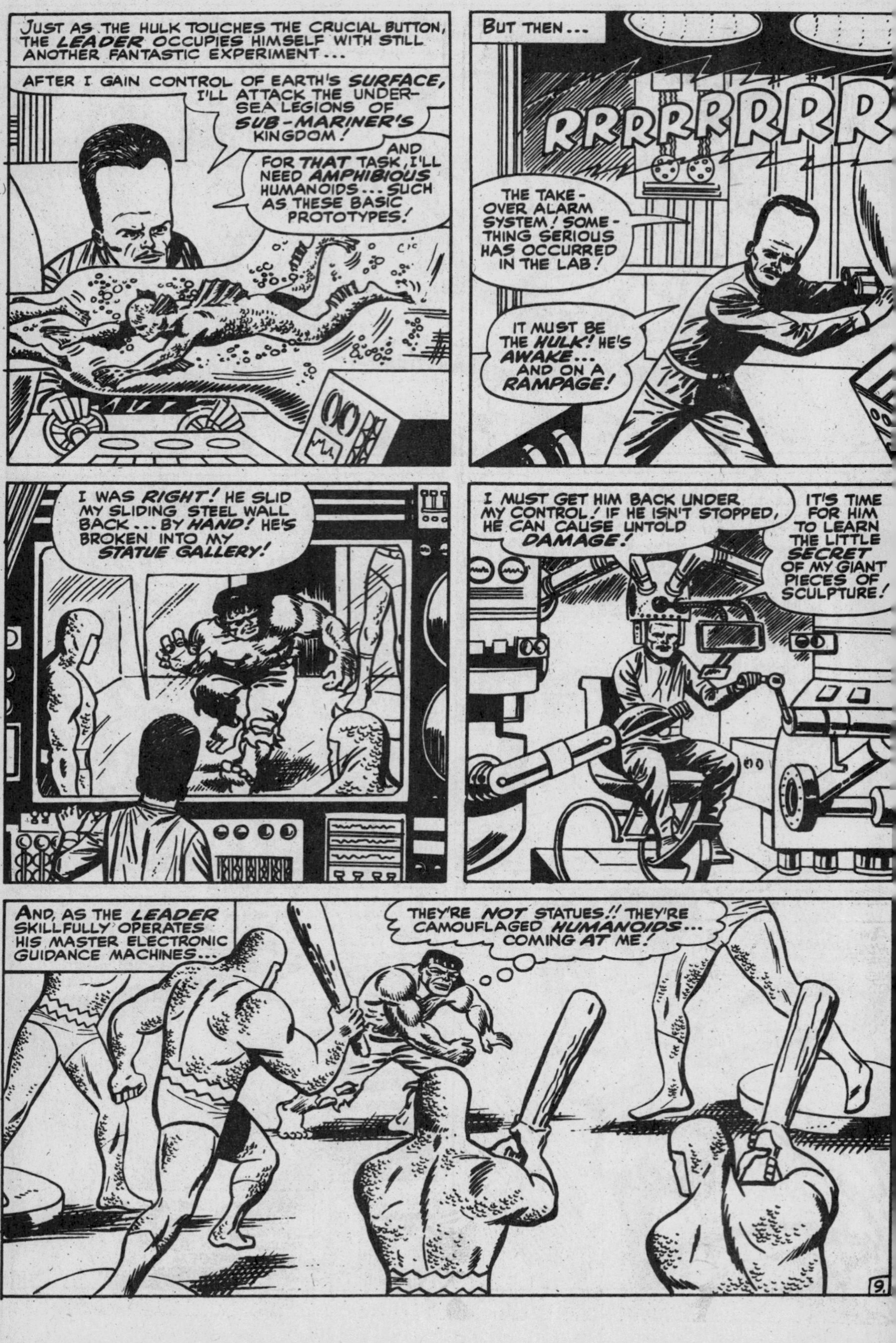
JUST AS THE HULK TOUCHES THE CRUCIAL BUTTON, THE LEADER OCCUPIES HIMSELF WITH STILL ANOTHER FANTASTIC EXPERIMENT...
AFTER I GAIN CONTROL OF EARTH'S SURFACE, I'LL ATTACK THE UNDER-SEA LEGIONS OF SUB-MARINER'S KINGDOM!
AND FOR THAT TASK, I'LL NEED AMPHIBIOUS HUMANOIDS... SUCH AS THESE BASIC PROTOTYPES!
BUT THEN...
RRRRRRRR
THE TAKE-OVER ALARM SYSTEM! SOMETHING SERIOUS HAS OCCURRED IN THE LAB!
IT MUST BE THE HULK! HE'S AWAKE... AND ON A RAMPAGE!
I WAS RIGHT! HE SLID MY SLIDING STEEL WALL BACK... BY HAND! HE'S BROKEN INTO MY STATUE GALLERY!
I MUST GET HIM BACK UNDER MY CONTROL! IF HE ISN'T STOPPED, HE CAN CAUSE UNTOLD DAMAGE!
IT'S TIME FOR HIM TO LEARN THE LITTLE SECRET OF MY GIANT PIECES OF SCULPTURE!
AND, AS THE LEADER SKILLFULLY OPERATES HIS MASTER ELECTRONIC GUIDANCE MACHINES...
THEY'RE NOT STATUES!! THEY'RE CAMOUFLAGED HUMANOIDS... COMING AT ME!
9

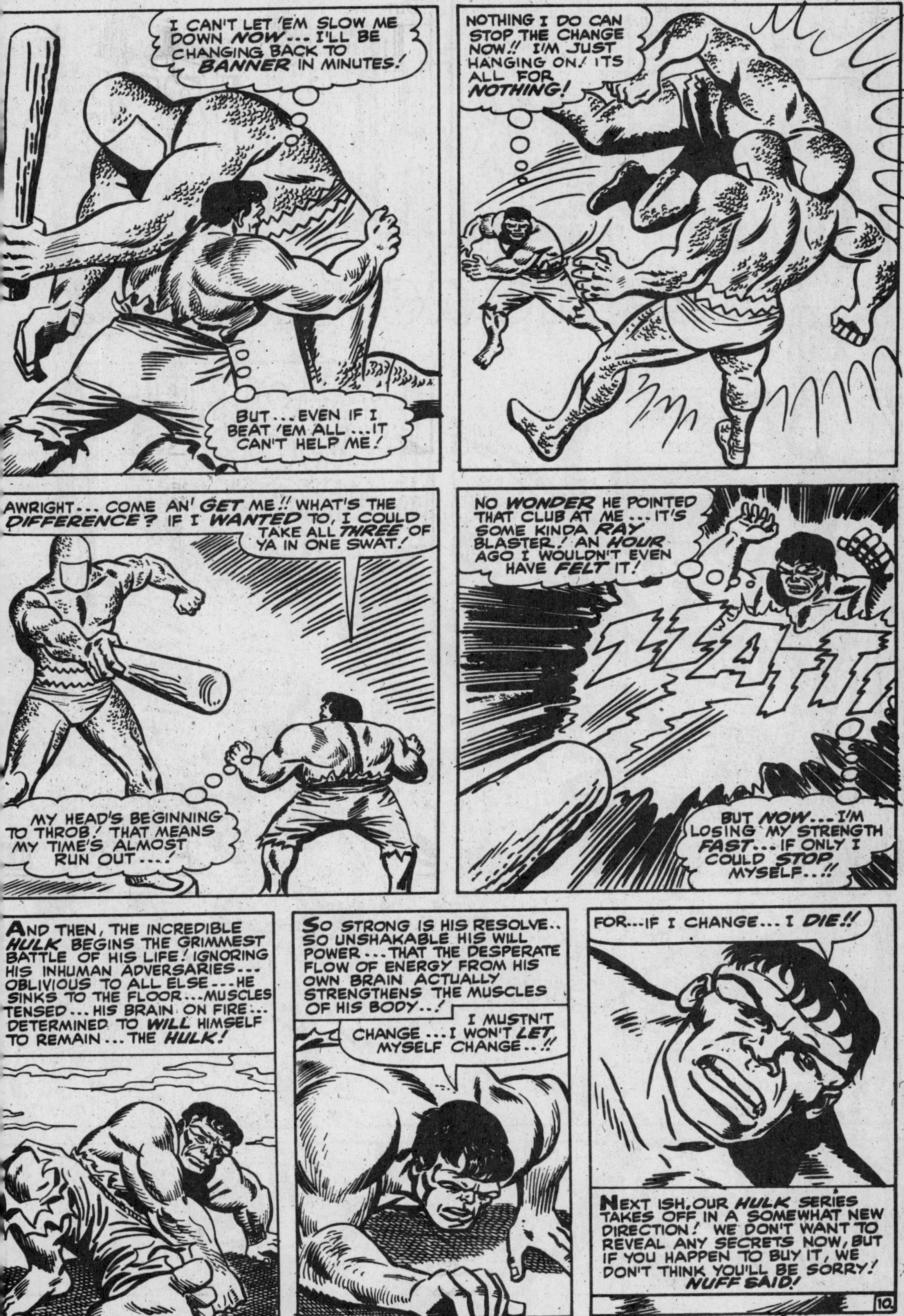
I CAN'T LET 'EM SLOW ME DOWN NOW... I'LL BE CHANGING BACK TO BANNER IN MINUTES!
BUT... EVEN IF I BEAT 'EM ALL... IT CAN'T HELP ME!
NOTHING I DO CAN STOP THE CHANGE NOW!! I'M JUST HANGING ON! ITS ALL FOR NOTHING!
AWRIGHT... COME AN' GET ME!! WHAT'S THE DIFFERENCE? IF I WANTED TO, I COULD TAKE ALL THREE OF YA IN ONE SWAT!
MY HEAD'S BEGINNING TO THROB! THAT MEANS MY TIME'S ALMOST RUN OUT...!
NO WONDER HE POINTED THAT CLUB AT ME... IT'S SOME KINDA RAY BLASTER! AN HOUR AGO I WOULDN'T EVEN HAVE FELT IT!
ZZAT
BUT NOW... I'M LOSING MY STRENGTH FAST... IF ONLY I COULD STOP MYSELF..!!
AND THEN, THE INCREDIBLE HULK BEGINS THE GRIMMEST BATTLE OF HIS LIFE! IGNORING HIS INHUMAN ADVERSARIES... OBLIVIOUS TO ALL ELSE... HE SINKS TO THE FLOOR... MUSCLES TENSED... HIS BRAIN ON FIRE... DETERMINED TO WILL HIMSELF TO REMAIN... THE HULK!
SO STRONG IS HIS RESOLVE.. SO UNSHAKABLE HIS WILL POWER... THAT THE DESPERATE FLOW OF ENERGY FROM HIS OWN BRAIN ACTUALLY STRENGTHENS THE MUSCLES OF HIS BODY..!
I MUSTN'T CHANGE... I WON'T LET MYSELF CHANGE..!!
FOR... IF I CHANGE... I DIE!!
NEXT ISH, OUR HULK SERIES TAKES OFF IN A SOMEWHAT NEW DIRECTION! WE DON'T WANT TO REVEAL ANY SECRETS NOW, BUT IF YOU HAPPEN TO BUY IT, WE DON'T THINK YOU'LL BE SORRY! NUFF SAID!
10.

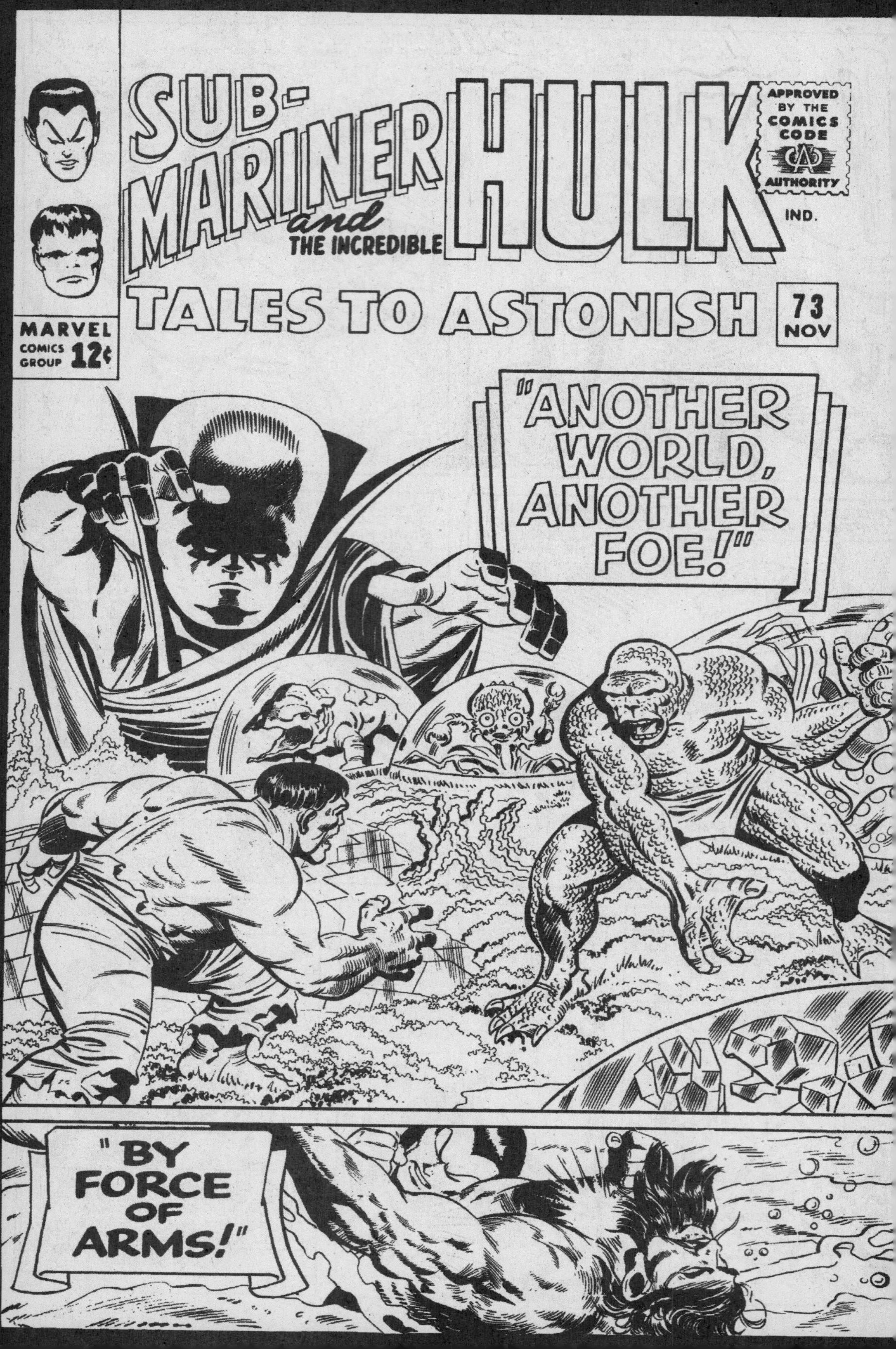

SUB-MARINER and THE INCREDIBLE HULK
APPROVED BY THE COMICS CODE AUTHORITY
IND.
TALES TO ASTONISH
73 NOV
MARVEL COMICS GROUP 12¢
"ANOTHER WORLD, ANOTHER FOE!"
"BY FORCE OF ARMS!"

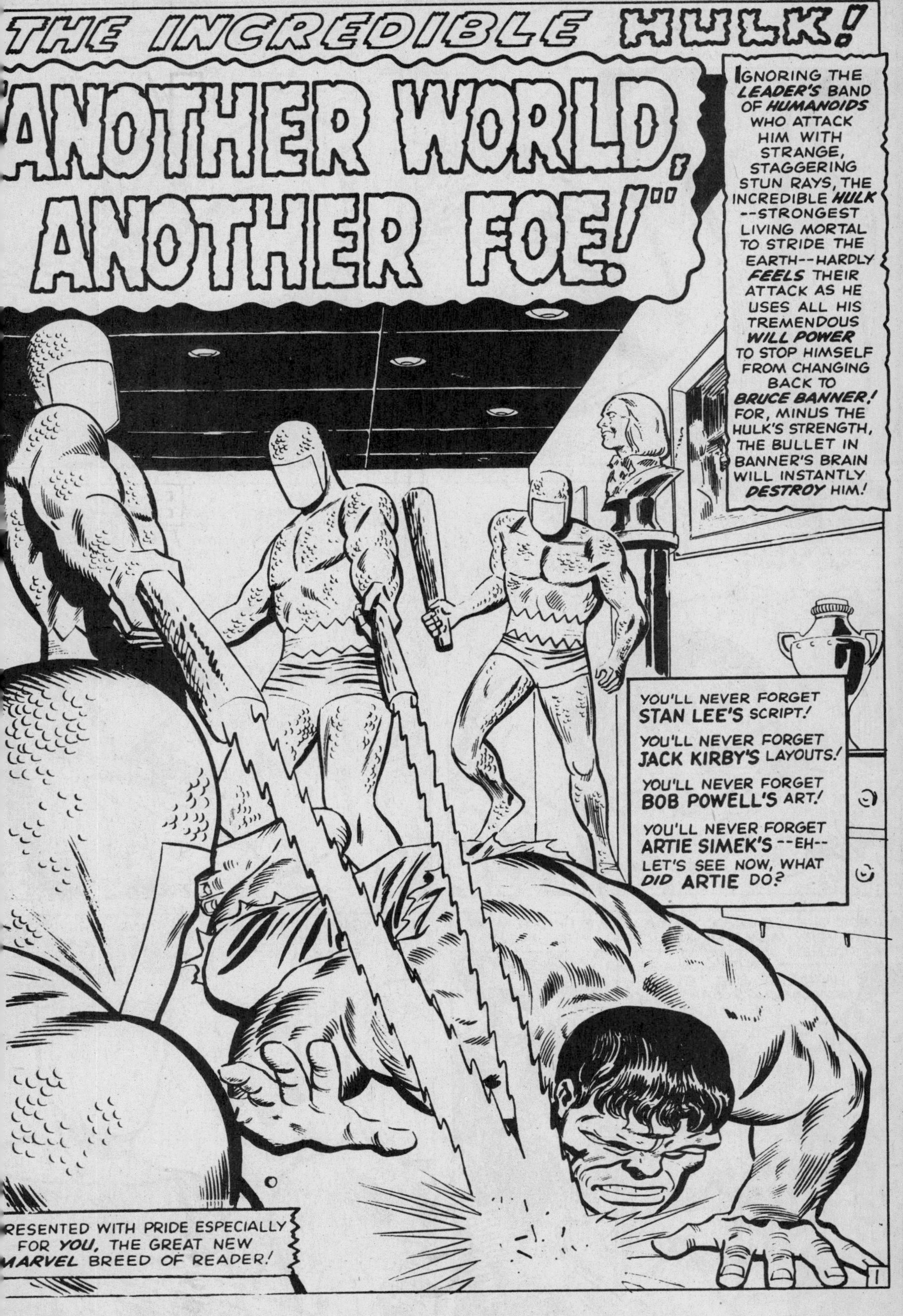
THE INCREDIBLE HULK!
"ANOTHER WORLD, ANOTHER FOE!"
IGNORING THE LEADER'S BAND OF HUMANOIDS WHO ATTACK HIM WITH STRANGE, STAGGERING STUN RAYS, THE INCREDIBLE HULK --STRONGEST LIVING MORTAL TO STRIDE THE EARTH--HARDLY FEELS THEIR ATTACK AS HE USES ALL HIS TREMENDOUS WILL POWER TO STOP HIMSELF FROM CHANGING BACK TO BRUCE BANNER! FOR, MINUS THE HULK'S STRENGTH, THE BULLET IN BANNER'S BRAIN WILL INSTANTLY DESTROY HIM!
YOU'LL NEVER FORGET STAN LEE'S SCRIPT!
YOU'LL NEVER FORGET JACK KIRBY'S LAYOUTS!
YOU'LL NEVER FORGET BOB POWELL'S ART!
YOU'LL NEVER FORGET ARTIE SIMEK'S --EH-- LET'S SEE NOW, WHAT DID ARTIE DO?
RESENTED WITH PRIDE ESPECIALLY FOR YOU, THE GREAT NEW MARVEL BREED OF READER!
1

RELENTLESSLY, THE EMOTIONLESS HUMANOIDS CONTINUE TO POUND THE GREEN GOLIATH WITH THEIR STAGGERING RAYS--UNTIL, FINALLY--

IT'S NO USE! I CAN'T KEEP CONCENTRATING ON PREVENTING THE *CHANGE*-- NOT WITH THOSE BLASTED *BOLTS* HITTING ME EVERY SECOND!

BUT, EVERY TIME MY ATTENTION IS DISTRACTED--I GET *WEAKER*--I GET CLOSER TO BECOMING BRUCE BANNER...

--AND *THAT* BRINGS ME CLOSER TO-- MY *FINISH!*

WHAT'S THE *USE??* WHY KEEP TRYING? IT'S PROBABLY THE BEST THING THAT COULD *HAPPEN* TO ME!

I'M NO GOOD TO *ANYONE* --INCLUDING *MYSELF!* THE WORLD HATES ME--FEARS ME-- ONLY *ANOTHER* MISFIT LIKE THE *LEADER*, WOULD WANT TO BE MY ALLY!

AS FOR THE *LEADER* HIMSELF, WE FIND HIM AT THAT VERY MOMENT, FRANTICALLY RACING TO THE SCENE...

THE DAMAGE IS UNBELIEVABLE! EVEN MY *HUMANOIDS* CAN'T STOP THE HULK!

ENOUGH! RETURN TO YOUR STATIONS! *I* SHALL DEAL WITH HIM MYSELF!

STRANGE! HE SEEMS TO BE *COLLAPSING!* AND YET, IT ISN'T FROM THE EFFECTS OF THE STUN RAYS!

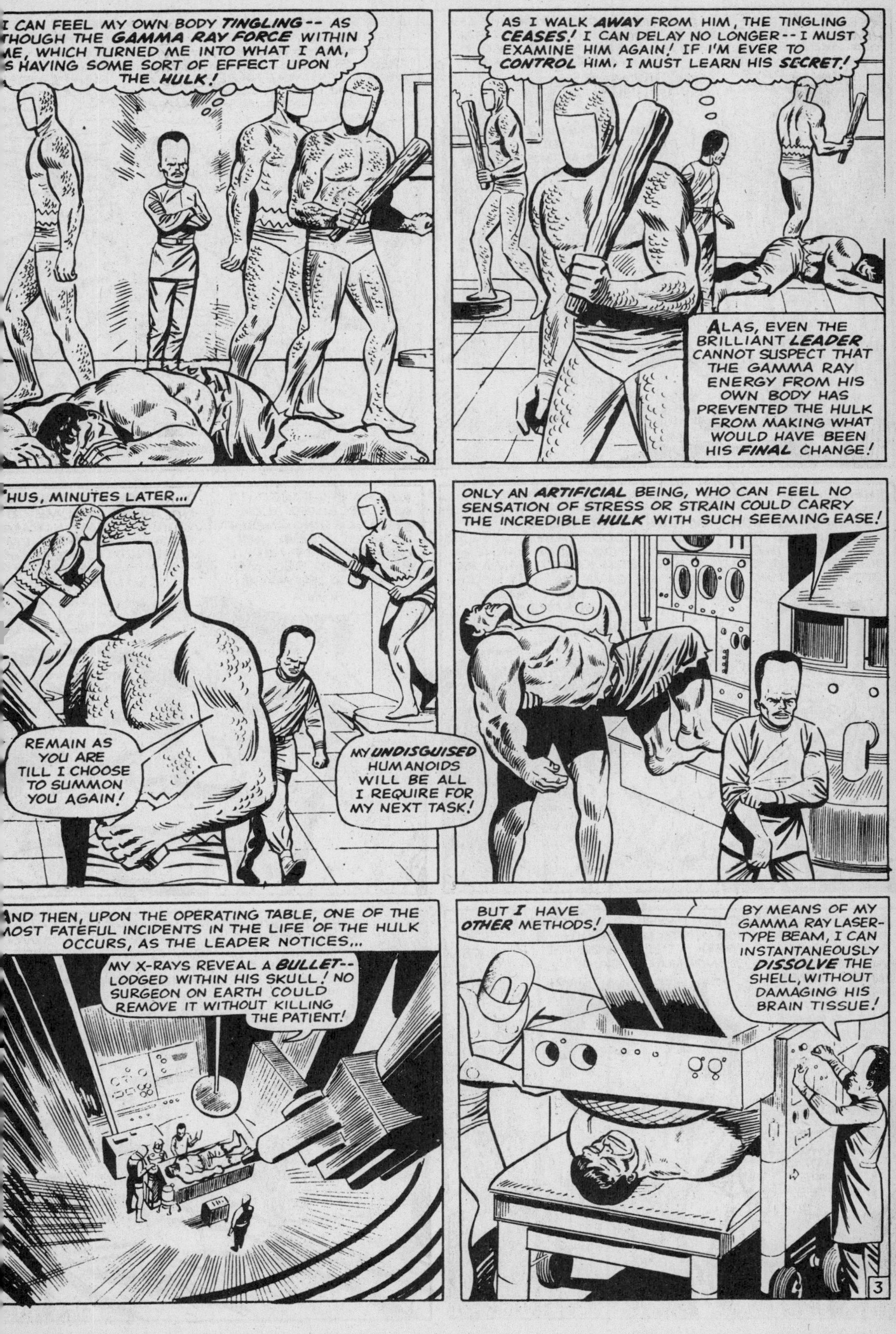
I CAN FEEL MY OWN BODY TINGLING-- AS THOUGH THE GAMMA RAY FORCE WITHIN ME, WHICH TURNED ME INTO WHAT I AM, IS HAVING SOME SORT OF EFFECT UPON THE HULK!
AS I WALK AWAY FROM HIM, THE TINGLING CEASES! I CAN DELAY NO LONGER-- I MUST EXAMINE HIM AGAIN! IF I'M EVER TO CONTROL HIM, I MUST LEARN HIS SECRET!
ALAS, EVEN THE BRILLIANT LEADER CANNOT SUSPECT THAT THE GAMMA RAY ENERGY FROM HIS OWN BODY HAS PREVENTED THE HULK FROM MAKING WHAT WOULD HAVE BEEN HIS FINAL CHANGE!
THUS, MINUTES LATER...
REMAIN AS YOU ARE TILL I CHOOSE TO SUMMON YOU AGAIN!
MY UNDISGUISED HUMANOIDS WILL BE ALL I REQUIRE FOR MY NEXT TASK!
ONLY AN ARTIFICIAL BEING, WHO CAN FEEL NO SENSATION OF STRESS OR STRAIN COULD CARRY THE INCREDIBLE HULK WITH SUCH SEEMING EASE!
AND THEN, UPON THE OPERATING TABLE, ONE OF THE MOST FATEFUL INCIDENTS IN THE LIFE OF THE HULK OCCURS, AS THE LEADER NOTICES...
MY X-RAYS REVEAL A BULLET-- LODGED WITHIN HIS SKULL! NO SURGEON ON EARTH COULD REMOVE IT WITHOUT KILLING THE PATIENT!
BUT I HAVE OTHER METHODS!
BY MEANS OF MY GAMMA RAY LASER-TYPE BEAM, I CAN INSTANTANEOUSLY DISSOLVE THE SHELL, WITHOUT DAMAGING HIS BRAIN TISSUE!
3

IT'S **DONE!** AND NOW, I'LL BATHE HIM WITH A FULL-INTENSITY SHOWER OF GAMMA RAYS-- TO BRING HIM BACK TO HIS FULL STRENGTH!

SOMETHING **HAPPENING**-- I-I FEEL DIFFERENT-- NEVER HAD SUCH A CONCENTRATED AMOUNT OF GAMMA RAYS BEFORE--!

HE'S MUTTERING DELIRIOUSLY! BUT-- I WONDER IF THIS TREATMENT **WILL** CHANGE HIM IN SOME WAY?

A SHORT TIME LATER, THE HEAVY EYELIDS OF T HULK SLOWLY OPEN, AND THEN...

YOU'RE STRONGER THAN **EVER!** I EXPECTED YOU TO BE UNCONSCIOUS FOR **DAYS**, BUT IT'S BEEN LESS THAN AN **HOUR!**

UNCONSCIOUS SCAR?? WHAT HAPPENED? TALK--!

AND THE LASER BEAM SCAR-- IT'S ALREADY DISAPPEARED!

I DIDN'T CHANGE BACK TO BANNER! I'VE GOT TO FIND OUT **WHY!**

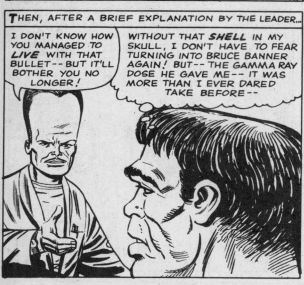

THEN, AFTER A BRIEF EXPLANATION BY THE LEADER...

I DON'T KNOW HOW YOU MANAGED TO **LIVE** WITH THAT BULLET-- BUT IT'LL BOTHER YOU NO LONGER!

WITHOUT THAT **SHELL** IN MY SKULL, I DON'T HAVE TO FEAR TURNING INTO BRUCE BANNER AGAIN! BUT-- THE GAMMA RAY DOSE HE GAVE ME-- IT WAS MORE THAN I EVER DARED TAKE BEFORE--

I ALWAYS FEARED IF I RECEIVED SUCH A STAGGERING AMOUNT IT WOULD **SEAL MY IDENTITY!** I'D NEVER BE ABLE TO BECOME **BRUCE BANNER** AGAIN!

WHAT **IRONY!** NOW THA IT'S **SAFE** FOR ME TO REVERT TO MY NORMA FORM-- I **CAN'T!** I'M DESTINED TO **REMAIN** THE HULK-- **FOREVER** WITH BANNER'S **BRAIN**

HE NEVER **SUSPECTED** I REALLY HAD **TWO** IDENTITIES! NOW, I'M JUST LIKE **HE** IS-- A GREEN-SKINNED FREAK! I'LL NEVER BE NORMAL AGAIN!

NEVER FORGET THAT IT WAS **I** WHO SAVED YOUR LIFE! I WAS **I** WHO REMOVED THAT DEADLY BULLET! YOU ARE ETERNALLY IN MY **DEBT!**

REPORT TO ME IN MY LABORATORY IN FIVE MINUTES!

HE'S **RIGHT!** I **DO** OWE HIM MY LIFE! I CAN'T EVER CHANGE **THAT!**

BUT-- WHAT KIND OF LIFE **IS** IT?? I'M DOOMED TO REMAIN THE MOST HATED-- THE MOST FEARED CREATURE TO WALK THE EARTH-- TO SPEND THE REST OF MY DAYS AND NIGHTS AS A GROTESQUE CARICATURE OF A HUMAN BEING-- AS AN UGLY, RAMPAGING **HULK!**

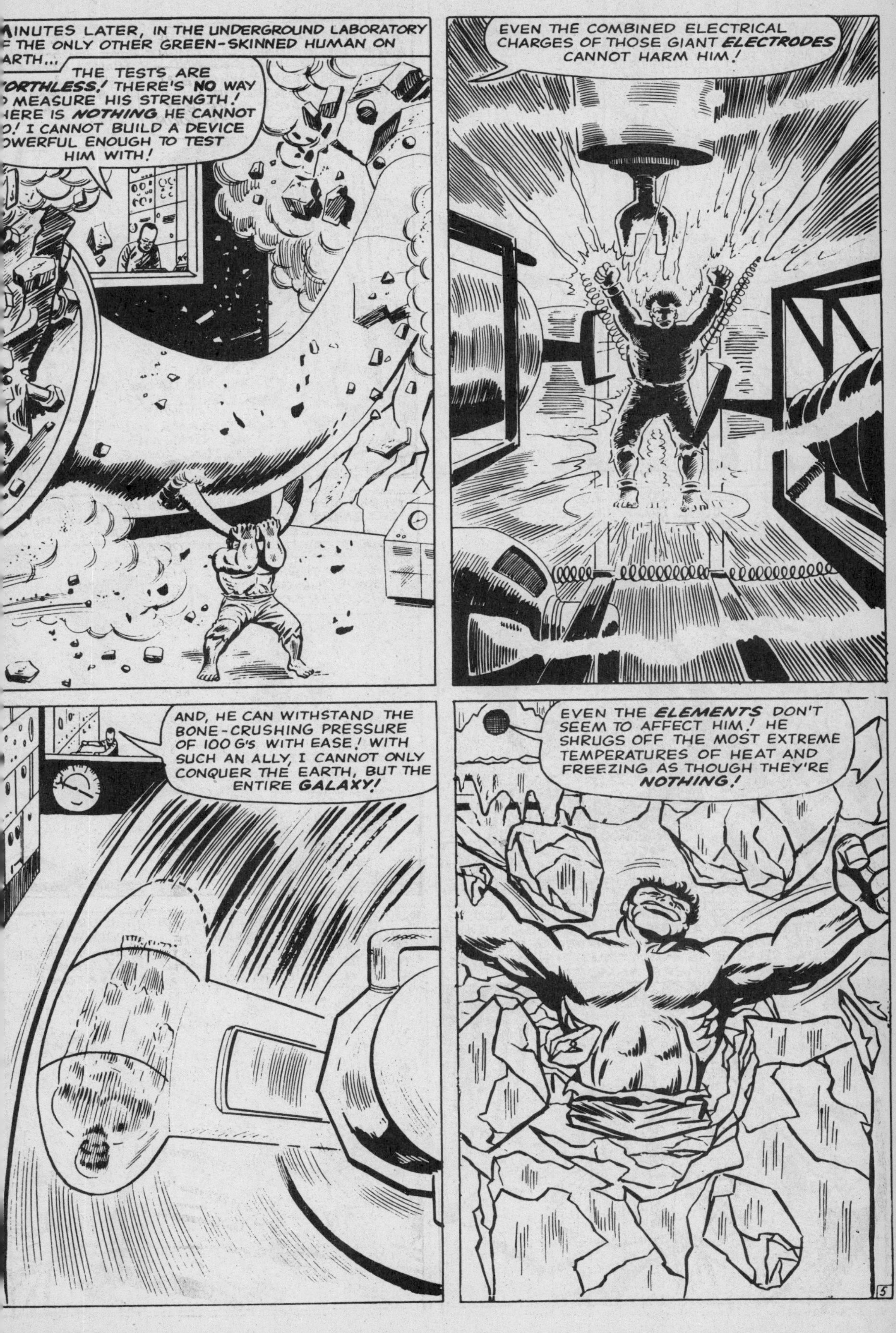
MINUTES LATER, IN THE UNDERGROUND LABORATORY OF THE ONLY OTHER GREEN-SKINNED HUMAN ON EARTH...
THE TESTS ARE WORTHLESS! THERE'S NO WAY TO MEASURE HIS STRENGTH! THERE IS NOTHING HE CANNOT DO! I CANNOT BUILD A DEVICE POWERFUL ENOUGH TO TEST HIM WITH!
EVEN THE COMBINED ELECTRICAL CHARGES OF THOSE GIANT ELECTRODES CANNOT HARM HIM!
AND, HE CAN WITHSTAND THE BONE-CRUSHING PRESSURE OF 100 G'S WITH EASE! WITH SUCH AN ALLY, I CANNOT ONLY CONQUER THE EARTH, BUT THE ENTIRE GALAXY!
EVEN THE ELEMENTS DON'T SEEM TO AFFECT HIM! HE SHRUGS OFF THE MOST EXTREME TEMPERATURES OF HEAT AND FREEZING AS THOUGH THEY'RE NOTHING!
5

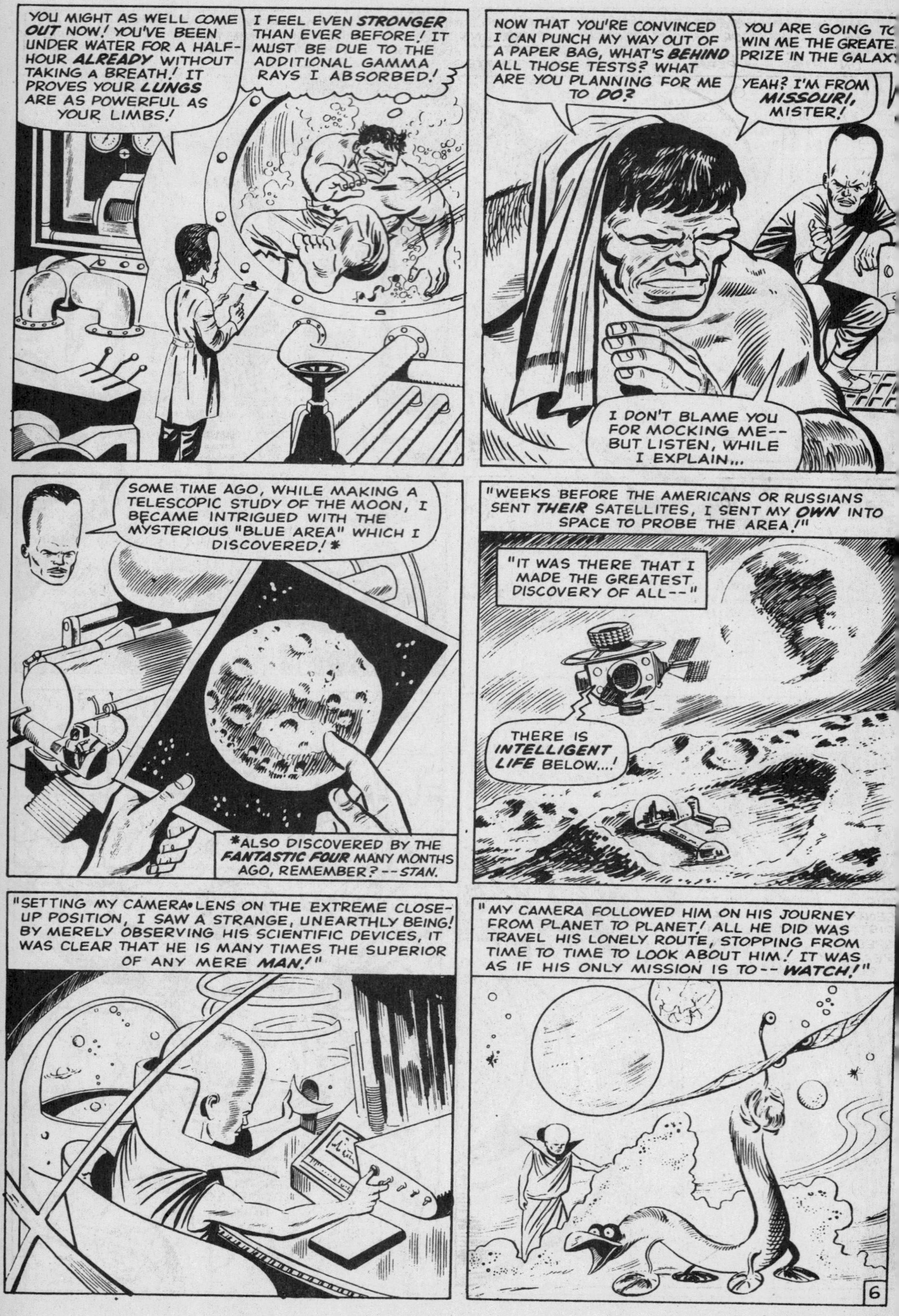
YOU MIGHT AS WELL COME OUT NOW! YOU'VE BEEN UNDER WATER FOR A HALF-HOUR ALREADY WITHOUT TAKING A BREATH! IT PROVES YOUR LUNGS ARE AS POWERFUL AS YOUR LIMBS!
I FEEL EVEN STRONGER THAN EVER BEFORE! IT MUST BE DUE TO THE ADDITIONAL GAMMA RAYS I ABSORBED!
NOW THAT YOU'RE CONVINCED I CAN PUNCH MY WAY OUT OF A PAPER BAG, WHAT'S BEHIND ALL THOSE TESTS? WHAT ARE YOU PLANNING FOR ME TO DO?
YOU ARE GOING TO WIN ME THE GREATE PRIZE IN THE GALAXY
YEAH? I'M FROM MISSOURI, MISTER!
I DON'T BLAME YOU FOR MOCKING ME-- BUT LISTEN, WHILE I EXPLAIN...
SOME TIME AGO, WHILE MAKING A TELESCOPIC STUDY OF THE MOON, I BECAME INTRIGUED WITH THE MYSTERIOUS "BLUE AREA" WHICH I DISCOVERED! *
*ALSO DISCOVERED BY THE FANTASTIC FOUR MANY MONTHS AGO, REMEMBER? --STAN.
"WEEKS BEFORE THE AMERICANS OR RUSSIANS SENT THEIR SATELLITES, I SENT MY OWN INTO SPACE TO PROBE THE AREA!"
"IT WAS THERE THAT I MADE THE GREATEST DISCOVERY OF ALL--"
THERE IS INTELLIGENT LIFE BELOW...!
"SETTING MY CAMERA LENS ON THE EXTREME CLOSE-UP POSITION, I SAW A STRANGE, UNEARTHLY BEING! BY MERELY OBSERVING HIS SCIENTIFIC DEVICES, IT WAS CLEAR THAT HE IS MANY TIMES THE SUPERIOR OF ANY MERE MAN!"
"MY CAMERA FOLLOWED HIM ON HIS JOURNEY FROM PLANET TO PLANET! ALL HE DID WAS TRAVEL HIS LONELY ROUTE, STOPPING FROM TIME TO TIME TO LOOK ABOUT HIM! IT WAS AS IF HIS ONLY MISSION IS TO-- WATCH!"
6

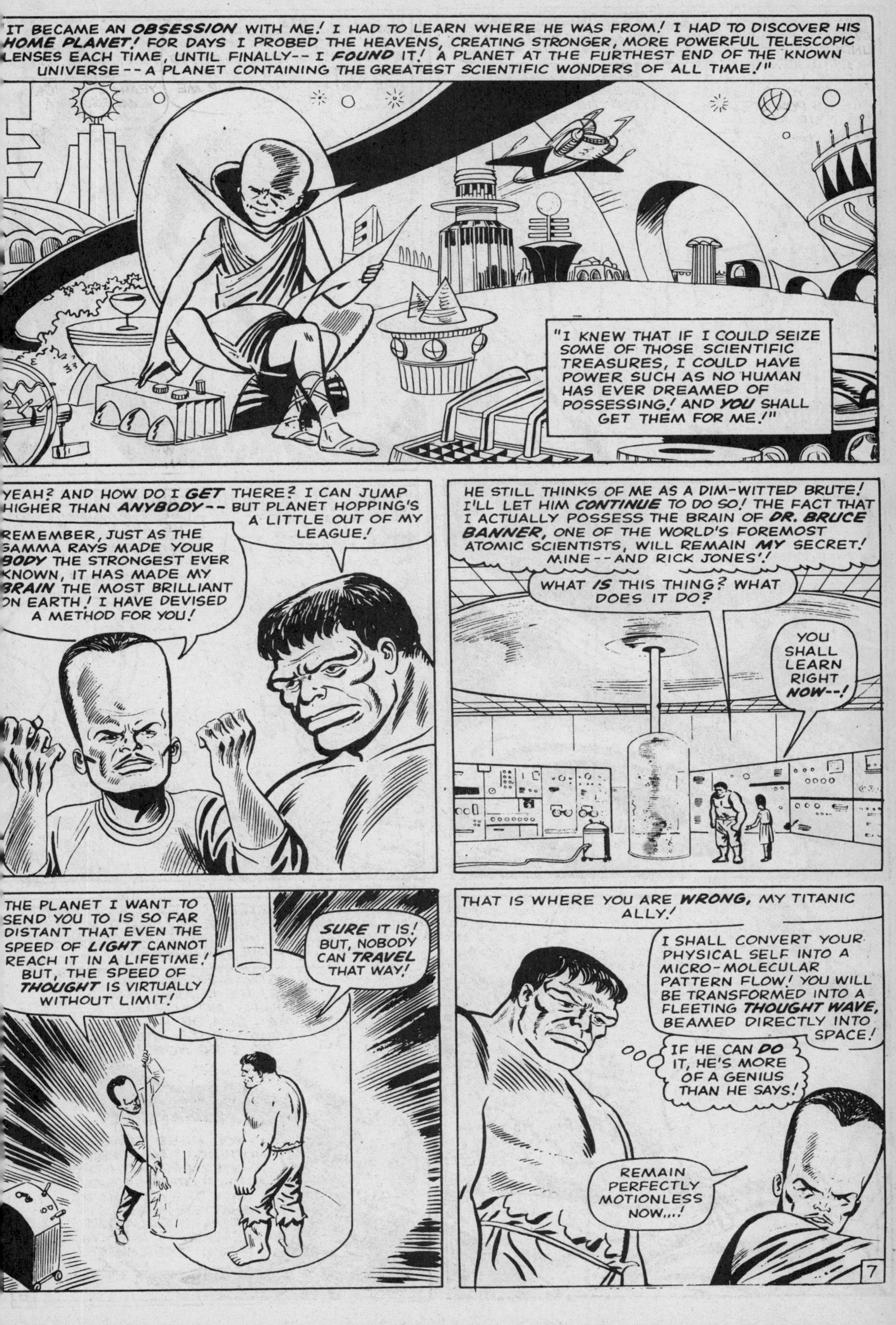
IT BECAME AN OBSESSION WITH ME! I HAD TO LEARN WHERE HE WAS FROM! I HAD TO DISCOVER HIS HOME PLANET! FOR DAYS I PROBED THE HEAVENS, CREATING STRONGER, MORE POWERFUL TELESCOPIC LENSES EACH TIME, UNTIL FINALLY-- I FOUND IT! A PLANET AT THE FURTHEST END OF THE KNOWN UNIVERSE--A PLANET CONTAINING THE GREATEST SCIENTIFIC WONDERS OF ALL TIME!"
"I KNEW THAT IF I COULD SEIZE SOME OF THOSE SCIENTIFIC TREASURES, I COULD HAVE POWER SUCH AS NO HUMAN HAS EVER DREAMED OF POSSESSING! AND YOU SHALL GET THEM FOR ME!"
YEAH? AND HOW DO I GET THERE? I CAN JUMP HIGHER THAN ANYBODY-- BUT PLANET HOPPING'S A LITTLE OUT OF MY LEAGUE!
REMEMBER, JUST AS THE GAMMA RAYS MADE YOUR BODY THE STRONGEST EVER KNOWN, IT HAS MADE MY BRAIN THE MOST BRILLIANT ON EARTH! I HAVE DEVISED A METHOD FOR YOU!
HE STILL THINKS OF ME AS A DIM-WITTED BRUTE! I'LL LET HIM CONTINUE TO DO SO! THE FACT THAT I ACTUALLY POSSESS THE BRAIN OF DR. BRUCE BANNER, ONE OF THE WORLD'S FOREMOST ATOMIC SCIENTISTS, WILL REMAIN MY SECRET! MINE--AND RICK JONES'!
WHAT IS THIS THING? WHAT DOES IT DO?
YOU SHALL LEARN RIGHT NOW--!
THE PLANET I WANT TO SEND YOU TO IS SO FAR DISTANT THAT EVEN THE SPEED OF LIGHT CANNOT REACH IT IN A LIFETIME! BUT, THE SPEED OF THOUGHT IS VIRTUALLY WITHOUT LIMIT!
SURE IT IS! BUT, NOBODY CAN TRAVEL THAT WAY!
THAT IS WHERE YOU ARE WRONG, MY TITANIC ALLY!
I SHALL CONVERT YOUR PHYSICAL SELF INTO A MICRO-MOLECULAR PATTERN FLOW! YOU WILL BE TRANSFORMED INTO A FLEETING THOUGHT WAVE, BEAMED DIRECTLY INTO SPACE!
IF HE CAN DO IT, HE'S MORE OF A GENIUS THAN HE SAYS!
REMAIN PERFECTLY MOTIONLESS NOW...!
7

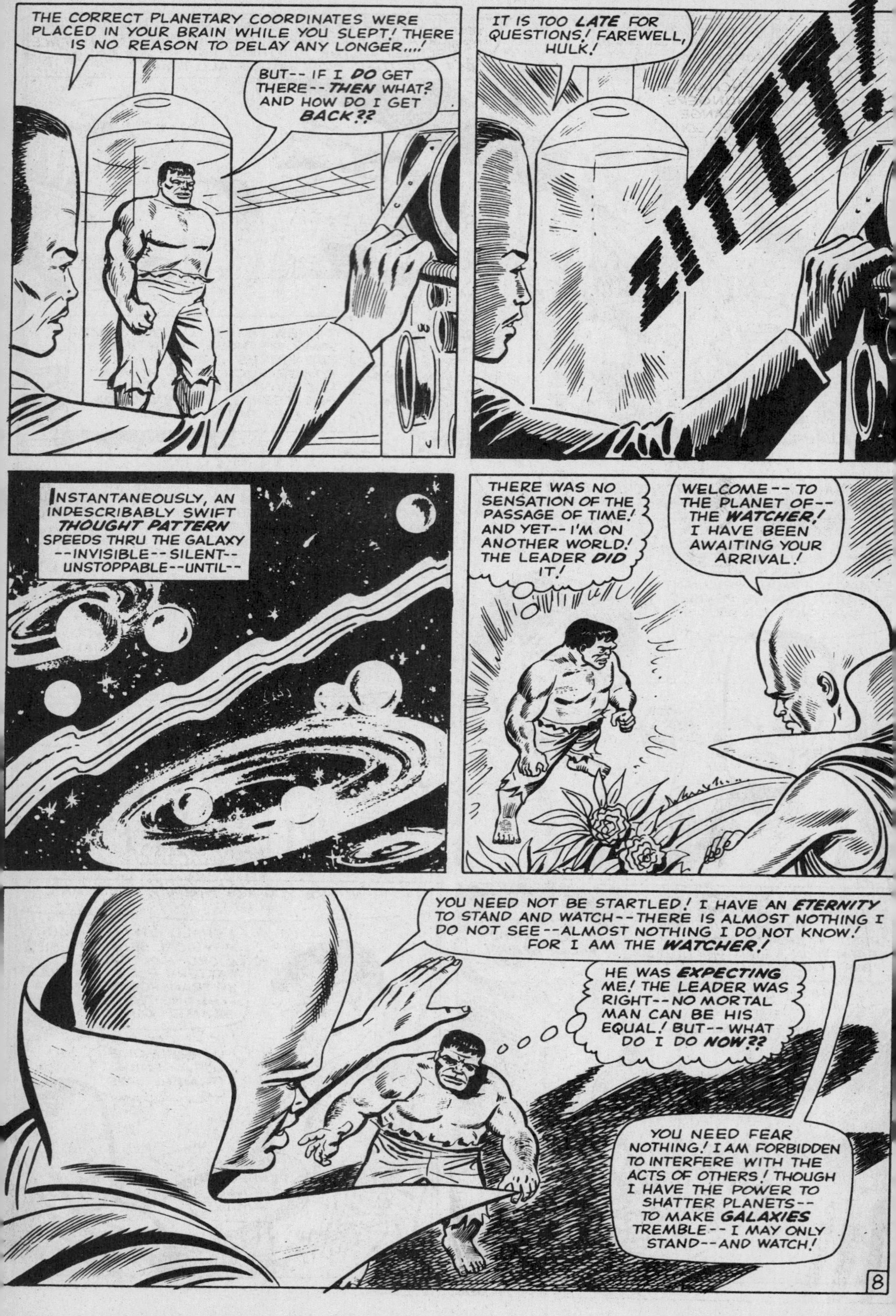
THE CORRECT PLANETARY COORDINATES WERE PLACED IN YOUR BRAIN WHILE YOU SLEPT! THERE IS NO REASON TO DELAY ANY LONGER....!
BUT-- IF I DO GET THERE--THEN WHAT? AND HOW DO I GET BACK??
IT IS TOO LATE FOR QUESTIONS! FAREWELL, HULK!
ZITTT!
INSTANTANEOUSLY, AN INDESCRIBABLY SWIFT THOUGHT PATTERN SPEEDS THRU THE GALAXY --INVISIBLE--SILENT-- UNSTOPPABLE--UNTIL--
THERE WAS NO SENSATION OF THE PASSAGE OF TIME! AND YET-- I'M ON ANOTHER WORLD! THE LEADER DID IT!
WELCOME-- TO THE PLANET OF-- THE WATCHER! I HAVE BEEN AWAITING YOUR ARRIVAL!
YOU NEED NOT BE STARTLED! I HAVE AN ETERNITY TO STAND AND WATCH--THERE IS ALMOST NOTHING I DO NOT SEE--ALMOST NOTHING I DO NOT KNOW! FOR I AM THE WATCHER!
HE WAS EXPECTING ME! THE LEADER WAS RIGHT--NO MORTAL MAN CAN BE HIS EQUAL! BUT-- WHAT DO I DO NOW??
YOU NEED FEAR NOTHING! I AM FORBIDDEN TO INTERFERE WITH THE ACTS OF OTHERS! THOUGH I HAVE THE POWER TO SHATTER PLANETS-- TO MAKE GALAXIES TREMBLE--I MAY ONLY STAND--AND WATCH!
8

BENEATH THE BRUTAL FORM OF THE HULK, THE KEEN, CURIOUS MIND OF DR. BANNER SEETHES WITH EXCITEMENT! LIKE A CHILD, LET LOOSE IN SOME ENCHANTED WONDERLAND, HE HUNGERS TO TAKE IN ALL THE STRANGE, UNEARTHLY SIGHTS AND SOUNDS OF THE FANTASTIC PLANET ON WHICH HE FINDS HIMSELF!

YOU MAY ROAM AT WILL, OBSERVING ALL THAT YOU DESIRE! I AM BOUND TO OFFER YOU NO INTERFERENCE!

MECHANICAL LIFE FORMS--FLORA AND FAUNA SUCH AS NO MAN COULD HAVE EVER *DREAMED* OF.!! THIS WORLD IS A SCIENTIFIC STOREHOUSE OF *TREASURES* BEYOND MEASURE!

ALMOST *NONE* OF THE ARTIFACTS YOU GAZE UPON ARE NATIVE TO THIS PLANET! THEY HAVE ALL BEEN *BROUGHT* HERE-- FOR FURTHER STUDY-- BY MYSELF! THEY ARE PART OF MY COLLECTION-- A COLLECTION I HAVE BEEN GATHERING FOR UNTOLD AGES!

THEY'RE TOTALLY BEYOND MY UNDERSTANDING! I CAN JUST BARELY *GUESS* THEIR PURPOSES-- THEIR FUNCTIONS!

THEN SUDDENLY, A MENTAL COMMAND RINGS OUT IN THE STILL-REELING BRAIN OF THE INCREDIBLE HULK-- THE COMMAND OF -- THE *LEADER!*

I AM WITH YOU STILL-- I CAN SEE WHAT YOU SEE-- HEAR WHAT YOU HEAR! MY PLAN IS BEARING FRUIT!

9

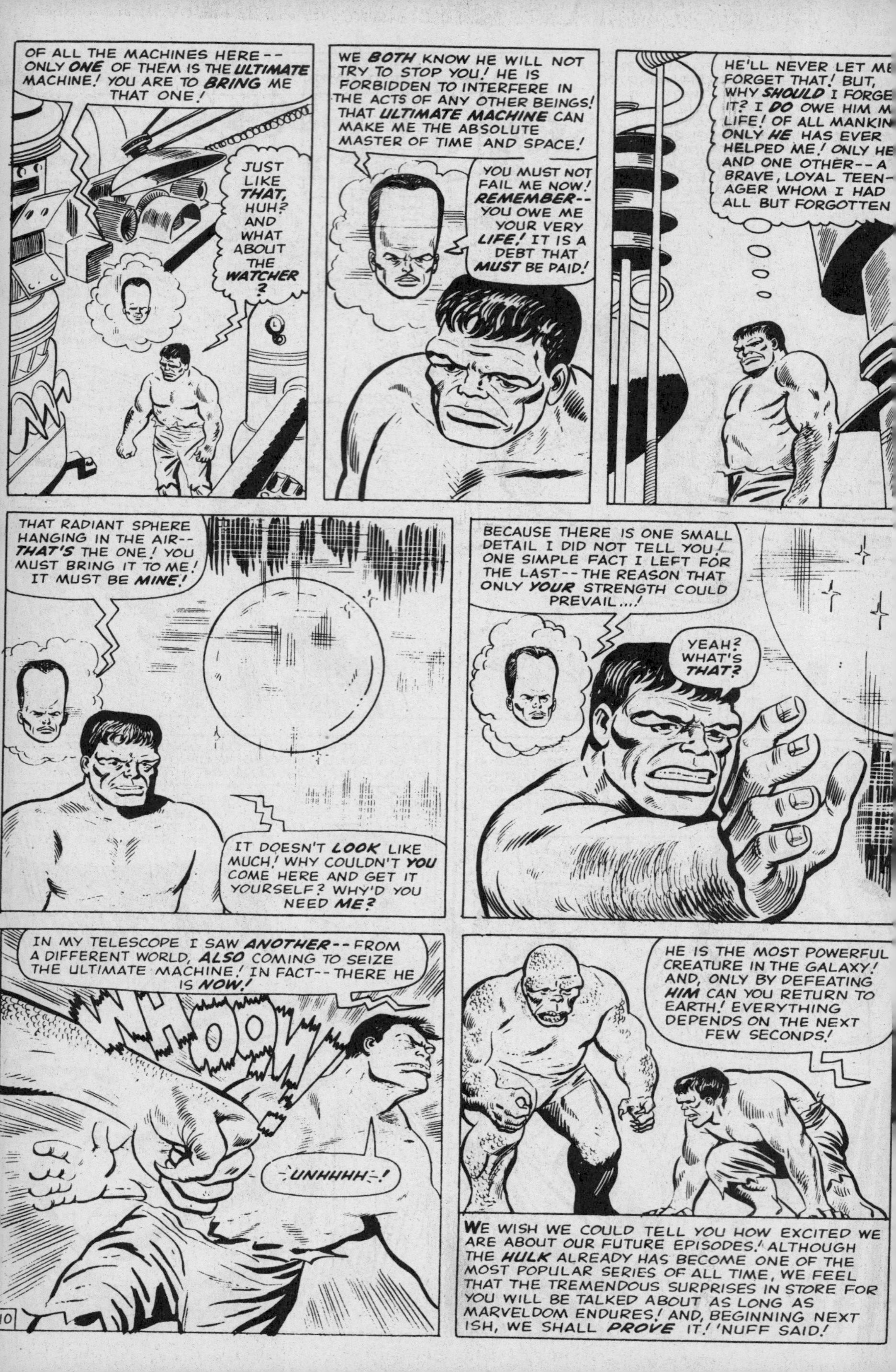
OF ALL THE MACHINES HERE-- ONLY ONE OF THEM IS THE ULTIMATE MACHINE! YOU ARE TO BRING ME THAT ONE!
JUST LIKE THAT, HUH? AND WHAT ABOUT THE WATCHER?
WE BOTH KNOW HE WILL NOT TRY TO STOP YOU! HE IS FORBIDDEN TO INTERFERE IN THE ACTS OF ANY OTHER BEINGS! THAT ULTIMATE MACHINE CAN MAKE ME THE ABSOLUTE MASTER OF TIME AND SPACE!
YOU MUST NOT FAIL ME NOW! REMEMBER-- YOU OWE ME YOUR VERY LIFE! IT IS A DEBT THAT MUST BE PAID!
HE'LL NEVER LET ME FORGET THAT! BUT, WHY SHOULD I FORGE IT? I DO OWE HIM M LIFE! OF ALL MANKIN ONLY HE HAS EVER HELPED ME! ONLY HE AND ONE OTHER-- A BRAVE, LOYAL TEEN-AGER WHOM I HAD ALL BUT FORGOTTEN
THAT RADIANT SPHERE HANGING IN THE AIR-- THAT'S THE ONE! YOU MUST BRING IT TO ME! IT MUST BE MINE!
IT DOESN'T LOOK LIKE MUCH! WHY COULDN'T YOU COME HERE AND GET IT YOURSELF? WHY'D YOU NEED ME?
BECAUSE THERE IS ONE SMALL DETAIL I DID NOT TELL YOU! ONE SIMPLE FACT I LEFT FOR THE LAST-- THE REASON THAT ONLY YOUR STRENGTH COULD PREVAIL...!
YEAH? WHAT'S THAT?
IN MY TELESCOPE I SAW ANOTHER-- FROM A DIFFERENT WORLD, ALSO COMING TO SEIZE THE ULTIMATE MACHINE! IN FACT-- THERE HE IS NOW!
WHOOM
-UNHHHH-!
HE IS THE MOST POWERFUL CREATURE IN THE GALAXY! AND, ONLY BY DEFEATING HIM CAN YOU RETURN TO EARTH! EVERYTHING DEPENDS ON THE NEXT FEW SECONDS!
WE WISH WE COULD TELL YOU HOW EXCITED WE ARE ABOUT OUR FUTURE EPISODES! ALTHOUGH THE HULK ALREADY HAS BECOME ONE OF THE MOST POPULAR SERIES OF ALL TIME, WE FEEL THAT THE TREMENDOUS SURPRISES IN STORE FOR YOU WILL BE TALKED ABOUT AS LONG AS MARVELDOM ENDURES! AND, BEGINNING NEXT ISH, WE SHALL PROVE IT! 'NUFF SAID!
10

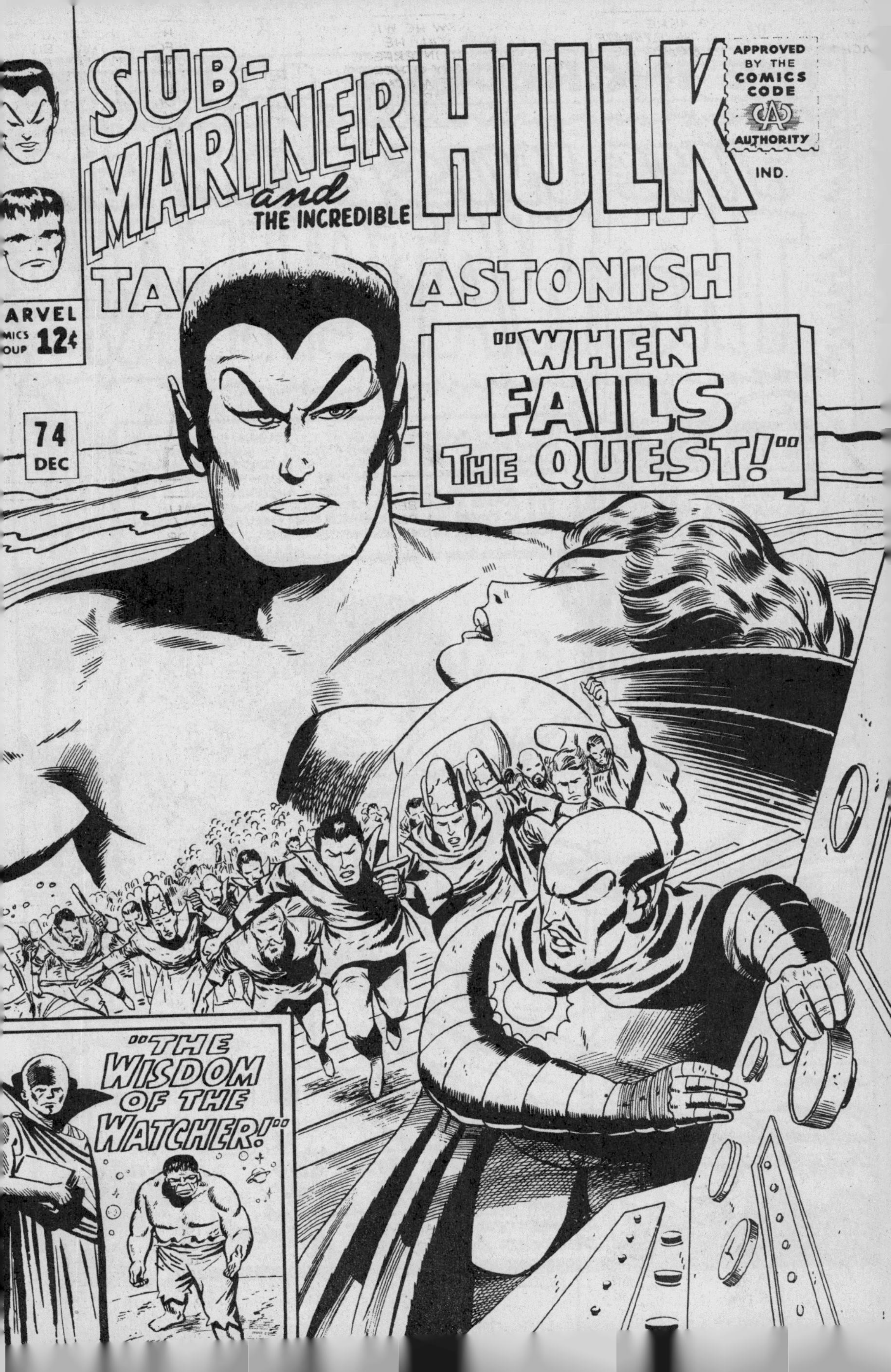
SUB-MARINER
and
THE INCREDIBLE HULK
APPROVED BY THE COMICS CODE AUTHORITY
IND.
TA ASTONISH
ARVEL
MICS
OUP
12¢
74
DEC
"WHEN FAILS THE QUEST!"
"THE WISDOM OF THE WATCHER!"

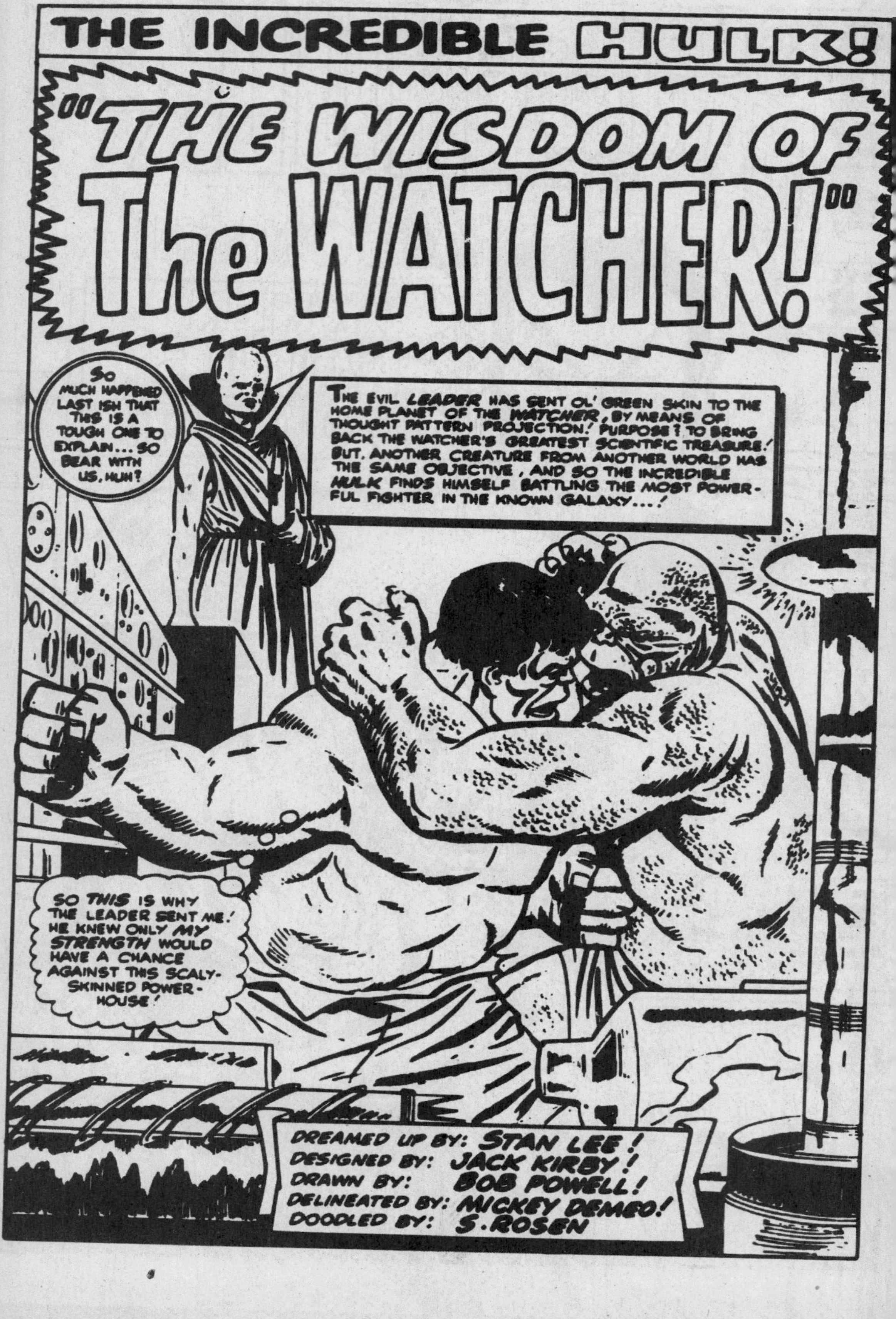
THE INCREDIBLE HULK!
"THE WISDOM OF The WATCHER!"
SO MUCH HAPPENED LAST ISH THAT THIS IS A TOUGH ONE TO EXPLAIN... SO BEAR WITH US, HUH?
THE EVIL LEADER HAS SENT OL' GREEN SKIN TO THE HOME PLANET OF THE WATCHER, BY MEANS OF THOUGHT PATTERN PROJECTION! PURPOSE? TO BRING BACK THE WATCHER'S GREATEST SCIENTIFIC TREASURE! BUT, ANOTHER CREATURE FROM ANOTHER WORLD HAS THE SAME OBJECTIVE, AND SO THE INCREDIBLE HULK FINDS HIMSELF BATTLING THE MOST POWERFUL FIGHTER IN THE KNOWN GALAXY...!
SO THIS IS WHY THE LEADER SENT ME! HE KNEW ONLY MY STRENGTH WOULD HAVE A CHANCE AGAINST THIS SCALY-SKINNED POWER-HOUSE!
DREAMED UP BY: STAN LEE!
DESIGNED BY: JACK KIRBY!
DRAWN BY: BOB POWELL!
DELINEATED BY: MICKEY DEMEO!
DOODLED BY: S. ROSEN

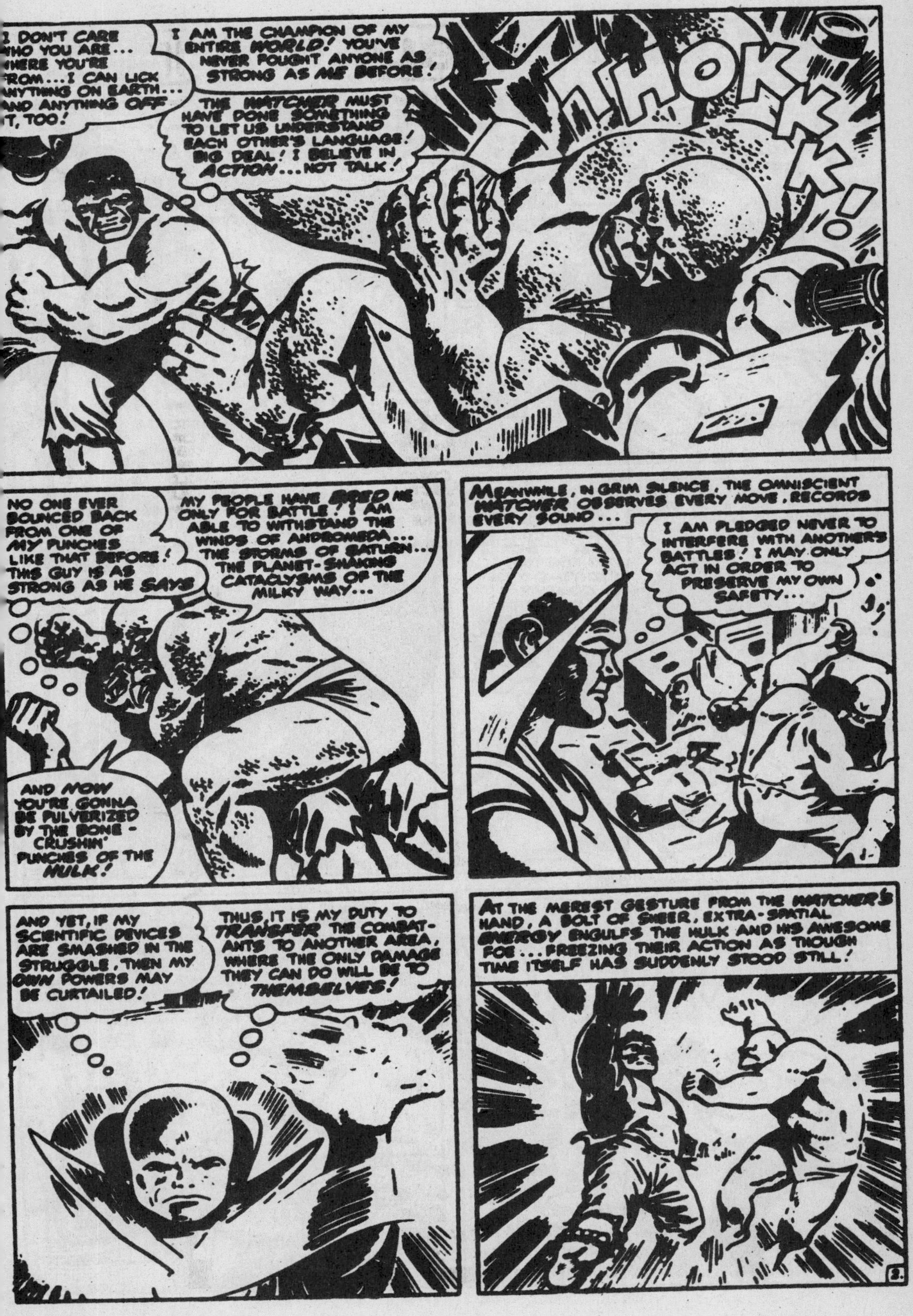
I DON'T CARE WHO YOU ARE... WHERE YOU'RE FROM... I CAN LICK ANYTHING ON EARTH... AND ANYTHING OFF IT, TOO!
I AM THE CHAMPION OF MY ENTIRE WORLD! YOU'VE NEVER FOUGHT ANYONE AS STRONG AS ME BEFORE!
THE WATCHER MUST HAVE DONE SOMETHING TO LET US UNDERSTAND EACH OTHER'S LANGUAGE! BIG DEAL! I BELIEVE IN ACTION... NOT TALK!
THOKK!
NO ONE EVER BOUNCED BACK FROM ONE OF MY PUNCHES LIKE THAT BEFORE! THIS GUY IS AS STRONG AS HE SAYS
MY PEOPLE HAVE BRED ME ONLY FOR BATTLE! I AM ABLE TO WITHSTAND THE WINDS OF ANDROMEDA... THE STORMS OF SATURN... THE PLANET-SHAKING CATACLYSMS OF THE MILKY WAY...
AND NOW YOU'RE GONNA BE PULVERIZED BY THE BONE-CRUSHIN' PUNCHES OF THE HULK!
MEANWHILE, IN GRIM SILENCE, THE OMNISCIENT WATCHER OBSERVES EVERY MOVE, RECORDS EVERY SOUND...
I AM PLEDGED NEVER TO INTERFERE WITH ANOTHER'S BATTLES! I MAY ONLY ACT IN ORDER TO PRESERVE MY OWN SAFETY...
AND YET, IF MY SCIENTIFIC DEVICES ARE SMASHED IN THE STRUGGLE, THEN MY OWN POWERS MAY BE CURTAILED!
THUS IT IS MY DUTY TO TRANSFER THE COMBATANTS TO ANOTHER AREA, WHERE THE ONLY DAMAGE THEY CAN DO WILL BE TO THEMSELVES!
AT THE MEREST GESTURE FROM THE WATCHER'S HAND, A BOLT OF SHEER, EXTRA-SPATIAL ENERGY ENGULFS THE HULK AND HIS AWESOME FOE... FREEZING THEIR ACTION AS THOUGH TIME ITSELF HAS SUDDENLY STOOD STILL!
2.

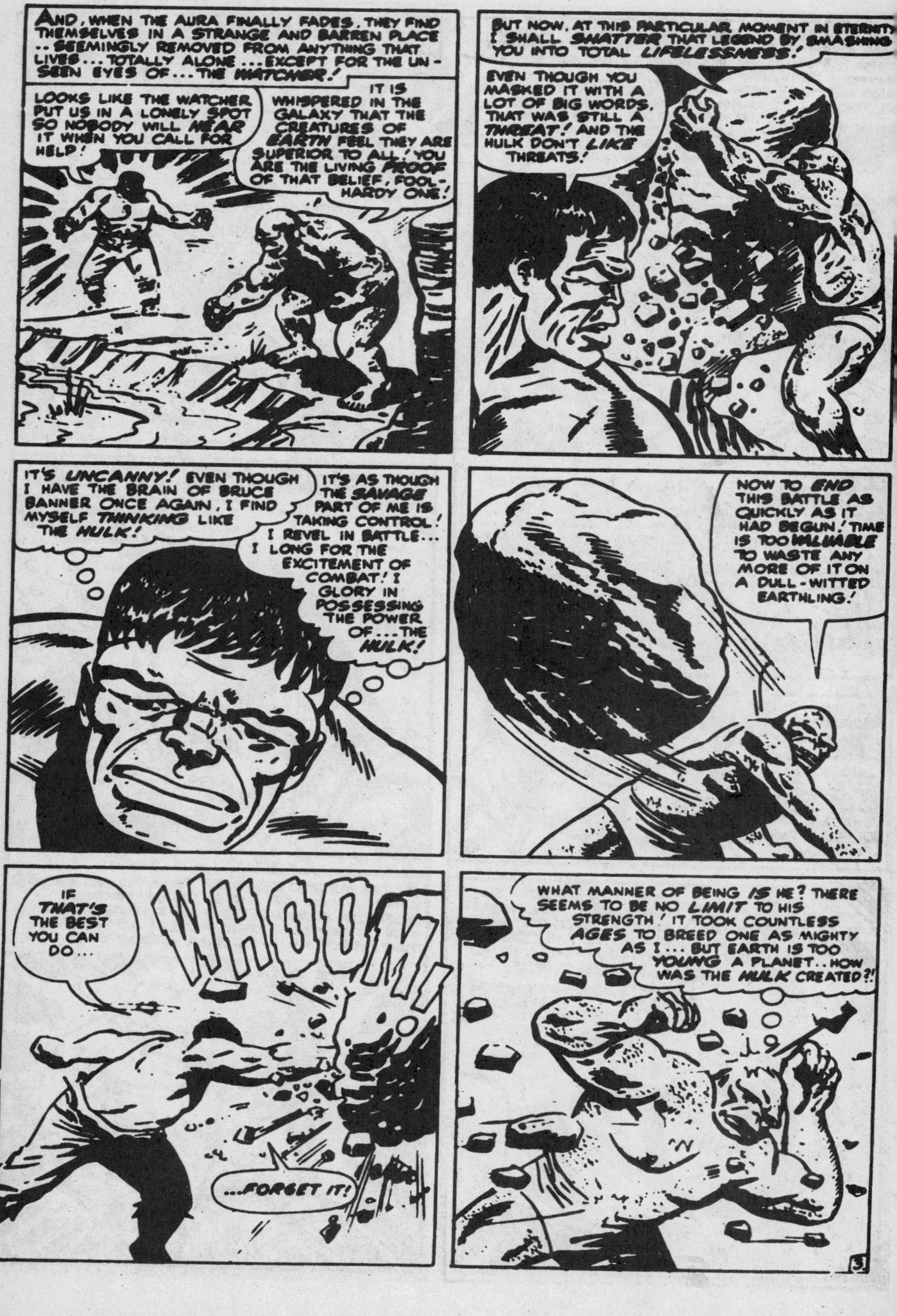

AND, WHEN THE AURA FINALLY FADES, THEY FIND THEMSELVES IN A STRANGE AND BARREN PLACE .. SEEMINGLY REMOVED FROM ANYTHING THAT LIVES... TOTALLY ALONE ... EXCEPT FOR THE UNSEEN EYES OF... THE WATCHER!
LOOKS LIKE THE WATCHER PUT US IN A LONELY SPOT SO NOBODY WILL HEAR IT WHEN YOU CALL FOR HELP!
IT IS WHISPERED IN THE GALAXY THAT THE CREATURES OF EARTH FEEL THEY ARE SUPERIOR TO ALL! YOU ARE THE LIVING PROOF OF THAT BELIEF, FOOL-HARDY ONE!
BUT NOW, AT THIS PARTICULAR MOMENT IN ETERNITY I SHALL SHATTER THAT LEGEND BY SMASHING YOU INTO TOTAL LIFELESSNESS!
EVEN THOUGH YOU MASKED IT WITH A LOT OF BIG WORDS, THAT WAS STILL A THREAT! AND THE HULK DON'T LIKE THREATS!
IT'S UNCANNY! EVEN THOUGH I HAVE THE BRAIN OF BRUCE BANNER ONCE AGAIN, I FIND MYSELF THINKING LIKE THE HULK!
IT'S AS THOUGH THE SAVAGE PART OF ME IS TAKING CONTROL! I REVEL IN BATTLE... I LONG FOR THE EXCITEMENT OF COMBAT! I GLORY IN POSSESSING THE POWER OF... THE HULK!
NOW TO END THIS BATTLE AS QUICKLY AS IT HAD BEGUN! TIME IS TOO VALUABLE TO WASTE ANY MORE OF IT ON A DULL-WITTED EARTHLING!
IF THAT'S THE BEST YOU CAN DO...
WHOOM!
...FORGET IT!
WHAT MANNER OF BEING IS HE? THERE SEEMS TO BE NO LIMIT TO HIS STRENGTH! IT TOOK COUNTLESS AGES TO BREED ONE AS MIGHTY AS I... BUT EARTH IS TOO YOUNG A PLANET... HOW WAS THE HULK CREATED?!
3

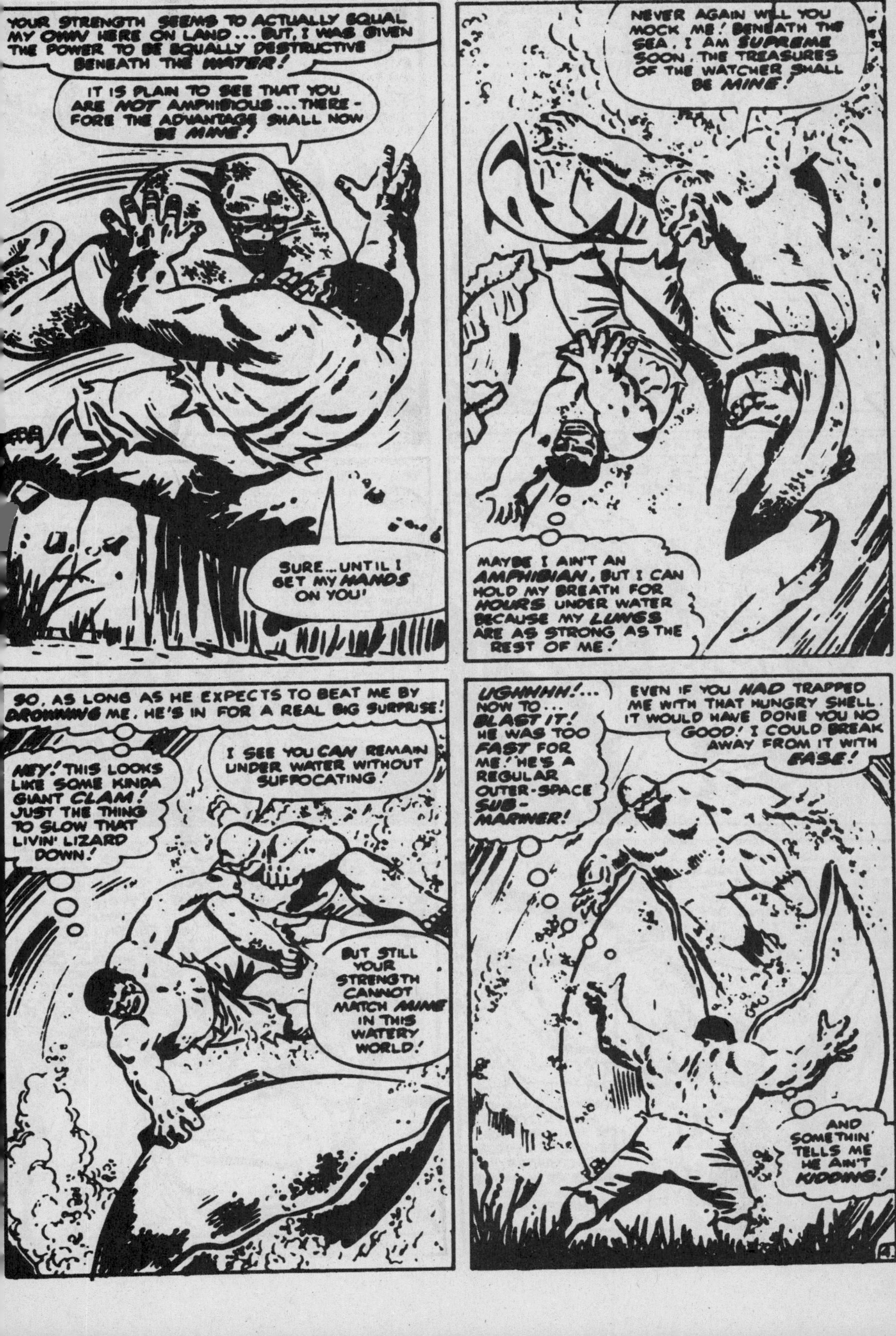
YOUR STRENGTH SEEMS TO ACTUALLY EQUAL MY OWN HERE ON LAND... BUT, I WAS GIVEN THE POWER TO BE EQUALLY DESTRUCTIVE BENEATH THE WATER!
IT IS PLAIN TO SEE THAT YOU ARE NOT AMPHIBIOUS... THERE-FORE THE ADVANTAGE SHALL NOW BE MINE!
SURE... UNTIL I GET MY HANDS ON YOU!
NEVER AGAIN WILL YOU MOCK ME! BENEATH THE SEA, I AM SUPREME. SOON, THE TREASURES OF THE WATCHER SHALL BE MINE!
MAYBE I AIN'T AN AMPHIBIAN, BUT I CAN HOLD MY BREATH FOR HOURS UNDER WATER BECAUSE MY LUNGS ARE AS STRONG AS THE REST OF ME!
SO, AS LONG AS HE EXPECTS TO BEAT ME BY DROWNING ME, HE'S IN FOR A REAL BIG SURPRISE!
HEY! THIS LOOKS LIKE SOME KINDA GIANT CLAM! JUST THE THING TO SLOW THAT LIVIN' LIZARD DOWN!
I SEE YOU CAN REMAIN UNDER WATER WITHOUT SUFFOCATING!
BUT STILL YOUR STRENGTH CANNOT MATCH MINE IN THIS WATERY WORLD!
UGHHHH!... NOW TO BLAST IT! HE WAS TOO FAST FOR ME! HE'S A REGULAR OUTER-SPACE SUB-MARINER!
EVEN IF YOU HAD TRAPPED ME WITH THAT HUNGRY SHELL, IT WOULD HAVE DONE YOU NO GOOD! I COULD BREAK AWAY FROM IT WITH EASE!
AND SOMETHIN' TELLS ME HE AIN'T KIDDING!
4

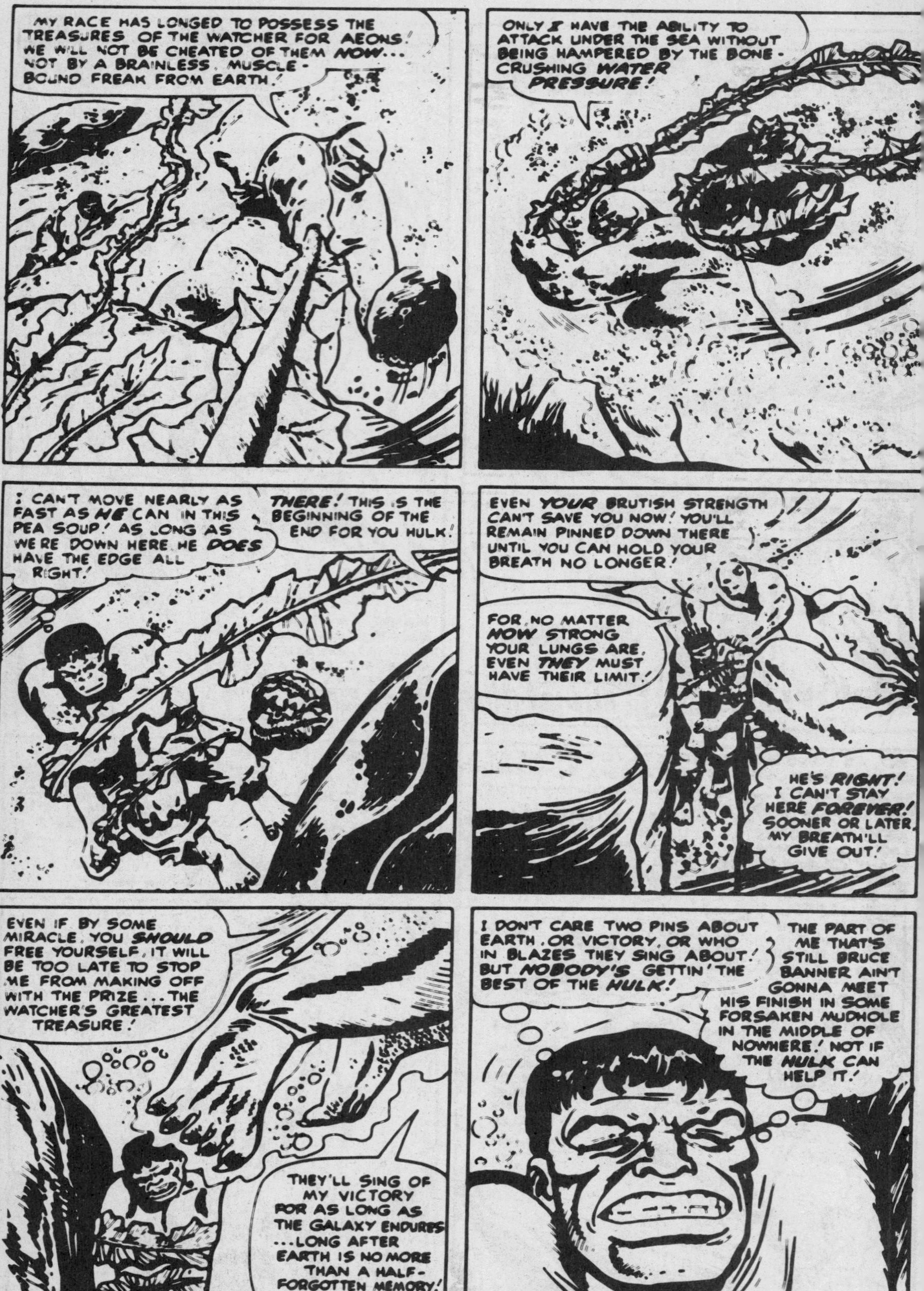
MY RACE HAS LONGED TO POSSESS THE TREASURES OF THE WATCHER FOR AEONS! WE WILL NOT BE CHEATED OF THEM NOW... NOT BY A BRAINLESS, MUSCLE-BOUND FREAK FROM EARTH!
ONLY I HAVE THE ABILITY TO ATTACK UNDER THE SEA WITHOUT BEING HAMPERED BY THE BONE-CRUSHING WATER PRESSURE!
I CAN'T MOVE NEARLY AS FAST AS HE CAN IN THIS PEA SOUP! AS LONG AS WE'RE DOWN HERE HE DOES HAVE THE EDGE ALL RIGHT!
THERE! THIS IS THE BEGINNING OF THE END FOR YOU HULK!
EVEN YOUR BRUTISH STRENGTH CAN'T SAVE YOU NOW! YOU'LL REMAIN PINNED DOWN THERE UNTIL YOU CAN HOLD YOUR BREATH NO LONGER!
FOR, NO MATTER NOW STRONG YOUR LUNGS ARE, EVEN THEY MUST HAVE THEIR LIMIT!
HE'S RIGHT! I CAN'T STAY HERE FOREVER! SOONER OR LATER, MY BREATH'LL GIVE OUT!
EVEN IF, BY SOME MIRACLE, YOU SHOULD FREE YOURSELF, IT WILL BE TOO LATE TO STOP ME FROM MAKING OFF WITH THE PRIZE... THE WATCHER'S GREATEST TREASURE!
THEY'LL SING OF MY VICTORY FOR AS LONG AS THE GALAXY ENDURES ...LONG AFTER EARTH IS NO MORE THAN A HALF-FORGOTTEN MEMORY!
I DON'T CARE TWO PINS ABOUT EARTH, OR VICTORY, OR WHO IN BLAZES THEY SING ABOUT! BUT NOBODY'S GETTIN' THE BEST OF THE HULK!
THE PART OF ME THAT'S STILL BRUCE BANNER AIN'T GONNA MEET HIS FINISH IN SOME FORSAKEN MUDHOLE IN THE MIDDLE OF NOWHERE! NOT IF THE HULK CAN HELP IT!

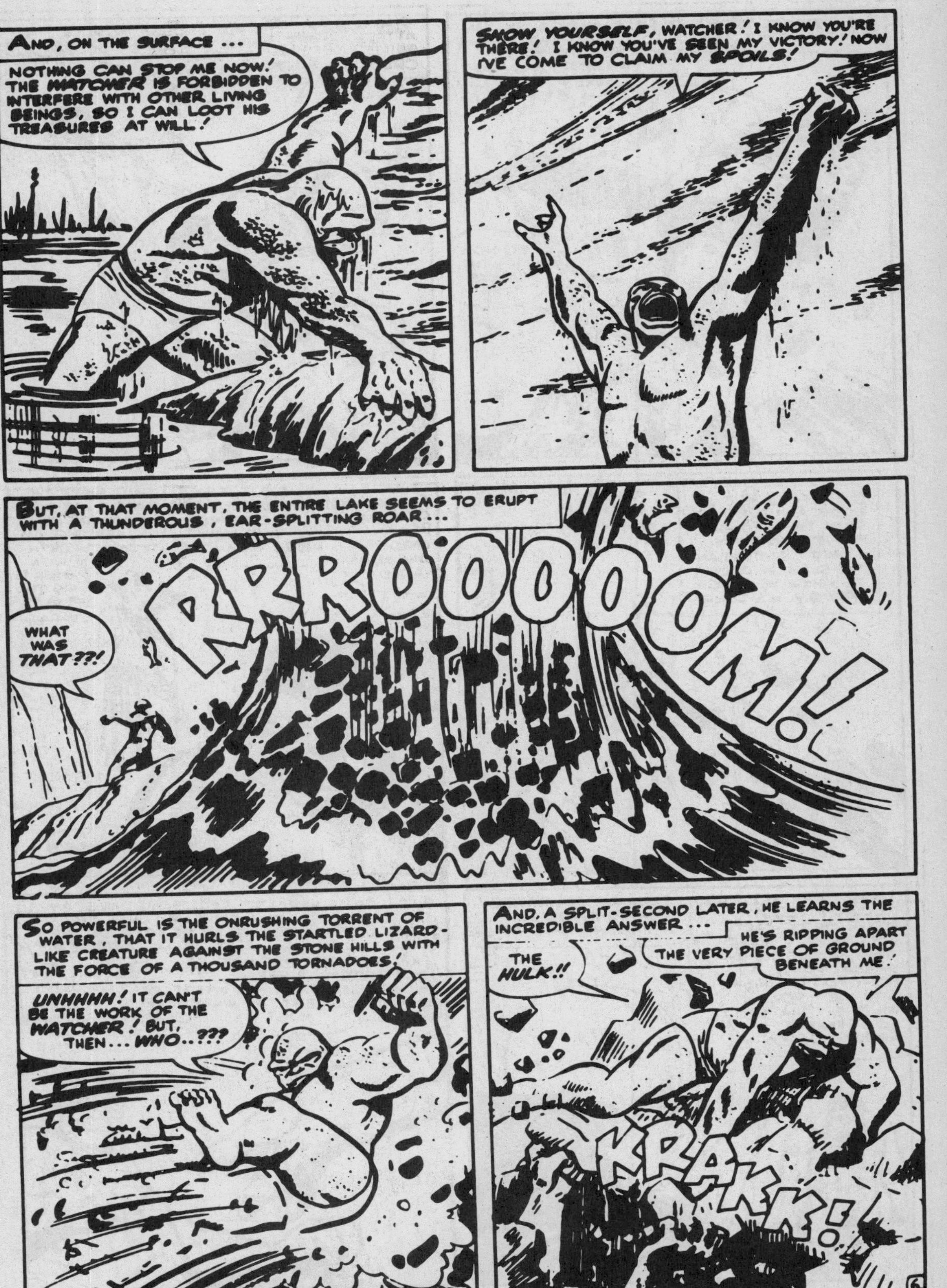
AND, ON THE SURFACE ...
NOTHING CAN STOP ME NOW! THE WATCHER IS FORBIDDEN TO INTERFERE WITH OTHER LIVING BEINGS, SO I CAN LOOT HIS TREASURES AT WILL!
SHOW YOURSELF, WATCHER! I KNOW YOU'RE THERE! I KNOW YOU'VE SEEN MY VICTORY! NOW I'VE COME TO CLAIM MY SPOILS!
BUT, AT THAT MOMENT, THE ENTIRE LAKE SEEMS TO ERUPT WITH A THUNDEROUS, EAR-SPLITTING ROAR...
RRROOOOOM!
WHAT WAS THAT???!
SO POWERFUL IS THE ONRUSHING TORRENT OF WATER, THAT IT HURLS THE STARTLED LIZARD-LIKE CREATURE AGAINST THE STONE HILLS WITH THE FORCE OF A THOUSAND TORNADOES!
UNHHHH! IT CAN'T BE THE WORK OF THE WATCHER! BUT, THEN... WHO...???
AND, A SPLIT-SECOND LATER, HE LEARNS THE INCREDIBLE ANSWER...
THE HULK!!
HE'S RIPPING APART THE VERY PIECE OF GROUND BENEATH ME.
KRAKK!
6

THEN, BEFORE THE STARTLED, SHAKEN ALIEN CAN MAKE ANOTHER MOVE...

YOU DID YOUR *WORST*, AND YOU WEREN'T ABLE TO STOP ME!

SO NOW IT'S THE *HULK'S* TURN!

SEE WHAT I MEAN ???

I PUT ENOUGH MUSCLE INTO THAT TOSS TO KEEP 'IM TRAVELLING FOR *DAYS!*

BUT BEFORE HE CAN ZOOM ANY FURTHER FROM THE WATCHER'S PLANET BOTH THE LIZARD CREATURE AND THE SLAB OF ROCK TO WHICH HE CLINGS *VANISH* IN MID AIR.

FFFFFFT!

WHAT *HAPPENED* TO 'IM? I DIDN'T THROW HIM *THAT* HARD!

NO. BUT IT WAS HARD ENOUGH TO CONVINCE ME THAT *YOU* WERE THE VICTOR.

THUS SINCE THE BATTLE HAS ENDED I TOOK THE LIBERTY OF SENDING HIM FORTHWITH BACK TO HIS OWN PLANET!

THE *WATCHER'S* VOICE.

I NEVER SAW ANYTHING I COULDN'T *BEAT*, EITHER ON THE EARTH.. OR OFF IT. I NEVER SAW ANYONE I DIDN'T WANNA TACKLE AND FIGHT TO THE FINISH WITH.. BUT *YOU*... WHAT IS IT THAT'S SO DIFFERENT ABOUT *YOU??*

I AM THE *WATCHER!* THAT IS *ENOUGH!* THAT ANSWERS ALL

BUT I CAME HERE TO *GET* SOMETHING! AND I CAN'T EVEN LET *YOU* STOP ME! UNTIL I BRING IT BACK TO HIM I'LL NEVER BE FREE OF THE *LEADER!*

EXPLANATIONS ARE NOT NECESSARY. I SEE ALL. I KNOW ALL. I SHALL NOT INTERFERE WITH YOUR QUEST. DO WHAT YOU MUST.

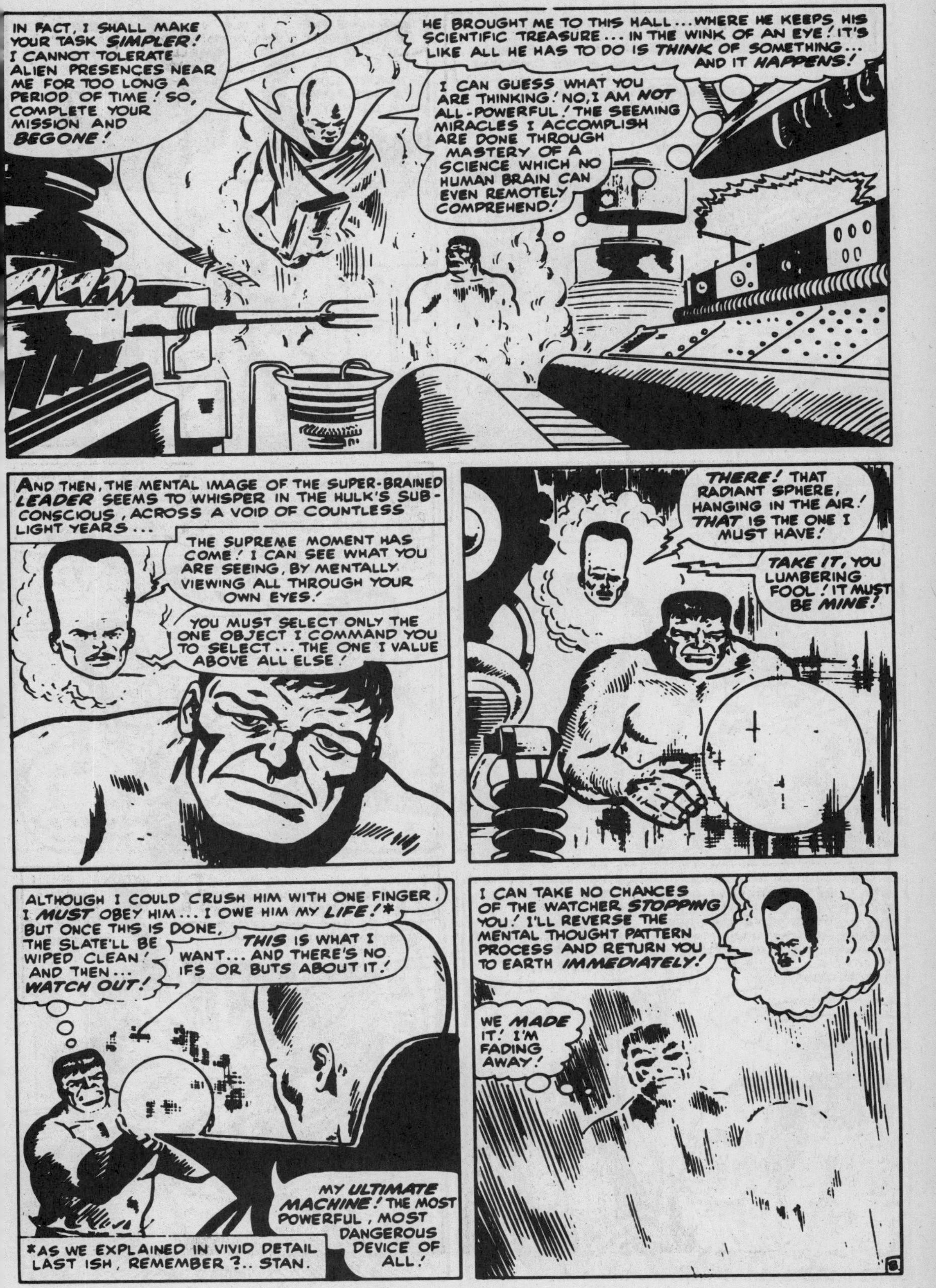
IN FACT, I SHALL MAKE YOUR TASK SIMPLER! I CANNOT TOLERATE ALIEN PRESENCES NEAR ME FOR TOO LONG A PERIOD OF TIME! SO, COMPLETE YOUR MISSION AND BEGONE!
HE BROUGHT ME TO THIS HALL... WHERE HE KEEPS HIS SCIENTIFIC TREASURE... IN THE WINK OF AN EYE! IT'S LIKE ALL HE HAS TO DO IS THINK OF SOMETHING... AND IT HAPPENS!
I CAN GUESS WHAT YOU ARE THINKING! NO, I AM NOT ALL-POWERFUL! THE SEEMING MIRACLES I ACCOMPLISH ARE DONE THROUGH MASTERY OF A SCIENCE WHICH NO HUMAN BRAIN CAN EVEN REMOTELY COMPREHEND!
AND THEN, THE MENTAL IMAGE OF THE SUPER-BRAINED LEADER SEEMS TO WHISPER IN THE HULK'S SUB-CONSCIOUS, ACROSS A VOID OF COUNTLESS LIGHT YEARS...
THE SUPREME MOMENT HAS COME! I CAN SEE WHAT YOU ARE SEEING, BY MENTALLY VIEWING ALL THROUGH YOUR OWN EYES!
YOU MUST SELECT ONLY THE ONE OBJECT I COMMAND YOU TO SELECT... THE ONE I VALUE ABOVE ALL ELSE!
THERE! THAT RADIANT SPHERE, HANGING IN THE AIR! THAT IS THE ONE I MUST HAVE!
TAKE IT, YOU LUMBERING FOOL! IT MUST BE MINE!
ALTHOUGH I COULD CRUSH HIM WITH ONE FINGER, I MUST OBEY HIM... I OWE HIM MY LIFE!* BUT ONCE THIS IS DONE, THE SLATE'LL BE WIPED CLEAN! AND THEN... WATCH OUT!
THIS IS WHAT I WANT... AND THERE'S NO IFS OR BUTS ABOUT IT!
MY ULTIMATE MACHINE! THE MOST POWERFUL, MOST DANGEROUS DEVICE OF ALL!
*AS WE EXPLAINED IN VIVID DETAIL LAST ISH, REMEMBER?.. STAN.
I CAN TAKE NO CHANCES OF THE WATCHER STOPPING YOU! I'LL REVERSE THE MENTAL THOUGHT PATTERN PROCESS AND RETURN YOU TO EARTH IMMEDIATELY!
WE MADE IT! I'M FADING AWAY!
8

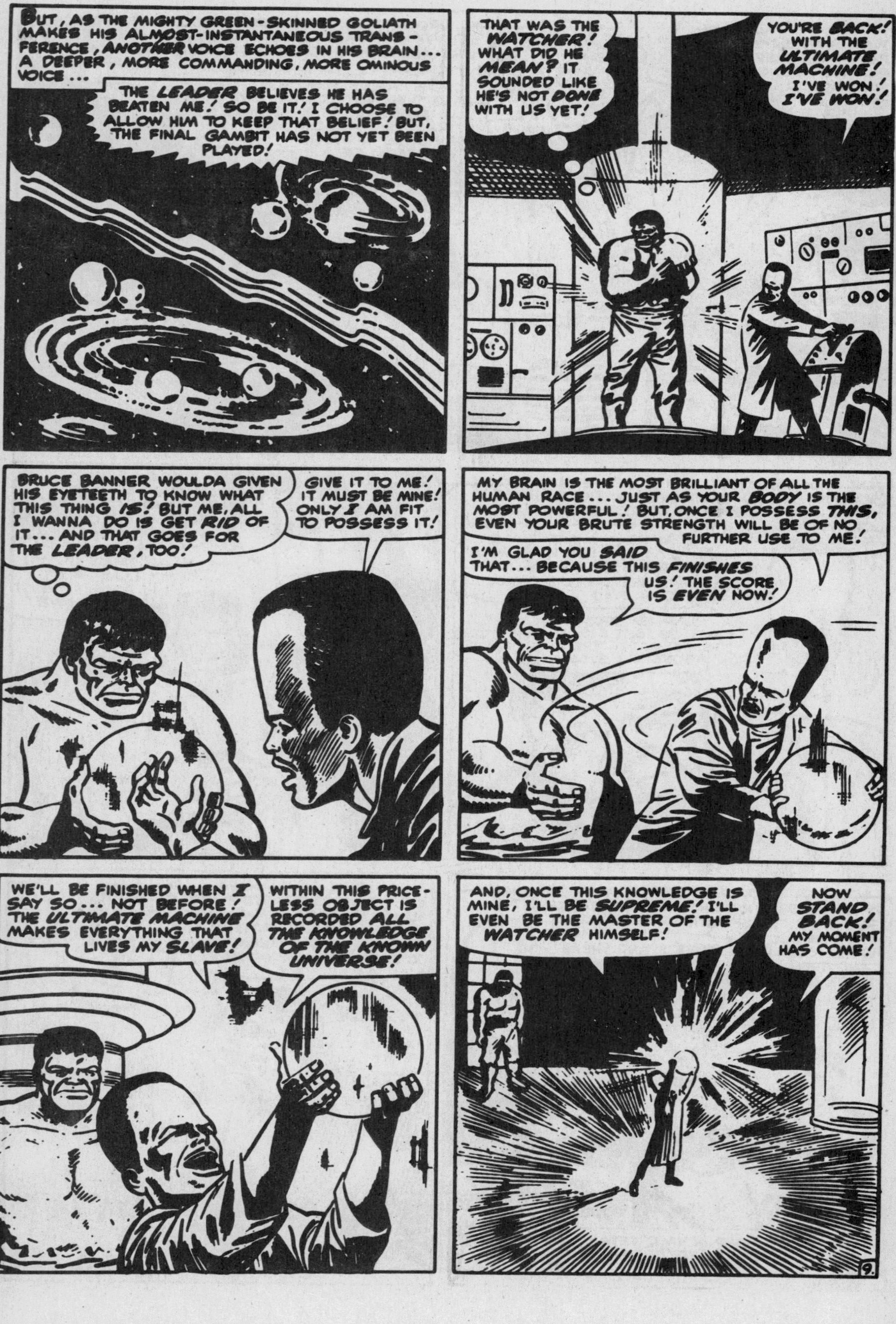
BUT, AS THE MIGHTY GREEN-SKINNED GOLIATH MAKES HIS ALMOST-INSTANTANEOUS TRANS-FERENCE, ANOTHER VOICE ECHOES IN HIS BRAIN... A DEEPER, MORE COMMANDING, MORE OMINOUS VOICE...
THE LEADER BELIEVES HE HAS BEATEN ME! SO BE IT! I CHOOSE TO ALLOW HIM TO KEEP THAT BELIEF! BUT, THE FINAL GAMBIT HAS NOT YET BEEN PLAYED!
THAT WAS THE WATCHER! WHAT DID HE MEAN? IT SOUNDED LIKE HE'S NOT DONE WITH US YET!
YOU'RE BACK! WITH THE ULTIMATE MACHINE! I'VE WON! I'VE WON!
BRUCE BANNER WOULDA GIVEN HIS EYETEETH TO KNOW WHAT THIS THING IS! BUT ME, ALL I WANNA DO IS GET RID OF IT... AND THAT GOES FOR THE LEADER, TOO!
GIVE IT TO ME! IT MUST BE MINE! ONLY I AM FIT TO POSSESS IT!
MY BRAIN IS THE MOST BRILLIANT OF ALL THE HUMAN RACE... JUST AS YOUR BODY IS THE MOST POWERFUL! BUT, ONCE I POSSESS THIS, EVEN YOUR BRUTE STRENGTH WILL BE OF NO FURTHER USE TO ME!
I'M GLAD YOU SAID THAT... BECAUSE THIS FINISHES US! THE SCORE IS EVEN NOW!
WE'LL BE FINISHED WHEN I SAY SO... NOT BEFORE! THE ULTIMATE MACHINE MAKES EVERYTHING THAT LIVES MY SLAVE!
WITHIN THIS PRICE-LESS OBJECT IS RECORDED ALL THE KNOWLEDGE OF THE KNOWN UNIVERSE!
AND, ONCE THIS KNOWLEDGE IS MINE, I'LL BE SUPREME! I'LL EVEN BE THE MASTER OF THE WATCHER HIMSELF!
NOW STAND BACK! MY MOMENT HAS COME!
9.

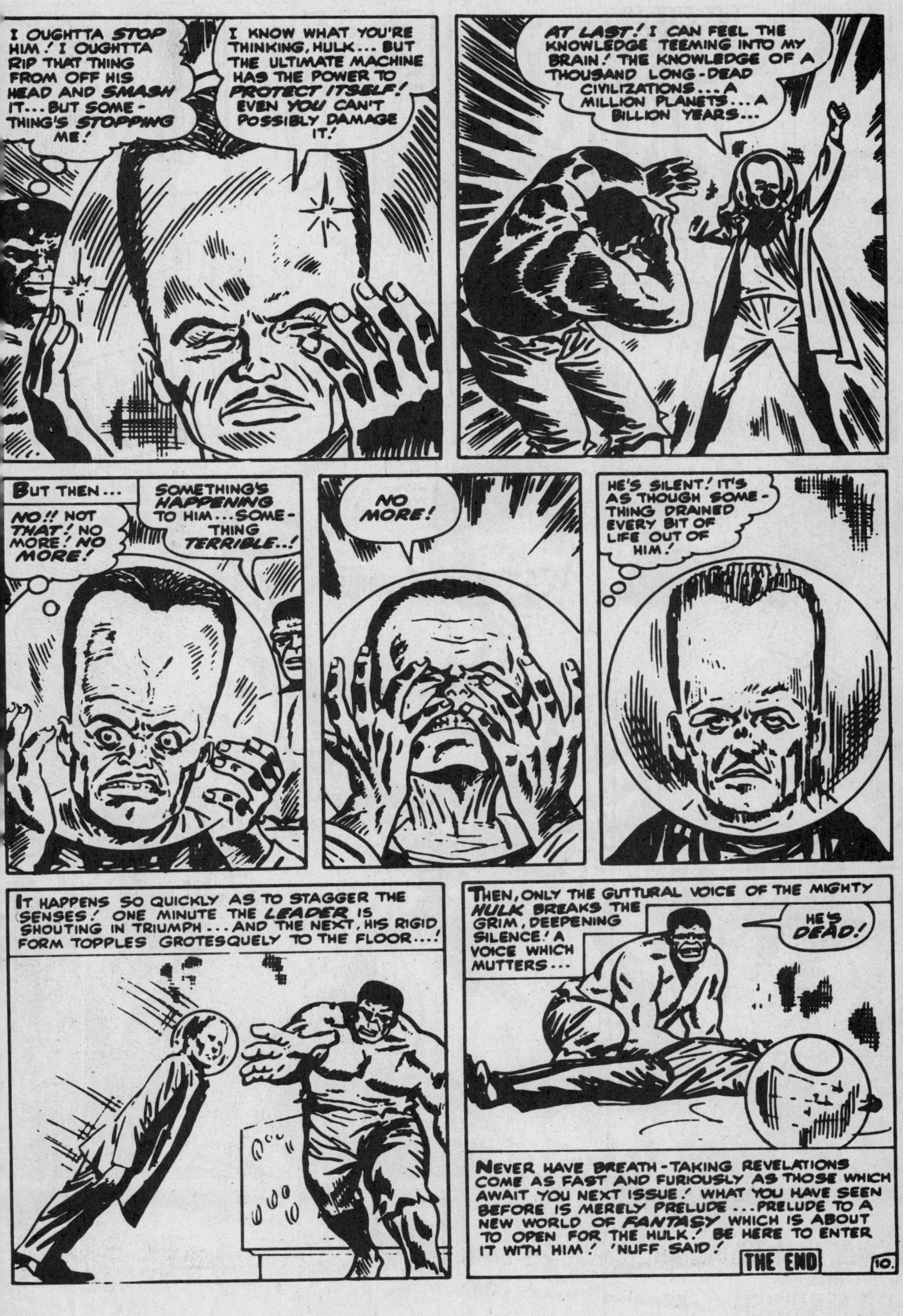

I OUGHTTA STOP HIM! I OUGHTTA RIP THAT THING FROM OFF HIS HEAD AND SMASH IT... BUT SOME-THING'S STOPPING ME!
I KNOW WHAT YOU'RE THINKING, HULK... BUT THE ULTIMATE MACHINE HAS THE POWER TO PROTECT ITSELF! EVEN YOU CAN'T POSSIBLY DAMAGE IT!
AT LAST! I CAN FEEL THE KNOWLEDGE TEEMING INTO MY BRAIN! THE KNOWLEDGE OF A THOUSAND LONG-DEAD CIVILIZATIONS... A MILLION PLANETS... A BILLION YEARS...
BUT THEN...
NO!! NOT THAT! NO MORE! NO MORE!
SOMETHING'S HAPPENING TO HIM... SOME-THING TERRIBLE..!
NO MORE!
HE'S SILENT! IT'S AS THOUGH SOME-THING DRAINED EVERY BIT OF LIFE OUT OF HIM!
IT HAPPENS SO QUICKLY AS TO STAGGER THE SENSES! ONE MINUTE THE LEADER IS SHOUTING IN TRIUMPH... AND THE NEXT, HIS RIGID FORM TOPPLES GROTESQUELY TO THE FLOOR...!
THEN, ONLY THE GUTTURAL VOICE OF THE MIGHTY HULK BREAKS THE GRIM, DEEPENING SILENCE! A VOICE WHICH MUTTERS...
HE'S DEAD!
NEVER HAVE BREATH-TAKING REVELATIONS COME AS FAST AND FURIOUSLY AS THOSE WHICH AWAIT YOU NEXT ISSUE! WHAT YOU HAVE SEEN BEFORE IS MERELY PRELUDE... PRELUDE TO A NEW WORLD OF FANTASY WHICH IS ABOUT TO OPEN FOR THE HULK! BE HERE TO ENTER IT WITH HIM! 'NUFF SAID!
THE END
10.

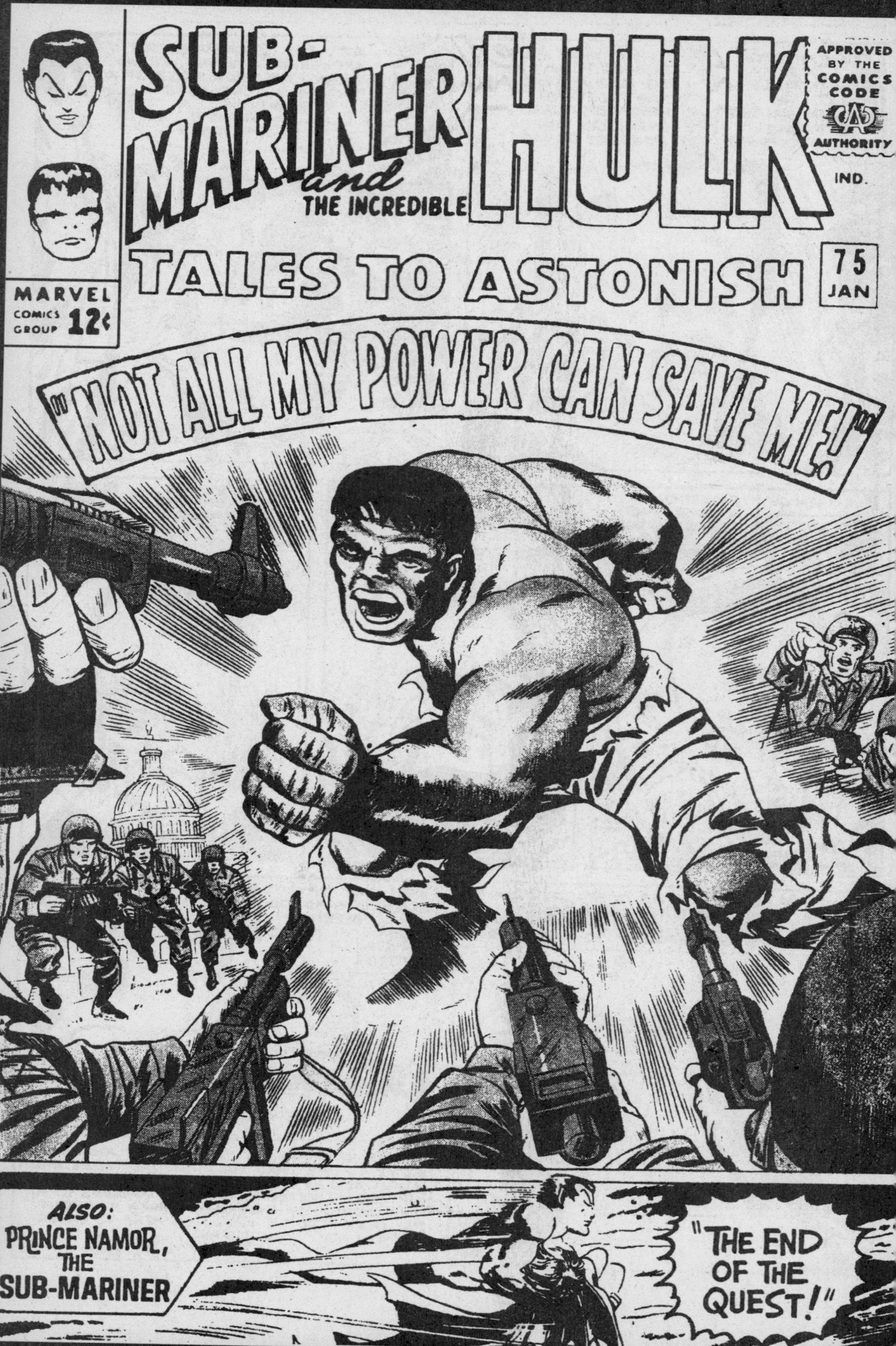

SUB-MARINER and THE INCREDIBLE HULK
APPROVED BY THE COMICS CODE AUTHORITY
IND.
TALES TO ASTONISH
75 JAN
MARVEL COMICS GROUP 12¢
"NOT ALL MY POWER CAN SAVE ME!"
ALSO: PRINCE NAMOR, THE SUB-MARINER
"THE END OF THE QUEST!"

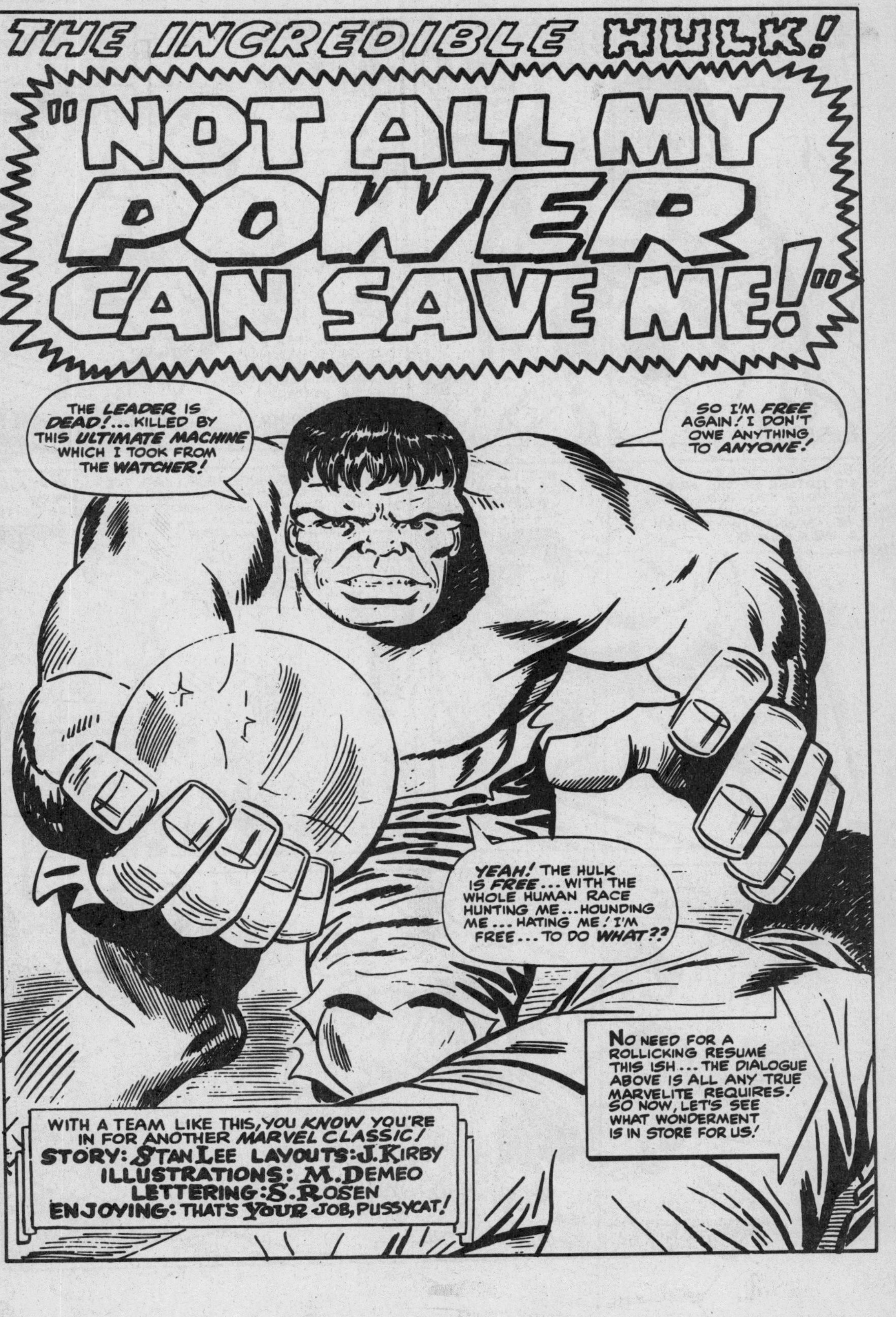
THE INCREDIBLE HULK!
"NOT ALL MY POWER CAN SAVE ME!"
THE LEADER IS DEAD!... KILLED BY THIS ULTIMATE MACHINE WHICH I TOOK FROM THE WATCHER!
SO I'M FREE AGAIN! I DON'T OWE ANYTHING TO ANYONE!
YEAH! THE HULK IS FREE... WITH THE WHOLE HUMAN RACE HUNTING ME... HOUNDING ME... HATING ME! I'M FREE... TO DO WHAT??
NO NEED FOR A ROLLICKING RESUMÉ THIS ISH... THE DIALOGUE ABOVE IS ALL ANY TRUE MARVELITE REQUIRES! SO NOW, LET'S SEE WHAT WONDERMENT IS IN STORE FOR US!
WITH A TEAM LIKE THIS, YOU KNOW YOU'RE IN FOR ANOTHER MARVEL CLASSIC!
STORY: STAN LEE LAYOUTS: J. KIRBY
ILLUSTRATIONS: M. DEMEO
LETTERING: S. ROSEN
ENJOYING: THAT'S YOUR JOB, PUSSYCAT!

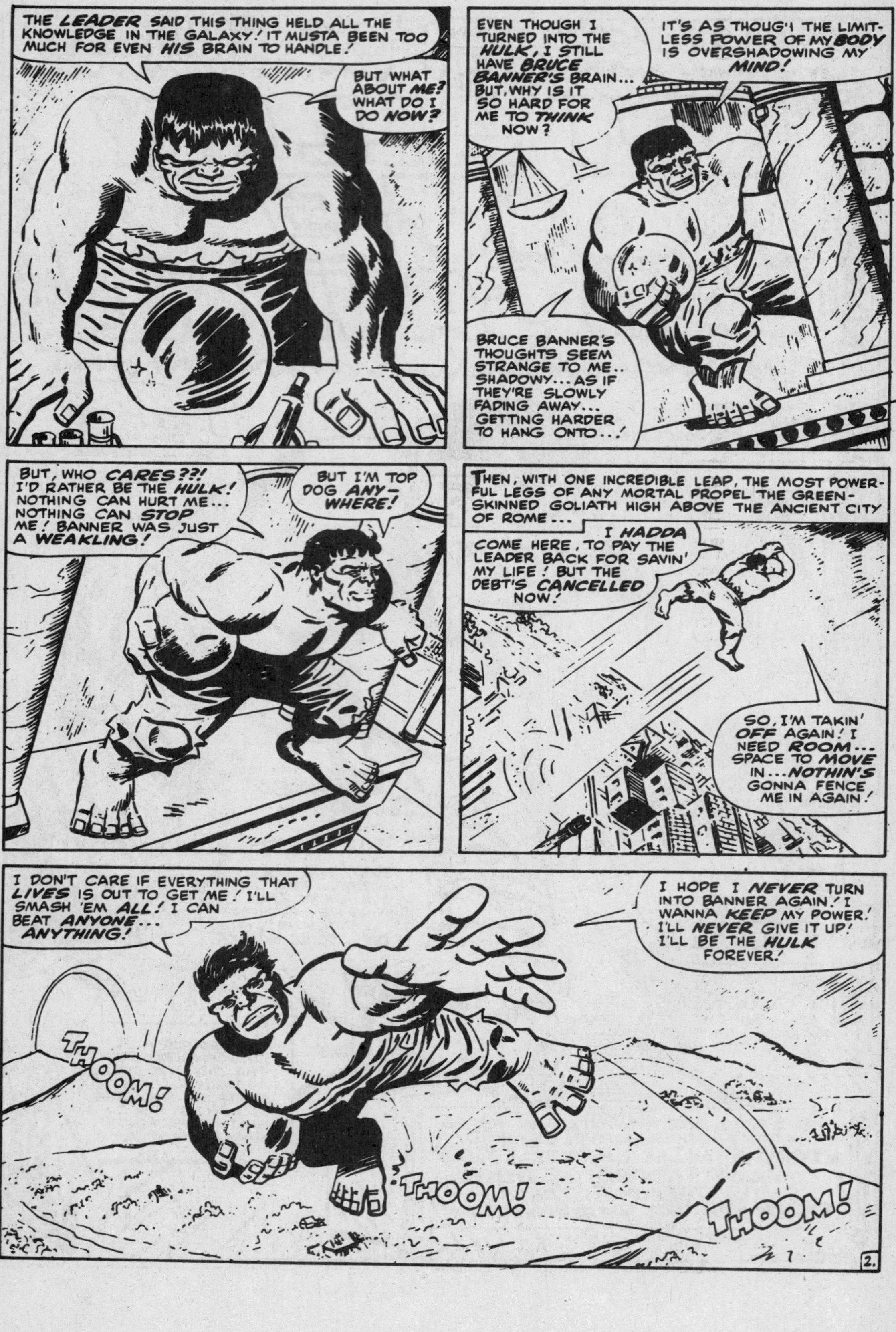
THE LEADER SAID THIS THING HELD ALL THE KNOWLEDGE IN THE GALAXY! IT MUSTA BEEN TOO MUCH FOR EVEN HIS BRAIN TO HANDLE!
BUT WHAT ABOUT ME? WHAT DO I DO NOW?
EVEN THOUGH I TURNED INTO THE HULK, I STILL HAVE BRUCE BANNER'S BRAIN... BUT, WHY IS IT SO HARD FOR ME TO THINK NOW?
IT'S AS THOUGH THE LIMITLESS POWER OF MY BODY IS OVERSHADOWING MY MIND!
BRUCE BANNER'S THOUGHTS SEEM STRANGE TO ME.. SHADOWY... AS IF THEY'RE SLOWLY FADING AWAY... GETTING HARDER TO HANG ONTO...!
BUT, WHO CARES??! I'D RATHER BE THE HULK! NOTHING CAN HURT ME... NOTHING CAN STOP ME! BANNER WAS JUST A WEAKLING!
BUT I'M TOP DOG ANYWHERE!
THEN, WITH ONE INCREDIBLE LEAP, THE MOST POWERFUL LEGS OF ANY MORTAL PROPEL THE GREEN-SKINNED GOLIATH HIGH ABOVE THE ANCIENT CITY OF ROME...
I HADDA COME HERE, TO PAY THE LEADER BACK FOR SAVIN' MY LIFE! BUT THE DEBT'S CANCELLED NOW!
SO, I'M TAKIN' OFF AGAIN! I NEED ROOM... SPACE TO MOVE IN... NOTHIN'S GONNA FENCE ME IN AGAIN!
I DON'T CARE IF EVERYTHING THAT LIVES IS OUT TO GET ME! I'LL SMASH 'EM ALL! I CAN BEAT ANYONE... ANYTHING!
I HOPE I NEVER TURN INTO BANNER AGAIN! I WANNA KEEP MY POWER! I'LL NEVER GIVE IT UP! I'LL BE THE HULK FOREVER!
THOOM!
THOOM!
THOOM!
2.

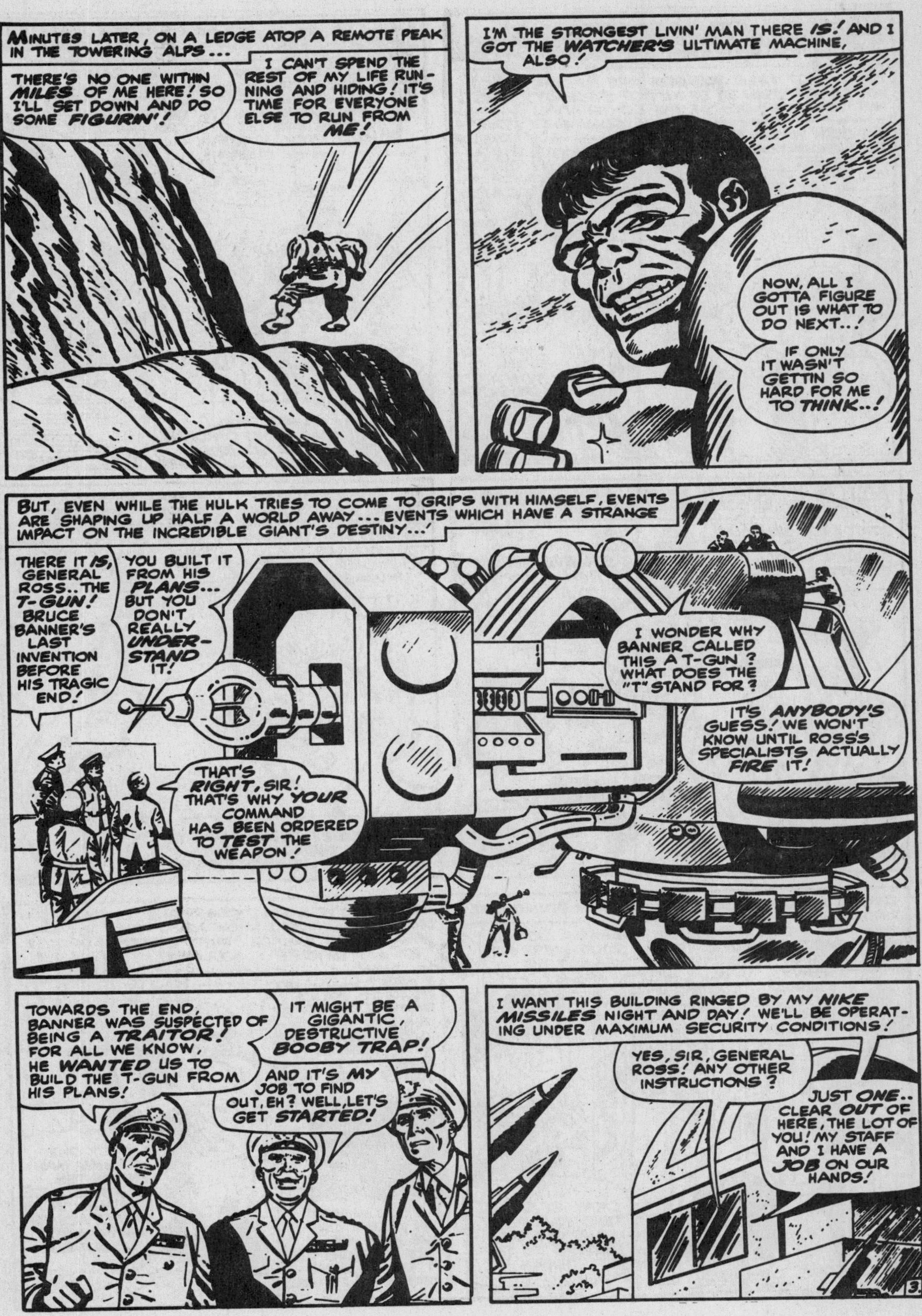
MINUTES LATER, ON A LEDGE ATOP A REMOTE PEAK IN THE TOWERING ALPS...
THERE'S NO ONE WITHIN MILES OF ME HERE! SO I'LL SET DOWN AND DO SOME FIGURIN'!
I CAN'T SPEND THE REST OF MY LIFE RUNNING AND HIDING! IT'S TIME FOR EVERYONE ELSE TO RUN FROM ME!
I'M THE STRONGEST LIVIN' MAN THERE IS! AND I GOT THE WATCHER'S ULTIMATE MACHINE, ALSO!
NOW, ALL I GOTTA FIGURE OUT IS WHAT TO DO NEXT..!
IF ONLY IT WASN'T GETTIN SO HARD FOR ME TO THINK..!
BUT, EVEN WHILE THE HULK TRIES TO COME TO GRIPS WITH HIMSELF, EVENTS ARE SHAPING UP HALF A WORLD AWAY... EVENTS WHICH HAVE A STRANGE IMPACT ON THE INCREDIBLE GIANT'S DESTINY...!
THERE IT IS, GENERAL ROSS.. THE T-GUN! BRUCE BANNER'S LAST INVENTION BEFORE HIS TRAGIC END!
YOU BUILT IT FROM HIS PLANS... BUT YOU DON'T REALLY UNDERSTAND IT!
THAT'S RIGHT, SIR! THAT'S WHY YOUR COMMAND HAS BEEN ORDERED TO TEST THE WEAPON!
I WONDER WHY BANNER CALLED THIS A T-GUN? WHAT DOES THE "T" STAND FOR?
IT'S ANYBODY'S GUESS! WE WON'T KNOW UNTIL ROSS'S SPECIALISTS ACTUALLY FIRE IT!
TOWARDS THE END, BANNER WAS SUSPECTED OF BEING A TRAITOR! FOR ALL WE KNOW, HE WANTED US TO BUILD THE T-GUN FROM HIS PLANS!
IT MIGHT BE A GIGANTIC, DESTRUCTIVE BOOBY TRAP!
AND IT'S MY JOB TO FIND OUT, EH? WELL, LET'S GET STARTED!
I WANT THIS BUILDING RINGED BY MY NIKE MISSILES NIGHT AND DAY! WE'LL BE OPERATING UNDER MAXIMUM SECURITY CONDITIONS!
YES, SIR, GENERAL ROSS! ANY OTHER INSTRUCTIONS?
JUST ONE.. CLEAR OUT OF HERE, THE LOT OF YOU! MY STAFF AND I HAVE A JOB ON OUR HANDS!
3.

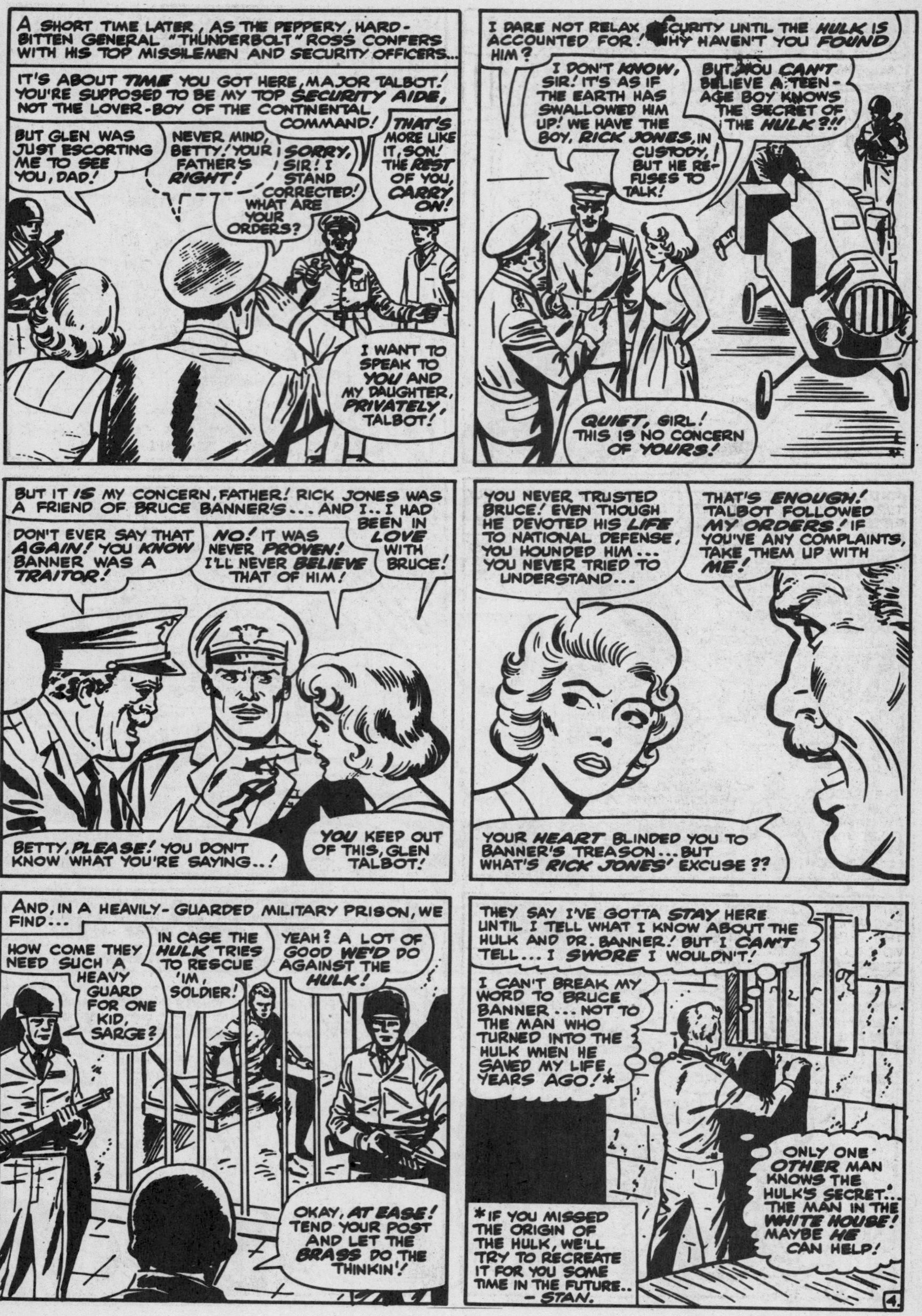
A SHORT TIME LATER, AS THE PEPPERY, HARD-BITTEN GENERAL "THUNDERBOLT" ROSS CONFERS WITH HIS TOP MISSILEMEN AND SECURITY OFFICERS...
IT'S ABOUT TIME YOU GOT HERE, MAJOR TALBOT! YOU'RE SUPPOSED TO BE MY TOP SECURITY AIDE, NOT THE LOVER-BOY OF THE CONTINENTAL COMMAND!
BUT GLEN WAS JUST ESCORTING ME TO SEE YOU, DAD!
NEVER MIND, BETTY! YOUR FATHER'S RIGHT!
SORRY, SIR! I STAND CORRECTED! WHAT ARE YOUR ORDERS?
THAT'S MORE LIKE IT, SON! THE REST OF YOU, CARRY ON!
I WANT TO SPEAK TO YOU AND MY DAUGHTER, PRIVATELY, TALBOT!
I DARE NOT RELAX SECURITY UNTIL THE HULK IS ACCOUNTED FOR! WHY HAVEN'T YOU FOUND HIM?
I DON'T KNOW, SIR! IT'S AS IF THE EARTH HAS SWALLOWED HIM UP! WE HAVE THE BOY, RICK JONES, IN CUSTODY, BUT HE REFUSES TO TALK!
BUT YOU CAN'T BELIEVE A TEEN-AGE BOY KNOWS THE SECRET OF THE HULK?!!
QUIET, GIRL! THIS IS NO CONCERN OF YOURS!
BUT IT IS MY CONCERN, FATHER! RICK JONES WAS A FRIEND OF BRUCE BANNER'S... AND I.. I HAD BEEN IN LOVE WITH BRUCE!
DON'T EVER SAY THAT AGAIN! YOU KNOW BANNER WAS A TRAITOR!
NO! IT WAS NEVER PROVEN! I'LL NEVER BELIEVE THAT OF HIM!
BETTY, PLEASE! YOU DON'T KNOW WHAT YOU'RE SAYING..!
YOU KEEP OUT OF THIS, GLEN TALBOT!
YOU NEVER TRUSTED BRUCE! EVEN THOUGH HE DEVOTED HIS LIFE TO NATIONAL DEFENSE, YOU HOUNDED HIM... YOU NEVER TRIED TO UNDERSTAND...
THAT'S ENOUGH! TALBOT FOLLOWED MY ORDERS! IF YOU'VE ANY COMPLAINTS, TAKE THEM UP WITH ME!
YOUR HEART BLINDED YOU TO BANNER'S TREASON... BUT WHAT'S RICK JONES' EXCUSE??
AND, IN A HEAVILY-GUARDED MILITARY PRISON, WE FIND...
HOW COME THEY NEED SUCH A HEAVY GUARD FOR ONE KID, SARGE?
IN CASE THE HULK TRIES TO RESCUE 'IM, SOLDIER!
YEAH? A LOT OF GOOD WE'D DO AGAINST THE HULK!
OKAY, AT EASE! TEND YOUR POST AND LET THE BRASS DO THE THINKIN'!
THEY SAY I'VE GOTTA STAY HERE UNTIL I TELL WHAT I KNOW ABOUT THE HULK AND DR. BANNER! BUT I CAN'T TELL... I SWORE I WOULDN'T!
I CAN'T BREAK MY WORD TO BRUCE BANNER... NOT TO THE MAN WHO TURNED INTO THE HULK WHEN HE SAVED MY LIFE, YEARS AGO!*
ONLY ONE OTHER MAN KNOWS THE HULK'S SECRET... THE MAN IN THE WHITE HOUSE! MAYBE HE CAN HELP!
*IF YOU MISSED THE ORIGIN OF THE HULK, WE'LL TRY TO RECREATE IT FOR YOU SOME TIME IN THE FUTURE.. — STAN.
4.

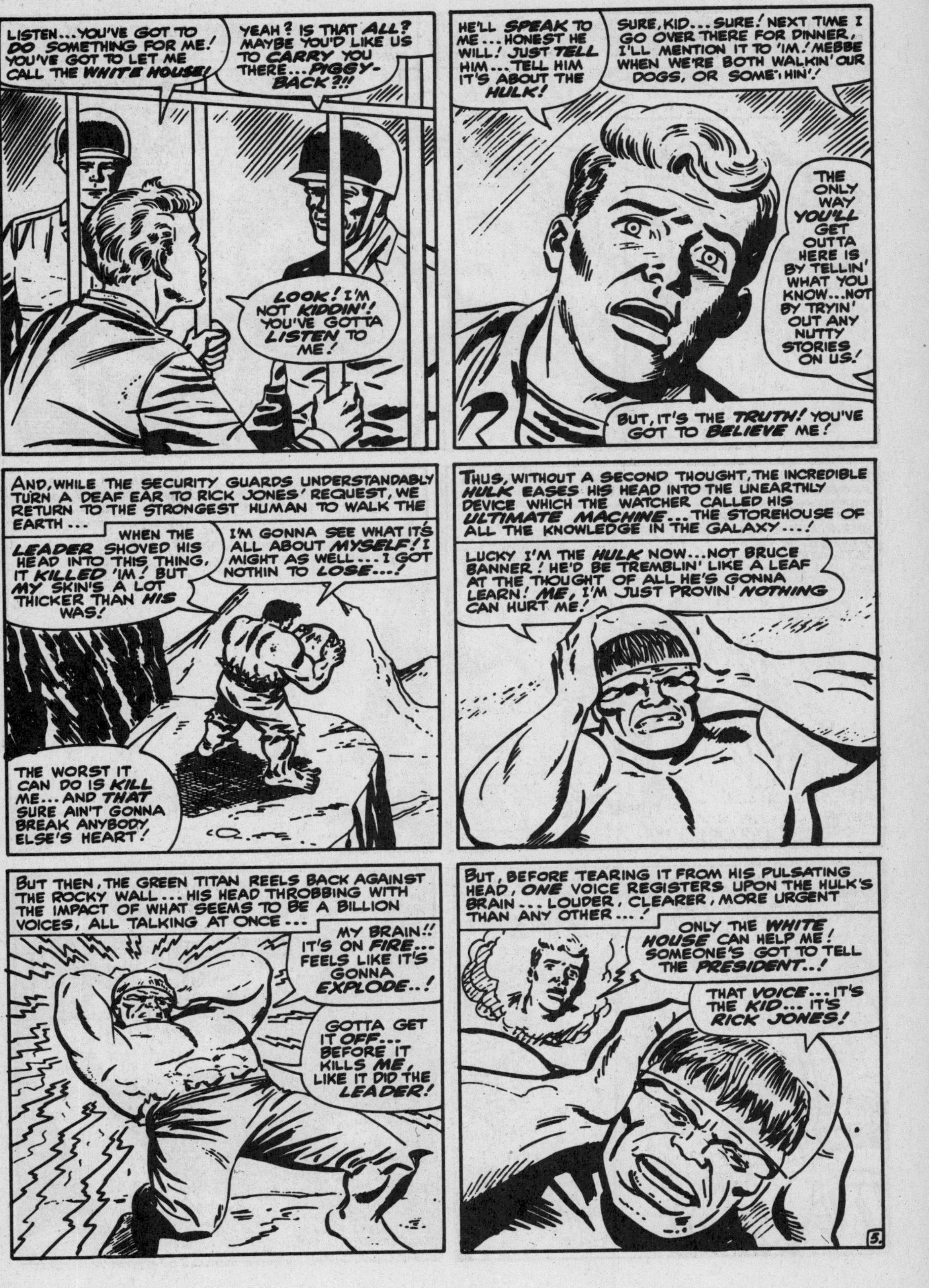

LISTEN...YOU'VE GOT TO DO SOMETHING FOR ME! YOU'VE GOT TO LET ME CALL THE WHITE HOUSE!
YEAH? IS THAT ALL? MAYBE YOU'D LIKE US TO CARRY YOU THERE...PIGGY-BACK?!!
LOOK! I'M NOT KIDDIN'! YOU'VE GOTTA LISTEN TO ME!
HE'LL SPEAK TO ME...HONEST HE WILL! JUST TELL HIM...TELL HIM IT'S ABOUT THE HULK!
SURE, KID...SURE! NEXT TIME I GO OVER THERE FOR DINNER, I'LL MENTION IT TO 'IM! MEBBE WHEN WE'RE BOTH WALKIN' OUR DOGS, OR SOME'HIN'!
THE ONLY WAY YOU'LL GET OUTTA HERE IS BY TELLIN' WHAT YOU KNOW...NOT BY TRYIN' OUT ANY NUTTY STORIES ON US!
BUT, IT'S THE TRUTH! YOU'VE GOT TO BELIEVE ME!
AND, WHILE THE SECURITY GUARDS UNDERSTANDABLY TURN A DEAF EAR TO RICK JONES' REQUEST, WE RETURN TO THE STRONGEST HUMAN TO WALK THE EARTH...
WHEN THE LEADER SHOVED HIS HEAD INTO THIS THING, IT KILLED 'IM! BUT MY SKIN'S A LOT THICKER THAN HIS WAS!
I'M GONNA SEE WHAT IT'S ALL ABOUT MYSELF! I MIGHT AS WELL...I GOT NOTHIN TO LOSE...!
THE WORST IT CAN DO IS KILL ME...AND THAT SURE AIN'T GONNA BREAK ANYBODY ELSE'S HEART!
THUS, WITHOUT A SECOND THOUGHT, THE INCREDIBLE HULK EASES HIS HEAD INTO THE UNEARTHLY DEVICE WHICH THE WATCHER CALLED HIS ULTIMATE MACHINE...THE STOREHOUSE OF ALL THE KNOWLEDGE IN THE GALAXY...!
LUCKY I'M THE HULK NOW...NOT BRUCE BANNER! HE'D BE TREMBLIN' LIKE A LEAF AT THE THOUGHT OF ALL HE'S GONNA LEARN! ME, I'M JUST PROVIN' NOTHING CAN HURT ME!
BUT THEN, THE GREEN TITAN REELS BACK AGAINST THE ROCKY WALL...HIS HEAD THROBBING WITH THE IMPACT OF WHAT SEEMS TO BE A BILLION VOICES, ALL TALKING AT ONCE...
MY BRAIN!! IT'S ON FIRE...FEELS LIKE IT'S GONNA EXPLODE..!
GOTTA GET IT OFF...BEFORE IT KILLS ME, LIKE IT DID THE LEADER!
BUT, BEFORE TEARING IT FROM HIS PULSATING HEAD, ONE VOICE REGISTERS UPON THE HULK'S BRAIN...LOUDER, CLEARER, MORE URGENT THAN ANY OTHER...!
ONLY THE WHITE HOUSE CAN HELP ME! SOMEONE'S GOT TO TELL THE PRESIDENT..!
THAT VOICE...IT'S THE KID...IT'S RICK JONES!
5.

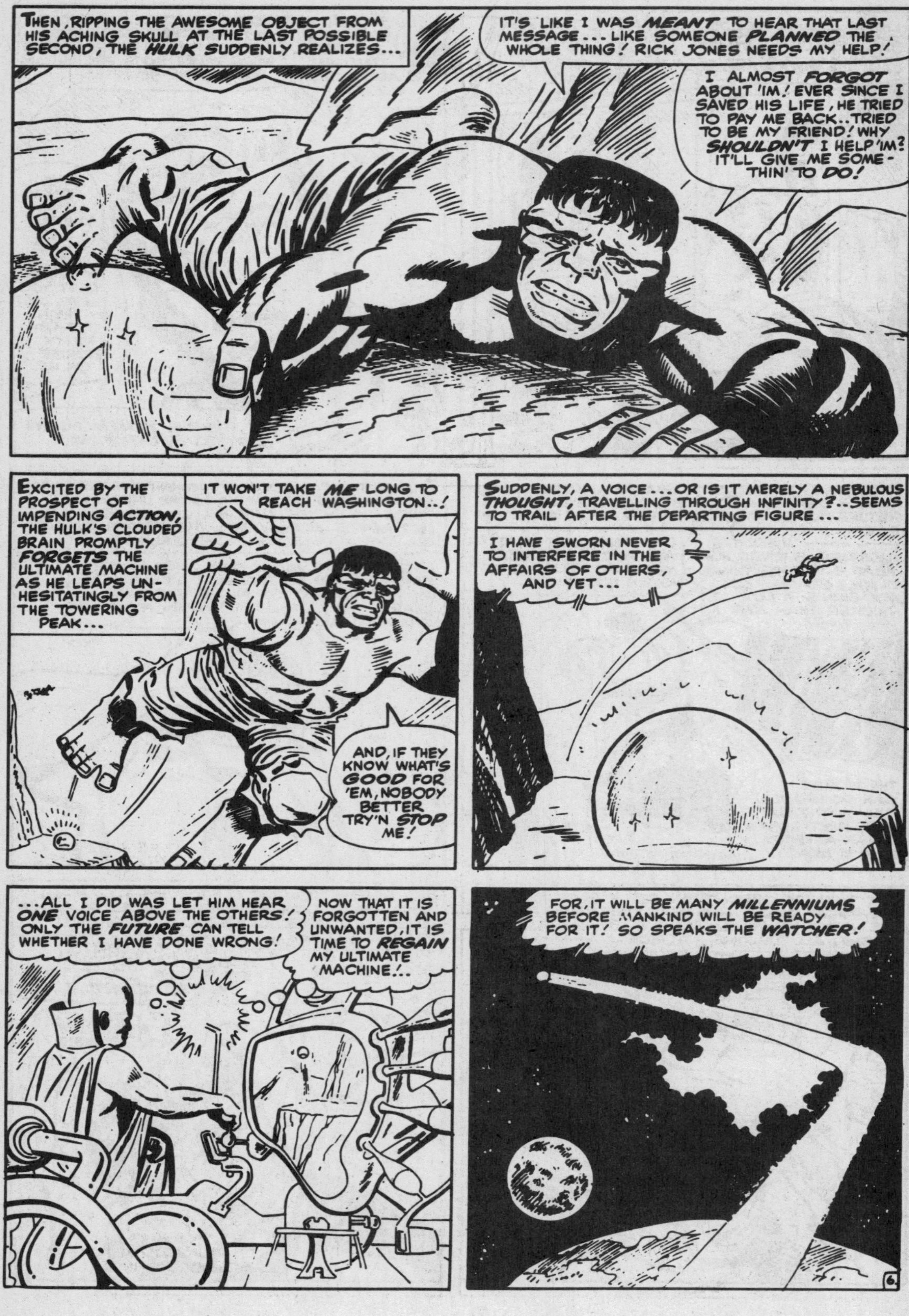
THEN, RIPPING THE AWESOME OBJECT FROM HIS ACHING SKULL AT THE LAST POSSIBLE SECOND, THE HULK SUDDENLY REALIZES...
IT'S LIKE I WAS MEANT TO HEAR THAT LAST MESSAGE... LIKE SOMEONE PLANNED THE WHOLE THING! RICK JONES NEEDS MY HELP!
I ALMOST FORGOT ABOUT 'IM! EVER SINCE I SAVED HIS LIFE, HE TRIED TO PAY ME BACK.. TRIED TO BE MY FRIEND! WHY SHOULDN'T I HELP 'IM? IT'LL GIVE ME SOME-THIN' TO DO!
EXCITED BY THE PROSPECT OF IMPENDING ACTION, THE HULK'S CLOUDED BRAIN PROMPTLY FORGETS THE ULTIMATE MACHINE AS HE LEAPS UN-HESITATINGLY FROM THE TOWERING PEAK...
IT WON'T TAKE ME LONG TO REACH WASHINGTON..!
AND, IF THEY KNOW WHAT'S GOOD FOR 'EM, NOBODY BETTER TRY'N STOP ME!
SUDDENLY, A VOICE... OR IS IT MERELY A NEBULOUS THOUGHT, TRAVELLING THROUGH INFINITY?.. SEEMS TO TRAIL AFTER THE DEPARTING FIGURE...
I HAVE SWORN NEVER TO INTERFERE IN THE AFFAIRS OF OTHERS, AND YET...
...ALL I DID WAS LET HIM HEAR ONE VOICE ABOVE THE OTHERS! ONLY THE FUTURE CAN TELL WHETHER I HAVE DONE WRONG!
NOW THAT IT IS FORGOTTEN AND UNWANTED, IT IS TIME TO REGAIN MY ULTIMATE MACHINE!..
FOR, IT WILL BE MANY MILLENNIUMS BEFORE MANKIND WILL BE READY FOR IT! SO SPEAKS THE WATCHER!
6

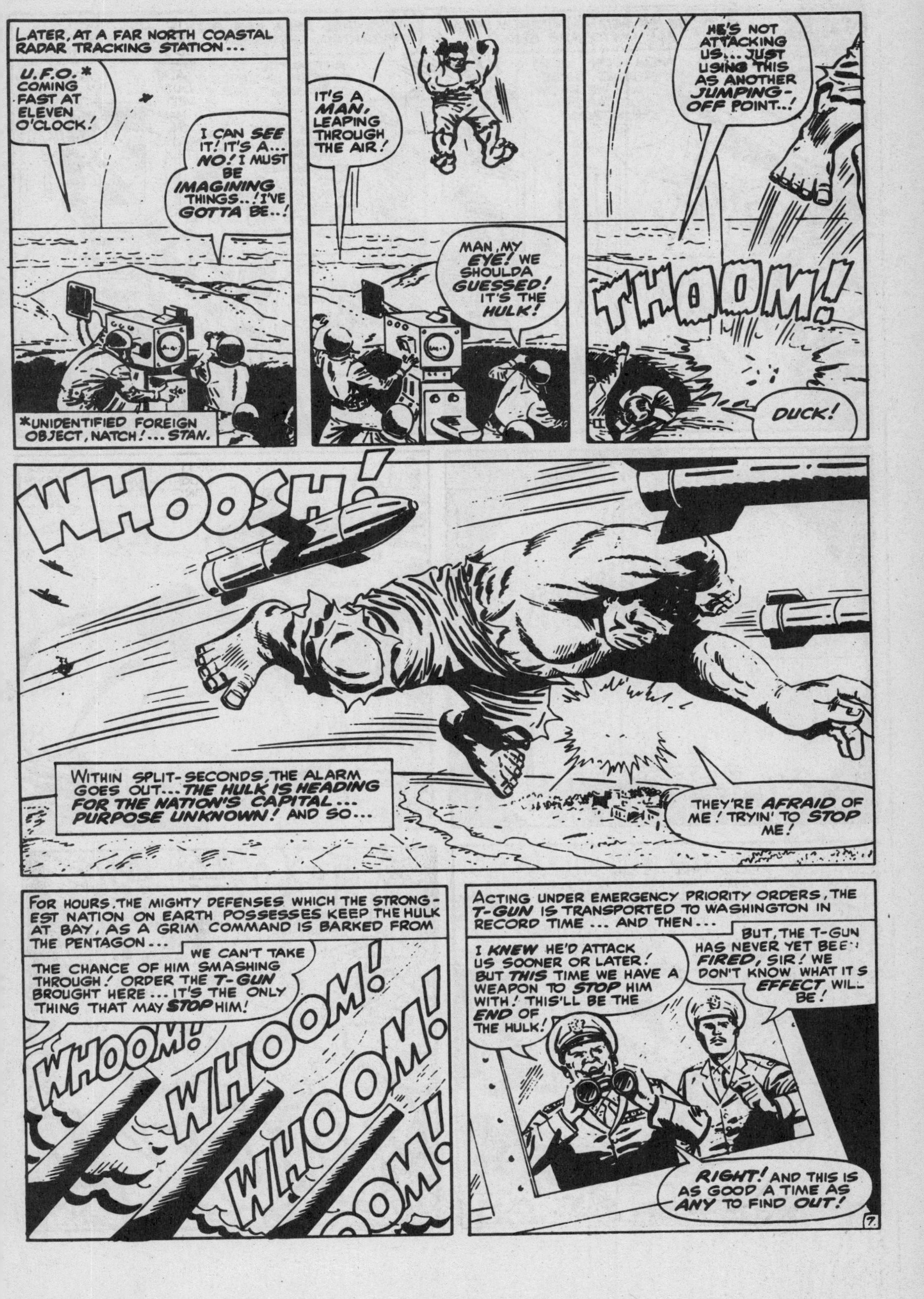

LATER, AT A FAR NORTH COASTAL RADAR TRACKING STATION...
U.F.O.* COMING FAST AT ELEVEN O'CLOCK!
I CAN SEE IT! IT'S A... NO! I MUST BE IMAGINING THINGS...! I'VE GOTTA BE..!
*UNIDENTIFIED FOREIGN OBJECT, NATCH!... STAN.
IT'S A MAN, LEAPING THROUGH THE AIR!
MAN, MY EYE! WE SHOULDA GUESSED! IT'S THE HULK!
HE'S NOT ATTACKING US... JUST USING THIS AS ANOTHER JUMPING-OFF POINT..!
THOOM!
DUCK!
WHOOSH!
WITHIN SPLIT-SECONDS, THE ALARM GOES OUT... THE HULK IS HEADING FOR THE NATION'S CAPITAL... PURPOSE UNKNOWN! AND SO...
THEY'RE AFRAID OF ME! TRYIN' TO STOP ME!
FOR HOURS, THE MIGHTY DEFENSES WHICH THE STRONGEST NATION ON EARTH POSSESSES KEEP THE HULK AT BAY, AS A GRIM COMMAND IS BARKED FROM THE PENTAGON...
WE CAN'T TAKE THE CHANCE OF HIM SMASHING THROUGH! ORDER THE T-GUN BROUGHT HERE... IT'S THE ONLY THING THAT MAY STOP HIM!
WHOOM! WHOOM! WHOOM! WHOOM!
ACTING UNDER EMERGENCY PRIORITY ORDERS, THE T-GUN IS TRANSPORTED TO WASHINGTON IN RECORD TIME ... AND THEN...
I KNEW HE'D ATTACK US SOONER OR LATER! BUT THIS TIME WE HAVE A WEAPON TO STOP HIM WITH! THIS'LL BE THE END OF THE HULK!
BUT, THE T-GUN HAS NEVER YET BEEN FIRED, SIR! WE DON'T KNOW WHAT ITS EFFECT WILL BE!
RIGHT! AND THIS IS AS GOOD A TIME AS ANY TO FIND OUT!
7

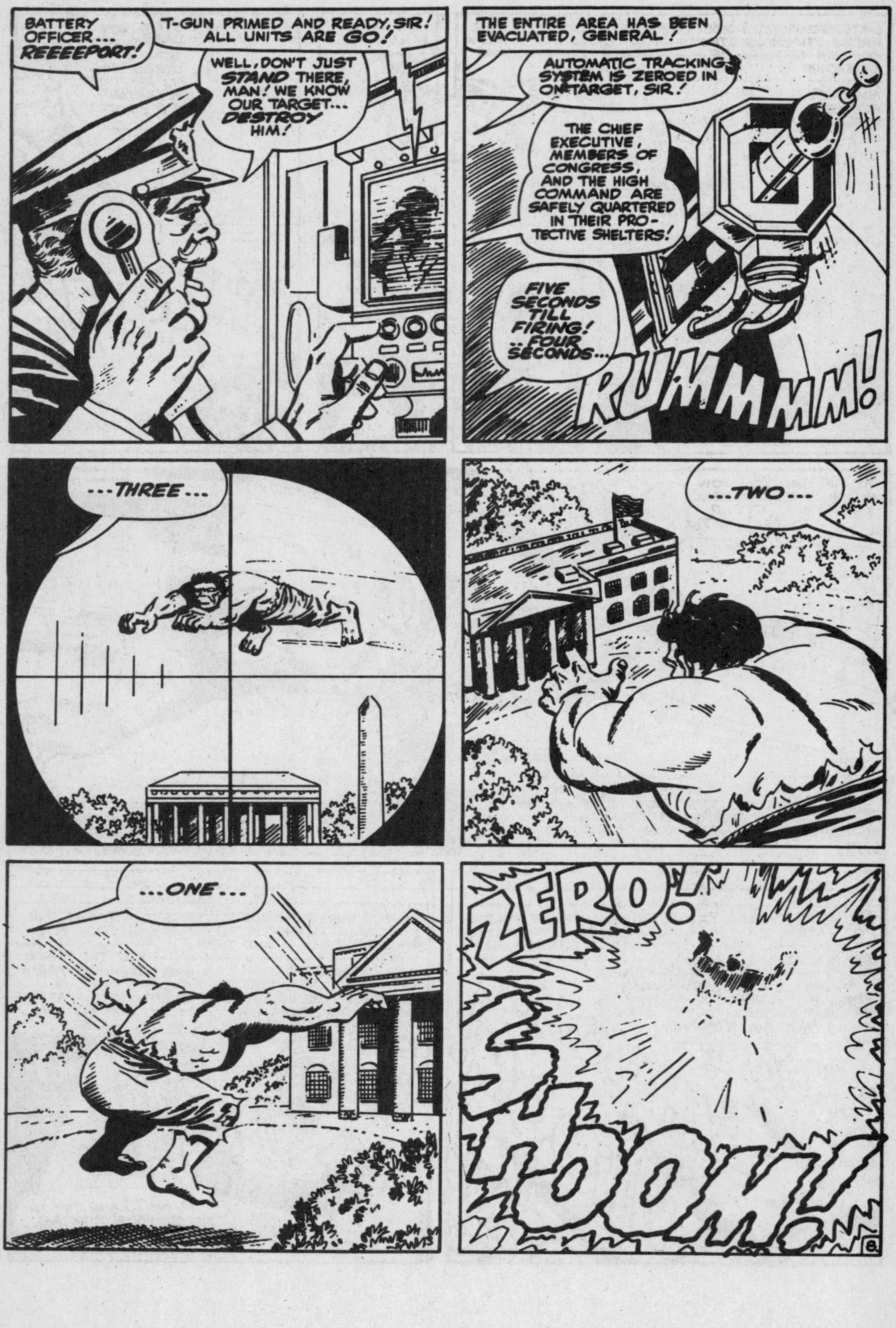
BATTERY OFFICER... REEEEEPORT!
T-GUN PRIMED AND READY, SIR! ALL UNITS ARE GO!
WELL, DON'T JUST STAND THERE, MAN! WE KNOW OUR TARGET... DESTROY HIM!
THE ENTIRE AREA HAS BEEN EVACUATED, GENERAL!
AUTOMATIC TRACKING SYSTEM IS ZEROED IN ON TARGET, SIR!
THE CHIEF EXECUTIVE, MEMBERS OF CONGRESS, AND THE HIGH COMMAND ARE SAFELY QUARTERED IN THEIR PROTECTIVE SHELTERS!
FIVE SECONDS TILL FIRING! ..FOUR SECONDS...
RUMMMMM!
...THREE...
...TWO...
...ONE...
ZERO!
FOOM!
8

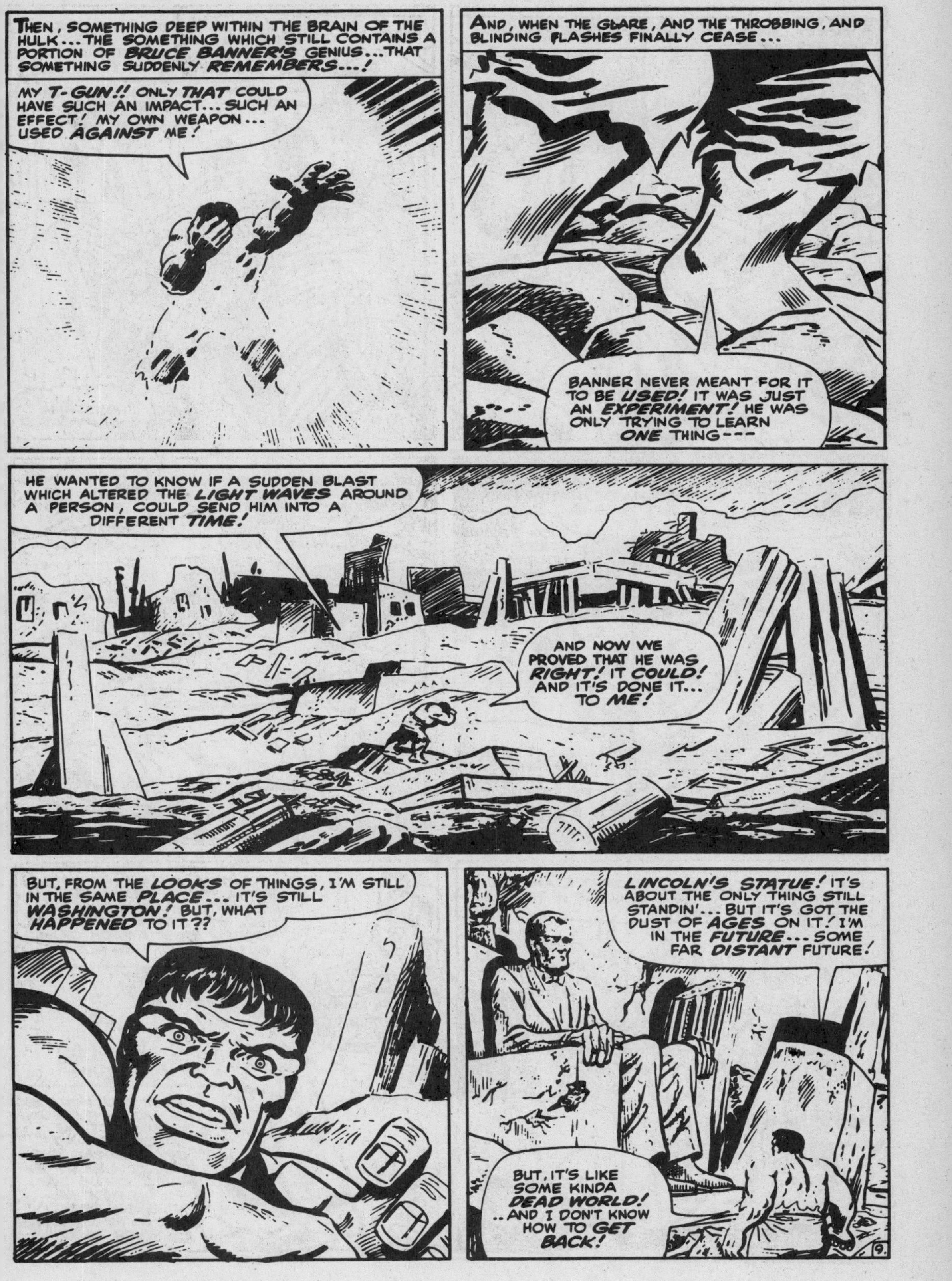
THEN, SOMETHING DEEP WITHIN THE BRAIN OF THE HULK... THE SOMETHING WHICH STILL CONTAINS A PORTION OF BRUCE BANNER'S GENIUS... THAT SOMETHING SUDDENLY REMEMBERS...!
MY T-GUN!! ONLY THAT COULD HAVE SUCH AN IMPACT... SUCH AN EFFECT! MY OWN WEAPON... USED AGAINST ME!
AND, WHEN THE GLARE, AND THE THROBBING, AND BLINDING FLASHES FINALLY CEASE...
BANNER NEVER MEANT FOR IT TO BE USED! IT WAS JUST AN EXPERIMENT! HE WAS ONLY TRYING TO LEARN ONE THING---
HE WANTED TO KNOW IF A SUDDEN BLAST WHICH ALTERED THE LIGHT WAVES AROUND A PERSON, COULD SEND HIM INTO A DIFFERENT TIME!
AND NOW WE PROVED THAT HE WAS RIGHT! IT COULD! AND IT'S DONE IT... TO ME!
BUT, FROM THE LOOKS OF THINGS, I'M STILL IN THE SAME PLACE... IT'S STILL WASHINGTON! BUT, WHAT HAPPENED TO IT??
LINCOLN'S STATUE! IT'S ABOUT THE ONLY THING STILL STANDIN'... BUT IT'S GOT THE DUST OF AGES ON IT! I'M IN THE FUTURE... SOME FAR DISTANT FUTURE!
BUT, IT'S LIKE SOME KINDA DEAD WORLD! ..AND I DON'T KNOW HOW TO GET BACK!
9

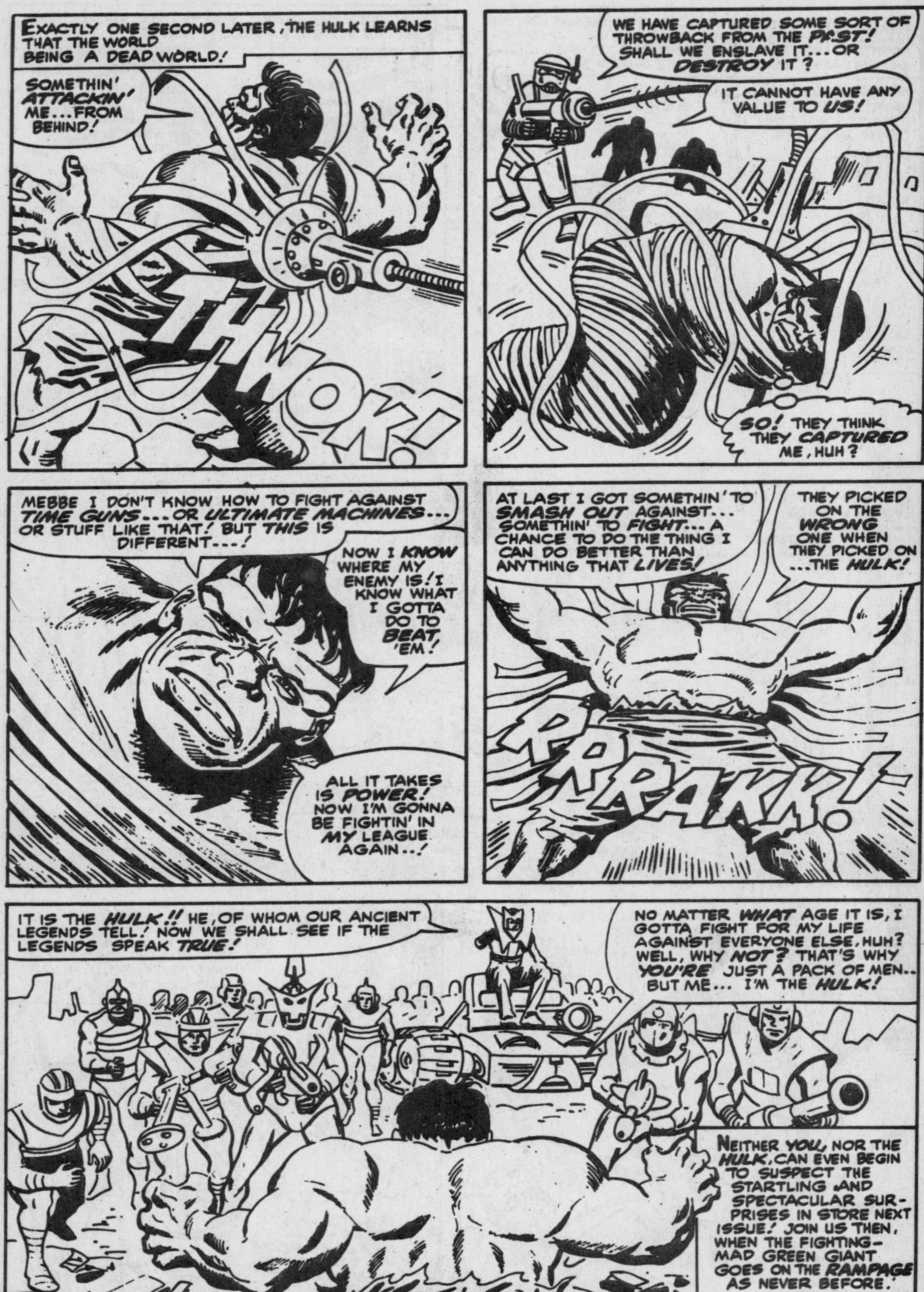
EXACTLY ONE SECOND LATER, THE HULK LEARNS THAT THE WORLD BEING A DEAD WORLD!
SOMETHIN' ATTACKIN' ME...FROM BEHIND!
THWOK!
WE HAVE CAPTURED SOME SORT OF THROWBACK FROM THE PAST! SHALL WE ENSLAVE IT...OR DESTROY IT?
IT CANNOT HAVE ANY VALUE TO US!
SO! THEY THINK THEY CAPTURED ME, HUH?
MEBBE I DON'T KNOW HOW TO FIGHT AGAINST TIME GUNS...OR ULTIMATE MACHINES...OR STUFF LIKE THAT! BUT THIS IS DIFFERENT...!
NOW I KNOW WHERE MY ENEMY IS! I KNOW WHAT I GOTTA DO TO BEAT 'EM!
ALL IT TAKES IS POWER! NOW I'M GONNA BE FIGHTIN' IN MY LEAGUE AGAIN..!
AT LAST I GOT SOMETHIN' TO SMASH OUT AGAINST... SOMETHIN' TO FIGHT... A CHANCE TO DO THE THING I CAN DO BETTER THAN ANYTHING THAT LIVES!
THEY PICKED ON THE WRONG ONE WHEN THEY PICKED ON ...THE HULK!
RRRAKK!
IT IS THE HULK!! HE, OF WHOM OUR ANCIENT LEGENDS TELL! NOW WE SHALL SEE IF THE LEGENDS SPEAK TRUE!
NO MATTER WHAT AGE IT IS, I GOTTA FIGHT FOR MY LIFE AGAINST EVERYONE ELSE, HUH? WELL, WHY NOT? THAT'S WHY YOU'RE JUST A PACK OF MEN.. BUT ME... I'M THE HULK!
NEITHER YOU, NOR THE HULK, CAN EVEN BEGIN TO SUSPECT THE STARTLING AND SPECTACULAR SURPRISES IN STORE NEXT ISSUE! JOIN US THEN, WHEN THE FIGHTING-MAD GREEN GIANT GOES ON THE RAMPAGE AS NEVER BEFORE!
10.

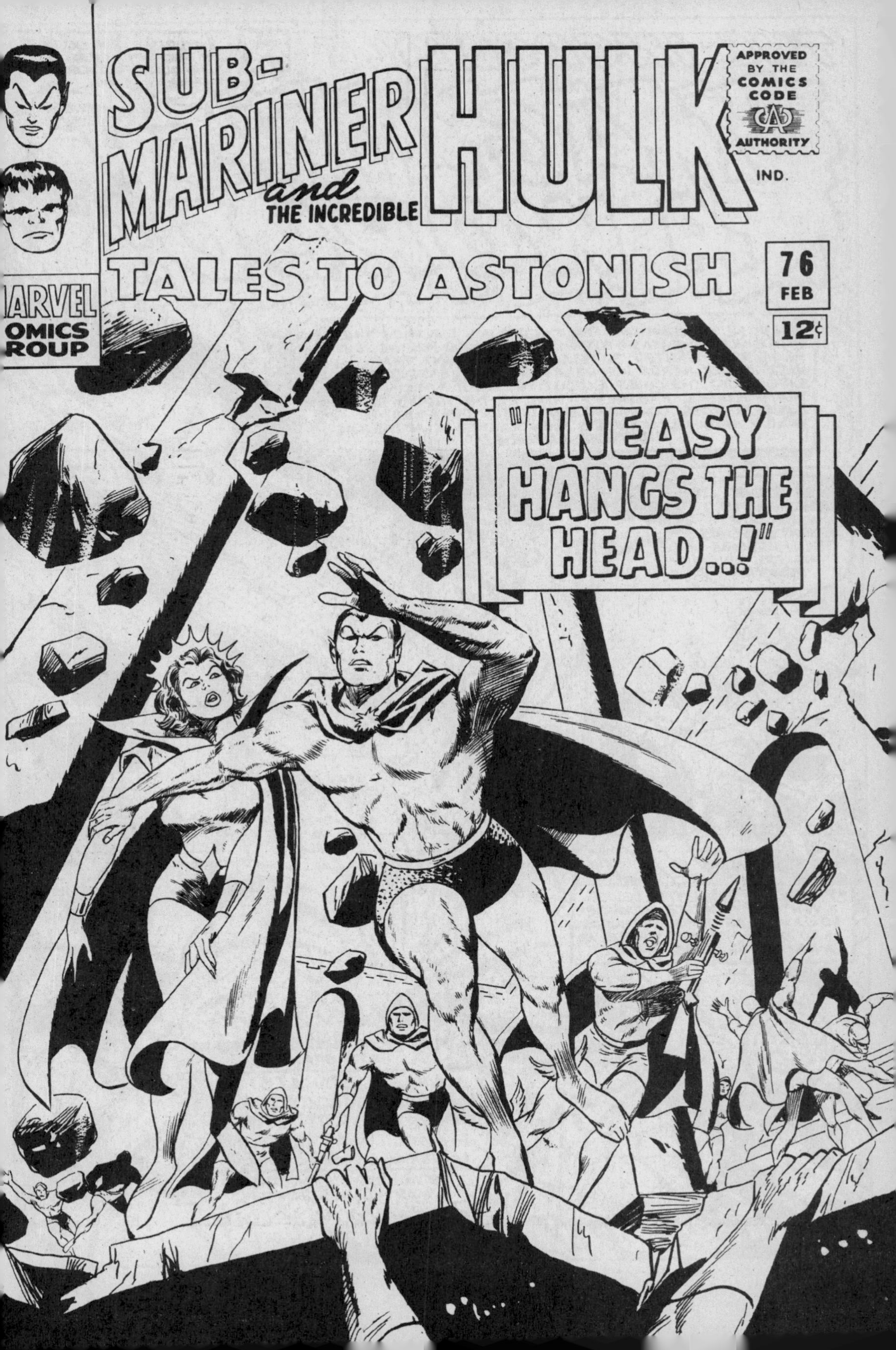

SUB-MARINER
and
THE INCREDIBLE
HULK
APPROVED BY THE COMICS CODE AUTHORITY
IND.
MARVEL COMICS GROUP
TALES TO ASTONISH
76
FEB
12¢
"UNEASY HANGS THE HEAD..!"

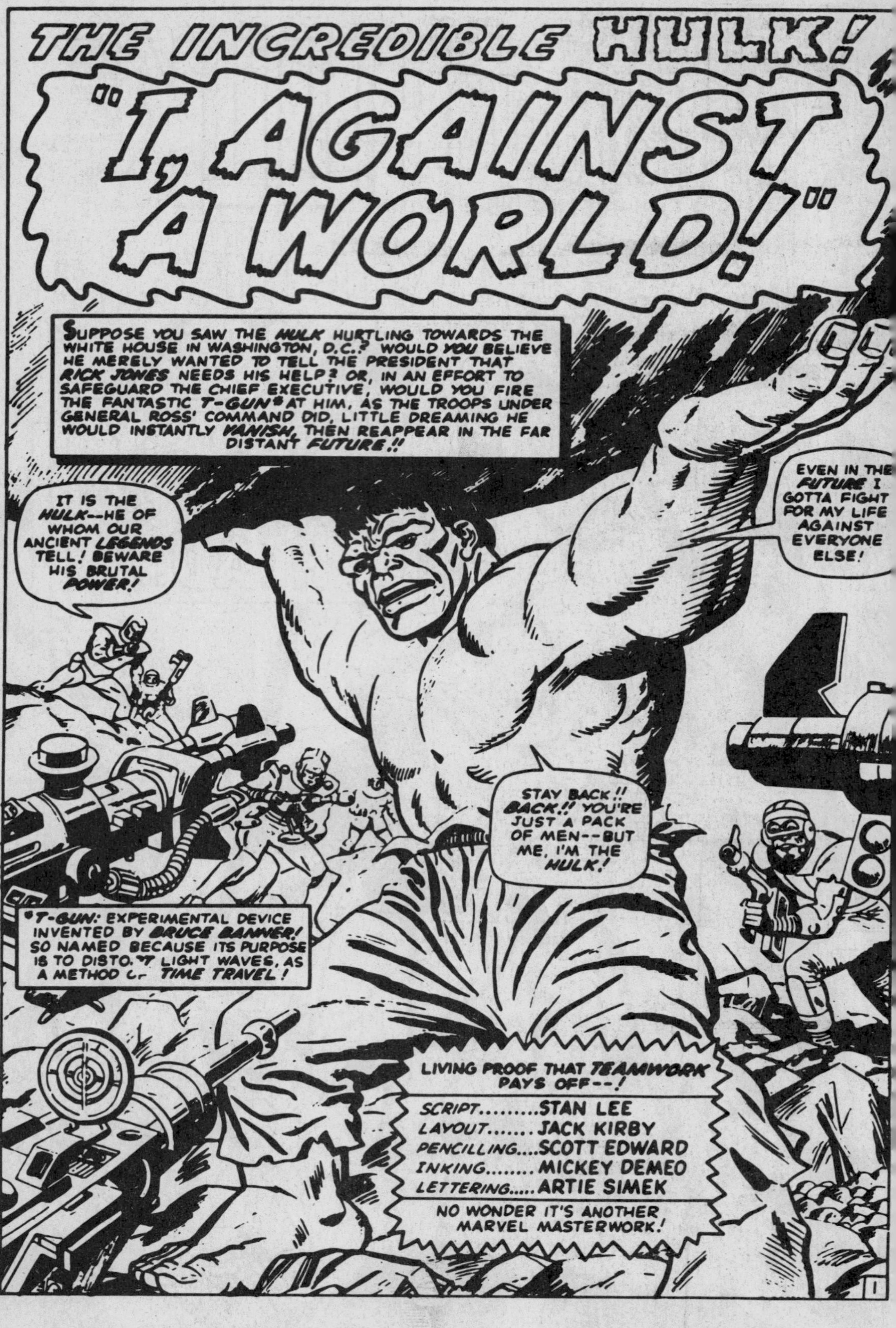

THE INCREDIBLE HULK!
"I, AGAINST A WORLD!"
SUPPOSE YOU SAW THE HULK HURTLING TOWARDS THE WHITE HOUSE IN WASHINGTON, D.C.? WOULD YOU BELIEVE HE MERELY WANTED TO TELL THE PRESIDENT THAT RICK JONES NEEDS HIS HELP? OR, IN AN EFFORT TO SAFEGUARD THE CHIEF EXECUTIVE, WOULD YOU FIRE THE FANTASTIC T-GUN* AT HIM, AS THE TROOPS UNDER GENERAL ROSS' COMMAND DID, LITTLE DREAMING HE WOULD INSTANTLY VANISH, THEN REAPPEAR IN THE FAR DISTANT FUTURE!!
IT IS THE HULK--HE OF WHOM OUR ANCIENT LEGENDS TELL! BEWARE HIS BRUTAL POWER!
EVEN IN THE FUTURE I GOTTA FIGHT FOR MY LIFE AGAINST EVERYONE ELSE!
STAY BACK!! BACK!! YOU'RE JUST A PACK OF MEN--BUT ME, I'M THE HULK!
*T-GUN: EXPERIMENTAL DEVICE INVENTED BY BRUCE BANNER! SO NAMED BECAUSE ITS PURPOSE IS TO DISTO..T LIGHT WAVES, AS A METHOD .. TIME TRAVEL!
LIVING PROOF THAT TEAMWORK PAYS OFF--!
SCRIPT.........STAN LEE
LAYOUT.......JACK KIRBY
PENCILLING....SCOTT EDWARD
INKING........MICKEY DEMEO
LETTERING.....ARTIE SIMEK
NO WONDER IT'S ANOTHER MARVEL MASTERWORK!
1

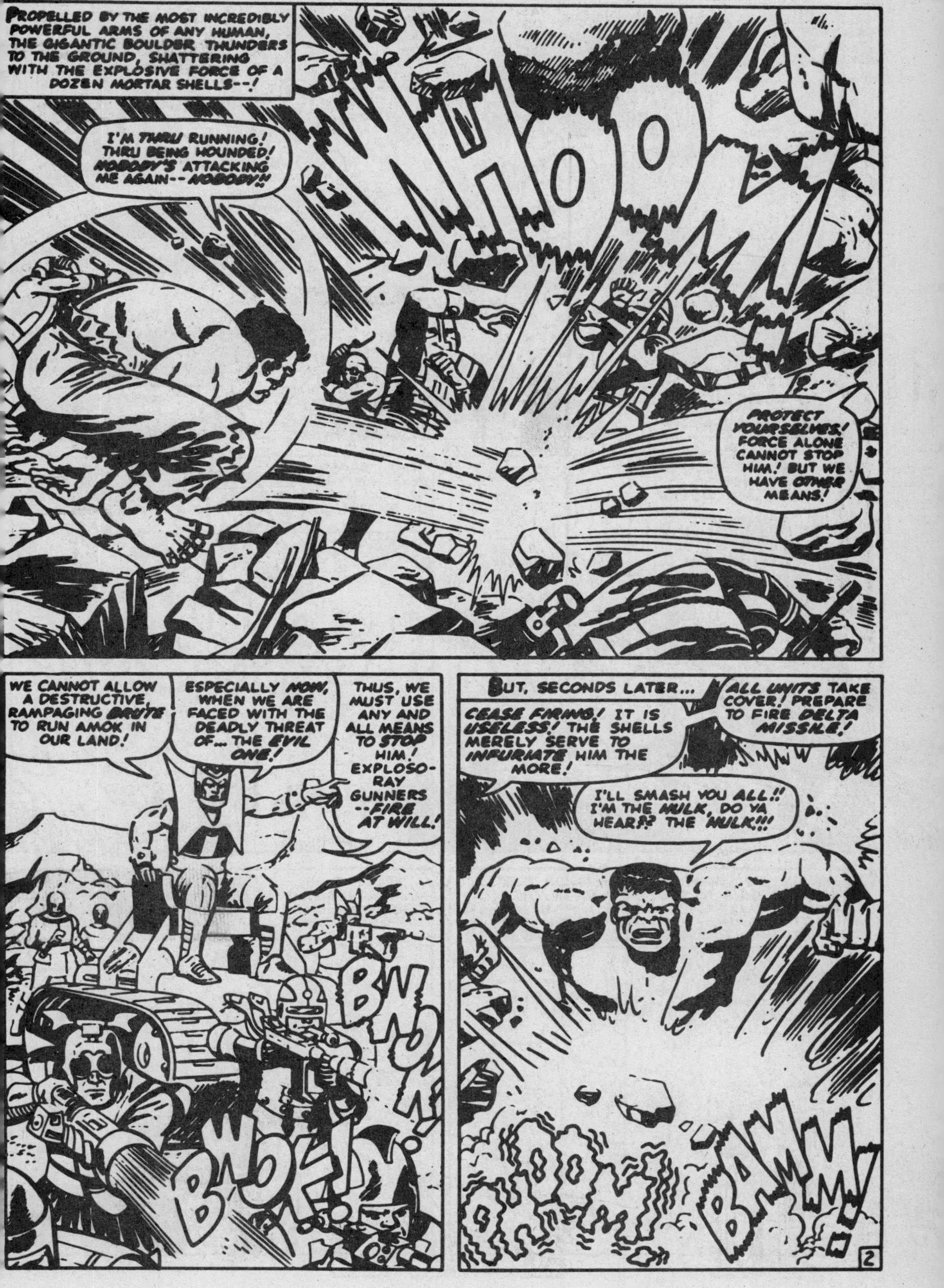
PROPELLED BY THE MOST INCREDIBLY POWERFUL ARMS OF ANY HUMAN, THE GIGANTIC BOULDER THUNDERS TO THE GROUND, SHATTERING WITH THE EXPLOSIVE FORCE OF A DOZEN MORTAR SHELLS--!
I'M THRU RUNNING! THRU BEING HOUNDED! NOBODY'S ATTACKING ME AGAIN--NOBODY!!
WHOOM!
PROTECT YOURSELVES! FORCE ALONE CANNOT STOP HIM! BUT WE HAVE OTHER MEANS!
WE CANNOT ALLOW A DESTRUCTIVE, RAMPAGING BRUTE TO RUN AMOK IN OUR LAND!
ESPECIALLY NOW, WHEN WE ARE FACED WITH THE DEADLY THREAT OF... THE EVIL ONE!
THUS, WE MUST USE ANY AND ALL MEANS TO STOP HIM! EXPLOSO-RAY GUNNERS --FIRE AT WILL!
BWOK
BWOOM
BUT, SECONDS LATER...
ALL UNITS TAKE COVER! PREPARE TO FIRE DELTA MISSILE!
CEASE FIRING! IT IS USELESS! THE SHELLS MERELY SERVE TO INFURIATE HIM THE MORE!
I'LL SMASH YOU ALL!! I'M THE HULK, DO YA HEAR?? THE HULK!!!
BOOM
BAMM!
2

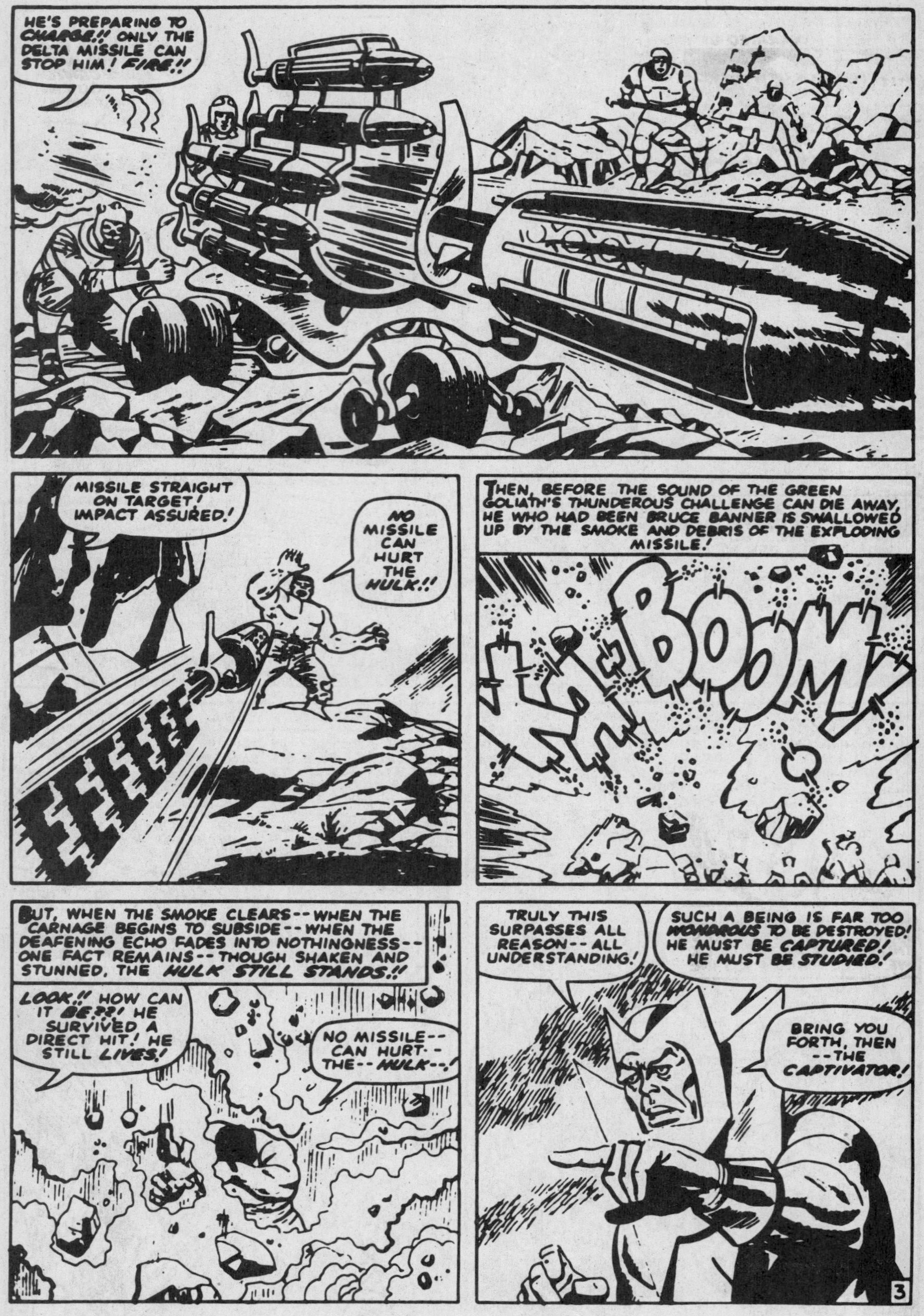
HE'S PREPARING TO CHARGE!! ONLY THE DELTA MISSILE CAN STOP HIM! FIRE!!
MISSILE STRAIGHT ON TARGET! IMPACT ASSURED!
NO MISSILE CAN HURT THE HULK!!
THEN, BEFORE THE SOUND OF THE GREEN GOLIATH'S THUNDEROUS CHALLENGE CAN DIE AWAY, HE WHO HAD BEEN BRUCE BANNER IS SWALLOWED UP BY THE SMOKE AND DEBRIS OF THE EXPLODING MISSILE!
KA-BOOM!
BUT, WHEN THE SMOKE CLEARS--WHEN THE CARNAGE BEGINS TO SUBSIDE--WHEN THE DEAFENING ECHO FADES INTO NOTHINGNESS--ONE FACT REMAINS--THOUGH SHAKEN AND STUNNED, THE HULK STILL STANDS!!
LOOK!! HOW CAN IT BE??! HE SURVIVED A DIRECT HIT! HE STILL LIVES!
NO MISSILE--CAN HURT--THE--HULK--!
TRULY THIS SURPASSES ALL REASON--ALL UNDERSTANDING!
SUCH A BEING IS FAR TOO WONDROUS TO BE DESTROYED! HE MUST BE CAPTURED! HE MUST BE STUDIED!
BRING YOU FORTH, THEN --THE CAPTIVATOR!
3

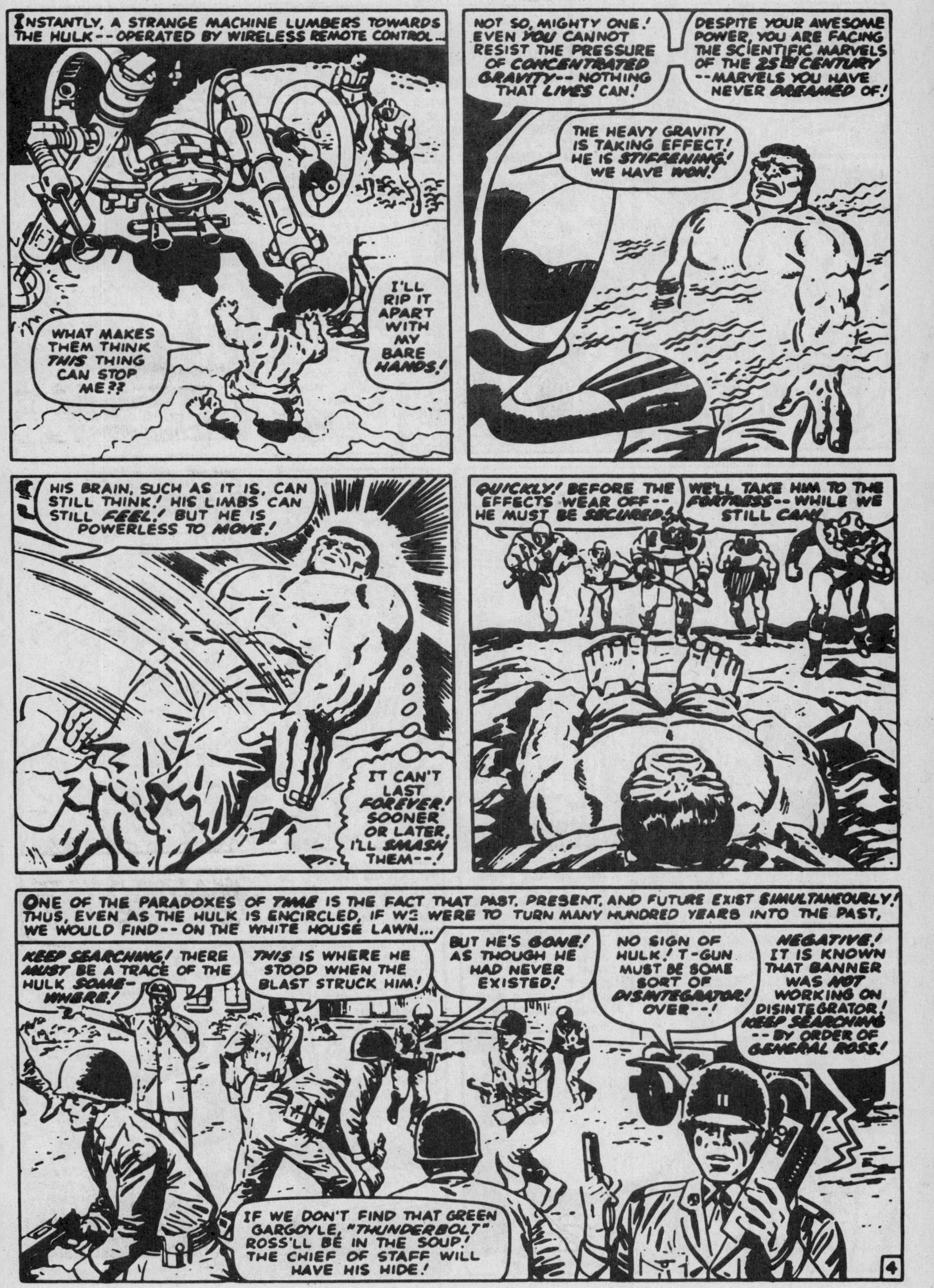
INSTANTLY, A STRANGE MACHINE LUMBERS TOWARDS THE HULK--OPERATED BY WIRELESS REMOTE CONTROL...
WHAT MAKES THEM THINK THIS THING CAN STOP ME??
I'LL RIP IT APART WITH MY BARE HANDS!
NOT SO, MIGHTY ONE! EVEN YOU CANNOT RESIST THE PRESSURE OF CONCENTRATED GRAVITY-- NOTHING THAT LIVES CAN!
DESPITE YOUR AWESOME POWER, YOU ARE FACING THE SCIENTIFIC MARVELS OF THE 25TH CENTURY --MARVELS YOU HAVE NEVER DREAMED OF!
THE HEAVY GRAVITY IS TAKING EFFECT! HE IS STIFFENING! WE HAVE WON!
HIS BRAIN, SUCH AS IT IS, CAN STILL THINK! HIS LIMBS CAN STILL FEEL! BUT HE IS POWERLESS TO MOVE!
IT CAN'T LAST FOREVER! SOONER OR LATER, I'LL SMASH THEM--!
QUICKLY! BEFORE THE EFFECTS WEAR OFF-- HE MUST BE SECURED!
WE'LL TAKE HIM TO THE FORTRESS-- WHILE WE STILL CAN!
ONE OF THE PARADOXES OF TIME IS THE FACT THAT PAST, PRESENT, AND FUTURE EXIST SIMULTANEOURLY! THUS, EVEN AS THE HULK IS ENCIRCLED, IF WE WERE TO TURN MANY HUNDRED YEARS INTO THE PAST, WE WOULD FIND--ON THE WHITE HOUSE LAWN...
KEEP SEARCHING! THERE MUST BE A TRACE OF THE HULK SOMEWHERE!
THIS IS WHERE HE STOOD WHEN THE BLAST STRUCK HIM!
BUT HE'S GONE! AS THOUGH HE HAD NEVER EXISTED!
NO SIGN OF HULK! T-GUN MUST BE SOME SORT OF DISINTEGRATOR! OVER--!
NEGATIVE! IT IS KNOWN THAT BANNER WAS NOT WORKING ON DISINTEGRATOR! KEEP SEARCHING --BY ORDER OF GENERAL ROSS!
IF WE DON'T FIND THAT GREEN GARGOYLE, "THUNDERBOLT" ROSS'LL BE IN THE SOUP! THE CHIEF OF STAFF WILL HAVE HIS HIDE!
4

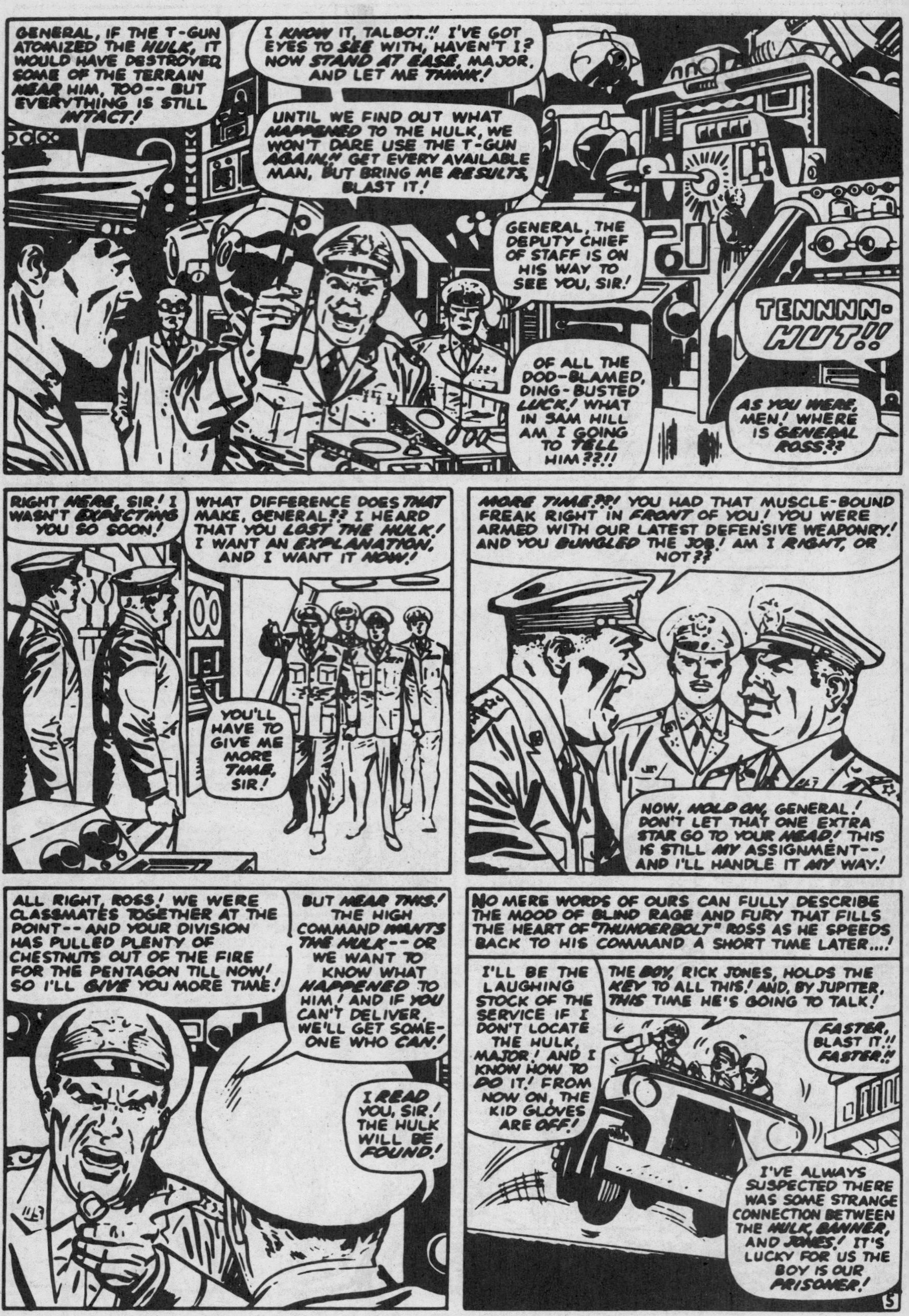
GENERAL, IF THE T-GUN ATOMIZED THE HULK, IT WOULD HAVE DESTROYED SOME OF THE TERRAIN NEAR HIM, TOO-- BUT EVERYTHING IS STILL INTACT!
I KNOW IT, TALBOT!! I'VE GOT EYES TO SEE WITH, HAVEN'T I? NOW STAND AT EASE, MAJOR, AND LET ME THINK!
UNTIL WE FIND OUT WHAT HAPPENED TO THE HULK, WE WON'T DARE USE THE T-GUN AGAIN!! GET EVERY AVAILABLE MAN, BUT BRING ME RESULTS, BLAST IT!
GENERAL, THE DEPUTY CHIEF OF STAFF IS ON HIS WAY TO SEE YOU, SIR!
TENNNN-HUT!!
OF ALL THE DOD-BLAMED, DING-BUSTED LUCK! WHAT IN SAM HILL AM I GOING TO TELL HIM??!!
AS YOU WERE, MEN! WHERE IS GENERAL ROSS??
RIGHT HERE, SIR! I WASN'T EXPECTING YOU SO SOON!
WHAT DIFFERENCE DOES THAT MAKE, GENERAL?? I HEARD THAT YOU LOST THE HULK! I WANT AN EXPLANATION, AND I WANT IT NOW!
YOU'LL HAVE TO GIVE ME MORE TIME, SIR!
MORE TIME??! YOU HAD THAT MUSCLE-BOUND FREAK RIGHT IN FRONT OF YOU! YOU WERE ARMED WITH OUR LATEST DEFENSIVE WEAPONRY! AND YOU BUNGLED THE JOB! AM I RIGHT, OR NOT??
NOW, HOLD ON, GENERAL! DON'T LET THAT ONE EXTRA STAR GO TO YOUR HEAD! THIS IS STILL MY ASSIGNMENT-- AND I'LL HANDLE IT MY WAY!
ALL RIGHT, ROSS! WE WERE CLASSMATES TOGETHER AT THE POINT-- AND YOUR DIVISION HAS PULLED PLENTY OF CHESTNUTS OUT OF THE FIRE FOR THE PENTAGON TILL NOW! SO I'LL GIVE YOU MORE TIME!
BUT HEAR THIS! THE HIGH COMMAND WANTS THE HULK-- OR WE WANT TO KNOW WHAT HAPPENED TO HIM! AND IF YOU CAN'T DELIVER, WE'LL GET SOMEONE WHO CAN!
I READ YOU, SIR! THE HULK WILL BE FOUND!
NO MERE WORDS OF OURS CAN FULLY DESCRIBE THE MOOD OF BLIND RAGE AND FURY THAT FILLS THE HEART OF "THUNDERBOLT" ROSS AS HE SPEEDS BACK TO HIS COMMAND A SHORT TIME LATER...!
I'LL BE THE LAUGHING STOCK OF THE SERVICE IF I DON'T LOCATE THE HULK, MAJOR! AND I KNOW HOW TO DO IT! FROM NOW ON, THE KID GLOVES ARE OFF!
THE BOY, RICK JONES, HOLDS THE KEY TO ALL THIS! AND, BY JUPITER, THIS TIME HE'S GOING TO TALK!
FASTER, BLAST IT!! FASTER!!
I'VE ALWAYS SUSPECTED THERE WAS SOME STRANGE CONNECTION BETWEEN THE HULK, BANNER, AND JONES! IT'S LUCKY FOR US THE BOY IS OUR PRISONER!
5

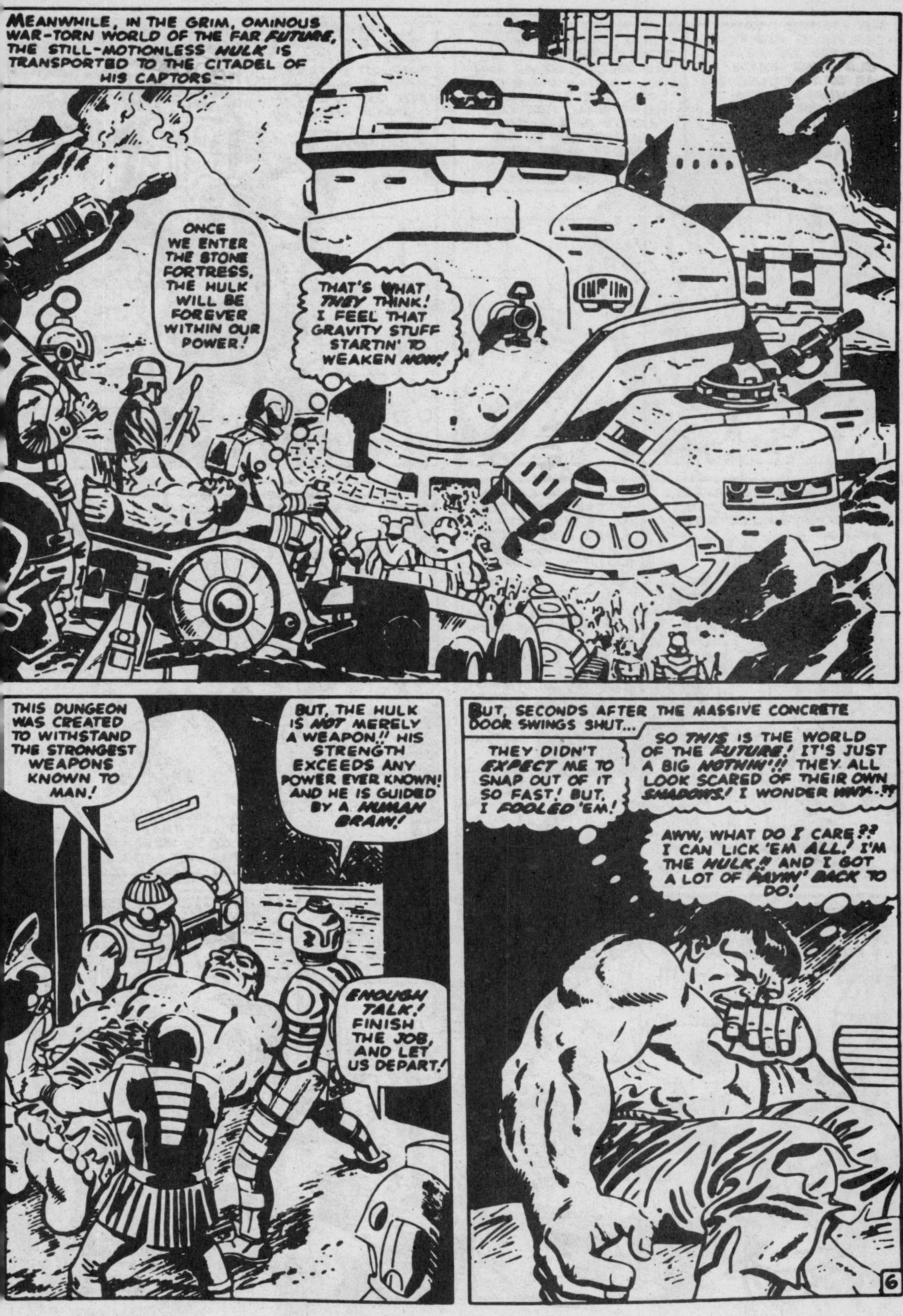

MEANWHILE, IN THE GRIM, OMINOUS WAR-TORN WORLD OF THE FAR FUTURE, THE STILL-MOTIONLESS HULK IS TRANSPORTED TO THE CITADEL OF HIS CAPTORS--
ONCE WE ENTER THE STONE FORTRESS, THE HULK WILL BE FOREVER WITHIN OUR POWER!
THAT'S WHAT THEY THINK! I FEEL THAT GRAVITY STUFF STARTIN' TO WEAKEN NOW!
THIS DUNGEON WAS CREATED TO WITHSTAND THE STRONGEST WEAPONS KNOWN TO MAN!
BUT, THE HULK IS NOT MERELY A WEAPON!! HIS STRENGTH EXCEEDS ANY POWER EVER KNOWN! AND HE IS GUIDED BY A HUMAN BRAIN!
ENOUGH TALK! FINISH THE JOB, AND LET US DEPART!
BUT, SECONDS AFTER THE MASSIVE CONCRETE DOOR SWINGS SHUT...
THEY DIDN'T EXPECT ME TO SNAP OUT OF IT SO FAST! BUT, I FOOLED 'EM!
SO THIS IS THE WORLD OF THE FUTURE! IT'S JUST A BIG NOTHIN'!! THEY ALL LOOK SCARED OF THEIR OWN SHADOWS! I WONDER WHY..??
AWW, WHAT DO I CARE?? I CAN LICK 'EM ALL! I'M THE HULK!! AND I GOT A LOT OF PAYIN' BACK TO DO!
6

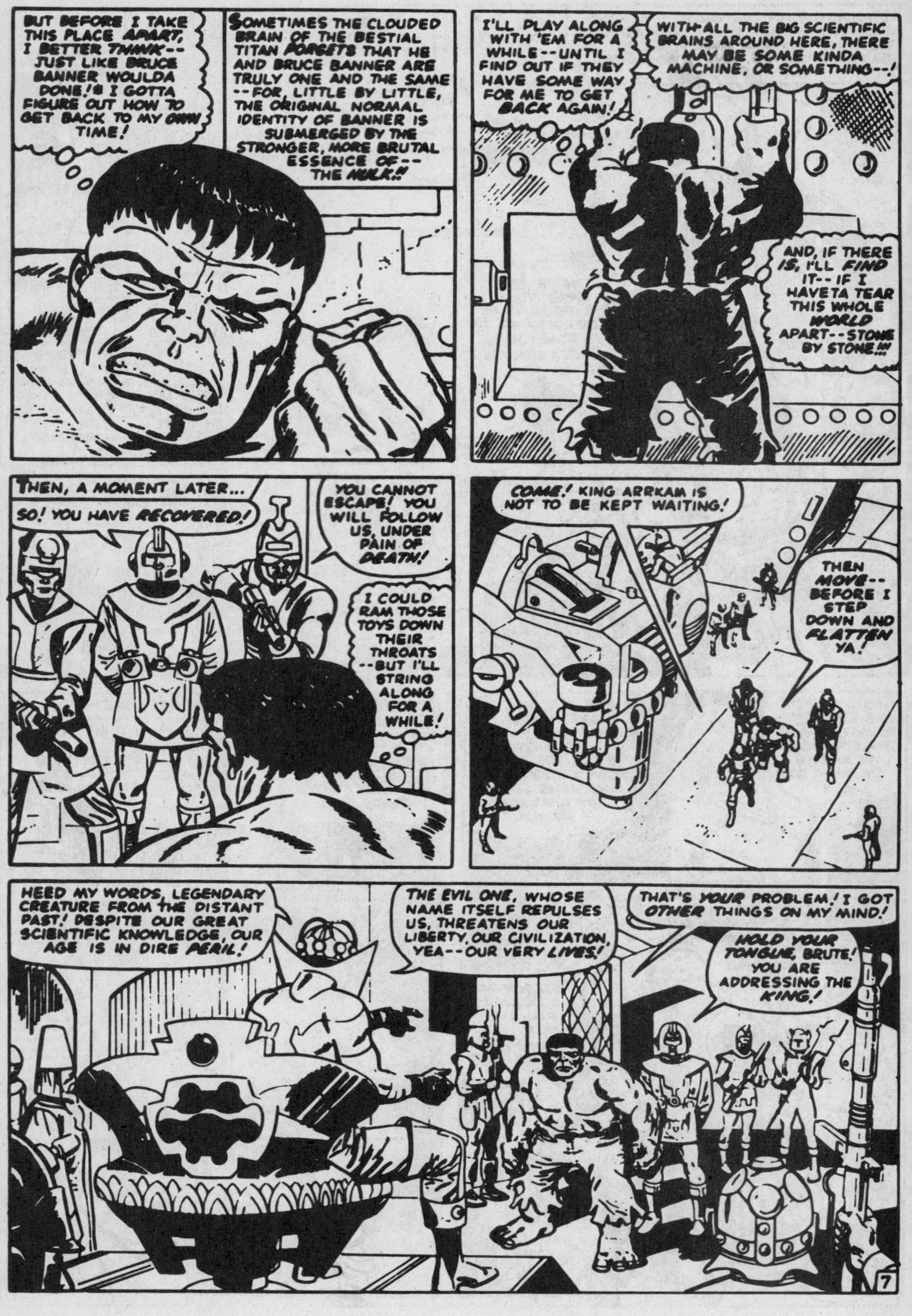
BUT BEFORE I TAKE THIS PLACE APART, I BETTER THINK-- JUST LIKE BRUCE BANNER WOULDA DONE!! I GOTTA FIGURE OUT HOW TO GET BACK TO MY OWN TIME!
SOMETIMES THE CLOUDED BRAIN OF THE BESTIAL TITAN FORGETS THAT HE AND BRUCE BANNER ARE TRULY ONE AND THE SAME --FOR, LITTLE BY LITTLE, THE ORIGINAL NORMAL IDENTITY OF BANNER IS SUBMERGED BY THE STRONGER, MORE BRUTAL ESSENCE OF-- THE HULK!!
I'LL PLAY ALONG WITH 'EM FOR A WHILE--UNTIL I FIND OUT IF THEY HAVE SOME WAY FOR ME TO GET BACK AGAIN!
WITH ALL THE BIG SCIENTIFIC BRAINS AROUND HERE, THERE MAY BE SOME KINDA MACHINE, OR SOMETHING--!
AND, IF THERE IS, I'LL FIND IT--IF I HAVETA TEAR THIS WHOLE WORLD APART--STONE BY STONE!!!
THEN, A MOMENT LATER...
SO! YOU HAVE RECOVERED!
YOU CANNOT ESCAPE! YOU WILL FOLLOW US, UNDER PAIN OF DEATH!
I COULD RAM THOSE TOYS DOWN THEIR THROATS --BUT I'LL STRING ALONG FOR A WHILE!
COME! KING ARRKAM IS NOT TO BE KEPT WAITING!
THEN MOVE-- BEFORE I STEP DOWN AND FLATTEN YA!
HEED MY WORDS, LEGENDARY CREATURE FROM THE DISTANT PAST! DESPITE OUR GREAT SCIENTIFIC KNOWLEDGE, OUR AGE IS IN DIRE PERIL!
THE EVIL ONE, WHOSE NAME ITSELF REPULSES US, THREATENS OUR LIBERTY, OUR CIVILIZATION, YEA--OUR VERY LIVES!
THAT'S YOUR PROBLEM! I GOT OTHER THINGS ON MY MIND!
HOLD YOUR TONGUE, BRUTE! YOU ARE ADDRESSING THE KING!
7

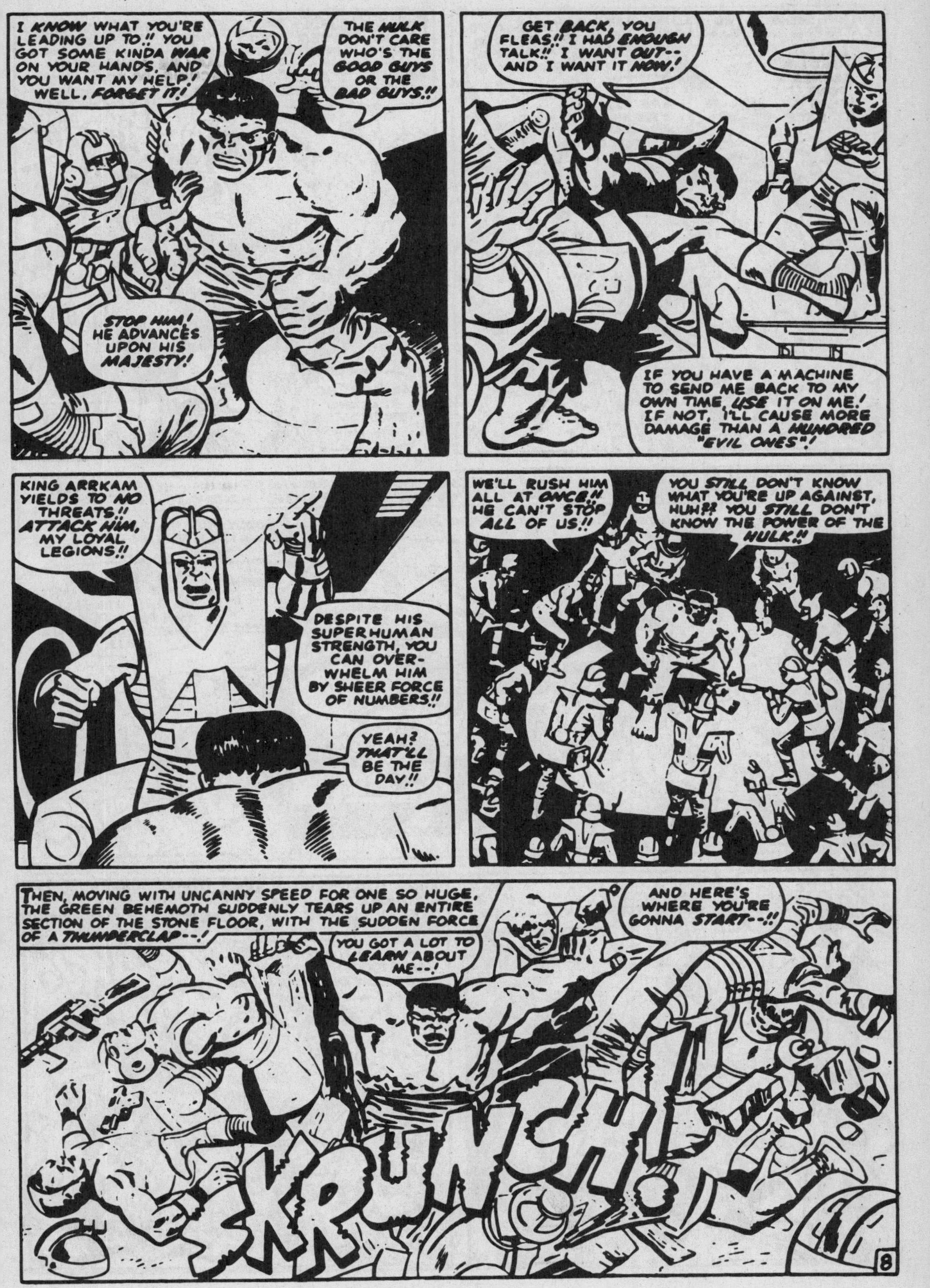

I KNOW WHAT YOU'RE LEADING UP TO!! YOU GOT SOME KINDA WAR ON YOUR HANDS, AND YOU WANT MY HELP! WELL, FORGET IT!
THE HULK DON'T CARE WHO'S THE GOOD GUYS OR THE BAD GUYS!!
STOP HIM! HE ADVANCES UPON HIS MAJESTY!
GET BACK, YOU FLEAS!! I HAD ENOUGH TALK!! I WANT OUT-- AND I WANT IT NOW!
IF YOU HAVE A MACHINE TO SEND ME BACK TO MY OWN TIME, USE IT ON ME! IF NOT, I'LL CAUSE MORE DAMAGE THAN A HUNDRED "EVIL ONES"!
KING ARRKAM YIELDS TO NO THREATS!! ATTACK HIM, MY LOYAL LEGIONS!!
DESPITE HIS SUPERHUMAN STRENGTH, YOU CAN OVER-WHELM HIM BY SHEER FORCE OF NUMBERS!!
YEAH? THAT'LL BE THE DAY!!
WE'LL RUSH HIM ALL AT ONCE!! HE CAN'T STOP ALL OF US!!
YOU STILL DON'T KNOW WHAT YOU'RE UP AGAINST, HUH?? YOU STILL DON'T KNOW THE POWER OF THE HULK!!
THEN, MOVING WITH UNCANNY SPEED FOR ONE SO HUGE, THE GREEN BEHEMOTH SUDDENLY TEARS UP AN ENTIRE SECTION OF THE STONE FLOOR, WITH THE SUDDEN FORCE OF A THUNDERCLAP--!
YOU GOT A LOT TO LEARN ABOUT ME--!
AND HERE'S WHERE YOU'RE GONNA START--!!
SKRUNCH!
8

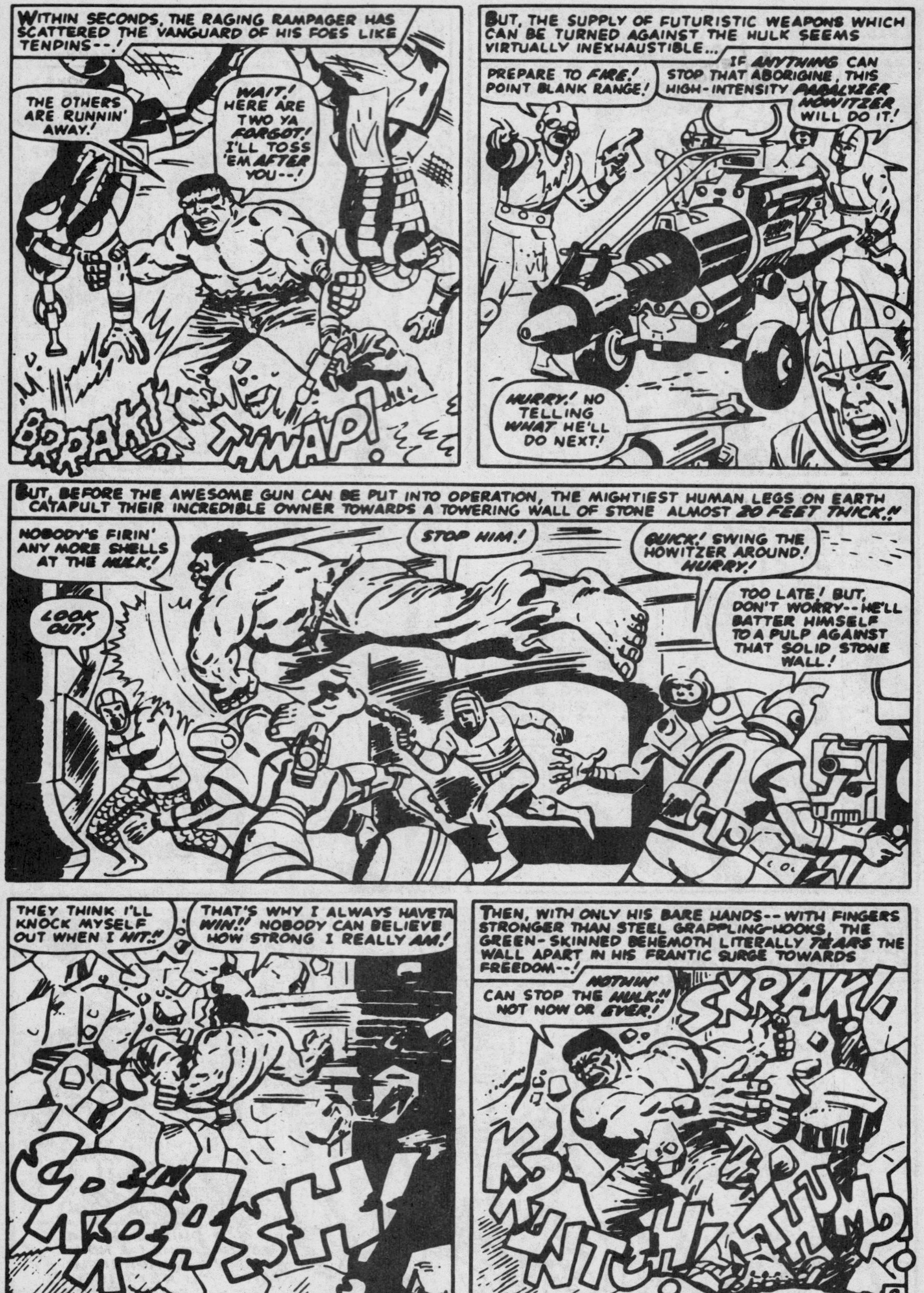

WITHIN SECONDS, THE RAGING RAMPAGER HAS SCATTERED THE VANGUARD OF HIS FOES LIKE TENPINS--!
THE OTHERS ARE RUNNIN' AWAY!
WAIT! HERE ARE TWO YA FORGOT! I'LL TOSS 'EM AFTER YOU--!
BRRAKK!
THWAP!
BUT, THE SUPPLY OF FUTURISTIC WEAPONS WHICH CAN BE TURNED AGAINST THE HULK SEEMS VIRTUALLY INEXHAUSTIBLE...
PREPARE TO FIRE! POINT BLANK RANGE!
IF ANYTHING CAN STOP THAT ABORIGINE, THIS HIGH-INTENSITY PARALYZER HOWITZER WILL DO IT!
HURRY! NO TELLING WHAT HE'LL DO NEXT!
BUT, BEFORE THE AWESOME GUN CAN BE PUT INTO OPERATION, THE MIGHTIEST HUMAN LEGS ON EARTH CATAPULT THEIR INCREDIBLE OWNER TOWARDS A TOWERING WALL OF STONE ALMOST 20 FEET THICK!!
NOBODY'S FIRIN' ANY MORE SHELLS AT THE HULK!
STOP HIM!
QUICK! SWING THE HOWITZER AROUND! HURRY!
LOOK OUT!
TOO LATE! BUT, DON'T WORRY--HE'LL BATTER HIMSELF TO A PULP AGAINST THAT SOLID STONE WALL!
THEY THINK I'LL KNOCK MYSELF OUT WHEN I HIT!!
THAT'S WHY I ALWAYS HAVETA WIN!! NOBODY CAN BELIEVE HOW STRONG I REALLY AM!
CRRAASH!
THEN, WITH ONLY HIS BARE HANDS--WITH FINGERS STRONGER THAN STEEL GRAPPLING-HOOKS, THE GREEN-SKINNED BEHEMOTH LITERALLY TEARS THE WALL APART IN HIS FRANTIC SURGE TOWARDS FREEDOM--!
NOTHIN' CAN STOP THE HULK!! NOT NOW OR EVER!
SKRAK!
KRUNTCH!
THUMP!
9

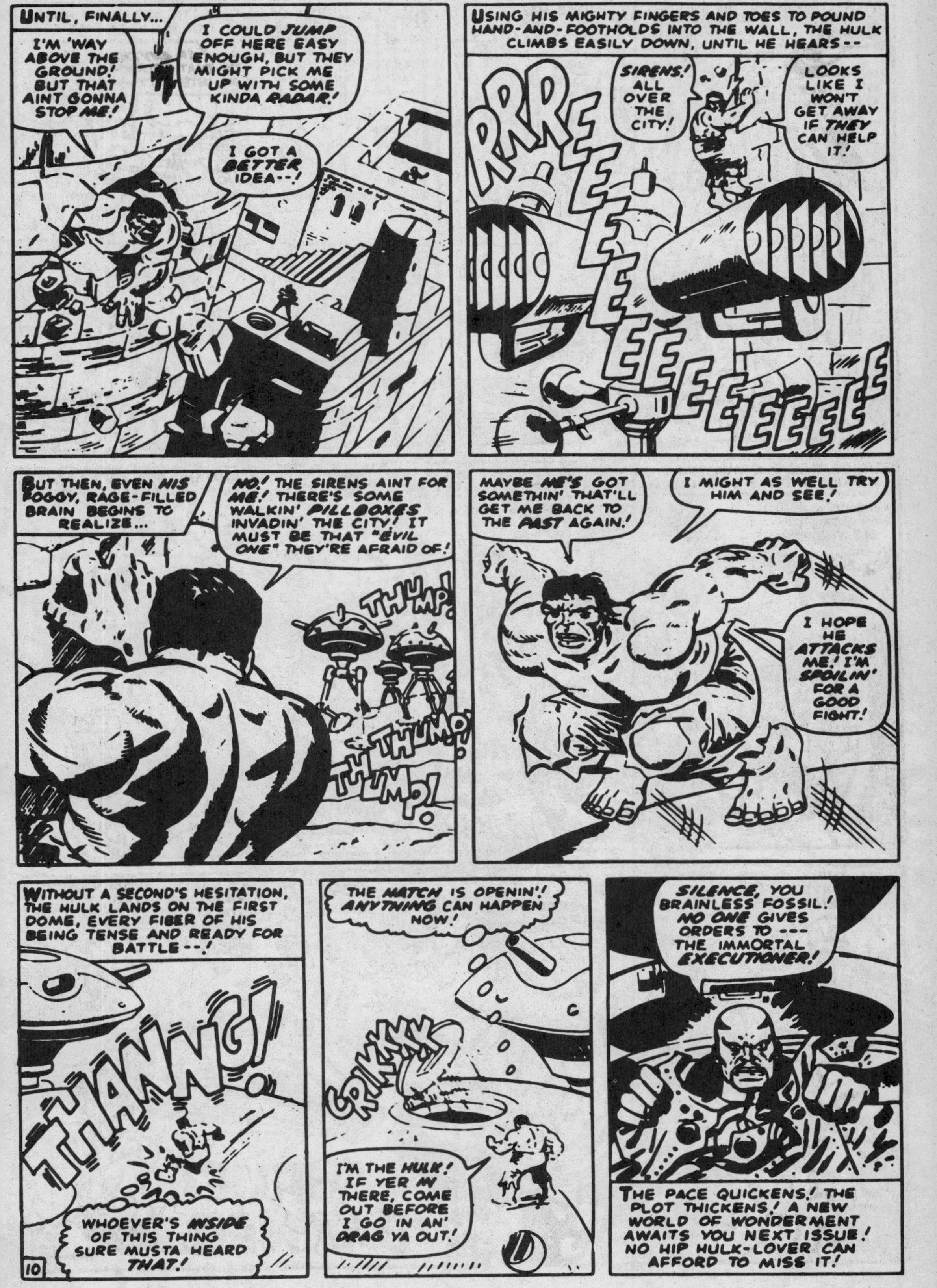
UNTIL, FINALLY...
I'M 'WAY ABOVE THE GROUND! BUT THAT AINT GONNA STOP ME!
I COULD JUMP OFF HERE EASY ENOUGH, BUT THEY MIGHT PICK ME UP WITH SOME KINDA RADAR!
I GOT A BETTER IDEA--!
USING HIS MIGHTY FINGERS AND TOES TO POUND HAND-AND-FOOTHOLDS INTO THE WALL, THE HULK CLIMBS EASILY DOWN, UNTIL HE HEARS--
SIRENS! ALL OVER THE CITY!
LOOKS LIKE I WON'T GET AWAY IF THEY CAN HELP IT!
RRREEEEEEEEEEEE
BUT THEN, EVEN HIS FOGGY, RAGE-FILLED BRAIN BEGINS TO REALIZE...
NO! THE SIRENS AINT FOR ME! THERE'S SOME WALKIN' PILLBOXES INVADIN' THE CITY! IT MUST BE THAT "EVIL ONE" THEY'RE AFRAID OF!
THUMP!
THUMP!
THUMP!
MAYBE HE'S GOT SOMETHIN' THAT'LL GET ME BACK TO THE PAST AGAIN!
I MIGHT AS WELL TRY HIM AND SEE!
I HOPE HE ATTACKS ME! I'M SPOILIN' FOR A GOOD FIGHT!
WITHOUT A SECOND'S HESITATION, THE HULK LANDS ON THE FIRST DOME, EVERY FIBER OF HIS BEING TENSE AND READY FOR BATTLE--!
THANNG!
WHOEVER'S INSIDE OF THIS THING SURE MUSTA HEARD THAT!
10
THE MATCH IS OPENIN'! ANYTHING CAN HAPPEN NOW!
CRIKKKK
I'M THE HULK! IF YER IN THERE, COME OUT BEFORE I GO IN AN' DRAG YA OUT!
SILENCE, YOU BRAINLESS FOSSIL! NO ONE GIVES ORDERS TO --- THE IMMORTAL EXECUTIONER!
THE PACE QUICKENS! THE PLOT THICKENS! A NEW WORLD OF WONDERMENT AWAITS YOU NEXT ISSUE! NO HIP HULK-LOVER CAN AFFORD TO MISS IT!

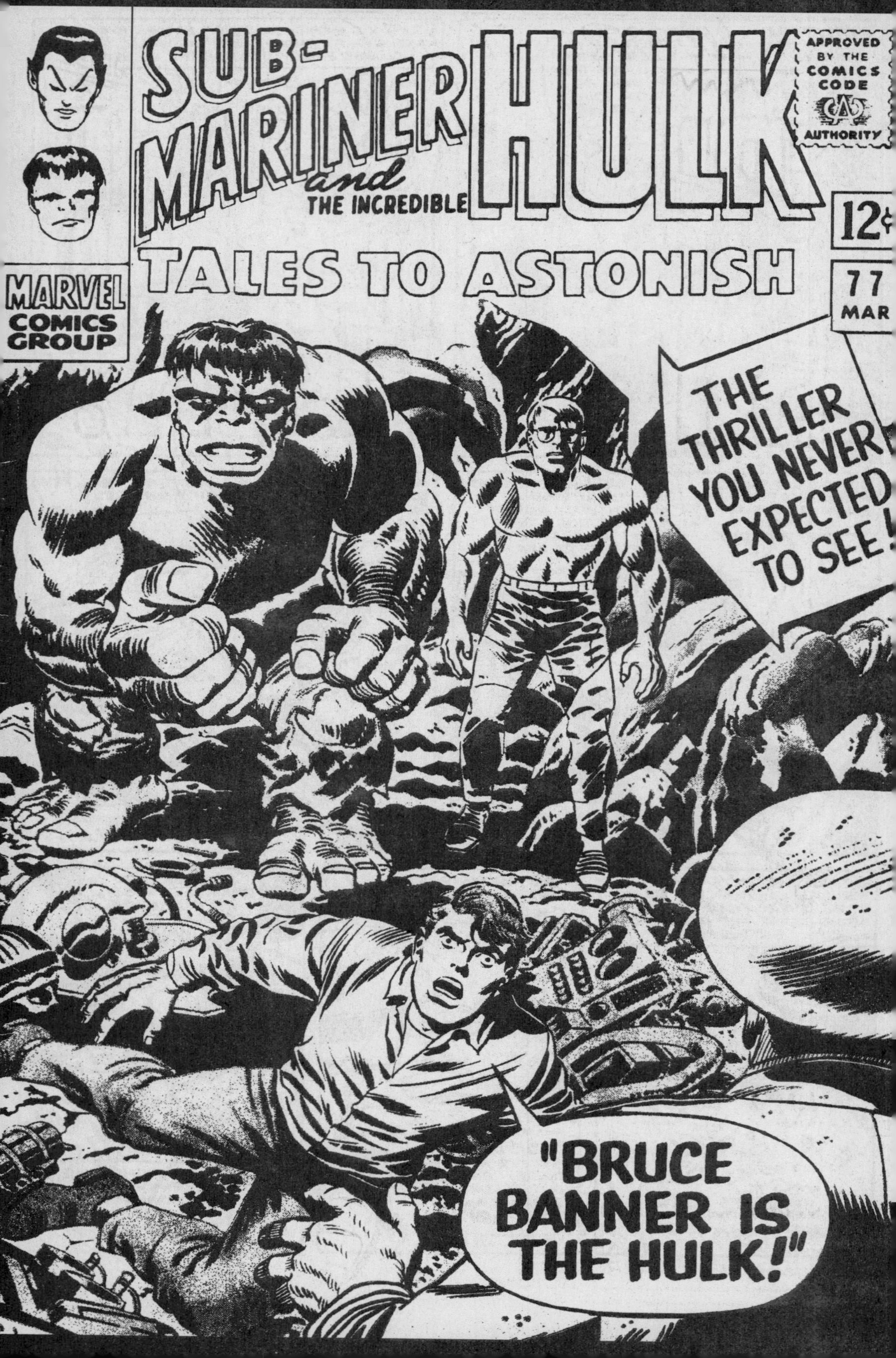
SUB-MARINER and THE INCREDIBLE HULK
TALES TO ASTONISH
APPROVED BY THE COMICS CODE AUTHORITY
12¢
77 MAR
MARVEL COMICS GROUP
THE THRILLER YOU NEVER EXPECTED TO SEE!
"BRUCE BANNER IS THE HULK!"

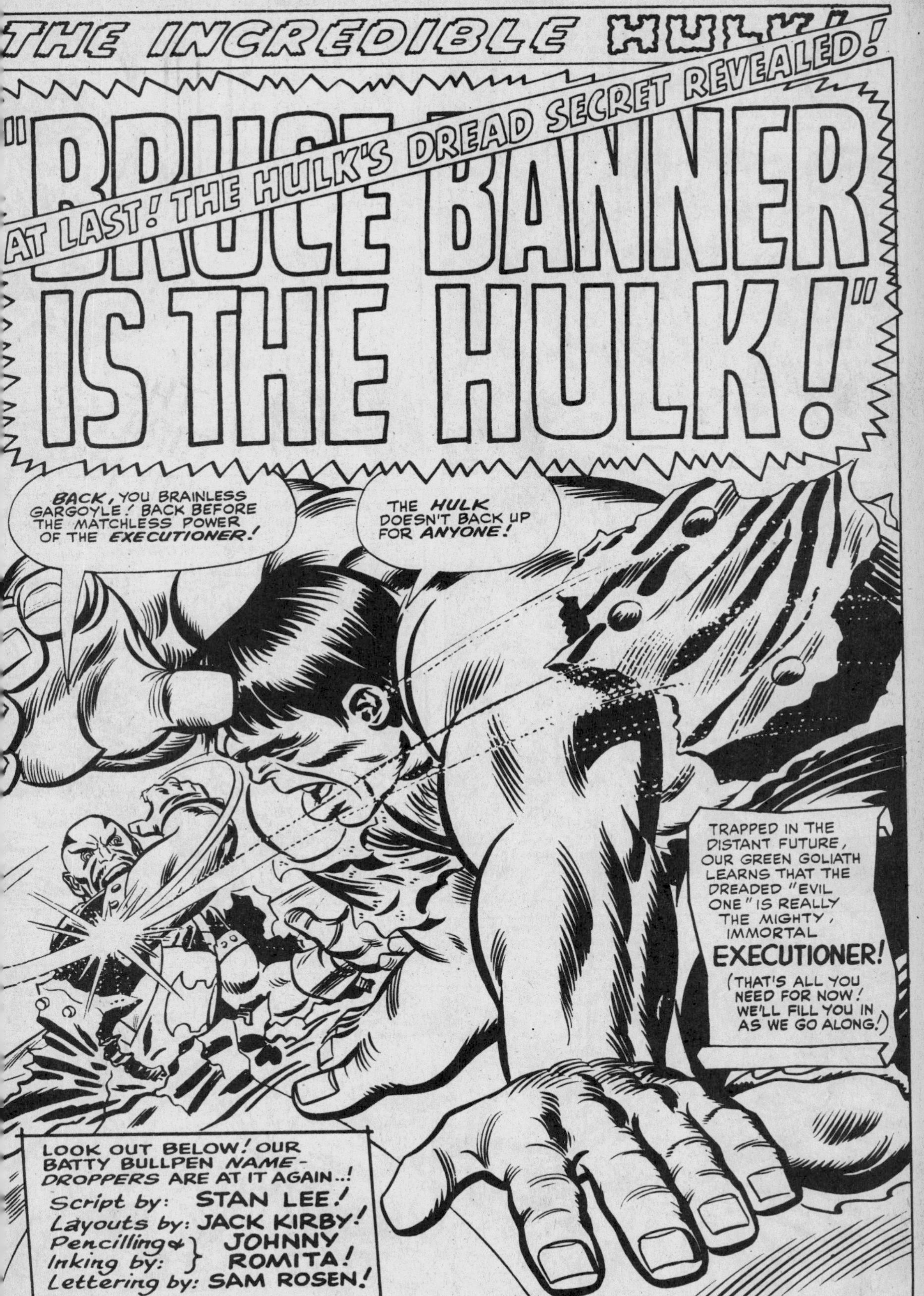
THE INCREDIBLE HULK!
AT LAST! THE HULK'S DREAD SECRET REVEALED!
"BRUCE BANNER IS THE HULK!"
BACK, YOU BRAINLESS GARGOYLE! BACK BEFORE THE MATCHLESS POWER OF THE EXECUTIONER!
THE HULK DOESN'T BACK UP FOR ANYONE!
TRAPPED IN THE DISTANT FUTURE, OUR GREEN GOLIATH LEARNS THAT THE DREADED "EVIL ONE" IS REALLY THE MIGHTY, IMMORTAL EXECUTIONER!
(THAT'S ALL YOU NEED FOR NOW! WE'LL FILL YOU IN AS WE GO ALONG!)
LOOK OUT BELOW! OUR BATTY BULLPEN NAME-DROPPERS ARE AT IT AGAIN..!
Script by: STAN LEE!
Layouts by: JACK KIRBY!
Pencilling & Inking by: JOHNNY ROMITA!
Lettering by: SAM ROSEN!

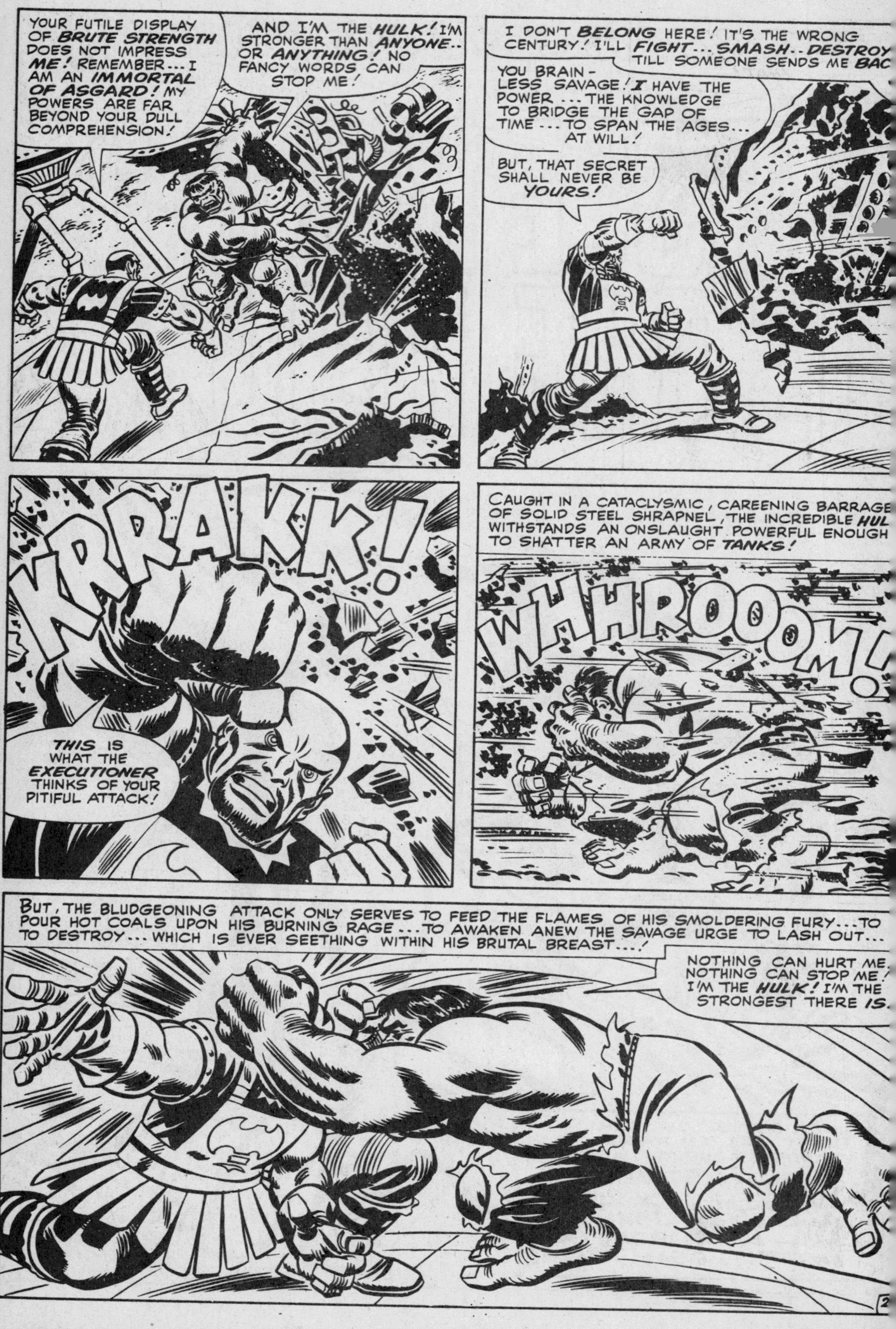
YOUR FUTILE DISPLAY OF BRUTE STRENGTH DOES NOT IMPRESS ME! REMEMBER... I AM AN IMMORTAL OF ASGARD! MY POWERS ARE FAR BEYOND YOUR DULL COMPREHENSION!
AND I'M THE HULK! I'M STRONGER THAN ANYONE... OR ANYTHING! NO FANCY WORDS CAN STOP ME!
I DON'T BELONG HERE! IT'S THE WRONG CENTURY! I'LL FIGHT... SMASH.. DESTROY TILL SOMEONE SENDS ME BAC
YOU BRAIN-LESS SAVAGE! I HAVE THE POWER ... THE KNOWLEDGE TO BRIDGE THE GAP OF TIME ... TO SPAN THE AGES... AT WILL!
BUT, THAT SECRET SHALL NEVER BE YOURS!
KRRAKK!
THIS IS WHAT THE EXECUTIONER THINKS OF YOUR PITIFUL ATTACK!
CAUGHT IN A CATACLYSMIC, CAREENING BARRAGE OF SOLID STEEL SHRAPNEL, THE INCREDIBLE HUL WITHSTANDS AN ONSLAUGHT POWERFUL ENOUGH TO SHATTER AN ARMY OF TANKS!
WHHROOOM!
BUT, THE BLUDGEONING ATTACK ONLY SERVES TO FEED THE FLAMES OF HIS SMOLDERING FURY... TO POUR HOT COALS UPON HIS BURNING RAGE ... TO AWAKEN ANEW THE SAVAGE URGE TO LASH OUT... TO DESTROY... WHICH IS EVER SEETHING WITHIN HIS BRUTAL BREAST...!
NOTHING CAN HURT ME, NOTHING CAN STOP ME! I'M THE HULK! I'M THE STRONGEST THERE IS.

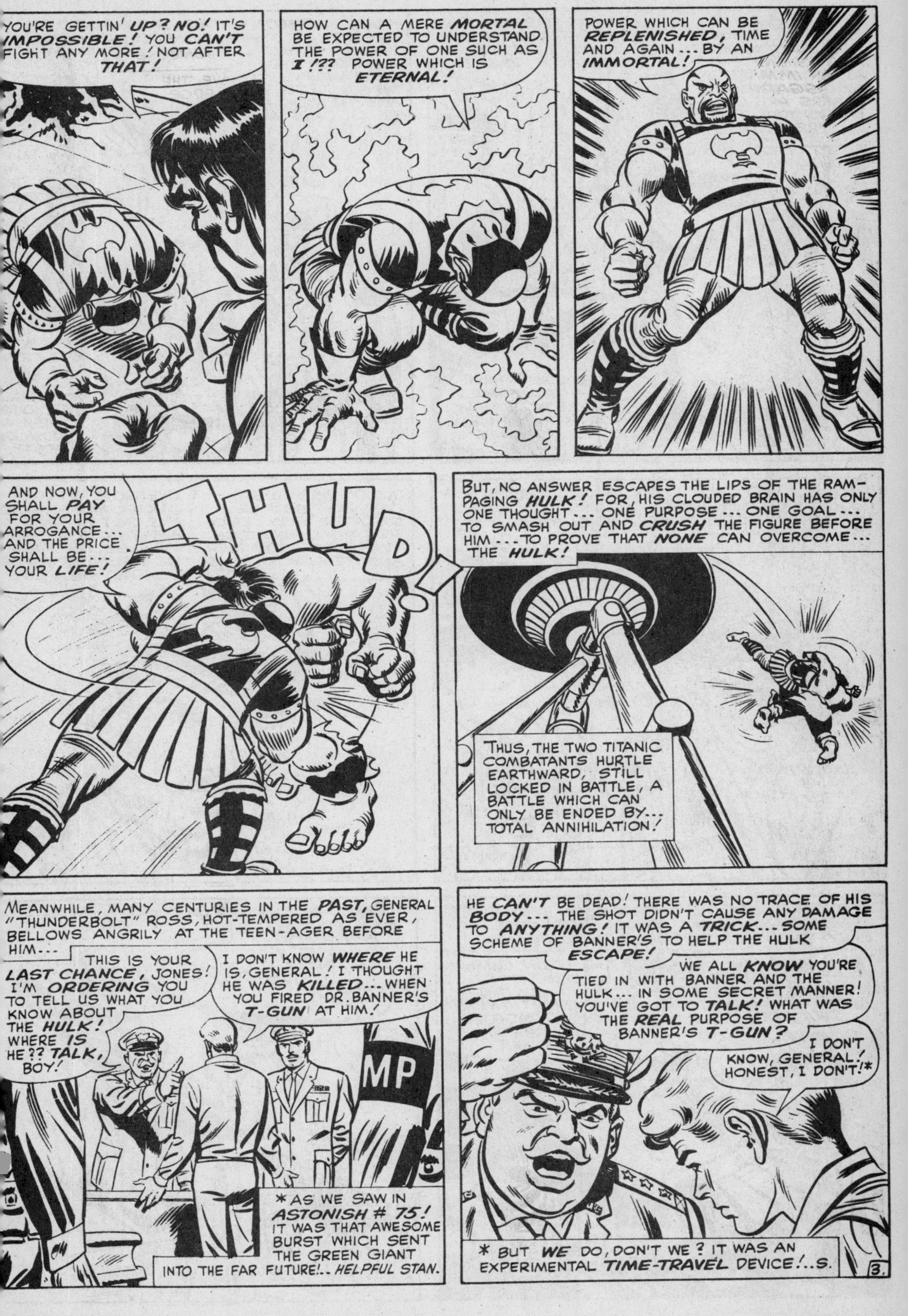
YOU'RE GETTIN' UP? NO! IT'S IMPOSSIBLE! YOU CAN'T FIGHT ANY MORE! NOT AFTER THAT!
HOW CAN A MERE MORTAL BE EXPECTED TO UNDERSTAND THE POWER OF ONE SUCH AS I!?? POWER WHICH IS ETERNAL!
POWER WHICH CAN BE REPLENISHED, TIME AND AGAIN... BY AN IMMORTAL!
AND NOW, YOU SHALL PAY FOR YOUR ARROGANCE... AND THE PRICE SHALL BE... YOUR LIFE!
THUD!
BUT, NO ANSWER ESCAPES THE LIPS OF THE RAMPAGING HULK! FOR, HIS CLOUDED BRAIN HAS ONLY ONE THOUGHT... ONE PURPOSE... ONE GOAL... TO SMASH OUT AND CRUSH THE FIGURE BEFORE HIM... TO PROVE THAT NONE CAN OVERCOME... THE HULK!
THUS, THE TWO TITANIC COMBATANTS HURTLE EARTHWARD, STILL LOCKED IN BATTLE, A BATTLE WHICH CAN ONLY BE ENDED BY... TOTAL ANNIHILATION!
MEANWHILE, MANY CENTURIES IN THE PAST, GENERAL "THUNDERBOLT" ROSS, HOT-TEMPERED AS EVER, BELLOWS ANGRILY AT THE TEEN-AGER BEFORE HIM...
THIS IS YOUR LAST CHANCE, JONES! I'M ORDERING YOU TO TELL US WHAT YOU KNOW ABOUT THE HULK! WHERE IS HE?? TALK, BOY!
I DON'T KNOW WHERE HE IS, GENERAL! I THOUGHT HE WAS KILLED... WHEN YOU FIRED DR. BANNER'S T-GUN AT HIM!
MP
*AS WE SAW IN ASTONISH # 75! IT WAS THAT AWESOME BURST WHICH SENT THE GREEN GIANT INTO THE FAR FUTURE!.. HELPFUL STAN.
HE CAN'T BE DEAD! THERE WAS NO TRACE OF HIS BODY... THE SHOT DIDN'T CAUSE ANY DAMAGE TO ANYTHING! IT WAS A TRICK... SOME SCHEME OF BANNER'S TO HELP THE HULK ESCAPE!
WE ALL KNOW YOU'RE TIED IN WITH BANNER AND THE HULK... IN SOME SECRET MANNER! YOU'VE GOT TO TALK! WHAT WAS THE REAL PURPOSE OF BANNER'S T-GUN?
I DON'T KNOW, GENERAL! HONEST, I DON'T!*
* BUT WE DO, DON'T WE? IT WAS AN EXPERIMENTAL TIME-TRAVEL DEVICE!..S.
3.

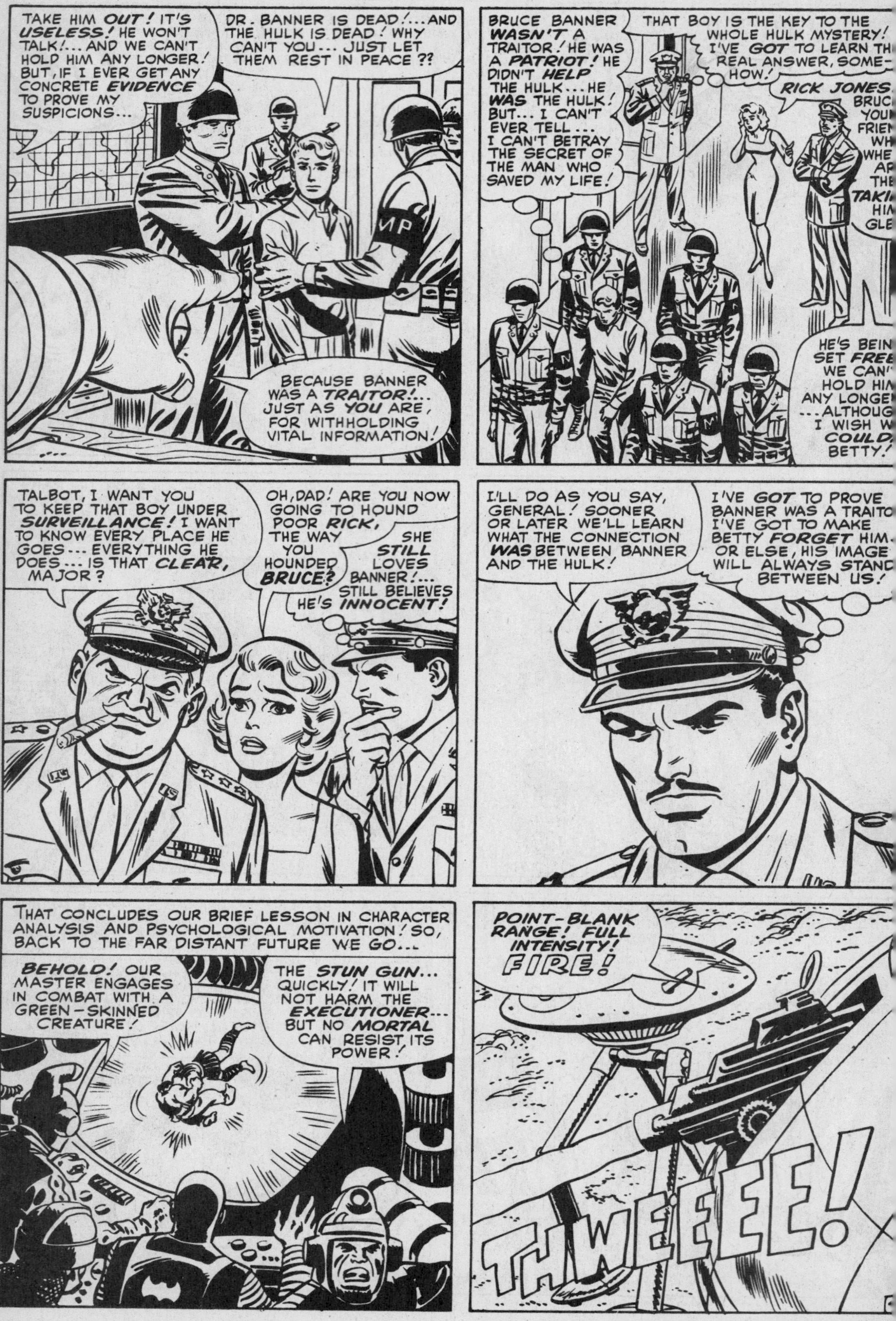
TAKE HIM OUT! IT'S USELESS! HE WON'T TALK!... AND WE CAN'T HOLD HIM ANY LONGER! BUT, IF I EVER GET ANY CONCRETE EVIDENCE TO PROVE MY SUSPICIONS...
DR. BANNER IS DEAD!... AND THE HULK IS DEAD! WHY CAN'T YOU... JUST LET THEM REST IN PEACE ??
BECAUSE BANNER WAS A TRAITOR!... JUST AS YOU ARE, FOR WITHHOLDING VITAL INFORMATION!
MP
BRUCE BANNER WASN'T A TRAITOR! HE WAS A PATRIOT! HE DIDN'T HELP THE HULK... HE WAS THE HULK! BUT... I CAN'T EVER TELL... I CAN'T BETRAY THE SECRET OF THE MAN WHO SAVED MY LIFE!
THAT BOY IS THE KEY TO THE WHOLE HULK MYSTERY! I'VE GOT TO LEARN TH REAL ANSWER, SOME-HOW!
RICK JONES
HE'S BEIN SET FREE WE CAN' HOLD HIM ANY LONGE ...ALTHOUG I WISH W COULD, BETTY!
TALBOT, I WANT YOU TO KEEP THAT BOY UNDER SURVEILLANCE! I WANT TO KNOW EVERY PLACE HE GOES... EVERYTHING HE DOES... IS THAT CLEAR, MAJOR?
OH, DAD! ARE YOU NOW GOING TO HOUND POOR RICK, THE WAY YOU HOUNDED BRUCE?
SHE STILL LOVES BANNER!... STILL BELIEVES HE'S INNOCENT!
I'LL DO AS YOU SAY, GENERAL! SOONER OR LATER WE'LL LEARN WHAT THE CONNECTION WAS BETWEEN BANNER AND THE HULK!
I'VE GOT TO PROVE BANNER WAS A TRAITO I'VE GOT TO MAKE BETTY FORGET HIM. OR ELSE, HIS IMAGE WILL ALWAYS STAND BETWEEN US!
THAT CONCLUDES OUR BRIEF LESSON IN CHARACTER ANALYSIS AND PSYCHOLOGICAL MOTIVATION! SO, BACK TO THE FAR DISTANT FUTURE WE GO...
BEHOLD! OUR MASTER ENGAGES IN COMBAT WITH A GREEN-SKINNED CREATURE!
THE STUN GUN... QUICKLY! IT WILL NOT HARM THE EXECUTIONER... BUT NO MORTAL CAN RESIST ITS POWER!
POINT-BLANK RANGE! FULL INTENSITY! FIRE!
THWEEEE!

AH! MY STUN BEAM... TO WHICH I MYSELF AM INVULNERABLE!

FOOOOM!

NOTHING THAT LIVES... EXCEPT AN IMMORTAL OF ASGARD... CAN WITHSTAND ITS SHATTERING FORCE!

ACADEMIC NOTE: THE SOUND EFFECT ABOVE IS PRONOUNCED "FOOM"! THE THIRD "O" IS SILENT! --STAN

WHAT?! YOU BEGIN TO RISE TO YOUR FEET?!!

I CANNOT TOLERATE A MERE MORTAL HAVING POWER WHICH IS ALMOST THE EQUAL OF MY OWN! NOW, MORE THAN EVER, MUST I BATTER YOU INTO TOTAL HELPLESSNESS!

DO YOUR WORST! WHAT'S THE DIFFERENCE? IT'S THE LAST CHANCE YOU'LL EVER GET!

FOR YOUR INSOLENCE ALONE, YOU SHALL PAY WITH YOUR LIFE!

THUD!

NOT FOR NOTHING AM I CALLED... THE EXECUTIONER!

ARRHHHH!

WHRAK!

AND NOW...I SHALL FINISH THE JOB!

YOU KNOCKED ME DOWN! NOBODY KNOCKS THE HULK DOWN! NOBODY!

WITH THAT, THE GREEN GOLIATH'S WORDS BECOME HOPELESSLY UNINTELLIGIBLE! SO CONSUMED WITH RAGE IS HE, THAT HE CANNOT SPEAK-- HE CANNOT THINK...HE CAN ONLY... HATE!

5

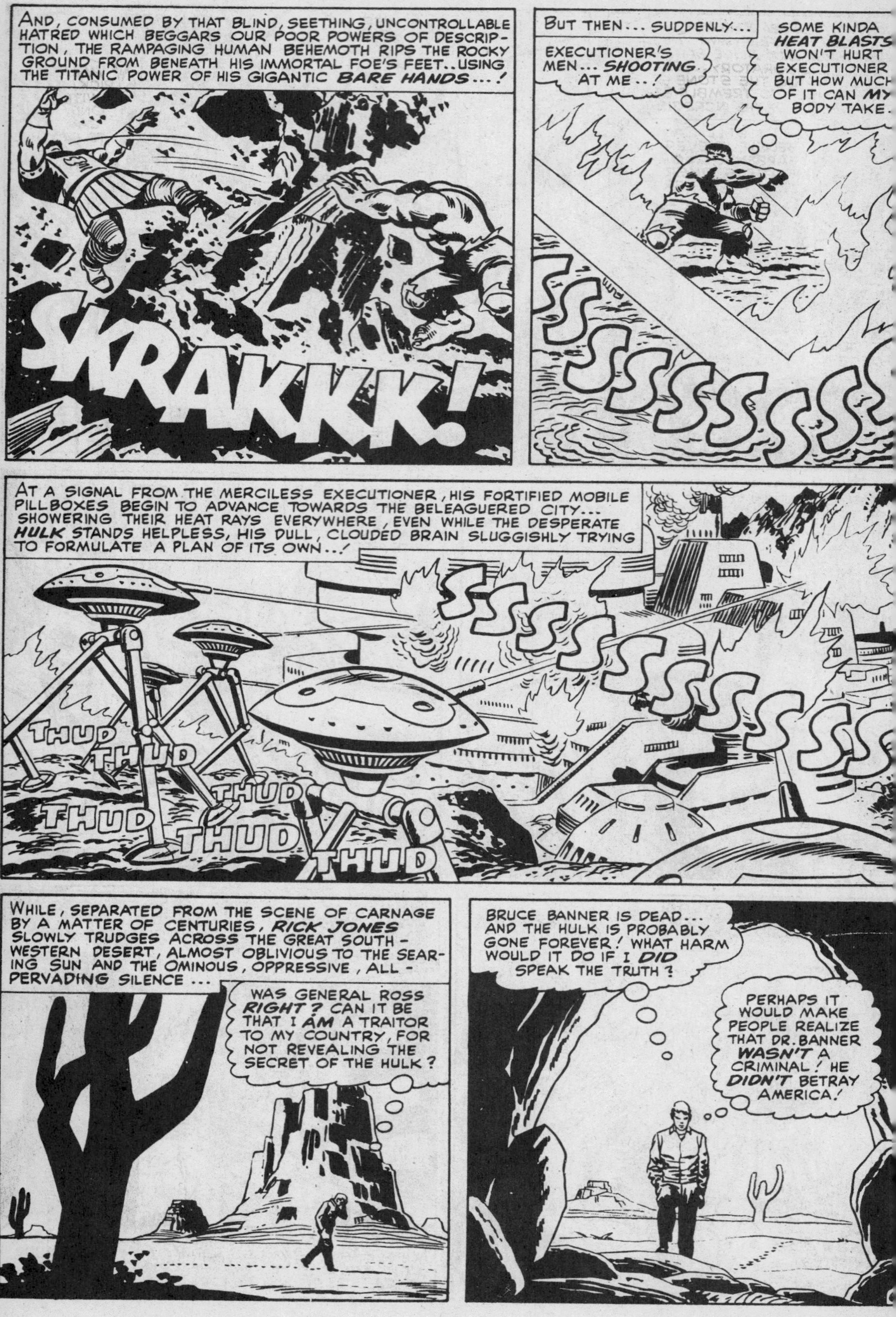

AND, CONSUMED BY THAT BLIND, SEETHING, UNCONTROLLABLE HATRED WHICH BEGGARS OUR POOR POWERS OF DESCRIPTION, THE RAMPAGING HUMAN BEHEMOTH RIPS THE ROCKY GROUND FROM BENEATH HIS IMMORTAL FOE'S FEET.. USING THE TITANIC POWER OF HIS GIGANTIC BARE HANDS...!
SKRAKKK!
BUT THEN... SUDDENLY...
EXECUTIONER'S MEN... SHOOTING. AT ME..!
SOME KINDA HEAT BLASTS WON'T HURT EXECUTIONER BUT HOW MUCH OF IT CAN MY BODY TAKE..
SSSSSSSS
AT A SIGNAL FROM THE MERCILESS EXECUTIONER, HIS FORTIFIED MOBILE PILLBOXES BEGIN TO ADVANCE TOWARDS THE BELEAGUERED CITY... SHOWERING THEIR HEAT RAYS EVERYWHERE, EVEN WHILE THE DESPERATE HULK STANDS HELPLESS, HIS DULL, CLOUDED BRAIN SLUGGISHLY TRYING TO FORMULATE A PLAN OF ITS OWN..!
SSSSSSSSSSSS
THUD THUD THUD THUD THUD THUD
WHILE, SEPARATED FROM THE SCENE OF CARNAGE BY A MATTER OF CENTURIES, RICK JONES SLOWLY TRUDGES ACROSS THE GREAT SOUTH-WESTERN DESERT, ALMOST OBLIVIOUS TO THE SEARING SUN AND THE OMINOUS, OPPRESSIVE, ALL-PERVADING SILENCE...
WAS GENERAL ROSS RIGHT? CAN IT BE THAT I AM A TRAITOR TO MY COUNTRY, FOR NOT REVEALING THE SECRET OF THE HULK?
BRUCE BANNER IS DEAD... AND THE HULK IS PROBABLY GONE FOREVER! WHAT HARM WOULD IT DO IF I DID SPEAK THE TRUTH?
PERHAPS IT WOULD MAKE PEOPLE REALIZE THAT DR. BANNER WASN'T A CRIMINAL! HE DIDN'T BETRAY AMERICA!

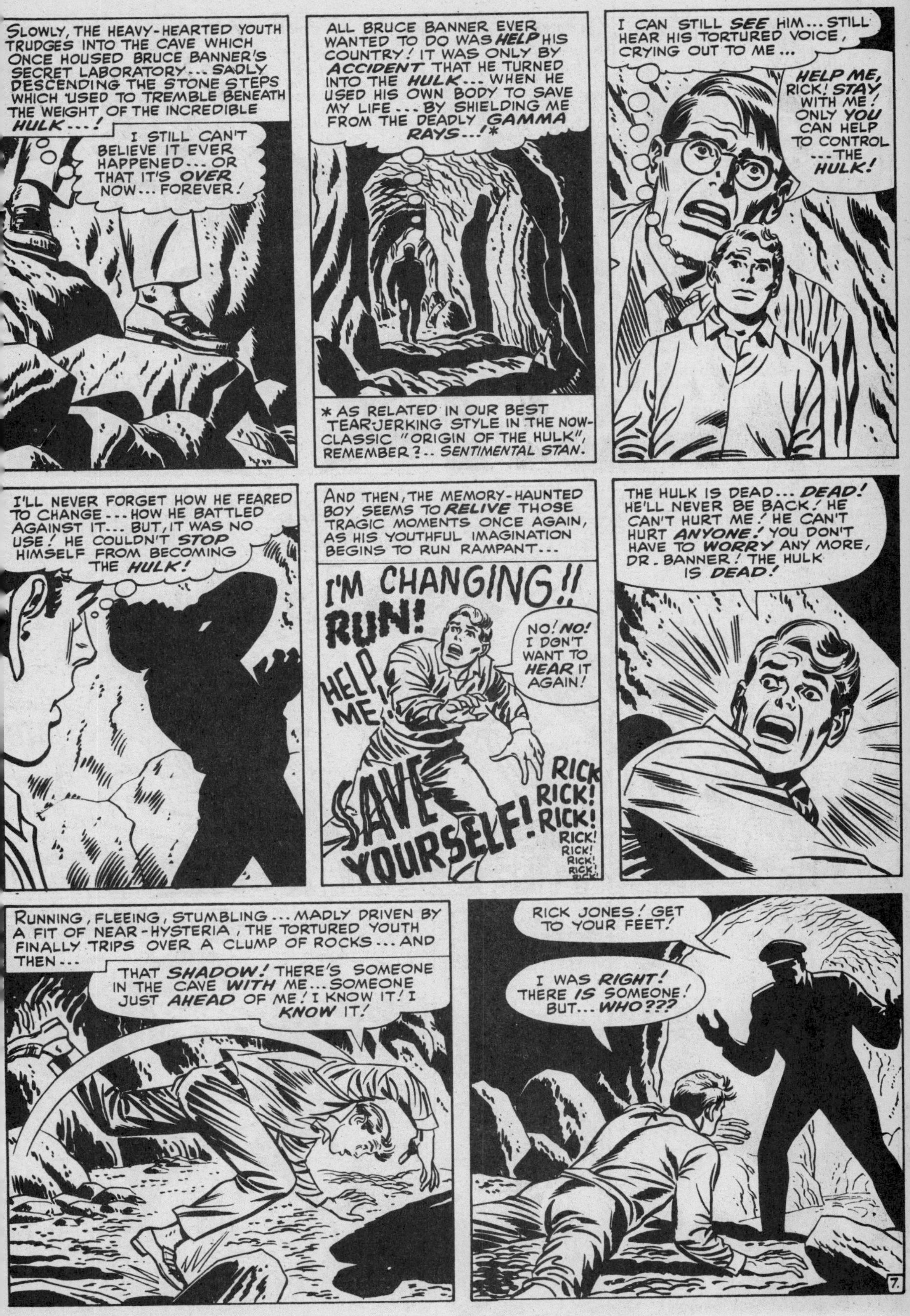

SLOWLY, THE HEAVY-HEARTED YOUTH TRUDGES INTO THE CAVE WHICH ONCE HOUSED BRUCE BANNER'S SECRET LABORATORY... SADLY DESCENDING THE STONE STEPS WHICH USED TO TREMBLE BENEATH THE WEIGHT OF THE INCREDIBLE HULK...!
I STILL CAN'T BELIEVE IT EVER HAPPENED... OR THAT IT'S OVER NOW... FOREVER!
ALL BRUCE BANNER EVER WANTED TO DO WAS HELP HIS COUNTRY! IT WAS ONLY BY ACCIDENT THAT HE TURNED INTO THE HULK... WHEN HE USED HIS OWN BODY TO SAVE MY LIFE... BY SHIELDING ME FROM THE DEADLY GAMMA RAYS..!*
* AS RELATED IN OUR BEST TEAR-JERKING STYLE IN THE NOW-CLASSIC "ORIGIN OF THE HULK", REMEMBER?.. SENTIMENTAL STAN.
I CAN STILL SEE HIM... STILL HEAR HIS TORTURED VOICE, CRYING OUT TO ME...
HELP ME, RICK! STAY WITH ME! ONLY YOU CAN HELP TO CONTROL ---THE HULK!
I'LL NEVER FORGET HOW HE FEARED TO CHANGE--- HOW HE BATTLED AGAINST IT... BUT, IT WAS NO USE! HE COULDN'T STOP HIMSELF FROM BECOMING THE HULK!
AND THEN, THE MEMORY-HAUNTED BOY SEEMS TO RELIVE THOSE TRAGIC MOMENTS ONCE AGAIN, AS HIS YOUTHFUL IMAGINATION BEGINS TO RUN RAMPANT...
I'M CHANGING!!
RUN!
HELP ME!
NO! NO! I DON'T WANT TO HEAR IT AGAIN!
SAVE YOURSELF!
RICK RICK! RICK! RICK! RICK! RICK! RICK!
THE HULK IS DEAD... DEAD! HE'LL NEVER BE BACK! HE CAN'T HURT ME! HE CAN'T HURT ANYONE! YOU DON'T HAVE TO WORRY ANY MORE, DR. BANNER! THE HULK IS DEAD!
RUNNING, FLEEING, STUMBLING... MADLY DRIVEN BY A FIT OF NEAR-HYSTERIA, THE TORTURED YOUTH FINALLY TRIPS OVER A CLUMP OF ROCKS... AND THEN...
THAT SHADOW! THERE'S SOMEONE IN THE CAVE WITH ME... SOMEONE JUST AHEAD OF ME! I KNOW IT! I KNOW IT!
RICK JONES! GET TO YOUR FEET!
I WAS RIGHT! THERE IS SOMEONE! BUT... WHO???
7.

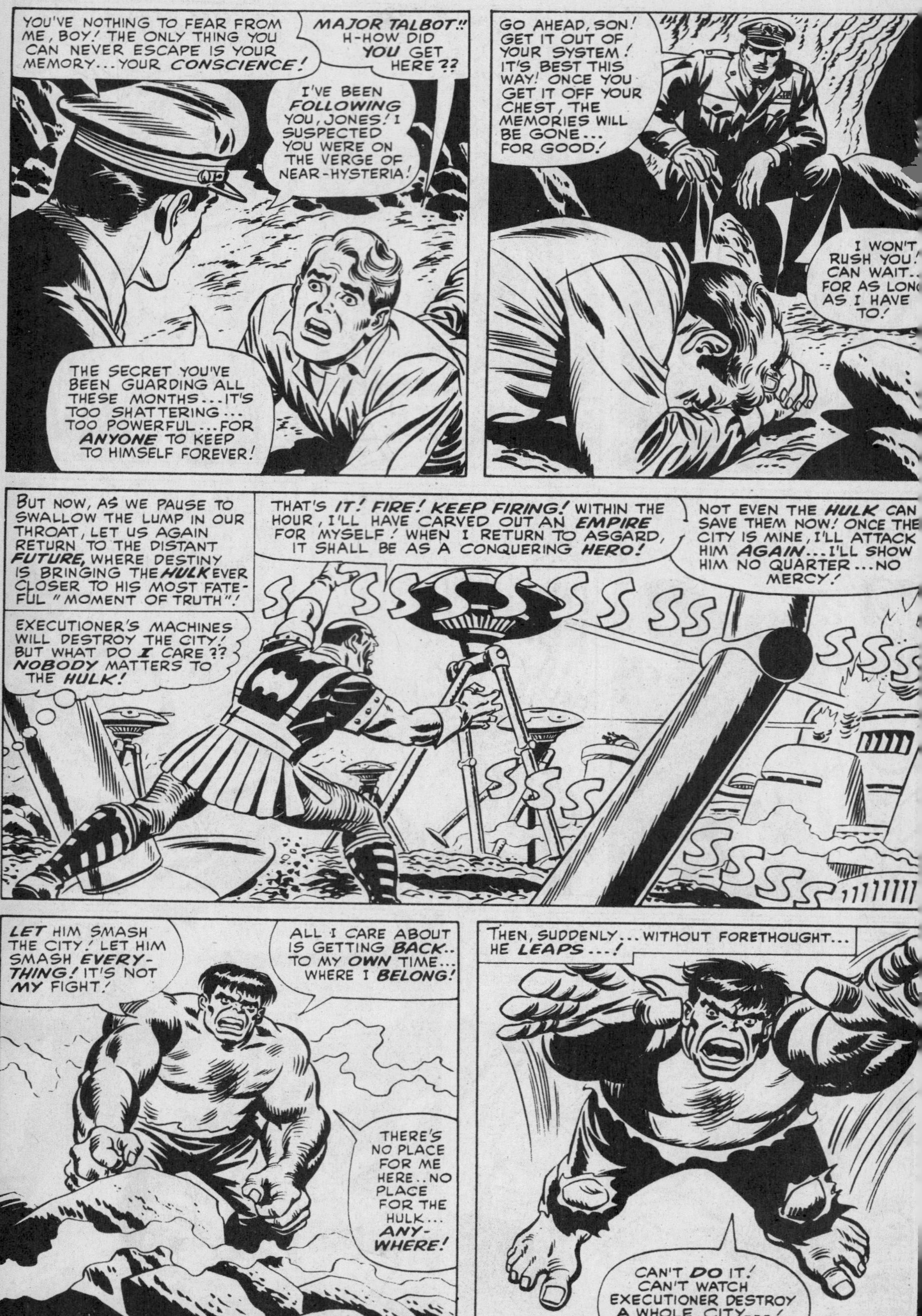

YOU'VE NOTHING TO FEAR FROM ME, BOY! THE ONLY THING YOU CAN NEVER ESCAPE IS YOUR MEMORY... YOUR CONSCIENCE!
MAJOR TALBOT!! H-HOW DID YOU GET HERE??
I'VE BEEN FOLLOWING YOU, JONES! I SUSPECTED YOU WERE ON THE VERGE OF NEAR-HYSTERIA!
THE SECRET YOU'VE BEEN GUARDING ALL THESE MONTHS... IT'S TOO SHATTERING... TOO POWERFUL... FOR ANYONE TO KEEP TO HIMSELF FOREVER!
GO AHEAD, SON! GET IT OUT OF YOUR SYSTEM! IT'S BEST THIS WAY! ONCE YOU GET IT OFF YOUR CHEST, THE MEMORIES WILL BE GONE... FOR GOOD!
I WON'T RUSH YOU! CAN WAIT... FOR AS LONG AS I HAVE TO!
BUT NOW, AS WE PAUSE TO SWALLOW THE LUMP IN OUR THROAT, LET US AGAIN RETURN TO THE DISTANT FUTURE, WHERE DESTINY IS BRINGING THE HULK EVER CLOSER TO HIS MOST FATEFUL "MOMENT OF TRUTH"!
EXECUTIONER'S MACHINES WILL DESTROY THE CITY! BUT WHAT DO I CARE?? NOBODY MATTERS TO THE HULK!
THAT'S IT! FIRE! KEEP FIRING! WITHIN THE HOUR, I'LL HAVE CARVED OUT AN EMPIRE FOR MYSELF! WHEN I RETURN TO ASGARD, IT SHALL BE AS A CONQUERING HERO!
NOT EVEN THE HULK CAN SAVE THEM NOW! ONCE THE CITY IS MINE, I'LL ATTACK HIM AGAIN... I'LL SHOW HIM NO QUARTER... NO MERCY!
SSSSSSSS
LET HIM SMASH THE CITY! LET HIM SMASH EVERYTHING! IT'S NOT MY FIGHT!
ALL I CARE ABOUT IS GETTING BACK.. TO MY OWN TIME... WHERE I BELONG!
THERE'S NO PLACE FOR ME HERE.. NO PLACE FOR THE HULK... ANYWHERE!
THEN, SUDDENLY... WITHOUT FORETHOUGHT... HE LEAPS...!
CAN'T DO IT! CAN'T WATCH EXECUTIONER DESTROY A WHOLE CITY...!
8.

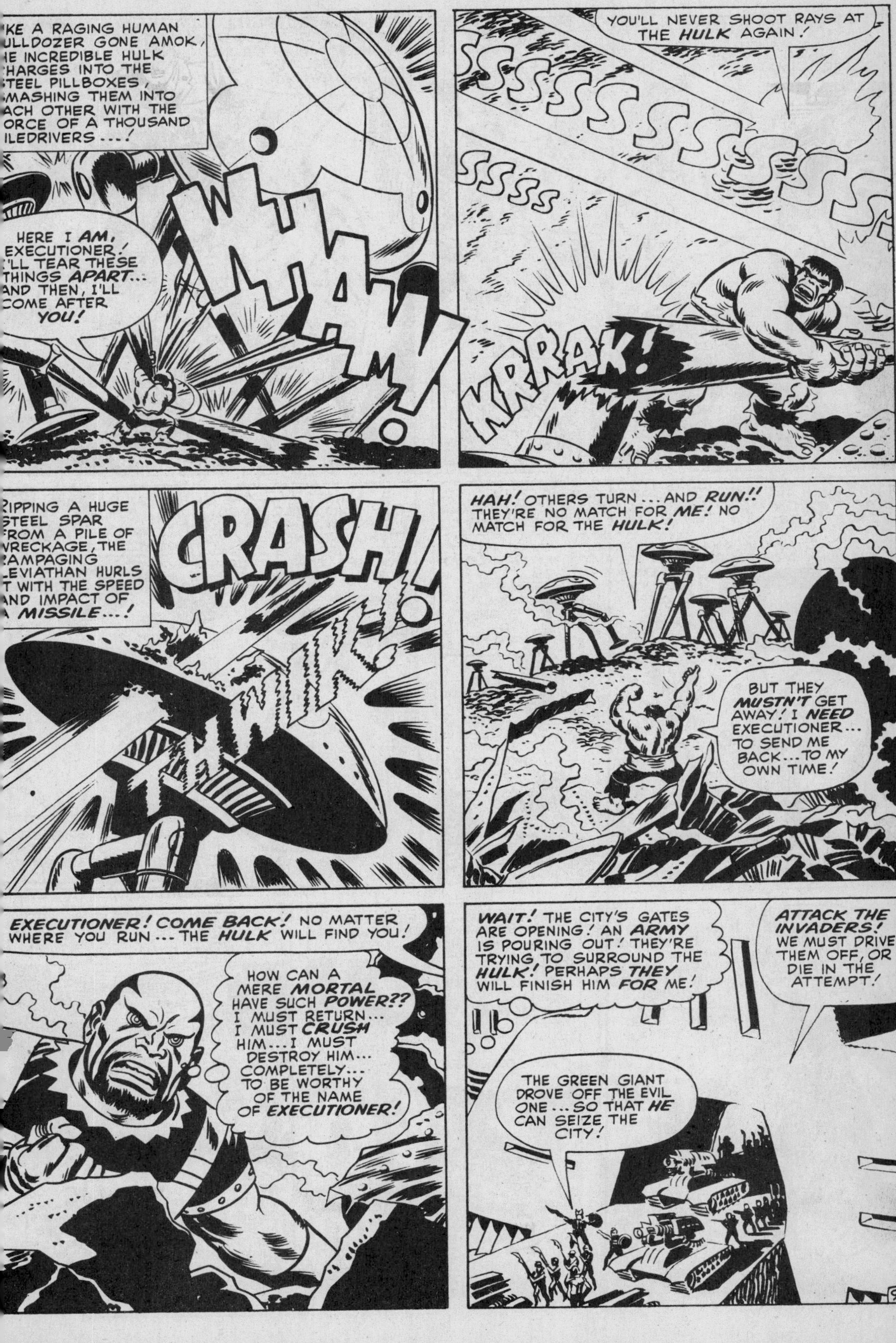
KE A RAGING HUMAN ULLDOZER GONE AMOK, HE INCREDIBLE HULK HARGES INTO THE TEEL PILLBOXES, MASHING THEM INTO ACH OTHER WITH THE ORCE OF A THOUSAND ILEDRIVERS...!
HERE I AM, EXECUTIONER! I'LL TEAR THESE THINGS APART... AND THEN, I'LL COME AFTER YOU!
WHAM!
YOU'LL NEVER SHOOT RAYS AT THE HULK AGAIN!
SSSSSSSSSS
SSSSS
KRRAK!
RIPPING A HUGE STEEL SPAR FROM A PILE OF WRECKAGE, THE RAMPAGING LEVIATHAN HURLS IT WITH THE SPEED AND IMPACT OF A MISSILE...!
CRASH!
THWUK!
HAH! OTHERS TURN... AND RUN!! THEY'RE NO MATCH FOR ME! NO MATCH FOR THE HULK!
BUT THEY MUSTN'T GET AWAY! I NEED EXECUTIONER... TO SEND ME BACK... TO MY OWN TIME!
EXECUTIONER! COME BACK! NO MATTER WHERE YOU RUN... THE HULK WILL FIND YOU!
HOW CAN A MERE MORTAL HAVE SUCH POWER?? I MUST RETURN... I MUST CRUSH HIM... I MUST DESTROY HIM... COMPLETELY... TO BE WORTHY OF THE NAME OF EXECUTIONER!
WAIT! THE CITY'S GATES ARE OPENING! AN ARMY IS POURING OUT! THEY'RE TRYING TO SURROUND THE HULK! PERHAPS THEY WILL FINISH HIM FOR ME!
ATTACK THE INVADERS! WE MUST DRIVE THEM OFF, OR DIE IN THE ATTEMPT!
THE GREEN GIANT DROVE OFF THE EVIL ONE... SO THAT HE CAN SEIZE THE CITY!
9.

SURRENDER OR DIE, MIGHTY ONE! YOU ARE FAR TOO POWERFUL TO BE PERMITTED TO ROAM FREE!

STAY BACK! NO ONE CAPTURES THE HULK! I'LL SMASH YOU ALL!

LOOK, SIRE... HIS BODY! SOMETHING WONDROUS IS HAPPENING TO IT!

THE PRIMITIVE BRUTE POSSESSES A MAGICAL POWER! HE IS SAVING HIMSELF BY VANISHING!

WHAT'S HAPPENING TO ME ?? THIS NEVER WAIT! NOW I KNOW WHEN THE T-GUN HIT ME! IT WAS THE SAME WAY...!

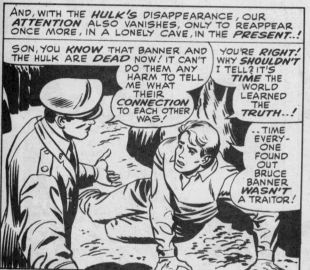

AND, WITH THE HULK'S DISAPPEARANCE, OUR ATTENTION ALSO VANISHES, ONLY TO REAPPEAR ONCE MORE, IN A LONELY CAVE, IN THE PRESENT...!

SON, YOU KNOW THAT BANNER AND THE HULK ARE DEAD NOW! IT CAN'T DO THEM ANY HARM TO TELL ME WHAT THEIR CONNECTION TO EACH OTHER WAS!

YOU'RE RIGHT! WHY SHOULDN'T I TELL? IT'S TIME THE WORLD LEARNED THE TRUTH...!

..TIME EVERYONE FOUND OUT BRUCE BANNER WASN'T A TRAITOR!

DR. BANNER WAS THE GREATEST GUY WHO EVER LIVED! HE NEVER WANTED TO DO ANYTHING WRONG...IT WAS ONLY BECAUSE HE SAVED MY LIFE THAT HE TURNED INTO ---THE HULK!

YOU MEAN...BANNER AND THE HULK...WERE ONE AND THE SAME!

THEN, THAT EXPLAINS WHY I NEVER SAW THEM TOGETHER... WHY BANNER COULD NEVER JUSTIFY HIS ABSENCES...!

JONES..WAIT! I WANT TO HEAR MORE..!

THERE ISN'T ANY MORE..!

ANYWAY, WHAT DIFFERENCE DOES IT MAKE NOW? THEY'RE BOTH ---DEAD...!

BUT WHAT IF THEY'RE NOT?! ALL WE KNOW ABOUT THE HULK IS THAT HE VANISHED--!

---AND IF HE SHOULD STILL BE ALIVE... THEN BANNER IS, TOO!

AS THE HEAVY-HEARTED TEEN-AGER LEAVES THE GLOOMY CAVE, FOLLOWED BY A STARTLED, WORRIED MAJOR TALBOT, NEITHER OF THEM NOTICES A STRANGE, MYSTIFYING OCCURRENCE---

FROM A SMALL PILE OF WRECKAGE IN THE MURKY SHADOWS, A MYSTERIOUS WHIRLWIND SEEMS TO FORM.

...SLOWLY AT FIRST, THEN FASTER AND FASTER, LIKE AN OMEN OF RETURNING LIFE! ONLY OUR NEXT ISSUE CAN TELL WHAT IT SIGNIFIES --- BUT, OF THIS WE CAN BE CERTAIN ... A NEW, SENSATIONAL CHAPTER IN THE LIFE OF THE HULK IS ABOUT TO BEGIN...AND WE SHALL THRILL TO EACH MOMENT OF IT...TOGETHER!

10

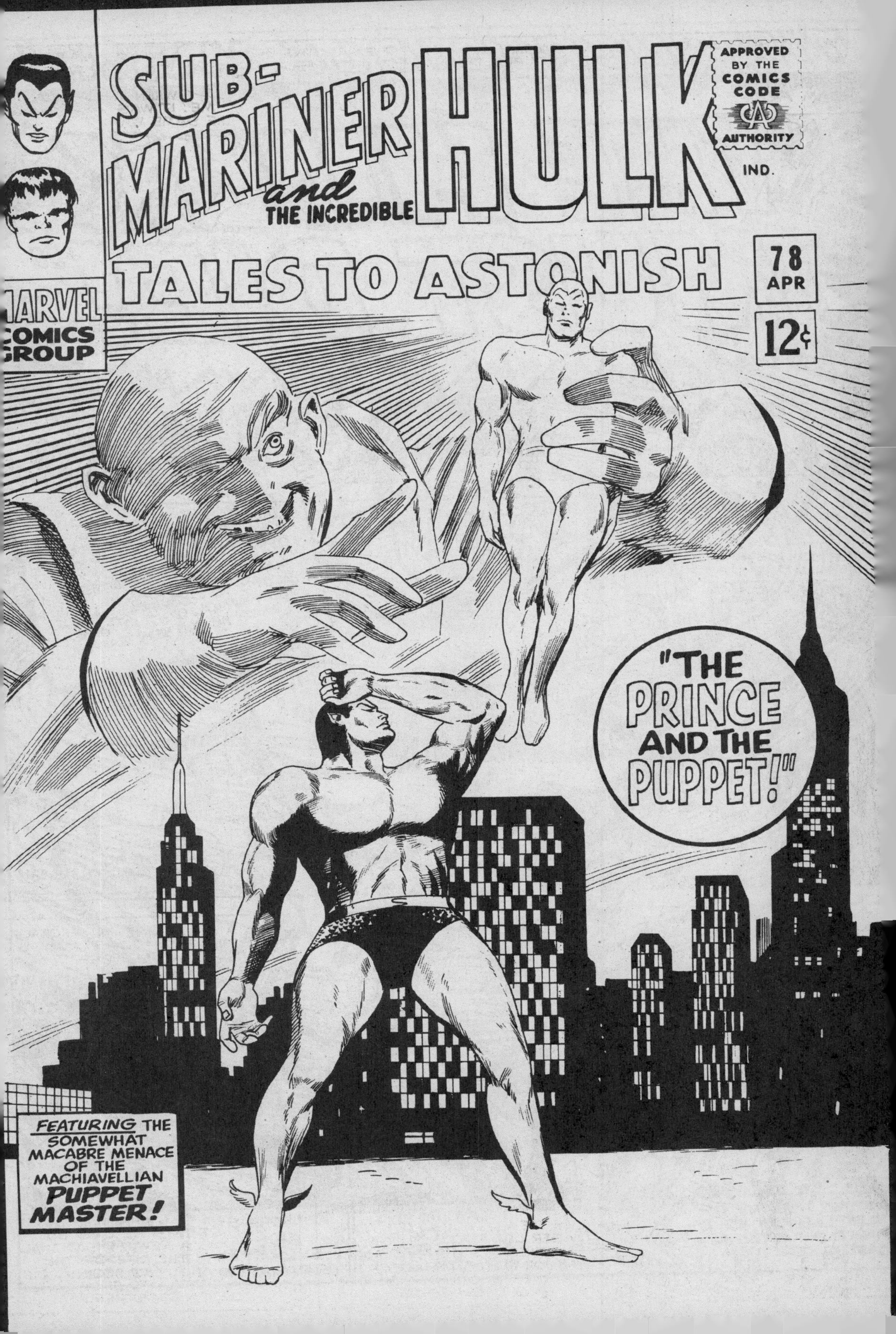

SUB-MARINER and THE INCREDIBLE HULK
APPROVED BY THE COMICS CODE AUTHORITY
IND.
TALES TO ASTONISH
78 APR
12¢
MARVEL COMICS GROUP
"THE PRINCE AND THE PUPPET!"
FEATURING THE SOMEWHAT MACABRE MENACE OF THE MACHIAVELLIAN PUPPET MASTER!

THE INCREDIBLE HULK!

"THE HULK MUST DIE!"

LAST ISH, THINKING THE HULK IS DEAD, RICK JONES FINALLY REVEALED HIS GREATEST SECRET... THE FACT THAT DR. BRUCE BANNER AND THE INCREDIBLE HULK ARE ACTUALLY ONE AND THE SAME! BUT, AS THE TEENAGER LEAVES THE HULK'S LONELY CAVE WITH A SHOCKED MAJOR GLEN TALBOT, NEITHER OF THEM REALIZES THAT THE GREEN TITAN IS SLOWLY RETURNING FROM THE FAR-DISTANT FUTURE, IN WHICH HE HAD BEEN TRAPPED...!

ANOTHER TRULY INSPIRED TALENT LINEUP BY MIGHTY MARVEL'S MASTERFUL CASTING DIRECTOR...

STORY BY:	LAYOUTS BY:	ARTWORK BY:	LETTERING BY:
STAN LEE (CERTAINLY!)	JACK KIRBY (NATURALLY!)	BILL EVERETT (SURPRISINGLY!)	SAM ROSEN (INEVITABLY!)

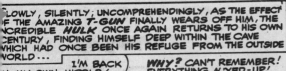

SLOWLY, SILENTLY, UNCOMPREHENDINGLY, AS THE EFFECT OF THE AMAZING *T-GUN* FINALLY WEARS OFF HIM, THE INCREDIBLE *HULK* ONCE AGAIN RETURNS TO HIS OWN CENTURY, FINDING HIMSELF DEEP WITHIN THE CAVE WHICH HAD ONCE BEEN HIS REFUGE FROM THE OUTSIDE WORLD...

I'M BACK IN MY OWN WORLD! MY OWN *CAVE!*

WHY? CAN'T REMEMBER! EVERYTHING 'N' XED-UP! HEAD HURTS! CAN'T THINK...!

WITH EACH PASSING SECOND, THE BRILLIANT BRAIN OF *BRUCE BANNER* BECOMES MORE CLOUDED... MORE DULLED... AS THE BESTIAL, SAVAGE MIND OF THE *HULK* ALL BUT OBLITERATES THE IDENTITY OF HIS OTHER SELF!

NO *NEED* TO THINK! I'M WHERE I *BELONG!* I'M STRONG AS EVER! I'M THE *HULK!*

THAT'S ALL THAT *MATTERS!*

NO DIFFERENCE *WHAT* WORLD I'M IN! MEN HATE ME.. HOUND ME.. HUNT ME!! NO PLACE TO REST... NO PLACE TO TURN....!

BUT I'M *STRONGEST* OF ALL! I GO *ANYWHERE!* I DO *ANYTHING!* NO ONE CAN STOP THE *HULK!*

THUS, WITH HIS BRUTISH BRAIN CONFUSED, BEWILDERED, BRIMMING WITH NAMELESS RAGE AGAINST EVERY-THING THAT LIVES, THE GREEN-SKINNED GIANT LEAVES THE SANCTUARY OF HIS CAVE, AS, SOME DISTANCE AWAY, A VOICE EXCLAIMS...

CHARLIE! LOOK! ON THAT RIDGE! IT'S *HIM!*

MAJOR TALBOT'S ORDER FOR AN AROUND-THE-CLOCK ALERT *PAID OFF!* THE HULK IS STILL ALIVE! WE'VE *FOUND* 'IM!

GIVE ME HIS EXACT LOCATION, RATE OF SPEED, AND ESTIMATED OBJECTIVE!

I'LL CONTACT THE BASE RIGHT *NOW!* BOY, WILL *THIS* SHAKE 'EM UP BACK THERE!

BUT, BEFORE THE MESSAGE IS RECEIVED AT THE SPRAWLING SOUTHWESTERN MISSILE COMMAND WE FIND...

GENERAL ROSS WANTED ME TO WELCOME YOU TO OUR BASE, DR. *ZAXON!* IT'S AN HONOR TO HAVE A SCIENTIST OF YOUR STATURE AS A REPLACE-MENT FOR BRUCE BANNER!

THANK YOU, MAJOR TALBOT! I SHALL ATTEMPT TO ERASE THE *BLOT* WHICH BANNER'S TREASON HAS GIVEN THE NAME OF SCIENCE!

DANGER

2

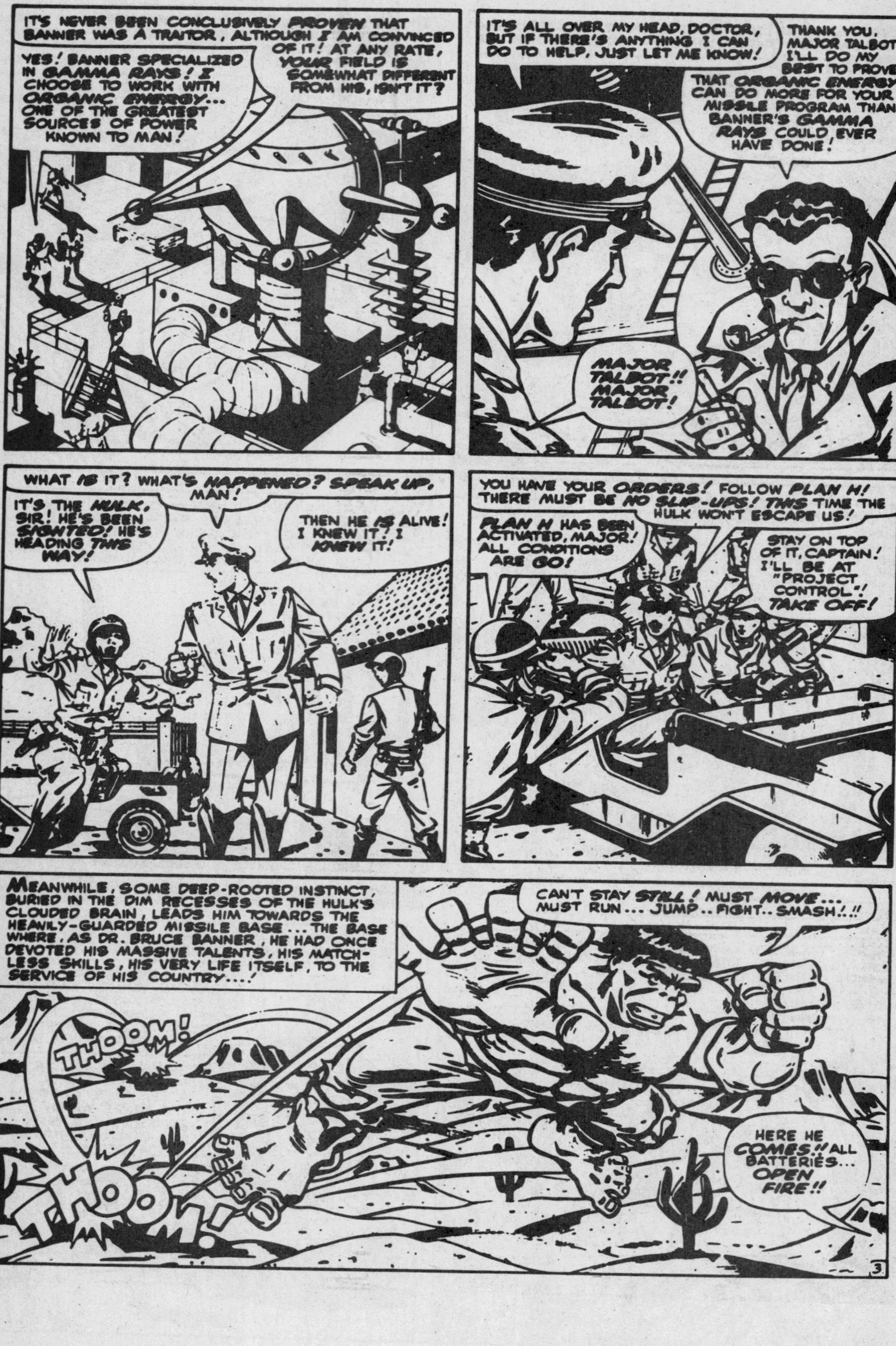
IT'S NEVER BEEN CONCLUSIVELY PROVEN THAT BANNER WAS A TRAITOR, ALTHOUGH I AM CONVINCED OF IT! AT ANY RATE, YOUR FIELD IS SOMEWHAT DIFFERENT FROM HIS, ISN'T IT?
YES! BANNER SPECIALIZED IN GAMMA RAYS! I CHOOSE TO WORK WITH ORGANIC ENERGY... ONE OF THE GREATEST SOURCES OF POWER KNOWN TO MAN!
IT'S ALL OVER MY HEAD, DOCTOR, BUT IF THERE'S ANYTHING I CAN DO TO HELP, JUST LET ME KNOW!
THANK YOU, MAJOR TALBOT! I'LL DO MY BEST TO PROVE THAT ORGANIC ENERGY CAN DO MORE FOR YOUR MISSLE PROGRAM THAN BANNER'S GAMMA RAYS COULD EVER HAVE DONE!
MAJOR TALBOT!! MAJOR TALBOT!
WHAT IS IT? WHAT'S HAPPENED? SPEAK UP, MAN!
IT'S THE HULK, SIR! HE'S BEEN SIGHTED! HE'S HEADING THIS WAY!
THEN HE IS ALIVE! I KNEW IT! I KNEW IT!
YOU HAVE YOUR ORDERS! FOLLOW PLAN H! THERE MUST BE NO SLIP-UPS! THIS TIME THE HULK WON'T ESCAPE US!
PLAN H HAS BEEN ACTIVATED, MAJOR! ALL CONDITIONS ARE GO!
STAY ON TOP OF IT, CAPTAIN! I'LL BE AT "PROJECT CONTROL"! TAKE OFF!
MEANWHILE, SOME DEEP-ROOTED INSTINCT, BURIED IN THE DIM RECESSES OF THE HULK'S CLOUDED BRAIN, LEADS HIM TOWARDS THE HEAVILY-GUARDED MISSILE BASE ... THE BASE WHERE, AS DR. BRUCE BANNER, HE HAD ONCE DEVOTED HIS MASSIVE TALENTS, HIS MATCHLESS SKILLS, HIS VERY LIFE ITSELF, TO THE SERVICE OF HIS COUNTRY...!
CAN'T STAY STILL! MUST MOVE... MUST RUN... JUMP.. FIGHT.. SMASH!..!!
THOOM!
THOOM!
HERE HE COMES!! ALL BATTERIES... OPEN FIRE!!
3

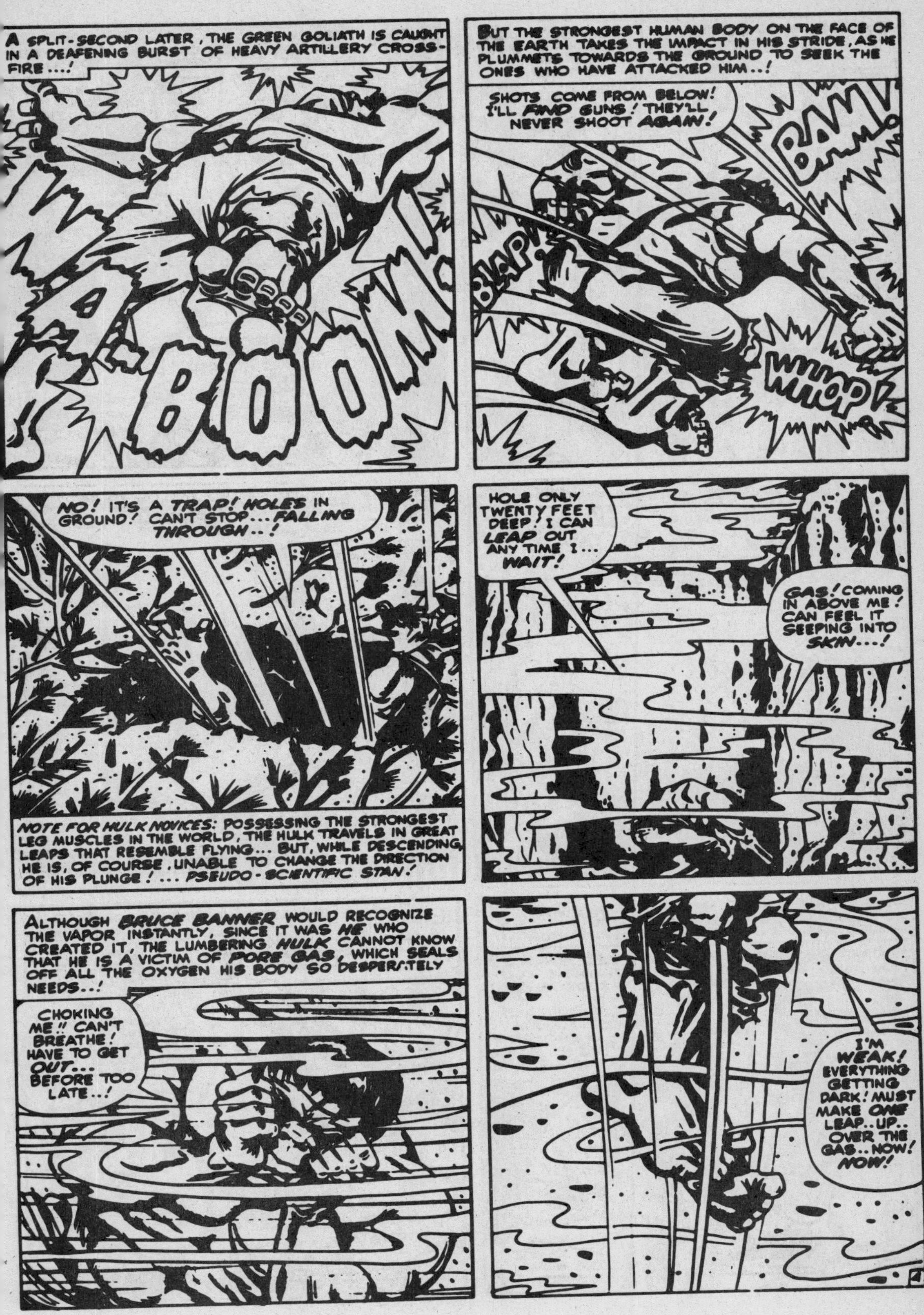
A SPLIT-SECOND LATER, THE GREEN GOLIATH IS CAUGHT IN A DEAFENING BURST OF HEAVY ARTILLERY CROSS-FIRE...!
BOOM!
BUT THE STRONGEST HUMAN BODY ON THE FACE OF THE EARTH TAKES THE IMPACT IN HIS STRIDE, AS HE PLUMMETS TOWARDS THE GROUND TO SEEK THE ONES WHO HAVE ATTACKED HIM..!
SHOTS COME FROM BELOW! I'LL FIND GUNS! THEY'LL NEVER SHOOT AGAIN!
BAM!
BLAP!
WHOP!
NO! IT'S A TRAP! HOLES IN GROUND! CAN'T STOP... FALLING THROUGH..!
NOTE FOR HULK NOVICES: POSSESSING THE STRONGEST LEG MUSCLES IN THE WORLD, THE HULK TRAVELS IN GREAT LEAPS THAT RESEMBLE FLYING... BUT, WHILE DESCENDING, HE IS, OF COURSE, UNABLE TO CHANGE THE DIRECTION OF HIS PLUNGE! ... PSEUDO-SCIENTIFIC STAN!
HOLE ONLY TWENTY FEET DEEP! I CAN LEAP OUT ANY TIME I... WAIT!
GAS! COMING IN ABOVE ME! CAN FEEL IT SEEPING INTO SKIN...!
ALTHOUGH BRUCE BANNER WOULD RECOGNIZE THE VAPOR INSTANTLY, SINCE IT WAS HE WHO CREATED IT, THE LUMBERING HULK CANNOT KNOW THAT HE IS A VICTIM OF PORE GAS, WHICH SEALS OFF ALL THE OXYGEN HIS BODY SO DESPERATELY NEEDS..!
CHOKING ME!! CAN'T BREATHE! HAVE TO GET OUT... BEFORE TOO LATE..!
I'M WEAK! EVERYTHING GETTING DARK! MUST MAKE ONE LEAP..UP.. OVER THE GAS..NOW! NOW!
4

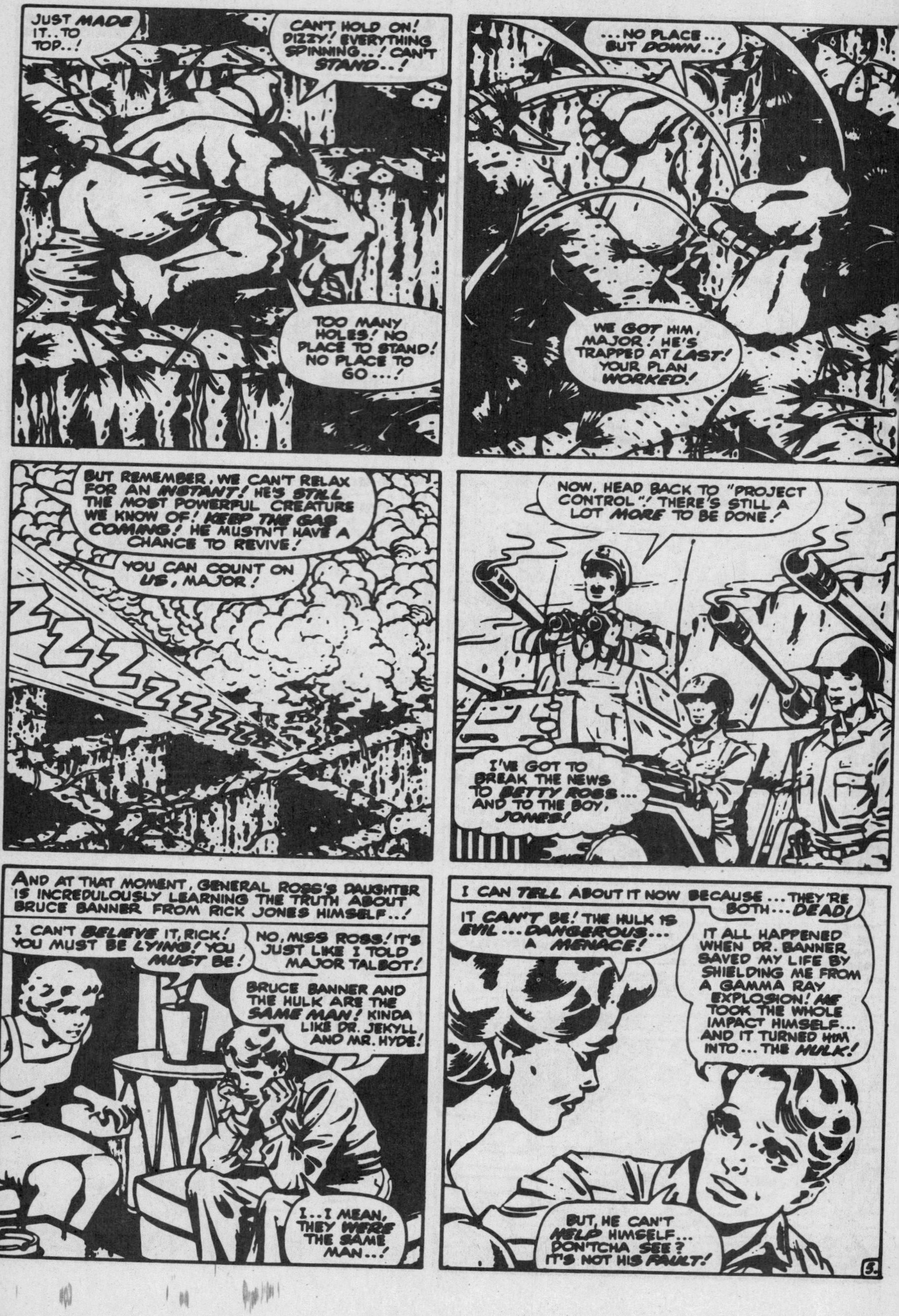
JUST MADE IT.. TO TOP..!
CAN'T HOLD ON! DIZZY! EVERYTHING SPINNING...! CAN'T STAND..!
TOO MANY HOLES! NO PLACE TO STAND! NO PLACE TO GO...!
...NO PLACE... BUT DOWN...!
WE GOT HIM, MAJOR! HE'S TRAPPED AT LAST! YOUR PLAN WORKED!
BUT REMEMBER, WE CAN'T RELAX FOR AN INSTANT! HE'S STILL THE MOST POWERFUL CREATURE WE KNOW OF! KEEP THE GAS COMING! HE MUSTN'T HAVE A CHANCE TO REVIVE!
YOU CAN COUNT ON US, MAJOR!
NOW, HEAD BACK TO "PROJECT CONTROL"! THERE'S STILL A LOT MORE TO BE DONE!
I'VE GOT TO BREAK THE NEWS TO BETTY ROSS... AND TO THE BOY, JONES!
AND AT THAT MOMENT, GENERAL ROSS'S DAUGHTER IS INCREDULOUSLY LEARNING THE TRUTH ABOUT BRUCE BANNER FROM RICK JONES HIMSELF...!
I CAN'T BELIEVE IT, RICK! YOU MUST BE LYING! YOU MUST BE!
NO, MISS ROSS! IT'S JUST LIKE I TOLD MAJOR TALBOT!
BRUCE BANNER AND THE HULK ARE THE SAME MAN! KINDA LIKE DR. JEKYLL AND MR. HYDE!
I..I MEAN, THEY WERE THE SAME MAN...!
I CAN TELL ABOUT IT NOW BECAUSE... THEY'RE BOTH... DEAD!
IT CAN'T BE! THE HULK IS EVIL... DANGEROUS... A MENACE!
IT ALL HAPPENED WHEN DR. BANNER SAVED MY LIFE BY SHIELDING ME FROM A GAMMA RAY EXPLOSION! HE TOOK THE WHOLE IMPACT HIMSELF... AND IT TURNED HIM INTO... THE HULK!
BUT, HE CAN'T HELP HIMSELF... DON'TCHA SEE? IT'S NOT HIS FAULT!
5.

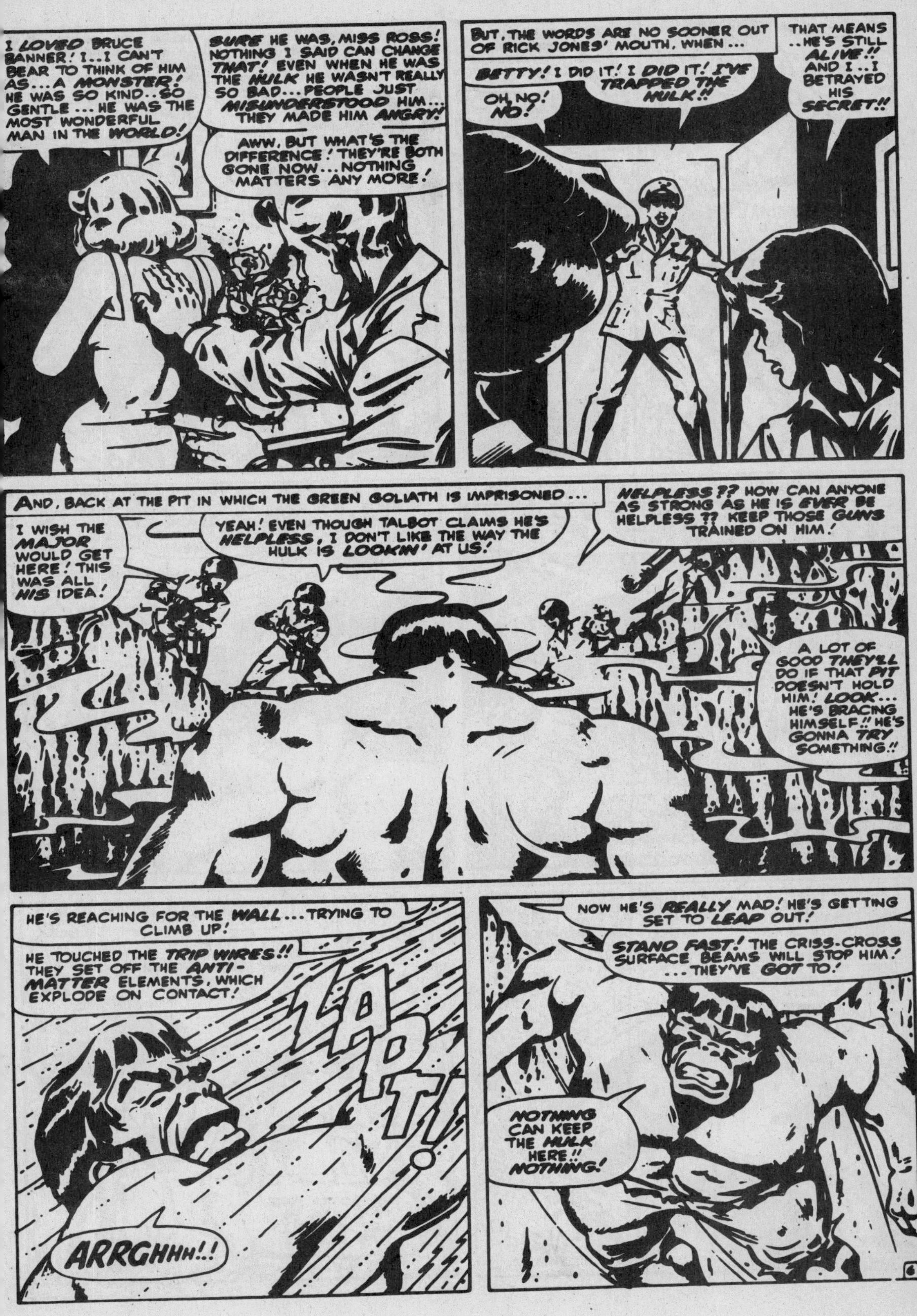
I LOVED BRUCE BANNER! I..I CAN'T BEAR TO THINK OF HIM AS... A MONSTER! HE WAS SO KIND..SO GENTLE ... HE WAS THE MOST WONDERFUL MAN IN THE WORLD!
SURE HE WAS, MISS ROSS! NOTHING I SAID CAN CHANGE THAT! EVEN WHEN HE WAS THE HULK HE WASN'T REALLY SO BAD...PEOPLE JUST MISUNDERSTOOD HIM... THEY MADE HIM ANGRY!
AWW, BUT WHAT'S THE DIFFERENCE! THEY'RE BOTH GONE NOW... NOTHING MATTERS ANY MORE!
BUT, THE WORDS ARE NO SOONER OUT OF RICK JONES' MOUTH, WHEN ...
BETTY! I DID IT! I DID IT! I'VE TRAPPED THE HULK!!
OH, NO! NO!
THAT MEANS ..HE'S STILL ALIVE!! AND I ..I BETRAYED HIS SECRET!!
AND, BACK AT THE PIT IN WHICH THE GREEN GOLIATH IS IMPRISONED ...
I WISH THE MAJOR WOULD GET HERE! THIS WAS ALL HIS IDEA!
YEAH! EVEN THOUGH TALBOT CLAIMS HE'S HELPLESS, I DON'T LIKE THE WAY THE HULK IS LOOKIN' AT US!
HELPLESS?? HOW CAN ANYONE AS STRONG AS HE IS EVER BE HELPLESS?? KEEP THOSE GUNS TRAINED ON HIM!
A LOT OF GOOD THEY'LL DO IF THAT PIT DOESN'T HOLD HIM! LOOK... HE'S BRACING HIMSELF!! HE'S GONNA TRY SOMETHING!!
HE'S REACHING FOR THE WALL... TRYING TO CLIMB UP!
HE TOUCHED THE TRIP WIRES!! THEY SET OFF THE ANTI-MATTER ELEMENTS, WHICH EXPLODE ON CONTACT!
ZAPT!
ARRGHHH!!
NOW HE'S REALLY MAD! HE'S GETTING SET TO LEAP OUT!
STAND FAST! THE CRISS-CROSS SURFACE BEAMS WILL STOP HIM! ...THEY'VE GOT TO!
NOTHING CAN KEEP THE HULK HERE!! NOTHING!
6

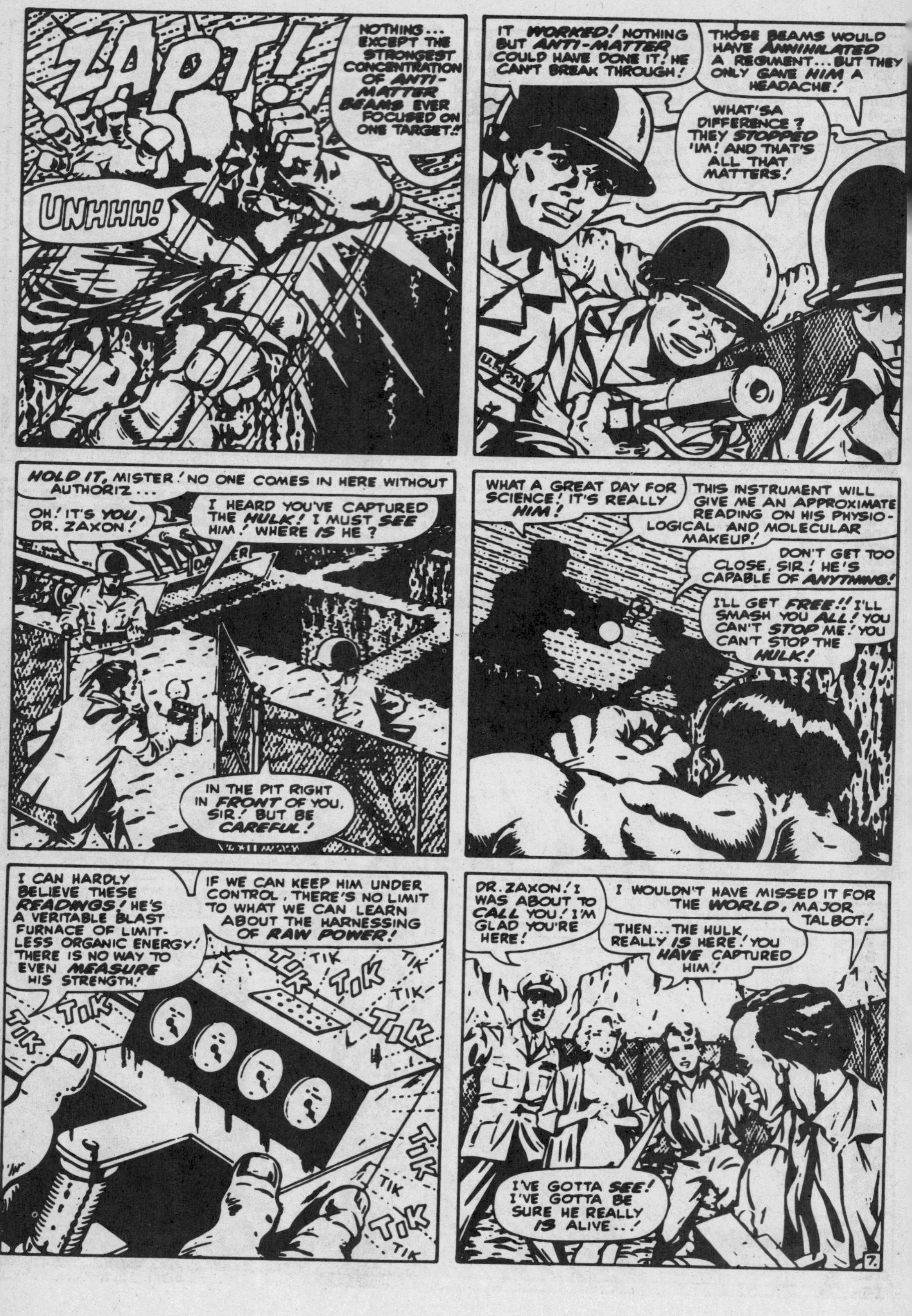
ZAPT!
NOTHING... EXCEPT THE STRONGEST CONCENTRATION OF ANTI-MATTER BEAMS EVER FOCUSED ON ONE TARGET!!
UNHHH!
IT WORKED! NOTHING BUT ANTI-MATTER COULD HAVE DONE IT! HE CAN'T BREAK THROUGH!
THOSE BEAMS WOULD HAVE ANNIHILATED A REGIMENT... BUT THEY ONLY GAVE HIM A HEADACHE!
WHAT'SA DIFFERENCE? THEY STOPPED 'IM! AND THAT'S ALL THAT MATTERS!
HOLD IT, MISTER! NO ONE COMES IN HERE WITHOUT AUTHORIZ...
OH! IT'S YOU, DR. ZAXON!
I HEARD YOU'VE CAPTURED THE HULK! I MUST SEE HIM! WHERE IS HE?
IN THE PIT RIGHT IN FRONT OF YOU, SIR! BUT BE CAREFUL!
WHAT A GREAT DAY FOR SCIENCE! IT'S REALLY HIM!
THIS INSTRUMENT WILL GIVE ME AN APPROXIMATE READING ON HIS PHYSIOLOGICAL AND MOLECULAR MAKEUP!
DON'T GET TOO CLOSE, SIR! HE'S CAPABLE OF ANYTHING!
I'LL GET FREE!! I'LL SMASH YOU ALL! YOU CAN'T STOP ME! YOU CAN'T STOP THE HULK!
I CAN HARDLY BELIEVE THESE READINGS! HE'S A VERITABLE BLAST FURNACE OF LIMITLESS ORGANIC ENERGY! THERE IS NO WAY TO EVEN MEASURE HIS STRENGTH!
IF WE CAN KEEP HIM UNDER CONTROL, THERE'S NO LIMIT TO WHAT WE CAN LEARN ABOUT THE HARNESSING OF RAW POWER!
TIK TIK TIK TIK TIK TIK TIK
DR. ZAXON! I WAS ABOUT TO CALL YOU! I'M GLAD YOU'RE HERE!
I WOULDN'T HAVE MISSED IT FOR THE WORLD, MAJOR TALBOT!
THEN... THE HULK REALLY IS HERE! YOU HAVE CAPTURED HIM!
I'VE GOTTA SEE! I'VE GOTTA BE SURE HE REALLY IS ALIVE...!
7.

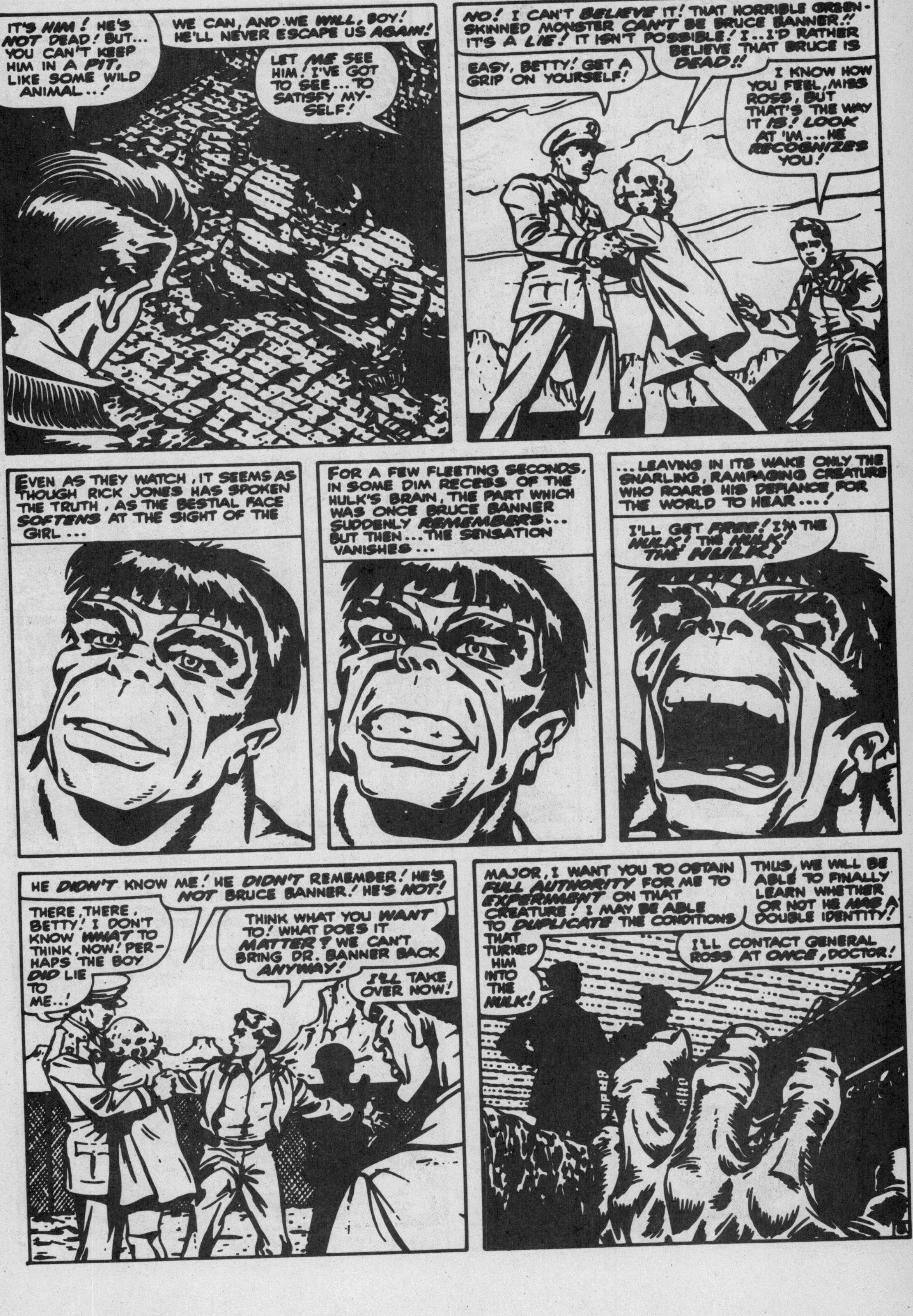

IT'S HIM! HE'S NOT DEAD! BUT... YOU CAN'T KEEP HIM IN A PIT, LIKE SOME WILD ANIMAL...!
WE CAN, AND WE WILL, BOY! HE'LL NEVER ESCAPE US AGAIN!
LET ME SEE HIM! I'VE GOT TO SEE... TO SATISFY MY-SELF!
NO! I CAN'T BELIEVE IT! THAT HORRIBLE GREEN-SKINNED MONSTER CAN'T BE BRUCE BANNER!! IT'S A LIE! IT ISN'T POSSIBLE! I..I'D RATHER BELIEVE THAT BRUCE IS DEAD!!
EASY, BETTY! GET A GRIP ON YOURSELF!
I KNOW HOW YOU FEEL, MISS ROSS, BUT THAT'S THE WAY IT IS! LOOK AT 'IM... HE RECOGNIZES YOU!
EVEN AS THEY WATCH, IT SEEMS AS THOUGH RICK JONES HAS SPOKEN THE TRUTH, AS THE BESTIAL FACE SOFTENS AT THE SIGHT OF THE GIRL...
FOR A FEW FLEETING SECONDS, IN SOME DIM RECESS OF THE HULK'S BRAIN, THE PART WHICH WAS ONCE BRUCE BANNER SUDDENLY REMEMBERS... BUT THEN... THE SENSATION VANISHES...
...LEAVING IN ITS WAKE ONLY THE SNARLING, RAMPAGING CREATURE WHO ROARS HIS DEFIANCE FOR THE WORLD TO HEAR...!
I'LL GET FREE! I'M THE HULK! THE HULK! THE HULK!
HE DIDN'T KNOW ME! HE DIDN'T REMEMBER! HE'S NOT BRUCE BANNER! HE'S NOT!
THERE, THERE, BETTY! I DON'T KNOW WHAT TO THINK, NOW! PERHAPS THE BOY DID LIE TO ME...!
THINK WHAT YOU WANT TO! WHAT DOES IT MATTER? WE CAN'T BRING DR. BANNER BACK ANYWAY!
I'LL TAKE OVER NOW!
MAJOR, I WANT YOU TO OBTAIN FULL AUTHORITY FOR ME TO EXPERIMENT ON THAT CREATURE! I MAY BE ABLE TO DUPLICATE THE CONDITIONS THAT TURNED HIM INTO THE HULK!
THUS, WE WILL BE ABLE TO FINALLY LEARN WHETHER OR NOT HE HAS A DOUBLE IDENTITY!
I'LL CONTACT GENERAL ROSS AT ONCE, DOCTOR!

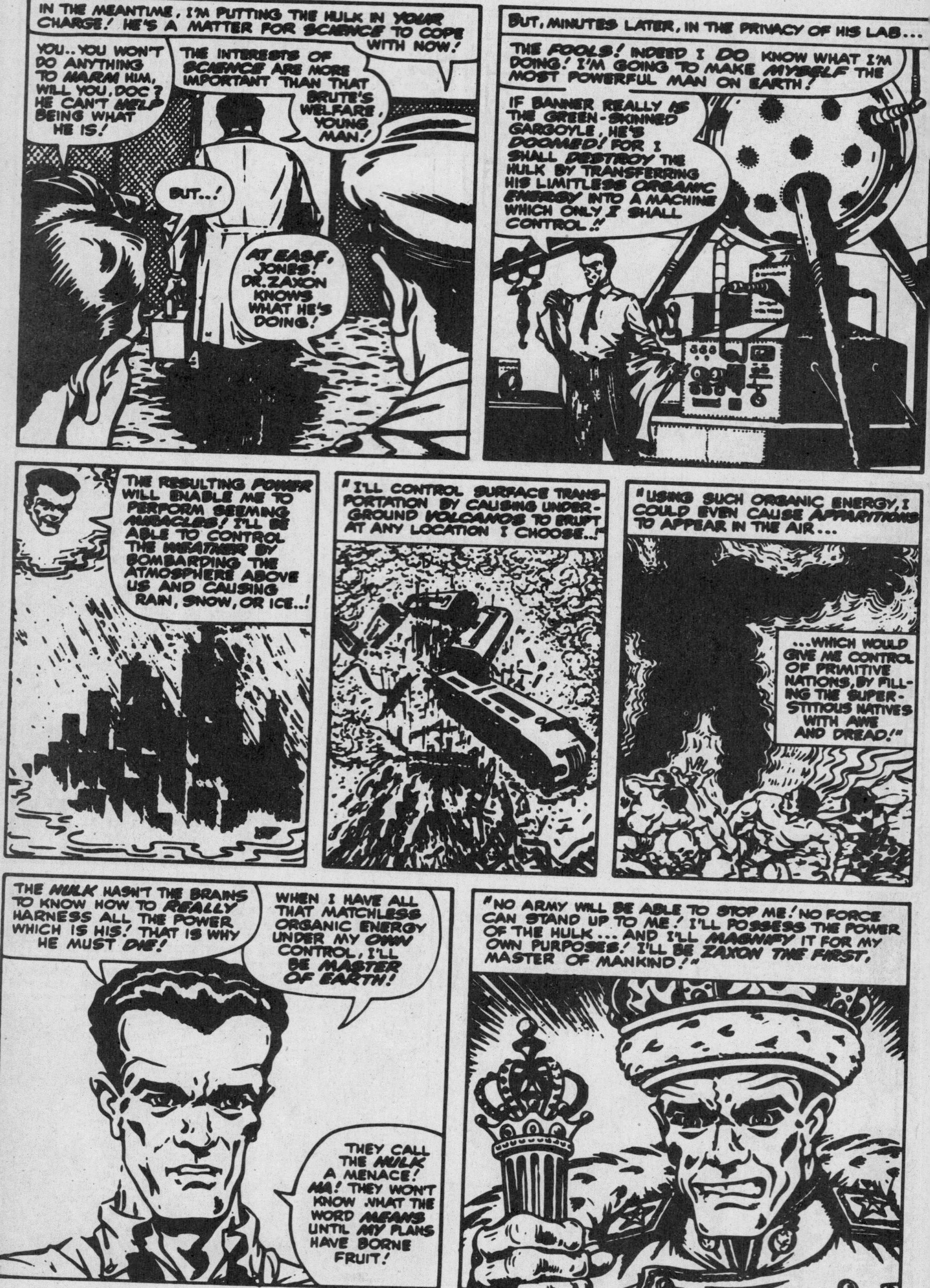

IN THE MEANTIME, I'M PUTTING THE HULK IN YOUR CHARGE! HE'S A MATTER FOR SCIENCE TO COPE WITH NOW!
YOU.. YOU WON'T DO ANYTHING TO HARM HIM, WILL YOU, DOC? HE CAN'T HELP BEING WHAT HE IS!
THE INTERESTS OF SCIENCE ARE MORE IMPORTANT THAN THAT BRUTE'S WELFARE, YOUNG MAN!
BUT...!
AT EASE, JONES! DR. ZAXON KNOWS WHAT HE'S DOING!
BUT, MINUTES LATER, IN THE PRIVACY OF HIS LAB...
THE FOOLS! INDEED I DO KNOW WHAT I'M DOING! I'M GOING TO MAKE MYSELF THE MOST POWERFUL MAN ON EARTH!
IF BANNER REALLY IS THE GREEN-SKINNED GARGOYLE, HE'S DOOMED! FOR I SHALL DESTROY THE HULK BY TRANSFERRING HIS LIMITLESS ORGANIC ENERGY INTO A MACHINE WHICH ONLY I SHALL CONTROL!!
THE RESULTING POWER WILL ENABLE ME TO PERFORM SEEMING MIRACLES! I'LL BE ABLE TO CONTROL THE WEATHER BY BOMBARDING THE ATMOSPHERE ABOVE US AND CAUSING RAIN, SNOW, OR ICE...!
"I'LL CONTROL SURFACE TRANSPORTATION BY CAUSING UNDERGROUND VOLCANOS TO ERUPT AT ANY LOCATION I CHOOSE...!
"USING SUCH ORGANIC ENERGY, I COULD EVEN CAUSE APPARITIONS TO APPEAR IN THE AIR...
...WHICH WOULD GIVE ME CONTROL OF PRIMITIVE NATIONS, BY FILLING THE SUPERSTITIOUS NATIVES WITH AWE AND DREAD!"
THE HULK HASN'T THE BRAINS TO KNOW HOW TO REALLY HARNESS ALL THE POWER WHICH IS HIS! THAT IS WHY HE MUST DIE!
WHEN I HAVE ALL THAT MATCHLESS ORGANIC ENERGY UNDER MY OWN CONTROL, I'LL BE MASTER OF EARTH!
THEY CALL THE HULK A MENACE! HA! THEY WON'T KNOW WHAT THE WORD MEANS UNTIL MY PLANS HAVE BORNE FRUIT!
"NO ARMY WILL BE ABLE TO STOP ME! NO FORCE CAN STAND UP TO ME! I'LL POSSESS THE POWER OF THE HULK... AND I'LL MAGNIFY IT FOR MY OWN PURPOSES! I'LL BE ZAXON THE FIRST, MASTER OF MANKIND!"
5.

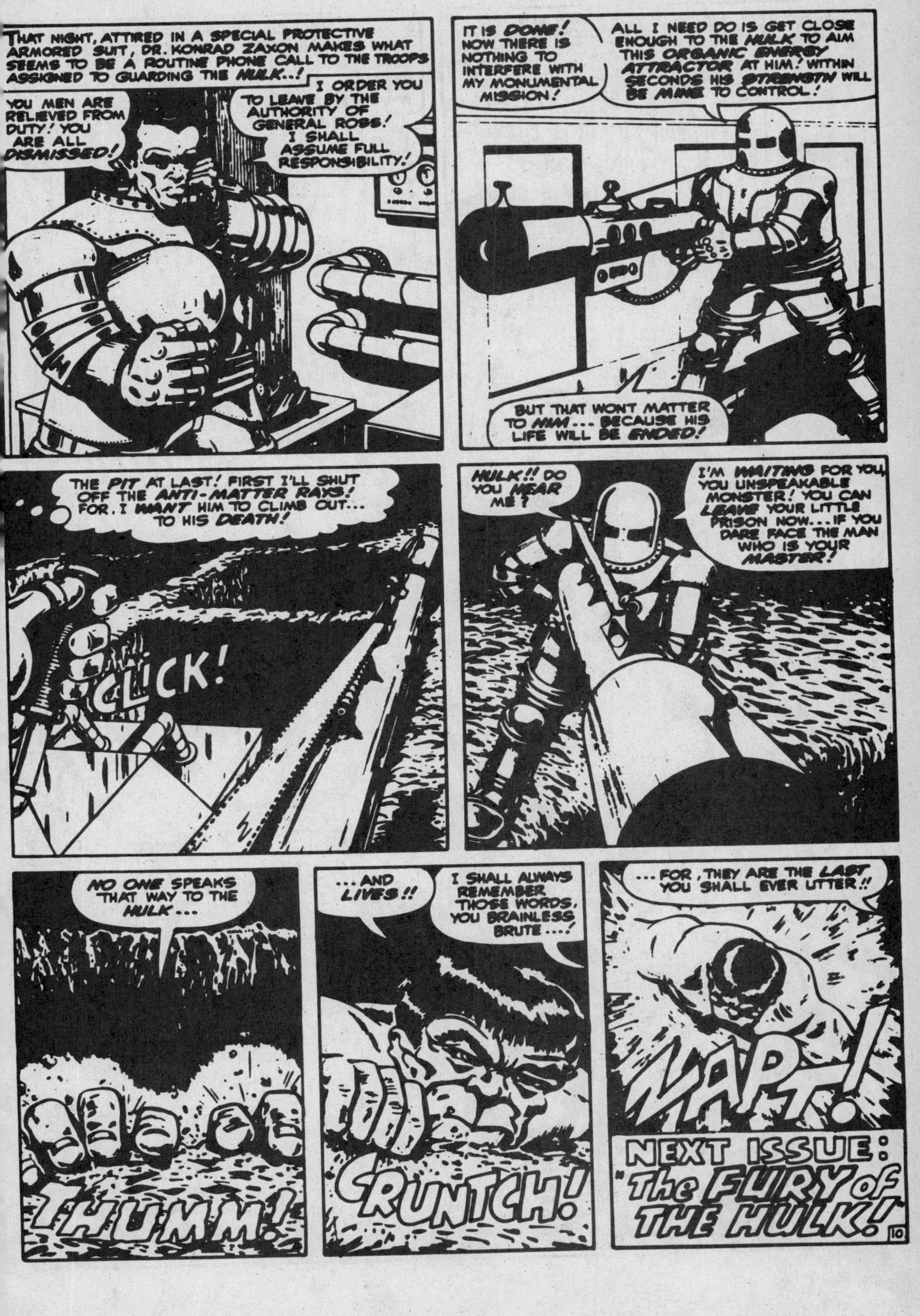
THAT NIGHT, ATTIRED IN A SPECIAL PROTECTIVE ARMORED SUIT, DR. KONRAD ZAXON MAKES WHAT SEEMS TO BE A ROUTINE PHONE CALL TO THE TROOPS ASSIGNED TO GUARDING THE HULK..!
YOU MEN ARE RELIEVED FROM DUTY! YOU ARE ALL DISMISSED!
I ORDER YOU TO LEAVE BY THE AUTHORITY OF GENERAL ROSS! I SHALL ASSUME FULL RESPONSIBILITY!
IT IS DONE! NOW THERE IS NOTHING TO INTERFERE WITH MY MONUMENTAL MISSION!
ALL I NEED DO IS GET CLOSE ENOUGH TO THE HULK TO AIM THIS ORGANIC ENERGY ATTRACTOR AT HIM! WITHIN SECONDS HIS STRENGTH WILL BE MINE TO CONTROL!
BUT THAT WONT MATTER TO HIM... BECAUSE HIS LIFE WILL BE ENDED!
THE PIT AT LAST! FIRST I'LL SHUT OFF THE ANTI-MATTER RAYS! FOR, I WANT HIM TO CLIMB OUT... TO HIS DEATH!
CLICK!
HULK!! DO YOU HEAR ME?
I'M WAITING FOR YOU, YOU UNSPEAKABLE MONSTER! YOU CAN LEAVE YOUR LITTLE PRISON NOW... IF YOU DARE FACE THE MAN WHO IS YOUR MASTER!
NO ONE SPEAKS THAT WAY TO THE HULK...
THUMM!
...AND LIVES!!
I SHALL ALWAYS REMEMBER THOSE WORDS, YOU BRAINLESS BRUTE...!
CRUNTCH!
...FOR, THEY ARE THE LAST YOU SHALL EVER UTTER!!
WAPT!
NEXT ISSUE: "The FURY of THE HULK!"
10

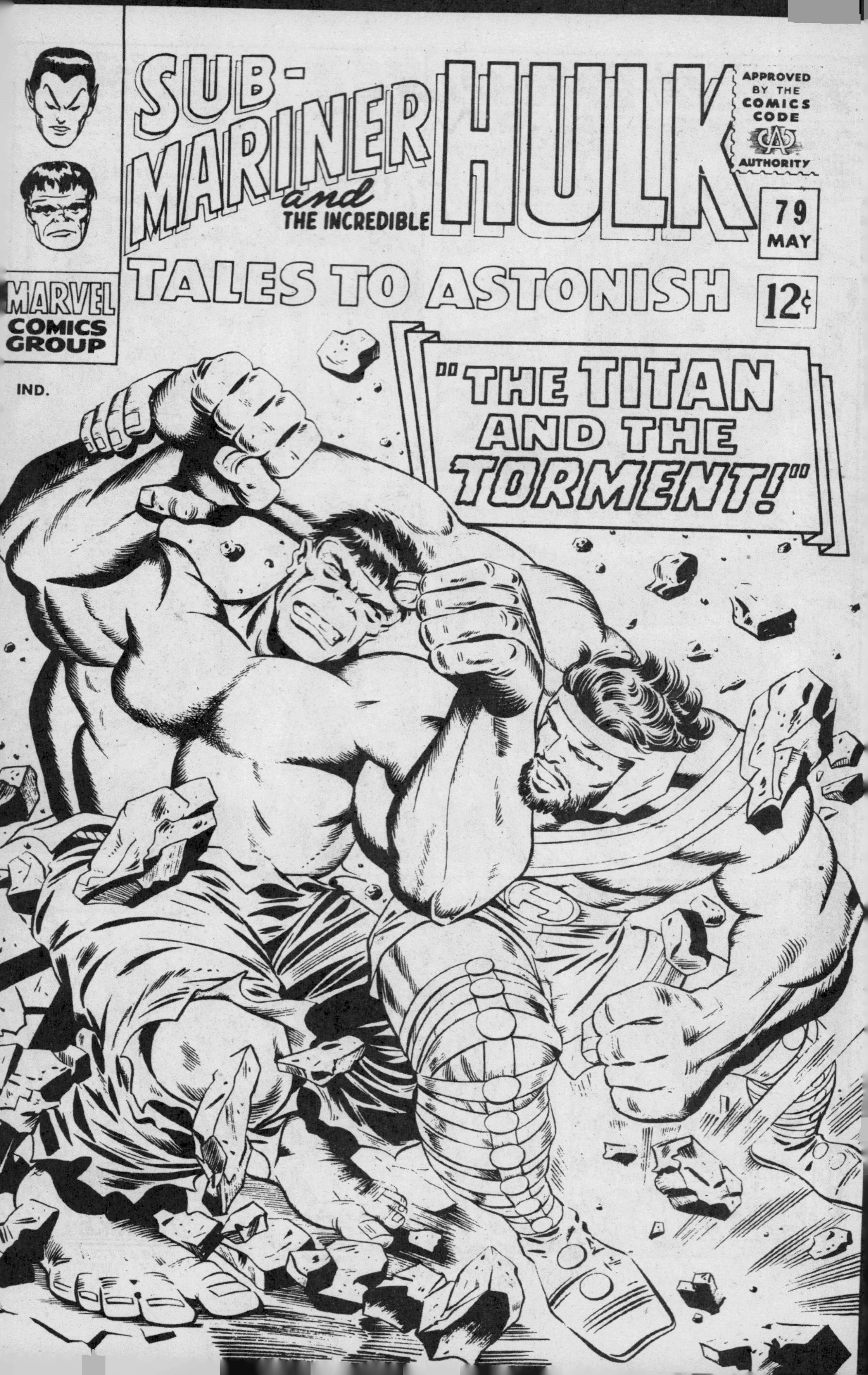

SUB-MARINER and THE INCREDIBLE HULK
TALES TO ASTONISH
APPROVED BY THE COMICS CODE AUTHORITY
79 MAY
12¢
MARVEL COMICS GROUP
IND.
"THE TITAN AND THE TORMENT!"

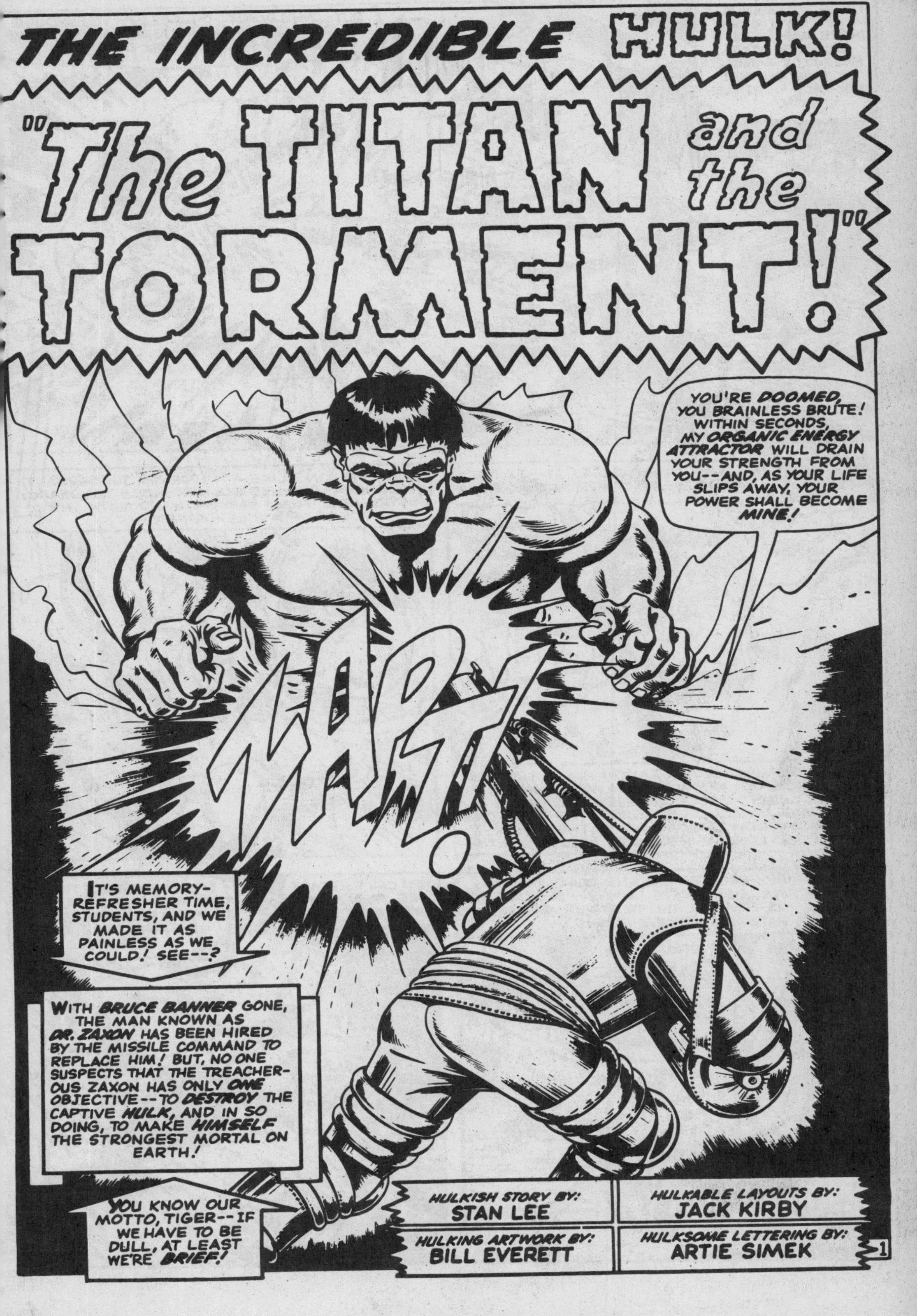
THE INCREDIBLE HULK!
"The TITAN and the TORMENT!"
YOU'RE DOOMED, YOU BRAINLESS BRUTE! WITHIN SECONDS, MY ORGANIC ENERGY ATTRACTOR WILL DRAIN YOUR STRENGTH FROM YOU--AND, AS YOUR LIFE SLIPS AWAY, YOUR POWER SHALL BECOME MINE!
ZAP!
IT'S MEMORY-REFRESHER TIME, STUDENTS, AND WE MADE IT AS PAINLESS AS WE COULD! SEE--?
WITH BRUCE BANNER GONE, THE MAN KNOWN AS DR. ZAXON HAS BEEN HIRED BY THE MISSILE COMMAND TO REPLACE HIM! BUT, NO ONE SUSPECTS THAT THE TREACHEROUS ZAXON HAS ONLY ONE OBJECTIVE--TO DESTROY THE CAPTIVE HULK, AND IN SO DOING, TO MAKE HIMSELF THE STRONGEST MORTAL ON EARTH!
YOU KNOW OUR MOTTO, TIGER--IF WE HAVE TO BE DULL, AT LEAST WE'RE BRIEF!
HULKISH STORY BY: STAN LEE
HULKABLE LAYOUTS BY: JACK KIRBY
HULKING ARTWORK BY: BILL EVERETT
HULKSOME LETTERING BY: ARTIE SIMEK
1

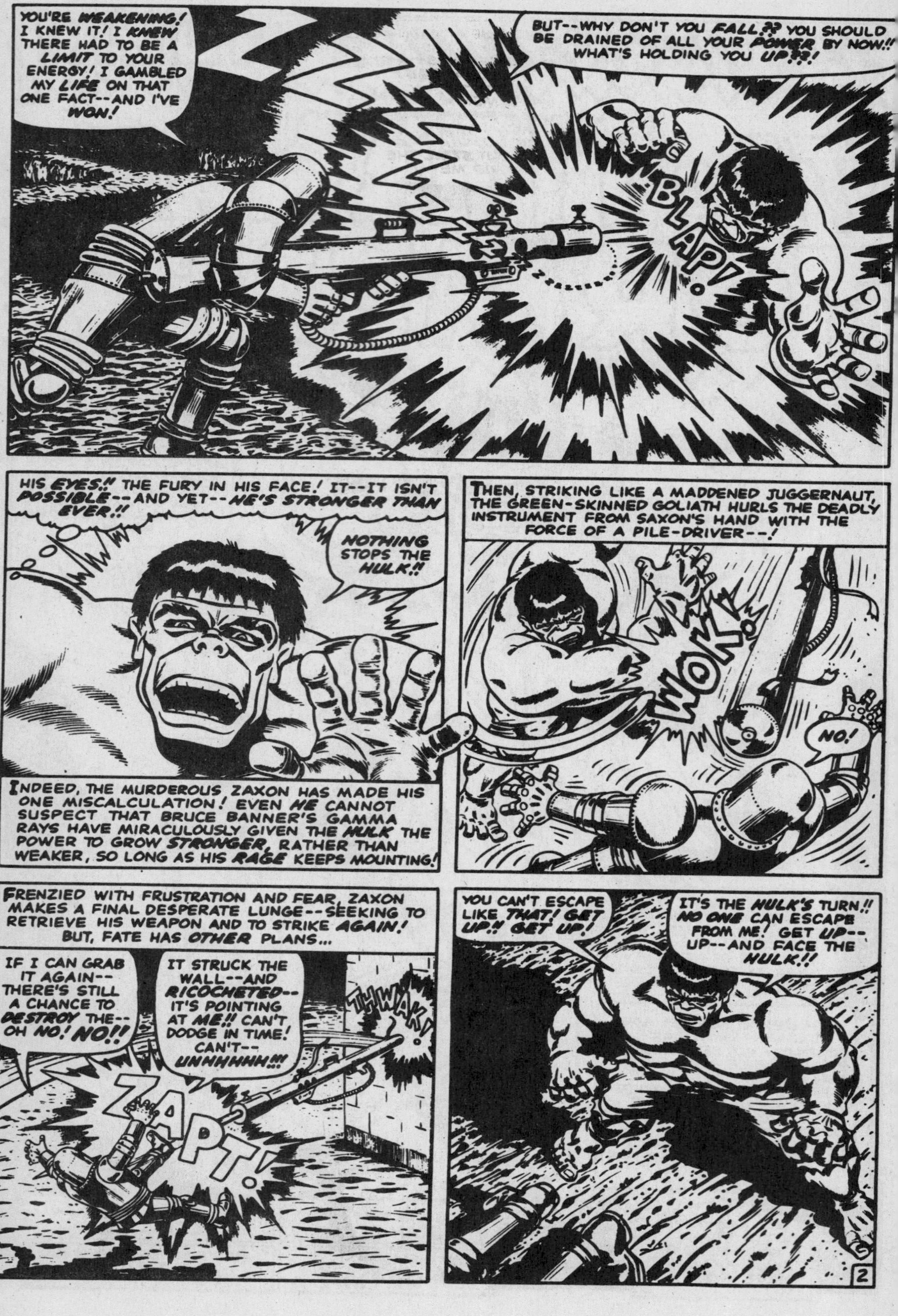
YOU'RE WEAKENING! I KNEW IT! I KNEW THERE HAD TO BE A LIMIT TO YOUR ENERGY! I GAMBLED MY LIFE ON THAT ONE FACT--AND I'VE WON!
BUT--WHY DON'T YOU FALL?? YOU SHOULD BE DRAINED OF ALL YOUR POWER BY NOW!! WHAT'S HOLDING YOU UP??!
BLAP!
HIS EYES!! THE FURY IN HIS FACE! IT--IT ISN'T POSSIBLE--AND YET--HE'S STRONGER THAN EVER!!
NOTHING STOPS THE HULK!!
INDEED, THE MURDEROUS ZAXON HAS MADE HIS ONE MISCALCULATION! EVEN HE CANNOT SUSPECT THAT BRUCE BANNER'S GAMMA RAYS HAVE MIRACULOUSLY GIVEN THE HULK THE POWER TO GROW STRONGER, RATHER THAN WEAKER, SO LONG AS HIS RAGE KEEPS MOUNTING!
THEN, STRIKING LIKE A MADDENED JUGGERNAUT, THE GREEN-SKINNED GOLIATH HURLS THE DEADLY INSTRUMENT FROM SAXON'S HAND WITH THE FORCE OF A PILE-DRIVER--!
WOK!
NO!
FRENZIED WITH FRUSTRATION AND FEAR, ZAXON MAKES A FINAL DESPERATE LUNGE--SEEKING TO RETRIEVE HIS WEAPON AND TO STRIKE AGAIN! BUT, FATE HAS OTHER PLANS...
IF I CAN GRAB IT AGAIN--THERE'S STILL A CHANCE TO DESTROY THE--OH NO! NO!!
IT STRUCK THE WALL--AND RICOCHETED--IT'S POINTING AT ME!! CAN'T DODGE IN TIME! CAN'T--UNHHHHH!!!
THWAK!
ZAPT!
YOU CAN'T ESCAPE LIKE THAT! GET UP!! GET UP!
IT'S THE HULK'S TURN!! NO ONE CAN ESCAPE FROM ME! GET UP--UP--AND FACE THE HULK!!
2

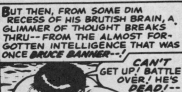

BUT THEN, FROM SOME DIM RECESS OF HIS BRUTISH BRAIN, A GLIMMER OF THOUGHT BREAKS THRU-- FROM THE ALMOST FORGOTTEN INTELLIGENCE THAT WAS ONCE *BRUCE BANNER*--!

CAN'T GET UP! BATTLE OVER! HE'S DEAD! -- NO ONE TO FIGHT NOW!

THEN, THE BESTIAL BRAIN CLOUDS OVER AGAIN-- AND ONLY ONE EMOTION REMAINS-- A SENSE OF TOWERING *RAGE*--!

ALWAYS MEN HUNT ME!! ALWAYS THEY TRY TO KILL ME!! WHY? WHY?? THEY'RE SO PUNY-- SO WEAK-- BUT STILL THEY HOUND ME--!

WHY? WHY MUST--?? UHH!! VOICES!

WHAT WAS GOIN' ON IN THERE?

IT MUST BE THE HULK!! HE MUSTA BROKEN FREE!

DON'T JUST STAND THERE! SOUND THE ALARM!!

BUT-- *DR. ZAXON* WAS IN THERE!! IF THE HULK BROKE LOOSE-- THEN--

A CHANCE!! WE'VE GOTTA DO SOMETHIN'!!

MEN COME!! BUT-- THEY WON'T FIND THE HULK!

THOOM!
THOOM!

HE'S LEAPING AWAY!

THOOM!

SECONDS LATER, AFTER THE STARTLED TROOPS HAVE PEERED OVER THE STEEL FENCE...

ZAXON'S DEAD!! THE HULK MUSTA KILLED 'IM! I'VE GOTTA NOTIFY MAJOR TALBOT!!

NOW WE KNOW FOR SURE THAT HE'S A KILLER!

WHAT IN BLAZES IS HE MADE OF?? BULLETS JUST BOUNCE OFF 'IM!!

CRACK

MEANWHILE, A SCENE TAKES PLACE SOME MILES AWAY WHICH IS DESTINED TO HAVE AN IMPORTANT EFFECT UPON THE STRANGE SAGA OF THE INCREDIBLE HULK--!

THAT'S IT, HERCULES! EAT ALL YOU WANT TO! YOU'VE GOT TO BE AT YOUR FIGHTING PEAK WHEN YOU MEET THE HEAD OF THE STUDIO, IN HOLLYWOOD!

HERCULES IS ALWAYS AT HIS FIGHTING PEAK! I EAT BECAUSE IT DOTH GIVE ME PLEASURE!

3

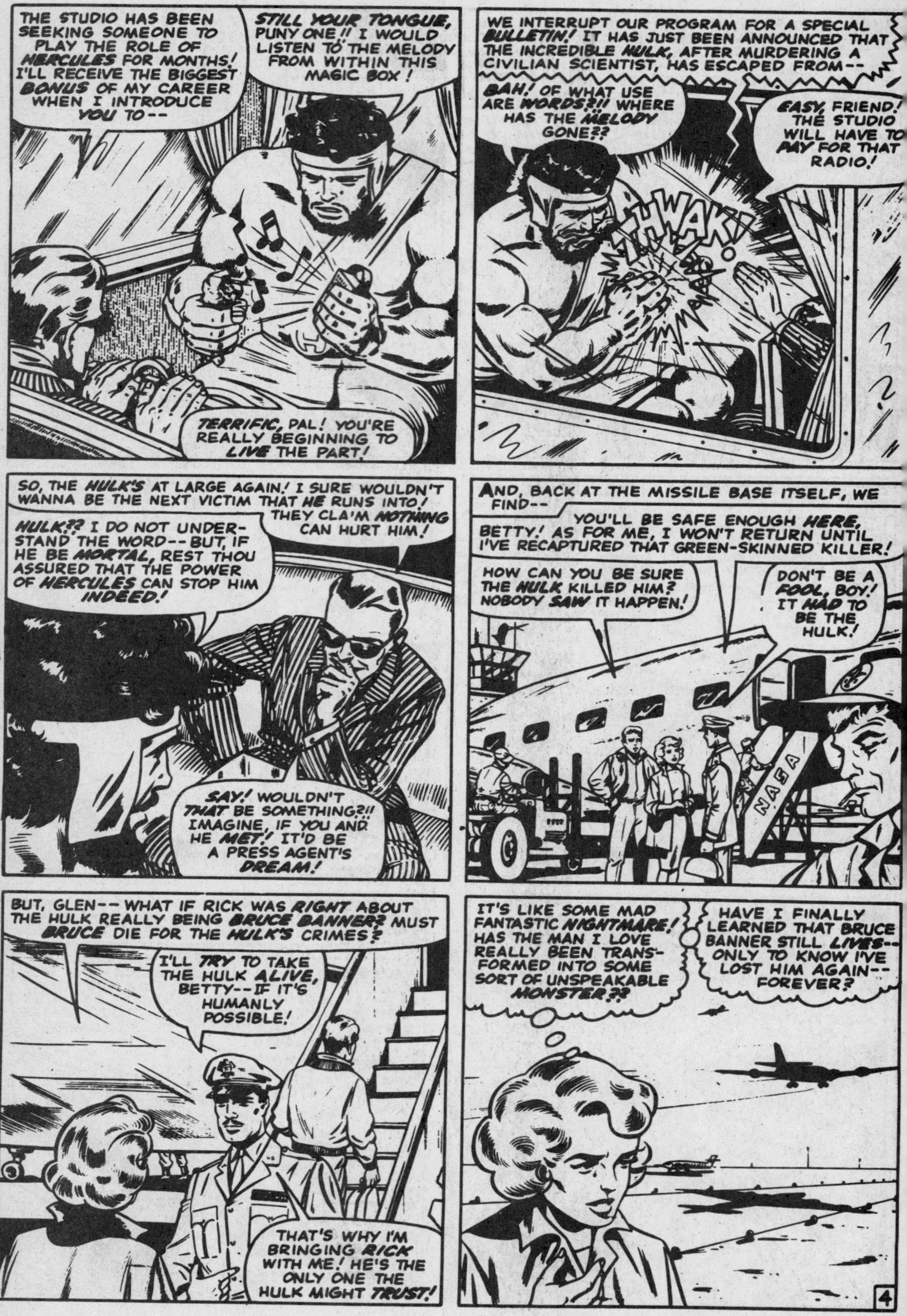
THE STUDIO HAS BEEN SEEKING SOMEONE TO PLAY THE ROLE OF HERCULES FOR MONTHS! I'LL RECEIVE THE BIGGEST BONUS OF MY CAREER WHEN I INTRODUCE YOU TO--
STILL YOUR TONGUE, PUNY ONE!! I WOULD LISTEN TO THE MELODY FROM WITHIN THIS MAGIC BOX!
TERRIFIC, PAL! YOU'RE REALLY BEGINNING TO LIVE THE PART!
WE INTERRUPT OUR PROGRAM FOR A SPECIAL BULLETIN! IT HAS JUST BEEN ANNOUNCED THAT THE INCREDIBLE HULK, AFTER MURDERING A CIVILIAN SCIENTIST, HAS ESCAPED FROM--
BAH! OF WHAT USE ARE WORDS?!! WHERE HAS THE MELODY GONE??
EASY, FRIEND! THE STUDIO WILL HAVE TO PAY FOR THAT RADIO!
THWAK!
SO, THE HULK'S AT LARGE AGAIN! I SURE WOULDN'T WANNA BE THE NEXT VICTIM THAT HE RUNS INTO! THEY CLA'M NOTHING CAN HURT HIM!
HULK?? I DO NOT UNDERSTAND THE WORD--BUT, IF HE BE MORTAL, REST THOU ASSURED THAT THE POWER OF HERCULES CAN STOP HIM INDEED!
SAY! WOULDN'T THAT BE SOMETHING?!! IMAGINE, IF YOU AND HE MET! IT'D BE A PRESS AGENT'S DREAM!
AND, BACK AT THE MISSILE BASE ITSELF, WE FIND--
YOU'LL BE SAFE ENOUGH HERE, BETTY! AS FOR ME, I WON'T RETURN UNTIL I'VE RECAPTURED THAT GREEN-SKINNED KILLER!
HOW CAN YOU BE SURE THE HULK KILLED HIM? NOBODY SAW IT HAPPEN!
DON'T BE A FOOL, BOY! IT HAD TO BE THE HULK!
NASA
BUT, GLEN--WHAT IF RICK WAS RIGHT ABOUT THE HULK REALLY BEING BRUCE BANNER? MUST BRUCE DIE FOR THE HULK'S CRIMES?
I'LL TRY TO TAKE THE HULK ALIVE, BETTY--IF IT'S HUMANLY POSSIBLE!
THAT'S WHY I'M BRINGING RICK WITH ME! HE'S THE ONLY ONE THE HULK MIGHT TRUST!
IT'S LIKE SOME MAD FANTASTIC NIGHTMARE! HAS THE MAN I LOVE REALLY BEEN TRANSFORMED INTO SOME SORT OF UNSPEAKABLE MONSTER??
HAVE I FINALLY LEARNED THAT BRUCE BANNER STILL LIVES--ONLY TO KNOW I'VE LOST HIM AGAIN--FOREVER?
4

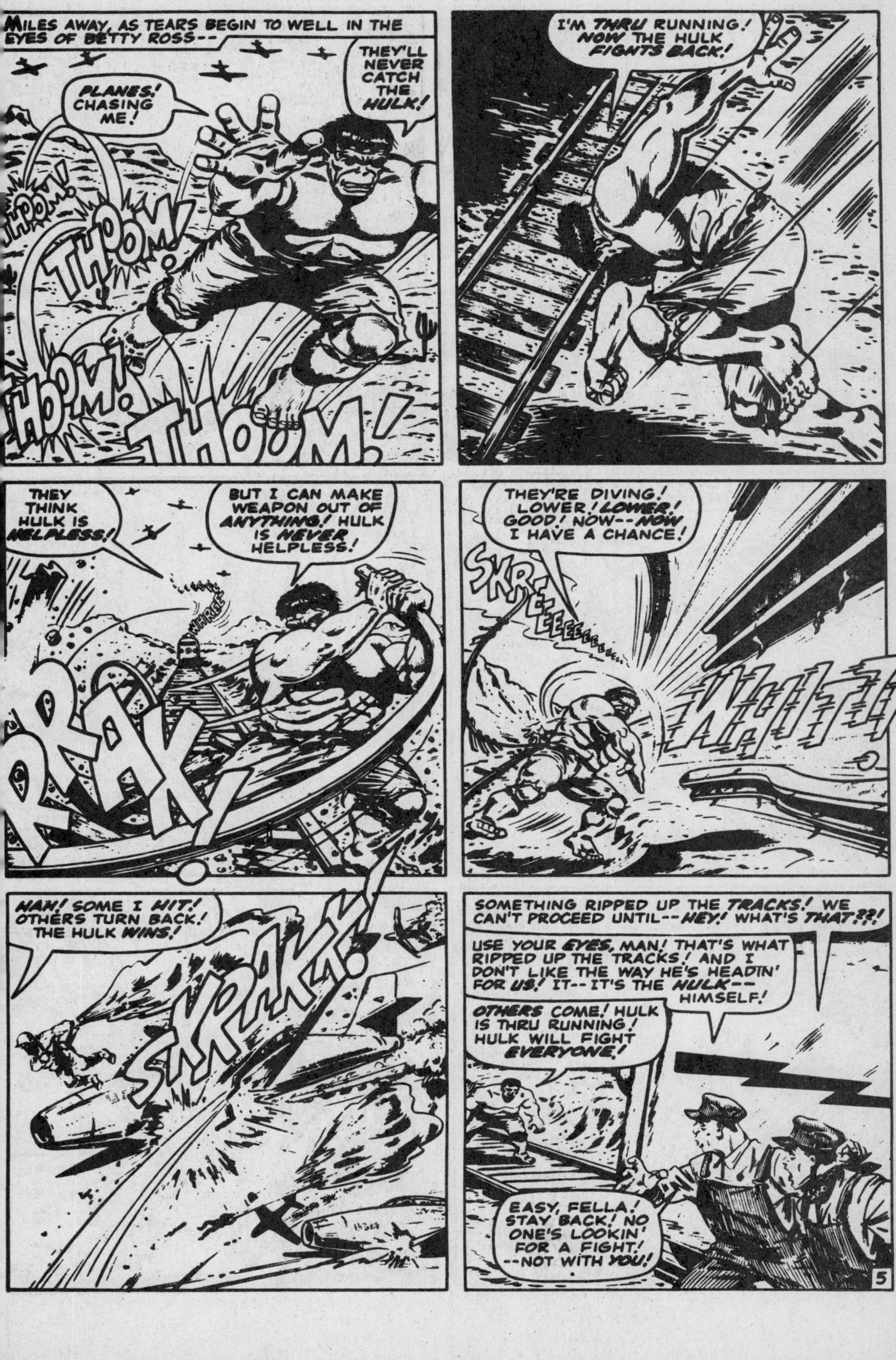
MILES AWAY, AS TEARS BEGIN TO WELL IN THE EYES OF BETTY ROSS--
PLANES! CHASING ME!
THEY'LL NEVER CATCH THE HULK!
THOOM!
THOOM!
THOOM!
I'M THRU RUNNING! NOW THE HULK FIGHTS BACK!
THEY THINK HULK IS HELPLESS!
BUT I CAN MAKE WEAPON OUT OF ANYTHING! HULK IS NEVER HELPLESS!
KRAK!
THEY'RE DIVING! LOWER! LOWER! GOOD! NOW--NOW I HAVE A CHANCE!
SKREEEEEE
MAN! SOME I HIT! OTHERS TURN BACK! THE HULK WINS!
SKRAKK!
SOMETHING RIPPED UP THE TRACKS! WE CAN'T PROCEED UNTIL--HEY! WHAT'S THAT??!
USE YOUR EYES, MAN! THAT'S WHAT RIPPED UP THE TRACKS! AND I DON'T LIKE THE WAY HE'S HEADIN' FOR US! IT-- IT'S THE HULK-- HIMSELF!
OTHERS COME! HULK IS THRU RUNNING! HULK WILL FIGHT EVERYONE!
EASY, FELLA! STAY BACK! NO ONE'S LOOKIN' FOR A FIGHT! --NOT WITH YOU!

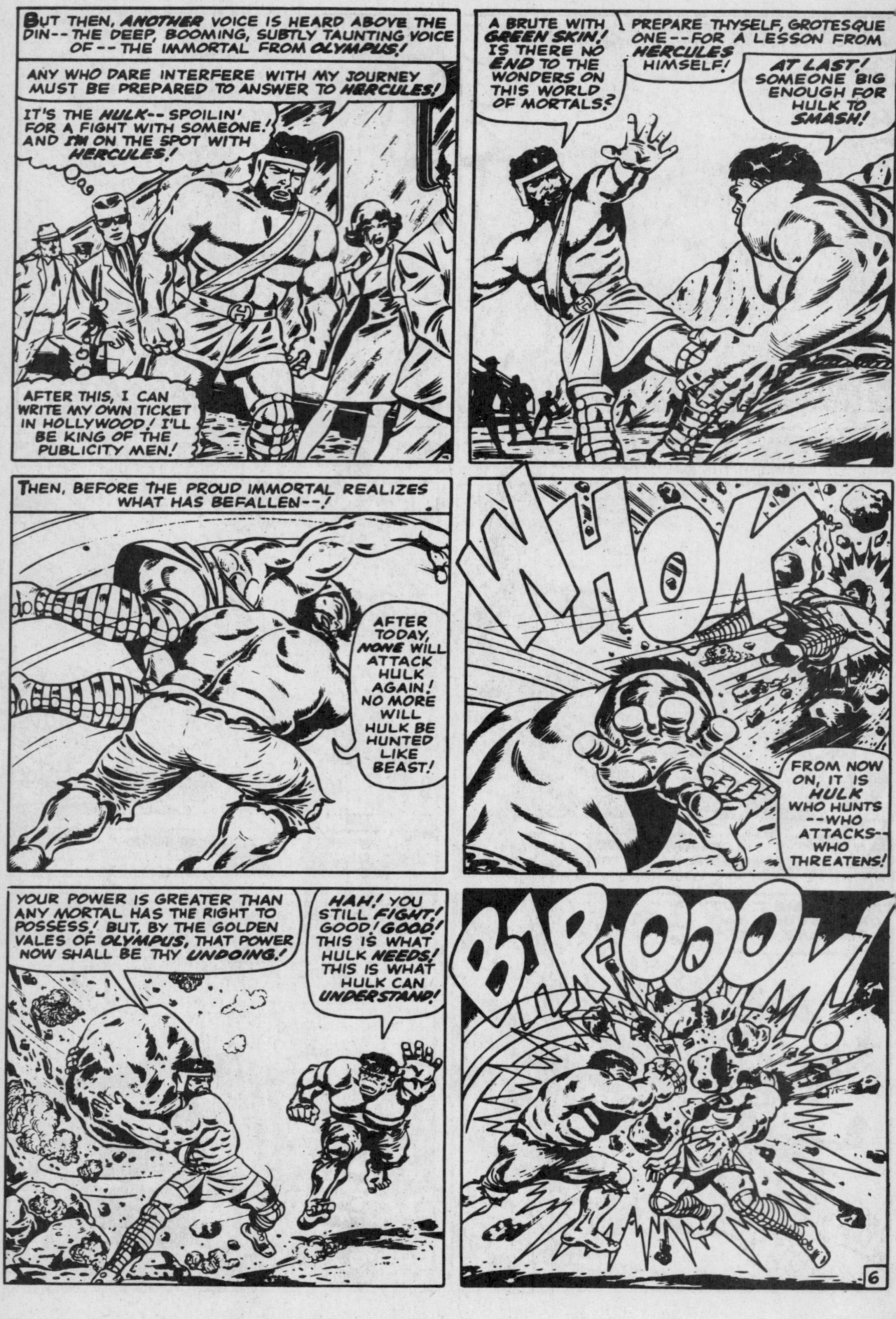

BUT THEN, ANOTHER VOICE IS HEARD ABOVE THE DIN--THE DEEP, BOOMING, SUBTLY TAUNTING VOICE OF--THE IMMORTAL FROM OLYMPUS!
ANY WHO DARE INTERFERE WITH MY JOURNEY MUST BE PREPARED TO ANSWER TO HERCULES!
IT'S THE HULK--SPOILIN' FOR A FIGHT WITH SOMEONE! AND I'M ON THE SPOT WITH HERCULES!
AFTER THIS, I CAN WRITE MY OWN TICKET IN HOLLYWOOD! I'LL BE KING OF THE PUBLICITY MEN!
A BRUTE WITH GREEN SKIN! IS THERE NO END TO THE WONDERS ON THIS WORLD OF MORTALS?
PREPARE THYSELF, GROTESQUE ONE--FOR A LESSON FROM HERCULES HIMSELF!
AT LAST! SOMEONE BIG ENOUGH FOR HULK TO SMASH!
THEN, BEFORE THE PROUD IMMORTAL REALIZES WHAT HAS BEFALLEN--!
AFTER TODAY, NONE WILL ATTACK HULK AGAIN! NO MORE WILL HULK BE HUNTED LIKE BEAST!
WHOOM
FROM NOW ON, IT IS HULK WHO HUNTS--WHO ATTACKS--WHO THREATENS!
YOUR POWER IS GREATER THAN ANY MORTAL HAS THE RIGHT TO POSSESS! BUT, BY THE GOLDEN VALES OF OLYMPUS, THAT POWER NOW SHALL BE THY UNDOING!
HAH! YOU STILL FIGHT! GOOD! GOOD! THIS IS WHAT HULK NEEDS! THIS IS WHAT HULK CAN UNDERSTAND!
B-R-OOOOM!
6

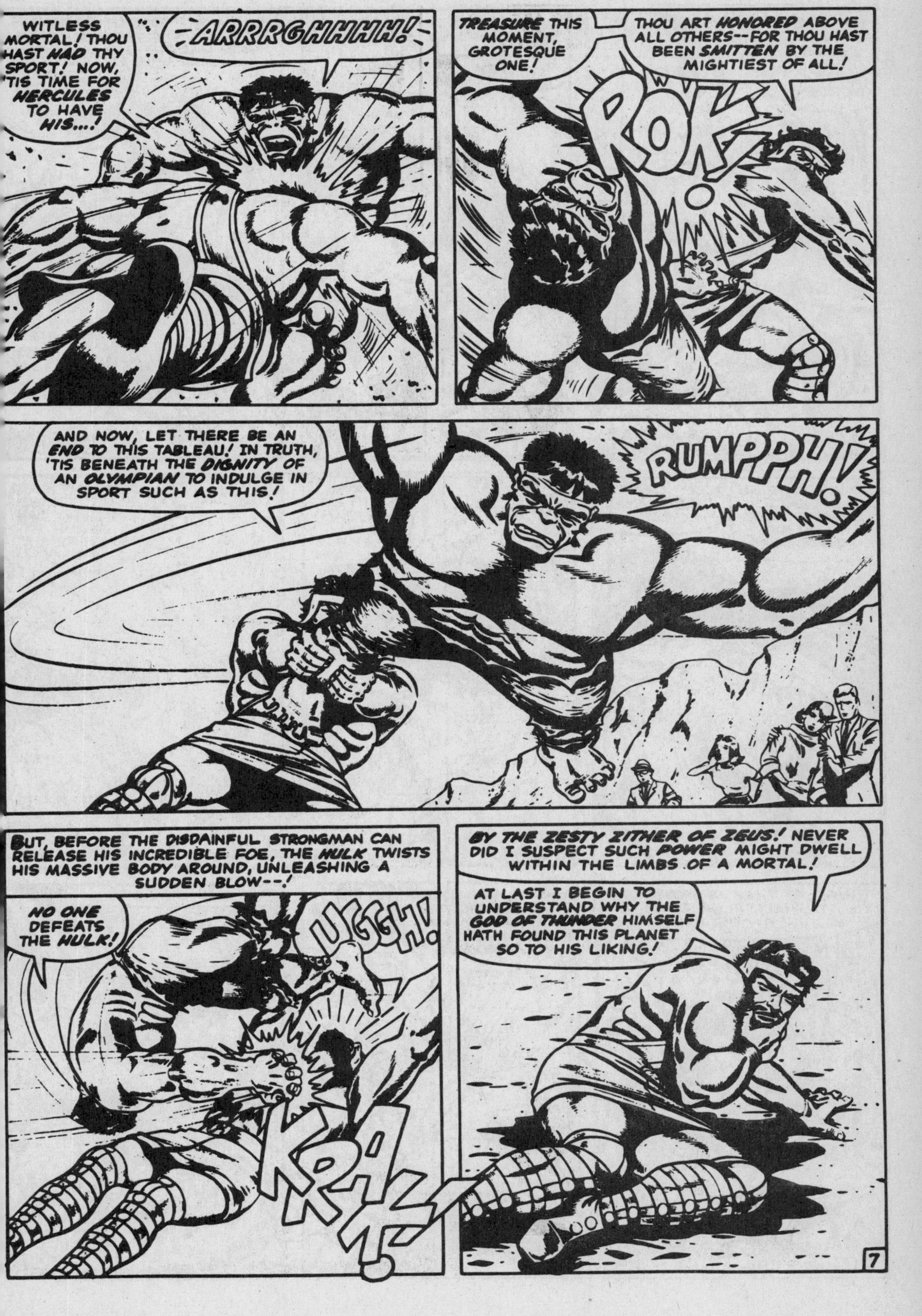
WITLESS MORTAL! THOU HAST HAD THY SPORT! NOW, 'TIS TIME FOR HERCULES TO HAVE HIS....!
ARRRGHHHHH!
TREASURE THIS MOMENT, GROTESQUE ONE!
THOU ART HONORED ABOVE ALL OTHERS--FOR THOU HAST BEEN SMITTEN BY THE MIGHTIEST OF ALL!
ROK
AND NOW, LET THERE BE AN END TO THIS TABLEAU! IN TRUTH, 'TIS BENEATH THE DIGNITY OF AN OLYMPIAN TO INDULGE IN SPORT SUCH AS THIS!
RUMPPH!
BUT, BEFORE THE DISDAINFUL STRONGMAN CAN RELEASE HIS INCREDIBLE FOE, THE HULK TWISTS HIS MASSIVE BODY AROUND, UNLEASHING A SUDDEN BLOW--!
NO ONE DEFEATS THE HULK!
UGGH!
KRAK!
BY THE ZESTY ZITHER OF ZEUS! NEVER DID I SUSPECT SUCH POWER MIGHT DWELL WITHIN THE LIMBS OF A MORTAL!
AT LAST I BEGIN TO UNDERSTAND WHY THE GOD OF THUNDER HIMSELF HATH FOUND THIS PLANET SO TO HIS LIKING!

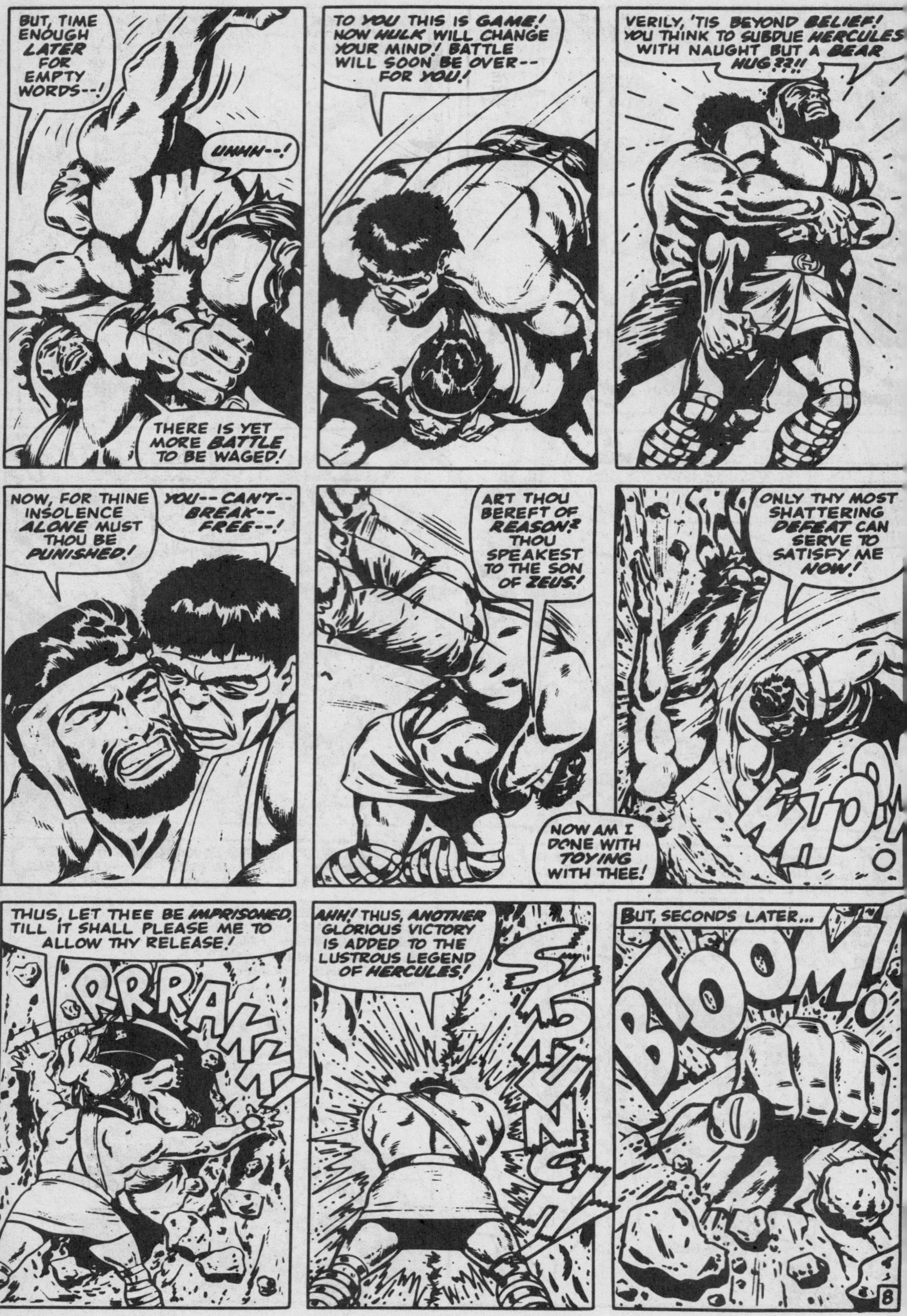
BUT, TIME ENOUGH LATER FOR EMPTY WORDS--!
UNHH--!
THERE IS YET MORE BATTLE TO BE WAGED!
TO YOU THIS IS GAME! NOW HULK WILL CHANGE YOUR MIND! BATTLE WILL SOON BE OVER-- FOR YOU!
VERILY, 'TIS BEYOND BELIEF! YOU THINK TO SUBDUE HERCULES WITH NAUGHT BUT A BEAR HUG??!!
NOW, FOR THINE INSOLENCE ALONE MUST THOU BE PUNISHED!
YOU-- CAN'T-- BREAK-- FREE--!
ART THOU BEREFT OF REASON? THOU SPEAKEST TO THE SON OF ZEUS!
ONLY THY MOST SHATTERING DEFEAT CAN SERVE TO SATISFY ME NOW!
NOW AM I DONE WITH TOYING WITH THEE!
WHOO
THUS, LET THEE BE IMPRISONED, TILL IT SHALL PLEASE ME TO ALLOW THY RELEASE!
RRRAKK!
AHH! THUS, ANOTHER GLORIOUS VICTORY IS ADDED TO THE LUSTROUS LEGEND OF HERCULES!
SHUNCH
BUT, SECONDS LATER...
BLOOM!
8

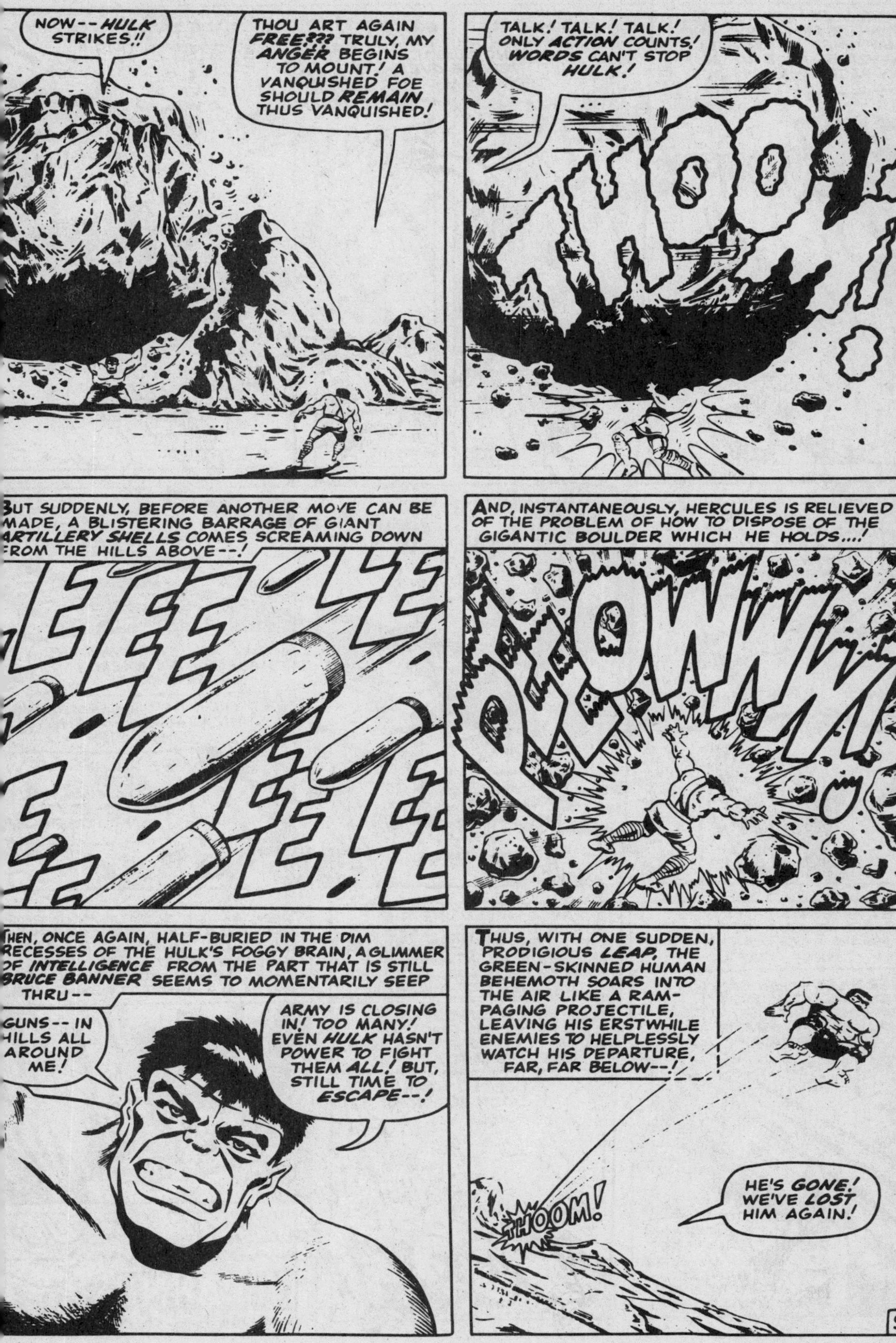

NOW--HULK STRIKES!!
THOU ART AGAIN FREE??? TRULY, MY ANGER BEGINS TO MOUNT! A VANQUISHED FOE SHOULD REMAIN THUS VANQUISHED!
TALK! TALK! TALK! ONLY ACTION COUNTS! WORDS CAN'T STOP HULK!
WHOOO!
BUT SUDDENLY, BEFORE ANOTHER MOVE CAN BE MADE, A BLISTERING BARRAGE OF GIANT ARTILLERY SHELLS COMES SCREAMING DOWN FROM THE HILLS ABOVE--!
AND, INSTANTANEOUSLY, HERCULES IS RELIEVED OF THE PROBLEM OF HOW TO DISPOSE OF THE GIGANTIC BOULDER WHICH HE HOLDS....!
THEN, ONCE AGAIN, HALF-BURIED IN THE DIM RECESSES OF THE HULK'S FOGGY BRAIN, A GLIMMER OF INTELLIGENCE FROM THE PART THAT IS STILL BRUCE BANNER SEEMS TO MOMENTARILY SEEP THRU--
GUNS-- IN HILLS ALL AROUND ME!
ARMY IS CLOSING IN! TOO MANY! EVEN HULK HASN'T POWER TO FIGHT THEM ALL! BUT, STILL TIME TO ESCAPE--!
THUS, WITH ONE SUDDEN, PRODIGIOUS LEAP, THE GREEN-SKINNED HUMAN BEHEMOTH SOARS INTO THE AIR LIKE A RAMPAGING PROJECTILE, LEAVING HIS ERSTWHILE ENEMIES TO HELPLESSLY WATCH HIS DEPARTURE, FAR, FAR BELOW--!
THOOM!
HE'S GONE! WE'VE LOST HIM AGAIN!

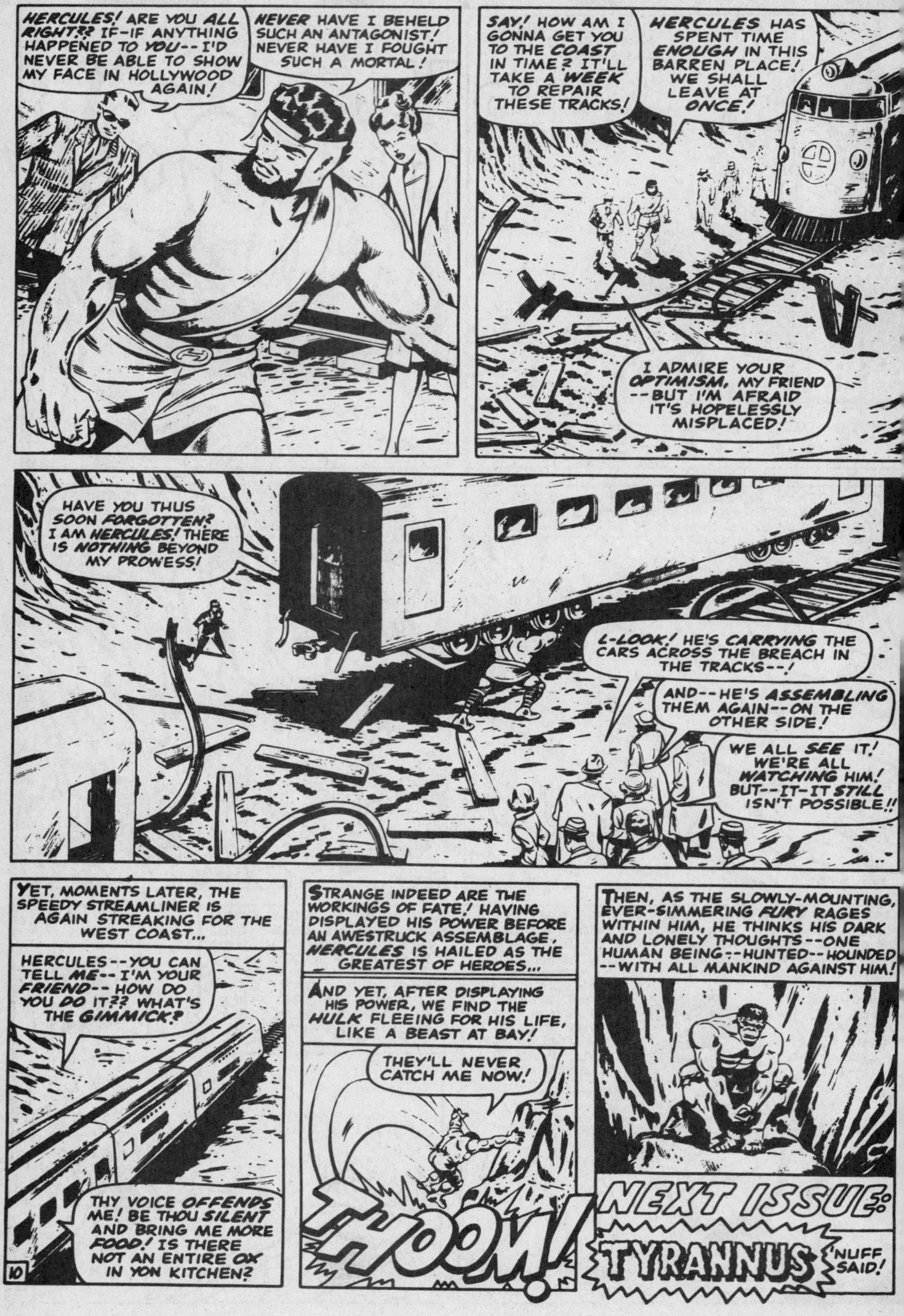
HERCULES! ARE YOU ALL RIGHT?? IF--IF ANYTHING HAPPENED TO YOU--I'D NEVER BE ABLE TO SHOW MY FACE IN HOLLYWOOD AGAIN!
NEVER HAVE I BEHELD SUCH AN ANTAGONIST! NEVER HAVE I FOUGHT SUCH A MORTAL!
SAY! HOW AM I GONNA GET YOU TO THE COAST IN TIME? IT'LL TAKE A WEEK TO REPAIR THESE TRACKS!
HERCULES HAS SPENT TIME ENOUGH IN THIS BARREN PLACE! WE SHALL LEAVE AT ONCE!
I ADMIRE YOUR OPTIMISM, MY FRIEND --BUT I'M AFRAID IT'S HOPELESSLY MISPLACED!
HAVE YOU THUS SOON FORGOTTEN? I AM HERCULES! THERE IS NOTHING BEYOND MY PROWESS!
L-LOOK! HE'S CARRYING THE CARS ACROSS THE BREACH IN THE TRACKS--!
AND--HE'S ASSEMBLING THEM AGAIN--ON THE OTHER SIDE!
WE ALL SEE IT! WE'RE ALL WATCHING HIM! BUT--IT-IT STILL ISN'T POSSIBLE!!
YET, MOMENTS LATER, THE SPEEDY STREAMLINER IS AGAIN STREAKING FOR THE WEST COAST...
HERCULES--YOU CAN TELL ME--I'M YOUR FRIEND--HOW DO YOU DO IT?? WHAT'S THE GIMMICK?
THY VOICE OFFENDS ME! BE THOU SILENT AND BRING ME MORE FOOD! IS THERE NOT AN ENTIRE OX IN YON KITCHEN?
10
STRANGE INDEED ARE THE WORKINGS OF FATE! HAVING DISPLAYED HIS POWER BEFORE AN AWESTRUCK ASSEMBLAGE, HERCULES IS HAILED AS THE GREATEST OF HEROES...
AND YET, AFTER DISPLAYING HIS POWER, WE FIND THE HULK FLEEING FOR HIS LIFE, LIKE A BEAST AT BAY!
THEY'LL NEVER CATCH ME NOW!
THOOM!
THEN, AS THE SLOWLY-MOUNTING, EVER-SIMMERING FURY RAGES WITHIN HIM, HE THINKS HIS DARK AND LONELY THOUGHTS--ONE HUMAN BEING--HUNTED--HOUNDED--WITH ALL MANKIND AGAINST HIM!
NEXT ISSUE...
TYRANNUS
'NUFF SAID!

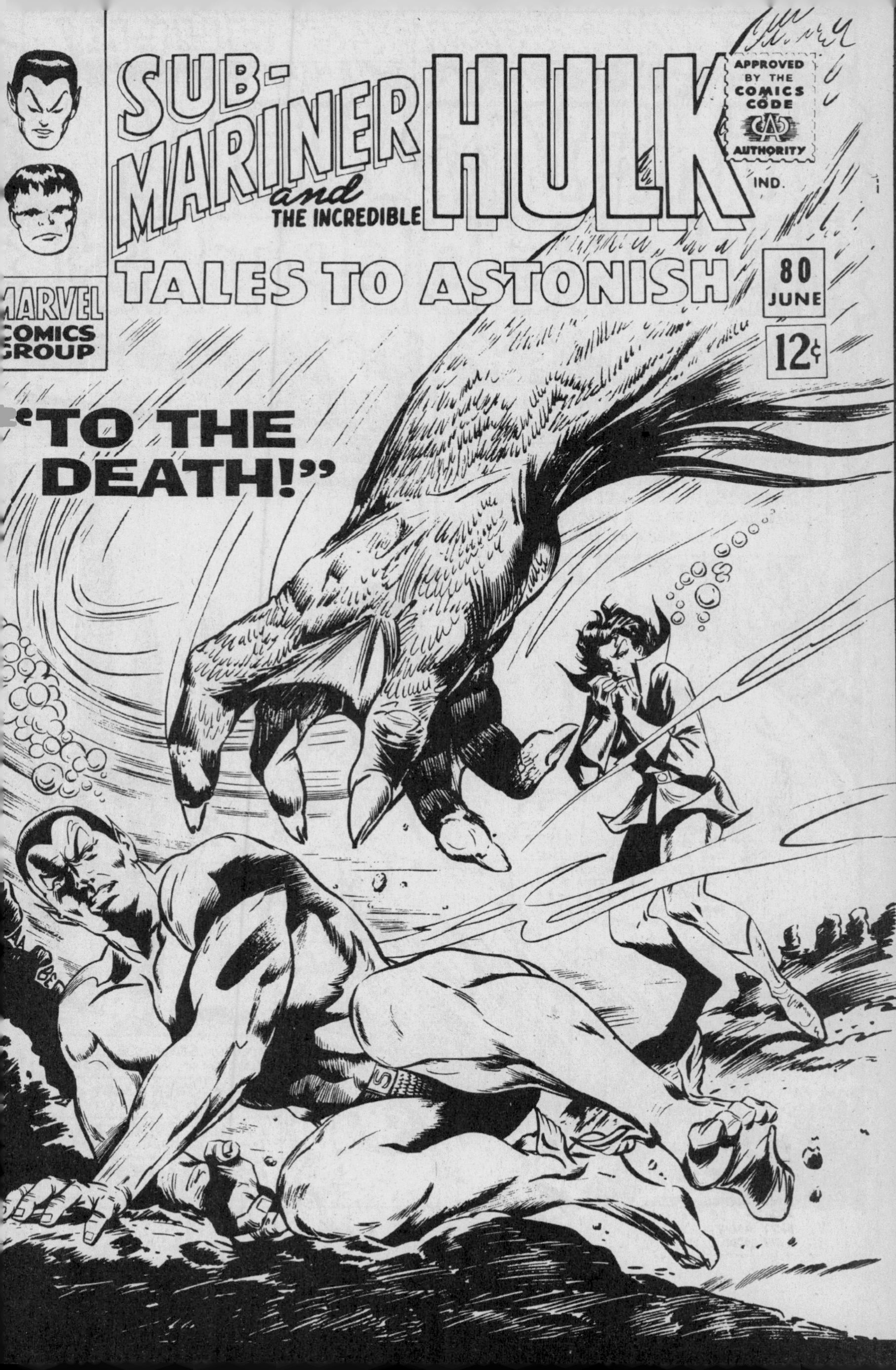
SUB-MARINER
and THE INCREDIBLE
HULK
APPROVED BY THE COMICS CODE AUTHORITY
IND.
TALES TO ASTONISH
80
JUNE
12¢
MARVEL COMICS GROUP
"TO THE DEATH!"

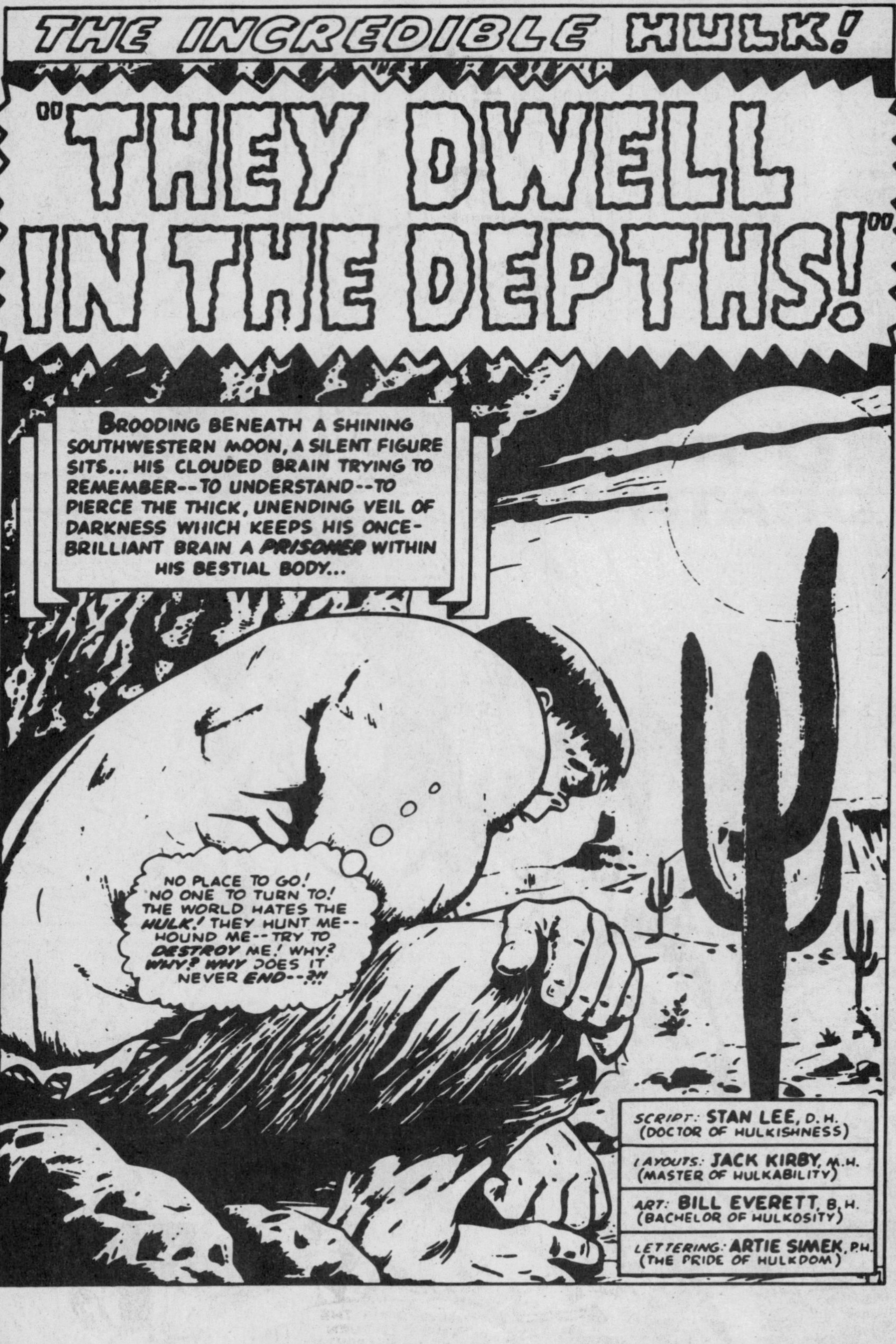
THE INCREDIBLE HULK!
"THEY DWELL IN THE DEPTHS!"
BROODING BENEATH A SHINING SOUTHWESTERN MOON, A SILENT FIGURE SITS... HIS CLOUDED BRAIN TRYING TO REMEMBER--TO UNDERSTAND--TO PIERCE THE THICK, UNENDING VEIL OF DARKNESS WHICH KEEPS HIS ONCE-BRILLIANT BRAIN A PRISONER WITHIN HIS BESTIAL BODY...
NO PLACE TO GO! NO ONE TO TURN TO! THE WORLD HATES THE HULK! THEY HUNT ME--HOUND ME--TRY TO DESTROY ME! WHY? WHY? WHY DOES IT NEVER END--?!!
SCRIPT: STAN LEE, D.H. (DOCTOR OF HULKISHNESS)
LAYOUTS: JACK KIRBY, M.H. (MASTER OF HULKABILITY)
ART: BILL EVERETT, B.H. (BACHELOR OF HULKOSITY)
LETTERING: ARTIE SIMEK, P.H. (THE PRIDE OF HULKDOM)

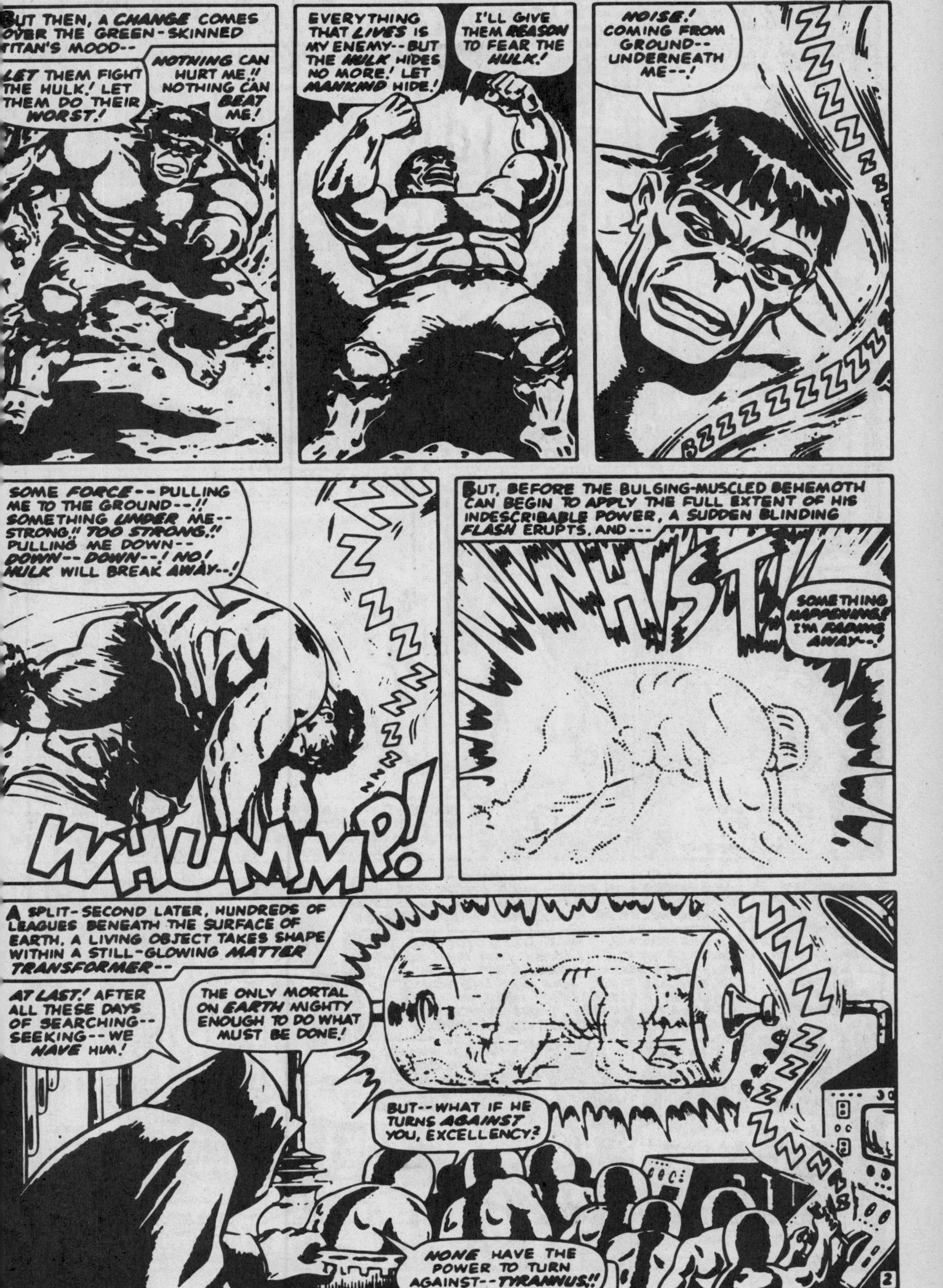

BUT THEN, A CHANGE COMES OVER THE GREEN-SKINNED TITAN'S MOOD--
LET THEM FIGHT THE HULK! LET THEM DO THEIR WORST!
NOTHING CAN HURT ME!! NOTHING CAN BEAT ME!
EVERYTHING THAT LIVES IS MY ENEMY--BUT THE HULK HIDES NO MORE! LET MANKIND HIDE!
I'LL GIVE THEM REASON TO FEAR THE HULK!
NOISE! COMING FROM GROUND--UNDERNEATH ME--!
SOME FORCE--PULLING ME TO THE GROUND--!! SOMETHING UNDER ME--STRONG!! TOO STRONG!! PULLING ME DOWN--DOWN--DOWN--! NO! HULK WILL BREAK AWAY--!
WHUMMP!
BUT, BEFORE THE BULGING-MUSCLED BEHEMOTH CAN BEGIN TO APPLY THE FULL EXTENT OF HIS INDESCRIBABLE POWER, A SUDDEN BLINDING FLASH ERUPTS, AND---
WHIST!
SOMETHING HAPPENING! I'M FADING AWAY--!
A SPLIT-SECOND LATER, HUNDREDS OF LEAGUES BENEATH THE SURFACE OF EARTH, A LIVING OBJECT TAKES SHAPE WITHIN A STILL-GLOWING MATTER TRANSFORMER--
AT LAST! AFTER ALL THESE DAYS OF SEARCHING--SEEKING--WE HAVE HIM!
THE ONLY MORTAL ON EARTH MIGHTY ENOUGH TO DO WHAT MUST BE DONE!
BUT--WHAT IF HE TURNS AGAINST YOU, EXCELLENCY?
NONE HAVE THE POWER TO TURN AGAINST--TYRANNUS!!

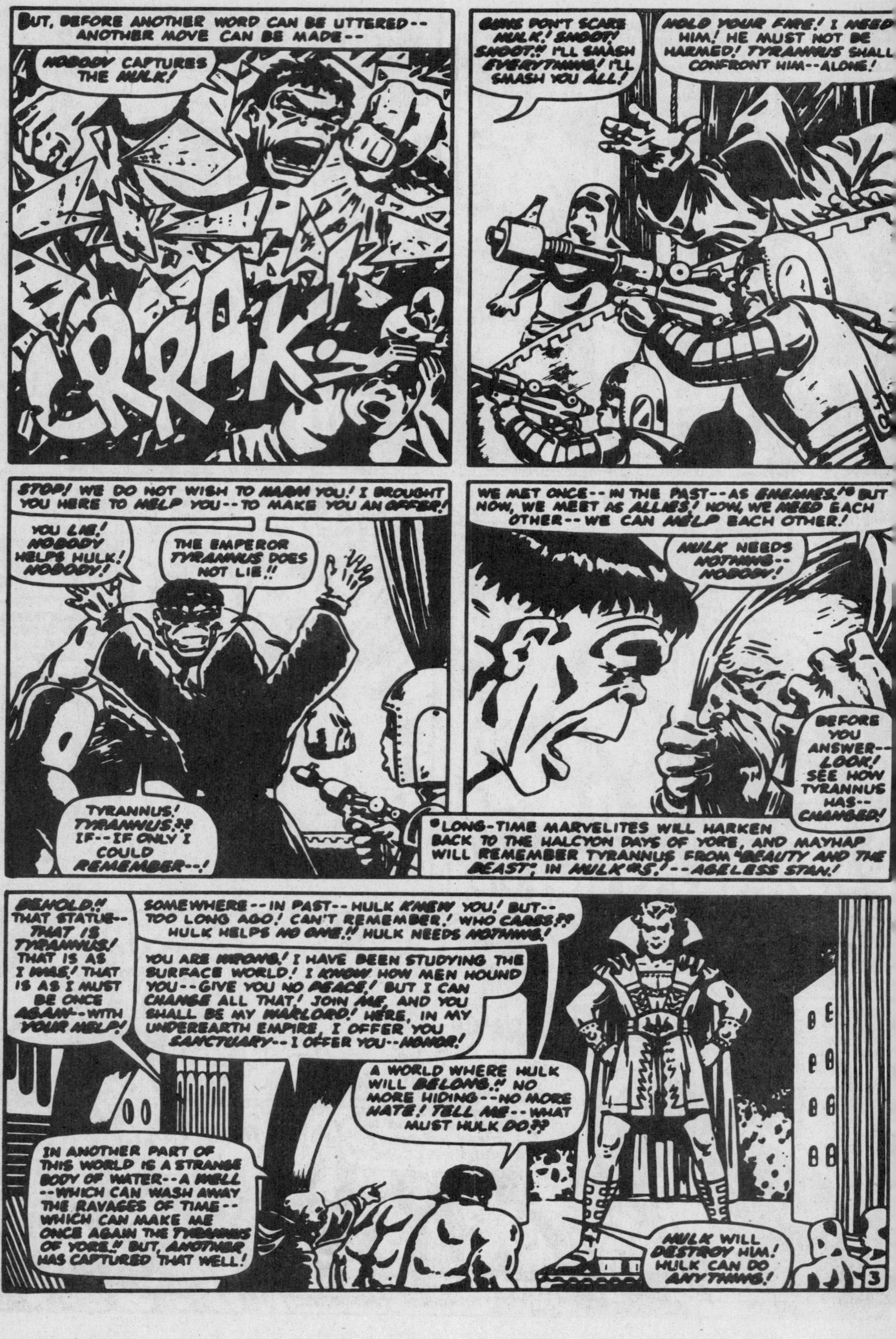

BUT, BEFORE ANOTHER WORD CAN BE UTTERED-- ANOTHER MOVE CAN BE MADE--
NOBODY CAPTURES THE HULK!
KRRAK!
GUNS DON'T SCARE HULK! SHOOT! SHOOT!! I'LL SMASH EVERYTHING! I'LL SMASH YOU ALL!
HOLD YOUR FIRE! I NEED HIM! HE MUST NOT BE HARMED! TYRANNUS SHALL CONFRONT HIM--ALONE!
STOP! WE DO NOT WISH TO HARM YOU! I BROUGHT YOU HERE TO HELP YOU--TO MAKE YOU AN OFFER!
YOU LIE! NOBODY HELPS HULK! NOBODY!
THE EMPEROR TYRANNUS DOES NOT LIE!!
TYRANNUS! TYRANNUS?? IF--IF ONLY I COULD REMEMBER--!
WE MET ONCE--IN THE PAST--AS ENEMIES!* BUT NOW, WE MEET AS ALLIES! NOW, WE NEED EACH OTHER--WE CAN HELP EACH OTHER!
HULK NEEDS NOTHING--NOBODY!
BEFORE YOU ANSWER--LOOK! SEE HOW TYRANNUS HAS--CHANGED!
*LONG-TIME MARVELITES WILL HARKEN BACK TO THE HALCYON DAYS OF YORE, AND MAYHAP WILL REMEMBER TYRANNUS FROM "BEAUTY AND THE BEAST", IN HULK #5! --AGELESS STAN!
BEHOLD!! THAT STATUE--THAT IS TYRANNUS! THAT IS AS I WAS! THAT IS AS I MUST BE ONCE AGAIN--WITH YOUR HELP!
SOMEWHERE--IN PAST--HULK KNEW YOU! BUT--TOO LONG AGO! CAN'T REMEMBER! WHO CARES?? HULK HELPS NO ONE!! HULK NEEDS NOTHING!
YOU ARE WRONG! I HAVE BEEN STUDYING THE SURFACE WORLD! I KNOW HOW MEN HOUND YOU--GIVE YOU NO PEACE! BUT I CAN CHANGE ALL THAT! JOIN ME, AND YOU SHALL BE MY WARLORD! HERE, IN MY UNDEREARTH EMPIRE, I OFFER YOU SANCTUARY--I OFFER YOU--HONOR!
A WORLD WHERE HULK WILL BELONG!! NO MORE HIDING--NO MORE HATE! TELL ME--WHAT MUST HULK DO??
IN ANOTHER PART OF THIS WORLD IS A STRANGE BODY OF WATER--A WELL--WHICH CAN WASH AWAY THE RAVAGES OF TIME--WHICH CAN MAKE ME ONCE AGAIN THE TYRANNUS OF YORE!! BUT, ANOTHER HAS CAPTURED THAT WELL!
HULK WILL DESTROY HIM! HULK CAN DO ANYTHING!

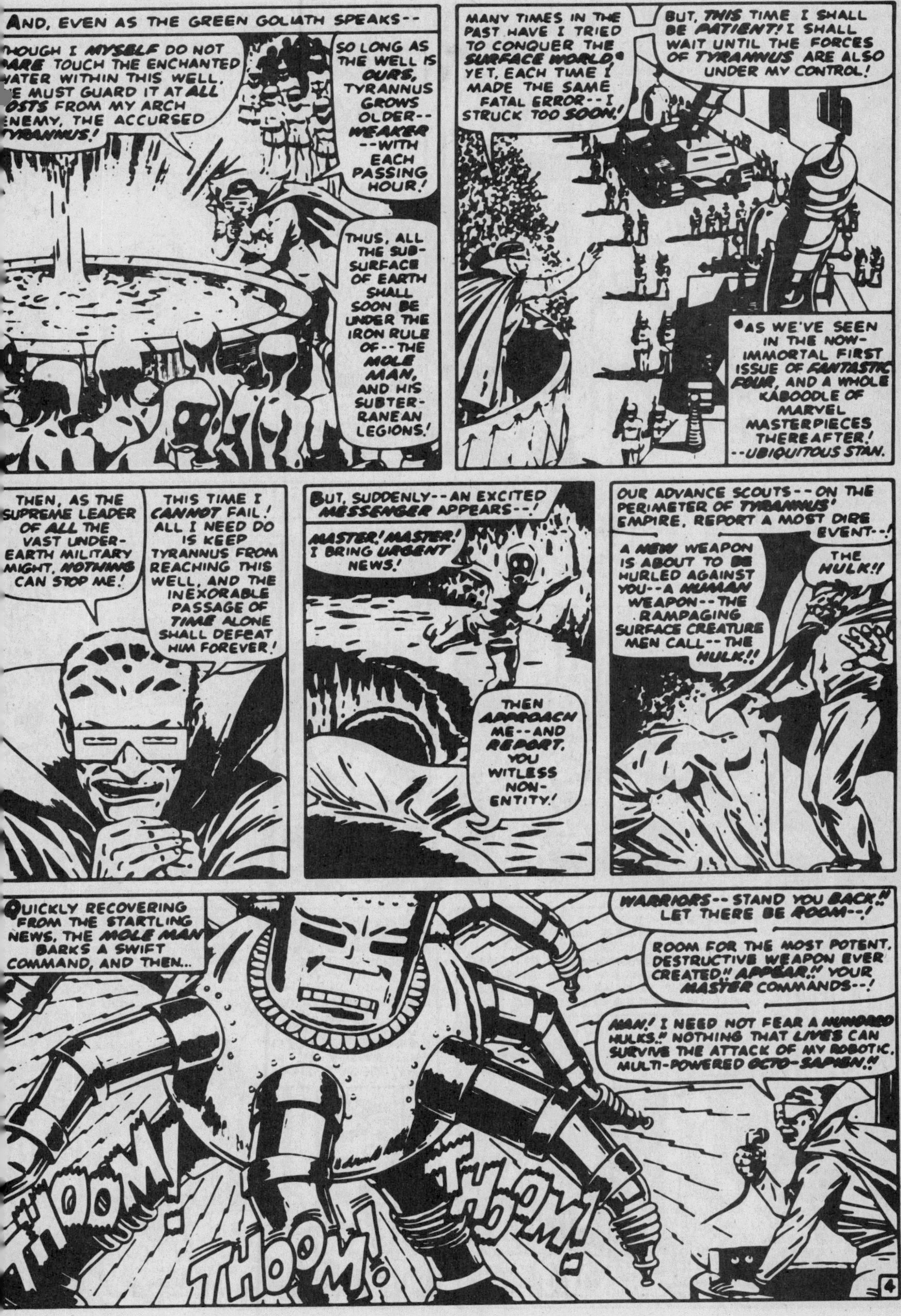
AND, EVEN AS THE GREEN GOLIATH SPEAKS--
THOUGH I MYSELF DO NOT DARE TOUCH THE ENCHANTED WATER WITHIN THIS WELL, WE MUST GUARD IT AT ALL COSTS FROM MY ARCH ENEMY, THE ACCURSED TYRANNUS!
SO LONG AS THE WELL IS OURS, TYRANNUS GROWS OLDER--WEAKER--WITH EACH PASSING HOUR!
THUS, ALL THE SUB-SURFACE OF EARTH SHALL SOON BE UNDER THE IRON RULE OF--THE MOLE MAN, AND HIS SUBTERRANEAN LEGIONS!
MANY TIMES IN THE PAST HAVE I TRIED TO CONQUER THE SURFACE WORLD,* YET, EACH TIME I MADE THE SAME FATAL ERROR--I STRUCK TOO SOON!
BUT, THIS TIME I SHALL BE PATIENT! I SHALL WAIT UNTIL THE FORCES OF TYRANNUS ARE ALSO UNDER MY CONTROL!
*AS WE'VE SEEN IN THE NOW-IMMORTAL FIRST ISSUE OF FANTASTIC FOUR, AND A WHOLE KABOODLE OF MARVEL MASTERPIECES THEREAFTER! --UBIQUITOUS STAN.
THEN, AS THE SUPREME LEADER OF ALL THE VAST UNDER-EARTH MILITARY MIGHT, NOTHING CAN STOP ME!
THIS TIME I CANNOT FAIL! ALL I NEED DO IS KEEP TYRANNUS FROM REACHING THIS WELL, AND THE INEXORABLE PASSAGE OF TIME ALONE SHALL DEFEAT HIM FOREVER!
BUT, SUDDENLY--AN EXCITED MESSENGER APPEARS--!
MASTER! MASTER! I BRING URGENT NEWS!
THEN APPROACH ME--AND REPORT, YOU WITLESS NON-ENTITY!
OUR ADVANCE SCOUTS--ON THE PERIMETER OF TYRANNUS' EMPIRE, REPORT A MOST DIRE EVENT--!
A NEW WEAPON IS ABOUT TO BE HURLED AGAINST YOU--A HUMAN WEAPON--THE RAMPAGING SURFACE CREATURE MEN CALL--THE HULK!!
THE HULK!!
QUICKLY RECOVERING FROM THE STARTLING NEWS, THE MOLE MAN BARKS A SWIFT COMMAND, AND THEN...
WARRIORS--STAND YOU BACK!! LET THERE BE ROOM--!
ROOM FOR THE MOST POTENT, DESTRUCTIVE WEAPON EVER CREATED!! APPEAR!! YOUR MASTER COMMANDS--!
MAN! I NEED NOT FEAR A HUNDRED HULKS!! NOTHING THAT LIVES CAN SURVIVE THE ATTACK OF MY ROBOTIC, MULTI-POWERED OCTO-SAPIEN!!
THOOM! THOOM! THOOM!
4

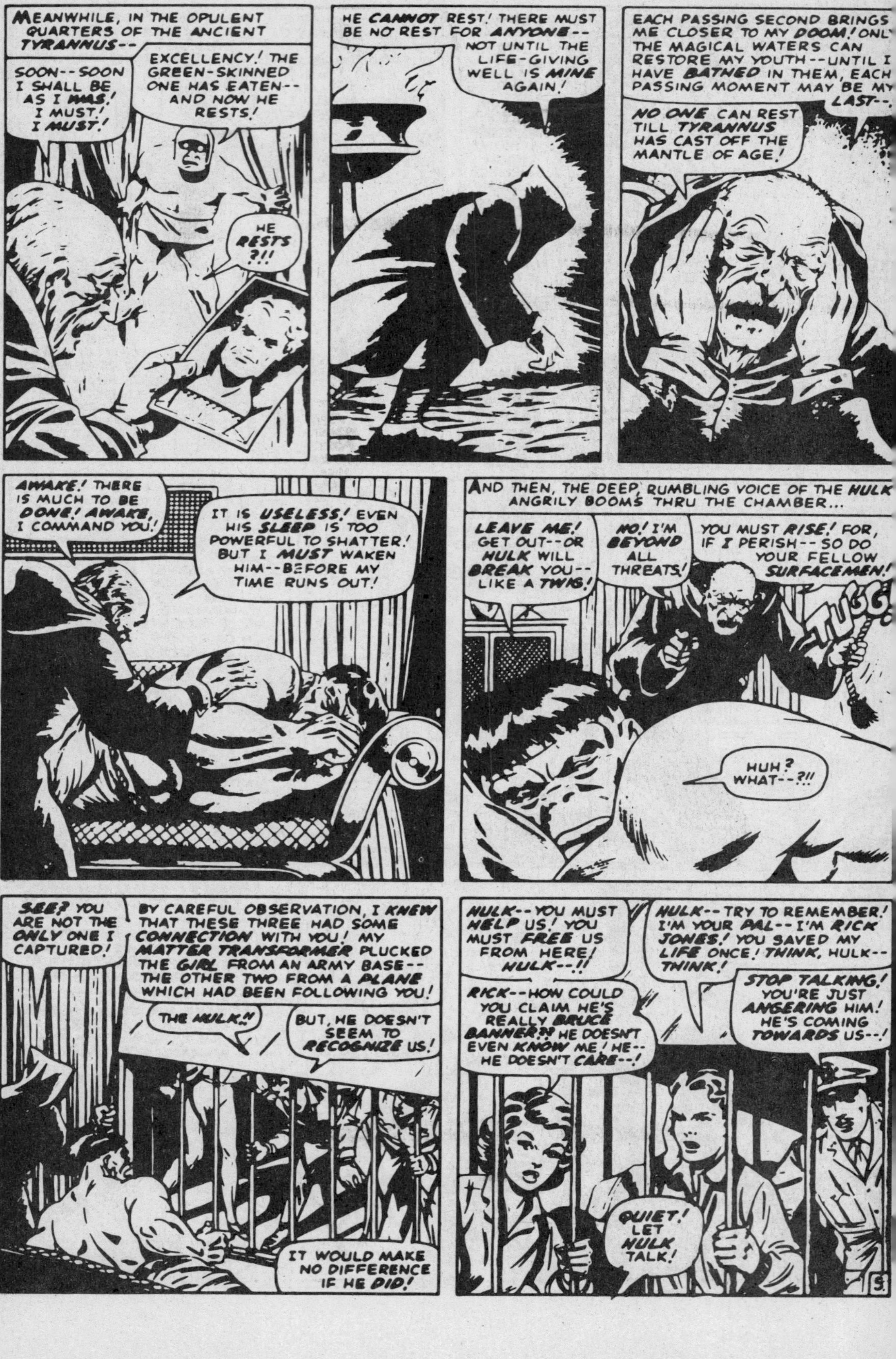
MEANWHILE, IN THE OPULENT QUARTERS OF THE ANCIENT TYRANNUS--
SOON--SOON I SHALL BE AS I WAS! I MUST! I MUST!
EXCELLENCY! THE GREEN-SKINNED ONE HAS EATEN--AND NOW HE RESTS!
HE RESTS?!!
HE CANNOT REST! THERE MUST BE NO REST FOR ANYONE--NOT UNTIL THE LIFE-GIVING WELL IS MINE AGAIN!
EACH PASSING SECOND BRINGS ME CLOSER TO MY DOOM! ONLY THE MAGICAL WATERS CAN RESTORE MY YOUTH--UNTIL I HAVE BATHED IN THEM, EACH PASSING MOMENT MAY BE MY LAST--.
NO ONE CAN REST TILL TYRANNUS HAS CAST OFF THE MANTLE OF AGE!
AWAKE! THERE IS MUCH TO BE DONE! AWAKE, I COMMAND YOU!
IT IS USELESS! EVEN HIS SLEEP IS TOO POWERFUL TO SHATTER! BUT I MUST WAKEN HIM--BEFORE MY TIME RUNS OUT!
AND THEN, THE DEEP, RUMBLING VOICE OF THE HULK ANGRILY BOOMS THRU THE CHAMBER...
LEAVE ME! GET OUT--OR HULK WILL BREAK YOU--LIKE A TWIG!
NO! I'M BEYOND ALL THREATS!
YOU MUST RISE! FOR, IF I PERISH--SO DO YOUR FELLOW SURFACEMEN!
TUGG
HUH? WHAT--?!!
SEE? YOU ARE NOT THE ONLY ONE I CAPTURED!
BY CAREFUL OBSERVATION, I KNEW THAT THESE THREE HAD SOME CONNECTION WITH YOU! MY MATTER TRANSFORMER PLUCKED THE GIRL FROM AN ARMY BASE--THE OTHER TWO FROM A PLANE WHICH HAD BEEN FOLLOWING YOU!
THE HULK!!
BUT, HE DOESN'T SEEM TO RECOGNIZE US!
IT WOULD MAKE NO DIFFERENCE IF HE DID!
HULK--YOU MUST HELP US! YOU MUST FREE US FROM HERE! HULK--!!
RICK--HOW COULD YOU CLAIM HE'S REALLY BRUCE BANNER?! HE DOESN'T EVEN KNOW ME! HE--HE DOESN'T CARE--!
HULK--TRY TO REMEMBER! I'M YOUR PAL--I'M RICK JONES! YOU SAVED MY LIFE ONCE! THINK, HULK--THINK!
STOP TALKING! YOU'RE JUST ANGERING HIM! HE'S COMING TOWARDS US--!
QUIET! LET HULK TALK!
5

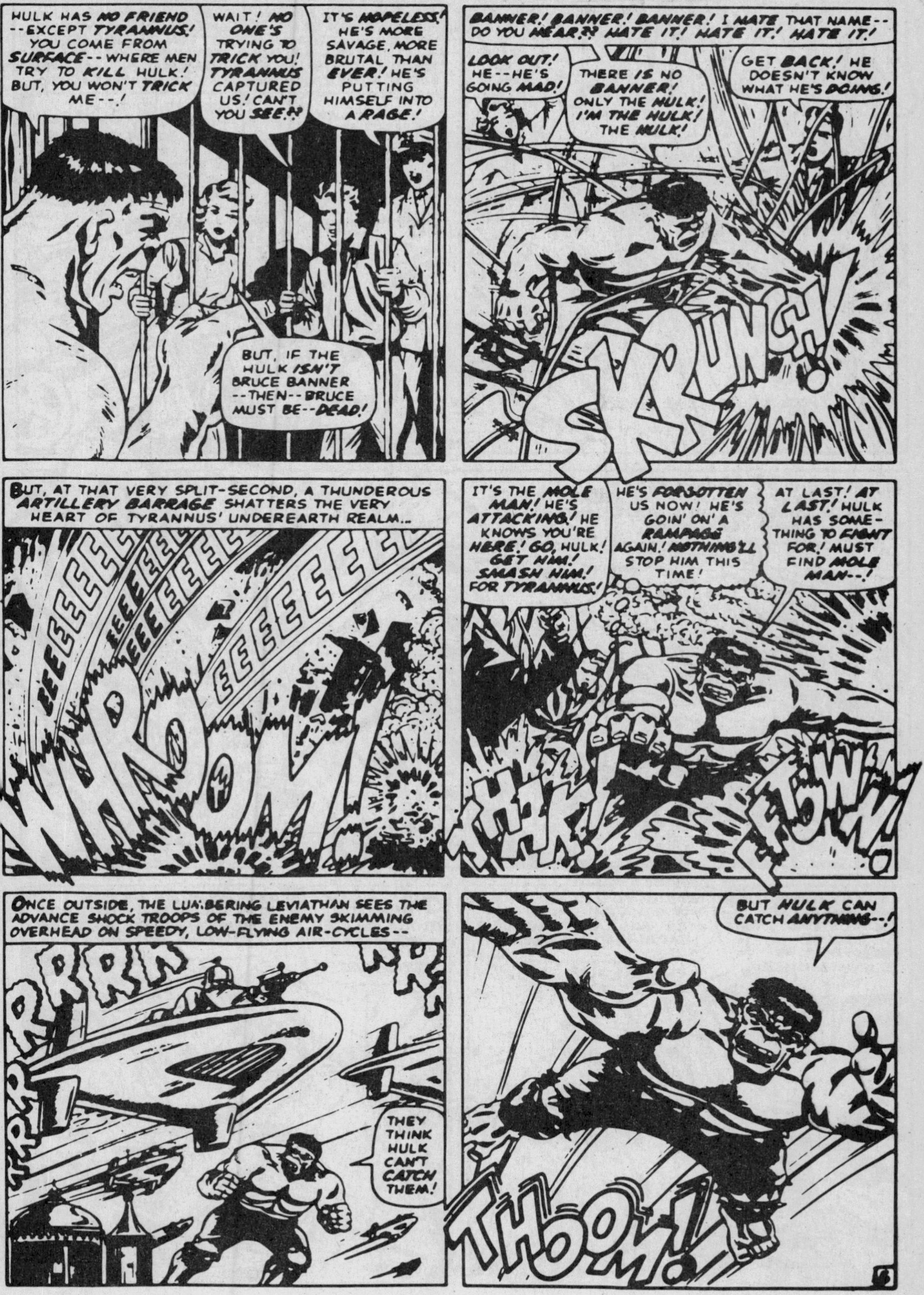

HULK HAS NO FRIEND --EXCEPT TYRANNUS! YOU COME FROM SURFACE--WHERE MEN TRY TO KILL HULK! BUT, YOU WON'T TRICK ME--!
WAIT! NO ONE'S TRYING TO TRICK YOU! TYRANNUS CAPTURED US! CAN'T YOU SEE?!
IT'S HOPELESS! HE'S MORE SAVAGE, MORE BRUTAL THAN EVER! HE'S PUTTING HIMSELF INTO A RAGE!
BUT, IF THE HULK ISN'T BRUCE BANNER --THEN--BRUCE MUST BE--DEAD!
BANNER! BANNER! BANNER! I HATE THAT NAME--DO YOU HEAR?! HATE IT! HATE IT! HATE IT!
LOOK OUT! HE--HE'S GOING MAD!
THERE IS NO BANNER! ONLY THE HULK! I'M THE HULK! THE HULK!
GET BACK! HE DOESN'T KNOW WHAT HE'S DOING!
SKRUNCH!
BUT, AT THAT VERY SPLIT-SECOND, A THUNDEROUS ARTILLERY BARRAGE SHATTERS THE VERY HEART OF TYRANNUS' UNDEREARTH REALM...
EEEEEEEEE
WHROOM!
IT'S THE MOLE MAN! HE'S ATTACKING! HE KNOWS YOU'RE HERE! GO, HULK! GET HIM! SMASH HIM! FOR TYRANNUS!
HE'S FORGOTTEN US NOW! HE'S GOIN' ON' A RAMPAGE AGAIN! NOTHING'LL STOP HIM THIS TIME!
AT LAST! AT LAST! HULK HAS SOME-THING TO FIGHT FOR! MUST FIND MOLE MAN--!
THAK!
FTOWN!
ONCE OUTSIDE, THE LUMBERING LEVIATHAN SEES THE ADVANCE SHOCK TROOPS OF THE ENEMY SKIMMING OVERHEAD ON SPEEDY, LOW-FLYING AIR-CYCLES--
RRRR
THEY THINK HULK CAN'T CATCH THEM!
BUT HULK CAN CATCH ANYTHING--!
THOOOM!

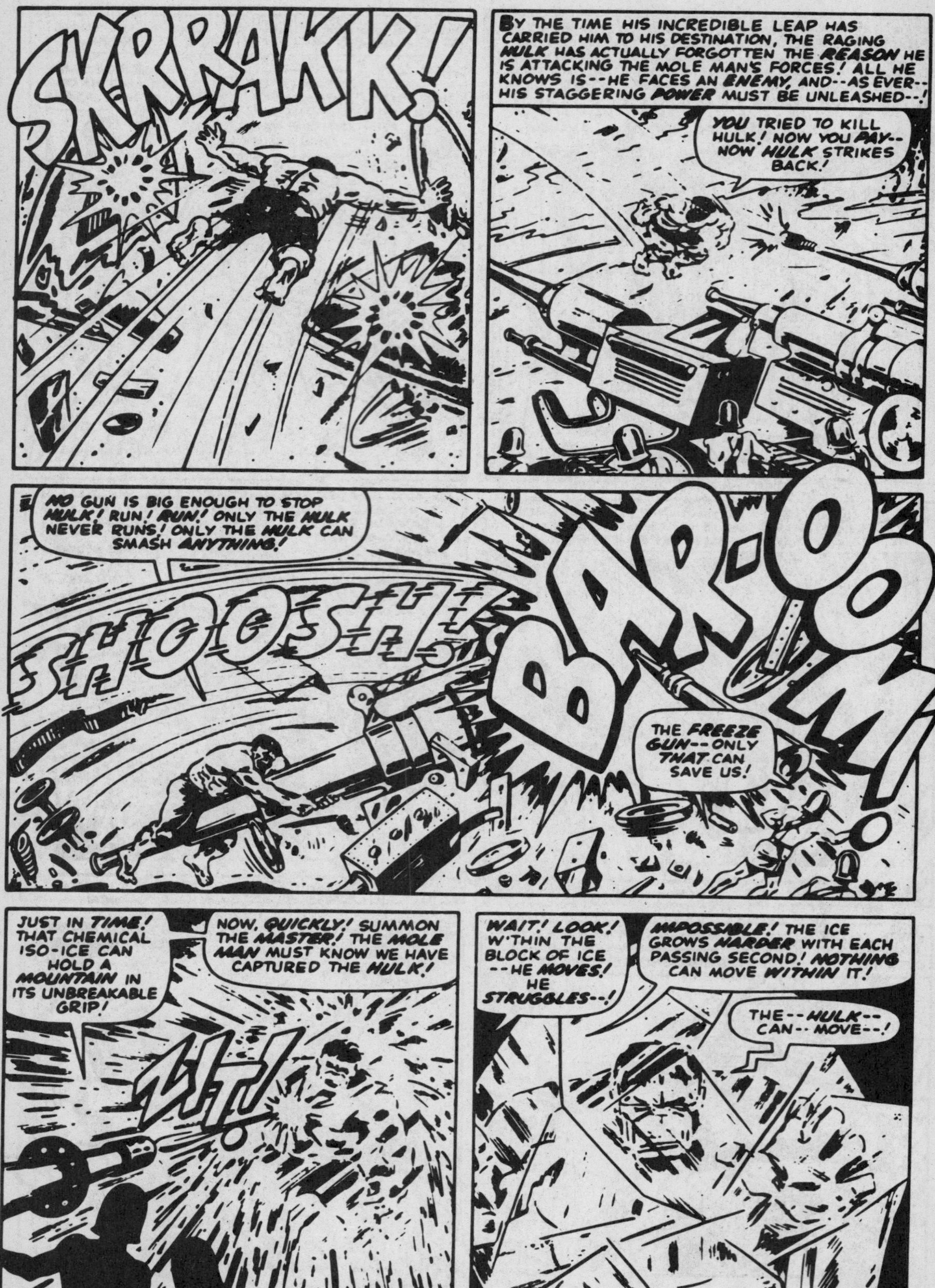
SKRRAKK!
BY THE TIME HIS INCREDIBLE LEAP HAS CARRIED HIM TO HIS DESTINATION, THE RAGING HULK HAS ACTUALLY FORGOTTEN THE REASON HE IS ATTACKING THE MOLE MAN'S FORCES! ALL HE KNOWS IS--HE FACES AN ENEMY, AND--AS EVER--HIS STAGGERING POWER MUST BE UNLEASHED--!
YOU TRIED TO KILL HULK! NOW YOU PAY--NOW HULK STRIKES BACK!
NO GUN IS BIG ENOUGH TO STOP HULK! RUN! RUN! ONLY THE HULK NEVER RUNS! ONLY THE HULK CAN SMASH ANYTHING!
SHOOSH!
BAR-OOM!
THE FREEZE GUN--ONLY THAT CAN SAVE US!
JUST IN TIME! THAT CHEMICAL ISO-ICE CAN HOLD A MOUNTAIN IN ITS UNBREAKABLE GRIP!
NOW, QUICKLY! SUMMON THE MASTER! THE MOLE MAN MUST KNOW WE HAVE CAPTURED THE HULK!
ZIT!
WAIT! LOOK! W'THIN THE BLOCK OF ICE--HE MOVES! HE STRUGGLES--!
IMPOSSIBLE! THE ICE GROWS HARDER WITH EACH PASSING SECOND! NOTHING CAN MOVE WITHIN IT!
THE--HULK--CAN--MOVE--!

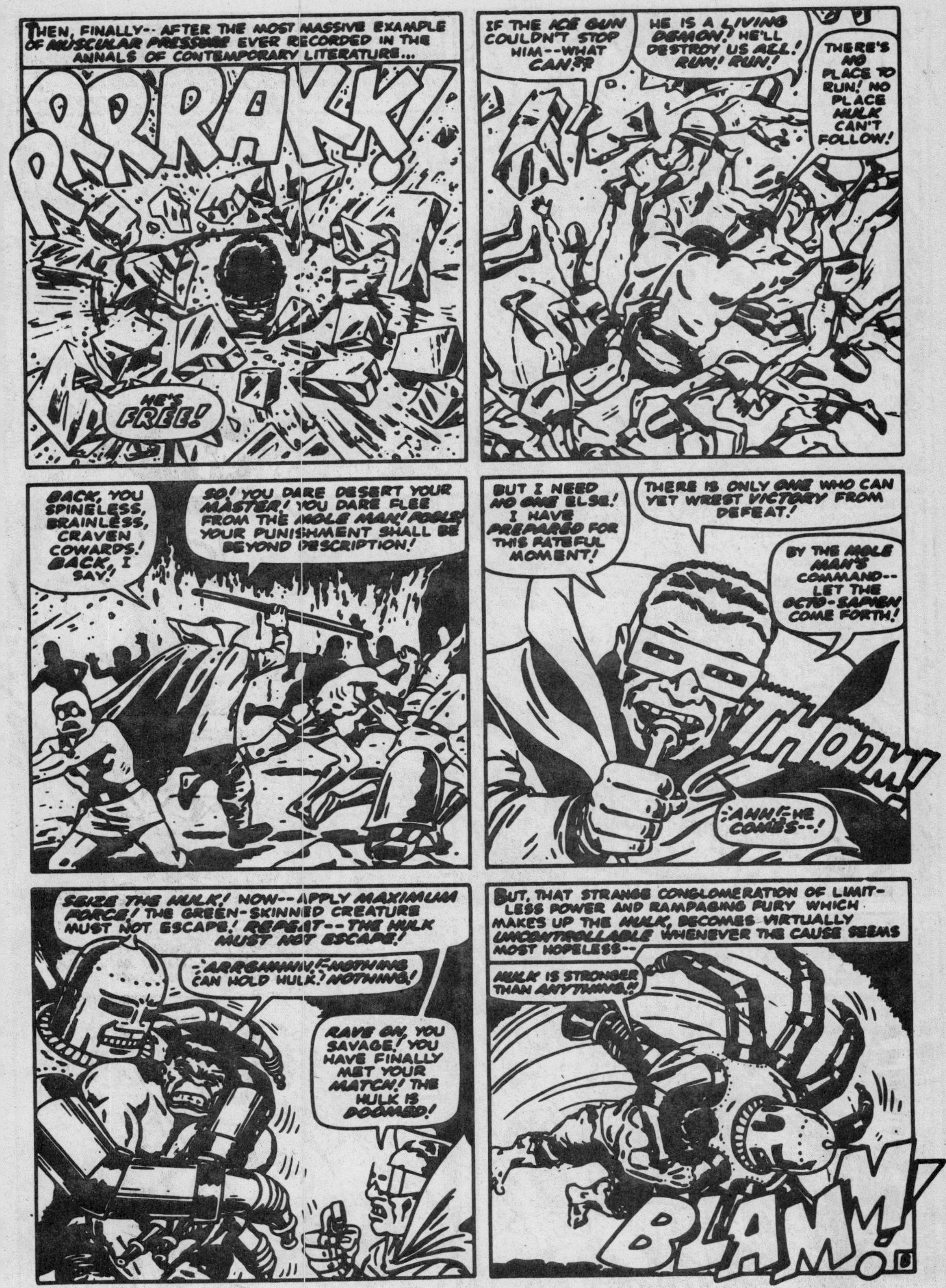
THEN, FINALLY-- AFTER THE MOST MASSIVE EXAMPLE OF MUSCULAR PRESSURE EVER RECORDED IN THE ANNALS OF CONTEMPORARY LITERATURE...
PPRRAKK!
HE'S FREE!
IF THE ICE GUN COULDN'T STOP HIM--WHAT CAN?!?
HE IS A LIVING DEMON! HE'LL DESTROY US ALL! RUN! RUN!
THERE'S NO PLACE TO RUN! NO PLACE HULK CAN'T FOLLOW!
BACK, YOU SPINELESS, BRAINLESS, CRAVEN COWARDS! BACK, I SAY!
SO! YOU DARE DESERT YOUR MASTER! YOU DARE FLEE FROM THE MOLE MAN! FOOLS! YOUR PUNISHMENT SHALL BE BEYOND DESCRIPTION!
BUT I NEED NO ONE ELSE! I HAVE PREPARED FOR THIS FATEFUL MOMENT!
THERE IS ONLY ONE WHO CAN YET WREST VICTORY FROM DEFEAT!
BY THE MOLE MAN'S COMMAND-- LET THE OCTO-SAPIEN COME FORTH!
THOOM!
AHH!--HE COMES--!
SEIZE THE HULK! NOW--APPLY MAXIMUM FORCE! THE GREEN-SKINNED CREATURE MUST NOT ESCAPE! REPEAT--THE HULK MUST NOT ESCAPE!
--ARRGHHH!--NOTHING CAN HOLD HULK! NOTHING!
RAVE ON, YOU SAVAGE! YOU HAVE FINALLY MET YOUR MATCH! THE HULK IS DOOMED!
BUT, THAT STRANGE CONGLOMERATION OF LIMITLESS POWER AND RAMPAGING FURY WHICH MAKES UP THE HULK, BECOMES VIRTUALLY UNCONTROLLABLE WHENEVER THE CAUSE SEEMS MOST HOPELESS--
HULK IS STRONGER THAN ANYTHING!!
BLAMM!
6

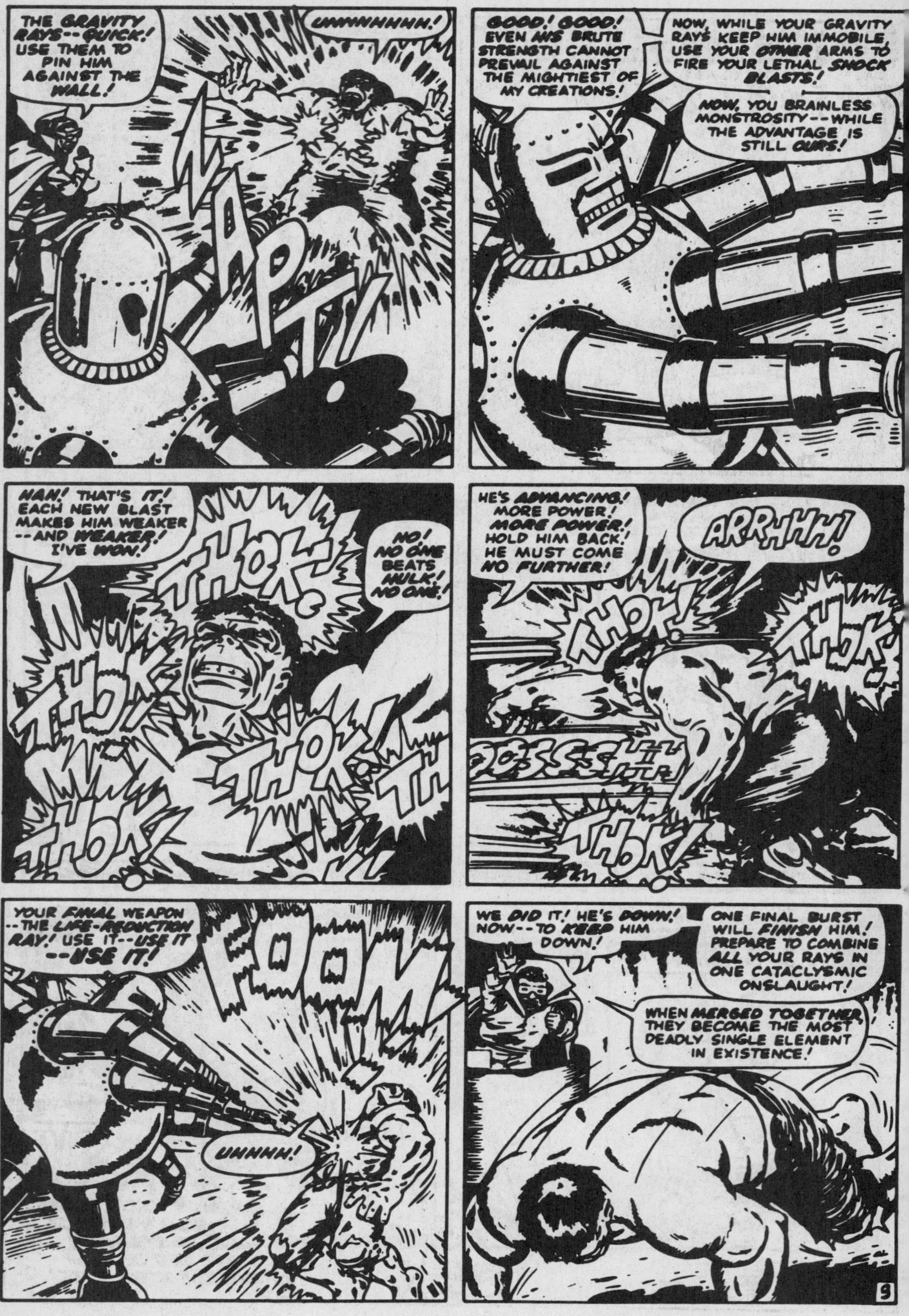
THE GRAVITY RAYS--QUICK! USE THEM TO PIN HIM AGAINST THE WALL!
UNNNHHHHH!
ZAPT!
GOOD! GOOD! EVEN HIS BRUTE STRENGTH CANNOT PREVAIL AGAINST THE MIGHTIEST OF MY CREATIONS!
NOW, WHILE YOUR GRAVITY RAYS KEEP HIM IMMOBILE, USE YOUR OTHER ARMS TO FIRE YOUR LETHAL SHOCK BLASTS!
NOW, YOU BRAINLESS MONSTROSITY--WHILE THE ADVANTAGE IS STILL OURS!
HAH! THAT'S IT! EACH NEW BLAST MAKES HIM WEAKER --AND WEAKER! I'VE WON!
THOK!
NO! NO ONE BEATS HULK! NO ONE!
THOK!
THOK!
THOK!
HE'S ADVANCING! MORE POWER! MORE POWER! HOLD HIM BACK. HE MUST COME NO FURTHER!
ARRHHH!
THOK!
THOK!
THOK!
YOUR FINAL WEAPON --THE LIFE-REDUCTION RAY! USE IT--USE IT --USE IT!
FOOOM
UNHHH!
WE DID IT! HE'S DOWN! NOW--TO KEEP HIM DOWN!
ONE FINAL BURST WILL FINISH HIM! PREPARE TO COMBINE ALL YOUR RAYS IN ONE CATACLYSMIC ONSLAUGHT!
WHEN MERGED TOGETHER, THEY BECOME THE MOST DEADLY SINGLE ELEMENT IN EXISTENCE!
9

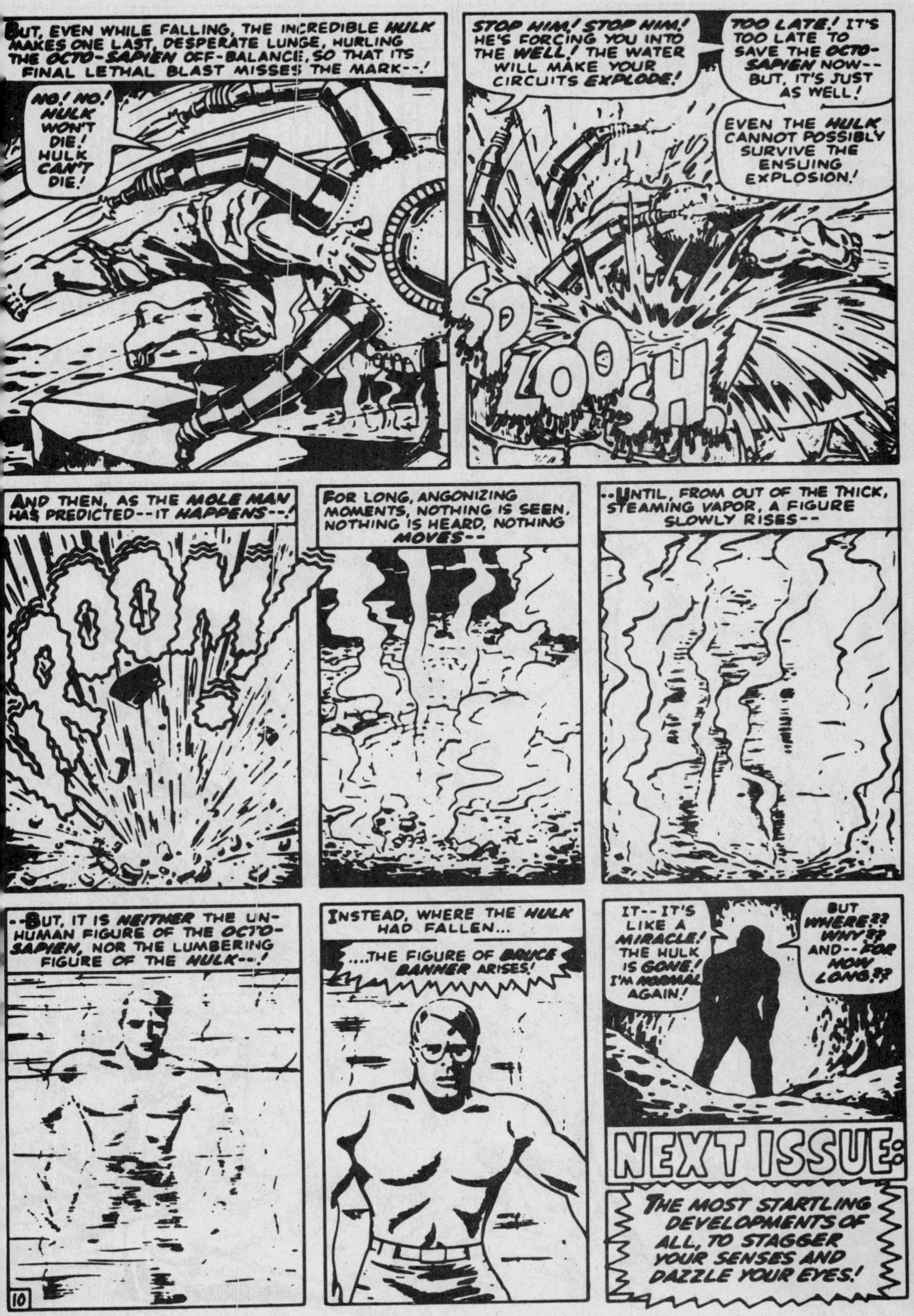

BUT, EVEN WHILE FALLING, THE INCREDIBLE HULK MAKES ONE LAST, DESPERATE LUNGE, HURLING THE OCTO-SAPIEN OFF-BALANCE, SO THAT ITS FINAL LETHAL BLAST MISSES THE MARK--!
NO! NO! HULK WON'T DIE! HULK CAN'T DIE!
STOP HIM! STOP HIM! HE'S FORCING YOU INTO THE WELL! THE WATER WILL MAKE YOUR CIRCUITS EXPLODE!
TOO LATE! IT'S TOO LATE TO SAVE THE OCTO-SAPIEN NOW-- BUT, IT'S JUST AS WELL!
EVEN THE HULK CANNOT POSSIBLY SURVIVE THE ENSUING EXPLOSION!
SPLOOSH!
AND THEN, AS THE MOLE MAN HAS PREDICTED--IT HAPPENS--!
BOOOM!
FOR LONG, ANGONIZING MOMENTS, NOTHING IS SEEN, NOTHING IS HEARD, NOTHING MOVES--
--UNTIL, FROM OUT OF THE THICK, STEAMING VAPOR, A FIGURE SLOWLY RISES--
--BUT, IT IS NEITHER THE UN-HUMAN FIGURE OF THE OCTO-SAPIEN, NOR THE LUMBERING FIGURE OF THE HULK--!
INSTEAD, WHERE THE HULK HAD FALLEN...
....THE FIGURE OF BRUCE BANNER ARISES!
IT--IT'S LIKE A MIRACLE! THE HULK IS GONE! I'M NORMAL AGAIN!
BUT WHERE?? WHY?? AND--FOR HOW LONG??
NEXT ISSUE:
THE MOST STARTLING DEVELOPMENTS OF ALL, TO STAGGER YOUR SENSES AND DAZZLE YOUR EYES!

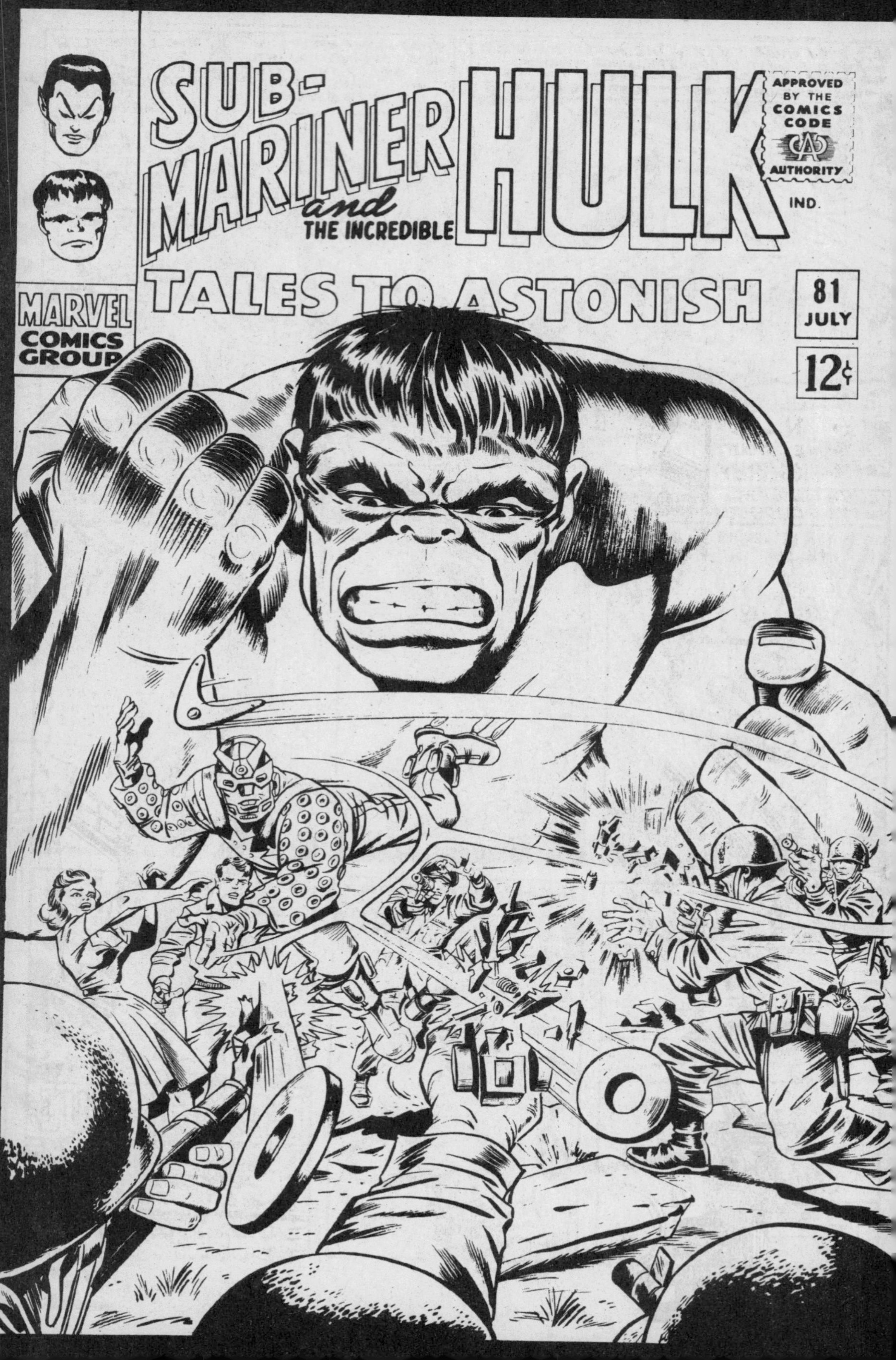
SUB-MARINER
and
THE INCREDIBLE HULK
APPROVED BY THE COMICS CODE AUTHORITY
IND.
MARVEL COMICS GROUP
TALES TO ASTONISH
81
JULY
12¢

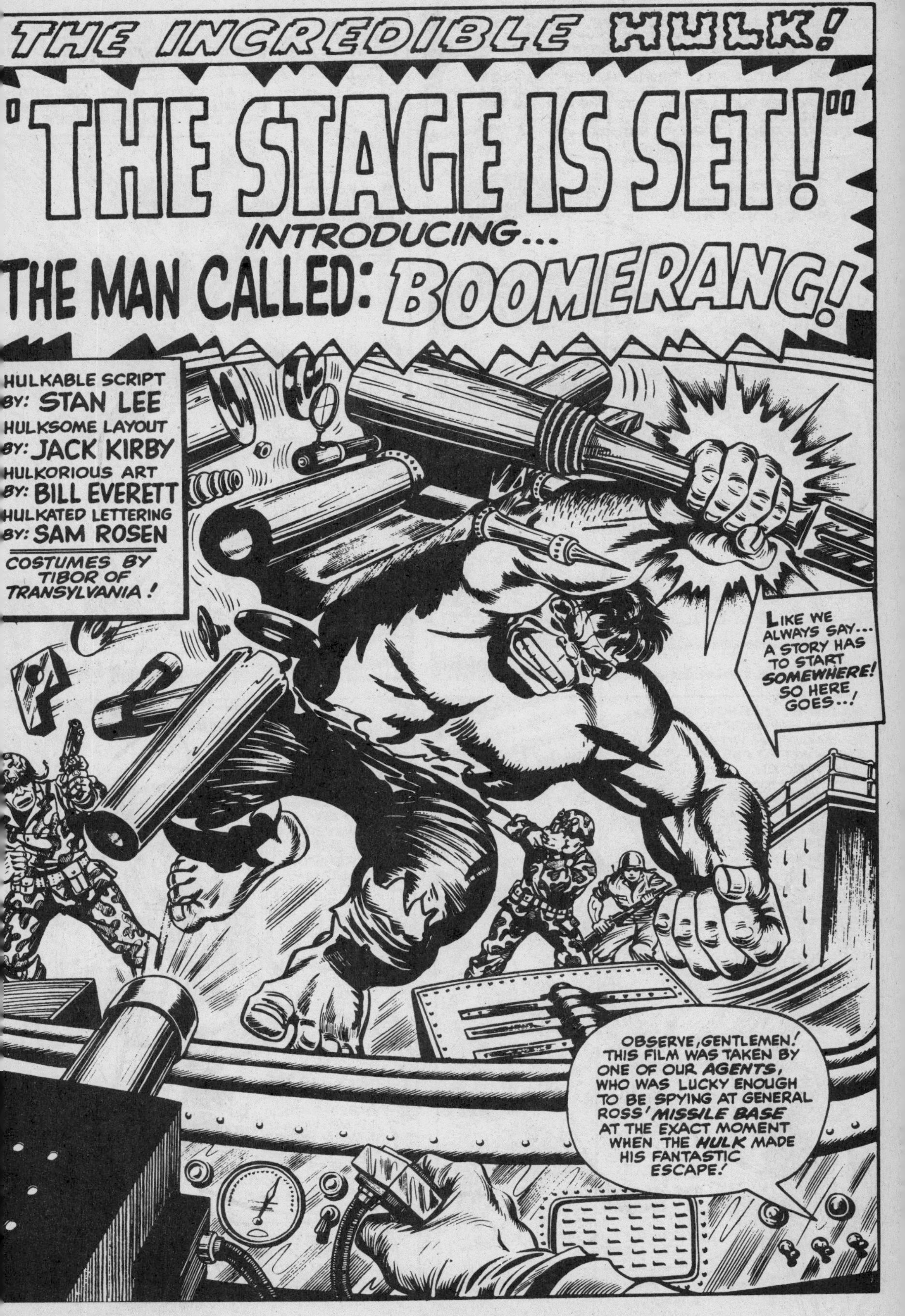
THE INCREDIBLE HULK!
"THE STAGE IS SET!"
INTRODUCING...
THE MAN CALLED: BOOMERANG!
HULKABLE SCRIPT BY: STAN LEE
HULKSOME LAYOUT BY: JACK KIRBY
HULKORIOUS ART BY: BILL EVERETT
HULKATED LETTERING BY: SAM ROSEN
COSTUMES BY TIBOR OF TRANSYLVANIA!
LIKE WE ALWAYS SAY... A STORY HAS TO START SOMEWHERE! SO HERE GOES...!
OBSERVE, GENTLEMEN! THIS FILM WAS TAKEN BY ONE OF OUR AGENTS, WHO WAS LUCKY ENOUGH TO BE SPYING AT GENERAL ROSS' MISSILE BASE AT THE EXACT MOMENT WHEN THE HULK MADE HIS FANTASTIC ESCAPE!

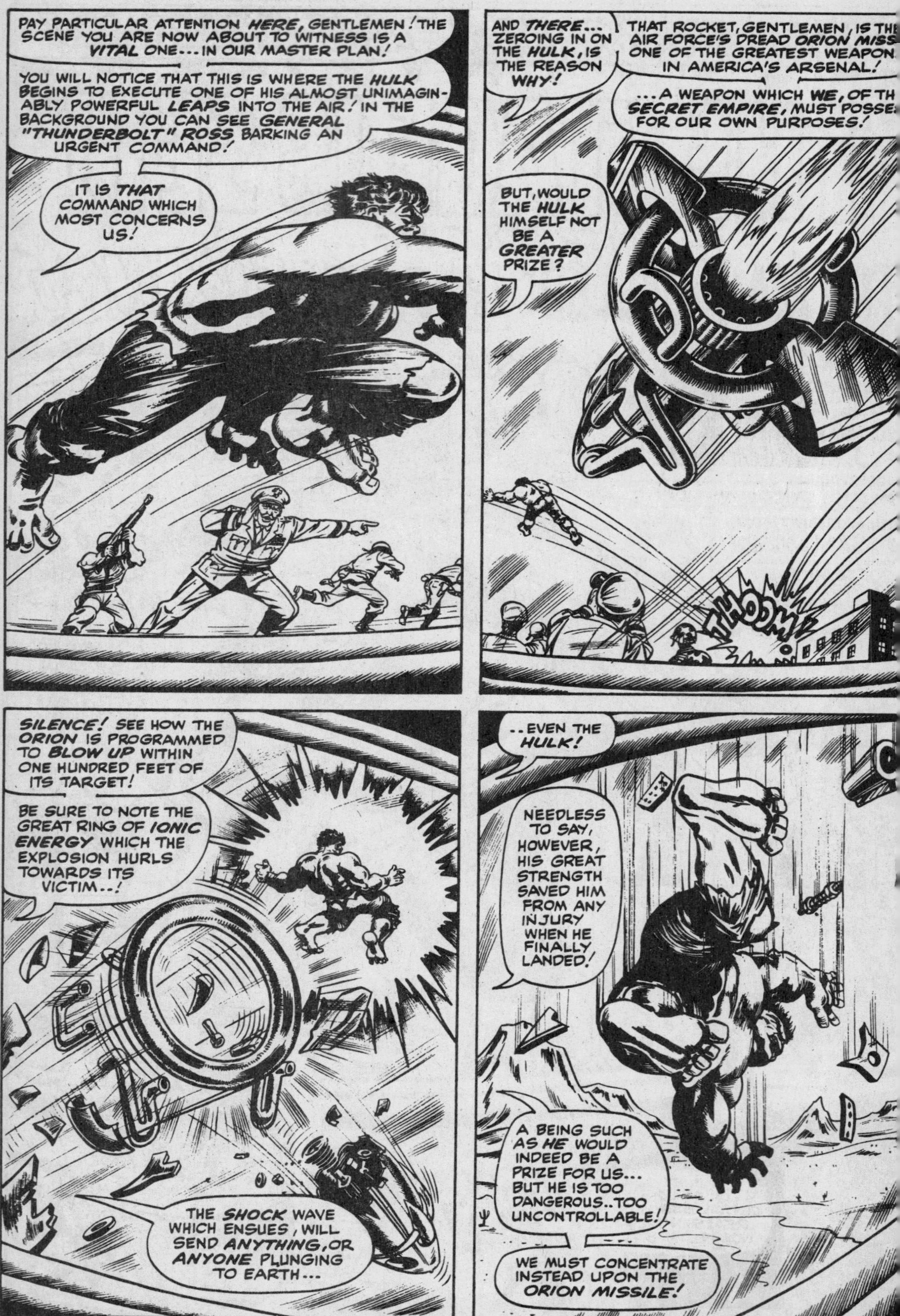
PAY PARTICULAR ATTENTION HERE, GENTLEMEN! THE SCENE YOU ARE NOW ABOUT TO WITNESS IS A VITAL ONE... IN OUR MASTER PLAN!
YOU WILL NOTICE THAT THIS IS WHERE THE HULK BEGINS TO EXECUTE ONE OF HIS ALMOST UNIMAGINABLY POWERFUL LEAPS INTO THE AIR! IN THE BACKGROUND YOU CAN SEE GENERAL "THUNDERBOLT" ROSS BARKING AN URGENT COMMAND!
IT IS THAT COMMAND WHICH MOST CONCERNS US!
AND THERE... ZEROING IN ON THE HULK, IS THE REASON WHY!
THAT ROCKET, GENTLEMEN, IS TH
AIR FORCE'S DREAD ORION MISS
ONE OF THE GREATEST WEAPON
IN AMERICA'S ARSENAL!
...A WEAPON WHICH WE, OF TH
SECRET EMPIRE, MUST POSSE
FOR OUR OWN PURPOSES!
BUT, WOULD THE HULK HIMSELF NOT BE A GREATER PRIZE?
THOOM!
SILENCE! SEE HOW THE ORION IS PROGRAMMED TO BLOW UP WITHIN ONE HUNDRED FEET OF ITS TARGET!
BE SURE TO NOTE THE GREAT RING OF IONIC ENERGY WHICH THE EXPLOSION HURLS TOWARDS ITS VICTIM..!
THE SHOCK WAVE WHICH ENSUES, WILL SEND ANYTHING, OR ANYONE PLUNGING TO EARTH...
..EVEN THE HULK!
NEEDLESS TO SAY, HOWEVER, HIS GREAT STRENGTH SAVED HIM FROM ANY INJURY WHEN HE FINALLY LANDED!
A BEING SUCH AS HE WOULD INDEED BE A PRIZE FOR US... BUT HE IS TOO DANGEROUS..TOO UNCONTROLLABLE!
WE MUST CONCENTRATE INSTEAD UPON THE ORION MISSILE!

Panel 1:
...HUS ENDS OUR TTLE FEATURE ILM, GENTLEMEN! TRUST YOU FOUND...EH, *EDUCATIONAL*!

INDEED IT *WAS* NUMBER FIVE! AS CHIEFS OF OPERATIONS FOR NORTH AMERICA, SOUTH AMERICA, AND EUROPE, IT IS *OUR JOB* TO SELECT AN AGENT TO OBTAIN THE MISSILE FOR OUR *SECRET EMPIRE*!

YOU ARE *RIGHT*, NUMBER SEVEN!

Panel 2:
THE ONLY *LOGICAL* CHOICE IS...THE *BOOMERANG*! IF ANYBODY CAN ACCOMPLISH THIS, IT IS *HE*!

I'LL CONTACT HIM AT ONCE...VIA OUR PRIVATE MICRO-WAVE-LENGTH!

KLIKKITY KLAK!

Panel 3:
MOMENTS LATER, IN ANOTHER CITY..IN ANOTHER STATE..

BOOMERANG SPEAKING! ELL ME THE DETAILS AND GIVE ME THE *PRICE*! VER!

WHO ARE YOU TALKING TO, FRED? JUST FIDDLING AROUND WITH MY CITIZENS BAND WALKIE-TALKIE, DOLL! I GET A REAL *CHARGE* OUT OF IT!

Panel 4:
TALK *FAST*...AND KEEP IT *LOW*! YOU HAVE EXACTLY *THIRTY SECONDS*!

YOU WERE SO *GLAMOROUS* A FEW SEASONS AGO WHEN YOU WERE A STAR *PITCHER*! WHAT A PITY THEY *SUSPENDED* YOU!

I DON'T MISS IT! I'VE FOUND MANY MORE *IMPORTANT* THINGS!

THE *ORION MISSILE*?!! I UNDERSTAND! I'LL DO IT! OVER AND OUT!

THE SPORTS WRITERS ALL SAID THAT YOU COULD HAVE BEEN THE *GREATEST*!

Panel 5:

BY THE WAY, HANDSOME...WHAT *ARE* ALL THOSE IMPORTANT THINGS YOU'RE ALWAYS TALKING ABOUT?

THERE'S SO MUCH ABOUT YOU THAT I DON'T KNOW...THAT I FEEL I'LL *NEVER* KNOW!

COME *OFF* IT, HONEY! YOU'RE MAKING ME SOUND LIKE A POOR MAN'S *JAMES BOND*!

I'VE JUST GOT A LOT OF CONFIDENTIAL *BUSINESS* DEALS IN THE WORKS, THAT'S ALL!

Panel 6:

AND NOW, *YOU'D* BETTER BE GOING, TOO, HONEY! SOMETHING CAME UP THAT I'VE GOT TO ATTEND TO *RIGHT AWAY*!

LET ME TAKE A RAIN CHECK ON THAT DINNER-DANCE AT ARTHUR'S!

ALL RIGHT, FRED..THERE'LL BE OTHER NIGHTS!

Panel 7:

BUT, IF YOU BREAK *ONE* MORE DATE WITH ME...IT'LL BE THE *LAST TIME*!

IF MY *LUCK* DOESN'T HOLD OUT ON THIS JOB, IT REALLY *WILL* BE THE LAST TIME!

WISH ME LUCK, LADY! IF THIS DEAL TURNS OUT OKAY, I'LL BE ON *EASY STREET* FOR LIFE!

I'LL CALL YOU FIRST CHANCE I GET!

FORGIVE ME IF I DON'T HOLD MY BREATH!

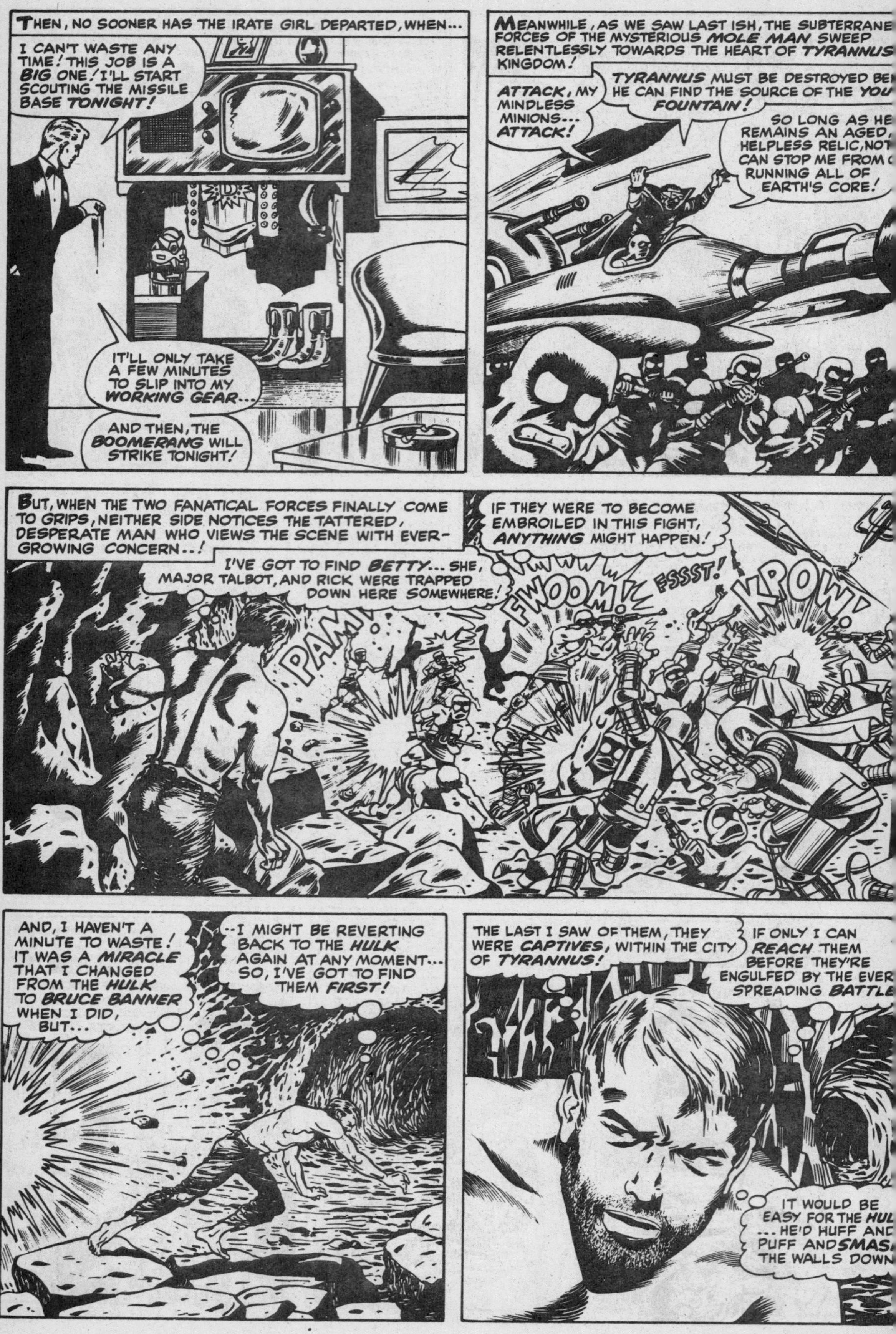
THEN, NO SOONER HAS THE IRATE GIRL DEPARTED, WHEN...
I CAN'T WASTE ANY TIME! THIS JOB IS A BIG ONE! I'LL START SCOUTING THE MISSILE BASE TONIGHT!
IT'LL ONLY TAKE A FEW MINUTES TO SLIP INTO MY WORKING GEAR...
AND THEN, THE BOOMERANG WILL STRIKE TONIGHT!
MEANWHILE, AS WE SAW LAST ISH, THE SUBTERRANE FORCES OF THE MYSTERIOUS MOLE MAN SWEEP RELENTLESSLY TOWARDS THE HEART OF TYRANNUS KINGDOM!
ATTACK, MY MINDLESS MINIONS... ATTACK!
TYRANNUS MUST BE DESTROYED BE HE CAN FIND THE SOURCE OF THE YOU FOUNTAIN!
SO LONG AS HE REMAINS AN AGED, HELPLESS RELIC, NOT CAN STOP ME FROM RUNNING ALL OF EARTH'S CORE!
BUT, WHEN THE TWO FANATICAL FORCES FINALLY COME TO GRIPS, NEITHER SIDE NOTICES THE TATTERED, DESPERATE MAN WHO VIEWS THE SCENE WITH EVER-GROWING CONCERN..!
IF THEY WERE TO BECOME EMBROILED IN THIS FIGHT, ANYTHING MIGHT HAPPEN!
I'VE GOT TO FIND BETTY... SHE, MAJOR TALBOT, AND RICK WERE TRAPPED DOWN HERE SOMEWHERE!
FWOOM!
FSSST!
KPOW!
PAM!
AND, I HAVEN'T A MINUTE TO WASTE! IT WAS A MIRACLE THAT I CHANGED FROM THE HULK TO BRUCE BANNER WHEN I DID, BUT...
--I MIGHT BE REVERTING BACK TO THE HULK AGAIN AT ANY MOMENT... SO, I'VE GOT TO FIND THEM FIRST!
THE LAST I SAW OF THEM, THEY WERE CAPTIVES, WITHIN THE CITY OF TYRANNUS!
IF ONLY I CAN REACH THEM BEFORE THEY'RE ENGULFED BY THE EVER SPREADING BATTLE
IT WOULD BE EASY FOR THE HUL ...HE'D HUFF AND PUFF AND SMAS THE WALLS DOWN

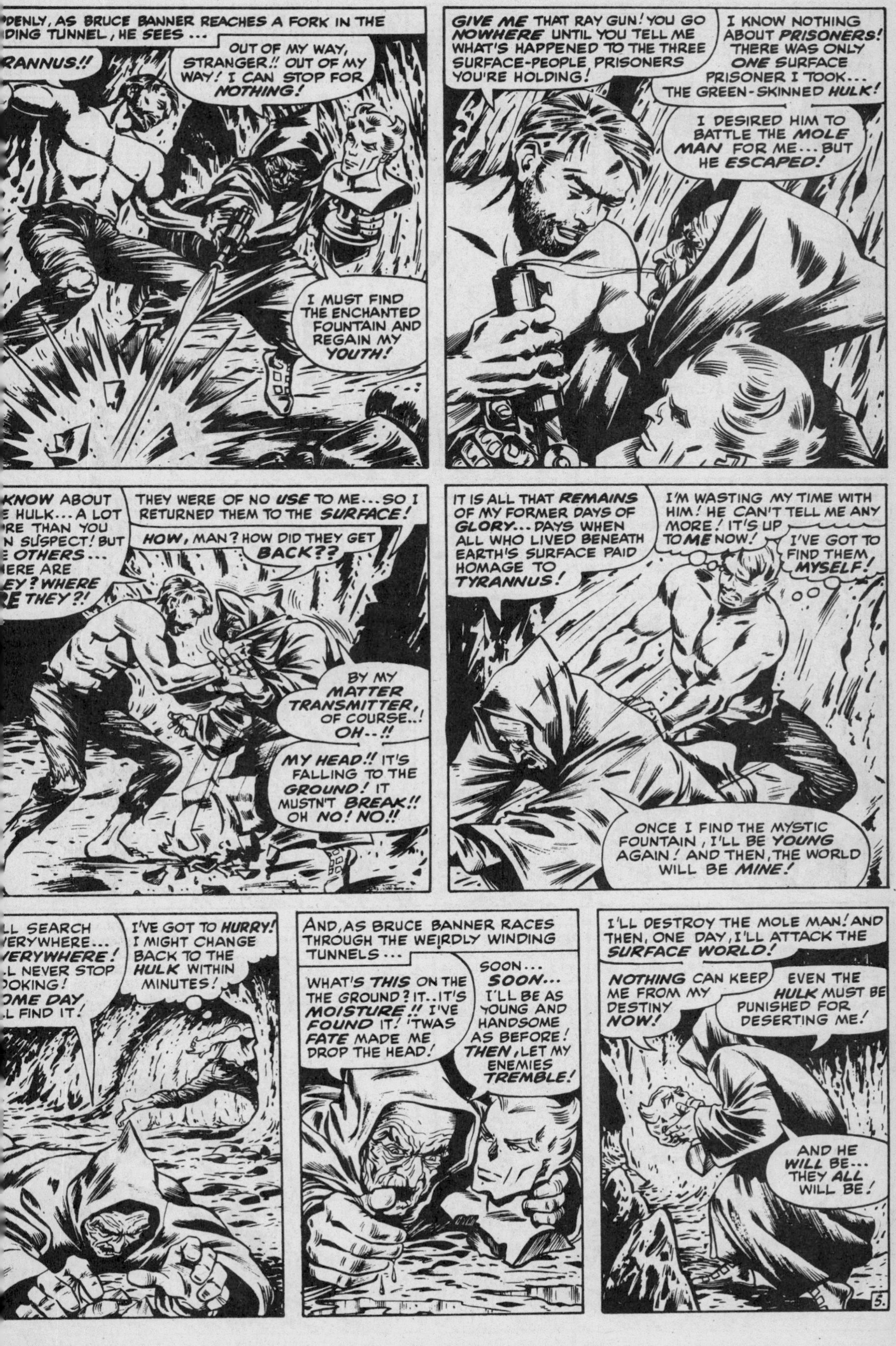

DDENLY, AS BRUCE BANNER REACHES A FORK IN THE
DING TUNNEL, HE SEES...
RANNUS!!
OUT OF MY WAY, STRANGER!! OUT OF MY WAY! I CAN STOP FOR NOTHING!
I MUST FIND THE ENCHANTED FOUNTAIN AND REGAIN MY YOUTH!
GIVE ME THAT RAY GUN! YOU GO NOWHERE UNTIL YOU TELL ME WHAT'S HAPPENED TO THE THREE SURFACE-PEOPLE PRISONERS YOU'RE HOLDING!
I KNOW NOTHING ABOUT PRISONERS! THERE WAS ONLY ONE SURFACE PRISONER I TOOK... THE GREEN-SKINNED HULK!
I DESIRED HIM TO BATTLE THE MOLE MAN FOR ME... BUT HE ESCAPED!
KNOW ABOUT
HULK... A LOT
RE THAN YOU
N SUSPECT! BUT
OTHERS...
ERE ARE
EY? WHERE
E THEY?!
THEY WERE OF NO USE TO ME... SO I RETURNED THEM TO THE SURFACE!
HOW, MAN? HOW DID THEY GET BACK??
BY MY MATTER TRANSMITTER, OF COURSE..! OH--!!
MY HEAD!! IT'S FALLING TO THE GROUND! IT MUSTN'T BREAK!! OH NO! NO!!
IT IS ALL THAT REMAINS OF MY FORMER DAYS OF GLORY... DAYS WHEN ALL WHO LIVED BENEATH EARTH'S SURFACE PAID HOMAGE TO TYRANNUS!
I'M WASTING MY TIME WITH HIM! HE CAN'T TELL ME ANY MORE! IT'S UP TO ME NOW!
I'VE GOT TO FIND THEM MYSELF!
ONCE I FIND THE MYSTIC FOUNTAIN, I'LL BE YOUNG AGAIN! AND THEN, THE WORLD WILL BE MINE!
LL SEARCH
ERYWHERE...
ERYWHERE!
L NEVER STOP
OKING!
OME DAY
L FIND IT!
I'VE GOT TO HURRY! I MIGHT CHANGE BACK TO THE HULK WITHIN MINUTES!
AND, AS BRUCE BANNER RACES THROUGH THE WEIRDLY WINDING TUNNELS...
WHAT'S THIS ON THE THE GROUND? IT.. IT'S MOISTURE!! I'VE FOUND IT! 'TWAS FATE MADE ME DROP THE HEAD!
SOON... SOON... I'LL BE AS YOUNG AND HANDSOME AS BEFORE! THEN, LET MY ENEMIES TREMBLE!
I'LL DESTROY THE MOLE MAN! AND THEN, ONE DAY, I'LL ATTACK THE SURFACE WORLD!
NOTHING CAN KEEP ME FROM MY DESTINY NOW!
EVEN THE HULK MUST BE PUNISHED FOR DESERTING ME!
AND HE WILL BE... THEY ALL WILL BE!
5.

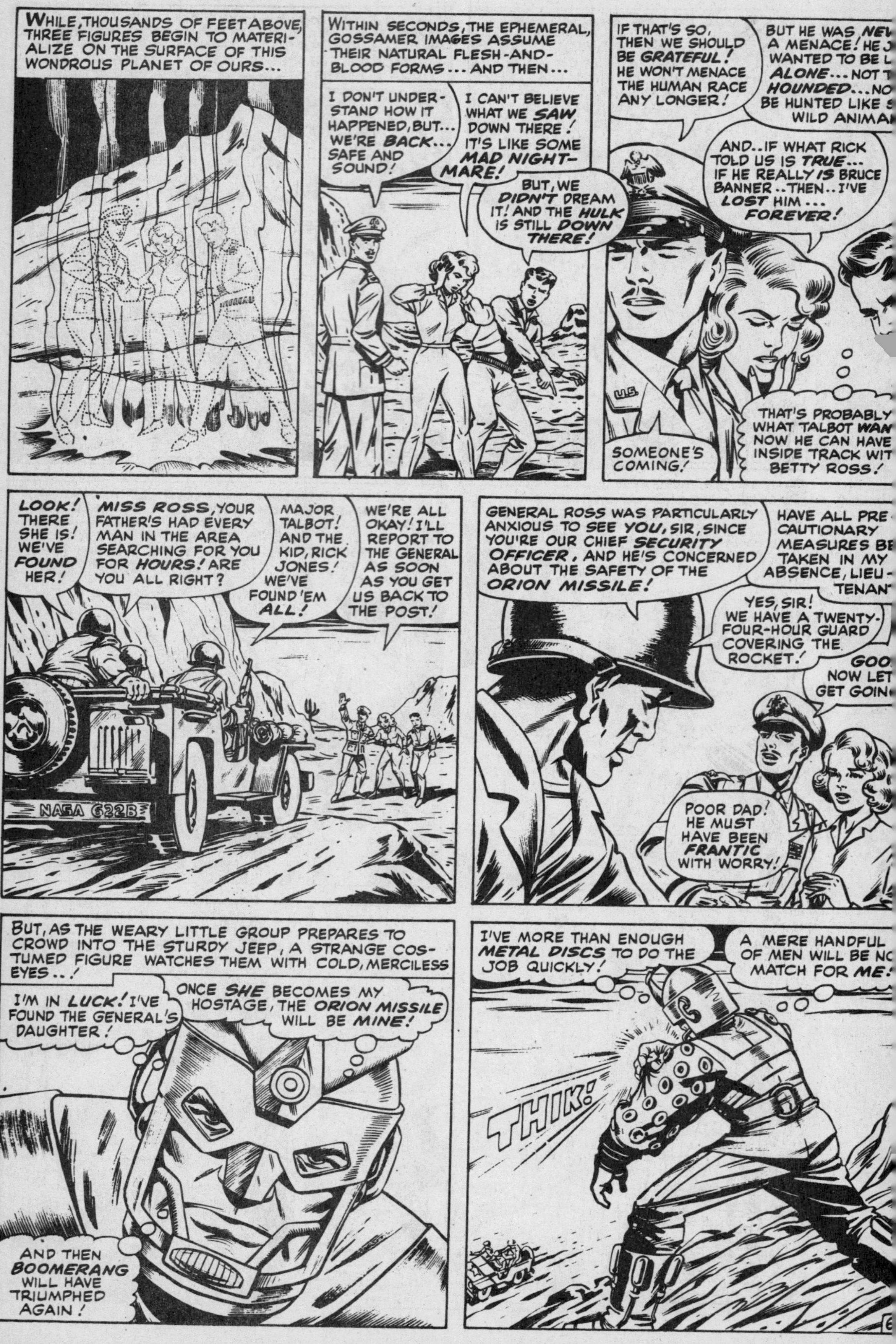
WHILE, THOUSANDS OF FEET ABOVE, THREE FIGURES BEGIN TO MATERIALIZE ON THE SURFACE OF THIS WONDROUS PLANET OF OURS...
WITHIN SECONDS, THE EPHEMERAL, GOSSAMER IMAGES ASSUME THEIR NATURAL FLESH-AND-BLOOD FORMS ... AND THEN ...
I DON'T UNDERSTAND HOW IT HAPPENED, BUT... WE'RE BACK... SAFE AND SOUND!
I CAN'T BELIEVE WHAT WE SAW DOWN THERE! IT'S LIKE SOME MAD NIGHTMARE!
BUT, WE DIDN'T DREAM IT! AND THE HULK IS STILL DOWN THERE!
IF THAT'S SO, THEN WE SHOULD BE GRATEFUL! HE WON'T MENACE THE HUMAN RACE ANY LONGER!
BUT HE WAS NEV A MENACE! HE J WANTED TO BE L ALONE... NOT T HOUNDED... NO BE HUNTED LIKE WILD ANIMA
AND.. IF WHAT RICK TOLD US IS TRUE... IF HE REALLY IS BRUCE BANNER.. THEN.. I'VE LOST HIM... FOREVER!
U.S.
THAT'S PROBABLY WHAT TALBOT WAN NOW HE CAN HAVE INSIDE TRACK WIT BETTY ROSS!
SOMEONE'S COMING!
LOOK! THERE SHE IS! WE'VE FOUND HER!
MISS ROSS, YOUR FATHER'S HAD EVERY MAN IN THE AREA SEARCHING FOR YOU FOR HOURS! ARE YOU ALL RIGHT?
MAJOR TALBOT! AND THE KID, RICK JONES! WE'VE FOUND 'EM ALL!
WE'RE ALL OKAY! I'LL REPORT TO THE GENERAL AS SOON AS YOU GET US BACK TO THE POST!
NASA 622B
GENERAL ROSS WAS PARTICULARLY ANXIOUS TO SEE YOU, SIR, SINCE YOU'RE OUR CHIEF SECURITY OFFICER, AND HE'S CONCERNED ABOUT THE SAFETY OF THE ORION MISSILE!
HAVE ALL PRE CAUTIONARY MEASURES BE TAKEN IN MY ABSENCE, LIEU-TENANT
YES, SIR! WE HAVE A TWENTY-FOUR-HOUR GUARD COVERING THE ROCKET!
GOO NOW LET GET GOIN
POOR DAD! HE MUST HAVE BEEN FRANTIC WITH WORRY!
BUT, AS THE WEARY LITTLE GROUP PREPARES TO CROWD INTO THE STURDY JEEP, A STRANGE COSTUMED FIGURE WATCHES THEM WITH COLD, MERCILESS EYES..!
I'M IN LUCK! I'VE FOUND THE GENERAL'S DAUGHTER!
ONCE SHE BECOMES MY HOSTAGE, THE ORION MISSILE WILL BE MINE!
AND THEN BOOMERANG WILL HAVE TRIUMPHED AGAIN!
I'VE MORE THAN ENOUGH METAL DISCS TO DO THE JOB QUICKLY!
A MERE HANDFUL OF MEN WILL BE NC MATCH FOR ME!
THIK!
6

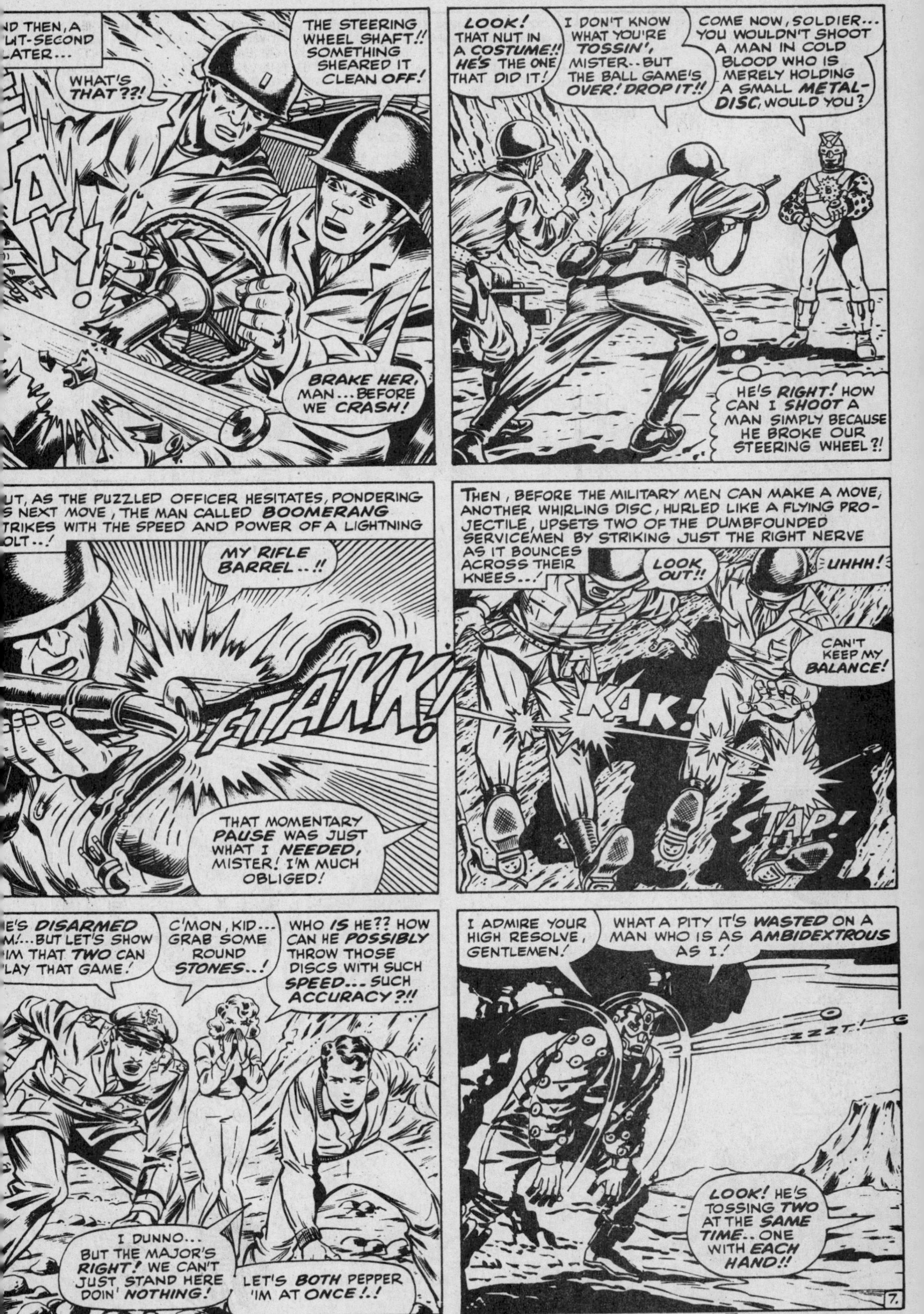
ND THEN, A
LIT-SECOND
LATER...
WHAT'S THAT??!
THE STEERING WHEEL SHAFT!! SOMETHING SHEARED IT CLEAN OFF!
BRAKE HER, MAN... BEFORE WE CRASH!
LOOK! THAT NUT IN A COSTUME!! HE'S THE ONE THAT DID IT!
I DON'T KNOW WHAT YOU'RE TOSSIN', MISTER--BUT THE BALL GAME'S OVER! DROP IT!!
COME NOW, SOLDIER... YOU WOULDN'T SHOOT A MAN IN COLD BLOOD WHO IS MERELY HOLDING A SMALL METAL-DISC, WOULD YOU?
HE'S RIGHT! HOW CAN I SHOOT A MAN SIMPLY BECAUSE HE BROKE OUR STEERING WHEEL?!
UT, AS THE PUZZLED OFFICER HESITATES, PONDERING S NEXT MOVE, THE MAN CALLED BOOMERANG TRIKES WITH THE SPEED AND POWER OF A LIGHTNING OLT..!
MY RIFLE BARREL..!!
FTANKK!
THAT MOMENTARY PAUSE WAS JUST WHAT I NEEDED, MISTER! I'M MUCH OBLIGED!
THEN, BEFORE THE MILITARY MEN CAN MAKE A MOVE, ANOTHER WHIRLING DISC, HURLED LIKE A FLYING PROJECTILE, UPSETS TWO OF THE DUMBFOUNDED SERVICEMEN BY STRIKING JUST THE RIGHT NERVE AS IT BOUNCES ACROSS THEIR KNEES...!
LOOK OUT!!
UHHH!
CAN'T KEEP MY BALANCE!
KAK!
STAP!
E'S DISARMED M!...BUT LET'S SHOW IM THAT TWO CAN LAY THAT GAME!
C'MON, KID... GRAB SOME ROUND STONES..!
WHO IS HE?? HOW CAN HE POSSIBLY THROW THOSE DISCS WITH SUCH SPEED... SUCH ACCURACY?!!
I DUNNO... BUT THE MAJOR'S RIGHT! WE CAN'T JUST STAND HERE DOIN' NOTHING!
LET'S BOTH PEPPER 'IM AT ONCE!.!
I ADMIRE YOUR HIGH RESOLVE, GENTLEMEN!
WHAT A PITY IT'S WASTED ON A MAN WHO IS AS AMBIDEXTROUS AS I!
ZZZT!
LOOK! HE'S TOSSING TWO AT THE SAME TIME.. ONE WITH EACH HAND!!
7.

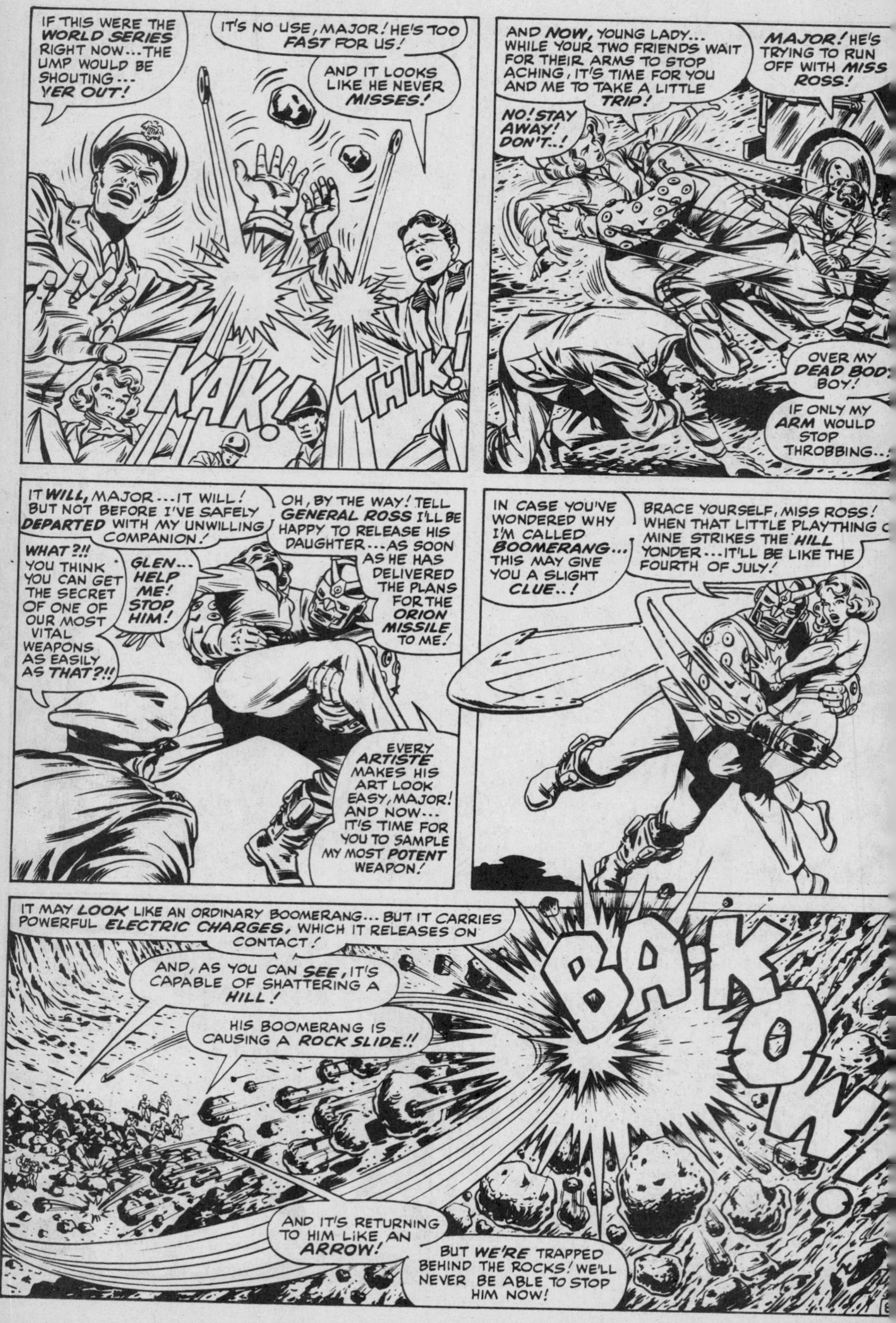
IF THIS WERE THE WORLD SERIES RIGHT NOW... THE UMP WOULD BE SHOUTING... YER OUT!
IT'S NO USE, MAJOR! HE'S TOO FAST FOR US!
AND IT LOOKS LIKE HE NEVER MISSES!
KAK!
THIK!
AND NOW, YOUNG LADY... WHILE YOUR TWO FRIENDS WAIT FOR THEIR ARMS TO STOP ACHING, IT'S TIME FOR YOU AND ME TO TAKE A LITTLE TRIP!
MAJOR! HE'S TRYING TO RUN OFF WITH MISS ROSS!
NO! STAY AWAY! DON'T..!
OVER MY DEAD BODY BOY!
IF ONLY MY ARM WOULD STOP THROBBING...!
IT WILL, MAJOR... IT WILL! BUT NOT BEFORE I'VE SAFELY DEPARTED WITH MY UNWILLING COMPANION!
OH, BY THE WAY! TELL GENERAL ROSS I'LL BE HAPPY TO RELEASE HIS DAUGHTER... AS SOON AS HE HAS DELIVERED THE PLANS FOR THE ORION MISSILE TO ME!
WHAT?!! YOU THINK YOU CAN GET THE SECRET OF ONE OF OUR MOST VITAL WEAPONS AS EASILY AS THAT?!!
GLEN... HELP ME! STOP HIM!
EVERY ARTISTE MAKES HIS ART LOOK EASY, MAJOR! AND NOW... IT'S TIME FOR YOU TO SAMPLE MY MOST POTENT WEAPON!
IN CASE YOU'VE WONDERED WHY I'M CALLED BOOMERANG... THIS MAY GIVE YOU A SLIGHT CLUE..!
BRACE YOURSELF, MISS ROSS! WHEN THAT LITTLE PLAYTHING OF MINE STRIKES THE HILL YONDER... IT'LL BE LIKE THE FOURTH OF JULY!
IT MAY LOOK LIKE AN ORDINARY BOOMERANG... BUT IT CARRIES POWERFUL ELECTRIC CHARGES, WHICH IT RELEASES ON CONTACT!
AND, AS YOU CAN SEE, IT'S CAPABLE OF SHATTERING A HILL!
HIS BOOMERANG IS CAUSING A ROCK SLIDE!!
BA-KROOW!
AND IT'S RETURNING TO HIM LIKE AN ARROW!
BUT WE'RE TRAPPED BEHIND THE ROCKS! WE'LL NEVER BE ABLE TO STOP HIM NOW!

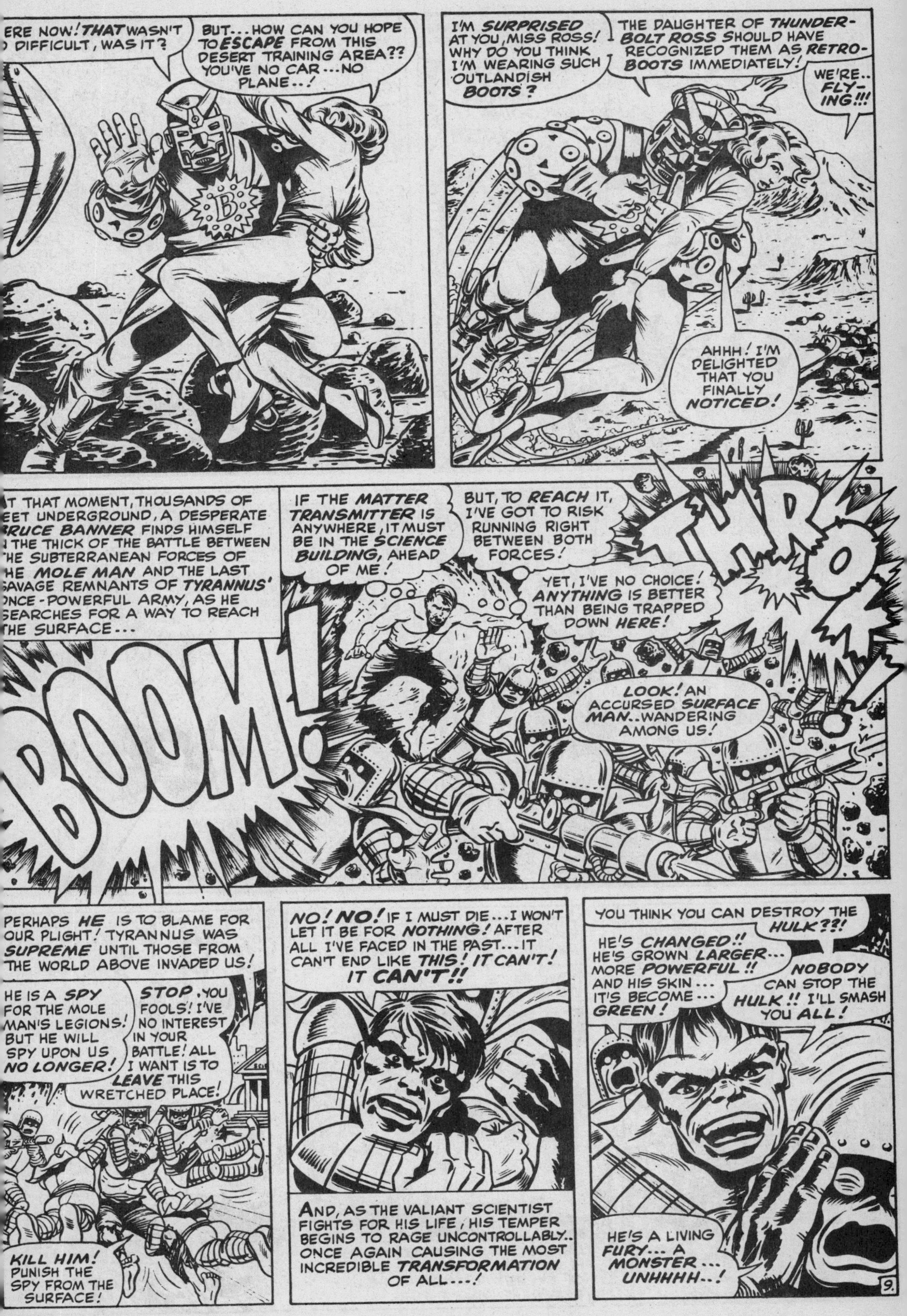
ERE NOW! THAT WASN'T
DIFFICULT, WAS IT?
BUT... HOW CAN YOU HOPE TO ESCAPE FROM THIS DESERT TRAINING AREA?? YOU'VE NO CAR... NO PLANE..!
I'M SURPRISED AT YOU, MISS ROSS! WHY DO YOU THINK I'M WEARING SUCH OUTLANDISH BOOTS?
THE DAUGHTER OF THUNDER-BOLT ROSS SHOULD HAVE RECOGNIZED THEM AS RETRO-BOOTS IMMEDIATELY!
WE'RE.. FLY-ING!!!
AHHH! I'M DELIGHTED THAT YOU FINALLY NOTICED!
AT THAT MOMENT, THOUSANDS OF FEET UNDERGROUND, A DESPERATE BRUCE BANNER FINDS HIMSELF IN THE THICK OF THE BATTLE BETWEEN THE SUBTERRANEAN FORCES OF THE MOLE MAN AND THE LAST SAVAGE REMNANTS OF TYRANNUS' ONCE-POWERFUL ARMY, AS HE SEARCHES FOR A WAY TO REACH THE SURFACE...
IF THE MATTER TRANSMITTER IS ANYWHERE, IT MUST BE IN THE SCIENCE BUILDING, AHEAD OF ME!
BUT, TO REACH IT, I'VE GOT TO RISK RUNNING RIGHT BETWEEN BOTH FORCES!
YET, I'VE NO CHOICE! ANYTHING IS BETTER THAN BEING TRAPPED DOWN HERE!
THRO!
BOOM!
LOOK! AN ACCURSED SURFACE MAN..WANDERING AMONG US!
PERHAPS HE IS TO BLAME FOR OUR PLIGHT! TYRANNUS WAS SUPREME UNTIL THOSE FROM THE WORLD ABOVE INVADED US!
HE IS A SPY FOR THE MOLE MAN'S LEGIONS! BUT HE WILL SPY UPON US NO LONGER!
STOP, YOU FOOLS! I'VE NO INTEREST IN YOUR BATTLE! ALL I WANT IS TO LEAVE THIS WRETCHED PLACE!
KILL HIM! PUNISH THE SPY FROM THE SURFACE!
NO! NO! IF I MUST DIE... I WON'T LET IT BE FOR NOTHING! AFTER ALL I'VE FACED IN THE PAST... IT CAN'T END LIKE THIS! IT CAN'T! IT CAN'T!!
AND, AS THE VALIANT SCIENTIST FIGHTS FOR HIS LIFE, HIS TEMPER BEGINS TO RAGE UNCONTROLLABLY.. ONCE AGAIN CAUSING THE MOST INCREDIBLE TRANSFORMATION OF ALL...!
YOU THINK YOU CAN DESTROY THE HULK??!
HE'S CHANGED!! HE'S GROWN LARGER... MORE POWERFUL!! AND HIS SKIN... IT'S BECOME... GREEN!
NOBODY CAN STOP THE HULK!! I'LL SMASH YOU ALL!
HE'S A LIVING FURY... A MONSTER... UNHHHH..!
9.

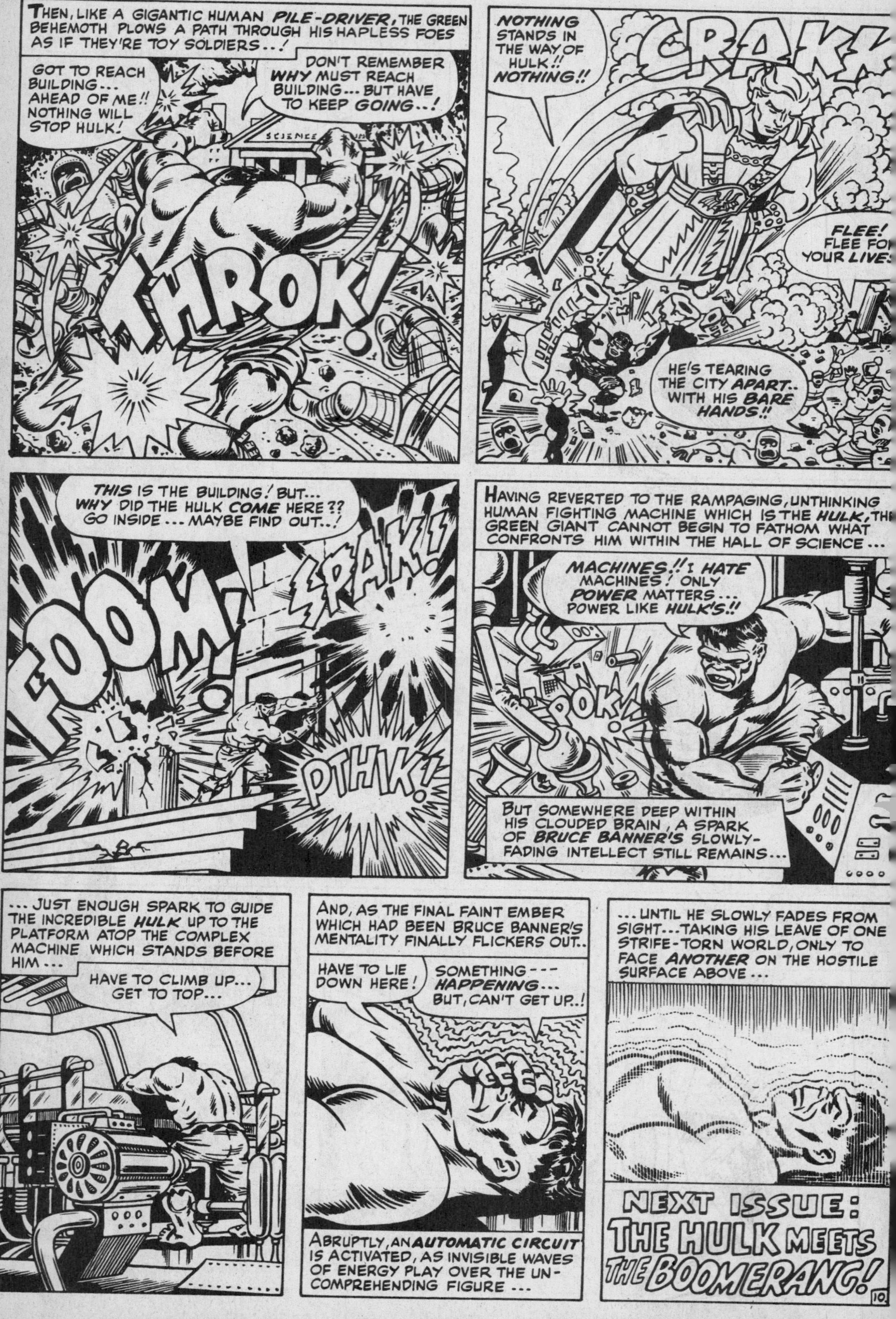

THEN, LIKE A GIGANTIC HUMAN PILE-DRIVER, THE GREEN BEHEMOTH PLOWS A PATH THROUGH HIS HAPLESS FOES AS IF THEY'RE TOY SOLDIERS..!
GOT TO REACH BUILDING... AHEAD OF ME!! NOTHING WILL STOP HULK!
DON'T REMEMBER WHY MUST REACH BUILDING... BUT HAVE TO KEEP GOING..!
SCIENCE
THROK!
NOTHING STANDS IN THE WAY OF HULK!! NOTHING!!
CRAKK
FLEE! FLEE FO YOUR LIVE
HE'S TEARING THE CITY APART.. WITH HIS BARE HANDS!!
THIS IS THE BUILDING! BUT... WHY DID THE HULK COME HERE?? GO INSIDE... MAYBE FIND OUT..!
FOOM!
SPAK!
PTHK!
HAVING REVERTED TO THE RAMPAGING, UNTHINKING HUMAN FIGHTING MACHINE WHICH IS THE HULK, TH GREEN GIANT CANNOT BEGIN TO FATHOM WHAT CONFRONTS HIM WITHIN THE HALL OF SCIENCE...
MACHINES!! I HATE MACHINES! ONLY POWER MATTERS... POWER LIKE HULK'S!!
POK
BUT SOMEWHERE DEEP WITHIN HIS CLOUDED BRAIN, A SPARK OF BRUCE BANNER'S SLOWLY-FADING INTELLECT STILL REMAINS...
...JUST ENOUGH SPARK TO GUIDE THE INCREDIBLE HULK UP TO THE PLATFORM ATOP THE COMPLEX MACHINE WHICH STANDS BEFORE HIM...
HAVE TO CLIMB UP... GET TO TOP...
AND, AS THE FINAL FAINT EMBER WHICH HAD BEEN BRUCE BANNER'S MENTALITY FINALLY FLICKERS OUT..
HAVE TO LIE DOWN HERE!
SOMETHING--- HAPPENING... BUT, CAN'T GET UP..!
ABRUPTLY, AN AUTOMATIC CIRCUIT IS ACTIVATED, AS INVISIBLE WAVES OF ENERGY PLAY OVER THE UN-COMPREHENDING FIGURE...
...UNTIL HE SLOWLY FADES FROM SIGHT...TAKING HIS LEAVE OF ONE STRIFE-TORN WORLD, ONLY TO FACE ANOTHER ON THE HOSTILE SURFACE ABOVE...
NEXT ISSUE: THE HULK MEETS THE BOOMERANG!
10

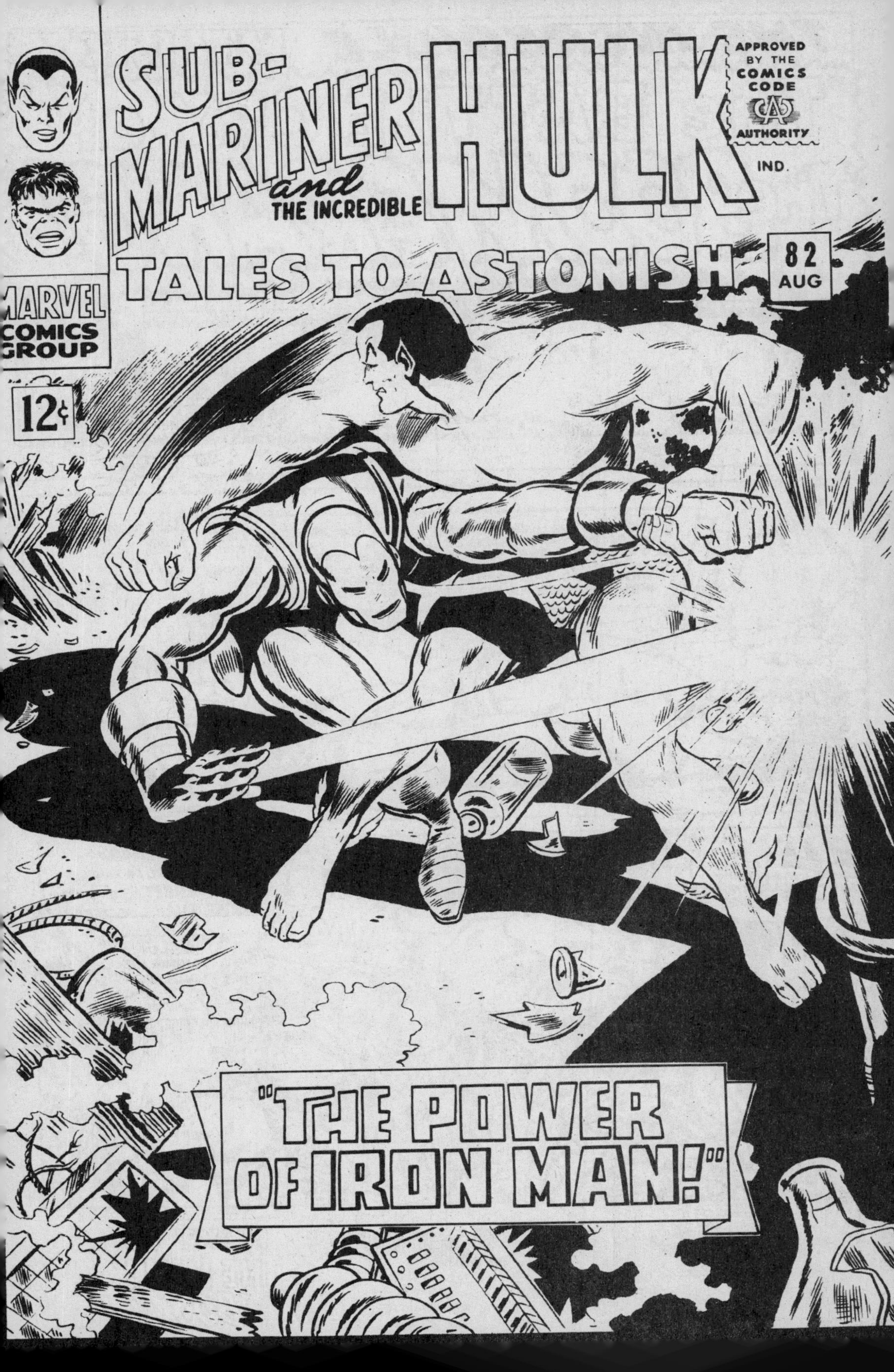
SUB-MARINER
and THE INCREDIBLE
HULK
APPROVED BY THE COMICS CODE CA AUTHORITY
IND.
TALES TO ASTONISH
82
AUG
MARVEL COMICS GROUP
12¢
"THE POWER OF IRON MAN!"

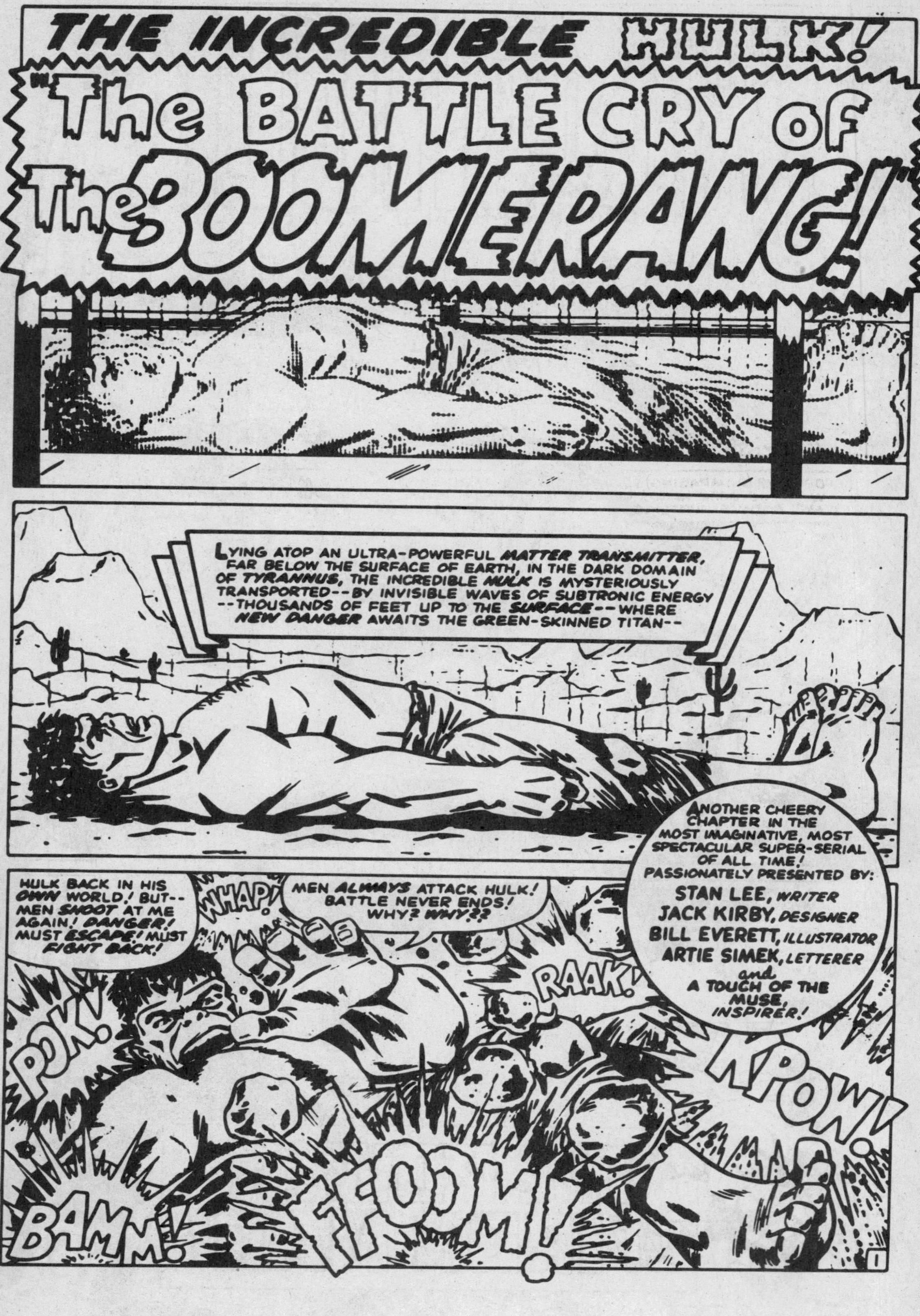
THE INCREDIBLE HULK!
"The BATTLE CRY of The BOOMERANG!"
LYING ATOP AN ULTRA-POWERFUL MATTER TRANSMITTER, FAR BELOW THE SURFACE OF EARTH, IN THE DARK DOMAIN OF TYRANNUS, THE INCREDIBLE HULK IS MYSTERIOUSLY TRANSPORTED--BY INVISIBLE WAVES OF SUBTRONIC ENERGY --THOUSANDS OF FEET UP TO THE SURFACE--WHERE NEW DANGER AWAITS THE GREEN-SKINNED TITAN--
ANOTHER CHEERY CHAPTER IN THE MOST IMAGINATIVE, MOST SPECTACULAR SUPER-SERIAL OF ALL TIME! PASSIONATELY PRESENTED BY:
STAN LEE, WRITER
JACK KIRBY, DESIGNER
BILL EVERETT, ILLUSTRATOR
ARTIE SIMEK, LETTERER
and A TOUCH OF THE MUSE, INSPIRER!
HULK BACK IN HIS OWN WORLD! BUT--MEN SHOOT AT ME AGAIN! DANGER! MUST ESCAPE! MUST FIGHT BACK!
WHAP!
MEN ALWAYS ATTACK HULK! BATTLE NEVER ENDS! WHY? WHY??
RAAK!
POK!
KPOW!
BAMM!
FFOOM!

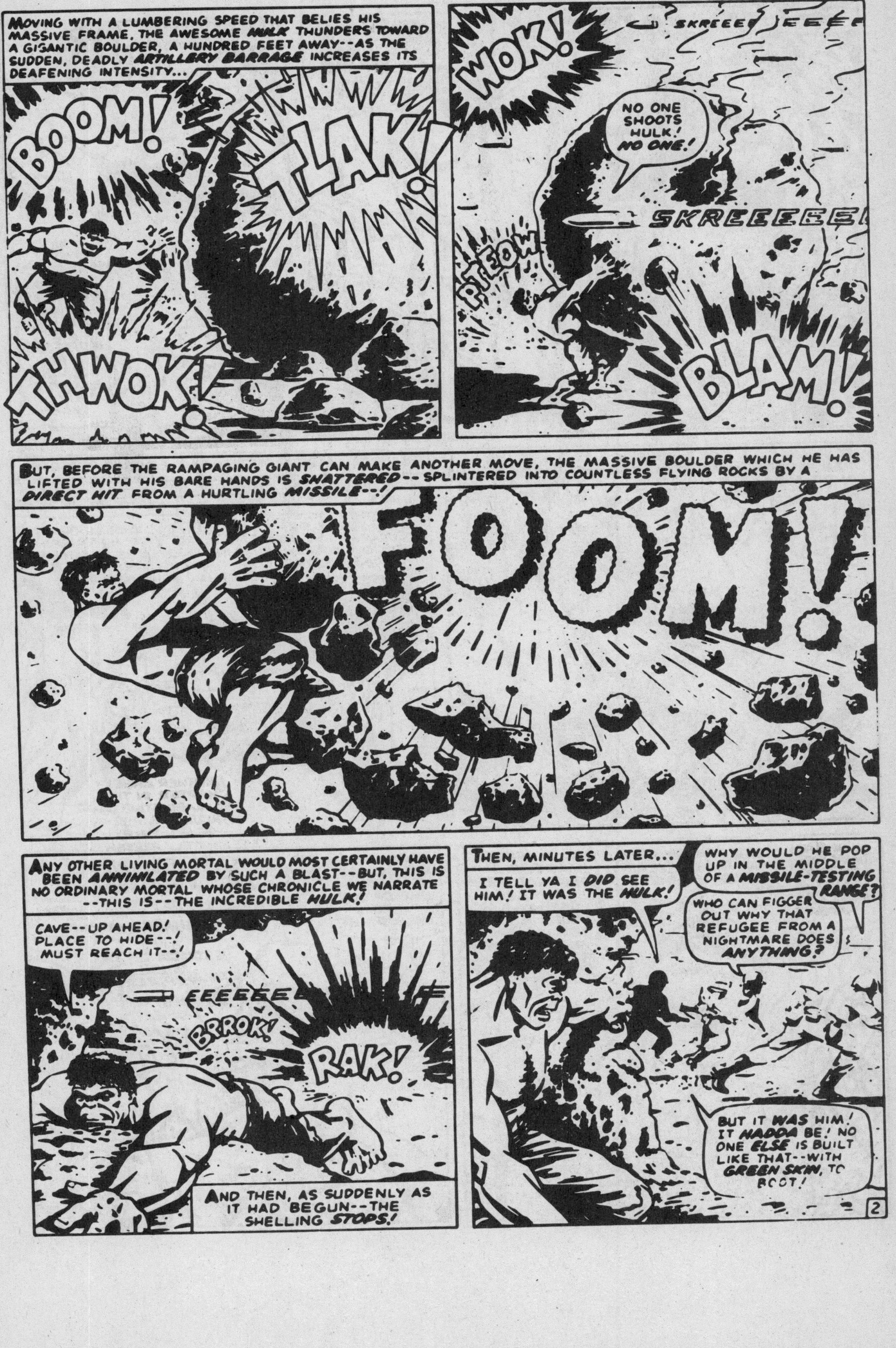
MOVING WITH A LUMBERING SPEED THAT BELIES HIS MASSIVE FRAME, THE AWESOME HULK THUNDERS TOWARD A GIGANTIC BOULDER, A HUNDRED FEET AWAY--AS THE SUDDEN, DEADLY ARTILLERY BARRAGE INCREASES ITS DEAFENING INTENSITY...
BOOM!
TLAK!
THWOK!
WOK!
SKREEEE
NO ONE SHOOTS HULK! NO ONE!
SKREEEEEE!
PTEOW
BLAM!
BUT, BEFORE THE RAMPAGING GIANT CAN MAKE ANOTHER MOVE, THE MASSIVE BOULDER WHICH HE HAS LIFTED WITH HIS BARE HANDS IS SHATTERED--SPLINTERED INTO COUNTLESS FLYING ROCKS BY A DIRECT HIT FROM A HURTLING MISSILE--!
FOOM!
ANY OTHER LIVING MORTAL WOULD MOST CERTAINLY HAVE BEEN ANNIHILATED BY SUCH A BLAST--BUT, THIS IS NO ORDINARY MORTAL WHOSE CHRONICLE WE NARRATE --THIS IS--THE INCREDIBLE HULK!
CAVE--UP AHEAD! PLACE TO HIDE--! MUST REACH IT--!
EEEEEE
BRROK!
RAK!
AND THEN, AS SUDDENLY AS IT HAD BEGUN--THE SHELLING STOPS!
THEN, MINUTES LATER...
I TELL YA I DID SEE HIM! IT WAS THE HULK!
WHY WOULD HE POP UP IN THE MIDDLE OF A MISSILE-TESTING RANGE?
WHO CAN FIGGER OUT WHY THAT REFUGEE FROM A NIGHTMARE DOES ANYTHING?
BUT IT WAS HIM! IT HADDA BE! NO ONE ELSE IS BUILT LIKE THAT--WITH GREEN SKIN, TO BOOT!
2

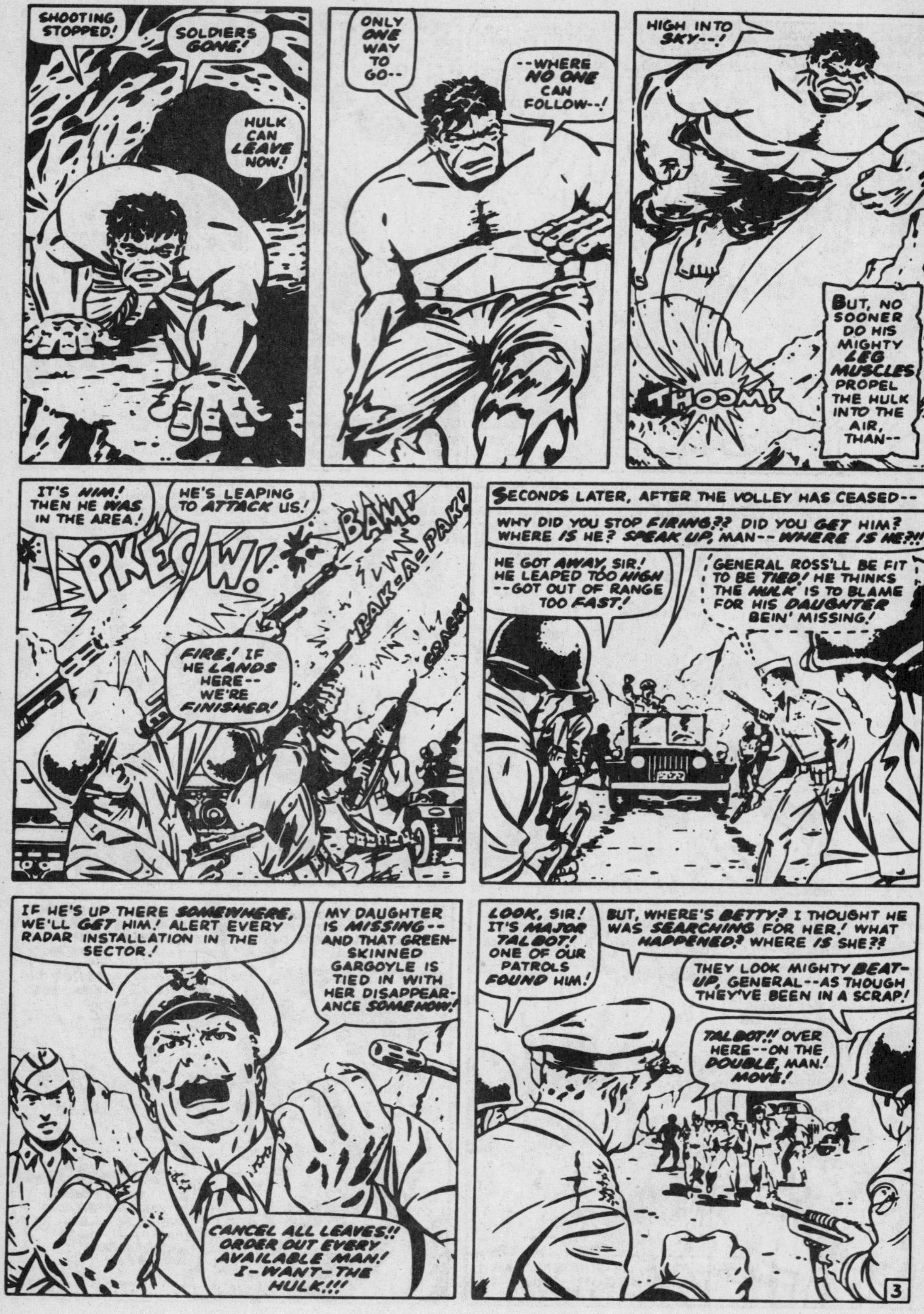
SHOOTING STOPPED!
SOLDIERS GONE!
HULK CAN LEAVE NOW!
ONLY ONE WAY TO GO--
--WHERE NO ONE CAN FOLLOW--!
HIGH INTO SKY--!
BUT, NO SOONER DO HIS MIGHTY LEG MUSCLES PROPEL THE HULK INTO THE AIR, THAN--
THOOM!
IT'S HIM! THEN HE WAS IN THE AREA!
HE'S LEAPING TO ATTACK US!
PKEOW!
BAM!
PAK-A-PAK!
PAK-A-PAK!
CRACK!
FIRE! IF HE LANDS HERE--WE'RE FINISHED!
SECONDS LATER, AFTER THE VOLLEY HAS CEASED--
WHY DID YOU STOP FIRING?? DID YOU GET HIM? WHERE IS HE? SPEAK UP, MAN--WHERE IS HE?!!
HE GOT AWAY, SIR! HE LEAPED TOO HIGH --GOT OUT OF RANGE TOO FAST!
GENERAL ROSS'LL BE FIT TO BE TIED! HE THINKS THE HULK IS TO BLAME FOR HIS DAUGHTER BEIN' MISSING!
IF HE'S UP THERE SOMEWHERE, WE'LL GET HIM! ALERT EVERY RADAR INSTALLATION IN THE SECTOR!
MY DAUGHTER IS MISSING--AND THAT GREEN-SKINNED GARGOYLE IS TIED IN WITH HER DISAPPEARANCE SOMEHOW!
CANCEL ALL LEAVES!! ORDER OUT EVERY AVAILABLE MAN! I-WANT-THE HULK!!!
LOOK, SIR! IT'S MAJOR TALBOT! ONE OF OUR PATROLS FOUND HIM!
BUT, WHERE'S BETTY? I THOUGHT HE WAS SEARCHING FOR HER! WHAT HAPPENED? WHERE IS SHE??
THEY LOOK MIGHTY BEAT-UP, GENERAL--AS THOUGH THEY'VE BEEN IN A SCRAP!
TALBOT!! OVER HERE--ON THE DOUBLE, MAN! MOVE!
3

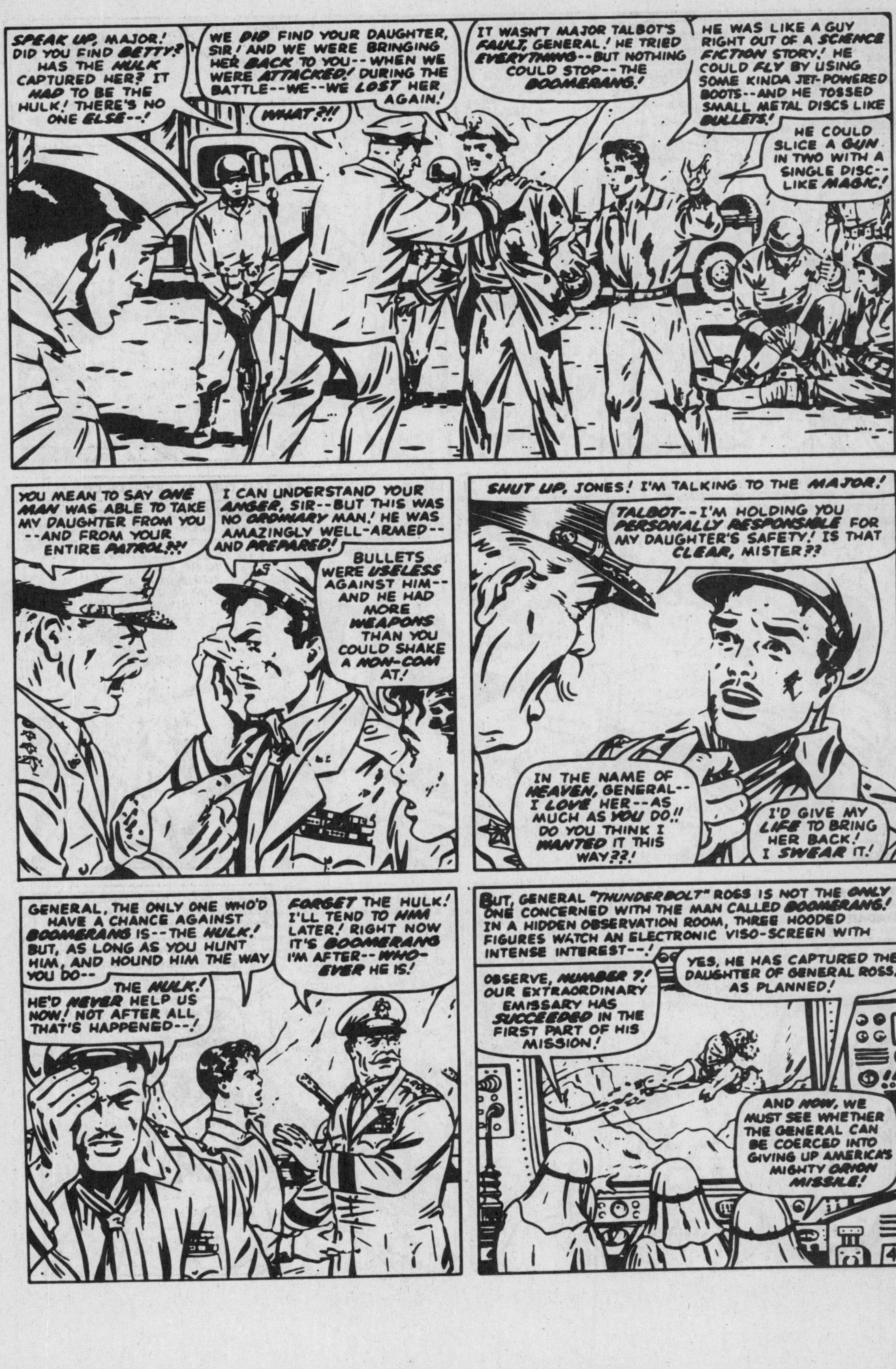

SPEAK UP, MAJOR! DID YOU FIND BETTY? HAS THE HULK CAPTURED HER? IT HAD TO BE THE HULK! THERE'S NO ONE ELSE--!
WE DID FIND YOUR DAUGHTER, SIR! AND WE WERE BRINGING HER BACK TO YOU--WHEN WE WERE ATTACKED! DURING THE BATTLE--WE--WE LOST HER AGAIN!
WHAT?!!
IT WASN'T MAJOR TALBOT'S FAULT, GENERAL! HE TRIED EVERYTHING--BUT NOTHING COULD STOP--THE BOOMERANG!
HE WAS LIKE A GUY RIGHT OUT OF A SCIENCE FICTION STORY! HE COULD FLY BY USING SOME KINDA JET-POWERED BOOTS--AND HE TOSSED SMALL METAL DISCS LIKE BULLETS!
HE COULD SLICE A GUN IN TWO WITH A SINGLE DISC--LIKE MAGIC!
YOU MEAN TO SAY ONE MAN WAS ABLE TO TAKE MY DAUGHTER FROM YOU --AND FROM YOUR ENTIRE PATROL??!
I CAN UNDERSTAND YOUR ANGER, SIR--BUT THIS WAS NO ORDINARY MAN! HE WAS AMAZINGLY WELL-ARMED--AND PREPARED!
BULLETS WERE USELESS AGAINST HIM--AND HE HAD MORE WEAPONS THAN YOU COULD SHAKE A NON-COM AT!
SHUT UP, JONES! I'M TALKING TO THE MAJOR!
TALBOT--I'M HOLDING YOU PERSONALLY RESPONSIBLE FOR MY DAUGHTER'S SAFETY! IS THAT CLEAR, MISTER??
IN THE NAME OF HEAVEN, GENERAL--I LOVE HER--AS MUCH AS YOU DO!! DO YOU THINK I WANTED IT THIS WAY??!
I'D GIVE MY LIFE TO BRING HER BACK! I SWEAR IT!
GENERAL, THE ONLY ONE WHO'D HAVE A CHANCE AGAINST BOOMERANG IS--THE HULK! BUT, AS LONG AS YOU HUNT HIM, AND HOUND HIM THE WAY YOU DO--
THE HULK! HE'D NEVER HELP US NOW! NOT AFTER ALL THAT'S HAPPENED--!
FORGET THE HULK! I'LL TEND TO HIM LATER! RIGHT NOW IT'S BOOMERANG I'M AFTER--WHO-EVER HE IS!
BUT, GENERAL "THUNDERBOLT" ROSS IS NOT THE ONLY ONE CONCERNED WITH THE MAN CALLED BOOMERANG! IN A HIDDEN OBSERVATION ROOM, THREE HOODED FIGURES WATCH AN ELECTRONIC VISO-SCREEN WITH INTENSE INTEREST--!
OBSERVE, NUMBER 7! OUR EXTRAORDINARY EMISSARY HAS SUCCEEDED IN THE FIRST PART OF HIS MISSION!
YES, HE HAS CAPTURED THE DAUGHTER OF GENERAL ROSS, AS PLANNED!
AND NOW, WE MUST SEE WHETHER THE GENERAL CAN BE COERCED INTO GIVING UP AMERICA'S MIGHTY ORION MISSILE!

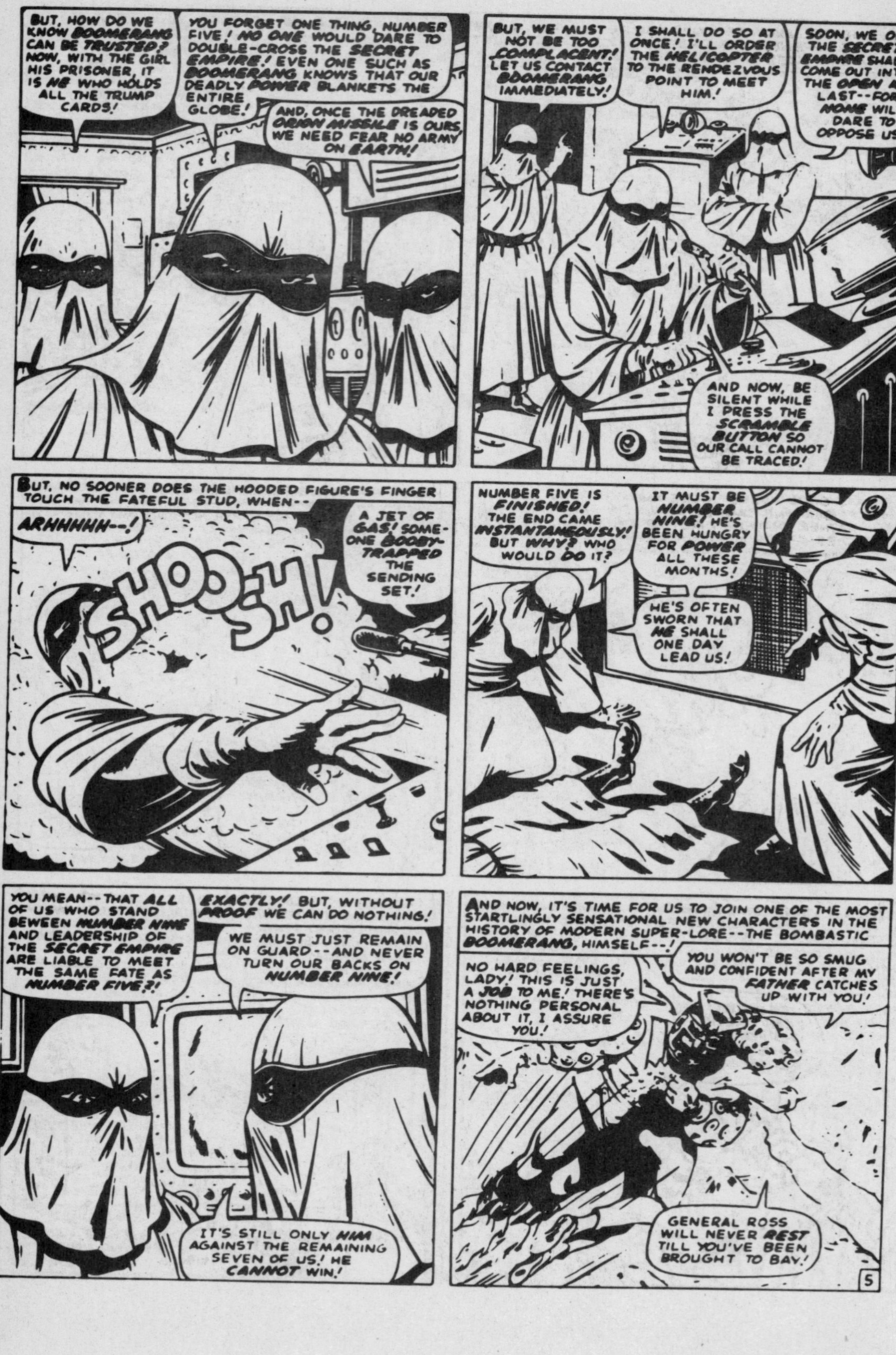
BUT, HOW DO WE KNOW BOOMERANG CAN BE TRUSTED? NOW, WITH THE GIRL HIS PRISONER, IT IS HE WHO HOLDS ALL THE TRUMP CARDS!
YOU FORGET ONE THING, NUMBER FIVE! NO ONE WOULD DARE TO DOUBLE-CROSS THE SECRET EMPIRE! EVEN ONE SUCH AS BOOMERANG KNOWS THAT OUR DEADLY POWER BLANKETS THE ENTIRE GLOBE!
AND, ONCE THE DREADED ORION MISSILE IS OURS, WE NEED FEAR NO ARMY ON EARTH!
BUT, WE MUST NOT BE TOO COMPLACENT! LET US CONTACT BOOMERANG IMMEDIATELY!
I SHALL DO SO AT ONCE! I'LL ORDER THE HELICOPTER TO THE RENDEZVOUS POINT TO MEET HIM!
SOON, WE OF THE SECRET EMPIRE SHALL COME OUT INTO THE OPEN AT LAST--FOR NONE WILL DARE TO OPPOSE US!
AND NOW, BE SILENT WHILE I PRESS THE SCRAMBLE BUTTON SO OUR CALL CANNOT BE TRACED!
BUT, NO SOONER DOES THE HOODED FIGURE'S FINGER TOUCH THE FATEFUL STUD, WHEN--
ARHHHHH--!
SHOO-SH!
A JET OF GAS! SOMEONE BOOBY-TRAPPED THE SENDING SET!
NUMBER FIVE IS FINISHED! THE END CAME INSTANTANEOUSLY! BUT WHY? WHO WOULD DO IT?
IT MUST BE NUMBER NINE! HE'S BEEN HUNGRY FOR POWER ALL THESE MONTHS!
HE'S OFTEN SWORN THAT HE SHALL ONE DAY LEAD US!
YOU MEAN--THAT ALL OF US WHO STAND BEWEEN NUMBER NINE AND LEADERSHIP OF THE SECRET EMPIRE ARE LIABLE TO MEET THE SAME FATE AS NUMBER FIVE?!
EXACTLY! BUT, WITHOUT PROOF WE CAN DO NOTHING!
WE MUST JUST REMAIN ON GUARD--AND NEVER TURN OUR BACKS ON NUMBER NINE!
IT'S STILL ONLY HIM AGAINST THE REMAINING SEVEN OF US! HE CANNOT WIN!
AND NOW, IT'S TIME FOR US TO JOIN ONE OF THE MOST STARTLINGLY SENSATIONAL NEW CHARACTERS IN THE HISTORY OF MODERN SUPER-LORE--THE BOMBASTIC BOOMERANG, HIMSELF--!
NO HARD FEELINGS, LADY! THIS IS JUST A JOB TO ME! THERE'S NOTHING PERSONAL ABOUT IT, I ASSURE YOU!
YOU WON'T BE SO SMUG AND CONFIDENT AFTER MY FATHER CATCHES UP WITH YOU!
GENERAL ROSS WILL NEVER REST TILL YOU'VE BEEN BROUGHT TO BAY!
5

Panel 1 (top left):

BUT, BEFORE ANOTHER WORD CAN BE UTTERED, A *NEW* FIGURE APPEARS ON THE HORIZON--PERHAPS THE MOST MENACING, MOST SPINE-CHILLING FIGURE OF ALL TIME--!

THE *HULK.!!!*

THOOM!

THOOM!

Panel 2 (top right):

HELP.!! HELP ME--PLEASE, HULK--PLEASE--!!

THAT *VOICE.!!* I *KNOW* IT! HULK MUST *HELP!*

GOT TO PUT ON MORE *SPEED*--GET OUT OF RANGE BEFORE HE CAN COME *AFTER ME!*

Panel 3 (middle left):

AS ALL GOOD *HULKOPHILES* KNOW, THE INCREDIBLE ONE CANNOT ACTUALLY *FLY,* BUT RATHER TRAVELS THRU THE AIR BY A SERIES OF TREMENDOUS *LEAPS!*

THOOM!

THEREFORE, HE MUST WAIT UNTIL HE *LANDS* BEFORE HE CAN TAKE TO THE AIR AGAIN, TO ATTEMPT *PURSUIT--!*

Panel 4 (middle right):

YET, ALTHOUGH THE GREEN BEHEMOTH REACHES HIS PREY LIKE A CANNONADING PROJECTILE, HE CANNOT DART AND WEAVE AND MANEUVER THE WAY *BOOMERANG* CAN!

YOU'RE *FAST,* BIG GUY--BUT YOU HAVEN'T A *CHANCE*-- BECAUSE YOU *CAN'T CHANGE DIRECTION!*

HULK WILL GET YOU.!! WAIT AND *SEE!*

Panel 5 (bottom left):

THEN, AS THE LONG, DESPERATE, SEEMINGLY UNEND- ING MINUTES FLY BY--

IT'S NO USE! I CAN'T KEEP IT UP *FOREVER!* AND HE DOESN'T GET *TIRED*--!

HE'S AS *FAST NOW* AS WHEN HE STARTED!

THOOM!

Panel 6 (bottom right):

CAN'T KEEP IT UP ANY LONGER WITHOUT ENDANGERING *YOU,* LADY! AND YOU'RE TOO *VALUABLE* TO ME!

SO I'LL LEAVE YOU *HERE,* WHILE I TACKLE HIM ON FOOT! I'VE STILL GOT THE WEAPONS TO *BEAT* 'IM!

DON'T *TRY* IT! HE'LL *KILL YOU!*

NO ONE *CAN* STAND UP TO THE *HULK!*

6

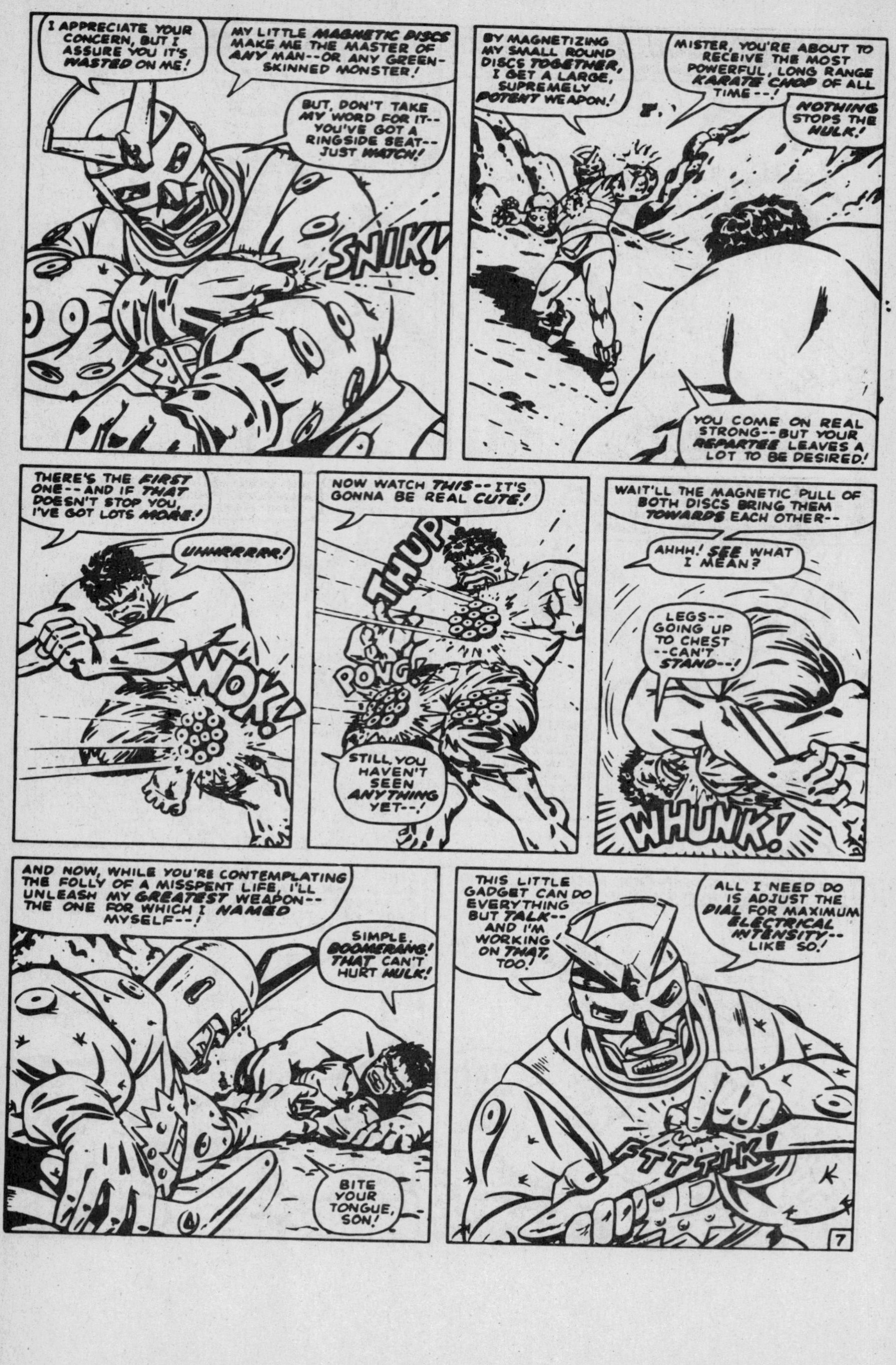

I APPRECIATE YOUR CONCERN, BUT I ASSURE YOU IT'S WASTED ON ME!
MY LITTLE MAGNETIC DISCS MAKE ME THE MASTER OF ANY MAN--OR ANY GREEN-SKINNED MONSTER!
BUT, DON'T TAKE MY WORD FOR IT--YOU'VE GOT A RINGSIDE SEAT--JUST WATCH!
SNIK!
BY MAGNETIZING MY SMALL ROUND DISCS TOGETHER, I GET A LARGE, SUPREMELY POTENT WEAPON!
MISTER, YOU'RE ABOUT TO RECEIVE THE MOST POWERFUL, LONG RANGE KARATE CHOP OF ALL TIME--!
NOTHING STOPS THE HULK!
YOU COME ON REAL STRONG--BUT YOUR REPARTEE LEAVES A LOT TO BE DESIRED!
THERE'S THE FIRST ONE--AND IF THAT DOESN'T STOP YOU, I'VE GOT LOTS MORE!
UHHRRRRR!
WOK!
NOW WATCH THIS--IT'S GONNA BE REAL CUTE!
THUP!
PONG!
STILL, YOU HAVEN'T SEEN ANYTHING YET--!
WAIT'LL THE MAGNETIC PULL OF BOTH DISCS BRING THEM TOWARDS EACH OTHER--
AHHH! SEE WHAT I MEAN?
LEGS--GOING UP TO CHEST--CAN'T STAND--!
WHUNK!
AND NOW, WHILE YOU'RE CONTEMPLATING THE FOLLY OF A MISSPENT LIFE, I'LL UNLEASH MY GREATEST WEAPON--THE ONE FOR WHICH I NAMED MYSELF--!
SIMPLE. BOOMERANG! THAT CAN'T HURT HULK!
BITE YOUR TONGUE, SON!
THIS LITTLE GADGET CAN DO EVERYTHING BUT TALK--AND I'M WORKING ON THAT, TOO!
ALL I NEED DO IS ADJUST THE DIAL FOR MAXIMUM ELECTRICAL INTENSITY--LIKE SO!
STTTIK!

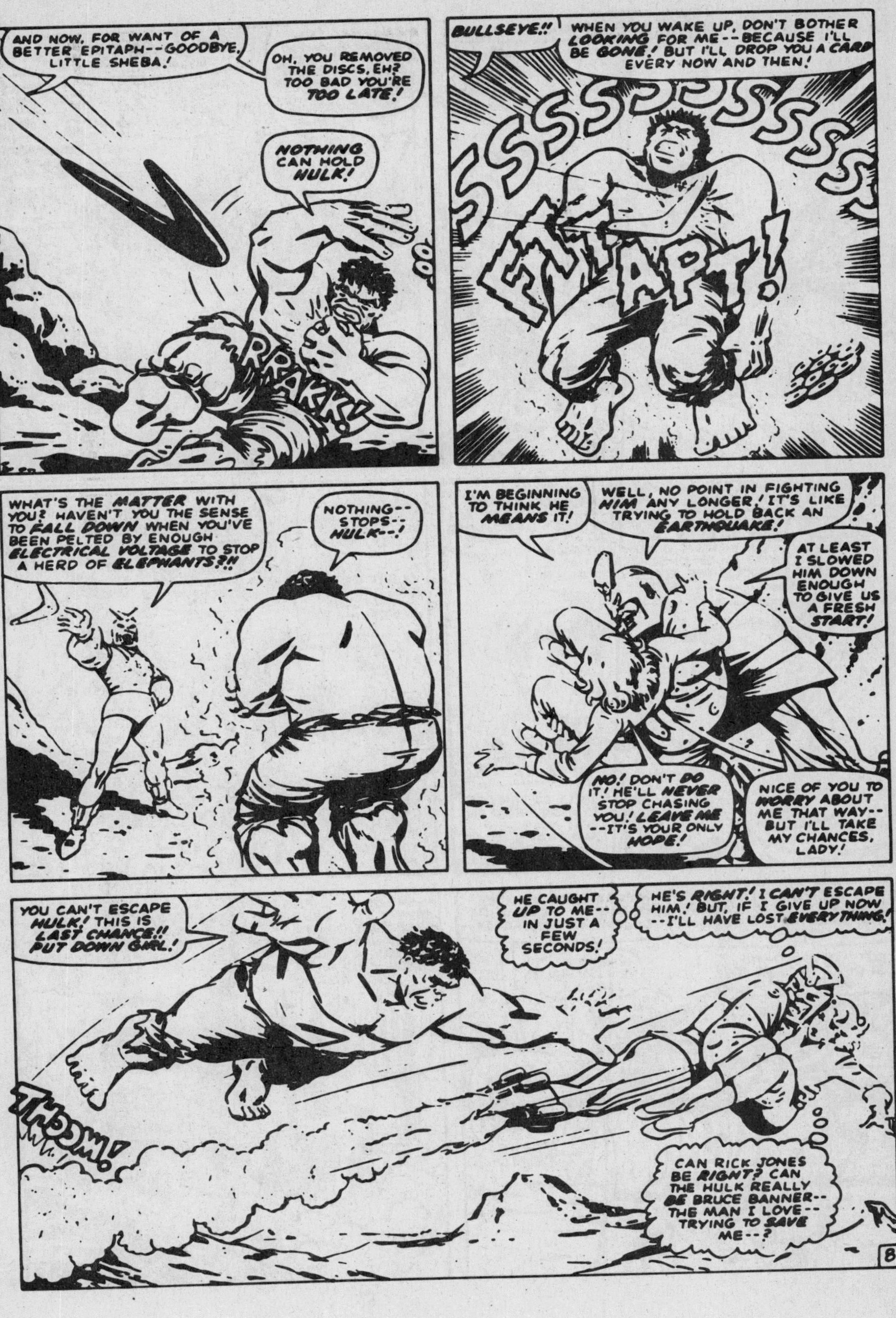
AND NOW, FOR WANT OF A BETTER EPITAPH--GOODBYE, LITTLE SHEBA!
OH, YOU REMOVED THE DISCS, EH? TOO BAD YOU'RE TOO LATE!
NOTHING CAN HOLD HULK!
RRAKK!
BULLSEYE!!
WHEN YOU WAKE UP, DON'T BOTHER LOOKING FOR ME--BECAUSE I'LL BE GONE! BUT I'LL DROP YOU A CARD EVERY NOW AND THEN!
SSSSSSSSSSSS
FTTTAPT!
WHAT'S THE MATTER WITH YOU? HAVEN'T YOU THE SENSE TO FALL DOWN WHEN YOU'VE BEEN PELTED BY ENOUGH ELECTRICAL VOLTAGE TO STOP A HERD OF ELEPHANTS?!!
NOTHING--STOPS--HULK--!
I'M BEGINNING TO THINK HE MEANS IT!
WELL, NO POINT IN FIGHTING HIM ANY LONGER! IT'S LIKE TRYING TO HOLD BACK AN EARTHQUAKE!
AT LEAST I SLOWED HIM DOWN ENOUGH TO GIVE US A FRESH START!
NO! DON'T DO IT! HE'LL NEVER STOP CHASING YOU! LEAVE ME--IT'S YOUR ONLY HOPE!
NICE OF YOU TO WORRY ABOUT ME THAT WAY--BUT I'LL TAKE MY CHANCES, LADY!
YOU CAN'T ESCAPE HULK! THIS IS LAST CHANCE!! PUT DOWN GIRL!
HE CAUGHT UP TO ME--IN JUST A FEW SECONDS!
HE'S RIGHT! I CAN'T ESCAPE HIM! BUT, IF I GIVE UP NOW--I'LL HAVE LOST EVERYTHING!
THOOM!
CAN RICK JONES BE RIGHT? CAN THE HULK REALLY BE BRUCE BANNER--THE MAN I LOVE--TRYING TO SAVE ME--?
8

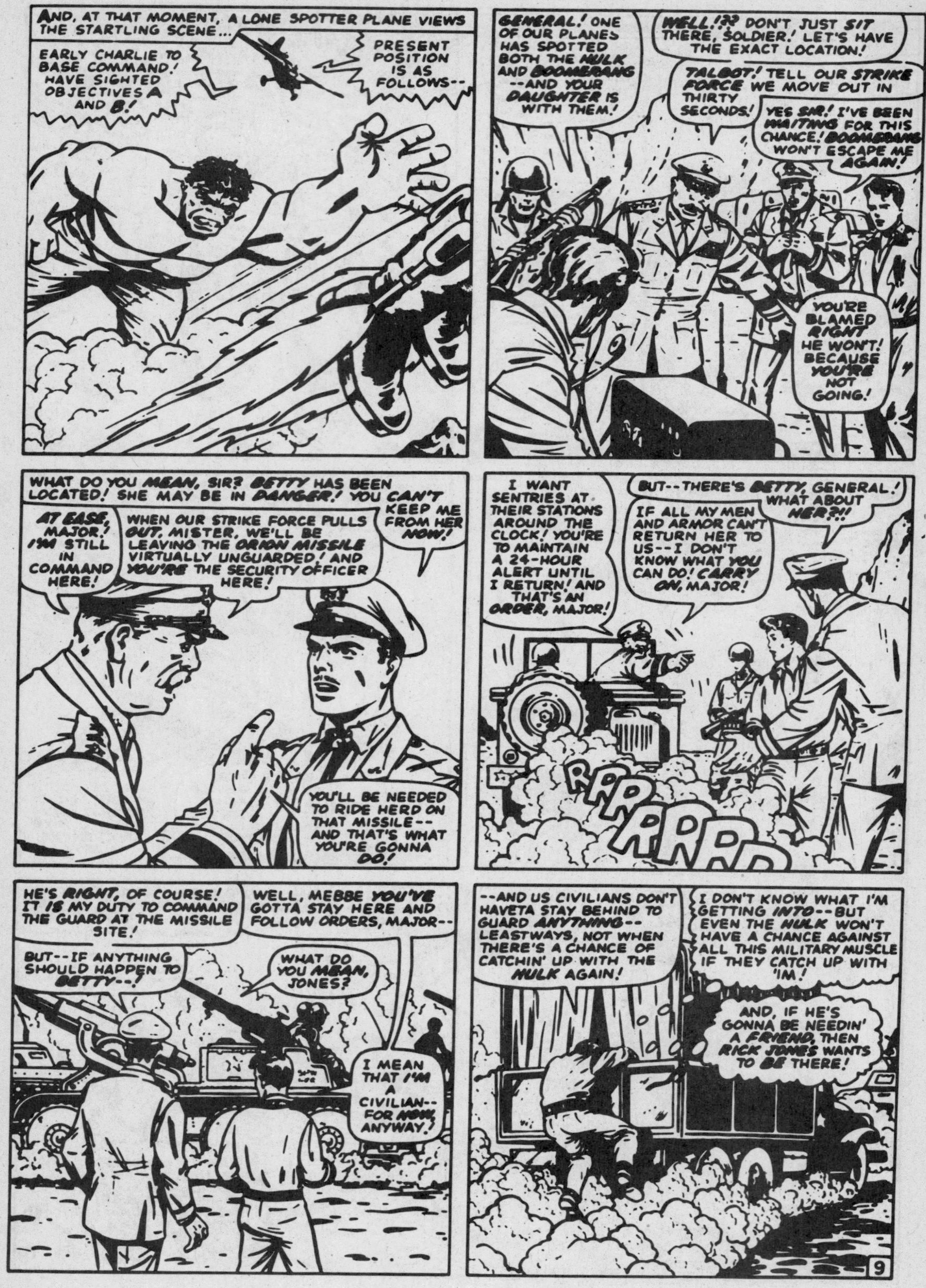
AND, AT THAT MOMENT, A LONE SPOTTER PLANE VIEWS THE STARTLING SCENE...
EARLY CHARLIE TO BASE COMMAND! HAVE SIGHTED OBJECTIVES A AND B!
PRESENT POSITION IS AS FOLLOWS--
GENERAL! ONE OF OUR PLANES HAS SPOTTED BOTH THE HULK AND BOOMERANG --AND YOUR DAUGHTER IS WITH THEM!
WELL!?? DON'T JUST SIT THERE, SOLDIER! LET'S HAVE THE EXACT LOCATION!
TALBOT! TELL OUR STRIKE FORCE WE MOVE OUT IN THIRTY SECONDS!
YES SIR! I'VE BEEN WAITING FOR THIS CHANCE! BOOMERANG WON'T ESCAPE ME AGAIN!
YOU'RE BLAMED RIGHT HE WON'T! BECAUSE YOU'RE NOT GOING!
WHAT DO YOU MEAN, SIR? BETTY HAS BEEN LOCATED! SHE MAY BE IN DANGER! YOU CAN'T KEEP ME FROM HER NOW!
AT EASE, MAJOR! I'M STILL IN COMMAND HERE!
WHEN OUR STRIKE FORCE PULLS OUT, MISTER, WE'LL BE LEAVING THE ORION MISSILE VIRTUALLY UNGUARDED! AND YOU'RE THE SECURITY OFFICER HERE!
YOU'LL BE NEEDED TO RIDE HERD ON THAT MISSILE-- AND THAT'S WHAT YOU'RE GONNA DO!
I WANT SENTRIES AT THEIR STATIONS AROUND THE CLOCK! YOU'RE TO MAINTAIN A 24-HOUR ALERT UNTIL I RETURN! AND THAT'S AN ORDER, MAJOR!
BUT--THERE'S BETTY, GENERAL! WHAT ABOUT HER?!!
IF ALL MY MEN AND ARMOR CAN'T RETURN HER TO US--I DON'T KNOW WHAT YOU CAN DO! CARRY ON, MAJOR!
RRRRRRRD
HE'S RIGHT, OF COURSE! IT IS MY DUTY TO COMMAND THE GUARD AT THE MISSILE SITE!
BUT--IF ANYTHING SHOULD HAPPEN TO BETTY--!
WELL, MEBBE YOU'VE GOTTA STAY HERE AND FOLLOW ORDERS, MAJOR--
WHAT DO YOU MEAN, JONES?
I MEAN THAT I'M A CIVILIAN-- FOR NOW, ANYWAY!
--AND US CIVILIANS DON'T HAVETA STAY BEHIND TO GUARD ANYTHING-- LEASTWAYS, NOT WHEN THERE'S A CHANCE OF CATCHIN' UP WITH THE HULK AGAIN!
I DON'T KNOW WHAT I'M GETTING INTO--BUT EVEN THE HULK WON'T HAVE A CHANCE AGAINST ALL THIS MILITARY MUSCLE IF THEY CATCH UP WITH 'IM!
AND, IF HE'S GONNA BE NEEDIN' A FRIEND, THEN RICK JONES WANTS TO BE THERE!
9

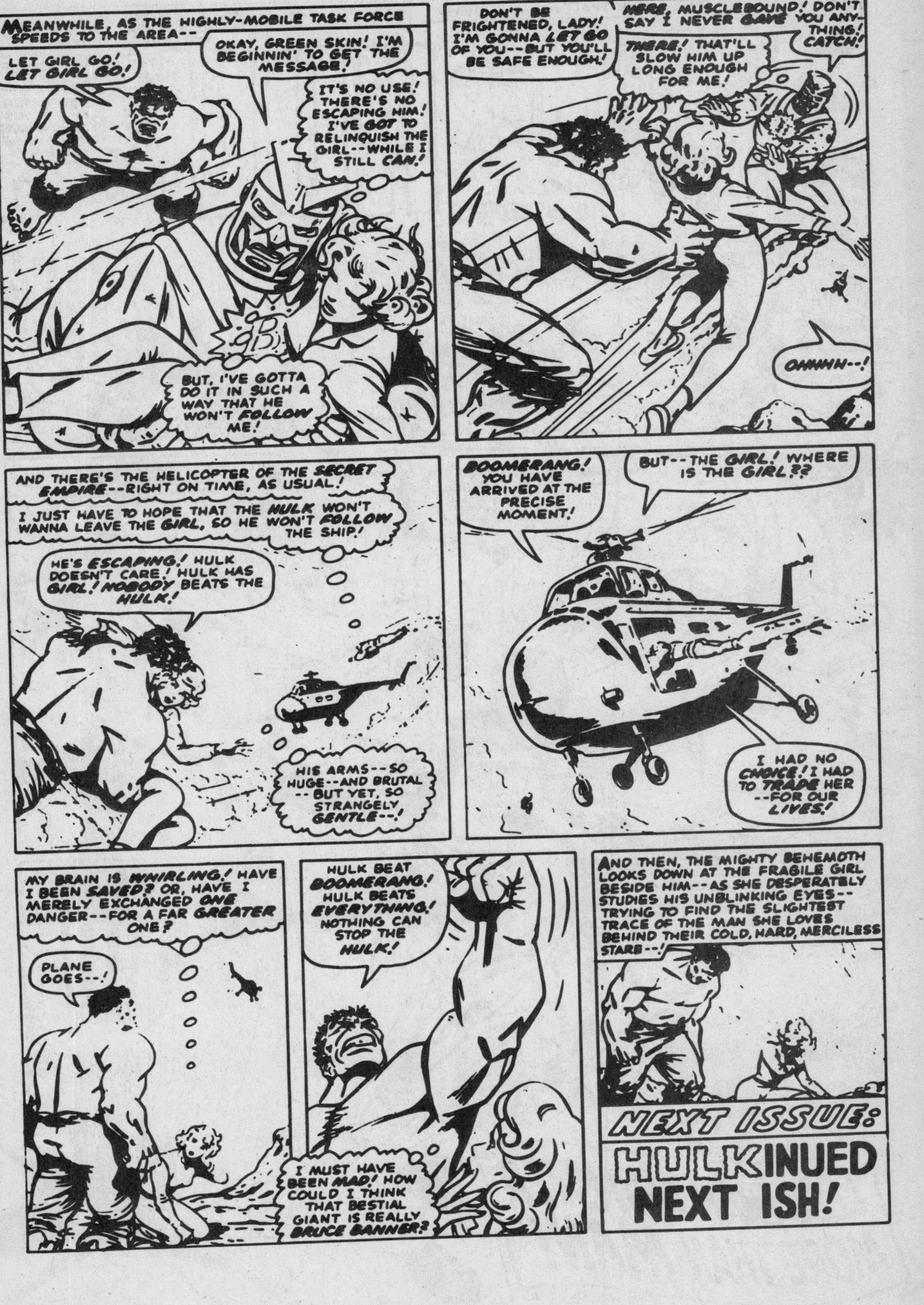
MEANWHILE, AS THE HIGHLY-MOBILE TASK FORCE SPEEDS TO THE AREA--
LET GIRL GO! LET GIRL GO!
OKAY, GREEN SKIN! I'M BEGINNIN' TO GET THE MESSAGE!
IT'S NO USE! THERE'S NO ESCAPING HIM! I'VE GOT TO RELINQUISH THE GIRL--WHILE I STILL CAN!
BUT, I'VE GOTTA DO IT IN SUCH A WAY THAT HE WON'T FOLLOW ME!
DON'T BE FRIGHTENED, LADY! I'M GONNA LET GO OF YOU--BUT YOU'LL BE SAFE ENOUGH!
HERE, MUSCLEBOUND! DON'T SAY I NEVER GAVE YOU ANYTHING! CATCH!
THERE! THAT'LL SLOW HIM UP LONG ENOUGH FOR ME!
OHHHH--!
AND THERE'S THE HELICOPTER OF THE SECRET EMPIRE--RIGHT ON TIME, AS USUAL!
I JUST HAVE TO HOPE THAT THE HULK WON'T WANNA LEAVE THE GIRL, SO HE WON'T FOLLOW THE SHIP!
HE'S ESCAPING! HULK DOESN'T CARE! HULK HAS GIRL! NOBODY BEATS THE HULK!
HIS ARMS--SO HUGE--AND BRUTAL--BUT YET, SO STRANGELY GENTLE--!
BOOMERANG! YOU HAVE ARRIVED AT THE PRECISE MOMENT!
BUT--THE GIRL! WHERE IS THE GIRL??
I HAD NO CHOICE! I HAD TO TRADE HER--FOR OUR LIVES!
MY BRAIN IS WHIRLING! HAVE I BEEN SAVED? OR, HAVE I MERELY EXCHANGED ONE DANGER--FOR A FAR GREATER ONE?
PLANE GOES--!
HULK BEAT BOOMERANG! HULK BEATS EVERYTHING! NOTHING CAN STOP THE HULK!
I MUST HAVE BEEN MAD! HOW COULD I THINK THAT BESTIAL GIANT IS REALLY BRUCE BANNER?
AND THEN, THE MIGHTY BEHEMOTH LOOKS DOWN AT THE FRAGILE GIRL BESIDE HIM--AS SHE DESPERATELY STUDIES HIS UNBLINKING EYES--TRYING TO FIND THE SLIGHTEST TRACE OF THE MAN SHE LOVES BEHIND THEIR COLD, HARD, MERCILESS STARE--!
NEXT ISSUE:
HULKINUED NEXT ISH!

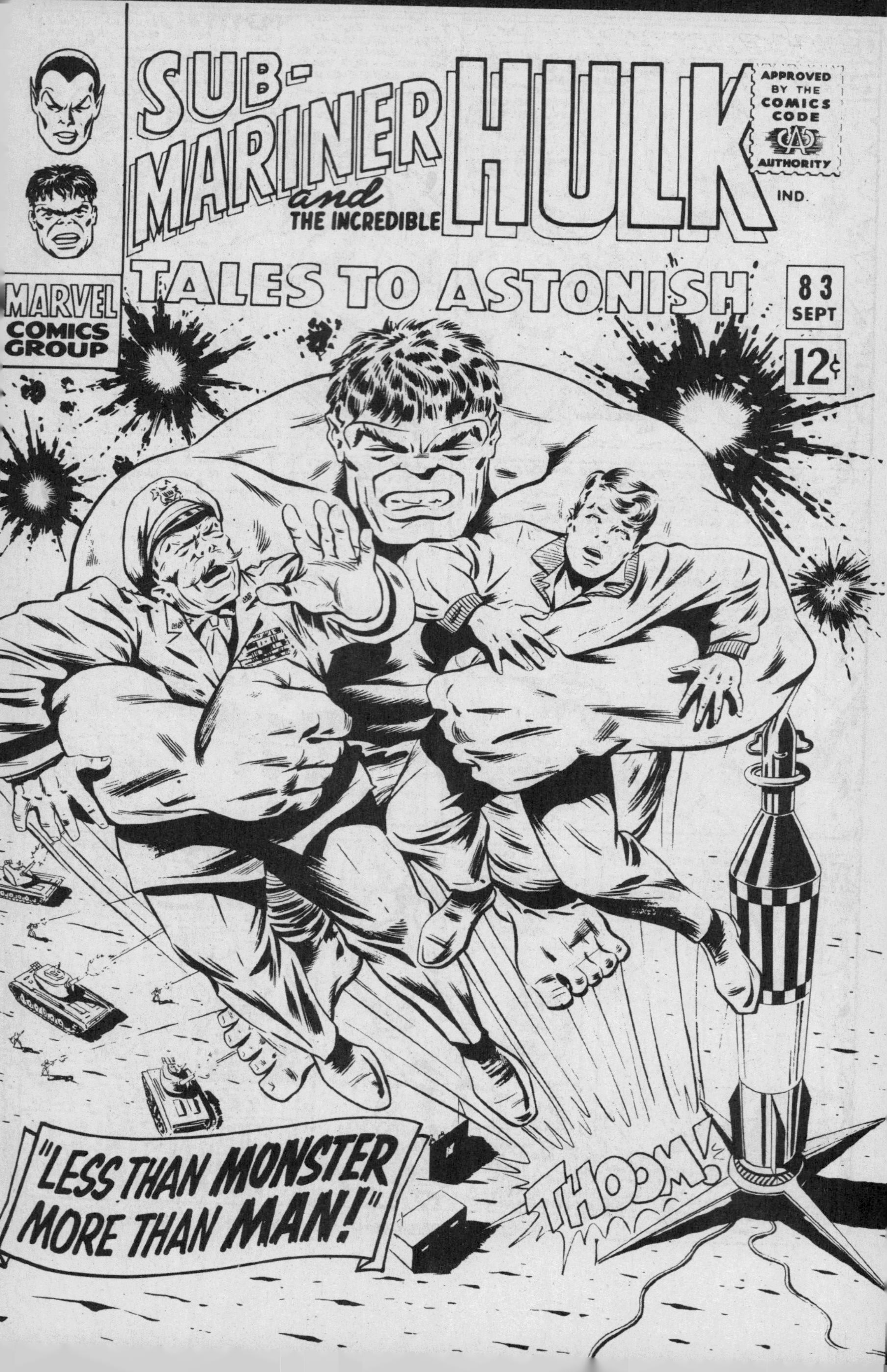
SUB-MARINER and THE INCREDIBLE HULK
TALES TO ASTONISH
MARVEL COMICS GROUP
APPROVED BY THE COMICS CODE AUTHORITY
IND.
83 SEPT
12¢
"LESS THAN MONSTER MORE THAN MAN!"
THOOM!

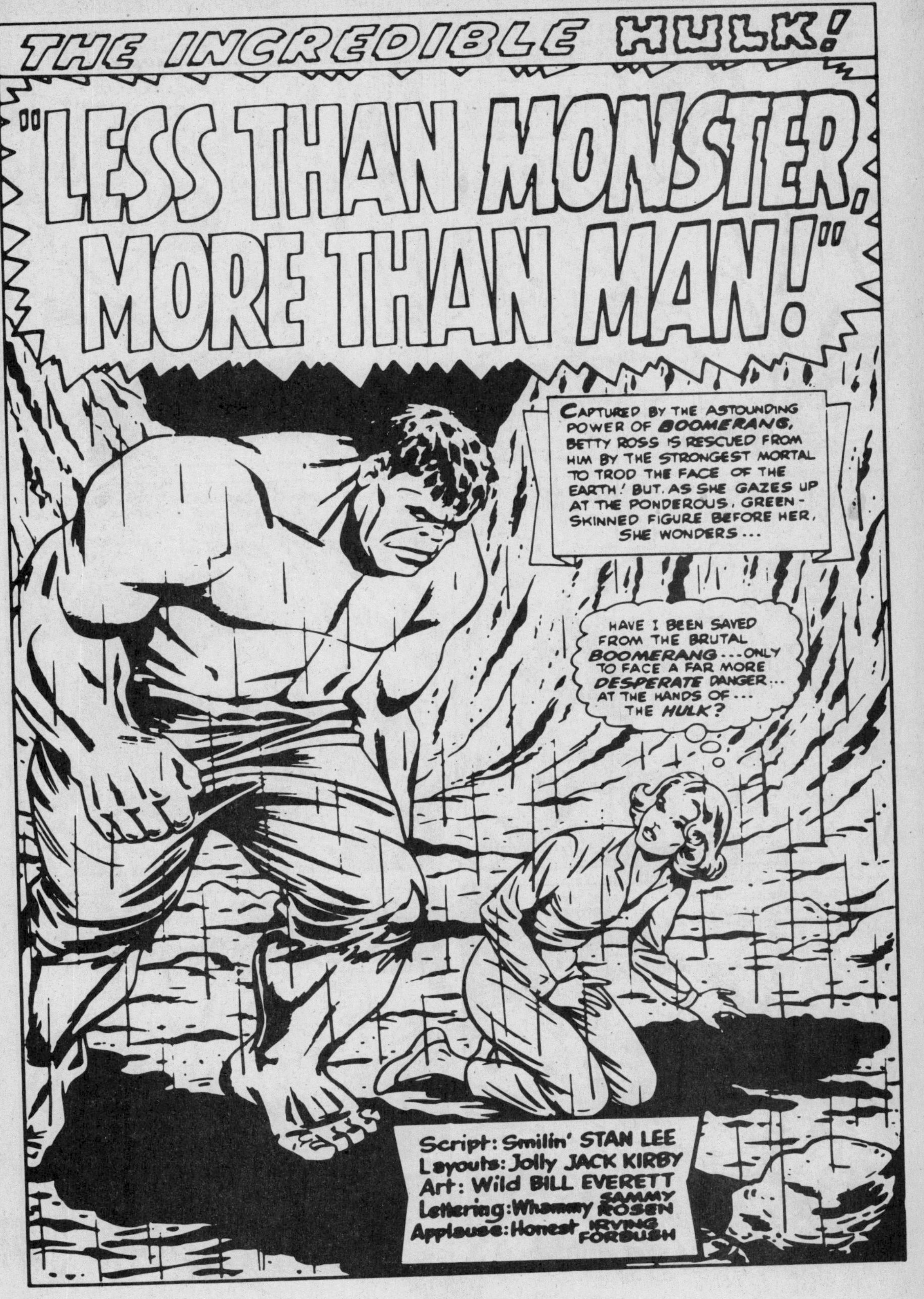
THE INCREDIBLE HULK!
"LESS THAN MONSTER, MORE THAN MAN!"
CAPTURED BY THE ASTOUNDING POWER OF BOOMERANG, BETTY ROSS IS RESCUED FROM HIM BY THE STRONGEST MORTAL TO TROD THE FACE OF THE EARTH! BUT AS SHE GAZES UP AT THE PONDEROUS, GREEN-SKINNED FIGURE BEFORE HER, SHE WONDERS...
HAVE I BEEN SAVED FROM THE BRUTAL BOOMERANG... ONLY TO FACE A FAR MORE DESPERATE DANGER... AT THE HANDS OF... THE HULK?
Script: Smilin' STAN LEE
Layouts: Jolly JACK KIRBY
Art: Wild BILL EVERETT
Lettering: Whammy SAMMY ROSEN
Applause: Honest IRVING FORBUSH

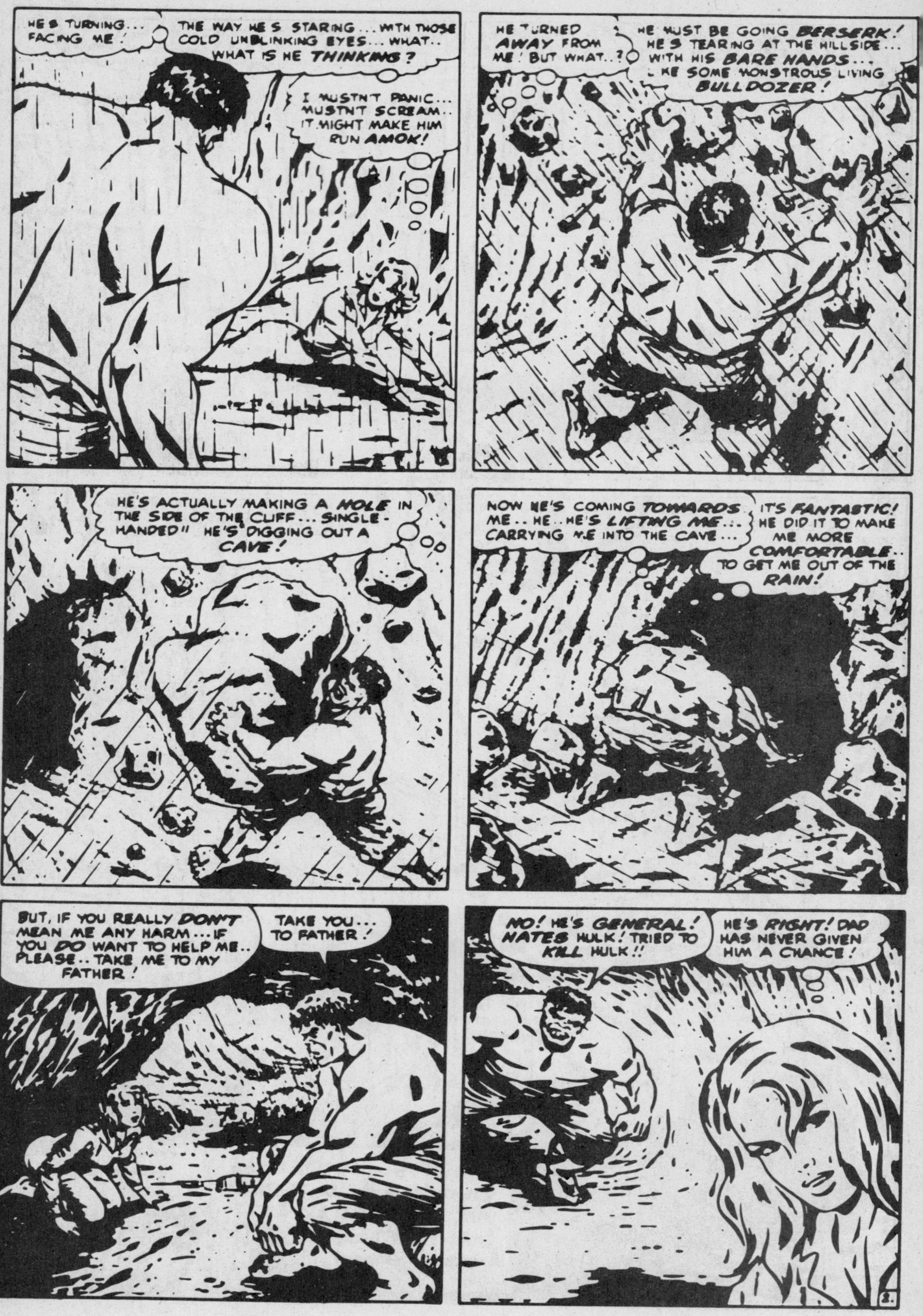
HE'S TURNING... FACING ME!
THE WAY HE'S STARING... WITH THOSE COLD UNBLINKING EYES... WHAT.. WHAT IS HE THINKING?
I MUSTN'T PANIC... MUSTN'T SCREAM... IT MIGHT MAKE HIM RUN AMOK!
HE TURNED AWAY FROM ME! BUT WHAT..?
HE MUST BE GOING BERSERK! HE'S TEARING AT THE HILLSIDE... WITH HIS BARE HANDS... LIKE SOME MONSTROUS LIVING BULLDOZER!
HE'S ACTUALLY MAKING A HOLE IN THE SIDE OF THE CLIFF... SINGLE-HANDED!! HE'S DIGGING OUT A CAVE!
NOW HE'S COMING TOWARDS ME.. HE.. HE'S LIFTING ME... CARRYING ME INTO THE CAVE...
IT'S FANTASTIC! HE DID IT TO MAKE ME MORE COMFORTABLE.. TO GET ME OUT OF THE RAIN!
BUT, IF YOU REALLY DON'T MEAN ME ANY HARM... IF YOU DO WANT TO HELP ME.. PLEASE.. TAKE ME TO MY FATHER!
TAKE YOU... TO FATHER!
NO! HE'S GENERAL! HATES HULK! TRIED TO KILL HULK!!
HE'S RIGHT! DAD HAS NEVER GIVEN HIM A CHANCE!

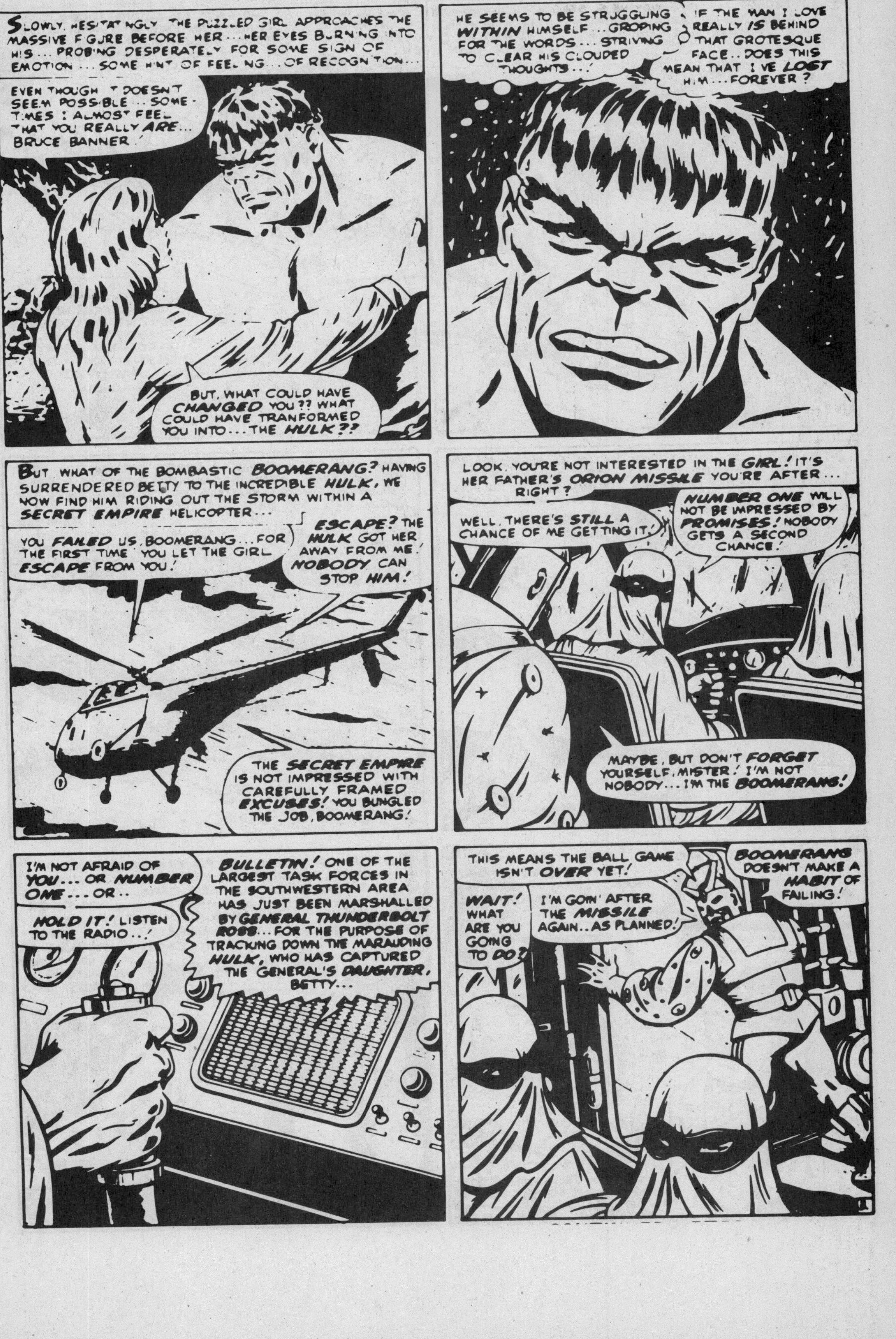
SLOWLY, HESITATINGLY, THE PUZZLED GIRL APPROACHES THE MASSIVE FIGURE BEFORE HER... HER EYES BURNING INTO HIS... PROBING DESPERATELY FOR SOME SIGN OF EMOTION... SOME HINT OF FEELING... OF RECOGNITION...
EVEN THOUGH IT DOESN'T SEEM POSSIBLE... SOMETIMES I ALMOST FEEL THAT YOU REALLY ARE... BRUCE BANNER!
BUT, WHAT COULD HAVE CHANGED YOU?? WHAT COULD HAVE TRANFORMED YOU INTO... THE HULK??
HE SEEMS TO BE STRUGGLING WITHIN HIMSELF... GROPING FOR THE WORDS... STRIVING TO CLEAR HIS CLOUDED THOUGHTS...!
IF THE MAN I LOVE REALLY IS BEHIND THAT GROTESQUE FACE.. DOES THIS MEAN THAT I'VE LOST HIM... FOREVER?
BUT WHAT OF THE BOMBASTIC BOOMERANG? HAVING SURRENDERED BETTY TO THE INCREDIBLE HULK, WE NOW FIND HIM RIDING OUT THE STORM WITHIN A SECRET EMPIRE HELICOPTER...
YOU FAILED US, BOOMERANG... FOR THE FIRST TIME YOU LET THE GIRL ESCAPE FROM YOU!
ESCAPE? THE HULK GOT HER AWAY FROM ME! NOBODY CAN STOP HIM!
THE SECRET EMPIRE IS NOT IMPRESSED WITH CAREFULLY FRAMED EXCUSES! YOU BUNGLED THE JOB, BOOMERANG!
LOOK, YOU'RE NOT INTERESTED IN THE GIRL! IT'S HER FATHER'S ORION MISSILE YOU'RE AFTER... RIGHT?
WELL, THERE'S STILL A CHANCE OF ME GETTING IT!
NUMBER ONE WILL NOT BE IMPRESSED BY PROMISES! NOBODY GETS A SECOND CHANCE!
MAYBE, BUT DON'T FORGET YOURSELF, MISTER! I'M NOT NOBODY... I'M THE BOOMERANG!
I'M NOT AFRAID OF YOU... OR NUMBER ONE... OR..
HOLD IT! LISTEN TO THE RADIO...!
BULLETIN! ONE OF THE LARGEST TASK FORCES IN THE SOUTHWESTERN AREA HAS JUST BEEN MARSHALLED BY GENERAL THUNDERBOLT ROSS... FOR THE PURPOSE OF TRACKING DOWN THE MARAUDING HULK, WHO HAS CAPTURED THE GENERAL'S DAUGHTER, BETTY...
THIS MEANS THE BALL GAME ISN'T OVER YET!
BOOMERANG DOESN'T MAKE A HABIT OF FAILING!
WAIT! WHAT ARE YOU GOING TO DO?
I'M GOIN' AFTER THE MISSILE AGAIN.. AS PLANNED!

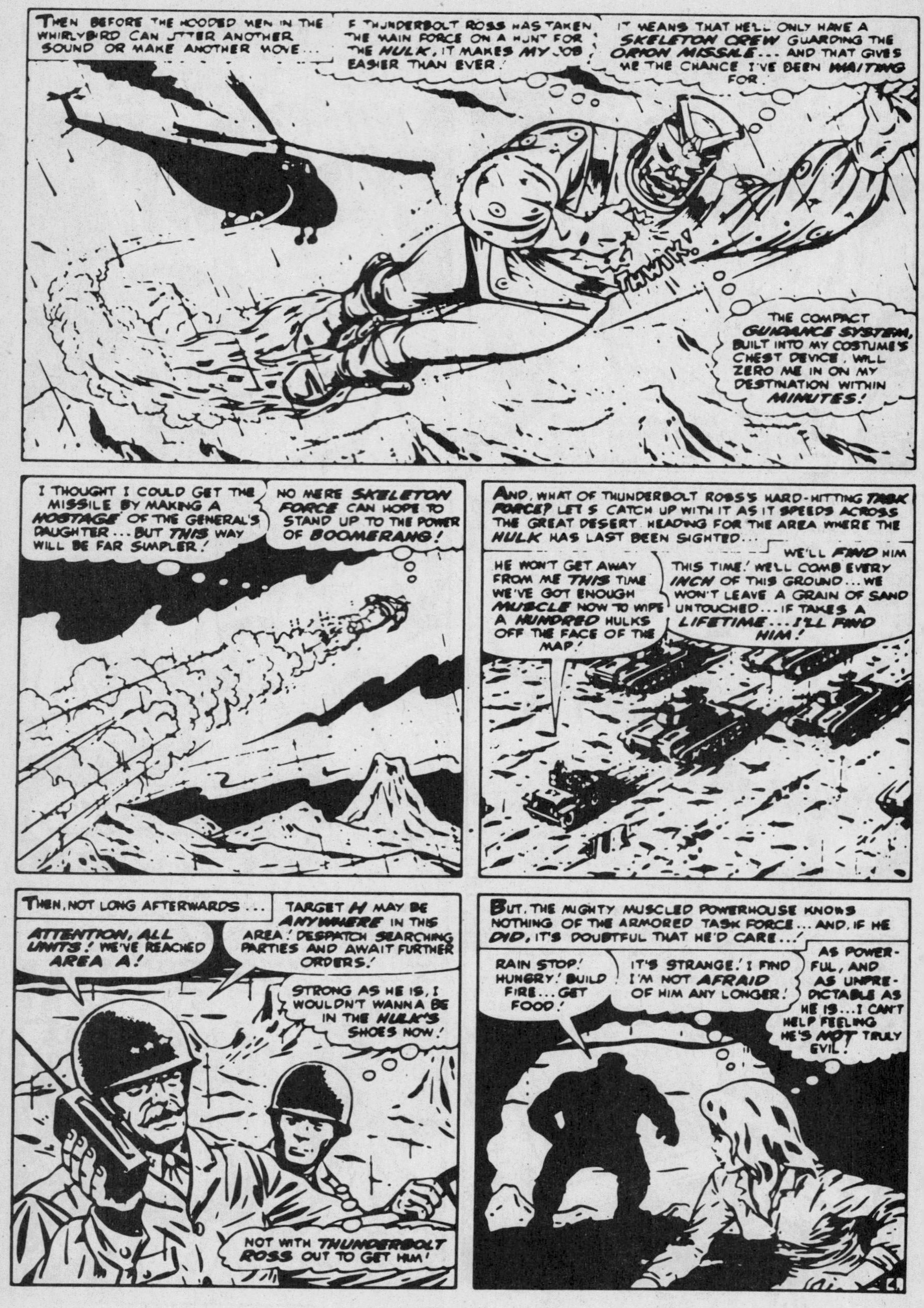

THEN BEFORE THE HOODED MEN IN THE WHIRLYBIRD CAN UTTER ANOTHER SOUND OR MAKE ANOTHER MOVE...
F THUNDERBOLT ROSS HAS TAKEN THE MAIN FORCE ON A HUNT FOR THE HULK, IT MAKES MY JOB EASIER THAN EVER!
IT MEANS THAT HE'LL ONLY HAVE A SKELETON CREW GUARDING THE ORION MISSILE... AND THAT GIVES ME THE CHANCE I'VE BEEN WAITING FOR.
THWIK!
THE COMPACT GUIDANCE SYSTEM, BUILT INTO MY COSTUME'S CHEST DEVICE, WILL ZERO ME IN ON MY DESTINATION WITHIN MINUTES!
I THOUGHT I COULD GET THE MISSILE BY MAKING A HOSTAGE OF THE GENERAL'S DAUGHTER... BUT THIS WAY WILL BE FAR SIMPLER!
NO MERE SKELETON FORCE CAN HOPE TO STAND UP TO THE POWER OF BOOMERANG!
AND, WHAT OF THUNDERBOLT ROSS'S HARD-HITTING TASK FORCE? LET'S CATCH UP WITH IT AS IT SPEEDS ACROSS THE GREAT DESERT HEADING FOR THE AREA WHERE THE HULK HAS LAST BEEN SIGHTED...
HE WON'T GET AWAY FROM ME THIS TIME WE'VE GOT ENOUGH MUSCLE NOW TO WIPE A HUNDRED HULKS OFF THE FACE OF THE MAP!
WE'LL FIND HIM THIS TIME! WE'LL COMB EVERY INCH OF THIS GROUND... WE WON'T LEAVE A GRAIN OF SAND UNTOUCHED... IF TAKES A LIFETIME... I'LL FIND HIM!
THEN, NOT LONG AFTERWARDS...
ATTENTION, ALL UNITS! WE'VE REACHED AREA A!
TARGET H MAY BE ANYWHERE IN THIS AREA! DESPATCH SEARCHING PARTIES AND AWAIT FURTHER ORDERS!
STRONG AS HE IS, I WOULDN'T WANNA BE IN THE HULK'S SHOES NOW!
NOT WITH THUNDERBOLT ROSS OUT TO GET HIM!
BUT, THE MIGHTY MUSCLED POWERHOUSE KNOWS NOTHING OF THE ARMORED TASK FORCE... AND, IF HE DID, IT'S DOUBTFUL THAT HE'D CARE...!
RAIN STOP! HUNGRY! BUILD FIRE... GET FOOD!
IT'S STRANGE! I FIND I'M NOT AFRAID OF HIM ANY LONGER!
AS POWERFUL, AND AS UNPREDICTABLE AS HE IS... I CAN'T HELP FEELING HE'S NOT TRULY EVIL!
4

WHEREVER HE'S SEEN... WHEREVER HE APPEARS... MEN *HUNT* HIM... AND *HOUND* HIM... AS THOUGH HE'S SOME *SAVAGE, WILD BEAST* OF PREY...

PERHAPS, IF HE WERE JUST GIVEN A *CHANCE*... IF EVEN ONE PERSON SHOWED SOME *FAITH*... SOME *TRUST* IN HIM...

...PERHAPS THINGS WOULD BE *DIFFERENT!*

THOSE TWO LARGE CHUNKS OF *FLINT ROCK* HE PICKED UP... WHAT'S HE GOING TO DO...?

STAY *BACK!* NEED FIRE! HULK MAKE FIRE!

P'TOOM!

HE... HE *SMASHED* THEM TOGETHER... WITH SUCH INDESCRIBABLE *FORCE*... THAT THE *FRICTION* ALONE CAUSED THE WOOD PILE TO BURST INTO FLAME!

WITH STRENGTH SUCH AS *HIS*, IS THERE *ANYTHING* HE CAN'T DO?

GIRL *WAIT!* HULK COMES *BACK!*

EASIER TO SEE *FOOD* FROM HIGH UP *HERE!*

THM!

BUT, NO SOONER HAS THE GREEN-SKINNED BEHEMOTH TAKEN TO THE AIR, WHEN...

MEN *SHOOT* AT HULK!

PEEOWWW!

PWEEEEEEEE!

KROW!

KRAK!

SPARROW PATROL! SPARROW PATROL! MAYDAY! MAYDAY! HULK SIGHTED! HULK SIGHTED!

BRING UP *HEAVY STUFF*... ON THE *DOUBLE!*

WEOW!

BRAAAA!

RAM!

BKOW!

WHILE, BACK AT THE BASE, *MAJOR GLEN TALBOT*, IN CHARGE OF THE SMALL, BUT *HEAVILY-ARMED* UNIT ASSIGNED TO GUARD THE VITAL *ORION MISSILE*, GOES ABOUT HIS DUTIES WITH *GLUM RESIGNATION*...

EVERY AVAILABLE MAN IS OUT HUNTING FOR THE *HULK*... AND FOR *BETTY ROSS*... THE GIRL I *LOVE!*

...WHILE *I'M* STUCK *HERE*... ON ROUTINE GUARD DETAIL... PLAYING NURSEMAID TO THAT *BLASTED MISSILE!*

IF ONLY THERE WAS SOME *WORD* ABOUT *BETTY!*

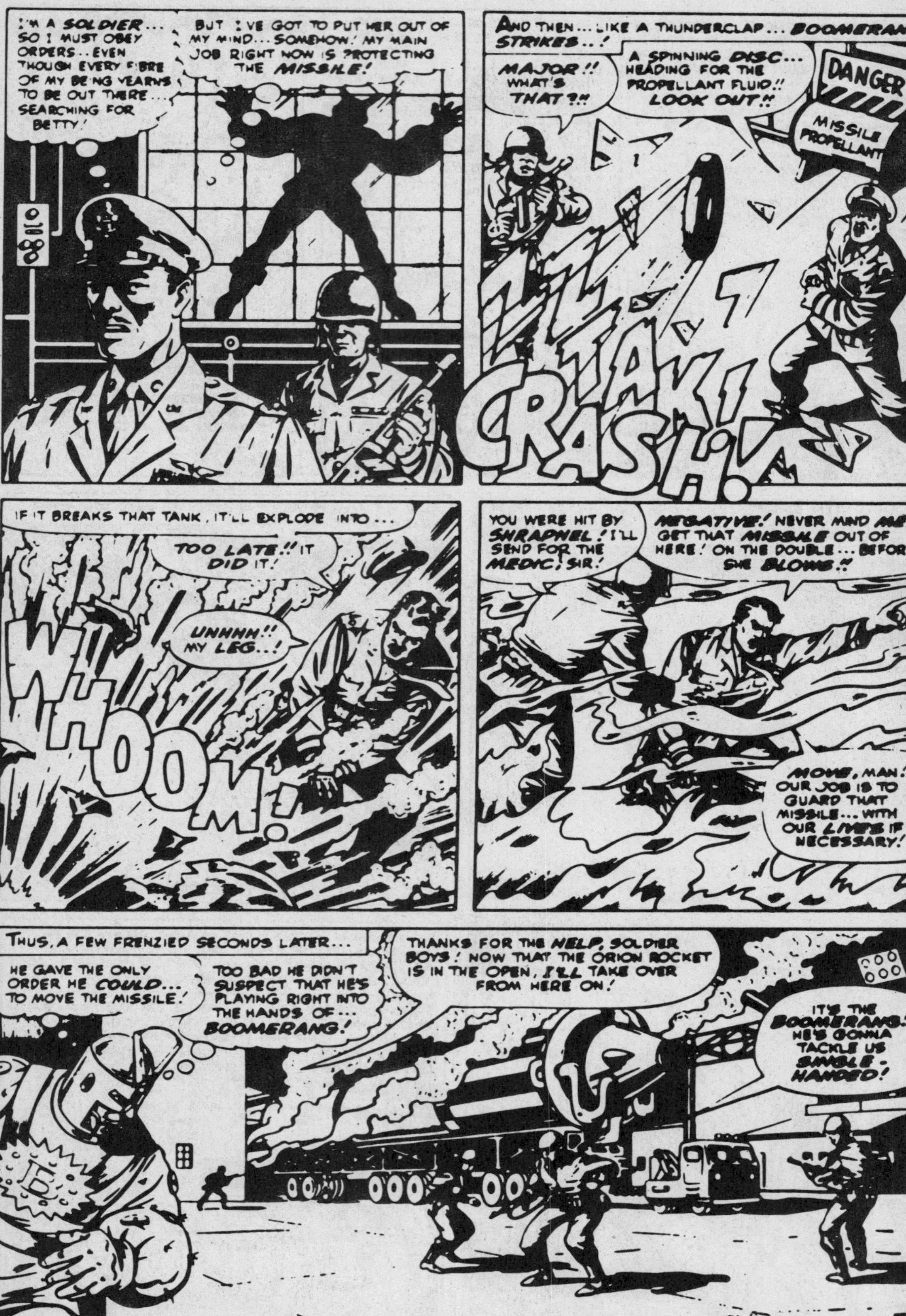
I'M A SOLDIER... SO I MUST OBEY ORDERS... EVEN THOUGH EVERY FIBRE OF MY BEING YEARNS TO BE OUT THERE... SEARCHING FOR BETTY!
BUT I'VE GOT TO PUT HER OUT OF MY MIND... SOMEHOW! MY MAIN JOB RIGHT NOW IS PROTECTING THE MISSILE!
AND THEN... LIKE A THUNDERCLAP... BOOMERANG STRIKES...!
MAJOR!! WHAT'S THAT?!!
A SPINNING DISC... HEADING FOR THE PROPELLANT FLUID!! LOOK OUT!!
DANGER
MISSILE PROPELLANT
TAK!
CRASH!
IF IT BREAKS THAT TANK, IT'LL EXPLODE INTO...
TOO LATE!! IT DID IT!
UNNHH!! MY LEG...!
WHOOOM!
YOU WERE HIT BY SHRAPNEL! I'LL SEND FOR THE MEDIC, SIR!
NEGATIVE! NEVER MIND ME! GET THAT MISSILE OUT OF HERE! ON THE DOUBLE... BEFORE SHE BLOWS!!
MOVE, MAN! OUR JOB IS TO GUARD THAT MISSILE... WITH OUR LIVES IF NECESSARY!
THUS, A FEW FRENZIED SECONDS LATER...
HE GAVE THE ONLY ORDER HE COULD... TO MOVE THE MISSILE!
TOO BAD HE DIDN'T SUSPECT THAT HE'S PLAYING RIGHT INTO THE HANDS OF... BOOMERANG!
THANKS FOR THE HELP, SOLDIER BOYS! NOW THAT THE ORION ROCKET IS IN THE OPEN, I'LL TAKE OVER FROM HERE ON!
IT'S THE BOOMERANG!! HE'S GONNA TACKLE US SINGLE-HANDED!
6

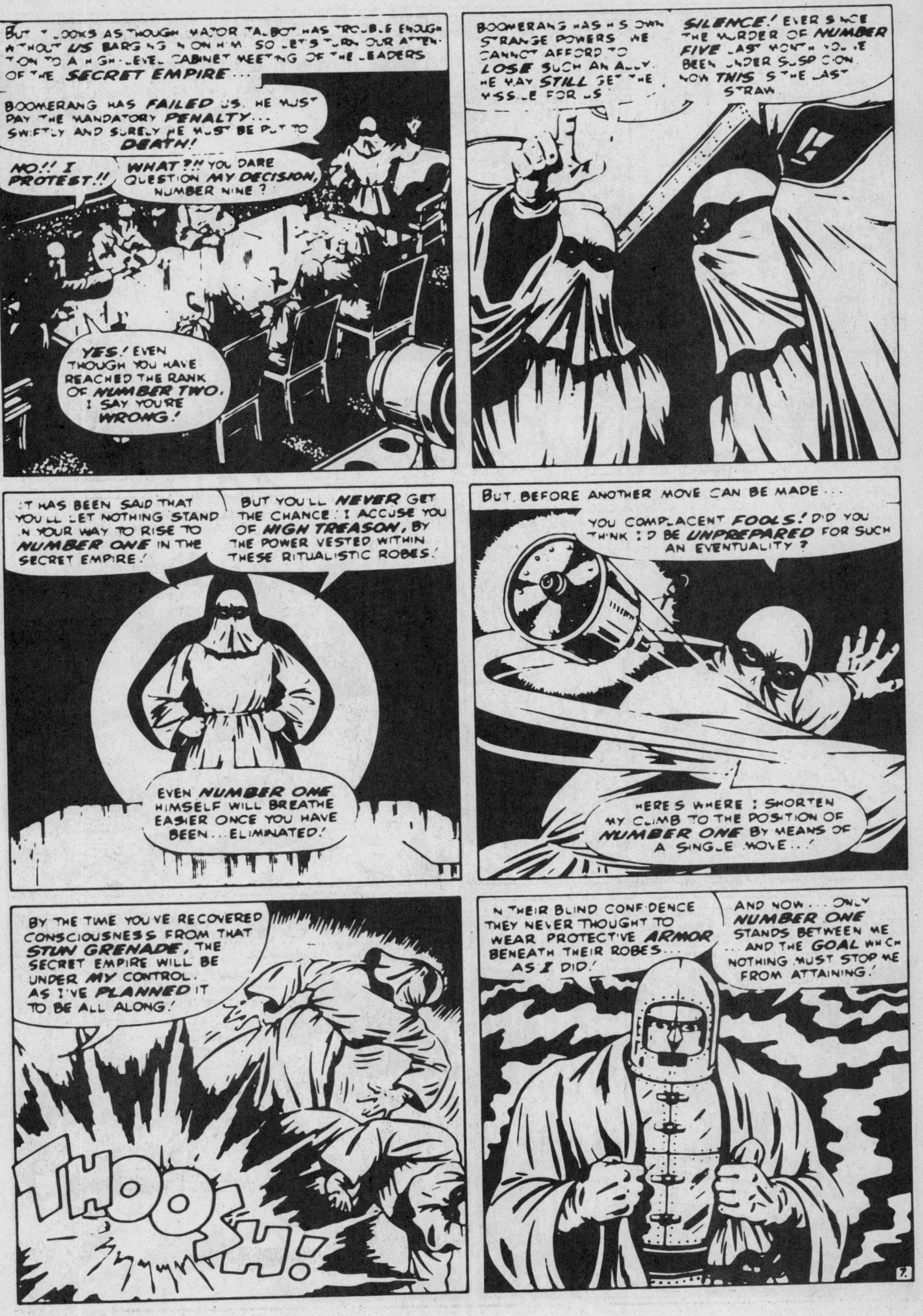

BUT IT LOOKS AS THOUGH MAJOR TALBOT HAS TROUBLE ENOUGH WITHOUT US BARGING IN ON HIM. SO LET'S TURN OUR ATTENTION TO A HIGH-LEVEL CABINET MEETING OF THE LEADERS OF THE SECRET EMPIRE...
BOOMERANG HAS FAILED US. HE MUST PAY THE MANDATORY PENALTY... SWIFTLY AND SURELY HE MUST BE PUT TO DEATH!
NO!! I PROTEST!!
WHAT?!! YOU DARE QUESTION MY DECISION, NUMBER NINE?
YES! EVEN THOUGH YOU HAVE REACHED THE RANK OF NUMBER TWO, I SAY YOU'RE WRONG!
BOOMERANG HAS HIS OWN STRANGE POWERS. WE CANNOT AFFORD TO LOSE SUCH AN ALLY. HE MAY STILL GET THE MISSILE FOR US!
SILENCE! EVER SINCE THE MURDER OF NUMBER FIVE LAST MONTH YOU'VE BEEN UNDER SUSPICION. NOW THIS IS THE LAST STRAW.
IT HAS BEEN SAID THAT YOU'LL LET NOTHING STAND IN YOUR WAY TO RISE TO NUMBER ONE IN THE SECRET EMPIRE!
BUT YOU'LL NEVER GET THE CHANCE! I ACCUSE YOU OF HIGH TREASON, BY THE POWER VESTED WITHIN THESE RITUALISTIC ROBES!
EVEN NUMBER ONE HIMSELF WILL BREATHE EASIER ONCE YOU HAVE BEEN... ELIMINATED!
BUT BEFORE ANOTHER MOVE CAN BE MADE...
YOU COMPLACENT FOOLS! DID YOU THINK I'D BE UNPREPARED FOR SUCH AN EVENTUALITY?
HERE'S WHERE I SHORTEN MY CLIMB TO THE POSITION OF NUMBER ONE BY MEANS OF A SINGLE MOVE...!
BY THE TIME YOU'VE RECOVERED CONSCIOUSNESS FROM THAT STUN GRENADE, THE SECRET EMPIRE WILL BE UNDER MY CONTROL, AS I'VE PLANNED IT TO BE ALL ALONG!
THOOSH!
IN THEIR BLIND CONFIDENCE THEY NEVER THOUGHT TO WEAR PROTECTIVE ARMOR BENEATH THEIR ROBES... AS I DID!
AND NOW... ONLY NUMBER ONE STANDS BETWEEN ME... AND THE GOAL WHICH NOTHING MUST STOP ME FROM ATTAINING!
7.

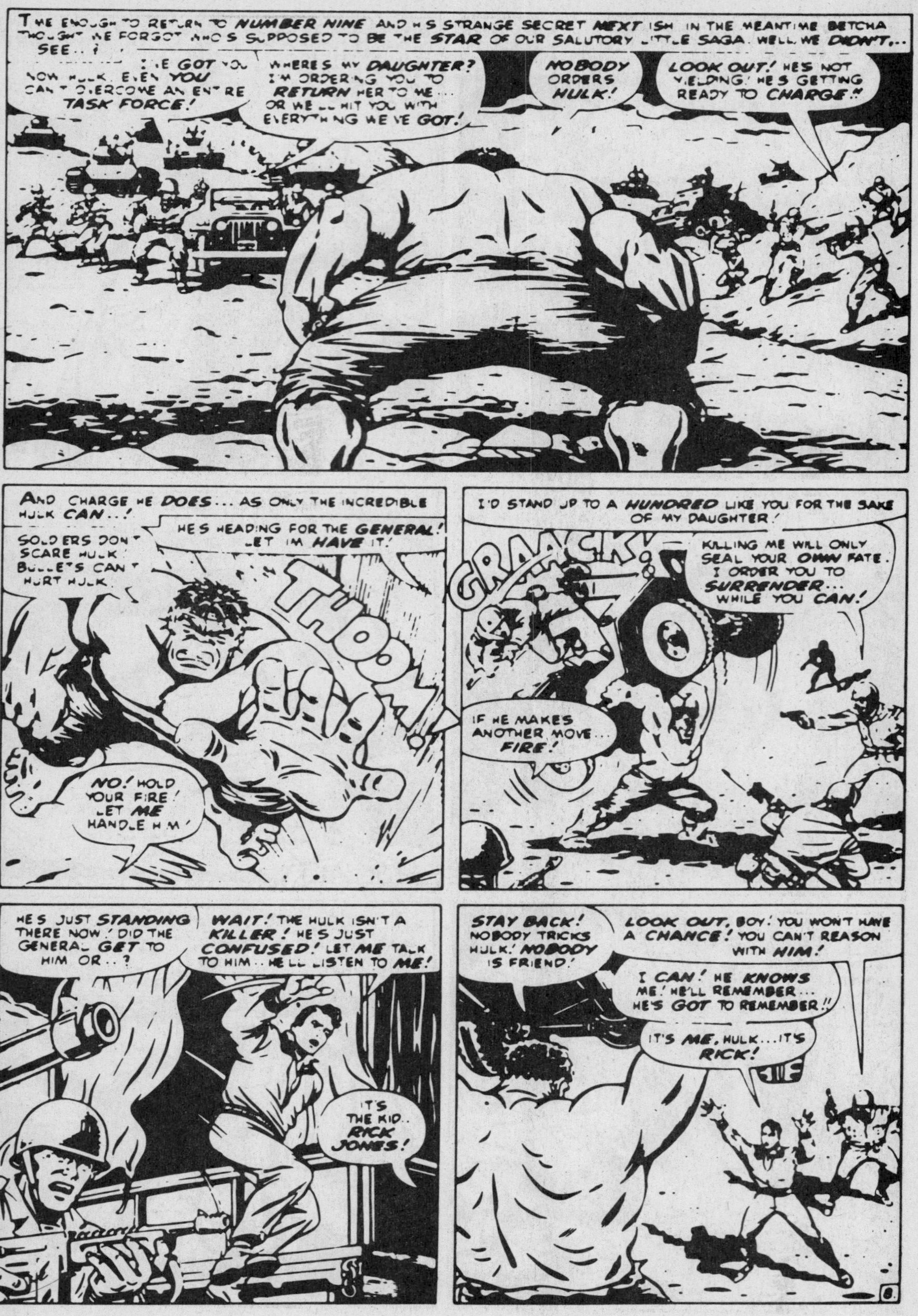

THE ENOUGH TO RETURN TO NUMBER NINE AND HIS STRANGE SECRET NEXT ISH. IN THE MEANTIME BETCHA THOUGHT WE FORGOT WHO'S SUPPOSED TO BE THE STAR OF OUR SALUTORY LITTLE SAGA. WELL, WE DIDN'T... SEE...!
WE GOT YOU NOW HULK. EVEN YOU CAN'T OVERCOME AN ENTIRE TASK FORCE!
WHERE'S MY DAUGHTER? I'M ORDERING YOU TO RETURN HER TO ME... OR WE'LL HIT YOU WITH EVERYTHING WE'VE GOT!
NOBODY ORDERS HULK!
LOOK OUT! HE'S NOT YIELDING! HE'S GETTING READY TO CHARGE!!
AND CHARGE HE DOES... AS ONLY THE INCREDIBLE HULK CAN...!
SOLDIERS DON'T SCARE HULK! BULLETS CAN'T HURT HULK.
HE'S HEADING FOR THE GENERAL! LET 'IM HAVE IT!
THOOM!
NO! HOLD YOUR FIRE! LET ME HANDLE HIM!
I'D STAND UP TO A HUNDRED LIKE YOU FOR THE SAKE OF MY DAUGHTER!
GRAACK!
KILLING ME WILL ONLY SEAL YOUR OWN FATE. I ORDER YOU TO SURRENDER... WHILE YOU CAN!
IF HE MAKES ANOTHER MOVE... FIRE!
HE'S JUST STANDING THERE NOW! DID THE GENERAL GET TO HIM OR..?
WAIT! THE HULK ISN'T A KILLER! HE'S JUST CONFUSED! LET ME TALK TO HIM.. HE'LL LISTEN TO ME!
IT'S THE KID.. RICK JONES!
STAY BACK! NOBODY TRICKS HULK! NOBODY IS FRIEND!
LOOK OUT, BOY! YOU WON'T HAVE A CHANCE! YOU CAN'T REASON WITH HIM!
I CAN! HE KNOWS ME! HE'LL REMEMBER... HE'S GOT TO REMEMBER!!
IT'S ME, HULK... IT'S RICK!
8

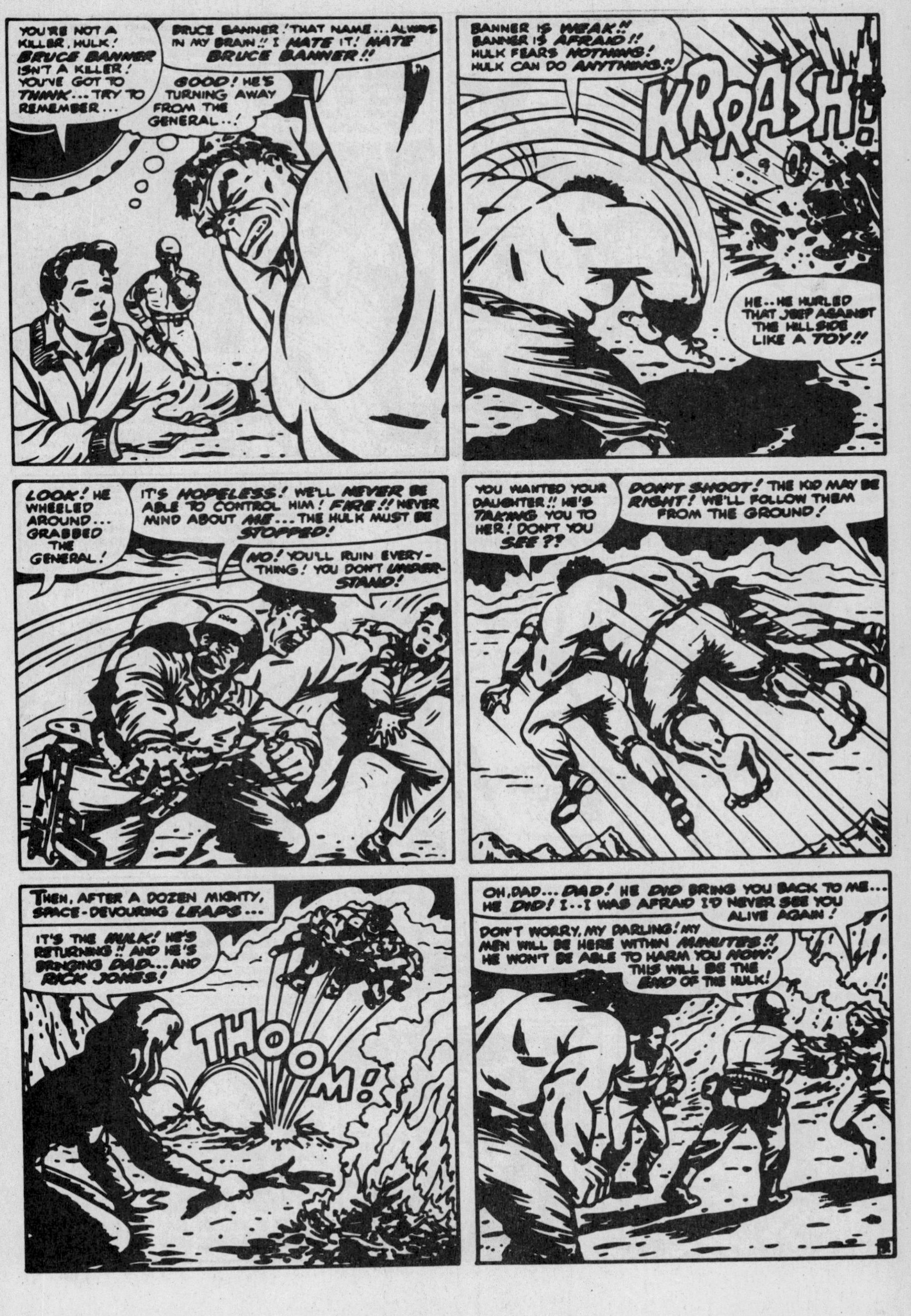
YOU'RE NOT A KILLER, HULK! BRUCE BANNER ISN'T A KILLER! YOU'VE GOT TO THINK... TRY TO REMEMBER...
BRUCE BANNER! THAT NAME... ALWAYS IN MY BRAIN!! I HATE IT! HATE BRUCE BANNER!!
GOOD! HE'S TURNING AWAY FROM THE GENERAL...!
BANNER IS WEAK!! BANNER IS AFRAID!! HULK FEARS NOTHING! HULK CAN DO ANYTHING!!
KRRASH!
HE... HE HURLED THAT JEEP AGAINST THE HILLSIDE LIKE A TOY!!
LOOK! HE WHEELED AROUND... GRABBED THE GENERAL!
IT'S HOPELESS! WE'LL NEVER BE ABLE TO CONTROL HIM! FIRE!! NEVER MIND ABOUT ME... THE HULK MUST BE STOPPED!
NO! YOU'LL RUIN EVERYTHING! YOU DON'T UNDERSTAND!
YOU WANTED YOUR DAUGHTER!! HE'S TAKING YOU TO HER! DON'T YOU SEE??
DON'T SHOOT! THE KID MAY BE RIGHT! WE'LL FOLLOW THEM FROM THE GROUND!
THEN, AFTER A DOZEN MIGHTY, SPACE-DEVOURING LEAPS...
IT'S THE HULK! HE'S RETURNING!! AND HE'S BRINGING DAD... AND RICK JONES!
THOOOM!
OH, DAD... DAD! HE DID BRING YOU BACK TO ME... HE DID! I... I WAS AFRAID I'D NEVER SEE YOU ALIVE AGAIN!
DON'T WORRY, MY DARLING! MY MEN WILL BE HERE WITHIN MINUTES!! HE WON'T BE ABLE TO HARM YOU NOW! THIS WILL BE THE END OF THE HULK!

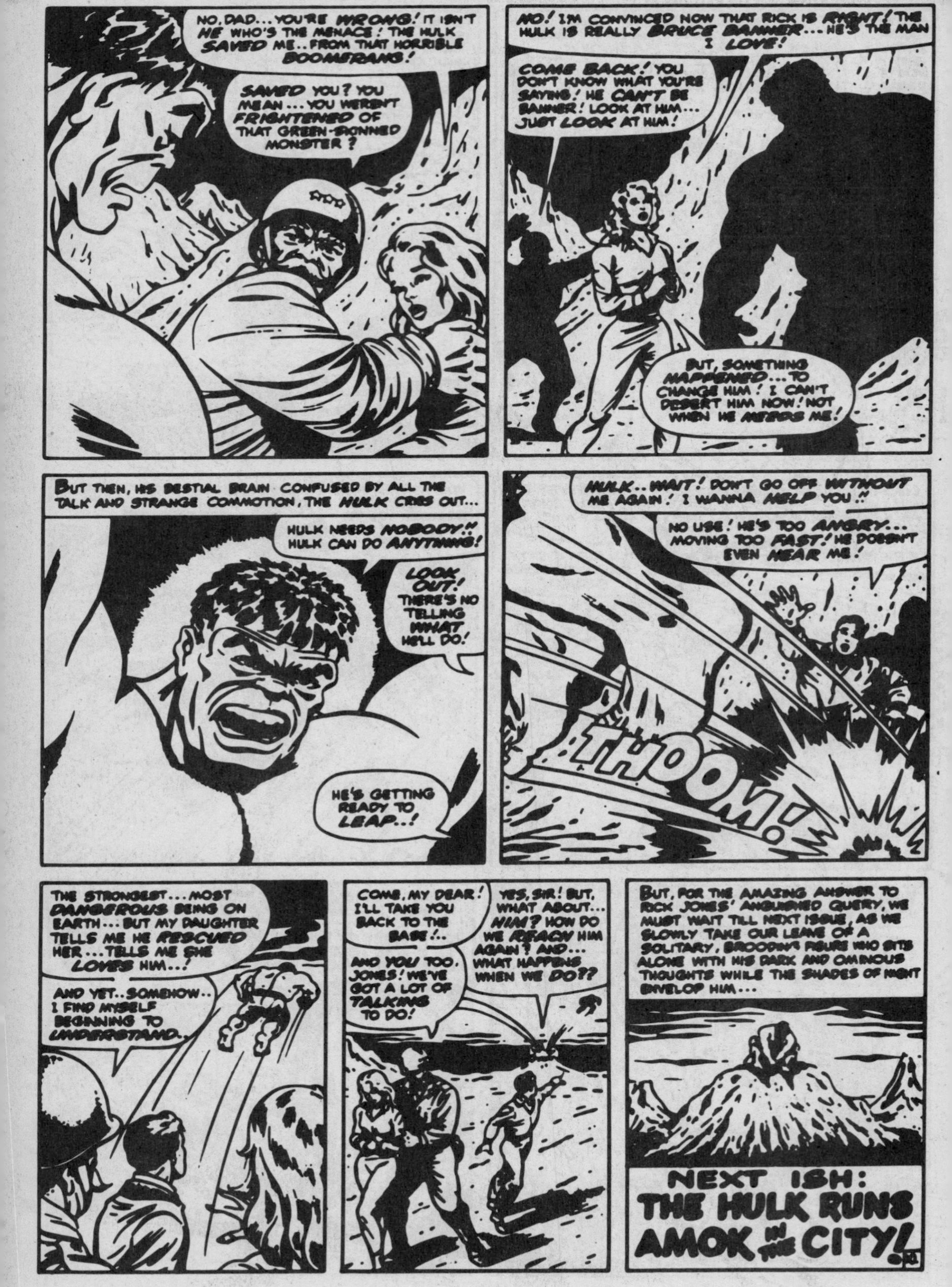
NO, DAD... YOU'RE WRONG! IT ISN'T HE WHO'S THE MENACE! THE HULK SAVED ME.. FROM THAT HORRIBLE BOOMERANG!
SAVED YOU? YOU MEAN... YOU WEREN'T FRIGHTENED OF THAT GREEN-SKINNED MONSTER?
NO! I'M CONVINCED NOW THAT RICK IS RIGHT! THE HULK IS REALLY BRUCE BANNER... HE'S THE MAN I LOVE!
COME BACK! YOU DON'T KNOW WHAT YOU'RE SAYING! HE CAN'T BE BANNER! LOOK AT HIM... JUST LOOK AT HIM!
BUT, SOMETHING HAPPENED... TO CHANGE HIM! I CAN'T DESERT HIM NOW! NOT WHEN HE NEEDS ME!
BUT THEN, HIS BESTIAL BRAIN CONFUSED BY ALL THE TALK AND STRANGE COMMOTION, THE HULK CRIES OUT...
HULK NEEDS NOBODY!! HULK CAN DO ANYTHING!
LOOK OUT! THERE'S NO TELLING WHAT HE'LL DO!
HE'S GETTING READY TO LEAP..!
HULK.. WAIT! DON'T GO OFF WITHOUT ME AGAIN! I WANNA HELP YOU!!
NO USE! HE'S TOO ANGRY... MOVING TOO FAST! HE DOESN'T EVEN HEAR ME!
THOOM!
THE STRONGEST... MOST DANGEROUS BEING ON EARTH... BUT MY DAUGHTER TELLS ME HE RESCUED HER... TELLS ME SHE LOVES HIM...!
AND YET.. SOMEHOW.. I FIND MYSELF BEGINNING TO UNDERSTAND..
COME, MY DEAR! I'LL TAKE YOU BACK TO THE BASE!..
AND YOU TOO, JONES! WE'VE GOT A LOT OF TALKING TO DO!
YES, SIR! BUT, WHAT ABOUT... HIM? HOW DO WE REACH HIM AGAIN? AND... WHAT HAPPENS WHEN WE DO??
BUT, FOR THE AMAZING ANSWER TO RICK JONES' ANGUISHED QUERY, WE MUST WAIT TILL NEXT ISSUE, AS WE SLOWLY TAKE OUR LEAVE OF A SOLITARY, BROODING FIGURE WHO SITS ALONE WITH HIS DARK AND OMINOUS THOUGHTS WHILE THE SHADES OF NIGHT ENVELOP HIM...
NEXT ISH:
THE HULK RUNS AMOK IN THE CITY!

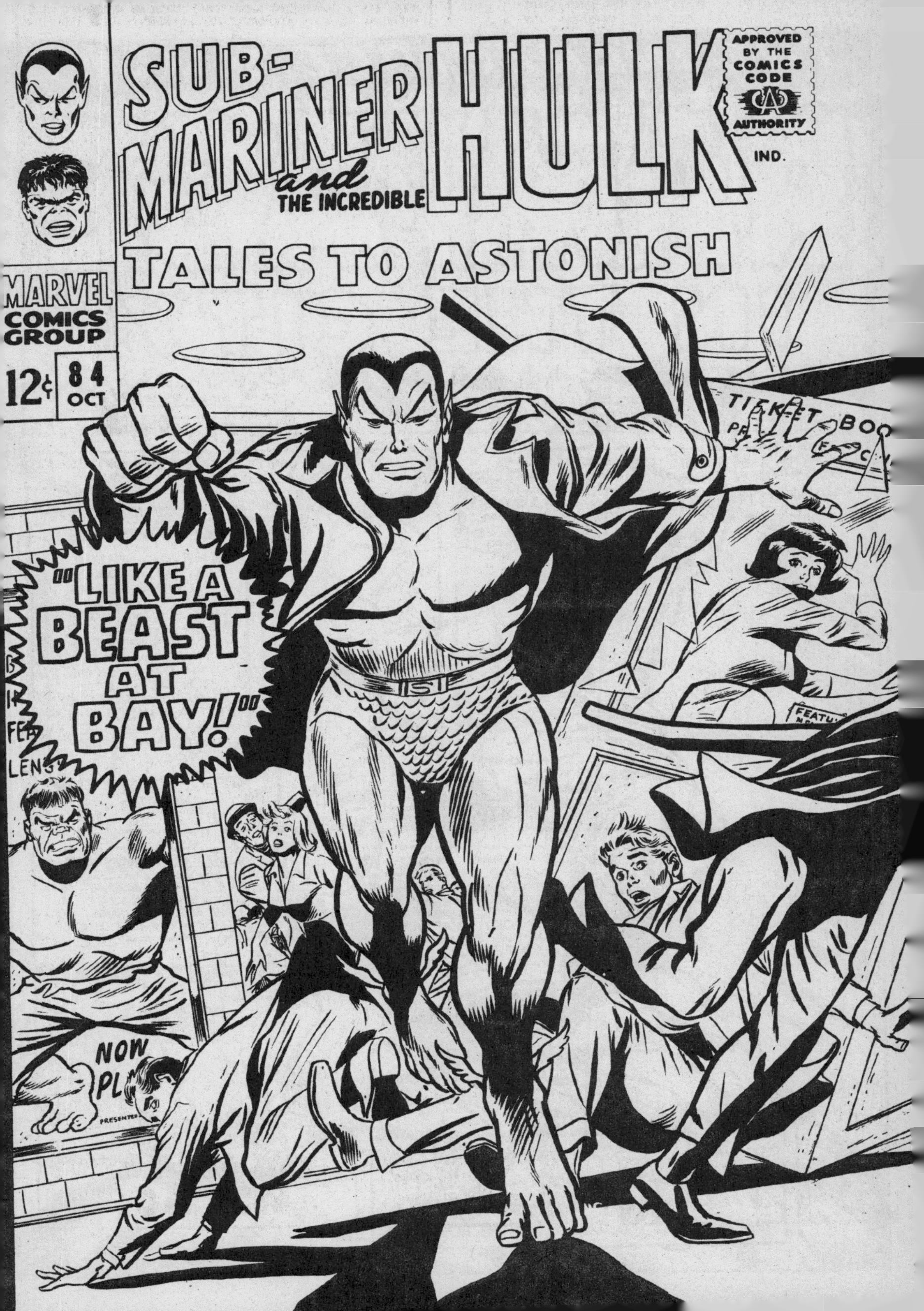
SUB-MARINER and THE INCREDIBLE HULK
APPROVED BY THE COMICS CODE AUTHORITY
IND.
TALES TO ASTONISH
MARVEL COMICS GROUP
12¢
84 OCT
"LIKE A BEAST AT BAY!"
TICKET BOO
NOW
PL
PRESENTED

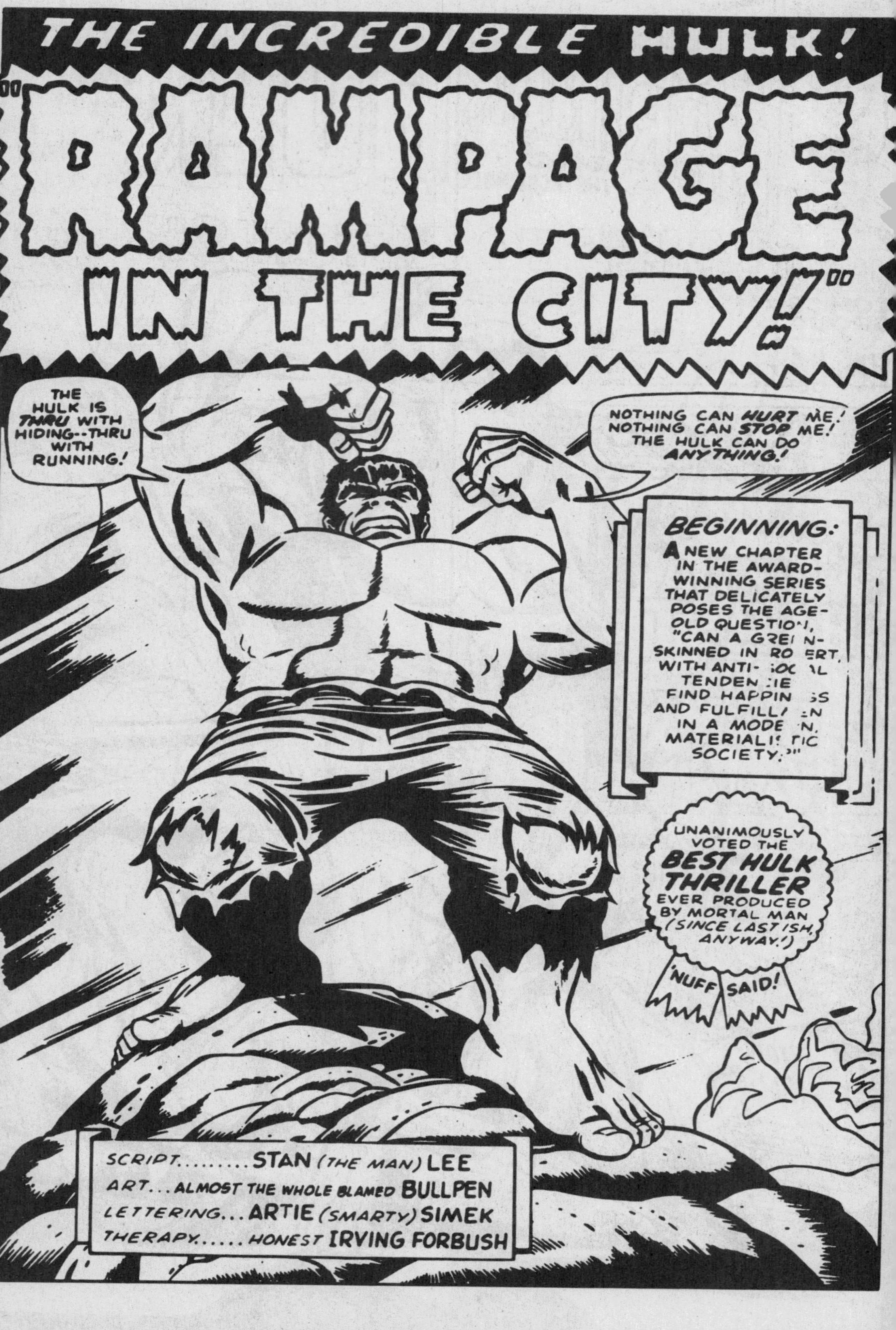
THE INCREDIBLE HULK!
"RAMPAGE IN THE CITY!"
THE HULK IS THRU WITH HIDING--THRU WITH RUNNING!
NOTHING CAN HURT ME! NOTHING CAN STOP ME! THE HULK CAN DO ANYTHING!
BEGINNING:
A NEW CHAPTER IN THE AWARD-WINNING SERIES THAT DELICATELY POSES THE AGE-OLD QUESTI N, "CAN A GREE N-SKINNED IN RO ERT, WITH ANTI- OCIAL TENDEN IE FIND HAPPIN SS AND FULFILL EN IN A MODE N, MATERIALI TIC SOCIETY?"
UNANIMOUSLY VOTED THE BEST HULK THRILLER EVER PRODUCED BY MORTAL MAN (SINCE LAST ISH, ANYWAY!)
'NUFF SAID!
SCRIPT........STAN (THE MAN) LEE
ART...ALMOST THE WHOLE BLAMED BULLPEN
LETTERING...ARTIE (SMARTY) SIMEK
THERAPY.....HONEST IRVING FORBUSH

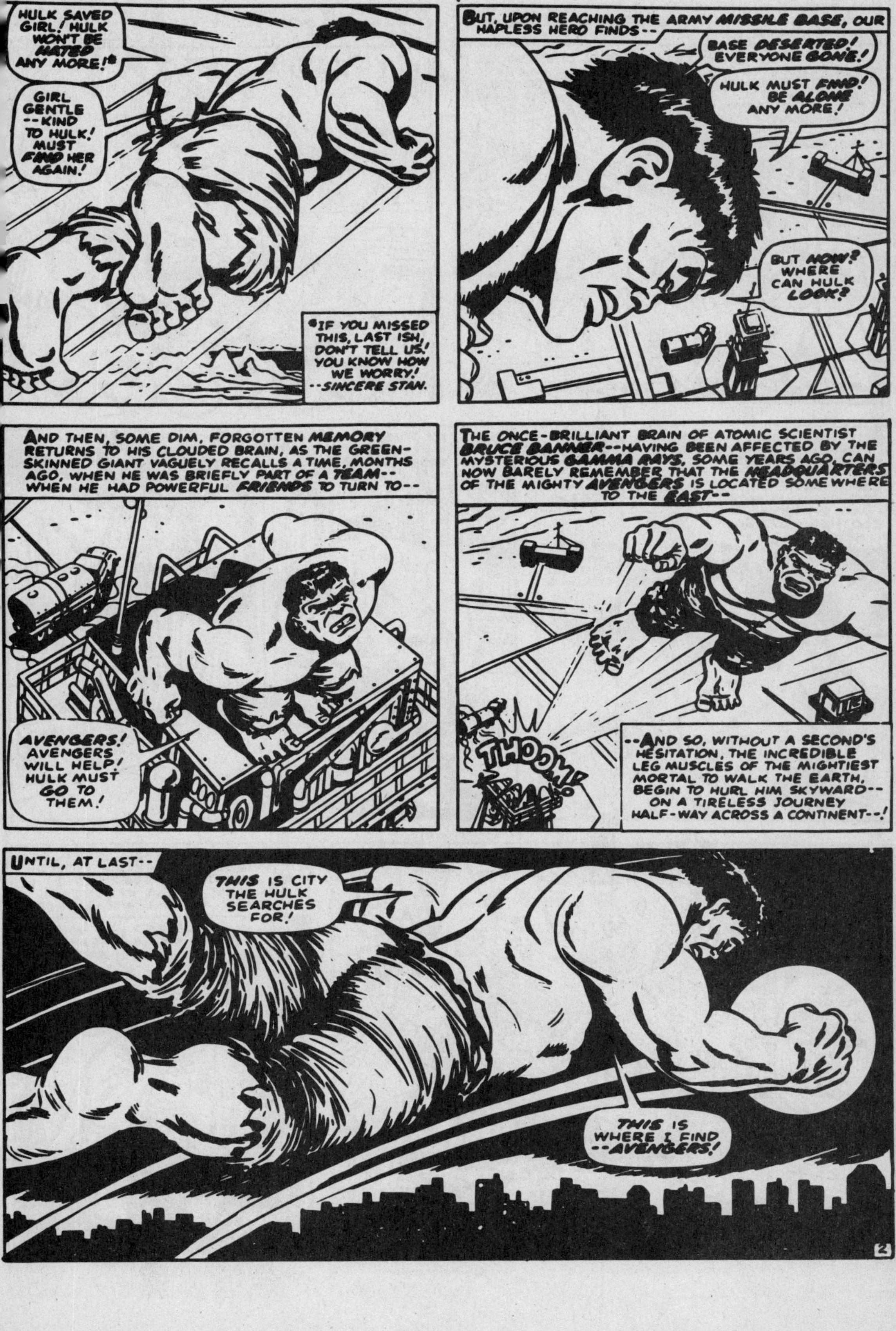

HULK SAVED GIRL! HULK WON'T BE HATED ANY MORE!*
GIRL GENTLE --KIND TO HULK! MUST FIND HER AGAIN!
*IF YOU MISSED THIS, LAST ISH, DON'T TELL US! YOU KNOW HOW WE WORRY! --SINCERE STAN.
BUT, UPON REACHING THE ARMY MISSILE BASE, OUR HAPLESS HERO FINDS--
BASE DESERTED! EVERYONE GONE!
HULK MUST FIND! BE ALONE ANY MORE!
BUT NOW? WHERE CAN HULK LOOK?
AND THEN, SOME DIM, FORGOTTEN MEMORY RETURNS TO HIS CLOUDED BRAIN, AS THE GREEN-SKINNED GIANT VAGUELY RECALLS A TIME, MONTHS AGO, WHEN HE WAS BRIEFLY PART OF A TEAM--WHEN HE HAD POWERFUL FRIENDS TO TURN TO--
AVENGERS! AVENGERS WILL HELP! HULK MUST GO TO THEM!
THE ONCE-BRILLIANT BRAIN OF ATOMIC SCIENTIST BRUCE BANNER--HAVING BEEN AFFECTED BY THE MYSTERIOUS GAMMA RAYS, SOME YEARS AGO, CAN NOW BARELY REMEMBER THAT THE HEADQUARTERS OF THE MIGHTY AVENGERS IS LOCATED SOME WHERE TO THE EAST--
THOOOM!
--AND SO, WITHOUT A SECOND'S HESITATION, THE INCREDIBLE LEG MUSCLES OF THE MIGHTIEST MORTAL TO WALK THE EARTH, BEGIN TO HURL HIM SKYWARD-- ON A TIRELESS JOURNEY HALF-WAY ACROSS A CONTINENT--!
UNTIL, AT LAST--
THIS IS CITY THE HULK SEARCHES FOR!
THIS IS WHERE I FIND --AVENGERS!
2

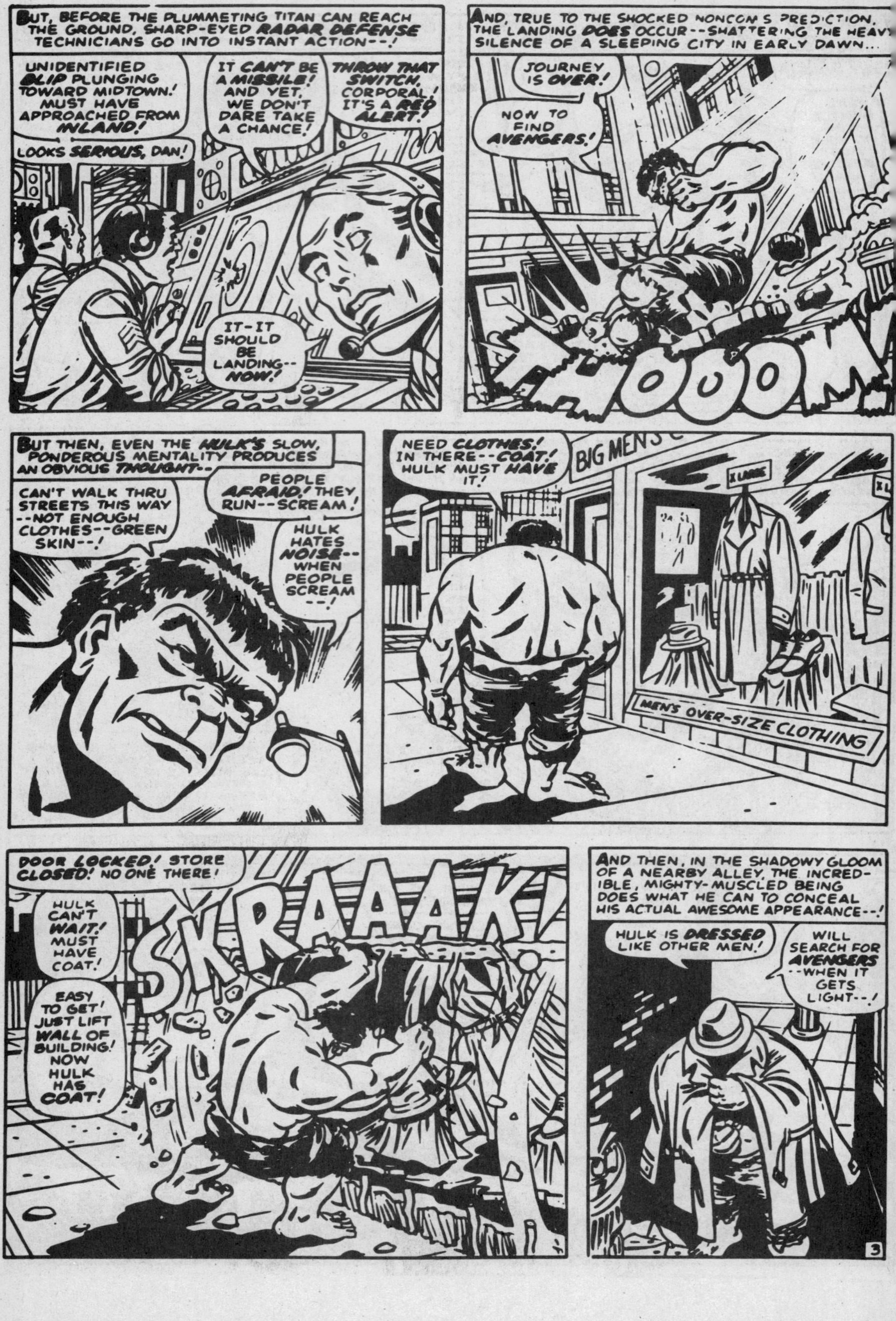
BUT, BEFORE THE PLUMMETING TITAN CAN REACH THE GROUND, SHARP-EYED RADAR DEFENSE TECHNICIANS GO INTO INSTANT ACTION--!
UNIDENTIFIED BLIP PLUNGING TOWARD MIDTOWN! MUST HAVE APPROACHED FROM INLAND!
LOOKS SERIOUS, DAN!
IT CAN'T BE A MISSILE! AND YET, WE DON'T DARE TAKE A CHANCE!
THROW THAT SWITCH, CORPORAL! IT'S A RED ALERT!
IT-IT SHOULD BE LANDING--NOW!
AND, TRUE TO THE SHOCKED NONCOM'S PREDICTION, THE LANDING DOES OCCUR--SHATTERING THE HEAVY SILENCE OF A SLEEPING CITY IN EARLY DAWN...
JOURNEY IS OVER!
NOW TO FIND AVENGERS!
THOOOOM
BUT THEN, EVEN THE HULK'S SLOW, PONDEROUS MENTALITY PRODUCES AN OBVIOUS THOUGHT--
CAN'T WALK THRU STREETS THIS WAY --NOT ENOUGH CLOTHES--GREEN SKIN--!
PEOPLE AFRAID! THEY RUN--SCREAM!
HULK HATES NOISE--WHEN PEOPLE SCREAM--!
NEED CLOTHES! IN THERE--COAT! HULK MUST HAVE IT!
BIG MEN'S
X LARGE
MEN'S OVER-SIZE CLOTHING
DOOR LOCKED! STORE CLOSED! NO ONE THERE!
HULK CAN'T WAIT! MUST HAVE COAT!
SKRAAAK!
EASY TO GET! JUST LIFT WALL OF BUILDING! NOW HULK HAS COAT!
AND THEN, IN THE SHADOWY GLOOM OF A NEARBY ALLEY, THE INCREDIBLE, MIGHTY-MUSCLED BEING DOES WHAT HE CAN TO CONCEAL HIS ACTUAL AWESOME APPEARANCE--!
HULK IS DRESSED LIKE OTHER MEN!
WILL SEARCH FOR AVENGERS--WHEN IT GETS LIGHT--!
3

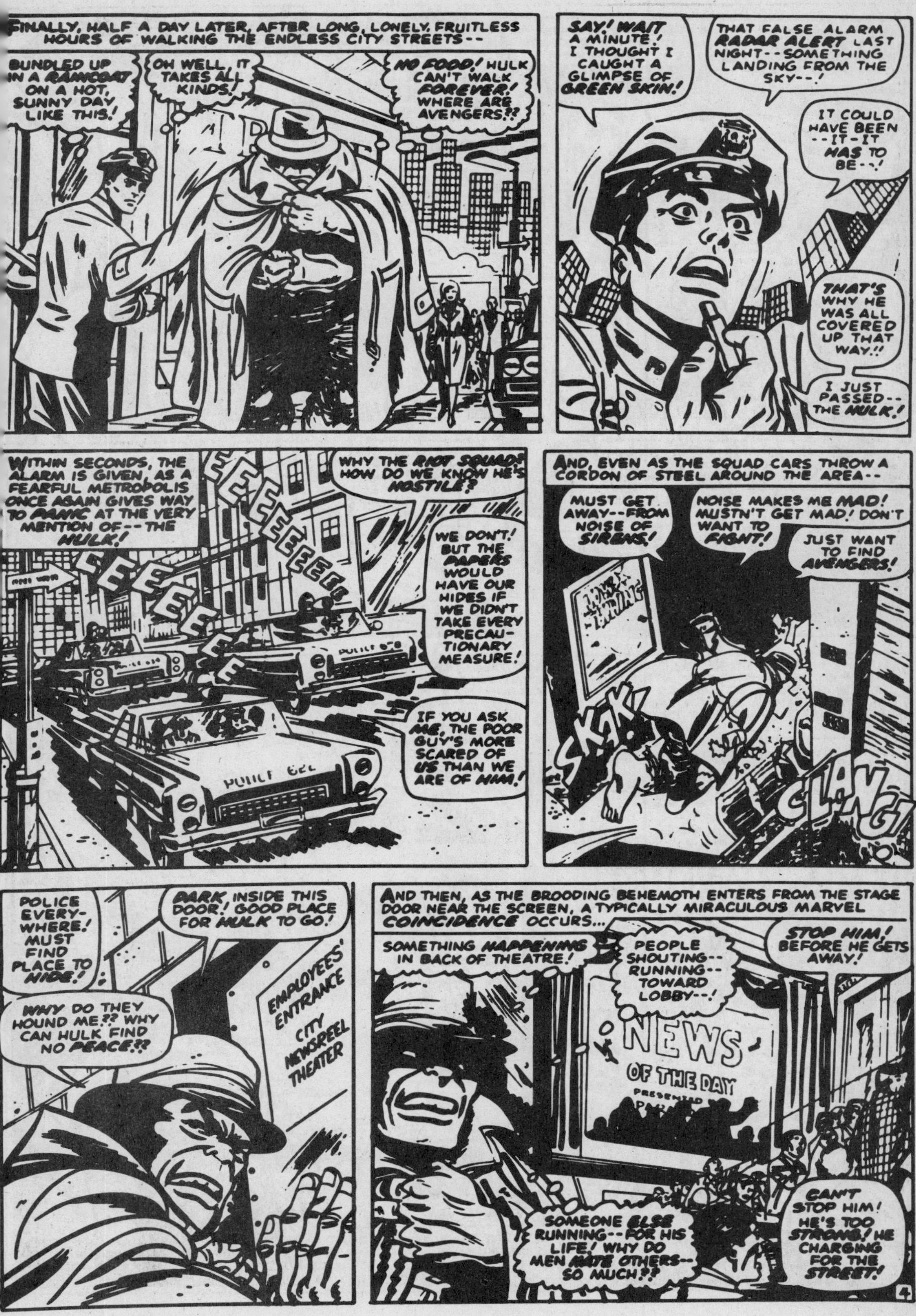

FINALLY, HALF A DAY LATER, AFTER LONG, LONELY, FRUITLESS HOURS OF WALKING THE ENDLESS CITY STREETS--
BUNDLED UP IN A RAINCOAT ON A HOT, SUNNY DAY LIKE THIS!
OH WELL, IT TAKES ALL KINDS!
NO FOOD! HULK CAN'T WALK FOREVER! WHERE ARE AVENGERS??
SAY! WAIT A MINUTE! I THOUGHT I CAUGHT A GLIMPSE OF GREEN SKIN!
THAT FALSE ALARM RADAR ALERT LAST NIGHT--SOMETHING LANDING FROM THE SKY--!
IT COULD HAVE BEEN--IT-IT HAS TO BE--!
THAT'S WHY HE WAS ALL COVERED UP THAT WAY!!
I JUST PASSED--THE HULK!
WITHIN SECONDS, THE ALARM IS GIVEN, AS A FEARFUL METROPOLIS ONCE AGAIN GIVES WAY TO PANIC AT THE VERY MENTION OF--THE HULK!
EEEEEEEEEEE
WHY THE RIOT SQUAD? HOW DO WE KNOW HE'S HOSTILE?
WE DON'T! BUT THE PAPERS WOULD HAVE OUR HIDES IF WE DIDN'T TAKE EVERY PRECAUTIONARY MEASURE!
IF YOU ASK ME, THE POOR GUY'S MORE SCARED OF US THAN WE ARE OF HIM!
AND, EVEN AS THE SQUAD CARS THROW A CORDON OF STEEL AROUND THE AREA--
MUST GET AWAY--FROM NOISE OF SIRENS!
NOISE MAKES ME MAD! MUSTN'T GET MAD! DON'T WANT TO FIGHT!
JUST WANT TO FIND AVENGERS!
SKRK
CLANG!
POLICE EVERYWHERE! MUST FIND PLACE TO HIDE!
DARK INSIDE THIS DOOR! GOOD PLACE FOR HULK TO GO!
WHY DO THEY HOUND ME?? WHY CAN HULK FIND NO PEACE??
EMPLOYEES' ENTRANCE
CITY NEWSREEL THEATER
AND THEN, AS THE BROODING BEHEMOTH ENTERS FROM THE STAGE DOOR NEAR THE SCREEN, A TYPICALLY MIRACULOUS MARVEL COINCIDENCE OCCURS...
SOMETHING HAPPENING IN BACK OF THEATRE!
PEOPLE SHOUTING--RUNNING--TOWARD LOBBY--!
STOP HIM! BEFORE HE GETS AWAY!
NEWS OF THE DAY
SOMEONE ELSE RUNNING--FOR HIS LIFE! WHY DO MEN HATE OTHERS--SO MUCH??
CAN'T STOP HIM! HE'S TOO STRONG! HE CHARGING FOR THE STREET!
4

AND THEN, THERE IN THE SHADOWS, WHERE HE STANDS--UNSEEN--UNNOTICED--A GLIMMER OF *RECOGNITION* FLICKERS IN THE HULK'S CONFUSED BRAIN--

THAT *FACE!* I *KNOW* HIM! I HAVE SEEN HIM --SOMEWHERE-- *FOUGHT* HIM-- SOMEWHERE! BUT I HAVE FOUGHT --SO *MANY*-- HOW CAN I BE *SURE*?!!

AND, BEFORE THE HULK CAN EVEN HOPE TO REMEMBER--THE EPISODE IS *ENDED*-- THE STRANGER IS *GONE!*

BUT, HE WHO HAD ONCE BEEN THE SHARP-WITTED, SUPREMELY INTELLIGENT *BRUCE BANNER*, NOW FINDS IT DIFFICULT TO RETAIN A THOUGHT FOR ANY APPRECIABLE LENGTH OF TIME! AND SO--

DON'T KNOW WHERE TO GO--WHAT TO DO! POLICE MUST NOT FIND ME!

HULK WILL STAY *HERE*-- IN DARK-- WHERE IT IS SAFE!

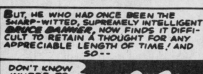

WAIT! ON SCREEN! WHAT IS-- *THAT*?!!

AND *THAT*, AS WE CAN PLAINLY SEE, IS ANOTHER CAPRICIOUS *COINCIDENCE*--TOO REMOTE TO OCCUR IN *FICTION*--BUT ALL TOO *POSSIBLE* IN THIS STARTLING WORLD WE LIVE IN--!

--YOU ARE NOW WITNESSING A FILM JUST RELEASED BY THE PENTAGON! IT WAS TAKEN BY A COMBAT PHOTOGRAPHER, AT THE SCENE OF OUR MOST CLOSELY- GUARDED SOUTHWESTERN MISSILE BASE!

THIS IS THE FIRST STARTLING FILM OF THE MAN CALLED *BOOMERANG*, AS HE SINGLE-HANDEDLY ATTEMPTED TO SABOTAGE AMERICA'S VITAL *ORION MISSILE!*

BOOMERANG! IT WAS *HIM* --WHO CAPTURED *GIRL!*

*THOSE OF YOU WHO READ OUR PAST FEW ISHES CAN SKIP THE NEXT PAGE, AS ITS PRIME PURPOSE IS TO BRING *NEWER* MARVEL- ITES UP TO DATE! JUST ANOTHER SUPER-SERVICE FROM YOUR BIG HEARTED BULLPEN'--- SANCTIMONIUS STAN

5

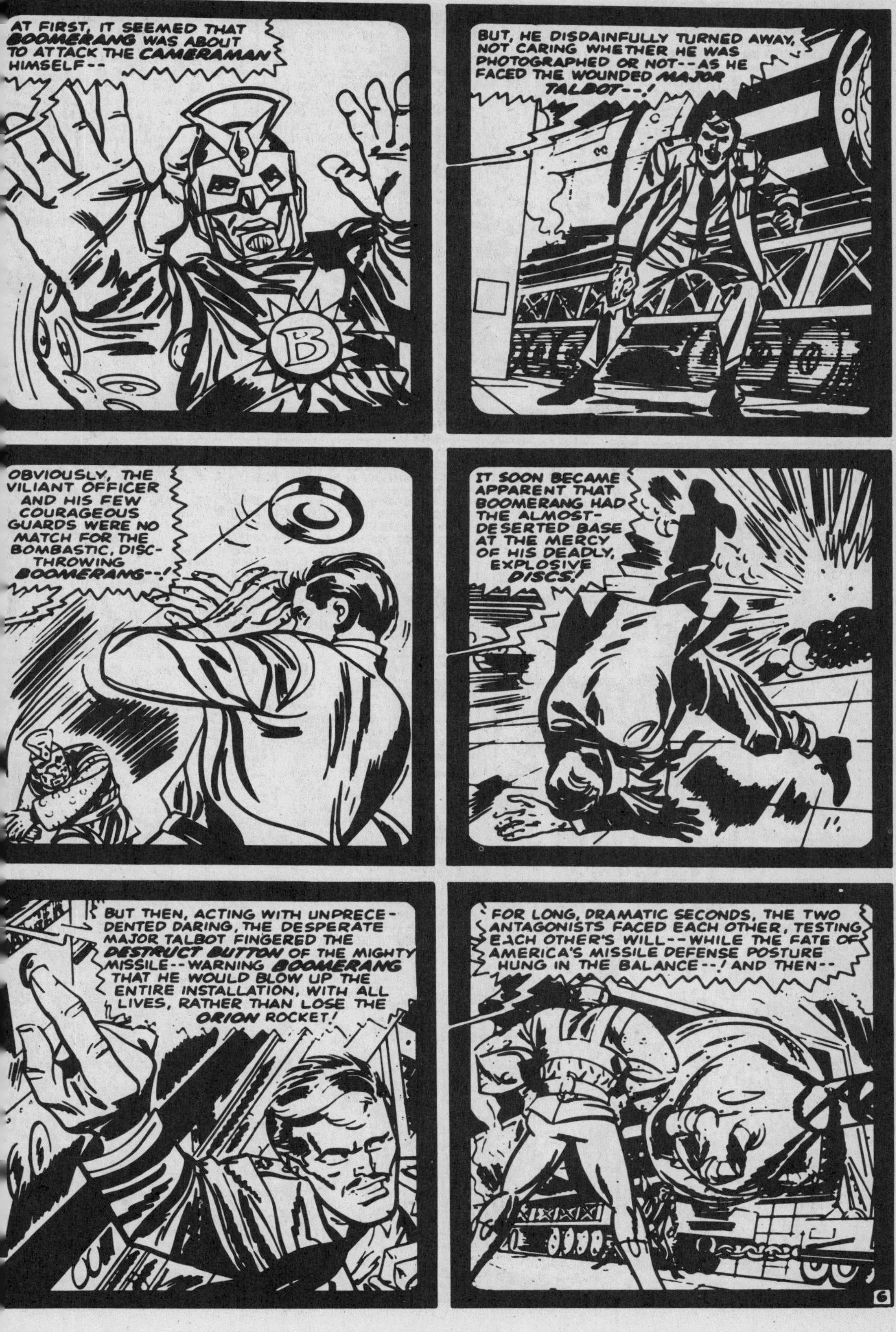
AT FIRST, IT SEEMED THAT BOOMERANG WAS ABOUT TO ATTACK THE CAMERAMAN HIMSELF--
BUT, HE DISDAINFULLY TURNED AWAY, NOT CARING WHETHER HE WAS PHOTOGRAPHED OR NOT--AS HE FACED THE WOUNDED MAJOR TALBOT--!
OBVIOUSLY, THE VILIANT OFFICER AND HIS FEW COURAGEOUS GUARDS WERE NO MATCH FOR THE BOMBASTIC, DISC-THROWING BOOMERANG--!
IT SOON BECAME APPARENT THAT BOOMERANG HAD THE ALMOST-DESERTED BASE AT THE MERCY OF HIS DEADLY, EXPLOSIVE DISCS!
BUT THEN, ACTING WITH UNPRECE-DENTED DARING, THE DESPERATE MAJOR TALBOT FINGERED THE DESTRUCT BUTTON OF THE MIGHTY MISSILE--WARNING BOOMERANG THAT HE WOULD BLOW UP THE ENTIRE INSTALLATION, WITH ALL LIVES, RATHER THAN LOSE THE ORION ROCKET!
FOR LONG, DRAMATIC SECONDS, THE TWO ANTAGONISTS FACED EACH OTHER, TESTING EACH OTHER'S WILL--WHILE THE FATE OF AMERICA'S MISSILE DEFENSE POSTURE HUNG IN THE BALANCE--! AND THEN--
6

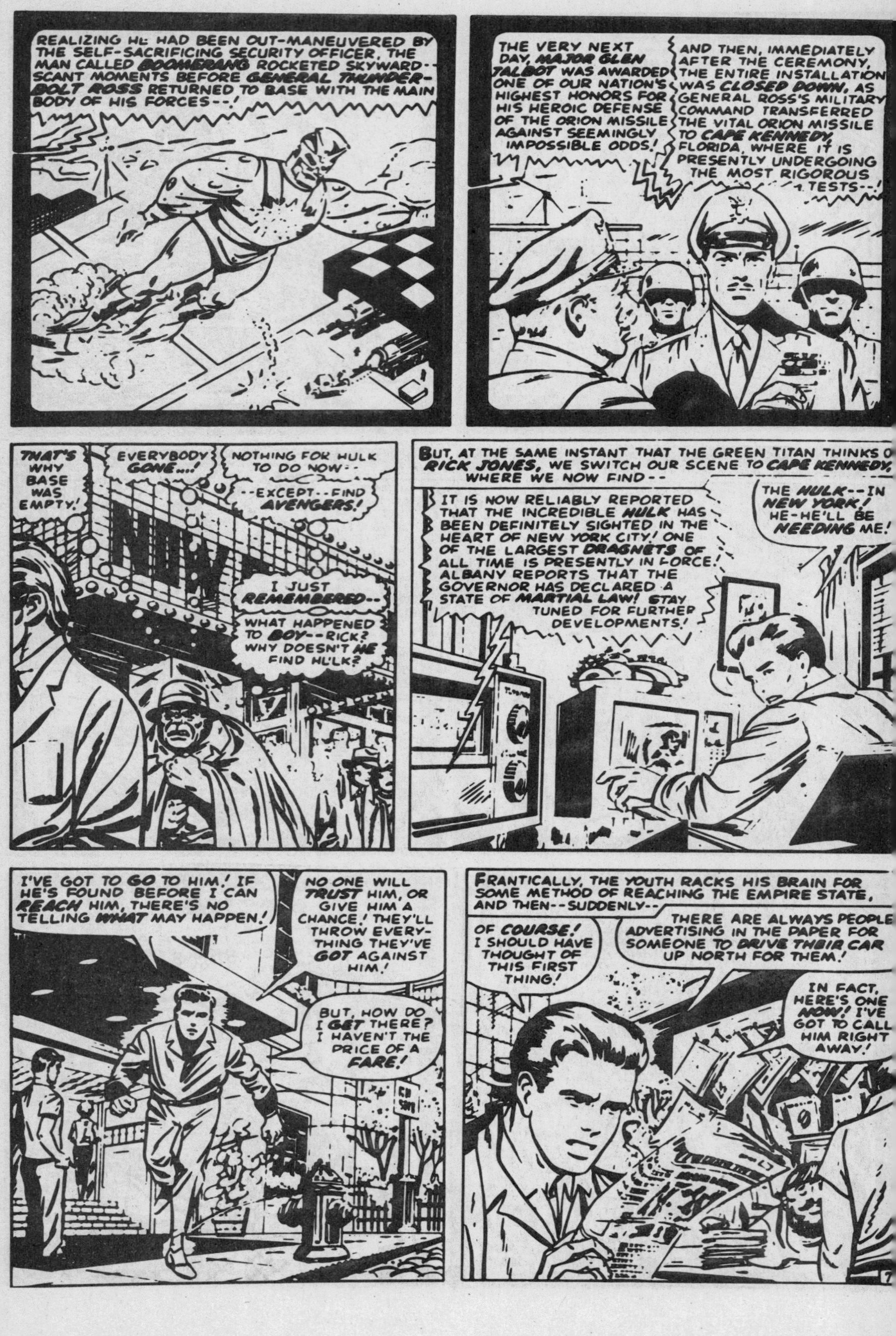

REALIZING HE HAD BEEN OUT-MANEUVERED BY THE SELF-SACRIFICING SECURITY OFFICER, THE MAN CALLED BOOMERANG ROCKETED SKYWARD-- SCANT MOMENTS BEFORE GENERAL THUNDERBOLT ROSS RETURNED TO BASE WITH THE MAIN BODY OF HIS FORCES--!
THE VERY NEXT DAY, MAJOR GLEN TALBOT WAS AWARDED ONE OF OUR NATION'S HIGHEST HONORS FOR HIS HEROIC DEFENSE OF THE ORION MISSILE AGAINST SEEMINGLY IMPOSSIBLE ODDS!
AND THEN, IMMEDIATELY AFTER THE CEREMONY, THE ENTIRE INSTALLATION WAS CLOSED DOWN, AS GENERAL ROSS'S MILITARY COMMAND TRANSFERRED THE VITAL ORION MISSILE TO CAPE KENNEDY, FLORIDA, WHERE IT IS PRESENTLY UNDERGOING THE MOST RIGOROUS TESTS--!
THAT'S WHY BASE WAS EMPTY!
EVERYBODY GONE...!
NOTHING FOR HULK TO DO NOW--
--EXCEPT--FIND AVENGERS!
I JUST REMEMBERED--
WHAT HAPPENED TO BOY--RICK? WHY DOESN'T HE FIND HULK?
BUT, AT THE SAME INSTANT THAT THE GREEN TITAN THINKS OF RICK JONES, WE SWITCH OUR SCENE TO CAPE KENNEDY, WHERE WE NOW FIND--
IT IS NOW RELIABLY REPORTED THAT THE INCREDIBLE HULK HAS BEEN DEFINITELY SIGHTED IN THE HEART OF NEW YORK CITY! ONE OF THE LARGEST DRAGNETS OF ALL TIME IS PRESENTLY IN FORCE! ALBANY REPORTS THAT THE GOVERNOR HAS DECLARED A STATE OF MARTIAL LAW! STAY TUNED FOR FURTHER DEVELOPMENTS!
THE HULK--IN NEW YORK! HE-HE'LL BE NEEDING ME!
I'VE GOT TO GO TO HIM! IF HE'S FOUND BEFORE I CAN REACH HIM, THERE'S NO TELLING WHAT MAY HAPPEN!
NO ONE WILL TRUST HIM, OR GIVE HIM A CHANCE! THEY'LL THROW EVERYTHING THEY'VE GOT AGAINST HIM!
BUT, HOW DO I GET THERE? I HAVEN'T THE PRICE OF A FARE!
FRANTICALLY, THE YOUTH RACKS HIS BRAIN FOR SOME METHOD OF REACHING THE EMPIRE STATE, AND THEN--SUDDENLY--
OF COURSE! I SHOULD HAVE THOUGHT OF THIS FIRST THING!
THERE ARE ALWAYS PEOPLE ADVERTISING IN THE PAPER FOR SOMEONE TO DRIVE THEIR CAR UP NORTH FOR THEM!
IN FACT, HERE'S ONE NOW! I'VE GOT TO CALL HIM RIGHT AWAY!
7

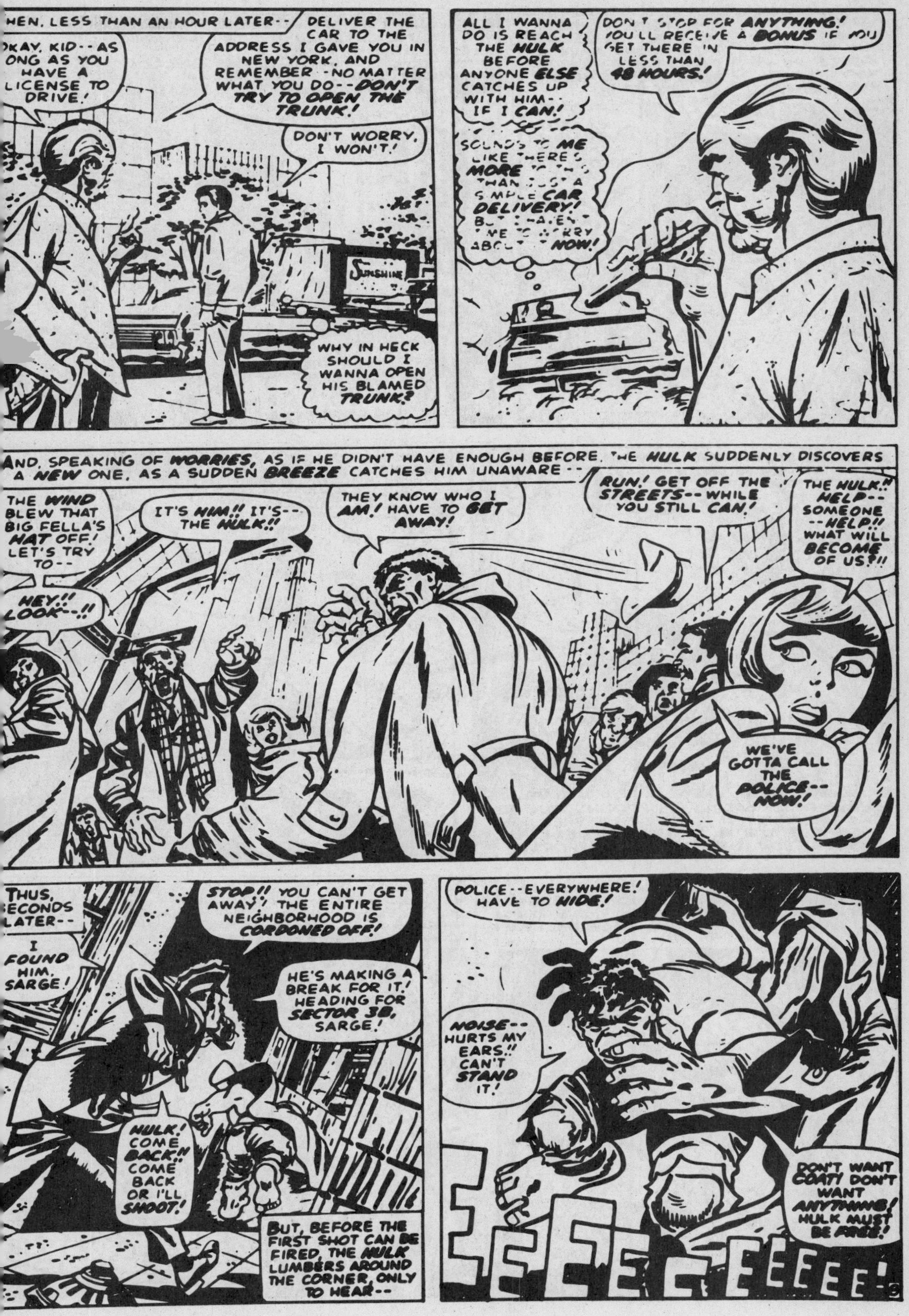
HEN, LESS THAN AN HOUR LATER--
OKAY, KID--AS ONG AS YOU HAVE A LICENSE TO DRIVE!
DELIVER THE CAR TO THE ADDRESS I GAVE YOU IN NEW YORK, AND REMEMBER --NO MATTER WHAT YOU DO--DON'T TRY TO OPEN THE TRUNK!
DON'T WORRY, I WON'T!
SUNSHINE
WHY IN HECK SHOULD I WANNA OPEN HIS BLAMED TRUNK?
ALL I WANNA DO IS REACH THE HULK BEFORE ANYONE ELSE CATCHES UP WITH HIM-- IF I CAN!
DON'T STOP FOR ANYTHING! YOU'LL RECEIVE A BONUS IF YOU GET THERE IN LESS THAN 48 HOURS!
SOUNDS TO ME LIKE THERE'S MORE TO THIS THAN JUST A SIMPLE CAR DELIVERY! NOW!
AND, SPEAKING OF WORRIES, AS IF HE DIDN'T HAVE ENOUGH BEFORE, THE HULK SUDDENLY DISCOVERS A NEW ONE, AS A SUDDEN BREEZE CATCHES HIM UNAWARE--
THE WIND BLEW THAT BIG FELLA'S HAT OFF! LET'S TRY TO--
HEY!! LOOK--!!
IT'S HIM!! IT'S-- THE HULK!!
THEY KNOW WHO I AM! HAVE TO GET AWAY!
RUN! GET OFF THE STREETS--WHILE YOU STILL CAN!
THE HULK!! HELP-- SOMEONE --HELP!! WHAT WILL BECOME OF US?!!
WE'VE GOTTA CALL THE POLICE-- NOW!
THUS, SECONDS LATER--
I FOUND HIM, SARGE!
STOP!! YOU CAN'T GET AWAY! THE ENTIRE NEIGHBORHOOD IS CORDONED OFF!
HE'S MAKING A BREAK FOR IT! HEADING FOR SECTOR 3B, SARGE!
HULK! COME BACK!! COME BACK OR I'LL SHOOT!
BUT, BEFORE THE FIRST SHOT CAN BE FIRED, THE HULK LUMBERS AROUND THE CORNER, ONLY TO HEAR--
POLICE--EVERYWHERE! HAVE TO HIDE!
NOISE-- HURTS MY EARS!! CAN'T STAND IT!
DON'T WANT COAT! DON'T WANT ANYTHING! HULK MUST BE FREE!
EEEEE-EEEEE!

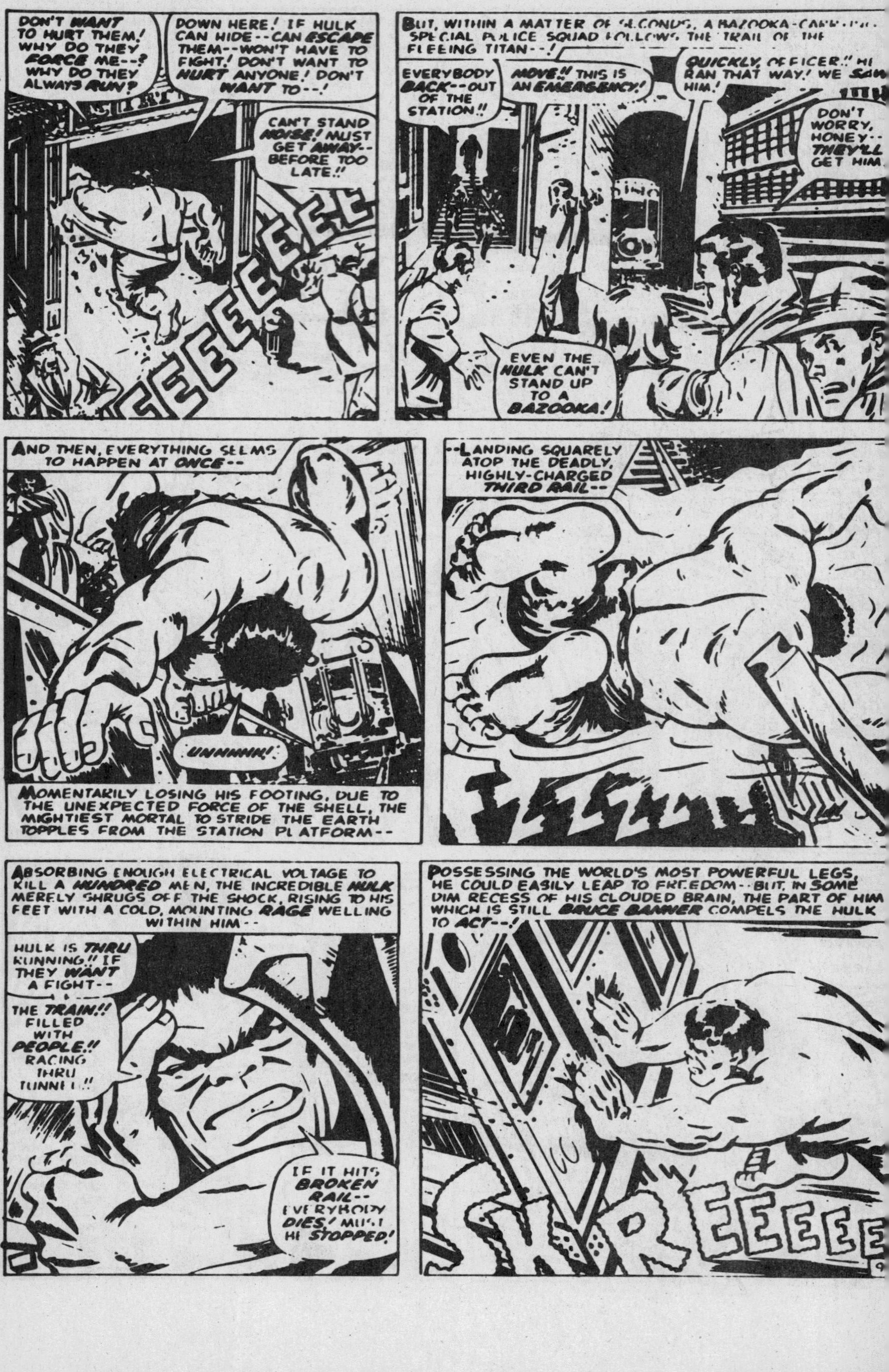
DON'T WANT TO HURT THEM! WHY DO THEY FORCE ME--? WHY DO THEY ALWAYS RUN?
DOWN HERE! IF HULK CAN HIDE--CAN ESCAPE THEM--WON'T HAVE TO FIGHT! DON'T WANT TO HURT ANYONE! DON'T WANT TO--!
CAN'T STAND NOISE! MUST GET AWAY--BEFORE TOO LATE.!!
BUT, WITHIN A MATTER OF SECONDS, A BAZOOKA-CARR SPECIAL POLICE SQUAD FOLLOWS THE TRAIL OF THE FLEEING TITAN--!
EVERYBODY BACK--OUT OF THE STATION!!
MOVE!! THIS IS AN EMERGENCY!
QUICKLY, OFFICER!! HE RAN THAT WAY! WE SAW HIM!
DON'T WORRY, HONEY--THEY'LL GET HIM.
EVEN THE HULK CAN'T STAND UP TO A BAZOOKA!
AND THEN, EVERYTHING SEEMS TO HAPPEN AT ONCE--
UNNNNH!
MOMENTARILY LOSING HIS FOOTING, DUE TO THE UNEXPECTED FORCE OF THE SHELL, THE MIGHTIEST MORTAL TO STRIDE THE EARTH TOPPLES FROM THE STATION PLATFORM--
--LANDING SQUARELY ATOP THE DEADLY, HIGHLY-CHARGED THIRD RAIL--
ABSORBING ENOUGH ELECTRICAL VOLTAGE TO KILL A HUNDRED MEN, THE INCREDIBLE HULK MERELY SHRUGS OFF THE SHOCK, RISING TO HIS FEET WITH A COLD, MOUNTING RAGE WELLING WITHIN HIM--
HULK IS THRU RUNNING!! IF THEY WANT A FIGHT--
THE TRAIN!! FILLED WITH PEOPLE!! RACING THRU TUNNEL!!
IF IT HITS BROKEN RAIL--EVERYBODY DIES! MUST BE STOPPED!
POSSESSING THE WORLD'S MOST POWERFUL LEGS, HE COULD EASILY LEAP TO FREEDOM--BUT, IN SOME DIM RECESS OF HIS CLOUDED BRAIN, THE PART OF HIM WHICH IS STILL BRUCE BANNER COMPELS THE HULK TO ACT--!
9

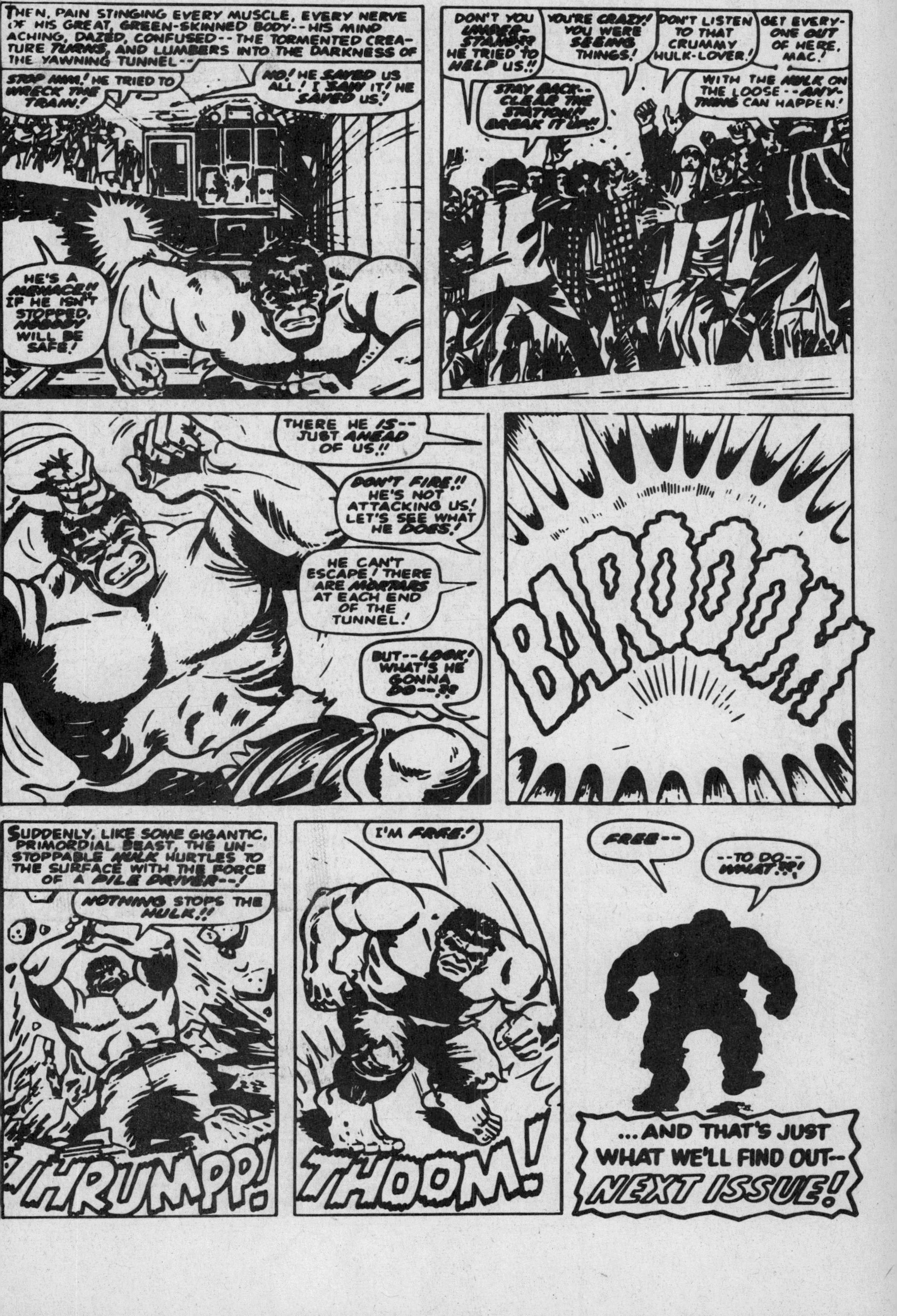
THEN, PAIN STINGING EVERY MUSCLE, EVERY NERVE OF HIS GREAT, GREEN-SKINNED BODY--HIS MIND ACHING, DAZED, CONFUSED--THE TORMENTED CREATURE TURNS, AND LUMBERS INTO THE DARKNESS OF THE YAWNING TUNNEL--
STOP HIM! HE TRIED TO WRECK THE TRAIN!
NO! HE SAVED US ALL! I SAW IT! HE SAVED US!
HE'S A MENACE!! IF HE ISN'T STOPPED, NOBODY WILL BE SAFE!
DON'T YOU UNDERSTAND?? HE TRIED TO HELP US!!
YOU'RE CRAZY! YOU WERE SEEING THINGS!
DON'T LISTEN TO THAT CRUMMY HULK-LOVER!
GET EVERYONE OUT OF HERE, MAC!
STAY BACK--CLEAR THE STATION!! BREAK IT UP!!
WITH THE HULK ON THE LOOSE--ANYTHING CAN HAPPEN!
THERE HE IS--JUST AHEAD OF US!!
DON'T FIRE!! HE'S NOT ATTACKING US! LET'S SEE WHAT HE DOES!
HE CAN'T ESCAPE! THERE ARE MORTARS AT EACH END OF THE TUNNEL!
BUT--LOOK! WHAT'S HE GONNA DO--?!
BAROOOM
SUDDENLY, LIKE SOME GIGANTIC, PRIMORDIAL BEAST, THE UNSTOPPABLE HULK HURTLES TO THE SURFACE WITH THE FORCE OF A PILE DRIVER--!
NOTHING STOPS THE HULK!!
THRUMPP!
I'M FREE!
THOOM!
FREE--
--TO DO--WHAT?!
...AND THAT'S JUST WHAT WE'LL FIND OUT--NEXT ISSUE!

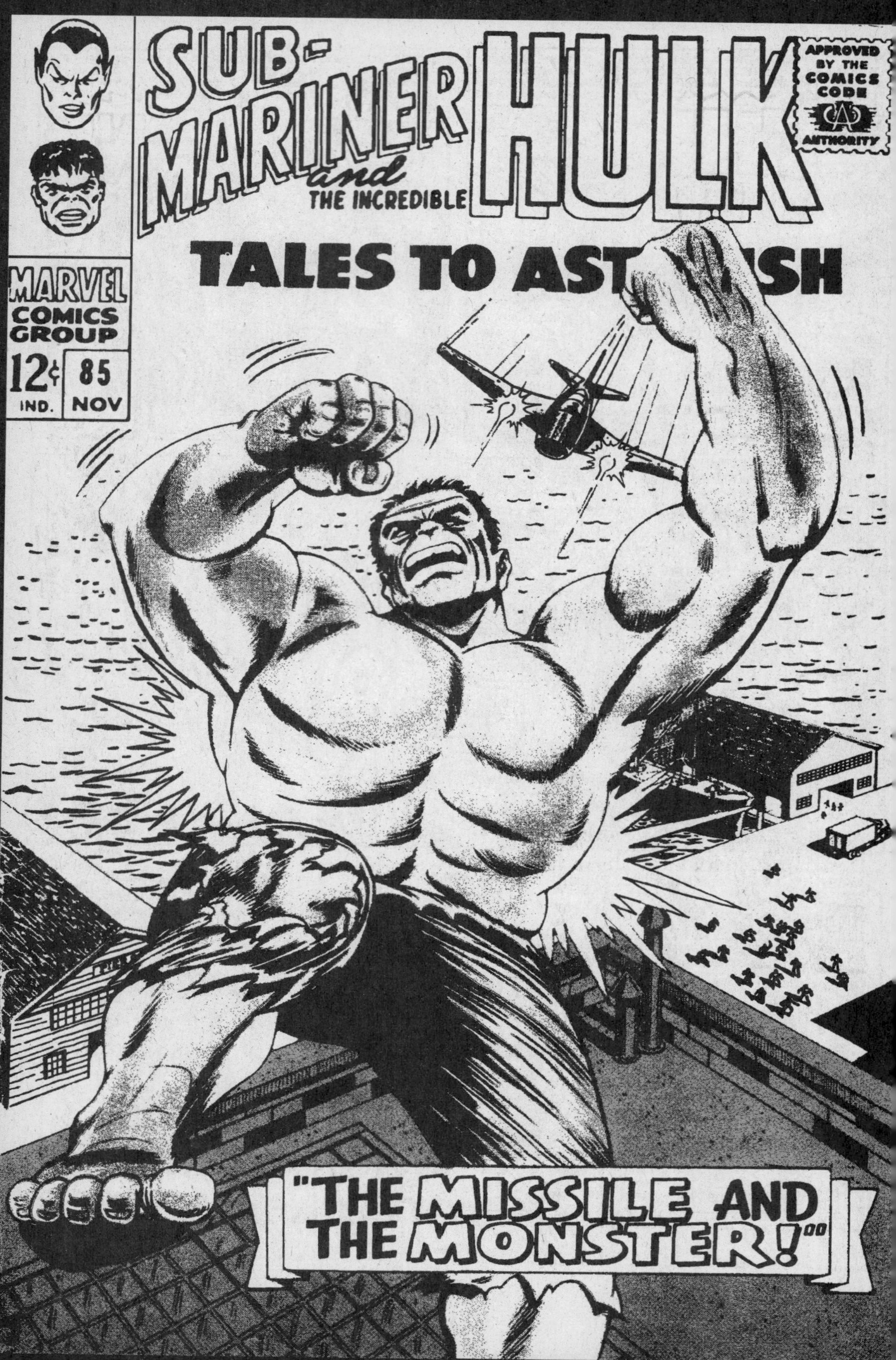
SUB-MARINER
and
THE INCREDIBLE HULK
APPROVED BY THE COMICS CODE CA AUTHORITY
TALES TO AST
SH
MARVEL COMICS GROUP
12¢ IND.
85 NOV
"THE MISSILE AND THE MONSTER!"

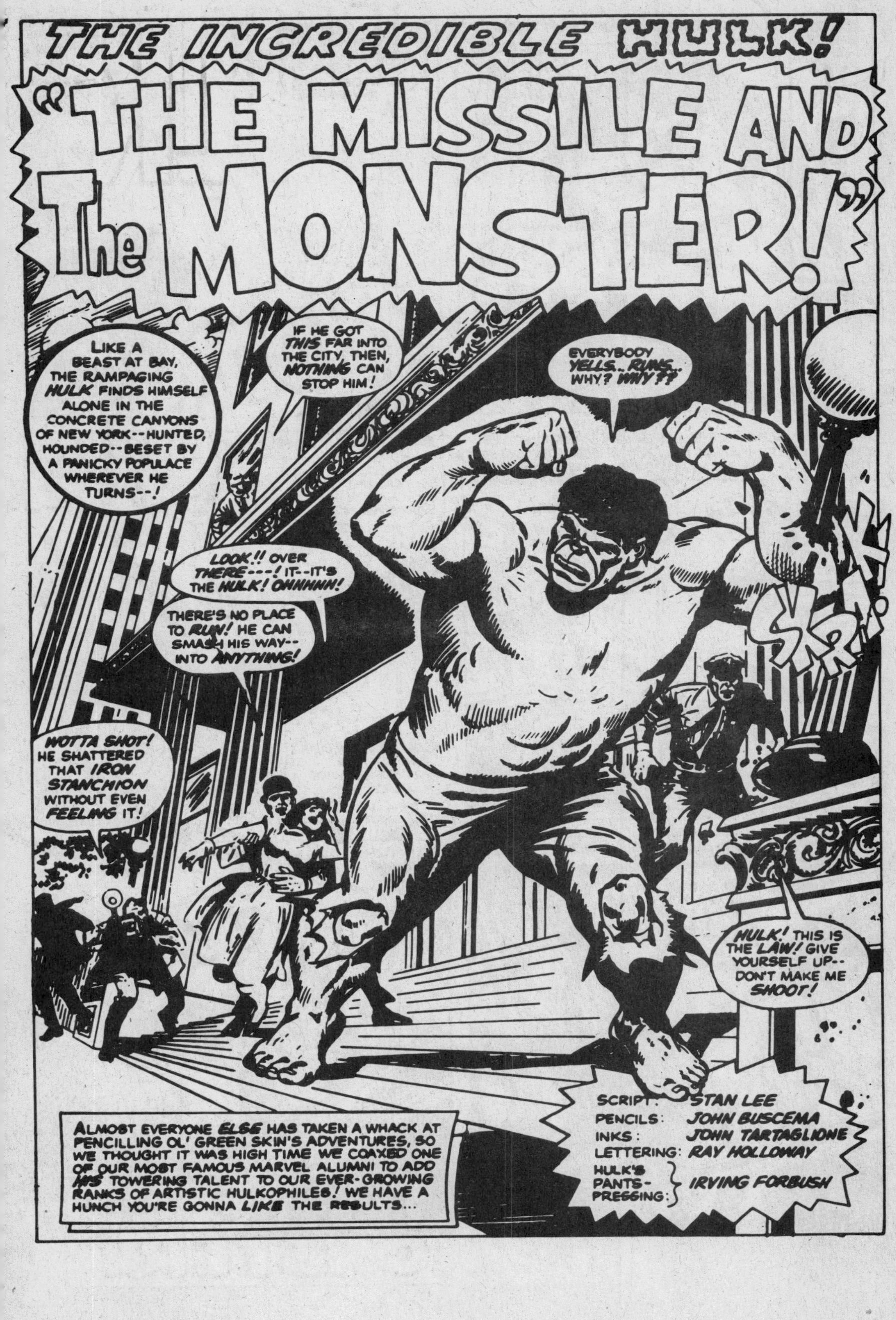
THE INCREDIBLE HULK!
"THE MISSILE AND The MONSTER!"
LIKE A BEAST AT BAY, THE RAMPAGING HULK FINDS HIMSELF ALONE IN THE CONCRETE CANYONS OF NEW YORK--HUNTED, HOUNDED--BESET BY A PANICKY POPULACE WHEREVER HE TURNS--!
IF HE GOT THIS FAR INTO THE CITY, THEN, NOTHING CAN STOP HIM!
EVERYBODY YELLS.. RUNS.. WHY? WHY?!
LOOK!! OVER THERE---! IT--IT'S THE HULK! OHHHHH!
THERE'S NO PLACE TO RUN! HE CAN SMASH HIS WAY--INTO ANYTHING!
WOTTA SHOT! HE SHATTERED THAT IRON STANCHION WITHOUT EVEN FEELING IT!
HULK! THIS IS THE LAW! GIVE YOURSELF UP--DON'T MAKE ME SHOOT!
ALMOST EVERYONE ELSE HAS TAKEN A WHACK AT PENCILLING OL' GREEN SKIN'S ADVENTURES, SO WE THOUGHT IT WAS HIGH TIME WE COAXED ONE OF OUR MOST FAMOUS MARVEL ALUMNI TO ADD HIS TOWERING TALENT TO OUR EVER-GROWING RANKS OF ARTISTIC HULKOPHILES! WE HAVE A HUNCH YOU'RE GONNA LIKE THE RESULTS...
SCRIPT: STAN LEE
PENCILS: JOHN BUSCEMA
INKS: JOHN TARTAGLIONE
LETTERING: RAY HOLLOWAY
HULK'S PANTS-PRESSING: IRVING FORBUSH

NOBODY SHOOTS THE HULK!

RUN! HE'S ABOUT TO ATTACK--!

NO! WE'RE ALMOST BENEATH HIS NOTICE!

HE'S LEAPING AWAY-- BUT- THE POWER-- THE FORCE OF HIS LEGS-- HE-HE TOOK OFF LIKE A MISSILE!

THOOM!

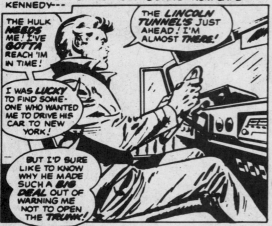

AND, EVEN AS THE INCREDIBLE GREEN GIANT HURTLES OVER THE CITY-- A WORRIED RICK JONES COMPLETES THE LAST LAP OF HIS FRANTIC DRIVE FROM CAPE KENNEDY---

THE HULK NEEDS ME! I'VE GOTTA REACH 'IM IN TIME!

THE LINCOLN TUNNEL'S JUST AHEAD! I'M ALMOST THERE!

I WAS LUCKY TO FIND SOME-ONE WHO WANTED ME TO DRIVE HIS CAR TO NEW YORK!

BUT I'D SURE LIKE TO KNOW WHY HE MADE SUCH A BIG DEAL OUT OF WARNING ME NOT TO OPEN THE TRUNK!

WHILE, BACK AT CAPE KENNEDY---

THAT FOOL BOY WILL BE REACHING HIS DESTINATION ANY MINUTE NOW!

I PLANNED TOO CAREFULLY FOR ANYTHING TO GO WRONG!

AFTER THE WAY I WARNED HIM, JONES WOULDN'T DARE TO OPEN THE CAR'S TRUNK!

SO I'D BETTER MAKE SURE THAT ALL IS IN READINESS!

CLICK!

NO ONE YET SUSPECTS WHAT'S BEHIND THIS INNOCENT-SEEMING DOOR--!

BUT, ONE DAY THE WORLD WILL KNOW!

AND, ON THAT DAY, IT WILL BE TOO LATE FOR THE GREATEST CITY ON EARTH TO SAVE ITSELF-- FROM INSTANT ANNIHILATION!

SO FAR, MY TIMING HAS BEEN PERFECT!

MY CAR WILL REACH NEW YORK EXACTLY AT H-HOUR--

--AT THE PRECISE MOMENT GENERAL ROSS GIVES THE ORDER TO LAUNCH THE ORION MISSILE!

2

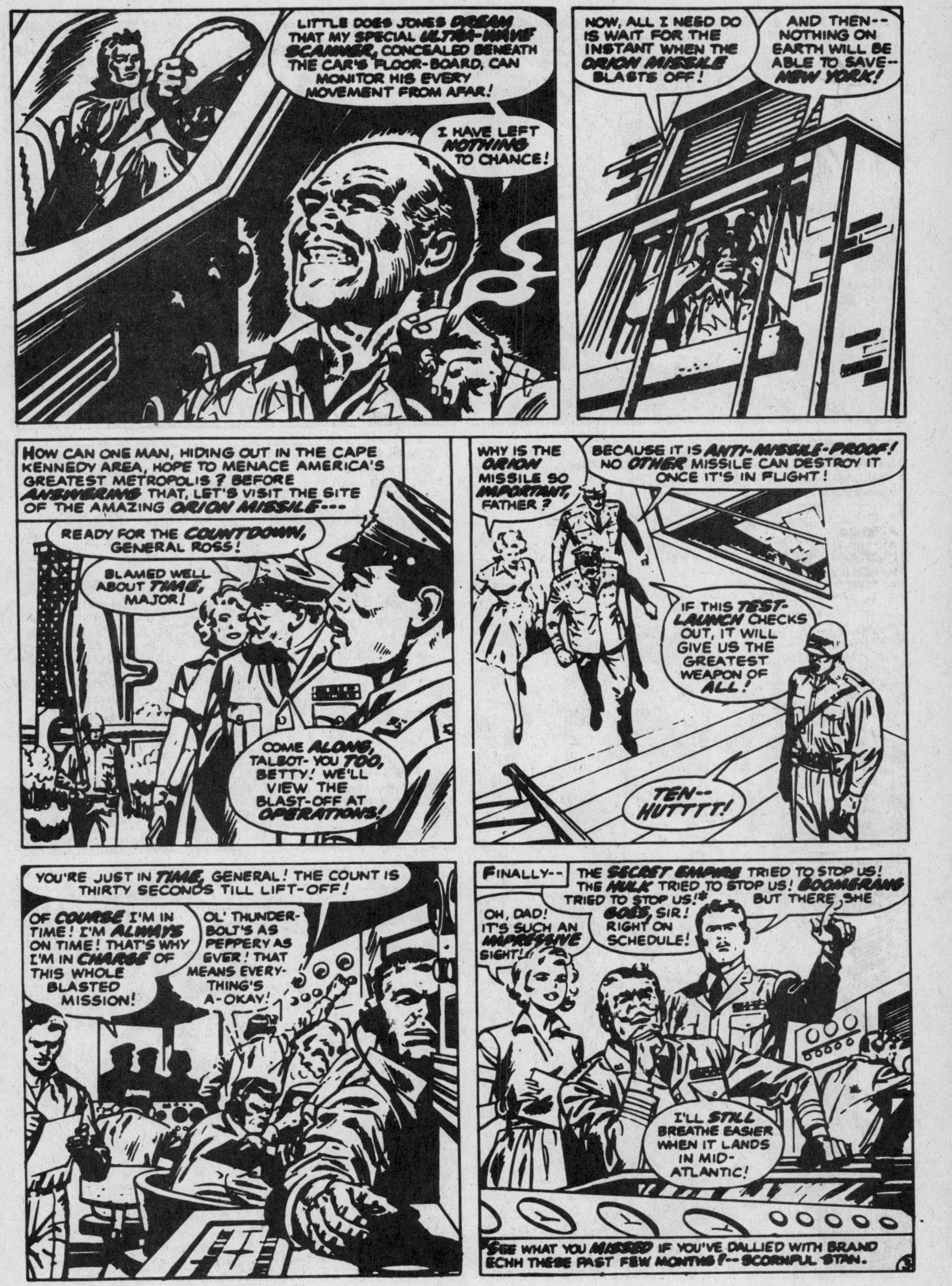
LITTLE DOES JONES DREAM THAT MY SPECIAL ULTRA-WAVE SCANNER, CONCEALED BENEATH THE CAR'S FLOOR-BOARD, CAN MONITOR HIS EVERY MOVEMENT FROM AFAR!
I HAVE LEFT NOTHING TO CHANCE!
NOW, ALL I NEED DO IS WAIT FOR THE INSTANT WHEN THE ORION MISSILE BLASTS OFF!
AND THEN-- NOTHING ON EARTH WILL BE ABLE TO SAVE-- NEW YORK!
HOW CAN ONE MAN, HIDING OUT IN THE CAPE KENNEDY AREA, HOPE TO MENACE AMERICA'S GREATEST METROPOLIS? BEFORE ANSWERING THAT, LET'S VISIT THE SITE OF THE AMAZING ORION MISSILE---
READY FOR THE COUNTDOWN, GENERAL ROSS!
BLAMED WELL ABOUT TIME, MAJOR!
COME ALONG, TALBOT- YOU TOO, BETTY! WE'LL VIEW THE BLAST-OFF AT OPERATIONS!
WHY IS THE ORION MISSILE SO IMPORTANT, FATHER?
BECAUSE IT IS ANTI-MISSILE-PROOF! NO OTHER MISSILE CAN DESTROY IT ONCE IT'S IN FLIGHT!
IF THIS TEST-LAUNCH CHECKS OUT, IT WILL GIVE US THE GREATEST WEAPON OF ALL!
TEN-- HUTTTT!
YOU'RE JUST IN TIME, GENERAL! THE COUNT IS THIRTY SECONDS TILL LIFT-OFF!
OF COURSE I'M IN TIME! I'M ALWAYS ON TIME! THAT'S WHY I'M IN CHARGE OF THIS WHOLE BLASTED MISSION!
OL' THUNDER-BOLT'S AS PEPPERY AS EVER! THAT MEANS EVERY-THING'S A-OKAY!
FINALLY--
THE SECRET EMPIRE TRIED TO STOP US! THE HULK TRIED TO STOP US! BOOMERANG TRIED TO STOP US!* BUT THERE SHE GOES, SIR! RIGHT ON SCHEDULE!
OH, DAD! IT'S SUCH AN IMPRESSIVE SIGHT!
I'LL STILL BREATHE EASIER WHEN IT LANDS IN MID-ATLANTIC!
*SEE WHAT YOU MISSED IF YOU'VE DALLIED WITH BRAND ECHH THESE PAST FEW MONTHS!-- SCORNFUL STAN.
3

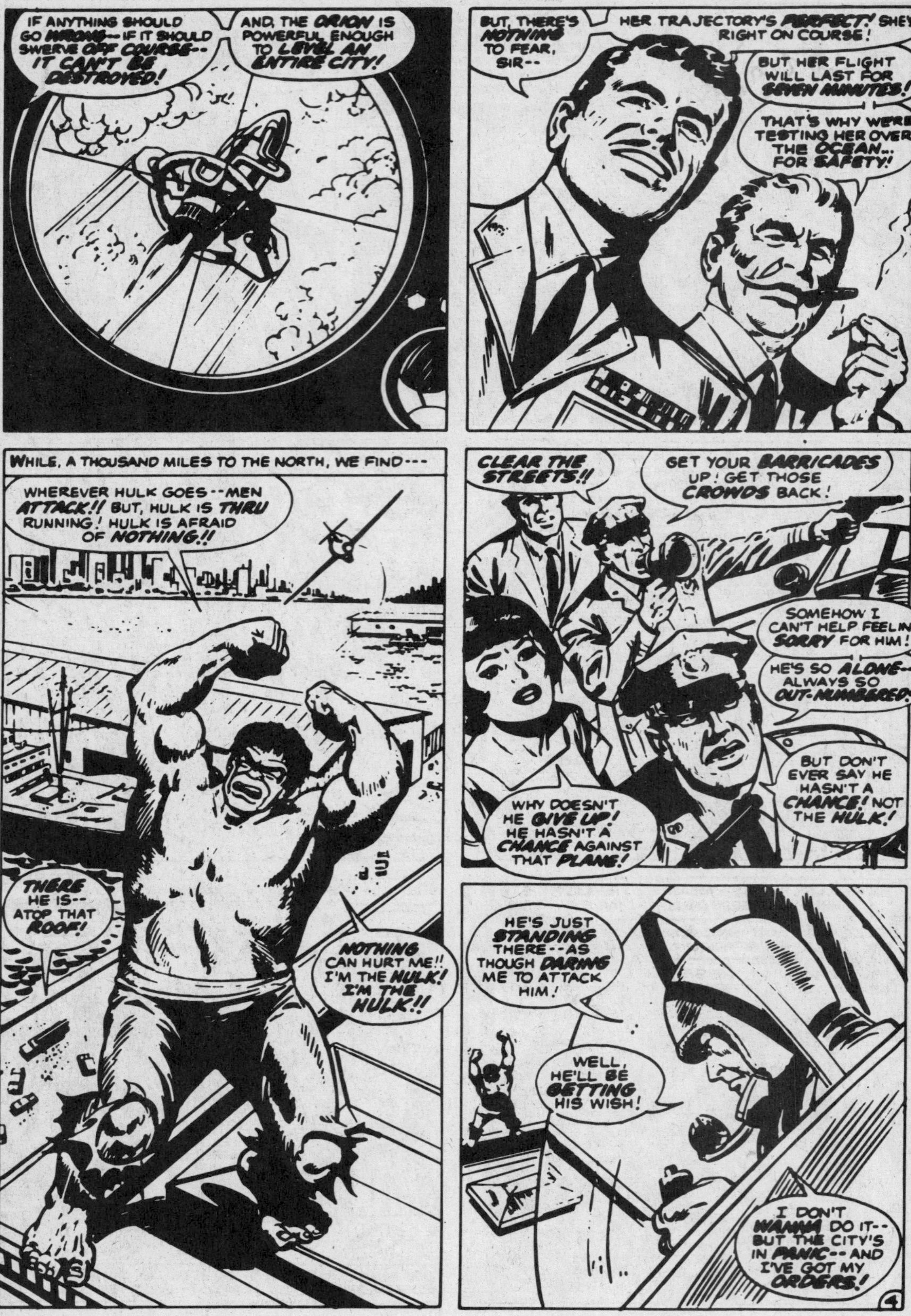
IF ANYTHING SHOULD GO WRONG-- IF IT SHOULD SWERVE OFF COURSE-- IT CAN'T BE DESTROYED!
AND, THE ORION IS POWERFUL ENOUGH TO LEVEL AN ENTIRE CITY!
BUT, THERE'S NOTHING TO FEAR, SIR--
HER TRAJECTORY'S PERFECT! SHE'S RIGHT ON COURSE!
BUT HER FLIGHT WILL LAST FOR SEVEN MINUTES!
THAT'S WHY WE'RE TESTING HER OVER THE OCEAN... FOR SAFETY!
WHILE, A THOUSAND MILES TO THE NORTH, WE FIND---
WHEREVER HULK GOES--MEN ATTACK!! BUT, HULK IS THRU RUNNING! HULK IS AFRAID OF NOTHING!!
THERE HE IS-- ATOP THAT ROOF!
NOTHING CAN HURT ME!! I'M THE HULK! I'M THE HULK!!
CLEAR THE STREETS!!
GET YOUR BARRICADES UP! GET THOSE CROWDS BACK!
SOMEHOW I CAN'T HELP FEELIN' SORRY FOR HIM!
HE'S SO ALONE-- ALWAYS SO OUT-NUMBERED!
WHY DOESN'T HE GIVE UP! HE HASN'T A CHANCE AGAINST THAT PLANE!
BUT DON'T EVER SAY HE HASN'T A CHANCE! NOT THE HULK!
HE'S JUST STANDING THERE--AS THOUGH DARING ME TO ATTACK HIM!
WELL, HE'LL BE GETTING HIS WISH!
I DON'T WANNA DO IT-- BUT THE CITY'S IN PANIC--AND I'VE GOT MY ORDERS!

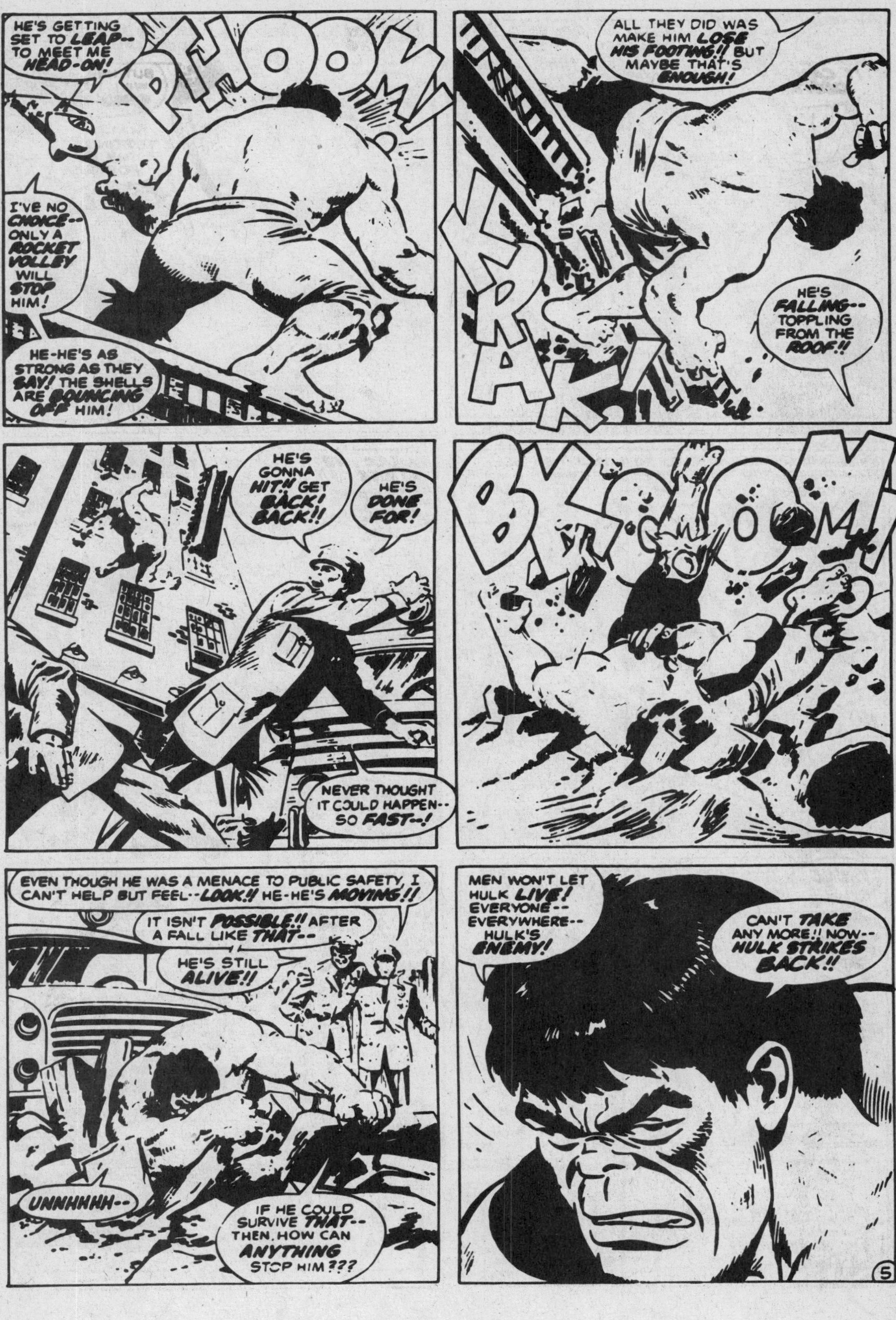
HE'S GETTING SET TO LEAP-- TO MEET ME HEAD-ON!
PTHOOM!
I'VE NO CHOICE-- ONLY A ROCKET VOLLEY WILL STOP HIM!
HE-HE'S AS STRONG AS THEY SAY! THE SHELLS ARE BOUNCING OFF HIM!
ALL THEY DID WAS MAKE HIM LOSE HIS FOOTING!! BUT MAYBE THAT'S ENOUGH!
KRAK!
HE'S FALLING-- TOPPLING FROM THE ROOF!!
HE'S GONNA HIT!! GET BACK! BACK!!
HE'S DONE FOR!
NEVER THOUGHT IT COULD HAPPEN-- SO FAST--!
BVOOOM!
EVEN THOUGH HE WAS A MENACE TO PUBLIC SAFETY, I CAN'T HELP BUT FEEL--LOOK!! HE-HE'S MOVING!!
IT ISN'T POSSIBLE!! AFTER A FALL LIKE THAT--
HE'S STILL ALIVE!!
UNNHHHH--
IF HE COULD SURVIVE THAT-- THEN, HOW CAN ANYTHING STOP HIM???
MEN WON'T LET HULK LIVE! EVERYONE-- EVERYWHERE-- HULK'S ENEMY!
CAN'T TAKE ANY MORE!! NOW-- HULK STRIKES BACK!!
5

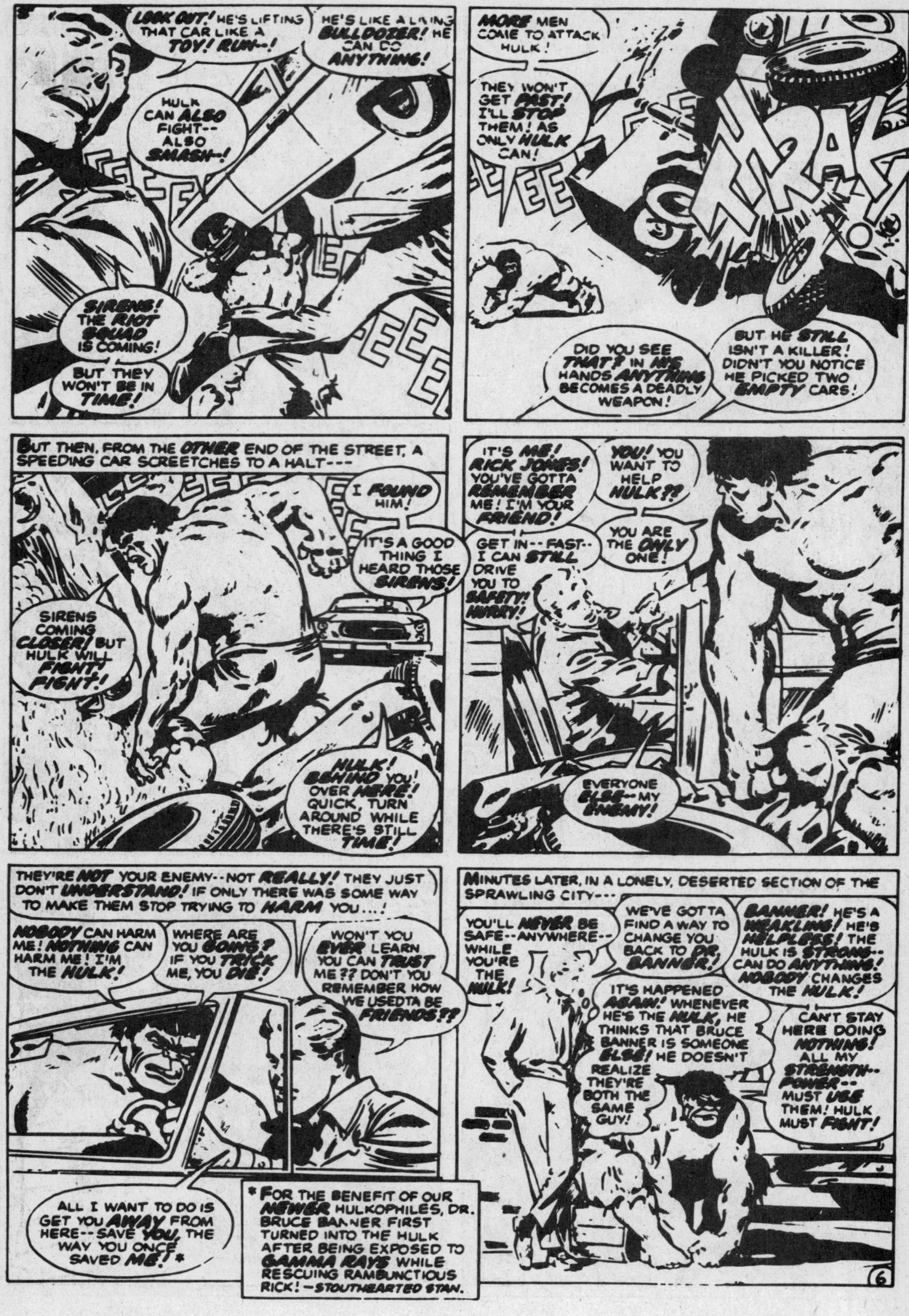

LOOK OUT! HE'S LIFTING THAT CAR LIKE A TOY! RUN--!
HE'S LIKE A LIVING BULLDOZER! HE CAN DO ANYTHING!
HULK CAN ALSO FIGHT-- ALSO SMASH--!
SIRENS! THE RIOT SQUAD IS COMING!
BUT THEY WON'T BE IN TIME!
MORE MEN COME TO ATTACK HULK!
THEY WON'T GET PAST! I'LL STOP THEM! AS ONLY HULK CAN!
THRAK!
DID YOU SEE THAT? IN HIS HANDS ANYTHING BECOMES A DEADLY WEAPON!
BUT HE STILL ISN'T A KILLER! DIDN'T YOU NOTICE HE PICKED TWO EMPTY CARS!
BUT THEN, FROM THE OTHER END OF THE STREET, A SPEEDING CAR SCREETCHES TO A HALT---
I FOUND HIM!
IT'S A GOOD THING I HEARD THOSE SIRENS!
SIRENS COMING CLOSER! BUT HULK WILL FIGHT! FIGHT!
HULK! BEHIND YOU! OVER HERE! QUICK, TURN AROUND WHILE THERE'S STILL TIME!
IT'S ME! RICK JONES! YOU'VE GOTTA REMEMBER ME! I'M YOUR FRIEND!
YOU! YOU WANT TO HELP HULK??
YOU ARE THE ONLY ONE!
GET IN-- FAST-- I CAN STILL DRIVE YOU TO SAFETY! HURRY!
EVERYONE ELSE-- MY ENEMY!
THEY'RE NOT YOUR ENEMY--NOT REALLY! THEY JUST DON'T UNDERSTAND! IF ONLY THERE WAS SOME WAY TO MAKE THEM STOP TRYING TO HARM YOU...!
NOBODY CAN HARM ME! NOTHING CAN HARM ME! I'M THE HULK!
WHERE ARE YOU GOING? IF YOU TRICK ME, YOU DIE!
WON'T YOU EVER LEARN YOU CAN TRUST ME?? DON'T YOU REMEMBER HOW WE USEDTA BE FRIENDS??
ALL I WANT TO DO IS GET YOU AWAY FROM HERE-- SAVE YOU, THE WAY YOU ONCE SAVED ME! *
* FOR THE BENEFIT OF OUR NEWER HULKOPHILES, DR. BRUCE BANNER FIRST TURNED INTO THE HULK AFTER BEING EXPOSED TO GAMMA RAYS WHILE RESCUING RAMBUNCTIOUS RICK! --STOUTHEARTED STAN.
MINUTES LATER, IN A LONELY, DESERTED SECTION OF THE SPRAWLING CITY---
YOU'LL NEVER BE SAFE--ANYWHERE-- WHILE YOU'RE THE HULK!
WE'VE GOTTA FIND A WAY TO CHANGE YOU BACK TO DR. BANNER!
BANNER! HE'S A WEAKLING! HE'S HELPLESS! THE HULK IS STRONG-- CAN DO ANYTHING! NOBODY CHANGES THE HULK!
IT'S HAPPENED AGAIN! WHENEVER HE'S THE HULK, HE THINKS THAT BRUCE BANNER IS SOMEONE ELSE! HE DOESN'T REALIZE THEY'RE BOTH THE SAME GUY!
CAN'T STAY HERE DOING NOTHING! ALL MY STRENGTH-- POWER-- MUST USE THEM! HULK MUST FIGHT!
6

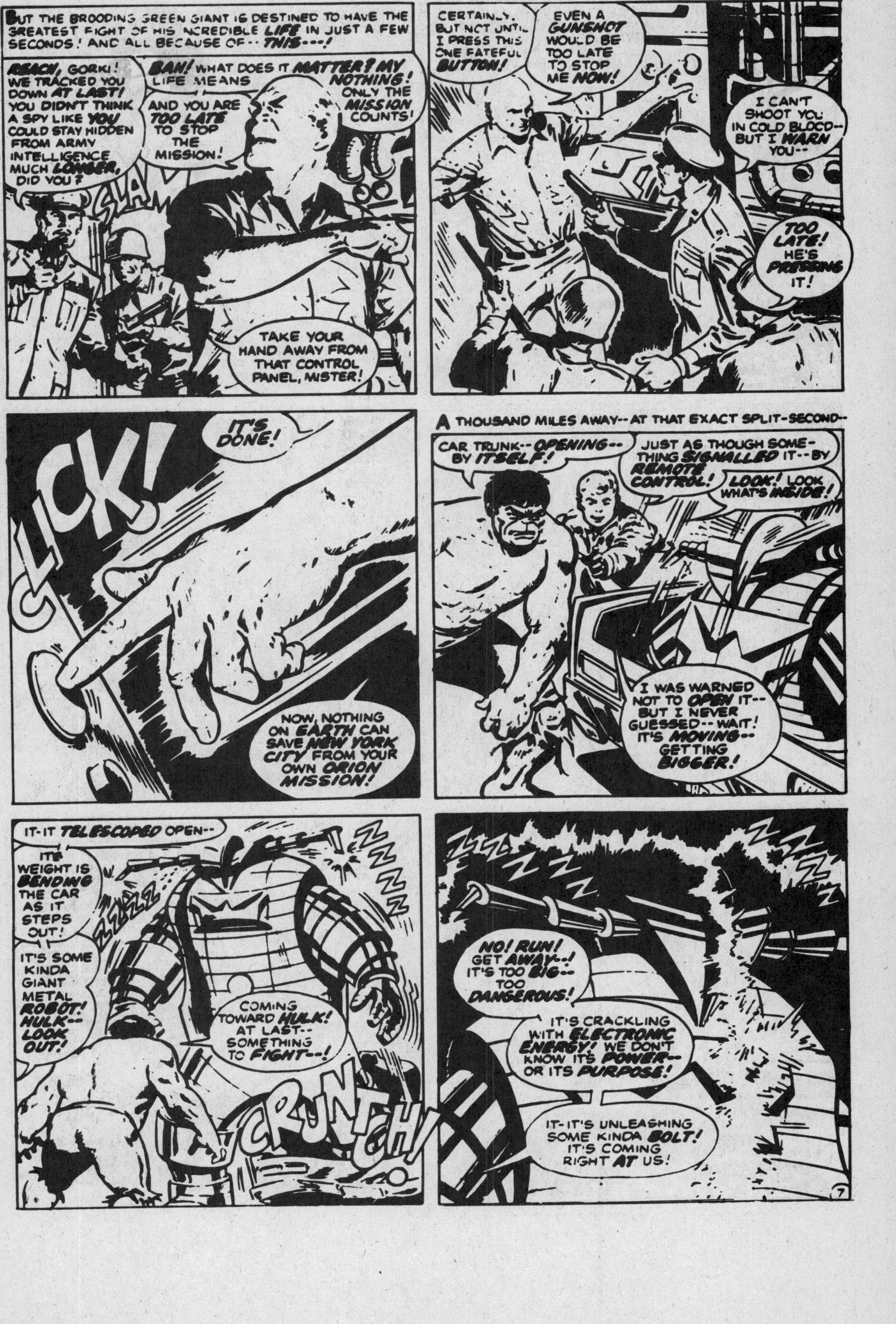

BUT THE BROODING GREEN GIANT IS DESTINED TO HAVE THE GREATEST FIGHT OF HIS INCREDIBLE LIFE IN JUST A FEW SECONDS! AND ALL BECAUSE OF-- THIS--!
REACH, GORKI! WE TRACKED YOU DOWN AT LAST! YOU DIDN'T THINK A SPY LIKE YOU COULD STAY HIDDEN FROM ARMY INTELLIGENCE MUCH LONGER, DID YOU?
BAH! WHAT DOES IT MATTER? MY LIFE MEANS NOTHING! ONLY THE MISSION COUNTS!
AND YOU ARE TOO LATE TO STOP THE MISSION!
SLAM
TAKE YOUR HAND AWAY FROM THAT CONTROL PANEL, MISTER!
CERTAINLY. BUT NOT UNTIL I PRESS THIS ONE FATEFUL BUTTON!
EVEN A GUNSHOT WOULD BE TOO LATE TO STOP ME NOW!
I CAN'T SHOOT YOU IN COLD BLOOD-- BUT I WARN YOU--
TOO LATE! HE'S PRESSING IT!
CLICK!
IT'S DONE!
NOW, NOTHING ON EARTH CAN SAVE NEW YORK CITY FROM YOUR OWN ORION MISSION!
A THOUSAND MILES AWAY-- AT THAT EXACT SPLIT-SECOND--
CAR TRUNK-- OPENING-- BY ITSELF!
JUST AS THOUGH SOMETHING SIGNALLED IT-- BY REMOTE CONTROL!
LOOK! LOOK WHAT'S INSIDE!
I WAS WARNED NOT TO OPEN IT-- BUT I NEVER GUESSED-- WAIT! IT'S MOVING-- GETTING BIGGER!
IT-IT TELESCOPED OPEN--
ITS WEIGHT IS BENDING THE CAR AS IT STEPS OUT!
IT'S SOME KINDA GIANT METAL ROBOT! HULK-- LOOK OUT!
COMING TOWARD HULK! AT LAST-- SOMETHING TO FIGHT--!
CRUNCH!
NO! RUN! GET AWAY--! IT'S TOO BIG-- TOO DANGEROUS!
IT'S CRACKLING WITH ELECTRONIC ENERGY! WE DON'T KNOW ITS POWER-- OR ITS PURPOSE!
IT-IT'S UNLEASHING SOME KINDA BOLT! IT'S COMING RIGHT AT US!

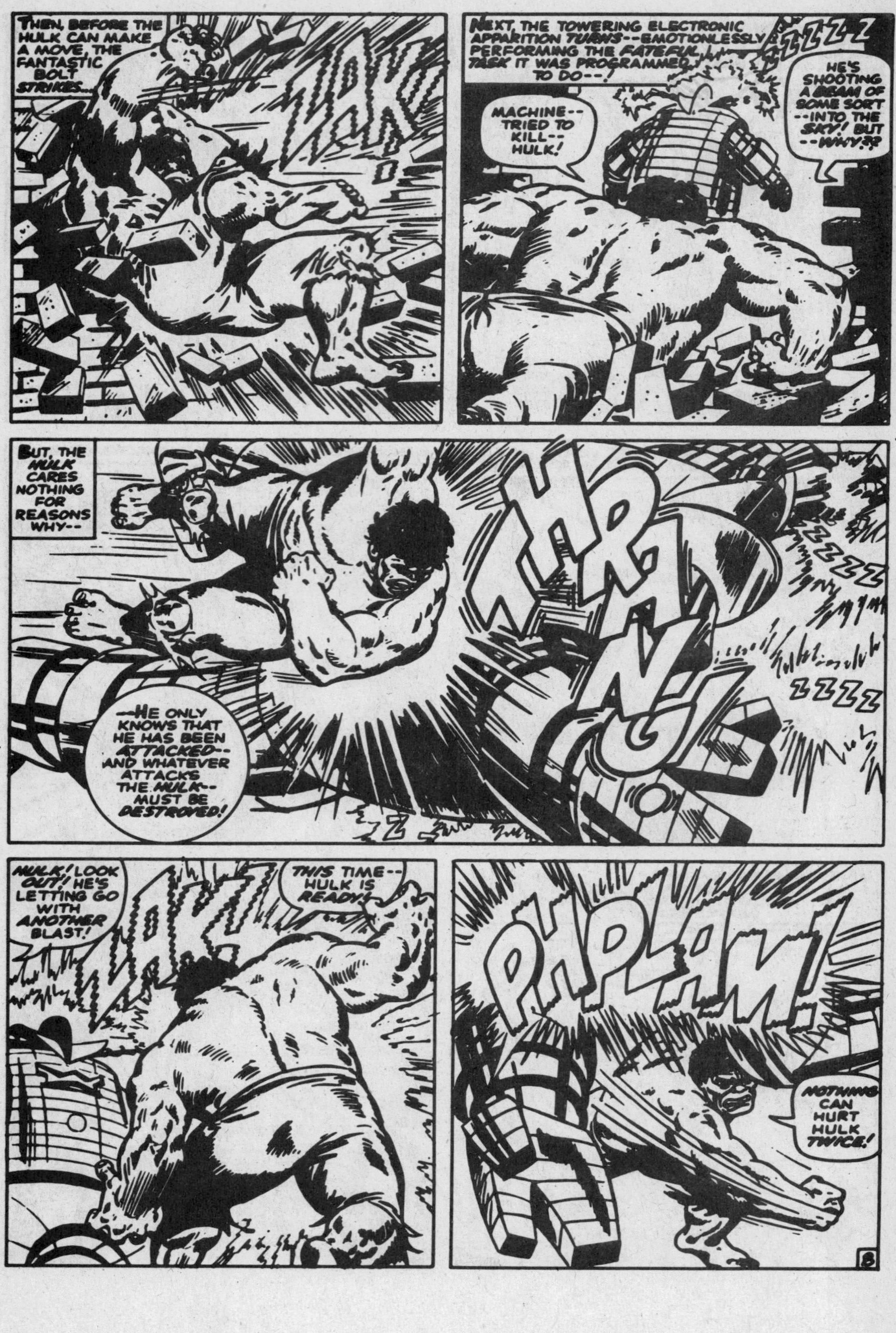
THEN, BEFORE THE HULK CAN MAKE A MOVE, THE FANTASTIC BOLT STRIKES...
NEXT, THE TOWERING ELECTRONIC APPARITION TURNS--EMOTIONLESSLY PERFORMING THE FATEFUL TASK IT WAS PROGRAMMED TO DO--!
MACHINE-- TRIED TO KILL-- HULK!
HE'S SHOOTING A BEAM OF SOME SORT --INTO THE SKY! BUT --WHY??
BUT, THE HULK CARES NOTHING FOR REASONS WHY--
--HE ONLY KNOWS THAT HE HAS BEEN ATTACKED--AND WHATEVER ATTACKS THE HULK--MUST BE DESTROYED!
ZZZZ
HULK! LOOK OUT! HE'S LETTING GO WITH ANOTHER BLAST!
THIS TIME--HULK IS READY!
PHPLAM!
NOTHING CAN HURT HULK TWICE!
8

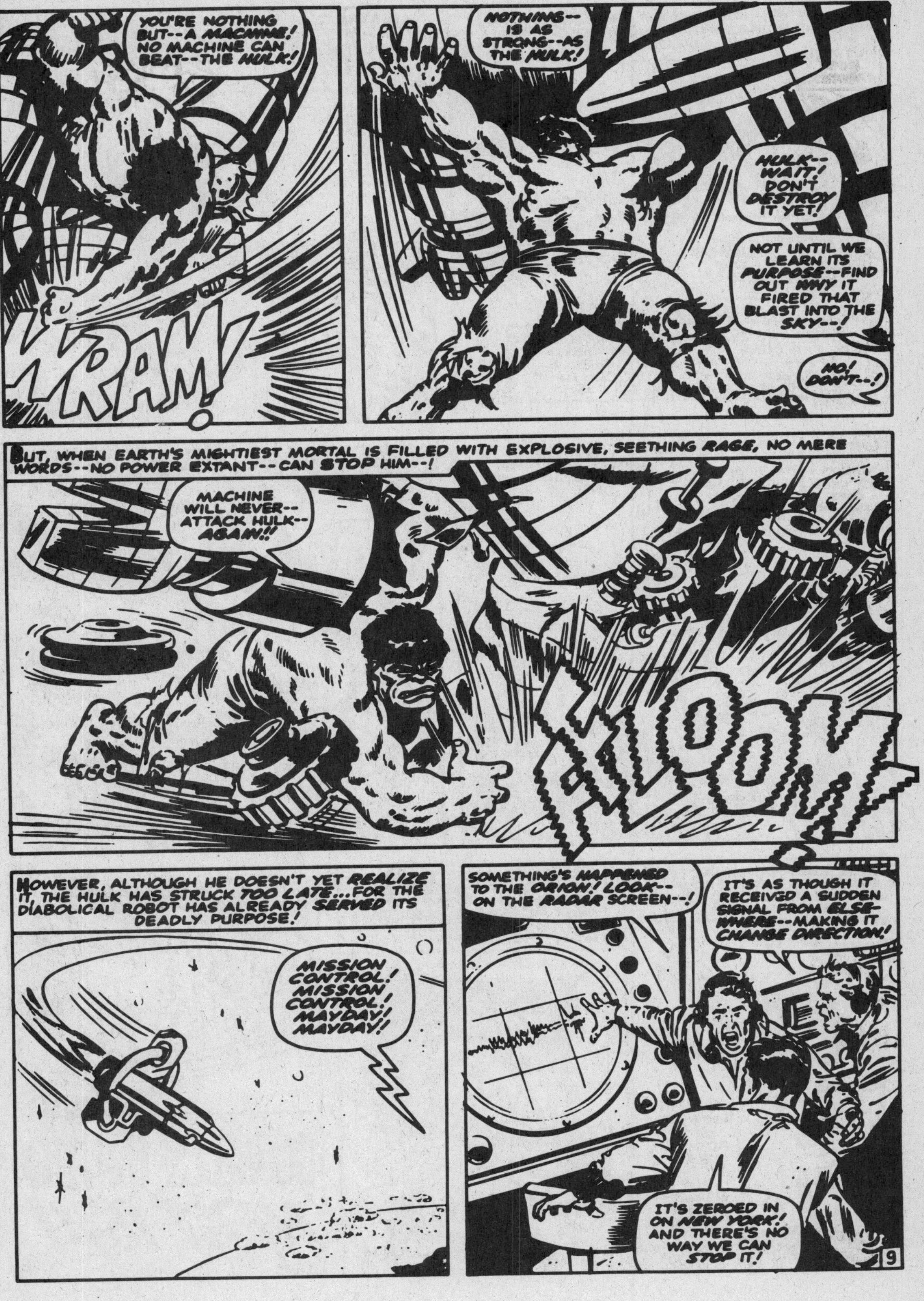
YOU'RE NOTHING BUT--A MACHINE! NO MACHINE CAN BEAT--THE HULK!
WRAM!
NOTHING--IS AS STRONG--AS THE HULK!
HULK--WAIT! DON'T DESTROY IT YET!
NOT UNTIL WE LEARN ITS PURPOSE--FIND OUT WHY IT FIRED THAT BLAST INTO THE SKY--!
NO! DON'T--!
BUT, WHEN EARTH'S MIGHTIEST MORTAL IS FILLED WITH EXPLOSIVE, SEETHING RAGE, NO MERE WORDS--NO POWER EXTANT--CAN STOP HIM--!
MACHINE WILL NEVER--ATTACK HULK--AGAIN!!
FALOOM!
HOWEVER, ALTHOUGH HE DOESN'T YET REALIZE IT, THE HULK HAS STRUCK TOO LATE...FOR THE DIABOLICAL ROBOT HAS ALREADY SERVED ITS DEADLY PURPOSE!
MISSION CONTROL! MISSION CONTROL! MAYDAY! MAYDAY!
SOMETHING'S HAPPENED TO THE ORION! LOOK--ON THE RADAR SCREEN--!
IT'S AS THOUGH IT RECEIVED A SUDDEN SIGNAL FROM ELSE-WHERE--MAKING IT CHANGE DIRECTION!
IT'S ZEROED IN ON NEW YORK! AND THERE'S NO WAY WE CAN STOP IT!
9

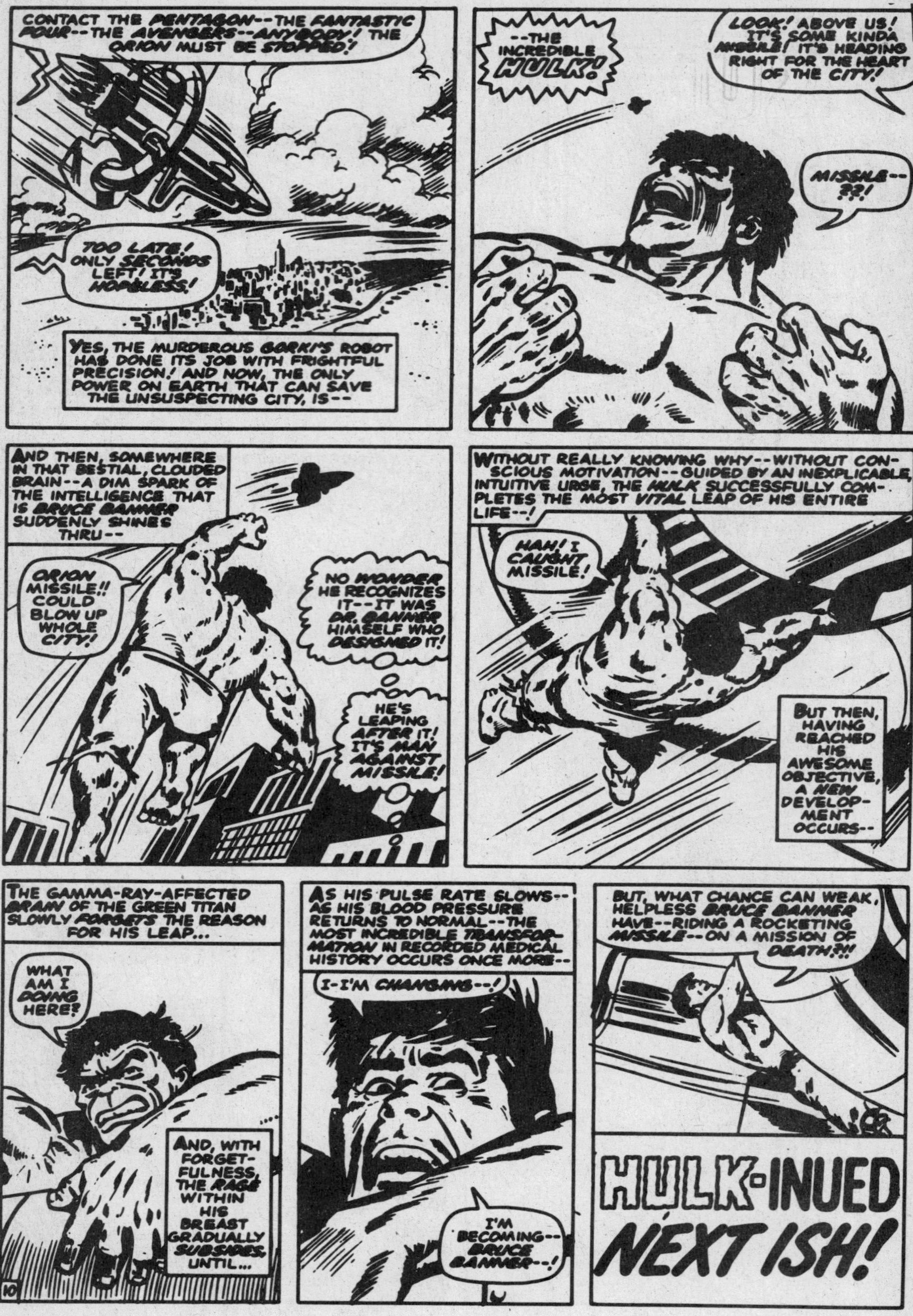

CONTACT THE PENTAGON--THE FANTASTIC FOUR--THE AVENGERS--ANYBODY! THE ORION MUST BE STOPPED!
TOO LATE! ONLY SECONDS LEFT! IT'S HOPELESS!
YES, THE MURDEROUS GORKI'S ROBOT HAS DONE ITS JOB WITH FRIGHTFUL PRECISION! AND NOW, THE ONLY POWER ON EARTH THAT CAN SAVE THE UNSUSPECTING CITY, IS--
--THE INCREDIBLE HULK!
LOOK! ABOVE US! IT'S SOME KINDA MISSILE! IT'S HEADING RIGHT FOR THE HEART OF THE CITY!
MISSILE--??!
AND THEN, SOMEWHERE IN THAT BESTIAL, CLOUDED BRAIN--A DIM SPARK OF THE INTELLIGENCE THAT IS BRUCE BANNER SUDDENLY SHINES THRU--
ORION MISSILE!! COULD BLOW UP WHOLE CITY!
NO WONDER HE RECOGNIZES IT--IT WAS DR. BANNER HIMSELF WHO DESIGNED IT!
HE'S LEAPING AFTER IT! IT'S MAN AGAINST MISSILE!
WITHOUT REALLY KNOWING WHY--WITHOUT CONSCIOUS MOTIVATION--GUIDED BY AN INEXPLICABLE, INTUITIVE URGE, THE HULK SUCCESSFULLY COMPLETES THE MOST VITAL LEAP OF HIS ENTIRE LIFE--!
HAH! I CAUGHT MISSILE!
BUT THEN, HAVING REACHED HIS AWESOME OBJECTIVE, A NEW DEVELOPMENT OCCURS--
THE GAMMA-RAY-AFFECTED BRAIN OF THE GREEN TITAN SLOWLY FORGETS THE REASON FOR HIS LEAP...
WHAT AM I DOING HERE?
AND, WITH FORGETFULNESS, THE RAGE WITHIN HIS BREAST GRADUALLY SUBSIDES, UNTIL...
10
AS HIS PULSE RATE SLOWS--AS HIS BLOOD PRESSURE RETURNS TO NORMAL--THE MOST INCREDIBLE TRANSFORMATION IN RECORDED MEDICAL HISTORY OCCURS ONCE MORE--
I-I'M CHANGING--!
I'M BECOMING--BRUCE BANNER--!
BUT, WHAT CHANCE CAN WEAK, HELPLESS BRUCE BANNER HAVE--RIDING A ROCKETING MISSILE--ON A MISSION OF DEATH?!!
HULK-INUED NEXT ISH!

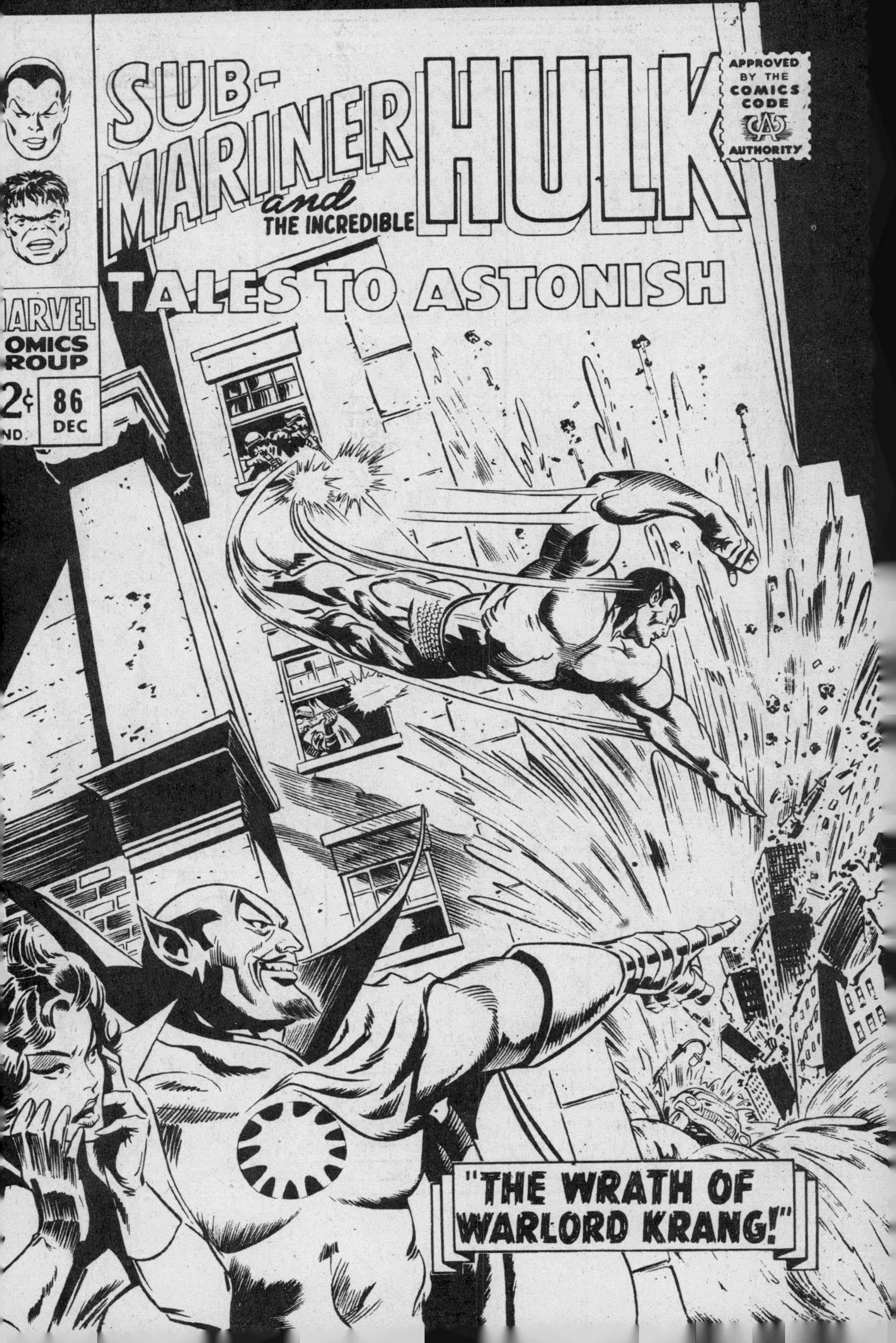

SUB-MARINER
and
THE INCREDIBLE HULK
TALES TO ASTONISH
APPROVED BY THE COMICS CODE AUTHORITY
ARVEL
OMICS
ROUP
2¢
86
DEC
ND.
"THE WRATH OF WARLORD KRANG!"

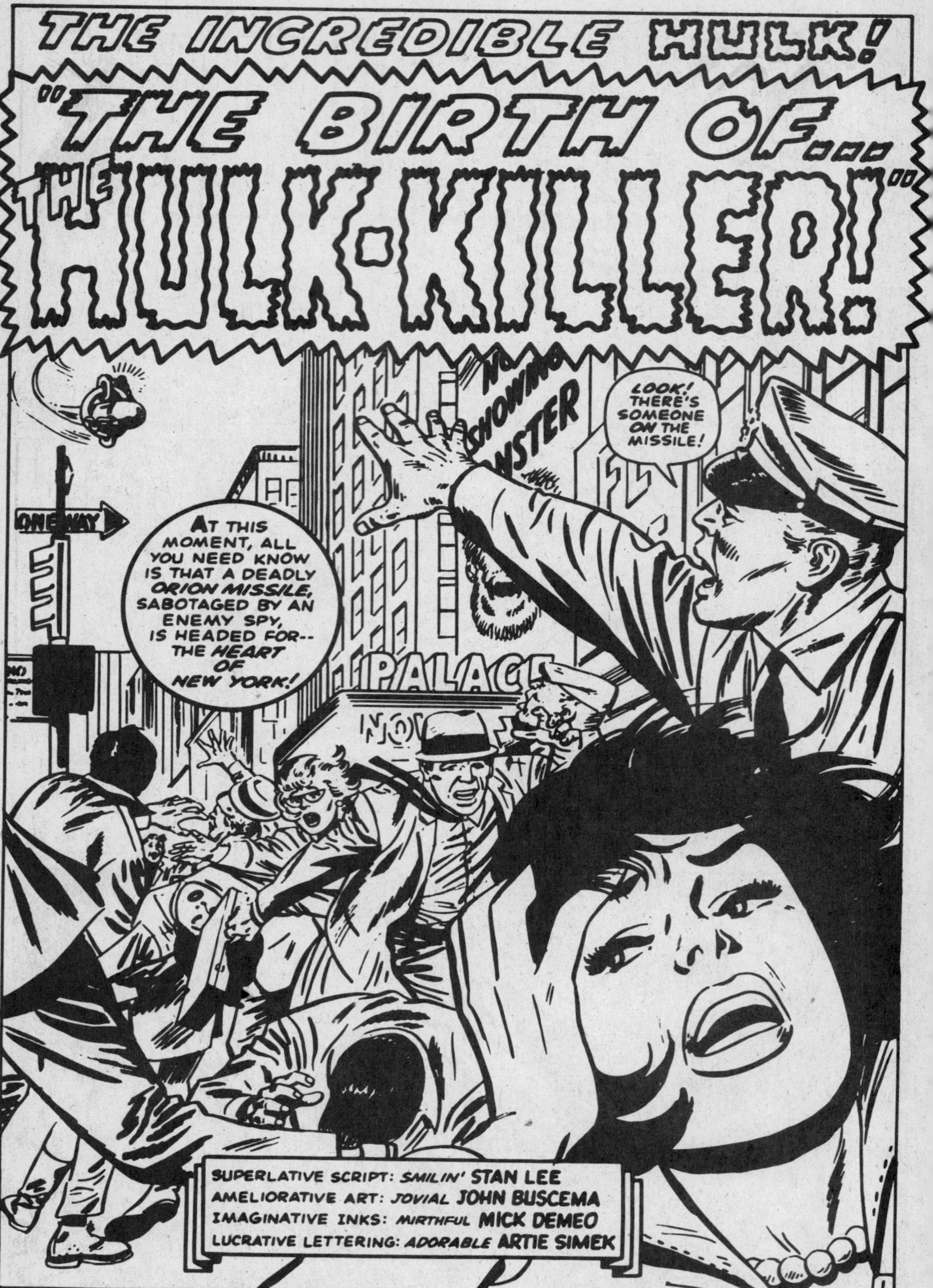
THE INCREDIBLE HULK!
"THE BIRTH OF... THE HULK-KILLER!"
ONE WAY
NO SHOWING
NSTER
LOOK! THERE'S SOMEONE ON THE MISSILE!
AT THIS MOMENT, ALL YOU NEED KNOW IS THAT A DEADLY ORION MISSILE, SABOTAGED BY AN ENEMY SPY, IS HEADED FOR-- THE HEART OF NEW YORK!
PALACE
SUPERLATIVE SCRIPT: SMILIN' STAN LEE
AMELIORATIVE ART: JOVIAL JOHN BUSCEMA
IMAGINATIVE INKS: MIRTHFUL MICK DEMEO
LUCRATIVE LETTERING: ADORABLE ARTIE SIMEK
1

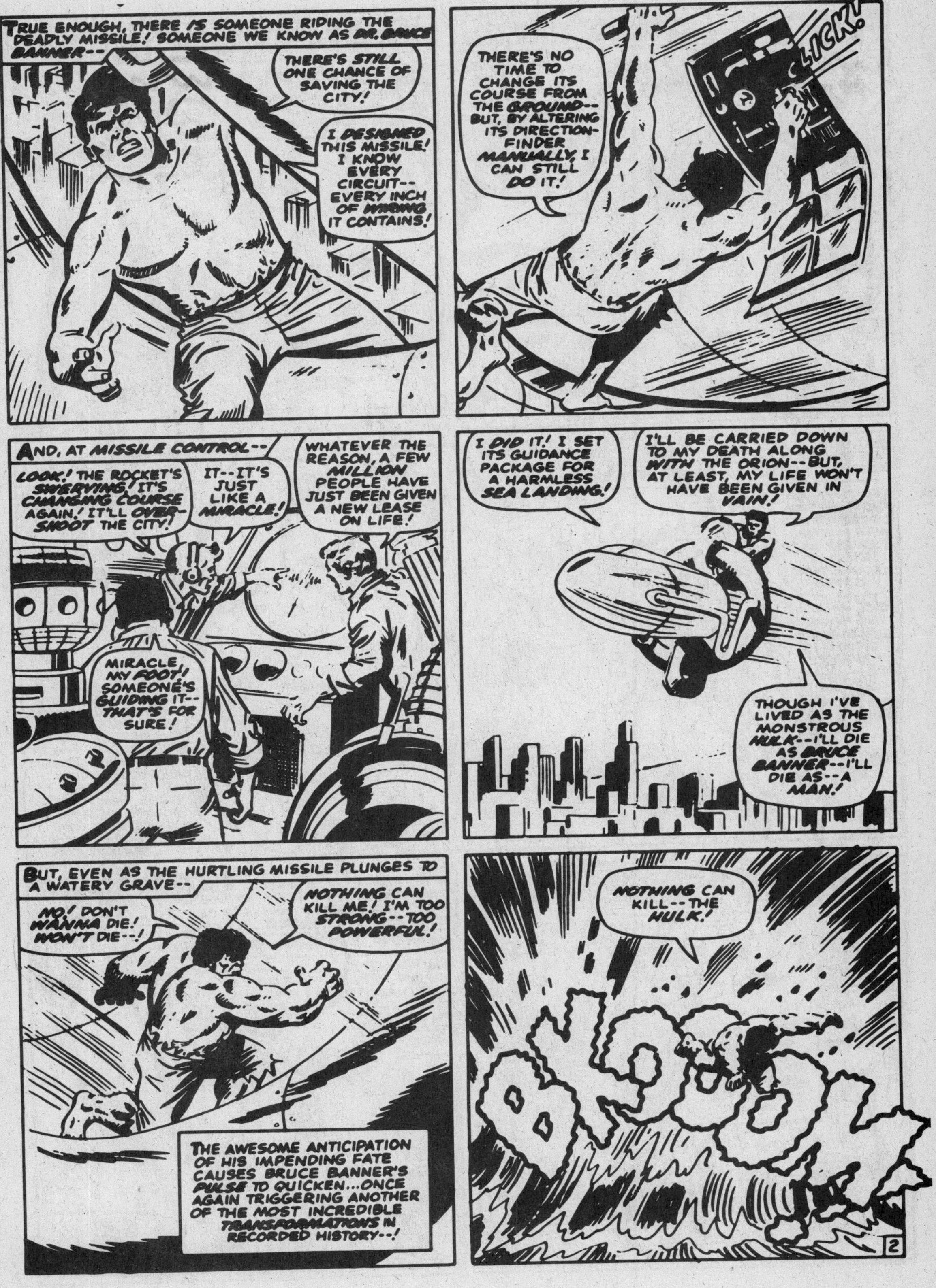
TRUE ENOUGH, THERE IS SOMEONE RIDING THE DEADLY MISSILE! SOMEONE WE KNOW AS DR. BRUCE BANNER--
THERE'S STILL ONE CHANCE OF SAVING THE CITY!
I DESIGNED THIS MISSILE! I KNOW EVERY CIRCUIT--EVERY INCH OF WIRING IT CONTAINS!
THERE'S NO TIME TO CHANGE ITS COURSE FROM THE GROUND--BUT, BY ALTERING ITS DIRECTION-FINDER MANUALLY, I CAN STILL DO IT!
CLICK!
AND, AT MISSILE CONTROL--
LOOK! THE ROCKET'S SWERVING! IT'S CHANGING COURSE AGAIN! IT'LL OVER-SHOOT THE CITY!
IT--IT'S JUST LIKE A MIRACLE!
WHATEVER THE REASON, A FEW MILLION PEOPLE HAVE JUST BEEN GIVEN A NEW LEASE ON LIFE!
MIRACLE, MY FOOT! SOMEONE'S GUIDING IT--THAT'S FOR SURE!
I DID IT! I SET ITS GUIDANCE PACKAGE FOR A HARMLESS SEA LANDING!
I'LL BE CARRIED DOWN TO MY DEATH ALONG WITH THE ORION--BUT, AT LEAST, MY LIFE WON'T HAVE BEEN GIVEN IN VAIN!
THOUGH I'VE LIVED AS THE MONSTROUS HULK--I'LL DIE AS BRUCE BANNER--I'LL DIE AS--A MAN!
BUT, EVEN AS THE HURTLING MISSILE PLUNGES TO A WATERY GRAVE--
NO! DON'T WANNA DIE! WON'T DIE--!
NOTHING CAN KILL ME! I'M TOO STRONG--TOO POWERFUL!
THE AWESOME ANTICIPATION OF HIS IMPENDING FATE CAUSES BRUCE BANNER'S PULSE TO QUICKEN...ONCE AGAIN TRIGGERING ANOTHER OF THE MOST INCREDIBLE TRANSFORMATIONS IN RECORDED HISTORY--!
NOTHING CAN KILL--THE HULK!
2

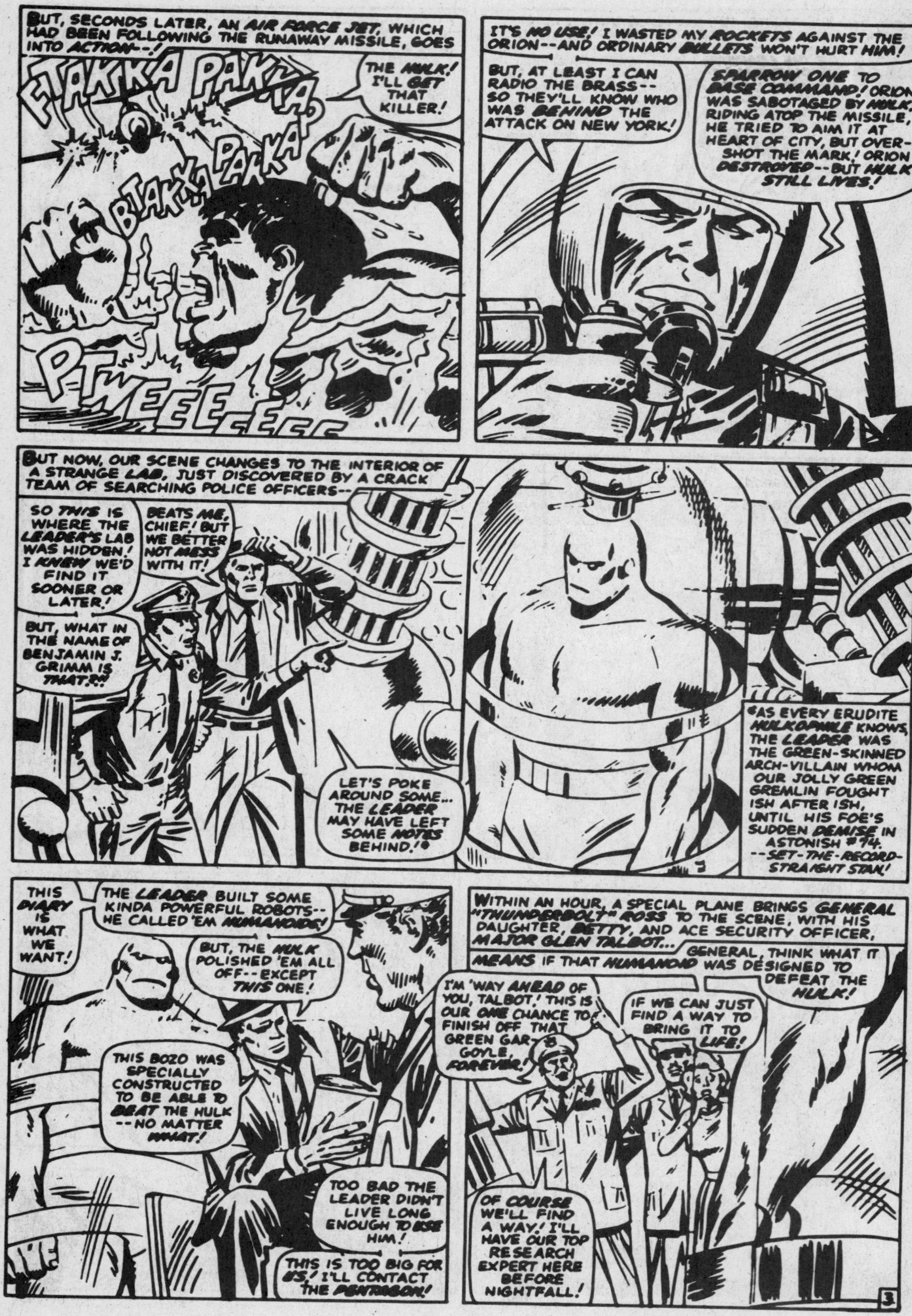
BUT, SECONDS LATER, AN AIR FORCE JET, WHICH HAD BEEN FOLLOWING THE RUNAWAY MISSILE, GOES INTO ACTION--!
TAKKA PAKKA
THE HULK! I'LL GET THAT KILLER!
PAKKA
P-TWEEEEEE
IT'S NO USE! I WASTED MY ROCKETS AGAINST THE ORION--AND ORDINARY BULLETS WON'T HURT HIM!
BUT, AT LEAST I CAN RADIO THE BRASS--SO THEY'LL KNOW WHO WAS BEHIND THE ATTACK ON NEW YORK!
SPARROW ONE TO BASE COMMAND! ORION WAS SABOTAGED BY HULK! RIDING ATOP THE MISSILE, HE TRIED TO AIM IT AT HEART OF CITY, BUT OVER-SHOT THE MARK! ORION DESTROYED--BUT HULK STILL LIVES!
BUT NOW, OUR SCENE CHANGES TO THE INTERIOR OF A STRANGE LAB, JUST DISCOVERED BY A CRACK TEAM OF SEARCHING POLICE OFFICERS--
SO THIS IS WHERE THE LEADER'S LAB WAS HIDDEN! I KNEW WE'D FIND IT SOONER OR LATER!
BEATS ME, CHIEF! BUT WE BETTER NOT MESS WITH IT!
BUT, WHAT IN THE NAME OF BENJAMIN J. GRIMM IS THAT?!
LET'S POKE AROUND SOME... THE LEADER MAY HAVE LEFT SOME NOTES BEHIND!*
*AS EVERY ERUDITE HULKOPHILE KNOWS, THE LEADER WAS THE GREEN-SKINNED ARCH-VILLAIN WHOM OUR JOLLY GREEN GREMLIN FOUGHT ISH AFTER ISH, UNTIL HIS FOE'S SUDDEN DEMISE IN ASTONISH #74. --SET-THE-RECORD-STRAIGHT STAN!
THIS DIARY IS WHAT WE WANT!
THE LEADER BUILT SOME KINDA POWERFUL ROBOTS--HE CALLED 'EM HUMANOIDS!
BUT, THE HULK POLISHED 'EM ALL OFF--EXCEPT THIS ONE!
THIS BOZO WAS SPECIALLY CONSTRUCTED TO BE ABLE TO BEAT THE HULK--NO MATTER WHAT!
TOO BAD THE LEADER DIDN'T LIVE LONG ENOUGH TO USE HIM!
THIS IS TOO BIG FOR US! I'LL CONTACT THE PENTAGON!
WITHIN AN HOUR, A SPECIAL PLANE BRINGS GENERAL "THUNDERBOLT" ROSS TO THE SCENE, WITH HIS DAUGHTER, BETTY, AND ACE SECURITY OFFICER, MAJOR GLEN TALBOT...
GENERAL, THINK WHAT IT MEANS IF THAT HUMANOID WAS DESIGNED TO DEFEAT THE HULK!
I'M 'WAY AHEAD OF YOU, TALBOT! THIS IS OUR ONE CHANCE TO FINISH OFF THAT GREEN GAR-GOYLE, FOREVER!
IF WE CAN JUST FIND A WAY TO BRING IT TO LIFE!
OF COURSE WE'LL FIND A WAY! I'LL HAVE OUR TOP RESEARCH EXPERT HERE BEFORE NIGHTFALL!
3

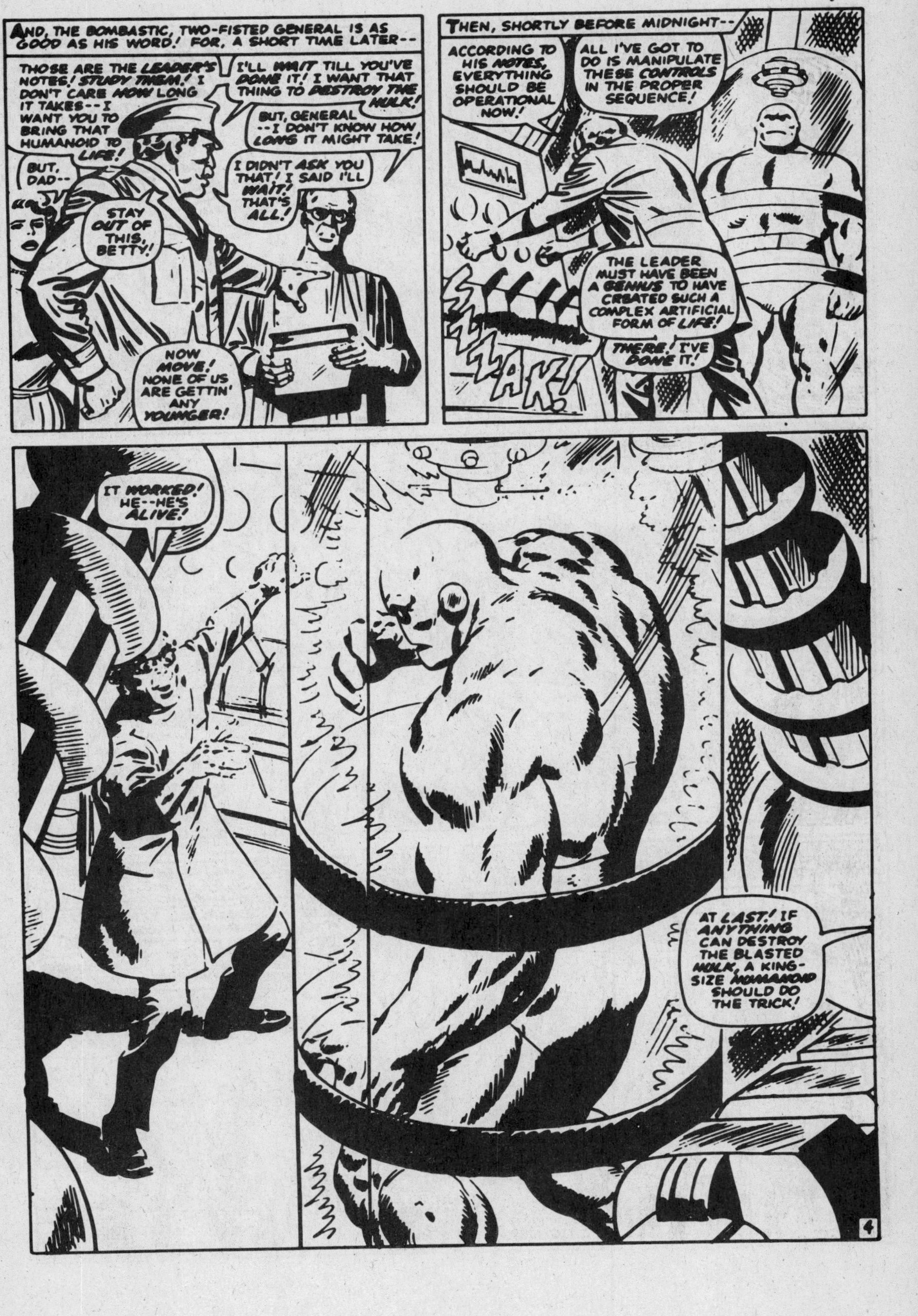
AND, THE BOMBASTIC, TWO-FISTED GENERAL IS AS GOOD AS HIS WORD! FOR, A SHORT TIME LATER--
THOSE ARE THE LEADER'S NOTES! STUDY THEM! I DON'T CARE HOW LONG IT TAKES--I WANT YOU TO BRING THAT HUMANOID TO LIFE!
I'LL WAIT TILL YOU'VE DONE IT! I WANT THAT THING TO DESTROY THE HULK!
BUT, GENERAL --I DON'T KNOW HOW LONG IT MIGHT TAKE!
BUT, DAD--
I DIDN'T ASK YOU THAT! I SAID I'LL WAIT! THAT'S ALL!
STAY OUT OF THIS, BETTY!
NOW MOVE! NONE OF US ARE GETTIN' ANY YOUNGER!
THEN, SHORTLY BEFORE MIDNIGHT--
ACCORDING TO HIS NOTES, EVERYTHING SHOULD BE OPERATIONAL NOW!
ALL I'VE GOT TO DO IS MANIPULATE THESE CONTROLS IN THE PROPER SEQUENCE!
THE LEADER MUST HAVE BEEN A GENIUS TO HAVE CREATED SUCH A COMPLEX ARTIFICIAL FORM OF LIFE!
THERE! I'VE DONE IT!
SZZZAK!
IT WORKED! HE--HE'S ALIVE!
AT LAST! IF ANYTHING CAN DESTROY THE BLASTED HULK, A KING-SIZE HUMANOID SHOULD DO THE TRICK!
4

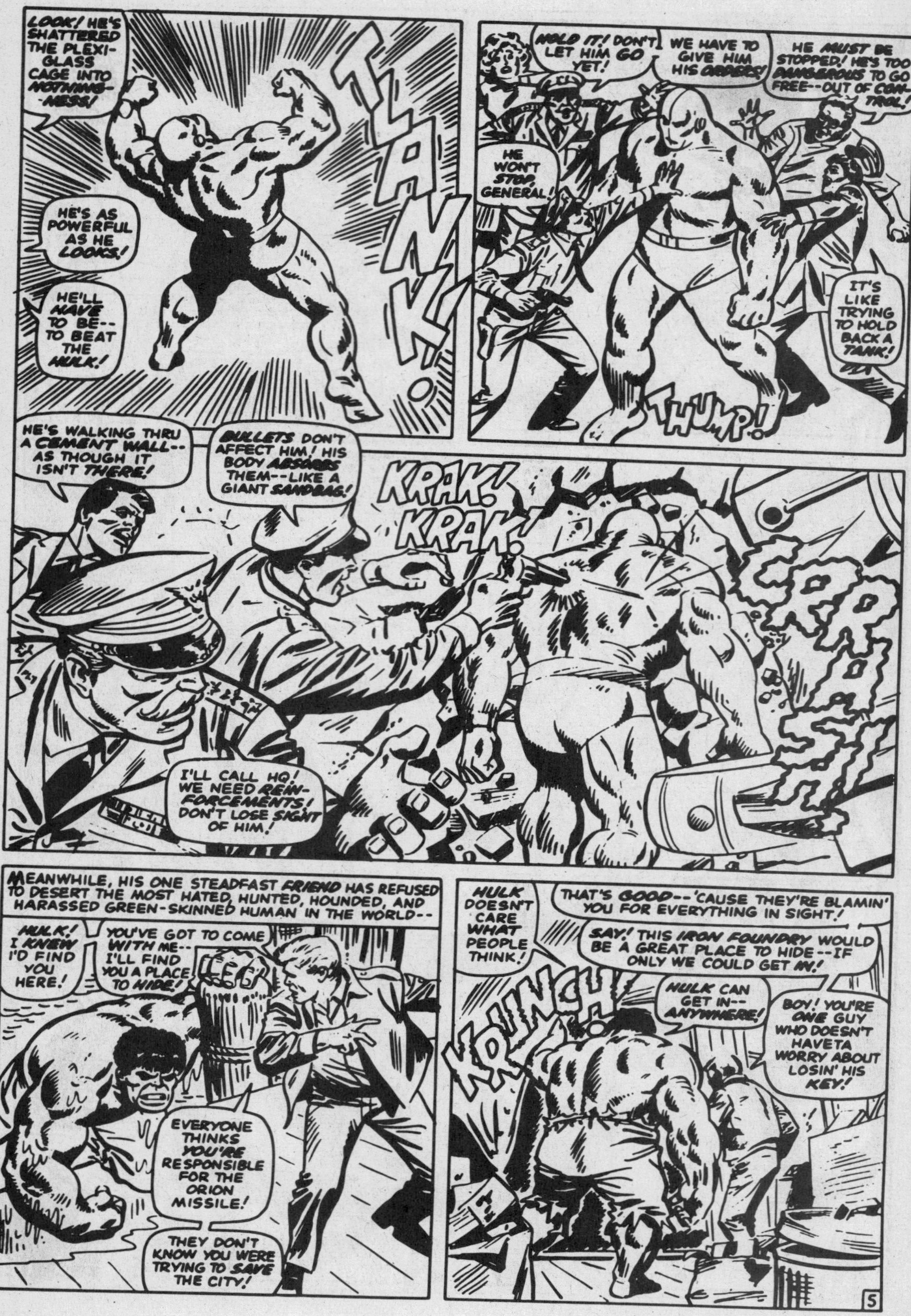
LOOK! HE'S SHATTERED THE PLEXI-GLASS CAGE INTO NOTHING-NESS!
TLANK!
HE'S AS POWERFUL AS HE LOOKS!
HE'LL HAVE TO BE-- TO BEAT THE HULK!
HOLD IT! DON'T LET HIM GO YET!
WE HAVE TO GIVE HIM HIS ORDERS!
HE MUST BE STOPPED! HE'S TOO DANGEROUS TO GO FREE--OUT OF CON-TROL!
HE WON'T STOP, GENERAL!
IT'S LIKE TRYING TO HOLD BACK A TANK!
THUMP!
HE'S WALKING THRU A CEMENT WALL-- AS THOUGH IT ISN'T THERE!
BULLETS DON'T AFFECT HIM! HIS BODY ABSORBS THEM--LIKE A GIANT SANDBAG!
KRAK! KRAK!
CRR
I'LL CALL HQ! WE NEED REIN-FORCEMENTS! DON'T LOSE SIGHT OF HIM!
MEANWHILE, HIS ONE STEADFAST FRIEND HAS REFUSED TO DESERT THE MOST HATED, HUNTED, HOUNDED, AND HARASSED GREEN-SKINNED HUMAN IN THE WORLD--
HULK! I KNEW I'D FIND YOU HERE!
YOU'VE GOT TO COME WITH ME-- I'LL FIND YOU A PLACE TO HIDE!
EVERYONE THINKS YOU'RE RESPONSIBLE FOR THE ORION MISSILE!
THEY DON'T KNOW YOU WERE TRYING TO SAVE THE CITY!
HULK DOESN'T CARE WHAT PEOPLE THINK!
THAT'S GOOD--'CAUSE THEY'RE BLAMIN' YOU FOR EVERYTHING IN SIGHT!
SAY! THIS IRON FOUNDRY WOULD BE A GREAT PLACE TO HIDE--IF ONLY WE COULD GET IN!
KRUNCH!
HULK CAN GET IN-- ANYWHERE!
BOY! YOU'RE ONE GUY WHO DOESN'T HAVETA WORRY ABOUT LOSIN' HIS KEY!
5

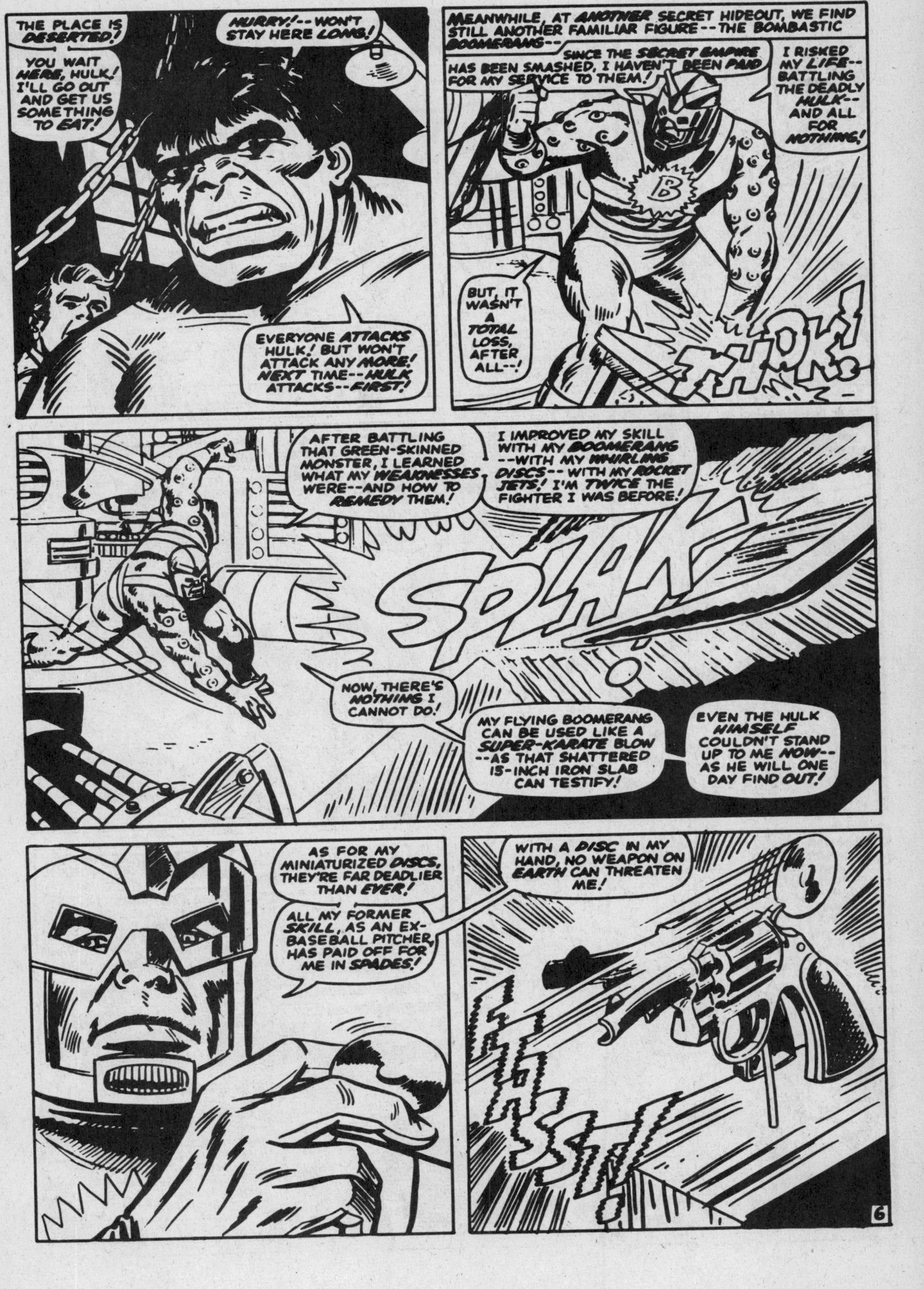

THE PLACE IS DESERTED!
YOU WAIT HERE, HULK! I'LL GO OUT AND GET US SOMETHING TO EAT!
HURRY!--WON'T STAY HERE LONG!
EVERYONE ATTACKS HULK! BUT WON'T ATTACK ANY MORE! NEXT TIME--HULK ATTACKS--FIRST!
MEANWHILE, AT ANOTHER SECRET HIDEOUT, WE FIND STILL ANOTHER FAMILIAR FIGURE--THE BOMBASTIC BOOMERANG--
SINCE THE SECRET EMPIRE HAS BEEN SMASHED, I HAVEN'T BEEN PAID FOR MY SERVICE TO THEM!
I RISKED MY LIFE--BATTLING THE DEADLY HULK--AND ALL FOR NOTHING!
BUT, IT WASN'T A TOTAL LOSS, AFTER ALL--!
THOK!
AFTER BATTLING THAT GREEN-SKINNED MONSTER, I LEARNED WHAT MY WEAKNESSES WERE--AND HOW TO REMEDY THEM!
I IMPROVED MY SKILL WITH MY BOOMERANGS --WITH MY WHIRLING DISCS--WITH MY ROCKET JETS! I'M TWICE THE FIGHTER I WAS BEFORE!
SPLAK!
NOW, THERE'S NOTHING I CANNOT DO!
MY FLYING BOOMERANG CAN BE USED LIKE A SUPER-KARATE BLOW --AS THAT SHATTERED 15-INCH IRON SLAB CAN TESTIFY!
EVEN THE HULK HIMSELF COULDN'T STAND UP TO ME NOW--AS HE WILL ONE DAY FIND OUT!
AS FOR MY MINIATURIZED DISCS, THEY'RE FAR DEADLIER THAN EVER!
ALL MY FORMER SKILL, AS AN EX-BASEBALL PITCHER, HAS PAID OFF FOR ME IN SPADES!
WITH A DISC IN MY HAND, NO WEAPON ON EARTH CAN THREATEN ME!
HISSSS!
6

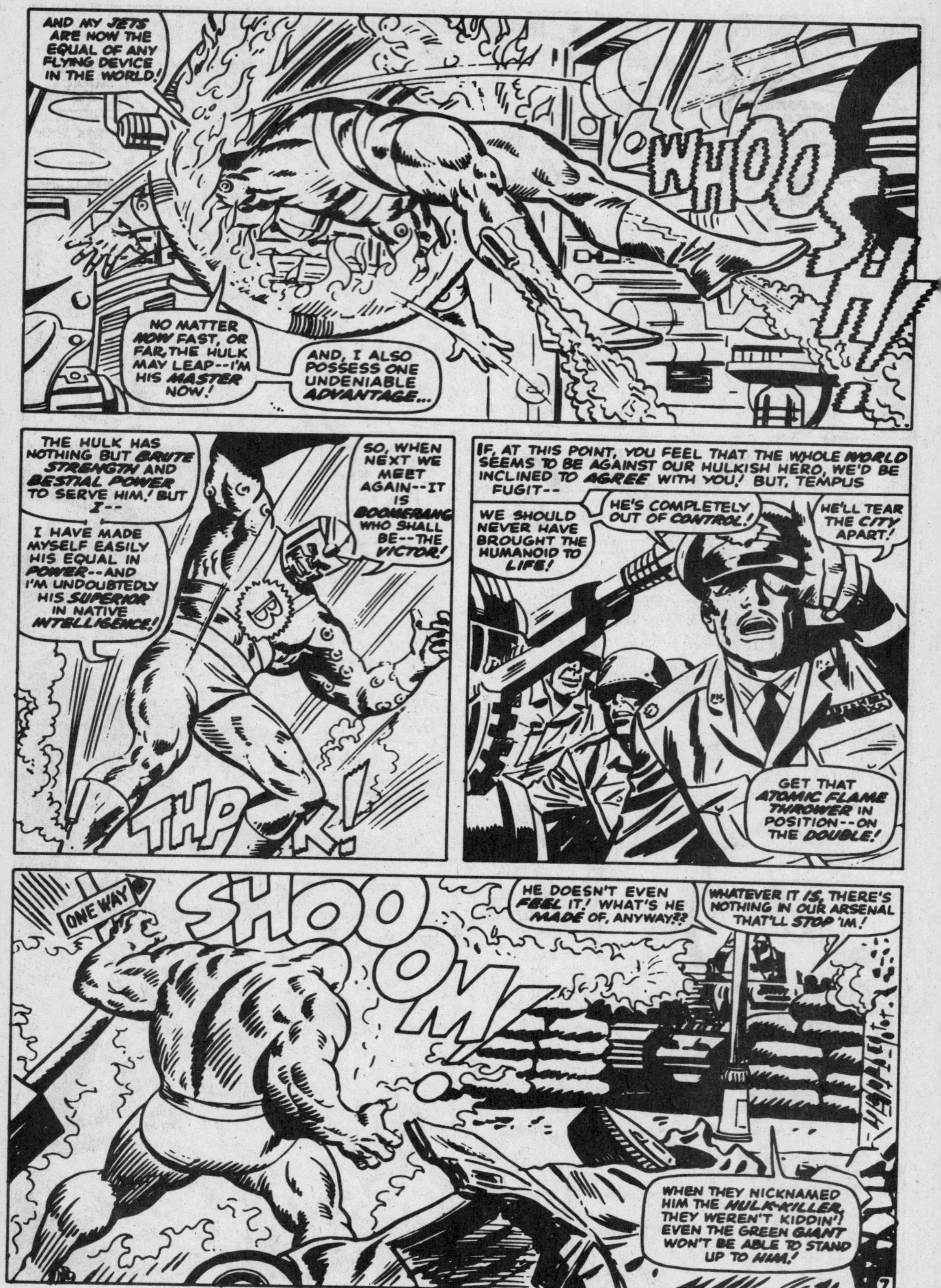
AND MY JETS ARE NOW THE EQUAL OF ANY FLYING DEVICE IN THE WORLD!
WHOOSH!
NO MATTER HOW FAST, OR FAR, THE HULK MAY LEAP--I'M HIS MASTER NOW!
AND, I ALSO POSSESS ONE UNDENIABLE ADVANTAGE...
THE HULK HAS NOTHING BUT BRUTE STRENGTH AND BESTIAL POWER TO SERVE HIM! BUT I--
I HAVE MADE MYSELF EASILY HIS EQUAL IN POWER--AND I'M UNDOUBTEDLY HIS SUPERIOR IN NATIVE INTELLIGENCE!
SO, WHEN NEXT WE MEET AGAIN--IT IS BOOMERANG WHO SHALL BE--THE VICTOR!
THPAK!
IF, AT THIS POINT, YOU FEEL THAT THE WHOLE WORLD SEEMS TO BE AGAINST OUR HULKISH HERO, WE'D BE INCLINED TO AGREE WITH YOU! BUT, TEMPUS FUGIT--
WE SHOULD NEVER HAVE BROUGHT THE HUMANOID TO LIFE!
HE'S COMPLETELY OUT OF CONTROL!
HE'LL TEAR THE CITY APART!
GET THAT ATOMIC FLAME THROWER IN POSITION--ON THE DOUBLE!
ONE WAY
SHOOOM!
HE DOESN'T EVEN FEEL IT! WHAT'S HE MADE OF, ANYWAY??
WHATEVER IT IS, THERE'S NOTHING IN OUR ARSENAL THAT'LL STOP 'IM!
WHEN THEY NICKNAMED HIM THE HULK-KILLER, THEY WEREN'T KIDDIN'! EVEN THE GREEN GIANT WON'T BE ABLE TO STAND UP TO HIM!

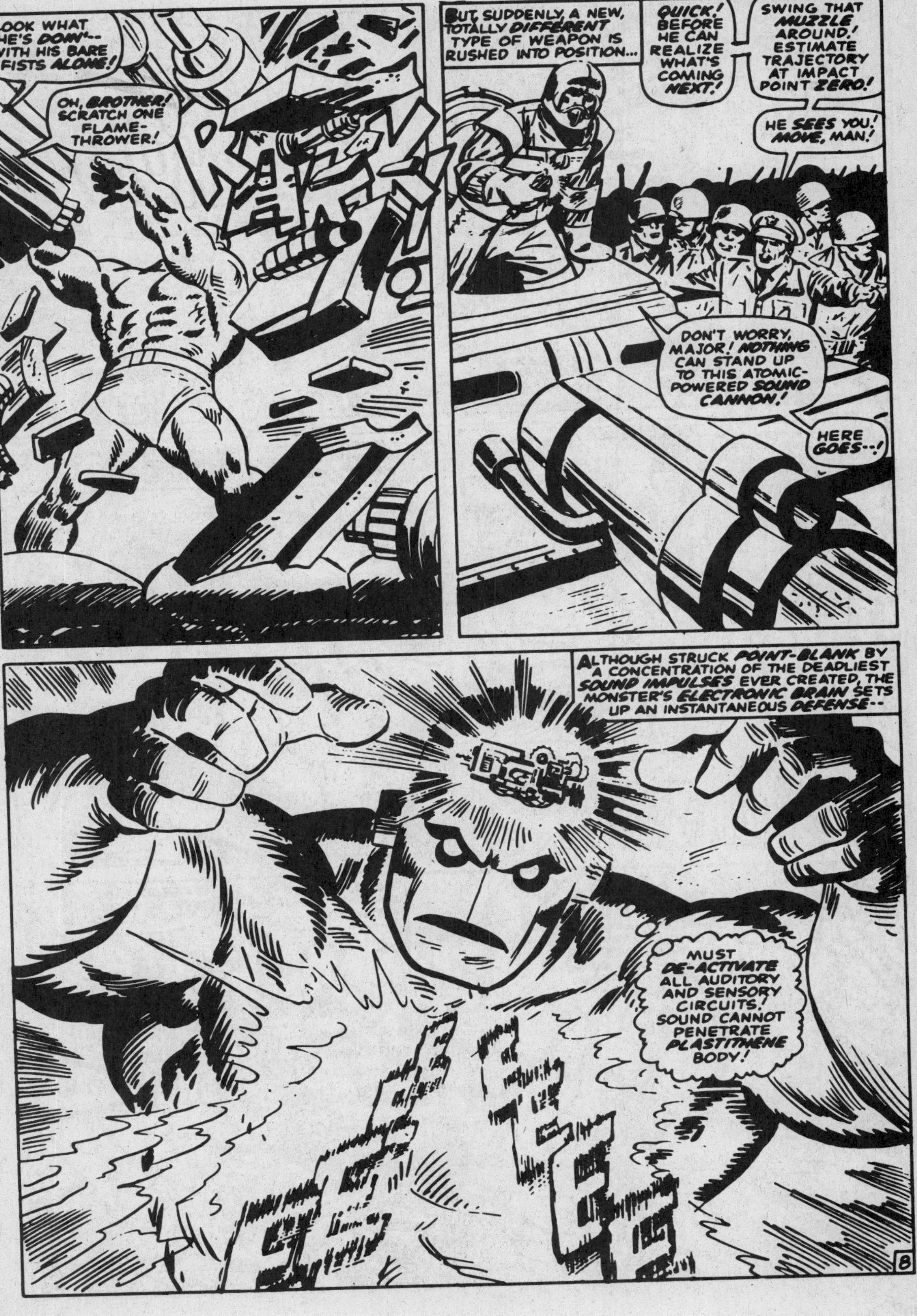
LOOK WHAT HE'S DOIN'-- WITH HIS BARE FISTS ALONE!
OH, BROTHER! SCRATCH ONE FLAME-THROWER!
BUT SUDDENLY, A NEW, TOTALLY DIFFERENT TYPE OF WEAPON IS RUSHED INTO POSITION...
QUICK! BEFORE HE CAN REALIZE WHAT'S COMING NEXT!
SWING THAT MUZZLE AROUND! ESTIMATE TRAJECTORY AT IMPACT POINT ZERO!
HE SEES YOU! MOVE, MAN!
DON'T WORRY, MAJOR! NOTHING CAN STAND UP TO THIS ATOMIC-POWERED SOUND CANNON!
HERE GOES--!
ALTHOUGH STRUCK POINT-BLANK BY A CONCENTRATION OF THE DEADLIEST SOUND IMPULSES EVER CREATED, THE MONSTER'S ELECTRONIC BRAIN SETS UP AN INSTANTANEOUS DEFENSE--
MUST DE-ACTIVATE ALL AUDITORY AND SENSORY CIRCUITS! SOUND CANNOT PENETRATE PLASTITHENE BODY!
8

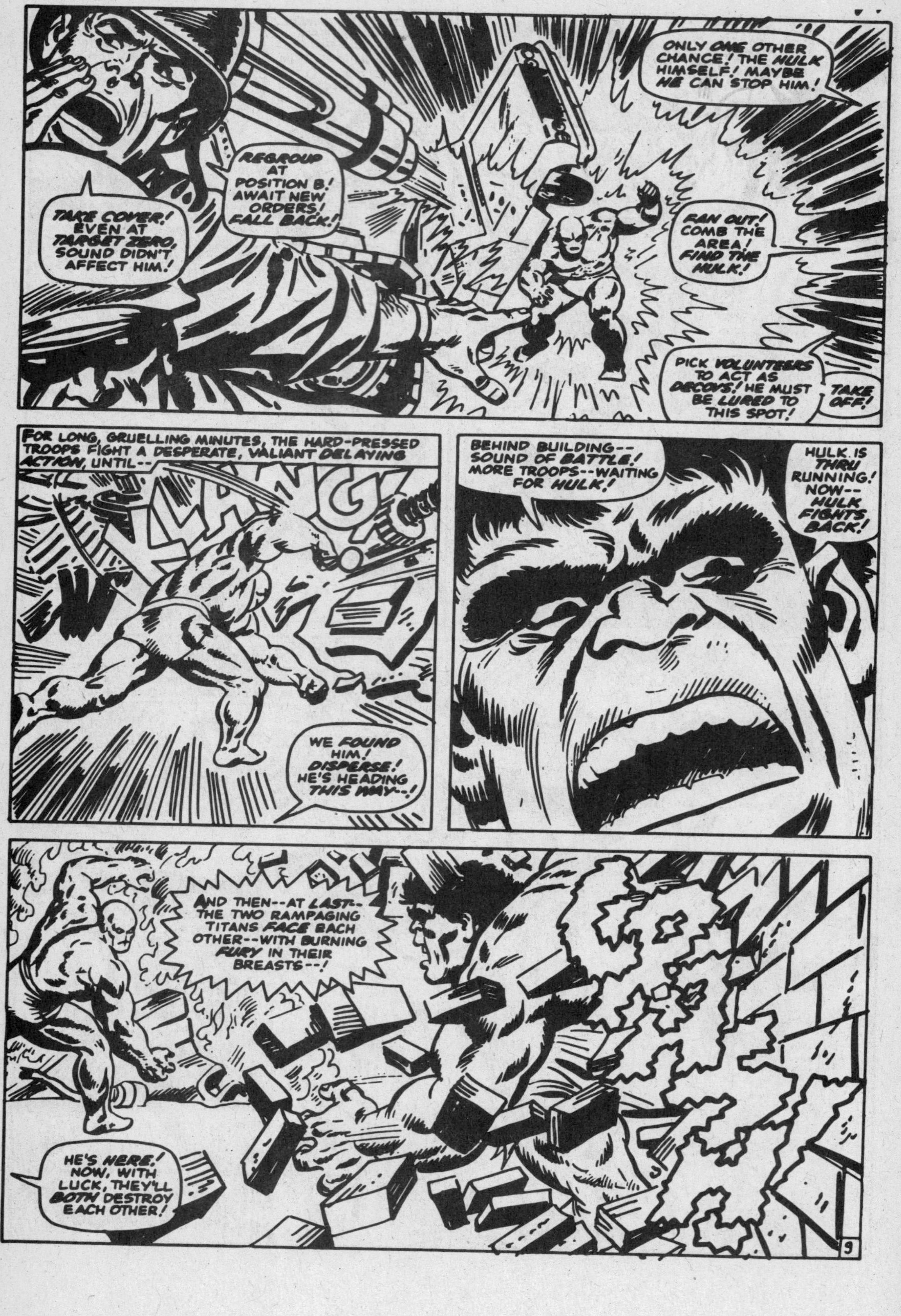
TAKE COVER! EVEN AT TARGET ZERO, SOUND DIDN'T AFFECT HIM!
REGROUP AT POSITION B! AWAIT NEW ORDERS! FALL BACK!
ONLY ONE OTHER CHANCE! THE HULK HIMSELF! MAYBE HE CAN STOP HIM!
FAN OUT! COMB THE AREA! FIND THE HULK!
PICK VOLUNTEERS TO ACT AS DECOYS! HE MUST BE LURED TO THIS SPOT!
TAKE OFF!
FOR LONG, GRUELLING MINUTES, THE HARD-PRESSED TROOPS FIGHT A DESPERATE, VALIANT DELAYING ACTION, UNTIL--
WE FOUND HIM! DISPERSE! HE'S HEADING THIS WAY--!
BEHIND BUILDING-- SOUND OF BATTLE! MORE TROOPS--WAITING FOR HULK!
HULK IS THRU RUNNING! NOW-- HULK FIGHTS BACK!
AND THEN--AT LAST-- THE TWO RAMPAGING TITANS FACE EACH OTHER--WITH BURNING FURY IN THEIR BREASTS--!
HE'S HERE! NOW, WITH LUCK, THEY'LL BOTH DESTROY EACH OTHER!
9

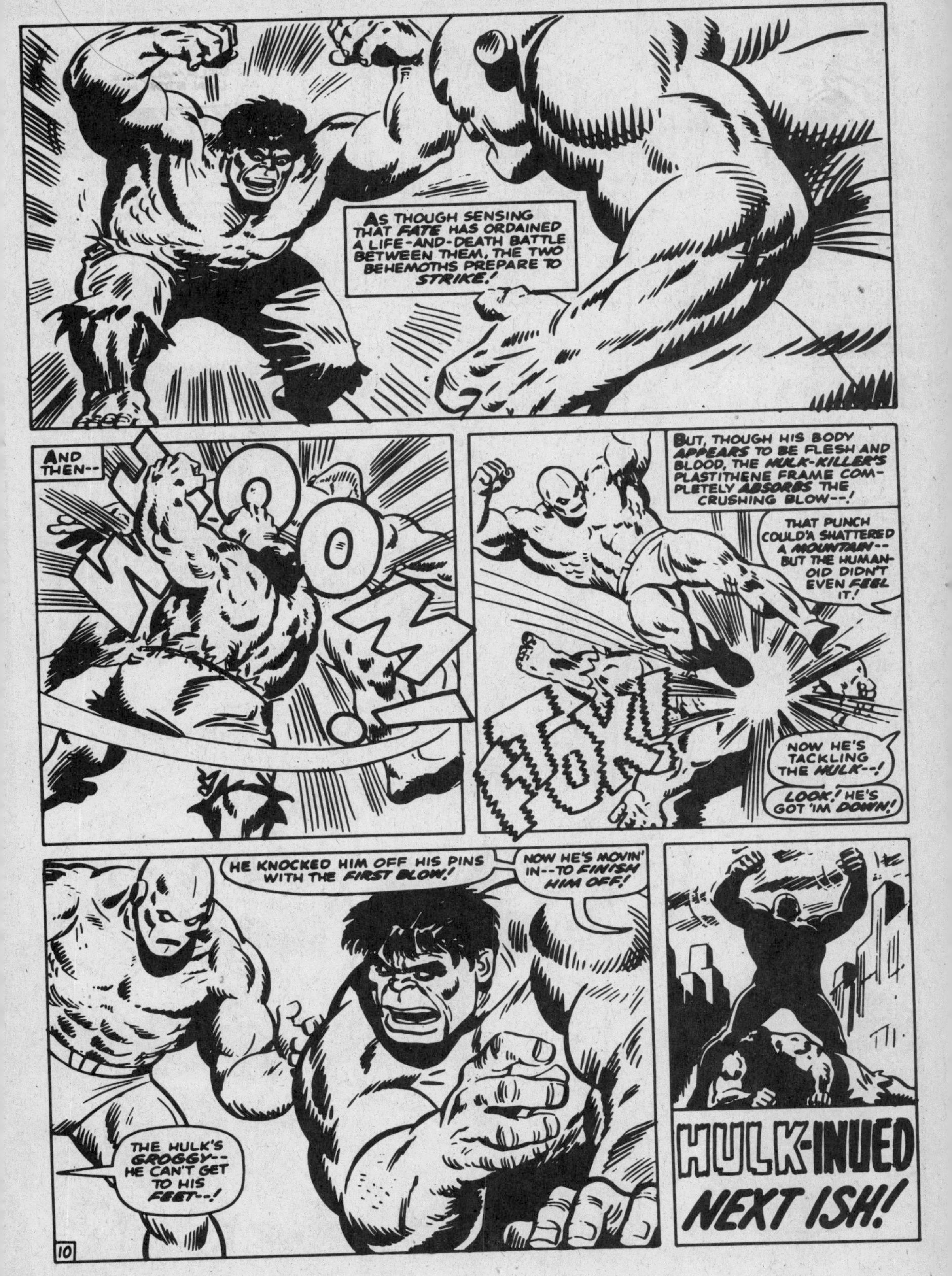
AS THOUGH SENSING THAT FATE HAS ORDAINED A LIFE-AND-DEATH BATTLE BETWEEN THEM, THE TWO BEHEMOTHS PREPARE TO STRIKE!
AND THEN--
BUT, THOUGH HIS BODY APPEARS TO BE FLESH AND BLOOD, THE HULK-KILLER'S PLASTITHENE FRAME COMPLETELY ABSORBS THE CRUSHING BLOW--!
THAT PUNCH COULD'A SHATTERED A MOUNTAIN-- BUT THE HUMANOID DIDN'T EVEN FEEL IT!
NOW HE'S TACKLING THE HULK--!
LOOK! HE'S GOT 'IM DOWN!
HE KNOCKED HIM OFF HIS PINS WITH THE FIRST BLOW!
NOW HE'S MOVIN' IN--TO FINISH HIM OFF!
THE HULK'S GROGGY-- HE CAN'T GET TO HIS FEET--!
HULK-INUED NEXT ISH!
10

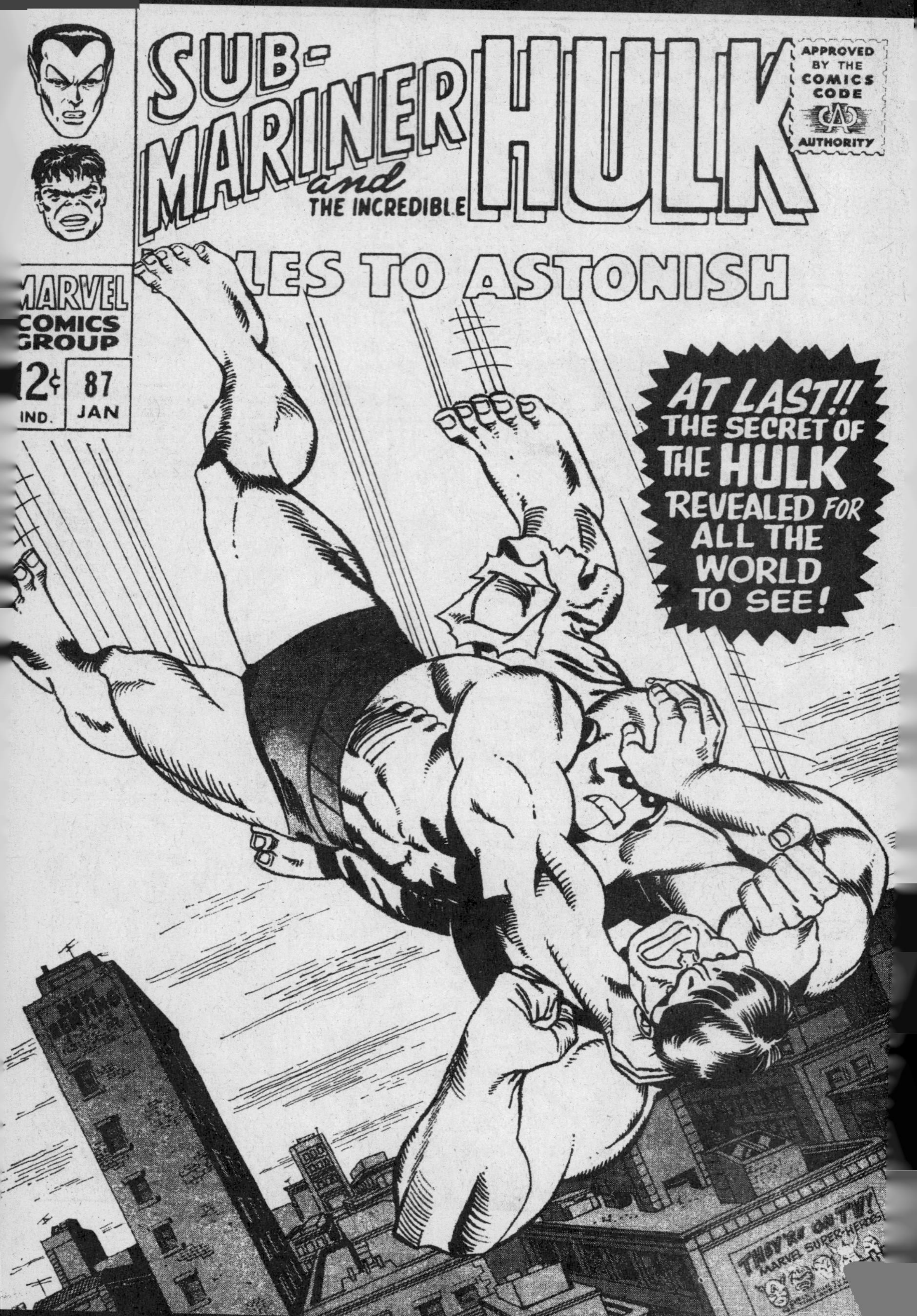
SUB-MARINER
and
THE INCREDIBLE HULK
APPROVED BY THE COMICS CODE AUTHORITY
LES TO ASTONISH
MARVEL COMICS GROUP
12¢ IND.
87 JAN
AT LAST!! THE SECRET OF THE HULK REVEALED FOR ALL THE WORLD TO SEE!
THEY'RE ON TV!
MARVEL SUPER-HEROES

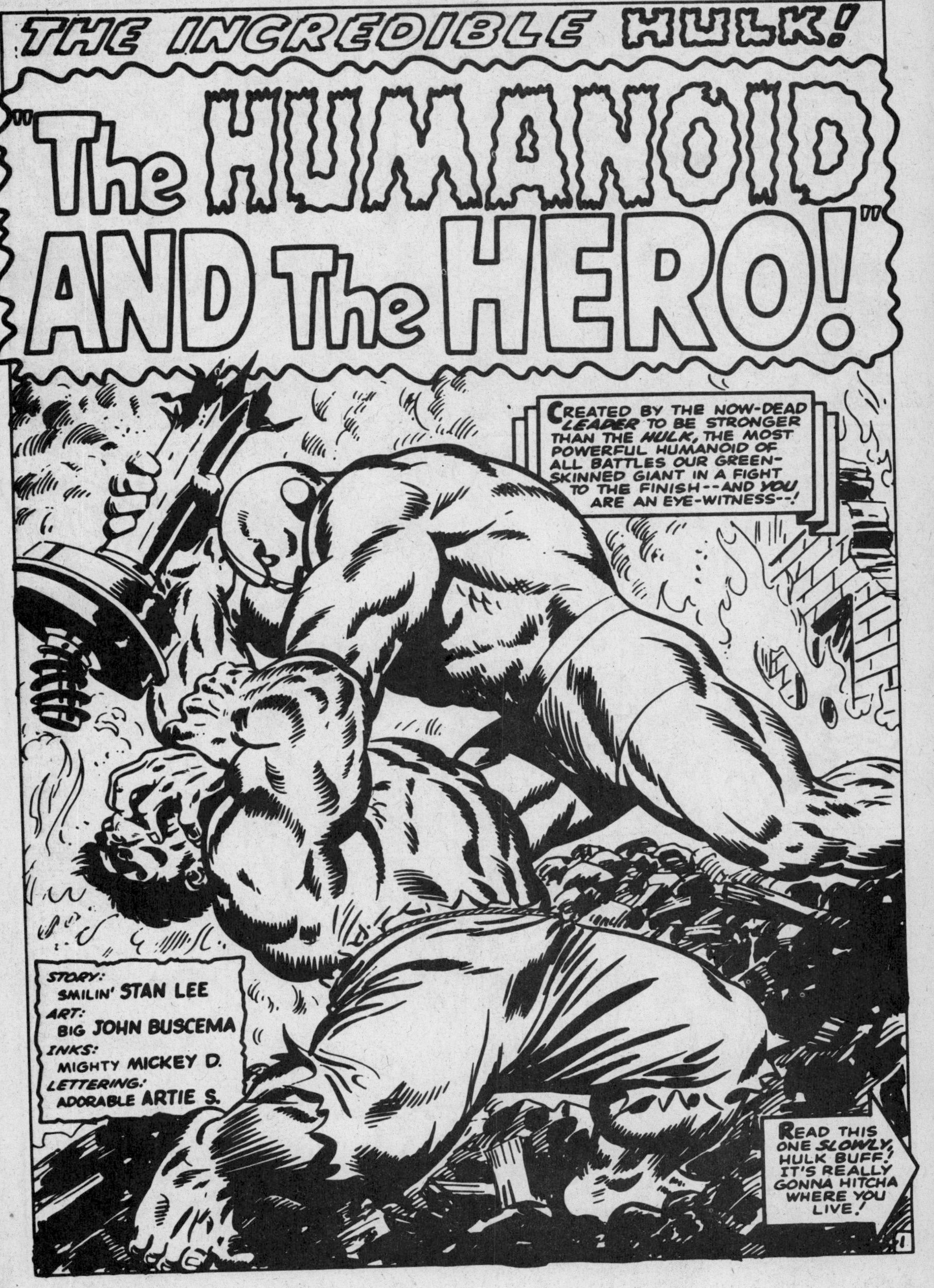
THE INCREDIBLE HULK!
"The HUMANOID AND The HERO!"
CREATED BY THE NOW-DEAD LEADER TO BE STRONGER THAN THE HULK, THE MOST POWERFUL HUMANOID OF ALL BATTLES OUR GREEN-SKINNED GIANT IN A FIGHT TO THE FINISH--AND YOU ARE AN EYE-WITNESS--!
STORY: SMILIN' STAN LEE
ART: BIG JOHN BUSCEMA
INKS: MIGHTY MICKEY D.
LETTERING: ADORABLE ARTIE S.
READ THIS ONE SLOWLY, HULK BUFF! IT'S REALLY GONNA HITCHA WHERE YOU LIVE!
1

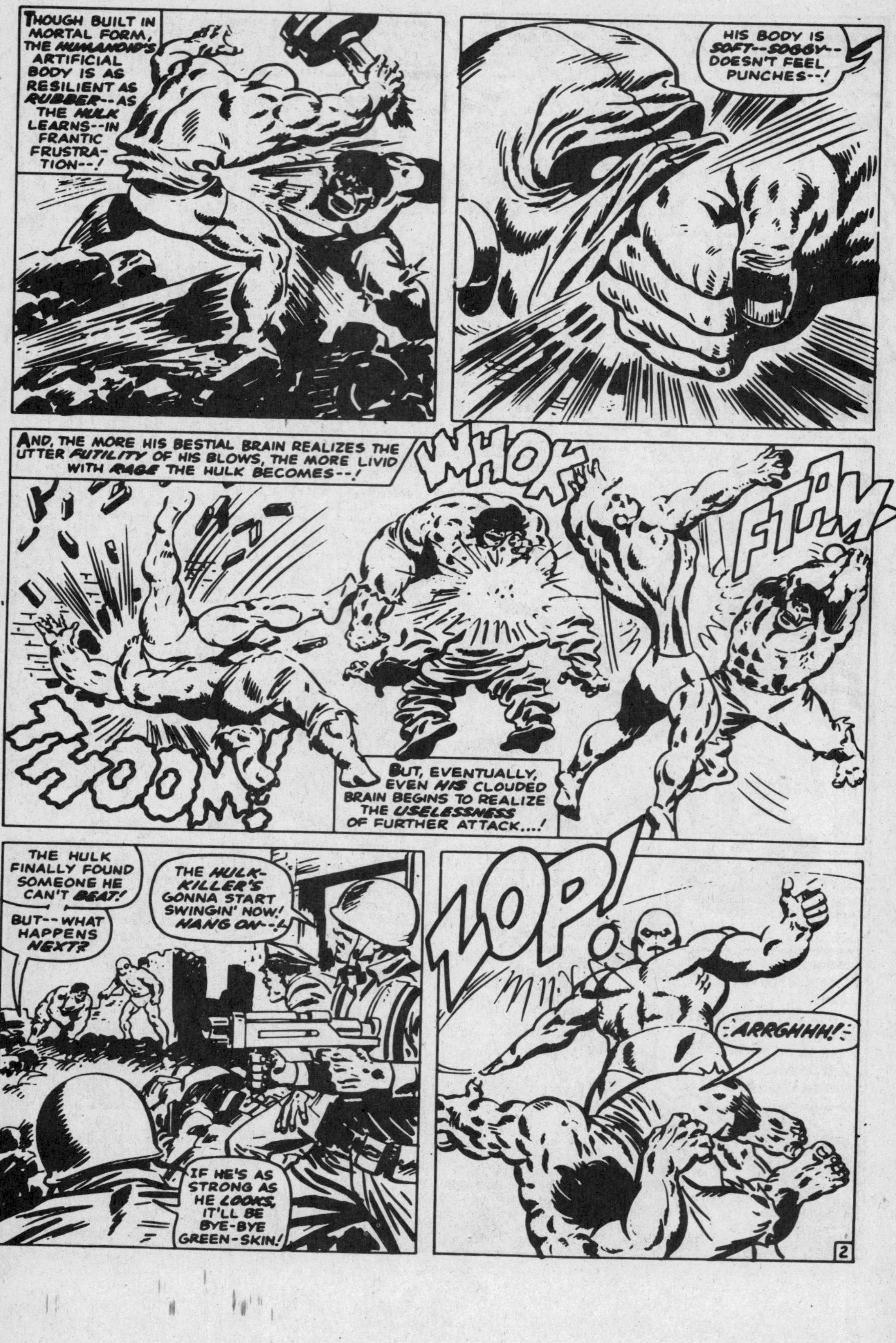

THOUGH BUILT IN MORTAL FORM, THE HUMANOID'S ARTIFICIAL BODY IS AS RESILIENT AS RUBBER--AS THE HULK LEARNS--IN FRANTIC FRUSTRATION--!
HIS BODY IS SOFT--SOGGY--DOESN'T FEEL PUNCHES--!
AND, THE MORE HIS BESTIAL BRAIN REALIZES THE UTTER FUTILITY OF HIS BLOWS, THE MORE LIVID WITH RAGE THE HULK BECOMES--!
WHOK
FTAW
THOOM
BUT, EVENTUALLY, EVEN HIS CLOUDED BRAIN BEGINS TO REALIZE THE USELESSNESS OF FURTHER ATTACK...!
THE HULK FINALLY FOUND SOMEONE HE CAN'T BEAT!
BUT--WHAT HAPPENS NEXT?
THE HULK-KILLER'S GONNA START SWINGIN' NOW! HANG ON--!
IF HE'S AS STRONG AS HE LOOKS, IT'LL BE BYE-BYE GREEN-SKIN!
ZOP!
ARRGHHH!

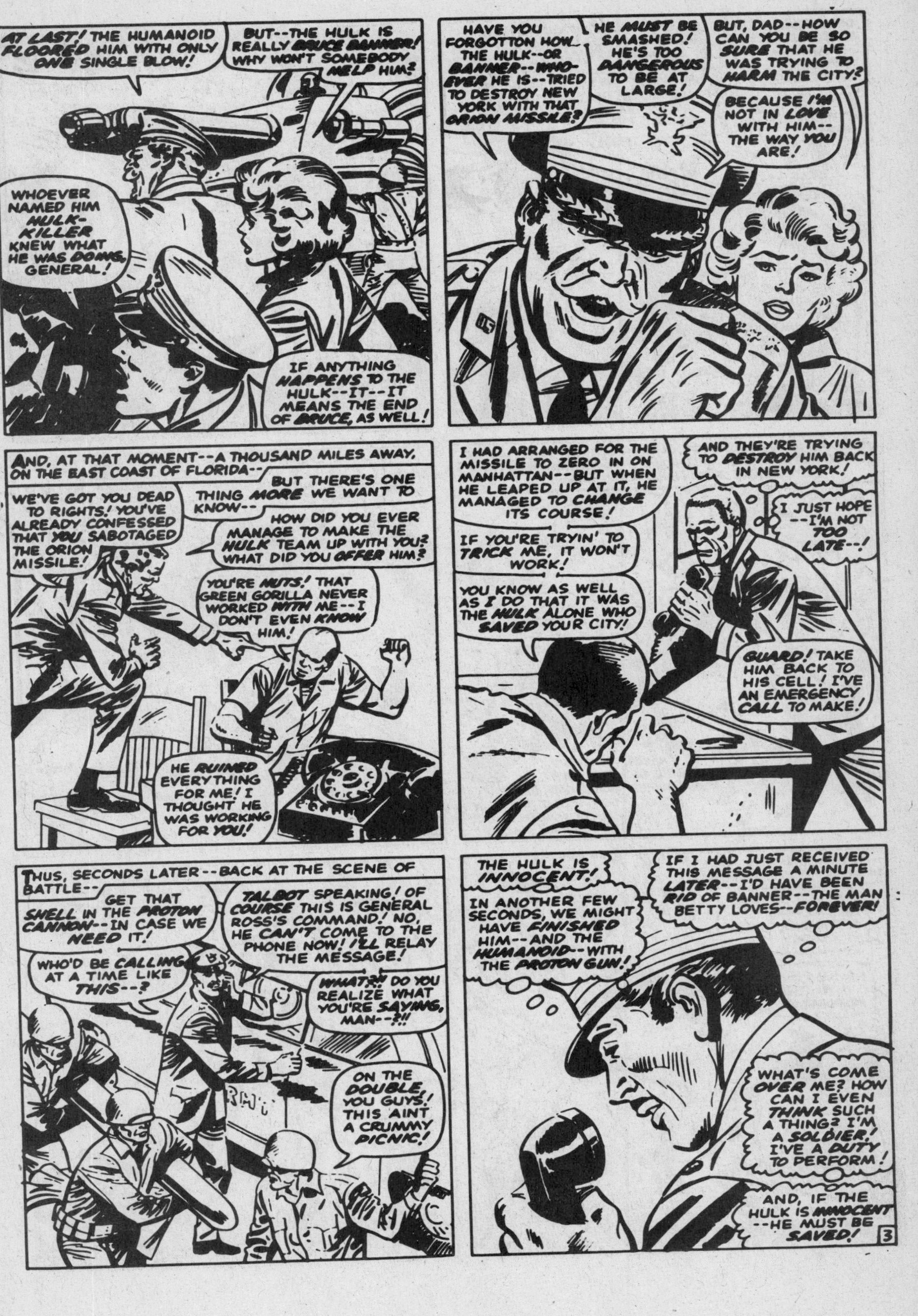
AT LAST! THE HUMANOID FLOORED HIM WITH ONLY ONE SINGLE BLOW!
BUT--THE HULK IS REALLY BRUCE BANNER! WHY WON'T SOMEBODY HELP HIM?
WHOEVER NAMED HIM HULK-KILLER KNEW WHAT HE WAS DOING, GENERAL!
IF ANYTHING HAPPENS TO THE HULK--IT--IT MEANS THE END OF BRUCE, AS WELL!
HAVE YOU FORGOTTON HOW THE HULK--OR BANNER--WHO-EVER HE IS--TRIED TO DESTROY NEW YORK WITH THAT ORION MISSILE?
HE MUST BE SMASHED! HE'S TOO DANGEROUS TO BE AT LARGE!
BUT, DAD--HOW CAN YOU BE SO SURE THAT HE WAS TRYING TO HARM THE CITY?
BECAUSE I'M NOT IN LOVE WITH HIM--THE WAY YOU ARE!
AND, AT THAT MOMENT--A THOUSAND MILES AWAY, ON THE EAST COAST OF FLORIDA--
WE'VE GOT YOU DEAD TO RIGHTS! YOU'VE ALREADY CONFESSED THAT YOU SABOTAGED THE ORION MISSILE!
BUT THERE'S ONE THING MORE WE WANT TO KNOW--
HOW DID YOU EVER MANAGE TO MAKE THE HULK TEAM UP WITH YOU? WHAT DID YOU OFFER HIM?
YOU'RE NUTS! THAT GREEN GORILLA NEVER WORKED WITH ME--I DON'T EVEN KNOW HIM!
HE RUINED EVERYTHING FOR ME! I THOUGHT HE WAS WORKING FOR YOU!
I HAD ARRANGED FOR THE MISSILE TO ZERO IN ON MANHATTAN--BUT WHEN HE LEAPED UP AT IT, HE MANAGED TO CHANGE ITS COURSE!
IF YOU'RE TRYIN' TO TRICK ME, IT WON'T WORK!
YOU KNOW AS WELL AS I DO THAT IT WAS THE HULK ALONE WHO SAVED YOUR CITY!
AND THEY'RE TRYING TO DESTROY HIM BACK IN NEW YORK!
I JUST HOPE --I'M NOT TOO LATE--!
GUARD! TAKE HIM BACK TO HIS CELL! I'VE AN EMERGENCY CALL TO MAKE!
THUS, SECONDS LATER--BACK AT THE SCENE OF BATTLE--
GET THAT SHELL IN THE PROTON CANNON--IN CASE WE NEED IT!
WHO'D BE CALLING AT A TIME LIKE THIS--?
TALBOT SPEAKING! OF COURSE THIS IS GENERAL ROSS'S COMMAND! NO, HE CAN'T COME TO THE PHONE NOW! I'LL RELAY THE MESSAGE!
WHAT?!! DO YOU REALIZE WHAT YOU'RE SAYING, MAN--?!!
ON THE DOUBLE, YOU GUYS! THIS AINT A CRUMMY PICNIC!
THE HULK IS INNOCENT!
IN ANOTHER FEW SECONDS, WE MIGHT HAVE FINISHED HIM--AND THE HUMANOID--WITH THE PROTON GUN!
IF I HAD JUST RECEIVED THIS MESSAGE A MINUTE LATER--I'D HAVE BEEN RID OF BANNER--THE MAN BETTY LOVES--FOREVER!
WHAT'S COME OVER ME? HOW CAN I EVEN THINK SUCH A THING? I'M A SOLDIER! I'VE A DUTY TO PERFORM!
AND, IF THE HULK IS INNOCENT --HE MUST BE SAVED!
3

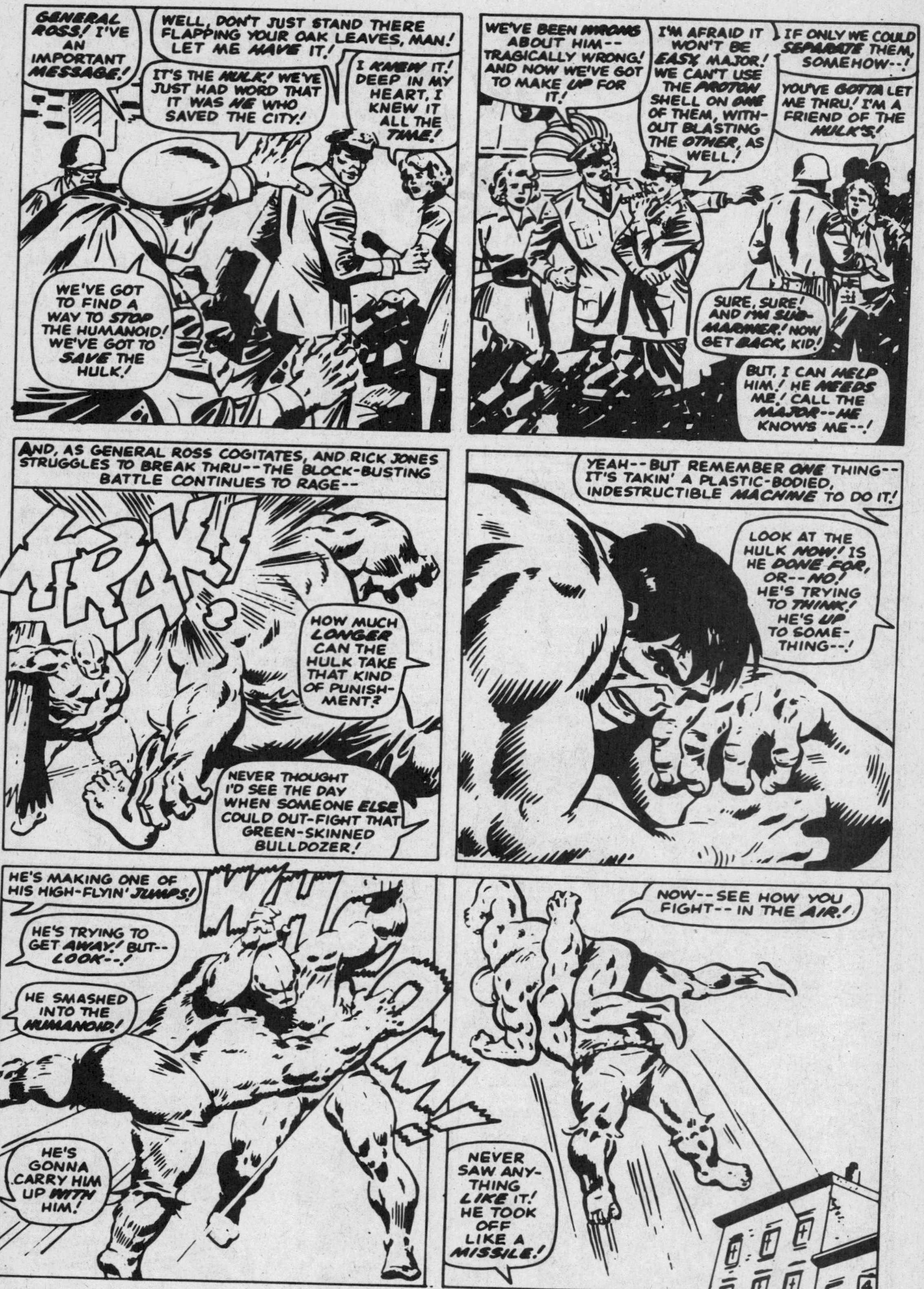
GENERAL ROSS! I'VE AN IMPORTANT MESSAGE!
WELL, DON'T JUST STAND THERE FLAPPING YOUR OAK LEAVES, MAN! LET ME HAVE IT!
IT'S THE HULK! WE'VE JUST HAD WORD THAT IT WAS HE WHO SAVED THE CITY!
I KNEW IT! DEEP IN MY HEART, I KNEW IT ALL THE TIME!
WE'VE GOT TO FIND A WAY TO STOP THE HUMANOID! WE'VE GOT TO SAVE THE HULK!
WE'VE BEEN WRONG ABOUT HIM-- TRAGICALLY WRONG! AND NOW WE'VE GOT TO MAKE UP FOR IT!
I'M AFRAID IT WON'T BE EASY, MAJOR! WE CAN'T USE THE PROTON SHELL ON ONE OF THEM, WITH-OUT BLASTING THE OTHER, AS WELL!
IF ONLY WE COULD SEPARATE THEM, SOMEHOW--!
YOU'VE GOTTA LET ME THRU! I'M A FRIEND OF THE HULK'S!
SURE, SURE! AND I'M SUB-MARINER! NOW GET BACK, KID!
BUT, I CAN HELP HIM! HE NEEDS ME! CALL THE MAJOR--HE KNOWS ME--!
AND, AS GENERAL ROSS COGITATES, AND RICK JONES STRUGGLES TO BREAK THRU--THE BLOCK-BUSTING BATTLE CONTINUES TO RAGE--
KRAK!
HOW MUCH LONGER CAN THE HULK TAKE THAT KIND OF PUNISH-MENT?
NEVER THOUGHT I'D SEE THE DAY WHEN SOMEONE ELSE COULD OUT-FIGHT THAT GREEN-SKINNED BULLDOZER!
YEAH--BUT REMEMBER ONE THING--IT'S TAKIN' A PLASTIC-BODIED, INDESTRUCTIBLE MACHINE TO DO IT!
LOOK AT THE HULK NOW! IS HE DONE FOR, OR--NO! HE'S TRYING TO THINK! HE'S UP TO SOME-THING--!
HE'S MAKING ONE OF HIS HIGH-FLYIN' JUMPS!
HE'S TRYING TO GET AWAY! BUT-- LOOK--!
HE SMASHED INTO THE HUMANOID!
HE'S GONNA CARRY HIM UP WITH HIM!
NOW--SEE HOW YOU FIGHT--IN THE AIR!
NEVER SAW ANY-THING LIKE IT! HE TOOK OFF LIKE A MISSILE!
4

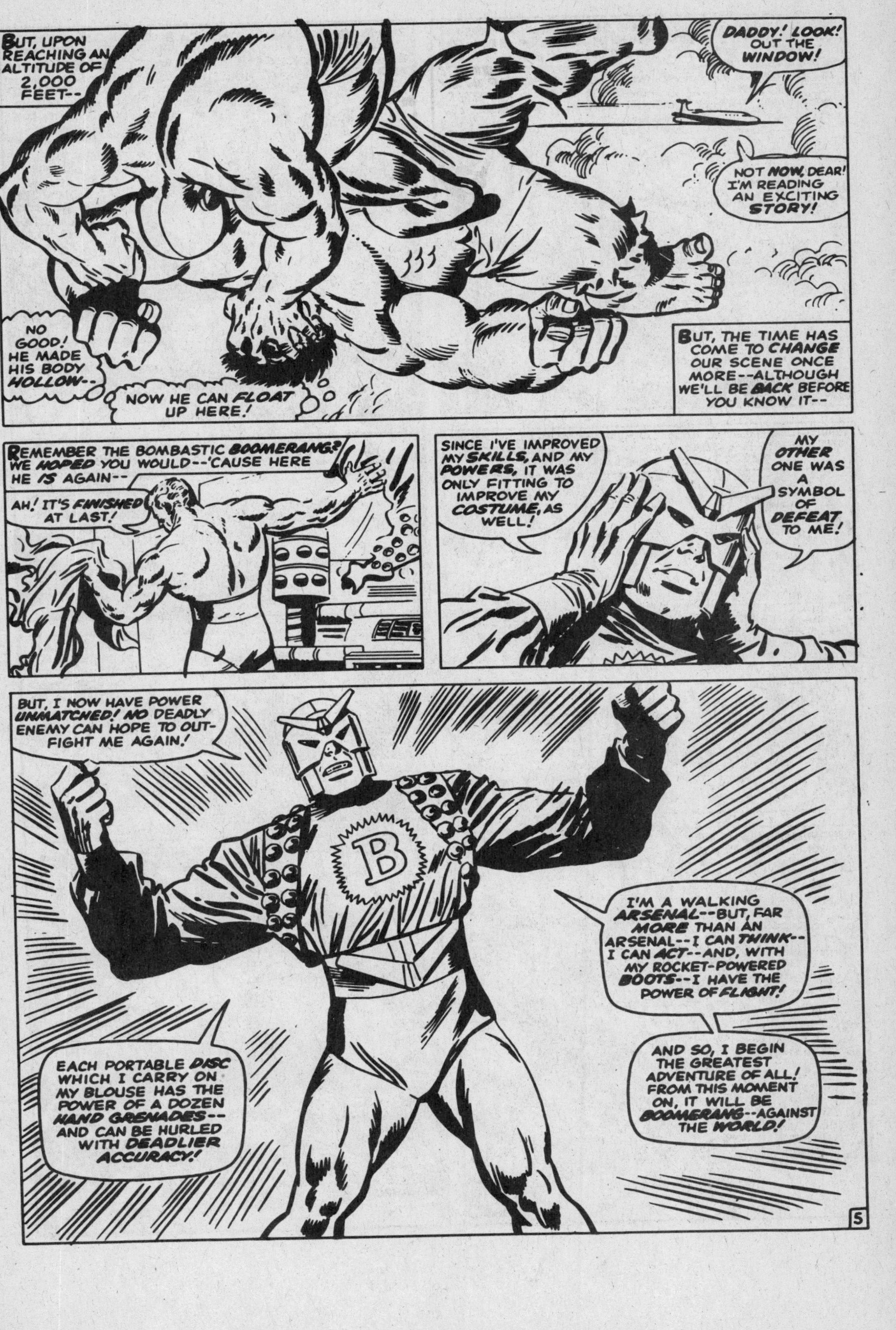

BUT, UPON REACHING AN ALTITUDE OF 2,000 FEET--
DADDY! LOOK! OUT THE WINDOW!
NOT NOW, DEAR! I'M READING AN EXCITING STORY!
NO GOOD! HE MADE HIS BODY HOLLOW--
NOW HE CAN FLOAT UP HERE!
BUT, THE TIME HAS COME TO CHANGE OUR SCENE ONCE MORE--ALTHOUGH WE'LL BE BACK BEFORE YOU KNOW IT--
REMEMBER THE BOMBASTIC BOOMERANG? WE HOPED YOU WOULD--'CAUSE HERE HE IS AGAIN--
AH! IT'S FINISHED AT LAST!
SINCE I'VE IMPROVED MY SKILLS, AND MY POWERS, IT WAS ONLY FITTING TO IMPROVE MY COSTUME, AS WELL!
MY OTHER ONE WAS A SYMBOL OF DEFEAT TO ME!
BUT, I NOW HAVE POWER UNMATCHED! NO DEADLY ENEMY CAN HOPE TO OUT-FIGHT ME AGAIN!
B
I'M A WALKING ARSENAL--BUT, FAR MORE THAN AN ARSENAL--I CAN THINK--I CAN ACT--AND, WITH MY ROCKET-POWERED BOOTS--I HAVE THE POWER OF FLIGHT!
EACH PORTABLE DISC WHICH I CARRY ON MY BLOUSE HAS THE POWER OF A DOZEN HAND GRENADES--AND CAN BE HURLED WITH DEADLIER ACCURACY!
AND SO, I BEGIN THE GREATEST ADVENTURE OF ALL! FROM THIS MOMENT ON, IT WILL BE BOOMERANG--AGAINST THE WORLD!
5

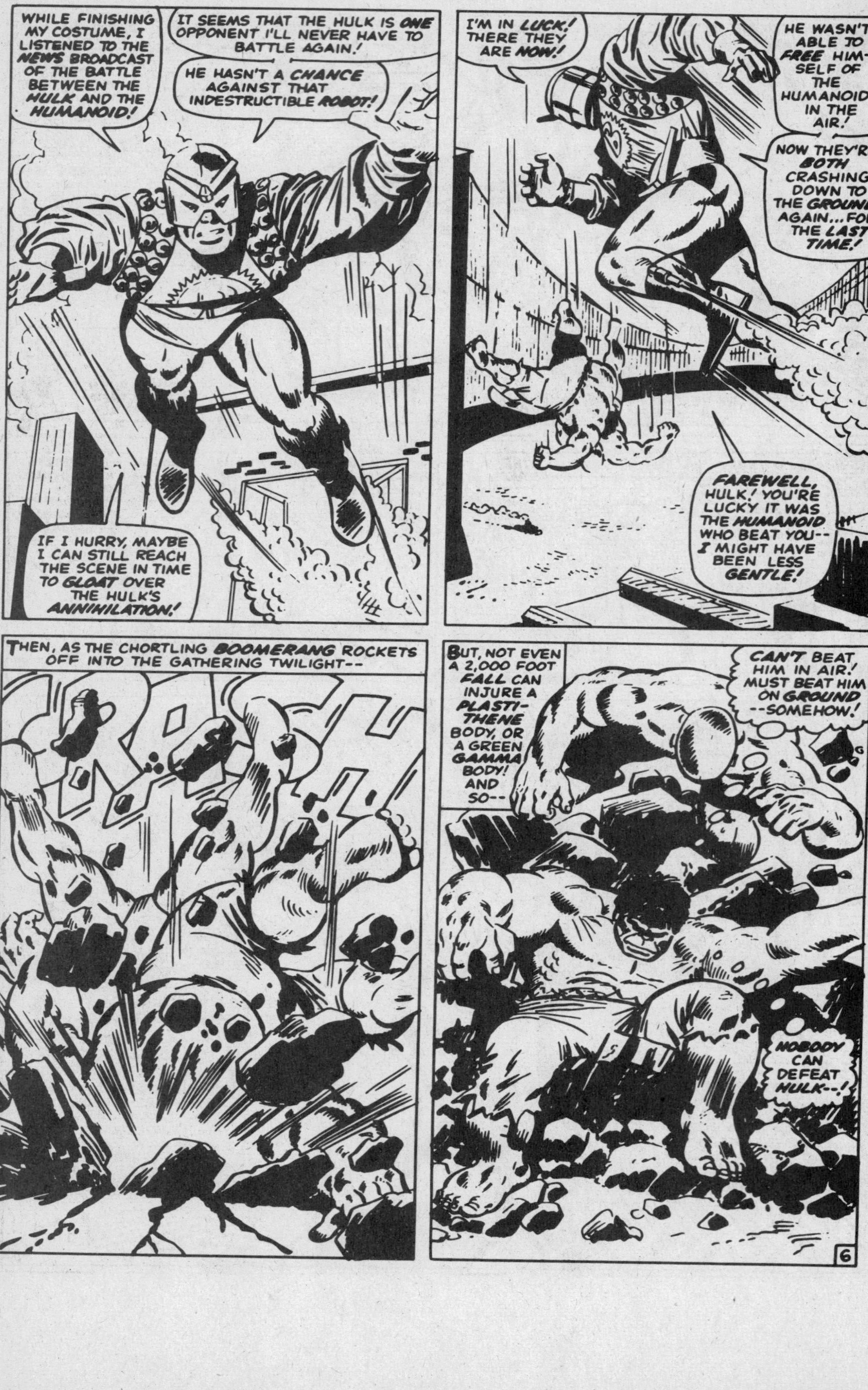
WHILE FINISHING MY COSTUME, I LISTENED TO THE NEWS BROADCAST OF THE BATTLE BETWEEN THE HULK AND THE HUMANOID!
IT SEEMS THAT THE HULK IS ONE OPPONENT I'LL NEVER HAVE TO BATTLE AGAIN!
HE HASN'T A CHANCE AGAINST THAT INDESTRUCTIBLE ROBOT!
IF I HURRY, MAYBE I CAN STILL REACH THE SCENE IN TIME TO GLOAT OVER THE HULK'S ANNIHILATION!
I'M IN LUCK! THERE THEY ARE NOW!
HE WASN'T ABLE TO FREE HIMSELF OF THE HUMANOID IN THE AIR!
NOW THEY'RE BOTH CRASHING DOWN TO THE GROUND AGAIN... FOR THE LAST TIME!
FAREWELL, HULK! YOU'RE LUCKY IT WAS THE HUMANOID WHO BEAT YOU-- I MIGHT HAVE BEEN LESS GENTLE!
THEN, AS THE CHORTLING BOOMERANG ROCKETS OFF INTO THE GATHERING TWILIGHT--
CRASH!
BUT, NOT EVEN A 2,000 FOOT FALL CAN INJURE A PLASTI-THENE BODY, OR A GREEN GAMMA BODY! AND SO--
CAN'T BEAT HIM IN AIR! MUST BEAT HIM ON GROUND --SOMEHOW!
NOBODY CAN DEFEAT HULK--!
6

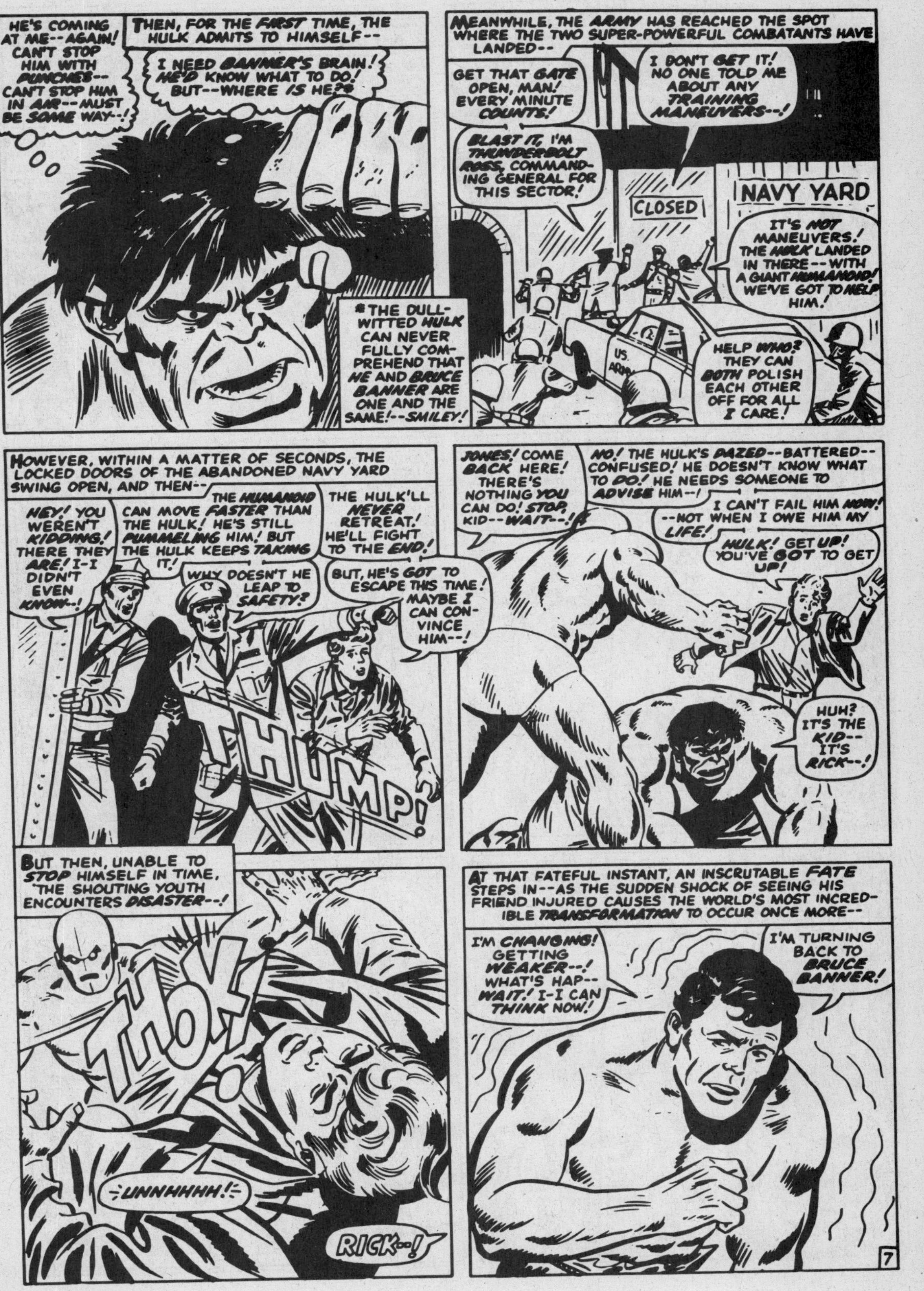
HE'S COMING AT ME--AGAIN! CAN'T STOP HIM WITH PUNCHES-- CAN'T STOP HIM IN AIR--MUST BE SOME WAY--!
THEN, FOR THE FIRST TIME, THE HULK ADMITS TO HIMSELF--
I NEED BANNER'S BRAIN! HE'D KNOW WHAT TO DO! BUT--WHERE IS HE?*
*THE DULL-WITTED HULK CAN NEVER FULLY COMPREHEND THAT HE AND BRUCE BANNER ARE ONE AND THE SAME!--SMILEY!
MEANWHILE, THE ARMY HAS REACHED THE SPOT WHERE THE TWO SUPER-POWERFUL COMBATANTS HAVE LANDED--
GET THAT GATE OPEN, MAN! EVERY MINUTE COUNTS!
I DON'T GET IT! NO ONE TOLD ME ABOUT ANY TRAINING MANEUVERS--!
BLAST IT, I'M THUNDERBOLT ROSS, COMMANDING GENERAL FOR THIS SECTOR!
CLOSED
NAVY YARD
IT'S NOT MANEUVERS! THE HULK LANDED IN THERE--WITH A GIANT HUMANOID! WE'VE GOT TO HELP HIM!
HELP WHO? THEY CAN BOTH POLISH EACH OTHER OFF FOR ALL I CARE!
HOWEVER, WITHIN A MATTER OF SECONDS, THE LOCKED DOORS OF THE ABANDONED NAVY YARD SWING OPEN, AND THEN--
HEY! YOU WEREN'T KIDDING! THERE THEY ARE! I-I DIDN'T EVEN KNOW--!
THE HUMANOID CAN MOVE FASTER THAN THE HULK! HE'S STILL PUMMELING HIM! BUT THE HULK KEEPS TAKING IT!
THE HULK'LL NEVER RETREAT! HE'LL FIGHT TO THE END!
WHY DOESN'T HE LEAP TO SAFETY?
BUT, HE'S GOT TO ESCAPE THIS TIME! MAYBE I CAN CONVINCE HIM--!
THUMP!
JONES! COME BACK HERE! THERE'S NOTHING YOU CAN DO! STOP, KID--WAIT--!
NO! THE HULK'S DAZED--BATTERED--CONFUSED! HE DOESN'T KNOW WHAT TO DO! HE NEEDS SOMEONE TO ADVISE HIM--!
I CAN'T FAIL HIM NOW! --NOT WHEN I OWE HIM MY LIFE!
HULK! GET UP! YOU'VE GOT TO GET UP!
HUH? IT'S THE KID--IT'S RICK--!
BUT THEN, UNABLE TO STOP HIMSELF IN TIME, THE SHOUTING YOUTH ENCOUNTERS DISASTER--!
THOK
-UNNHHHH!-
RICK--!
AT THAT FATEFUL INSTANT, AN INSCRUTABLE FATE STEPS IN--AS THE SUDDEN SHOCK OF SEEING HIS FRIEND INJURED CAUSES THE WORLD'S MOST INCREDIBLE TRANSFORMATION TO OCCUR ONCE MORE--
I'M CHANGING! GETTING WEAKER--! WHAT'S HAP-- WAIT! I-I CAN THINK NOW!
I'M TURNING BACK TO BRUCE BANNER!
7

THEN, AS THE *HUMANOID* STANDS IDLY BY--*PONDERING ITS NEXT MOVE*--

RICK! ARE YOU ALL *RIGHT*, SON? WHY DID YOU *RUN* BETWEEN US THAT WAY?

HE'S NOT *HURT*, BANNER! MERELY *STUNNED!*

BRUCE! IT'S *YOU!*

TRIED TO *HELP*--TO GET YOU TO RUN *AWAY*--!

NOW THERE CAN BE NO *DOUBT!* THE *HULK* ISN'T A *MONSTER*--HE *NEVER WAS!* HE WAS ALWAYS *YOU!*

--*WHEW!*--FEEL LIKE I BEEN KICKED BY A *MULE!*

MAJOR! THE *HUMANOID'S* STARTING TO *ADVANCE* TOWARDS US! WHAT'LL WE DO, SIR?

ALERT THE *PROTON GUN* CREW! PREPARE FOR *FIRING!*

WAIT! IT'S TOO *POWERFUL*--TOO *DANGEROUS!* THERE MAY BE A *BETTER WAY!*

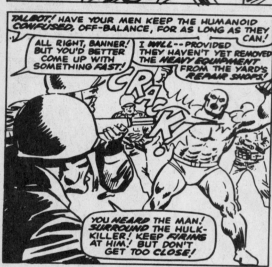

TALBOT! HAVE YOUR MEN KEEP THE HUMANOID *CONFUSED*, *OFF-BALANCE*, FOR AS LONG AS THEY CAN!

ALL RIGHT, BANNER! BUT YOU'D BETTER COME UP WITH SOMETHING *FAST!*

I WILL--*PROVIDED* THEY HAVEN'T YET *REMOVED* THE *HEAVY EQUIPMENT* FROM THE YARD'S *REPAIR SHOPS!*

CRACK!

YOU *HEARD* THE MAN! *SURROUND* THE HULK-KILLER! KEEP *FIRING* AT HIM! BUT DON'T GET TOO *CLOSE!*

YOU'VE *GOT* TO DO IT, BRUCE! YOU'VE GOT TO SHOW THE WORLD WHAT *I* ALREADY *KNOW*--THAT YOU'RE *NOT* A MENACE! YOU'RE ON THE *SIDE* OF MANKIND!

THERE'S ONLY *ONE* WAY TO STOP THE HUMANOID! HE'S *NOT ALIVE!* HE'S *BASICALLY A MACHINE!*

AND, *ANY* MACHINE CAN BE *IMMOBILIZED!*

RICK! TELL THE GENERAL TO LINE UP AS MANY *TECHNICIANS* AS HE CAN! MEN WHO KNOW THEIR JOB--AND CAN MOVE *FAST!*

I'M RIGHT *BEHIND* YOU, BLAST IT! I'LL GET THE MEN!

BUT, WHAT'S YOUR *PLAN?* WHAT CAN *YOU* DO WHAT ALL OUR *WEAPONS* COULDN'T?

THE HUMANOID IS MORE THAN A GIANT, *INDESTRUCTIBLE* MENACE, GENERAL! HE'S THE CREATION OF ONE OF THE MOST *DANGEROUSLY BRILLIANT BRAINS* THAT EVER LIVED!

AND, THE WAY TO *FIGHT* HIM ISN'T MERELY BY *BRUTE FORCE*--BUT BY APPLYING SOME UNEXPECTED *COUNTER-INTELLIGENCE!*

ALL RIGHT, MISTER! YOU'LL *HAVE* YOUR CHANCE! AND, FOR *YOUR* SAKE, I HOPE IT *WORKS!*

WHILE, A FEW HUNDRED YARDS AWAY--

SKRAKK--

IT'S LIKE SHOOTING INTO A *SACK* OF SAND! HE DOESN'T MEAN A *THING!*

LOOK OUT! HE'S GETTING READY TO *RUSH* US!

WHATEVER BANNER'S GONNA *DO*--HE BETTER DO IT *FAST!*

8

BOOK! HE'S TOSSIN' THAT HUNK A *IRON* AT US LIKE IT'S A *PEBBLE!*

BLAM!

WHEW! IF THAT THING EVER *CONNECTED*--!

WHERE'S *BANNER?* WHAT'S HE DOIN' IN THERE?

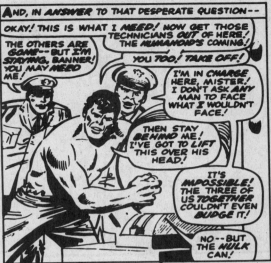

AND, IN ANSWER TO THAT DESPERATE QUESTION--

OKAY! THIS IS WHAT I *NEED!* NOW GET THOSE TECHNICIANS *OUT* OF HERE! THE *HUMANOID'S* COMING!

THE OTHERS ARE *GONE*--BUT I'M *STAYING*, BANNER! YOU MAY *NEED* ME!

YOU *TOO!* TAKE *OFF!*

I'M IN *CHARGE* HERE, MISTER! I DON'T ASK *ANY* MAN TO FACE WHAT I *WOULDN'T* FACE!

THEN STAY *BEHIND* ME! I'VE GOT TO *LIFT* THIS OVER HIS HEAD!

IT'S *IMPOSSIBLE!* THE THREE OF US *TOGETHER* COULDN'T EVEN *BUDGE* IT!

NO--BUT THE *HULK* CAN!

BUT YOU'RE *NOT* THE HULK ANY *MORE!* YOU'RE *BANNER!* HAVE YOU GONE *MAD?*

I *HOPE* SO! IT'S WHAT I'M COUNT-ING ON!

I'VE GOT TO GET *MAD* ENOUGH, IN THE NEXT TWO SECONDS, TO INCREASE MY *PULSE RATE*--!

IT'S *WORKING!* I CAN *FEEL* IT! STAND BACK! *BACK! BACK!*

I *KNEW*--THE SIGHT OF HIM-- WOULD DO IT--!

NOW--IF ONLY-- I CAN--*REMEMBER*--

--REMEMBER--WHAT I'M SUPPOSED--TO *DO*--!

THE *MACHINE!* YOU WANTED TO *LIFT* IT OVER HIS HEAD!

MACHINE! THAT'S *RIGHT!* MUST GET *MACHINE....*

LOOK! HE'S *LIFTING* IT! AS THOUGH IT'S *WEIGHTLESS!*

WHATEVER *BANNER* DID TO IT--IT'S LOADED WITH *POWER!*

MUST *LIFT* IT--OVER HEAD--

THE *HUMANOID* LOOKS *CONFUSED!*--DOESN'T KNOW WHAT'LL HAPPEN *NEXT!*

9

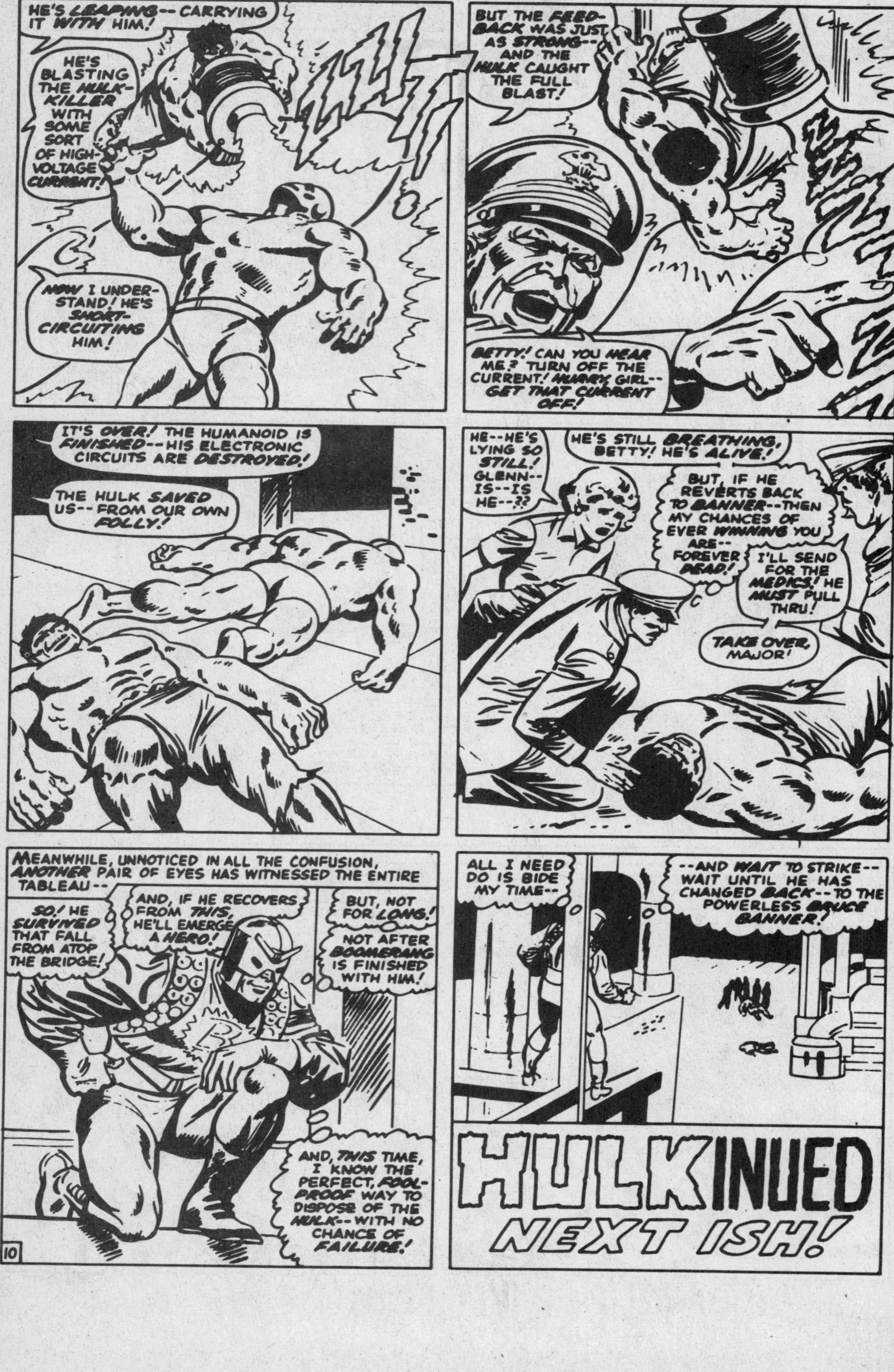

HE'S LEAPING--CARRYING IT WITH HIM!
HE'S BLASTING THE HULK-KILLER WITH SOME SORT OF HIGH-VOLTAGE CURRENT!
NOW I UNDERSTAND! HE'S SHORT-CIRCUITING HIM!
BUT THE FEED-BACK WAS JUST AS STRONG--AND THE HULK CAUGHT THE FULL BLAST!
BETTY! CAN YOU HEAR ME? TURN OFF THE CURRENT! HURRY, GIRL--GET THAT CURRENT OFF!
IT'S OVER! THE HUMANOID IS FINISHED--HIS ELECTRONIC CIRCUITS ARE DESTROYED!
THE HULK SAVED US--FROM OUR OWN FOLLY!
HE--HE'S LYING SO STILL! GLENN--IS--IS HE--??
HE'S STILL BREATHING, BETTY! HE'S ALIVE!
BUT, IF HE REVERTS BACK TO BANNER--THEN MY CHANCES OF EVER WINNING YOU ARE--FOREVER DEAD!
I'LL SEND FOR THE MEDICS! HE MUST PULL THRU!
TAKE OVER, MAJOR!
MEANWHILE, UNNOTICED IN ALL THE CONFUSION, ANOTHER PAIR OF EYES HAS WITNESSED THE ENTIRE TABLEAU--
SO! HE SURVIVED THAT FALL FROM ATOP THE BRIDGE!
AND, IF HE RECOVERS FROM THIS, HE'LL EMERGE A HERO!
BUT, NOT FOR LONG!
NOT AFTER BOOMERANG IS FINISHED WITH HIM!
AND, THIS TIME, I KNOW THE PERFECT, FOOL-PROOF WAY TO DISPOSE OF THE HULK--WITH NO CHANCE OF FAILURE!
10
ALL I NEED DO IS BIDE MY TIME--
--AND WAIT TO STRIKE--WAIT UNTIL HE HAS CHANGED BACK--TO THE POWERLESS BRUCE BANNER!
HULKINUED NEXT ISH!

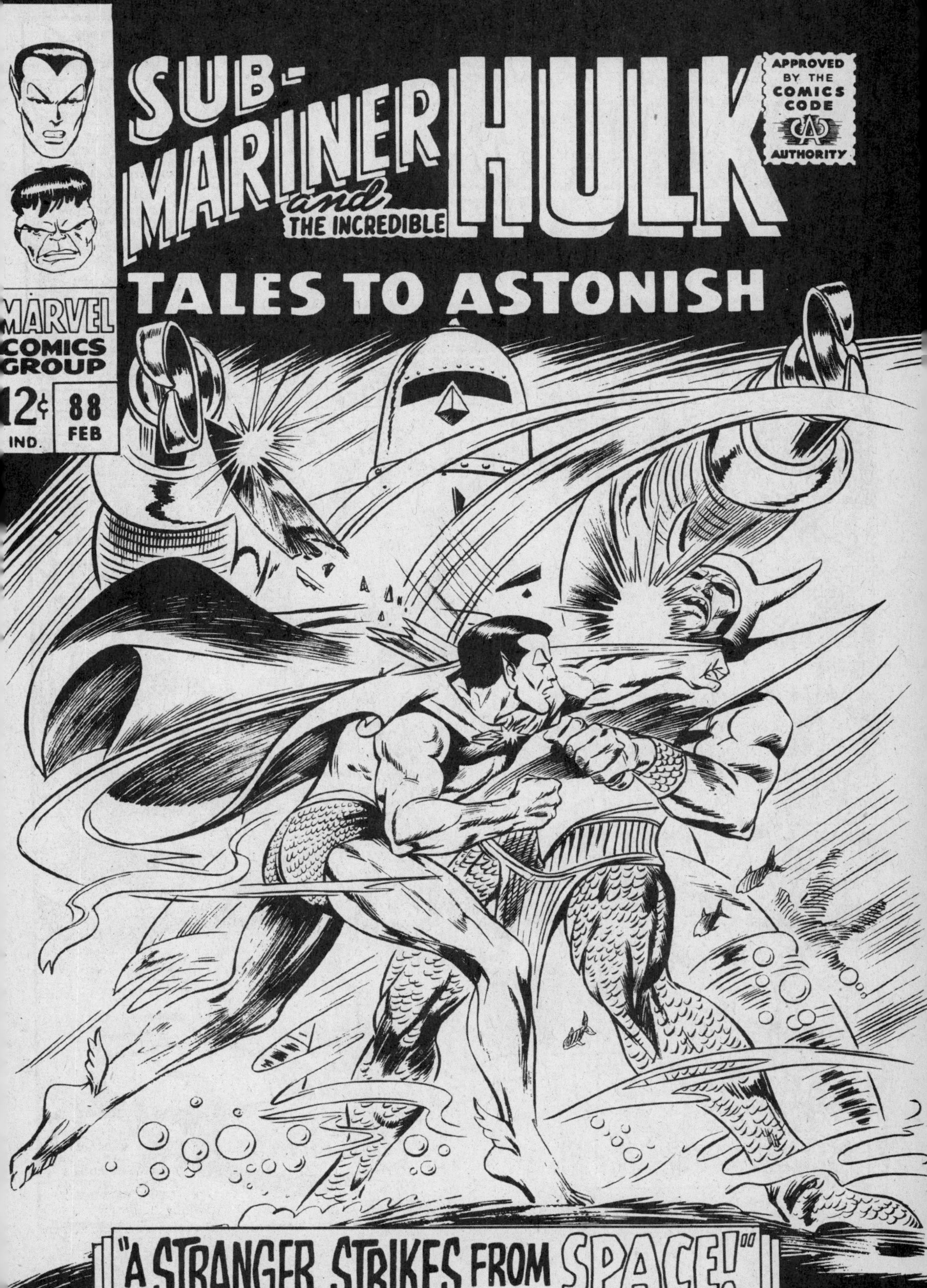

SUB-MARINER and THE INCREDIBLE HULK
APPROVED BY THE COMICS CODE AUTHORITY
TALES TO ASTONISH
MARVEL COMICS GROUP
12¢ IND.
88 FEB
"A STRANGER STRIKES FROM SPACE!"

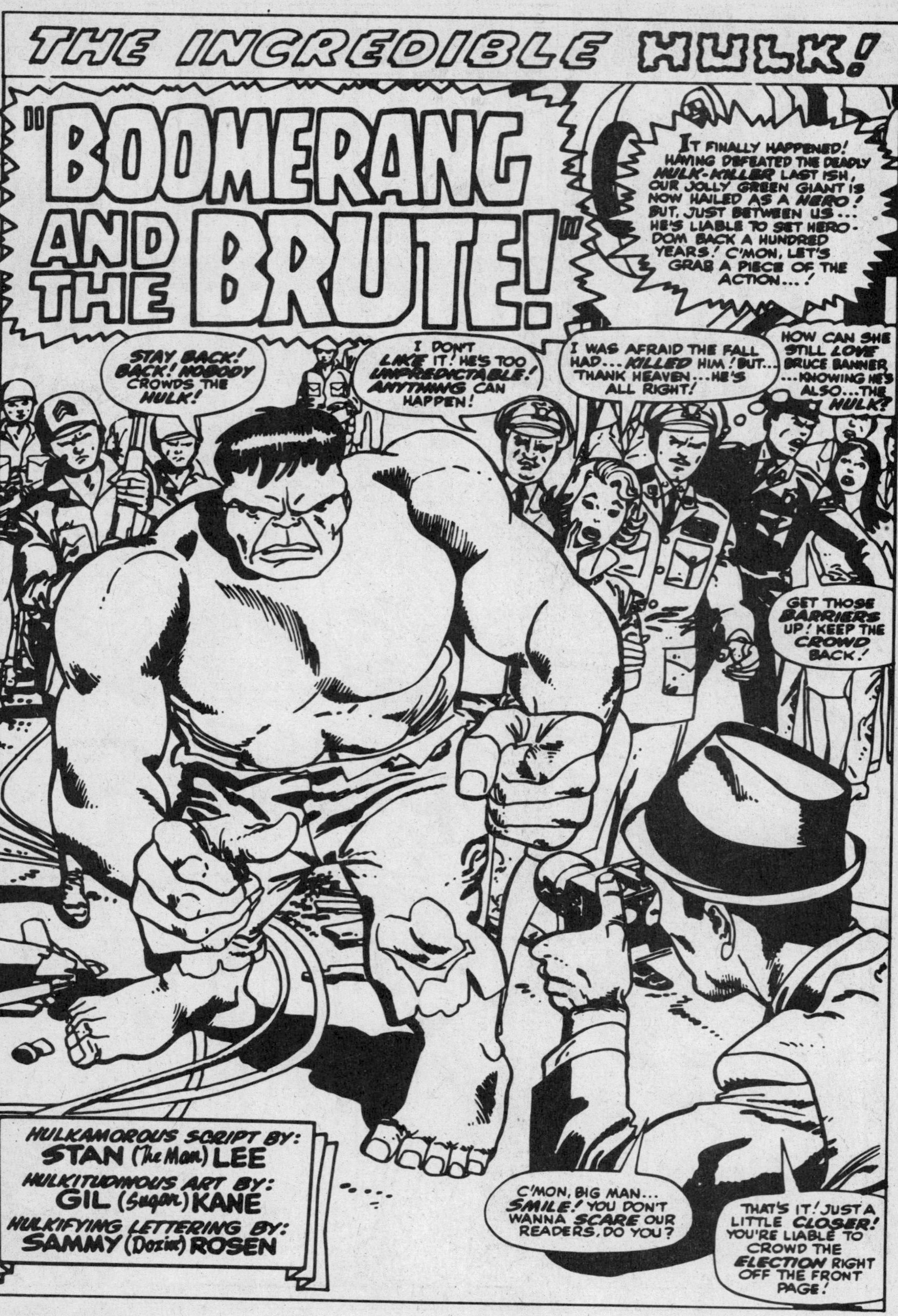
THE INCREDIBLE HULK!
"BOOMERANG AND THE BRUTE!"
IT FINALLY HAPPENED! HAVING DEFEATED THE DEADLY HULK-KILLER LAST ISH, OUR JOLLY GREEN GIANT IS NOW HAILED AS A HERO! BUT, JUST BETWEEN US... HE'S LIABLE TO SET HERO-DOM BACK A HUNDRED YEARS! C'MON, LET'S GRAB A PIECE OF THE ACTION...!
STAY BACK! BACK! NOBODY CROWDS THE HULK!
I DON'T LIKE IT! HE'S TOO UNPREDICTABLE! ANYTHING CAN HAPPEN!
I WAS AFRAID THE FALL HAD... KILLED HIM! BUT... THANK HEAVEN... HE'S ALL RIGHT!
HOW CAN SHE STILL LOVE BRUCE BANNER ...KNOWING HE'S ALSO... THE HULK?
GET THOSE BARRIERS UP! KEEP THE CROWD BACK!
HULKAMOROUS SCRIPT BY: STAN (The Man) LEE
HULKITUDINOUS ART BY: GIL (Sugar) KANE
HULKIFYING LETTERING BY: SAMMY (Dozin') ROSEN
C'MON, BIG MAN... SMILE! YOU DON'T WANNA SCARE OUR READERS, DO YOU?
THAT'S IT! JUST A LITTLE CLOSER! YOU'RE LIABLE TO CROWD THE ELECTION RIGHT OFF THE FRONT PAGE!

LIGHTS *BLINDING* HULK! CAN'T *SEE*!.. GO...OR HULK *SMASH!*

FLLASHH!

OKAY, PAL..OKAY! YOU SURE DON'T HAVETA TELL ME *TWICE!*

GLEN...WHAT WILL *HAPPEN* TO HIM NOW? HOW DO WE MAKE HIM TURN BACK TO *BRUCE BANNER?*

TOO MUCH *NOISE!* TOO MANY *PEOPLE!*

IT'S *ANYBODY'S* GUESS, BETTY! NO ONE *KNOWS!*

DON'T GET TOO *CLOSE!* HE MIGHT DO *ANYTHING!*

YOU MUSTN'T *MIND* ALL THIS! YOU'RE A *HERO* NOW! YOU WON'T BE *HOUNDED* ANYMORE!

EVERYONE *LOOKS*.. EVERYONE *CROWDS* CLOSER!

KEEP *AWAY* FROM HULK!

BETTY! BE *CARE-FUL!* HE ISN'T *BRUCE BANNER* NOW!

HE'D NEVER HURT *ME*... I *KNOW* IT!

As the excited crowd continues to mill around the most *incredible* living mortal on earth, the epoch-making scene is televised throughout the nation, where it is viewed with rapt fascination by all...

HE'S *PROVEN* HIMSELF AT LAST!

NOW, THERE CAN BE NO DOUBT IN *ANYONE'S* MIND THAT THE HULK WAS *NEVER* A THREAT TO AMERICA'S SECURITY!

THE POOR, LUMBERING BRUTE! HE WAS GUILTY ONLY OF BEING *FEARED*.. AND *MIS-UNDERSTOOD!*

AND, WITHIN THAT *MONSTROUS BODY*, THE BRILLIANT BRAIN OF OUR *GREATEST ATOMIC SCIENTIST* IS HELD PRISONER!

WE MUST SPARE NO EFFORT TO *FREE* HIM... TO MAKE *DR. BRUCE BANNER* NORMAL ONCE AGAIN!

I WANT TO SEND A *MESSAGE* TO GENERAL ROSS! YES, *THUNDER-BOLT* ROSS... IN CHARGE OF *OPERATION HULK*...

MEANWHILE, BACK IN NEW YORK...

THEY HAVEN'T NOTICED *BOOMERANG* YET, THANKS TO THE CONCEALING *SHADOWS* UP HERE!

THERE'S *STILL* TIME FOR ME TO FIND A WAY TO *DESTROY THE HULK!*

ONE OF MY SMALL, EXPLOSIVE *DISCS* WILL DO THE TRICK!

ALL I NEED DO IS *ANGER* HIM...MAKE HIM GO ON A *RAMPAGE* AGAIN!

ARGNNN!

SKLEAST!

FLLASHH!

2

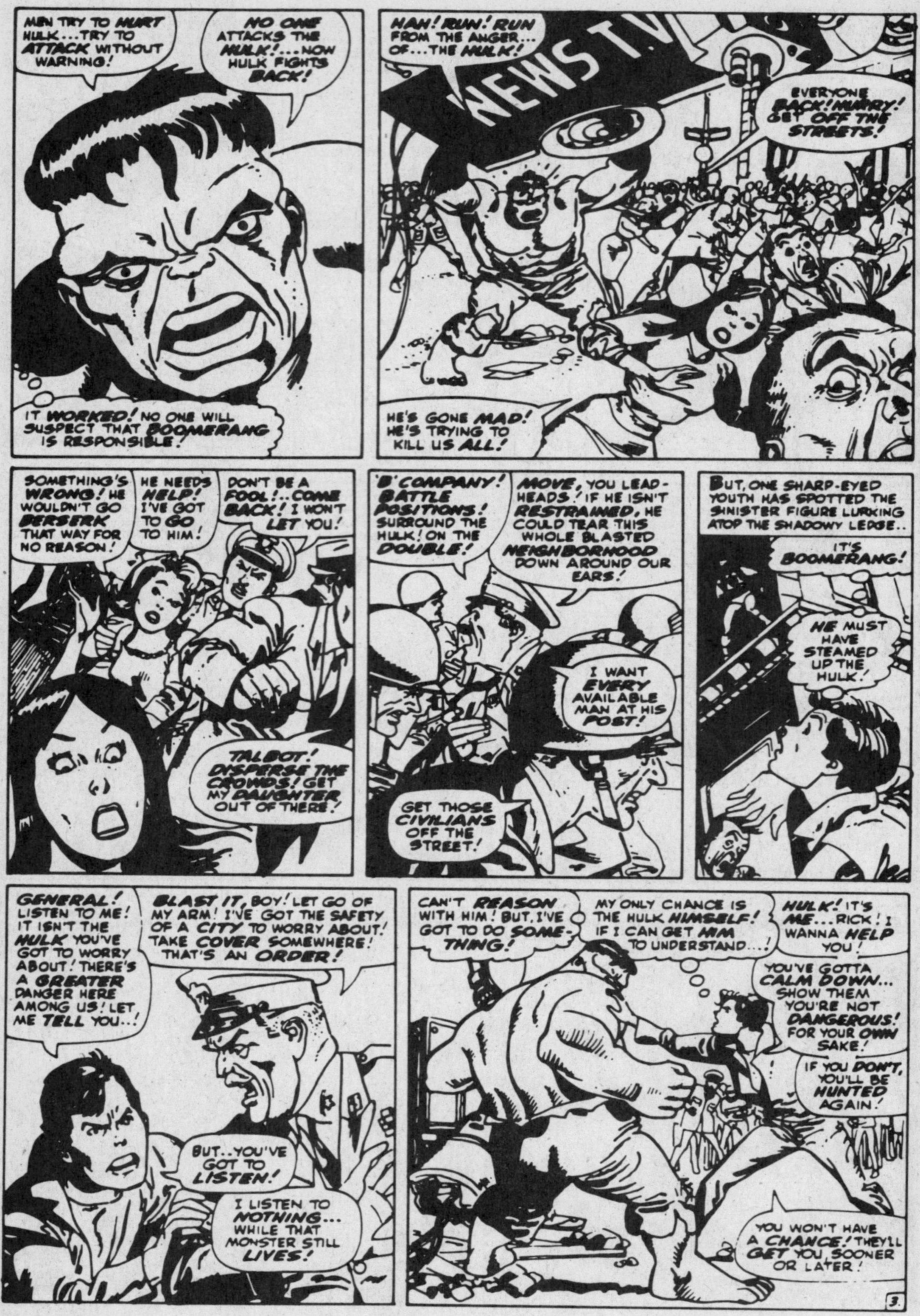
MEN TRY TO HURT HULK...TRY TO ATTACK WITHOUT WARNING!
NO ONE ATTACKS THE HULK!...NOW HULK FIGHTS BACK!
IT WORKED! NO ONE WILL SUSPECT THAT BOOMERANG IS RESPONSIBLE!
HAH! RUN! RUN FROM THE ANGER OF...THE HULK!
NEWS T.V.
EVERYONE BACK! HURRY! GET OFF THE STREETS!
HE'S GONE MAD! HE'S TRYING TO KILL US ALL!
SOMETHING'S WRONG! HE WOULDN'T GO BERSERK THAT WAY FOR NO REASON!
HE NEEDS HELP! I'VE GOT TO GO TO HIM!
DON'T BE A FOOL!..COME BACK! I WON'T LET YOU!
TALBOT! DISPERSE THE CROWDS! GET MY DAUGHTER OUT OF THERE!
'B' COMPANY! BATTLE POSITIONS! SURROUND THE HULK! ON THE DOUBLE!
MOVE, YOU LEAD-HEADS! IF HE ISN'T RESTRAINED, HE COULD TEAR THIS WHOLE BLASTED NEIGHBORHOOD DOWN AROUND OUR EARS!
I WANT EVERY AVAILABLE MAN AT HIS POST!
GET THOSE CIVILIANS OFF THE STREET!
BUT, ONE SHARP-EYED YOUTH HAS SPOTTED THE SINISTER FIGURE LURKING ATOP THE SHADOWY LEDGE..
IT'S BOOMERANG!
HE MUST HAVE STEAMED UP THE HULK!
GENERAL! LISTEN TO ME! IT ISN'T THE HULK YOU'VE GOT TO WORRY ABOUT! THERE'S A GREATER DANGER HERE AMONG US! LET ME TELL YOU...!
BLAST IT, BOY! LET GO OF MY ARM! I'VE GOT THE SAFETY OF A CITY TO WORRY ABOUT! TAKE COVER SOMEWHERE! THAT'S AN ORDER!
BUT...YOU'VE GOT TO LISTEN!
I LISTEN TO NOTHING... WHILE THAT MONSTER STILL LIVES!
CAN'T REASON WITH HIM! BUT, I'VE GOT TO DO SOME-THING!
MY ONLY CHANCE IS THE HULK HIMSELF! IF I CAN GET HIM TO UNDERSTAND...!
HULK! IT'S ME...RICK! I WANNA HELP YOU!
YOU'VE GOTTA CALM DOWN... SHOW THEM YOU'RE NOT DANGEROUS! FOR YOUR OWN SAKE!
IF YOU DON'T, YOU'LL BE HUNTED AGAIN!
YOU WON'T HAVE A CHANCE! THEY'LL GET YOU SOONER OR LATER!

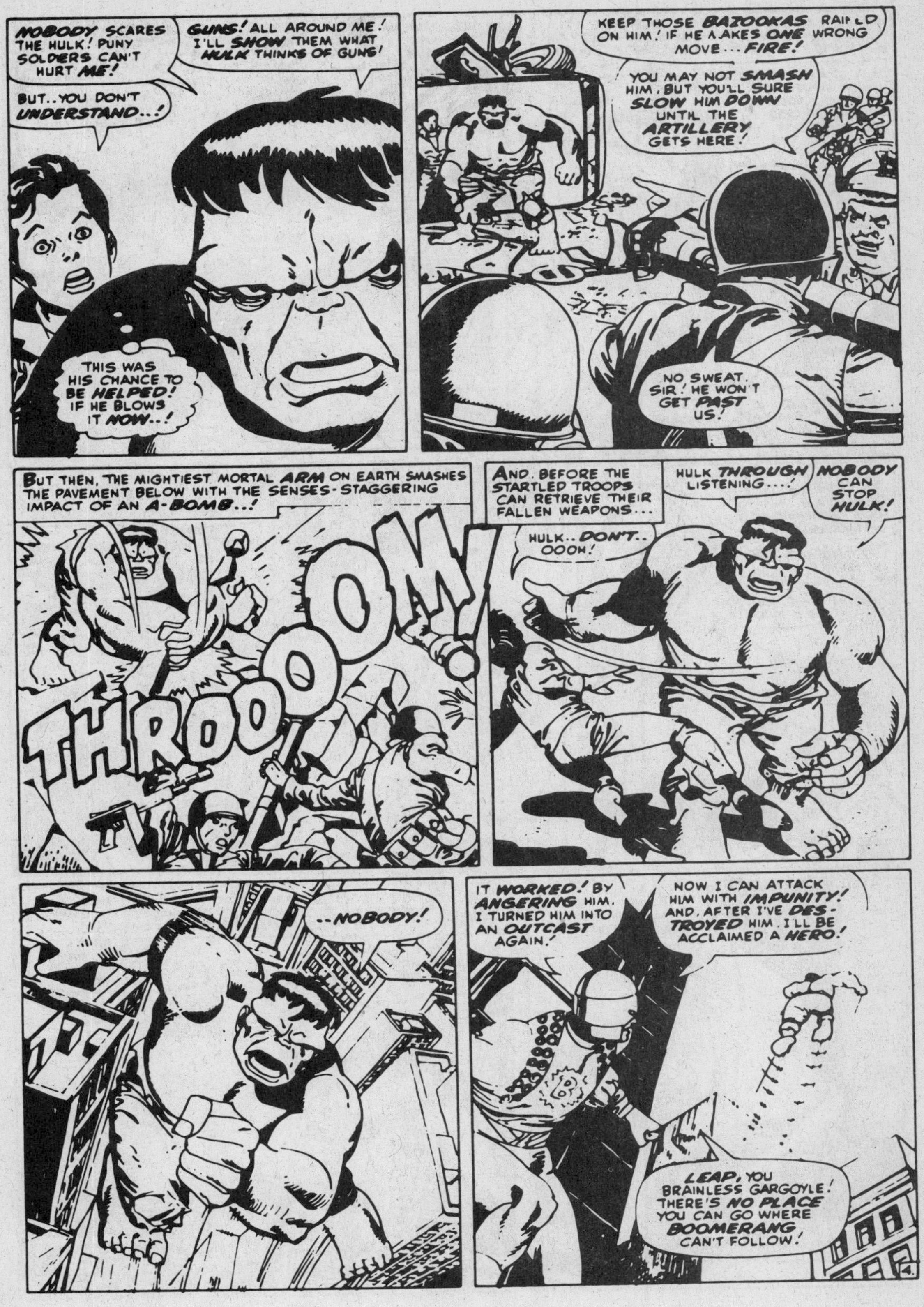

NOBODY SCARES THE HULK! PUNY SOLDERS CAN'T HURT ME!
GUNS! ALL AROUND ME! I'LL SHOW THEM WHAT HULK THINKS OF GUNS!
BUT.. YOU DON'T UNDERSTAND..!
THIS WAS HIS CHANCE TO BE HELPED! IF HE BLOWS IT NOW..!
KEEP THOSE BAZOOKAS RAI LD ON HIM! IF HE A AKES ONE WRONG MOVE... FIRE!
YOU MAY NOT SMASH HIM, BUT YOU'LL SURE SLOW HIM DOWN UNTIL THE ARTILLERY GETS HERE!
NO SWEAT, SIR! HE WON'T GET PAST US!
BUT THEN, THE MIGHTIEST MORTAL ARM ON EARTH SMASHES THE PAVEMENT BELOW WITH THE SENSES-STAGGERING IMPACT OF AN A-BOMB..!
THROOOOM!
AND, BEFORE THE STARTLED TROOPS CAN RETRIEVE THEIR FALLEN WEAPONS...
HULK THROUGH LISTENING....!
NOBODY CAN STOP HULK!
HULK.. DON'T.. OOOH!
--NOBODY!
IT WORKED! BY ANGERING HIM, I TURNED HIM INTO AN OUTCAST AGAIN!
NOW I CAN ATTACK HIM WITH IMPUNITY! AND, AFTER I'VE DESTROYED HIM, I'LL BE ACCLAIMED A HERO!
LEAP, YOU BRAINLESS GARGOYLE! THERE'S NO PLACE YOU CAN GO WHERE BOOMERANG CAN'T FOLLOW!
4.

HE GOT *AWAY!* BUT, I'LL *FIND* HIM! I'LL TRACK HIM DOWN IF IT TAKES THE REST OF MY *LIFE!* NOBODY CAN DEFY THE ARMY... THE LAW..

BUT, *DAD!* HE DOESN'T KNOW WHAT HE'S *DOING!* YOU CAN'T PUNISH *BRUCE BANNER* FOR THE DEEDS OF THE *HULK!*

HOW DO WE KNOW BANNER *ISN'T* RESPONSIBLE, BETTY?

WE KNOW SO LITTLE *ABOUT* THE HULK! WHAT IF BANNER *IS* IN CONTROL OF HIM...ALL THE TIME?

GENERAL ROSS! I HAVE AN URGENT DISPATCH FOR YOU...FROM *WASHINGTON!*

A *WHITE HOUSE COURIER!* WHAT DOES *THIS* MEAN?

DON'T JUST *SIT* THERE, MAN! LET ME *HAVE* IT!

SKREEEEE

IT'S CLASSIFIED *TOP PRIORITY,* SIR! FOR YOUR *IMMEDIATE ATTENTION!*

IT CONCERNS THE *HULK!*

I *SUSPECTED* AS MUCH!

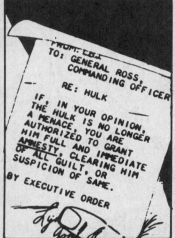

FROM: FBI
TO: GENERAL ROSS, COMMANDING OFFICER

RE: HULK

IF, IN YOUR OPINION, THE HULK IS NO LONGER A MENACE, YOU ARE AUTHORIZED TO GRANT HIM FULL AND IMMEDIATE AMNESTY, CLEARING HIM OF ALL GUILT, OR SUSPICION OF SAME.

BY EXECUTIVE ORDER

SO...IT'S UP TO *ME!* IF IN MY OPINION, THE HULK IS NO LONGER A MENACE...!

JUST A SHORT *HALF HOUR* AGO, MY ANSWER MIGHT HAVE BEEN *DIFFERENT!* BUT, NOW...

AND, EVEN AS THE *PARDON* WHICH MIGHT HAVE BEEN HIS FLOATS IRONICALLY TO THE GROUND, A *NEW* DANGER ARISES TO THREATEN THE SORELY-HARASSED GREEN GIANT...

AND *NOW,* HULK.. IT WILL BE JUST *YOU* AND ME...

BUT, BEFORE THE DAY IS ENDED, IT WILL BE ONLY... *ME!*

5.

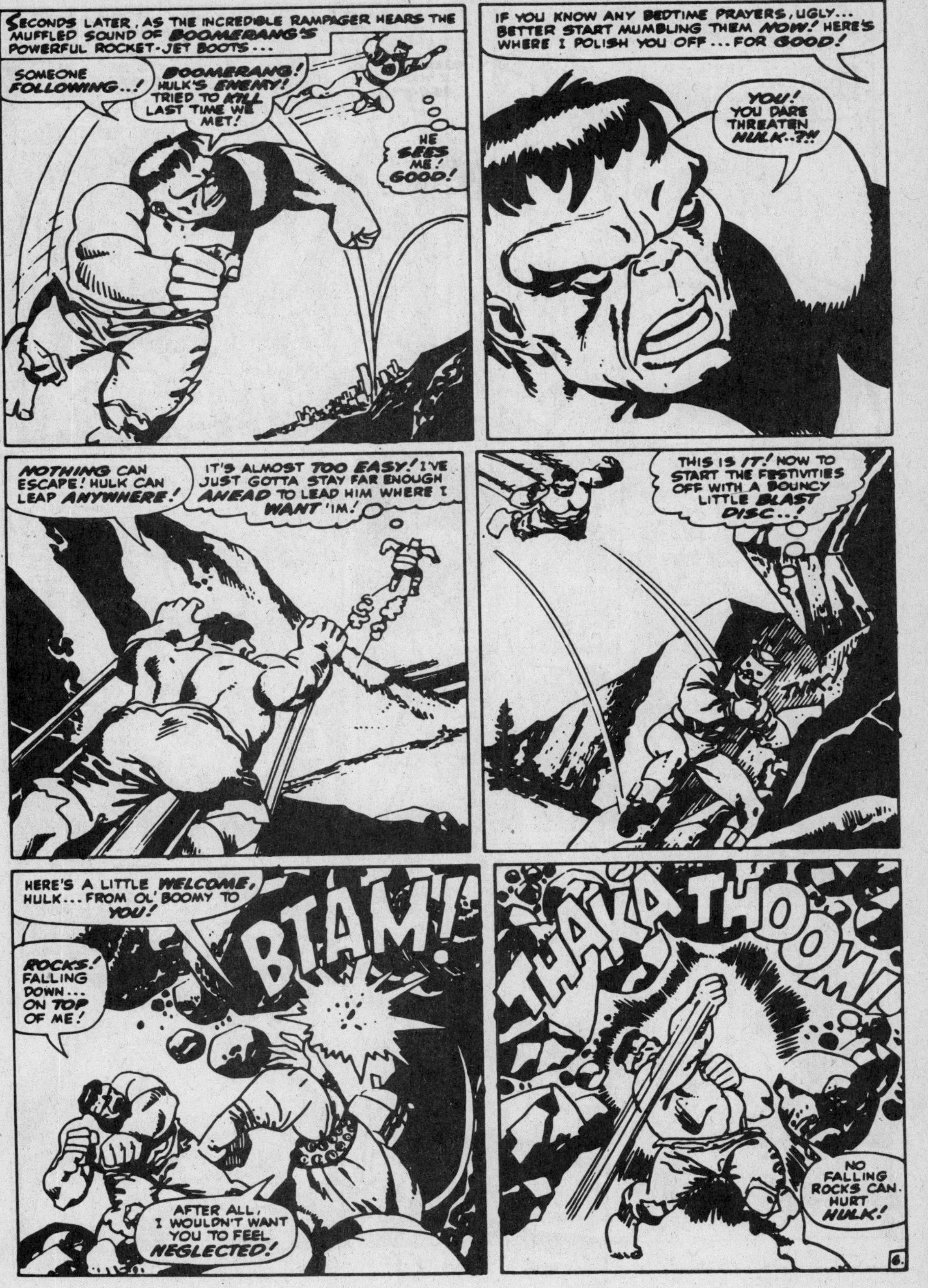
SECONDS LATER, AS THE INCREDIBLE RAMPAGER HEARS THE MUFFLED SOUND OF BOOMERANG'S POWERFUL ROCKET-JET BOOTS...
SOMEONE FOLLOWING..!
BOOMERANG! HULK'S ENEMY! TRIED TO KILL LAST TIME WE MET!
HE SEES ME! GOOD!
IF YOU KNOW ANY BEDTIME PRAYERS, UGLY... BETTER START MUMBLING THEM NOW! HERE'S WHERE I POLISH YOU OFF... FOR GOOD!
YOU! YOU DARE THREATEN HULK..?!!
NOTHING CAN ESCAPE! HULK CAN LEAP ANYWHERE!
IT'S ALMOST TOO EASY! I'VE JUST GOTTA STAY FAR ENOUGH AHEAD TO LEAD HIM WHERE I WANT 'IM!
THIS IS IT! NOW TO START THE FESTIVITIES OFF WITH A BOUNCY LITTLE BLAST DISC..!
THK
HERE'S A LITTLE WELCOME, HULK... FROM OL' BOOMY TO YOU!
BTAM!
ROCKS! FALLING DOWN... ON TOP OF ME!
AFTER ALL, I WOULDN'T WANT YOU TO FEEL NEGLECTED!
THAKA THOOM!
NO FALLING ROCKS CAN HURT HULK!
6.

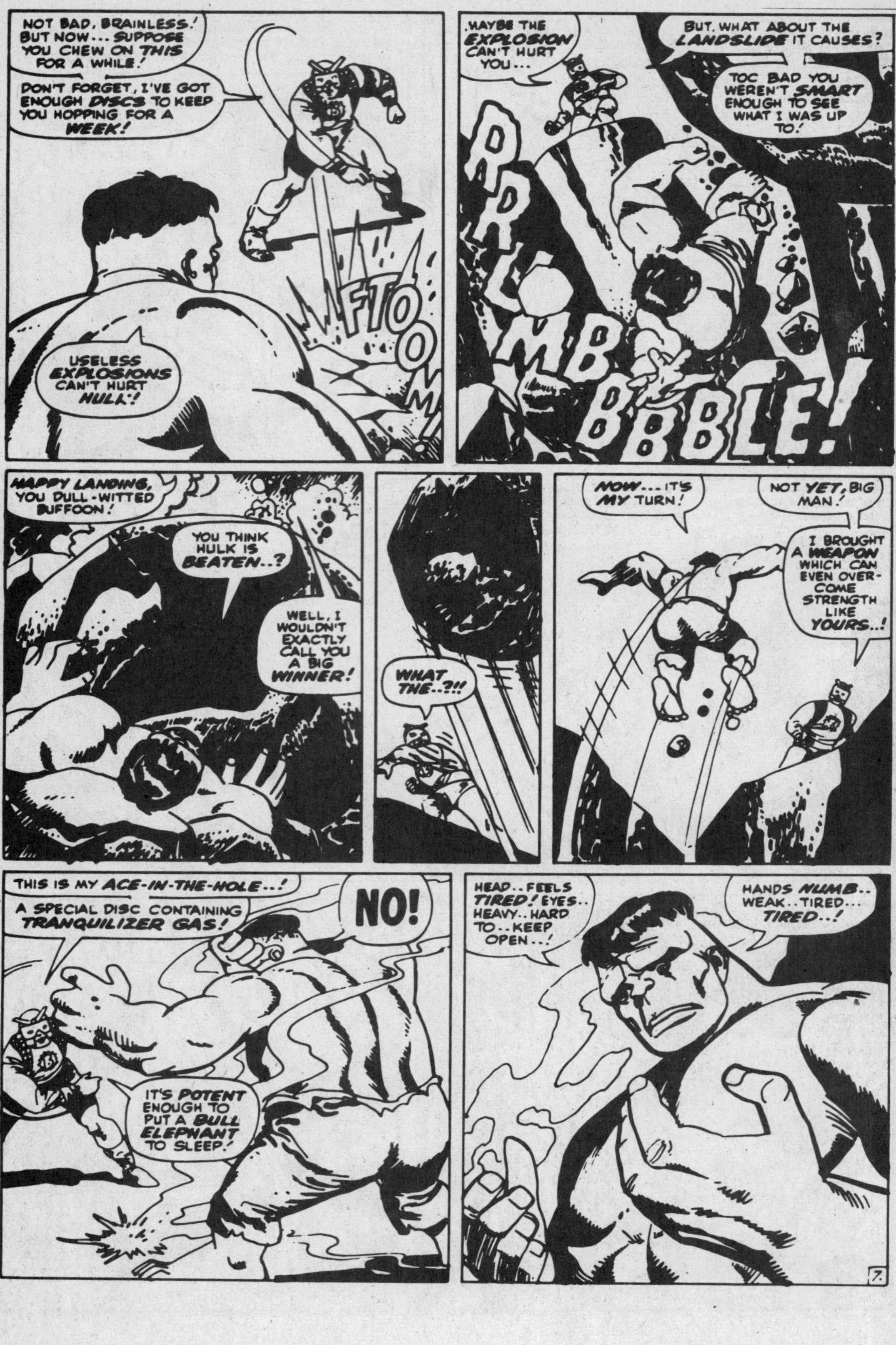
NOT BAD, BRAINLESS! BUT NOW... SUPPOSE YOU CHEW ON THIS FOR A WHILE!
DON'T FORGET, I'VE GOT ENOUGH DISCS TO KEEP YOU HOPPING FOR A WEEK!
FTOOOM
USELESS EXPLOSIONS CAN'T HURT HULK!
MAYBE THE EXPLOSION CAN'T HURT YOU...
BUT, WHAT ABOUT THE LANDSLIDE IT CAUSES?
TOO BAD YOU WEREN'T SMART ENOUGH TO SEE WHAT I WAS UP TO!
RRUMBBBBBLE!
HAPPY LANDING, YOU DULL-WITTED BUFFOON!
YOU THINK HULK IS BEATEN..?
WELL, I WOULDN'T EXACTLY CALL YOU A BIG WINNER!
WHAT THE..?!!
NOW... IT'S MY TURN!
NOT YET, BIG MAN!
I BROUGHT A WEAPON WHICH CAN EVEN OVER-COME STRENGTH LIKE YOURS..!
THIS IS MY ACE-IN-THE-HOLE..!
A SPECIAL DISC CONTAINING TRANQUILIZER GAS!
NO!
IT'S POTENT ENOUGH TO PUT A BULL ELEPHANT TO SLEEP!
HEAD.. FEELS TIRED! EYES.. HEAVY.. HARD TO.. KEEP OPEN..!
HANDS NUMB.. WEAK.. TIRED... TIRED..!
7.

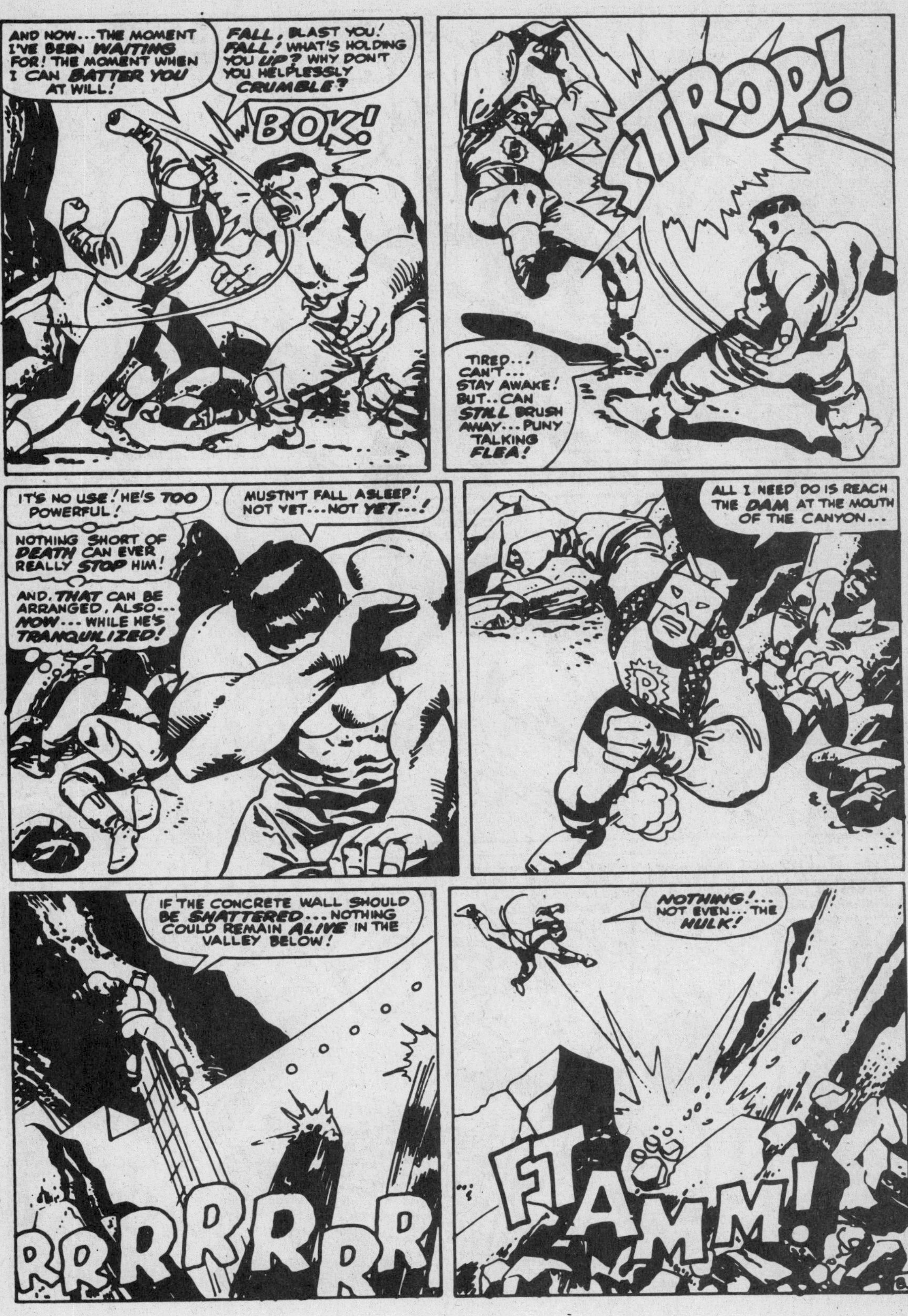

AND NOW... THE MOMENT I'VE BEEN WAITING FOR! THE MOMENT WHEN I CAN BATTER YOU AT WILL!
FALL, BLAST YOU! FALL! WHAT'S HOLDING YOU UP? WHY DON'T YOU HELPLESSLY CRUMBLE?
BOK!
STROP!
TIRED..! CAN'T... STAY AWAKE! BUT.. CAN STILL BRUSH AWAY... PUNY TALKING FLEA!
IT'S NO USE! HE'S TOO POWERFUL!
MUSTN'T FALL ASLEEP! NOT YET... NOT YET...!
NOTHING SHORT OF DEATH CAN EVER REALLY STOP HIM!
AND, THAT CAN BE ARRANGED, ALSO... NOW... WHILE HE'S TRANQUILIZED!
ALL I NEED DO IS REACH THE DAM AT THE MOUTH OF THE CANYON...
IF THE CONCRETE WALL SHOULD BE SHATTERED... NOTHING COULD REMAIN ALIVE IN THE VALLEY BELOW!
RRRRRRR
NOTHING!... NOT EVEN... THE HULK!
FTAMM!

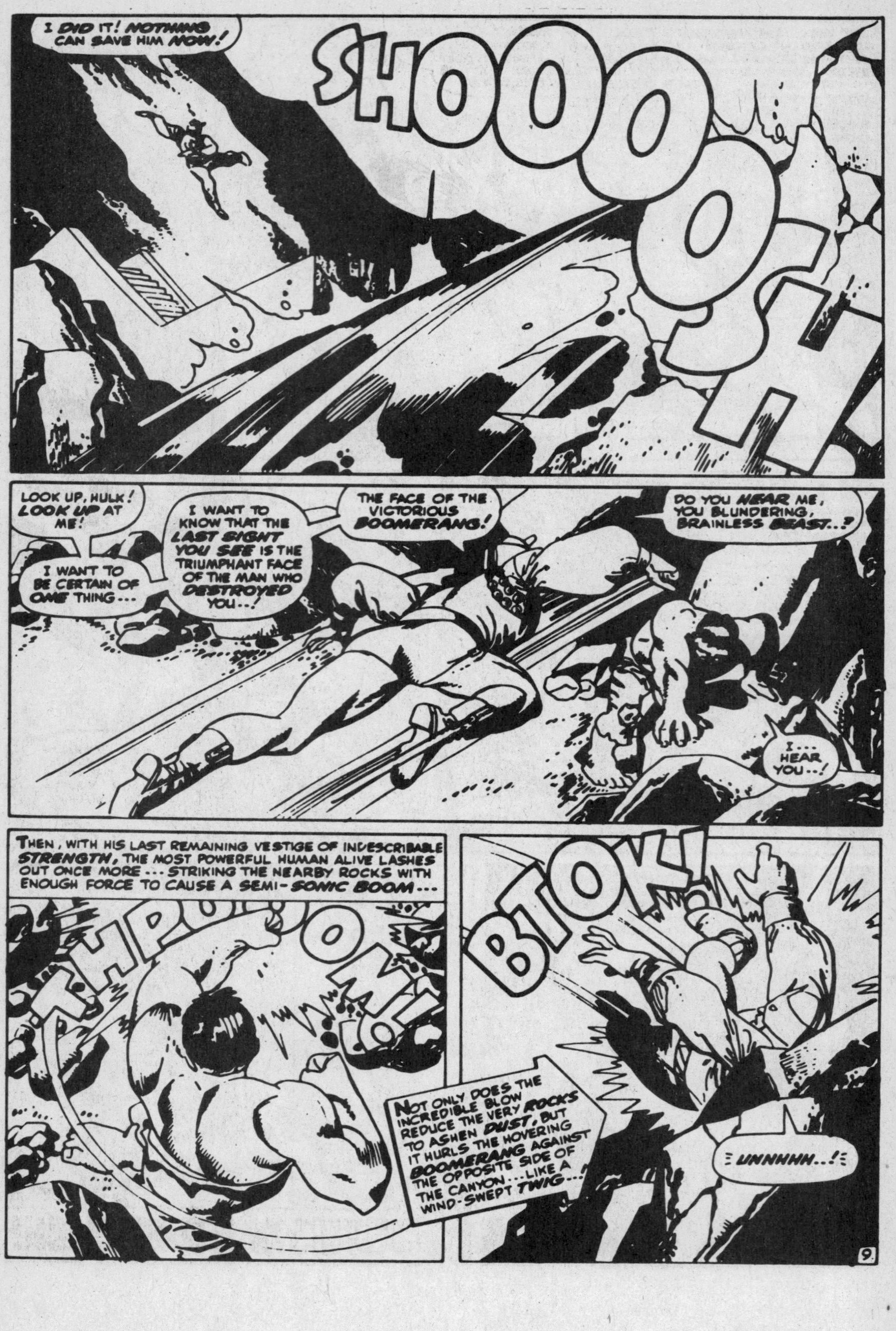
I DID IT! NOTHING CAN SAVE HIM NOW!
SHOOOOOSH!
LOOK UP, HULK! LOOK UP AT ME!
I WANT TO BE CERTAIN OF ONE THING...
I WANT TO KNOW THAT THE LAST SIGHT YOU SEE IS THE TRIUMPHANT FACE OF THE MAN WHO DESTROYED YOU...!
THE FACE OF THE VICTORIOUS BOOMERANG!
DO YOU HEAR ME, YOU BLUNDERING, BRAINLESS BEAST..?
I... HEAR YOU...!
THEN, WITH HIS LAST REMAINING VESTIGE OF INDESCRIBABLE STRENGTH, THE MOST POWERFUL HUMAN ALIVE LASHES OUT ONCE MORE... STRIKING THE NEARBY ROCKS WITH ENOUGH FORCE TO CAUSE A SEMI-SONIC BOOM...
THPOOOOM!
BTOK!
NOT ONLY DOES THE INCREDIBLE BLOW REDUCE THE VERY ROCKS TO ASHEN DUST, BUT IT HURLS THE HOVERING BOOMERANG AGAINST THE OPPOSITE SIDE OF THE CANYON... LIKE A WIND-SWEPT TWIG...
UNNHHHH...!
9

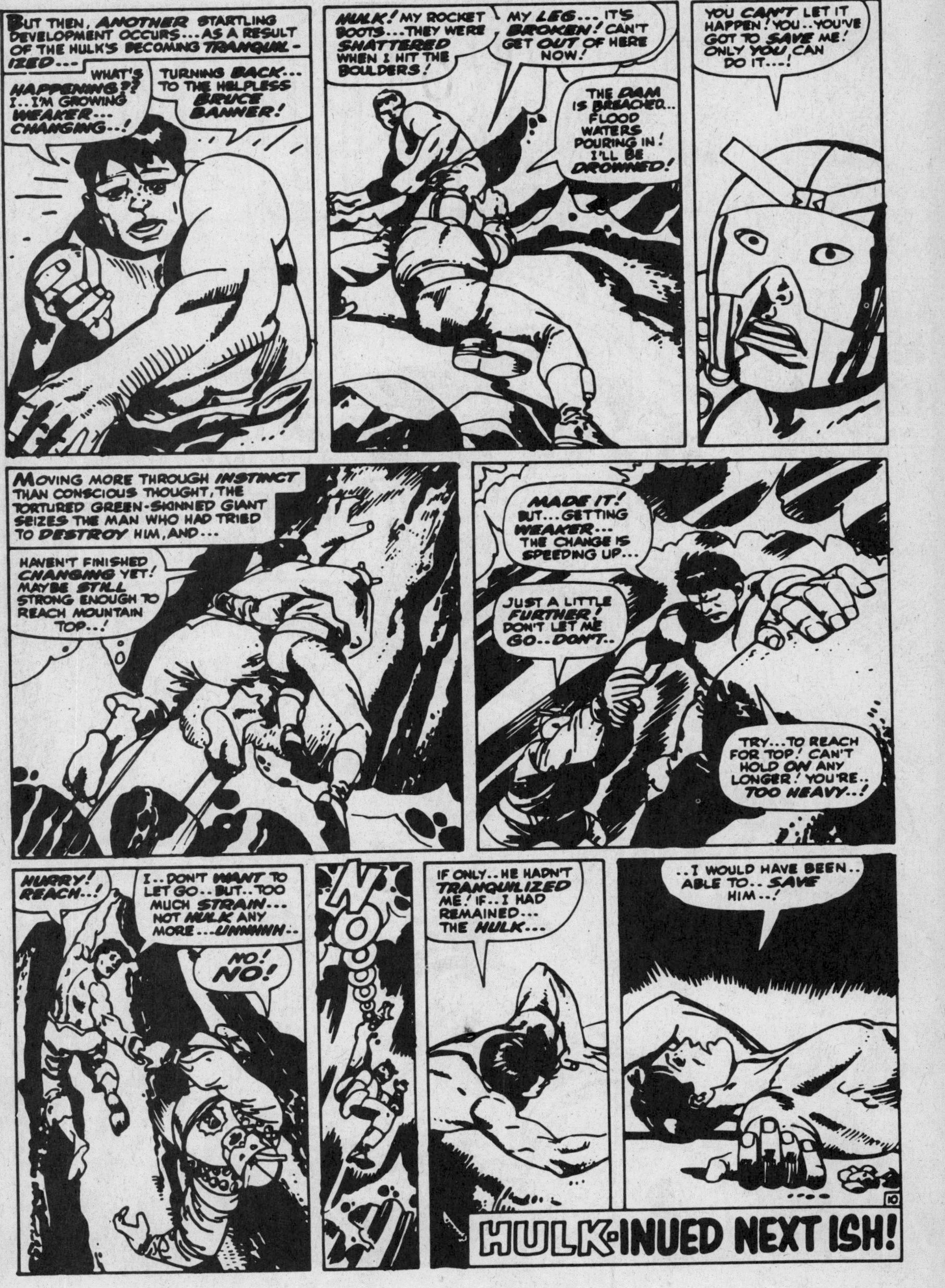
BUT THEN, ANOTHER STARTLING DEVELOPMENT OCCURS...AS A RESULT OF THE HULK'S BECOMING TRANQUILIZED...
WHAT'S HAPPENING?? I..I'M GROWING WEAKER... CHANGING..!
TURNING BACK...TO THE HELPLESS BRUCE BANNER!
HULK! MY ROCKET BOOTS...THEY WERE SHATTERED WHEN I HIT THE BOULDERS!
MY LEG...IT'S BROKEN! CAN'T GET OUT OF HERE NOW!
THE DAM IS BREACHED...FLOOD WATERS POURING IN! I'LL BE DROWNED!
YOU CAN'T LET IT HAPPEN! YOU...YOU'VE GOT TO SAVE ME! ONLY YOU CAN DO IT...!
MOVING MORE THROUGH INSTINCT THAN CONSCIOUS THOUGHT, THE TORTURED GREEN-SKINNED GIANT SEIZES THE MAN WHO HAD TRIED TO DESTROY HIM, AND...
HAVEN'T FINISHED CHANGING YET! MAYBE STILL STRONG ENOUGH TO REACH MOUNTAIN TOP..!
MADE IT! BUT...GETTING WEAKER... THE CHANGE IS SPEEDING UP...
JUST A LITTLE FURTHER! DON'T LET ME GO..DON'T..
TRY...TO REACH FOR TOP! CAN'T HOLD ON ANY LONGER! YOU'RE.. TOO HEAVY..!
HURRY! REACH..!
I..DON'T WANT TO LET GO..BUT..TOO MUCH STRAIN... NOT HULK ANY MORE...UMMMNH..
NO! NO!
NOOOOOOO
IF ONLY..HE HADN'T TRANQUILIZED ME! IF..I HAD REMAINED... THE HULK...
..I WOULD HAVE BEEN.. ABLE TO..SAVE HIM..!
10
HULK-INUED NEXT ISH!

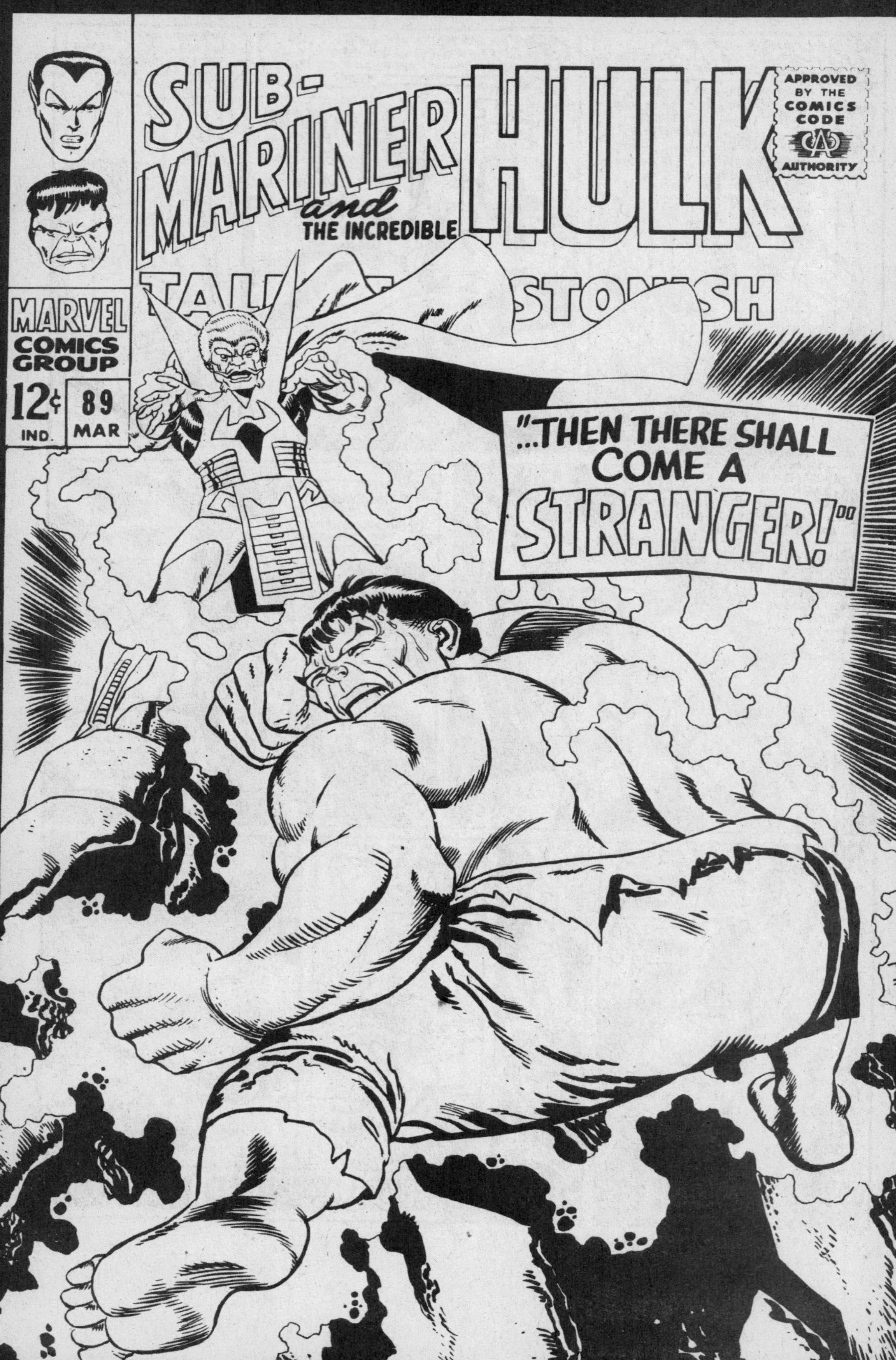
SUB-MARINER and THE INCREDIBLE HULK
TALES TO ASTONISH
APPROVED BY THE COMICS CODE AUTHORITY
MARVEL COMICS GROUP
12¢ IND.
89 MAR
"...THEN THERE SHALL COME A STRANGER!"

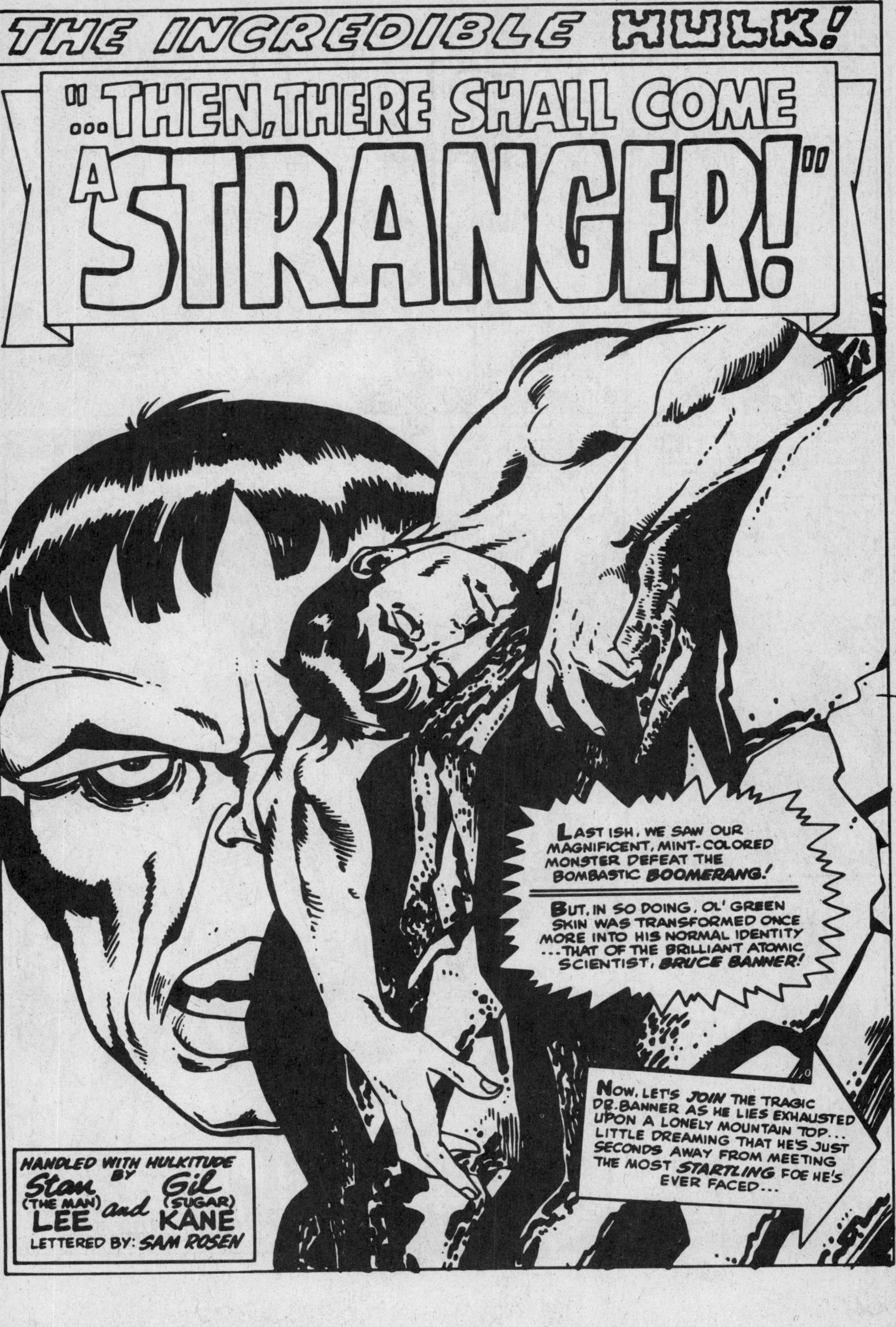
THE INCREDIBLE HULK!
"...THEN, THERE SHALL COME A STRANGER!"
LAST ISH, WE SAW OUR MAGNIFICENT, MINT-COLORED MONSTER DEFEAT THE BOMBASTIC BOOMERANG!
BUT, IN SO DOING, OL' GREEN SKIN WAS TRANSFORMED ONCE MORE INTO HIS NORMAL IDENTITY ...THAT OF THE BRILLIANT ATOMIC SCIENTIST, BRUCE BANNER!
NOW, LET'S JOIN THE TRAGIC DR. BANNER AS HE LIES EXHAUSTED UPON A LONELY MOUNTAIN TOP... LITTLE DREAMING THAT HE'S JUST SECONDS AWAY FROM MEETING THE MOST STARTLING FOE HE'S EVER FACED...
HANDLED WITH HULKITUDE BY Stan (THE MAN) LEE and Gil (SUGAR) KANE
LETTERED BY: SAM ROSEN

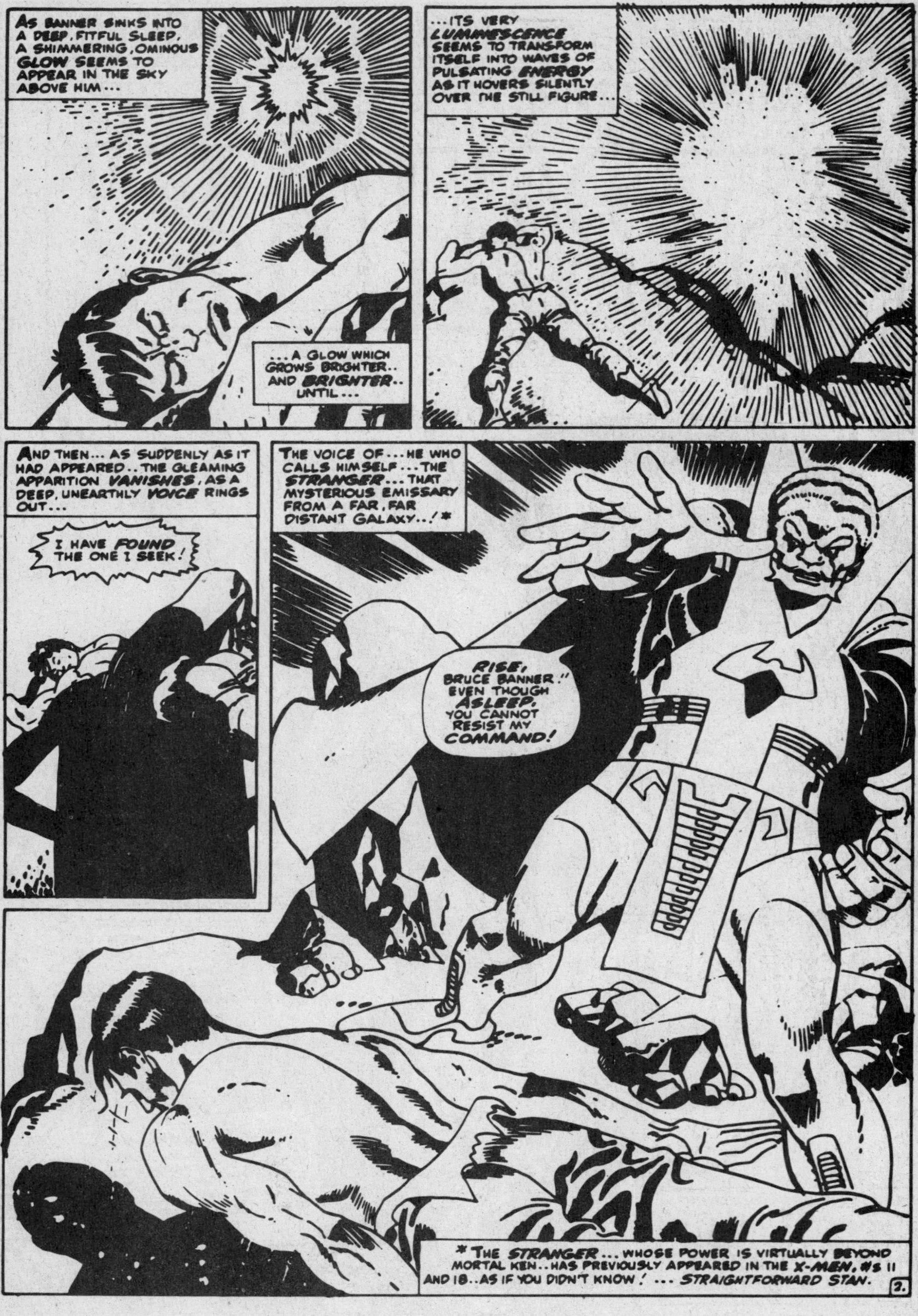

AS BANNER SINKS INTO A DEEP, FITFUL SLEEP, A SHIMMERING, OMINOUS GLOW SEEMS TO APPEAR IN THE SKY ABOVE HIM...
...A GLOW WHICH GROWS BRIGHTER... AND BRIGHTER.. UNTIL...
...ITS VERY LUMMESCENCE SEEMS TO TRANSFORM ITSELF INTO WAVES OF PULSATING ENERGY AS IT HOVERS SILENTLY OVER THE STILL FIGURE...
AND THEN... AS SUDDENLY AS IT HAD APPEARED.. THE GLEAMING APPARITION VANISHES, AS A DEEP, UNEARTHLY VOICE RINGS OUT...
I HAVE FOUND THE ONE I SEEK!
THE VOICE OF... HE WHO CALLS HIMSELF... THE STRANGER... THAT MYSTERIOUS EMISSARY FROM A FAR, FAR DISTANT GALAXY...! *
RISE, BRUCE BANNER!! EVEN THOUGH ASLEEP, YOU CANNOT RESIST MY COMMAND!
* THE STRANGER... WHOSE POWER IS VIRTUALLY BEYOND MORTAL KEN.. HAS PREVIOUSLY APPEARED IN THE X-MEN, #S 11 AND 18.. AS IF YOU DIDN'T KNOW! ... STRAIGHTFORWARD STAN.
2.

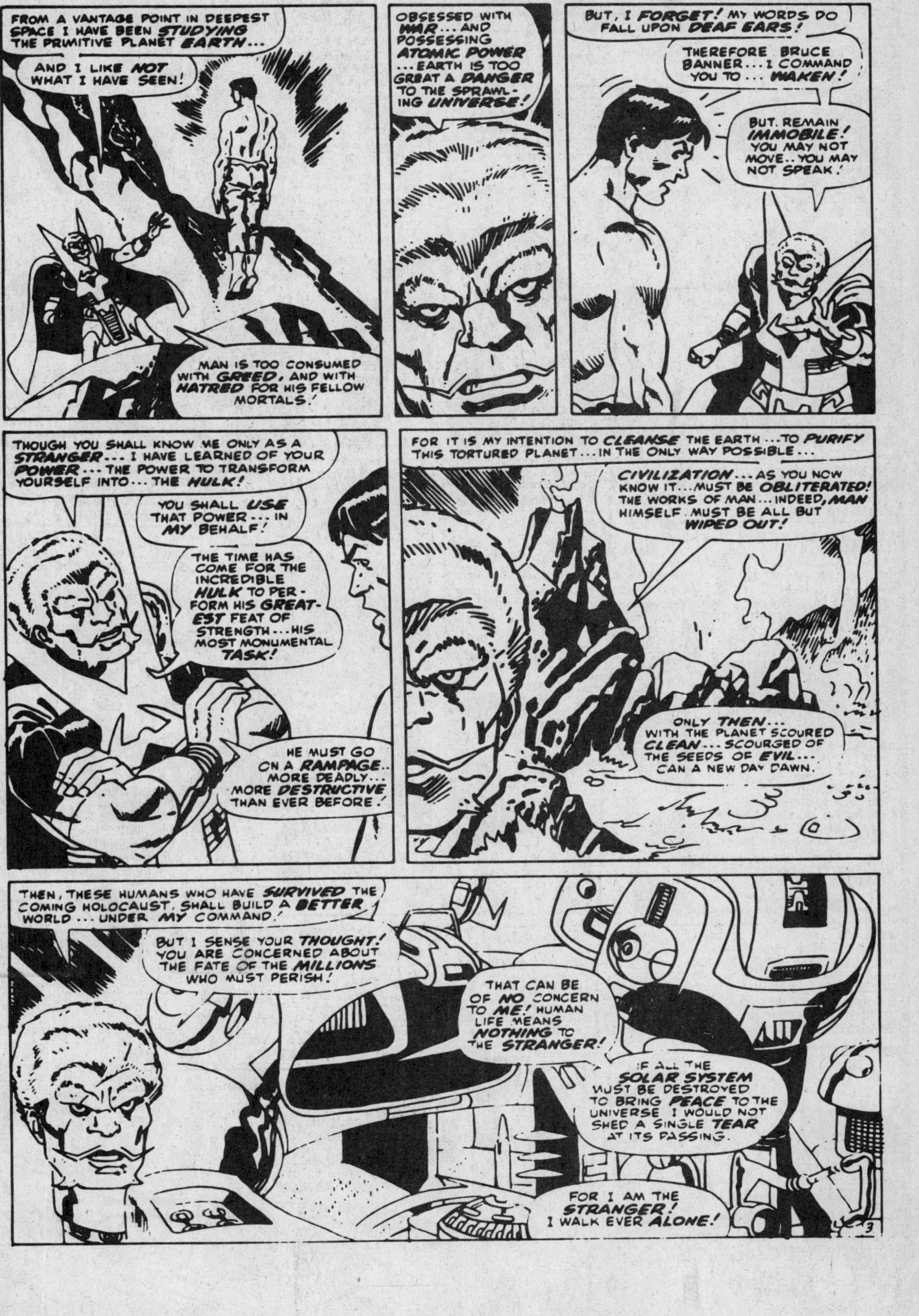
FROM A VANTAGE POINT IN DEEPEST SPACE I HAVE BEEN STUDYING THE PRIMITIVE PLANET EARTH...
AND I LIKE NOT WHAT I HAVE SEEN!
MAN IS TOO CONSUMED WITH GREED, AND WITH HATRED FOR HIS FELLOW MORTALS!
OBSESSED WITH WAR... AND POSSESSING ATOMIC POWER ...EARTH IS TOO GREAT A DANGER TO THE SPRAWLING UNIVERSE!
BUT, I FORGET! MY WORDS DO FALL UPON DEAF EARS!
THEREFORE BRUCE BANNER... I COMMAND YOU TO... WAKEN!
BUT, REMAIN IMMOBILE! YOU MAY NOT MOVE.. YOU MAY NOT SPEAK!
THOUGH YOU SHALL KNOW ME ONLY AS A STRANGER... I HAVE LEARNED OF YOUR POWER... THE POWER TO TRANSFORM YOURSELF INTO... THE HULK!
YOU SHALL USE THAT POWER... IN MY BEHALF!
THE TIME HAS COME FOR THE INCREDIBLE HULK TO PERFORM HIS GREATEST FEAT OF STRENGTH...HIS MOST MONUMENTAL TASK!
HE MUST GO ON A RAMPAGE.. MORE DEADLY... MORE DESTRUCTIVE THAN EVER BEFORE!
FOR IT IS MY INTENTION TO CLEANSE THE EARTH ...TO PURIFY THIS TORTURED PLANET... IN THE ONLY WAY POSSIBLE...
CIVILIZATION... AS YOU NOW KNOW IT... MUST BE OBLITERATED! THE WORKS OF MAN... INDEED, MAN HIMSELF MUST BE ALL BUT WIPED OUT!
ONLY THEN... WITH THE PLANET SCOURED CLEAN... SCOURGED OF THE SEEDS OF EVIL... CAN A NEW DAY DAWN.
THEN, THESE HUMANS WHO HAVE SURVIVED THE COMING HOLOCAUST, SHALL BUILD A BETTER WORLD... UNDER MY COMMAND!
BUT I SENSE YOUR THOUGHT! YOU ARE CONCERNED ABOUT THE FATE OF THE MILLIONS WHO MUST PERISH!
THAT CAN BE OF NO CONCERN TO ME! HUMAN LIFE MEANS NOTHING TO THE STRANGER!
IF ALL THE SOLAR SYSTEM MUST BE DESTROYED TO BRING PEACE TO THE UNIVERSE I WOULD NOT SHED A SINGLE TEAR AT ITS PASSING.
FOR I AM THE STRANGER! I WALK EVER ALONE!
3

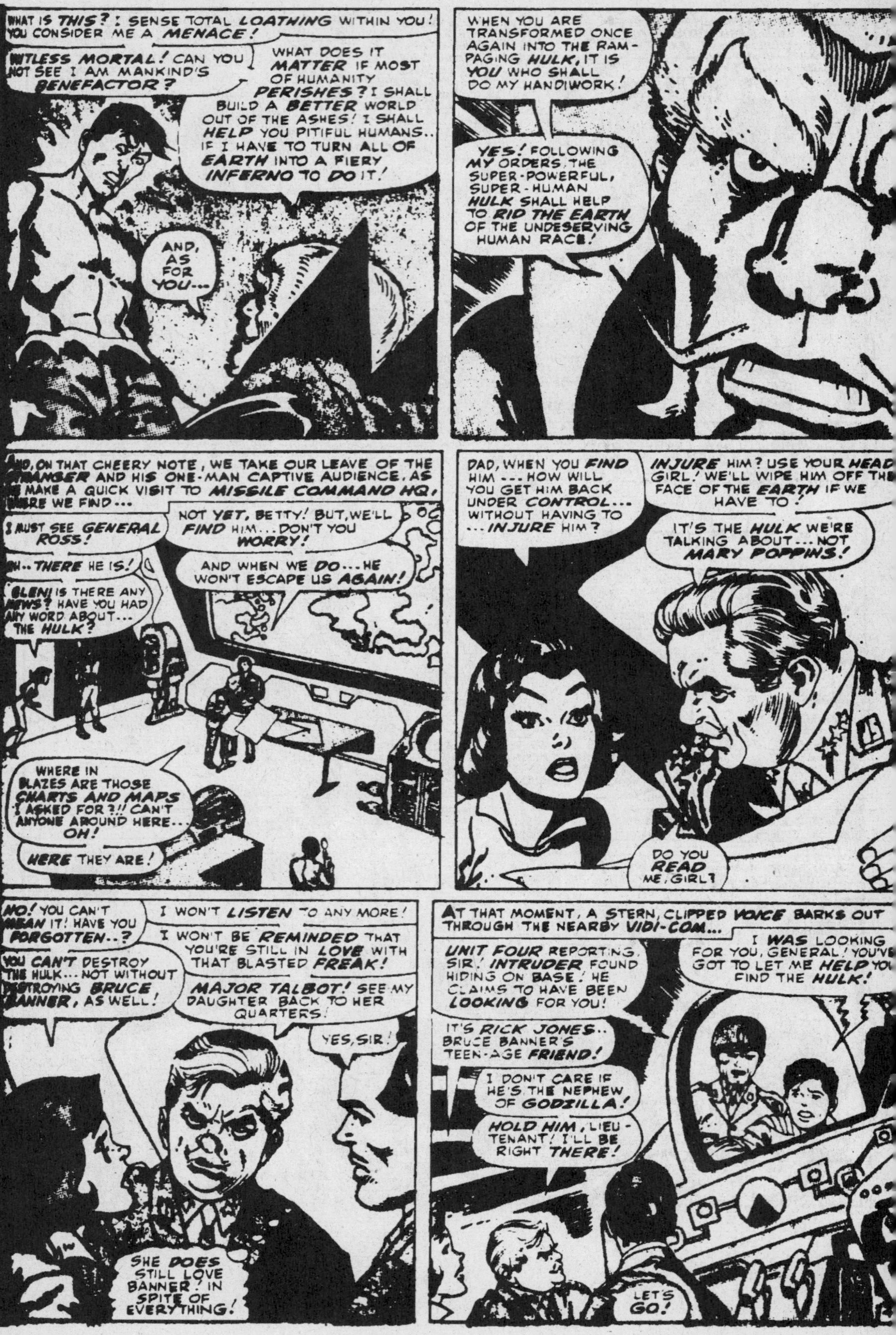
WHAT IS THIS? I SENSE TOTAL LOATHING WITHIN YOU! YOU CONSIDER ME A MENACE!
WITLESS MORTAL! CAN YOU NOT SEE I AM MANKIND'S BENEFACTOR?
WHAT DOES IT MATTER IF MOST OF HUMANITY PERISHES? I SHALL BUILD A BETTER WORLD OUT OF THE ASHES! I SHALL HELP YOU PITIFUL HUMANS.. IF I HAVE TO TURN ALL OF EARTH INTO A FIERY INFERNO TO DO IT!
AND, AS FOR YOU...
WHEN YOU ARE TRANSFORMED ONCE AGAIN INTO THE RAMPAGING HULK, IT IS YOU WHO SHALL DO MY HANDIWORK!
YES! FOLLOWING MY ORDERS, THE SUPER-POWERFUL, SUPER-HUMAN HULK SHALL HELP TO RID THE EARTH OF THE UNDESERVING HUMAN RACE!
AND, ON THAT CHEERY NOTE, WE TAKE OUR LEAVE OF THE STRANGER AND HIS ONE-MAN CAPTIVE AUDIENCE, AS WE MAKE A QUICK VISIT TO MISSILE COMMAND HQ, WHERE WE FIND...
I MUST SEE GENERAL ROSS!
NOT YET, BETTY! BUT, WE'LL FIND HIM... DON'T YOU WORRY!
AND WHEN WE DO... HE WON'T ESCAPE US AGAIN!
OH.. THERE HE IS!
GLEN! IS THERE ANY NEWS? HAVE YOU HAD ANY WORD ABOUT... THE HULK?
WHERE IN BLAZES ARE THOSE CHARTS AND MAPS I ASKED FOR?!! CAN'T ANYONE AROUND HERE... OH!
HERE THEY ARE!
DAD, WHEN YOU FIND HIM --- HOW WILL YOU GET HIM BACK UNDER CONTROL... WITHOUT HAVING TO ...INJURE HIM?
INJURE HIM? USE YOUR HEAD, GIRL! WE'LL WIPE HIM OFF THE FACE OF THE EARTH IF WE HAVE TO!
IT'S THE HULK WE'RE TALKING ABOUT... NOT MARY POPPINS!
DO YOU READ ME, GIRL?
NO! YOU CAN'T MEAN IT! HAVE YOU FORGOTTEN..?
YOU CAN'T DESTROY THE HULK... NOT WITHOUT DESTROYING BRUCE BANNER, AS WELL!
I WON'T LISTEN TO ANY MORE!
I WON'T BE REMINDED THAT YOU'RE STILL IN LOVE WITH THAT BLASTED FREAK!
MAJOR TALBOT! SEE MY DAUGHTER BACK TO HER QUARTERS!
YES, SIR!
SHE DOES STILL LOVE BANNER! IN SPITE OF EVERYTHING!
AT THAT MOMENT, A STERN, CLIPPED VOICE BARKS OUT THROUGH THE NEARBY VIDI-COM...
UNIT FOUR REPORTING, SIR! INTRUDER FOUND HIDING ON BASE! HE CLAIMS TO HAVE BEEN LOOKING FOR YOU!
I WAS LOOKING FOR YOU, GENERAL! YOU'VE GOT TO LET ME HELP YOU FIND THE HULK!
IT'S RICK JONES.. BRUCE BANNER'S TEEN-AGE FRIEND!
I DON'T CARE IF HE'S THE NEPHEW OF GODZILLA!
HOLD HIM, LIEUTENANT! I'LL BE RIGHT THERE!
LET'S GO!

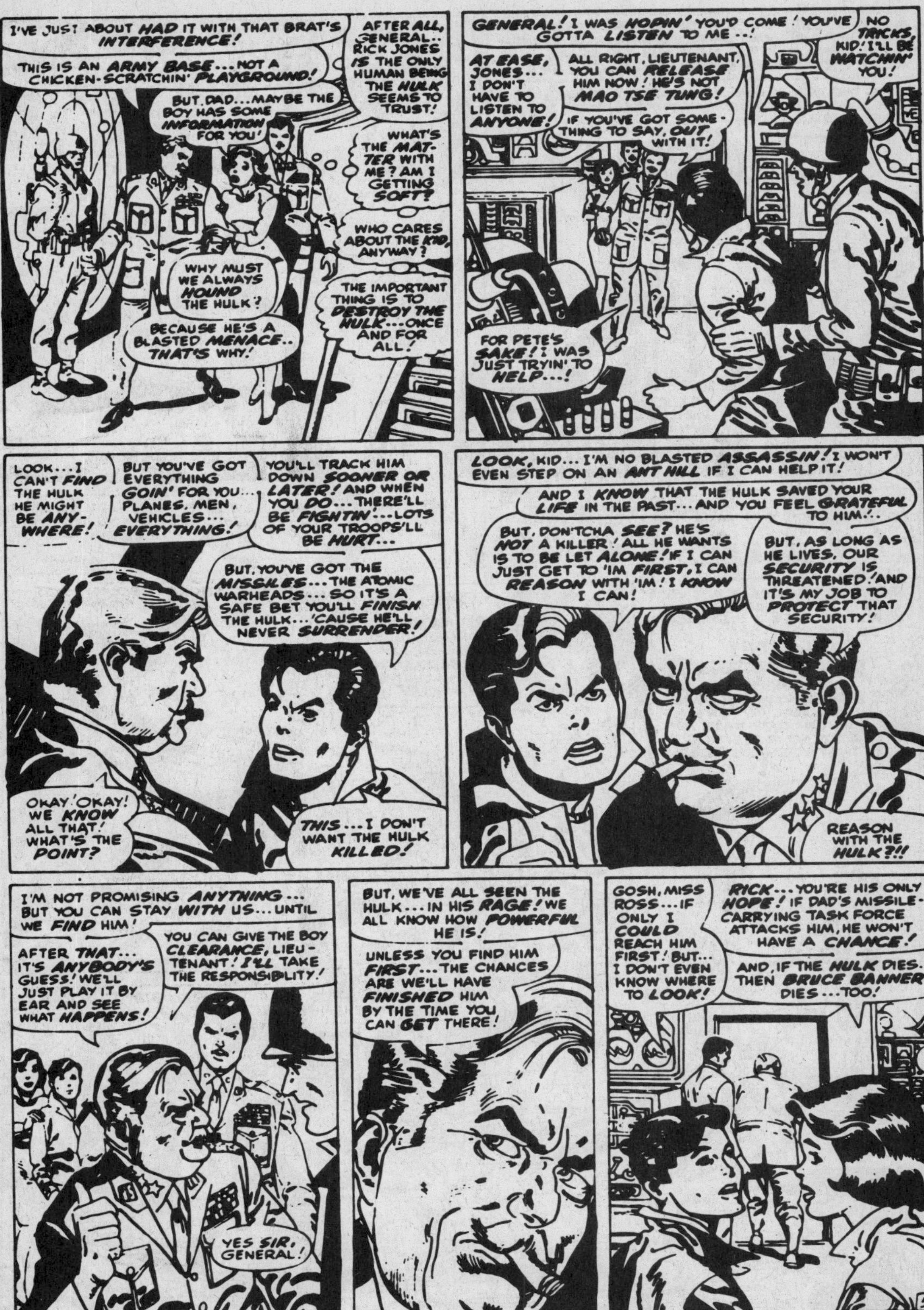
I'VE JUST ABOUT HAD IT WITH THAT BRAT'S INTERFERENCE!
THIS IS AN ARMY BASE... NOT A CHICKEN-SCRATCHIN' PLAYGROUND!
BUT, DAD... MAYBE THE BOY HAS SOME INFORMATION FOR YOU!
AFTER ALL, GENERAL.. RICK JONES IS THE ONLY HUMAN BEING THE HULK SEEMS TO TRUST!
WHAT'S THE MATTER WITH ME? AM I GETTING SOFT?
WHO CARES ABOUT THE KID, ANYWAY?
WHY MUST WE ALWAYS HOUND THE HULK?
BECAUSE HE'S A BLASTED MENACE.. THAT'S WHY!
THE IMPORTANT THING IS TO DESTROY THE HULK... ONCE AND FOR ALL!
GENERAL! I WAS HOPIN' YOU'D COME! YOU'VE GOTTA LISTEN TO ME..!
NO TRICKS, KID! I'LL BE WATCHIN' YOU!
AT EASE, JONES... I DON'T HAVE TO LISTEN TO ANYONE!
ALL RIGHT, LIEUTENANT, YOU CAN RELEASE HIM NOW! HE'S NOT MAO TSE TUNG!
IF YOU'VE GOT SOMETHING TO SAY, OUT WITH IT!
FOR PETE'S SAKE! I WAS JUST TRYIN' TO HELP...!
LOOK... I CAN'T FIND THE HULK HE MIGHT BE ANYWHERE!
BUT YOU'VE GOT EVERYTHING GOIN' FOR YOU... PLANES, MEN, VEHICLES... EVERYTHING!
YOU'LL TRACK HIM DOWN SOONER OR LATER! AND WHEN YOU DO... THERE'LL BE FIGHTIN'... LOTS OF YOUR TROOPS'LL BE HURT...
BUT, YOU'VE GOT THE MISSILES... THE ATOMIC WARHEADS... SO IT'S A SAFE BET YOU'LL FINISH THE HULK... 'CAUSE HE'LL NEVER SURRENDER!
OKAY! OKAY! WE KNOW ALL THAT! WHAT'S THE POINT?
THIS... I DON'T WANT THE HULK KILLED!
LOOK, KID... I'M NO BLASTED ASSASSIN! I WON'T EVEN STEP ON AN ANT HILL IF I CAN HELP IT!
AND I KNOW THAT THE HULK SAVED YOUR LIFE IN THE PAST... AND YOU FEEL GRATEFUL TO HIM..
BUT, DON'TCHA SEE? HE'S NOT A KILLER! ALL HE WANTS IS TO BE LET ALONE! IF I CAN JUST GET TO 'IM FIRST, I CAN REASON WITH 'IM! I KNOW I CAN!
BUT, AS LONG AS HE LIVES, OUR SECURITY IS THREATENED! AND IT'S MY JOB TO PROTECT THAT SECURITY!
REASON WITH THE HULK?!!
I'M NOT PROMISING ANYTHING... BUT YOU CAN STAY WITH US... UNTIL WE FIND HIM!
AFTER THAT... IT'S ANYBODY'S GUESS! WE'LL JUST PLAY IT BY EAR AND SEE WHAT HAPPENS!
YOU CAN GIVE THE BOY CLEARANCE, LIEUTENANT! I'LL TAKE THE RESPONSIBILITY!
YES SIR, GENERAL!
BUT, WE'VE ALL SEEN THE HULK... IN HIS RAGE! WE ALL KNOW HOW POWERFUL HE IS!
UNLESS YOU FIND HIM FIRST... THE CHANCES ARE WE'LL HAVE FINISHED HIM BY THE TIME YOU CAN GET THERE!
GOSH, MISS ROSS... IF ONLY I COULD REACH HIM FIRST! BUT... I DON'T EVEN KNOW WHERE TO LOOK!
RICK... YOU'RE HIS ONLY HOPE! IF DAD'S MISSILE-CARRYING TASK FORCE ATTACKS HIM, HE WON'T HAVE A CHANCE!
AND, IF THE HULK DIES.. THEN BRUCE BANNER DIES... TOO!
5.

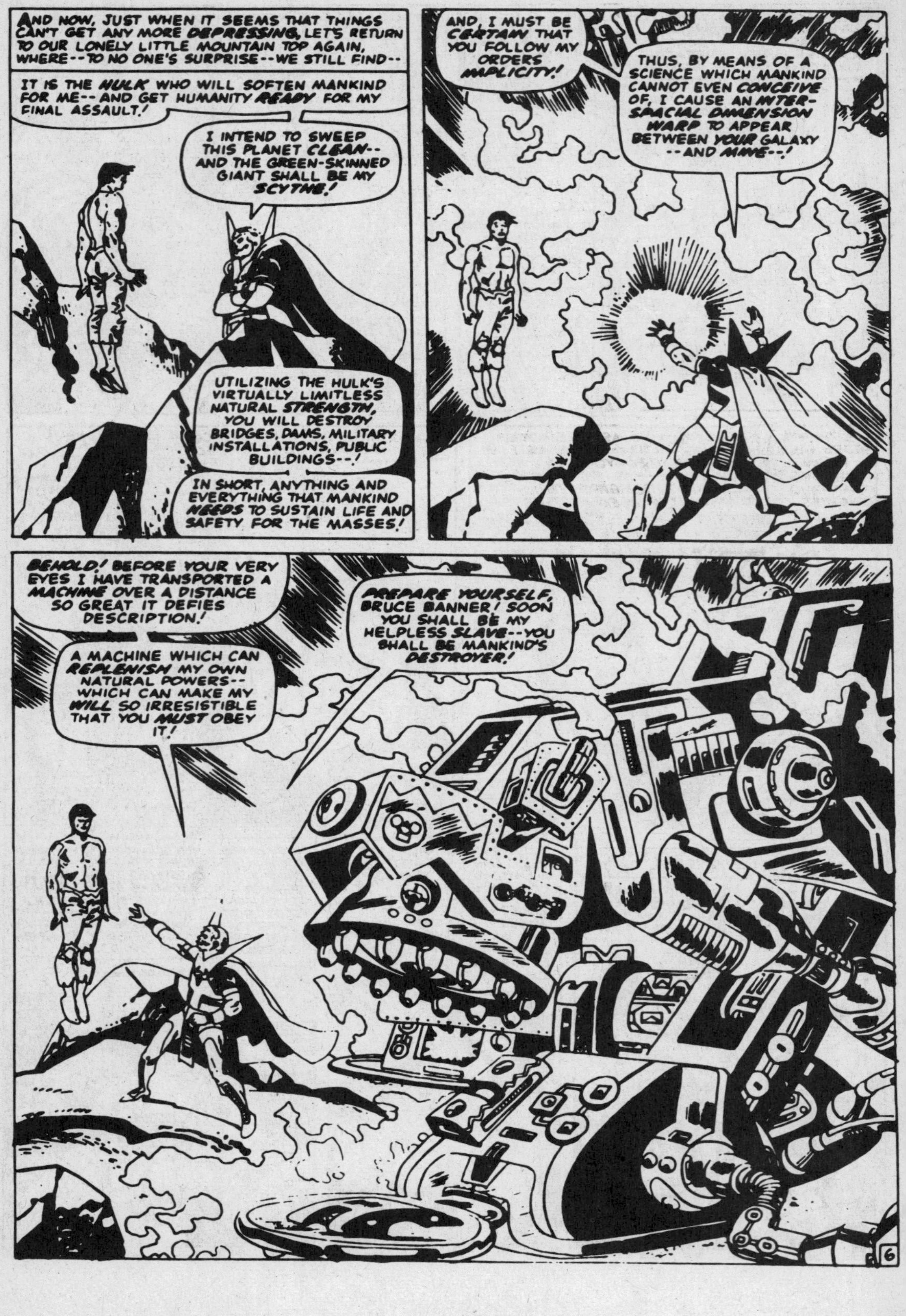

AND NOW, JUST WHEN IT SEEMS THAT THINGS CAN'T GET ANY MORE DEPRESSING, LET'S RETURN TO OUR LONELY LITTLE MOUNTAIN TOP AGAIN, WHERE--TO NO ONE'S SURPRISE--WE STILL FIND--
IT IS THE HULK WHO WILL SOFTEN MANKIND FOR ME--AND GET HUMANITY READY FOR MY FINAL ASSAULT.!
I INTEND TO SWEEP THIS PLANET CLEAN--AND THE GREEN-SKINNED GIANT SHALL BE MY SCYTHE!
UTILIZING THE HULK'S VIRTUALLY LIMITLESS NATURAL STRENGTH, YOU WILL DESTROY BRIDGES, DAMS, MILITARY INSTALLATIONS, PUBLIC BUILDINGS--!
IN SHORT, ANYTHING AND EVERYTHING THAT MANKIND NEEDS TO SUSTAIN LIFE AND SAFETY FOR THE MASSES!
AND, I MUST BE CERTAIN THAT YOU FOLLOW MY ORDERS IMPLICITY!
THUS, BY MEANS OF A SCIENCE WHICH MANKIND CANNOT EVEN CONCEIVE OF, I CAUSE AN INTER-SPACIAL DIMENSION WARP TO APPEAR BETWEEN YOUR GALAXY --AND MINE--!
BEHOLD! BEFORE YOUR VERY EYES I HAVE TRANSPORTED A MACHINE OVER A DISTANCE SO GREAT IT DEFIES DESCRIPTION!
A MACHINE WHICH CAN REPLENISH MY OWN NATURAL POWERS--WHICH CAN MAKE MY WILL SO IRRESISTIBLE THAT YOU MUST OBEY IT!
PREPARE YOURSELF, BRUCE BANNER! SOON YOU SHALL BE MY HELPLESS SLAVE--YOU SHALL BE MANKIND'S DESTROYER!
6

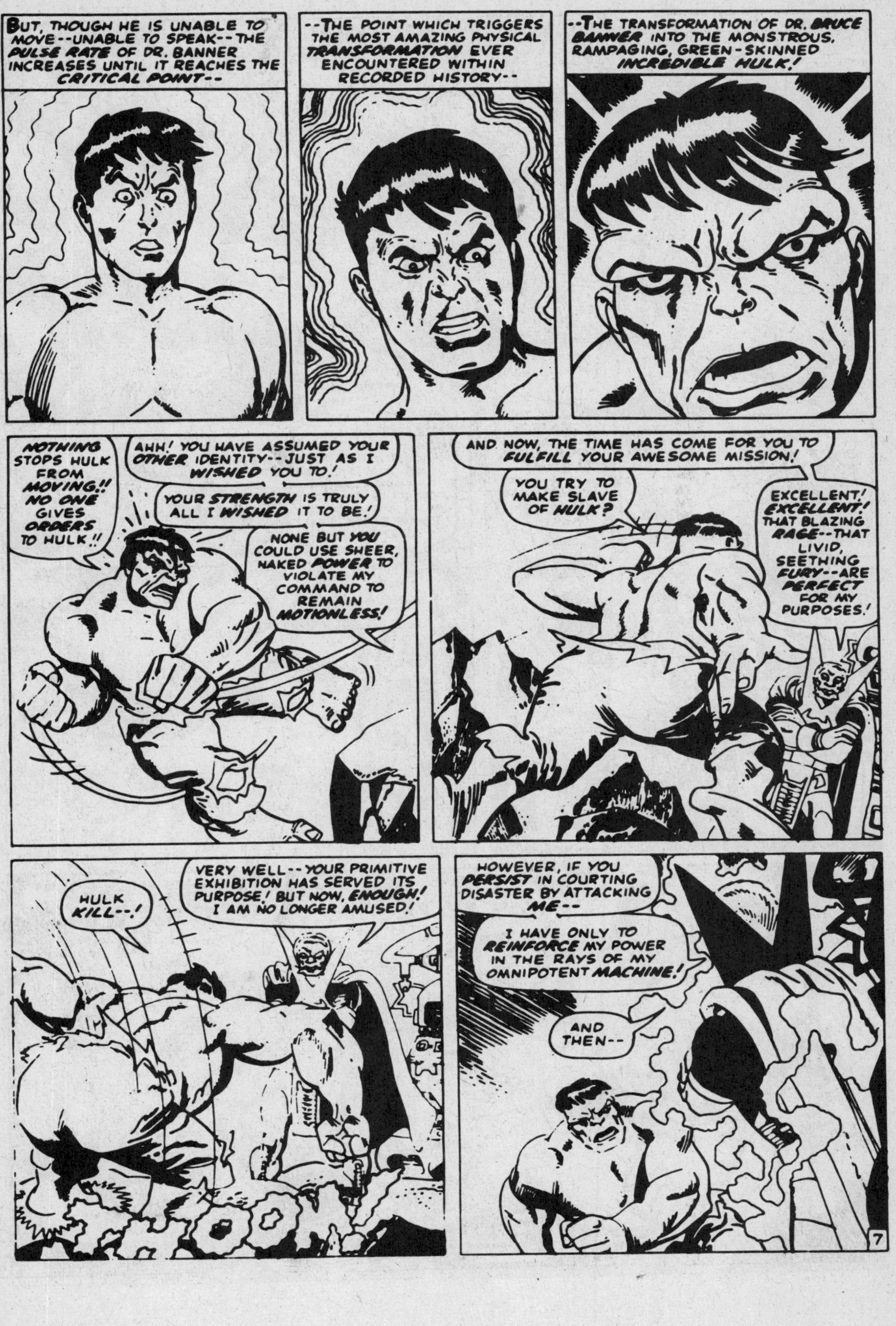

BUT, THOUGH HE IS UNABLE TO MOVE--UNABLE TO SPEAK--THE PULSE RATE OF DR. BANNER INCREASES UNTIL IT REACHES THE CRITICAL POINT--
--THE POINT WHICH TRIGGERS THE MOST AMAZING PHYSICAL TRANSFORMATION EVER ENCOUNTERED WITHIN RECORDED HISTORY--
--THE TRANSFORMATION OF DR. BRUCE BANNER INTO THE MONSTROUS, RAMPAGING, GREEN-SKINNED INCREDIBLE HULK!
NOTHING STOPS HULK FROM MOVING!! NO ONE GIVES ORDERS TO HULK!!
AHH! YOU HAVE ASSUMED YOUR OTHER IDENTITY--JUST AS I WISHED YOU TO!
YOUR STRENGTH IS TRULY ALL I WISHED IT TO BE!
NONE BUT YOU COULD USE SHEER, NAKED POWER TO VIOLATE MY COMMAND TO REMAIN MOTIONLESS!
AND NOW, THE TIME HAS COME FOR YOU TO FULFILL YOUR AWESOME MISSION!
YOU TRY TO MAKE SLAVE OF HULK?
EXCELLENT! EXCELLENT! THAT BLAZING RAGE--THAT LIVID, SEETHING FURY--ARE PERFECT FOR MY PURPOSES!
HULK KILL--!
VERY WELL--YOUR PRIMITIVE EXHIBITION HAS SERVED ITS PURPOSE! BUT NOW, ENOUGH! I AM NO LONGER AMUSED!
HOWEVER, IF YOU PERSIST IN COURTING DISASTER BY ATTACKING ME--
I HAVE ONLY TO REINFORCE MY POWER IN THE RAYS OF MY OMNIPOTENT MACHINE!
AND THEN--
7

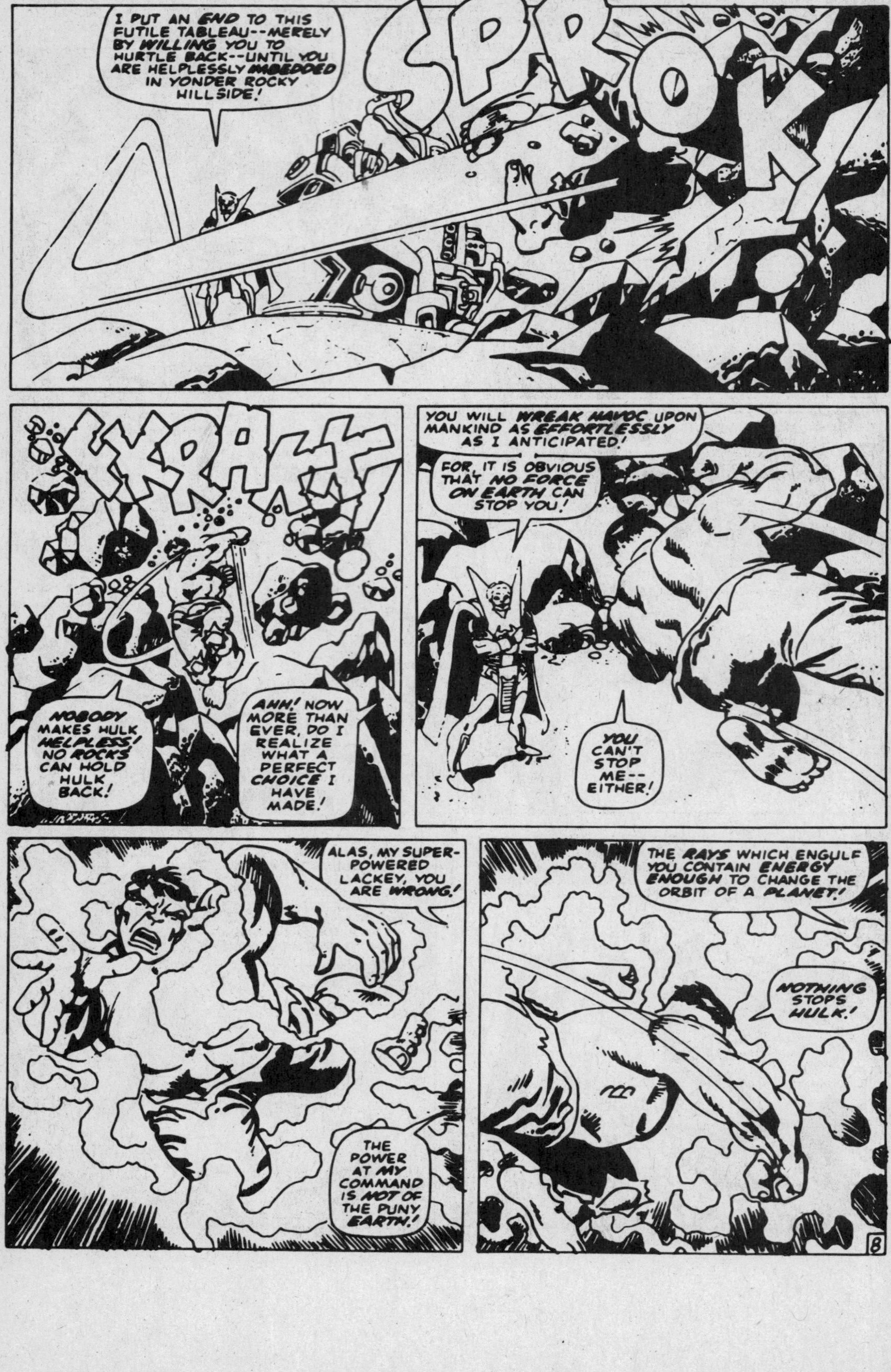

I PUT AN END TO THIS FUTILE TABLEAU--MERELY BY WILLING YOU TO HURTLE BACK--UNTIL YOU ARE HELPLESSLY IMBEDDED IN YONDER ROCKY HILLSIDE!
SPROK!
SKRAK!
NOBODY MAKES HULK HELPLESS! NO ROCKS CAN HOLD HULK BACK!
AHH! NOW MORE THAN EVER, DO I REALIZE WHAT A PERFECT CHOICE I HAVE MADE!
YOU WILL WREAK HAVOC UPON MANKIND AS EFFORTLESSLY AS I ANTICIPATED!
FOR, IT IS OBVIOUS THAT NO FORCE ON EARTH CAN STOP YOU!
YOU CAN'T STOP ME--EITHER!
ALAS, MY SUPER-POWERED LACKEY, YOU ARE WRONG!
THE POWER AT MY COMMAND IS NOT OF THE PUNY EARTH!
THE RAYS WHICH ENGULF YOU CONTAIN ENERGY ENOUGH TO CHANGE THE ORBIT OF A PLANET!
NOTHING STOPS HULK!
8

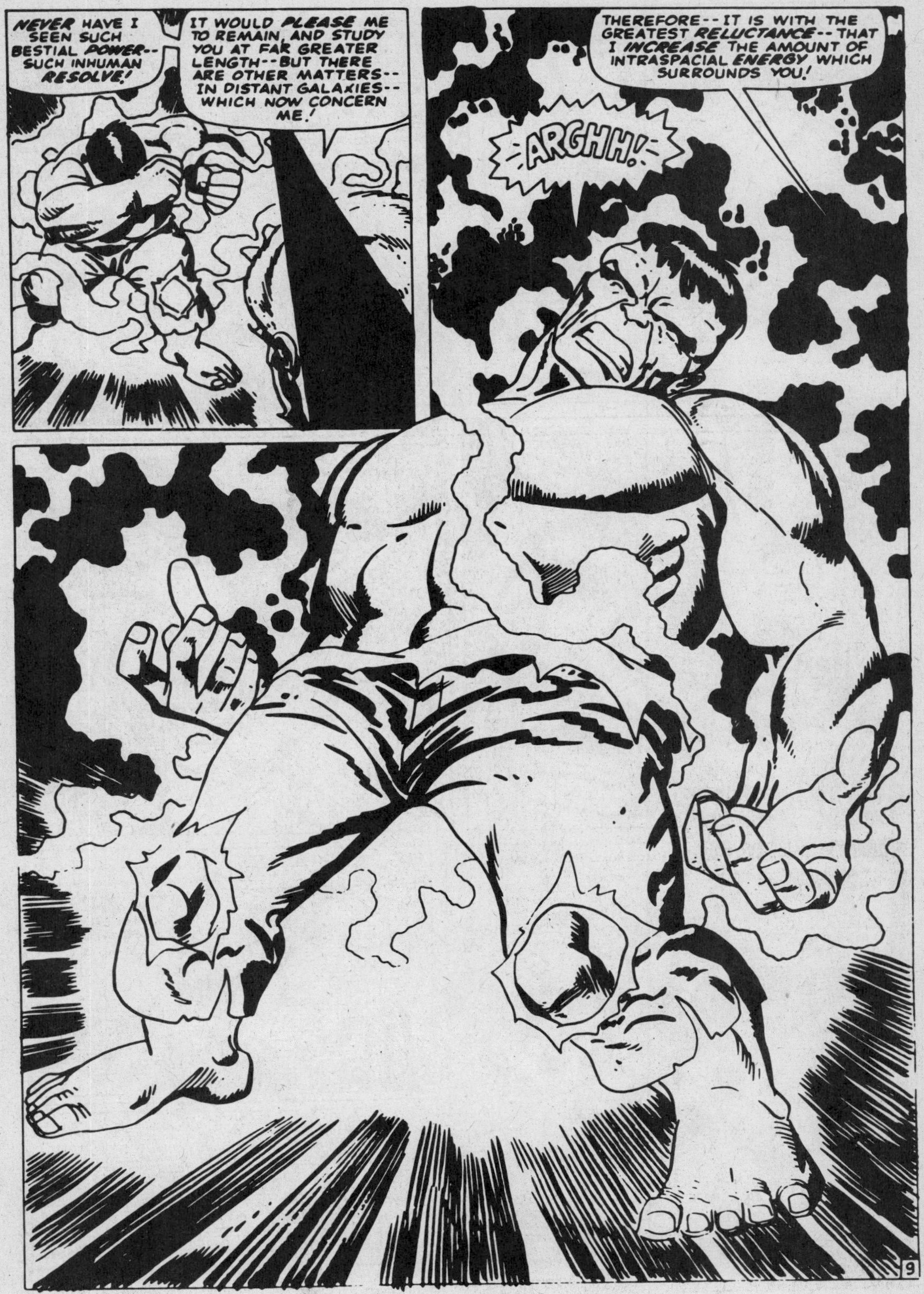
NEVER HAVE I SEEN SUCH BESTIAL POWER-- SUCH INHUMAN RESOLVE!
IT WOULD PLEASE ME TO REMAIN, AND STUDY YOU AT FAR GREATER LENGTH--BUT THERE ARE OTHER MATTERS-- IN DISTANT GALAXIES-- WHICH NOW CONCERN ME!
THEREFORE--IT IS WITH THE GREATEST RELUCTANCE--THAT I INCREASE THE AMOUNT OF INTRASPACIAL ENERGY WHICH SURROUNDS YOU!
ARGHH!
9

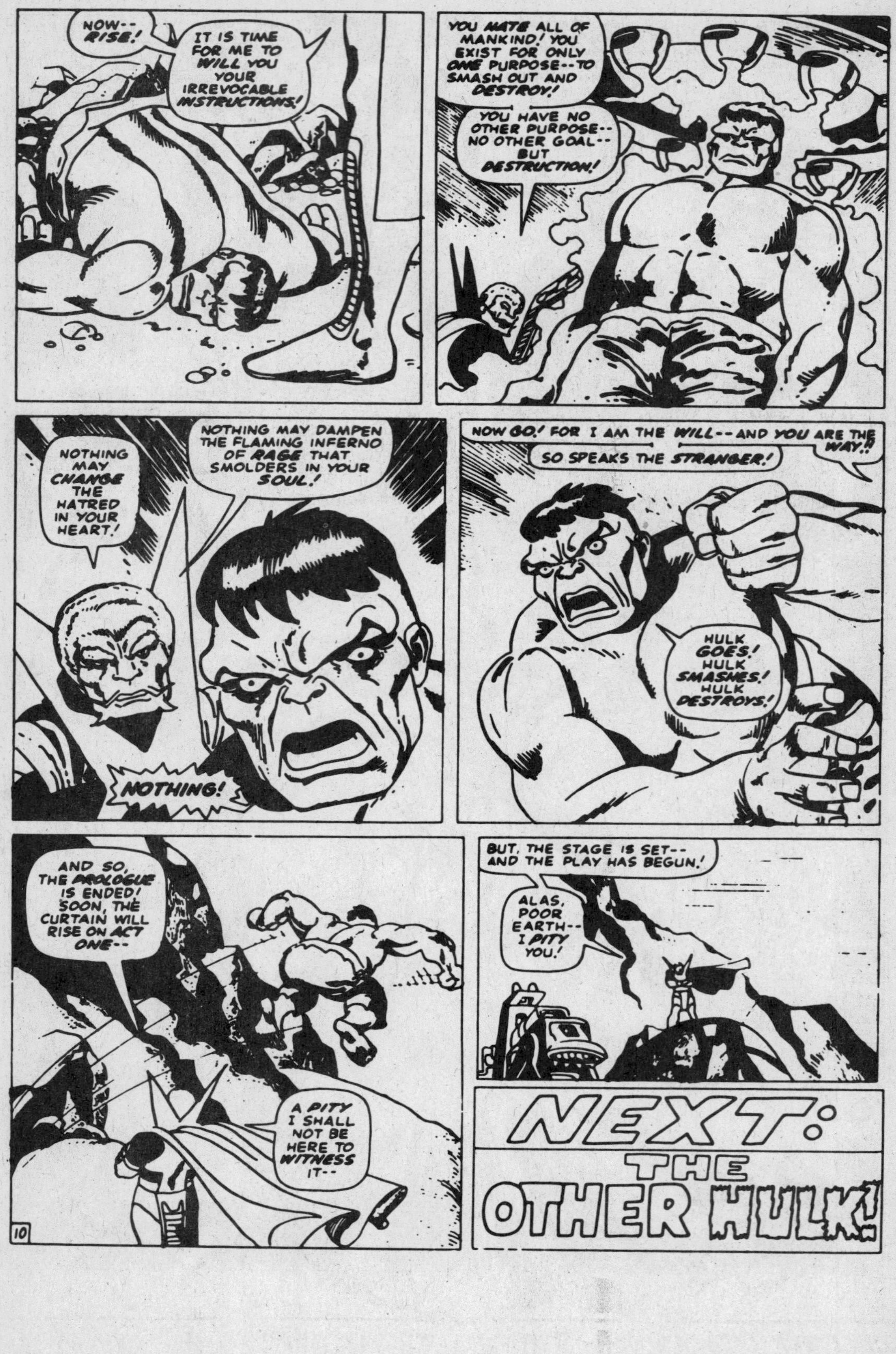
NOW-- RISE!
IT IS TIME FOR ME TO WILL YOU YOUR IRREVOCABLE INSTRUCTIONS!
YOU HATE ALL OF MANKIND! YOU EXIST FOR ONLY ONE PURPOSE--TO SMASH OUT AND DESTROY!
YOU HAVE NO OTHER PURPOSE-- NO OTHER GOAL-- BUT DESTRUCTION!
NOTHING MAY CHANGE THE HATRED IN YOUR HEART!
NOTHING MAY DAMPEN THE FLAMING INFERNO OF RAGE THAT SMOLDERS IN YOUR SOUL!
NOTHING!
NOW GO! FOR I AM THE WILL--AND YOU ARE THE WAY!!
SO SPEAKS THE STRANGER!
HULK GOES! HULK SMASHES! HULK DESTROYS!
AND SO, THE PROLOGUE IS ENDED! SOON, THE CURTAIN WILL RISE ON ACT ONE--
A PITY I SHALL NOT BE HERE TO WITNESS IT--
10
BUT, THE STAGE IS SET-- AND THE PLAY HAS BEGUN!
ALAS, POOR EARTH-- I PITY YOU!
NEXT: THE OTHER HULK!

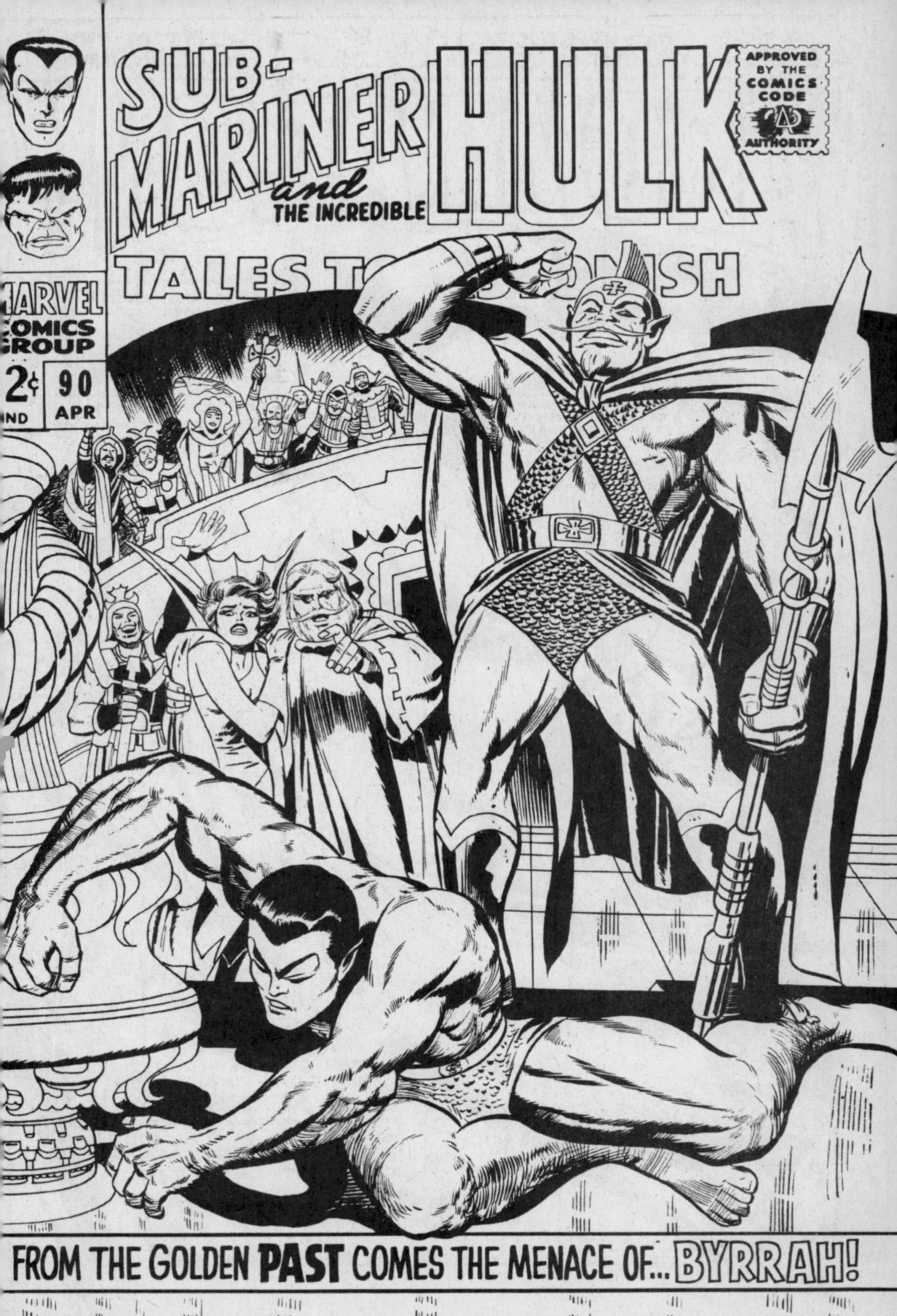
SUB-MARINER and THE INCREDIBLE HULK
TALES TO ASTONISH
APPROVED BY THE COMICS CODE AUTHORITY
MARVEL COMICS GROUP
12¢ 90 APR
IND
FROM THE GOLDEN PAST COMES THE MENACE OF... BYRRAH!

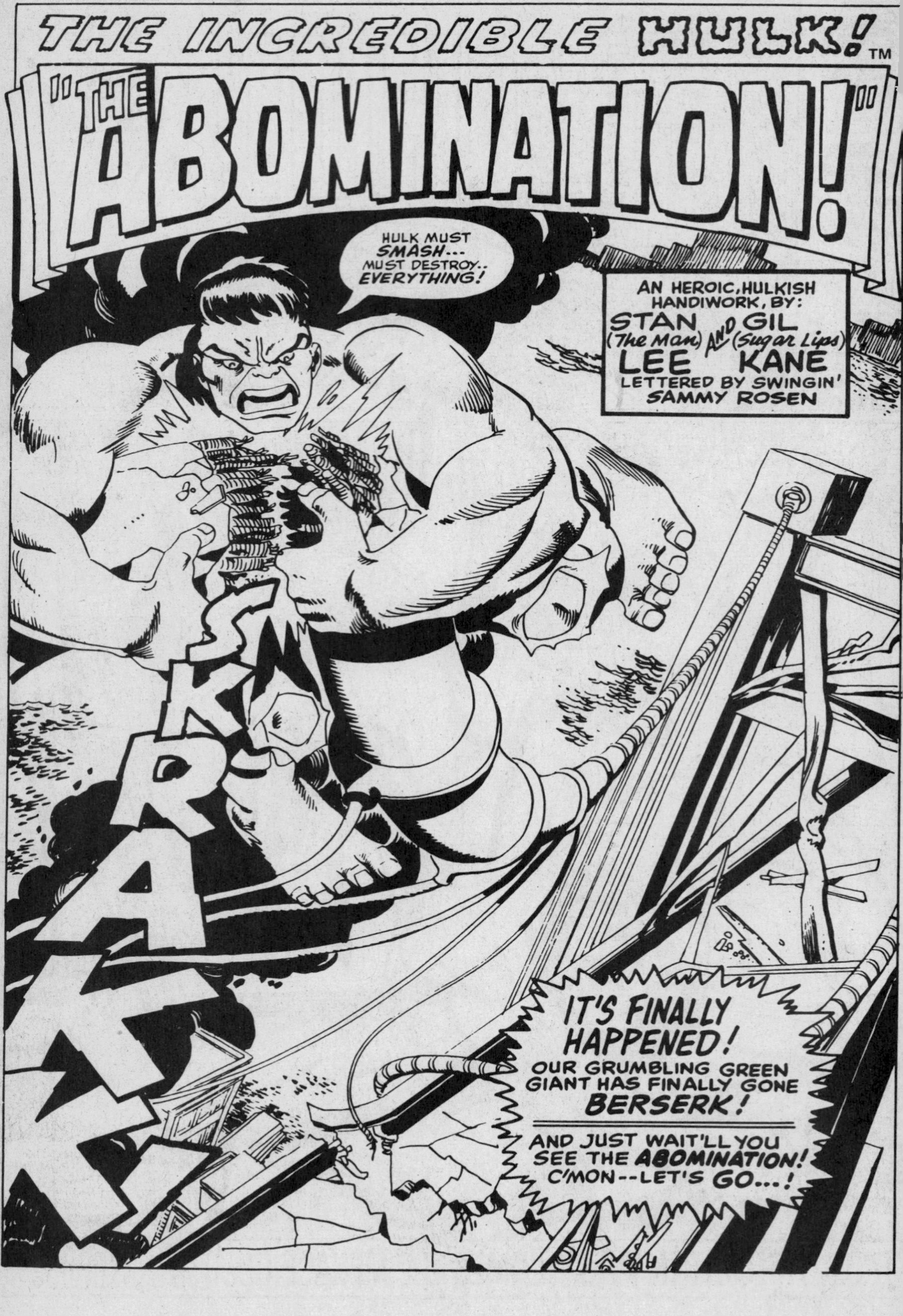
THE INCREDIBLE HULK! TM
"THE ABOMINATION!"
HULK MUST SMASH... MUST DESTROY.. EVERYTHING!
AN HEROIC, HULKISH HANDIWORK, BY: STAN (The Man) LEE AND GIL (Sugar Lips) KANE LETTERED BY SWINGIN' SAMMY ROSEN
KRAK
IT'S FINALLY HAPPENED! OUR GRUMBLING GREEN GIANT HAS FINALLY GONE BERSERK!
AND JUST WAIT'LL YOU SEE THE ABOMINATION! C'MON--LET'S GO...!

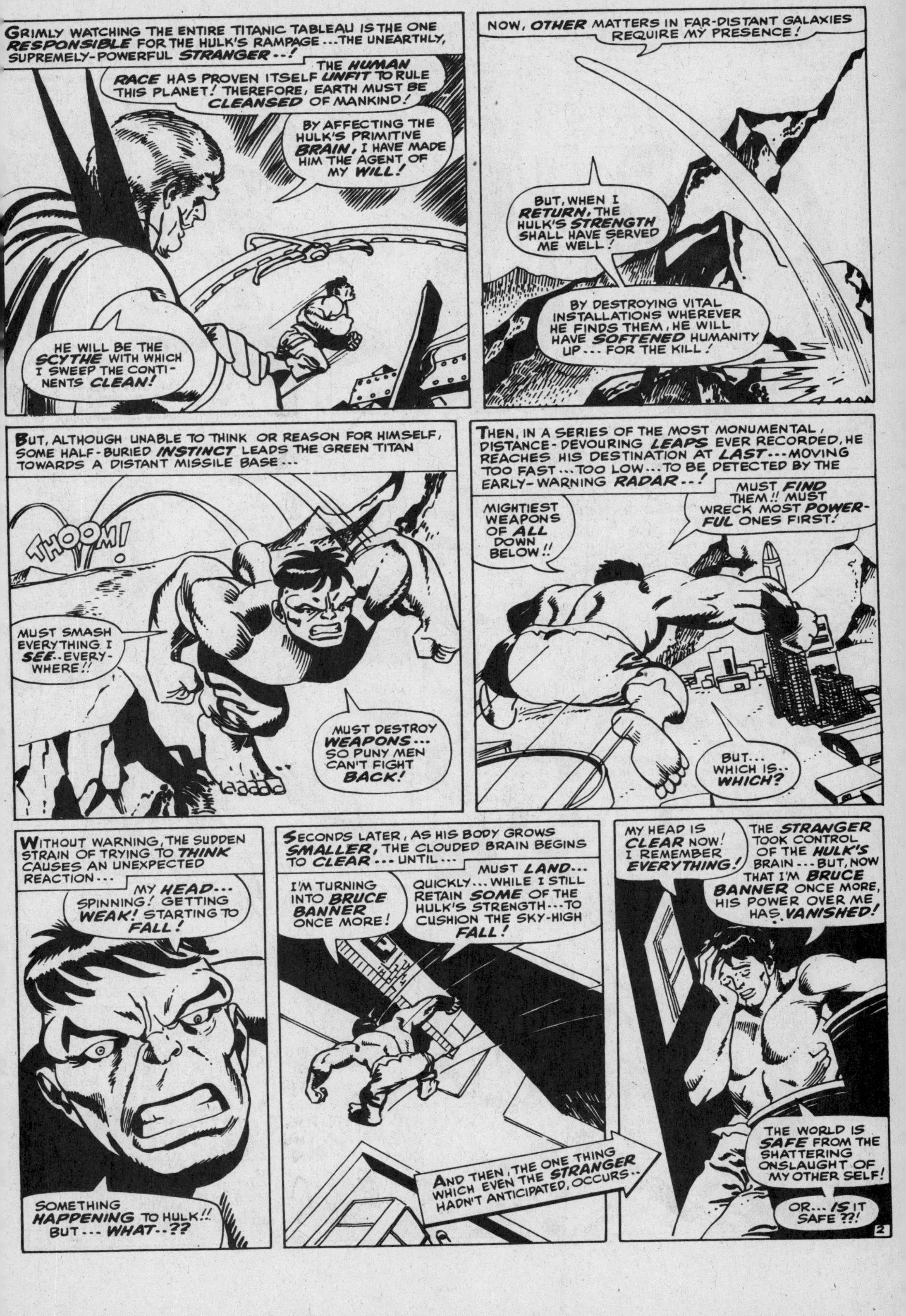
GRIMLY WATCHING THE ENTIRE TITANIC TABLEAU IS THE ONE RESPONSIBLE FOR THE HULK'S RAMPAGE ... THE UNEARTHLY, SUPREMELY-POWERFUL STRANGER--!
THE HUMAN RACE HAS PROVEN ITSELF UNFIT TO RULE THIS PLANET! THEREFORE, EARTH MUST BE CLEANSED OF MANKIND!
BY AFFECTING THE HULK'S PRIMITIVE BRAIN, I HAVE MADE HIM THE AGENT OF MY WILL!
HE WILL BE THE SCYTHE WITH WHICH I SWEEP THE CONTI-NENTS CLEAN!
NOW, OTHER MATTERS IN FAR-DISTANT GALAXIES REQUIRE MY PRESENCE!
BUT, WHEN I RETURN, THE HULK'S STRENGTH SHALL HAVE SERVED ME WELL!
BY DESTROYING VITAL INSTALLATIONS WHEREVER HE FINDS THEM, HE WILL HAVE SOFTENED HUMANITY UP ... FOR THE KILL!
BUT, ALTHOUGH UNABLE TO THINK OR REASON FOR HIMSELF, SOME HALF-BURIED INSTINCT LEADS THE GREEN TITAN TOWARDS A DISTANT MISSILE BASE ...
THOOM!
MUST SMASH EVERYTHING I SEE.. EVERY-WHERE!!
MUST DESTROY WEAPONS... SO PUNY MEN CAN'T FIGHT BACK!
THEN, IN A SERIES OF THE MOST MONUMENTAL, DISTANCE-DEVOURING LEAPS EVER RECORDED, HE REACHES HIS DESTINATION AT LAST ... MOVING TOO FAST ... TOO LOW ... TO BE DETECTED BY THE EARLY-WARNING RADAR--!
MIGHTIEST WEAPONS OF ALL DOWN BELOW!!
MUST FIND THEM!! MUST WRECK MOST POWER-FUL ONES FIRST!
BUT... WHICH IS.. WHICH?
WITHOUT WARNING, THE SUDDEN STRAIN OF TRYING TO THINK CAUSES AN UNEXPECTED REACTION ...
MY HEAD... SPINNING! GETTING WEAK! STARTING TO FALL!
SOMETHING HAPPENING TO HULK!! BUT ... WHAT--??
SECONDS LATER, AS HIS BODY GROWS SMALLER, THE CLOUDED BRAIN BEGINS TO CLEAR ... UNTIL ...
I'M TURNING INTO BRUCE BANNER ONCE MORE!
MUST LAND... QUICKLY... WHILE I STILL RETAIN SOME OF THE HULK'S STRENGTH--TO CUSHION THE SKY-HIGH FALL!
AND THEN, THE ONE THING WHICH EVEN THE STRANGER HADN'T ANTICIPATED, OCCURS..
MY HEAD IS CLEAR NOW! I REMEMBER EVERYTHING!
THE STRANGER TOOK CONTROL OF THE HULK'S BRAIN ... BUT, NOW THAT I'M BRUCE BANNER ONCE MORE, HIS POWER OVER ME HAS VANISHED!
THE WORLD IS SAFE FROM THE SHATTERING ONSLAUGHT OF MY OTHER SELF!
OR... IS IT SAFE ??!
2

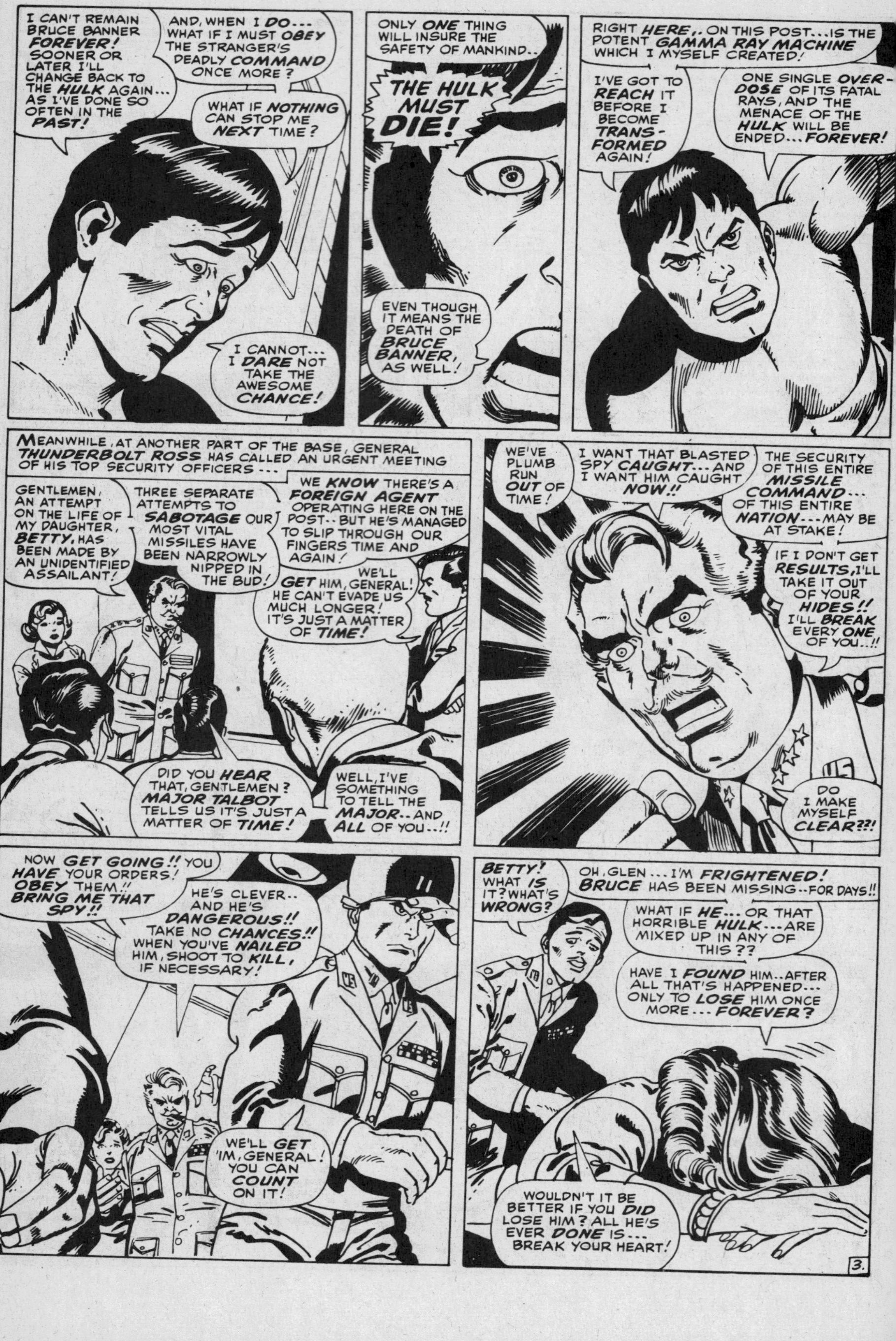

I CAN'T REMAIN BRUCE BANNER FOREVER! SOONER OR LATER I'LL CHANGE BACK TO THE HULK AGAIN... AS I'VE DONE SO OFTEN IN THE PAST!
AND, WHEN I DO... WHAT IF I MUST OBEY THE STRANGER'S DEADLY COMMAND ONCE MORE?
WHAT IF NOTHING CAN STOP ME NEXT TIME?
I CANNOT... I DARE NOT TAKE THE AWESOME CHANCE!
ONLY ONE THING WILL INSURE THE SAFETY OF MANKIND..
THE HULK MUST DIE!
EVEN THOUGH IT MEANS THE DEATH OF BRUCE BANNER, AS WELL!
RIGHT HERE,. ON THIS POST... IS THE POTENT GAMMA RAY MACHINE WHICH I MYSELF CREATED!
I'VE GOT TO REACH IT BEFORE I BECOME TRANS-FORMED AGAIN!
ONE SINGLE OVER-DOSE OF ITS FATAL RAYS, AND THE MENACE OF THE HULK WILL BE ENDED... FOREVER!
MEANWHILE, AT ANOTHER PART OF THE BASE, GENERAL THUNDERBOLT ROSS HAS CALLED AN URGENT MEETING OF HIS TOP SECURITY OFFICERS---
GENTLEMEN, AN ATTEMPT ON THE LIFE OF MY DAUGHTER, BETTY, HAS BEEN MADE BY AN UNIDENTIFIED ASSAILANT!
THREE SEPARATE ATTEMPTS TO SABOTAGE OUR MOST VITAL MISSILES HAVE BEEN NARROWLY NIPPED IN THE BUD!
WE KNOW THERE'S A FOREIGN AGENT OPERATING HERE ON THE POST-- BUT HE'S MANAGED TO SLIP THROUGH OUR FINGERS TIME AND AGAIN!
WE'LL GET HIM, GENERAL! HE CAN'T EVADE US MUCH LONGER! IT'S JUST A MATTER OF TIME!
DID YOU HEAR THAT, GENTLEMEN? MAJOR TALBOT TELLS US IT'S JUST A MATTER OF TIME!
WELL, I'VE SOMETHING TO TELL THE MAJOR.. AND ALL OF YOU..!!
WE'VE PLUMB RUN OUT OF TIME!
I WANT THAT BLASTED SPY CAUGHT... AND I WANT HIM CAUGHT NOW!!
THE SECURITY OF THIS ENTIRE MISSILE COMMAND... OF THIS ENTIRE NATION--- MAY BE AT STAKE!
IF I DON'T GET RESULTS, I'LL TAKE IT OUT OF YOUR HIDES!! I'LL BREAK EVERY ONE OF YOU..!!
DO I MAKE MYSELF CLEAR??!
NOW GET GOING!! YOU HAVE YOUR ORDERS! OBEY THEM!! BRING ME THAT SPY!!
HE'S CLEVER.. AND HE'S DANGEROUS!! TAKE NO CHANCES!! WHEN YOU'VE NAILED HIM, SHOOT TO KILL, IF NECESSARY!
WE'LL GET 'IM, GENERAL! YOU CAN COUNT ON IT!
BETTY! WHAT IS IT? WHAT'S WRONG?
OH, GLEN... I'M FRIGHTENED! BRUCE HAS BEEN MISSING--FOR DAYS!!
WHAT IF HE... OR THAT HORRIBLE HULK--- ARE MIXED UP IN ANY OF THIS??
HAVE I FOUND HIM.. AFTER ALL THAT'S HAPPENED--- ONLY TO LOSE HIM ONCE MORE--- FOREVER?
WOULDN'T IT BE BETTER IF YOU DID LOSE HIM? ALL HE'S EVER DONE IS--- BREAK YOUR HEART!
3.

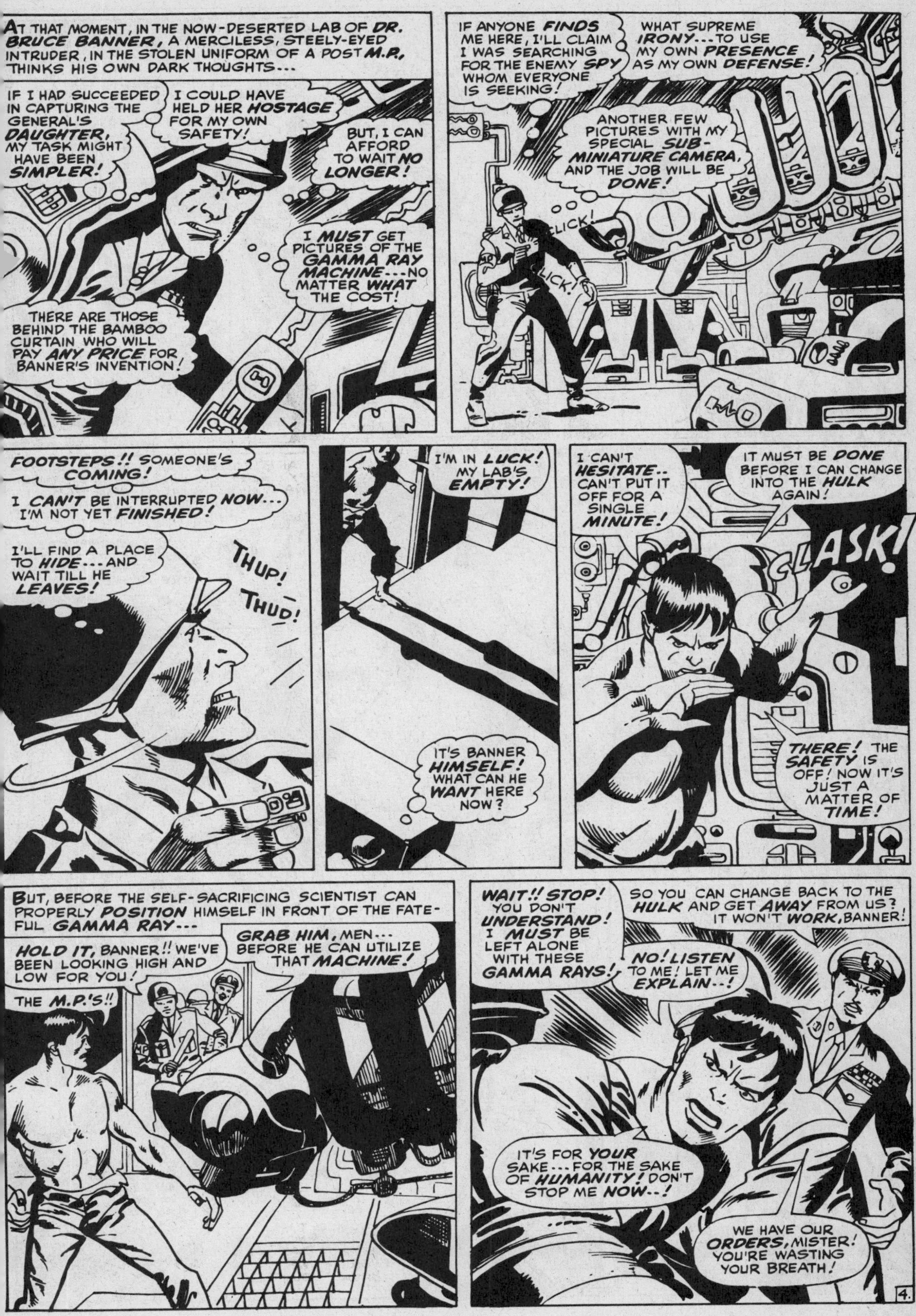
AT THAT MOMENT, IN THE NOW-DESERTED LAB OF DR. BRUCE BANNER, A MERCILESS, STEELY-EYED INTRUDER, IN THE STOLEN UNIFORM OF A POST M.P., THINKS HIS OWN DARK THOUGHTS...
IF I HAD SUCCEEDED IN CAPTURING THE GENERAL'S DAUGHTER, MY TASK MIGHT HAVE BEEN SIMPLER!
I COULD HAVE HELD HER HOSTAGE FOR MY OWN SAFETY!
BUT, I CAN AFFORD TO WAIT NO LONGER!
I MUST GET PICTURES OF THE GAMMA RAY MACHINE---NO MATTER WHAT THE COST!
THERE ARE THOSE BEHIND THE BAMBOO CURTAIN WHO WILL PAY ANY PRICE FOR BANNER'S INVENTION!
IF ANYONE FINDS ME HERE, I'LL CLAIM I WAS SEARCHING FOR THE ENEMY SPY WHOM EVERYONE IS SEEKING!
WHAT SUPREME IRONY---TO USE MY OWN PRESENCE AS MY OWN DEFENSE!
ANOTHER FEW PICTURES WITH MY SPECIAL SUB-MINIATURE CAMERA, AND THE JOB WILL BE DONE!
CLICK!
CLICK!
FOOTSTEPS!! SOMEONE'S COMING!
I CAN'T BE INTERRUPTED NOW... I'M NOT YET FINISHED!
I'LL FIND A PLACE TO HIDE... AND WAIT TILL HE LEAVES!
THUP!
THUD!
I'M IN LUCK! MY LAB'S EMPTY!
IT'S BANNER HIMSELF! WHAT CAN HE WANT HERE NOW?
I CAN'T HESITATE.. CAN'T PUT IT OFF FOR A SINGLE MINUTE!
IT MUST BE DONE BEFORE I CAN CHANGE INTO THE HULK AGAIN!
CLASK!
THERE! THE SAFETY IS OFF! NOW IT'S JUST A MATTER OF TIME!
BUT, BEFORE THE SELF-SACRIFICING SCIENTIST CAN PROPERLY POSITION HIMSELF IN FRONT OF THE FATEFUL GAMMA RAY---
HOLD IT, BANNER!! WE'VE BEEN LOOKING HIGH AND LOW FOR YOU!
GRAB HIM, MEN... BEFORE HE CAN UTILIZE THAT MACHINE!
THE M.P.'S!!
WAIT!! STOP! YOU DON'T UNDERSTAND! I MUST BE LEFT ALONE WITH THESE GAMMA RAYS!
SO YOU CAN CHANGE BACK TO THE HULK AND GET AWAY FROM US? IT WON'T WORK, BANNER!
NO! LISTEN TO ME! LET ME EXPLAIN--!
IT'S FOR YOUR SAKE... FOR THE SAKE OF HUMANITY! DON'T STOP ME NOW--!
WE HAVE OUR ORDERS, MISTER! YOU'RE WASTING YOUR BREATH!
4.

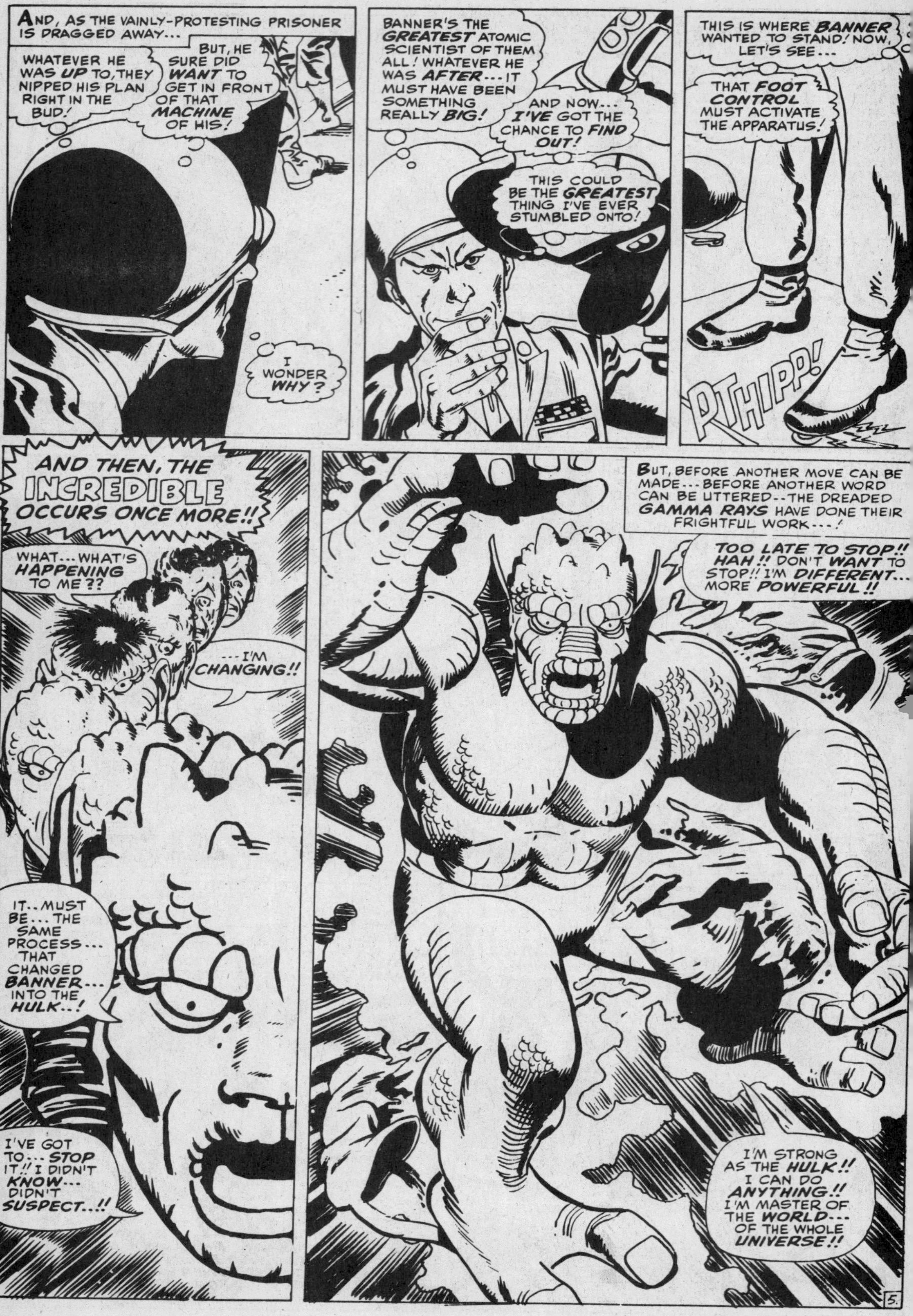

AND, AS THE VAINLY-PROTESTING PRISONER IS DRAGGED AWAY...
WHATEVER HE WAS UP TO, THEY NIPPED HIS PLAN RIGHT IN THE BUD!
BUT, HE SURE DID WANT TO GET IN FRONT OF THAT MACHINE OF HIS!
I WONDER WHY?
BANNER'S THE GREATEST ATOMIC SCIENTIST OF THEM ALL! WHATEVER HE WAS AFTER... IT MUST HAVE BEEN SOMETHING REALLY BIG!
AND NOW... I'VE GOT THE CHANCE TO FIND OUT!
THIS COULD BE THE GREATEST THING I'VE EVER STUMBLED ONTO!
THIS IS WHERE BANNER WANTED TO STAND! NOW, LET'S SEE...
THAT FOOT CONTROL MUST ACTIVATE THE APPARATUS!
PTHIPP!
AND THEN, THE INCREDIBLE OCCURS ONCE MORE!!
WHAT... WHAT'S HAPPENING TO ME??
---I'M CHANGING!!
IT.. MUST BE... THE SAME PROCESS... THAT CHANGED BANNER... INTO THE HULK..!
I'VE GOT TO... STOP IT!! I DIDN'T KNOW... DIDN'T SUSPECT..!!
BUT, BEFORE ANOTHER MOVE CAN BE MADE--- BEFORE ANOTHER WORD CAN BE UTTERED--THE DREADED GAMMA RAYS HAVE DONE THEIR FRIGHTFUL WORK---!
TOO LATE TO STOP!! HAH!! DON'T WANT TO STOP!! I'M DIFFERENT... MORE POWERFUL!!
I'M STRONG AS THE HULK!! I CAN DO ANYTHING!! I'M MASTER OF THE WORLD--- OF THE WHOLE UNIVERSE!!
5.

NO ONE can stand *UP* to me!! NO ONE can *STOP* me! I AM INVINCIBLE!

AND THEN, WITHOUT *REALIZING* IT, THE NEWLY-CREATED MONSTROUS BEING UNWITTINGLY SAVES HIS OWN LIFE..!

I'LL *SMASH* THE MACHINE... SO THAT NO ONE *ELSE* CAN EVER BE AS *POWERFUL* AS *I*!!

--FOR, HAD HE BEEN BOMBARDED BY THE INDESCRIBABLY POTENT *RAYS* JUST A FEW SECONDS *LONGER*, THE FORMER SPY WOULD HAVE SUFFERED THE SAME FATE WHICH *BRUCE BANNER* HAD INTENDED FOR THE *HULK*..

THUBOOM!

HAH!! NOW, THERE ARE ONLY *TWO* OF US...*ME*..AND THE BRAINLESS GREEN *HULK!*

BUT, SOON ONLY *ONE* WILL REMAIN !!

FOR, ONCE I DESTROY *HIM*...MY STRENGTH WILL BE THE *GREATEST!* MY POWER WILL BE *SUPREME!*

NOW, ALL THAT REMAINS TO DO IS... *FIND HIM!*

BTAM!

AND, *FIND HIM I WILL*--!!

80

THERE'S ROOM FOR ONLY *ONE* LIVING, GREEN-SKINNED *POWERHOUSE* HERE ON EARTH...*

AND THAT ONE IS *ME!!*

6

*AS WE HAVE SEEN, THE MYSTERIOUS *GAMMA RAYS* AFFECT EVERYONE THEY TOUCH IN A *DIFFERENT* MANNER! MANY MONTHS AGO, THEY GAVE THE NOW-DEAD *LEADER* THE MOST *BRILLIANT MIND* ON EARTH! WHEN THEY TRANSFORMED *BRUCE BANNER* INTO T[HE] *HULK*, THEY SUBSTITUTED *POWER* FOR INTELLIGENCE.. NOW..THEY HAVE CREATED THE *ABOMINATION* YOU SEE BEFORE

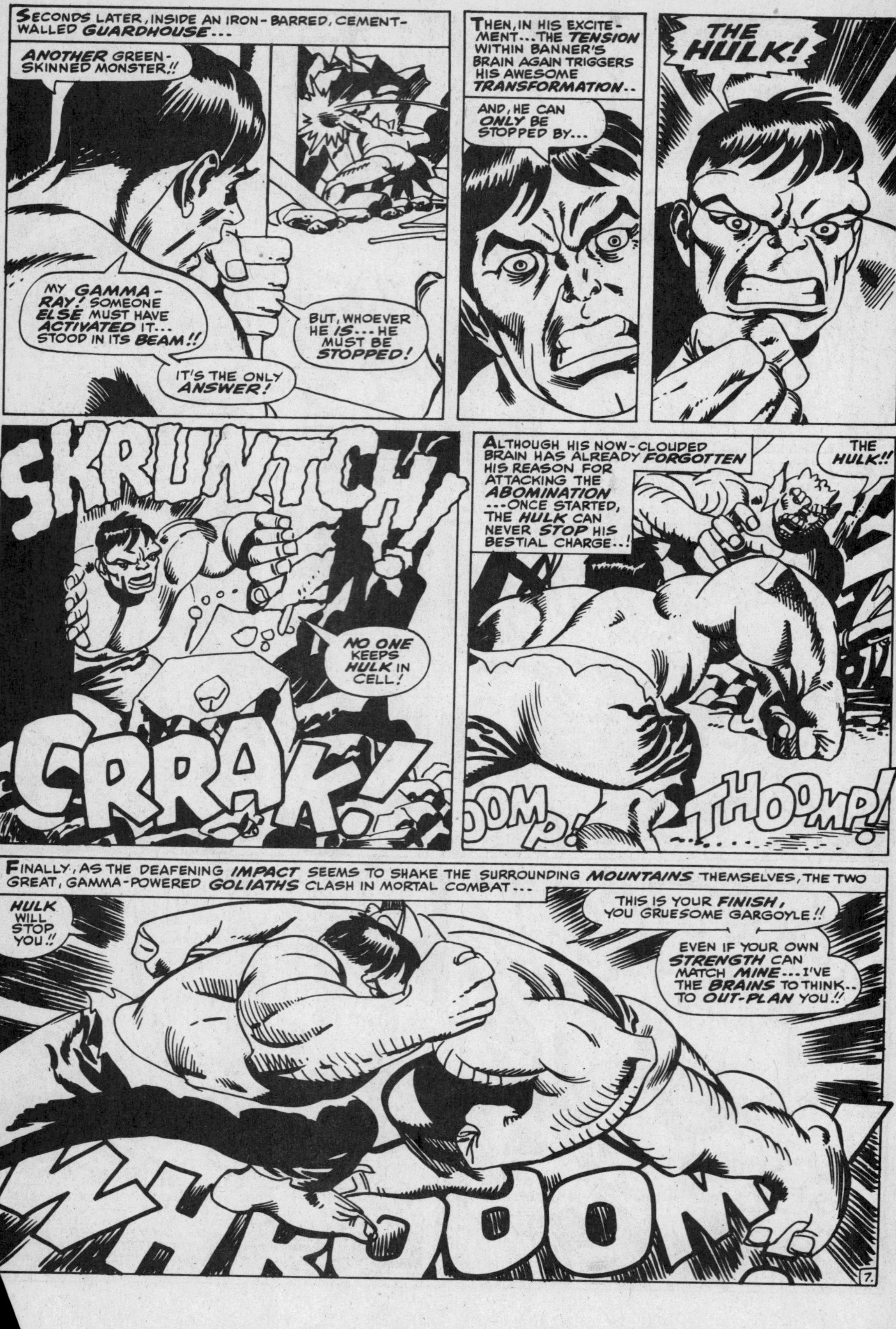

SECONDS LATER, INSIDE AN IRON-BARRED, CEMENT-WALLED GUARDHOUSE...
ANOTHER GREEN-SKINNED MONSTER!!
MY GAMMA-RAY! SOMEONE ELSE MUST HAVE ACTIVATED IT... STOOD IN ITS BEAM!!
BUT, WHOEVER HE IS... HE MUST BE STOPPED!
IT'S THE ONLY ANSWER!
THEN, IN HIS EXCITEMENT... THE TENSION WITHIN BANNER'S BRAIN AGAIN TRIGGERS HIS AWESOME TRANSFORMATION..
AND, HE CAN ONLY BE STOPPED BY...
THE HULK!
SKRUNTCH!
NO ONE KEEPS HULK IN CELL!
CRRAK!
ALTHOUGH HIS NOW-CLOUDED BRAIN HAS ALREADY FORGOTTEN HIS REASON FOR ATTACKING THE ABOMINATION ...ONCE STARTED, THE HULK CAN NEVER STOP HIS BESTIAL CHARGE...!
THE HULK!!
DOOMP!
THOOMP!
FINALLY, AS THE DEAFENING IMPACT SEEMS TO SHAKE THE SURROUNDING MOUNTAINS THEMSELVES, THE TWO GREAT, GAMMA-POWERED GOLIATHS CLASH IN MORTAL COMBAT...
HULK WILL STOP YOU!!
THIS IS YOUR FINISH, YOU GRUESOME GARGOYLE!!
EVEN IF YOUR OWN STRENGTH CAN MATCH MINE... I'VE THE BRAINS TO THINK.. TO OUT-PLAN YOU!!
KRADOOM

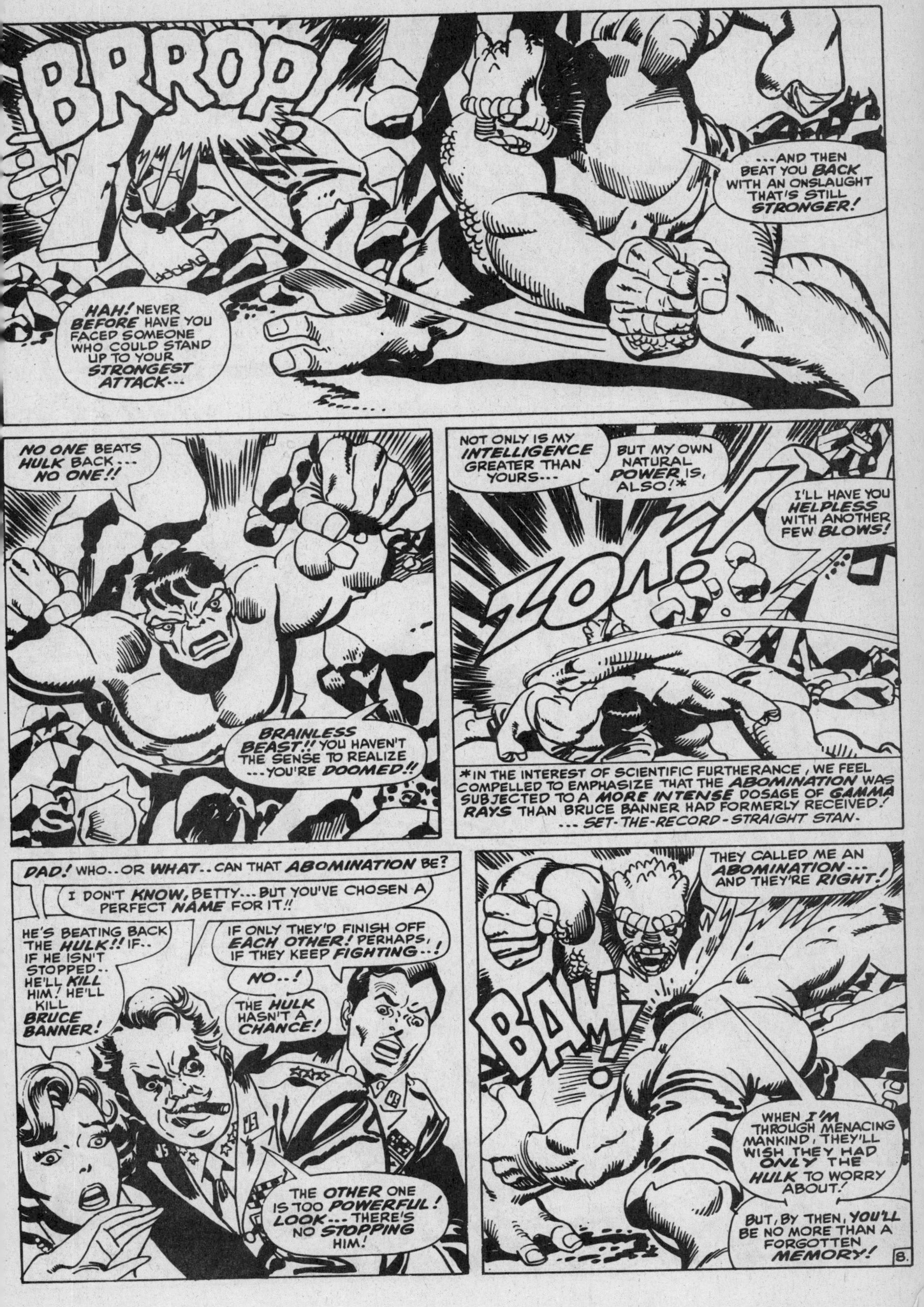
BRROP!
HAH! NEVER BEFORE HAVE YOU FACED SOMEONE WHO COULD STAND UP TO YOUR STRONGEST ATTACK...
...AND THEN BEAT YOU BACK WITH AN ONSLAUGHT THAT'S STILL STRONGER!
NO ONE BEATS HULK BACK... NO ONE!!
BRAINLESS BEAST!! YOU HAVEN'T THE SENSE TO REALIZE ...YOU'RE DOOMED!!
NOT ONLY IS MY INTELLIGENCE GREATER THAN YOURS...
BUT MY OWN NATURAL POWER IS, ALSO!*
I'LL HAVE YOU HELPLESS WITH ANOTHER FEW BLOWS!
ZOK!
*IN THE INTEREST OF SCIENTIFIC FURTHERANCE, WE FEEL COMPELLED TO EMPHASIZE THAT THE ABOMINATION WAS SUBJECTED TO A MORE INTENSE DOSAGE OF GAMMA RAYS THAN BRUCE BANNER HAD FORMERLY RECEIVED! ---SET-THE-RECORD-STRAIGHT STAN.
DAD! WHO..OR WHAT..CAN THAT ABOMINATION BE?
I DON'T KNOW, BETTY... BUT YOU'VE CHOSEN A PERFECT NAME FOR IT!!
HE'S BEATING BACK THE HULK!! IF.. IF HE ISN'T STOPPED.. HE'LL KILL HIM! HE'LL KILL BRUCE BANNER!
IF ONLY THEY'D FINISH OFF EACH OTHER! PERHAPS, IF THEY KEEP FIGHTING..!
NO..!
THE HULK HASN'T A CHANCE!
THE OTHER ONE IS TOO POWERFUL! LOOK... THERE'S NO STOPPING HIM!
THEY CALLED ME AN ABOMINATION... AND THEY'RE RIGHT!
BAM!
WHEN I'M THROUGH MENACING MANKIND, THEY'LL WISH THEY HAD ONLY THE HULK TO WORRY ABOUT!
BUT, BY THEN, YOU'LL BE NO MORE THAN A FORGOTTEN MEMORY!
8.

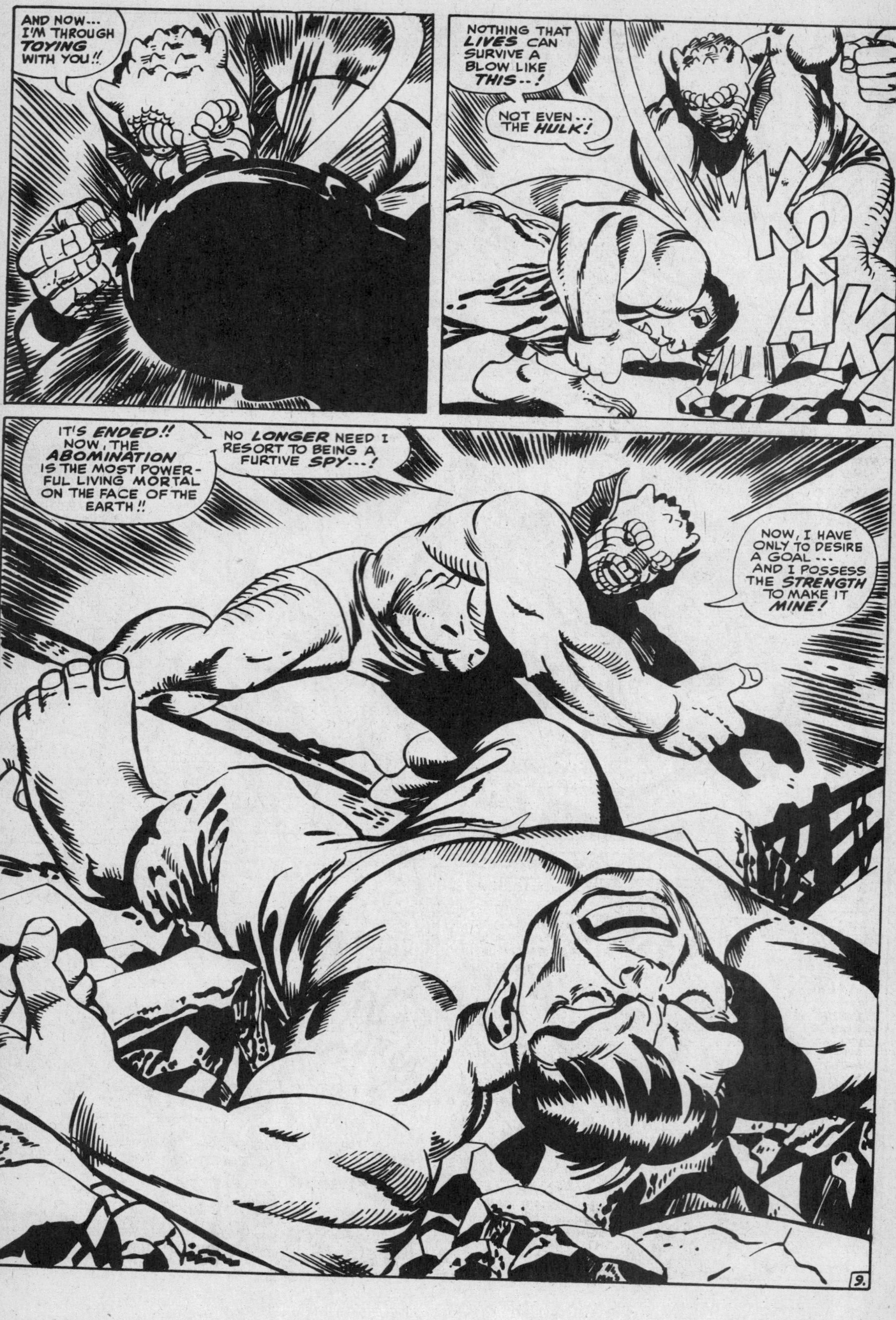
AND NOW... I'M THROUGH TOYING WITH YOU!!
NOTHING THAT LIVES CAN SURVIVE A BLOW LIKE THIS--!
NOT EVEN... THE HULK!
KRAK
IT'S ENDED!! NOW, THE ABOMINATION IS THE MOST POWERFUL LIVING MORTAL ON THE FACE OF THE EARTH!!
NO LONGER NEED I RESORT TO BEING A FURTIVE SPY...!
NOW, I HAVE ONLY TO DESIRE A GOAL... AND I POSSESS THE STRENGTH TO MAKE IT MINE!
9.

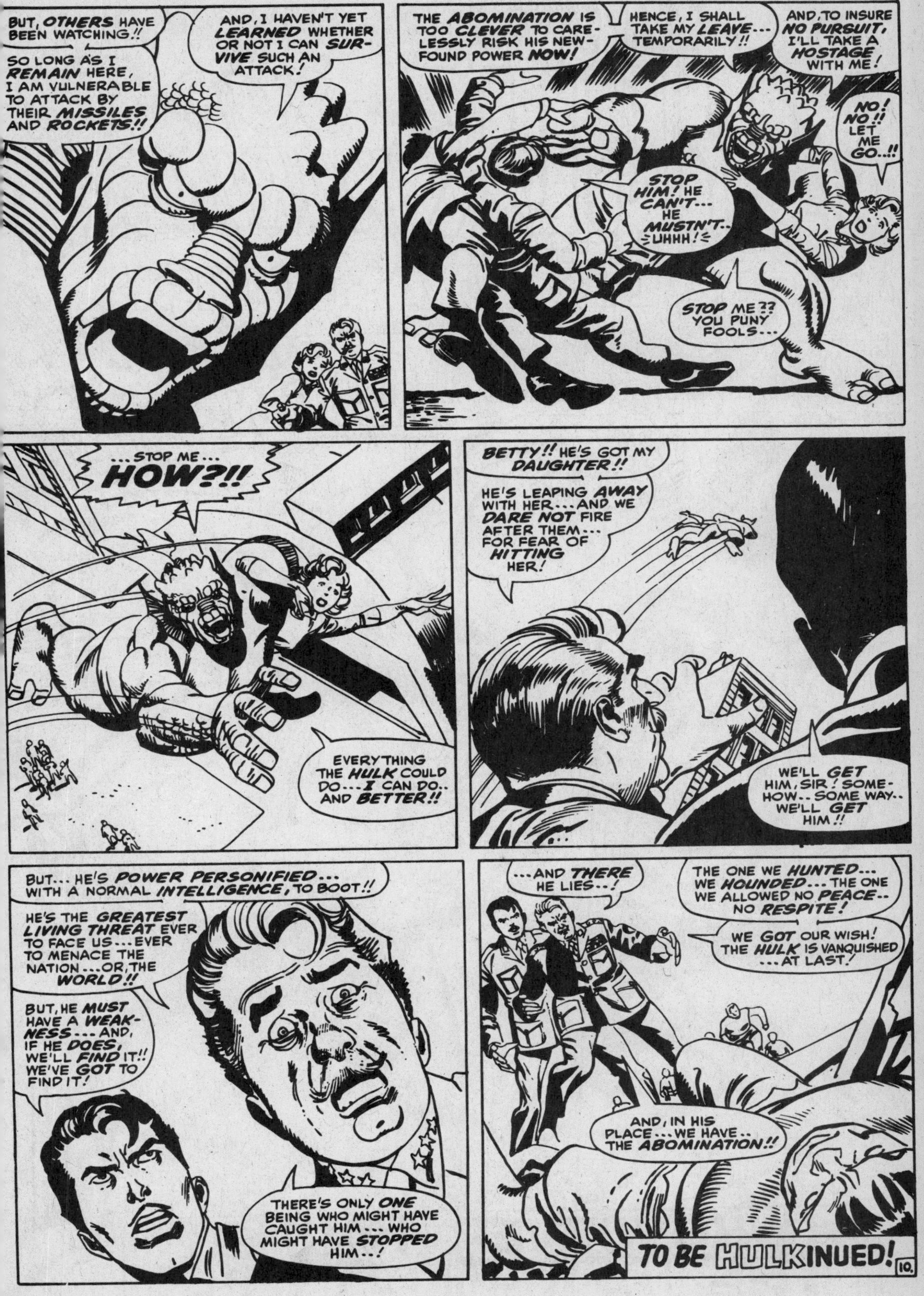
BUT, OTHERS HAVE BEEN WATCHING!!
SO LONG AS I REMAIN HERE, I AM VULNERABLE TO ATTACK BY THEIR MISSILES AND ROCKETS!!
AND, I HAVEN'T YET LEARNED WHETHER OR NOT I CAN SURVIVE SUCH AN ATTACK!
THE ABOMINATION IS TOO CLEVER TO CARELESSLY RISK HIS NEW-FOUND POWER NOW!
HENCE, I SHALL TAKE MY LEAVE... TEMPORARILY!!
AND, TO INSURE NO PURSUIT, I'LL TAKE A HOSTAGE WITH ME!
NO! NO!! LET ME GO..!!
STOP HIM! HE CAN'T... HE MUSTN'T... UHHH!
STOP ME?? YOU PUNY FOOLS...
...STOP ME... HOW?!!
EVERYTHING THE HULK COULD DO... I CAN DO.. AND BETTER!!
BETTY!! HE'S GOT MY DAUGHTER!!
HE'S LEAPING AWAY WITH HER... AND WE DARE NOT FIRE AFTER THEM... FOR FEAR OF HITTING HER!
WE'LL GET HIM, SIR! SOMEHOW.. SOME WAY.. WE'LL GET HIM!!
BUT... HE'S POWER PERSONIFIED... WITH A NORMAL INTELLIGENCE, TO BOOT!!
HE'S THE GREATEST LIVING THREAT EVER TO FACE US... EVER TO MENACE THE NATION... OR, THE WORLD!!
BUT, HE MUST HAVE A WEAKNESS... AND, IF HE DOES, WE'LL FIND IT!! WE'VE GOT TO FIND IT!
THERE'S ONLY ONE BEING WHO MIGHT HAVE CAUGHT HIM... WHO MIGHT HAVE STOPPED HIM..!
...AND THERE HE LIES..!
THE ONE WE HUNTED... WE HOUNDED... THE ONE WE ALLOWED NO PEACE.. NO RESPITE!
WE GOT OUR WISH! THE HULK IS VANQUISHED ...AT LAST!
AND, IN HIS PLACE... WE HAVE.. THE ABOMINATION!!
TO BE HULKINUED!
10.

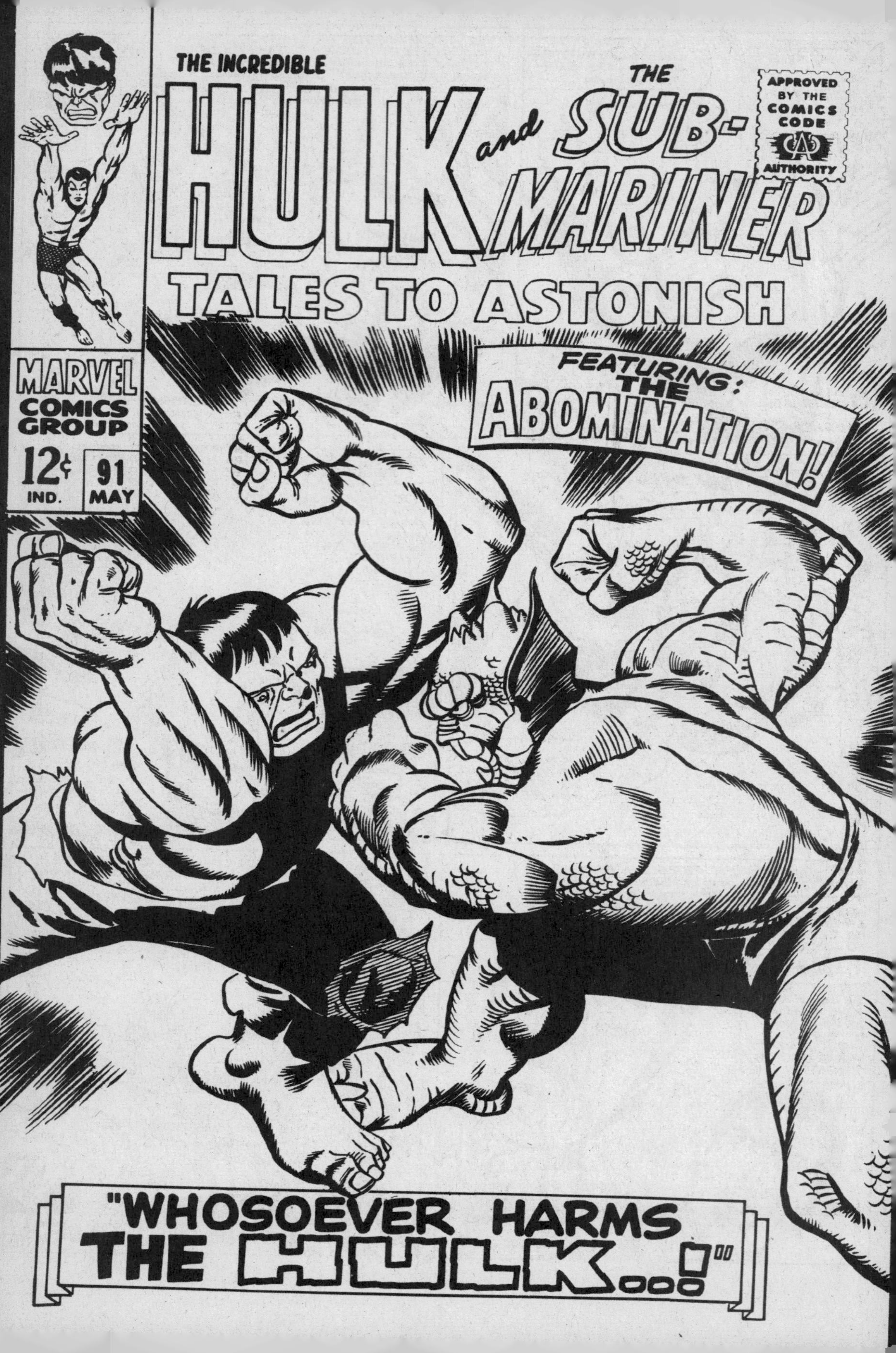
THE INCREDIBLE
HULK and THE SUB-MARINER
TALES TO ASTONISH
APPROVED BY THE COMICS CODE AUTHORITY
MARVEL COMICS GROUP
12¢ IND.
91 MAY
FEATURING: THE ABOMINATION!
"WHOSOEVER HARMS THE HULK...!"

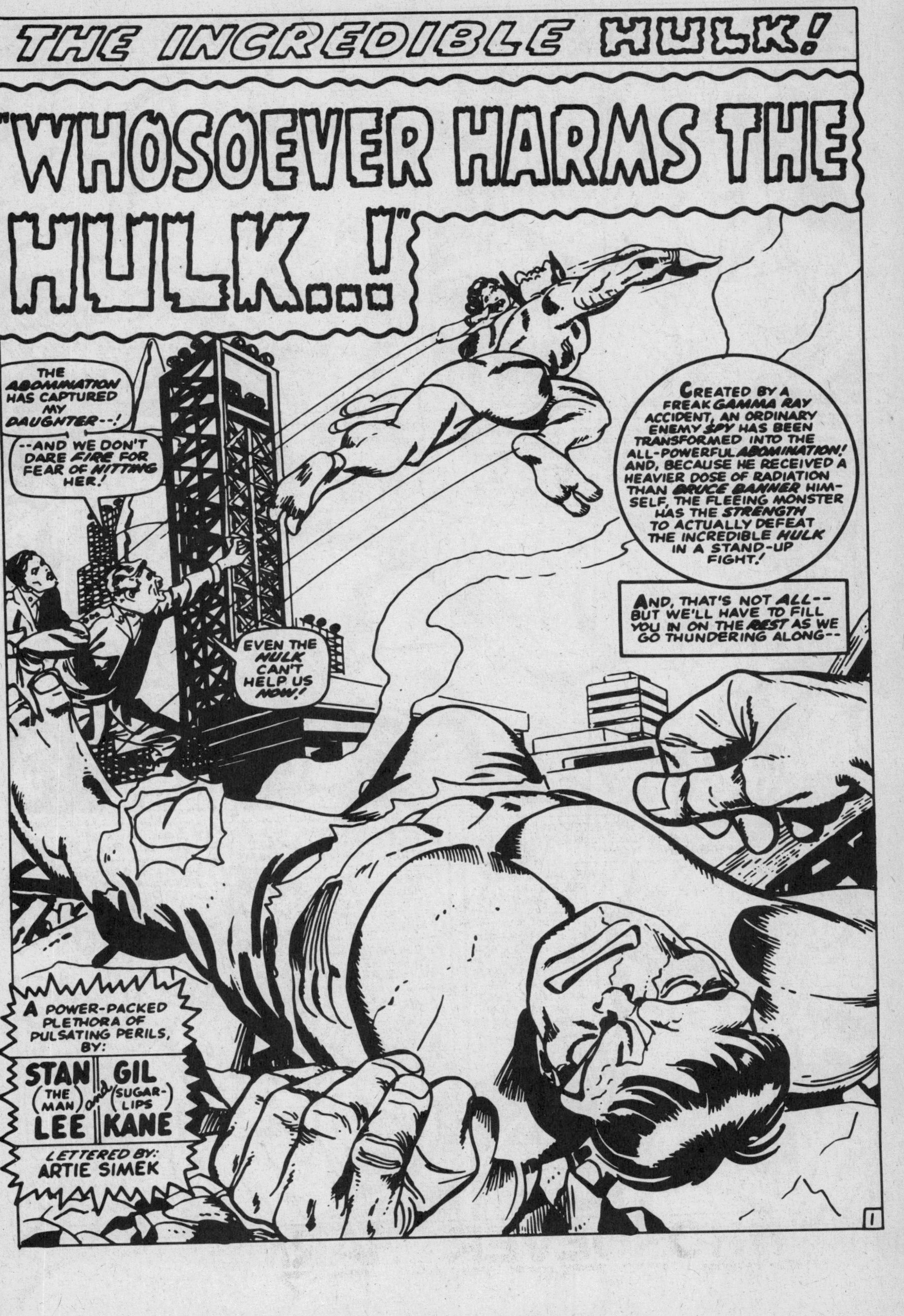
THE INCREDIBLE HULK!
"WHOSOEVER HARMS THE HULK..!"
THE ABOMINATION HAS CAPTURED MY DAUGHTER--!
--AND WE DON'T DARE FIRE FOR FEAR OF HITTING HER!
CREATED BY A FREAK GAMMA RAY ACCIDENT, AN ORDINARY ENEMY SPY HAS BEEN TRANSFORMED INTO THE ALL-POWERFUL ABOMINATION! AND, BECAUSE HE RECEIVED A HEAVIER DOSE OF RADIATION THAN BRUCE BANNER HIMSELF, THE FLEEING MONSTER HAS THE STRENGTH TO ACTUALLY DEFEAT THE INCREDIBLE HULK IN A STAND-UP FIGHT!
AND, THAT'S NOT ALL-- BUT WE'LL HAVE TO FILL YOU IN ON THE REST AS WE GO THUNDERING ALONG--
EVEN THE HULK CAN'T HELP US NOW!
A POWER-PACKED PLETHORA OF PULSATING PERILS, BY:
STAN (THE MAN) LEE and GIL (SUGAR-LIPS) KANE
LETTERED BY: ARTIE SIMEK
1

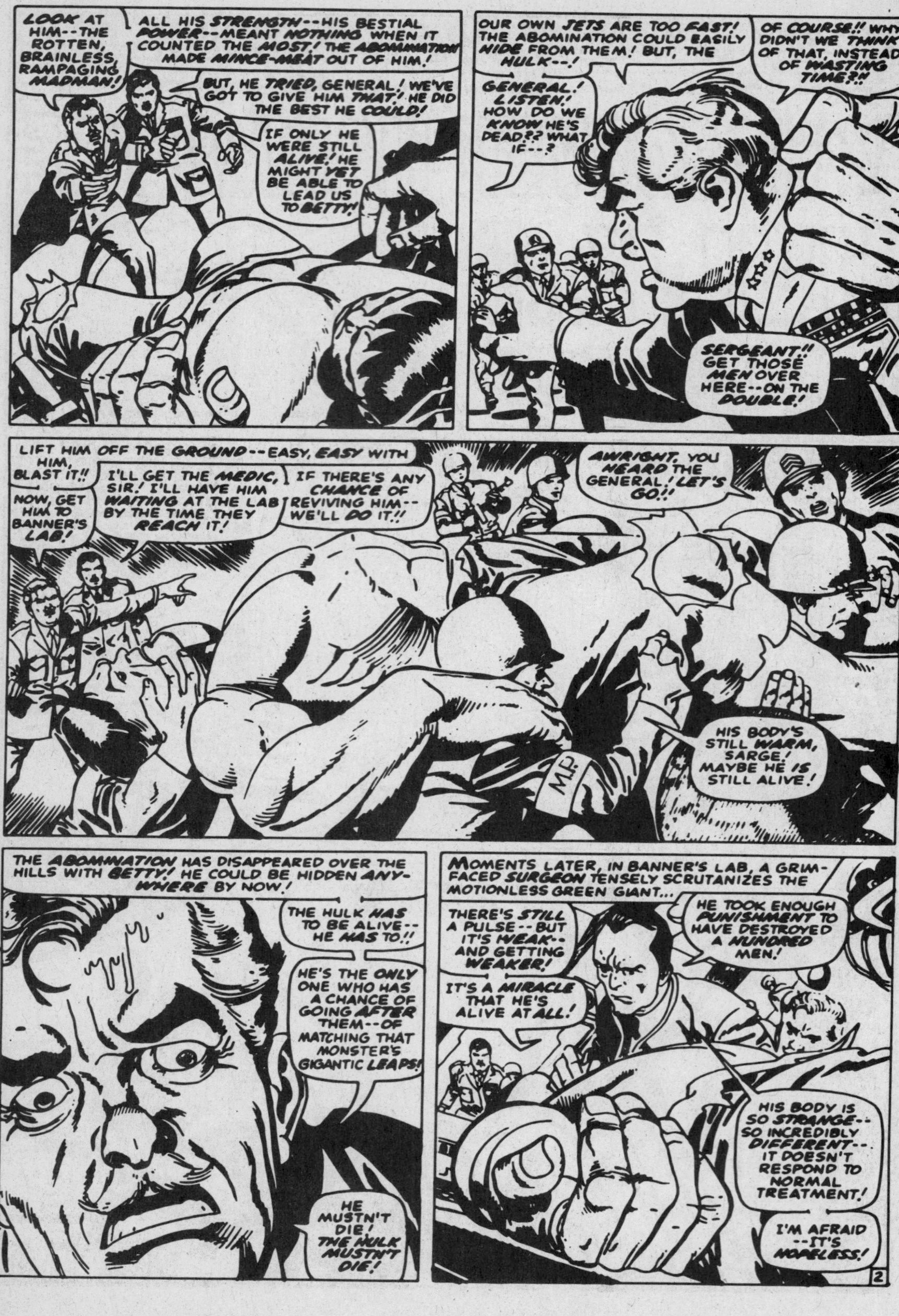
LOOK AT HIM--THE ROTTEN, BRAINLESS, RAMPAGING MADMAN!
ALL HIS STRENGTH--HIS BESTIAL POWER--MEANT NOTHING WHEN IT COUNTED THE MOST! THE ABOMINATION MADE MINCE-MEAT OUT OF HIM!
BUT, HE TRIED, GENERAL! WE'VE GOT TO GIVE HIM THAT! HE DID THE BEST HE COULD!
IF ONLY HE WERE STILL ALIVE! HE MIGHT YET BE ABLE TO LEAD US TO BETTY!
OUR OWN JETS ARE TOO FAST! THE ABOMINATION COULD EASILY HIDE FROM THEM! BUT, THE HULK--!
GENERAL! LISTEN! HOW DO WE KNOW HE'S DEAD?? WHAT IF--?
OF COURSE!! WHY DIDN'T WE THINK OF THAT, INSTEAD OF WASTING TIME?!!
SERGEANT!! GET THOSE MEN OVER HERE--ON THE DOUBLE!
LIFT HIM OFF THE GROUND--EASY, EASY WITH HIM, BLAST IT!!
NOW, GET HIM TO BANNER'S LAB!
I'LL GET THE MEDIC, SIR! I'LL HAVE HIM WAITING AT THE LAB BY THE TIME THEY REACH IT!
IF THERE'S ANY CHANCE OF REVIVING HIM--WE'LL DO IT!!
AWRIGHT, YOU HEARD THE GENERAL! LET'S GO!!
M.P.
HIS BODY'S STILL WARM, SARGE! MAYBE HE IS STILL ALIVE!
THE ABOMINATION HAS DISAPPEARED OVER THE HILLS WITH BETTY! HE COULD BE HIDDEN ANYWHERE BY NOW!
THE HULK HAS TO BE ALIVE--HE HAS TO!!
HE'S THE ONLY ONE WHO HAS A CHANCE OF GOING AFTER THEM--OF MATCHING THAT MONSTER'S GIGANTIC LEAPS!
HE MUSTN'T DIE! THE HULK MUSTN'T DIE!
MOMENTS LATER, IN BANNER'S LAB, A GRIM-FACED SURGEON TENSELY SCRUTANIZES THE MOTIONLESS GREEN GIANT...
THERE'S STILL A PULSE--BUT IT'S WEAK--AND GETTING WEAKER!
HE TOOK ENOUGH PUNISHMENT TO HAVE DESTROYED A HUNDRED MEN!
IT'S A MIRACLE THAT HE'S ALIVE AT ALL!
HIS BODY IS SO STRANGE--SO INCREDIBLY DIFFERENT--IT DOESN'T RESPOND TO NORMAL TREATMENT!
I'M AFRAID--IT'S HOPELESS!
2

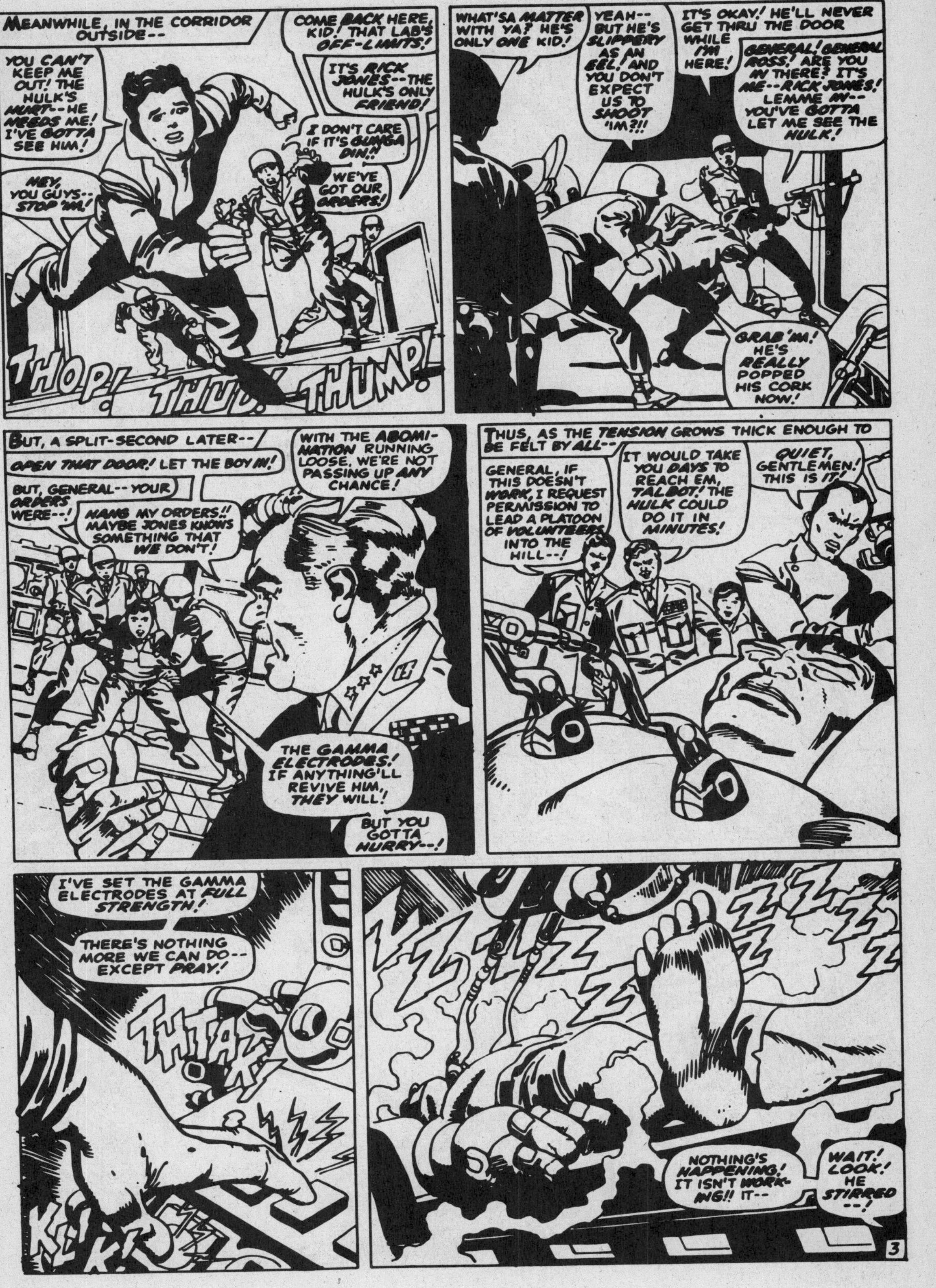
MEANWHILE, IN THE CORRIDOR OUTSIDE--
YOU CAN'T KEEP ME OUT! THE HULK'S HURT--HE NEEDS ME! I'VE GOTTA SEE HIM!
COME BACK HERE, KID! THAT LAB'S OFF-LIMITS!
IT'S RICK JONES--THE HULK'S ONLY FRIEND!
I DON'T CARE IF IT'S GUNGA DIN!!
WE'VE GOT OUR ORDERS!
HEY, YOU GUYS--STOP 'IM!
THOP! THUD! THUMP!
WHAT'SA MATTER WITH YA? HE'S ONLY ONE KID!
YEAH--BUT HE'S SLIPPERY AS AN EEL! AND YOU DON'T EXPECT US TO SHOOT 'IM?!!
IT'S OKAY! HE'LL NEVER GET THRU THE DOOR WHILE I'M HERE!
GENERAL! GENERAL ROSS! ARE YOU IN THERE? IT'S ME--RICK JONES! LEMME IN--YOU'VE GOTTA LET ME SEE THE HULK!
GRAB 'IM! HE'S REALLY POPPED HIS CORK NOW!
BUT, A SPLIT-SECOND LATER--
OPEN THAT DOOR! LET THE BOY IN!
BUT, GENERAL--YOUR ORDERS WERE--!
HANG MY ORDERS!! MAYBE JONES KNOWS SOMETHING THAT WE DON'T!
WITH THE ABOMINATION RUNNING LOOSE, WE'RE NOT PASSING UP ANY CHANCE!
THE GAMMA ELECTRODES! IF ANYTHING'LL REVIVE HIM, THEY WILL!
BUT YOU GOTTA HURRY--!
THUS, AS THE TENSION GROWS THICK ENOUGH TO BE FELT BY ALL--
GENERAL, IF THIS DOESN'T WORK, I REQUEST PERMISSION TO LEAD A PLATOON OF VOLUNTEERS INTO THE HILL--!
IT WOULD TAKE YOU DAYS TO REACH EM, TALBOT! THE HULK COULD DO IT IN MINUTES!
QUIET, GENTLEMEN! THIS IS IT!
I'VE SET THE GAMMA ELECTRODES AT FULL STRENGTH!
THERE'S NOTHING MORE WE CAN DO--EXCEPT PRAY!
THTAZ-AK!
KLIK! KLIK!
NOTHING'S HAPPENING! IT ISN'T WORKING!! IT--
WAIT! LOOK! HE STIRRED--!
3

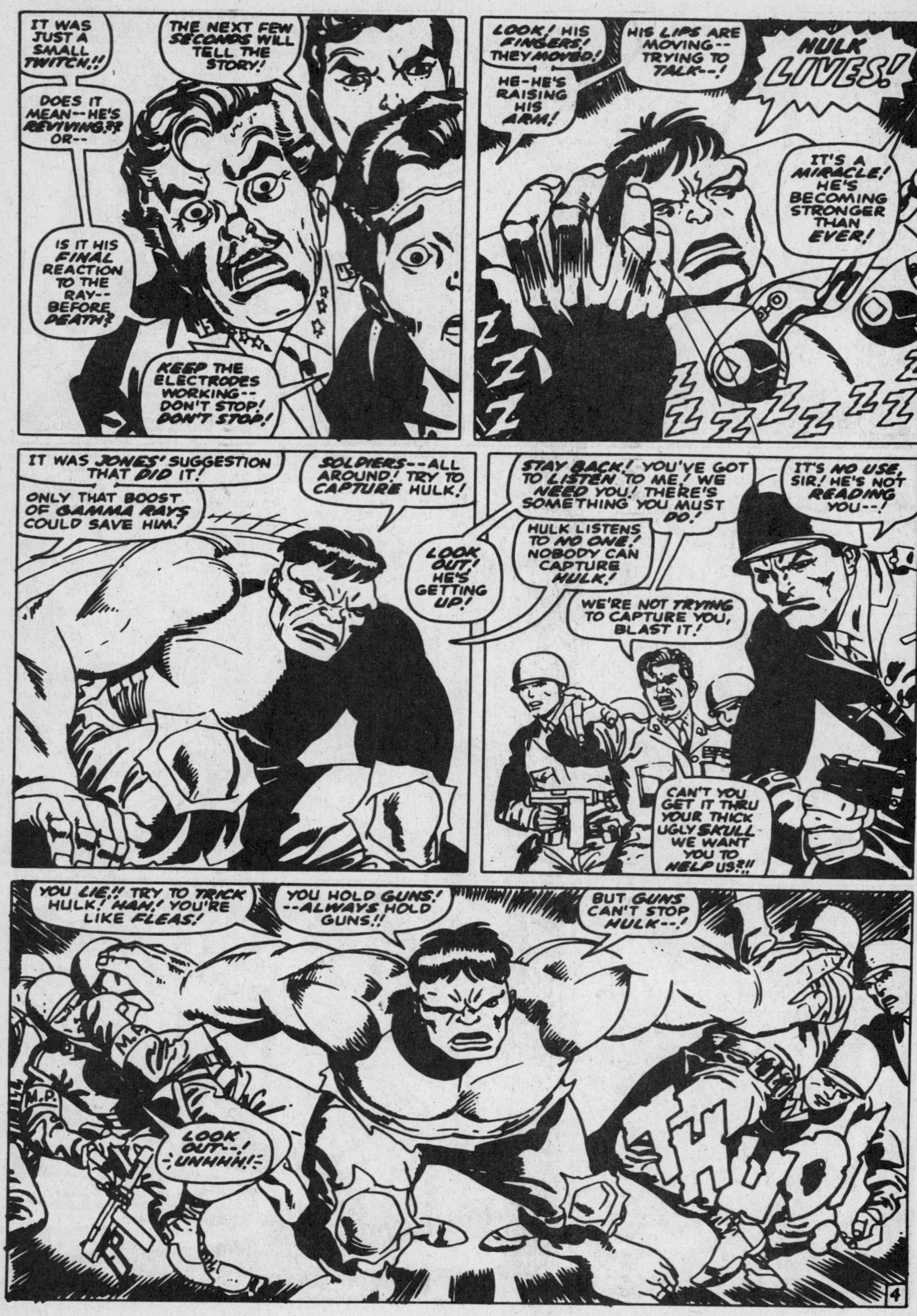
IT WAS JUST A SMALL TWITCH!!
THE NEXT FEW SECONDS WILL TELL THE STORY!
DOES IT MEAN--HE'S REVIVING?? OR--
IS IT HIS FINAL REACTION TO THE RAY--BEFORE DEATH?
KEEP THE ELECTRODES WORKING--DON'T STOP! DON'T STOP!
LOOK! HIS FINGERS! THEY MOVED!
HE-HE'S RAISING HIS ARM!
HIS LIPS ARE MOVING--TRYING TO TALK--!
HULK LIVES!
IT'S A MIRACLE! HE'S BECOMING STRONGER THAN EVER!
IT WAS JONES' SUGGESTION THAT DID IT!
ONLY THAT BOOST OF GAMMA RAYS COULD SAVE HIM.
SOLDIERS--ALL AROUND! TRY TO CAPTURE HULK!
LOOK OUT! HE'S GETTING UP!
STAY BACK! YOU'VE GOT TO LISTEN TO ME! WE NEED YOU! THERE'S SOMETHING YOU MUST DO!
HULK LISTENS TO NO ONE! NOBODY CAN CAPTURE HULK!
IT'S NO USE, SIR! HE'S NOT READING YOU--!
WE'RE NOT TRYING TO CAPTURE YOU, BLAST IT!
CAN'T YOU GET IT THRU YOUR THICK UGLY SKULL WE WANT YOU TO HELP US?!!
YOU LIE!! TRY TO TRICK HULK! HAH! YOU'RE LIKE FLEAS!
YOU HOLD GUNS! --ALWAYS HOLD GUNS!!
BUT GUNS CAN'T STOP HULK--!
M.P.
M.P.
LOOK OUT--! --UNHHH!--
THUD!
4

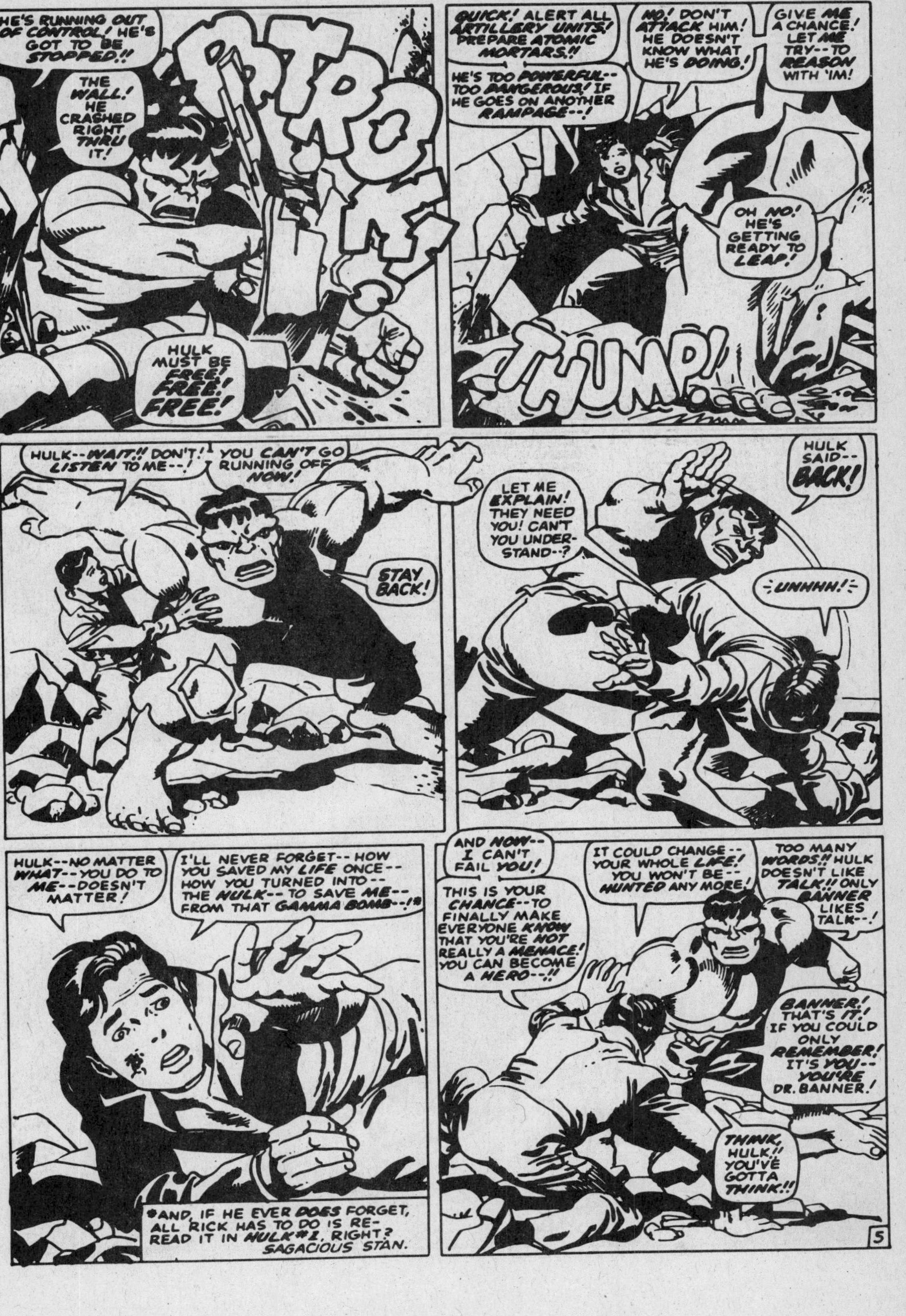
HE'S RUNNING OUT OF CONTROL! HE'S GOT TO BE STOPPED!!
THE WALL! HE CRASHED RIGHT THRU IT!
HULK MUST BE FREE! FREE! FREE!
QUICK! ALERT ALL ARTILLERY UNITS! PREPARE ATOMIC MORTARS!!
HE'S TOO POWERFUL-- TOO DANGEROUS! IF HE GOES ON ANOTHER RAMPAGE--!
NO! DON'T ATTACK HIM! HE DOESN'T KNOW WHAT HE'S DOING!
GIVE ME A CHANCE! LET ME TRY--TO REASON WITH 'IM!
OH NO! HE'S GETTING READY TO LEAP!
THUMP!
HULK--WAIT!! DON'T! LISTEN TO ME--!
YOU CAN'T GO RUNNING OFF NOW!
STAY BACK!
LET ME EXPLAIN! THEY NEED YOU! CAN'T YOU UNDER-STAND--?
HULK SAID-- BACK!
UNNHH!
HULK--NO MATTER WHAT--YOU DO TO ME--DOESN'T MATTER!
I'LL NEVER FORGET--HOW YOU SAVED MY LIFE ONCE--HOW YOU TURNED INTO--THE HULK--TO SAVE ME--FROM THAT GAMMA BOMB--!*
*AND, IF HE EVER DOES FORGET, ALL RICK HAS TO DO IS RE-READ IT IN HULK #1, RIGHT? SAGACIOUS STAN.
AND NOW-- I CAN'T FAIL YOU!
THIS IS YOUR CHANCE--TO FINALLY MAKE EVERYONE KNOW THAT YOU'RE NOT REALLY A MENACE! YOU CAN BECOME A HERO--!!
IT COULD CHANGE--YOUR WHOLE LIFE! YOU WON'T BE--HUNTED ANY MORE!
TOO MANY WORDS!! HULK DOESN'T LIKE TALK!! ONLY BANNER LIKES TALK--!
BANNER! THAT'S IT! IF YOU COULD ONLY REMEMBER! IT'S YOU-- YOU'RE DR. BANNER!
THINK, HULK!! YOU'VE GOTTA THINK!!
5

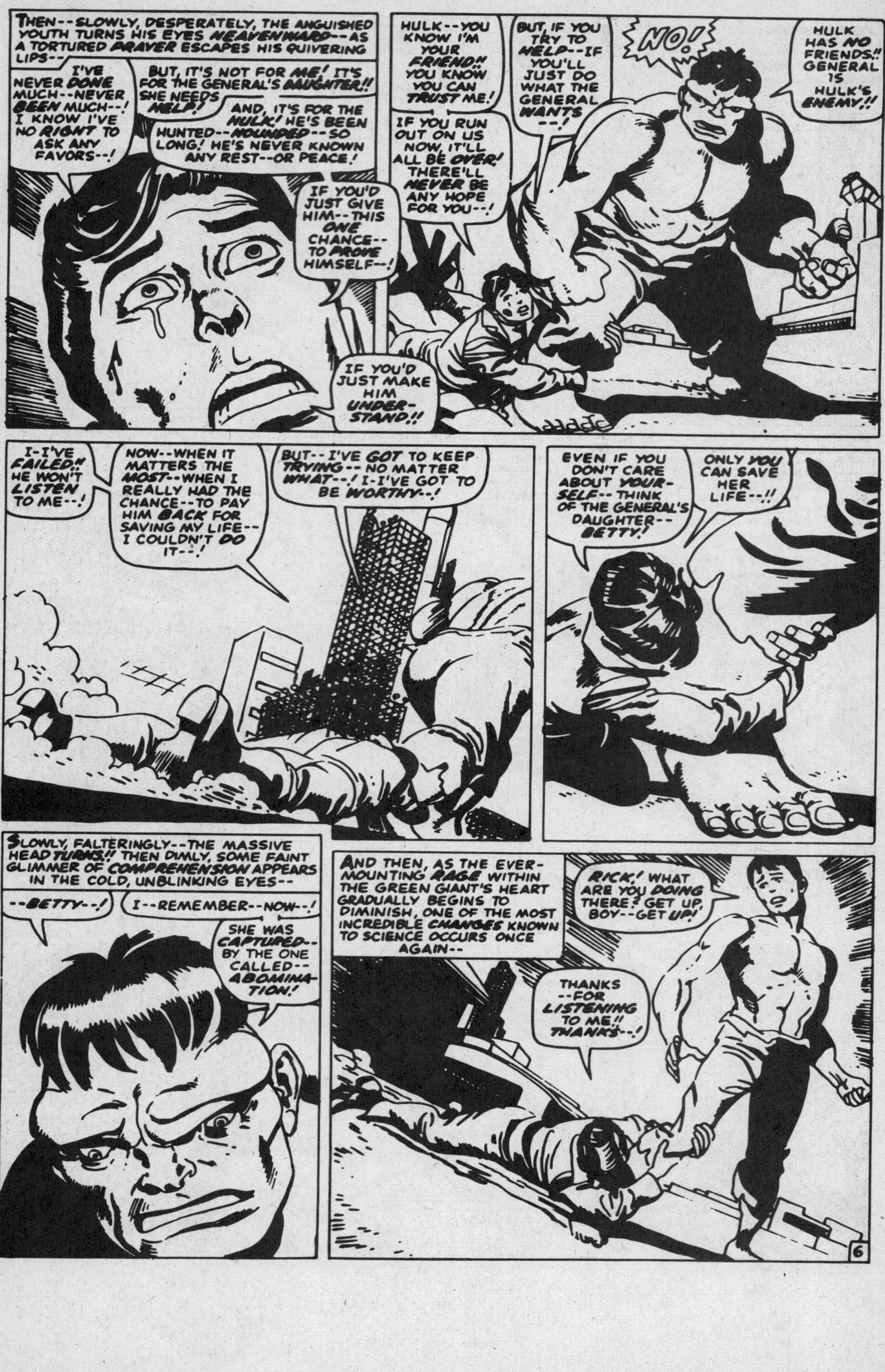

THEN--SLOWLY, DESPERATELY, THE ANGUISHED YOUTH TURNS HIS EYES HEAVENWARD--AS A TORTURED PRAYER ESCAPES HIS QUIVERING LIPS--
I'VE NEVER DONE MUCH--NEVER BEEN MUCH--! I KNOW I'VE NO RIGHT TO ASK ANY FAVORS--!
BUT, IT'S NOT FOR ME! IT'S FOR THE GENERAL'S DAUGHTER!! SHE NEEDS HELP!
AND, IT'S FOR THE HULK! HE'S BEEN HUNTED--HOUNDED--SO LONG! HE'S NEVER KNOWN ANY REST--OR PEACE!
IF YOU'D JUST GIVE HIM--THIS ONE CHANCE--TO PROVE HIMSELF--!
IF YOU'D JUST MAKE HIM UNDER-STAND!!
HULK--YOU KNOW I'M YOUR FRIEND!! YOU KNOW YOU CAN TRUST ME!
BUT, IF YOU TRY TO HELP--IF YOU'LL JUST DO WHAT THE GENERAL WANTS--!
IF YOU RUN OUT ON US NOW, IT'LL ALL BE OVER! THERE'LL NEVER BE ANY HOPE FOR YOU--!
NO!
HULK HAS NO FRIENDS!! GENERAL IS HULK'S ENEMY!!
I-I'VE FAILED!! HE WON'T LISTEN TO ME--!
NOW--WHEN IT MATTERS THE MOST--WHEN I REALLY HAD THE CHANCE--TO PAY HIM BACK FOR SAVING MY LIFE--I COULDN'T DO IT--!
BUT--I'VE GOT TO KEEP TRYING--NO MATTER WHAT--! I-I'VE GOT TO BE WORTHY--!
EVEN IF YOU DON'T CARE ABOUT YOUR-SELF--THINK OF THE GENERAL'S DAUGHTER--BETTY!
ONLY YOU CAN SAVE HER LIFE--!!
SLOWLY, FALTERINGLY--THE MASSIVE HEAD TURNS!! THEN DIMLY, SOME FAINT GLIMMER OF COMPREHENSION APPEARS IN THE COLD, UNBLINKING EYES--
--BETTY--!
I--REMEMBER--NOW--!
SHE WAS CAPTURED--BY THE ONE CALLED--ABOMINA-TION!
AND THEN, AS THE EVER-MOUNTING RAGE WITHIN THE GREEN GIANT'S HEART GRADUALLY BEGINS TO DIMINISH, ONE OF THE MOST INCREDIBLE CHANGES KNOWN TO SCIENCE OCCURS ONCE AGAIN--
RICK! WHAT ARE YOU DOING THERE? GET UP, BOY--GET UP!
THANKS--FOR LISTENING TO ME!! THANKS--!
6

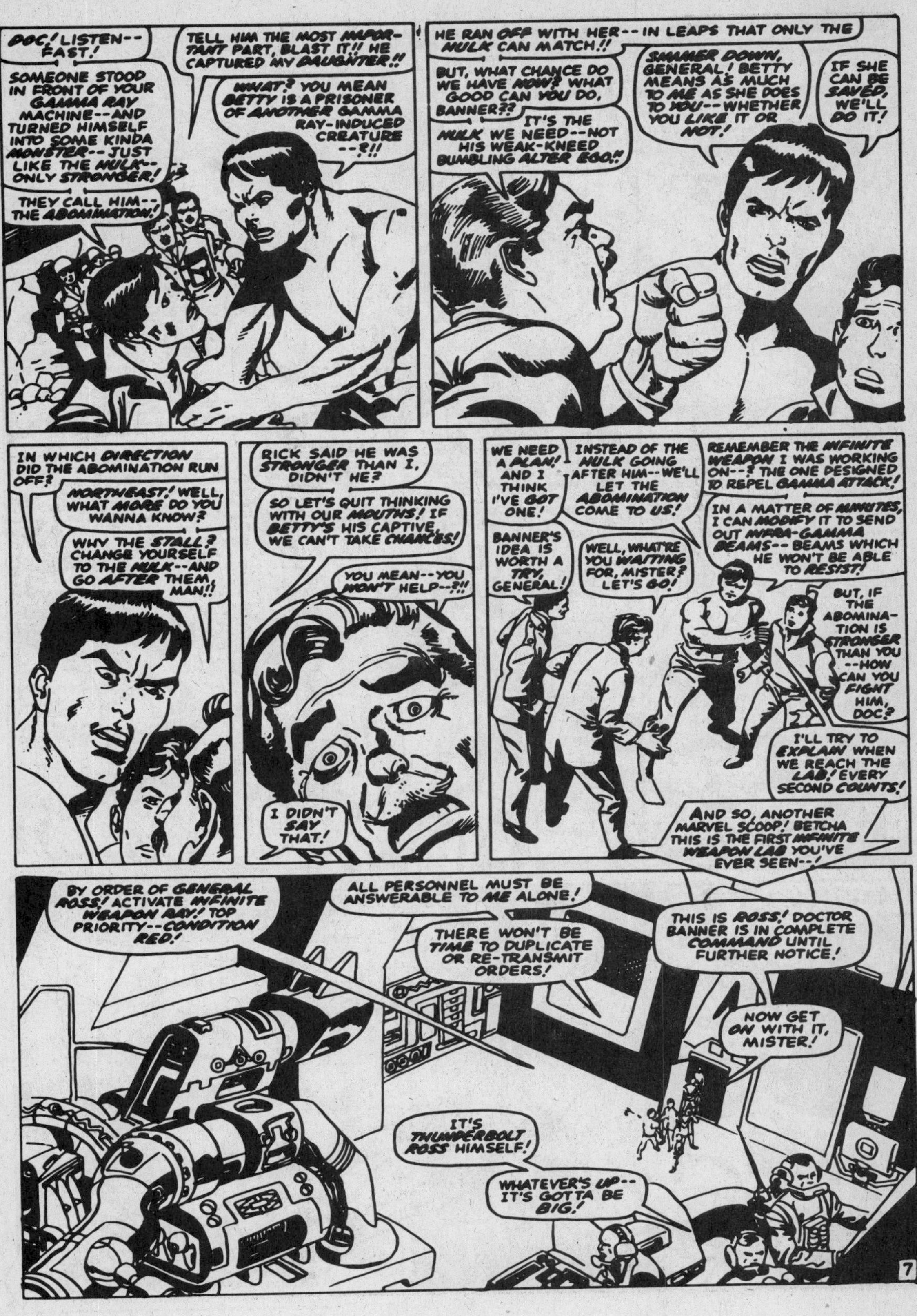
DOC! LISTEN--FAST!
SOMEONE STOOD IN FRONT OF YOUR GAMMA RAY MACHINE--AND TURNED HIMSELF INTO SOME KINDA MONSTER--JUST LIKE THE HULK--ONLY STRONGER!
THEY CALL HIM--THE ABOMINATION!
TELL HIM THE MOST IMPORTANT PART, BLAST IT!! HE CAPTURED MY DAUGHTER!!
WHAT? YOU MEAN BETTY IS A PRISONER OF ANOTHER GAMMA RAY-INDUCED CREATURE--?!!
HE RAN OFF WITH HER--IN LEAPS THAT ONLY THE HULK CAN MATCH!!
BUT, WHAT CHANCE DO WE HAVE NOW? WHAT GOOD CAN YOU DO, BANNER??
IT'S THE HULK WE NEED--NOT HIS WEAK-KNEED BUMBLING ALTER EGO!!
SIMMER DOWN, GENERAL! BETTY MEANS AS MUCH TO ME AS SHE DOES TO YOU--WHETHER YOU LIKE IT OR NOT!
IF SHE CAN BE SAVED, WE'LL DO IT!
IN WHICH DIRECTION DID THE ABOMINATION RUN OFF?
NORTHEAST! WELL, WHAT MORE DO YOU WANNA KNOW?
WHY THE STALL? CHANGE YOURSELF TO THE HULK--AND GO AFTER THEM, MAN!!
RICK SAID HE WAS STRONGER THAN I, DIDN'T HE?
SO LET'S QUIT THINKING WITH OUR MOUTHS! IF BETTY'S HIS CAPTIVE, WE CAN'T TAKE CHANCES!
YOU MEAN--YOU WON'T HELP--?!!
I DIDN'T SAY THAT!
WE NEED A PLAN! AND I THINK I'VE GOT ONE!
INSTEAD OF THE HULK GOING AFTER HIM--WE'LL LET THE ABOMINATION COME TO US!
REMEMBER THE INFINITE WEAPON I WAS WORKING ON--? THE ONE DESIGNED TO REPEL GAMMA ATTACK!
IN A MATTER OF MINUTES, I CAN MODIFY IT TO SEND OUT INFRA-GAMMA BEAMS--BEAMS WHICH HE WON'T BE ABLE TO RESIST!
BANNER'S IDEA IS WORTH A TRY, GENERAL!
WELL, WHAT'RE YOU WAITING FOR, MISTER? LET'S GO!
BUT, IF THE ABOMINATION IS STRONGER THAN YOU--HOW CAN YOU FIGHT HIM, DOC?
I'LL TRY TO EXPLAIN WHEN WE REACH THE LAB! EVERY SECOND COUNTS!
AND SO, ANOTHER MARVEL SCOOP! BETCHA THIS IS THE FIRST INFINITE WEAPON LAB YOU'VE EVER SEEN--!
BY ORDER OF GENERAL ROSS! ACTIVATE INFINITE WEAPON RAY! TOP PRIORITY--CONDITION RED!
ALL PERSONNEL MUST BE ANSWERABLE TO ME ALONE!
THERE WON'T BE TIME TO DUPLICATE OR RE-TRANSMIT ORDERS!
THIS IS ROSS! DOCTOR BANNER IS IN COMPLETE COMMAND UNTIL FURTHER NOTICE!
NOW GET ON WITH IT, MISTER!
IT'S THUNDERBOLT ROSS HIMSELF!
WHATEVER'S UP--IT'S GOTTA BE BIG!
7

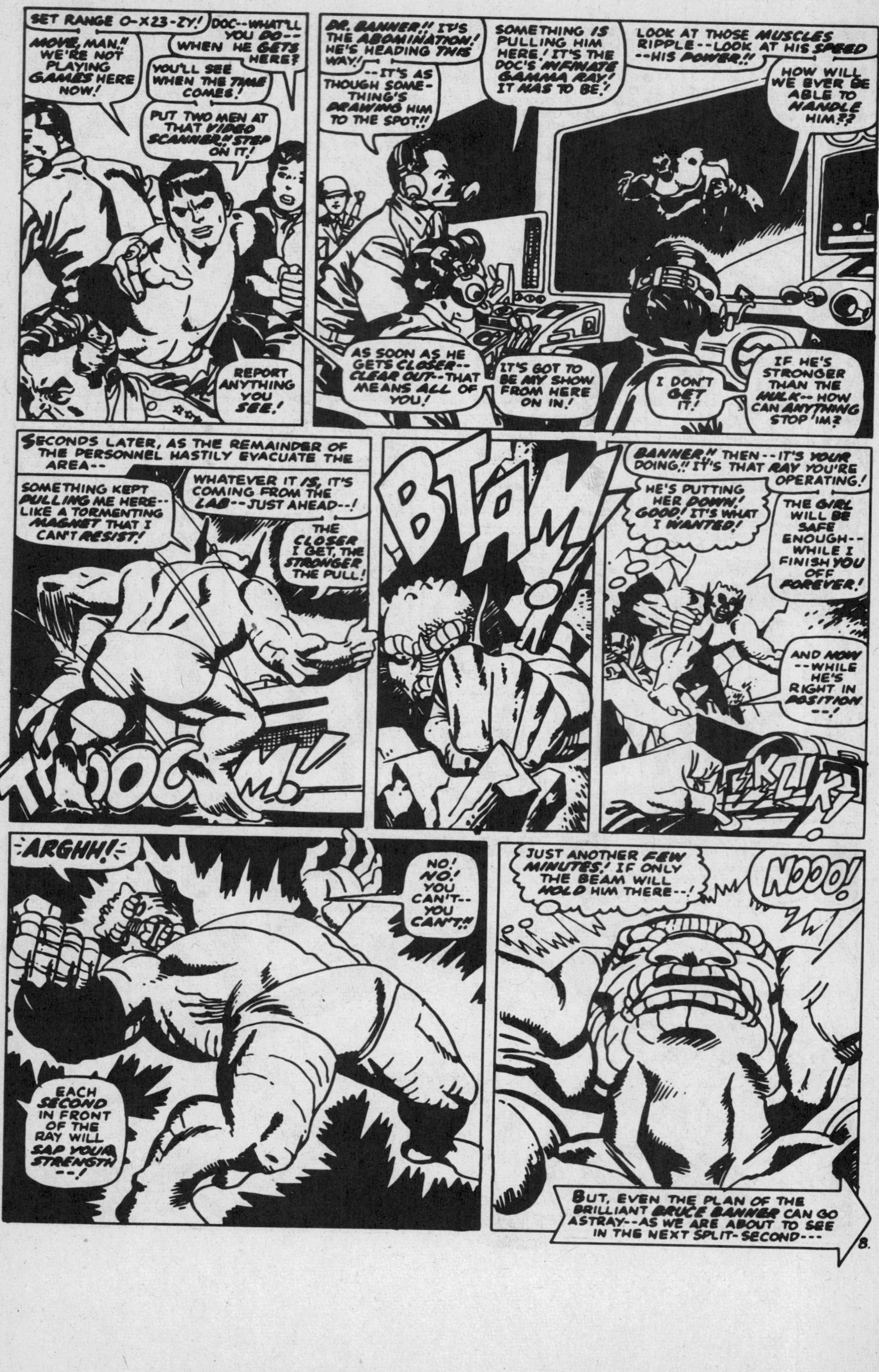
SET RANGE O-X23-ZY!
MOVE, MAN!! WE'RE NOT PLAYING GAMES HERE NOW!
DOC--WHAT'LL YOU DO--WHEN HE GETS HERE?
YOU'LL SEE WHEN THE TIME COMES!
PUT TWO MEN AT THAT VIDEO SCANNER!! STEP ON IT!
REPORT ANYTHING YOU SEE!
DR. BANNER!! IT'S THE ABOMINATION! HE'S HEADING THIS WAY!
--IT'S AS THOUGH SOMETHING'S DRAWING HIM TO THE SPOT!!
SOMETHING IS PULLING HIM HERE! IT'S THE DOC'S INFINITE GAMMA RAY! IT HAS TO BE!
LOOK AT THOSE MUSCLES RIPPLE--LOOK AT HIS SPEED--HIS POWER!!
HOW WILL WE EVER BE ABLE TO HANDLE HIM??
AS SOON AS HE GETS CLOSER--CLEAR OUT--THAT MEANS ALL OF YOU!
IT'S GOT TO BE MY SHOW FROM HERE ON IN!
I DON'T GET IT!
IF HE'S STRONGER THAN THE HULK--HOW CAN ANYTHING STOP 'IM?
SECONDS LATER, AS THE REMAINDER OF THE PERSONNEL HASTILY EVACUATE THE AREA--
SOMETHING KEPT PULLING ME HERE--LIKE A TORMENTING MAGNET THAT I CAN'T RESIST!
WHATEVER IT IS, IT'S COMING FROM THE LAB--JUST AHEAD--!
THE CLOSER I GET, THE STRONGER THE PULL!
THOOOM!
BTAM
BANNER!! THEN--IT'S YOUR DOING!! IT'S THAT RAY YOU'RE OPERATING!
HE'S PUTTING HER DOWN! GOOD! IT'S WHAT I WANTED!
THE GIRL WILL BE SAFE ENOUGH--WHILE I FINISH YOU OFF FOREVER!
AND NOW--WHILE HE'S RIGHT IN POSITION--!
KLIK
ARGHH!
NO! NO! YOU CAN'T--YOU CAN'T!!
EACH SECOND IN FRONT OF THE RAY WILL SAP YOUR STRENGTH--!
JUST ANOTHER FEW MINUTES! IF ONLY THE BEAM WILL HOLD HIM THERE--!
NOOO!
BUT, EVEN THE PLAN OF THE BRILLIANT BRUCE BANNER CAN GO ASTRAY--AS WE ARE ABOUT TO SEE IN THE NEXT SPLIT-SECOND---

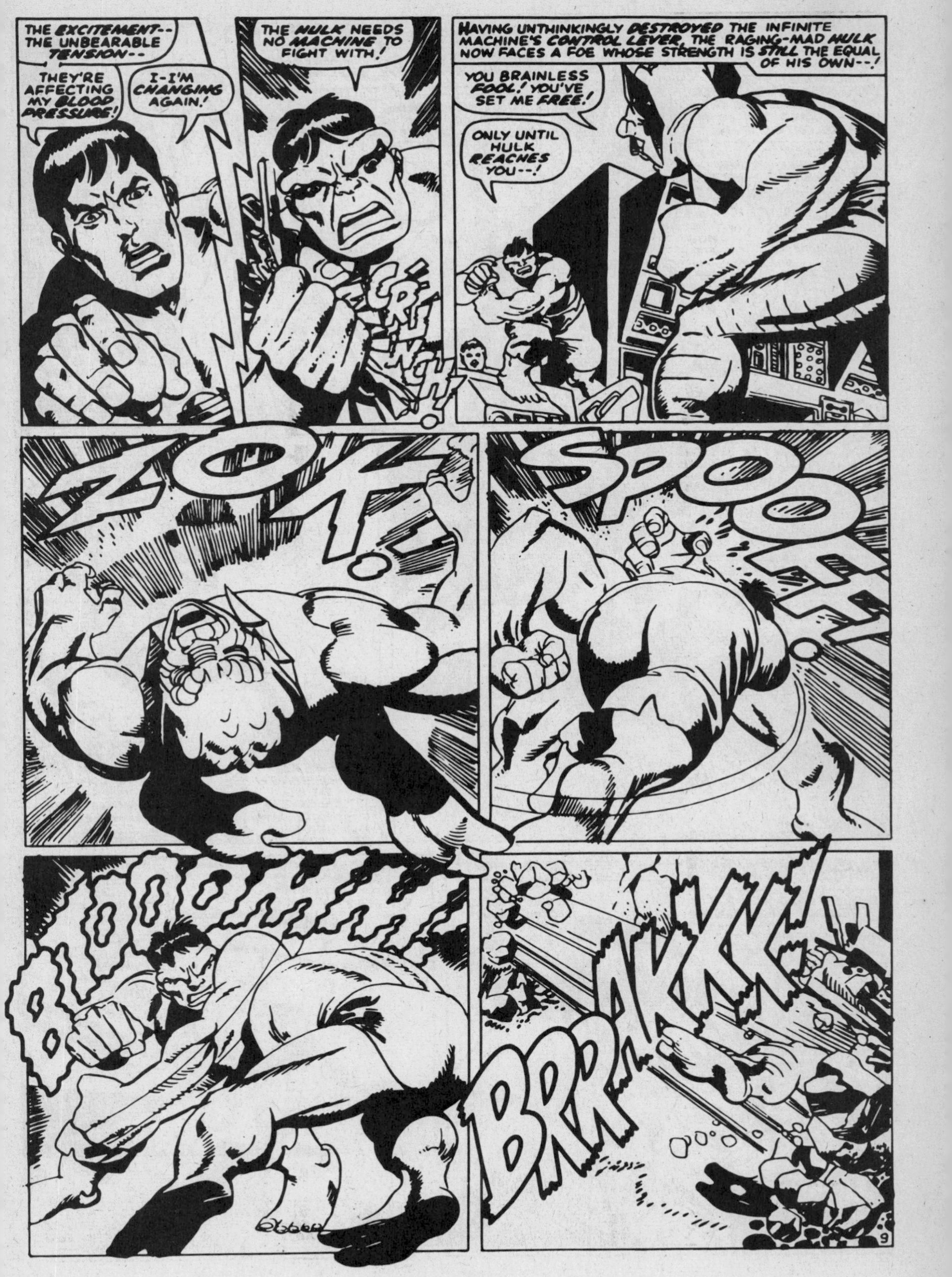
THE EXCITEMENT-- THE UNBEARABLE TENSION--
THEY'RE AFFECTING MY BLOOD PRESSURE!
I-I'M CHANGING AGAIN!
THE HULK NEEDS NO MACHINE TO FIGHT WITH!
CRUNCH!
HAVING UNTHINKINGLY DESTROYED THE INFINITE MACHINE'S CONTROL LEVER, THE RAGING-MAD HULK NOW FACES A FOE WHOSE STRENGTH IS STILL THE EQUAL OF HIS OWN--!
YOU BRAINLESS FOOL! YOU'VE SET ME FREE!
ONLY UNTIL HULK REACHES YOU--!
ZOK!
9

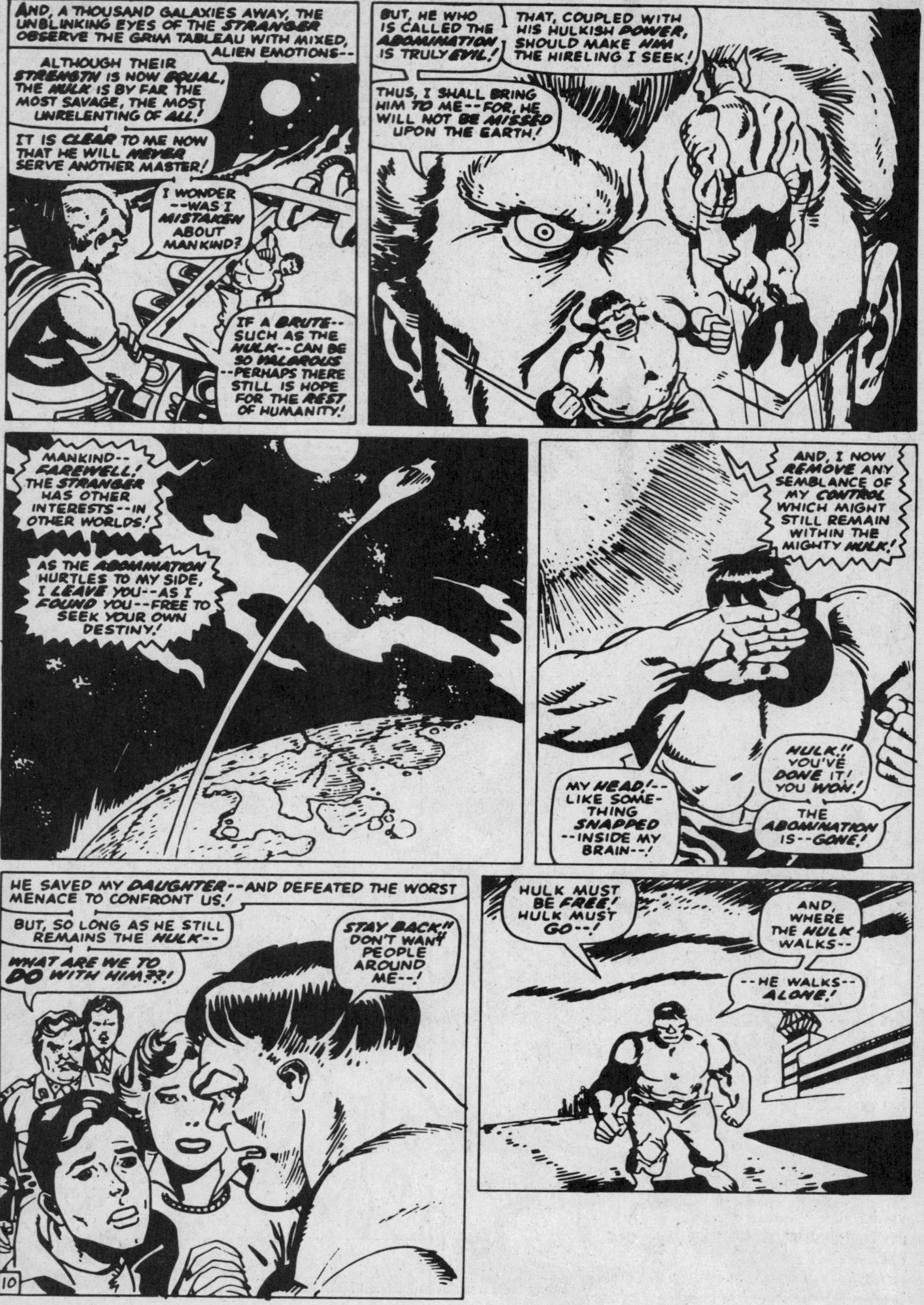

AND, A THOUSAND GALAXIES AWAY, THE UNBLINKING EYES OF THE STRANGER OBSERVE THE GRIM TABLEAU WITH MIXED, ALIEN EMOTIONS--
ALTHOUGH THEIR STRENGTH IS NOW EQUAL, THE HULK IS BY FAR THE MOST SAVAGE, THE MOST UNRELENTING OF ALL!
IT IS CLEAR TO ME NOW THAT HE WILL NEVER SERVE ANOTHER MASTER!
I WONDER --WAS I MISTAKEN ABOUT MANKIND?
IF A BRUTE-- SUCH AS THE HULK--CAN BE SO VALOROUS --PERHAPS THERE STILL IS HOPE FOR THE REST OF HUMANITY!
BUT, HE WHO IS CALLED THE ABOMINATION IS TRULY EVIL!
THAT, COUPLED WITH HIS HULKISH POWER, SHOULD MAKE HIM THE HIRELING I SEEK!
THUS, I SHALL BRING HIM TO ME--FOR, HE WILL NOT BE MISSED UPON THE EARTH!
MANKIND-- FAREWELL! THE STRANGER HAS OTHER INTERESTS--IN OTHER WORLDS!
AS THE ABOMINATION HURTLES TO MY SIDE, I LEAVE YOU--AS I FOUND YOU--FREE TO SEEK YOUR OWN DESTINY!
AND, I NOW REMOVE ANY SEMBLANCE OF MY CONTROL WHICH MIGHT STILL REMAIN WITHIN THE MIGHTY HULK!
MY HEAD!-- LIKE SOME- THING SNAPPED --INSIDE MY BRAIN--!
HULK!! YOU'VE DONE IT! YOU WON!
THE ABOMINATION IS--GONE!
HE SAVED MY DAUGHTER--AND DEFEATED THE WORST MENACE TO CONFRONT US!
BUT, SO LONG AS HE STILL REMAINS THE HULK--
WHAT ARE WE TO DO WITH HIM??!
STAY BACK!! DON'T WANT PEOPLE AROUND ME--!
HULK MUST BE FREE! HULK MUST GO--!
AND, WHERE THE HULK WALKS--
--HE WALKS-- ALONE!
10

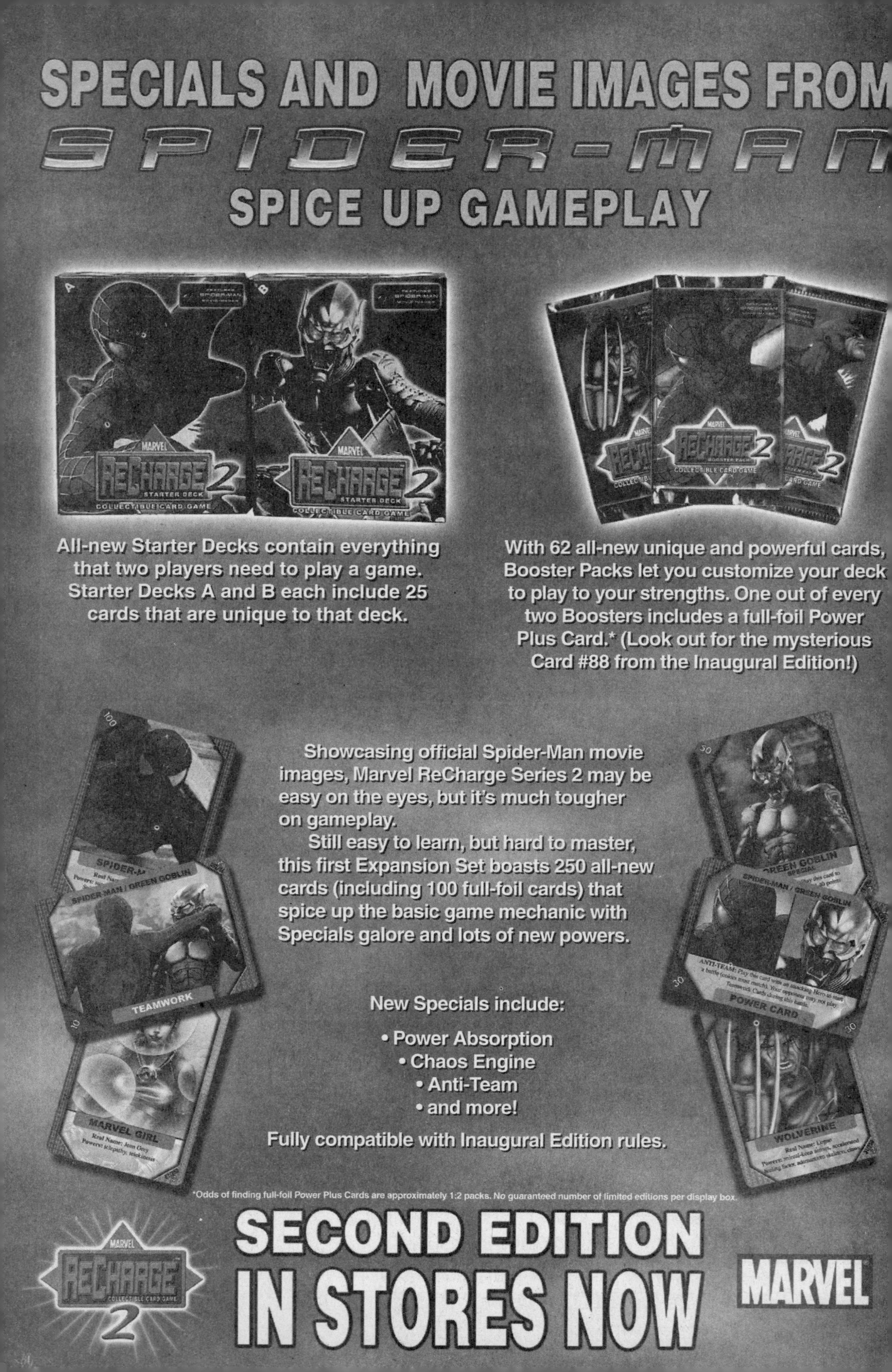
SPECIALS AND MOVIE IMAGES FROM
SPIDER-MAN
SPICE UP GAMEPLAY
MARVEL
RECHARGE 2
STARTER DECK
COLLECTIBLE CARD GAME
BOOSTER PACK
All-new Starter Decks contain everything that two players need to play a game. Starter Decks A and B each include 25 cards that are unique to that deck.
With 62 all-new unique and powerful cards, Booster Packs let you customize your deck to play to your strengths. One out of every two Boosters includes a full-foil Power Plus Card.* (Look out for the mysterious Card #88 from the Inaugural Edition!)
Showcasing official Spider-Man movie images, Marvel ReCharge Series 2 may be easy on the eyes, but it's much tougher on gameplay.
Still easy to learn, but hard to master, this first Expansion Set boasts 250 all-new cards (including 100 full-foil cards) that spice up the basic game mechanic with Specials galore and lots of new powers.
SPIDER-MAN / GREEN GOBLIN
TEAMWORK
MARVEL GIRL
GREEN GOBLIN
POWER CARD
WOLVERINE
New Specials include:
• Power Absorption
• Chaos Engine
• Anti-Team
• and more!
Fully compatible with Inaugural Edition rules.
*Odds of finding full-foil Power Plus Cards are approximately 1:2 packs. No guaranteed number of limited editions per display box.
SECOND EDITION
IN STORES NOW
MARVEL